LITERARY HISTORY OF CANADA
Canadian Literature in English

LITERARY HISTORY OF CANADA

Canadian Literature
in English

General Editor
CARL F. KLINCK

Editors
ALFRED G. BAILEY, CLAUDE BISSELL,
ROY DANIELLS, NORTHROP FRYE,
DESMOND PACEY

UNIVERSITY OF TORONTO PRESS

©UNIVERSITY OF TORONTO PRESS 1965
REPRINTED WITH CORRECTIONS 1966

Printed in the U.S.A.

Contents

INTRODUCTION ix

PART I: NEW FOUND LANDS

1. The Voyagers   DAVID GALLOWAY   3
2. Explorers by Land (to 1860)   VICTOR G. HOPWOOD   19
3. Explorers by Sea: The West Coast   VICTOR G. HOPWOOD   41

PART II: THE TRANSPLANTING OF TRADITIONS

4. Overture to Nationhood   ALFRED G. BAILEY   55
5. Settlement
    I. Newfoundland (1715–1880)   FRED COGSWELL   68
    II. The Maritime Provinces (1720–1815)   FRED COGSWELL   71
    III. The Canadas (1763–1812)   JAMES AND RUTH TALMAN   83
6. Haliburton   FRED COGSWELL   92
7. Literary Activity in the Maritime Provinces (1815–1880)   FRED COGSWELL   102
8. Literary Activity in the Canadas (1812–1841)   CARL F. KLINCK   125
9. Literary Activity in Canada East and West (1841–1880)   CARL F. KLINCK   145
10. Folktales and Folk Songs   EDITH FOWKE   163
11. Literary Publishing   H. PEARSON GUNDY   174

PART III: THE EMERGENCE OF A TRADITION

12. Confederation to the First World War   ROY DANIELLS   191
13. Historical Writing in Canada (to 1920)   KENNETH N. WINDSOR   208

CONTENTS

14. The Growth of Canadian English — M. H. SCARGILL — 251
15. New Forces: New Fiction (1880–1920) — GORDON ROPER — 260
16. The Kinds of Fiction (1880–1920) — GORDON ROPER, RUPERT SCHIEDER, AND S. ROSS BEHARRIELL — 284
17. Writers of Fiction (1880–1920) — GORDON ROPER, S. ROSS BEHARRIELL, AND RUPERT SCHIEDER — 313
18. Essays and Travel Books
    I. Essays (1880–1920) — BRANDON CONRON — 340
    II. Travel Books (1880–1920) — ELIZABETH WATERSTON — 347
19. Nature Writers and the Animal Story — ALEC LUCAS — 364
20. Lampman and Roberts — ROY DANIELLS — 389
21. Crawford, Carman, and D. C. Scott — ROY DANIELLS — 406
22. Minor Poets (1880–1920) — ROY DANIELLS — 422
23. Philosophical Writings (to 1910) — JOHN A. IRVING (ADAPTED BY A. H. JOHNSON) — 431
24. Scientific Writings — A. VIBERT DOUGLAS — 445
25. Literature of Protest — FRANK W. WATT — 457

PART IV: THE REALIZATION OF A TRADITION

26. The Writer and his Public — DESMOND PACEY — 477
27. Canadian History and Social Sciences since 1920
    I. The Writing of Canadian History — WILLIAM M. KILBOURN — 496
    II. Writing in the Social Sciences — HENRY B. MAYO — 519
28. Literary Scholarship — MILLAR MACLURE — 529
29. Religious and Theological Writings — VERY REV. JAMES S. THOMSON — 551
30. Philosophical Writings (1910–1964)
    I. The Achievement of G. S. Brett — JOHN A. IRVING — 576
    II. Other Philosophers — A. H. JOHNSON — 586
31. Travel Books on Canada (1920–1960) — ELIZABETH WATERSTON — 598
32. Essays and Autobiography
    I. Essays (1920–1960) — BRANDON CONRON — 609
    II. Autobiography — JAY MACPHERSON — 616
33. Children's Books — MARJORIE MCDOWELL — 624
34. Drama and Theatre — MICHAEL TAIT — 633

CONTENTS vii

35. Fiction (1920–1940)   DESMOND PACEY   658
36. Fiction (1940–1960)   HUGO MCPHERSON   694
37. Poetry (1920–1935)   MUNRO BEATTIE   723
38. Pratt   MUNRO BEATTIE   742
39. Poetry (1935–1950)   MUNRO BEATTIE   751
40. Poetry (1950–1960)   MUNRO BEATTIE   785

CONCLUSION   NORTHROP FRYE   821

BIBLIOGRAPHY AND NOTES   853

THE CONTRIBUTORS   868

ACKNOWLEDGMENTS   873

INDEX   877

Introduction

THIS *Literary History of Canada* (Canadian Literature in English) is a cooperative project which began in 1957. Its Editors have had two principal aims: to publish a comprehensive reference book on the (English) literary history of this country, and to encourage established and younger scholars to engage in a critical study of that history both before and after the appearance of the book.

The programme for basic research into the literature in English which led to this book has taken six years to complete and has been carried out by many hands. From the beginning, the task of survey and assessment was seen to be beyond the scope of any one man. The book now being published has in fact been written by the Editors and twenty-nine other scholars, all of whom are named in the list of *Contributors* at the end of the book. They faced conditions different from those prevailing in contemporary scholarship in American literature or in general Canadian history: Canadian literary history and criticism (in English) had been provided with a much narrower base of authenticated information. The amount of primary research needed to establish a foundation for this work, especially with reference to all periods before 1920, has been unusually large for a subject of such national significance.

The terms in the sub-title "Canadian . . . in English" require definition. Although "Canadian" has a clear reference in external matters, it often has to be qualified when the reference is an internal one and the context is historical, sociological or cultural. "English-Canadian" and "French-Canadian" are commonly used to emphasize a "bicultural," certainly a bilingual, situation in a land settled by people of many different origins. We have employed "Canadian literature in English" here, rather than "English-Canadian literature," because the former term puts the name of this country first and suggests unity rather than division. "Canadian literature in French" will receive parallel treatment in the *Histoire de la littérature canadienne-française*, directed by Dean Léopold Lamontagne of Laval, assisted by Professors Paul Wyczynski of Ottawa and Albert LeGrand of Montreal. The time will come, one may hope, when it will be possible to make a comparative study of both literatures. In the meantime, the Editors of this volume devoted to Canadian literature in

English have the satisfaction and honour of knowing that a translation of their work into French by Dean Maurice Lebel will soon appear.

Now the term "Canadian." Referring to our thought, culture, and especially the art of writing, Northrop Frye has said that Canada is "an environment, the place where something has happened." It has been our task to discover what kind of "place" Canada was and is, and what has happened here in the realm of literature and of closely associated writings. "Canadian" has been broadly used for whoever or whatever is native, or has been naturalized, or has a distinct bearing upon the native—that is on people or events which had their focus here, although one could insist in some other context upon employing the label of the author's home country, as one might in referring to the New World novels of John Galt, known as a novelist of Scotland.

Historically, Canada was a number of "places." After the power of France in the northern part of North America fell before General Wolfe in 1759, the noun "Quebec" and the adjective "Canadian" were used to designate the old French colony and (from 1774 to 1791) also the "Old North West." After 1791 there were two Canadas, Lower (the old province) and Upper (now called Ontario); but between 1841 and 1867 there was once more a single Canada, with East (Quebec) and West (Ontario) sections. The British Atlantic provinces of Nova Scotia and New Brunswick did not bear the name of Canada before 1867, the date of Confederation with Quebec and Ontario by the British North America Act. Other colonies in the East joined later: Prince Edward Island in 1873 and Newfoundland not until 1949. In the farther Canadian West new provinces were formed as settlement progressed: Manitoba in 1870, British Columbia in 1871, Saskatchewan and Alberta in 1905. There are still Territories extending beyond the provinces. Canada is now the name for the whole northern half of the continent, except Alaska; it refers to the units and their common area and identity. Historically, the name often groups them all together in spite of what they were called in their own right in the period before federation.

The Editors and contributors have not joined in a chauvinistic hunt for "the great Canadian novel" or even for "Canadianism." They wish to demonstrate, not to argue about, what and how much has grown up in Canada. Their attitude resembles that of the painter Homer Watson, expressed on September 30, 1930, in a letter to Mr. Arthur Lismer: "Myself being so much Canadian, why should I think of trying to be Canadian? . . . Things form naturally, not by forcing. . . . I was born amid the hardwood trees and noted the beech, oak and elm, as native as the jack pine. And the trees mentioned are not as those of England. There is a difference which I hope anyone with a [discerning] mind will see."

Our writers have recognized no embargo upon foreign subject-matter, no restriction upon intellectual trade. "Canadian" culture has concerned itself, for example, with the classics, Freud, and international affairs as well as with Huron Indians or Montreal's social problems. The report given here has tried to show how the best writing in this country has reflected local, national, and universal matters which have engaged our serious thought. If we do not launch out from a studied knowledge of ourselves and of our own ways, no one else will.

That writing of intellectual and artistic quality has a history in Canada cannot be doubted; but readers may still have some misgivings about the title, "literary history." If a study with any foundation was to be made, "literary" had to be employed in a generic sense. Authors and books of slight importance could not be set aside without investigation; this volume may give some names their first and last mention in a discussion of Canadian literature. Descriptive reference, however, without the addition of a specific claim for artistic value, must not be construed as anything more than an illustration of what was in the "environment." Whenever values are being critically assessed, "literary" is used, of course, in its restricted meaning.

This book treats, not only works generically classified as "literature," but also, chiefly in separate chapters, other works which have influenced literature or have been significantly related to literature in expressing the cultural life of the country. Canadian achievements in writing on philosophy, general history, the social sciences, religion and theology, and the natural sciences have been outlined. It would be too much to claim that we have here the intellectual history of Canada, even with restriction to the humanities, but the book does deal with much that would have to be taken into account in such a desirable production.

"Literary history" has been chosen as a main title instead of "history of literature" because the latter carries too limited a suggestion of a review of books. Each term indicates that temporal sequence is not to be neglected; but the latter would not have conveyed fully the purpose of noting whatever germinates, grows, continues, recurs, or becomes distinctive, perhaps unique. This volume represents a positive attempt to give a history of Canada in terms of writings which deserve more or less attention because of significant thought, form, and use of language. It also aims to contribute to criticism by offering reasons for singling out those works regarded as the best.

The divisions and periods of this history have not been arbitrarily imposed, but have rather been discovered in the light of the evidence. Literary history need not match exactly the main lines of political events, and uneven progress in different genres can upset any pre-established system of dates for groups of chapters. No formula was laid down for the approach to, and the internal organization of, these chapters. It was suspected that some ready-made categories and descriptive headings hitherto solemnly accepted in Canadian literary history might prove to be part of the folklore, and thus hamper basic research.

It seemed better to allow the systematic process of finding, sifting, and interpreting facts to dictate the approaches, methods of classification, critical concepts, and descriptive styles most appropriate to the truth as the respective authors saw it. The styles in the various chapters differ, of course, for other reasons: the contributors are experienced writers, proficient in their own idioms; they were free of cumbersome regulations, and *con amore* responsive to the spirit and shape of their discoveries. Differences in interpretation and opinion expressed by various contributors have been respected, for each bears the authority of dedication and research.

Flexibility, freshness, and authenticity were placed in the balance against strict orderliness, but an order emerged. Four major Parts were recognized (as they are set forth in the Table of Contents). Part I was necessary to supply the framework, to show how the Old World grew in knowledge of the New Found Lands through the accounts of voyages and explorations. Part II, from the beginning of settlement to the decade after the British North America Act of 1867, had to record a period of "literary activity" rather than of production of memorable imaginative works; it called for more historical description than critical assessment. Part III, from the early years of Confederation to the end of the First World War, a period in which literary products accumulated, required much pioneer work of sifting. Part IV, from 1920 to 1960, covers a period in which critical evaluation of the best known authors had to be made; it demanded at times extended treatment of their work.

These four Parts mark the shape and suggest the pattern of a volume possessed of unity although there are many chapters and dozens of contributors. Introductory chapters (4, 12, and 26) for Parts II, III, and IV effect further consolidation. Each of these historical essays was written by an editor after the evidence of all the component chapters was at hand, the tone had been established, and the threads to be drawn together were visible. In addition, a critical Conclusion was written by Northrop Frye after the manuscript for the rest of the book was complete.

For the sake of convenience, long discussions on a major topic, for example "Fiction (1880–1920)," were cut into two or three chapters; short discussions on limited topics were joined with other short ones. The aims of this project could not have been realized, and the volume would have gone beyond all bounds, if it had been necessary to include biographical data and a large bibliographical appendix. For details about the lives of Canadian men and women the reader may consult Dr. W. S. Wallace's *The Macmillan Dictionary of Canadian Biography* (1963); successive volumes of the comprehensive *Dictionary of Canadian Biography* will soon begin to appear. Wherever it was possible, dates of authors' lives were inserted in the text of this *Literary History*, especially for writers no longer alive.

The "Bibliographical Notes" which follow the text are brief and highly selective; they were appended only if the author of a chapter felt that they were essential. The entire omission of notes for certain other chapters means only that these contributors rely upon the reader to seek out the numerous sources recorded in bibliographies of Canadian literature, especially in Reginald Eyre Watters' *A Check List of Canadian Literature and Background Materials, 1628–1950* (Toronto, 1959), which is virtually a companion volume. It is a record of books. Professor Watters and Dr. Inglis F. Bell will shortly publish *On Canadian Literature, 1906–1960*, "A Check List of Articles, Books and Theses on English-Canadian Literature, Its Authors and Language." The "Index" of this *Literary History* will be useful for reference and cross-reference, but also uniquely for tracing authorship of books known to the searcher only by titles. Some items in the Index and in the text of chapters will inevitably require correction. Assistance in this regard provided by readers, researchers, and critics will be welcome and will be acknowledged if communications are addressed to the General Editor in care of the University of Toronto Press.

It was possible to wait a reasonable number of years for thorough research and preparation of most of the manuscripts, but certain contributors, whom we were fortunate in enlisting during the last year, rendered full service under the shadow of the deadline. Among these were Professors Henry B. Mayo, and Allison H. Johnson. Since Professor John Irving could not complete his chapters on Philosophical Writings because of illness, Professor Johnson quickly adapted and revised, with Professor Irving's permission, two of the latter's earlier articles on this subject and added a section on recent books of philosophy. Time has also been a factor in decisions about a terminal date (roughly 1960) for books to be included in the discussion in various chapters. A few contributors have attempted to review publications which appeared as late as 1964.

The Editors and contributors were assisted by other persons named in the notes and a host of helpers insufficiently acknowledged and described as a group of colleagues, students, academic officials, librarians, representatives of foundations, publishers, wives, and secretaries. All of these were singularly possessed of patience and all are remembered with admiration and gratitude. No editor or other writer received any payment for his labours or fees for his manuscript, but each one has the satisfaction of knowing that the six years of preparation of the *Literary History of Canada* have seen a remarkable growth of interest in, and many scholarly recruits for, the critical study of Canadian literature. Almost all who have written chapters have other books and articles now in progress on topics which emerged during the course of their research.

The loyal service of the writers and the support provided by the Humanities Research Council of Canada and the Canada Council can never be suitably acknowledged. During every year of preparation the Humanities Research

Council provided funds for occasional meetings and other ordinary expenses. The encouragement given by that Council was also invaluable. The Canada Council made twenty-two separate short-term grants in aid of research to individuals who were working for the *Literary History*; not one application was refused. It was a heart-warming experience of scholarly co-operation and of national recognition of our literature—for which all concerned deserve our personal thanks.

Such support has been carried over into publication. The Editors gratefully acknowledge a substantial grant-in-aid for this purpose from the Humanities Research Council of Canada, using funds provided by the Canada Council. The Publications Fund of the University of Toronto Press similarly receives our thanks for a large grant-in-aid, and the Press itself for friendly assistance since 1957. Mr. Marsh Jeanneret, Director of the Press, and the late Dr. George Brown gave encouragement and help from the day on which the project was initiated. The editorial competence, dedication, and firmness of Miss Francess Halpenny, Editor of the Press, have made this almost her own book; she deserves thanks and praise, but no blame for errors perpetrated by others. Many other publishers named in the "Acknowledgments" have made a generous contribution by allowing free use of copyright material.

For the Editors
CARL F. KLINCK

October 10, 1964

PART I

New Found Lands

1. The Voyagers

DAVID GALLOWAY

I. THE PRELUDE

THE NEW WORLD was not discovered; it just grew. Plato's *Lost Atlantis* in the western ocean beyond the Pillars of Hercules, St. Brandan's Isle, the Earthly Paradise, the Fortunate Islands, and the Islands of the Blest, are all part of man's longing to find a Never-Never Land in the reality of dreams. Throughout the Middle Ages these legendary islands floated dimly beyond the fringes of the known world across the Western Seas. Human aspirations are etched in the early fourteenth-century poem, "The Land of Cockayne," "Fur in see bi west Spaygne," where there is a kind of satirical, anti-clerical, pre-Rabelaisian Big Rock Candy Mountain in which the rivers are of oil, milk, honey, and wine, and water is used for washing only. In some medieval maps and manuscripts the Earthly Paradise appears in Asia or Africa, but after Christopher Columbus it is often identified with the west, and Columbus thought that he was near it when he reached the mouth of the Orinoco.

Accounts of early travellers to the New World tell tales of mountains whose sands sparkle with gold, and of natives who "seeme to lyue in that goulden worlde of the whiche owlde wryters speake so much: wherin men lyued simplye and innocentlye without inforcement of lawes, without quarrellinge Iudges and libelles. . . ."[1]* Such ideal pictures live in the work of many sixteenth- and seventeenth-century writers. For Robert Greene, Cuba is ". . . a Region so inricht / With Savours sparkling from the smiling heavens." For Edmund Waller, writing of Bermuda about forty years later, "Heaven sure has kept this spot of Earth uncursed / To show how all things were created first."[2] Donne, as we might expect, in "Love's Progress" places the Fortunate Islands in his mistress's lips, and places "my America! my new-found-land" even nearer to paradise. The realities, of course, were not always so delectable, and early travellers also tell spine-tingling tales of "People called *Cannibales* or *Anthropophagi*, which are accustomed to eate mans fleshe." If the Earthly Paradise, El Dorado, the Seven Cities of Cibola, and King Solomon's Ophir were never actually discovered, lands where "neyther the coldnesse of

*The references required for this chapter are incorporated with the Bibliographical Notes.

wynter is sharpe . . . nor the heate of sommer intollerable" seemed to contain riches beyond the dreams of avarice.

In the minds of men who saw their fondest dreams beyond the setting sun, what is now Canada was, in the sixteenth century, a mere footnote to the countries of perpetual spring farther south. If Canada resembles any of the legendary lands of the Middle Ages, it probably resembles *Ultima Thule*. In a general sense, *Ultima Thule* was simply the "farthest land," and more often than not the Ancients had placed it in the land of the Midnight Sun. For various writers it later became Ireland, the North Pole, the Orkneys, the Shetlands, Norway, or the Faroes. For Sir Francis Bacon, Seneca's prediction in *Medea*, "The time will come . . . When men no more shall unknown courses measure, / For round the world no 'farthest land' shall be," led to America. Although there was no widespread identification of Thule with the New World, it was generally recognized to be a cold northern land, and often it was placed somewhere near the routes which men were later to follow in search of the Northwest Passage.

Historians, writing of the New World in the sixteenth century, often give the impression that the Elizabethans, fired by the voyagers' reports, dreamed of golden opportunities in America. True, the New World represented aspects of men's dreams, but men would still have dreamed even if it had not gradually taken physical shape in the sixteenth century. The New World is important to us because we live in it, but the vast majority of Elizabethans took no interest in America as an object of colonization, trade, or missionary endeavour; in the creative imagination of the age, as judged by its literature, America is comparatively unimportant. In the web of Elizabethan life the strands of the New World are few, and such interest as there was, was expressed by a tiny minority of dedicated men such as Richard Hakluyt, John Dee, Sir Francis Walsingham, and some of the voyagers themselves. Historians, who have often been the victims of that "gigantic optical illusion" of which Professor Butterfield writes in *The Whig Interpretation of History*, have organized past history "by reference to the present" and have made inferences "from a particular series of abstractions from the past—abstractions which by the very principle of their origin beg the very questions that the historian is pretending to answer" (p. 30). That arch-Whig of historians, G. M. Trevelyan, for example, sees Richard Hakluyt as one of the two most influential writers in the age of Shakespeare, and writes that "Hakluyt, in narrating the deeds of our explorers and seamen, directed across the ocean the thoughts of adventurous youth, of scholars, statesmen and merchants and of all who had money to invest. Even up-country squires and farmers began to dream of boundless expanses of virgin soil, waiting since the dawn of time to be broken by the English plough." (*Illustrated English Social History*, II, 52.)

The absolute importance of Richard Hakluyt has blinded historians to his relative importance in the age in which he lived. His *Principal Navigations, Voyages, Traffiques and Discoveries of the English Nation* (1598–1600) is so important to subsequent generations because much of his material is unique; most of it was unknown to the reading public until he printed it. However, the number of his readers has probably been over-estimated.[3]

There are, of course, many incidental references to the New World in the literature of the sixteenth century, and tags such as the "wealth of the Indies" are quite common. But in assessing the importance of the New World to the creative imagination, historians have often quoted a few well-known passages *ad nauseam* as though they were typical. J. Holland Rose, and R. B. Nye and J. E. Morpurgo, for example, quote Maria's description of Malvolio— "He does smile his face into more lines than is in the new map with the augmentation of the Indies"—as an indication of the groundlings' interest in the New World.[4] In fact there is no record of a public performance of *Twelfth Night* at all, although the play was performed at Court and in the Hall of the Middle Temple. So what has been taken to be an indication of widespread knowledge of a map in the *Principal Navigations*, based on Molineux's globe which stood in the Hall of the Middle Temple, could well be an allusion directed specifically at the Court or the Inns of Court.[5]

It is, of course, impossible to assess popular interest in events by counting allusions to them; the tavern talk of the day is silent, and the ordinary seamen are mute and inglorious. But if we are trying to assess popular interest in a subject, the broadside ballad might provide us with a key. There are, apparently, more ballads about the Revolt of the Northern Earls in 1569 alone than there are about the entire New World in the sixteenth and seventeenth centuries.[6] The popular imagination as expressed in the ballad seems to have been fired more by a single spectacular event at home than by the birth of a whole new world overseas.

If the impact of the New World as a whole on the creative imagination of the Elizabethan age was less significant than is commonly supposed, the impact of what is now Canada was definitely insignificant. In contrast to the first voyage of Christopher Columbus, who found, in Espaniola, a land of perpetual spring, the Cabots, on their first voyage, found a sterner, harder land. Prominent in accounts of subsequent voyages to Canada, in fact, are descriptions of struggles against the elements. The time available for the completion of a northern voyage is limited. The little ships leave Dartmouth and St. Malo, Harwich and Honfleur, in April or May; they must be back by October, and over them hang the urgent shadows of the coming winter. In the voyages to Virginia and the Indies there is no such sense of urgency, and whatever the dangers of sailing to the south, there is no danger of having to experience the frozen horrors which Cartier endured in the St. Lawrence winter of 1535–36.

From its very beginnings, the "literature" of Canada was stamped by a struggle against the climate and against the land itself. For Northrop Frye, reviewing A. J. M. Smith's *Book of Canadian Poetry* in the *Canadian Forum* four centuries later, "the outstanding achievement of Canadian poetry is in the evocation of stark terror. Not a coward's terror, of course; but a controlled vision of the causes of cowardice. The immediate source of this is obviously the frightening loneliness of a huge and thinly settled country."

Scant as references to Canada are, the country seems to have made its appearance in English literature earlier than did the warmer and wealthier lands to the south. The voyages of the Norsemen, unknown to Europe as a whole, may have been known to the seamen of Bristol, who were making regular visits to Iceland by the end of the fifteenth century. The voyages of the Cabots, of the Company Adventurers of the New Found Lands, of John Rut, and—no doubt—of others of whom no trace remains, seemed to herald a dawn of colonial expansion in the northern part of North America. The dawn was a false one and nothing was done for another half a century, but some of these voyages do seem to find dim reflection in Tudor literature. The interlude *Hickscorner* (written *c.* 1510) contains a reference to the 'new founde Ilande,' and a comparatively extended treatment appears in John Rastell's *A New Interlude and a mery of the nature of the iiij elements* (1519?).[7] In 1517, John Rastell, brother-in-law of Sir Thomas More, had set out for North America, but his "mariners, / False of promise and dissemblers," had put him ashore in Ireland. Rastell's "interlude" "may be accepted as the first work in modern geography of English authorship." In the hundred lines or so in which he deals with the "new lands," we have a glimpse of "Canadians" as they appeared to an intelligent man of the court of Henry VIII:

> And what a great meritorious deed
> It were to have the people instructed,
> To live more virtuously,
> And to learn to know of men the manner,
> And also to know God their Maker,
> Which as yet live all beastly.

In these lines appears a strain which was later to be developed in the promotion literature of colonization. Moreover, in the copper that the natives have, in the "Great abundance of woods," and in the "Fish they have so great plenty," can be dimly seen the ingredients of Canada's economic future.

When we contrast the amount of material that was published in Spain about the Spanish colonies, however, with the meagre scraps that were published in England about North America, Canada remains very much the poor relation of the American dream. Throughout the sixteenth century many of the northern voyagers, in fact, regarded Canada as a nuisance—an obstacle which lay across the path which led to the golden gates of Cathay.

The accounts of the voyagers themselves, the most direct expression of the New World, are, of course, the base upon which Canadian literary history in the sixteenth and seventeenth centuries must rest. Hakluyt's *Principal Navigations* (1598–1600) have been called, in Froude's well-worn phrase, "the Prose Epic of the modern English nation." Epic in scope and action they undoubtedly are, taken as a whole; as literature, they vary a great deal, although about one third have "significant literary merit."[8]

Some of the narratives of the voyagers to Canada, such as Christopher Hall's account of Frobisher's first voyage to the Northwest (1576; Hakluyt, Everyman ed., V, 131–37), Silvester Wyet's account of a voyage to "the Bay of Saint Laurence" (1594; Hakluyt VI, 98–100), and Charles Leigh's account of his voyage with "divers other to Cape Briton and the Isle of Ramea" (1597; Hakluyt VI, 100–14) are of the practical, log-book, journal-jotting variety. Dangers and excitements seldom ruffle the matter-of-fact surface of the style, although some of the details about the Indians, the vegetation, and the wild life are interesting enough in themselves. In contrast, George Best's "discourse" of Frobisher's voyages (1576, 1577, 1578; Hakluyt V, 170–276), and Edward Haye's account of Gilbert's last voyage (1583; Hakluyt VI, 1–42), are among the most lively in Hakluyt.

Like most of the accounts, Best's contains much unexciting detail, but it also contains what is, perhaps, the earliest effective description of a battle with the Canadian elements:

There arose a sudden terrible tempest at the Southeast, which blowing from the maine sea, directly upon the place of the Streites, brought together all the yce a seaboorde of us upon our backes. . . . And again some where so fast shut up and compassed in amongst an infinite number of great countreys and Islands of yce, that they were faine to submit themselves and their ships to the mercy of the unmercifull yce, . . . for plankes of timber of more than three inches thicke, and other things of greater force and bignesse, by the surging of the sea and billowe, with yce were shivered and cut in sunder, . . . that our ships, even those of greatest burdens, with the meeting of contrary waves of the sea, were heaved up betweene Islands of yce, a foote welneere out the sea above their watermark, having their knees and timbers within boord both bowed and broken therewith. . . . And albeit, by reason of the fleeting yce, which were dispersed here almost the whole sea over, they were brought many times to the extreamest point of perill, mountaines of yce tenne thousand times scaping them scarce one ynch, which to have striken had bene their present destruction. . . . (Hakluyt, V, 238–39)

Best's account shows a humour and a humanity lacking in most of the others. He clearly admires Frobisher, but he does not suppress the fact that one of the "salvages" "hurt the Generall in the buttocke with an arrow, who the rather speedily fled backe. . . ." The savages are treated as human beings—if somewhat recalcitrant and "subtill" ones—and Best's description of the touching devotion between a captive man and a captive woman, "so that (I thinke) the one would hardly have lived without the comfort of the other," strikes the tender notes of an incipient idyll of love. In an age when the hardships of the ordinary seaman went largely unrecorded, we learn that "we lost in all the voyage only one man, besides one that dyed at sea, which was sicke before he came aboord, and was so desirous to follow this enterprise, that he rather chose to dye theerin, then not to be one to attempt so notable a voyage."

Unlike Best, Haye introduces a moralizing, religious tone into his treatment of Gilbert's last voyage, but the account has, on the whole, a restrained simplicity with few rhetorical devices. The disasters of the voyage are the work of God, and over the expedition hang hints of a tragically inevitable conclusion. One passage almost hints at a preview of the scene in Shakespeare's *Antony and Cleopatra* (IV.iv), when Antony's soldiers hear "hautboys . . . under the stage" and fear that ". . . the god Hercules, whom Antony lov'd, / Now leaves him."

> The evening was faire and pleasant, yet not without token of storme to ensue, and most part of this Wednesday night, like the Swanne that singeth before her death, they in the Admiral, or Delight, continued in sounding of Trumpets, with Drummes, and Fifes: also winding the Cornets, Haughtboyes: and in the end of their jolitie, left with the battell and ringing of dolefull knels. (Hakluyt, VI, 28)

Haye's account has a dying fall and music at the close, and Gilbert passes through his travail, before finally meeting his Maker, "sitting abaft with a booke in his hand," and crying "out unto us in the Hind (so oft as we did approch within hearing) We are as neere to heaven by sea as by land."

The voyagers' accounts, plain, concrete, and incisive as they usually are, are relatively free from the rhetoric and conceit which are so characteristic of Elizabethan prose as a whole. Many of the accounts were, of course, written by seamen and merchants with no pretensions to literary skill, but "this plainness of style" extends to "the writings of university-trained men" who "were aware of the literary fashions of their age, but did not give way to them in their narratives." The accounts "are the unstudied and natural outpourings of men's expressions of what they saw and did. Men told these tales for what was in them rather than to achieve any special effect."[9] Descriptions of landscapes are especially bare and unadorned, and part of the reason is that there were simply no techniques available to writers at that time which they could use to describe natural scenery. "When the feeling for landscape was still in its simplest stages, so that the eye of painter and engraver, fascinated by space and sky, simple forms and elementary masses, was not yet trained to render the specific, the unusual, and the scientifically exact, small wonder that the writers of voyage literature were equally unskilled to describe in words what perhaps had vividly impressed them."[10]

If none of the accounts of sixteenth-century voyages to Canada can compare, as literature, with Sir Walter Raleigh's account of Guiana, some of them do rank high as voyage literature. They show the first attempts, in the English language, to come to grips with the vast loneliness of Canada, and with the vaster loneliness of the seas around her coasts.

Ballad writers were sometimes inspired by the exploits of the Elizabethan seamen, but the New World, when it appears, is usually incidental to the struggle with Spain. The few ballads about the Northwest have a pathetic minor key quality, compared to the more full-blooded expressions of Drake's adventures in the Caribbean. The second half of a ballad (c. 1584) about Drake's return from his voyage around the world refers to the loss of Sir Humphrey Gilbert on his way back from the "New-found-land" in 1583.

> Gallants all of British blood,
> Why do ye not saile on th'ocean flood?
> I protest ye are not worth a philberd,
> Compared with Sir Humphry Gilberd?
>
> For he walkt forth in a rainy day,
> To the New-found-land he took his way,
> With many a gallant fresh and green;
> Ne never came home again. God bless the Queen.[11]

The quality of the verse as a whole does not suggest that the last line is ironical.

On May 20, 1577, there was entered in the Stationers' *Register*, a ballad (now lost) called "Ffullers ffarewell to master Ffourbousier and the other gentlemen adventurers whoe labour to discouer the right passage to Catay," while a "thing" on Frobisher was entered six weeks later, on July 1. A poem called "Thomas Ellis in praise of Frobisher,"[12] which seems to refer to Frobisher's expedition of 1577, makes a few oblique references to such things as "countrise strange" and "men of savage kind," and compares Frobisher to Jason; but the golden fleece, of course, turned out to be mere dross after all.

II. THE SETTLEMENTS

When Queen Elizabeth died, on March 24, 1603, most of the hopes represented by the voyages of men like Sir Humphrey Gilbert and John Davis, and by the laborious compilations of Richard Hakluyt, Preacher, were still the stuff of dreams.

> .... Sir Humfrey Gilbert sure,
> and all his troupe is gone.
> But whether, no man knowes. . . .

Ever since—and perhaps before—John Cabot had come back from his voyage of 1497 and found the seas full of fish, fishermen from France, Spain, Portugal, and England had cast their nets on the Grand Bank and in the Bay of St. Lawrence. Some of them had even wintered on the shores, but the sixteenth century passed without permanent settlement.

With the formation of the Royal Council for Virginia in 1606, and the first permanent settlement at Jamestown in the following year, there seems to follow a period of popular interest in colonization. Several ballads, sermons, and pamphlets in praise of "the noble enterprise" came from the London printing presses. "The persons interested in Virginia increase daily," wrote Zuñiga, the Spanish Ambassador, to his King in a letter dated March 28, 1608. "R. Rich, Gent., one of the voyage," gives us in *Newes from Virginia* (1610) what is perhaps the first real affirmation of faith in the future of colonization in ballad literature.

> Let England know our willingnesse,
> For that our worke is good,
> We hope to plant a nation,
> Where none before hath stood.

The Virginia voyages were undoubtedly talked about a great deal in the years immediately before and after the founding of Jamestown, but it is easy to over-estimate the enthusiasm which they aroused. Their "literature" is propaganda, rather than the spontaneous expression of interest in a subject which had caught the popular imagination. Much of it represents an effort to combat scepticism and hostility. R. Rich's confidence is tempered by the "scandall" and "false report" which have attended his voyage, and by the discomfort and discontent of the colonists. A sermon of Daniel Price, preached on Sunday, May 28, 1609, includes a "reproofe of those that traduce the Honourable Plantation of Virginia."[13] Even Michael Drayton's "Ode to the Virginian Voyage," which is quoted so frequently, as though it were typical of poetic enthusiasm, is, in fact, the only known poem of real literary merit on the Virginian expedition by a major poet.

In spite of their many hardships, the colonists in Virginia clung on, to be joined on the American coast by the Pilgrim Fathers in 1620. In what is now Canada, in the meantime, three permanent settlements had been founded before the independent, God-fearing, Puritans had landed on Plymouth Rock. The French had already settled at Port Royal (1605) and Quebec (1608), and the English at Cupar's Cove in Newfoundland (1610).

The cultural—and even the political—history of English Canada in the seventeenth century is sparse, desultory, and shadowy compared to that of French Canada and the New England colonies. There is nothing in the English language which can compare in detail and in literary quality with the accounts of the early French settlements given by Lescarbot[14] and Champlain,[15] and nothing later in the century which can compare with the vast bulk and minute fascination of the *Jesuit Relations*.[16] Short histories of Canada, when dealing with the seventeenth century, often devote about ninety per cent of their pages to the French. Lescarbot was probably the first European to write verse, and he staged the first dramatic production, in North America. His fastidious regard for detail does not allow him to overlook the humming-bird, which supplants the wren as the smallest bird in poetry:

> *Niridau* oiselet délicat de nature,
> Qui de l'abeille prend la tendre nourriture
> Pillant de nos jardins les odorantes fleurs,
> Et des rives des bois les plus rares douceurs.

Lescarbot's pageant, *Théâtre de Neptune*, written especially for the Sieur de Poutrincourt's return to Port Royal, was presented "sur les flots du Port Royal" on the 14th day of November, 1606. Ten months later, on September 5 and 30, 1607, "*Hamlet* and *Richard*" were acted on Captain William Keeling's ship, the *Dragon*, off Sierra Leone. The very fact that Lescarbot could write and organize his entertainment in the wilderness and that Shakespeare could be acted on a cramped ship off the Guinea coast should warn us against being too dogmatic about "first performances." Long before *Hamlet* and *Théâtre de Neptune* were written, amateur actors may have fretted their hours on improvised stages in North America and signified nothing to posterity.

It is unlikely, nevertheless, that much literature was written, or that plays were performed, in Acadia by the French settlers who followed Lescarbot and de Poutrincourt. Although the ritual of the Church may have helped to satisfy incipient dramatic instincts, the churches and priests, like the settlers, were scattered, and even by the end of the century the two thousand Acadians of the Port Royal, Chignecto, and Minas areas were still concerned mainly with simple physical needs. Even in the more populous and concentrated society of the fortress of Quebec itself, attempts to produce Corneille, Racine, and Molière were short-lived. "The theatre was not a vigorous form of artistic expression in Quebec until recent years, because of the Jansenist element in French-Canadian Catholicism, which also gave a puritanical tone to society in other respects."[17]

Narrow as the culture of New France may have been during the second half of the seventeenth century, "the colony showed some signs of breaking through the narrow intellectual limits which had been imposed by frontier toil, and ignorance and clerical control."[18] In Quebec there were at least some of the trappings of a cultural life—a Jesuit college with a faculty of theology, private libraries of three and four thousand volumes, a fairly good assortment of recent and contemporary literature, church choirs, an organ, and a developing tradition of folk song. "Of the seven to ten thousand songs collected in the Province of Quebec in recent years nine tenths are derived from songs brought to Quebec before 1673."[19]

Narrowly theological and utilitarian as the taste of New England also often seems, it produced, by the end of the seventeenth century, a culture which New France could not rival. Religious opposition to plays persisted in New England as it did in New France, but, farther south, in Charleston, the first professional actors to perform in the colonies offered a play in 1703. By the year 1701, there were universities at Cambridge (1636), Williamsburg (1693), and New Haven (1701). Three years after the founding of Harvard a printing press was set up in Cambridge (1639), to be followed by presses in Philadelphia (1685) and New York (1693); whereas the first result of a printing press in Canada was the *Halifax Gazette* of 1752, and there is no conclusive evidence of printing in New France until 1764. The first newspaper in the American colonies, however, appeared in Boston in 1690, and by 1735 there were five newspapers in the town. By the early eighteenth century, Edward Taylor (*c.* 1645-1729) had written—even if he had not published—the best poetry in New England before the nineteenth century.

In the sparse, primitive English settlements in Newfoundland, Nova Scotia, and Isle St. Jean (Prince Edward Island), however, the taste for learning hardly existed. During the seventeenth century there were no printing presses, no bookstores, no colleges, no centres of population, and, apparently, no Edward Taylors. There was no Cotton Mather who, in his *Magnalia, Christi Americana* (1702), produced at great length and in great detail "the Ecclesiastical History of New England, from its First Planting in the year 1620, unto the Year of our Lord, 1692."

Meagre as English literary achievements in, and about, Canada were, English literature was written in Canada as soon—or nearly as soon—as it was in the American colonies to the south. In it there are no elaborate prospects of El Dorados, but there are modest hints of promised lands. Those men who had favoured colonization in the days of Elizabeth had naturally been concerned not to give the impression that life was one long battle against the elements. Anthony Parkhurst, in a letter to Richard Hakluyt (1578; Hakluyt V, 343-49), had said that "Newfoundland is in a temperate climate and not so cold as foolish mariners doe say. . . ." Sir George Peckham, in "A true Reporte of the late Discoveries . . ." (Hakluyt VI, 42-78), had stressed "manifold benefits, commodities and pleasures heretofore unknowen" and had talked of the "wholesome air and fertile soil." Frobisher commended Peckham's "report" in, for him, the unusual medium of verse: "A pleasaunt ayre, a sweete and firtell soile, / A certaine gaine, a never dying praise."[20] John

Guy, the founder of the Cupar's Cove settlement and its first governor, writing home from the Cove in a letter dated May 16, 1611, speaks in a quiet, modestly optimistic manner of a temperate winter in which "not onely men may safely inhabit here without any neede of Stove, but Navigation may be made to and fro from England to these parts at any time of the yeare." Guy's letter may be read in the volumes of *Purchas His Pilgrimes*, published originally in 1625 (in the edition of 1905–7, XIX, 410–16).

In spite of the hardships of the early days of the colony, the twenty years following Guy's settlement were to produce bursts of minor poetic activity on the parts of some of the leading colonists. Among the "divers honourable persons and others who have undertaken to helpe advance his Majesties Plantation in the New-found-land," was "the Worshipfull William Vaughan of Tarracod, in the Countie of Carmarthen, Doctor of Civill Law." Vaughan (*c.* 1575–1641) had already published *The Golden Grove* (1600), a general guide to morals, politics, and literature, in which he had shown himself to have at least one admirable quality for a colonist by denouncing plays as folly and wickedness. In 1622 the fantastic Welshman may have visited Newfoundland, although it is unlikely that he did so, where he had bought a grant of land in 1616, "and hath in two severall yeers sent thither divers men and women." In 1626, in England, he published *The Golden Fleece*, partly in verse, partly in prose, to encourage emigration.

Prefixed to the book were commendatory verses by Guy, and by Captain John Mason (1586–1635). Guy, in a burst of poetic optimism, foresaw "A trade more rich than Jason brought to Greece / From Colchos land," and Mason wrote of ". . . how my heart doth leap with joy to hear / Our New-found Isle by Britons prized dear!" Mason, classical scholar, governor of the colony from 1615 to 1621, and later founder of New Hampshire (1629), had already published his *Briefe Discourse of the New-found-land* (1620) to encourage settlement. He too tried to counter the rumour that the winters were unbearable, although he admitted that the mosquitoes were a nuisance in summer. Sir Richard Whitbourne (fl. 1579–1626) also, in *A Discourse and Discovery of Newfoundland*, published in the same year (1620; reprinted in part in Purchas XIX), had described the colony and assured prospective settlers that "even in Winter, it is as pleasant and helthfull as England is." For him, too, the mosquitoes were troublesome, but mainly to "loytering people . . . when they find any such lying lazily or sleeping in the Woods. . . ." The old sea dog, author, judge, and colonial governor, had made his first trip to Newfoundland in 1580, had seen Gilbert "take possession of that Countrie in the Harbour of St. Johns" (1583), had commanded a ship of his own against the Spanish Armada, and, after many more voyages, had been to Newfoundland again in 1618. Safe in port at Exmouth, writing his *Discourse*, he can be forgiven if he remembers "a strange Creature . . . in the Harbour of Saint Johns, which very swiftly came swimming towards me, . . . whether it were a Marmaide or no, I leave it for others to judge." Whitbourne's *Discourse*—conceited, humorous, tongue-in-cheek—is one of the most charming records of early Newfoundland.

How much of *The Golden Fleece* Sir William Vaughan—or Orpheus Junior as he called himself—might have written in Newfoundland, we do not know, but we are virtually certain that Robert Hayman (1575–1629), who succeeded Captain John Mason as governor, did indeed write his contribution to Canadian literature there, because all of his "Epigrams and other small parcels, both Morall and Divine" were "Composed and done at Harbor-Grace in Britaniola, anciently called Newfound-land." Hayman's *Quodlibets, Lately Come Over from New Britaniola, Old Newfound-land* (1628), is probably the first book of original English verse written on the North American continent.[21]

Hayman dedicates his "few bad unripe Rimes" to Charles I. Several of his friends, including Vaughan and George Wither, wrote poetic forewords. Wither cries: "Behold, e'en from these uncouth shores, among / Unpeopled woods, and hills these straines were sung." Over the 350 "epigrams and other small parcels" hangs an air of rustic urbanity—a moralizing on the ways of men in the Old World, recollected in the tranquillity of the New. There are epigrams in rhymed iambics on God, religion, papists, fools, drunkards, liars, doctors, merchants, tobacco, universities, mayors, and usurers; there are epigrams on John Donne, Ben Jonson, and Michael Drayton "whose unwearied old muse still produceth new dainties"; there are epigrams on our old friends, Mason, Vaughan, and Whitbourne, and on others who have laboured in the cause of Newfoundland. There is a charming nostalgic memory of Sir Francis Drake whom Hayman remembers from his boyhood in Totnes. Over a span of forty years or so, he recalls Drake's "walking up Totnes long Street," giving him "*a* faire red *Orange*," kissing him, and saying "*God blesse my boy*: / Which I record with comfort to this day." Drake had no children.

Hayman's sentiments about Newfoundland, in verse, are often similar to those of Mason, Guy, and Whitbourne, in prose. The four elements are "wholesome," "sweet," and "rich." The winter is ". . . short, wholesome, constant clear, / Not thicke, unwholesome, shuffling, as 'tis here," and although Newfoundland cannot compare with England for "cloaths, company, buildings faire," a man may find peace of mind:

> Alwayes enough, most times some what to spare,
> With little paines, lesse toyle, and lesser care,
> Exempt from taxings, ill newes, Lawing, feare,
> If cleane, and warme, no matter what you weare,
> Healthy, and wealthy, if men carefull are. . . .

In spite of such delights Hayman is conscious of the eternal problem of getting English women to live in Canada:

> Sweet creatures, did you truely understand
> The pleasant life you'd live in *Newfound-land*,
> You would with *teares* desire to be brought thither. . . .

The tiny renaissance—or naissance—of literature in English in Newfoundland was short-lived. Modest as it was in quantity and quality, however, we have to wait until after the coming of the Loyalists towards the end of the eighteenth century before anything better developed in Canada.

In 1621, the year Robert Hayman probably became governor of Newfoundland, King James I made an enormous grant of land between the Gaspé Peninsula and what is now Maine to his fellow Scotsman, Sir William Alexander (1567?–1640), later Earl of Stirling. Alexander almost immediately made a sub-grant to Sir Robert Gordon of Lochinvar (1580–1656) in Cape Breton or New Galloway. There were several vigorous attempts at settlement, complicated by rivalries among the settlers themselves and by war with France. The dispute about Nova Scotia–Acadia, in fact, was only the symptomatic beginning of the long and bitter struggle for Canada as a whole.

Hayman had been optimistic about Alexander's projects, when, in *Quodlibets*, he had written: "Old *Scotland* you made happy by your birth, / *New-Scotland* you will make a happy earth." But the Scots of Nova Scotia inspired even less of literary merit than the English and Welsh of Newfoundland. Lochinvar's *Encouragements for such as shall have intention to be undertakers of the New Plantation of Cape Breton* . . . (1625) is precise, clear, and practical, but undistinguished; Alexander's *An Encouragement to Colonies* (1624) is scholarly and pedantic and lacks the inspiration of direct experience. Alexander was, of course, a poet, but most of his poetry was written before James's grant of 1621 and shows no debt to the New World, although his *Encouragement* does seem, at times, to be fired by his poetic imagination. In 1613 he had written an addition to Sir Philip Sidney's prose romance, *Arcadia*, and "the curious reader can detect some traces of the influence of the *Arcadia* in the brocaded prose of Alexander's *Encouragement to Colonies*."[22]

While the settlers of Newfoundland and Nova Scotia were trying to lay foundations, others were still building castles in the air of the Northwest. Hard as life in pioneer settlements is, the good settler has an essentially domestic mind which leads him to clear woods, build houses, and till the soil. But the New World was also built by those who moved through unpathed waters and unmapped forests. The strains run through American life and through human nature itself.

The dream of a northwestern passage to Cathay persisted. "The desire of Riches in some, of Knowledge in others, hath long wheted mens industries, to finde out a more compendious way to the East Indies . . ." (Purchas, XIV, 297). For Henry Briggs, the mathematician, in his *Treatise on the North-West Passage to the South Sea*, . . . (1622), the way lay through the ever-beckoning Strait of Anian "where are seated (as they fable) the large kingdomes of Cebola and Quivira, having great and populous Cities of civill people; whose houses are said to bee five stories high . . ." (Purchas, XIV, 424).

The dream ended for a long time in the frozen reality of the northern seas. After a winter of smouldering hatreds and personal feuds, Henry Hudson's men baulked at the terrors of bleak rocks shrouded in frost and mist, and set their captain adrift in an open boat. Button, Hall, Baffin, Bylot, Hawkridge, Luke Foxe, and Thomas James were all to follow Hudson to the Northwest. But with the return of Foxe and James, who had sailed independently and met one another, in August 1631, near Cape Henrietta Maria, at the western entrance to James Bay, the voyages were over for more than a century until Captain Christopher Middleton set out, once more, in 1742.

If the voyagers to the Northwest did not gain their ultimate objective, at least they left many of their names on the map of Canada. If they are not great literature themselves, the voyagers' accounts at least helped to inspire great literature later on, "and as we read [Coleridge's "The Ancient Mariner"] we catch again the very savour of countless phrases in Hakluyt, Purchas and James." "That stubborn and pious old Bristol seaman, Captain Thomas James had provided in his *Strange and Dangerous Voyage*, with a certain grim satisfaction in his hardships, the raw material for a new *Inferno*, all ice; and Coleridge could no more have escaped in Bristol the shade of his ancient fellow-townsman than the Wedding-Guest could have given the ancient mariner the slip."[23]

It is natural that with the English settlements established—however precariously—in Newfoundland and Nova Scotia, and with the establishment of "The Governor and Company of Adventurers of England trading into Hudson's Bay," after 1670, information about Canada in England should increase. But the information takes the form largely of petitions from the colonists to the government at home, acts to encourage trade, treaties with, and accounts of war against, France. The "literature" on Canada, in fact, becomes more "official" and moves away from such charm as is found in Whitbourne, where facts and sound practical advice mingle with fancies and quaint conceits.

As the seventeenth century goes on the New World finds more factual and informed expression in England. Sir Francis Bacon was one of the first writers to put the voyagers' accounts to critical tests, and he significantly acknowledges having taken one piece of information from "an intelligent merchant who had carried out a colony to Newfoundland." References to

Canada in literature proper are still meagre, although the ones that there are tend to become more specific. Thomas Heywood in *Londons Peaceable Estate* (1639) refers to "Harber-grace in Newfoundland," and William Drummond of Hawthornden, poet-friend of Sir William Alexander, in an *Entertainment of King Charles* (1633), speaks of one of the characters as having "attyre . . . of divers coloured feathers, which shew her to bee an American, and to represent new Scotland."[24]

In the ballad literature of the seventeenth century Canada is not mentioned at all, and, oddly enough, while there are half-a-dozen ballads on Cromwell's war with Spain in the West Indies, there are none—or at least none have survived—on England's struggles with France in Canada (but see p.856, l. 31).

It is natural, perhaps, that interest in the New World as a subject for literature should still concentrate on the Indies, the long-standing rivalry between England and Spain, and the cruelty of the Spaniards to the natives. Spanish cruelty had dramatic possibilities and was a convenient vehicle in which to express the idea of "the noble savage." It is easier to visualize innocent, primitive man in the sun-lit lands of the south, than to picture him squatting squalidly through a long Canadian winter. In the work of several English writers the Spanish conqueror became a symbol of the corrupt civilization which degraded natural man, hitherto happy in his long, golden days of nature. On the whole, the "noble savage" reached greater theoretical and philosophical expression in France than he did in England, in the writings of such men as Montaigne, Montesquieu, and Rousseau. In that gay, charming, anti-clerical, half-charlatan Baron Lahontan, in fact, France produced both a voyager and "un 'philosophe,' qui dépasse en hardiesse bien des 'philosophes.' "[25]

In England, however, the noble savage appears on the stage in Sir William D'Avenant's *The Cruelty of the Spaniards in Peru* (1658), which shows us the happy state of the natives before the Spaniards arrive, and even shows us —in dumb show—one Spaniard "basting an Indian Prince which is roasted at an artificial fire." In Sir Robert Howard's *The Indian Queen* (written in 1662) and in John Dryden's sequel, *The Indian Emperor* (first acted in 1665), the selfless innocence of Indian life is once more contrasted with the rapacity of the "civilized" Spaniards.

The seventeenth century seems to have produced no literary work with Canada as its main subject, and even the plays of John Crowne (1640?-1703?), who spent seven or eight years in Nova Scotia and New England, show no trace of Canadian influence.

At last, however, John Dennis (1657-1734) moves the noble savage to Canada in his play *Liberty Asserted* (1704), "a Satyr upon Arbitrary Power, a Satyr upon the Government of the French." The play deals with the struggle, in Canada, between the French and Hurons on one side and the English and

Iroquois on the other. There is no local colour, however, and Canada is merely described, in Dennis's preface, as "a vast Tract Land in Northern America, on the Back of New England and New York." Ulamor, the General of the Five Nations, is a very noble savage indeed, and a fast friend of the gallant English General Beaufort. Both Ulamor and Beaufort love Irene, the daughter of chief Zephario of the Angians, but Beaufort nobly renounces his sweetheart in favour of his friend and, as Zephario says:

> The English always were a gallant nation,
> And foes to Force and friends to Liberty.

After a peace, the French under Frontenac perfidiously break their word, but when Frontenac discovers that Ulamor is really his son by the Huron Princess, Sakia, even that hardened old warrior relents, repudiates the tyranny of his government, and accepts Ulamor's offer—"I'll make thee King of all Canadian France."

The play, which seems to have been quite popular, has a promising dramatic situation, a tightly knit plot, and moving moments often shattered by lines of appalling banality. Canada, in name if not in spirit, had made its début on the London stage.

Six years after the first performance of *Liberty Asserted*, the London public had a chance to satisfy its curiosity about the noble savage at first hand when four Iroquois "Kings of Canada" visited England. (Indians had, of course, been brought back to England occasionally from the time of the Cabots, and frequently from about the beginning of the seventeenth century.) The four kings had an audience with Queen Anne, dined with the Duke of Ormonde, were "mightily pleased with their reception at Whitehall," saw a literally riotous performance of *Macbeth* at the Haymarket Theatre, and did not "refuse a Glass of Brandy or strong Liquor from any hands that offer it." In short, they received the kind of hospitality that an Englishman expects to find in America today. Ballads, pamphlets, poems, dramatic epilogues, engravings of the kings themselves, poured from the press. Addison, Steele, Swift, and Defoe wrote about them. A group of young bloods even called themselves "mohocks" and acted in a natural manner which terrified the citizens and brought the young bloods into conflict with the authorities.[26]

Canada had now made a definite literary and physical impact on the old world of England. But, for English literature in the eighteenth century, Canada was merely a minor vehicle, and the elemental force of the country lay tamed under literary forms and conventions. The early voyagers—plain and crude as their accounts usually were—are the real forefathers of later poets such as Earle Birney, for it is they who held in their "morning's hand / the welling and wildness of Canada, the fling of a nation."

2. Explorers by Land
to 1860

VICTOR G. HOPWOOD

I. EUROPEAN AND FRENCH-CANADIAN BACKGROUND

UNLIKE EUROPEAN CONSCIOUSNESS, which goes back directly to ritual and myth, Canadian consciousness, particularly that of English-speaking Canada, was born literate and historical. Thus the growth of European literature can be seen as a statement and restatement of myth within a continuous community, while Canadian literature faces from the start the problem of creating from the record according to a sense of history. The contrast is particularly sharp for those elements of consciousness which correspond to the foundation myths of primitive society and their expression in epic and related literature. The proto-form of our still largely unwritten foundation literature is the record of our explorers, fur traders, and pioneers.

Our explorers and fur traders left much fair to excellent writing, although the bulk of what they produced is simply historical source material. Few people were actually engaged in exploration and the fur trade, but of these a large proportion were literate since both activities require records, the ubiquitous log or journal from which more subtle forms of writing can evolve. Further, there was an interest in the homelands in discoveries, and a guaranteed market for accounts of them.

Canadian culture is marked by the parallel growth of two Canadian literatures, one in English and one in French. Each began within a parent European literature, slowly developed its own characteristics, and took its departure from its mother culture in the European metropolis. In the case of English Canadian literature at least, the new literature was modified by the influence of the more quickly maturing extension of British culture to the south.

Even before Canada was actually settled by Europeans the story of French exploration in North America appeared in English literature. Florio's translation (1580) of Jacques Cartier's account of the first two of his three voyages to Canada in the early sixteenth century reappears in the second edition of Hakluyt's *Principal Navigations* (1598–1600) along with such English voyages as those of John Cabot and Humphrey Gilbert. Hakluyt added a translation of the third voyage.

Today, every Canadian school child hears the story, either in English or in French, of how Jacques Cartier first found the great gulf he named for St. Lawrence, and a country called Canada. On his second voyage he sailed up the St. Lawrence, and wrote in his chronicle, "On both shores of it we began to see as goodly a countrey as possibly can with eye be seene," and thus started the historical process of creating an image of the new land. From Cartier's account of his voyages numerous events have become part of Canadian consciousness—Cartier raising the fleur-de-lis and cross, Cartier seizing two friendly Indians to take home as exhibits, Cartier's party nearly dying of scurvy during the winter until the Indians showed them how to make medicine from the "anneda" tree, possibly the white cedar or *arbor vitae*. And along with such stories, occasional phrases echo from Cartier's chronicle, such as the later translation of his description of the Labrador shore, "the land that God gave Cain."

The second great English collection of voyages, *Purchas His Pilgrimes* (1625), contains a translation of Champlain's account of his first voyage to North America in 1603, *Des Sauvages*. In the same collection also appears the tragic story of Henry Hudson.

Samuel de Champlain (1570?–1635) is certainly the central figure and writer of the French exploration of Canada inland from the sea. He was responsible, personally and through his agents, for the basic exploration of the St. Lawrence and its tributaries. From that valley, French explorers spread out to the Mississippi and the Gulf of Mexico, to Hudson Bay, to the prairies and the foot of the Rockies. After the British conquest, French-Canadian voyageurs pressed on with the explorers of the North West Company to the Arctic and the Pacific. The St. Lawrence became the portal of half a continent, the symbol of a nation's founding, expansion, and unity, a recurring theme in the poetry and romance of the new country.

After Purchas published Champlain's account of his first visit to the St. Lawrence, no more of his writings were translated into English until the nineteenth century. Nevertheless, the story of Champlain entered English-Canadian consciousness through various interpreters and popularizers. In the translations are found memorable images of the founding of Canada, all expressed in grave and unassuming narrative: the raising of buildings at Quebec, the fateful campaign against the Iroquois, the winter with the Hurons. From these and other incidents of the struggle of Champlain to establish New France emerges our picture of Champlain himself, the prototype in Canadian consciousness of the French administrator, pioneer, soldier, and explorer. Companion figures to Champlain in this tradition are the later explorers, La Salle and La Vérendrye.

The missionary explorer is a second major type, originating in the *Jesuit Relations,* a series of narratives, set down mainly between 1632 and 1679 by various members of the Jesuit order, telling of the progress of their missions. Written by men trained to observe and record, the *Relations* are basic documents of Canadian literature, history, ethnology, and geography. The character and quality of the writings are as varied as the men who wrote them: often crude, but frequently vivid in description and expressive of powerful feeling; sometimes wearisome in detail, but often dramatic in conflict and story. At their best, the *Relations* are well described by the man who first Englished them in full at the end of the nineteenth century, Reuben Gold Thwaites:

> [The narrator's] meaning is seldom obscure. We gain from his pages a vivid picture of life in the primeval forest, as he lived it; we seem to see him upon his long canoe journeys, squatted amidst his dusky fellows, working his passage at the paddles, and carrying cargoes upon the portage trail; we see him the butt and scorn of the savage camp, sometimes deserted in the heart of the wilderness, and obliged to wait for another flotilla or to make his way alone as best he can. Arrived at last, at his journey's end, we often find him vainly seeking for shelter in the squalid huts of the natives, with every man's hand against him, but his own heart open to them all. We find him, even when at last domiciled in some faraway village, working against hope to save the unbaptized from eternal damnation; we seem to see the rising storm of opposition, invoked by native medicine men,—who to his seventeenth century imagination seem devils indeed,—and at last the bursting climax of superstitious frenzy which sweeps him and his before it.

Thwaites's description touches on the dramatic heart of the *Relations*, the conflict between the Jesuits' evangelical zeal and the beliefs of primitive nomads, between feudal theology and Stone Age superstition. From this matrix emerge the various figures of the drama—Lalemant, the gentle martyr; Brébeuf, the lion of the faith; Marquette, the proselytizing pathfinder of the wilderness. Behind the devotion and the strength we can see the more problematical qualities which helped produce the many martyrdoms, such as the over-zealousness of Father Jogues and the *donné* Goupil in teaching Iroquois children to make the sign of the cross against the wishes of their parents.

The most famous part of the Jesuit chronicles is the tragic story of the victims of the French-Dutch struggle, the Huron Indians and Jesuit missionaries massacred by the Iroquois. Short English versions of this story were available even before general translation, and the story itself has been the inspiration for literary works in English as well as French, including the poems "Père Lalement" by Marjorie Pickthall and *Brébeuf and his Brethren* by E. J. Pratt.

His ability to grasp the conflicts in the life of New France made the American historian Francis Parkman the outstanding interpreter of early French-Canadian society to readers of English. Parkman's work has been preeminent because of his wide acquaintance with the original sources, his direct experience of the Indian reaction to Europeans, and his gift for vigorous description, in addition to his strong sense of character and drama. Modern historians tend to be sceptical of imaginative attempts like Parkman's to make the past live, but the fact is that it is Parkman's Champlain, Frontenac, Father Jogues, La Salle, and Pontiac which have become fixed in the minds of English-speaking Canadians.

Unlike the political and religious explorers, the majority of French fur traders left indifferent narratives or none at all. The *coureurs de bois*, often illiterate, and frequently operating illegally, had seldom the ability or the desire to record their wanderings and transactions. Among them were many important explorers and historical figures, but we are concerned with two only, Radisson and Groseilliers, for their adventures are contained in a manuscript which may well be the first primary account in English of Canadian land exploration.

II. FROM THE BAY

Pierre Esprit Radisson's *Voyages* were written in England in 1668–69 to impress Charles II and various courtiers and merchants. The manuscript of the *Voyages* that has survived is either an original in Radisson's English or a translation from a lost manuscript in French. In the latter case, the founders of the Hudson's Bay Company paid for a translation of almost dazzling illiteracy. English syntax and diction have seldom been murdered as wildly as in Radisson's *Voyages*, a fact which seems to give them a life all their own. They describe an uncertain number of fur-trading journeys taking place at uncertain dates early in the second half of the seventeenth century.

The *Voyages* express a great new insight into the geography of the continent in the form of a traveller's narrative as admirable for its qualities as fiction as for its real adventures and its ideas. Radisson in his third voyage makes a doubtful claim to have been with Médard Chouart des Groseilliers on his trip to Lake Michigan and beyond. In the fourth voyage he makes a dubious assertion that Groseilliers and he reached the Northern Sea from Lake Superior. In spite of the mixed truth and fancy, Radisson's story contains a new and brilliant concept—that the centre of North American fur production was more accessible by Hudson Bay than by the St. Lawrence. The idea was not acceptable in New France, and the two *coureurs de bois* went to England for support. The outcome was the founding of the Hudson's Bay Company.

The psychology of the *coureur de bois* is well expressed by Radisson, for example in the contempt he shows for some faint-hearted Frenchmen who turned back to civilization when confronted with the Iroquois. He describes these men as "Gaillards" who only desire to do well, and then proceeds to contrast their idle boasting with the deeds of real woodsmen. Elsewhere, in a few words, he conveys the individualism of the trader, the eager welcome of the Indians to the bringer of invaluable European goods, and the power the goods gave the trader over the Indian:

> We weare Cesars, being nobody to contradict us. We went away free from any burden, whilst those poore miserable thought themselves happy to carry our Equipage, for the hope that they had that we should give them a brasse ring, or an awle, or an needle.

Radisson also expresses the vision of what America was to mean to the multitudes of Europe, though it is hard to guess how much is fancy in his description of the country south of the Great Lakes.

> The Europeans fight for a rock in the sea against one another. . . . Contrarywise those kingdoms are so delicious & under so temperat a climat, plentifull of all things, the earth bringing foorth its fruit twice a yeare, the people live long & lusty & wise in their way. What conquest would that bee att litle or no cost; what laborinth of pleasure should millions of people have, instead that millions complaine of misery & poverty!

Radisson's first two voyages deal with his adventures as a youth in the wilds of North America. Although they are not as important historically as the third and fourth voyages, as dramatic adventure stories they are scarcely to be surpassed. The first voyage constitutes a superb example of the story of escape from death by adoption, of which the Pocahontas and John Smith tale is the American prototype. The stories of John Tanner, Alexander Henry, and John Jewitt are later Canadian versions. After adoption, escape, recapture, and re-acceptance by the Mohawks, Radisson went with some young braves on a hunting and war party to the west of the Appalachians. Few if any white men had yet penetrated that wilderness, and, more important, Radisson saw his adventures on this journey practically from the point of view of an Indian. Radisson's final escape from the Mohawks, and his later return in his second voyage to Iroquois territory, this time with the Jesuits, is as wild an adventure as the rest of his career.

Radisson's English manuscripts also had their share of adventures. They came into the hands of Samuel Pepys, the diarist, and were in a part of his collection which was being used for waste paper by a London shopkeeper when they were saved by Richard Rawlinson in 1750. Eventually Rawlinson's collection became the property of the Bodleian Library at Oxford, where the Radisson manuscripts lay unnoticed until nearly 1885, when they were published.

The charter of the company formed to exploit the inspiration of Groseilliers and Radisson is not in itself a literary document, but its words are quotable and have attained some literary fame. Even the name, "Company of Adventurers trading into Hudson's Bay," has helped to cast a glamour over a basically commercial enterprise. The terms of the charter (1670) have a certain legal grandiloquence in their bestowal of almost kingly powers. The

Latin motto, *Pro pelle cutem*, has had the power to provoke speculation on its origin and meaning, ranging from variations on Juvenal (*pro cute pellum*) and the Vulgate book of Job (*pellum pro pelle*) through the idea of barter (skin for skin), to the facetious "Either way we skin you." E. E. Rich suggests that it refers to the process of making felt for beaver hats and means the skin for the fur.

After the Radisson papers and the charter, the early literature on the Hudson's Bay Company is disappointingly dull. In the 1740's, Arthur Dobbs, Henry Ellis, and others published attacks on the Company for its monopoly and alleged its failure to fulfil the obligation in its charter to carry out exploration. The Company's attempt to vindicate itself brought a counter-attack from Joseph Robson, an English mason who had worked at Fort Churchill. Robson's *An Account of Six Years Residence in Hudson's Bay* (1752) is memorable for a certain eloquence in its animus against the Company which had "for eighty years slept at the edge of a frozen sea." The same volume also contains several contributions to the mythology of Henry Kelsey (d. 1729), including the statement that the Indians called him "Little Giant" for shooting a grizzly bear.

The most complete known journal of Kelsey came to light in the papers of Arthur Dobbs in 1926 and was published by the Public Archives of Canada in 1929. It can barely be classified as literature, although much romance attaches to the adventures it tells. In 1690 "the boy Henry Kelsey" joined a band of Indians and travelled with them to the prairies, staying inland two winters. He was probably the first white man to see the Canadian prairies, to kill a grizzly bear, and to see an Indian buffalo hunt.

Kelsey is unique among explorers in providing a verse introduction to his journal, perhaps the first English verse written in mainland Canada. Poetry will never be Kelsey's chief title to fame, but occasional doggerel couplets are vigorous, such as these on the grizzly:

> His skin to gett I have used al ye ways I can
> He is mans food & he makes food of man
> His hide they would not me it preserve
> But said it was a god & they should Starve

Kelsey's journal, the introduction in verse, and an appendix on the beliefs of the Indians he met, are the earliest descriptions we have of the Plains Indians. There are not only sharp observations but also occasional touches of reserved humour, for example, with the medicine men who "by their singing will pretend to know w^t ye firmament of heaven is made of," some claiming to "have been there & seen it."

Antony Henday journeyed in 1754 to the prairies between what is now Calgary and Edmonton, nearly within sight of the Rockies. Henday's superiors were sceptical of his account, partly because he described the Plains Indians as having horses. His journal was published in 1907, by the Royal Society of Canada, from a copy in the Public Archives. It is clearly written and extremely matter of fact. Here is an entry describing a meeting with a band of the later dreaded Blackfeet:

16 [May, 1755] Friday. Paddled 30 Miles N.b.E. when we came to 30 tents of Archithinue Natives: I talked with them as I did with the others; but all to no purpose. Our Indians traded a great many Furs from them. They have the finest Horses I have yet seen here, and are very kind people.

This is a typical entry in the journal of an explorer or fur trader. Its form is like, and probably based on, the ship's log; it states daily, as relevant, the course travelled, weather, surrounding country, and incidents of discovery or trade. A useful record, it is usually tedious, all bare facts, all equal. Exploration tends to be repetitive, and the fourth or fifth adventure with a bear, boring, at least in the telling. If journals are to become interesting to the ordinary reader, they need suppression of repetitive detail, expansion with incident and description, and development of direction and purpose. The account may then be called a "narrative."

The model, and one of the best narratives of Canadian land exploration, is Hearne's *Journey from Prince of Wales's Fort in Hudson's Bay to the Northern Ocean*, published in 1795. It begins a series of major narratives, notably by Mackenzie, Henry, Harmon, Thompson, and Ross, all conforming more or less to a pattern. They are written in the first person, are factual, and derive their interest from the novelty of their material, their story of endurance, adventure, and discovery, and the incidental insight given into the character of the author.

In his dedication, Hearne (1745–1792) rightly describes his style as "plain and unadorned." Its other virtues include clarity, definiteness of statement, sure choice of appropriate detail, combined with quick and unfaltering transitions and a firm but not obtrusive prose rhythm.

Hearne's book describes his two failures and final success (1769, 1770, 1771–72) in walking across the Canadian Barrens to the mouth of the Coppermine River on the shore of the Arctic Ocean. From each of his two failures, Hearne drew the appropriate lesson. Indeed, one of Hearne's outstanding characteristics was his ability to learn both from his own experience and from the people he travelled with and among. This capacity, combined with expressive power, becomes a literary quality in an explorer's narrative, since, almost by definition, exploration literature expresses the experience of seeking and finding the geographical unknown. Here in Hearne's words is how a Chipewyan leader analysed Hearne's difficulties after his second failure:

He attributed all our misfortunes to the misconduct of my guides, and the very plan we pursued, by the desire of the Governor, in not taking any women with us on this journey, was, he said, the principal thing that occasioned all our wants: "for," said he, "when all the men are heavy laden, they can neither hunt nor travel to any considerable distance; and in case they meet with success in hunting, who is to carry the produce of their labour?"

In effect, Hearne adopted the Indian method of travelling to reach the unknown coppermines. He placed himself under the protection of an Indian of some standing, and lived the Indian life, following the nomadic wanderings of the band for fish and animals, while it worked its way generally towards his goal.

Hearne's *Journey* is interesting not only as adventure but also as keen and accurate observation of nature. Hearne was alert both to the facts and to many ridiculous travellers' tales which had been accepted as true. His description of the beaver and his debunking of the surrounding mythology are noteworthy. He analyses the beaver's anatomy, for example, and points out that:

> It would be as impossible for a beaver to use its tail as a trowel, except on the surface of the ground on which it walks, as it would have been for Sir James Thornhill to have painted the dome of St. Paul's cathedral without the assistance of scaffolding.

The historian Brebner has called Hearne's account of his journey "one of the classics of the literature of exploration," partly because of the author's "odd, judicious literary artistry," but also because it "conveys unconsciously a portrait 'in the round' of a very likeable and inquisitive, if somewhat timorous man." R. Glover in a recent edition of Hearne's work supports Brebner's opinion, except for the inappropriate word, "timorous." Nevertheless, the word points to something essential in Hearne's character, although grossly misrepresenting it. Hearne was willing to achieve his purpose by surrendering his command to the purposes of others. Possessed of the courage, persistence, and understanding to reach his goal, he still had an aversion to any struggle to bend others to his will. There was also a touch of the sceptic in his outlook, an attitude reinforced by eighteenth-century French rationalism or Humean scepticism. Hearne approached his difficulties with "philosophy" and found something corresponding to his own view in the attitude of the Indians. The result of his undogmatic attitude, almost at times complaisance, is a realistic yet sympathetic and discerning account of Indian life.

The *Journey* is one of the most sophisticated early journals and narratives, perhaps as the result of a bent more speculative and literary than was common among fur traders. Hearne is frequently moved to compare European and Indian ways, to comment on the effects of environment and custom on the outlook of people, and to raise such questions as whether Indians really benefit from European trade. There is also, one suspects, a touch of Dickens' fat boy in Hearne; he seems to like taking advantage of his cosmopolitan outlook to make his readers' flesh creep with accounts of outlandish foods and customs. He takes apparent relish, for example, in comparing the dish the Indians made of the contents of a caribou's stomach to a Scotch haggis.

Even before publication the literary and scientific importance of Hearne's journals was recognized by the French geographer La Pérouse, who was in command of the French ships to whom Hearne surrendered Prince of Wales's Fort (Fort Churchill) in 1782. La Pérouse returned the captured manuscript to Hearne, stipulating that he publish it as soon as he returned to England.

A few other eighteenth-century documents on Hudson Bay deserve notice. Mathew Cocking's journal of a trip to the prairies in 1772, published in 1908, is similar to Henday's. Isham and Graham, stay-at-home factors on the Bay, wrote accounts of the region's natural history, Indians, and fur trade. James Isham's *Observations on Hudson's Bay*, published by the Hudson's Bay Record Society in 1949, contains much information and the occasional piece of lively writing, such as the speech of an interior Indian on coming to trade:

> we Livd. hard Last winter and in want. the powder being short measure and bad, I say!—tell your Servants to fill the measure and not to put their finger's within the Brim, take pity of us, take pity of us, I say!

Andrew Graham's account of the Bay is still unpublished. In some ways it repeats that of Isham, although the natural history sections are more extensive. Both Graham and Isham indicate a continuing connection among a few of the Hudson's Bay Company employees with scientific organizations such as the Royal Society and the Edinburgh Society.

In general, however, by the end of the eighteenth century, a few years after the conquest of New France, the initiative in the exploration of the interior of Canada passed from Hudson Bay to the new British traders in Montreal. At the same time, the exploration of the northwest coast of America was beginning.

III. FROM MONTREAL

The merchants of Montreal who came to control trade up the St. Lawrence after the British conquest were from both Britain and the American colonies. Alexander Henry the elder (1739–1824), a New Englander fired by French-Canadian accounts of the fur trade, was one of the first white men to venture to the western Great Lakes after 1759. His *Travels and Adventures in Canada and the Indian Territories between the Years 1760 and 1776* (1809) is probably the most skilfully written fur-trader's narrative. Henry had a story to tell and made the most of it; as a result his book not only achieved immortality in its own right, but parts of its most exciting sections were incorporated almost word for word into Parkman's history of the Pontiac war.

At Michilimackinac in 1763 Henry saw the massacre of the English garrison which followed the famous game of baggataway or lacrosse. He himself avoided immediate death but was later captured, only to be spared again, this time by the intercession of an Indian friend who claimed him as a brother and then helped him to escape. The later parts of Henry's *Travels and Adventures*, while not so bloodcurdling, are still well written and interesting. When he describes being lost in the woods or crossing the prairies without food, he uses events, scenery, and thoughts to build up a strong feeling of anxiety and urgency. He reports the customs and legends of the Indians with sympathy and keen observation. Among the early writers he carried one of the lightest baggages of civilized preconceptions. To use social workers' jargon, he was not "judgmental"; he was, rather, almost pure adventurer. He reports what he sees objectively, with a certain amount of amusement, but nevertheless appreciatively:

The bear being dead, all my assistants approached, and all, but more particularly my old mother (as I was wont to call her), took her [the bear's] head in their hands, stroking and kissing it several times; begging a thousand pardons for taking away her life: calling her their relation and grandmother; and requesting her not to lay the fault upon them, since it was truly an Englishman that had put her to death.

Alexander Mackenzie's *Voyages from Montreal through the Continent of North America to the Frozen and Pacific Oceans in 1789 and 1793*, which was published earlier (London, 1801) than Henry's book, quickly went through three editions and aroused great interest. For example, Marshal Bernadotte claimed that the *Voyages* were smuggled into France and translated for him at Napoleon's command to provide information essential to a planned attack on Canada via Louisiana. Among the books Napoleon had on St. Helena were the three volumes of the French edition.

The "from Montreal" in Mackenzie's title was like a gauntlet thrown down by the Montreal traders in reply to the "from Prince of Wales's Fort" of Hearne's *Journey* published in 1795. It reflects the crescendo of opposition to the Hudson's Bay Company from the "peddlers from Quebec" who in 1787 sank their differences to form the North West Company. The voyages of Mackenzie were in a sense the first fruit of that amalgamation.

Mackenzie's *Voyages* opens with a history of the fur trade, probably written by the explorer's cousin Roderick, valuable to the historian but colourless. Yet even this matter-of-fact document grows lyrical over the beauties of the historic Methy Portage. The second and the third parts of Mackenzie's book are in journal form. The third, the most interesting, describes the crossing of the Rocky Mountains to the Pacific Ocean, where Mackenzie painted on a rock near Bella Coola the famous words, "Alexander Mackenzie, from Canada by land the twenty-second of July, one thousand seven hundred and ninety-three." Here Mackenzie unknowingly missed meeting Vancouver by only six weeks.

The *Edinburgh Review* of October 1802 touches shrewdly upon the attraction of Mackenzie's *Voyages*. It brings out, indeed, a thread of Canadian literature which runs from its very beginning right through to the present.

> There is something in the idea of traversing a vast and unknown continent, that gives an agreeable expansion to our conceptions; and the imagination is insensibly engaged and inflamed by the spirit of adventure, and the perils and the novelties that are implied in a voyage of discovery. . . . His narrative, if sometimes minute and fatiguing, is uniformly distinct and consistent; his observations, though not numerous, are sagacious and unassuming; and the whole work bears an impression of correctness and veracity, that leaves no unpleasant feeling of doubt or suspicion in the mind of the reader.

Mackenzie himself had a fair idea of the literary quality of his own book. In his preface, he carefully put aside any claim to "the charms of embellished narrative, or animated description." What he did claim was "the approbation due to simplicity and to truth." It is a claim which readers have found every reason to allow, although recent research adds an ironic footnote on the matter of simplicity. A preserved copy of parts of his original journal shows that the version published by Mackenzie contained a number of "improvements." These were made by William Combe, the creator of Dr. Syntax, who had previously edited Meares's voyages. An example is the description of a portage as "very commodious" which Mackenzie had called "good."

The power of Mackenzie's journal resides mainly in its story and the force of character of the man who wrote it. Prosaic and repetitive, it is nevertheless an account which enlarges the horizons of human knowledge and reveals the man, the very type of pushing Scot who has contributed much to Canadian development. Mackenzie overcame human and natural opposition by sheer drive. He had imagination, but it was not sensitivity; it was rather a compelling vision of what single-minded ambition could achieve.

Simon Fraser's journals describing the exploration of the Fraser River in 1808 possess to a superlative degree the best qualities of Mackenzie's journal. The brief account by Fraser (1776–1862) of his thousand-mile journey to the sea and back was included in a much-edited form in L. F. R. Masson's *Les Bourgeois de la Compagnie du Nord-Ouest* (1889). In 1960 a text of all the known *Journals and Letters*, properly edited by W. Kaye Lamb, was published. Some of Fraser's descriptive passages have been frequently quoted as catching the force of the river or the immensity of its chasm. The power of his description comes, not so much from diction or imagery, as from the sense of appropriate activity on the part of Fraser and his men—activity which in its turn is the key to our sense of Fraser's character. Anyone who has seen the Fraser River in its canyons must find it hard to believe that any human had the hardihood deliberately to descend it in a birchbark canoe or the power to command twenty-three other men to accompany him.

It being absolutely impossible to carry the canoes by land, yet sooner than to abandon them, all hands without hesitation embarked, as it were *à corps perdu* upon the mercy of the Stygian tide. Once engaged the die was cast, and the great difficulty consisted in keeping the canoes in the medium, or *fil d'eau*, that is to say, clear of the precipice on one side, and of the gulphs formed by the waves on the other. However, thus skimming along like lightning, the crews cool and determined, followed each other in awful silence. And [when] we arrived at the end we stood gazing on our narrow escape from perdition. After breathing a little, we continued our course to a point where the Indians were encamped.

Fraser's writing, as shown above, is blunt in statement, despite its clichés. The French expressions are in no sense an affectation. French was probably then the main language of the fur trade in *le pays d'en haut*, a sparsely settled Babel of half a continent, where English and some Gaelic were spoken by the masters, French by the bulk of the employees, and a score of languages and dialects by the native Indians.

Daniel Williams Harmon (1778–1845) was, like Alexander Henry, a Yankee adventurer in the Canadian fur trade, but far less colourful. His *Journal of Voyages and Travels in the Interior of North America* (1820), reporting his years, 1800–1819, in the Northwest, is generally marked by neither literary skill nor heroic endeavour. It is notable, however, for containing in its routine pages an intimate record of an inner struggle against the common practice of the traders of abandoning their Indian wives on returning to civilization.

My intention now is, to keep her as long as I remain in this uncivilized part of the world; and when I return to my native land, I shall endeavour to place her under the protection of some honest man, with whom she can pass the remainder of her days in this country, much more agreeably, than it would be possible for her to do, were she to be taken down into the civilized world, to the manners, customs and language of which, she would be an entire stranger.

Harmon's complaisance was eventually shaken by the death of a son and by his Puritan conscience. The outcome was a religious conversion and a rejection of his earlier intention.

We have wept together over the early departure of several children, and especially, over the death of a beloved son. We have children still living, who are equally dear to us both. How could I spend my days in the civilized world, and leave my beloved children in the wilderness? The thought has in it the bitterness of death. How could I tear them from a mother's love, and leave her to mourn over their absence, to the day of her death?

Alexander Henry the younger (d. 1814), the nephew of the author of *Travels and Adventures*, like Harmon kept a journal in detail for the whole length of time, 1799–1814, that he spent in the western fur trade. A transcript has survived, which was edited and published by Elliott Coues in 1897 as *New Light on the Early History of the Greater North-West*. The frankness of the author on all matters is sometimes the result of prurience rather than objectivity, but the journal has many interesting anecdotes and much information.

The pre-eminence of David Thompson's *Narrative of his Explorations in Western America 1784–1812* among travel literature is emerging belatedly but definitely, as has his genius as a mapmaker and explorer. Thompson never completed his *Narrative*, in spite of his constant rewriting of the work between 1846 and 1851. For some parts there are three versions as narrative in addition to the original journal record and some reports to the North West Company. Through the various versions it is possible to see his struggle to subordinate the great mass of his information to the narrative form, a process never finished, but carried to the point where Thompson's writing is the major primary work in English on the exploration of Canada. It is available in the edition prepared by J. B. Tyrrell and published by the Champlain Society in 1916 and in a more complete form in 1962.

One of the colleagues of Thompson (1770–1857), Dr. J. J. Bigsby, in *The Shoe and Canoe* (1850) describes him as a conversationalist, and indeed it is almost possible to hear the voice of the story-teller himself as we read the *Narrative*. Says Bigsby:

No living person possesses a tithe of his information respecting the Hudson's Bay countries. . . . Never mind his Bunyan-like face and cropped hair; he has a very powerful mind, and a singular faculty of picture-making. He can create a wilderness and people it with warring savages, or climb the Rocky Mountains with you in a snow-storm, so clearly and palpably, that only shut your eyes and you hear the crack of the rifle, or feel the snow-flakes melt on your cheeks as he talks.

As an example of Thompson's image-making power, here, from his *Narrative*, is the description of how the old Piegan chief, Sarkamappee, introduced Thompson as a boy to a young war chief. The meeting can almost be seen, and the words of the old man take on a mythic quality.

the war chief . . . gave me his left hand, and I gave him my right hand, upon which he looked at me, and smiled as much as to say a contest would not be equal; at his going away the same took place. . . . The old man now remarked to me that as we proceed [ed] on, we should see a great many Indians who had never seen a white man, as very few of them went to the trading houses. If one of our people offers you his left give him your left hand, for the right hand is no mark of friendship. This hand wields the spear, draws the Bow and the trigger of the gun; it is the hand of death. The left hand is next to the heart, and speaks truth and friendship, it holds the shield of protection, and is the hand of life.*

Thompson's descriptions of people, events, and scenes are direct and rich in detail. He uses figures of speech only occasionally, although probably more

*This quotation is taken directly from Thompson's manuscript in the Ontario archives.

often than the other explorers. Where he does use them, they are apt and forceful. More often than not they are in the mouths of one of the many characters who fill his pages, as in the above example.

The lesser units of Thompson's narration are brief descriptions or anecdotes, such as might be found in the author's speech. There are scores of interesting tales in his pages, each like a good nut, full of meat. Many a brief page or two contains what could be the kernel of a whole novel in its graphic description of events and shrewd revelation of character. Some of the anecdotes have a condensed epic quality which contributes to the character of the work as a whole. The following passage is an example of such quality, and also of Thompson's humour and his ability to catch the flavour of dialogue.

They soon broke silence, and Cartier [a Salish Indian chief] mildly said, You know our law is, that a man that seduces a woman must be killed; I said I have no objection to your law, to what purpose do you tell me this; the Orator then spoke, my daughter with her mother has always sat quietly in my Tent, until these few days past, when one of your men has been every day, while we are hunting, to my tent with beads and rings to seduce my daughter. Looking round on my men, he said he is not here, (on their entering my servant had gone into my room, I knew it must be him; the men and myself were every day too much fatigued to think of women.) But wherever he is, we hope you will give him to us that he may die by our law. I told them I had no inclination to screen the Man, but as they were much in want of guns and ammunition for hunting and to protect themselves from their enemies, if they wished me to return with those articles, and various others, they must give me a Man to take his place, otherwise I could not return; they looked at each other, and said we cannot find a man capable, besides his going among strange people where he may be killed; very well, then if you kill my man I cannot return to you, but shall stay with the Peeagans, your enemies; then what is to be done, exclaimed the Orator. I replied, let him live this time, and as you are noted for being a good gelder of Horses; if this Man ever again enters your Tent, geld him, but let him live; at this proposition they laughed, and said, well let him live, but so sure as he comes to seduce our women, we shall geld him; after smoking, they retired in good humour. But my men, all young and in the prime of life, did not at all relish the punishment.

The larger units of the book are the dozen or more major journeys and explorations which Thompson made, with visits to or life among new groups of people. These journeys give a picture of the life and customs of the Cree, Chipewyan, Assiniboine, Blackfeet, Mandan, Chippewa, Kootenae, and Interior and Coast Salish. Some sections record Indian myths, folklore, and beliefs; others describe animals and plants and their place in Indian life. Thompson's account of these matters must be considered to be especially authoritative, as he spent half a lifetime among the Indians, was the first white man to see some of them, and got most of his information directly in the language of several of the tribes.

All of Thompson's journeys and explorations fit into a panorama of tremendous scope, greater than that of any comparable North American work, stretching over twenty-eight years, including service in both the Hudson's Bay Company and the North West Company, and ranging from London to Hudson Bay, Reindeer Lake, the sources of the Mississippi, and the mouth of the Columbia. The unity of the whole work is both that of an epoch and that of the story of a fourteen-year-old charity-school boy who made himself into a great scientific geographer, able to say on the completion of his exploration of the Columbia:

Thus I have fully completed the survey of this part of North America from sea to sea, and by almost innumerable astronomical Observations have determined the positions of the Mountains, Lakes and Rivers, and other remarkable places on the northern part of this Continent; the Maps of all of which have been drawn and laid down in geographical position, being now the work of twenty-seven years.

The story of Jacob Astor's Pacific Fur Company establishment, Astoria, is best known as told by the American, Washington Irving. In his *Astoria* (1836) he refers, rather condescendingly, to "literary" and "scribbling" clerks although he drew rather heavily on their memoirs with only a perfunctory acknowledgment. Two such clerks were Gabriel Franchère (1786-1863) and Ross Cox (1793-1853).

Franchère's *Relation d'un voyage à la côte du Nord-Ouest de l'Amerique Septentrionale* (1820), covering the years 1810-14, was translated into English in 1854. With the exception of a few purple passages, perhaps introduced by his editor, its easy direct style is most appropriate to the simple almost archetypal story which it tells: a voyage from New York around the Horn to the mouth of the Columbia, adventures while trading for furs, and a journey by canoe across the continent to Montreal.

Cox's *Adventures on the Columbia River* (1832), referring to his service first with the Pacific Fur Company and then the North West Company, was written in later life after the author had returned to Ireland. There his work included journalism, an occupation reflected in the style of the book, which is not improved by the fashionable loading with allusions and quotations. As an historical source, Cox is unreliable, for he wrote largely from memory and hearsay. As a story of adventure, however, his book is quickly and easily told, and contains some humour.

Alexander Ross (1783-1856) is unusual among the fur traders in having written a series of books. Like Franchère and Cox, he was a clerk among the Astorians, and his *Adventures of the First Settlers on the Oregon or Columbia River* (1848) tells much the same story. It is a rambling and racy book, written with a keen eye for character. Ross had a satirical gift, and he did not spare either Astor's direction from New York of the affairs of the settlement or the officers of his fur company who carried them out. But it was not until Ross was describing Astoria after it had become Fort George, in *The Fur Hunters of the Far West* (1855), that his satire really flowered. Ross lost his seniority twice: once when the North West Company absorbed Astoria during the War of 1812, and again when the Nor'Westers joined the Hudson's Bay Company in 1821. To him in each case the villain was the bureaucracy of the North West Company; both the decadence and the romance of its last years appear in his pages:

The Bourgeois is therefore carried on board his canoe upon the back of some sturdy fellow generally appointed for this purpose. He seats himself on a convenient feather bed, somewhat low in the centre of his canoe, his gun by his side, his little cherubs fondling around him, and his faithful spanial lying at his feet.

No sooner is he at his ease than his pipe is presented by his attendant. He then puffs the Indian leaf in curling clouds. His silken banner undulates over the stern of his painted vessel. Then the bending paddles are plied, and the fragile craft speeds through the currents with a degree of fleetness not to be surpassed. Yell upon yell from the hearty crew proclaims the prowess and adroitness.

The books of Ross, Franchère, Cox, and the later *Traits of American Indian Life* (1853) and *Snake Country Journals* (1950) of Peter Skene Ogden (1794–1854) have a new subject-matter in the expeditions of armed parties of company trappers into Indian territory, according to the American system of obtaining furs. The change of atmosphere from Thompson to these men is instructive. Henry, Harmon, and Thompson seem at home among the Indians. The new men, brave as they were, seemed to walk with their fingers to the trigger, expecting and nerved for armed conflict. There is danger and adventure enough in these expeditions, but the sense of enlarging the known world that is found in Hearne, Mackenzie, and Thompson is gone.

Ross's last book, *The Red River Settlement* (1856), tells of the hardships of the settlers who were brought to the prairies after 1811 by Lord Selkirk, and who became the pawns of the Hudson's Bay Company in the last ten years of near civil war between the two great fur companies. Ross writes as if the Hudson's Bay Company charter was not only royal but divine. However, one-sidedness allowed for, the book is a moving account of the settlers and their difficulties, both natural and man-made, before and after the joining of the companies.

The Red River Settlement marks the beginning of the end of the rule of the fur trade over western Canada, although its dead hand was to linger on till after Confederation. After Ross's works there are few documents of the fur trade which can be considered literature. Samuel Black's *Rocky Mountain Journal* (1955) of his explorations in 1824 into the Finlay and Stikine River country is prolix, florid, and hard to read, although it contains some interesting description, especially of geological formations. The works of George Simpson (1787?–1860), Governor-in-chief of Rupert's Land, are routine and philistine and reflect a way of life which had lost its mission and become a matter of cost accounting. What other people say about George Simpson is more interesting than his own writing. John M'Lean's *Twenty-Five Years' Service in the Hudson's Bay Territory* (1849) gives an unofficial picture of the great man's rule and of company posts from Labrador to New Caledonia. Letitia Hargrave's *Letters* (1947) are lively, intimate, and discerning, but are less concerned with travel than domestic matters; her husband was chief factor at York Factory and she lived there 1840-51. The first missionary journals and letters, such as those of John West (1775?-1845) and Pierre Jean de Smet (1801-1873), indicate the end of the hegemony of the traders. When the painter Paul Kane (1810-1871) travelled west in 1846-48 he was consciously in search of the images of an epoch before it faded forever. *Wanderings of an Artist* (1859) is a lively and unpretentious portrait of the artist as a preserver of history, and at the same time it is the swan song of the "Old Northwest." Only a few years later, when Viscount Milton and Dr. Cheadle, an irrepressible tourist team, wrote their jaunty travelogue, *The North-west Passage by Land* (1865), the emphasis has changed from furs and exploration to settlement, mining, roads, and railways.

IV. THE NORTHWEST PASSAGE

In 1818, the search for the Northwest Passage was renewed with the voyage of John Ross (1777-1856); the Canadian Arctic became, as Jeanette Mirsky suggests in *To the Arctic!*, the stage for a drama which entered its climax thirty years later with the loss of the Franklin expedition and the beginning of ten years of search for it, after which the stage lights were dimmed for generations. The simile of a drama is apt, not only because many of the central characters appear and reappear throughout the four decades between curtains, but also because character and event lock in a chain leading to the Franklin catastrophe. Because of this unity, almost that of a plot, the voluminous literature of the nineteenth-century search for the Northwest Passage has a power over the imagination which in most cases is not intrinsic in the individual works.

John Ross's *Voyage of Discovery* (1819) set the pattern for the opening chapters of the voyages to follow. He rediscovered Baffin Bay, thus refurbishing the tarnished name of its original discoverer and restoring it to the map; he described the cliffs of crimson snow on the Greenland shore; he met and observed the famous group of West Greenland Eskimos whom he called "Arctic Highlanders." Unfortunately he imagined seeing a range of mountains closing off Lancaster Sound and his passage to the west. William Parry (1790-1855), in command of the second ship, did not make the same mistake; he was sent out again the following year.

The liveliest part of Parry's *Journal of a Voyage for the Discovery of a Northwest Passage . . . 1819-20* (1821) describes sailing right over what

Ross called "Crocker's Mountains" and westward through thirty degrees, almost halfway to Cook's nearest point of exploration east from Bering Strait. After the hopes, the noise, and the excitement, the ships were stopped by winter and had first to find and then cut an entrance into a harbour till spring: "The seamen, who are always fond of doing things in their own way, took advantage of a fresh northerly breeze, by setting some boats' sails upon the pieces of ice, a contrivance which saved both time and labour."

Some dramatic and publishing history arises out of Parry's winter in the ice, since the officers produced a number of London plays, including Garrick's *Miss in her Teens*. For Christmas they produced their own operetta, *Northwest Passage*, with F. W. Beechey as stage manager. Edward Sabine edited a weekly paper, the *North Georgia Gazette and Winter Chronicle*, certainly the first literary magazine in the Canadian Arctic, but there is little to glean from its combination of youthful facetiousness and pious reflections. Beechey (1796–1856) and Sabine (1788–1883) wrote books on their various Arctic experiences.

Parry and Ross both made further voyages into the Arctic, less significant than Parry's first as exploration, but more interesting for first descriptions of Canadian Eskimos north of Hudson Bay. Ross and Parry were verbose sermonizers, whose books are saved by the intrinsic interest of their material and their sincerity.

Parallel to Parry's and Ross's voyages were a number of land journeys from the interior of Canada to and along the Arctic coast. The most famous of these is the first by John Franklin (1786–1847), in 1819–22, reported in his *Journey to the Polar Sea* (1823). His *Narrative of a Second Expedition* (1828), is of lesser interest.

Like many of the best narratives of exploration, Franklin's are organized around a geographical hypothesis—in this case the existence and continuity of a North American Arctic coastline. Subordination to such a purpose is broken in the first book by an unnecessary introduction giving largely secondhand information about the travel to the point where actual exploration began. This slowness in getting to the intellectually significant and therefore exciting events is typical of the Arctic narratives of the time. The concluding third of Franklin's *Journey* becomes absorbing because of the speed and intensity of the events which he describes. The struggle to live, involving both starvation and cannibalism, is one of the most intense ever recorded. Franklin, with part of his expedition, survived—in spite of almost complete ignorance of life in the region—to set down an indelible image of the hostility to man of the Arctic.

Powerful as Franklin's description is when taken at its face value, it becomes even more dramatic when read with irony as well as sympathy, for we see in his *Journey* the seeds of his final disaster. A certain stiffness in the verbal quality in Franklin's writing, combined with a constant exhibition of fortitude and will power, raises the question whether the extreme horror of the events was not partly brought about by the character of the leader plus the rigidity of naval discipline. Such critical reading does not remove Franklin's major work from its place among the best told and most thrilling narratives of exploration. It does, however, point to the difference between a British naval officer's image of the Arctic and the developing Canadian one. The exploration of Canada's Arctic, like her Pacific coast, was in its beginning mainly a British enterprise which only gradually took on a Canadian character. And it was only as the experience of the Canadian frontier was transferred to the Arctic, and the knowledge of the Eskimos was incorporated into that experience, that our Arctic began to become "friendly" to civilized man. Even now, the image of the Arctic as a home for man has only won a beachhead in Canadian consciousness in contrast to Franklin's *Erebus* and *Terror*.

Franklin's journeys were in part written by his subordinates: Hood, Back (1796–1878), and John Richardson (1787–1865). The latter two afterwards conducted their own expeditions of which they wrote accounts, which did much to reinforce Franklin's image of the north. George Back's *Narrative of the Arctic Land Expedition to the Mouth of the Great Fish River* (1836), describing an attempt in 1833–35 to find Ross, lost on his second expedition, is among the more readable of the travel books of the period, in spite of Victorian diction and roundabout sentence structure. One reason is Back's sense of scenery. He was a landscape artist of considerable ability who had the gift of putting what he saw into words. Also, he was a much easier character than Franklin, enjoyed whatever company he was in, relished conversation and anecdote, and had some facility in catching them in words. His writing is cumulative in effect rather than strikingly apt in individual phrase and therefore hard to illustrate by quotation. What follows indicates the man and his prose at its relatively unimpeded best.

I took upon me the part of amusing the Esquimaux, by sketching their likenesses and writing down their names. This gratified them exceedingly; but their merriment knew no bounds when I attempted, what was really no easy task, to pronounce what I had written.

The works of two fur-trader explorers, Thomas Simpson and John Rae, introduce a more indigenous image of the Arctic. That their writing is little known is testimony to the dominance, even to this day, of the Franklin view.

Thomas Simpson (1808–1840), nephew of George, demonstrated how explorers could live off the country in the Arctic. His *Narrative of the Discoveries on the North Coast of America, 1836–39* (1843) published posthumously, tells of his four years of exploration in the Arctic, in which he not only traced hundreds of miles of unknown coast, but demonstrated that Arctic explorers could live almost completely on the resources of the country. His *Narrative* is competently written but strangely muted for so strident, egotistical, and persistent a personality. Part of the lack of drama is the result of his very capability as a wilderness traveller, a competence which prevented crises of the Franklin type. It is noticeable, however, that the writing, always clear and usually without affectation, becomes more expressive in the later parts. Simpson's character finds full expression in his letters which are outstanding for colour, forcefulness, and aphoristic derogatory characterization of his associates.

John Rae (1813–1893), as modest as Simpson was egotistic, is now becoming recognized as one of the greatest of Arctic explorers. His *Narrative of an Expedition to the Shores of the Arctic Sea in 1846 and 1847* (1850) describes the first successful wintering off the land north of the tree line by white men. Rae's writing is very plain, but it improves with each reading because of its economy, intellectual clarity, and sympathy with nature and men.

When Franklin set sail on his last expedition in 1845, all but a few miles of the Northwest Passage were known. Franklin's men felt confident that the explorer's prize of the centuries would fall to them and the splendidly equipped *Erebus* and *Terror*. They sailed into Lancaster Sound, never to be seen alive again by civilized men. Fourteen years later, and after the failure of nearly forty search expeditions, Leopold M'Clintock found the first of their corpses.

British naval officers commanded most of the rescue expeditions, and usually published official accounts, in addition to which their subordinates often prepared unofficial versions. For the most part these volumes are hard to tell one from another. With a few notable exceptions they are written in turgid prose expressing high moral purpose and a determinaton to conquer the Arctic; they are boy scoutish without a boy scout's understanding of how to cope with the wilderness.

The main discovery of the Franklin search was the Northwest Passage, although it was not actually navigated. In an expedition of 1850–54, Robert McClure sailed the *Investigator* from Bering Strait to within twenty-five miles of Parry's farthest exploration from the east, only to be forced to abandon his ship in the ice. He and his crew completed the passage—on foot. The story is edited by J. Sherard Osborn in *Discovery of the North-West Passage* (1856); and told by Alexander Armstrong, in *A Personal Narrative of the Discovery of the Northwest Passage* (1857), and J. A. Miertsching. The last was a Swiss Moravian missionary who spoke Eskimo; his book was published in German (*Reise-Tagebuch*, 1855) and translated into French (*Journal de M. Miertsching*, 1857).

Joseph René Bellot, a French volunteer, accompanied one of the expeditions sent out personally by Lady Franklin. Bellot's *Journal d'un voyage aux mers polaires* (1851), translated into English as *Memoirs* (1855), is one of the few flashes of gaiety in the final Franklin gloom. Although his work has little interest as history and science, it does present, as Leslie H. Neatby says, "a lively picture of a gay and intelligent Frenchman amid a shipload of Scottish Calvinists."

Two of the outstanding books on the search, *The Grinnell Expedition* (1854) and *Arctic Explorations: The Second Grinnell Expedition* (1857), are those by Elisha Kent Kane, the medical officer for the first and the commander of the second American expedition. Kane's prose is balanced and cadenced according to mid-nineteenth-century ideas of rhetoric, slightly verbose, but made tense by sudden colloquial statements—Kane's personality bursting through the Philadelphia norms.

Having begun to apply the approach of the American frontiersman to the Arctic search in the first expedition, Kane went on in the second to become a master of Eskimo technique. The Pennsylvania gentleman took to the life of the Greenland "Etahs" as though born to it, describing his contact with it frankly, vividly, and sometimes amusingly:

The kotluk of each matron was glowing with a flame sixteen inches long. A flipper-quarter of walrus, which lay frozen on the floor of the netek, was cut into steaks; and the kolupsuts began to smoke with a burden of ten or fifteen pounds apiece. . . . I broke my fast on a handful of frozen liver-nuts that Bill brought me, and, bursting out into a profuse perspiration, I stripped like the rest, threw my well-tired carcass across Mrs. Eider-duck's extremities, put her left-hand baby under my armpit, pillowed my head on Myouk's somewhat warm stomach, and thus, an honored guest and in the place of honor, fell asleep.

Kane's reporting is lively, but his intellectual comprehension of his savage environment is even more outstanding. Had there been a Kane among Franklin's officers, their story might have been different. As it is, Kane's hopes for the lost expedition twist in the heart like knives:

My mind never realizes the complete catastrophe, the destruction of all Franklin's crews. I picture them to myself broken into detachments, and my mind fixes itself on one little group of some thirty, who have found the open spot of some tidal eddy, and, under the teachings of an Esquimaux, or perhaps one of their own Greenland whalers, have set bravely to work, and trapped the fox, speared the bear, and killed the seal and walrus and whale. I think of them ever with hope.

How different the real story! The first definite information was brought back by the John Rae mentioned earlier. Here is what the Eskimos told him, according to his report in the British Parliamentary papers of 1855:

In the spring . . . a party of "white men," amounting to about forty, were seen travelling southward over the ice, and dragging a boat with them. . . . by signs the natives were made to understand that their ship, or ships, had been crushed by ice, and that they were now going to where they expected to find deer to shoot. . . . At a later date the same season . . . the bodies of some thirty persons were discovered on the continent, and five on an island near it. . . .

From the mutilated state of many of the corpses, and the contents of the kettles, it is evident that our wretched countrymen had been driven to the last resource,—cannibalism,—as a means of prolonging existence.

Rae's report roused horror when it was made public, and Rae was forced to defend his conclusions and his own integrity in a set of magazine articles which could be taken as models of closely reasoned argument. One set of such articles appeared in Dickens's *Household Words*.

The final solution of the Franklin mystery—a vindication of Rae's conclusions in all essentials—is told in Leopold M'Clintock's *The Voyage of the 'Fox' in the Arctic Seas* (1859). The story it tells is at once a summing-up of the Franklin expedition and search, and the most thrilling and the best-written of all the nineteenth-century books concerned with the Northwest Passage. Here is M'Clintock's arrival at the scene of the disaster:

The skeleton—now perfectly bleached—was lying upon its face, the limbs and smaller bones either dissevered or knawed away by small animals. . . . This poor man seems to have selected the bare ridge top, as affording the least tiresome walking, and to have fallen upon his face in the position in which we found him.

It was a melancholy truth that the old woman spoke when she said, "They fell down and died as they walked along."

M'Clintock's outstanding characteristic, which enabled him both to solve the Franklin mystery and to write a good book, was straightforward intelligence interested in everything. Nothing seems to escape his attention—men, dogs, wild life, the weather, the ice, the ship—all are set down in unencumbered quick marching prose. His description of the escape of the *Fox* from pack ice shows his observation, his style, and his affection for his ship—a feeling one would expect to find expressed frequently in sailor's narratives, but which turns out to be surprisingly rare.

Our bow is very strongly fortified, well plated externally with iron, and so very sharp that the ice-masses, repeatedly hurled against the ship by the swell as she rose to meet it, were thus deprived of their destructive force; they struck us obliquely, yet caused the vessel to shake violently, the bells to ring, and almost knocked us off our legs. On many occasions the engines were stopped dead by ice choking the screw; once it was some minutes before it could be got to revolve again. Anxious minutes those!

. . . What a release ours has been, not only from eight months' imprisonment, but from the perils of that one day! Had our little vessel been destroyed after the ice broke up, there remained no hope for us. . . . Should I ever have to pass through such an ice-covered, heaving ocean again, let me secure a passage in the 'Fox.'

3. Explorers by Sea: The West Coast

VICTOR G. HOPWOOD

TWO CENTURIES before James Cook arrived in 1778 at Nootka, the wave of Renaissance exploration broke just south of what is now British Columbia, leaving the northwest coast of America to be wrapped in myths as thick as its own fogs. The nearest authentic approach was Drake's in 1579, recorded both in Hakluyt's *Voyages* and in *The World Encompassed by Sir Francis Drake* (1628), the latter written by Drake's nephew of the same name and based on the notes of Francis Fletcher, the chaplain on the voyage.

After discovering Cape Horn and pillaging Spanish ports and shipping in the Pacific in one of history's most successful voyages of piracy, Drake explored north in the *Golden Hind*, hoping to return to England by the fabled Northwest Passage, safe from pursuit. The westward trend of the land led Drake to conclude that there was no Northwest Passage, and bad weather added the corollary that if it did exist, it was unnavigable. Here is Francis Fletcher's account:

The very roapes of our ship were stiffe, and the raine which fell was an unnatural congealed and frozen substance. . . . there followed most vile, thicke and stinking fogges against which the sea prevailed nothing. . . . Adde hereunto, that though we searched the coast diligently, even unto the 48 deg., yet found we not the land to trend so much as one point in any place towards the East, but rather running on continually North-west, as if it went directly to meet with Asia.

The *Golden Hind* therefore returned south and then sailed west across the Pacific, to make the first English circumnavigation of the world and to introduce a pattern for real and fictional voyages in English literature, echoing from its own time down to the character in T. S. Eliot's "Sweeney among the Nightingales" who leaves the estuary of "the River Plate," passes through "the hornèd gate" and reappears, leaning in through branches which "circumscribe a golden grin."

Purchas published in 1625 Michael Lok's story of the apocryphal or semi-apocryphal voyage in 1592 of a Greek, Apostolos Valerianos, usually called Juan de Fuca, supposedly a pilot in the service of Spain. De Fuca claimed to have been searching the Pacific coast for the Straits of Anian when he entered a broad inlet between 47° and 48°, "sayling therein more than twentie dayes" before arriving at a "very much broader Sea." At the entrance of his strait, De Fuca said, there was "a great Hedland or Iland, with an exceeding high Pinacle, or spired Rocke, like a piller thereupon." De Fuca thus added a new myth to geography—the Sea of the West, which turned out in the end surprisingly like the Gulf of Georgia and Puget Sound.

For the next century and a half, the west coast has its epics in fictitious voyages and its poems in the works of imaginative cartographers. As late as 1761, Thomas Jefferys republished a map by De l'Isle, showing the Sea of the West with the fabulous city of Quivira on its eastern coast, which almost touches the sources of the Mississippi. North of the Sea of the West, De l'Isle drew the strait supposedly discovered by Bartholomew de Fonte for Spain, according to a letter published in 1708 as his in the London *Monthly Miscellany*. De Fonte's maze of imaginary lakes and straits eventually led back to Hudson Bay. De Fonte's letter itself is probably a straight-faced imitation, such as Defoe might have written, of a traveller's tale. Amid such fantasies and speculations, it is only natural that Jonathan Swift should place his land of Brobdingnag in the neighbourhood of Vancouver Island and that the following parts of *Gulliver's Travels* should be located in the North Pacific. For those who like to see mysterious correspondences, the Indian myth of giant men, Sasquatches, in southwestern British Columbia, should prove intriguing.

About the middle of the eighteenth century, information began to reach western Europe of the explorations and trade of the Russians across Siberia and the North Pacific to Alaska. The great story is that of the expeditions under Vitus Bering (1725–30, 1733–42), including the tragedy of his death in 1741. The naturalist on the last expedition, the German G. W. Steller, wrote an account that stands out for lively and sympathetic description of animals, and especially for the earliest description of the sea otter, "a beautiful and pleasing animal, cunning and amusing in its habits, and at the same time ingratiating and amorous," copulating "in the human manner." The story of the shipwrecked expedition on the Commander Islands rings like a prophecy of the role of the sea otter in the international commercial struggle to come. The castaways lived in a savage state of disorder and misery

on account of envy and ill-will, making the animals shy by constant pursuit both day and night, and from the beginning driving them from the neighborhood. In the chase of these animals everyone tried to defraud everybody else and in every way and manner to cheat the more the nearer spring approached and the hope rose of being able to transport the skins to Kamchatka with great profit.

Reviving European interest in the unknown North Pacific was indicated by an article published in 1761 by the French sinologist, De Guignes, translating an ancient Chinese account by a priest Hui Shan of a voyage in the fifth century A.D. to what was identified as the North Pacific coast from Kamchatka to Mexico. The date of the possible but unauthenticated voyage is about the same as that of the legendary but not impossible voyage of the Irish priest Brendan across the Atlantic.

Spanish exploration, which had been dormant north of California for a century and a half, was renewed in answer to the rumours of the Russian challenge. On July 18, 1774, the missionary Fray Juan Crespi, who accompanied Juan Perez on a voyage to the northern end of the Queen Charlotte Islands, became the first European to record a view of any part of British Columbia. Two days later, a few miles farther north, near the northern tip of the Queen Charlotte Islands, a canoe came out from shore, giving white men their first sight of the Haida Indians.

While they were still some distance from the bark we heard them singing, and by the tone we knew them to be heathen, for they sing the same song as those from San Diego to Monterey. They drew near the frigate and we saw there were eight men and a boy in the canoe, seven of them rowing, while the eighth, who was painted, was standing up in the attitude of dancing, and, throwing feathers on the water.

A translation of Crespi's journal for this voyage is included in H. E. Bolton's book, *Fray Juan Crespi* (1927).

In 1778, James Cook (1728–1779) arrived from the Sandwich Islands (Hawaii), which he had discovered, to conclude his third great voyage of world exploration. Cook's explorations, in contrast to those of the Spanish, were made public. His two previous voyages had brought much of Oceania out of the dark of speculation into the light of knowledge. For Australians and New Zealanders he has become a national and literary symbol. It is surprising that he has not been given the same recognition in Canadian literature, since his historical role was similar, and his connection with Canada prolonged. He made his name as a surveyor in the estuary of the St. Lawrence River and in Newfoundland, after taking part in the captures of Louisbourg and Quebec.

Cook's narration is plain and modest, tending to conceal the fact that his voyages were adventures continually probing into the unknown areas of the world, more remote and difficult of access than Robinson Crusoe's island. In an age when the seamen were customarily flogged for even small offences, Cook maintained discipline with relatively few and mild punishments. Instead of keel-hauling sailors who undressed during the long voyages, he encouraged his crews to change and wash their frequently damp and filthy clothing— clothing which he was careful to see was adequate to the exposures of his voyages. He also first introduced the systematic use of foods that prevented scurvy. He won the loyalty of his crews, and men and officers enlisted for voyage after voyage. They created a legend about their captain, saying he could smell land when asleep and leap out of bed to appear on deck to meet some peril of the sea. Add his improvements in navigation and map-making, and we can realize that the west coast of Canada was brought into the light of modern knowledge by one of the geniuses of the modern world, a Newton or Darwin of geography.

In spite of matter-of-factness, Cook's narratives of his explorations caught the imagination of Europe. Coleridge's response to them is well known; their influence upon the writing of "The Ancient Mariner" is evident from a passage from *A Voyage to the Pacific Ocean . . . in the Years 1776–80* (1784), occurring as Cook on his third expedition was making his first approach to the shores of western North America, off the coast of Oregon:

Some parts of the sea seemed covered with a kind of slime; and some small sea animals were swimming about. The most conspicuous of which, were of the gelatinous, or *medusa* kind, almost globular; and another sort smaller, that had a white, or shining appearance, and were very numerous. Some of these last were taken up, and put into a glass cup, with some salt water, in which they appeared like small scales, or bits of silver, when at rest, in a prone situation. When they began to swim about, which they did, with equal ease, upon their back, sides, or belly, they emitted the brightest colours of the most precious gems, according to their position with respect to the light. Sometimes they appeared quite pellucid, at other times assuming various tints of blue, from a pale sapphirine, to a deep violet colour; which were frequently mixed with a ruby, or opaline redness; and glowed with a strength sufficient to illuminate the vessel and water. These colours appeared most vivid when the glass was held to a strong light; and mostly vanished, on the subsiding of the animals to the bottom, when they had a brownish cast. But with candle light, the colour was, chiefly, a beautiful, pale green, tinged with a burnished gloss; and, in the dark, it had a faint appearance of glowing fire. They proved to be a new species of *oniscus*, and, from their properties, were, by Mr. Anderson (to whom we owe this account of them), called *oniscus fulgens*; being probably, an animal which has a share in producing some sorts of that lucid appearance, often observed near ships at sea, in the night.

Proceeding up the coast, Cook found the harbour of Nootka, whose name was soon to be world famous. He described the mountains and forests of Vancouver Island, and the Indians of Nootka. After their first greeting of the ships, the natives

lay at a little distance from the ship, and conversed with each other in a very easy manner; nor did they seem to shew the least surprize or distrust. Some of them, now and then, got up, and said something after the manner of their first harangues; and one sung a very agreeable air, with a degree of softness and melody which we could not have expected; the word *haela*, being often repeated as the burden of the song. . . . the canoes began to come off in greater numbers; and we had, at one time, thirty-two of them near the ship, carrying from three to seven or eight persons each, both men and women. . . . One canoe was remarkable for a singular head, which had a bird's eye and bill, of an enormous size, painted on it.

Leaving Nootka, Cook went north up the coast, passing through Bering Strait and crossing back and forth between the northern coasts of Siberia and Alaska, trying to find a way through the Arctic ice. These explorations in the Bering Sea almost, but not quite, wrote finished to the geographic myth of the Northwest Passage. They also contributed further to Coleridge's poetic myth, for the account tells of the ice-blink, the fog and snow, the surrounding of the ship by pack ice, and the tacking back and forth to escape.

Cook's death in a fight with the natives of Hawaii in 1779 meant that the conclusion of this third voyage was told by James King. The voyage as a whole, like the second, was edited for official publication by John Douglas, later Bishop of Salisbury. Probably for political reasons as well as problems in editing and producing the lavish volumes, the official version was not published until 1784. Although all of the officers and crew had been commanded to surrender any private diaries of the voyage, private accounts were also published because of public interest, including those by John Rickman, William Ellis, and John Ledyard. Today, at last, an edition of Cook's journals based on his unedited manuscripts is being published by the Hakluyt Society under the editorship of J. C. Beaglehole.

The immediate effect of the publication of Cook's explorations was to open up the pursuit, almost to extinction, of the sea otter. The beauty of the gentle and sociable animal's fur made it a fitting garment for mandarins and wealthy merchants, and established a trade triangle of Northwest America, China, and Europe or the United States. Nootka Sound for a brief quarter of a century became a crossroads of trade and the centre of a major international political struggle. The world attention on Nootka meant that accounts of a considerable number of west coast voyages were published and records of many others preserved, of which a number have either some literary quality or the potential of becoming legend.

Cook's third voyage also established the structural pattern of the literature on British Columbia immediately following. Numerous accounts tell of a voyage from Europe or the eastern United States into Oceania, often touching at Hawaii, of bartering for furs on the northwestern shores of America, to be exchanged in China for luxury goods for the home market. Most voyages ranged the world, with the crux of the venture in the North Pacific. None of the wanderers settled in the New World, and most returned to tell their story and realize their profits in the original metropolis.

France was among the nations most stimulated by the publication of Cook's explorations, but the French Revolution and the following wars prevented many actual voyages to the Northwest Pacific. The first and most famous was in 1786, recorded in *Voyage round the World by La Pérouse* (1798, from the French original of Milet-Mureau); there is a brief part on the British Columbia coast. Like other French voyages, its structure follows that of

Cook's. C. P. C. Fleurieu compiled a description of the first French venture into the maritime fur trade in *A Voyage round the World Performed during the Years, 1790, 1791, and 1792 by Etienne Marchand* (English translation, 1801), written after Marchand's death. The book is remarkable for Marchand's perception, expressed rather loquaciously, of the aesthetic qualities of the Haida buildings and sculptures on North Island:

Can we avoid being astonished to find them so numerous on an island which is not perhaps more than six leagues in circumference, where population is not extensive, and among a nation of hunters? And is not our astonishment increased, when we consider the progress this people have made in architecture? What instinct, or rather what genius it has required to conceive and execute solidly, without the knowledge of the succours by which mechanism makes up for the weakness of the improved man, those edifices, those heavy frames of buildings of fifty feet in extent by eleven in elevation?

Mémoires du capitaine Péron (1824) tells the adventures of a French officer on an American ship, among them the rescue from the penal colony at Botany Bay of a number of prisoners, one of them Thomas Muir the Scottish reformer. The description of trading for sea otter skins is enlivened with anecdotes, including that of the sole survivor of a Boston ship seized by the Haida.

The first traders were usually British. The associated captains, Portlock and Dixon, published voyages independently in 1789, valuable for the historian, although pedestrian as writing (Portlock, *A Voyage round the World, but more particularly to the North-West Coast of America*; Dixon's book bears the same title). For literature, Nathaniel Portlock's voyage is significant because his crew included the seaman John Nicol.

The Life and Adventures of John Nicol, Mariner was set down from conversations by John Howell, an editor of more than ordinary literary tact, in 1822 and published by W. Blackwood in the same year. The story has the immediacy of first-hand experience, combined with an aptness of expression and a narrative speed which indicates that the old sailor had polished it through many tellings. It is a unique forecastle prose Aeneid of what is now the British Commonwealth of Nations. After visiting Quebec, Newfoundland, and the waters of Greenland, and serving against American privateers during the Revolution, Nicol sailed for the northwest coast in 1795 as a cooper and brewer with Captain Portlock. He observed that the Indians thought the captain a lesser man than the smith, who

was a smart young fellow, and kept the Indians in great awe and wonder. They thought the coals were made into powder. I have seen them steal small pieces, and bruise them, then come back. When he saw this, he would spit upon the anvil while working the hot iron, and give a blow upon it; they would run away in fear and astonishment when they heard the crack.

After returning to England, Nicol sailed in the crew of a ship to Botany Bay, Australia, carrying women prisoners, by one of whom he had a son. For years Nicol wandered the sea, in trade and battle, striving to return to his Sarah, only to find that she had escaped from the penal colony and could not be traced.

George Dixon's *Voyage* is livelier than Portlock's and makes some pretensions to style, not altogether successful, by taking the form of a series of letters signed by the initials of Dixon's supercargo, William Beresford. The letters describe trade in the Queen Charlotte Islands, which were named after Dixon's ship. They also describe the wretched condition in which Portlock and Dixon found John Meares and his crew on the Alaska coast, asserting that scurvy had been assisted by drunkenness, a statement which provoked a war of pamphlets betwen Dixon and Meares, notable for their virulence.

John Meares's *Voyages Made in the Years 1788 and 1789 . . . to the North West Coast of America . . .* (1790), ghosted by William Combe, is lively in description and forceful in argument, although these qualities are diluted with bombast, promotional rhetoric, and sentimental cliché. The narrative played a significant part in the struggle over Nootka which brought Britain and Spain almost to war. Meares was stronger on the persuasive lie and wily stratagem than on the truth, and when all else failed him, he used violence if he could get away with it. Thus there is both a detective and a human interest in the documents which surround him, particularly the polemics with Dixon and the differing accounts of how his ships were seized by the Spaniards in 1789. The version of this incident to be found in the diary of the Spanish commandant at Nootka, Martinez, is as partisan as Meares's.

Where his own interests were not involved, Meares was among the most perceptive recorders of the people and events of the west coast, and his writing at its best is sharply focussed, as can be seen in his description of the launching at Friendly Cove of the *North West America*, the first ship built in the area for which it was named.

On the firing of a gun, the vessel started from the ways like a shot. Indeed she went off with so much velocity, that she had nearly made her way out of the harbour; for the fact was, that not being very much accustomed to this business, we had forgotten to place an anchor and cable on board, to bring her up, which is the usual practice on those occasions: the boats, however, soon towed her to her intended station; and in a short time the North West America was anchored close to the Iphigenia and the Felice.

Meares tried to appropriate to himself the discovery of the Strait of Juan de Fuca, actually found by Charles Barkley. Captain Barkley was accompanied by his wife, Mrs. Frances Hornby Barkley, the first white woman on the west coast. She kept what is described as a "lively and entertaining diary," which was unfortunately destroyed in a fire; only quotations from and paraphrases of parts of it survive, one of which describes the above-mentioned discovery.

The founding figure for Canada's west coast is George Vancouver (1757–1798), second only to Cook among the explorers and mappers of the North Pacific. Where Cook sketched in bold outline the coast from Oregon north, Vancouver methodically filled in the details and mapped, named, and described many of the intricate waterways, islands, and headlands of the British Columbia, Washington, and Alaska coast. Vancouver's prose in his *Voyage of Discovery to the North Pacific Ocean, 1790–95* (1801) is clear but rather ponderous and uneconomical, based on accurate observation but lacking in drama and imagination. Its pace is slowed by sentences such as "Little remains further to add respecting the station we had just quitted, but to state the general satisfaction that prevailed on leaving a region so truly desolate and inhospitable." Whereas the Renaissance accounts of voyages treated geography and nautical detail boldly, Vancouver, even more than Cook, dwelt upon them to the point of wearying the ordinary reader. As a result, stories such as those of John Nicol or John Jewitt have greater immediacy than Vancouver's officially authorized narrative.

Vancouver's narrative does have its moments of excitement, for example, when he was sailing up Howe Sound, thinking for a few hours that he had breached the barrier of the coast mountains; but, in general, his story is interesting because of the massiveness of his achievement and because its events are surrounded by an aura of later history which makes his progress a succession of significant moments. By far the most interesting and human parts of Vancouver's story are those dealing with his meetings with the Spaniards. The warm friendship between Vancouver and Quadra, representatives as they were of contending powers, shines through the impersonal account.

> Senr. Quadra had very earnestly requested that I would name some port or island after us both, to commemorate our meeting and the very friendly intercourse that had taken place and subsisted between us. Conceiving no spot so proper for this denomination as the place where we had first met, which was nearly in the center of a tract of land that had first been circumnavigated by us . . . I named that country the island of QUADRA and VANCOUVER.

The first half of the name has been lost, and thereby more than half of the namers' intention.

The pleasant impression that Vancouver gives of his relations with the Spanish is confirmed by the narrative usually attributed to Espinosa of the surveying expedition of the two small schooners, the *Sutil* and the *Mexicana*, commanded by Galiano and Valdes. The expedition made outstanding contributions to the mapping of the waters inside the Strait of Juan de Fuca and left many Spanish names in British Columbia waters. The narrative contrasts very favourably with Vancouver's in its freedom from non-essential detail, and its observation and description of Indian life.

A number of unpublished and unofficial logs and narratives of Vancouver's ships, the *Discovery* and the *Chatham,* give a more human account of the expedition and a less Olympian and more choleric picture of its leader. There is a lively and uninhibited anonymous *Chatham* narrative, which includes a description of natives at Tahiti connected with the *Bounty* mutiny (Bligh was with Cook on his third voyage) and an account of the exploration up the Columbia River by the boats of the *Chatham.* Thomas Manby's journal gives a facile and flowery account of the pleasures of Tahiti and the Sandwich Islands, and an outspoken version of Vancouver's actions.

Archibald Menzies, the naturalist of the expedition, emerges from the multiple references of the various accounts as a most likable character, testy at times with Vancouver's arbitrary commands, but ordinarily a kindly and attentive surgeon. Menzies' own journal has been published in part by the British Columbia Archives (1923). Other naturalists have given Menzies' name to many of the plants which he first observed and described, notably the beautiful broad-leaved evergreen, the Menzies arbutus or madrona.

Against Vancouver's great accomplishments must be placed his failure to recognize the mouth of the fabled River of the West, passing it in April 1792 with the comment, "not considering this opening worthy of more attention". Within two weeks Robert Gray in the *Columbia* entered the estuary and named the river for his ship, making the outstanding American discovery on the west coast of America.

There are a number of accounts connected with the *Columbia,* and these have been collected into one volume, *Voyages of the "Columbia" to the Northwest Coast,* by F. W. Howay (Massachusetts Historical Society, 1941). In one way or another, each version reflects the heightening strife between traders and Indians. The narrative of John Hoskins, the supercargo, tells how Captain Kendrick of the *Columbia*'s consort, the *Lady Washington,* provoked a later attack: "He took Coyah, tied a rope round his neck, whipt him, painted his face, cut off his hair, took away from him a great many skins, and then turned him ashore." Hoskins's telling of the voyage unfortunately breaks off before the discovery of the river. Unfinished as it is, it still gives a forthright description of relations aboard ship as well as with the Indians. John Boit's log reveals that even the *Columbia*'s great discovery was marred by the savagery of the maritime fur trade:

At length a large Canoe with at least 20 Men in her got within ½ pistol shot of the quarter, and with a Nine pounder, loaded with langerege and about 10 Musketts, loaded with Buck shot, we dash'd her all to peices, and no doubt kill'd every soul **in her.**

The discovery of the Columbia River marks dramatically the increasing participation of the Americans in the sea fur trade. Accounts of their voyages published at the time are few, and tend to be unofficial, since each captain was interested in keeping his source of furs to himself. One account is that of John Jewitt, a British blacksmith, one of the two survivors of the *Boston*, whose crew was massacred in 1803 by the Nootka Indians led by their chief, Maquinna, who appears in many accounts, beginning with Captain Cook. While a captive, Jewitt secretly kept a diary which was published in a small edition in 1807. This was later edited for him by Richard Alsop of Connecticut into a longer work, *Narrative of the Adventures and Sufferings of John R. Jewitt* (1815). Jewitt's narrative belongs with those of Radisson and Henry in telling a story of survival by adoption. The story itself is fast moving and dramatic, the observation sharp, and the writing vigorous. When Maquinna's harpoons several times failed him, Jewitt made one of steel, with which the chief succeeded in taking a whale:

The bringing in of this fish exhibited a scene of universal festivity. As soon as the canoes appeared at the mouth of the Cove, those on board with them singing a triumph to a slow air, to which they kept time with their paddles, all who were on shore, men, women, and children, mounted the roofs of their houses to congratulate the king on his success, drumming most furiously on the planks, and exclaiming *Wocash—wocash, Tyee*!

The various Indians emerge clearly and distinctly from Jewitt's narrative, which, under the circumstances, shows considerable understanding of and liking for his captors. There is more than a hint in the story that Jewitt actually found life with the Indians pleasant. Perhaps some of his disparaging comments were made for the benefit of his New England public. Jewitt's own outlook is indicated by his editor's statement some years after the book was published that "he feared he had done Jewitt but little good in furnishing him with a vagabond mode of earning a livelihood, by hawking his book from a wheelbarrow through the country."

Another unofficial record of a trading voyage was kept by a seaman, Stephen Reynolds. His log for 1810–14 was expertly edited by F. W. Howay and published in 1938. The *Voyage of the New Hazard* is a forecastle view of the sea-otter trade in its decline. Predatory from the beginning, and conducted among a warlike people, it became increasingly violent and piratical as the competition increased, the furs became scarcer, and the Indians more hostile and better armed. The condition of half war, half trade emerges starkly in entries such as the following: "A canoe came alongside; the captain threw a billet of wood at her and stove her"; "Sold all shrowton [oolichan oil] and two slaves: one slave five skins, one three"; "fired a volley of musquetry, blunderbusses, and a broadside of large guns"; "tried to run them [two canoes] down with vessel, but wind light they got in shore safe."

If the relations with the Indians were near open war, the life aboard ship was brutal to a state of near civil war. Reynolds's log records a continuous series of arbitrary blows, floggings, cattings, puttings in irons, deprivings of rations, and mastheadings. The violence combined with the abbreviated ship's log style gives an essentially illiterate book something of the compelling power of art.

Mr. Gale ordered reef out trysail. Jack and Pace not hearing did not go aft. Gale jawed them, called them sons of bitches, etc., was very censorious. Jack said he was neither son of bitch nor boozer upon which Gale struck and clinched him. Jack made his defense and soon got the better, when Gale called on the boatswain, who took Jack away, who ran forward, Gale after him, got a handspike and struck him two or three times. Pace took the handspike away; he got it again and after Pace with it. The captain hearing the noise came up; struck Jack and Pace several times with the end of a rope and his fist. After the trysail was hoisted the criminals were sent to the mastheads till eight o'clock, when Gale called them down, made them take off their jackets and gave them a severe rope's-ending.

As the massacre of the sea otter came to its end, the ships deserted Nootka and other centres of the maritime fur trade, leaving no permanent mark save a cluster of legends. Between the voyages of the traders and the explorations of Cook and Vancouver, it had become certain for the ships of the times, in the words of Earle Birney:

> that there is no clear Strait of Anian
> to lead us easy back to Europe.

Ahead was rediscovery from the land and the "long endeavour to be joined."

PART II

The Transplanting of Traditions

4. Overture to Nationhood

ALFRED G. BAILEY

LONG BEFORE there were any people of English speech in what is now Canada, Englishmen had begun to frequent the coasts of North America. The fishery in the New-found-land and the northwest passage to Cathay had engaged the attention of Elizabethans, especially those of the West Country, in that legendary age of voyagings overseas. It has been the custom to think of maritime enterprise as the most characteristic aspect of the history of the period. It comes then as something of a surprise to learn, as we do from Professor Galloway in a preceding chapter, that the new world beyond the western ocean had so slight an impact upon the literature of the period. Hakluyt's compilation, of course, did something to bring the narratives of voyages to the attention of those who shared an interest in exploration with the navigators themselves. Yet valuable as these narratives are from this point of view, not all were possessed of sufficient merit to warrant consideration as literature.

Just as monastic chronicles grew from Easter tables, it is evident that the narratives of the seafarers often represented a development from the ship's log. Details of the new lands and of the people who inhabited them are generally meagre. In part this seems to be because of the limitations of current prose style. But it was also because the contest with Spain engrossed the attention of the age. Not until the early decades of the seventeenth century were permanent colonies established in the New World. Even then Virginia was more often the subject of minutes of trading companies, and of reports of propagandists, than it was an inspiration to the poets, and, with some exceptions, it did not itself become, during its first century, the seed plot of an indigenous literature. In this regard the contrast with the New England colonies was sharp. There the Pilgrims and the Puritans, stirred to the depths by the spiritual crisis of the time, wrote histories and theological treatises with the eye of God upon them. Whether in simple narratives such as Bradford's account of the founding of Plymouth or in the doctrinal disputations of John Cotton, Peter Bulkeley, and Roger Williams, the consciousness of being engaged in the building of a new heaven and a new earth was a constant factor.

All these developments were outside the territories that go to make up the present Canadian Dominion. Yet it is an illusion that literary and other cultural phenomena can be fitted to a procrustean bed of territorial nationalism. We make no concession to this illusion when we note the relevance of the New England achievement to the religious and literary stirrings of the Nova Scotian Yankees, much later, in the era of the Revolution.

These pre-revolutionary settlements did not take shape until long after the English had established outposts and colonies in Newfoundland and on the shores of Hudson Bay. The English began to frequent the coasts of Newfoundland in increasing numbers after 1550, in pursuit of the dry fishery, that nursery of seamen and source of "England's treasure by foreign trade." The technique of this method, in contrast to that of the green fishery, required the formation of semi-permanent settlements. Gradually these became more numerous, and eventually permanent. It is germane to the processes of literary history to remark that we would scarcely be concerned with the case of Newfoundland but for the stroke of a politician's pen that in 1949 brought that island in as the tenth Canadian province. By this fortuitous and, in some senses, irrelevant event the content of Canadian literature was increased, slightly enriched, and partially altered. The confederation of the island with the Dominion may serve to remind us of the degree of artificiality characterizing what we are accustomed to refer to as "Canadian" literature.

Canadians must nevertheless accept with gratitude the four centuries of living in Newfoundland, and the writing that came out of it, with which they are now most properly identified. They must equally regret the prolonged dearth that followed upon a remarkable succession of early seventeenth-century governors of literary tastes, notably Hayman, and other learned persons, products of the Mother Country, who happily engaged in the promotion of colonization in those days. Settlement might have borne fruit in a transference of creative effort if exploitation by rapacious merchants and the tyrannous rule of the admirals on the station had not debased the inhabitants, frustrating the normal growth of institutions, prolonging illiteracy, and isolating them from all humanizing influences except those that they could engender for themselves. The growth of balladry, and of new and distinctive forms of speech, is a testimony to the ability of man to improve upon adversity.

Twentieth-century scholars, in looking back upon the early history of Canada, may find it difficult to draw an inference of inevitability from what they see. The Dominion as we now know it could not have been predicted by the generations of men, both French and English, who began the task of laying its foundations in the seventeenth century. That it might have turned out to be quite a different thing, with ethnic and territorial components at variance with those of the present, may serve to warn us against the habit of reading back the modern mystique of Canadianism into earlier epochs in which it must of necessity be quite alien. The reader will therefore not be asked to join in pursuit of the *ignis fatuus* of the "distinctively Canadian" in the writings of the Scots who gave their name to Nova Scotia, but touched only momentarily upon the course of its early history. Neither, for identical reasons, will the narratives pertaining to the successive English conquests of Acadia detain us. Samuel Argall in 1613, the Kirkes in 1628, Thomas Temple and William Crowne (father of the playwright John Crowne) in 1654, and Phips in 1690, are indicative of a persistent English, and New England, interest in the region, but they cannot claim our attention as facts of immediate significance to the theme with which we are concerned in this volume. The narrative of the captivity of John Gyles among the Malecite Indians of the river St. John in the 1690's, however, is not without merit and relevance and a time would come when the New Englanders would claim and even occupy the coasts of Acadia in their drive to possess and exploit the wealth of adjacent fisheries, making records of their material and spiritual dispositions which in the proper place must evoke some passing comment.

For the moment a development of equal concern must engage our attention. We must seek for the beginnings of literary effort and activity among the peoples of English speech who by 1670 had begun the attempt to outflank the French in their pursuit of the beaver and other fur-bearing animals across the central reaches of the North American continent. At the moment in 1607 when Champlain and DeMonts forsook Acadia for Quebec, the French became committed to the control and exploitation of the valley of the St. Lawrence and of the tremendous hinterland to which it led. Almost at the same time that the English replaced the Dutch as masters of the Hudson Valley (1664) they began from their posts on Hudson Bay their inroads upon the northern flank of the great route to the interior which the French had developed in the face of almost insuperable difficulties. It all began with the defection of a French *coureur de bois* of romantic memory. In 1668 Pierre Esprit Radisson, enraged at the French governor, Argenson, who "did grease his Chopps" with the trader's hard-earned proceeds, turned up in England, accompanied by Groseilliers, with the proposal that eventuated in the founding of the Hudson's Bay Company. It has not been possible to determine whether Radisson's account of his adventures in the interior of North America was composed in English by himself or was rendered from the French by an anonymous translator. Whether original or not, it cannot be claimed as a representative example of Restoration prose. As Professor Hopwood has noted, its very illiteracy appears to have imparted to it a kind of primitive vitality, and in this regard, though in different degree, it has something in common with the narrative of Henry Kelsey, the boy who, a generation later, was the first writer of English verse on the Canadian mainland, and so far as is known the earliest to see and describe the Canadian prairie. For all its imperfections Kelsey's work, like that of Radisson, is enhanced in value because of the infrequency with which the merchant adventurers took pen in hand for any but the most mundane purposes. Not until 1754 do we encounter another record of exploration, that of Antony Henday, worthy of mention in a literary history; and not before 1795 did there appear a work of positive literary value, Hearne's relation of his journey to the shores of the Arctic sea. Detachment, sympathy with tribal custom, and insight comparable to that of a trained anthropologist, qualities of the man himself, informed his work and made it memorable.

Hearne stands out for his intrinsic merits and not because the contributions made by the men of Hudson Bay are, from a literary standpoint, so few in number. A greater volume of significant work, by contrast, came out of the North Pacific late in the eighteenth century, at a time when official explorations and claims by Russian, Spaniard, Englishman, and American, and the mounting conflict over the sea otter trade, drew men of many backgrounds to hazard their lives and fortunes in those distant waters. The memory of Drake's exploit, and the hope of finding the Strait of Anian leading back to Europe, had never been entirely lost; but something like two centuries divided the voyage of the Elizabethan, and the accounts of his enterprise, from the new men whose names are linked with Nootka Sound, the renewal of imperialist rivalry, and the later trials and excitements of geographical discovery. In his chapter on the literature of exploration in the North and West, Professor Hopwood has clearly revealed to us the pre-eminence over all others of James Cook, the greatness of his achievement and the worth of his narrative. For the writings of Captain George Vancouver one cannot make similar claims, since unhappily they do not match in literary importance the events which are narrated in such painstaking and meticulous detail. Other men who were in no way the equals of either of the two great captains were nonetheless the authors of unforgettable tales of the strife and hardships of the sea, and of the strange ways of the coast tribes, throwing at times a lurid light upon the beginnings of Canada's west coast province.

II

Very different in character from all this was the literary activity that already had begun to be evident in the old provinces of Nova Scotia and Quebec in the wake of the British Conquest. Port Royal, in what the French called Acadia, had in 1710 surrendered to a British force composed largely of New Englanders, a half-century before the final act in the drama of conquest was brought to an end by the capitulation of Montreal. The Treaty of Utrecht had confirmed the British in their possession of Nova Scotia in 1713, but between that event and the Treaty of Paris, which in 1763 transferred the sovereignty of the St. Lawrence to its new masters, the province by the sea had continued to be vulnerable to the intermittent, but always to be feared, hostilities of the French forces detached for operations in that area. The menace of Louisbourg, and the terror of massacre and torture at the hands of France's Indian allies, hindered, if they did not altogether prevent, a movement of people from New England into the northeastern area as a corollary of the expansion of the fishery in Nova Scotian waters. Only with the implementation of Governor Shirley's "Great Plan" for the destruction of French strongholds, and the transportation of the hapless Acadians, were those dangers at last removed. The conquest of such key points as Beauséjour (1755) and Louisbourg (1758), and the scattered military actions that followed, were recorded in such "illiterate" diaries as that of Sergeant Burrell, stationed in 1758 at Fort Frederick at the mouth of the St. John, as well as the more polished efforts of Abijah Willard, Joshua Winslow, and other officers engaged in those campaigns. Neither these nor the diary of Simeon Perkins, valuable as the latter may be as a source for the period of the American War, can compare with the devotional writings of Henry Alline from a literary point of view.

Professor Cogswell has drawn our attention to the need to take into account the pervasive influence of evangelical pietism upon the life of the people of the Maritime Provinces. It was to have been expected that the Great Awakening in the British colonies to the southward, and especially the disturbances created by Jonathan Edwards in his attempt to revive the Puritan theocracy, would have affected in some degree the several thousands of Yankee settlers who had found their way into the province of Nova Scotia by the beginning of the Revolutionary War. The great work of Henry Alline was to free large numbers of them from the fear of eternal damnation. His style is not quite equal to the gospel of charity and loving-kindness that it was his purpose to impart. But sincerity and depth of feeling carried him a long way beyond any other contributor to the devotional literature of the time. The Puritan temper appears to have had the general effect of stultifying rather than stimulating the growth of literary expression in these provinces throughout the greater part of the nineteenth century. Again it would appear that one must make an exception in the case of Alline. That religion was the all-absorbing interest of Maritimers of three and four generations ago is borne out by the large numbers of books devoted to the subject in any libraries which are still to be found in the old houses throughout the countryside.

Less remote from today seem the worldly gentry of the Loyalist migration who came in such numbers to the old province of Nova Scotia at the conclusion of the War of Independence, submerging for the time being, or so it might have appeared, the Whiggish and Puritan Yankees who had already established themselves to the eastward. It seems remarkable that a group containing such a large proportion of university graduates and members of the learned professions should have failed, with a few exceptions, to express in memorable terms something of the cataclysmic experience through which they had passed, especially when their triumphant opponents made such noteworthy contributions to the literature of political science. Perhaps they were left empty by the ruin of the War. Perhaps it was that, as champions of a counter-revolution that failed of its purpose, they looked to a past that had never existed for comfort and illumination. Understandably they could not rejoice in the new world of man-come-into-his-own that to many, on both sides of the Atlantic, seemed heralded by the birth of the Republic. They sought to realize their own ideals in the new areas of settlement into which they migrated. Though they were not all Tories by any means their coming greatly strengthened the conservatism of what remained of the Empire on North American soil. Their social attitudes, formed before and during the Revolutionary War, they brought with them from the old colonies to the new. Thus it is that colonial New York, New Jersey, the Carolinas, and the other lands they left behind them, are a part of the Canadian past, as is seventeenth-century Quebec; more so than Huronia of which hardly a trace remains, except archaeologically, and as a source of alien inspiration, frequently historiographical and sometimes literary.*

There was a sense in which Edward Winslow, Jacob Bailey, James Moody, Jonathan Odell, and other makers of what literature there was in the Maritimes were to have no successors. Reared, as many of them were, in colonies that had grown to something approaching metropolitan status, they were

---

*If one wished to state the matter sociologically, one could say that modern Canadians of British origin belong to the same "in-group" as the eighteenth-century New York Loyalists. But to all modern Canadians, even the remnants of the Huron-Wyandot themselves, the seventeenth-century Hurons are an "out-group." The Huron language is no longer spoken and the Huron culture is virtually extinct. The United Empire Loyalist is one of the great strands of a continuous Canadian tradition. The Hurons were deliberately selected for comparison in this chapter because they constitute the example *par excellence* of discontinuity in Canadian cultural history. Although the Loyalists originated outside present Canadian territory and the catastrophe that overwhelmed the Hurons in the 1640's occurred on Canadian soil, the territorial impact is not a direct one as it would be on the lower animals, but is experienced by man through the filter of his culture (in the anthropological sense). This is a literary history, and literature is the expression of a culture. The cultural frame of reference is therefore more fundamental than the territorial, and the Hurons are as "exterior" to us as are the medieval Persians. On the other hand it is worth mentioning in passing that there is a sense in which the Huron catastrophe is the most crucial event in Canadian history. They were much more numerous than the few thousand French in the Canada of the 1640's. If they had been left to multiply as did the English and the French, Canada today might well be a largely Indian state as is Mexico.

forced by the exigencies of the wilderness in which they found refuge to revert to the most primitive conditions imaginable. In the Thirteen Colonies a class structure had evolved and a degree of sophistication had come to mark the mental outlook of the educated and the well-to-do. While the majority of the Loyalists were not of this class, attempts on the part of the "gentry" to establish large estates were by no means lacking. The often extensive grants did not encourage the grouping of dwellings into villages and towns. North of the Bay of Fundy, in that part of the back country of Nova Scotia that was in 1784 erected into the province of New Brunswick, "useful men from New England" were fewest in number. Professor W. S. MacNutt, in a recent history of the province, states: "There was nothing to compel a man to live in proximity to and in emulation of his neighbours. The element that explained the remarkable local initiative of New England, the orderly development of townships that thrust responsibility as well as privileges upon individuals, was completely absent in New Brunswick." The hard labour of the frontier, absence of schools, isolation from stimulating contacts, in many cases a stultifying orthodoxy in the spheres of politics and religion, all combined to discourage, if they did not entirely prevent, a recourse to literary expression on the part of the generations immediately following that of the Migration. Not only in this but in other aspects of provincial culture, notably in architectural style, a deterioration was observable, which was not altogether attributable to the taste of the Victorians.

Students of Nova Scotian attitudes and institutions, as these took shape in the two decades that separated the end of the Seven Years' War from the coming of the Loyalists, will always be beholden to the late Professor Brebner for his admirable, and probably definitive, study of the Yankee populations who, in that interval, established their settlements, largely in the southwestern part of the peninsula nearest New England. The Nova Scotian Yankee had emerged as a variant of the New England Yankee by the beginning of the Revolutionary War. Caught between two competing imperial systems, he strove, sometimes ineffectually, for neutrality. His desire not to make irrevocable decisions in the matter of allegiance, together with the substantial material benefits to be derived from forswearing independence of Great Britain, engendered in him the well-known habits of "moderation" and "harmony" in the face of public questions. He was inclined to be a Whig while not being a rebel, and was thus able to accommodate himself, when the time came, to those Loyalists who settled in the parts that remained Nova Scotian when New Brunswick and Cape Breton were set apart in 1784. He exercised a leavening influence upon the Loyalists who themselves were not all political quietists, so that the whole people when the moment came would stand upon their rights without, at the same time, having recourse to extreme measures.

The province of Nova Scotia experienced a fivefold increase in population from 1784 to 1837, a considerable accumulation of capital from a widening range of industrial and commercial undertakings, from privateering on the high seas, and an enlargement of the means of intelligence through the establishment of schools and colleges, libraries and periodicals. Thomas McCulloch cultivated a zeal for education among the Scottish settlers in the eastern part of the province, while King's College at Windsor, serving the Anglican community, awoke among certain of the students, notably Thomas Chandler Haliburton, a taste for literature that was at once detached and urbane. These characteristics of the provincial Tory underlie the satires and caricatures through which Haliburton hoped to spur his countrymen to emulate the enterprise, both industrial and intellectual, of the Massachusetts Yankees. He was making, in essence, a response to a political challenge, an attempt in new and favourable circumstances to vindicate the choice which the Loyalists had made long before in the cataclysmic year of 1776, the choice between conformity with the principles of the Revolution and exile in a strange land. What he could not bring himself to see was that the only solution for Nova Scotia's continuing ills was to find a peaceful substitute for the American Revolution, an equitable middle ground between independence and subordination to a distant metropolis. It was the glory of Howe, with his political acumen, his clear perception of principles, his tact and moderation, that he was able, against bitter political opposition from the Tory oligarchy of Halifax, to bring to fruition an arrangement for provincial self-government, within the framework of the Empire, which accorded with the historic temper of his people. Howe's poems are relatively commonplace, but in the course of the great contest in which he became engaged he drafted a body of political statements that are forthright and terse, trenchant and perceptive. It is arguable that with the achievement of responsible government Howe's work was done, and that the province went forward to face the ordeal of confederation in circumstances that evoked no comparable literary response.

Later in the nineteenth century Prince Edward Island became the home of a poet, John Hunter-Duvar, whom the anthologists of recent decades have not forgotten, but no movement of national significance arose in the small island province. Almost from its founding to the moment of its confederation with Canada in 1873 its people were the victims of an intransigent system of absentee land ownership that depressed all aspects of provincial life.

No such conditions were to be found in New Brunswick but that province experienced an adverse set of circumstances that were peculiarly its own. It was difficult for a sense of provincial identity, or a common purpose, to emerge in a land of which the different parts were so isolated from one another, and among a people who had been so uprooted as were the Loyalist exiles. They had, as we have seen, been compelled to revert to the most primitive conditions of living in the early years of settlement following immediately upon the migrations at the conclusion of the War of Independence. The adoption of policies by the Imperial Government that affected adversely the prospects of the province, was followed, from the first decade of the nineteenth century onward, by the rise of the timber trade that gave New Brunswick almost its first and for a long time its only accession of wealth. But though it brought prosperity it did so at a cost. The trade was unsettling and retarded the growth of stable communities in which schools and related amenities could develop.

Better times for New Brunswick were in the offing when the momentary depression which had ensued as a consequence of the repeal by Great Britain of the duties on foreign timber, which had protected colonial produce, was followed by an attempt to diversify the economy. With railway building, reciprocity of trade with the United States, responsible government, and a series of educational reforms, the society of the province gathered momentum and a spirit of self-reliance began to replace the traditional sense of dependence on the Mother Country that had been so marked a characteristic in previous generations. King's College, New Brunswick, stemming originally from the Fredericton Academy of 1785, was renamed the University of New Brunswick and placed on a broader foundation than had hitherto proved possible. It was this institution more than any other that was responsible for the development of the Fredericton school of poets. The Loyalist satirist Jonathan Odell had been among the founders of the college, and as the century advanced the Anglican and Tory society of Fredericton was found to be congenial to a number of persons of literary tastes. Much poetry and prose —the name of James De Mille comes to mind—was written elsewhere in the province, some of it having been competently done; but most of it is no longer read and is known only to antiquaries. On the other hand the poetry of Carman and Roberts had a seminal influence upon the course of Canadian literature. The scholars of the University provided an intellectual preparation without which it could not have been written. George R. Parkin and Canon Roberts, themselves products of the University, made essential contributions. On his return from Oxford in 1875, Parkin awakened in his receptive pupils a love of Keats and the Pre-Raphaelite poets. The father of Charles G. D. Roberts instilled in his son a pride in the new land that the Fathers of Confederation had, in the face of formidable odds, succeeded in bringing into being. It was no accident that the son was the first to celebrate the birth of the new Dominion in memorable verse. Graduating in the year of triumph of Sir John Macdonald's National Policy, he first tried his hand at school teaching in Chatham and Fredericton. When in 1883, at the request of Goldwin

Smith, he moved to Toronto to edit the new periodical, *The Week*, he took a step which was to hasten the growth of a literary movement that can be seen in retrospect to have embodied an impulse reflective of the new nationality.

III

The province of Ontario in which Roberts was to find himself in 1883 had, with Quebec, passed through trying circumstances, involving periodic reorganizations not always unmarked by turbulence, in the course of its earlier history. Largely uninhabited at the time of Wolfe's victory on the Plains of Abraham in 1759, it was to have no substantial population of English speech until the close of the Revolutionary War when Loyalists and frontier farmers from western New York moved on to its empty but fertile acres, prompted in some cases more by a besetting land hunger than by any particular desire to alter their allegiance. It was called Upper Canada in 1791. Years before, at the close of the Seven Years' War in 1763, when what are now Quebec and Ontario were an entity, the English were hardly more than a handful of officials who came to administer the newly conquered territory inhabited by some sixty thousand French Canadians. They were supplemented by a few traders, largely of Yankee and Scottish origin, but containing other elements as well, the most influential of whom were intent upon the pursuit of the fur trade. Nowhere, not even in the towns of Quebec and Montreal, could the English-speaking be expected to be numerous enough to form a society for some time to come. Those who celebrated Wolfe's victory in verse in the pages of English periodicals may never have come to Canada at all, and the authors of the logs of the Conquest were mostly transients in alien surroundings, as were almost all of the military and civilian elements who followed them for a generation afterwards. Some were inclined to feel unhappy in the province, like Attorney-General Maseres who wrote with such clarity of insight on the institutions of the colony. Not so the English novelist, Mrs. Brooke, who resided for a time in Quebec and who could write amusingly of social occasions, including the flirtations of the military and seigneurial classes. A striking feature of her work, as noted by Dr. and Mrs. Talman in their chapter on the beginnings of literary activity in Canada, is her sensitive and extended treatment of topography and scenery, which suggests to them almost a work of description and travel. Even the poets who first appeared display a similar bias, and seem related to the travel writers of the period. On the whole, however, it was a literature of information rather than a literature of imagination, concerned with society more than with nature, often embodying statistical compilations of social and economic data relating to the newly acquired territory and its inhabitants.

The traders, on the other hand, must be treated as a class by themselves. Alexander Henry's narrative of the Pontiac rising is touched with the imagination of the artist; and in chapter 2 preceding, Professor Hopwood has reappraised David Thompson at his true worth. By contrast Alexander Mackenzie and Simon Fraser tell plain tales of tremendous feats of endurance. These Nor'westers were trying to achieve on the basis of the St. Lawrence and Great Lakes system an economy that was continental in scope, thus anticipating the territorial limits of the later Dominion. In the end, in the face of competition from Hudson Bay and the American traders, they failed; but long before they were forced into amalgamation with their northern competitors, the old fur-trading metropolis of Montreal had begun to develop the new staples of timber and wheat. By the 1820's it had become evident that canals, banks, an efficacious system of commercial law, and favourable legislation, would all be needed if the possibilities of the new industries were to be realized. In the course of endeavouring to attain their objective the mercantile classes of Lower Canada (as the settled part of what is now the province of Quebec was called from 1791 to 1840) collided with the agrarian party who were largely French-Canadian. Frustration, deadlock, and finally, in 1837, rebellion, all combined to accentuate in the English of Lower Canada their sense of identity with the Mother Country. A self-conscious colonialism became the keynote of their endeavours and was reflected in their newspapers and in the new periodical literature that began to make its appearance in the twenties. The middle-class piety and sentiment of contemporary England, tempered by compatible American influences, were exemplified by the leading periodical of the time. Begun in 1838, Montreal's *Literary Garland* did not consciously encourage a nativist trend, but represented "a detour in the development of a national literature," as Professor Klinck once aptly observed. He characterized Mrs. Traill as having approached slowly, through Nature's door, acceptance of life in Canada West. Susanna Moodie, her more inflexible sister, consciously resisted an idiom, apposite to her North American milieu, that would have required forswearing the standards upon which her life, like that of the class from which she came, had hitherto stood.

Contemporary support from Canada West, lately called Upper Canada, for such periodicals as the *Garland* was limited by the character of that section of the new united province. A low degree of literacy characterized the American farmers, partly Loyalist, who in the first years constituted the bulk of the population. The peaceful absorption of the province into the American union was forestalled by the Americans themselves through their invasion in 1812–1814; but successful resistance meant acquiescing in the rule of an irresponsible oligarchy which thereafter was able to enhance its power by treating its political opponents as enemies of the British connection and by denying reforms that were necessary to the progressive development of the country. The struggle that culminated in rebellion in 1837 was marked by the vigorous journalism of such men as William Lyon Mackenzie, but on the whole there was little forthcoming from either side that is of interest to the student of Canadian literary history. Neither did the great wave of immigration from the British Isles that peopled the wild lands of the province in the thirties and forties contribute much that was immediately favourable to its cultural advancement. Deriving largely from the fringes of British society, and thus containing only a small proportion of persons of learning and cultivation, the immigrants were in addition forced to come to terms with the Canadian back country. This experience accentuated in them a materialistic outlook and bred too often an indifference to education, which were offset only in the course of time through the efforts of such men as Egerton Ryerson, Archdeacon Strachan, and those who aided and applauded them.

In the meantime, apart from the work of several Scottish poet-journalists, and of members of such families as the Moodies, Traills, Stewarts, and Langtons, largely of the Trent valley, the student in search of literary values need not look much beyond the novels of Major John Richardson. Native-born, and on what was still a turbulent frontier, he caught and rendered in literary form the life of the Indian tribes and the pageantry of war; but the indifference which he experienced at the hands of his fellow Canadians in the decade following the Rebellions of 1837 confirms the existence of the limitations already suggested.

Only with the mid-century were the handicaps of the earlier decades at length overcome. Through the occupation of all good arable land by the fifties, together with the building of the railways, the growth of manufacturing, and the accumulation of investment capital, encouragement was given to the formation of a pattern of institutional consolidation and expansion, of which the federation of the provinces in 1867 was the crowning effect. The development of technological skills, evident in many fields including the application of steam power to the printing press, combined with specialized professional knowledge fostered by new university foundations to promote the publishing of books and periodicals for which the demand was suddenly enlarged. The exploration of the Canadian past, and of the French régime in particular, which had been begun with such effect at an earlier day by Mrs. Leprohon, was in 1877 carried to a level of achievement in *The Golden Dog* that brought its author, William Kirby, much popular acclaim. The deliberate fostering of a national spirit by the Canada First movement in the sixties and seventies, under the inspiration of the martyred McGee, helped to focus the aspirations of the time and exerted a quickening influence on all aspects of Canadian writing. Poems published in 1868 by Charles Mair were regarded as embodying the new spirit, and the young poet, Archibald Lampman, while an undergraduate at Trinity, found in the poetry of the New Brunswicker, Charles Roberts, assurance that Canadians were not helplessly situated on the outskirts of civilization where no art and no literature could be. In actuality much work of literary value had already been achieved in Ontario, but with the advent of the school of Roberts, Lampman, Carman, Campbell, and Scott, the formative period of Canadian literary history may be regarded as having passed into one of a national achievement from which the country has never seriously receded, and from which it has advanced to the ampler perspectives of our own day.

5. Settlement

I. Newfoundland 1715–1880

FRED COGSWELL

THE DEVELOPMENT of literature in the three Maritime Provinces followed a coherent pattern. Writing in the pioneer stage in the eighteenth century consisted mainly of the diaries and journals of soldiers and others. Two movements near the end of the century, the "new light" religion of Henry Alline and the Loyalist migration, provided the impetus and shape for the development of a native literature of substantial proportions in the nineteenth century.

The pattern of the development of literature in Newfoundland was tragically different. Although the first permanent settlement had been established upon the island as early as 1610, the colony in its growth was at least a century behind the Maritimes. The reasons are to be found in the nature of the economy and political control of Newfoundland.

Newfoundland's economy was centred around fishing and fur trading rather than agriculture, and the direction of the colony was controlled by private concerns in Great Britain and by the naval authority. The latter was only interested in the preservation of naval bases, and the former in procuring for their enterprises in the colony the cheapest possible labour from the lowest classes in Great Britain and Ireland. Education and the provision of social amenities, beyond the reach of the colonists themselves, were left to the missionaries, and the eighteenth century was not one in which an evangelical spirit pervaded the Anglican church.

As a result of exploitation and neglect until near the close of the eighteenth century, the Newfoundland colonists sank into illiteracy and barbarism. This illiteracy of most Newfoundlanders had two striking effects upon their culture. It compelled them to preserve and add to the vigorous popular ballad tradition which they had brought with them from the British Isles. Secondly, here alone the English language was not fixed by the printed word, and proliferated into new vocabulary and phraseology extremely interesting to the linguist.

The late eighteenth and early nineteenth centuries brought some amelioration of the social conditions in Newfoundland. The growth of the Methodist missions, their stimulation of the Anglican Society for the Preservation of the

Gospel in Foreign Parts, and the increased activity of Roman Catholic missions all played their part in raising the moral and educational standards among the Islanders. A further impetus was given by the establishment of a local legislative authority in 1832 and by public assistance to the schools in 1843. Nevertheless, the standard of education by 1880 had not reached a sufficiently high level to give rise to and support a native literature.

The literature of Newfoundland from 1715 to 1880 is therefore, with a few exceptions, a continuation of the literature of discovery written by Europeans about the New World.

Cesar François Cassini (1714–1784), of the celebrated Italian family of scientists, visited Newfoundland during the course of a series of experiments to observe the transit of Venus. His observations on the island are recorded in his *Voyage to Newfoundland in 1768* which was translated into English in 1778.

The most important eighteenth-century writer was George Cartwright (1732–1819). Born of an ancient family in Nottinghamshire, Cartwright had fought under Clive in India and under the Marquis of Granby in Europe. Unable to support himself upon his retirement half-pay, Captain Cartwright engaged in trading, fishing, and trapping activities in Labrador from 1766 to 1792.

The literary fruits of Cartwright's enterprise were *A Journal of Transactions and Events of Nearly Sixteen Years on the Coast of Labrador*, published by subscription in three volumes at Newark in 1792, and containing *Labrador: A Poetical Epistle*, later reprinted at St. John's in 1882. Cartwright's *Journal*, much admired by Coleridge and Southey, contains the unvarnished day-by-day jottings of a Pepysian man with a passion for hunting and little sense of discrimination. It is a mine of information about the fur trade, the fisheries, the Indians, the Eskimos, and social conditions on a sordid frontier. It is also an unconscious revelation of a contradictory but powerful personality.

Labrador: A Poetical Epistle condenses into heroic couplets some of the more innocuous material of the *Journal*. Although it does not escape from the dangers inherent in poetic diction, the poem is enthusiastic and charming. It is completely without that sense of bleakness and isolation in the landscape that some critics have seen as characteristic of Canadian writing. The following lines are typical:

> So cutting cold, now blust'ring Boreas blows,
> None can with naked Face, his blasts oppose.
> But well wrapp'd up, we travel out secure,
> And find Health's blessings, in an Air so pure.

Lewis Amadens Anspach (fl. 1799–1822) wrote two books on Newfoundland, *A Summary of the Laws of Commerce and Navigation* (1809) and *A History of the Island of Newfoundland and the Coast of Labrador*

(1819). The latter book is regarded as the most meritorious of the pioneer histories of the colony. Lieutenant Edward Chappell (1792–1861) of the Royal Navy contributed, in 1818, his *Voyage of His Majesty's Ship Rosamond to Newfoundland and the Southern Coast of Labrador.*

W. E. Cormack (1796–1868) was a native-born Newfoundlander. His father, a prominent St. John's merchant, had him educated in Edinburgh, and Cormack upon his return interested himself in the geography, geology, flora and fauna of the island. Despite opposition occasioned by the reluctance of those in authority to have publicity given to the conditions of the Indians in the interior, he became in 1822 the first white man to make an east to west overland crossing of Newfoundland. His *Narrative of a Journey across the Island of Newfoundland in 1822* first appeared in the *Edinburgh Philosophical Journal* during 1823 and 1824 and has since been thrice reprinted in book form. It is competent narrative containing useful information about the interior of Newfoundland and showing its author's courage, powers of endurance, and humanitarianism. After this exploit, Cormack interested himself in preserving the Beothok Indians, then on the verge of extinction. His "Report of W. E. Cormack's Journey in Search of Red Indians in Newfoundland" appeared in the *New Philosophical Journal* during 1828–29 and is the source of much that is known about that ill-fated race.

Sir Richard Henry Bonnycastle (1791–1847), while commander of the Royal Engineers in Newfoundland, compiled a survey of the island, *Newfoundland in 1842*, published in London in the same year. Far more attractive as a writer was Joseph Beete Jukes (1811–1869). Jukes, one of England's leading geologists, was commissioned to make a geological survey of Newfoundland and incorporated his findings in *Report on the Geology of Newfoundland* (1839). His *Excursions in and about Newfoundland during the Years 1839 and 1840*, published in two volumes in London in 1842, is the most readable nineteenth-century book on Newfoundland. Written in a graceful, easy style, the book abounds in vivid observation and anecdote.

Although one would not expect to find *belles-lettres* flourishing in Newfoundland during the period under discussion, they are represented by two writers, Philip Tocque (1814–1899) and Moses Harvey (1820–1901).

Philip Tocque was born in Carbonear and during his early manhood was an Anglican school-teacher. Past middle age, he studied divinity in Connecticut and was ordained as an Anglican priest in 1864. He is the author of three books, *Wandering Thoughts, or Solitary Hours* (1846), *Newfoundland as it was and as it is* (1878), and *Kaleidoscope Echoes* (1895). *Wandering Thoughts,* written during a short residence on the north coast of Newfoundland, comprises useful information and moralizing addressed to a juvenile audience and grouped loosely under such general topics as "The Past," "The Night Walk," "The Ocean," "Winter," "Temperance," etc. It must have provided much interesting reading to the audience for which it was designed; today it has no value as literature.

Moses M. Harvey was an Irish Presbyterian clergyman who settled in Newfoundland and was for more than twenty years pastor of St. Andrew's Free Presbyterian Church in St. John's. A strenuous local historian and *littérateur*, Harvey produced several books, of which the most important are *Newfoundland* (1883), a rather pedestrian history written in collaboration with Joseph Hatton, and *Lectures, Literary and Biographical* (1864). The latter book consists of lectures delivered to the Literary Institute of St. John's on such subjects as "Edmund Burke and Oliver Goldsmith," "Wit and Humor," "English, Scotch and American," and "Ireland—Her History and People." These lectures evince a wide knowledge and range of reading on the part of their creator but are commonplace in thought and turgidly over-ornate in style.

Newfoundland's sole nineteenth-century writer of verse of any importance was Henrietta Prescott (d. 1875), daughter of Admiral Sir Henry Prescott, Governor of Newfoundland from 1836 to 1841. Her *Poems, Written in Newfoundland* (1839) by their direct simplicity and conventional treatment of domestic themes show her as one of the more attractive followers of Felicia Hemans. Only a half-dozen of her several hundred poems relate to Newfoundland, and these are interesting chiefly for Miss Prescott's whole-hearted appreciation of the natural beauty of the island in all its seasons. In the bleakness of a Newfoundland winter, she can write:

> And let us look upon the snow, as white and pure it lies,
> When the vales are gently sloping, or the hill's tall summits rise;
> Let us mark each branch and twig in the frequent "silver-frost,"
> And confess that, e'en now, the trace of Beauty is not lost. . . .
>
> When we see the smile of peace and health on each beloved face,—
> Oh! *then*, we'll say, "Our lot hath fallen in a goodly place."

II. The Maritime Provinces 1720–1815

FRED COGSWELL

THE MARITIME PROVINCES were principally French settlements throughout the first half of the eighteenth century. Port Royal was garrisoned by English troops after 1710, but it was not until 1749 that the first permanent English settlement was established at Halifax. Eleven years later, a number of New England frontiersmen were settled on lands vacated by Acadians around the shores of Minas Basin and at Sheffield and Maugerville on the St. John River.

Shortly afterward, other emigrants settled in Prince Edward Island, around the Isthmus of Chignecto, and at Pictou. The main impetus for settlement, however, did not come until the close of the American War of Independence. At that time, more than thirty thousand Loyalist refugees tried to establish a new home in the Maritimes, the chief areas of their settlement being Shelburne and Annapolis in Nova Scotia and the valleys of the St. John and St. Croix rivers in New Brunswick.

The coming of the Loyalists transformed what was essentially a scattered frontier of New England farmers, giving it a varied class structure, a multiplication of specialized trades, a temporary influx of capital, and a new political and cultural orientation. Maritime literature between 1720 and 1815 also breaks into two sharply marked and well-defined periods: Pre-Loyalist and Loyalist. The latter, however, was not exclusive. Literature far different in tone from that of the Loyalists was produced between 1783 and 1815, on the one hand by British officials and soldiers and on the other hand by nonconformist religionists.

PRE-LOYALIST LITERATURE (1720–1783)

Early eighteenth-century literature involving the Maritime Provinces was a continuation of the literature of exploration and consisted mainly of the journals and personal narratives of a few individuals who found themselves briefly in that region. These accounts, usually written by semi-literate frontiersmen or soldiers, were simple, unimaginative narratives, interesting for the details which they gave of Indian and French settlements but no more literature than the bulk of the narratives of an earlier period now found in Hakluyt's *Voyages* or Purchas's *Pilgrimes*.

The most interesting of these narratives is the *Memoirs of Odd Adventures* (1736). This is an account of the sufferings and hardships endured by John Gyles (1677–1755) while a captive of the Malecite Indians in the St. John River valley between the years 1689 and 1698. It is noteworthy as a record of the fortitude and endurance of a small boy under hopeless conditions and for the picture which it contains of the perilous and squalid life of the Malecite bands of the late seventeenth century. Skimpier in its details and more articulate in style is the *Journal* of John Witherspoon (17??), which relates its author's experiences as a prisoner of the French and Indians in Acadia during the Seven Years' War.

Although Samuel Curwen (1715–1802), a distinguished Loyalist judge of Massachusetts, did not settle in the Maritimes, his *Journal and Letters* (1864) contains first-hand accounts of the siege of Louisbourg, at which he was present during the years 1744 and 1755. The mediocre verse narratives of George Cockings (d. 1802), *War: An Heroic Poem* (1762) and *The*

American War (1781), also touch upon the naval campaigns in Acadia during the Seven Years' War.

Gamaliel Smethurst (17??–17??), who established a permanent home in Nova Scotia and who ultimately became Controller of Customs and Deputy Surveyor General for that province, was a man of some education; consequently his two volumes, *A Narrative of an Extraordinary Escape out of the Hands of the Indians in the Gulf of St. Lawrence* (1760) and *A Providential Escape after a Shipwreck in Coming from the Island of St. John* (1774), make greater pretensions to literary style than the plain narratives of Gyles and Witherspoon and the laconic notations of Curwen and Cockings.

One other writer who was in Nova Scotia before 1760 deserves mention. John Adams was brought as a boy to Annapolis Royal and lived there until the time of his graduation from Harvard College. After graduation, he was ordained to preach at the Newport, Rhode Island, Congregational Church and remained in New England for the remainder of his life. It is difficult, therefore, to accept the claim of some Nova Scotian authorities that Canadian literature begins with the publication in 1745 in New England of his *Poems on Various Occasions*.

After 1760, prose and verse began to be produced by permanent settlers in the Maritimes. As a child of the New England frontier, Nova Scotia preserved its parent's basic characteristics. Among these was a high degree of literacy. Reading and writing, however, were prized because they were useful in conducting business and because without them an individual was cut off from reading the Bible and the devotional literature which consumed the interest of most of the members of the community during their leisure hours.

The religion of the Nova Scotian Yankee was a Congregationalism that united democracy in church administration with theological tyranny. It was dominated by the concept of a God whose arbitrary will destined each member of the human race irrevocably either to delight or to damnation. In this most important matter affecting existence, the believer was powerless to act on his own behalf. In the scattered rural communities, the minds and spirits of the young were tormented by fear, often for many years, before they accepted finally their preordained positions as members of the elect or the reprobate. Belief in Calvinism was a closed circle out of which few dared to step, guarded as it was by learned tomes liberally garnished with scriptural quotation. The thought of most Nova Scotian divines was, understandably, derivative from the great Calvinistic writers of New England and Scotland, and their sermons, hymns, and tracts are second-rate as theology and literature. One man of genius, Henry Alline, did appear and his work and writings have been more influential than those of any other single individual in shaping the cultural life of the Maritime Provinces.

HENRY ALLINE (1748–1784)

In *The Life and Journal of the Rev. Mr. Henry Alline*, published at Boston in 1806, Alline has set forth, in a tone and spirit remarkably similar to those of Jonathan Edwards' *Personal Narrative*, what is essentially an autobiography of the soul. He is careful, however, to link the spiritual events in his life to the physical details in such a way as to interest the psychologist (part of Alline's *Journal* found its way into William James's *The Varieties of Religious Experience*) and to provide the reader with an adequate picture of his personality. Further evidence of the career, personality, and impact of Alline is provided in many books written by his contemporaries or by those who visited the Maritimes shortly after his death. Most notable of these are *The Narrative of a Mission, to Nova Scotia, New Brunswick, and the Somers Islands, with a Tour to Lake Ontario* (1816) by Joshua Marsden, *Memoir of the Rev. James MacGregor* (1859) by George Patterson, and *A Narrative of the Life and Christian Experience of Mrs. Mary Bradley . . . Written by Herself* (1849) (see below). All these sources concur as to Alline's goodness, the warmth of his personality, and the eloquence and persuasiveness of his preaching.

Henry Alline was born at Newport, Rhode Island, the child of a strict Calvinist household. His formal education ended at the age of eleven when, in 1760, his parents and their seven children moved to a farm at Falmouth, Nova Scotia. For the next fifteen years, Henry Alline was to work with his father on the family farm, but he already kept inside himself a rich and secret inner life.

Alline's inner life began at the age of eight, when through his sister's fears during a thunderstorm, he came to realize that "God" and "death" and "hell" were not mere words but dire facts which at any moment he might be called upon to face. Fear sharpened his zest for religious reading and made keener his understanding of church doctrine. With understanding came an incurable emotional revulsion against a Being who would knowingly damn His creatures as a mere demonstration of the strength of His will. To worship such a God was blasphemy, and young Alline sought through years of prayer and meditation in secret to find a God nearer to his heart's desire. None came, and Alline as a young man abandoned himself to the less carnal forms of worldly enjoyment, becoming a leader in the card parties and frolics of the neighbourhood. One evening when Alline was on the way to a party of pleasure, his God came to him in a dramatic and visual manner. After that, Alline became a pious young man and, receiving a call from God to preach, he hesitated only long enough to assure himself that the voice he heard was not the voice of the devil. He set about preparing to obey the call.

Alline was reluctant to begin preaching because of his lack of a university education, but after an unsuccessful attempt to return to New England to study, he set his hand to the ministry with a concentration that was to take up every waking moment for the rest of his life. From 1776 to 1783, Henry Alline traversed, on horseback and in all weathers, the length and breadth of the then settled areas of the Maritime Provinces, preaching, often several times a day, wherever he could find an audience. Worn out prematurely by his labours but still tireless in spirit, Alline set out to bring the light to New England in August 1783, and at the close of January 1784, he expired of exhaustion in New Hampshire.

The only solace and relaxation which Henry Alline allowed himself was writing on religious themes. The essence of his theology is set out at length in his *Two Mites on Some of the Most Important Points of Divinity,* published at Halifax in 1781, which although not so superficially attractive as the *Life and Journal,* is in aim and execution a far more considerable book.

In *Two Mites,* Alline arranges the results of his meditation and reading into a compact, acutely reasoned, and happily illustrated system of theology. The Bible, the works of Milton, J. W. Fletcher, Edward Young, and William Law are cited to support arguments and positions adopted out of psychological compulsion on the part of the author. Alline's entire theology stems from his conviction that God must be lovable, just, and good. Salvation must come from the free choice of the individual and not by the arbitrary will of God; otherwise, God is a tyrant. It must not come easily; otherwise it would have little meaning. At no time, however, during the life of the individual can it be impossible. With salvation comes union of the individual soul with the Holy Ghost. By this union the soul is strengthened to persevere in good works and gladdened by the restoration of the kind of pristine happiness enjoyed by Adam before the Fall. Each salvation is a deeply felt personal experience, and there is no other way to achieve it, either by good works or by the following of prescribed ritual. A church organization and the rites of the church exist for the mutual sustenance of church members and should be decided by the members collectively, but the form of these rites is not in itself of sufficient importance to cause disunion or lack of charity among church members.

Alline did not lack intellectual daring and ingenuity in setting forth and defending his theology. He believed in Adam's fall from grace. He also believed that it was unjust to condemn a man for any sin but his own. He solved the dilemma by concluding that Adam's wrong choice was made in eternity and concurred in by all the souls of the human race present there with Adam. These souls, as a consequence of sin, became separated from God in eternity into the fallen world of time. As a result of the descent of Christ into that world as mediator, they there enjoy an ever present opportunity of redemption should they avail themselves of it.

Alline's eclectic theology was a disruptive element in the churches of the Maritimes, combatting on the one hand the fatalism of Calvinism and on the other the over-emphasis upon morality and ritual. It did much, however, to release individuals from the grip of fear and to bring a warm-hearted humanity and a more attractive concept of God to religion. He himself founded no church organization, for he felt that Christianity existed through the spirit only. He is, however, the spiritual ancestor of the Baptist church in the Maritimes, and his influence, temporarily eclipsed by the rise of worldliness as an aftermath of the Loyalist migration, reasserted itself in the puritanism of the nineteenth century and lives on today, almost undiminished, in the various evangelical sects that dominate the religious life of the rural Maritimes.

Alline's published sermons, of which *A Gospel Call to Sinners* (1797) is a representative example, are respectable examples of religious homily—marked chiefly by the fervour and eloquence of the joyous passages which occur in them. Alline, however, is more noted as a poet than as a sermon-writer.

His *Hymns and Spiritual Songs* (1802) parallels and exemplifies the theology contained in *Two Mites*. Although cramped by a formal pattern and diction, and marred by the occasional grammatical lapse, Alline's hymns are intense, dignified, and sincere, and often show a depth and originality of thought seldom seen in British hymns of the late eighteenth century. A good example is the opening hymn "On Man's Fall," in which Alline's dogma of the Kabbalistic Adam is set forth in verse:

> When Adam stood in light
> For trial, I was there;
> Between eternal day and night,
> And did my will declare.
>
> For when the choice was made
> I gave my full consent;
> In quest of other lovers stray'd,
> And from my father went.
>
> Then down with him I fell,
> And have no cause to say
> *Imputed guilt sinks me to hell*,
> I threw my self away.
>
> The countless race first stood
> In Adam all as one,
> Nor could a part forsake their God
> While others stood alone. . . .

Alline was a giant among pygmies. His uneducated followers lacked his acuteness of intellect and his sense of proportion. Only one of them deserves remembrance and that for one work. Benjamin Cleveland (1733–1790), of the family from which Grover Cleveland was descended, wrote the hymn beginning:

> O could I find from day to day
> A nearness to my God.

LOYALIST LITERATURE (1783–1815)

The Loyalist migrations ensured the speedy conquest of the frontier in the Maritimes Provinces; they also provided an élite whose Anglicanism, emphasis upon classical education, and conservative political views were in marked contrast to the attitudes of the Puritan farmers. They did not, however, at once provide the Maritimes with a literature. Although many Loyalists had been educated at universities and were fond of literature and although a few had established reputations as writers, they did not easily or readily come to terms with their new environment. The cultural fruits of their presence in the Maritimes did not ripen until the nineteenth century, by which time they were considerably modified by a resurgence of frontier puritanism.

The bulk of Loyalist literature was composed either before the Loyalists settled in the Maritimes or shortly afterward. It falls into two classes. The first of these—the journals, diaries, and letters of Loyalists describing their adventures and exploits during the American War of Independence—resembles the earlier literature of exploration and like that literature is primarily interesting for the light which it throws upon the history of the times. The second and more formal class of literature comprises the satirical verses composed by Tories during the American War of Independence. This is technically superior to the prose narrative and often both ingenious and clever. It is, however, too ill natured in tone and prejudiced in outlook for its appeal to outlast the audience of fellow Tories for which it was composed. In many ways, of course, the literature under discussion in this section belongs more properly to a literary history of the United States than of Canada. It is no accident that the finest poem composed by a Loyalist poet, "To Cordelia" by Joseph Stansbury, was a heart-felt rejection of the Maritime Provinces.

The journals and letters of the Loyalists are fascinating both for the adventures they contain and for the diversity of characters which their autobiographical details disclose. Sometimes, for non-literary reasons and in isolated passages, they approach literature. *The Narrative of Col. David Fanning* is a case in point. It was published posthumously in a mangled form in Richmond, Virginia, in 1862, and restored to its original from the author's Mss. by A. W. Savary in the *Canadian Magazine,* 1907–8. David Fanning (1754–1825), twice wounded and fourteen times taken prisoner in North

Carolina, was a child of civil war and knew no other life than violence until his settlement in New Brunswick at its close. Unimaginative and plodding in style, but doggedly honest, Fanning occasionally produces such a paragraph as Defoe might have envied. The following is a good example:

... my negro took up my rifle and came within ten yards and set himself down and took aim at my head, but luckily the ball missed my head about one inch, but it split my hat. I then got up and went towards him, when he ran at me with the gun and struck at my head. But I fended it off with my arms. He however broke the stock, forward of the lock. I knowing myself weak, I turned and ran sixty yards, but found myself not able to run. I got my feet entangled in some vines and unfortunately fell, and he came to me and with the barrel of my rifle he struck at me many times. I lay on my back and fended his strokes with my heels until he had knocked all the bottoms of my feet to blisters. His great eagerness to kill me put him much out of wind. I accidentally got hold of the gun barrel and he tried to bite my hand for some time. During the time of his trying to bite me, I knocked all his fore teeth out. ...

Circumstances had made Fanning a vindictive tiger. It is a welcome relief to turn to the journals and letters of older men, who had a recognized place of honour in settled communities, and who had acquired before the outbreak of hostilities a nobler and more civilized outlook than that of the Carolina frontier. One cannot read Lieutenant James Moody's *Narrative of his Exertions and Sufferings in the Cause of the Government since the Year 1776* (originally published in 1782, enlarged 1783) without realizing one's self in the presence of a true hero. Moody settled in Nova Scotia and died there in 1809. Less heroic certainly, but human and attractive are *The Winslow Papers, A.D. 1776-1826* (1901), the edited correspondence of Edward Winslow (1746–1815), a distinguished Loyalist who rose after his exile from the United States to the highest judicial position in New Brunswick. They have the added merit of revealing the feelings and aspirations of the Loyalists after they had settled in their new home.

The most readable of Loyalist documentary literature is *The Frontier Missionary: A Memoir of the Life of the Rev. Jacob Bailey* (1853). Jacob Bailey (1731–1808) is no hero but a timid human being caught in circumstances beyond his control, and the distresses of his last days in an American colony and of his flight to Nova Scotia are movingly related. The editor, William S. Bartlett, includes in an appendix in mutilated form one poem of Bailey's. Its undoubted merit makes one wish that the editor had included others. Bailey's manuscripts are, however, available at the Nova Scotia Archives and deserve editing and publishing at some time in the future.

Although Mather Byles, Jr. (1734–1814) was considered by his contemporaries to have possessed much of his father's poetical skill, the most celebrated Loyalist poets who settled in the Maritimes were Joseph Stansbury (1750–1809) and Jonathan Odell (1737–1818). Their work is most readily available in *The Loyal Verses of Joseph Stansbury and Doctor Jonathan Odell* (1860).

Both Stansbury and Odell were educated in a convention of strict adherence to a set poetical vocabulary and a traditionally sanctioned mechanical form. As a result the poems of one could as easily have been written by the other, despite the extreme differences of temperament that existed between them. They are of four kinds: public songs in the tradition of James Thomson's "Rule Britannia"; satires within a narrative framework; squibs and epigrams; and occasional poems. Both Stansbury's and Odell's patriotic songs are respectable verse within a now-dead tradition; the justice and cleverness of the satires do not outweigh the difficulties presented to the modern reader by the numerous local and contemporary allusions which must have been the chief reasons for their popularity in their own time; the squibs and epigrams, particularly Odell's upon Benjamin Franklin, are cold-bloodedly clever. The most readable and living work of Stansbury and Odell are the few occasional poems which they wrote primarily for the consolation of their own families. Odell's lines in celebration of his daughter's fifth birthday, and Stansbury's plaintive letter to his wife from Nova Scotia,

> —another way
> My fondest hopes and wishes lay,

are all that remain today of human interest out of many hours of meditation and careful composition on the part of two above-average late eighteenth century craftsmen.

OTHER WRITERS (1715–1815)

Although the Loyalists, through their numbers and the preponderance of educated professional men among them, imposed a new cultural pattern upon the Maritime Provinces, they by no means account for all the writers nor did they succeed in establishing a complete hegemony.

Many colonial officials and their families and many soldiers, quite independent of Loyalist influence, were stationed in the Maritimes between 1780 and 1820, and some of these occasionally produced work which can be regarded as literature. Among the Mss. of Lord Dalhousie (1770–1838) preserved at Register House, Edinburgh, are several graceful and witty occasional verses composed during his governorship of Nova Scotia between 1816 and 1819. A generation earlier may be noted the work of Griselda Tongue, the daughter of William Cotnam Tongue, a prominent late eighteenth century Nova Scotian official. Miss Tongue passed her short life at Windsor,

Nova Scotia, and left behind a small sheaf of verses that, despite their sentimentality and narrow range, have something of the charm of the work of William Cowper that inspired them. These verses were preserved by Beamish Murdoch in an appendix to his *History of Nova Scotia* (1865–67).

Little is known of Thomas Daniel Cowdell apart from the autobiographical data which appear in his first book of poems, *The Nova Scotia Minstrel*, first published in Dublin in 1809. From this we learn that he was born in Ireland, orphaned at an early age, emigrated to America, and there married a Scottish woman. After the couple had had eight children they returned to Great Britain where Cowdell published an account of his life in Nova Scotia and of the places visited in Great Britain on his return journey. The poems, written for the most part in octosyllabic couplets, have little to recommend them except the charm that comes of naïveté. By far the best of Cowdell's verse are "Indian Hymn" and "The Contented Indian," two dialect poems expressing what the author conceives to be the sentiments of the Micmac Indians.

Cowdell's second book, *A Poetical Account of the American Campaigns of 1812 and 1813* (1815) is a jingoistic survey of events during the War of 1812, reflecting the partisan spirit and the anxiety of contemporary British colonials. The following lines are representative:

> Thus Canada, with coarse inflated strain,
> The Yankees brawl and threaten thy domain,
> Would fain their dregs, with thy pure worth unite,
> To their equality thy sons invite.
> Thou know'st, when men are equal, 'tis in crime.

In Fredericton, Lieutenant Adam Allan (1757–1823) occupied much of his leisure in translating into standard English Allan Ramsay's Scots pastoral comedy "The Gentle Shepherd." Allan's translation was published as *The New Gentle Shepherd* in London (1798). Allan added to this translation an original poem in heroic couplets descriptive of the Grand Falls on the St. John River. This poem, unpolished and rough in versification, has a vigour and a fidelity to observation which is refreshing.

The most important non-Loyalist writer who lived in the Maritimes during this period was William Cobbett (1766–1835). Between the years 1784 and 1791, Cobbett was stationed with the British garrison at Fredericton. There he rose to the rank of Sergeant Major, and there he engaged in that course of self-education which was to bear such celebrated literary results in later life. Cobbett's reminiscences of his years in New Brunswick are scattered through his writings but occur most notably in *The Life and Adventures of Peter Porcupine* (1796) and in *Advice to Young Men* (1830). They are by far the most readable sketches now extant of life in the Maritimes during the late eighteenth century.

Less important as literature than the writing of officials and soldiers but more symptomatic of the future development of the Maritime Provinces was the continuation of religious writing. Although dimmed by the coming of the Loyalists, the light kindled by Henry Alline and his Baptist followers did not die out. At the turn of the century, it was to be augmented by the activity of British missions.

The Anglican missionaries for the most part remained in the areas settled by the Loyalists, with whom they were akin in spirit. The Presbyterians were most successful in the Scottish colonies of Pictou, Prince Edward Island, and Cape Breton. The Baptists and Methodists vied for the spiritual allegiance of the areas colonized by pre-Loyalists and of the non-Roman Catholic portions of the growing frontier settlements throughout the Maritimes. Their success ensured the continuity of the puritanism of the original Yankee settlers— a puritanism which despised all other forms of literature than those of moral and devotional tracts and verse. During the nineteenth century, these nonconformists were to challenge the political and cultural supremacy of the Anglican Tories and were to modify Maritime secular literature in the direction of their prejudices without, unfortunately, adding to it the fervour and intensity which they gave to their religious devotions. *A Narrative of the Life and Christian Experience of Mrs. Mary Bradley* (1849) recounts the experiences of a young woman (b. 1771) on a frontier where the chief source of interest, apart from daily routine, was the sermons preached by such men as Henry Alline, James MacGregor, and Joshua Marsden. *A Narrative* is the product of a sentimental and limited mind, but it demonstrates graphically the pre-eminent place held by religion in a pioneer community and the perplexities caused by the conflicting dogmas of its travelling exponents.

The sermons and religious tracts of James MacGregor (1759–1830) were preserved by posthumous publication in 1859. The major literary figure among Maritime missionaries, however, was Joshua Marsden.

JOSHUA MARSDEN (1777–1837)

Joshua Marsden was one of five missionaries sent out by the Methodist Church in England to the Maritime Provinces. He remained there from 1799 to 1807, travelling by water and upon horseback to the remotest districts. A detailed account of his mission is given in a series of letters entitled *The Narrative of a Mission, to Nova Scotia, New Brunswick, and the Somers Islands, with a Tour to Lake Ontario* (1816). Joshua Marsden was a man of good family and education. He must have been possessed of considerable personal charm since, during his sojourn in the Maritimes, he married, in the teeth of family hostility, the niece of the redoubtable Bishop Samuel Seabury. His letters, obviously composed from a running journal, reveal an initial sense of inadequacy and of antipathy to the frontier gradually yielding to confidence and love. Here and there in his work, striking sentences like the following occur:

There is, sir, a solitary loneliness in the woods of America to which no language can do adequate justice. It seems a shutting out of the whole moral creation. . . .

Interspersed among the letters are poetical effusions which, although metrically skilful, are stereotyped in thought and expression. The best of these is "A Farewell to Nova Scotia and New Brunswick," of which the following stanza is a sample:

> The spring just peeps upon thee and is fled,
> Short-liv'd thy summers are, severe thy clime,
> And frost and sea-fog bind around thy head
> A chaplet, this of snow, and that of rime;
> Yes, all the landscape terribly sublime
> Displays the rigours of a wintery wild;
> Yet I in thee hath cheerly past my time,
> Around my cot, the snow-clad season smil'd
> For I was preaching *Him*, who every care beguiled.

In 1815, Marsden published in England *The Backslider, a Descriptive Moral Poem, in Four Books*, in heroic couplets of considerable polish. Before embarking upon his theme, a sharp analysis of the psychological processes in the corruption of a good man, the poet describes the land where the poem was written:

> In this cold climate, where rough Boreas blows,
> Pours his fierce hail, and spreads his dazzling snows,
> Disrobes the green-wood, chills the solar beam,
> And shakes his icy-sceptre o'er the stream,
> Let me beguile stern winter's frigid ire,
> With books divine, a friend, and maple fire;
> Or cheat the night-storm terrible and fierce!
> With purest sweets of fancy-pleasing verse.

Joshua Marsden must have cheated many night-storms, for his other published books, most of them obviously composed during his residence in the Maritimes, include: *Leisure Hours; or, Poems, Moral, Religious & Descriptive* (1812); *The Mission* (1816); *Amusements of a Mission; or, Poems, Moral, Religious, and Descriptive, Interspersed with Anecdotes, Written during a Residence Abroad* (1818); and *Poems on Methodism* (1848). There are also two moral prose narratives: *Grace Displayed: An Interesting Narrative of the Life, Conversion, Christian Experience, Ministry and Missionary Labours of —— ——* (1813) and *Sketches of the Early Life of a Sailor, Now a Preacher of the Gospel* (1820).

Marsden's verse is superior to his prose and shows considerable talent; it fails to achieve its potential excellence mainly because Marsden kept it ever subordinate to his primary calling as a publicist for the Methodist church.

III. The Canadas 1763–1812

JAMES J. AND RUTH TALMAN

The period 1763–1812 saw little English writing in those parts which in 1792 became Upper and Lower Canada. For this dearth there are several explanations. Obviously, at first, the English-speaking population was small and almost entirely without pretensions to literary attainment. Indeed, if we are to believe Francis Maseres, whose letters represent some of the earliest writing in the period, the province was a "very dull and disagreeable place to live in."

The Loyalist migration, while adding greatly to the English-speaking population, did not add anything to its literary capacity. The immigrants did not come from those elements in society which wrote creatively. Indeed, many could not write, and those who could were too busy to do so, or did not have the inclination or competence to put their thoughts on paper. Most writing took the form of petitions to the Government. Non-Loyalist English-speaking immigrants differed from their Loyalist contemporaries only in their inability to secure land as Loyalist claimants.

With the large part of the population made up as it was, writing was left to the few literate immigrants and visitors from the United Kingdom. This writing took the form of one novel, a few poems, some printed sermons, travel accounts, diaries, and at least a couple of morbid items—broadsides purporting to present the confessions and last words of those about to be hanged. A few diaries and letters, not intended at the time for publication, have come down to us as representative of what people were thinking and saying.

The first English writer of note in Canada, after France ceded Canada to Great Britain, was Francis Maseres (1731–1824). He was born in London of Huguenot ancestry. After a distinguished career at Clare College, Cambridge, he graduated in 1752. In 1753 he published the first of a series of mathematical works he produced throughout his life. A year later he entered the practice of law. This profession led him to Quebec, as Attorney General, in 1766, where he remained until 1769. Before his arrival in Canada he wrote a pamphlet entitled *Considerations on the Expediency of Procuring an Act of Parliament for the Settlement of the Province of Quebec* (London, 1766). This was his first publication on Canadian affairs.

As Attorney General, Maseres drew up several reports for the Lieutenant-

Governor and Council on judicial and economic matters in the colony. His most significant report was that "concerning The State of the Laws and the Administration of Justice in that Province." This report and others, published by Maseres in *A Collection of Several Commissions* (London, 1772), are invaluable records of their time.

In the courts Maseres was less successful than he was as a writer. By May 1768 he was thoroughly discouraged with the country. The climate troubled him and he did not admire the scenery. But, he concluded: "What is worse than all, there are few agreeable people here to converse with." He left Canada in 1769 and never returned. In spite of his strictures, he did not lose his interest in the country. A bibliography of his writings, limited only to those items clearly attributable to him, for he wrote much anonymously, reveals a thorough-going knowledge of the country. His letters, edited with an excellent biographical introduction by W. S. Wallace in 1919, provide an early sample of Canadian literature.

One of the strong qualities of Maseres as a writer was his ability to enable his readers to see people as he saw them. For example, his description of a visiting official: "He is a well-bred agreeable man but not a lawyer; and he has a pompous way of talking that seems borrowed from the house of commons cant about the constitution &c, without having precise Ideas of what he would say." As Dr. Wallace has written, Maseres' letters give a "fresh and vivid picture of Canada" during the years 1766–68. Maseres died in England in 1824.

The only novel of the period is *The History of Emily Montague* by Frances Brooke (1724–1789), which was published in England in 1769. *Emily Montague* may truly claim to be the earliest Canadian novel—and, indeed, the earliest novel emanating from the North American continent, as nothing that can be described as a novel had appeared up to this time in the American colonies. Although published in England, the novel was undoubtedly written in Canada and most of its action takes place in a Canadian setting.

Frances Brooke, born Frances Moore, in Stubton, Lincolnshire, married the Reverend Dr. John Brooke in 1756 and joined him in Quebec in 1763 after he became chaplain of the garrison and Deputy to the Auditor General. There she resided for five years and came to know well both the French seigneurs of the city surroundings and officers of the British garrison and British officials.

Mrs. Brooke was peculiarly fitted to write of English–French Canada. Already she had published several novels and plays in England and had established a position in the English literary generation that followed Richardson and Fielding; also she was well acquainted with France, and had published a translation of a French romance. She was thus prepared to give a sympathetic portrayal of both facets of the Canadian scene.

Emily Montague is written in the epistolary style popular in the period.

It consists of 228 letters, written among a group of friends in Canada and England, which unfold the gentle and not very eventful love story of the principal characters, Emily Montague and Colonel Ed. Rivers. Two subordinate pairs of lovers, one in Quebec, one in England, add variety of character. Emily and her Colonel are interesting enough examples of the high cultural and moral "sensibility" much prized by novelists of that time. Emily's friend, Arabella Fermor, a coquette, shows a more sprightly wit. The letters are pleasing, written in an easy, lively style, and give a vivid picture of the society of the small provincial capital, with its afternoon drives and evening parties, balls, and one unforgettable sketch of a sleigh-ride over the ice and snow of the frozen St. Lawrence.

In one respect *Emily Montague* differs from all other novels of its genre. Here we have no violence—none of the abductions, seductions, duels, highwaymen, or ghosts that we find in other such romances, and, indeed, in Frances Brooke's English-based novels. In *Emily Montague,* except for the stumbling blocks in the course of true love, the story runs smoothly and unsensationally. Its sensation is provided by its setting: Canadian forests and rivers, Indians and habitants, waterfalls and snows. Is it a novel only, or might it be classed also with description and travel literature?

More popular than fiction, apparently, was poetry, for the period provides at least four long descriptive poems. The first of these, *Abram's Plains*, by Thomas Cary (1751–1823), was printed privately in Quebec in 1789. The poem, 568 lines in rhyming couplets, was patterned, according to its Preface, on "the harmonious Thompson [James Thomson, author of *The Seasons*]." Cary expressed admiration for Pope but could not help feeling a preference for Thomson "so strikingly unparalleled and inimitable" were the beauties of his numbers. At the same time Cary admitted that before he began his poem he re-read "Pope's *Windsor-Forest* and Dr. Goldsmith's *Deserted Village*, with the view of endeavouring, in some degree, to catch their manner of writing."

Abram's Plains, although derivative in style, is truly Canadian in content. Beginning with an invocation to the Plains "Where . . . I sit and court the Muse," Cary goes on to a description of the whole St. Lawrence system: "cold Superior"; Huron, "distinguish'd by its thund'ring bay"; Michigan; Erie; "thy dread fall, Niagara"; Montreal, with a reference to the fur trade; Quebec, with a description of its surrounding forest and mention of the shipbuilding industry; and so on, through the Gulf to the coasts of Labrador. In passing, Cary describes the settlers, with their fields and villages; Indians, Eskimos; buffalo, carriboo [*sic*], wolf, otter; fish, with a neatly sketched picture of the fishing through the ice of the St. Lawrence. In short, an epitome of the Canadian scene as it appeared in his time, though it is doubtful if Cary could actually have seen Eskimos.

Cary came to Quebec from England before 1787 and was working as a clerk in a government office when he published his poem. In 1797 he established a subscription library and later, in 1805, he founded the *Quebec Mercury* in the columns of which he continued his literary activity. He died in Quebec in 1823.

Another poem, similar in type, was *Canada, a Descriptive Poem*, written at Quebec in 1805, and presumably published in 1806. Heretofore this poem has been described as anonymous, but it now appears to have been written by Cornwall Bayley (1784–1807), a precocious undergraduate of Christ's College, Cambridge, who left England for Quebec in 1804, evidently travelling via the United States. His preface is dated Quebec, February, 1806. The author entreats "the candid reader to make allowances for the inexperience of a youth." He thoughtfully supplies a Plan of the poem, a useful device as its references are fairly obscure. The Plan gives an idea of what the poet attempted to describe:

The view from Cape Diamond . . . —The animal and vegitable [*sic*] productions of the Country—The Indians with some conjectures upon their origin and former state—The colonization of Canada by the French Missionaries—Its conquest by the British in 1759—The Death of Wolfe—The repulse of the American army under Montgomery—Reflections upon Democracy—and the usual evils of a Revolution—Illustrated by France—The Contrast presented in the innocent manners of the Canadians—Their Civil and Religious liberties—Their manners and customs described, as varying according to the seasons—Upper Canada introduced—Lakes —Falls of Niagara—Reflections upon Great Britain and her Colonies—Address to the St. Lawrence—its rivers—towns and villages—Panegyric upon Quebec—Its General Hospital—The Nuns—Their amusements &c. The poem concludes with a tribute of praise to the females of the Province.

This seems a comprehensive effort for a youth of twenty-one.

Another poet writing in, and of, Quebec was Stephen Dickson (b. 1761?), a graduate of the University of Dublin, who came to America apparently after being implicated in the Irish rebellion of 1798. He spent only a few months in Quebec, but published there early in 1799 *The Union of Taste and Science, a Poem: to which are subjoined a few Elucidating Notes*, a poem in praise of Governor Prescott and his wife, written in heroic couplets, in stanzas of irregular length. The poem represents Mrs. Prescott as Taste and the Governor as Science, and is filled with fulsome flattery toward its subjects, classical and current allusions, elaborate figures of speech and imagery. Dickson took the precaution of adding notes to explain his allusions. This small volume is, incidentally, a fine example of early Canadian printing.

A fourth descriptive poem, published in England, almost took on the attributes of a traveller's guide in verse. This was *Quebec Hill; or, Canadian Scenery: A Poem in Two Parts* (London, 1797). The author, J. Mackay, is an unknown. He does say, however, "By far the greatest part of the Poem was written in Canada, where the Writer has spent a considerable portion of his time." He adds, "The Author is sensible that the Poem might have been rendered, what some men of learning term, more poetical, if less attention had been paid to veracity; but, to lovers of truth, no apology is necessary on this head, and, to those of a contrary disposition, none is due."

The poem includes, among other subjects, a description of Niagara Falls, an account of the death of Wolfe, and lines on the fever and ague of Upper Canada. Some moralizing is thrown in. In the end the author admitted that he had not been won over by Canada:

> Now, having sung Canadian woods and vales,
> Its Summer's heat, and Winter's frigid gales,
> Let me remark, as climates I compare,
> And manners note, 'tis Britain I prefer.
> Dear isle! where temp'rate years their empire hold,
> Free from extremes of ardent heat or cold.

Beyond these four longer poems very little verse remains, except for fugitive items in the newspapers. One commonly recurring form of doggerel was the annual carrier's address, bringing New Year's greetings from the newspaper carrier or the printer's boy to the customers. These verses appeared yearly in the *Quebec Gazette* and other Canadian newspapers. The first in English was printed in the *Quebec Gazette* in January 1781. The verses, which have no literary merit, are sometimes comparable to the modern greeting-card verse; sometimes satirical; sometimes an undisguised hint for a New Year's tip. Similar verses were published to celebrate special occasions, such as the opening of a theatre in Quebec.

Of poetic drama we have one example, by Barnabas Bidwell (1763–1833), who came to Upper Canada from Massachusetts in 1810. During his senior year at Yale in 1784 he published a tragedy, *The Mercenary Match*, which was acted by his fellow students. According to the *Dictionary of American Biography*, the work was distinguished by the general smoothness of its blank verse and the felicity of its phrasing, qualities seldom found in eighteenth-century American plays. This work can scarcely qualify Bidwell as a Canadian playwright. He is said also, however, to have contributed eleven sketches to Robert Gourlay's *Statistical Account of Upper Canada* (London, 1822). These surely would stamp him as a Canadian writer.

Two writers of sermons deserve mention: Alexander Spark (1762–1819) and Jacob Mountain (1749–1825). Spark came to Quebec from Scotland in 1780 and officiated for many years at the Scotch Church (St. Andrew's Presbyterian Church). Though a profound scholar and an excellent writer, Spark left only a few sermons and orations, typical of their class and period in their figurative and rhetorical language. Mountain, born in England, where he held several livings, was appointed first Anglican bishop of Quebec in 1793. In England he wrote poems and sermons. His sole Canadian publication was a thanksgiving sermon published in Quebec in 1799.

Spark, besides his pastoral duties, engaged in journalism. From 1792 to

1794 he supervised the *Quebec Gazette,* and during this period he also edited the *Quebec Magazine,* a monthly journal which was devoted mainly to reprinting papers, alternately in English and French, from European and American periodicals, and contemporary classics. Its original material was mostly on agricultural matters.

Since Canada was a country new to English writers accounts of travel comprise a large part of its early literature. One early travel writer was the Montreal merchant Alexander Henry (1739–1824). His book *Travels and Adventures in Canada and the Indian Territories between the Years 1760 and 1776* (New York, 1809) has become a Canadian classic. This exciting story, besides offering a great deal of valuable geographical information and many curious details of the customs and manners of the Indians, provides an autobiography of the writer, describing his "intrepidity" when placed in "many trying and perilous situations."

Travel literature is represented also by the journal of John Lees. Lees (fl 1764–1775), a Quebec merchant, born in Scotland, was engaged in the fur trade in the upper country. He wrote a journal describing his travels in 1768 from Boston to Detroit and back by the Great Lakes and St. Lawrence to Montreal. His journal (published only in 1911) is a tightly packed storehouse of information about the country he traversed, the people he met, distances, prices, and other such straightforward material. With nothing imaginative about it, and not much grace of style, it is nevertheless of value to the historian of the period.

A similar journey, some years later, was described by George Heriot (1766–1844) in his *Travels through the Canadas* (London, 1807). It provides an account of the topography, climate, scenery, and settlements of both provinces. Heriot's descriptions are careful, detailed, and exact—pedestrian rather than evocative. He dealt with economic conditions, agriculture, and colonial administration, and showed himself a thoughtful observer. His book is not a mere tourist's diary, but a comprehensive picture of the country and its inhabitants. It is copiously illustrated with plates made from his own drawings, which show charm and considerable skill.

Heriot came to Canada from England and served as a clerk in the Ordnance Department at Quebec. From 1800 to 1816 he was Deputy Postmaster General of British North America. He wrote also a *History of Canada,* published in London in 1804. This work was largely based on Charlevoix and is not significant.

Probably the best-known description of Upper and Lower Canada was written by Irish-born Isaac Weld, junior (1774–1856), whose *Travels through the States of North America and the Provinces of Upper and Lower Canada, during the years 1795, 1796, and 1797,* was first published in London in 1799. Several other editions followed, and the work was translated into Dutch, Italian, French, and twice into German.

Weld spent from July to the end of October of 1796 in Upper and Lower Canada, and managed to travel as far west as the Detroit River, with the purpose of obtaining information as to the state of those provinces, and of determining from his own immediate observations "how far the present condition of the British dominions in America might be inferior, or otherwise, to that of the people of the States." His work is in the form of thirty-eight letters, of which sixteen deal with Canada. Weld's descriptions are graphic but do not present as intimate a picture as those of Lambert, who followed him.

He scarcely seems to have become enamoured of America, for his concluding words were, "my thoughts are solely bent upon returning to my native land, now dearer to me than ever . . . I shall speedily take my departure from this Continent, well pleased at having seen as much of it as I have done; but I shall leave it without a sigh, and without the slightest wish to revisit it."

By far the most comprehensive travel account written during this period was *Travels through Lower Canada and the United States of North America in the years 1806, 1807 and 1808*, by John Lambert. Its popularity in Britain was evidenced by the number of editions it went through. The first edition, in three volumes, was published in London in 1810; the second, in two volumes, in London and Edinburgh in 1813, and again in London in 1814; and the third, also in two volumes, in London and Edinburgh in 1814.

Lambert, about whom little is known, arrived at Quebec in the autumn of 1806 and "after residing a twelvemonth in Canada" visited the United States. He returned to Montreal early in May 1808, before he sailed for England. In his account of his tour through Lower Canada and part of the United States his object was to describe the people as he found them; "to remove the veil of unjust prejudices and the gloss of flattery."

In a style discursive and anecdotal he gave an intimate picture of life and manners in Quebec, not always in flattering terms. His account of the Canadian theatre shows something of the cultural development of the colony.

> There is, indeed, a building at Quebec called a Theatre, and also one at Montreal; but the persons who perform, or rather attempt to perform there, are as bad as the worst of our strolling actors; yet they have the conscience to charge the same price nearly as the London theatres. Sometimes the officers of the army lend their assistance to the company; but I have seen none, except Colonel Pye, and Captain Clark of the 49th, who did not murder the best scenes of our dramatic poets. It may be easily conceived how despicably low the Canadian theatricals must be, when boys are obliged to perform the female characters: the only actress being an old superannuated demirep, whose drunken Belvideras, Desdemonas, and Isabellas, have often *enraptured* a Canadian audience.

The quality of literature, in his opinion, was little better. "The state of literature and the arts," he said, "did not improve very rapidly after the conquest of the country by the English. The traders and settlers, who took up their abode among the French, were ill qualified to diffuse a taste for the arts and sciences, unless indeed it was the *science* of barter, and the *art* of gaining cent. per cent. upon their goods."

A morbid type of broadside seems to have been popular in Quebec. The *Quebec Gazette* on November 21, 1783, announced that the dying speech and confessions of two convicted murderers and robbers were to be published on the following Saturday. Again, in 1785, the confession of another criminal, hanged for stealing, was published. This type of literature was reminiscent of a type which was popular in Britain earlier in the century. Unfortunately the texts have not been preserved, but undoubtedly they would be similar to others which are extant.

Most of the foregoing literary activity took place in the Lower province as it was a settled community while Upper Canada was still in a much earlier stage of development. One interesting item that appeared early in Upper Canada—indeed, it was the first unofficial publication printed in that colony—was *Thoughts on the Education of Youth* by Richard Cockrel (1783?–1829), a teacher of mathematics at Newark (Niagara-on-the-Lake). This was a pamphlet, "Printed by G. Tiffany, and sold at his Book-Store," 1795. Cockrel shows some surprisingly modern pedagogical ideas, which would not be out of place in a modern P.T.A. meeting. "It behoves every master of a school to become acquainted as early as possible with the disposition of his pupils: soft words are sufficient in order to induce some boys to diligence, some will not do without threats, and others will never make any progress without now and then being brought to the birchen altar." "If masters would also use proper means to gain the affections of children, I am sure they might be successful and more happy in their situations." He made specific recommendations as to the size of classes and methods of presentation; he thought there should be no homework during holidays; rules of politeness should be taught; parents should keep children from the streets; and lastly he queried, "Do parents interest themselves as they ought?"

Contemporary for a time with Cockrel, Elizabeth Posthuma (Gwillim) Simcoe (1766–1850), the wife of Lieutenant Governor John Graves Simcoe, kept a diary which ran from September 17, 1791, to October 16, 1796. This was a day-to-day record from the time the Simcoes left England until they returned. The diary gives a great deal of information on travel, and on the life and people of Upper Canada. The first edition of the diary, edited by John Ross Robertson, was published only in 1911.

The name of D'Arcy Boulton (1759–1834) is not well known in the history of Upper Canada. Boulton was born in England and came to Canada about 1797. He was successively Solicitor General, Attorney General, and judge of assize. Service as Judge of the Queen's Bench was not as likely to lead to fame as other activities, but Boulton's *Sketch of His Majesty's*

Province of Upper Canada (London, 1805) shows the author to have been a lucid and well-qualified writer. He began with a general account of the colony and its political organization and divisions, and followed with a particular account of each township. His views may be appreciated when it is stated that rather than rhapsodizing over the beauties of Niagara Falls he remarked on the mills which the falls might be used to operate.

In 1890 Lady Matilda Edgar edited the Ridout Letters covering the years 1805 to 1815, under the title *Ten Years of Upper Canada*. The greater part of the collection consists of letters between Thomas Ridout (1754–1824) and his sons, George (1791–1871) and Thomas G. (1792–1861). The volume, consequently, is by way of being the work of a composite Ridout author. All were careful observers and could write with facility. Thomas Ridout, born in England, had led an eventful life. He migrated to Maryland and engaged in trade there during the American Revolution, after which he was captured by Indians and spent several months as their prisoner. On his escape he settled in Upper Canada, where he became Surveyor General and a member of the Legislative Council. He thus was closely associated with the early history of the colony. The letters printed range over many subjects —events, people, business, agriculture, and battles. A brief but well-written narrative of Thomas Ridout's captivity among the Shawanese in 1788 was included by the editor.

Canadian writing between 1763 and 1812 may not bulk large in quantity or high in quality. Small, however, as the output may have been our information regarding the country would be sorely depleted were it not for the writers mentioned above. Without them Canada would surely be the poorer.

6. Haliburton

FRED COGSWELL

IN THE TWO DECADES following 1815, the Maritime Provinces underwent a prolonged period of social and economic crisis. The emigrants from New England and Great Britain were hard put to it to maintain their old ways of behaviour and system of values in an economy that was going to pieces before their eyes. For with the close of the Napoleonic Wars, the artificially stimulated markets in timber and agricultural produce collapsed. With the deflation of a temporarily thriving economy, the unspectacular but steady revenues of officialdom became a prize to be fought for, and the resultant political agitation—behind the fine phrases in which it was cloaked—was in reality a naked struggle for assured economic survival on the part of its participants.

Nova Scotia, the most advanced colony and the one which had most benefited by the struggle in Europe, felt most keenly the altered circumstances, and at least two individuals in Nova Scotia possessed some insight into the nature of these pressures which were convulsing their society. Thomas McCulloch in the 1820's saw the thriftlessness and immorality increasing upon the frontier as a threat to the maintainance of religious values. A decade later, Thomas Haliburton shared McCulloch's vision, and added to it his discovery of the underlying motives of the political struggle, whose outcome in his opinion could not possibly solve the colony's ills. Both writers attempted to convert their neighbours to their ways of thinking by putting the situation as they saw it before them in fictitious but realistic terms. Out of their efforts, the first serious realistic Canadian prose fiction was born.

That this fiction did not take the form of the contemporary novel is understandable. The contemporary novel was regarded as a vehicle of escape from life, either to the medieval past of glamour or terror, or to the sentimental intrigues of a hypothetical European aristocracy. Consequently, McCulloch and Haliburton turned backward in time to the eighteenth century and modelled their work essentially upon the essay form as perfected by Addison and Steele.

Each letter in *The Letters of Mephibosheth Stepsure*, each chapter in *The Clockmaker*, is a selection of incidents from rural or urban Nova Scotian life designed to illustrate a moral or a social vice. The continuity between chapters is not arrived at through an over-riding unity of plot, as in the novel proper, but by a continuation of character and tone from chapter to chapter as in the essays of *The Spectator*.

Thomas McCulloch (1776–1843), a Scotsman, became Presbyterian minister at Pictou, Nova Scotia, in the early days of the nineteenth century. For more than forty years he was to play a leading role in the educational and theological life of Nova Scotia. He also found time to write fiction of limited, but genuine, talent. His collection of historical sketches, *Auld Eppie's Tales*, was designed as a counter-blast to the anti-Presbyterian bias of *Old Mortality*, but William Blackwood, the Edinburgh publisher, was too timid to publish it in competition with Sir Walter Scott. McCulloch's *William and Melville* was published in Edinburgh by Oliphant in 1826. Although its two novelettes contain accurate, if unsavoury, accounts of life in contemporary Halifax, they are basically temperance tracts, and their leading characters are wooden and unprepossessing. McCulloch belongs in a literary history for one book, *Letters of Mephibosheth Stepsure*, printed serially in the *Acadian Recorder*, and declined in 1828 by the timid Blackwood on the grounds of the coarseness of its humour. It was reissued in book form in Halifax in 1860.

In sixteen letters, Mephibosheth Stepsure—in his youth a lame orphan—describes his plodding rise to respectability and affluence in the community of Pictou by a combination of hard work, abstinence, religiosity, and cunning. Akin to Mephibosheth in ideology, practice, and prosperity are his wife, Dorothy, and her mother; his son, Abner; his cousin, Harrow; and a hard-featured Scots emigrant, Saunders Scantocreesh. Favoured by God, these devout Presbyterians listen to the spiritual admonitions of Dr. Drone. Against these faithful sheep of the congregation are the goats—all who succumb to the lure of a gambling economy and to the thriftlessness and dissipations of the frontier. In letter after letter, the rake's progress of the local citizens is described and their ultimate hardships are recounted.

There is much to repel the modern reader in *The Letters of Mephibosheth Stepsure*. Christian ethics, one feels, ought to be an end in themselves and not a means of making money, and to a healthy nature cold-blooded gloating over the misfortunes and failures of others is never pleasant. The book also has technical flaws. The characters—Trot, Whinge, Sham, Clippet—are, as their names suggest, caricatures; the episodes are often farce; and the use again and again of the same plot situations is monotonous. To compensate for these defects, *The Letters of Mephibosheth Stepsure* possess a marvellously unified tone and sensibility, a robust realism, a lack of prudishness, and a sustained, almost Swiftian, irony.

Besides being a creditable pioneer attempt at literature, the *Letters* had a seminal importance. They suggested the idea for the letters which Joseph Howe wrote in the *Nova Scotian* a few years later. They also showed Thomas Chandler Haliburton the possibilities for literature that lay in the local scene. Haliburton's debt to McCulloch has been greatly exaggerated recently; nevertheless *The Letters of Mephibosheth Stepsure* was one of many avenues that led to *The Clockmaker*.

By birth and education, Thomas Chandler Haliburton (1796–1865) was completely representative of early community leaders in the Maritimes. His father, William H. O. Haliburton, the son of a pre-Loyalist and staunch Tory, was clerk of the peace for Hants County, Nova Scotia, and afterwards a judge of the Inferior Court of Common Pleas. His mother, Lucy Chandler Grant Haliburton, was the daughter of parents who had given their lives for the Crown during the American War of Independence. The family was Anglican, and Haliburton attended King's College, Windsor, then the training ground for the Tory and Anglican professional men who dominated the social and economic life of the Maritimes.

From his father Haliburton acquired the philosophic basis of his Tory politics. He received from his mother the emotional prejudices connected with them and a violent dislike of the United States. During his early years at the Bar and as a member of the Nova Scotian Legislative Assembly between 1826 and 1829, Haliburton nevertheless intermittently indulged impulses radically at odds with his position and training. Among causes which he championed were the removal of the disabilities preventing Roman Catholics from holding office, common school education at state expense, and a permanent grant for Pictou Academy. All these were anathema to his Tory friends.

Gradually Haliburton found his position in the Legislative Assembly becoming untenable. Tactlessly outspoken and possessing a great gift for ridicule, he threw all his strength into any issue he supported and gored his friends and foes in turn. He had, however, too great a sense of worldly advantage to go over irretrievably to the party of Reform. His political friends accordingly took the first opportunity to get rid of a troublesome ally by offering him the judgeship that fell vacant upon his father's death in 1829. Haliburton was a judge of the Court of Common Pleas until its abolition in 1841. He then became a Supreme Court judge of Nova Scotia until retirement in 1854. Haliburton neither disgraced nor adorned the judicial office. Removed from direct contact with parliament, the fires of radicalism in him died, and in his old age he condemned the very causes which as a young man he had supported so eloquently.

Haliburton had visited England several times, and decided in 1856 to settle there permanently. From 1859 to 1865, the year of his death, he was

Tory M.P. for Launceston and opposed in the British parliament both the "little England" policy of William Gladstone and the aspirations of the British North American colonies for greater independence.

A complete hedonist, Haliburton was the uxorious husband of two wives, and a connoisseur of good drink, good food, good conversation, pretty women, and fast horses. His bluff heartiness, however, concealed a cold eye to personal profit in any friendship. Like the eighteenth-century country squires he resembled, he saw little but absurdity in any religion that went beyond Sunday attendance at the Anglican church, and like Joseph Howe he was completely out of sympathy with the emotional glories and sectarian disputes that characterized the religious life of contemporary Nova Scotia. Haliburton had little faith in abstract pretensions to virtue and enjoyed exposing the wolf of self-interest that lurked behind the sheep's clothing of idealism in private and public life. As free from prudishness as Smollett, he had an indecorous sense of humour which he indulged in conversation and sometimes allowed to creep into his writing.

Although successful in his private life, Haliburton in his later work developed a vein of melancholy that cannot be entirely accounted for by the inroads that he made upon his constitution. It stemmed paradoxically from a frustrated idealism. Although cynical of the ideals of other men, Haliburton himself was tied emotionally to a cause that was doomed. Haliburton believed passionately in the Toryism of Edmund Burke, and it was his misfortune to live through its decay in both Britain and America—partly from the onslaught of Liberal opportunists but mainly because of an inner loss of conviction on the part of the Tories themselves. Haliburton mistrusted Sir Robert Peel. He found the word "Conservative" merely the word "Liberal" writ large, and he hated it accordingly. He saw himself become an anachronism in a world where even gentlemen preferred *laissez-faire* to *noblesse oblige*; his despair only made him become more stubborn and extreme in the statement of his views. There runs throughout Haliburton's career a supreme irony; men read him for his humour and disregarded what to him was the *raison d'être* of everything he ever wrote.

Haliburton began his writing to make Nova Scotians and the rest of the world aware of the heritage and resources of the colony. He partly accomplished his purpose with the publication of *A General Description of Nova Scotia* (1823) and *An Historical and Statistical Account of Nova Scotia* (1829). Both books are praiseworthy pioneering ventures, well proportioned in arrangement and dignified and straightforward in style, and they represent a vast amount of individual research. They brought Haliburton only a local reputation, although *An Historical and Statistical Account* was, many years later, to provide the theme for Longfellow's poem *Evangeline*. It was *The Clockmaker; or, The Sayings and Doings of Samuel Slick, of*

Slickville, which began serially in the *Nova Scotian* in 1835 and was published in book form in three series (Halifax, 1836; London, 1838, 1840), that launched Haliburton upon his literary career.

The circumstances behind the writing of *The Clockmaker* are as follows. During Haliburton's years as a member of the Legislative Assembly, he had belonged to the Literary Club of Halifax and there had become a friend of Joseph Howe, then editor of the *Nova Scotian* and only just beginning his political career. Howe's local pride led him to publish Haliburton's *An Historical and Statistical Account of Nova Scotia* at a loss. Howe also, taking an example from the popularity of the *Letters of Mephibosheth Stepsure,* had ridden the length and breadth of Nova Scotia on horseback, examining the state of the colony and its people and reporting his findings to his own newspaper. A common love of Nova Scotia and a common concern over its lack of prosperity united Howe and Haliburton. One of the results of this concern was the publication of *The Clockmaker* in Howe's paper despite the difference in political opinions which had by 1834 begun to cloud the relations between the two friends.

As early as 1776, Hector St. Jean de Crèvecœur had commented in *Letters of an American Farmer* on the undue reliance of Nova Scotians upon government patronage rather than upon their own industry. Throughout the period of the Loyalist emigration and the Napoleonic Wars, this attitude in Nova Scotia had deepened into a set way of life. With the close of twenty years of speculative prosperity, Nova Scotia found herself in 1815 without capital or markets and with a population which had acquired habits ill suited to a life of meagre income and sober farming. The economic distress of the 1820's culminated in political agitation. Haliburton saw the Reform movement as a cloak for the ambitions of those who wished to supplant the present office-holders in their revenues. The salvation of Nova Scotia could only come, he felt, through a marked change in the habits of its people. He would have them emulate the thrift, hard work, and ingenuity of their Yankee neighbours, and his principal reason for writing *The Clockmaker* was to persuade them to do so. Although Howe disapproved of Haliburton's politics, he was sufficiently in accord with the main purpose of the book to give it his enthusiastic support.

Haliburton was particularly well qualified to comment upon Nova Scotia. He had spent seven years in doing research for *An Historical and Statistical Account*. As a judge on circuit, he observed large areas of the colony and became thoroughly acquainted with the conditions and the people of the county towns. All that remained was to determine the form into which his knowledge and observation were to be poured. That the appeal would be humorous was certain. Haliburton's most effective weapon in the Legislative Assembly had been ridicule, and he had noted the sensation caused a decade before by the *Letters of Mephibosheth Stepsure* and the even greater sensation being produced currently in New England by Seba Smith's *Life and Writings of Major Jack Downing, of Downingsville, Away Down East, in the State of Maine* (1833).

Haliburton borrowed from McCulloch the device—really as old as the Greeks and the Romans—of coining names suggestive of character; from Seba Smith he borrowed that of using vernacular speech and of exploiting the eccentricities of Yankee character. In *The Clockmaker*, however, he surpassed both McCulloch and Smith in imaginative conception and execution.

The Clockmaker, like a picaresque novel, is episodic. The narrator, a thinly disguised Haliburton, and Sam Slick, a Yankee clockmaker, travel about Nova Scotia, and their seemingly chance encounters and observations provide the material for anecdote and conversation. There is no development of plot within the work as a whole, but each chapter is unified in that its incidents and comments exemplify a theme. Each chapter is a lay sermon illustrated by pointed anecdote and often culminating in a homely but original and apt epigrammatic text. With no rising curve of suspense to attract and hold attention, *The Clockmaker* has nevertheless gone through at least seventy editions since the first was published in 1836, and has appeared in the United States, in England, and on the Continent. It has done so as a result of its author's brilliant use of characterization, anecdote, language, and point of view.

Only one of the characters in *The Clockmaker* really counts. The Squire and Mr. Hopewell are either foils to Sam Slick or pegs on which to hang Tory arguments, and the characters met intermittently are types who can usually be summed up in a surname. Human interest is sustained in chapter after chapter of a very long narrative by the vanity, resourcefulness, and linguistic ability of that Yankee jack-of-all-trades, Sam Slick.

The character of Slick has been objected to on the grounds that his attitude and actions are not consistent throughout Haliburton's several works about him, that his speech reflects the dialects of many localities rather than one, that he is in fact paste rather than diamond, a stage character and not a credible human being. It is quite true that the Sam Slick of *The Clockmaker* is not the Sam Slick of *The Attaché; or, Sam Slick in England* (1843), intended for a different audience. In the latter book, the peaceful Yankee pedlar has become a thin-skinned, pugnacious braggadocio. Perhaps critics of the change have not sufficiently noticed that Americans abroad are not always the same as Americans at home. Both Sam Slicks are consistent within the limits of the books in which they appear. In point of fact, Sam Slick's versatility is an artistic reflection of the spirit of New England. The Yankees were the Greeks of the New World, and Slick is a folk hero, an Odysseus of their commercial frontier. In their excursions by land and sea, the Yankees not only acquired knowledge of men and affairs, but they also picked up their language where they found it, appropriating picturesque phrases much as they appropriated ideas that could later be turned into dollars and cents. In Haliburton's time, Slick was a credible New Englander; if he is a stage character today, he is one at least in the same brilliant sense as the characters of Molière and Dickens.

By his use of Sam Slick in *The Clockmaker*, Haliburton preserves a fine balance in assessing Americans, British, and Nova Scotian colonists. His judgments, like those of most great humorists, are essentially ambivalent. He admired the British for their institutions, achievements, and because he was of their stock. He disliked them because they refused to alter traditional ways of doing things and because they patronized colonists. He disliked the Americans because of their bragging, their opportunism, and because they had beaten the British. He admired their thrift, industry, shrewdness, and practicality. Haliburton saw in the Nova Scotians a people of essentially British virtues. They were, however, ruining themselves by extravagance and by sacrificing their private affairs to the pursuit of pleasure, politics, and religion. Sam Slick serves both as an unconscious example of American crudity and as a model to demonstrate to Nova Scotians how they should employ themselves. His praise of Britain is usually confined to secondhand accounts of the opinions of his clergyman and is often qualified by his own disagreement. Out of Sam Slick's comment and action in *The Clockmaker* emerges an ideal Nova Scotian life founded upon Burkean principles and unified by practicality and common sense. The satire becomes universal because individual and local personalities are kept subordinate to the central theme.

Whether of character, situation, or language, the humour in *The Clockmaker* depends upon the reader's enjoyment of the exposure of human weakness or incongruity. Although often coarse, it is not savage or cruel. Despite its theme, *The Clockmaker* is an essentially happy book. At this stage in his life, Haliburton was secure in his enjoyment of life and in his faith that his gospel for Nova Scotia would ultimately prevail.

Haliburton united two incongruous elements in the style of *The Clockmaker*. The narrative parts are written in the formal English of eighteenth-century prose. In Sam Slick's conversations, Haliburton becomes a prose poet, daring in metaphor, building up adjectival climaxes without fear of barbarisms, and utilizing all the local resources of dialect. The use of dialect did for Haliburton what the use of lowland Scots did for Burns. It gave him his crowning touch of individuality and lifted him above the ruck of popular writers like Theodore Hook and Charles Lever whose works superficially resemble his own.

The Clockmaker was Haliburton's most popular book. He followed it in

1843 with *The Attaché; or, Sam Slick in England*, which contained much hard-hitting criticism of English society. Haliburton's British audience proved much less disposed to laugh at themselves than they had been to laugh at Nova Scotian colonists and Yankees. Less popular still, but deservedly so, were the final Sam Slick books: *Sam Slick's Wise Saws and Modern Instances; or, What He Said, Did, or Invented* (1853) and *Nature and Human Nature* (1855).

All four books keep the same structure and for their interest depend upon Sam Slick, the freshness of their anecdotes, and the justice of the viewpoint displayed in them. Few readers can absorb more than sixteen hundred pages of almost continuous monologue by one character without becoming weary of his mannerisms. Few writers can fill up as many pages with humorous anecdote and remain fresh and funny. Haliburton told his best stories first, and after *The Attaché* there is a considerable decline in the quality of the anecdotes presented. Still worse, Haliburton gradually lost the perspective necessary to the humorist. In *The Clockmaker*, he could allow himself to be worsted by Sam Slick and laugh. In less than ten years, his consciousness that his political ideals were doomed prevented Haliburton from further self-laughter. The more strongly the forces of history turned against Toryism, the more extreme became his satire in its favour until the effect of his humour was vitiated by partisan distortion. *The Attaché*, good as it is, is marred by extreme statement. Worst of all, in the last two Sam Slick books, Haliburton shows signs of exchanging the role of social critic for that feeblest of vaudeville roles—the mere teller of funny stories.

Although the Sam Slick books made Haliburton's reputation, they do not comprise all his fiction. Two books in which the professional humorist triumphs over the deeper satirist of human society are *The Letter-Bag of the Great Western; or, Life in a Steamer* (1840) and *The Season Ticket* (1860), the latter published after his move to England.

The first of these reminds one of Smollett's *Humphrey Clinker* and Galt's *The Ayrshire Legatees*. It is a collection of letters purporting to have been written by passengers aboard the *Great Western* en route from Liverpool to Halifax. Haliburton's avowed purpose was to popularize steam travel between England and Nova Scotia, but he completely fails to bring his imagination to this task, so that *The Letter-Bag* throughout remains as crude propaganda. He spends his ingenuity instead on rather juvenile "high jinks" and on burlesquing the national and religious mannerisms which Anglo-Saxons of a certain type automatically assign to "foreigners." Although it contains some fine comic passages, *The Letter-Bag* is too extreme in its caricature and too gross in its humour to rank very high as literature.

Railway travel in the British Isles is the matter of *The Season Ticket*. Here the subject is treated with more understanding and depth and is enlarged to include the whole subject of transportation within the British Empire. Haliburton saw improved transportation as vital to the unification and development of the Empire and advocated, among other projects of a far-seeing nature, the building by the British government of a railway to link the isolated British North American colonies. *The Season Ticket* is by far a more considerable book than *The Letter-Bag*. At the same time, neither incidents nor characters are so lively and entertaining as those of the Sam Slick books.

The Old Judge (1849) is Haliburton's valedictory to a Nova Scotia he failed to convert to his own way of thinking. Sombre, realistic, balanced in its judgments, it is the most satisfying of all Haliburton's books although it lacks the surface brilliance of *The Clockmaker*. It is constructed upon a pattern similar to that of *The Clockmaker* but more diversified. Nova Scotia is seen through the eyes of an educated British tourist who visits his friend, the Old Judge, and is squired around Nova Scotia by another friend, Lawyer Barclay. The tourist's observations and encounters are supplemented by the observations and reminiscences of his friends and the other characters who are incidentally introduced. The most interesting of these last is Stephen Richardson, a Nova Scotian eccentric. In the sketches of men and women, in the account of melodramatic events at lonely frontier outposts, and in his background descriptions, Haliburton unveils in *The Old Judge* an unsuspected facet of romantic feeling and talents of a high order for serious fiction. Had he considered it worthwhile, he might have become Canada's first major novelist.

Although *The Old Judge* is not lacking in the political bias and humour that characterized Haliburton's work, it is a sad book—full of regret for a way of life that was passing and masking its bitterness with ironic dignity. In its range, it is easily the best portrait of early nineteenth-century life in British North America; in human insight and interest, it is matched only by Susanna Moodie's *Roughing it in the Bush*.

Haliburton did not confine himself to fiction. He was a vigorous historian and writer of political tracts, publishing in addition to the works mentioned earlier, *The Bubbles of Canada* (1839), *A Reply to the Report of the Earl of Durham* (1839), *Rule and Misrule of the English in America* (1851), *An Address on the Present Condition, Resources and Prospects of British North America* (1857), and *Speech of the Hon. Mr. Justice Haliburton, M.P., in the House of Commons, on Tuesday, the 21st of April, 1860 on the Repeal of the Differential Duties on Foreign and Colonial Wood* (1860). *Rule and Misrule of the English in America* is a good thesis history; none of the other publications mentioned above are of more than specialist interest.

Haliburton is also important as an anthologist of American humour. He collected unusual stories and articles from United States newspapers, journals, and books, and published the results of his work in two books, *Traits of American Humour by Native Authors* (1852) and *The Americans at Home; or, Byeways, Backwoods, and Prairies* (1854). The prestige of his name made them popular in Great Britain and enabled many readers to sample for the first time a wide variety of New World writing. For these pioneer anthologies as well as for his own writing, Haliburton deserves the title given him by Artemus Ward, "the father of American humour." His labours prepared a reading public for the work of Mark Twain and Stephen Leacock.

Much of Haliburton's work is dated. Many of his favourite mannerisms, like the pun, have gone out of style. The smart Yankee is no longer a novelty to readers. There are, however, in his best work enough humour and wise comment of a universal nature to make it worth reading today. Haliburton must continue to vie with Stephen Leacock as Canada's greatest humorist.

In his own time, there was no question of Haliburton's greatness. For a decade he rivalled Dickens in popularity, and he was the first colonial to be honoured by Oxford University (1858) for literary merit. It is typical of colonial diffidence that Haliburton's work was thought of much more highly in both Great Britain and the United States than it was in his own province of Nova Scotia.

7. Literary Activity in the Maritime Provinces
1815-1880

FRED COGSWELL

I. GENERAL INTRODUCTION

WRITING IN THE MARITIMES between 1815 and 1880 is more significant when considered as history or sociology than it is when considered as literature. Literature, like a tree, is an organic growth and dependent for its size and configuration upon soil and climate. Both environment and cultural heritage were powerful limiting factors in the shaping of Maritime literature.

The environment was that of a few cities and many towns, strategically located with respect to transport; each was surrounded by a slowly growing hinterland of clearings where were provided the sinews of their economic life: lumber, farm produce, fish, and a few minerals. Each city or town was dominated by one or two leading families, but within its economic and social structure, it was amazingly diversified. Craftsmen and local industries supplied the homely demands of the rural areas and the luxury demands of the town magnates. There was a pride in craftsmanship and a self-sufficiency which remain in the Maritimes as attitudes although the social patterns which supported them have for the most part passed away.

The effect of the population distribution for literature was to hold down the numbers of those who would normally be expected to respond to or create it, and to restrict them to the members of a particular class. Pioneer conditions circumscribe life within a struggle for material possessions, and most Maritimers spent the nineteenth century in the shadow of the frontier. With few exceptions, education outside of the towns was limited or non-existent, and the literacy of the rural population was of a functional kind. Outside written literature, a vigorous oral tradition of folk literature in English, French, and Gaelic and the hymns of the various churches gave some spice to leisure hours and neighbourhood gatherings.

In the cities and towns most inhabitants—whether professional men or artisans—were more literate. Education was higher in calibre and more readily available. Publishing facilities existed, for the presses of local newspapers were always glad to print tracts and books of verse at their authors' expense. Both Halifax and Saint John made contacts, by means of public lectures and the drama, with the more sophisticated centres of the United States and Great Britain. Nevertheless, most inhabitants—whether professional men or artisans—spent their time in making money. The uncertainty of an economy where demand and price were fixed by fluctuating foreign parliaments and markets made constant attention to the acquiring of capital essential. This meant that only a very small segment of the population had the education, the interest, and the leisure to write. Literature was almost exclusively the property of lawyers, schoolteachers, clergymen, journalists, and their wives and daughters.

This narrow base for the creation and support of literature explains the almost complete absence of dramatic compositions, the scarcity of *belles-lettres*, and the paucity of Maritime prose in general. Other factors, however, must explain the great volume of poetry published by Maritime writers throughout the nineteenth century. For example, at least 108 books of verse were published between 1825 and 1880 in the Maritimes, and 32 books were published elsewhere by Maritime authors. Practically every newspaper had its poetry corner, containing verse little inferior to that currently being published in book form.

To understand the predominance of verse over prose, one must grasp the nature of the Loyalists in their hopes and in their failure. For good or evil, their spirit dominated the cultural life of the Maritimes throughout the century.

The Loyalists desired a stable, pyramidal society. At the top was to be a gentry—officials, great merchants, estate owners, professional men. Supporting the gentry and guided by it were to be, subtly graded, various smaller merchants, artisans, small farmers, tenants, and servants. Every man was to know his place, but there was to be a place for every man. All were to be united emotionally by the twin symbols, the Church and the Crown. Because they had been unwilling to see the spirit of the frontier supplant the spirit of eighteenth-century England, the Loyalists had fled to an even wilder frontier—and found themselves trapped in it.

When the expenses of the French wars forced England to abandon the subsidies which alone would have made aristocracy possible in the Maritimes, most Loyalist families sank into conditions of extreme poverty, and their children reverted to the materialism and illiteracy of the frontier. A few favoured families stood firm by monopolizing the civil appointments in the colonies. But all, whether they had means and education to support their pretensions or not, clung to their traditions. Among continuing values was an admiration—often without understanding—of poetry as a prestige symbol. Prose was common, but only the well-born and the well-educated, as their ancestors had been, could properly appreciate poetry. Unfortunately, the most valued quality of a poetry so conceived and appreciated was apt to be its decoration, conventionally moral and derivative of the fashions in the motherland.

A second prestige symbol among Loyalist families was a classical education. They could not afford much, but as soon as they could, the Loyalists founded academies and small colleges in various centres throughout the Maritimes. Here the élite were to acquire the rudiments of Greek, Latin, rhetoric, and the English classics. A few of them even carried on the habit of translation after their schooldays were done. For example, William Blowers Bliss (1795–1874) issued *Translations from Catullus, Horace, etc.*, from a Halifax press in 1872. The same year, Silas Tertius Rand (1810–1889) published several Baptist hymns turned into Latin verse among the miscellaneous poems of *The Dying Indian's Dream*. So strong was the respect for classical literature in the Maritimes that even Moses Hardy Nickerson, a self-educated radical, fills up several pages of *Carols of the Coast* (1892) with translations from the Latin. Other poets who did not translate directly used the Latin and Greek classics as models for their verse.

This non-utilitarian respect for education and this careful following of models kept Maritime writers from the barbarisms perpetrated by many frontiersmen elsewhere. At the same time, they inculcated the principle of imitation at the expense of originality, leading writers to rely too greatly upon forms of literature designed to meet conditions other than their own.

Cultural borrowing is particularly dangerous when the cultures concerned are disparate. Such Maritime poets as Peter Fisher, Oliver Goldsmith, James Hogg, Joseph Howe, William Martin Leggett, and David Palmer adopted the forms of a poetry already out of date in England. These were the heroic couplet, the public song, and Miltonic blank verse. Of these only the public song—a minor genre at best—proved transplantable. The heroic couplet, designed to express the sensibilities of an urban élite and demanding a professional polish, came off badly when applied to the frontier by amateur poets. Miltonic blank verse had become by the early nineteenth century imitative and mediocre in its own land.

The successors of this generation of Maritime poets borrowed from the great English romantics. Romantic forms and techniques had been developed to resolve the tensions of a complex society going through its time of troubles. Maritime poets fitted them to platitudinous and decorative verse on general themes to satisfy a society whose concepts were narrow and homogeneous.

One cannot help feeling that the emotional drive behind most Maritime poets was neither self nor social realization; it was rather a pathetic attempt to prove that the colonies, although separate in space from the motherland, were still indivisibly one with British culture. Local pride that verse was being written at all led to enthusiastic reviews in the local newspapers. Poets had no incentive to self-examination and improvement, and theme and occasion became the all too sufficient guides for the judgment of poetry.

Professionalism was necessarily absent through the greater part of the century. Prose writers wrote when they felt that they had something useful to say, and poets wrote as a genteel hobby. Not until the late 1860's did two writers, James De Mille and May Agnes Fleming, sit down cold-bloodedly to write for money. Seldom has any literature been so exclusively the province of the amateur.

The great defect of the amateur is that only incidentally is he concerned with form. A classical education had taught both Thomas McCulloch and Thomas Chandler Haliburton how to construct good sentences and proper paragraphs; their greatest defects lie in the larger formal aspects of their work. The form of literature which suffered most from the amateurism of its perpetrators was the novel which, before De Mille, was consistently feeble, wooden, and amateurish.

Most Maritime poets had received a classical education, and contemporary verse forms were straightforward and metrical. These factors kept their work from becoming doggerel, but the blight of amateurism was conspicuously present. A genuine poet achieves the unique expression of his personality through form—a way of putting words together which is the product of intense search and concentration. Maritime poets were too easily satisfied; the result is a sameness of expression which, when joined to a sameness of attitude and theme, makes essentially flavourless verse.

Maritime poets were further limited by the relatively restricted and homogeneous society in which they lived. They wrote in straightforward sentences and did not strain for the unusual phrase or image because their thought was limited. Their world was one of moral and aesthetic blacks and whites. What is most characteristic of their work is that each writer was absolutely certain as to the truth of what he was stating. Such certainty produces rhetoric rather than poetry, and rhetoric is more susceptible than genuine poetry to changes of fashion and taste. When one is certain of truth, one does not torture one's imagination to find fresh ways to express it—the readiest and least ambiguous are the best. The final effect upon the reader of Maritime poetry is one of impersonality—the dominance of a convention beyond which the poets never ventured. Too many poems might quite as easily have been written by other Maritime poets as by their authors.

It is not surprising, therefore, that Maritime poets achieved their best work in light and occasional verse. James De Mille's "Sweet Maiden of Passamaquoddy" springs readily to mind, as do John Hunter-Duvar's "The Emigration of the Fairies" and Richard Huntingdon's "The Memory of the

Red Man." By far the most attractive works of Joseph Howe, Moses Hardy Nickerson, Matthew Richey Knight, and James Arminius Richey are their occasional poems and epigrams.

No society is altogether homogeneous, of course. The most significant writing in the Maritimes sprang from an attempt by Maritime writers to resolve basic conflicts which over a period of years appeared in their society. These tensions are three in number.

The first in time was the conflict between orderly habits of life acquired in Britain and the British colonies in America and the shiftless, gambling economy imposed on the emigrants by their new environment. This tension found its fullest expression in prose in the *Letters of Mephibosheth Stepsure* by Thomas McCulloch, published in the *Acadian Recorder* in 1820 and 1821, in poetry in *The Lay of the Wilderness* (1833) by "A Native of New Brunswick" (Peter Fisher). In their zeal to persuade readers to industry and a more strict application to farming, McCulloch and Fisher gave realistic, if exaggerated, pictures of living conditions in New Brunswick and Nova Scotia.

A similar concern for industry and order in business and agriculture informs the social surveys published in the *Nova Scotian* newspaper in the 1820's and 1830's by Joseph Howe and *The Clockmaker* (1833) and other writings of Thomas Chandler Haliburton. In the work of Howe and Haliburton, however, the conflict between old ways and new merges with the political struggle for responsible government which from 1830 to 1840 adds a note of one-sided realism to a good deal of Maritime prose. The political polemic of the Maritimes makes intelligent use of the ideological bases provided by British thinkers, but only Haliburton, who saw a naked struggle for power underlying political ideologies, was able to create from this source of tension a literature of lasting value.

The third tension—that between Christianity and the crude hedonism of the frontier—was resolved by a puritanism as extreme as the excesses against which it recoiled. Unfortunately for literature, this puritanism became imbedded in the intellectual life of the Maritimes. The Baptist church, founded by the poet Henry Alline, succeeded in capturing a segment of Halifax intellectuals headed by Edmund Crawley. From the founding of Horton Academy (later Acadia College) in 1828, this religion acquired and maintained a position of leadership in the Maritimes that its sectarian rivals could not ignore. The strongest manifestation of puritanism by mid-century was the rise of the temperance movement which soon expanded to become interdenominational in scope.

The result of attempts to express temperance polemics in literary forms devised by the Romantics and Victorians was incongruity, bathos, and sentimentality. Alexander Kent Archibald's adaptation of the technique of

Byron's *Don Juan* to support the temperance movement in *Poems* (1848) is an excellent example of incongruity. S. C. Fulton's *Red Tarn, or the Vision of the Lake; a Thrilling Temperance Poem in Fourteen Cantos* (1873), in its opening vision of a lake of the alcoholically damned, achieves a turgid grandeur, but it too soon sinks to bathos and puerile rhetoric. The following from *Vesper Chimes* (1872) by Phebe Mills deserves quotation as a sample of the sentimentality that pervades a host of poems on the temperance movement:

> ... Alas for all her glowing dreams,
> Her new-found joys where are they now?
> Upon her cheek shame's hectic gleams,
> A hot flush mantles o'er her brow.
> What is it rends her feelings so?
> What is it wounds her woman's pride?
> Ah, she has learned the truth to know,
> She is a moderate drinker's bride.

The direct impact of puritanism produced hundreds of prose tracts and several novels, of which the *William and Melville* (1826) of Thomas McCulloch is the most distinguished. All are too extreme in their view of reality and too crude in their form to have more than a functional value.

Not a tension within the society of the Maritimes but an alternate source of culture was the presence of a large Scottish element. The Scottish community delighted in the nostalgic sentiment, the pungent satire, and the radical independence of Robert Burns, and many of its members tried to transfer these qualities to the poetry of their own localities. The result was a body of lowland Scots verse surpassing in realism and pith the achievement of those who clung to the more genteel Victorian colonial tradition.

All these factors were not sufficient in themselves to establish a realistic tradition in Maritime literature. On any frontier, men and women are tempted to use their leisure to escape from what they feel to be harsh and confining conditions; on a frontier in which the community gives its emotional allegiance to another land and another mode of living, they are tempted irresistibly. The first novel and the first book of verse published by native-born writers in the Maritimes demonstrate this truth. Julia Catherine Beckwith made the sub-title of her romance, *St. Ursula's Convent, or the Nun of Canada; Containing Scenes from Real Life* (1824) a misnomer. The book contains merely the day-dreams of a schoolgirl who had read too many British romances. Oliver Goldsmith's *The Rising Village* (1825) describes the pioneer homes of Nova Scotia as if they really were the neat English cottages which the author would have liked them to be. Reading and writing in the Maritimes during the nineteenth century were diversions—the vicarious fulfilments of frustrated hopes.

Apart from a few political pamphlets, the literary impact of Confederation upon the Maritimes was slight. The union ran counter to the spirit of local independence which had been slowly developing throughout the century; it also opposed the spirit of colonialism which was the Maritimer's principal cultural heritage. Confederation was adopted enthusiastically only by those financiers and politicians who had engineered it, and the thirteen years between 1867 and 1880 did not allow more than the tentative growth of a national consciousness. Symptoms, however, of the Canadian nationalism which was later to burgeon in the work of Roberts and others occur here and there in Maritime poetry. Examples are Robert Murray's hymn "From Ocean unto Ocean," V. H. Nelson's "My Own Canadian Home," and Frederick Augustus Dixon's pageant-play, *A Masque, Entitled "Canada's Welcome."*

As has been shown, men and women in the Maritimes did not always write for the right reasons. The society in which they lived and the models that they chose tended to produce at best a respectable mediocrity. Yet their very limitations gave to their work certain positive advantages.

The tone of life in the Maritimes was healthy, optimistic, and remarkably free from cynicism, pessimism, and sensationalism, and the literature reflects the spirit of a people still capable of responding with human warmth to ideal virtues and simple situations—a people whose lives were centred in the home, the occupation, and the church, and who did not require violence to stimulate their appetites. The Maritime writer never questioned that life, love, beauty were enduring gifts of God and that their opposites would be overcome by time and struggle. If the expression of his beliefs was often banal, his sincerity deserves respect.

The very deference which the educated gave to British literature ensured that they read it avidly. There was relatively little cultural lag on this section of the American frontier. Moses Hardy Nickerson sprang to the defence of Lord Byron at the time of the posthumous invasion of that poet's privacy by Harriet Beecher Stowe. A. D. McNeill's "Evolution" is a long poem in very good "In Memoriam" metre in defence of Darwin. In *Poems of Ten Years, 1877–1887*, Matthew Richey Knight, Methodist minister at Boiestown, New Brunswick, defends the British journalist W. T. Stead against clerical attack at the time of his exposure of the "White Slave" traffic in England. In fact, Maritime writers throughout the century dealt with the latest political and intellectual events in Britain with a liberality greater than that which they normally applied to their own *milieu*.

The general respect given to literature in the Maritimes encouraged young men and women to read and to create it. It was only a question of time before writers of genius would transcend, in part at least, the limitations of Maritime environment and cultural heritage. One such writer, as already noted, did emerge in Thomas Chandler Haliburton, whose prose sketches were recognized in Great Britain and the United States as comparable with those created by men of their own nationality. The poets had to wait longer, but the premature death in Fredericton of Peter John Allan was compensated by the development of Roberts and Carman in the 1880's. Throughout the nineteenth century, the Maritime Provinces were the seed-bed where a national poetry might arise if it were to arise at all.

II. THE NOVEL IN THE MARITIMES

No pioneer community has ever produced a major novelist or a major novel. Perhaps the most sophisticated of all literary forms, the novel has been a late-flowering expression of every culture in which it has appeared. It demands a maximum of self-awareness, a differentiated social structure, a demanding and discriminating audience, and a professional attention to technique. The Maritime Provinces lacked these conditions. In fact, many Maritimers as puritans regarded the novel as anathema. The few novels produced were the work of amateurs, and not until after 1810 did professional novelists emerge.

Maritime nineteenth-century works of fiction may be classified into two schools. The first comprises those novels which were written to popularize moralistic doctrines. To this group belong the *William and Melville* of Thomas McCulloch, the work in Halifax of the Herbert sisters, and that in New Brunswick of Sarah French, the pioneer writer of juvenile literature. The titles of the works provide a good indication of their contents. Sarah Herbert (1824–1844) wrote *Agnes Mailard: A Temperance Tale*. Mary Herbert (fl. 1859–1865) produced three novels: *Scenes in the Life of a Halifax Belle* (1859), *Woman as She Should Be; or, Agnes Wiltshire* (1861), and *Young Man's Choice* (1869). Sarah French published *Letters to a Young Lady on Leaving School and Entering the World* (1855) and *A Book for the Young* (1856).

These writers deserve respect for sincerity of intention, and they provide genuine insights into contemporary social conditions. Unfortunately, in their moral and religious zeal they allow their opinions concerning what ought to be to triumph over what in all likelihood would occur were the events of their novels to be transferred to real life. As a result, their plots appear contrived and unnatural. The characters are drawn in too unrelieved whites and blacks to be convincing, and moral earnestness is never leavened by humour.

The second, and far more numerous, group of writers of fiction produced either historical or society novels, more amateurish in technique but as escapist in content as the popular British fiction then being published by Bentley or Colburn.

Julia Catherine (Beckwith) Hart (1796–1867) wrote *St. Ursula's Convent;*

or, The Nun of Canada (1824). This book's sole claim to attention is that it was the first work of fiction to be written by a native-born English-speaking Canadian and the first to be published in what is now Canada. Mrs. Hart, who was Julia Beckwith when she wrote it, was a schoolgirl in Fredericton. She had read about the world of fashionable society in Paris and London, and she had a lively imagination. The best that can be said for her work is that it is no worse than that done by such novelists as Lady Blessington, who certainly had far better opportunities to know and do better. While living in the United States, Mrs. Hart produced a second novel, *Tonnewonte; or, The Adopted Son of America* (1831), slightly better than the first. A third novel exists in manuscript.

Two Saint John writers, John K. Laskey and Douglas S. Huyghue, may be mentioned briefly. Laskey's *Alathea; or, The Roman Exile* (1840) and Huyghue's two novels, *Argimou, a Legend of the Micmac* (1847) and *Nomads of the West; or, Ellen Clayton* (1850), are stereotyped in character, rhetorical in style, and melodramatic in plot.

Agatha Armour (d. 1891) of Fredericton wrote four novels under the direct influence of *East Lynne*. These are *Marion Wilburn* (n.d.), *Sylvia Leigh; or, The Heiress of Glenmarle* (1880), *Lady Rosamond's Secret* (1880), and *Marguerite Verne; or, Scenes from Canadian Life* (1886). *Lady Rosamond's Secret* is of interest to local historians as it contains sketches of Fredericton society during the governorship of Sir Howard Douglas.

Thomas Barlow Smith (1839–1933), a crotchety Nova Scotian seaman, wrote novels after his retirement. Experiences drawn from his own life and travels form vivid but incongruous patches against the romantic façade of *The Young Lion of the Woods; or, A Story of Early Colonial Days* (1889); *Rose Carney, a Story of Ever Shifting Scenes on Land and Sea* (1890); and *Seraph on the Sea; or, The Career of a Highland Drummer Boy* (1891).

Two books deserve mention as exceptions to the moralistic and melodramatic trends in amateur fiction in the Maritimes. The first of these is *The Mysterious Stranger,* published in London in 1817 and afterwards pirated several times in the United States. The book was actually designed as biography rather than as fiction, and it presents an illusion of reality much more vividly than any of the works mentioned above. *The Mysterious Stranger* was written by Walter Bates (1780–1842), Loyalist sheriff of Kings County, New Brunswick, a man with little interest in literature. So amazing, however, were the exploits of Henry More Smith as confidence man, jail-breaker, and horse-thief, that Bates took pen in hand to write his story. Its subject, the simplicity of its style, and the seeming truth of its background make *The Mysterious Stranger* still a readable book. One feels that it achieves its modest success because its author was not sufficiently acquainted with popular British fiction to spoil it by imitation.

The second work in prose fiction produced in the Maritimes before 1880 that contains touches of local realism was the anonymous *Miramichi*, published in Boston in 1863. Despite flaws in plotting, characterization, and style, the book does give some indication of what it was like to be living in New Brunswick during the middle years of the nineteenth century.

All the works discussed above were by amateurs, none of whom produced more than three novels in a lifetime. The term novelist, during the first eighty years of the nineteenth century, can only be applied to two writers in the Maritimes who gave to the novel something of the care and attention which it deserved and who largely depended upon it for their incomes.

The more financially successful of the two was May Agnes Fleming (née Early), a Saint John housewife (1840–1880). During the depression of the 1870's, she earned from the Street & Smith Company of New York as much as $10,000 a year. Mrs. Fleming received this princely income for writing no less than forty-two novels—primarily designed for serial publication— within the space of seventeen years. Undoubtedly she was Canada's first spectacularly successful professional novelist. Fifteen of Mrs. Fleming's novels appeared in book form during her lifetime, and twenty-seven were published after her death, which should constitute some kind of record in posthumous publication.

Apart from facility, there is little remarkable in Mrs. Fleming's work. As professional in her technique as Mrs. Channing, her English counterpart, she introduced into the high-born English society of her novels characters from Canada and the United States, and she was very careful to construct the plot of each novel so that some of the action would occur in Canada. By so doing, she indicates that although her books were designed primarily for United States and British sales, she was mindful of the local pride of a Canadian audience.

Within a very minor convention, Mrs. Fleming's novels are exciting, readable, and remarkably even in quality. A few which may be mentioned as having been very popular in their own time are: *The Dark Secret; or, The Mystery of Fontelle Hall* (1875), *Guy Earlscourt's Wife* (1872), *Lost for a Woman* (1880), *Noreen's Revenge* (1875), *The Actress' Daughter* (1886), and *Estella's Husband; or, Thrice Lost, Thrice Won* (1891).

There is both greater variety and a waste of a very real talent in the work of James De Mille (1833–1880).

De Mille was born in Saint John, educated at Horton Academy, Acadia College, and Brown University (M.A. 1854). He had travelled widely in Europe as a young man before establishing himself as a bookseller in Saint

John. When his bookselling business failed, De Mille turned to teaching and held the posts of professor of Classics at Acadia College (1860–64) and professor of English at Dalhousie College (1864–80). De Mille was, in the opinion of those who knew him, a brilliant and ambitious scholar. He composed a good textbook upon rhetoric and a bad poetical exercise in it, "Behind the Veil," which was published posthumously in 1893. At the time of his death, De Mille was being considered for the chair of rhetoric at Harvard College.

De Mille was a man of extraordinary energy possessed of a wide range of interests. He left behind him a considerable reputation as a host and a teller of witty stories. As a means of supplementing his academic salary, he turned to fiction, and—mainly for the American firm of Harper Brothers—wrote thirty books in less than twenty years.

De Mille's fiction can be classified into five groups: the B.O.W.C. Series, the Dodge Club Series, popular melodramatic novels, historical romances, and the anomalous *A Strange Manuscript Found in a Copper Cylinder*.

Neither the melodramatic nor the historical novels deserve detailed consideration. *Cord and Creese* (1869) and *The Cryptogram* (1871) are representative examples of the first. In these works, lurid incidents and highly coloured characters are woven into plots of great complexity and considerable ingenuity at the expense of the reader's credibility. The stories, however, are related with an energy and verve that are worthy of greater subjects. Typical historical romances are *Helena's Household: A Tale of Rome in the First Century* (1867) and *The Lily and the Cross: A Tale of Acadia* (1874). In these, chunks of undigested history are crudely combined with the typical insipid love affairs of the cardboard heroes and heroines of romance.

The four books of the B.O.W.C. (Brethren of the White Cross) series are *The B.O.W.C.: A Book for Boys* (1869), *The Boys of Grand Pré School* (1870), *Picked up Adrift* (1872), *The Treasure of the Sea* (1873). In this series, books were written for the first time in Canada that appealed to the authentic interests of young people and were at the same time readable and free from overt didacticism. De Mille drew upon his experiences as a schoolboy at Horton Academy for the characters, the background, and many of the incidents, and his lively style and acute sense of humour must have made the B.O.W.C. series a joy for the young people of his time. The writing of books for young people has since become a literary art, and by comparison the B.O.W.C. series now seems dated. It was, however, a commendable pioneer enterprise.

The Dodge Club; or, Italy in 1859 (1860), which initiated the Young Dodge Club series, represents the merging of two influences, *Pickwick Papers* and *Innocents Abroad*. De Mille took the idea of his plot from Dickens, but it is Twain's humour that dominates the book. Based upon incident rather than upon character, the humour of De Mille is inferior to most of Haliburton's. Occasional passages occur, however, which indicate what De Mille might have done had he been less facile and more careful in his composition. For example, there are few scenes in Canadian literature more delightfully droll than that in which the American Senator and the Italian countess discuss the poetry of Isaac Watts.

De Mille wrote into *The Dodge Club* and its inferior successors experiences gained during his tour of Europe in 1850 and 1851. As a result, the book does convey an authentic picture of travelling conditions in mid-century France and Italy. The characters are stage types, designed not to interfere with the incidents upon which the author depends for the popularity of his work. The love interest is slight, but it is saved from sentimentality by the light-hearted, almost flippant, treatment which De Mille gives to the romantic passages. Much of *The Dodge Club* is in fact a clever parody upon the melodramatic novel in which De Mille was so proficient, and it is mainly for this reason that the book achieves a shallow and superficial success.

A Strange Manuscript Found in a Copper Cylinder was published posthumously. It is indebted to Rider Haggard and to Jules Verne. From Haggard, De Mille took the technical device of telling his story by means of a chance-recovered manuscript; from Verne, he borrowed the method of making the manuscript appear more credible by having an audience of its readers discuss its marvels in the light of contemporary linguistic, palaeontological, and racial theories. This pseudo-scientific commentary is interspersed with the action and is thus designed to make the book more suspenseful as well as more credible. Although ingenious, the commentary is often more boring than convincing and takes up a disproportionate number of pages. The characters are lacking in life. Few readers could become involved in the fate of the hero, Adam More; his sweetheart, Alma; and her rival, Layelah. Despite these flaws, *A Strange Manuscript Found in a Copper Cylinder* is De Mille's most original and powerful work and is by far the most interesting novel to be written in the Maritimes before 1880.

Its greatest virtue is De Mille's imaginative conception of the Kosekim, a society of kindly cannibals who revere darkness, poverty, and death. Few ideas are so pregnant with possibilities for satire. De Mille, unfortunately, does not quite make the most of this one. His ingenious reversal of the values of contemporary Western life enables him to show human nature as a constant, independent of ideology, and he exploits with telling irony man's tendency to reject the absolute in favour of conformity. Nevertheless, he sacrifices an idea that might have produced another *Gulliver's Travels* for the sake of an adventure story. *A Strange Manuscript* is a good adventure story despite the tedious comments upon the manuscript and despite the satirical diversions. De Mille's accounts of bizarre adventure and fantastic landscapes are models of vivid narration. The book fails to achieve greatness only because its author attempted in its composition to do too many things at once.

III. BELLES-LETTRES AND DRAMA IN THE MARITIMES

This section will appear to be disproportionately brief; however, one result of the sparseness and wide distribution of population in the Maritimes was the relative absence of a basis to support dramatic compositions and *belles-lettres*. It is true that Halifax, Saint John, and occasionally Chatham, were visited by many of the great dramatic companies which played in New York and Boston, but the repertoires of these professional companies had no room for the works of local dramatists. Many amateur theatrical productions took place in the towns of the Maritimes, but the local players, none too confident of their acting ability, invariably chose plays whose established popularity was a guarantee of at least a modicum of success. The puritan ethos of the Maritimes also did not encourage the writing of plays. In consequence, all the drama in the Maritimes which found its way into print was designed for reading rather than for acting.

Prose drama, even when not designed for stage production, was almost non-existent. A fragment of a prose play was published in the *New Brunswick Courier* of Saint John for February 23, 1833. This was a crude and vigorous attack upon Sir Archibald Campbell, the Lieutenant Governor, and various members of his government for their conduct in the distribution of Crown lands.

Verse dramatists were scarcely more prolific. All that deserve consideration are a fragmentary romantic play included in *The Poetical Remains* (1853) of Peter John Allan (see below); two closet dramas, *The Enamorado* (1879) and *De Roberval* (1888) by John Hunter-Duvar (1830–1899); and three plays by Frederick Augustus Dixon (1843–1912), the most considerable of which was the wooden *A Masque, Entitled "Canada's Welcome": Shown Before His Excellency the Marquis of Lorne and Her Royal Highness Princess Louise on Feb. 24th, 1879, at the Opera House*. *De Roberval* is by far the most ambitious of these plays and is the only one that deserves serious literary consideration.

John Hunter-Duvar, who will re-appear in the discussion of poetry below, was a student of Renaissance history and literature and a collector of rare books. Largely for his own amusement he composed closet dramas, of which two only were ever published. In *De Roberval* Duvar tried to present the picture of a strong man marred by pride, to parade his learning of the details of Renaissance life in Europe, and to pay a graceful tribute to Sir

John A. Macdonald, to whom the book in which the play appears is dedicated. Unable to combine these ingredients dramatically, Duvar forces them into his play at the expense of the action. The tedious clowning, imitative of the Elizabethans at their worst, furnishes a further brake upon the development of the plot, and Duvar's mingling of slang and poetic language leads often to bathos:

> Delightful! Write me down a pirate bold.
> Sang dieu! I'll be Rollo o'er again,
> And lay hands on another Normandy.

At the same time, *De Roberval* is one of the first attempts to incorporate into a major literary form the nascent Canadian nationalism, and here and there throughout its pages are scattered passages that in their apt use of language surpass any other blank verse produced in Canada before the twentieth century. No playwright need be ashamed of lines like the following:

> I saw a savage once from Africa;
> Black as a lump of charcoal, kettle black,
> But fat as any high Church dignitary,
> And greasy as a friar mendicant;
> Bohemians bought her for a kind of show,
> As a descendant of the Queen of Sheba. . . .

The scarcity and short life of literary magazines in the Maritimes during the nineteenth century prevented the development of any considerable tradition in *belles-lettres*. A small body of work of seriousness, integrity, and concern for style may be found in *Poems and Essays* (1874) by Joseph Howe (1804–1873), *Thistledown* (1875) by Alexander Rae Garvie (1839–1875), and *Stewart's Literary Magazine* (1867–1872), published in Saint John by George Stewart (1848–1906), a distinguished essayist and journalist and the only Canadian member of the International Literary Congress of Europe.

Maritime literary prose in the nineteenth century was Sunday writing in Sunday clothes. It consisted mainly of essays in which the results of the author's reading and meditation on general topics were gathered together and decorated with lofty language and suitable figures of speech. It is serious, manly, dignified, but at the same time impersonal and inflexible.

Joseph Howe was primarily a politician and orator and secondarily a poet. As these, he will be dealt with elsewhere in this volume. The prose of *Poems and Essays* must, however, be treated as *belles lettres*. It consists of a moral tale, "The Locksmith of Philadelphia," and the text of five lectures, "Shakespeare," "Eloquence," "The Moral Influence of Women," "The Howe Festival," and "The Adornment of Ottawa." Most of the lectures were given to various Mechanics Institutes and illustrate Howe's mastery of a highly allusive rhetorical style—a style in which reminiscences drawn from many literary sources are cleverly combined with personal opinion and experience. They do not talk down to their audience, and their successful reception does credit to the intelligence of the working man in the Maritimes during the nineteenth century. None of Howe's essays is a classic, but all are respectable productions and provide eloquent testimonies to his breadth of learning and intelligence.

The ten essays in Alexander Rae Garvie's *Thistledown* show a keen eye for the details of physical description and a genuine love of Maritime landscape. They also demonstrate by frequent allusion and quotation the breadth of Garvie's reading in the English and French classics. Without being distinguished for originality of thought and style, such essays as "About Plagiarism," "Skating," "A Reverie," and "About Titles" are surprisingly polished productions to issue from a rural manse in New Brunswick in the nineteenth century.

IV. POETRY IN THE MARITIMES

Oliver Goldsmith's *The Rising Village* (1825), to be discussed more fully below, established a vogue in the Maritimes for narrative poetry written in couplets, involving local history and legend, and combining some account of pioneer conditions with a good deal of moralizing about the joys of rural life. This pattern was perpetuated in Peter Fisher's *The Lay of the Wilderness* (1833), and Joseph Howe's "Acadia," also to be discussed below, and continued to be written as late as *Allan Gray and His Doubts* (1881) by "A Lover of the Truth." It produced no masterpieces, but the following representatives are interesting for the light that they throw upon what Maritime poets considered as significant material for literature.

Mrs. I. S. Prowse's *The Burning Forest: A Tale of New Brunswick* (1830) is a graphic description of the plight of human beings caught in a forest fire. William Charles McKinnon (d. 1862) published *The Battle of the Nile: A Poem in Four Cantos* (1844) as an exercise in youthful colonial patriotism. Cassie Fairbanks' *The Long House: A Poem, Partly Founded on Fact* (1859), written in octosyllabic couplets, is a melodramatic account of a local murder. All narrative writers did not, however, use couplets. The Reverend Joseph Clinch wrote his lengthy but dull biblical narrative, *The Captivity of Babylon* (1840), in Spenserian stanzas, and Charles Windsor Hall used blank verse to deal with the expulsion of the Acadians in *Legends of the Gulf* (1870).

Pierce Stevens Hamilton (1826-1893) constructed a more elaborate framework in which to house the tales of Acadian history and legend contained in *The Feast of Saint Anne and Other Poems* (1878). The device is Chaucerian: a picnic party attends a Micmac celebration of the Feast of Saint Anne and its members agree to relate in turn various stories from Nova Scotia's past. Although the stories, composed in ballad stanzas, are vigorous, the framework is clumsily handled and the blank verse in which the balance of the poem is composed is rhetorical and poor.

A more sophisticated pattern for narrative verse was employed briefly by Arthur Sladen in Saint John and by Alexander Kent Archibald (b. 1803) in Nova Scotia. In their most substantial work, both these men adapted the verse form and mannerisms of Lord Byron's *Don Juan* to local themes. "Midnight Rambles" and "Angela" in Archibald's *Poems* (1848) reproduce something of Byron's stanzaic brilliance but fail to preserve the difficult balance between digression and narrative that made his work a success. The two narratives of *The Conflagration* (1838) by Arthur Sladen (mis-spelled Slader on the title-page) suffer from the same defect.

Byron was a short-lived influence upon satire in the poetry of the Maritimes, but throughout the nineteenth century Maritime writers—whether or not they wrote in lowland Scots—drew inspiration from the verses and attitude of Robert Burns. The work of John LePage (d. 1895), *The Island Minstrel*, published in Charlottetown in two volumes, 1860 and 1867, and the many volumes of Andrew Shiels (1793–1879), the Cape Breton blacksmith, are not sufficiently polished in form and phrase to make worthwhile for a reader the detailed study of local and political issues necessary to give them point. William Murdoch (1823–1887), the hermit of Partridge Island, includes in his *Poems and Songs* (1860) many poems of point and polish, of which the following stanza is a good example:

> God pity, then, the poor blue-noses,
> Their cheeks like flour, their nebs like roses;
> They puff they grue, and swallow doses
>   To heat their wame,
> Till oft when night their business closes
>   They hiccup hame. . . .

Although they did not write in lowland Scots, two Nova Scotians, Moses Hardy Nickerson (1846–1943) and David Fleming Little (d. 1881), were satirists in the school of Burns. Nickerson's *Carols of the Coast* (1892) and *Songs of Summerland* (1927) and Little's *Poems* (1881) contain many local satires and epigrams of more than passing interest. Little's verse, sharpened by frustration in love and the shadow of impending death by tuberculosis, exhibits an independence of outlook combined with an intensity of feeling that is all too rare in the poetry of the Maritimes before 1880. One feels that Burns himself would have approved the spirit and execution of "Bunson's Belief," Little's most considerable poem.

Religious satire in verse was too extreme in its outlook to have value in literature. Two exceptions occur. Between 1857 and 1862 James Arminius

Richey published five volumes of scholarly verse which contain many manly and skilful satires constructed in defence of Anglicanism against its more extreme opponents. The anonymous *No Sect in Heaven,* published in Saint John in 1868, is a clever and refreshing attack upon sectarian bigotry in its more absurd manifestations.

By 1850, the lyric had become the dominant literary form in the Maritimes. As stated earlier, Maritime lyric poets were handicapped by the puritan ethos, the uniformity of society, the colonialism, the materialism, and the isolation of a thinly populated frontier. As a result, they initiated no tradition of their own but followed either the Victorian tradition of poetic decoration and moral edification or the lowland Scots tradition of which Burns's "The Cotter's Saturday Night" and "To Mary in Heaven" are exemplars. No Maritime lyricist developed a personal style, and the work of most is a pastiche derived from not necessarily congruous sources. Nevertheless, the work of even the meanest or the most orthodox of Maritime poets holds scattered glints of interest. For example, a Halifax phrenologist, John Salter, published *The Poetical Works of John Salter* (1852). This volume contains as contemptible doggerel as was ever printed, but in it are a few dialect sketches of Negro life in Halifax that are grossly authentic and linguistically exciting. Mrs. J. P. Grant's *Stray Leaves: A Collection of Poems* (1865) is the epitome of Victorian provincialism, but it too contains a few poems, notably "Snowshoing" and "Tobogging" (*sic*), which are unpretentious and exact descriptions of local customs and landscape.

It is difficult for the historian to point out landmarks where all the trees are of nearly the same height. Although certainly not more worthy than others of the name of poets, a few Maritime writers deserve mention for their greater literary knowledge and the higher degree of polish which they gave to their verses.

Amos Henry Chandler (b. 1837) was a New Brunswick physician who, in conjunction with Charles Pelham Mulvaney, published *Lyrics, Songs, and Sonnets* (1880). Chandler's contributions show a marked influence of Shelley. His philosophic poems on nature display considerable power of phrase and control over intricate metrical form. They also make use of the Westmoreland landscape to a limited extent. Unfortunately, they lack the intensity of inner conviction required to save them from rhetoric.

Matthew Arnold and Thomas Carlyle are the principal influences upon the work of Matthew Richey Knight (b. 1854), of Boiestown, New Brunswick. Knight's *Poems of Ten Years, 1877-1887* (1887), contain a few good sonnets, several Landor-like epigrams, and a fragment, "Thomas Carlyle," happily conceived in the style and spirit of its subject.

The best of the sentimental followers of Burns were John Murdoch Harper (1845-1919), Robert Murdoch (b. 1836), and John Steele. In his own time, John McPherson (1817-1845) attracted the greatest degree of critical attention. This, however, was more because of his unhappy career as a self-educated farm labourer than because of his verses. *Poems, Descriptive and Moral* (1852), although competently executed, are disappointingly banal in subject, language, and sentiment.

Cursory mention may perhaps be given to the following Maritime lyricists and their works: John S. Allen (1841-1923), *From Apollyonville to the Holy City: A Poem* (1880); Margaret Gill Currie (b. 1843), *John Saint John and Anna Gray: A Romance of Old New Brunswick* (n.d.) and *Gabriel West and Other Poems* (1866); Archibald Gray, *Shades of the Hamlet, and Other Poems* (1852) and *Bubbles from the Deep* (1873); James Haynes, *Poems* (1864); James Hogg (1800-1866), *Poems, Religious, Moral, and Sentimental* (1825); Clotilda Jennings (d. 1895), *Linden Rhymes* (1854) and *North Mountain Near Grand-Pré* (1883); William Martin Leggett (1813-1863), *The Forest Wreath: A Collection of Lyrics* (1833); David Palmer (1780-1866), *New Brunswick and Other Poems* (1869); and Hiram Ladd Spencer (1829-1915), *Poems* (1850), *A Song of the Years, and a Memory of Acadia* (1889), and *The Fugitives* (1909).

Oliver Goldsmith

Although Oliver Goldsmith (1794-1861) only briefly wrote poetry, two circumstances have given him a disproportionate importance in Canadian literature. In the first place, he was the namesake and grand-nephew of the Anglo-Irish poet, Oliver Goldsmith; secondly, his *The Rising Village: A Poem* was the first volume of verse ever published in Canada by a native-born Canadian to receive serious attention at the hands of critics and literary historians.

The son of a Loyalist official, Goldsmith was born in Saint Andrews, New Brunswick, but within two years the family moved to Halifax. After teaching his son the rudiments of reading, writing, and arithmetic, Oliver Goldsmith's father destined him to a variety of occupations in turn. Goldsmith was employed successively in the naval hospital, an ironmonger's shop, a bookseller's shop, a lawyer's office, and a wholesale firm. In 1809, his father decided to send him to the Halifax Grammar School, but within a year he had procured for his son an ensigncy in the Nova Scotia Fencibles. Before Oliver could join that regiment, his father again changed his mind, made him resign his commission, and entered him in the Commissariat at Halifax as a volunteer.

This last choice proved fortunate, and Oliver Goldsmith followed until his death in 1861 the career of a successful colonial administrator. During a year spent in England in 1817 and 1818, Oliver Goldsmith became conscious of the deficiencies of his education, and upon his return to Halifax set conscientiously to work to repair them by reading and study. Although he never mastered Latin and Greek, he did manage to learn French and Spanish and to read widely in English literature.

In 1822, the Halifax Garrison organized a theatrical company, and Goldsmith was chosen to play the part of Tony Lumpkin in his great-uncle's play, *She Stoops to Conquer*. Inspired by the coincidence, Goldsmith composed a successful verse prologue to the play and followed it with a more serious imitation of *The Deserted Village*.

When *The Rising Village: A Poem* appeared in London in 1825, Goldsmith became so disappointed by the invidious comparisons that English critics made with his great-uncle's work that he lost all further interest in poetic composition. He did, however, re-issue the poem, along with a few occasional pieces, in a volume entitled *The Rising Village, with Other Poems*, published in Saint John in 1834. Goldsmith's only other work in literature was a manuscript autobiography, published for the first time in 1943 by the Ryerson Press.

The 570 lines of *The Rising Village* fall into three divisions. The first third of the poem traces in general terms the growth of a colony from the hardships of the early settlers to the settled calm enjoyed by their descendants. The final section paints an illusory picture of contemporary Nova Scotian prosperity. Sandwiched between and bearing little organic relation to either part is the pathetic story of Flora and Albert.

In his skilful use of balance and antithesis, Goldsmith demonstrates how carefully he had studied his great-uncle's work. Unfortunately, he borrowed tamely every conceivable trite phrase and hackneyed rhyme that had found its way into the eighteenth-century British couplet. As a result, his otherwise respectable lines are studded with clichés. Only in a few excursions into local description does his verse become more than a literary mosaic. The following is an example of his style at its best:

> Here, nails and blankets, side by side, are seen,
> There, horses' collars, and a large tureen;
> Buttons and tumblers, fish-hooks, aprons and knives,
> Shawls for young damsels, flannel for old wives;
> Woolcards and stockings, hats for men and boys,
> Mill-saws and fenders, silks and children's toys;
> All useful things, and joined with many more,
> Compose the well-assorted country store.

Goldsmith's additions to the 1834 volume comprise a few short occasional pieces and religious exercises in verse and a handful of love lyrics. All are undistinguished and make the reader view Goldsmith's early retirement from verse-making without regret.

Peter Fisher

A comparison of subject-matter and attitude in three rare anonymous books—*Sketches of New Brunswick* (1825), *Notitia of New Brunswick*

(1838) and *The Lay of the Wilderness: A Poem in Five Cantos,* by "A Native of New Brunswick" (1833)—would indicate that they were written by the same author. The first two are known to be the work of Peter Fisher of Saint Anne's (Fredericton), New Brunswick's pioneer historian.

The son of Ludovic (Lewis) Fisher, a New Jersey Loyalist of German descent, Peter Fisher (1782-1848) was born at Staten Island where the family were awaiting evacuation to New Brunswick. Fisher, who received a good education from the distinguished pioneer schoolmaster, Bealing Stephens Williams, combined great powers of observation and a good memory with commercial shrewdness and tremendous physical strength. While operating an extensive lumber business and raising a large family of distinguished sons, Fisher found time to gather materials for his histories and to incorporate into them and into his verse accurate descriptions of the social conditions of a New Brunswick in the grip of a lumbering economy. Although they are too unpolished to be significant as literature, his poem and his histories provide the best insights we have into living conditions in New Brunswick in the first forty years of the nineteenth century.

The Lay of the Wilderness is less literary than *The Rising Village.* Lacking the devices of balance and antithesis, Fisher's lines often degenerate into doggerel. Nor is the narrative intrinsically more interesting or better managed than that in Goldsmith's poem. *The Lay of the Wilderness* does, however, contain two ingredients conspicuously lacking in Goldsmith's work. One is an awareness of the democratic difference between life in a North American colony and life in Great Britain; the other is the uncompromising bluntness with which Fisher depicts the degeneracy of the Loyalist officers who attempted to settle on the upper St. John River. The failure of their settlement is sharply contrasted with the spectacular success achieved at Woodstock by a settlement of disbanded N.C.O.'s and privates.

Joseph Howe

Joseph Howe (1804-1873) was the greatest of all Maritimers. The self-educated son of a pioneer Nova Scotian printer, he won his way upward in society by unflagging energy and superior intelligence. A lustful, healthy, many-sided individual, Howe rivalled Benjamin Franklin in the versatility of his achievements. His career as a politician, orator, and prose writer is dealt with elsewhere in this volume. Howe himself was fondest of writing poetry. "Poetry," as he put it, "was my first love, but politics was the hag I married."

Howe's poetry, composed at odd moments snatched from a busy life, was published posthumously in *Poems and Essays* (1874). Its longest poem is the incomplete narrative, "Acadia," dealing with the perils of early settlement in Nova Scotia. The moralizing at the beginning and end of the poem is conventional and dull, but the central narrative differs from those of

Goldsmith by its vigour and fast pace. Howe's couplets are technically superior to Fisher's but less polished than Goldsmith's. They are, however, forthright and straightforward and bear more distinctly than the work of the other poets the marks of a personality.

Howe's other poems include heavy moralizing on "poetic" themes in a diction old-fashioned even for his time, occasional poems, and songs. The occasional poems are surprisingly effective. Howe could turn a graceful compliment or a clever epigram when the occasion offered. His finest verse is contained in the songs. These have the dignity, balance, and fine phrasing that characterized the public songs of England in the days of "Rule, Britannia." Few better patriotic poems have been written in Canada than "Song for the 8th of June" and "The Flag of Old England." Unfortunately, these have lost their magic since the spirit of British colonialism to which they appealed has given place to the spirit of Canadian nationalism.

Peter John Allan

Most of Peter John Allan's brief life (1825–1848) was spent in Fredericton, where his father was chief medical officer. Of commanding physique and endowed with unusual beauty and intellect, Allan embodied in his personality the romantic temperament at its best, and his death by fever at the age of twenty-three was a loss to the cause of poetry in the Maritimes. Had he lived, he might have established thirty years earlier the kind of poetic renaissance that Roberts and Carman were to create in the 1880's and 1890's. The posthumously published *Poetical Remains of Peter John Allan* (1853) indicate that Allan had begun to imitate his British models in the same spirit and with the same concern for technical perfection as Roberts was later to do. The book is a more immature and chaotic *Orion*.

Byron, Shelley, and Tennyson were Allan's masters, and he had learned their lessons with respect to the construction of stanza, line, and phrase although he had not, however, even begun to master the archetectonics of a long work. His major faults, however, were those of a young man to whom reading had brought more vivid experiences than had life. He is too ready to create literature out of other literature rather than out of his own experience, and there is little of his local background embodied in his work.

Alexander Rae Garvie

Of Scottish ancestry, Alexander Rae Garvie (1836–1875) was born in Demerara in British Guiana and died at Montreal. The greater part of his life, however, was spent in the Maritimes—mainly New Brunswick—as a Presbyterian clergyman. Garvie was shy and retiring by nature but an omnivorous reader and such a delightful companion to his intimate friends that George Stewart, Jr., likens him to Charles Lamb.

Garvie's essays in *Thistledown* (1875) have already been dealt with. His verse is largely lyrical, sober, reflective, and moralistic. Although skilful in its handling of metre, it is undistinguished in its phrasing. Exceptions are the sonnet, "Best of All Trees I Love the Stately Sombre Pines," a dignified expression of the stern grandeur of his religion, and the stoic "An Epitaph":

> How went my youth? Alas! bitter truth!
> It waned like the moon into clouds uncouth,
> Which hung over dawning dark omens of rain.
>
> How went my age? Turn thou the torn page,
> And read, writ in blood, Death's final mortgage—
> Signed, sealed and delivered in presence of Pain.

Garvie's most interesting poem is his narrative, "Allan Gray," the story of a love between two boys which ends in the tragic death of one of them. "Allan Gray" in some respects foreshadows the much greater treatment of this theme contained in Earle Birney's *David*. The tone of the poem is right throughout, but the effect is partly muffled by commonplace diction.

John Hunter-Duvar

John Hunter-Duvar (1830-1899) was a Scotsman of French ancestry who, after having been stationed for most of his life in the army in British North America, finally settled at "Hernewood, Fortune Cove, Prince Edward Island." There he commanded the Prince County battalion of active militia and for ten years served as Supervisor of Fisheries for the Government of Canada.

Like his drama, which has already been dealt with, Duvar's poems are the exercises of the leisure of a gentleman and are distinguished more for grace of execution than for any relevance they possess to the environment of Prince Edward Island at the time of their composition.

De Roberval, a Drama (1888) contains scattered songs and also two longer poems, "The Emigration of the Fairies," and "The Triumph of Constancy, a Romaunt." The latter is a moral fable in verse on a medieval theme. It is consistent in subject, sensibility, and language, and were it placed within the frame of *The Earthly Paradise*, it might easily pass as the work of William Morris.

"The Emigration of the Fairies" is Duvar's poetic masterpiece. The conception of this poem is original and happy. A bit of earth on which fairies still exist is washed from its native England during a storm, drifts across the Atlantic, and comes to rest at Hernewood, where Duvar gives the little people a second home. This device enables Duvar to describe the beauties and dangers of an Atlantic crossing, to contrast the old land with the new while paying graceful tributes to both, and to indulge his bizarre fancy with descriptions of objects upon a liliputian scale. By truncating Byron's *ottava rima* to a six-line stanza, Duvar found a form to fit his theme perfectly. Although the poem lacks modulation and possesses wit and fancy rather than feeling and imagination, "The Emigration of the Fairies" is the most technically successful and the most aesthetically satisfying poem to be published in the Maritimes before 1890.

In addition to the plays *The Enamorado* and *DeRoberval*, and the very rare *John a' Var: His Lays* (n.d.), Duvar left behind in newspapers and periodicals a good deal of fugitive verse. One poem, "Making an Acadian Farm," deserves rescue for the clarity with which it expresses the division in the Maritime soul between colonialism and frontier pride:

> Here dwelt the Squire . . .
> Self-reliant, as became his race,
> He set himself to see what he might do.
> And summing up his knowledge, found he knew
> Of trading nothing, and of farming little,
> But much of the great glory of the woods;
> So mainly fancy-led he took a stretch
> Of forest land, full of acclivities,
> With winding brooklets running at the base;
> And in the process of his clearing laid
> By bit and bit his English knowledge by;
> Saw zig-zag fences, without hate, and learned
> The science of the handling of the hoe,
> The handy shift and rude Colonial ways,
> And watched so long the swinging of the axe,
> He almost learned himself to chop a tree;
> He made himself a roughish kind of farm
> And called it by a fond ancestral name.
>
> Where once the stumps had been grew apple trees,
> And grass and grain and a rude garden place,
> And in the course of time the orchard fruits
> Grew red-cheeked in the sun; and specimens
> Of planted trees for landscape—beech and elm—
> And some imported—lime and sycamore,
> Became umbrageous, and lent dignity;
> While round the circuit of the whole domain
> Was left a margin of the old rough woods,
> Wherein the intersecting timber-roads
> Were under-brushed and trimmed to bridle-paths,
> At which the Squire—a setter at his heels—
> Would frequent take his rides in Spring or Fall,
> Beneath the red flame of the maple bush,
> Or in the yellow rain of beechen leaves;
> And musing, with full heart, would grateful say,—
> "Dear Lord! the land is fair to look upon,
> Although it is not like my English home!"

8. Literary Activity in the Canadas
1812-1841

CARL F. KLINCK

"A CANADIAN," Arthur L. Phelps has said, "is one who is increasingly aware of being American in the continental sense without being American in the national sense." The story of literary activity in the Canadas (Upper and Lower) from 1812 to 1880 supplements the social and political history of a period during which this part of North America absorbed settlers, largely from Britain, and ensured separation from the United States, at first by war and later by the formation of a new Dominion (1867). Among the factors making for cultural independence in this North American country were the presence of the co-operating *canadien* French, local solutions to local problems, the waves of new, direct British immigration, and closer ties with Britain than the United States had desired after the Revolution.

Literary *activity*, even if it is not to have qualitative status as literature, had a part to play in the positive development of a separate people, with much that became characteristically their own in attitudes, sensitivity, turns of thought and phrase, subject-matter, allusions, symbols, myths and legends. Many such images will be mentioned in chapters 8 and 9, and the composite image is of no small importance. The literary sources of this inheritance will now be traced in this chapter under two divisions, (I) Lower Canada: Quebec city and Montreal from the War of 1812 until the Union of the provinces (1812–1841) and (II) Upper Canada during the same period. In chapter 9 there are two more divisions, (I) Genteel colonialism in Canada East (Quebec) and Canada West (Ontario) (1841–1855) and (II) the Confederation era in central Canada (1855–1880).

I. LOWER CANADA: QUEBEC CITY AND MONTREAL (1812–1841)

At the time of the American War of 1812–1814, when naval and military forces supplied a temporary increase, the normal English-speaking population of the cities of Quebec and Montreal was estimated at about three thousand in each centre. As John Lambert saw them in Quebec (*Travels through Lower Canada and the United States*, 2nd ed., 1814), these people were the British and North American English who dominated the colony, consisting principally of government officials, military officers, and legal and ecclesiastical dignitaries, along with merchants, practitioners in medicine, shopkeepers, and traders. In Montreal there were fewer officials and more traders, especially those in the business of furs. These, of course, made up only a fraction of the population, for the British had not come fifty years earlier into an empty land. Lower Canada (in our day the province of Quebec) was almost wholly French in language, culture, religion, and laws. The term "Canadian" was equivalent to "*canadien*," that is North American French, and the image of Canada was made up of seigneurs, habitants, black-clothed clergy, advocates, *coureurs de bois, voyageurs*, French Hurons at Lorette, Gallic gaiety, rides in *calèches* or sleighs, folk singing, farm labour, lumbering, church-going, and villages scattered along the banks of the St. Lawrence. The English image, significant of power but also picturesque, included vice-regal display, military colour and bustle, polite sport, harbours full of transatlantic ships, vast stores for continental trade and development, political quarrelling, and high social life.

From the outside it was customary to regard Quebec and Montreal as subjects for literature in terms of war because of Wolfe and Montcalm; of age because of memories of the *ancien régime*; of primitivism because of the proximity to sublime scenery and harmless Indians; of forest adventure because of the visible product of furs; and of pleasurable "roughing it" because of Thomas Moore's "Canadian Boat Song" ("Faintly as tolls the evening chime"), published in 1806. From the inside the continuous involvement of two languages and peoples was more obvious. This complex internal situation can be illustrated from the journalistic works of John Neilson (1776–1848), who succeeded his uncle as editor of the venerable and influential Quebec *Gazette*. Beyond the range of current news were domestic affairs and daily living, fit subjects for poetry, as in the writings of a Montreal law-student Levi Adams. His social observations were warmer than Mrs. Frances Brooke's and his description of French Canadians at home places him in a line continued now in English through William Henry Drummond (1854–1907) to Roger Lemelin (the Plouffe family of the 1950's). Adams (who died in 1832) was partly lost under a pseudonym, but an attempt to revive knowledge of him seems justified by the results.

The indisputable fact is that Adams's name appeared on the title-page of *Jean Baptiste* (Montreal, 1825). The place of publication is worth noting with regard to all these early books since a Canadian imprint was rare. *The Charivari*, published in Montreal a year earlier and attributed to "Launcelot Longstaff"—a misleading pseudonym—appears now because of internal evidence to be by the same hand as *Jean Baptiste*. Both are comic, but sympathetic, narratives of the wooing and wedding of elderly French-Canadian bachelors. The treatment was suggested by Byron's *Beppo* to this native Canadian who, during Byron's lifetime, attempted adaptations of nearly the whole of that noble lord's poetic cycle: the melodies, the Eastern tales, the dramas, and the burlesques. The local reviewers, then beginning their own careers, congratulated their townsman on building, as David Chisholme said in the *Canadian Review* (July 1824), "upon the domestic habits and social pastimes of a virtuous people." Several claims to priority among the poets of the Canadas may be made for Adams. In addition to the books mentioned, he published eight poems (several very long ones), an essay, and two stories in the Montreal *Canadian Magazine* and *Canadian Review*. A large volume, 306 pages in length, *Tales of Chivalry and Romance* (Edinburgh, 1826), a puzzle to bibliographers, has been identified by the present writer as belonging to Adams. It stands with Oliver Goldsmith's *The Rising Village* (London, 1825) and Major Richardson's *Tecumseh* (London, 1828) among the first books of poetry published in the United Kingdom by native-born British North Americans.

If Mrs. Anne Cuthbert (Rae) Fleming (d. 1860) had been born in Canada, full claims for priority could have been made for her. The author of *A Year in Canada, and Other Poems* (Edinburgh, 1816) came to this country from Aberdeen, Scotland, in 1815 or 1816, after she had separated from her first husband, a Mr. Knight. The book gave her name as Anne Cuthbert Knight. She later became a resident of Montreal when she married James Fleming, brother of the financial celebrity John Fleming (1786?–1832). Her Goldsmithian poem, "A Year in Canada," deserves recognition as a very early and most thoughtful, if somewhat condescending, treatment of rural life and manners in Lower and Upper Canada (especially in Glengarry). In many ways she anticipates (but not in prose) the later works of Mrs. Traill, Mrs. Anna Jameson, and Mrs. Moodie. When she became a teacher in Montreal, Mrs. Fleming published chiefly school books, including *Views of Canadian Scenery for Canadian Children* (1843).

Official literature, of course, operated on a pretentious level, especially in Quebec city; name, rank, British background, and political connections received unusual respect. Yet even here there was a strong dash of North Americanism, illustrated neatly in the career of the Hon. William Smith (1769–1847), author of a *History of Canada*, printed in Quebec in 1815 but not issued until it was enlarged in 1826. Smith's father, from whom he inherited a position in the ruling class, had been a Loyalist from the American colony of New York. The son collected early records of Quebec—a special interest centred on this side of the Atlantic, although not resulting, Mrs. Leprohon asserted in her *Antoinette de Mirecourt* (1864), in a due respect for the French upper classes and habitants. Smith's correspondence with the Earl of Dalhousie shows that he helped the Governor General to plan and establish in 1824 the Literary and Historical Society of Quebec, an organization still in existence today. British paternalism had one of its better moments when the Earl called for "the formation of a Society, not entirely 'Antiquarian' but Historical rather and Canadian." The term "Canadian" was here formally baptized into the English realm of letters.

The Society's charter members, "men, eminent for rank, erudition and genius," included François-Xavier Garneau, who later interpreted Canadian history for his own people, and Joseph Bouchette (1774–1841), the native-born Surveyor General and famous author of *A Topographical Description of the Province of Lower Canada* (1815). But French-Canadian participation, except in the case of Bouchette, was infrequently realized, even after partial union with a rival society in 1829. Bouchette, however, and his fellow scientists, particularly the Army and Navy's practical professionals, skilled in mathematics, physics, geology, and hydrography—the explorers of this era—dominated the Society and its early *Transactions*. They are given credit for encouraging the official geological survey of Canada.

The first of the Society's *Historical Documents* did not come out until 1838. It is possible to read in them the literary efforts of the gentlemanly amateurs, who made certain that Canadian poets would know the local robin better than the foreign nightingale. Mrs. William Sheppard of Woodfield wrote papers on shells and song birds; her husband and the Countess of Dalhousie on Canadian plants; John Wilkie on the grammar of the Huron language; and Dr. Walter Henry on the ways of the salmon. Outside the Society, Robert Christie (1788–1856) also illustrated this tendency to treat the familiar, the practical, and the immediate. His history of Lower Canada was printed in instalments, eventually in six volumes, covering chiefly periods through which he himself lived; he presented in it an invaluable collection of copies of despatches, speeches, newspaper articles, and the like regarding matters as important as the events leading up to the rebellion of 1837, the coming of Lord Durham, and the achievement of responsible government.

Military men were the spice of Quebec society, and, after the Napoleonic and American War, the colony received some liberally educated half-pay officers who contributed to the vast store of British campaign literature. *Haverhill; or, Memoirs of an Officer in the Army of Wolfe* (London, 1831), by the American James Athearn Jones, is an example of the persistence of the earlier Conquest material and the deliberately bookish treatment of stock situations. Dr. Walter Henry, the salmon expert, however, in *Trifles from my Portfolio* (1839), "by a staff surgeon," showed himself to be the "Tiger" Dunlop of the lower province. Henry was a stylist and perhaps a conscious romantic, for he built up a picture of himself as officer, young lover, traveller, participant in historic events, physician, and naturalist. He had indeed been at St. Helena when Napoleon died; he had also had twenty-nine years of military service in the Peninsula, France, the East Indies, and Nepal. In addition, he was able to make a vivid report of the rebellion years in Upper and Lower Canada. Like Dunlop, Henry gives the reader a strong sense of being present at great events beside a remarkable companion.

Quebec was not the place to expect philosophical radicalism, but there was at least one man whom European upheavals had sent to the city and its reading public. *The Enquirer*, a periodical which began in May 1821 and lasted one year, was edited by "C.D.E.," whom W. Kaye Lamb has identified as Chevalier Robert-Anne D'Estimauville de Beaumouchel (1754–1831), author also of *Cursory View of the Local, Social, Moral and Political State of the Colony of Lower Canada* (1829). C.D.E. was a native Canadian, long a resident abroad, who returned to Quebec in 1812 in his fifty-eighth year. His series on "My Own Life" in the rare files of the *Enquirer* should be his claim to remembrance; Samuel Hull Wilcocke printed part of it in the *Scribbler* of December 18, 1823. This man, Wilcocke said, was "no bad writer himself." The Chevalier gave an account of his experiences in London "in the latter end of 1779 and in 1781" when he was "intimately acquainted with the respectable family of the three Brothers Sharp, with Dr. John Jebb and the celebrated Thos. Holcroft." But he was converted, he said, from the "alluring rights of man" to "Heavenly philanthropy," discovered through the "gospel." Levi Adams was younger, and shared the romantic enthusiasm of Byron for the oppressed people of Europe, especially in Greece and Spain. In "The Fall of Constantinople" he celebrated the "former fame and freedom" of Greece; and in "The Guerilla Bride" and "Ode to Spain" he deplored the lost "soul of honour" among the modern Spaniards. In a preface there was a reference to his own "sojourn" in their country.

The Church of England had its stalwarts in Quebec in the persons of its first three bishops, the Right Reverend Jacob Mountain, Charles James Stewart, and George Jehoshaphat Mountain (Bishop of Montreal, 1836–50, and of Quebec, 1850–63). The second two deserve to be remembered for their literary works, Bishop Stewart for his missionary reports of Upper and Lower Canada, and the younger Bishop (G.J.) Mountain (1789–1863) for his many published sermons, and his later unaffected account of his canoe trip in 1844 from Lachine to the church's mission at the Red River, in Prince Rupert's Land. This cultured traveller, following the route of the fur traders, gave his report with humility, accuracy, and vividness in his *Journal* (1845) and *Songs of the Wilderness* (1846). The "songs," written by "one whose habits of poetry were formed only in youth," give the impression of a Bryant actually in the wilderness. Few colonial versifiers were more sincere in describing native flowers, waterfowl, *voyageurs*, Indian life, fireflies, and mosquitoes ("mementos of the fall!"). The preface to the *Songs* expressed this churchman's opposition to currently fashionable verse which, he professed, ran "counter, in many particulars, to my own tastes and to my own predilections—perhaps I should say, my own prejudices." A generation earlier, he had been opposed by prejudices on the fashionable side, for his father and he had been criticized by an irresponsible, temperamental, but clever young Irishman, Adam Kidd, who liked Stewart and hated the Mountains.

Kidd (1802–1831), evidently a friend of the Percevals at Spencer Wood, had been no model student in the church's school of instruction for candidates for holy orders. For a life of this kind he had been ill prepared by his own romantic travels in the wake of Thomas Moore and perhaps by a weakness for Indian girls. Kidd's rebellion took the form of the first consciously symbolic narrative by a Canadian, explained—or obscured—by his own note printed in *The Huron Chief* (Montreal, 1830). He said that he had suffered "an accidental fall from the cloud-capped brows of a dangerous Mountain, over which I had heedlessly wandered, with that open carelessness which is so peculiarly the characteristic of poetic feeling." This seemed for a long time to refer romantically to Slievegallin in his native Ireland! Sufficient proof is now available to show that the mountain was one of the episcopal Mountains, whom Kidd then proceeded to compare in a long Indian idyll—heavily documented from Heckewelder and other "Indian" authorities—with Skenandow, chieftain of the Hurons, whose home was a natural mountain. The episcopal father-image suffers in Kidd's comparison with the father-image of the pagan sage Skenandow, and missionary activity is regarded as supererogatory for those who are by nature good.

The Montreal *Gazette* of May 30, 1830, reported entertainingly how Kidd, a year before his early death, solicited subscriptions for his book from door to door, asking half a crown before publication and another half a crown on delivery. If Kidd's preface may be trusted, he sold 1500 copies in advance; the total would have been nearly £190, and again as much on delivery. Many persons must have subscribed in ignorance of the "Mountain" reference; the *Gazette* reviewer did not allude to it.

Indians were known to Kidd in their very persons at Lorette, near Quebec city, but another poet, William Fitz Hawley (1804–1855), author of *Quebec, The Harp, and Other Poems* (Montreal, 1829), appears to have prepared himself for *The Unknown, or Lays of the Forest* (Montreal, 1831) by reading Campbell, Moore, and Byron, perhaps confusing Indians with characters in Mediterranean metrical narratives—a risk one took with romance in those days. Hawley's lays are located in Italy, Persia, Arabia, and Greece. The "forest" of the sub-title belongs only to the framework (the introduction and conclusion) of the tales; and the inhabitants of this forest near Three Rivers, a noble old man, a lost Leonie, and a mysterious stranger, are stock figures drawn from Eastern or Indian romances. Hawley confessed in his first book that he had not reached "the polished strains of Campbell, the wild energy of Byron, nor the magic wand of Moore, wreathed with flowers, and glittering with gems." In "To Maia," one of his "Other Poems," he did achieve the magic he desired, but in general he proved that foreign muses did not, or did not yet, rest comfortably on the slopes of Mount Royal.

Society verse with an eighteenth-century, and timeless, flavour was written with great success by Adam Kidd in poems like his address to Miss——— (whom he loved "for a minute"), his "Epitaph" on a drunken parson, and his lines "To the Countess of D———e" (undoubtedly Dalhousie):

> Oh! do not curse the humble bard—
> He's poor enough without it—
> For if he said your heart is hard,
> There's very few will doubt it.

Gustavus William Wicksteed, a charter member of the Literary Society, lived longer and also achieved a reputation for polite versifying. Quebec had often received tributes for its gay, social life: from Peter Kalm in 1749, Frances Brooke in the 1760's, John Lambert in the early 1800's, and John Galt in 1827. In that last year Galt wrote a piece for the amateur theatre and "Tiger" Dunlop "performed the Highlander beyond anything [Galt] ever saw on the regular stage." The festivities of the vice-regal court, the military, and the wealthy families of Quebec were rivalled in Montreal by the feasts of the kings of the fur trade. The hospitality accorded Washington Irving by some partners in the North West Company in 1803 was remembered as evidence of the "perfect romance" of the life of a trapper or fur trader when he wrote *Astoria* in 1836. Irving had, in turn, provided hints for Canadian writers who knew the gay and witty *Salmagundi* (1807), a series of Addisonian essays set in New York and written by Irving, Irving's brother William, and James Kirke Paulding. *The Charivari* (Montreal, 1824), probably by Levi Adams, employed a Salmagundian pseudonym, "Lancelot Lo[a]ngstaff." Another name from these New York essays, "Jeremy Cockloft," had been used in 1811 on a title-page to stand for the author of *Cursory Observations Made in Quebec*, probably the work of a Bermudian, who, as William Toye has recently pointed out, also published a minor epic, *Britannia, a Poem*.

Cultural criticism in Lower Canada may have been encouraged by the example of *Salmagundi*, the influence of the Philadelphia *Port Folio*, and especially by the second series of *Salmagundi*, edited by Paulding in 1819-20. Witty discussion was by no means everyone's forte; didacticism always has stalwarts, and not only among old men like the Chevalier D'Estimauville, who wrote *Cursory View*. Edward Lane, a younger man, introduced his "few remarks . . . on the religion, manners, customs, etc. of the Canadians" into a conventional and contrived romance of a Byronic hero who seeks a runaway wife and a lost son in Canada. This was called *The Fugitives; or, A Trip to Canada* (London, 1830), and the author described himself as "formerly a resident of Lower Canada." Lane has not been securely identified; perhaps he was the Edward Lane who served as a catechist (1833-34) at Rivière du Loup en Haut, near Sorel and Three Rivers, in the diocese of Quebec during the episcopate of Charles James Stewart. If this is so, one must indeed reckon with the literary influence of the Society for the Propagation of the Gospel in Foreign Parts. On the S.P.G.'s roll as teachers for a short time were Lane and the poet Adam Kidd, and as priests for longer periods the poet Adam Hood Burwell, Bishop J. G. Mountain, and the Rev. Joseph Abbott (1789-1863), who turned his memoranda for emigrants into a kind of novel, entitled *Philip Musgrave* (1846).

Yet another effort in social criticism, supplementing the newspapers, was a semi-monthly magazine in Montreal, *The Literary Miscellany*, edited by Henry John Hagan, which began in November 1822 and disappeared in June 1823. It had a "pedagogical air," said Samuel Hull Wilcocke of the *Scribbler*, who was himself a Salmagundian of a coarse variety, tempered not in New York but in the arena of British journalism. The issues of his ephemeral rival, the *Literary Miscellany*, Wilcocke explained, "were too much occupied with newspaper controversy, and newspaper criticism, both objects that are, in most cases, beneath the dignity of an essayist."

The great contemporary literary journals, the *Edinburgh Review,* the *Quarterly Review* (London) and especially *Blackwood's Edinburgh Magazine,* proved that Scots could be Salmagundians, on every level from academic wit to outrageous practical joking. David Chisholme and Dr. A. J. Christie, however, Wilcocke's other rivals as editors of Montreal literary journals, were not graduates of the Wilson-Lockhart-Maginn-Hogg-"Tiger" Dunlop school. These immigrants, recently arrived in Canada (Chisholme in 1822 and Christie in 1817), were courageously, and perhaps naively, determined to make the large and handsome issues of their magazines not unworthy Canadian parallels of the Edinburgh models. They were practical and sober men; it was no mean achievement to get these issues printed. Chisholme (1796-1842), a protégé of the Earl of Dalhousie, subsequently published *The Lower Canada Watchman* (Kingston, 1829) and was editor of the *Montreal Gazette* (1837-42). It was he who edited *The Canadian Magazine and Literary Repository*, a monthly, through seven numbers, from July 1823 until February 1824. Then he left this project and edited *The Canadian Review and Literary and Historical Journal*, which had a history of five numbers, appearing irregularly and ending in September 1826. Dr. A. J. Christie (d. 1843) had practised medicine, edited the Montreal *Herald* from 1819 to

1822 and the Montreal *Gazette* from 1823 to 1824; he had also published *The Emigrant's Assistant; or, Remarks on the Agricultural Interest of the Canadas* (1821). Christie succeeded Chisholme as editor of the *Canadian Magazine* in February 1824 and carried it into 1825.

These two editors wished to avoid giving their journals a colonial appearance. They reprinted, as North American editors habitually did, from British publications (the *New Monthly Magazine* is acknowledged), but they did so with more discretion than later Victorian editors displayed in seeking decorative fillers. The *Canadian Magazine*, for example, printed in its first numbers extracts from an account of Captain William Parry's expedition into the Arctic regions, a review of Captain John Franklin's *Narrative of a Journey to the Shores of the Polar Sea*, and chapters from Scott's *Quentin Durward*, along with "Original Papers" on the fur trade of Canada, the Lachine Canal, the history of Montreal from the time of Cartier, the establishment of an English theatre in Montreal, and "The Fall of Constantinople" by Levi Adams. The *Canadian Review* began in July 1824 with articles on the Quebec Literary and Historical Society, the settlement of the townships of Lower Canada, the influence of literature, the education and duties of a Canadian merchant, the wars of Canada, the history of the aborigines, and the fur trade; there were also reviews of John Howison's *Sketches of Upper Canada*, of *St. Ursula's Convent*, and of *The Charivari*, together with at least three poems which may be attributed to Levi Adams. The *Review* was kept, as Carl Ballstadt has estimated in an unpublished thesis (Western Ontario, 1959), 77 per cent Canadian in content.

The *Magazine* and the *Review* offer a parallel to *Salmagundi*, principally to ideas in the second series, because Paulding gave the impression that authors in the United States were as self-conscious, as eager to establish local identity, and as defiant of some British fashions as Chisholme and Christie—and Wilcocke—were. Paulding's essay on "National Literature" is the showpiece for this attitude. He opposed fiction which offended an American sense of decency and reality. There was no need for literary reliance upon superstition or ghosts, fairies and goblins; wonder could be excited and feelings aroused by struggles and situations within the experience of Americans.

"Real life is fraught with adventures," Paulding wrote, "to which the wildest fictions scarcely afford a parallel." On the basis of such convictions the *Canadian Magazine* of April 1824 approved of *The Widow of the Rock* (1824), a book of poems by Mrs. Margaret Blennerhasset, and the *Canadian Review* praised Adams's *The Charivari*. For similar reasons, *St. Ursula's Convent* (1824) by a Canadian woman, Julia Catherine Beckwith (Mrs. Hart) (1796–1867), was denounced as a "Quintessence of Novels and Romances." Wilcocke turned to this same book as one of the "miseries" of a reviewer and expressed the wish that the author had made a novel of the true story of six Canadian nuns from Sandwich, in Upper Canada, who were captured by pirates off Cuba, retaken by a British cruiser, and forwarded to New Orleans by an American vessel!

The maturity and shrewdness of Samuel Hull Wilcocke (1766?–1833) were coupled with the audacity to descend into the blackest depths of gossip and vilification. His pseudonym, "Lewis Luke MacCulloh, Esquire," was a very thin disguise. The weekly *Scribbler* (1821–27), his "blasted blue book," along with its companion, *The Free Press* (at first, published in Burlington, Vermont, 1822–23), had the notoriety of a scandal sheet in its own time; it was fated for oblivion after that during a century and a half, and now for professorial resurrection. Wilcocke could be painstaking enough to record acceptably the debates of the Lower Canada legislature for 1828–29, but he could also employ the tactics of vicious English journalism. "Tiger" Dunlop's paper, the *Telescope* (1825), published in London, England, in this lawless period of the *Age*, did not sink so low, even (apparently) with some efforts by his helpers, Lockhart and Maginn. Dunlop had not suffered as Wilcocke had.

The latter had been brought to Montreal about 1817, at the age of fifty, to support Edward Ellice, the "Bear" (pseud. "Mercator"), a partner in the North West Company, in a major "contest between the Earl of Selkirk and the Hudson's Bay Company, on one side, and the North-West Company on the other." More than thirty books on this controversy (which resulted in the supremacy of the Hudson's Bay Company) were published, and Wilcocke edited at least four of them. Either his own company turned against him, or he stole from them—as was alleged—and he claimed that he was "infamously used, grossly oppressed, and falsely accused." Illegal capture of him by the company's agents on United States territory caused an international incident, and resulted in Wilcocke's living precariously just over the United States border while he edited the Montreal *Scribbler* and the *Free Press*. These uninhibited vehicles criticizing Montreal officialdom, business, and society exposed and terrified the inhabitants of the city, who could expect to be recognized in ludicrous or compromising situations under names like Sir Frederick Brute, Lord Goddamnhim, the Hon. Tory Loverule, Rev. Moral Police, and McRavish, McKilliway & Co.

Although it was very uneven, the *Scribbler* functioned as a literary review, exhibiting Wilcocke's unusual background of reading and his flexible style. It demanded weekly issues from its harassed editor, yet it ran through ten volumes while other periodicals grew up and collapsed. Wilcocke could claim to be "the first that regularly assumed the critic's chair in Canada" and his journal to be the first to acquire "the dignity of appearing bound in volumes on the shelves of a library." Chisholme and Christie gambled on the existence of a cultivated reading public; Wilcocke scratched the surface of what he found.

An American colony in Montreal—recently identified by Lawrence M. Lande in *Old Lamps Aglow* (1957)—served as a North American influence. Harman and Margaret Blennerhasset, who had come originally from Ireland, had turned from the United States to this Canadian city for refuge and employment during the years 1819-22; Aaron Burr's wild expedition to fight the Spanish, conquer Mexico, and found a southern empire had failed, leaving the Blennerhassets disgraced and deprived of their great paradisal mansion on an island in the Ohio River near Parkersburg, Virginia. Mrs. Blennerhasset (1778-1842) gave expression to her sensations of exile and loss in *The Widow of the Rock and Other Poems, By a Lady* (Montreal, 1824). "A Negro's Benevolence" and other poems were presumably additions by her husband. Her title-poem was typically a frontier idyll of vanished happiness—of a young pioneer wife who went mad when her husband was killed by rattlesnakes. This remains as an instructive example of a process worth observing in early North American verse, the conventional tale or lyric hides and sublimates a real-life history similar in feeling although different in detail. Margaret Blennerhasset's heart, it is clear, was back in her own happy mansion, described in "The Desert[ed] Isle," a poem which concluded (in the Canadian version) with lines attacking Jefferson and anarchic Democracy.

In this American group there were also Charlotte Sweeny of Vermont and her husband Robert Sweeny, who had emigrated from Ireland about 1820 and who in December 1840 lost his life duelling with a Major Ward, while defending, so the legend goes, the honour of his beautiful wife. His epigrams and poetic "trifles light as air" were published in *Remnants* (Montreal, 1835) and in *Odds and Ends* (Montreal, 1836), the latter "a Canadian reprint" of a New York edition (1826). Of "A. Bowman," publisher of *Hours of Childhood and Other Poems* (Montreal, 1820), little is known; he was probably also the author, and therefore the hard-working American patriot described in the Preface. He may be identified with the Ariel Bowman who was a bookseller and started the *Canadian Times* in Montreal in January 1823, with Edward V. Sparhawk, a local publisher, as editor. The paper gave offence to the French-Canadians and was stopped by order of the Assembly at Quebec in October of that year. Even less is known about John H. Willis, who may also have been of American origin. Lawrence Lande reports that he was "a civil servant by profession, and an artist by inclination." His talent for sentimental social verse was described as "making my Muse beseem a Harlequin" on the title-page of his book, *Scraps and Sketches; or, The Album of a Literary Lounger* (Montreal, 1831).

Irish wit and story-telling which might have enlivened the literary society of Quebec or Montreal may be found in *The Emigrant, a Poem, in Four Cantos* (Montreal, 1842) by Standish O'Grady (b. 1793), a farmer near Sorel. He was the very image of a displaced person: an Irishman who had had no real desire to emigrate, as he did in 1836; a Protestant in French

Canada who regretted that he could not live in Upper Canada; a clergyman and graduate of Trinity College, Dublin, who made no success of farming. "A Canadian stud horse," he said, "with one miserable cow were the only remnant of my stock which survived the winter." His poem, *The Emigrant*, shows, therefore, less adaptation to life in the Canadas than appears in other immigrant "epics," Adam Hood Burwell's "Talbot Road" (1818), William Kirby's *The U.E.* (written 1846), and Alexander MacLachlan's *The Emigrant* (1861). The theme of exile or homesickness for the Old Land was not as common in Canadian colonial writing as one has been taught to believe. David Moir ("Delta"), who wrote the famous "Canadian Boat Song" for *Blackwood's Magazine* (September 1829),

> Fair these broad meads—these hoary woods are grand;
> But we are exiles from our fathers' land,

had never been in Canada. Among the early immigrants themselves, the theme was exploited mainly in the works of the small minority who had lost more by coming than they had gained by staying in this country.

O'Grady employed the heroic couplet of Pope or Goldsmith with facility in discursive, satiric, mournful, or sententious passages. His copious, gossipy notes make one wish that he had rounded out an essay in prose. Mr. and Mrs. Sawtell, friends of his in Sorel who were kind to him in sickness, had a somewhat more fashionable taste in verse; Mrs. M. Ethelind Sawtell's *The Mourner's Tribute; or, Effusions of Melancholy Hours* (Montreal, 1840) suggests the more sentimental tendencies of Cowper, Moore, Thomas Campbell, and Mrs. Hemans. In her solemn moods, idealistic elevation, and occasional felicitous references to the scenes about her, she belonged with the ladies who dominated the *Literary Garland*, the Montreal journal which first printed her title-poem (1839). For cultured people like her, in the towns as well as the cities, the emergence of the *Garland* marked the beginning of a new period.

II. UPPER CANADA (1812–1841)

West of Montreal, north of the St. Lawrence, Lake Ontario, and Lake Erie, there were many more Americans, or North Americans, living beside British immigrants and a very few Frenchmen in the separate British colony known since 1791 as Upper Canada. Here the waves of continental population movements were strongly felt and the cultural situation was far less stable. At the time of the War of 1812, the Loyalists of the post-Revolution era were still loyal, but they were North American in origin and not all of British stock. Moreover, they constituted, as Michael Smith pointed out in his *Geographical View of the Province of Upper Canada* (1813), only one-fifth of the 80,000 inhabitants; another three-fifths were non-Loyalist natives of the United States or their children; only one-fifth were direct British immigrants or their children. The early settlement of Upper Canada was clearly a part of the continental push westward. To the south, Americans had moved before 1800 from Virginia and the Carolinas into and beyond Kentucky. Farther north, there was a movement from Kentucky and Pennsylvania into southern Ohio, Indiana, and Illinois, and, still farther north, from New York and New England into northern Ohio, Michigan, and Upper Canada along the Great Lakes.

In his *Literature of the Middle Western Frontier* (1925), Ralph Leslie Rusk has named Lexington, Kentucky, from about 1779 to the 1820's, and after that Cincinnati, Ohio, as the cultural capitals. Detroit and Chicago were still small forts vulnerable to Tecumseh's Indians in the War of 1812; the town of Buffalo, on the way to the port of New York, stood nearest the early Upper Canadian towns of Niagara, Dundas, Hamilton, and York (Toronto after 1834). Cobourg and Belleville were farther to the east, as was Kingston, the most populous of these centres until the enormous burst of British immigration came in the 1830's and effected significant changes. When that decade ended, the settlers from Britain would outnumber those of North American origin, and the English-speaking residents of the combined Canadas would match the total of those who spoke French. By resisting invasion in war and subsequently becoming a goal of British emigration, Upper Canada remained a unique island in the American "Old Northwest"—retaining British rule, keeping up cultural relationships with the Old Land, and possessing a governmental system which would be adjusted (after a small rebellion) to provincial responsibility and the complexion of a non-aristocratic society.

When the period began, during the War of 1812, reality on the Niagara and Detroit borders offered literature some Indian–frontier imagery exceeding romantic fancies. Canadian writers (except Major John Richardson) and British readers generally have neglected this surfeit of the spectacular, this almost incredible profusion of New World "Gothic" material. Historical documentation has taken none of the storybook lustre from the gallant General Brock, the wise and brave Tecumseh, redcoats attempting forest warfare, American invaders, sharp-shooting mounted Kentuckians, sturdy Canadian militiamen, harassed settlers, navies battling on Lake Erie, and particularly Indians capable of strategic fighting or brutal massacre. The best treatment of this material is in Major Richardson's *War of 1812* (Brockville, 1842), enhanced by A. C. Casselman's editing in 1902. This autobiographical and documented history of the campaigns around Detroit is much better reading than Richardson's uninspired effort in fiction, *The Canadian Brothers* (1840) or his early metrical romance, *Tecumseh; or, The Warrior of the West* (written about 1823; published in London, 1828). This Byronic poem's only rival was Levi Adams's "Tecumthé," which was printed in the *Canadian*

Review in December 1824 and occupied about a third of the pages in *Tales of Chivalry and Romance* (Edinburgh, 1826).

Richardson's masterpiece, *Wacousta* (London, 1832) was not directly about this same war of 1812–14, of which Richardson was a veteran. Instead, he exercised his instructed fancy upon an earlier Indian struggle, Pontiac's siege of Detroit (1763), in which his grandfather Askin had played a part along with Major Robert Rogers, author of *Ponteach* (1766). Richardson (1796–1852), born at Queenston and reared at Fort Malden, was taken into Colonel Procter's 41st Regiment at the age of 15 or 16, fought in Procter's, Brock's, and Tecumseh's battles, and was captured at Moraviantown, where the great chieftain died. As a British officer, during the following twenty years in England, Barbados, Spain, and probably Paris, he learned the art of writing and published his experiments in a metrical romance (*Tecumseh*), a pseudo-moral exposure of sin in Paris (*Ecarté*, a novel, 1829), and a witty verse satire on fashionable moustaches and beards (*Kensington Gardens in 1830*).

After he returned to Canada, early in 1838, as a temporary correspondent for *The Times*, he rehashed his quarrels with military officers in a number of books, and produced a remarkably valuable autobiography, *Eight Years in Canada* (1847). Canadians seemed to be forgetting Richardson's boyhood war, while the United States was experiencing a revival of interest in the 1812–14 struggle, as old Indian fighters campaigned for the vice-presidency (Colonel Richard M. Johnson, 1836–40) and even the presidency (General William Henry Harrison, 1840–41). Hopeful of a better reception on the American side of the border, Richardson prepared some of his romances as thrillers for the cheap paperback market, where a few of them lasted until the 1880's. *The Canadian Brothers* was Americanized into *Matilda Montgomerie*, and two new ones, *Hardscrabble* (1850) and *Wau-nan-gee* (1852), gave an account of the fall and the massacre of Chicago. In 1847 or 1848 Richardson had moved to New York City, where he died in 1852, destitute and neglected.

Wacousta remains his best work: a Gothic tale of a feud carried by Englishmen from the Old to the New World. Wacousta is no Indian, except in acquired Indian habits, but the savages—nothing like Cooper's symbolic creatures—are there as they had impressed themselves on Richardson's soul. The book is poetic and a romance in a sense which does not belong to Cooper, for *Wacousta* is essentially a complex of vivid external equivalents (shrieks, surprises, terrors) for the outrages of mind and heart experienced by Richardson when he was a boy at war in the forests of the Canadian border.

In spite of such evidence, early English-speaking Upper Canada must be seen in proper perspective not as a vast hunting-ground of beyond-the-law frontiersmen, but as the home of settlers, *canadiens*, Loyalists, Mennonites, British colonists, New Englanders, and other North Americans. While in practice the system of land tenure was open to abuses and contradictions until well beyond the Rebellion era, the beginnings of law and order had been introduced after 1791 under principles laid down by Governor Simcoe and his able Surveyor General, D. W. Smith. The axe-and-plough pioneers are not without interest; they deserve something better than the caricatures often drawn of them. The first distinction to be made is between the early North American settlers and the British immigrants of the 1830's, 1840's, and 1850's. Richardson belonged to the early group and was one of those who felt lost in the deluge. Colonel Thomas Talbot, however, the baron of the Lake Erie shore, immortalized by Mrs. Anna Jameson in *Winter Studies and Summer Rambles in Canada* (1838) and Edward Ermatinger in *The Life of Colonel Talbot* (1859), breasted the waves. Closely associated with Talbot was Mahlon Burwell, the surveyor, and Mahlon's brother, Adam Hood Burwell (1790–1849), native-born (at Fort Erie) of Loyalist parents.

Adam Burwell began publishing poems in Upper Canadian newspapers as soon as these were revived after the American invasions. Wilcocke's *Scribbler* and the *Canadian Review* also accepted his offerings from 1821 to 1825. Among his poems dating back to 1816–18, and therefore slightly earlier than Oliver Goldsmith's *The Rising Village*, is "Talbot Road," a long, vigorous account of the Lake Erie barony. The elegance of neo-classicism, so conspicuously lacking in this world of forest homes, was curiously and uniquely supplied by the stock phrases and "poetic diction" of Thomas Campbell, James Thomson, Gray, and Goldsmith. Henry Scadding, indeed, was reminded of Drayton's *Polyolbion*. Burwell devised no native idiom for the natural scenery which he enjoyed and which spoke to him of God and man in the manner of the evangelical tradition. Elegance gave way in his later work to raw emotion and finally to Irvingite mysticism. It was either religion or politics which occupied the pioneer when his axe and plough were at rest.

The first ripples preceding the waves of British immigration brought adventurers, fanatics, and sometimes martyrs. Cawdell, Gourlay, and Mackenzie are, respectively, examples vivid enough to become lasting pioneer images. All were writers, James Martin Cawdell (1781?–1842) being so obscurely, because *The Wandering Rhymer* (York, 1826) and *The Roseharp* (1835) were only vague promises of performance. As he drifted down the various levels of decadent gentility, Cawdell lampooned Francis Gore, the lieutenant governor, and then in 1818 addressed to Gore's successor, Sir Peregrine Maitland, a *Memorial* which is a *tour de force* of autobiography, a pathetic joke, a serious burlesque of requests for easy preferment. The *Memorial* exists, far from public view, in the Public Archives of Canada and in a reprint by Adam Shortt in the *Canadian Historical Review* (1920). While Cawdell was lackadaisical in promoting schemes for colonization, Robert Fleming Gourlay (1778–1863) went too far, too fast, in his campaign against evils. His famous trial at Niagara in August 1819, in his second year in Upper Canada, yielded John Charles Dent a remarkable opening chapter for his book (1885) on the Upper Canadian Rebellion. Gourlay carried his own trouble back and forth across the Atlantic. His *Statistical Account of Upper Canada* (1822) and *The Banished Briton and Neptunian* (1843) are miscellanies of pamphlets, letters, petitions, and exhortations.

William Lyon Mackenzie (1795–1861) emigrated to York, Upper Canada, at the age of 24, and edited *The Colonial Advocate* first at Queenston in 1824 and then at York until 1834. He became unquestionably one of the major figures in colonial history, a complex man who could be pictured as a martyr or a fanatic, certainly a reformer, no less a "firebrand," a self-made man, an unwilling rebel, an ineffective leader, a blessing to Canadians in spite of himself. The *Selected Writings* of this man, recently (1960) edited by Margaret Fairley, reinforces the opinion that his early training, vast reading, alert observation, passion for facts, and powerful, popular style made him a Canadian William Cobbett. His essays on education, public works, agriculture, and publishing, as well as on politics, recreate vividly the early life of the settlements and rising towns.

A review of the newspapers is impossible in this limited space; Upper Canada had eight weeklies in 1825, thirty-eight in 1836, and its first successful dailies in the early 1850's. Out of the newspaper print-shops came the first pamphlets and books. Charles Fothergill at York published almanacs and James Lynne Alexander's poem, *Wonders of the West* (1825). At Kingston, Hugh C. Thomson of the *Herald* was very enterprising; Mrs. Hart's *St. Ursula's Convent* (1824) came from his press. At Ancaster, near Hamilton, George Gurnett (1792?–1861), who had lived in Richmond, Virginia, when Edgar Allan Poe was there as a boy in his teens, set up the *Gore Gazette* (1827–28), which printed some native poetry. The *Gore Gazette* led in 1833 to the short-lived *Canadian Literary Magazine* (York), of which Gurnett was the publisher. Three fortnightly publications attempted at nearby Hamilton failed between 1831 and 1833. A monthly *Canadian Magazine* at York ran into only four numbers in 1833; its publisher was Robert Stanton, and its editor was William Sibbald, "Late of the 1st or Royal Reg't," son of Mrs. Susan Sibbald, who later lived at "Eildon Hall," near Jackson's Point. The *Christian Guardian,* founded at York by the Rev. Egerton Ryerson as a weekly journal for the Wesleyan Methodists, began in 1829 its century-long honourable career.

The most interesting publication of the thirties was certainly Gurnett's *Canadian Literary Magazine* (three issues, 1833), expertly edited by John Kent under conservative, perhaps vice-regal, auspices. His contributors were promising *littérateurs* such as Mrs. Susanna Moodie, Dr. "Tiger" Dunlop, and Robert Douglas Hamilton, all British-trained authors who had published before arriving in Canada. Young Henry Scadding, whom he was teaching at Upper Canada College, impressed Kent. The "Editor's Address" sounded a hopeful note: "I did not expect to find the Canadians an ignorant people. . . . I find them advanced in civilization, beyond my expectations."

The population of Upper Canada rose between 1823 and 1840 from approximately 130,000 to 450,000 persons. Most of the increase must be attributed to immigration from Britain, which added to the total number of agricultural settlers, but also to that of the half-pay officers, gentlewomen, officials, younger sons, clergymen, lawyers, and especially young journalists—people like John Kent and the contributors to his magazine. Along with them came—and went—travellers, men and women of similar standing in society, some of whom enjoyed reputations and status in the great British journals, notably John Howison, Captain Frederick Marryat, Captain Basil Hall, Thomas Hamilton, Mrs. Anna Jameson, and Sir Francis Bond Head (a lieutenant governor). Less prominent (but equally interesting now) were Sir George Head, Lieutenant Francis Hall, Edward A. Talbot, John Mactaggart, Adam Fergusson, Isaac Fidler, John MacGregor, Andrew Picken, Patrick Shirreff, Thomas William Magrath, Thomas Need, and Alfred Domett. All of these and others of special note, William Lyon Mackenzie, John Galt, Dr. Dunlop, and Mrs. Traill wrote travel and emigrant books to the total of approximately one hundred dated between 1815 and 1840. With one exception—Thomas Rolph's *A Brief Account* (Dundas, U.C., 1836)—these were not published in Canada but in Britain. If these volumes reached Canada, they arrived chiefly—as Mrs. Moodie pointed out—in the baggage of emigrants who had purchased them before leaving the home ports. The market was in the British Isles among people hungry for useful details about the colony; realism was preferred above romanticizing.

Travel books may be called literature of quality if they perform the higher literary functions of fiction and achieve something of form, that is, if they go beyond "statistical accounts" and settlers' handbooks to create the myth of the new country, and at the same time show affinity with journals, sketches, essays, autobiographies, extended anecdotes, and other ordered narratives. Such fiction led to novels of manners in this age and place, when North American matter-of-factness was paralleled in Britain by a rising middle-class distrust of exotic romances. The vogue of Dickens was yet to come, but Scotland had an earlier writer, John Galt (1779–1839), who exhibited brilliantly what the novel could be if it did not become aristocratic, Gothic, historical, or even sentimental. His *Annals of the Parish* (1821) and *The Ayrshire Legatees* (1821) were in the long tradition of the Addisonian essay, of Defoe, Smollett, and Maria Edgeworth. Galt's intimate realistic descriptions of lowland Scottish characters (not without malicious touches) made fiction, as Mrs. Margaret Oliphant alleged, "of facts scarcely modified at all save by the machinery of story-telling."

By a rare coincidence, Galt came to Upper Canada in 1826 to be superintendent of the Canada Company's colonization scheme, and stayed until 1829. *Lawrie Todd* (1830) and *Bogle Corbet* (1831), his "Canadian novels," written after his return to England, were addressed to the British and American public as well as the Canadian. The action of *Lawrie Todd* is set in northern New York state, near enough to Guelph and Goderich to make Galt's Canadian experiences serve the text. He had his era's flair for large-scale planning; in some ways this was to be the comprehensive emigrant and travel book for this broad band of the American-Canadian Northwest. All the "forms" of travel literature were to coalesce in a novel. His habit of using "familiar models" accounted for his creation of Zerobabel L. Hoskins, a dialect-speaking Yankee character (five years before Sam Slick), and his use of Grant Thorburn's autobiography, which he literally purchased from Thorburn for exploitation ("a little poetical") in *Lawrie Todd*. *Bogle Corbet*, a sequel demanded by publishers, was meant to be more directly helpful to Canadian immigrants. Half of it was set in Glasgow, London, and Jamaica and the rest in Upper Canada near the Debit (that is, the Credit) River. Some of the Scottish passages rank with Galt's best efforts in witty description. Observation, ingenuity, humour, the right tone, reliable detail, and general applicability made these novels popular, though only for a few decades. No one has attempted to annotate their many allusions. Yet, as long as *Lawrie Todd* had a vogue, it advanced the cause of realistic fiction in the Canadas.

The Scots, Irish, English, and Yankees thronging Canadian ports, roads, forests, and villages included many "stage" types, whose living images can be recovered from the voluminous travel literature. Among these Dr. William "Tiger" Dunlop (1792–1848) was a prime character, willing to pose or to put himself on paper. His "Recollections of the American War" in the *Literary Garland* of 1847 excelled all such memoirs except Walter Henry's, and far surpassed Henry's in humour and charm. His own gifts for entertainment, combined with conscious employment of the manners of the *Blackwood's* circle (he played tiger to their leopard, scorpion, and boar), made him the most celebrated conservative literary man in Upper Canada. Coarse, candid, and realistic, he liked the frontier, and turned his merry bachelor life at "Gairbraid" into a legend. His *Statistical Sketches of Upper Canada* (1832) was famous for its sections on climate, "field-sports," cookery, and the like. This array of topics, impishly planned to suggest an Old Countryman's polite inquiries, was handled with an unspecified amount of buffoonery and burlesque. Dunlop thus persuaded his old friends, the Scottish reviewers, and, no doubt, a host of emigrants that Canada was a pleasant place. Admiration outlived him, and two women, Robina and Kathleen Lizars, revealed their love affair with his memory in a book, almost a novel, *In the Days of the Canada Company, 1825–1850* (1896). The "almost-novel" is precisely his place, for the good-natured sketch-cum-novel is the principal indigenous contribution to the literature of manners from Dunlop and Mrs. Traill to Stephen Leacock.

Dunlop was the untamed male in the backwoods; Mrs. Anna Brownell Jameson (1794–1860), a distinguished visitor, was the sophisticated feminist. *Winter Studies and Summer Rambles in Canada* (London, 1838), a remarkable book of travel, observation, and research, exhibited Mrs. Jameson's extra-curricular entertainment while she was attempting to make a settlement with her estranged husband, Robert S. Jameson, head of the legal profession in Upper Canada. She was always the accomplished European gentlewoman, the popular British author of *Loves of the Poets* (1829), *Memoirs of Celebrated Female Sovereigns* (1831), and *Characteristics of Women* (1831), the last of these being a contribution to Shakespeare criticism. She saw Colonel Talbot, colonial housewives, the Schoolcrafts of Mackinaw, and the squaws with a discerning feminine eye. "Few European women of refined and civilized habits" had taken such risks as she had in the northern waters, and none had recorded them. Her controlled sentiment, shrewd comments, delightful style, and an "impertinent leaven of egotism" gave Upper Canada one of the masterpieces of North American travel literature and a remarkable document of womanly independence.

For Mrs. Catharine Parr Traill (1802–1899) and Mrs. Susanna Moodie, refined ladies who adopted the life of settlers' wives, the problem of describing the country was not so easy. Their traditional idiom of ideas and words did not fit daily marginal living in the bush near Cobourg and Peterborough. A defence could be set up by use of stock words with inflexible interpretations, or surrender could be announced by a change of idiom with the risk of unpredictable responses. In the latter direction lay a fresh North American literature, but also, they felt, the destruction of their social order. Mrs. Traill, who lived thirty years in England and sixty-five years in Canada, gave in slowly because she suspected that the law and order of her new world was founded in a sublimely regulated nature rather than, as at home, in a fully regulated society. She began her report in *The Backwoods of Canada* (London, 1836), a book which became so popular that N. P. Willis extracted fifty-eight large pages from it to accompany the W. H. Bartlett prints in *Canadian Scenery* (1842). She continued her description in "Forest Gleanings," published serially (1852–53) in the *Anglo-American Magazine* of Toronto. And she won distinction as a naturalist in such books as *Canadian Wild Flowers* (1869), *Studies of Plant Life in Canada* (1885), and *Pearls and Pebbles* (1894).

Mrs. Traill brought a sense of immediacy, cheerful realism, controlled sentiment, shrewd comment, and a delightfully honest style to the series of autobiographical letters (addressed to her mother and friends in England) which made up the *Backwoods* volume. She established the image of the settler in the bush. Her chapter headings alone suggest some details: "the ocean voyage/ majestic and mighty river/ up the river to Montreal/ impressions of city and country/ first problems of backwoods/ Peterborough and environs/ journey through the woods/ settling on the land/ building a log-house/ winter in Canada/ problems of new settlers/ clearing the land/ Indian neighbours/ Canadian wild flowers/ Canada, the land of hope/ summer and its visitors/ some ills and troubles/ increasing home comforts/ the Mackenzie rebellion/ bush weddings."

Mrs. Moodie's *Roughing It* (London, 1852) belonged to the same period; Susanna lived in the bush near Cobourg and on the Otonabee, in eastern Ontario, from 1832 to 1840. She wrote occasional "Canadian" poems and sketches at least as early as 1838, and published the first of these sketches in the *Literary Garland* of 1847. She took more time than Mrs. Traill in making literature of the backwoods life, although she was personally less patient. *Roughing It* was primarily the result of nursing her tensions. This she did while she celebrated her escape (after 1840) and became a social critic. Her ideal was the home she had known in Suffolk, where she, Elizabeth, Agnes, Sara, Jane, Catharine, and Samuel Strickland—six sisters and one brother—had practised polite living and instructive writing in an evangelical and sentimental atmosphere not yet called "Victorian." Agnes had become the most famous of them, with *Lives of the Queens of England* (1840–48).

Susanna (Mrs. Moodie) advocated and illustrated such an English life for Canadians in a series of "English" novels in *The Literary Garland* (1838–51) of Montreal; in the *Victoria Magazine* (1847–48), "a cheap periodical for the Canadian people" which she edited with her husband at Belleville; and summarily and explicitly in *Life in the Clearings* (1853). So much experience with the craft of story-telling prepared her to carry emigrant fiction a step beyond John Galt's *Lawrie Todd* in the direction of the apprenticeship novel, a record of personal development rather than a survey of other people's lives. There are indeed many characters in *Roughing It* but they are all revealed as they rub against Mrs. Moodie, and as they add something to the image of herself—the suffering, learning author-heroine. Her liveliness, guileful humour, crafty rhetoric, mimicry of dialogue, polite "roughing," and romancing about herself were almost too successful. The settlers themselves resented her stubborn superiority, and thought that she exaggerated and distorted the truth for gullible outsiders. Her books were not popular in the Canadas until she publicly adopted all Canadians, and Canada itself, in a preface to her first edition in this country (in 1871, after Confederation). Since then she has been regarded, much too uncritically, as the typical settler's wife.

9. Literary Activity in Canada East and West
1841-1880

CARL F. KLINCK

I. GENTEEL COLONIALISM (1841–1855)

MONTREAL WAS THE NATURAL CENTRE for literary activity about 1840. The rebellion of 1837 was over, the two Canadas were united politically in 1841, and in December 1838 the Montreal *Literary Garland* had begun publication. A decade of transatlantic immigration toward the near west (Upper Canada) had strengthened the British foundation of literary endeavour. In the United States, especially in the eastern cities, there was a vogue of gentility, not unaptly described as English and Victorian, upheld by a polite reaction against the cruder aspects of western expansion. It was a world for women. John Lovell published *The Literary Garland*; John Gibson was editor; and men of the literary clubs, even rugged souls like Dunlop and Richardson, contributed. But the substance and tone were set by invincible ladies of Old British or Bostonian origin upon the pattern of the popular annuals or gift-books of the 1820's and their inevitable consequence, monthly journals, of which Godey's *Lady's Book*, begun in 1830, was the most famous.

The Montreal *Garland* bore a typical gift-book title, barely escaping a name like *Amulet, Iris,* or *Dew-Drop,* and the contents were consistently described as "gems" or "flowers." Every "boudoir from the Atlantic to Lake Erie" was to have them. In such precious pieces American *mores* allowed some eroticism. Sentimental romance had been taken over by female authors who were beguiling their sisters with wishful excitement, captivating menfolk by delicate attitudes, teaching good conduct by suggesting and deploring seduction, and thus delaying the rise of serious fiction. Poets like Letitia E. Landon served a similar popular demand, yet L.E.L. was copied in the respectable journals almost as much as Mrs. Hemans and Mrs. Lydia H. Sigourney. In Hemans and Sigourney the *Garland* probably found suitable models of taste, writers who could measure out excitement and instruction in acceptable proportions. This the editors also attempted to accomplish through fiction and verse in terms of middle-class morality, evangelical religion, superior status, high fashion, and English modes of thought.

The *Garland* kept up its own supply of didactically charged society tales, together with the inevitable biblical narratives, dramatic sketches and poems. The temptation to be English in the aristocratic or upper-gentlefolk manner was, of course, especially strong in the British colonies, where class distinctions lived a precarious life among only the favoured few. W. D. Howells would have seen much positive harm being done by literature catering to the dreams of this minority. The life portrayed was obviously foreign to most Canadian readers, who had shared in these things neither before nor after emigration. As the expression of a social goal or as a palliative it was deplorable. In literature, idealism must clothe itself in a certain dress, and the *Garland*'s garments wafted a strong perfume of artificiality to men and women on the farms and in the towns. The settlers were too literate and practical to be content with condescension or escapism; and the exotic was not well calculated to affect their religious lives. As a cultural experiment, the *Garland* had the commendable purpose of overcoming colonial rawness, of being a genteel supplement to the popular education which W. L. Mackenzie and the Rev. Egerton Ryerson demanded. As an aid to the development of a national literature, it taught certain skills, but it was a parlour game. It encouraged amenable native talent, but it made only feeble attempts to discover a native norm in content, treatment, or quality.

It was Anglo-Bostonian rather than Anglo-Canadian. "We were certain," the editor wrote in January 1843, "that the seed of Old England and of New England, which had been sown in Canada, could not be unproductive." The Old English tone was supplied by Mrs. Moodie, who had published *Enthusiasm and Other Poems* (1831) before leaving her homeland in 1832, and by Mrs. McLachlan, wife of a colonel of the Royal Engineers. But Eastern American contributions in the same mood were made by two Bostonian ladies living in Montreal. These two were, by a happy chance, daughters of Hannah Webster Foster (1759–1840), one of the earliest exponents of the sentimental novel in America, author of *The Coquette; or, the History of Eliza Wharton* (1797). The daughters had published New World historical romances in Boston in the 1820's, before they came to Canada. Their names and works were spread all over the pages of the *Garland*: Mrs. Eliza L. Cushing (1794–1886) contributed at least seventy varied items and finally became editor; Mrs. Harriet V. Cheney wrote poems and prose sketches in the early and the late period of the *Garland*'s existence. Another sister, Miss T. D. Foster (Mrs. Henry Giles), sent in, probably from Boston, her valuable articles on the culture of the Latin countries of Europe. The *Garland* was almost "entirely the produce of Canadian talent," but it was only rarely, as in Mrs. Moodie's "Canadian" poems, devoted to distinctively native subject-matter.

The *Literary Garland* was "done to death" in 1851 by the competitive American journals which it imitated; it was also ready for death because of something insecure in its British connections. The contemporary English period which it reflected had an "interim" quality; it favoured minor writers and period pieces. No one knows what a rejuvenated *Garland* would have become in the 1860's, when strong political nationalism in Canada found corresponding vigour in the major Victorian literary forces of George Eliot; Tennyson the Poet Laureate; Longfellow, the American more than half adopted by Britain; Keats, reborn in Tennyson and the Pre-Raphaelites; and Arnold, whose serene "culture" promised support against the excesses of North American republicanism, of which even Emerson and Whitman seemed to bear the marks.

Cultural tenacity was the clue to everything in the *Garland*. "The literature of a country," James Holmes wrote in August 1840, "is the *measure* of its progress towards refinement." Literature was also a *means* to that end. The Garland's programme was not meant to be nostalgic; it was optimistically designed to build a better North American world along lines of evangelical middle-class piety prevailing over any relics of Jacobinism, Regency licentiousness, or unschooled behaviour. Whether these authors began with home thoughts, fashionable manners, foreign history, biblical situations, war, Indians, love, loss, sacrifice, flowers, or illimitable works of God, they ended up with lessons in religious and social propriety. The monotony of the *Garland* poems, which were admirable enough in execution, was due to lack of tension, to a strategy concerned less with word-structure than with making the ideas come out right in cadences nicely adjusted to resolution in the purposes of God and Anglo-Bostonian society. The clergy, ranking also as cultural and religious arbiters, lent their support as the Rev. Edward Hartley Dewart (1828–1908) did in *Selections from Canadian Poets* (Montreal, 1864).

His excellent critical introduction was in effect a summing-up of genteel principles. Yet Dewart searched for more than Canadian talent in the generation of the 1860's; he gathered verses on Canadian themes inspired by incipient nationalism. His *Selections*, the first and last general anthology compiled before Confederation, represented Canadian poets alone, without any admixture of borrowed song. Collectively, these poets described their country's scenery, seasons, and weather with more love than realism, and they presented human beings responding ideally to typical situations. The book is panoramic, charming, and promising, indicative of considerable talent and craftsmanship at work during the last decade of colonial status.

Charles Sangster and Charles Heavysege, two of Dewart's major poets, were capable of winning recognition from a few genteel reviewers in the eastern United States and in Britain—and therefore in Canada. Both were lonely writers, self-made, striving hard for excellence in style which they knew was above them, Sangster looking to Byron, Scott, Milton, and Tennyson, and Heavysege looking to the Bible and Shakespeare. Sangster (1822–1893), born in Kingston, Upper Canada, lived in humble circumstances all his life, whether he worked in the Ordnance Office at Kingston, in newspaper establishments at Amherstburg or Kingston, or in the civil service department at Ottawa. During the 1850's he produced at least 450 pages of poetry; *The St. Lawrence and the Saguenay* was published at Kingston in 1856, and *Hesperus* in 1860 at Montreal. Sangster was not content with the world he viewed around him; he insisted on idealizing and ornamenting it:

> And so I love my art; chiefly, because
> Through it I rev'rence Nature, and improve
> The tone and tenor of the mind He gave.

Only in some sonnets "written in the Orillia Woods" and in occasional stanzas did his stock diction happily subside. Generally it is the echoes (managed by something more than dilettantism) and not Sangster's elaborations of ideas that reach toward profundity and power. Dewart's period piece of criticism made these claims for Sangster: "the richness and extent of his contributions, the originality and descriptive power he displays, the variety of Canadian themes on which he has written with force and elegance, his passionate sympathy with the beautiful in nature, and the chivalrous and manly patriotism which finds an utterance in his poems." This statement, by omission, emphasizes Sangster's deficiencies—he lacked a fresh approach and fresh human interest.

Charles Heavysege (1816–1876), an immigrant from England to Montreal in 1853, displayed in his *Revolt of Tartarus*, a Miltonic epic (published in England, 1852), the uncertainties of solitary, bookish, high-brow poeticizing in an English, and (soon) a North American, plebeian environment. Reliance upon the Old Testament and Shakespeare was part of the tradition. Chatham's Abraham Holmes, a satirist, could refer humorously to his Belinda "whose neck was like the tower of David, and head like Mount Carmel," but Heavysege would incorporate such a reference into impassioned imagery. Heavysege was solemnly in earnest, without the range and humour of his contemporary Herman Melville, whose American *Moby Dick* (1851) was biblical and Shakespearean in its own way, and showed its author, as Heavysege's works also did, at odds with God. For such an interpretation of Heavysege—appealing to criticism in our own day—one must remain indebted to Thomas R. Dale and his unpublished thesis on Heavysege (Chicago, 1951).

This poet did his best work in a single decade, while he was a cabinet-maker in Hilton's factory in Montreal (1853–60) and in his first years as a reporter (after 1860) on the Montreal *Transcript* and the *Daily Witness*. His books consisted of *The Revolt of Tartarus* (reprinted in Montreal, 1855);

Sonnets (1855); *Saul*, a Shakespeare-like closet drama of 135 scenes based on the biblical account of King Saul (1857 and 1859); *Count Filippo; or, The Unequal Marriage*, an "Italian" five-act tragedy of love and intrigue (1860); and *Jephthah's Daughter*, again a poetic narrative full of long speeches (1865). *Saul* was his best and representative work, and it was the one around which Coventry Patmore in the *North British Review* (1858) consolidated the view that Heavysege's theme was, as the angel said, "Faith lacking, all his [Saul's] works fell short." In all of Heavysege, however, Thomas Dale finds guarded "suggestions of divine injustice," of God's will as "a capricious and vindictive power." There is "not a grand denunciation in the manner of Blake or Shelley, nor an appeal from Christianity to Paganism in the manner of Swinburne or Hardy." But Dale draws attention to "the careful selection of damaging incident in the Biblical poems, and the complete silence maintained on such matters as divine mercy and happiness in a future life; the psychological truth of his tortured human characters, and the stony bleakness of the natural and supernatural forces which hem them in." Such an understanding of Heavysege is scarcely available to readers who see only anthologies containing a few of the very good sonnets and some extracts from the rhetorical speeches of the fallen angel Malzah, the evil spirit of Saul, a character creation which Patmore thought was equalled in our language only in Caliban and Ariel.

The genteel writers did not have it all to themselves. Before leaving the period from 1841 to 1855, one must look at some Victorian rebels, and at some others who thought they were only old-fashioned, or merely "down to earth." The latter, of course, were close to the bulk of the population, for most colonists read nothing if they did not scan newspapers in shops and taverns. One work which originated in the political world of journalism, *How I Came to be Governor of the Island of Cacona* (Montreal, 1852) by "the Hon. Francis Thistleton"—properly William Henry Fleet of the Montreal *Transcript*—qualifies as satiric fiction ridiculing a vulnerable foreign aristocrat, Lieutenant Governor Sir Francis Bond Head, himself an essayist of considerable charm and author of *A Narrative* (1839).

At least one journal, *The Magic Lantern* of Montreal (1848), attempted overt opposition to the *Garland*'s "romantic young ladies" who "expended their sentimentality upon the public." There were rumblings even within the pages of the *Garland*. Carl Ballstadt has drawn attention to the contributions of "W.P.C." of Williamstown (the town of the Northwesters near Cornwall). In an article on "Our Literature, Present and Prospective" (May 1848), W.P.C. regretted that "of late, our manner of reading has, I fear, included too much of the ideal and romantic, and too little of the real and practical." He recommended, as an antidote to foreign sentimental literature, more devotion to native historical writing and national songs; W.P.C. is thus in the line leading to Thomas D'Arcy McGee. Another significant line may be called the popular-academic, emerging in the 1850's with *The Canadian Journal*, and leading to *The British American Magazine*, *The Canadian Monthly*, and *The Week*. An uncertain beginning had been made as early as the 1840's through the efforts of the Rev. Dr. John McCaul, Vice-President and Professor of classics, logic, rhetoric and *belles-lettres* in King's College, Toronto (and later Vice-Chancellor of the University of Toronto). He thought in terms of twining lovely flowers with the maple leaf when he edited *The Maple Leaf or Canadian Annual, a Literary Souvenir* (1847–49). Although he relied upon European subject-matter, he insisted upon text and engravings which were the "produce" of Canada: "the only hands, which should weave the garland, should be those of her children by birth or by adoption."

Belinda; or, The Rivals: A Tale of Real Life (Detroit, 1843) sprang from a radically different environment. This burlesque of sentimental fiction was prepared in the west, at or near Chatham, where fashionable life, if there was any, was exposed to frontier irreverence and Wesleyan reproof. So few copies are extant that one may suspect confiscation of the rest by irate neighbours whose "real life" found its way into the book. The anonymous author, Abraham S. Holmes, a young law student and journalist, was the son of a well-known Wesleyan preacher and teacher of American origin. It is likely that both Holmes's coarseness and his polish were deliberately assumed. Excuses could be found for poor taste on the part of this author; the American Old Northwest (north and west of Cincinnati) had produced scarcely any native books of fiction except Mrs. Caroline M. Kirkland's *A New Home* (1839), published in Philadelphia. But Holmes may need no excuses. His creation of one of the rare true coquettes in North American fiction since Arabella Fermor (Emily Montague's friend in Frances Brooke's novel, 1769) looks like originality. Holmes's Belinda was not one of the many young ladies seduced by their own feelings and by unscrupulous men— to teach moral lessons, of course—in the hundreds of sentimental novels which were an American fad from Mrs. Foster's time until the Civil War. Miss Marilyn Davis, in a thesis on *Belinda* (University of Western Ontario, 1963), has pointed out that Holmes's heroine is not a victim, but an aggressor—seducing even her creator.

Coquetry is one of the lively arts: capturing it in words, as Holmes has done, requires Belinda's or Eve's own skill. Burlesquing it and, at the same time, standing up as a Methodist took a good deal of doing. Holmes's main equipment consisted of a flair for language, an uneasy conscience about rhetoric, a sophomoric delight in mimicry, a hodge-podge stock of quotations, a sharp eye for misconduct, and enough objectivity (legal and/or journalistic) for ironic dramatization. The disappearance of all but two copies has denied a host of posthumous admirers to a coquette who "at church . . . had the indescribable pleasure of seeing all her beaux together." Chatham's gift to the fiction of the early wild West, who got half a dozen men without a gun, lost the fame her sins deserved because of her author's literary promiscuity.

The *Anglo-American Magazine* (Toronto, 1852-55) may be reckoned among the folksy, rather than the genteel, forces. Its editor was the Rev. Robert Jackson MacGeorge (1811?-1884), known as "Solomon of Streetsville" because of his popular exposure of follies in the *Streetsville Weekly Review*. Associated with him editorially was Gilbert Auchinleck, author of a *History of the War of 1812* which, along with Mrs. Traill's *Forest Gleanings*, was the magazine's principal contribution to formal literature. The rest of it was gossipy in the old-fashioned Scottish way of "Noctes Ambrosianae" and other *Blackwood's* articles. MacGeorge spoke out against "twaddle," "slipslop romances," and "the gentle insipidity of the *Ladies Magazine*," and put his extensive knowledge of literature at the service of his public. *Uncle Tom's Cabin; or, Life among the Lowly*, in the year of its appearance (1852) transcended all his prejudices.

This American novel by Harriet Beecher Stowe affected all levels of literature just when the railroad expansion of the 1850's was linking Upper Canadian cities closely and rapidly with the great American centres. Little more than a half century had brought this change from the small-boat economy of Thomas Moore's time. British immigration to Upper Canada was subsiding. Everything favoured an immense extension of the cultural influence of the United States, if war between the states could be prevented. *Uncle Tom's Cabin* broke the high-middle-class monopoly which Mrs. Moodie and Mrs. Cushing stood for, and brought evangelical piety and sentiment into a broad, popular literary domain. Dickens's novels alone could not have effected this literary revolution in the Canadas.

It should be noted also that here another humanitarian force had been operating, especially on the level of the newspaper poets, among the Scots devoted to the school of Robert Burns. Of these, the acknowledged master was Alexander McLachlan (1818-1896), whom Dewart praised as "the sweetest and most intensely human of all our Canadian bards." The author of *Lyrics* (1858), *The Emigrant and Other Poems* (1861) and (later) *Poems and Songs* (1874) had come as a poor young man from Glasgow in 1840 and had committed himself to rural life in central Canada West. Dewart's selections from McLachlan seem calculated to show that this poet was not ungenteel, but his popular reputation depended upon such songs as "Acres of His Own," "Up, and be a Hero," "Young Canada, or, Jack's as Good as his Master," and "The Man Who Rose from Nothing." Not all Scots were or remained humble, but there was a poor man's Scottish tradition integrated with the earlier equalitarian tradition of the North American pioneer. It was given support by *Uncle Tom's Cabin*, the story of persons much more "lowly."

The "dialect" versifiers had long been active, with the help of fraternal societies and the local newspaper editors, in strengthening real or mystic bonds of nostalgia for either Scotland or Ireland and in fostering rather deliberate literature of exile which can be mistakenly interpreted as indicating dissatisfaction with Canada. Rightly understood, their verses were hymns of Scottish and Irish conquest, signs that Canada was theirs (and, they might have said, not Mrs. Moodie's). Many of them were prospering, going up in the world, and, if they were at times understandably homesick, they could share their sentiments. There were many of them, too many to name; but a sense of their variety and their enterprise may be gained by reference to three men who formed a bridge between those who repeated verses from home but wrote nothing, and the later generations who echoed sentiments in verses about ancestral lands which they had never seen.

Old Country "idiom" is a step beyond simple "dialect" and the term describes best what men like Stephens, Menzies, and MacQueen brought into the seedbed of Canadian writing. William S. Stephens (1809–1861) of Owen Sound, an immigrant from Northern Ireland in early boyhood, became a public phenomenon by the ease and frequency with which he composed impromptu verses in an eighteenth-century manner. When the "Hamilton mountain" was set as a poetical "task" for him by a lady about 1840, he opened on a description of Creation with unmated primeval creatures seeking companions. George Menzies (1796?–1847), who established the *Woodstock Herald*, had published verses when he was a gardener in Scotland; his *Poems*, containing a record of sorrowful thoughts, were published posthumously in Woodstock (1850) and in Aberdeen (1854). Thomas MacQueen (1803–1861), editor of the *Bathurst Courier* before he founded the *Huron Signal* in 1849, published three books of verse in Scotland and only one poem, "Our Own Broad Lake," in Canada. One of his books described him as "The Cottage Philosopher," since he was greatly given to "observations on morals and politics"; he had been a mason in Barkip, near Beith, and had dedicated himself to elevating the minds of the working classes.

II. THE CONFEDERATION ERA (1855–1880)

In Toronto, late in 1855, during "boom times," a great Railway Festival was held, which J. M. S. Careless in *Brown of the Globe* (p. 212) has called "really a public jubilee for the railway god himself." "And in the summer of 1856," Professor Careless continues (p. 229), "as a group of Toronto business men took active steps to open communications with the North West, Brown and his journal began a powerful campaign to awaken Canadians to the value and potentialities of the great Hudson's Bay territories." A travel book of the time, William H. G. Kingston's *Western Wanderings* (London, 1856), described Toronto as a city of colleges, public buildings, and polite society, and the home of the artist Paul Kane.

Not as apparent, but also very significant for literary vision was a shift in the policy of *The Canadian Journal: A Repertory of Industry, Science and Art*, founded in Toronto in August 1852, under the editorship of Henry Youle Hind, by the Canadian Institute as "a publication devoted to the Arts and Sciences of practical life." The journal in itself had been an important step in communication between those engaged in scientific and in industrial pursuits: to "assist, lighten and elevate the labours of the mechanic" and to "afford information to the manufacturer." The universities had had a place in the scheme; eight new institutions had been founded in the Canadas since the American War: McGill in Montreal (1821), Queen's in Kingston (1827), Victoria in Cobourg (1841), Bishop's in Lennoxville (1843), Ottawa in Ottawa (1848), and three Toronto colleges, King's (1827), Trinity (1851), and St. Michael's (1852). The University of Toronto was given its name in 1850 and reconstituted in 1853.

In January 1856 the *Canadian Journal* began a new series with a new purpose; the university men had taken over, to help to give recognized or independent existence to the sciences of Canada, to provide "a medium of communication" for subjects which could not be "profitably treated of in a popular form." In effect it became a learned, not a "mechanical," journal, with "departments" served almost wholly by Toronto professors, E. J. Chapman, James Bovell, Daniel Wilson, H. Y. Hind, Henry Croft, J. B. Cherriman, and the Rev. G. C. Irving. Other scholarly contributors were also welcome: in September 1857, for example, the Rev. A. Constable Geikie made a detailed survey of neologisms in "Canadian English." In February 1856 a similar journal, restricted more narrowly to science, was born in Montreal under the name of *The Canadian Naturalist* (later called *The Canadian Naturalist and Geologist*), sponsored by the Natural History Society of Montreal and supported chiefly by McGill professors. The leading authors in the early days were Elkanah Billings (the editor), Principal (later Sir) William Dawson, Sir William E. Logan (head of the Canadian Geological Survey, organized in 1842), T. Sterry Hunt, and Charles Smallwood. The Earl of Dalhousie's dreams for learned societies and publications were coming true. In content and style, of course, these journals were wholly different from the *Literary Garland*.

The *Canadian Journal* (Toronto), did not disregard the humanities. Daniel

Wilson (1816–1892) (later Sir Daniel, and President of the University of Toronto) dealt with English literature, but also history, ethnology and archaeology, since he was expert in these matters, having written a notable book, *The Archaeology and Prehistoric Annals of Scotland* (1851), two years before he came to Toronto. Many years later he put all these things together, along with Shakespeare's *The Tempest*, in *Caliban: The Missing Link* (1873). Meanwhile, he commented upon current British and American books, with one eye open for Canadiana. In a few learned reviews he established academic literary criticism in the Canadas.

It was a significant moment when, in January 1858, Wilson devoted a long article to Charles Sangster's *The St. Lawrence and the Saguenay,* McLachlan's *Poems*, Carroll Ryan's *Oscar*, and Professor E. J. Chapman's *A Song of Charity*. Wilson was fair, not snobbish, when he found most of Sangster's and Chapman's words and "music" to be regrettably "old worldish." For these men, no less than for Tennyson, he said, the nineteenth century could be "as fresh an *el dorado* as America was to Cortes or Pizaro." He believed that "its politics, its geology, its philosophy, its utopian aspirations, its homely fashions and fancies, all yield to his [Tennyson's] eye suggestive imagery rich with pregnant thought." These would come to the New World poet, he believed, if the poet would see "things as they are." "It is not," he added, "a 'Hiawatha' song we demand." Nor, another review indicated, was it *Leaves of Grass* by a Canadian Whitman that he desired. The *Canadian Journal* had little more to say in this period about the country's *belles lettres*, but Wilson's vision for the Canadian poet was not lost in the universities.

The *British American Magazine* (Toronto, 1863–64) was evidently planned to bring scholarly perception in matters of Canadian literature to a public broader than the restricted membership of the Institute. Henry Youle Hind (1823-1908), a noted explorer, chemist, geologist, and professor at Trinity College, Toronto, who had been first editor of the *Canadian Journal*, now joined Graeme Mercer Adam (1839–1912), an enterprising publisher, in founding the *British American*—a learned-popular magazine. The table of contents looked as if Hind and Adam had possessed, four years before its time, Henry J. Morgan's *Bibliotheca Canadensis* (1867)—an impressive 400-page volume of bio-bibliographical sketches of pre-Confederation authors —and had solicited contributions from the most promising among them. The best-known among those represented were Mrs. Moodie, Mrs. Traill, Mrs. Leprohon, the Rev. Dr. Scadding, Daniel Wilson, Thomas D'Arcy McGee, and Charles Mair.

Along with conscientious surveys of general literature, including the broad range of contemporary British and American journals, the *British American* printed original writings which reveal that the awakening of Canadian cultural life generally assigned to the 1870's and 1880's was actually under way in the 1860's. Looking backward and forward, one can see this complex of Canadian literary interests in existence even before Confederation. Mrs. M. J. H. Holiwell's serial novel, "The Settler's Daughter" (1863), a step from immigration literature toward the commonplace small-town novel, and Thomas D'Arcy McGee's pleas for "British American Nationality," both published in the *British American* (August and October 1863), are examples of what had become articulate since the demise of the *Garland*.

Thomas D'Arcy McGee (1825-1868) was the chief orator and literary man, as Sir John A. Macdonald was the leading politician, among the founding "Fathers of Confederation," who brought Ontario, Quebec, New Brunswick, and Nova Scotia into a national union by the British North America Act of 1867. "Our next census—in 1870—will find us over 4,000,000 souls," McGee told the Montreal Literary Club on November 4, 1867, in an address on "The Mental Outfit of the New Dominion" (the "incipient new nation"). He did not live until the census total was announced, a half million below his guess, but he raised the spirits of Canadians as he had never failed to do since he had settled in Montreal ten years before. On May 2, 1860, "standing before an enchanted legislature," as the Right Honourable Arthur Meighen later described it, McGee had spoken of the Northern Nation:

I look to the future of my adopted country with hope, though not without anxiety; I see in the not remote distance one great nationality bound, like the shield of Achilles, by the blue rim of Ocean. . . . I see a generation of industrious, contented, moral men, free in name and in fact,—men capable of maintaining, in peace and in war, a Constitution worthy of such a country.

McGee's phrases have become part of the Canadian language. His own accents were Irish. Ireland, which had given him life, also in a sense gave him a martyr's death, for he was shot down in Ottawa in April 1868 by a lurking assassin because he had denounced the Fenians, those of the American Irish who had turned the quarrels of their Old Country into a movement threatening the peace of Canada. McGee's whole-hearted adoption of the cause of Canadian nationalism during the last ten years of his life never quite freed him from his ties to Ireland itself. There too he had passionately wished a new nation to be born, and he had taken his place in the famous "Young Ireland" group of the 1840's, which replaced the Repeal Association of Daniel O'Connell and included Charles Gavan Duffy, Thomas Davis, John Mitchell and Samuel Ferguson (who became a link with the Irish Literary Revival of Yeats's generation). Most of them were literary men, and literature played an important part in their programme. They were the founders of the *Nation*, a Dublin newspaper (1842-48). McGee was associated with them from 1846 to 1848, and for a time edited the *Nation*. Like Duffy, he was driven into exile; the former had a notable public career in Australia, and McGee in

Canada, after a spell of vigorous Irish and Roman Catholic journalism in the United States (1848–57).

McGee's efforts on behalf of his people in the United States are generally understood, but his earlier leadership in the "Young Ireland" group of 1846–48 has not been sufficiently emphasized with regard to Canada's literary history. McGee, the young journalist who came to the Dublin *Nation* prepared to become a historian of the Irish people, learned from Duffy and Davis (who died in 1845) the theory and practice of "national poetry" which he later adapted to Canadian needs. In an unpublished thesis (University of Western Ontario, 1956), Miss Kathleen M. O'Donnell has demonstrated the existence of a programme devised by these men, calling for the use of literary works, principally historical works and ballads, in reviving or creating a nation and in giving it a "mental outfit." They said this in many ways: "to advance the cause of Nationality by all the aids, which literary as well as political talent could bring to its advocacy"—"to create and foster public opinion in Ireland, and to make it racy of the soil"—to teach "the native muse to become English in language without growing un-Irish in character."

For national ballads they had a formula, which Miss O'Donnell finds employed in McGee's own *Canadian Ballads* (Montreal, 1858), dedicated to Duffy in Australia, "in memory of Old Times." Duffy had published in 1845 *The Ballad Poetry of Ireland*. Fifteen of McGee's poems were ready after a year of his research into Canadian life and history; and, as if to justify his Irish formula, a number of them became immediate and lasting favourites, especially "Sebastian Cabot to his Lady," "Jacques Cartier," "The Arctic Indian's Faith" and "Our Ladye of the Snow!" McGee's ballads became the fashion. They evidently suited nicely the temperament of the Montreal Irish such as Mrs. Leprohon (Rosanna Mullins). It is interesting to speculate how much he did by such ballads about storm and ice to let the world form exciting or unfavourable opinions about the climate of British North America.

The ballads were only part of his programme, for he threw himself into public life as editor of *The New Era* (1857), member of the legislature for ten years, Father of Confederation, lecturer, orator, and advocate of Canadian culture. Meanwhile, he completed and published in New York, Toronto, Quebec, and London a half-dozen books on Canadian or Irish subjects, including a two-volume *Popular History of Ireland* (1864). He frequently gave lectures on literary topics—such as Shakespeare, Milton, Burke, Thomas Moore, Irish literature, Scottish poets, and the Robert Burns Centennial; these have been gathered into a collection of his *Speeches and Addresses* (1937) by the Honourable Charles Murphy. A large volume of his poems was issued in 1869 by Mrs. Mary Anne Sadlier (1820–1913), wife of James Sadlier, McGee's New York publisher. The editing was done *con amore*, since Mrs. Sadlier was bound by many ties to McGee's Canada. As Mary

Anne Madden, she had emigrated from Ireland to Montreal about 1847 and had written verses for the *Literary Garland* under the initials "M.A.M." This was only the beginning of her career; in the United States, after 1850, she became a prolific novelist, famous for stories of Irish emigration, especially *The Blakes and Flanagans* (1855).

The personal note is appropriate because Montreal gave opportunities for literary men to meet and encourage one another. This point is made in an otherwise undistinguished volume, *Poems by George Murray* (Montreal, 1912), prepared by John Reade, literary editor of the Montreal *Gazette* and author of *The Prophecy of Merlin, and Other Poems* (1870). Murray (1830–1910), classical master in the Montreal High School, was a graduate of King's College, London, and of Oxford. The selections in Murray's *Poems* opened with "How Canada was Saved" (written according to McGee's formula), which in 1874 had won the *Montreal Witness*'s prize for "the best ballad on any subject in Canadian history." In the "biographical sketch" Reade wrote about a literary club on Cathcart Street, of which Murray was secretary; the membership included D'Arcy McGee and Charles Heavysege, and probably the latter's friend George Martin. On the day of McGee's funeral, the club marched in a body to the grave, "each member wearing a badge of suitable device." Murray was also a leading spirit in the Athenaeum Club (begun in 1876), the Shakespeare Club, the Pen and Pencil Club, and the Royal Society of Canada (of which he was a charter member in 1882).

Rosanna Eleanor Mullins (Mrs. J. L. Leprohon) (1829–1879), by virtue of her best books, *The Manor House of De Villerai* (1859) and *Antoinette de Mirecourt* (1864), belongs to the 1860's, although she joined the contributors to the *Literary Garland* in 1846 and her *Poetical Works* were published posthumously in 1881. If she was born in 1829—the date accepted by Brother Adrian (Henry Deneau) in his unpublished thesis (University of Montreal, 1948)—then her fifteen poems, one sketch, and five serial novels appeared in the *Garland* while she was between seventeen and twenty-two years of age, the bright hope for a second generation of sentimental *Garland* romancers. Melodrama and tugging heartstrings she learned too well, but she also learned to write dialogue that was rarely lengthy, tedious, or pompous. And she found subject-matter ideally suited to her desires, re-creation of the life of the "oldest aristocracy" in the land, the French-Canadian seigneurs of the Conquest era—French society in Montreal, as it were, supplementing Mrs. Brooke's English society in Quebec. Rosanna's family was wealthy; her command of French was perfect; and J. L. Leprohon, whom she married in 1851, knew those people who preserved French family traditions.

She was able to give Canadian historical fiction new life and a richer social content, so that Heavysege imitated her (*The Advocate*, 1865) and William Kirby (*The Golden Dog*, 1877) profited by her success. This result was almost wholly due to *Antoinette de Mirecourt,* written and published in English, and also popular in French translation. *Le Manoir de Villerai* became virtually a French book because the *Family Herald,* in which it appeared, was discontinued, while Edouard L. de Bellefeuille's translation (1861), frequently reprinted in French, remained. Like *Antoinette,* Mrs. Leprohon's poems (in the posthumous edition by John Reade) have the mid-Victorian tone and diction of the *Literary Garland,* Dewart's selections, Tennyson, and Longfellow. They also have unmistakably the accents of Montreal and the new nation. Very few of the themes one associates with D'Arcy McGee, Charles Mair, Isabella Crawford, and Wilfred Campbell were left without a parallel tribute by Mrs. Leprohon; the transition from the pioneer verse of Mrs. Moodie to that of the early "Dominion" poets is nowhere more clearly shown than in Mrs. Leprohon's "Jacques Cartier's First Visit to Mount Royal," "A Canadian Summer Evening" "The White Canoe," "Red Rock Camp: A Tale of Early Colorado," and "An Afternoon in July."

William Kirby (1817–1906), also a romancer and poet, seems old-fashioned by comparison; his dedication to Canadian subject-matter was combined with literary manners derived from Goldsmith, the Tennyson of the *Idylls,* Sir Walter Scott, and Dumas the elder. Although he was an immigrant from England, he was temperamentally a Loyalist of the Niagara border, intent on making neo-Loyalists of British Canadians of the second or third generation, for whom nationalism rather than antiquarianism could raise an interest in pre-immigrant history. Kirby married into a Loyalist family, edited the Niagara *Mail* (1850–63), indulged in local historical research, became a public figure, corresponded with great men, and kept his eye on Tennyson, the Poet Laureate. Kirby came to Canada when the *Literary Garland* began, but he never contributed to it. *The U.E.: A Tale of Upper Canada in XII Cantos* was written in 1846, but published at Niagara in the *Mail* office in 1859. The cantos were in rhyming couplets, as were some of the idylls collected with others in blank verse in *Canadian Idylls* (Toronto, 1881, and enlarged later). On taking up *The U.E.,* one wishes Kirby well; one tries to read again; and one is still disappointed. The historical material of the Niagara Loyalists failed to find an appropriate form. The idyll had no life to lend this Canadian antique material, and even Isabella Crawford's near-genius was defeated by this genre in *Malcolm's Katie* (1884).

Scott and Dumas provided models more readily suited to North American history, as every writer of Wild West stories knows. Kirby, of course, turned toward the east, and found subject-matter more spectacular and popular than that of the Niagara frontier. In *The Golden Dog* (1877), a romance of Quebec in the days of Louis XV, Kirby pre-empted the history of the *ancien régime,* in which Mrs. Leprohon had set her *Manor House of de Villerai.* Kirby spread his net wider, painted on a broader canvas, produced an eventful story rather than a social period piece, and addressed readers in whom the nationalism of the Confederation period had instilled more regard for history. He had kept his eyes open for glamorous material; there were historical details concerning the Chateau of Beaumanoir, the Castle of St. Louis, the Intendant Bigot, Peter Kalm, Philibert, de Repentigny, de la Galissonière, La Corriveau, and "Le Chien d'Or." Parkman noted in a letter to James Macpherson Le Moine that Kirby had "*well* read" Le Moine's series of *Maple Leaves* (1863 and later). The romancer had also gained information from a young Niagara girl, who was the "living model," as Lorne Pierce said in his biography of Kirby, for Amelia de Repentigny. Kirby did not fail in telling a lively story, happily full of realistic detail. Images of Canadian life piled up rapidly under such auspices. But the development of anything native in Canadian romance was probably hindered by this example given by Kirby of ready success with European models.

While Kirby was reporting the past of Quebec, Charles Mair (1838–1917), born at Lanark in the Ottawa valley, was stepping westward, toward the far reaches of the continent. It was chiefly in the period after 1880 that he contributed to the historical and descriptive prose of the West, although his own experiences began with the first Riel rebellion of 1869–1870. Fascinating accounts of travel in the territories west and north of Ontario had been written before this time, especially between 1845 and 1860 by Bishop George J. Mountain (1845), Henry Youle Hind (geologist and explorer), Paul Kane (*Wanderings of an Artist*, 1859), and Robert Michael Ballantyne, the Scottish author of *Hudson's Bay; or, Life in the Woods of America* (1848) and many other boys' books upon which generations of young Britons built their ideas of greater Canada.

Mair's youthful verse in *Dreamland and Other Poems* (1868), a year after the founding of the Dominion, had promised nothing but a bookish career, begun in the grammar school at Perth and at Queen's University: here he was under the spell of Keats. Mair's important relationship with the men of the "Canada First" Movement at Ottawa—William A. Foster, Robert J. Haliburton, George T. Denison, and Henry J. Morgan—was too recent to affect *Dreamland*. Critics have justly found, as A. J. M. Smith has done, "a good deal of accurate observation and precise description" in these verses, but Mair's early stock diction is roughly like Sangster's in the 1850's, without Sangster's carefulness or taste. Mair might have been expected to begin where the popular poets of Dewart's *Selections* (1864) left off, moving tentatively toward Canadian authenticity, although still overwhelmed by popular English models. For Mair, however, the models were academic.

There must have been other young men in the 1860's fired at school or college by a study of Keats, Shelley, Shakespeare, Poe, perhaps Coleridge —especially the Keats of "Flora, and old Pan" happily linked to classical learning and undomesticated by Victorian accretions. Mair's *Dreamland* is evidence of what the universities could do for the poets; academic poetry, superficially at first a hindrance to Canadian literary emancipation (threatening loss of identity and a cultural lag), brought a new and inspiring freedom to Mair at Perth and Kingston before 1868. But Mair was not the man to make brilliant adaptations born of poetic insight. So *Dreamland* remains an item of literary history, throwing light, incidentally, upon the meaning of an often-quoted passage from one of Lampman's essays, in which the latter reported the excitement he experienced at Trinity College on first reading Charles G. D. Roberts's *Orion* (1880). The study of classical and English literature in more than one college in Canada was leading young men to Keats as an emancipating influence. New Brunswick's Roberts taught Lampman nothing in 1881 that Mair had not applied more explicitly to Canadian scenes before 1868: Roberts only overcame Lampman's reluctance to try his wings.

In other respects also the "immigrant" colleges of central Canada were as progressive and poetically inspiring as the Loyalist colleges of the Maritime Provinces. The infectious spirit of "Canada First," which was still strong in Toronto when Roberts sojourned there in 1883, had swept Mair off his feet in 1868, and this also was at the outset "an intellectual movement." Claude Bissell has drawn attention to William A. Foster's "Address to the Canadian National Association" (1875) (see Foster's *Canada First*, 1890, p. 77). Foster quoted with approval a "recent reviewer" who saw the "Canada First" movement as "a direct product, in some measure, of that higher culture which the universities and colleges of our land are steadily promoting." In Toronto not only the colleges were a leaven, but Mr. Goldwin Smith, a former Regius Professor at Oxford, had the stature of a Matthew Arnold. Even Isabella Valancy Crawford, who had not attended college, was warmed by the glow.

The impact of the new culture upon the poets was not confined to dipping Canadian details in Keatsian diction or to constructing national songs. British North American anti-republicanism was strong and many were ready to echo Daniel Wilson's "Not *Hiawatha*!" as well as "Not Whitman!" But the border was open, and influences from the United States freely contributed to another, more complex, growth of Canadian poetic imagery which could cope simultaneously with neo-Greekish myths and concepts of nature, Indian lore, theories of evolution, liberal theology, and primitive religion. Wilfred Campbell (1858–1918) finds his place in Canadian literary history as the exemplar of this development. Thoroughly imbued with Longfellow while he was a youth in Wiarton, Campbell moved on to University and Wycliffe Colleges in Toronto (1880–82), the city in which Daniel Wilson had recently prepared an adventure into the areas of poetic anthropology in *Caliban: The Missing Link* (1873). For two years thereafter, Campbell studied at the Episcopal Theological School in Cambridge, Massachusetts, near Harvard

University. Twenty years later, in his book *The Dread Voyage* (1893), the fruits of his preparation were fully evident, for *Hiawatha, Caliban,* (Sir) Edward B. Tylor's *Primitive Culture* (1871), and John Fiske's *Myths and Myth-makers* (1872) had led to Campbell's experiments in imagery of primitive nature and primitive religion; this was several generations before Sir James Frazer's *The Golden Bough* (1890-1915) enriched the poetry of the McGill group of the late 1920's. It is instructive to observe the similarity of Campbell's "The Mother" (*Harper's,* 1891) and "The Mother's Soul," also called "The Butterfly" (1883), of Isabella Crawford, who lived only in the environs of the Toronto colleges.

Very near was also the home of Goldwin Smith (1823-1910), a former professor at Oxford and Cornell, a great journalist and an indefatigable commentator, who settled in Toronto in 1871 at the age of forty-seven and after 1875 lived at "The Grange." A succession of literary-political magazines were taken under his wing. The first of these was the *Canadian Monthly and National Review* (1872-78), planned by the "Canada First" group before he arrived. Until late in 1874 he was its principal support in money, articles, and prestige; its editor, Graeme Mercer Adam, adopted Smith's unpopular, but yet influential, ideas on national independence. In poetry, however, Smith was definitely not radical. He indulged in verse translations from the Latin poets or the *Greek Anthology,* and he probably helped the universities to draw readers to the classics, which were undergirding the poetry of the young academic poets. His own taste in poetic selections stopped short at Tennyson, perhaps later at Matthew Arnold. It was in the first volume (May 1872) of the *Canadian Monthly* that William Dawson LeSueur described the spirit of the times:

If Mr. Arnold were wholly Greek, of what interest would he be to us? He could be but the echo of that original inspiration the direct products of which are yet in our hands. But if, with that breadth and calmness of manner which distinguished the great minds of Greek antiquity, he can present to us the living ideas and issues of today, then indeed is there food for the mind, as well as for the aesthetic sense, in his writings.

In performing the "function of criticism," Smith did not match Arnold's "disinterestedness," but his magazine *The Canadian Monthly* was, as Elisabeth Wallace has said in *Goldwin Smith, Victorian Liberal* (1957), "the nearest equivalent to such British periodicals as the *Fortnightly* and *Contemporary Review*." He wrote better than any one of his contributors, but their level, in prose, was high. Smith's own breadth was reflected in sections on "Current Literature," "Book Reviews," and "Literary Notes"; the reader could feel that Toronto shared in the culture of contemporary Britain, even in its fine art and its music. Generally speaking the young Canadian Greeks were not yet ready to publish in the 1870's. Native commonplace realism, however, happily demonstrated its persistence in the works of "Fidelis," Miss Agnes Maule Machar (1837–1927) of Kingston, who began her career with good history and readable fiction in *For King and Country: A Story of 1812* (in the *Canadian Monthly* and in book form in 1874).

The thin showing of *belles-lettres* by native authors was offset by a lively presentation of the nation's history and current affairs, for this was the magazine's true purpose. "*The Canadian Monthly* owed its existence," Smith said, "to the shortlived glow of national feeling which passed through the veins of the community on the morning of Confederation. . . . Then, as the movement in which it had originated flagged, the shadow of doom began to fall upon it . . . against English and American competition, patriotic feeling alone could hold its ground, and of this the limit has been seen." This obituary for the *Canadian Monthly* appeared in *The Bystander* of January 1883. In the late 1870's the *Monthly* had become *Rose Belford's* (1878–82). Smith kept on writing, always with a journalistic vehicle, and typically as "Bystander." From time to time in the 1880's he had his own journal with that very title (1880–81; 1883; 1889–90). In the meantime he founded *The Week* (1883–96).

The 1870's, therefore, may be seen as a period of transition, a time for gathering strength. Early in the productive decade which followed, before *The Week* began publication, the Royal Society of Canada was founded (1882) at the suggestion of the Marquess of Lorne (afterwards Duke of Argyll), Governor General of Canada. Smith, Dawson, Kirby, George Murray, Le Moine, Reade, Sangster, and Daniel Wilson were among the charter members. Almost sixty years had passed since the Earl of Dalhousie had organized the Literary and Historical Society of Quebec. The English literature of the Canadas had played its part in the building of the country's culture. A regional character had been formed and a national character was emerging out of trial and error, tradition and independence, observation and insight, during years of preparation.

10. Folktales and Folk Songs

EDITH FOWKE

FOLKTALES AND FOLK SONGS are our unwritten prose and poetry: they are handed down orally from generation to generation, exist in many different forms, and tend to lose their folk quality once they are frozen in print. As the literature of an unlettered people, they often reflect more clearly than printed literature the culture and development of a country in its early stages.

I. THE FOLKTALE

"Folktale" is a general term used to include all types of traditional narrative—myth, legend, fairy tale, animal story, and fable—and Indians, French Canadians, and English Canadians alike have delighted to tell them.

The Indians and Eskimos were particularly prolific story-tellers, and thousands of their tales have been collected and published. Certain stories were common to tribes all across the continent, while others were found only among the tribes of one region: for example, among the Eskimos of the far north, or the Indians of the Pacific Coast, the Plains, the Great Lakes, or the Maritimes.

Most of the Indian tribes have some "creation myths" or sacred legends in which they tell tales of their beginnings. Usually these are built around a culture hero: Glooscap of the Micmacs, Manabozho of the Algonkins, the Raven of the Pacific tribes, or the Old Man of the Plains. The most common myth tells how the culture hero, floating on a raft on primeval waters, sends down some animal, usually the muskrat, to bring up a few grains of sand, and out of that he makes the earth. Most tribes also have tales about the origin of light, fire, the seasons, the winds, the sun and moon. Usually the hero steals fire and light from some enemy who is keeping them from mankind.

There are also many stories about calamities that destroy the world. The most frequent is a great flood, but other tales tell how the world was destroyed, or almost destroyed, by fire, blizzards, or drought and a very widespread one tells of the efforts of various animals to free the sun, which has been trapped by some hostile power. In another tale the hero, like

Phaeton in Greek mythology, is permitted to carry the sun and almost burns up the earth.

The Indians also like to tell of trips to other worlds. The most famous tale is of a girl who finds herself in the upper world and marries a star who forbids her to dig in a certain place; when she disobeys, she sees her old home below and is seized with a longing to return; secretly, often with supernatural help, she prepares a rope and descends. Other stories suggest the European tales of Cupid and Psyche and the Swan Maiden, telling of a hero who climbs to the upper world in search of his supernatural wife, and finds her only after surviving many perils. Less common is the tale of a descent to the land of the dead, which closely parallels the Greek myth of Orpheus and Eurydice.

Many Indian stories remind us of familiar European fairy tales: one from the west coast, "The Deserted Children," resembles "Hansel and Gretel," with elements of "Jack and the Beanstalk." However, many Indian tales are very un-fairy-tale-like, for they deal both realistically and imaginatively with the processes of procreation and evacuation. So frequent are such themes that most anthologists find it necessary to note that they have eliminated them from the tales they publish. The anthologists prefer the more romantic legends that account for famous landmarks or that explain the various characteristics of birds and animals.

The first to note the Indian tales in Canada were the Jesuit Fathers. During the second half of the seventeenth century they recorded a number of Huron and Algonkin tales in the *Jesuit Relations*. Later, priests such as Father Lacombe and Father Petitot noted tales of the western and northern tribes. The first to record any tales in English was Henry Rowe Schoolcraft who served as Indian agent among the Ojibwas of the Great Lakes between 1812 and 1842. His tales inspired Longfellow's *Hiawatha*, although the actual Ojibwa culture hero was not Hiawatha but Manabozho; Hiawatha was a historical Iroquois leader of the sixteenth century.

In the half-century after Schoolcraft many others followed his example. Indian agents, missionaries, doctors, and teachers noted down the tales they heard and printed them, sometimes translating the narratives literally, more often retelling them in a style they thought would be of greater interest to the reading public. The most important of these early collectors was the Rev. S. T. Rand, whose *Legends of the Micmacs* (1894) is still a basic reference.

Then towards the end of the nineteenth century, the amateur collectors were succeeded by the specialists: anthropologists, ethnologists, and folklorists, who published literal translations of the tales they collected from particular tribes. Among the important regional collections are James Teit's *Traditions of the Thompson River Indians of British Columbia* (1898), *Folk-Tales of Salishan and Sahaptin Tribes* edited by Franz Boaz (1917), *Sacred Stories of the Sweet Grass Cree* by L. Bloomfield (1930), *The Micmac Indians of Eastern Canada* by W. D. and R. S. Wallis (1955), and several volumes by

Canada's foremost folklorist, Dr. Marius Barbeau, notably *Haida Myths Illustrated in Argillite Carvings* (1953) and *Huron-Wyandot Traditional Narratives in Translations and Native Texts* (1960).

Using the tales actually collected from the Indians as raw materials, many authors have published books in which the tales are rewritten or adapted for popular consumption. Pauline Johnson's *Legends of Vancouver* (1911) gives a rather romantic treatment of the ancient tales, and Cyrus MacMillan's *Canadian Wonder Tales* (1918) and *Canadian Fairy Tales* (1922) emphasize the fanciful elements. More representative are such general anthologies as *The Corn Goddess and Other Tales from Indian Canada* by Diamond D. Jenness (1956) and *Indian Legends of Canada* by Ethel May Clark (1960).

The second largest group of Canadian folktales was brought to New France by the seventeenth-century colonists. Along the St. Lawrence the medieval "romans de la Table Ronde" were handed down from generation to generation, and until recent times it was the custom to engage good story-tellers to entertain the men who spent the winter working in the lumber camps along the North Shore. Many of the old European tales—such as "The Seven-headed Dragon," "John the Bear," "Little Poucet," "The White Cat," "Cinderella," "Jack the Trickster," and "The Master Thief"—were picked up by the Indians who retold them in their turn. Especially popular were the tales of Petit Jean (or Ti-Jean, or Bon-Jean) whose cunning and trickery made up for his puny size: these may have inspired the lumberjack tales of Paul Bunyan.

Naturally most of the French-Canadian tales have been printed in French, and there are few literal English translations. However, various authors have given their versions of the most popular tales. Early samples appeared in W. P. Greenough's *Canadian Folk-Life and Folk-Lore* (1897) and in J. M. Le Moine's *The Legends of the St. Lawrence* (1898). Sometimes the tales were retold in simulated "habitant" dialect, as in P. A. W. Wallace's *Baptiste Larocque* (1923) and in some of W. H. Drummond's poems.

A good sampling of the European inheritance preserved in French Canada is found in *The Golden Phoenix* (1958), Michael Hornyansky's adaptation of eight tales collected by Dr. Barbeau. Some of these originated in the Orient, with roots that go far back in history: "The Thief of Valenciennes" had travelled from Arabia to Egypt by the sixth century B.C., and "The Golden Phoenix" (or "Le Grand Sultan") travelled to Europe from China thousands of years ago. Others, like "The Princess of Tomboso" and "The Fairy Quite Contrary," are very similar to the tales Grimm and Andersen told.

Of the legends that have taken root in Quebec and acquired a local flavour, Dr. Barbeau reports that the best are: "The Handsome Dancer" or "Rose Latulippe," in which the Devil attends a dance; "The Black Hen," about a soul for sale at a crossroads; "The Witch Canoe" or "La Chasse-Gallerie" which flies through the air with a gang of shanty boys; "The Black Horse," in which the Devil helps to build a parish church; "The Buried Treasures of Portneuf County"; "The Church Bell of Caughnawaga"; "The Midnight Mass of Père de la Brosse"; and "The Great Serpent of Lorette" or "Wolverine." All of these he has retold in *The Tree of Dreams* (1955), and the same themes turn up repeatedly in other collections.

Although the early British settlers also brought many European tales to Canada with them, they did not preserve them nearly as well as the French. Dr. Helen Creighton, a prolific Nova Scotia collector, notes that traditional tales in English are very scarce in that province, and W. J. Wintemberg, who collected various forms of folklore in Ontario in the early part of this century, noted that "folk tales are mostly of the noodle variety": that is, anecdotes about stupid fellows.

Of the more localized tales, Nova Scotia has many telling of buried gold and phantom ships, of ghosts and haunted houses, which Dr. Creighton drew upon for her *Bluenose Ghosts* (1957). Although the Americans claim Paul Bunyan, Canadian shanty boys from the Maritimes to the Pacific told tales of the mighty lumberjack and his Blue Ox, and Dr. J. D. Robins retold some of the Ontario yarns in *Logging with Paul Bunyan* (1957). In western Canada, the *Alberta Folklore Quarterly*, which flourished briefly in 1945 and 1946, published some local legends and characteristic tall tales; an American, Robert Gard, published some of the folktales he gathered in Alberta in his *Johnny Chinook* (1954).

Some folktales found their way into other literary forms. William Kirby's historical novel of old Quebec, *The Golden Dog* (1877), incorporates various elements of French-Canadian folklore, and the legend of the *corriveau* plays an important part in his plot. In *Mountain Cloud* (1944) Dr. Barbeau gives a fictional account of an Indian brave, based on the ritual and folklore of the west coast Indians. In the Maritimes, in the early nineteenth century, Thomas Chandler Haliburton made free use of many New England tales in his stories of the Yankee peddler, Sam Slick, and in Alberta in the twentieth, the redoubtable Bob Edwards localized and embroidered many tall tales to enliven the columns of his *Calgary Eye-Opener*. Poets have also borrowed from folklore, the most widely known example being Pauline Johnson's "Legend of the Qu'Appelle"; in a different idiom, Anne Wilkinson's "A Folk Tale" uses the traditional form to achieve a strikingly modern effect. However, on the whole our poets tend to draw their mythology from classical rather than Canadian sources.

II. THE FOLK SONG

Before the white man came to Canada our great plains and forests resounded to the chants of the Indians, and in the frozen north the Eskimos sang in their dance-houses during the long Arctic nights. Indeed, song entered more intimately into the life of the Indians than into that of any white nation, for they believed that the invisible voice could reach the invisible power that permeates nature and thereby bring them success in their undertakings. Thus song was an essential part of everything they did, entering into every important personal experience and every social ritual. As Miss Alice Fletcher, one of the earliest collectors of Indian songs, put it: "In his sports, in his games, when he wooed, and when he mourned . . . the Indian sang in every experience of life from the cradle to the grave."

Indian songs were very short and were usually made up either of a few words repeated again and again or of meaningless syllables. Usually they were not complete in themselves but formed part of a story or a ceremony: for example, prayers for rain, warriors' songs, dirges for the dead, songs of welcome, and hymns of victory. They are very important to an understanding of Indian culture, but as they largely defy translation, they have little bearing on Canada's literary history.

With the founding of New France, the Canadian wilderness echoed to the many songs which the pioneer settlers brought from their homeland and made part of their daily lives on this continent. In the words of Marius Barbeau, "Threshing and winnowing in the barns moved to the rhythm of work tunes, as did spinning, weaving, and beating the wash by the fireside."

The *coureurs de bois* and the fur traders sang as they pushed their way across the new continent, adapting the stately ballads of the French court to the rhythm of their paddles, and their singing made a strong impression on all who heard them. European visitors, explorers, traders, and early settlers frequently referred to the *voyageurs'* songs: Mrs. John Graves Simcoe describes them in her *Diary* (1792–96), as does John Mactaggart in *Three Years in Canada* (1829), Mrs. Anna Jameson in *Winter Studies and Summer Rambles in Canada, 1836–7*, R. M. Ballantyne in *Hudson Bay* (1843), and John J. Bigsby in *The Shoe and Canoe* (1850). Captain George Back noted some *voyageur* songs while on an Arctic expedition to the Coppermine River in 1823, and these were printed in London as *Canadian Airs,* the first Canadian folk songs ever published.

The second man to record any French folk songs on this continent was Edward Ermatinger, who noted eleven typical paddling songs while working for the Hudson's Bay Company between 1818 and 1828. These indicate that the songs of the *habitants* along the St. Lawrence and of the *voyageurs* in the west alike belonged largely to the common stock of traditional songs brought over by the early colonists in the seventeenth century—an impression confirmed by the first substantial collection of French-Canadian songs published by Ernest Gagnon in 1865. Indeed, Dr. Barbeau estimates that nineteen out of twenty of all French-Canadian songs are ancient.

Two well-known poems, both known by the title of "Canadian Boat Song," are the direct result of the *voyageurs'* songs. The first, composed by the Irish poet Thomas Moore after his visit to Canada in 1804, was inspired by a song the boatmen sang when rowing him down the St. Lawrence; the other, sometimes known as "The Lone Shieling," was published anonymously in *Blackwood's Edinburgh Magazine* for September 1829, under the title "Canadian Boat-Song (from the Gaelic)," although it is not a translation of any known Gaelic song and is not really a boat song but a lament. There has been considerable debate about its authorship, but it was probably written by David Macbeth Moir as a result of letters sent to him by John Galt when he visited Canada in 1827.

One of the earliest New World songs was the Indian carol, "Jesous Ahatonhia," which Father Brébeuf wrote in 1641 for the Hurons attending the Jesuit mission at Fort Ste Marie. A century later it was translated into French and sung in Quebec, and in 1926 J. E. Middleton wrote his own English interpretation which has become widely known as "The Huron Carol." This is perhaps the most truly Canadian of our songs, for it is the only one known to have been sung in Indian, French, and English.

The earliest song about a Canadian incident is said to be "Petit rocher de la haute montagne," sometimes known as "La plainte du coureur-de-bois." Its hero was a trapper, Cadieux, who died in saving his family from an Iroquois ambush on the Ottawa River in 1709. Soon afterwards the legend of Cadieux became widely popular among the *voyageurs* both as a tale and as a song, and many narratives of the fur trade mention it.

Occasionally the French Canadians composed new words to traditional tunes, the most familiar being "Vive la Canadienne!" a lively toast to the Canadian girl, and "Un Canadien errant," which A. Gérin-Lajoie wrote to express the feelings of a Canadian lad who fled to the United States after the Papineau rebellion of 1837. Other native French-Canadian songs catch the flavour of rural Quebec, for example, "Le Bal chez Boulé" which describes a country dance; "Youpe, Youpe sur la rivière," which tells of a *habitant* lad who goes to call on his girl and is rebuffed for being too fickle; and "Dans les Chantiers" and "Les Raftsmen," which describe life in the lumber camps.

In western Canada the Métis produced a prairie bard, Pierre Falcon, who composed songs that were very popular with the *voyageurs* throughout the nineteenth century. The most famous, usually known as "Falcon's Song," describes the Battle of Seven Oaks in 1816. Louis Riel also composed a number of verses, some of which have come down to us, as have also a few other Métis songs reflecting the early days on the prairies. Samples of these appear in Margaret Arnett MacLeod's little volume, *Songs of Old Manitoba* (1959).

The heritage of French-Canadian songs is incredibly rich: some 30,000 songs are now in the collections of the National Museum at Ottawa and the Archives de Folklore at Université Laval, and more are being added yearly. Naturally most of the published collections are in French, but a good sampling of the most popular French songs have appeared in English translations. Two nineteenth-century Canadian poets produced small volumes: G. T. Lanigan's *National Ballads of Canada* (1865) and William McLennan's *Songs of Old Canada* (1886). More recent books which give the songs in both French and English include *Canadian Folk Songs Old and New* by John Murray Gibbon (1928), *Folk Songs of Quebec* by Fowke and Johnston (1957), *Chantons un peu* by Alan Mills (1961), and four of Dr. Barbeau's numerous collections: *Folk Songs of French Canada* (1928), *Folk Songs of Old Quebec* (1935), *Roundelays* (1958), and *Jongleur Songs of Old Quebec* (1962). The last volume contains a detailed bibliography of French-Canadian songs.

When the English, Scots, and Irish began to settle in Canada they brought with them thousands of the songs then current in the British Isles, and most of these continued to be sung well into this century. Many of *The English and Scottish Popular Ballads* catalogued by Francis James Child have survived in Newfoundland, Nova Scotia, and Ontario, the most popular being "Barbara Allen," "Lady Isabel and the Elf Knight," "The Golden Vanity," "Little Musgrave and Lady Barnard," "The Farmer's Curst Wife," "Lord Thomas and Fair Annet," "The Cruel Mother," and "Young Beichan." Sometimes ballads have been preserved here that have disappeared in their homeland: for example, in Nova Scotia Dr. Helen Creighton collected "Robin Hood's Progress to Nottingham" of which the American folklorist Phillips Barry wrote: "Not a trace of this ballad has been found anywhere for three hundred years," and of her "False Knight upon the Road" he said: "Your version may be one of the oldest versions of any traditional English or Scottish ballad."

In addition to the medieval ballads, hundreds of the more recent broadside ballads were brought over from Britain and lovingly handed down in Canada: tales of highwaymen ("Brennan on the Moor" and "Bold Turpin") and pirates ("The Flying Cloud" and "Bold Manan"), of true love ("Burns and His Highland Mary" and "Pretty Polly Oliver") and false love ("The Girl I Left Behind" and "The Butcher Boy"), of famous battles ("The Plains of Waterloo" and "The Heights of Alma") and cruel murders ("The Ship's Carpenter" and "The Wexford Girl"). Again, many that have survived in oral tradition here have been forgotten in their homeland, as have also some beautiful versions of Old Country love songs such as "The Morning Dew," "She's Like the Swallow," and "The False Young Man."

Of the native English-Canadian ballads, two of the oldest describe General

Wolfe's victory and death on the Plains of Abraham. Then the United Empire Loyalists brought some songs to Canada, including "Revolutionary Tea" which pictures the outbreak of the American Revolution as a scrap between mother and daughter. The War of 1812 inspired a boastful ditty, "Come All You Bold Canadians," which describes General Brock's victory over General Hull at the Battle of Detroit, and two songs celebrate the victory of the British *Shannon* over the American *Chesapeake* in 1813. When William Lyon Mackenzie's American supporters raided Canada in 1838, the troops who routed them composed another boastful ditty, "The Battle of the Windmill," which was sung around Cornwall for many generations, and the Fenian raids of 1866 produced a Canadian parody of "Tramp, Tramp, Tramp, the Boys are Marching"—a song which later Canadian soldiers adapted for use in the Saskatchewan Rebellion, the Boer War, and World War I.

While such songs give the reactions of those who took part in colourful or dramatic events in Canada's history, the larger number of native Canadian songs reflect the daily lives of the ordinary people. Few of these rate high as poetry: at best they are vivid and lusty pictures of the rustic life; at worst, pedestrian doggerel. However, all those that have survived had something that appealed to the unlettered men and women who preserved them: they lived on because they said something that these people felt to be worth repeating. Some were humorous ditties about jails or sprees or local incidents; some told of murders or tragic accidents or riots. They were, in effect, a form of local history that gained more than local currency by being spread through the lumber camps or the fishing fleets. For example, the Nova Scotia ballad of the *Saladin* mutiny is still remembered in Ontario, as is a "Come-all-ye" describing a Twelfth of July riot that took place in Montreal in 1877. The Miramichi fire of 1825, the Birchall murder case of 1890, and the Halifax explosion of 1917 are still vivid in the folk memory. As a group these native songs are inferior to the older British ballads which have been polished by their passage through the centuries, but they are a significant expression of life in early Canada.

Many of the native songs were inspired by occupations. For some three hundred years the inhabitants of the small coastal villages of Newfoundland and Nova Scotia have been singing, adapting, and composing sea songs: sailors' shanties, accounts of whaling, sealing, or cod-fishing trips, and ballads about shipwrecks or brave deeds upon the high seas. Some are humorous, like "We'll Rant and We'll Roar like True Newfoundlanders"—a fisherman's adaptation of an old British sea song—and some are tragic, like "The Loss of the *Eliza*" or "The Ghostly Sailors," but all reflect the feelings of a people whose life is shaped by the sea.

Lumbering has also played a big part in Canada's history ever since the British navy ordered Canadian timber for its ships during the Napoleonic

Wars. All through the nineteenth century gangs of roving shanty-boys were spending their winters in snow-swept camps where they had to make their own entertainment. The songs they sang were numerous and varied, but the most characteristic fell into three groups: those describing the life and work in the camps ("Hogan's Lake" or "Turner's Camp"), those telling of death in the woods or on the rivers ("The Jam on Gerry's Rocks" or "Peter Emberley"), and those telling what happened when the shanty-boys headed for the bright lights in the spring with their winter's pay in their pockets ("The Grand Hotel" or "When the Shanty-Boy Comes Down").

Farmers produced fewer songs because their work was more solitary, and folk songs need an audience. However, the early settlers did compose some verses describing their life, usually couched in the form of complaints. In Ontario "The Scarborough Settler" longed to leave "Canada's muddy creeks" for "auld Scotia's glens," and out west "The Alberta Homesteader" complained that he was "starving to death on a government claim."

Cowboy songs were popular in Alberta, but most of them were merely borrowed from the United States: the early Canadian ranches were stocked with cattle driven up from Texas along the Old Chisholm Trail, and with them came American cowboys and their songs.

The gold-seekers of the Cariboo and Klondike also sang of their hopes and disappointments, but few of their songs have survived. Some verses that may have been traditional are included in *Sawney's Letters and Cariboo Rhymes* (1868) and *Rhymes of the Miner* edited by E. L. Chicanot (1937). The most popular ditty to come out of the Canadian north, "When the Ice Worms Nest Again," apparently originated with the Klondike balladeer, Robert Service, but it was transformed by the prospectors and trappers who sang it in varying forms all across northern Canada.

Two other poems by known poets were taken over by the folk and turned into songs: "The Wreck of the *Julie Plante*" by W. H. Drummond, and "The Walker of the Snow" by C. D. Shanly. Reversing the process, some authors have borrowed snatches of folk songs to add colour to their fiction or historical narratives, as in Kirby's *The Golden Dog*, or Slater's *The Yellow Briar*, and the old ballads play a leading role in Thomas Raddall's fine short story, "Blind MacNair."

Songs in the folk-song idiom are still being written, and some of them are passing into oral tradition. The best modern examples are "The Squidjiggin' Ground" which Arthur Scammell wrote in 1928 and which quickly became Newfoundland's favourite song, and "The Blackfly Song" written by Wade Hemsworth in 1949, which is increasingly popular in Ontario.

Samples of the different kinds of English-Canadian songs may be found in various volumes in addition to those that have already been mentioned. The earliest published collection appears to be James Murphy's *Songs and*

Ballads of Newfoundland, Ancient and Modern (1902), which gives an interesting assortment of the local songs composed by island bards. More significant is the work of Dr. W. Roy Mackenzie, a Nova Scotia–born English professor who collected a rich variety of Maritime songs during the early part of this century. In 1919 he described his adventures in a delightful book, *The Quest of the Ballad*, and in 1928 his collection appeared as *Sea Songs and Ballads from Nova Scotia*—a volume so well annotated that it is still a major reference for British and American folklorists.

After Dr. Mackenzie's pioneer work, collecting in Nova Scotia was taken up by Helen Creighton of Dartmouth who has continued to glean a rich harvest there for over thirty years. The best of the four-thousand-odd songs in her collection have appeared in three books: *Songs and Ballads from Nova Scotia* (1932), *Traditional Songs from Nova Scotia* (1950), and *Maritime Folk Songs* (1962). The other important Maritime collector, Louise Manny of Newcastle, is preparing a book of New Brunswick lumberjack songs, *Songs of Miramichi*, which she collected under the sponsorship of Lord Beaverbrook, and Edward D. Ives of the University of Maine has published a book about New Brunswick's famous traditional singer, *Larry Gorman: The Man That Made the Songs* (1964), as well as *Twenty-one Songs from Prince Edward Island* (1964).

The first major collections in Newfoundland were made not by Canadians but by visiting folklorists from the United States and Britain. In 1929 two young Americans, Elizabeth Bristol Greenleaf and Grace Yarrow Mansfield, visited the island as "the Vassar College folklore expedition" and published *Ballads and Sea Songs of Newfoundland* in 1933. They included songs of both British and New World origin, but when Miss Maud Karpeles of the English Folk Dance and Song Society visited the island in 1929 and 1930, she was interested primarily in the old British songs to be found there, and published some of these as *Folk Songs from Newfoundland* (1934). Gerald S. Doyle, a St. John's businessman, helped to preserve many of the native Newfoundland ditties by publishing several editions of a small paper-backed booklet, *Old-Time Songs of Newfoundland*, in which verses about the adventures of the local fishermen were interspersed with advertisements for patent medicines. More recently, Kenneth Peacock, a young Ottawa musician, spent a number of summers on the island recording songs for the National Museum, and published his collection as *Songs from the Newfoundland Outports* (1965). Dr. MacEdward Leach, a leading American folklorist, has also collected in Newfoundland and Labrador and has published *Ballads and Songs of the Lower Labrador Coast* (1965).

In addition to these regional collections, a broader selection of songs from across the country may be found in *Folk Songs of Canada* by Fowke and Johnston (1954) and *Canada's Story in Song* by Fowke, Mills, and Blume (1960).

Although books help to preserve the words and melodies, they cannot adequately convey the way our traditional songs were sung. They were normally sung solo and unaccompanied, and the melody was adapted from stanza to stanza to accommodate variations in the metre. Fortunately it is now possible to hear folk songs as they were actually sung by the folk on an increasing number of records. Most of these have been issued by the Folkways Record Corporation and include: "Folk Songs of Ontario" (FM 4005), "Folk Music in Nova Scotia" (FM 4006), "Irish and British Songs from the Ottawa Valley" (FM 4051), "Lumberjack Songs from the Ontario Shanties" (FM 4052), "Songs of the Miramichi" (FM 4053), "Maritime Folk Songs" (FE 4307), "Songs of the Great Lakes" (FE 4018) and "Folk Music of Saskatchewan" (FE 4312).

In pioneer days, and in rural areas until quite recently, traditional storytellers and folk singers were the main source of entertainment, and their tales and songs were cherished. With the coming of radio and television, their audience has been lost, and the old lore is fast disappearing. Many songs and stories still remain to be gathered from those who learned them in their youth, but the number who remember them is growing smaller each year. However, those that have been collected already and those that may still be garnered will provide a rich store upon which our future novelists, poets, historians, and sociologists may draw. The things that made the folktales and folk songs dear to many generations of our forefathers have much to tell us about our people and our past.

11. Literary Publishing

H. PEARSON GUNDY

AS EVERY CANADIANA COLLECTOR soon discovers, a much larger corpus of literary work has been produced in Canada than is generally known to the common, even well-informed reader. Much of it, to be sure, is now unread and all but unreadable, for the dross greatly outweighs the fine ore. Wilfred Eggleston, in *The Frontier and Canadian Letters* (1957), sums up Canadian writing of substance before 1900 as comprising "a few collections of poetry, three or four historical works, a few humorous sketches, an essay or two, but not a single novel or play." The rest he dismisses as "crude, derivative, imitative, dull and stodgy"—a harsh indictment which, as the present work shows, leaves out of consideration much that merits critical attention. No objective reassessment of our literary past, however, can transform low-lying plateaux into mountain peaks.

Was Canada, then, so devoid of talent, or were latent literary gifts thwarted before they had a chance to mature? Why, in a country which had printers and publishers for a hundred and fifty years before the present century, were our inglorious Miltons mute? Explanations and excuses have been multiplied: the harshness of pioneer times, the struggle to push our frontiers westward, our long and lingering colonial status, the overshadowing influence of a dynamic and powerful neighbour, our ingrained sectionalism, our retarded sense of identity, our sparse population, our indifference to the fine arts and, by contrast, the homage we have paid to wealth as a measure of success and social prestige. These are among the familiar reasons given for the paucity of our national literary heritage. Canadian publishers have also been made a convenient scapegoat. "Authorship without publishers is like the voice of one crying in the wilderness," cried William Kirby, in 1883. Timid, unadventurous, intent only on big names and safe markets, so we are told, our publishers have been content to promote popular British and American authors to the impoverishment of authorship in Canada.

There is doubtless some measure of truth or half-truth in all of these points, but too often they have been offered as airy generalizations based on insufficient or inconclusive evidence. In this chapter we shall examine the publisher–author relationship as it developed in Canada to determine, if we can, whether the conditions of publishing advanced or retarded Canadian literary expression.

For the first half-century after 1751, when the printing press was established in what is now Canada at Halifax, all printing and publishing was done by weekly newspaper offices and by the government which made use of them. Even after the government established its own printing offices, much work was let out on contract, and the King's (or Queen's) printers did private printing as well. When bookstores made their appearance in the early years of the last century, the more enterprising of them combined bookselling with publishing in the English tradition. The actual printing might still be done in a newspaper office, but the bookseller assumed the financial risk of publication, normally protecting himself by an advance subscription list. By the third decade of the century some of the larger bookstores had their own printing departments and were in lively competition with the newspaper presses.

With a later start than Montreal as a centre of English-language publishing, Toronto by mid-century was already overtaking the larger metropolis and was soon to become the publishing capital of English-speaking Canada. Maritime publishers supplied local needs but never succeeded in competing for the central market. In the west, apart from newspaper and job printing, there was little attempt at literary publication before the present century.

Newspaper offices, government printing departments, and bookstores were thus the direct forerunners of Canadian publishing houses which emerged in the latter years of the nineteenth century, commonly combining book publishing with the wholesale book trade, magazine publishing, or the manufacture of stationery. The development of publishing was, in broad outline, slow and unspectacular from 1751 to 1900; it was a relatively small, dispersed industry, gradually centring in Toronto, but without great capital behind it, hampered in its growth by severe business depressions in the 1850's and 1870's and, as we shall see, by copyright anomalies which so trammelled publishing houses that even the fittest found it hard to survive.

In her *Bibliography of Canadian Imprints, 1751–1800* (1952) Marie Tremaine describes over 1,200 separate publications of Canadian presses in the eighteenth century. Official government documents form the great bulk of this output, followed by ecclesiastical and legal works, almanacs, and a wide range of pamphlets, but very little that could be classed as *belles lettres*. As the English traveller, John Lambert, wrote in 1809, in his *Travels through Lower Canada and the United States* (1810), "The state of literature, the arts, and science in Canada can scarcely be said to be at a low ebb, because they were never known to flow."

Our first literary awakening is commonly attributed to Howe, Haliburton, and their coterie in Halifax during the late 1820's and 1830's. There were, however, unmistakable earlier signs of literary interest, even if the results were meagre. Some early Maritime verse had been published in Boston and Albany, and a narrative poem on the War of 1812 by Thomas Cowdell was issued from the newspaper press of John Howe in Halifax in 1815. Five years later a Montreal bookseller, Ariel Bowman, brought out a slim volume of his own verse, *Hours of Childhood and Other Poems*. In Upper Canada, Hugh C. Thomson, editor and proprietor of the *Upper Canada Herald*, published two booklets of verse in 1822, *Poems* by "Peter Pindar" (of which no copy seems to have survived) and a rhyming defence of the jury system grandiloquently addressed "To the Liege Men of Every British Colony and Province in the World" by "A Friend to his Species." Forsaking verse for prose fiction, Thomson published in 1824 the first novel by a native-born Canadian, *St. Ursula's Convent; or, The Nun of Canada*, whose anonymous author, Julia Catherine Hart (née Beckwith) was the wife of a Kingston bookbinder.

Two periodicals had appeared before 1800, the *Nova Scotia Magazine* (1789-92) and the *Quebec Magazine* (1792-94) though both were essentially miscellanies of reprinted articles and extracts. John Strachan's *Christian Examiner* (1819-20), first published in Kingston, then transferred to York, was an early attempt at an indigenous literary magazine not confined in content to religious themes. Equally transitory were two other early journals, the *Enquirer* (Quebec, 1821-22) and the *Literary Miscellany* (Montreal, 1822-23).

The founding by Lord Dalhousie of the Quebec Literary and Historical Society in 1824 stimulated a flurry of literary interest in the lower province. Some minor volumes of verse had already appeared in addition to the periodicals above mentioned. Then followed two new literary magazines edited by experienced journalists and published by two rival Montreal bookstore proprietors, Joseph Nickless and H. H. Cunningham.

The *Canadian Magazine and Literary Repository* was the first to appear, in July 1823, printed on the newspaper press of Nahum Mower for Nickless the bookseller. The editor, whose name is not given, was David Chisholme, a young Scotsman with legal training and a flair for writing, a *protégé* of the Earl of Dalhousie who brought him out to Canada in 1822. In a long introduction he outlined his editorial policy: ". . . it shall form one of the most prominent parts of our labours to select and transfer into our pages . . . such articles as we may deem of importance, in promoting the diffusion of useful knowledge throughout this country. . . . Besides selected articles from other publications, we intend that this work shall also contain *original* matter of such a local and general character as shall render it at once useful and entertaining to all classes of society. . . . A due proportion of our pages shall be allotted for the selection of published and unpublished verse. . . ."

There was no noticeable change in this policy when Chisholme was superseded, in February 1824, by Dr. A. J. Christie, the editor of the Montreal *Gazette*. The educational mission of the magazine was re-emphasized in volume II:

> Ignorance is the means of perpetuating national antipathies, of keeping alive the remembrance of unreasonable jealousy and suspicion. Let light arise among the people, and these bitter animosities will die. Why should the inhabitants of Canada consider themselves as of two distinct nations? Though their ancestors were descended from different originals, have not they themselves, the most serious reasons for unanimity and concord? Do they not breathe the same air? Are they not nourished by the same benignant soil; and all enriched by the commerce of the same River? Are they not protected by the same Government? Have they not the same laws, the same rights, and one common interest? The happiness of one cannot be injured without impairing that of the other. The welfare of both is promoted by the same means. Though their languages are different, their interests cannot be separated. (P. 136)

In July 1824 a rival publication made its appearance, Cunningham's periodical, the *Canadian Review and Literary and Historical Journal* (shortened after the first issue to *Canadian Review and Magazine*). Closely resembling the *Canadian Magazine* in format, the *Review* was edited by Christie's predecessor, David Chisholme, whose leading article was on the newly formed Quebec Literary and Historical Society, "so similar in its objects," he observed, "to our own pursuits."

This innocent comparison roused the ire of Dr. Christie—"The meridian sun to a farthing rushlight!" In a corrosive review of the new journal in his own volume III ("the public as well as ourselves will be woefully disappointed when they come to read this work") he read Chisholme a lecture on the pitfalls of conducting a literary journal in Canada:

> That there are men of genius and talent in this country will not be denied; but it is no less true that they seldom devote much of their time to literary composition. Deeply engaged in other avocations, although good judges of what they *read*, but few of them can spare time for *writing*. From this cause the conductor of a periodical publication in Canada has a heavier task to perform than in older countries ... [and] is more dependent upon his own talents and resources. (P. 113)

Ironically, however, Chisholme succeeded in drawing more widely on native contributors than Christie, and was able to keep the *Canadian Review and Magazine* going for a full year after his rival's publisher had been forced to suspend publication. The final issue ran an article (intended to be continued) on "Writers and Literature of Canada," a pretentious title which, the author wryly admits, would "at first view excite a smile ... if confined to the productions of native talent"; instead, it dealt with accounts of explorations and the *Jesuit Relations*.

Unimpressive as were the results of this early, self-conscious urge to launch

Canadian literature, it is worth noting that its promoters in widely separated parts of the country were newspaper and bookstore publishers. With little or no prospect of financial gain, they attempted to provide an outlet for writers on a higher literary level than that of the common weeklies. What was lacking were sufficient subscribers, and, above all, an author whose gift of imagination was matched by fresh and vigorous powers of expression. Such a man Joseph Howe was soon to discover in Halifax.

Among the lively young writers whom Howe gathered about him as editor of the *Novascotian* in 1828, was Thomas Chandler Haliburton, eloquent member of the House of Assembly for Annapolis. His first important work, *An Historical and Statistical Account of Nova Scotia* (1829) was published by Howe in two formidable octavo volumes at a heavy financial loss. Readers of this work could scarcely have foreseen the exuberant creator of Sam Slick. But Howe knew his author, and persuaded him to contribute some light sketches to "The Club," a regular feature of the *Novascotian*. Haliburton warmed to the task and produced something new in Canadian journalism. The sayings and doings of the Yankee clock pedlar, Sam Slick of Slickville, for the first time brought international popularity and acclaim to a Canadian writer. Howe re-published the original series as *The Clockmaker* in book form in 1836, now a rare edition much sought by collectors. The success of this book helped to offset Howe's loss on the earlier publication, but there was no possibility of copyright protection. There were, indeed, at that time no imperial or colonial copyright acts, and no vestige of international agreement. Moreover Howe's small newspaper press was not equipped to meet the demands of a "best seller" or even a second best. Subsequent volumes in the Sam Slick series were first published in the United States, in England, and in France.

Howe's other literary publications fell short of his own contributions in verse and prose to the *Novascotian* which, curiously enough, he never re-issued in book form.

Oliver Goldsmith, Howe's fellow townsman, found an English publisher, John Sharpe of London, for his *Rising Village* (1825). The poem was reprinted in its entirety in the *Canadian Review and Magazine*, February 1826, but not until eight years later was it re-issued with additional poems. This first Canadian edition was published by a Saint John bookseller, John McMillan, in 1834. The firm of J. & A. McMillan was soon to become the leading bookstore publisher in New Brunswick, and a close rival to the newspaper press of Henry Chubb, the publisher in 1825 of James Hogg's *Poems, Religious, Moral and Sentimental*. Other Maritime poets and prose writers appeared in the pages of various short-lived literary periodicals: the *New Brunswick Religious and Literary Journal* (Saint John, 1829-30), the *Halifax Monthly Magazine* (1830-31), *The Bee* (Pictou, 1835-38) or the *Colonial Pearl* (Halifax, 1837-40).

There were several bookstore publishers in Halifax during this period, the most active of which was the firm of A. & W. Mackinlay, whose bookshop on Granville Street was well stocked and well patronized. The Mackinlays, however, were less interested as publishers in *belles-lettres* than in school texts, theological tracts, and works of practical reference on the geology and geography of the province. For literary achievement in such subjects, Alexander Monro, in a work on *New Brunswick* (1855), commends the Nova Scotians, but adds a caveat against the circulation of "novels and other light trash of literature," calculated, he believed, "to corrupt the morals and retard the intellectual advancement of the people."

The publishing trend in the Canadas up to mid-century was similar to that of the Maritimes. In Upper Canada two literary journals made brief appearances at York in 1833. The *Canadian Literary Magazine*, published by George Gurnett, was well edited by John Kent, a teacher at Upper Canada College lately arrived from England, who, according to his "Editor's Address" in the first number, found Canadians "advanced in civilization beyond [his] expectation" and who invited "the support of every individual who feels a desire that Canada should possess a literature of its own"—support evidently not forthcoming. The other periodical, also stillborn, was the *Canadian Magazine*, printed and published by the King's Printer, Robert Stanton, and edited by W. Sibbald. It was to be a forum for writers on religion, science, literature, morality, agriculture, and was also to include fiction. Too ambitious for a small provincial capital, the journal expired before the end of 1833.

The following year, when York was incorporated as Toronto, two bookstores were established which soon became the largest in Upper Canada, the one run by a reformer, James Lesslie, the other by a Tory, Henry Rowsell. The Lesslie family, long established as booksellers in Dundee, Scotland, had come out to Canada in the 1820's and settled in Kingston and Dundas. When the father died, James Lesslie consolidated the family business in Toronto. He set up a printing department as well, issued a good many miscellaneous books and pamphlets, but threw most of his energy into a reform newspaper, the *Examiner*, finally bought out by George Brown of the *Globe*. Henry Rowsell, who enjoyed the patronage of Sir Francis Bond Head, Bishop Strachan, and the governing clique, was also a prolific publisher of pamphlets, tracts, yearbooks, law journals, and occasional volumes of minor verse. His chief excursion into *belles-lettres* was *The Maple Leaf; or, Canadian Annual* (1847–49) a literary annual under the editorship of the Rev. John McCaul, Professor of Classics in King's College (later the University of Toronto). The only Canadian feature of the first issue was the title and the fact that all the contributors were Canadians "by birth or adoption." There were articles on the Coliseum, the castles of Europe and Asia, on Val D'Ossola, interspersed with poems which betrayed their Canadian origin only by their limping metre. In format the volume was handsome in the ornate taste of the times, with a maple leaf design heavily printed in gold leaf on the hard covers, an engraved title-page in red and black, and ten full-page engravings to illustrate the text. In a preface to the second volume, 1848, the editor confessed to a miscalculation. He had supposed colonial readers would be most interested in "the scenes and subjects of the Old World," but in point of fact "both near and distant friends regretted the absence from the volume of the characteristics of 'the maple leaf.' " In the next, and final volume, editor and publisher sought, with some success, to produce a distinctively Canadian annual.

One of the verse contributors to the *Maple Leaf* was the bookseller-publisher Samuel Thompson, whose autobiography, *Reminiscences of a Canadian Pioneer* (1884), throws some revealing light on writing and publishing in the middle of the last century. Thompson was a friend of the Todd brothers, Alfred and Alpheus, and brought out the latter's *The Practice and Privileges of the Two Houses of Parliament* (1840), the first such work by a Canadian to be accepted as authoritative not only in the colonies but in Great Britain. Later Thompson became Queen's Printer, suffered bankruptcy, and was bought out by two of his employees, Robert Hunter and George M. Rose. The Hunter, Rose firm became one of the earliest fully-fledged publishing houses in Canada. (The firm was taken over in 1948 by Sir Isaac Pitman & Sons (Canada) Limited.)

More venerable in years than Hunter, Rose & Co. was the Methodist Book and Publishing House (now the Ryerson Press) which had its origin in the hand-press on which Egerton Ryerson in 1829 published the *Christian Guardian*. From the beginning this church press issued secular as well as religious books, and did much to encourage Canadian writing, but up to the period of Confederation it was essentially a periodical rather than a book-publishing house.

Two Montreal firms which began in the mid-1830's provided outlets for Canadian writers and did a good deal to extend literary interest in the two Canadas: Armour & Ramsay, booksellers, stationers and publishers, and John Lovell, printer and publisher.

Andrew Armour and Hew Ramsay conducted a large business with branches in Kingston, Hamilton, and Toronto. One of their shrewdest strokes was to persuade English magazine publishers to issue special colonial editions at a discount, after their normal runs were off the press, in order to compete with cheap American pirated reprints. They did so at some risk as a letter from them to Messrs. Blackwood & Sons, Edinburgh, of March 7, 1843, indicates (National Library of Scotland Ms. 4063); the letter concludes: ". . . have the goodness not to use our name, as it might lead us into unpleasant altercations both with the press here who are greatly in favour of the United States cheap editions as well as the agents who dispose of them." In 1838 Armour & Ramsay published Major John Richardson's *Personal*

Memoirs, the first of his works to appear under a Canadian imprint. The author then projected a revised subscription edition of his novel *Wacousta*, advertising himself as "the first and only writer of historical fiction the country has yet produced." But although his advertisements ran in the provincial press from May to November 1838, the response was too meagre to tempt Ramsay and Armour or any other Canadian publisher. The revised edition of *Wacousta* was set aside until a New York publisher brought it out in 1851. (Lovell finally issued a Canadian edition in 1868.) Meanwhile, however, Armour & Ramsay published a subscription edition of *The Canadian Brothers; or, The Prophecy Fulfilled* (2 vols., 1840). Richardson then determined to become his own publisher by setting up a press in Brockville from which he issued a weekly, the *New Era or Canadian Chronicle*; in this he published serially a new novel, *Jack Brag in Spain*, and the first series (all that was published) of *The War of 1812*. Publication of the latter in book form was made possible by a grant from the government. Richardson was disappointed in his hope that it would be used as a school text, and in the apathy of the reading public. He reported that only thirty copies were sold and when he sent the remainder to be auctioned off in Kingston a bidder was found for only one copy at sevenpence halfpenny. H. H. Cunningham, however, had sufficient confidence in the author to bring out two more of his works, *Eight Years in Canada* (1847) and *The Guards in Canada* (1848).

Another publisher who provided an outlet for Richardson and other writers was John Lovell of Montreal and Toronto. An Irishman by birth, he had come to Canada in 1820 at the age of 10, served his apprenticeship as a printer in Montreal, and in 1835 became an independent job printer. He then branched out into newspaper and periodical publishing, obtained government printing contracts, opened an office in Toronto, and specialized in the publication of gazetteers and directories for which there was a ready market.

In 1838 Lovell and his brother-in-law, John Gibson, launched the *Literary Garland*, the first successful Canadian literary journal, which lasted for thirteen years until 1851. One of Lovell's innovations was to pay his contributors. Susanna Moodie, in a familiar passage of *Roughing It in the Bush*, records her astonishment on receiving an invitation to contribute articles, short stories, and verse, with the promise of remuneration. "Such an application," she wrote, "was like a gleam of light springing up in the darkness. I had never been able to turn my thoughts toward literature during my sojourn in the bush. . . . I actually shed tears of joy over the first twenty-dollar bill I received from Montreal."

Other contributors to the *Literary Garland* included Major John Richardson, Mrs. Anna Jameson, Catharine Parr Traill, Charles Sangster, Mrs. Leprohon, and Mrs. Elizabeth Cushing (who edited the final volume after the death of Gibson). At a time when book publication in Canada was costly and hazardous, Lovell provided a forum for writers both native and immigrant in the pages of the *Garland* without which the literary record of the 1840's would have been even more arid than it is. Although neither publisher nor editor can be said to have discovered major literary talent, their journal maintained a respectable standard in the genteel tradition of the times.

Lovell was, perhaps, the only Canadian publisher of the last century who commissioned an author to write two novels for publication. The writer was Ebenezer Clemo, an impecunious English inventor who was then stranded in Montreal, and his novels (if such they may be called), both published under the pseudonym "Maple Knott" in 1858, were *The Life and Adventures of Simon Seek*, and *Canadian Homes; or, The Mystery Solved*. But as neither has any claim to literary merit, Lovell's gesture savours more of philanthropy than the encouragement of promising talent. There can be no doubt, however, that John Lovell did try to stimulate an interest in Canadian letters. Over a period of some fifty years he sought to bring before Canadian readers short stories, novels, and verse by Canadians. A dozen or more writers of fiction and a score of poets and poetasters appeared under the Lovell imprint. The very names of most of them are now forgotten—J. A. Phillips, A. L. Spedon, G. B. Chapin, H. S. Caswell, Frank Johnson, Augusta Baldwin, H. F. Darnell, Mrs. J. P. Grant, Henry Patterson, Kate Douglas Ramage and others. The more successful Canadian writers of fiction at the popular level, such as James De Mille and May Agnes Fleming, published all their work in the United States. The one Lovell author (apart from such public men as Thomas D'Arcy McGee and Joseph Howe) to achieve prominence in Canadian literary annals was William Kirby, the first edition of whose *Golden Dog* was published by the Lovell firm in 1877 at Rouses Point, N.Y., shortly before this American branch of the publishing house went bankrupt. But for a literary harvest so meagre after a lifetime of publishing, John Lovell cannot justly be blamed. On his part there was neither lack of critical discernment nor failure to provide financial incentives for creative writing. A publisher may encourage but can scarcely be expected to create writers.

After the demise of the *Literary Garland*, other efforts were made in the second half of the century to revive interest in Canadian letters. Six or eight literary magazines appeared in the Maritimes, in Quebec, and in Upper Canada, all of them short-lived. Typical of these was Thomas Maclear's *Anglo-American Magazine*, 1852-55. A Toronto bookstore-publisher, Maclear, in the prospectus for his new journal, deplored the flood of American magazines which were "little calculated to form or improve the literary taste" of Canadians. What was needed was a national, literary monthly, written by Canadians for Canadians. The *Anglo-American* scaled no literary heights, but it introduced Sangster to its readers, published some lively articles and stories, and impressed the English visitor to Toronto, W. H. G. Kingston, as "a very creditably conducted periodical" (to quote his *Western Wanderings; or,*

Pleasure Tour in the Canadas, London, 1856). It was soon to fall a victim to a severe financial depression, however, and its epitaph was "many subscribers but few subscriptions." The Maclear firm was later bought out by two former employees who, in 1869, formed the Copp, Clark Publishing Co.

The largest wholesale bookdealer and publisher in Toronto in the 1860's and 1870's was James Campbell & Son. The firm had a contract with the Department of Education to supply Canadian school texts written or edited by Canadians. Campbell's general line included a series of religious biographies, sermons, travel books, and an occasional volume of verse. The James Campbell & Son imprint became well known from Toronto to Halifax; their books were neat, well-printed volumes, superior in format and presswork to the average book published in Canada at the time. But as the firm regularly advertised that they were "prepared to furnish estimates to authors for the publication of their Mss.," it may be assumed that at least some titles on their list were published at the risk not of James Campbell & Son but of the aspiring authors.

This attitude towards native writers on the part of a large and respected publishing house bears out the contention of Rev. E. H. Dewart in his Introduction to *Selections from Canadian Poets* (Montreal: Lovell, 1864) that Canadian authors were under a severe disability:

> There is probably no country in the world, making equal pretensions to intelligence and progress, where the claims of native literature are so little felt, and where every effort in poetry has been met with so much coldness and indifference, as in Canada. . . . Our mental wants [are] supplied by the brain of the Mother Country, under circumstances that utterly preclude competition. . . . Booksellers, too, because they make sure sales and large profits on British and American works, which have already obtained popularity, seldom take the trouble to judge of a Canadian book on its merits, or use their influence to promote its sale.

For publishers the problem was not merely promotion of their Canadian authors but the impossibility of obtaining effective copyright protection as the law then stood. American publishers, if they so desired, could reprint any book published in Canada without compensation to the author or the original publisher. With equal impunity they regularly reprinted British books in cheap editions for the home market and for export to Canada. Against this piratical practice there was no redress.

Canadian copyright was based on the Imperial Copyright Act of 1842, as amended in 1847. This forbade the reprinting of British books in the colonies but permitted the import of American reprints on payment of a duty of 12½ per cent as compensation to British authors in lieu of royalties. Moreover an American author, by establishing temporary residence in Canada and sending a few advance copies of his latest book to England for "first publication," could obtain full protection under the Imperial Act against the reprinting of his work in Canada. A Canadian author's copyright in Great Britain, however, was forfeited if the original form of publication in Canada was deemed to be inferior to British standards.

Naturally this discriminatory legislation was considered intolerable by Canadian publishers who bent every effort to seek federal protection. The difficulty was, however, that the British Act took precedence over any colonial copyright law. Thus a Canadian Copyright Act of 1872 which legalized the reprinting of British authors on payment to them of 12½ per cent of the wholesale price was reserved by Westminster and never became law. This prompted John Lovell and Graeme Mercer Adam, a Toronto publisher, to go to London and place before the Board of Trade their case in seeking an amendment to the Imperial Copyright Act. Although they received a sympathetic hearing, British publishers effectively blocked any action.

The next stratagem was to devise a Canadian Act which would not contravene the provision of the Imperial Act but would specify the conditions under which American authors could obtain copyright in Canada. They had to be "domiciled" (not merely "resident") in Canada, and their books had to be printed (normally from imported stereotyped plates) in Canada. This Act, which obtained royal assent in 1875, was a half-way measure which still left Canadian publishers at a disadvantage in competition with British copyright publishers and with the American publishers of piratical reprints. The whole situation might have been rectified if the United States and Canada had signed the Berne International Copyright Convention of 1886, but neither country saw fit to do so. The United States Chase Act of 1891 made provision for limited reciprocal copyright, but in order to qualify for more than temporary copyright, foreign books had to be wholly manufactured in the United States. It was this requirement that prevented the United States from subscribing to the Berne Convention.*

The depressing effect of copyright restriction on Canadian publishing in the nineteenth century can readily be documented. George Maclean Rose, head of the Hunter, Rose Publishing Company, stated in 1884, in a letter to the Editor of *Books and Notions* (Toronto):

After many years' experience in the publishing business I have come to the conclusion that it is almost useless to attempt building up a large and profitable publishing trade in our country, unless our government takes the matter of copyright in hand. . . . As the British Copyright Act is at present understood and worked it is all one sided, that is, it gives the United States author and publisher entire possession of our markets.

*The British Copyright Acts of 1842 and 1847 were superseded by the 1911 Act which enabled Canada to formulate her own copyright laws. In 1952 a new Universal Copyright Convention was sponsored by the United Nations. The United States became a participating member in 1954 (the manufacturing requirement still holds for her own citizens or domiciliaries), and Canada, after a long delay, in August 1962.

In the same year and in the same periodical, Mercer Adam had, a few months earlier, made the following observation:

> The ethical influence of literary piracy on the book trade of America would be a subject for curious enquiry. Not the least of its evil effects is to be seen in the shrivelling up of native literature, and in the degeneracy of the modern publishing firms, who from preying upon British authors have descended to preying upon one another. Another harmful result is the lowering of public taste in the mechanical artistry of bookmaking. . . .

Adam's own career as publisher was frustrated by the British surrender of the Canadian book market to the United States, yet he persevered in advocating a literary revival in Canada with all the fervour of an evangelist. As J. E. Collins said of him in *The Week* (Aug. 28, 1884): "Mr. G. Mercer Adam has always been identified with our literature, saying good words for it when it hardly deserved good words, and blowing breath into its nostrils when it looked so like a corpse."

A Scot by birth, Adam had come to Toronto in 1858 at the age of 19 to enter the retail book trade. Seven years later he established the *British American Review* (after the failure in 1863 of the *British Canadian Review* in Quebec). It ran for two years but then folded up for lack of support. Meanwhile Adam had entered the book publishing field, and in 1867 formed, with J. H. Stevenson, the publishing house of Adam, Stevenson & Co. Together they launched an ambitious programme of bringing out Canadian books and acting as agents for British publishers. Almost single-handed, in 1872, Mercer Adam edited and published a trade journal, the *Canada Bookseller,* the twelve issues of which supply much information on the book trade and publishing industry of the time.

Adam saw encouraging signs that the intellectual and material progress which had led to Confederation would create a new national literature. To provide an incentive for native talent, he proposed to inaugurate a national review. He spoke, cautiously, about it in the *Canada Bookseller* for March 1872:

> There has been of late a general awakening of national life, which has probably extended to the literary and scientific sphere. . . . To deal with Canadian questions and to call forth Canadian talent will be the first aim of the *Canadian Monthly.* . . . Mr. Goldwin Smith has consented both to contribute regularly and to assist in conducting the magazine.

The initial success of the *Canadian Monthly and National Review* surpassed Adam's expectations; it soon became the most influential periodical of its kind to have appeared in Canada. Adam, Stevenson & Co. expanded their business to become what the *Toronto Directory* for 1873 described as a "great publishing house . . . a monument of the reading and literary ability of the Dominion." The partners had over-reached themselves, however, and in 1876, the firm was forced into bankruptcy. The *Monthly* was taken over by another publisher and continued, with Mercer Adam as editor (after a year's absence in New York), as *Rose-Belford's Canadian Monthly* until 1882.

C. P. Mulvany in *Toronto: Past and Present* (1884) attributed the demise of the *Canadian Monthly* to the indifference of Rose, Belford, the publishers, who ceased to pay the contributors. "With scant appreciation and no reward, Mr. Adam laboured for years to keep life in the *Canadian Monthly* whose publishers showed little inclination to second his efforts. . . . Owing to the course pursued by the publishers, the contributions were unpaid for. . . . "

When a new journal, *The Week*, appeared in 1883 under the editorship of Charles G. D. Roberts, Mercer Adam became a regular contributor. His disenchantment is reflected in an article he wrote for the issue of June 12, 1884, entitled "An Interregnum in Literature," commenting upon the decline of literary interest in the country and the decay of the better-class book trade. "The colonial status and the anomalies of the literary copyright law which surrenders the native book-market to the American publisher, are further obstacles to literary progress." Nevertheless *The Week* lasted for thirteen years and published some of the earliest verse of Roberts, Carman, Lampman, Duncan Campbell Scott, and many others.

William Kirby raised his voice in protest against the copyright laws in a paper read before the newly formed Royal Society of Canada in May 1883. Up to 1842, he maintained, authorship and publishing in Canada had as fair a chance of success as in the United States, but the Imperial Act put an end to all possible competition in Canada with American pirates. "Thus," he says, according to the report in the Quebec *Morning Chronicle* of February 1–4, 1884, "between the upper and lower millstones of British copyright publishers and American piratical publishers of British books, the business of book publishing in Canada has been ground to powder. . . . I say our clever men and women are waiting impatiently for the restoration of literary work in Canada by a due and needful encouragement of our publishing industries. . . . When that is done we shall see what forces are at work among us."

Without doubt Kirby over-simplified the problem and its solution. What was needed was not only untrammelled publishers but a literary climate of opinion and an interested public response, both of which were lacking at the time and could scarcely be produced by legislation.

One Canadian publisher who refused to be daunted by the prophets of gloom was the Reverend William Briggs. Appointed Book Steward of the Methodist Book and Publishing House in 1878, he determined to master a new vocation for which his theological training had scarcely prepared him. A man of great organizing ability, he had sound business instincts and an unlimited faith in Canadian enterprise. He soon belied Adam and Kirby by making publishing pay. At the same time he trained a succession of energetic young bookmen, several of whom later left the mother house to establish their own publishing firms, thus broadening the base of the publishing industry in Canada. In the same year that Kirby reported Canadian publishing "ground to powder," Briggs reported in *Books and Notions* for July that his house had printed during the year 245,023 books and pamphlets (i.e., copies), representing 31,071,070 pages; the number of books bound was 211,714. This placed the Methodist Book and Publishing House well ahead of other book publishers in Canada.

No other Canadian publisher in the closing decades of the last century did as much as William Briggs to stimulate literary talent and promote Canadian literature from coast to coast. Year after year, for the forty years he was in office (he retired in 1918), literary works by Canadian writers, especially the poets, appeared under the William Briggs imprint. William Kirby, Thomas O'Hagan, Sir James Edgar, Charles G. D. Roberts, Frederick George Scott, J. W. Bengough, Theodore H. Rand, Charles Mair, Catharine Parr Traill, and many others of lesser note were represented on the Briggs' lists by the turn of the century, and the real harvest was yet to come in the years of the Ryerson Press. This was a remarkable achievement for a Methodist minister in charge of a church publishing house at a time when other publishers were going bankrupt or barely managing to survive.

What, then, can be said in conclusion about the publisher-author relation in Canada up to 1900? We have seen that in the early period printer-publishers sought to provide outlets for native writers in newspapers, periodicals, and occasional subscription books. In this there was little thought or expectation of financial gain. Production costs were high and potential readers few and scattered. Literary journals appeared and disappeared but succeeded in producing a not inconsiderable body of Canadian writing, much of it uneven in quality. Book publication was a dubious financial risk which few publishers, whether newspaper proprietors or booksellers, could afford without the safeguard of a subscription list. The onus was usually on the author to produce this guarantee, a condition which doubtless discouraged all but the most determined writers.

From the mid-forties onward an increasing flood of cheap American books and pirated reprints of British authors further depressed the writing market in Canada. The reading public was content with the standard British and American authors of the day and showed little interest in supporting a native literature.

In the third quarter of the century, an expanded and more literate public provided a potential market for Canadian books, but copyright restrictions gave little or no protection to authors or publishers in Canada, and remedial legislation was reserved. Publishing increased in volume but was largely confined to non-literary productions. *Belles-lettres* continued to lag behind.

Confederation brought about a new access of patriotic and national sentiment and encouraged publishers to expect the first fruits of a literary harvest, a harvest which largely failed, however, to mature. Journals continued to provide a forum for literary talent, but Canada's ablest writers, with a few notable exceptions, became expatriates and had their work published outside of Canada.

William Briggs, Hunter, Rose & Co., Copp, Clark, W. J. Gage, and a few other houses with specialized publishing interests survived into the present century; others well known in their day were forced into bankruptcy. Under adverse conditions they did what they could to encourage and foster a native literature, and cannot be held accountable for the lowly estate of Canadian letters in these years.

To what extent copyright reform a century ago would have revolutionized Canadian book publishing, created markets for Canadian writers, and produced a golden literary harvest may be debated but never resolved.

PART III
The Emergence of a Tradition

12. Confederation to the First World War

ROY DANIELLS

THE YEAR 1885 saw the failure of Louis Riel's second rebellion and the completion of steel on the Canadian Pacific Railway's transcontinental line. These were outward signs of the growing strength of the Canadian nation. Nationalism as a sentiment found expression in the Canada First movement whose aims had been made explicit when in 1871 W. A. Foster spoke to a Toronto audience on "Canada First; or, Our New Nationality," urging them to believe that "all the requirements of a higher national life are here available."

In the late eighties, nevertheless, the air was filled with debate which produced, not clarification, but further confusion. A strong sentiment for commercial union with the United States provoked violent reaction from convinced imperialists. Assertions of French nationalism, sharpened by resentment at the execution of Riel, were countered by the British nationalism of Ontario, which spread to Manitoba. The prime minister of Nova Scotia openly advocated the secession of his province from the Dominion. American pressures upon Canada led to a reiteration of Macdonald's National Policy, the protection of Canadian independence by tariffs and railways. "A British subject I was born, a British subject I will die" was the substance of his manifesto before the Conservative electoral victory of 1891.

What gave pattern and purpose to the confused drama was the desire in almost every segment of Canadian opinion to achieve national unity. Though good commercial reasons existed for reciprocity with the United States, and though Goldwin Smith confidently anticipated annexation, the sentiment of national independence inevitably prevailed. Both Quebec and Ontario desired a viable Canadian nation though with very different ends in view.

The desire for national unity was, in terms of economics, a desire to weld together the visibly diverse regions of this northern half of the continent in which uniquely abundant natural resources could support a full-scale economy if transport were made available. Independence of the United States and association with Britain in the Empire were generally and increasingly regarded as essential to the realization of this plan. A sure instinct for national survival led to the ideological suppression of elements of discord. The concept of reciprocity was never clarified but allowed to disintegrate under the pressure of Macdonald's National Policy. The provinces established in 1884 the fact that their legislatures had sovereign powers in those matters which had been put within their jurisdiction, but at the time concessions of this sort served to strengthen federal unity. The disruptive opposition of capital and labour never came to a head until after the First World War, nor to the majority of middle-class nineteenth-century citizens did it appear more than the greedy outcry of workmen for what they had not earned, or as *Grip*, Canada's equivalent of *Punch*, saw it in 1877, "Hooray for general suffrage, Communism, free lunches, free drinks, free everything, general distribution of property...."

As the century drew to a close, Canadians became increasingly absorbed by the effort of economic expansion. The old National Policy, of eastern industrialization and western settlement held together by a transcontinental railway, was at last realized as a heartening actuality. Even the northwest prairies were opening to the wheat farmer and from still farther north and west came news of Pacific gold rushes. The economic strength and future potential of Canada were becoming obvious just when the Boer War and the Alaska boundary dispute accentuated Canadian desires for independence, under the Crown. The cloud which was to grow into a world war was still small upon the horizon.

Economic progress in the early twentieth century did not bring with it a commensurate growth of Canadian sensibility. The carefully nurtured, rather self-conscious, English-language culture of Ontario, built up with loving devotion in the 1870's and 1880's, held its ground. In Quebec, however, Henri Bourassa, the clerical leaders, and the editors of *Le Devoir* were uniting to promote quite another version of nationalist sentiment. An immigration of continental Europeans flowed into the Canadian prairies. British immigrants, knowing nothing and caring nothing about Ontario, came by tens of thousands to the far West. Throughout the West the Ontario tradition was becoming diffuse and attenuated. And in the East labour movements began to preach a social gospel of a new and potentially explosive kind.

The World War of 1914–18 evoked and absorbed the energies of Canadian patriotism as nothing else could have done, and of necessity the full effect of its strains became apparent only after the armistice. It was in August 1919, in the year of the Winnipeg general strike, that a Liberal convention, in Ottawa, selected as the new party leader William Lyon Mackenzie King. His victory in the election of 1921 was the beginning of a new set of tactics in the ceaseless effort to realize that national unity which had been implicit in Confederation.

There is no simple correspondence between an objective record of political, social, and economic events, on the one hand, and on the other, a criticism of the arts, whose creation and appreciation are suffused with subjectivity. Keats overheard and passed on the revelation that whatever the imagination apprehends as Beauty is also Truth; Coleridge's remedy for public grievances was "Let us become a better people." It is hard to forge direct links between such assertions and the Battle of Waterloo or the Reform Bill. In Canada, during the four decades following 1880, poetry is the supreme art, yet a direct connection between the best poems and contemporary events hardly exists. Some readers who care about Canada are disturbed by this apparent anomaly; they would like to have the poems spring from significant social thought. Lampman invites brief consideration in this context. He was a reader of Ruskin, Morris, and Mill; he believed in socialism as the ultimately desirable, though not immediately feasible form of government for Canada; he debated with his friends such problems as women's rights, George's single tax, and the conflict between science and religion; his distaste for party politicians and routine church-going he took no pains to conceal. But it has been observed that his poems of social criticism were "constructed rather than conceived," and that upon his best verse his secular liberalism had "directly, no bearing whatever." There remains an understandable and undispelled regret that Lampman did not move on to more modern poetic techniques, that he was denied the resources of radicalism or naturalism, and that his intellectual capacities and social insights were affected accordingly. But it can be argued that Lampman should not be expected to employ the selective literary sensibility of the late nineteenth century and simultaneously to act as a cutting edge of socio-political ideology. Lampman, furthermore, really did find peace, happiness, and renewed strength in nature: it seems certain that in nature, during the nineteenth century, strength, peace and happiness were to be found. The concluding lines of "An Old Lesson from the Fields" deserve to be accepted as his testament:

> O Light, I cried, and heaven with all your blue;
> O earth with all your sunny fruitfulness,
> And ye tall lilies of the wind-vexed field,
> What power and beauty life indeed might yield
> Could we but cast away its conscious stress,
> Simple of heart, becoming even as you!

(A creative mind expanding to achieve engagement with the full range of practical issues in its contemporary world is not likely to produce a memorable art-form: Augustine had no strategy for raising the siege of Hippo; Dante wrote in exile, Milton in defeat; neither Chaucer nor Shakespeare nor Wordsworth could envisage what their societies needed in the way of institutional reform.)

It is unfashionable at the moment to oppose the argument that culture appears by extrusion from everyday communal living. Sociological and political preoccupations obscure the concept of culture as a body of experience based upon traditional standards. The phrase "literary culture" has almost ceased to have a meaning. It is therefore natural to praise the "socially significant" poet at the expense of other levels of sensibility, intuition, or vision. What needs to be reasserted in any study of nineteenth-century Canada is the primacy and autonomy of cultural tradition at that time.

The *Canadian Monthly* of 1874 took the trouble to reprint, from the *Contemporary Review*, Mr. Gladstone's article on the Shield of Achilles. This piece, glowing with Gladstone's enthusiasm for the ancient world, was written by a lover of Homer for other lovers of Homer needing no introduction to the delights of wrestling with a difficult passage. The Ontario reader is therefore revisiting a *locus classicus* in the company of an eminent Englishman, an ex-prime minister, and a known scholar. The continuity of cultural tradition is abundantly apparent, as Gladstone's mind ranges over the Mediterranean scene "full of all things glorious, beautiful, and strong."

Wölfflin has observed that "Anyone who concerns himself exclusively with the subject-matter of works of art will be completely satisfied with it; yet the moment we want to apply artistic standards of judgment in the criticism of works of art we are forced to try to comprehend formal elements which are unmeaning and inexpressible in themselves." In an analogous way the student of Canada after Confederation will encounter a great deal of politics, many economic considerations, and a sequence of personalities and events sufficient to engage his whole attention. But he will need other avenues of approach if he is to reach the centre of Canadian consciousness.

A small group of periodicals published in Toronto furnishes a reliable conspectus of the central English literary tradition in Canada. These are the *Canadian Monthly*, the *Week* and the *Canadian Magazine*.

The *Canadian Monthly and National Review* (1872–78) which continued as *Rose-Belford's Canadian Monthly* (1878–82) was edited, with a lacuna of two years, by Graeme Mercer Adam, an ardent nationalist. By his own writing and by his selection of contributors he became one of the founders of the post-Confederation literary renaissance. The *Canadian Monthly* expressed the ideals of the Canada First Movement and was devotedly supported by Goldwin Smith. Its homogeneity over the decade of its life is remarkable; published in Toronto and consciously dedicated to nationalist ideals, it embodied the central sentiment of English-speaking Canada; in the quantity and quality of its ideas and in the range of its interests it had no rivals. Whatever their subject, its pages are never less than lucid, dignified, and persuasive. A small degree of historical imagination or sympathetic rapport will take today's reader of these volumes back into a golden world of high Victorian sensibility.

The ingredient of fiction was small but important. From cautious beginnings in the first volume (a serial story of Irish life and a few translations from French and German) we move to such a full-blown novel as ran from November 1880 to June 1881, crammed with striking incidents and stretched into long dramatic suspense, all in Wilkie Collins's best manner. The selection of this body of fiction shows a consistent regard for literary style and an intermittent desire to escape the local Canadian scene. England and the Mediterranean are preferred settings; romantic sentiment and melodramatic action are desired ingredients. Fairly strong moral and religious overtones make themselves heard, ranging in quality from the pervasive Christian faith of "Fidelis" to the stereotyped scenes of Collins—"the baffled Jesuit turned furiously on the dying man."

History, too, is a repository of exemplary wisdom. An account of George Fox and Quakerism ends with a summary appraisal: "It has exemplified the subtlety, pervasiveness and power of truth and love, and so strengthened all men's faith in their reality and ultimate victory." An editorial in 1872 reviews historical events common to Britain, Canada, and the United States and concludes: "It is possible that the hour of Canadian nationality may be drawing near. If so, let us prepare to found the nation, not in ingratitude but in truth and honour."

How deliberate and conscious were the aims of the founders of the *Monthly* is revealed on their first page. The magazine will deal with Canadian questions and call forth Canadian talent; it will nevertheless seek in all quarters for the means of interesting and instructing its readers; the utmost latitude of subject and expression is to be allowed, with the exception of party politics and party theology, "nor will anything be admitted which can give just offence to any portion of the community." The managers of the magazine have a national object in view and will endeavour to preserve throughout "a tone beneficial to the national character and worthy of the nation."

This desire to preserve, justify, and substantiate national unity imparts to these volumes an extraordinary unity of topic and tone. Criticism is constructive; love of country is everything from deep affection for the terrain itself to patriotic pride over memories of Lundy's Lane; the very book reviews shine like stars in a moral firmament. A world is created, its centre in the Canadian home, its middle distance the loved landscape of Canada, its protecting wall the circle of British institutions, associations, and loyalties. Across this welcome breastwork the United States, now neither menacing nor necessarily hostile, is to be viewed, and more exciting because less familiar, the great outposts of the civilization of continental Europe—France, Italy, Germany, and behind these the splendours of ancient Greece and Rome. It is a world as centripetal as that of Sherlock Holmes and as little liable to be shaken by irruptions of evil. There is recurring acknowledgment but little understanding of the culture of French Canada and of the implications of bi-culturalism; the natural vista from Ontario is into the immensity of the West, extending itself to the Pacific. The Indian is seen through the eyes of paternalism: "The thoughtful treatment of our Indians by the Hudson Bay Company, in the first instance, has tended to make them as peaceful and industrious as they are. It remains now for our Government to keep them strictly to an understanding that their rights will be secured to them as they are to the whites; but that in return for such treatment they must submit to the rule of life which the white man's law prescribes."

The solid agglutinative core of the magazine consists of articles on Canadian scenes and places, Canadian history, and Canadian culture. The direct approach of the writers is wholly delightful and a measure of the practical quality of their patriotism. Canada, one writer argues, is at bottom the creation of the labourer who clears the land for a farm. The merchant appears, to supply him; the magistrate to interpret the law; then the men of science and ministers of religion. Finally the statesman labours to "form his compact community or nation with the least amount of evil." To Canada national sentiment is an absolute necessity and its first principle is patriotism. But Canada needs the power to confer Canadian citizenship. The article concludes with a list of proposals aimed at securing Canadian unity and self-sufficiency; for example, French should be made compulsory in the common schools. The historian and politician J. G. Bourinot contributed a lengthy analysis of Canadian intellectual development up to 1880. It is a highly perceptive bi-cultural review, ending with a vision of "a future full of promise for literature as for industry."

National communities have an inevitable ritual in which the story of their heroes and the tales of their famous battles are rehearsed. A fine instance is the historical sketch of the War of 1812 written by the redoubtable "Fidelis" for the issue of July 1874. It has the true ring of heroic story, rising to its climax with the death of Brock: "Queenston Heights, where his death occurred, and where his memorial column stands, is, no less than the Plains of Abraham, one of Canada's sacred places, where memories akin to those of Thermopylae and Marathon may well move every Canadian who has a heart to feel them."

"Fidelis," or Agnes Maule Machar, was born in Kingston in 1837 and died there exactly ninety years later. She was a prolific contributor to the *Canadian Monthly* from 1873 onward and a superbly representative and summary figure. To the last volume, in 1882, she contributed not only articles on Sophocles but poems (one an Advent Hymn) and a plea for co-education in the universities. Her tenacity of purpose, her consistency of aim, her articulateness, and her ability to fuse religious, patriotic, and cultural interests give her all the force of a legend, and the prolongation of her literary work well into this century is in accord with the persistence of post-Confederation values until the period of the First World War.

The poetic contributions, which were numerous, will be discussed in a later chapter.

The *Canadian Monthly* went out of existence in 1882 and the void left by its passing was partially filled by the establishment, in the next year, of *The Week*, published in Toronto and edited by Charles G. D. Roberts. Its prospectus promised "faithfully to reflect and summarize the intellectual, social and political movements of the day" and, disdaining party leanings, to further "the free and healthy development of the Nation." Goldwin Smith backed the new magazine and contributed to it. G. Mercer Adam, "Fidelis," "Seranus," and other familiar names reappear. The continuity of the tradition is very real, although Roberts was less happy in his editorial office than Adam had been and soon abandoned it. *The Week* went out of existence in 1896 but *The Canadian Magazine*, 1893–1939, was already carrying on the tradition though with less *élan*. Founded and edited by the journalist J. G. Mowat, it too was published in Toronto. Its initial announcement would equally well have suited the old *Monthly*: "While the pages of the Magazine will be open to the expression of a wide diversity of opinions, and opinions with which the Magazine does not agree, the policy will be steadily pursued of cultivating Canadian patriotism and Canadian interests, and of endeavouring to aid in the consolidation of the Dominion on a basis of national self-respect and a mutual regard for the rights of the great elements which make up the population of Canada."

Another landmark of cultural publication is the collection of poems edited by William D. Lighthall as *Songs of the Great Dominion* in 1889. (An English edition appeared in the same year and another English edition, with a change of title, in 1892.) Lighthall's introduction and his choice of poems have a firmness of stance which gave his early readers the shock of recognition and won for his book a wide regard. He begins:

The poets whose songs fill this book are voices cheerful with the consciousness of young might, public wealth and heroism. Through them, taken all together, you may catch something of great Niagara falling, of brown rivers rushing with foam, of the crack of the rifle in the haunts of the moose and caribou, the lament of vanished races singing their death-song as they are swept on to the cataract of oblivion, the rural sounds of Arcadias just rescued from surrounding wildernesses by the axe, shrill war whoops of Iroquois battle, proud traditions of contest with the French and the Americans, stern and sorrowful cries of valour rising to curb rebellion. The tone of them is *courage*. . . .

He goes on to a lyrical praise of the landscape and natural resources of the country. His description of Canada is everywhere superlative:

> Her population is about five million souls. Her Valley of the Saskatchewan alone, it has been scientifically computed, will support eight hundred millions. In losing the United States, Britain lost the *smaller* half of her American possessions; the Colony of the Maple Leaf is about as large as Europe.

There is more, however, to Lighthall's love of Canada than a vision of geographical or material greatness:

> But what would material resources be without a corresponding greatness in man? Canada is also imperial in her traditions. Her French race are still conscious that they are the remnants of a power which once ruled North America from Hudson's Bay to the Gulf of Mexico. Existing English Canada is the result of simply the noblest epic migration the world has ever seen:—more loftily epic than the retirement of Pius Æneas from Ilion,—the withdrawal, namely, out of the rebel Colonies, of the thirty-five thousand United Empire Loyalists after the War of the Revolution. . . . Canada has, of historic right, a voice also in the Empire of today, and busies herself not a little in studying its problems. For example, the question whether the Empire will last is being asked. Her history has a reply to that:—IT WILL IF IT SETS CLEARLY BEFORE IT A DEFINITE IDEAL THAT MEN WILL SUFFER AND DIE FOR; and such an Ideal—worthy of long and patient endeavour—may be found in broadminded advance towards the voluntary Federation of Mankind.

It is hard to imagine a more perfect manifesto, articulating as it does a sense of the magnificence of the landscape, a vision of manifest destiny, an epic feeling for the heroic past, and a shining desire for moral excellence. The relation of English-speaking Canada to Quebec, to the Empire, to the United States, and to native Indian races has an air of being realized with the clarity of a cameo.

In compiling his anthology, Lighthall explicitly disclaims a purely literary aim. He is looking only for poetry that illustrates the country and its life "in a distinctive way." In 1889 he was a young lawyer living in Montreal, thirty-two years of age, a product of McGill University. In due course he became a K.C. and embarked on a long career of public service and of authorship. He exhibits a confidence and an enthusiasm which reflect the powerfully corporate Loyalist sentiment of the period.

The poems are grouped under headings which summarize Lighthall's intention: the Imperial spirit, the new nationality, the Indian, the *voyageur* and *habitant,* settlement life, sports and free life, the spirit of Canadian history, places, seasons. A few pieces by Crawford, Lampman, Carman, and D. C. Scott, filled with an appreciation of nature, stand above the general undistinguished level. Lighthall was fully aware that he was sacrificing poetic quality for representative national sentiment. This latter he perfectly reflects. It is the product of a high colonial culture.

The central concepts of this culture are precisely indicated in Lighthall's introduction. A vigorous spirit of expansion looks out on a magnificent, underdeveloped, and inviting terrain stretching into the boundless West. The past is a story of intense and successful struggle to conquer, to colonize, and to defend the country. The French have been defeated, the Americans repulsed, and the rebellions quelled. The French exist as remnants of a great power. The Americans have but the smaller half of what was British America. The Indians are a vanishing race. Destiny is at the service of English Canadians, whose epic virtues, derived from the heroism of the Loyalists, are equal to the double effort of creating the reality of national unity "from sea to sea" and clarifying, for the whole British Empire, its task of leading the advance towards a Federation of Mankind.

The formulated attitude towards French Canada, which to say the least imperfectly covered the ambiguities of the situation, is once more exhibited by Lighthall himself, under the transparent pseudonym of Wilfred Chateauclair, in *The Young Seigneur* (Montreal, 1888). In this slight story he intends "to map out a future for the Canadian nation." He draws an idyllic picture of the grandeur and beauty of the St. Lawrence valley, the virtues of the *habitant,* and the aspirations of those French Canadians who combine hereditary capacities for leadership with liberal politics, progressive ideas, and a firm morality. The idealism of Lighthall and his desire to see Canada become "The Perfect Nation" are simply an intense and poetically clairvoyant variant of the general Canadian hope. To French Canadians he says, "Identify yourselves with a nation vaster than your race, and cultivate your talents to put you at its head." These highlights of his story throw into relief dark shadows of ultramontane clerical bigotry and rampant political fraud.

The Golden Age of high colonialism in Ontario endures for about a quarter-century, from 1871–72, when the Canada First movement took shape, the *Canadian Monthly* began its course, and the first organization of the C.P.R. Company was effected, to 1896–97, when the economic depression came to an end, *The Week* ceased publication, and Laurier took office as prime minister.

The brazen age of prosperity which followed is also conveniently and fairly accurately seen as a quarter-century, terminating with the repatriation of Canadian soldiers after the First World War and the symbolic first publication of the *Canadian Forum* in October 1920. By this time the ideology of high colonialism had suffered marked diminution and decline, though never to the point of disintegration.

Several questions at once arise. Why did the fact of Confederation prove so powerful (though brief) a stimulus to Canada's literary culture? Why does the land, in the sense of terrain, play so dominant a role in Canadian experience? To what extent is periodical publication a reliable guide to cultural sensibility? How may we assess changes in this sensibility between, say, 1880 and the end of the First World War?

Students of English literature are often puzzled by what might be called the Waterloo effect—that is, the enormous but undefinable influence upon British morale and British creativeness induced by the long sustained effort of the Napoleonic Wars. It is plain for all to see yet it can never be properly documented. It is a kind of extra dimension to British life, "As every child can tell." Something similar happened to Elizabethans when the Armada was deflected and defeated.

The fact of Confederation created a field of force in the English-Canadian mind which brought Wolfe, the emigration of Loyalists, "Queenston Heights and Lundy's Lane," the repulse of the Fenians, the defeat of rebels in 1837 (and of Riel in 1870) into alignment. "Fidelis" and Lighthall, in comparing such events to Thermopylae, Marathon, or Æneas leaving Ilion to found another kingdom, were saying literally what they and thousands of others felt. It is the same sentiment as enables a contributor to the *Encyclopaedia Britannica* to say simply that Alfred is the noblest of the English kings.

Such considerations are above party politics or provincial interest; they are above sectionalism of any kind, whether of race, religion, or region. They give urgency, conviction, and a certain vagueness to patriotic utterance throughout the period. Men of all parties were powerfully if imprecisely impressed with the vastness of Canadian territory, the drama of Canada's history, and the potential future greatness of their country. What afflicted Macdonald, who had the stature of heroism, was the discrepancy between the vision of Canada's greatness and the meanness of political manipulation needed to realize it. "Send me better men to work with and I will be a better man."

Typical of patriotic writing in the *Canadian Monthly* is an article in 1874 on "The Massacre at the Cedars." American claims are disproved, American propaganda reprehended: "The publication of the original documents renders it possible to ascertain the real facts as they occurred, and Canadians, the more narrowly they enquire into the doings of their forefathers, will have the more reason to be proud of the early history of their country."

Typical also is a determination not to confuse a commitment to the British cultural tradition with uncritical admiration of British politics and society. The defeat of a strike of English farm labourers in 1874 is recorded in the *Monthly* with the bitter comment, "Combating privation in his industrial war, the peasant has shown something of the same stubborn valour with which, when in arms for his country, he has often held the post of duty upon the blood-stained hillside. . . . But the columns which he encountered on this occasion were columns which could not be rolled back like those which mounted to the attack at Waterloo. . . . Against overpowering wealth and territorial influence, with hunger as their sword, no valour or endurance can prevail."

The desire for Canadian national unity was intense and sustained. This ensured that the rational Goldwin Smith, with his Manchester-school liberalism, would always be odd man out. His eloquent desire to see Anglo-Saxon culture established in Canada brought him into the main stream of criticism and literature. His advocacy of continental union, his scepticism as to the nation-building potential of the C.P.R., his failure to grasp that French Canadians intended to remain French: these lapses kept him out of the main stream of Canadian political thought.

It has often been noticed that in the decades following Confederation the supreme art in Canada is poetry and that the best poems concern themselves with Canadian natural surroundings. This may be thought incompatible with the kind of Canada First aims we have just reviewed; yet, remembering the analogy of Romantic writing in England, we can perhaps concede that the Canadian poets chose with instinctive wisdom. It is not Lampman alone who, believing profoundly in his country, finds in landscape the intuition of its goodness and greatness. "It is in Nature," says one of Lighthall's characters watching the sun rise on the St. Lawrence, "that I can love Canada most, and become renewed into efforts for the good of her human sons." Those who turned to nature were not evading but seeking the true Canada. The only thing Canadians possessed that other people did not was the top half of the American continent. This presented the Golden Age with its most pressing problem, the achievement of transport as a means towards political and economic unity. Wolseley's difficulty was not to overcome Riel but to reach Fort Garry. The industrial problem of Canada was the long haul, for raw materials and for the finished product. The Canadian terrain was an enormous and irreducible fact as Lord Dufferin discovered when he travelled thousands of miles through the United States to reach the western side of his own territory. In ways that are not always rationally clear and through channels of expression often far from logically explicit Canadian feeling about the terrain of Canada made itself powerfully felt. Then, as now, the geological, geographical, topographic, and lyric features of the Canadian landscape were the fundamental facts of Canadian experience.

There are several reasons why the texture of Canada's literary *milieu* in the three decades following Confederation can be reliably sampled in the pages of the *Canadian Monthly*, *The Week*, and the *Canadian Magazine*. Newspapers, preoccupied with party politics, did not hold a clear mirror to national consciousness. Book publication was hazardous and for economic reasons failed to cover the true range of Canadian interests. The small group of Toronto periodicals is therefore peculiarly significant. Toronto was fortunate in having Goldwin Smith, who in turn was fortunate in Adam, the ideal editor. The image they projected upon the pages of the *Monthly* remained in focus for the rest of the century. This simplification of the pattern may appear to ignore not only Quebec but also the Maritimes and the successive frontiers of the West. The influence of French culture upon English was, however, tenuous and destined to become neither dominant nor subservient nor even contributory; the historical clarification has been towards a polarity. As for the prairies and the seaboards, Canadian cultural experience has always declined to follow the American form. The representative attitudes are not realized regionally or on the frontier, they are shaped and conserved at the centre, which in the present context and for the period under review is Ontario. S. D. Clark has shown how centrifugal forces were resisted, as tending towards American continentalism and towards the weakening of Canadian sovereignty. At this time moreover the provincial economies were all vulnerable and could only hope for stability and growth within the concept of national integration. The same was true of the cultural nexus in each of the English-speaking provinces.

To turn from the confused politics and desperate economics of the period to the world of ideas and values projected by Adam and his fellow contributors is a delightful as well as an illuminating experience. Book reviews and critical articles combine into a complex, lucid, and rewarding pattern. The climate of opinion never really changes: Canadian independence, for example, is advocated in terms of cultivating "A strong feeling of patriotism as opposed to mere loyalty," and this shift implies neither radical nor revolutionary thinking.

Moral earnestness is everywhere dominant. The period of pioneer settlement is conceived as Canada's "heroic age." The prospect of political independence brings biblical phrases to the pen: "it does not yet appear what we shall be." The reviewer of a book on Kant wants to keep the intellectual advantages of both Kant and Herbert Spencer. As a consequence of this kind of high seriousness, no real dialectic is allowed to develop. Exposition is a pervasive method of reviewing, but argument—as the whole cavalcade of Victorian problems rides by—is muted by the conscious need to recognize both orthodox Christian piety and the new liberal rationalism. The synthesis achieved is sufficiently liberal and sufficiently moral to make of George Eliot the Canadian reviewers' ideal novelist. A dynamic acceptance of the principle of moral regeneration, a constant realistic insight into character and conduct, a capacity to picture middle-class living: George Eliot had them all in abundance.

It follows that realism, whether in fiction, in drama, or in painting, was felt as a means to realize the ideal. An article on science and art begins with the words of Victor Cousin, "La vraie beauté est la beauté idéale, et la beauté idéale est un reflet de l'infini." Realism in drama is expected to serve other ends than its own. The sensational novel is condemned as untrue to moral and social actuality. In comments upon science, there is the same desire to reconcile objective inquiry with a conservation of ideal values: an article on Darwin praises him as "a reverent believer in the Unknown Power, from whom all Life proceeds" and goes on to say that "if the Church disagrees with Science, so much the worse for the Church."

The ingredients of high colonialism can be assessed fairly accurately. There is a real desire for cultural achievement, to match commercial achievement: "Canadian ships, freighted with the products of Canadian industry, are to be found floating in almost every sea. How many foreign nations know anything of Canadian thought or scholarship?" At the same time the vital necessity of cultural stimulus from outside is eagerly acknowledged. Cultural independence is, with a different time sequence, in the same class of desiderata as political independence. As the monarchical principle had been central to the plan of confederation, had made possible the concept of independence within the Empire, and had provided a safeguard against the "absorptive presence" of the United States, so the principle of loyalty to British cultural tradition provided a *milieu* within which Canadians could hope in time to achieve a national nexus. In the meantime British models were accorded the sincerest form of flattery. The *Canadian Monthly* had before it the example of the *Fortnightly Review*. This visible dependence upon British tradition, however, had no element of subservience. Misrepresentation of Canadian opinion in London journals, failure to guard Canadian interests on the part of British diplomats, ineptitude in the class of immigrant known as the remittance man: all were canvassed without hesitation. British aggression in Afghanistan and acts of brutality in the suppression of the Indian Mutiny were roundly condemned.

French and German literatures are given, on a lesser scale, the same earnest attention. Not only is fiction reviewed or translated; there are serious articles dealing with such key figures as Voltaire, Diderot (whose materialism is attacked), and Goethe (whose sense of the divine is admired). There is a lively interest in the standard American writers—Emerson, Holmes, Howells, and Whittier.

During the four or five decades under review, Romanticism gave ground to Realism; concepts of evolution belatedly permeated the public mind; collectivism gained recognition as a social fact; a pervasive materialism of outlook accompanied the economic boom which, beginning about 1896, lasted well into the war years. Book reviews in the periodicals provide a useful index to cultural change. The *Canadian Monthly*, during 1872, reviewed four biographies, including those of Wesley and Dickens; six books on literature and language, including works of Longfellow, Macaulay, and Aytoun; five historical works, whose subjects ranged from Mary Queen of Scots to the American Civil War; two works on science, including one by Huxley; five books on religion and morals, including Morley's *Voltaire* which is so treated; a few novels and travel books; and a reprint of *Roughing It in the Bush*. The general tone may be judged from the remark, "We begin almost to long for a biography, if it were possible of some one who *did not* rise in life, but, ignobly content with the humble state to which he was called, found happiness in duty and affection." The *Canadian Magazine*, during 1883, offers reviews covering the same general range of interests but reduced in number, truncated to become mere notes and generally inferior in range of ideas and critical style. Biography is represented by a life of Senator John Macdonald, a successful and generous business man. Two travel books, totally unimportant; a history of Bering and one of Columbus; an Ontario biography and the story of the Parliament Buildings in Toronto: these account for history and geography. The best poet reviewed is Edwin Arnold; in fiction we are on the level of Verne, Henty, and Lew Wallace; language is represented by a book on punctuation, science by a report of the Hamilton Association. Nor do critical articles come to any effective rescue of the world of ideas: Roberts is praised for "Ave," Tennyson and Browning for their concept of a future life, Kingsley for the allegory of *Water Babies*. Emerson is noticed twice, once in conjunction with Bacon and Cicero in praise of friendship. Having achieved in its review columns the lowest possible level consistent with its professed aims, the *Canadian Magazine* appears to have found a reliable formula. The books chosen for review continue with few exceptions to be mediocre and the reviews themselves trivial. Without being lost, the tradition is everywhere weakened and cheapened.

For this decline there appears to be no one explanation. The *Canadian Monthly,* when it ceased publication in 1882, gave as its reasons "our inchoate state as a nation," competition from England and America, "the indifference of our people to higher literature," lack of encouragement from the press and from public men, and the loss of steady patriotism in the excitements of "the political game." As the literate public became larger it appears to have become less literary. Though statistics are lacking, it is clear that English-speaking Canadians taking a cultural view of life were at no time very numerous, even in Ontario. Smith, Adam, and their friends made a brave and sustained effort, but never can so much have been owed by so few to so few.

If must be remembered that, although Toronto was the centre of Canadian publishing, a cultural impulse which produced some of Canada's best writing originated in Fredericton, the city memorable for Roberts and Carman. A. G. Bailey has identified this impulse as the second of two "creative moments" of the Maritimes, the first being centred in Nova Scotia, which in the 1830's and 1840's had produced Howe and Haliburton. The development in New Brunswick came a generation later, in Fredericton. Here Loyalist traditions persisted; the very isolation of the community from the expansive and disruptive development of the timber industry was a safeguard of intellectual pursuits and of the values of a class structure. In 1859, the University of New Brunswick was created on the basis of King's College, which had received its charter in 1826 and was in turn based on a college which had been in existence for over sixty years. Charles G. D. Roberts's father and Sir George Parkin, who taught Roberts and his cousin Bliss Carman, were themselves pupils of Baron d'Avray, professor of modern languages, remembered also as founder of the first provincial normal school, editor of a newspaper, and superintendent of education. A continuous tradition reached back to the 1780's when Royal Engineers had laid out the town for incoming Loyalists and Governor Carleton had made it his capital. In Fredericton the conservation of British values and the preservation of a colonial culture were no deterrents to the acceptance of nineteenth-century liberal ideas and Romantic literature.

The emergence of Roberts and Carman, together with others of their group, from the town and countryside of Fredericton in the 1880's has implications relevant to the whole of Canadian literature. It appears that even a small community may furnish the "critical mass" needed for a literary expansion; that preservation of social and cultural forms may be as significant in some contexts as innovation is in others; that when environmental influences have all been acknowledged there remains the fact that like answers to like, that poets are inspired, guided, and given models by other poets: the image of Parkin reading Keats, Rossetti, and Swinburne to his boys can never be effaced. Here was the origin of Canada's "dolce stil nuovo" and the source of our first national literary movement.

The pattern of periodical publication in Ontario appears with equal clarity, though on another scale, if we compare the three New Brunswick periodicals, *Stewart's Quarterly* (Saint John, 1867–72), the *Maritime Monthly* (Saint John, 1873–75) and the *New Brunswick Magazine* (Saint John, 1898–1905).

Stewart's Quarterly has a strong resemblance to the original *Canadian Monthly* and serves to demonstrate how pervasive, throughout the Canadian provinces, was the spirit of high colonialism. It is significant that George Stewart, its editor and proprietor, became in due course, after its demise, the editor of *Rose-Belford's Canadian Monthly* and of a newspaper in Quebec. It must have been difficult for Stewart to strike the right note for his Maritime clientele, as some changes of sub-title indicate, but he strove to preserve a balance among Canadian, British, European, and American elements and to find space for fiction, poetry, articles, and reviews.

Perhaps the most notable feature of his magazine is the sense of historical continuity which it induces. There is a continuous effort to recall the past and to establish tradition. A natural concomitant is an almost unfailing note of practicality and earnestness. There are articles on Canadian archives, on fishing rights, on the old forts of Acadia, on Newfoundland and the far Northwest, on Canadian worthies, on French and Indian wars, on the Canadian army of the future—calling for a uniting of "courage as was displayed by the men who led the Six Hundred at Balaclava, with the hand of science which the chiefs of that fatal yet glorious day failed to grasp." The British connection is tightened by warmly appreciative articles on Scott and Carlyle, Thackeray and Dickens, and minor figures. English literature is covered, period by period, in long and loving accounts. London papers, Oxford colleges, the Royal Family, the beauties of Scotland complete the picture, and the reader, on a tour of the field of Waterloo, is brought to the very scene: "Tread lightly, for beneath your feet is the dust of heroes." American tradition gets more scattered attention, though there is acknowledgment of the great (Columbus, Lincoln) and of the immediately popular (Mark Twain, Bret Harte). Attention to Europe is significant, if sporadic: we are told of Spanish history, Hungarian music, and Paris after the siege. Bach, Handel, and Mendelssohn receive serious attention.

Fiction is less prominent than one would expect, probably from lack of local talent. Brief stories of hazards in the bush or on the ice are interspersed with romantic, moral, or comical tales of local life: all are so slight as to infer no recognition of an art of fiction. Poetry is similarly sketchy: standard Victorian sentiments are versified about the seasons, the names of fair ladies, or historical events. Homer, Anacreon, Pindar appear, translated or adapted. In critical articles such names as McLachlan, Sangster, and Heavysege receive patriotic praise. An interest in science is apparent, though articles on scientific subjects are few. A revealing remark appears in a dialogue: "I have managed to read Lamb, Matthew Arnold, Keats, Longfellow, Browning, Bryant, Tennyson, Sydney Smith, Dickens and Whittier, and they are 'Household Words' by my fireside." But the speaker is now immersed in the reading of science.

There are many literary notices, particularly of English and American periodicals, but few reviews and these painfully restricted in outlook. Stewart, like Mercer Adam, seems to have laboured against difficult odds. Twenty issues appeared, growing from forty pages to ninety, and then he gave up: "The work has been somewhat arduous, as any man of experience knows; and though our labours have not been crowned with pecuniary success, we hope, as a literary venture, our work has not been altogether thrown away. Our aim has been to furnish a good, sound, healthy literature for the people of this 'incipient northern nation.' "

The *Maritime Monthly,* which appeared in 1873, approximated its predecessor in both style and content. Yet there is an indefinable relaxation of the spirit of high colonialism, a loss of centrality, a loss of the formal elements of composition. A Halifax contributor lays down the plan of Canadian literature as it should be: Canada has no aristocracy of blood, no oppression, no revolting forms of vice or corruption; "the delineator of Canadian life must picture the quiet scenes of industry, the simple incidents of ordinary life, the joys, sorrows, hopes, disappointments, successes and failures which are incident to men in the common routine of life."

The *New Brunswick Magazine*, which first appeared in 1898, made the Maritime provinces its special field and admitted that its aim was not a literary one, but the "diffusion of information in respect to the country and its people." Although many of its comments on old military manoeuvres, shipwrecks, history of settlement, derivation of words and the like can still be read with interest, the glory has departed. In the last few issues, even the historical material dwindles, and is replaced by an ever-increasing quantity of light fiction.

Within a decade and a half of Confederation several other journals were thrown up by the rising tide of nationalism; for example, the *Canadian Literary Journal* (Toronto), the *Harp* (Montreal), the *New Dominion Monthly* (Montreal). None, however, created a cultural pattern as significant, as consistent, and (even under abrasive neglect) as durable as the sequences we have discussed. The same may be said of the group established around the turn of the century in the Maritimes and in the West: the *Canada-West Magazine* (Winnipeg), the *Manitoban* (Winnipeg), *Acadiensis* (Saint John), the *New Brunswick Magazine* (Saint John), the *Prince Edward Island Magazine* (Charlottetown). In Toronto, the precarious *Bystander* (1880, 1883, 1889-90) and *Nation* (1874-76) of Goldwin Smith were extensions of his older and more solid enterprise of the *Canadian Monthly*, already discussed. Most other journals were either organs of particular churches or popular magazines or in the academic tradition of the universities.

Political radicalism, during the period under review, found literary expression which will be dealt with in a subsequent chapter.

To turn the pages of the old *Canadian Monthly* is to enter a lost world. Courage and loyalty were its pre-eminent virtues; it demonstrated that liberal views, critical standards, and religious faith could strengthen one another. A handful of people set themselves to form the ideas of a new nation. Inevitably limited by remoteness from great centres, unavoidably prejudiced and in the face of many dangers unable to develop a full dialectic, they achieved a vision of national greatness and an intellectual method more serviceable, more coherent, more beautiful than any other in English-Canadian history. From their record, in the phrase of D. C. Scott, "Rises the hymn of triumph and courage and comfort, Adeste Fideles."

13. Historical Writing in Canada
to 1920

KENNETH N. WINDSOR

IN THE pre-Confederation period the English-speaking community in Canada could not take much satisfaction in the achievement of its historians. In 1866, the year before the publication of his *Bibliotheca Canadensis*, Henry J. Morgan complained that, with the exception of F.-X. Garneau (1809–1866), Canadian historians "have no reason, as a general rule, to plume themselves upon the elaborate nature of their productions." This was also the opinion of J. Castell Hopkins (1864–1923) in his *Encyclopaedia* at the turn of the century. After considering the substantial achievements of French-Canadian historians in the early period, he confessed that "literary progress in English-speaking Canada had been much slower and less productive," and explained that "The competition of other interests and pursuits was keener and the characteristic physical activity of the race greater. The natural result was comparative indifference to anything except political controversy, through the medium of popular journals, or the ever present charm of English standard works."

I

Some of the earliest historical writing is found in those compendia of useful information, the Statistical Accounts, doubtless prepared in imitation of Sir John Sinclair's massive *Statistical Account of Scotland*, which was drawn up, as the title-page indicates, "from the communications of the ministers of the different parishes." There is a historical introduction and a good deal of historical information in Robert Gourlay's famous *Statistical Account of Upper Canada* published in 1822. Convinced that more accurate information about Canada was needed in the mother country, Gourlay (1778–1863) addressed 31 questions "to the Resident Landowners of Upper Canada" and urged each township to reply. Of the same type are the very useful compilations of Joseph Bouchette (1774–1841), culminating in his two-volume *The British Dominions in North America; or, A Topographical and Statistical Description of the Provinces of Lower and Upper Canada, New Brunswick,*

Nova Scotia, the Islands of Newfoundland, Prince Edward, and Cape Breton ... published in London in 1831. Bouchette was surveyor-general of Lower Canada from 1804 to the Act of Union and vice-president of the venerable Literary and Historical Society of Quebec founded by Lord Dalhousie in 1824. *The British Dominions in North America*, which contains a lengthy historical introduction, was written "to demonstrate the intrinsic worth of those vast and flourishing regions of the British Empire" and "to establish their importance to the mother country, the advantage of the mother country to them, and consequently the mutual benefits conferred, upon both parts of the empire, by their union, under a liberal and enlightened system of colonial policy." Also in English is Pierre de Sales Laterrière's *A Political and Historical Account of Lower Canada with Remarks on the Present Situation of the People* published anonymously in England in 1830. Dr. Laterrière (1785–1834) deplores the lack of information in England about the political crisis in Lower Canada and challenges the policy and pretentions of the oligarchy as expressed by John Fleming (1786?–1832) in his *Political Annals of Lower Canada* (1828). Like Gourlay, Laterrière had his remedies, particularly the abolition of the Legislative Council.

The most significant historical work in this rather awkward genre is Thomas Chandler Haliburton's *An Historical and Statistical Account of Nova Scotia* which was printed, in two volumes, by Joseph Howe in 1829. The first volume, a *History of Nova Scotia*, is one of the most impressive pieces of historical writing produced in Canada in the nineteenth century and it marks, with the appearance of Howe's *Rambles* in the previous year, a most significant advance in Canadian letters. (See also chapter 6, above.) The *Account* was compiled while Haliburton was a busy young lawyer and member of the Legislative Assembly living in Annapolis Royal, without the benefit of public or private libraries. The motive of compilation was largely patriotic. In Great Britain, he said later, "this valuable and important Colony was not merely wholly unknown, but misunderstood and misrepresented. Every book of Geography, every Gazetteer and elementary work that mentioned it, spoke of it in terms of contempt or condemnation." About the history, he wrote to Judge Peleg Wiswall in 1824, "When I . . . called the work I had in hand the history of the Country, I did not mean to apply it in the usual acceptation as a narrative of political events, but in a more enlarged sense as an account of whatever might be found in the Colony." But Haliburton's concept of history is not so broad as he suggests. It is the picturesque and romantic incidents which hold his creative attention: the exploration of the country and the competition for empire. About the latter he said, "These occurrences resemble duels, for which the parties for political purposes sought our wilderness as the most convenient place of Rendevous." The narrative stops at the Peace of Paris; as he put it himself, "After that period the 'short and simple annals of the poor' afford no materials for a continuation, and a history of the province subsequent to that epoch would be about as interesting as one of Dalhousie settlement." Throughout, Haliburton's style is elegant and his comments judicious, as can readily be seen in his discussion of the expulsion of the Acadians. Stopping his narrative as he does in 1763, he has little opportunity to express his intensely Tory point of view. He admitted in his preface, "I have drawn freely, wherever it suited my purpose, and in some instances have copied entire passages" from a "great number of authors," whom he lists. And this, according to the practice of the day, when footnotes were few and far between, was the extent of his acknowledgment to those who had gone before. For Howe the book proved a "ruinous speculation." "It cumbered my office for two years," he wrote, "involved me in heavy expenses for wages, and in debts for paper, materials, binding and engraving. . . . None sold abroad. The Book, though fairly printed, was wretchedly bound, the engravings were poor, and I was left with about 1000 copies, scattered about, unsaleable on my hands."

It should be pointed out, however, that Haliburton's *Historical and Statistical Account* was not the earliest book in this form dealing with Nova Scotia. The honour goes to *A Geographical History of Nova Scotia; Containing an Account of the Situation, Extent, and Limits thereof; As also of the various Struggles between the Two Crowns of England and France for the Possession of that Province* . . . , published anonymously in London in 1749. The information is based, so the preface states, partly on Charlevoix and partly on the author's own observations. It is a modest book of some 100 pages and is generally regarded as the first history in English relating to Canada.

The first book of this kind describing New Brunswick was Peter Fisher's *Sketches of New Brunswick; Containing an Account of the First Settlement of the Province, with a Brief Description of the Country, Climate, Productions, Inhabitants, Government, Rivers, Towns, Settlements, Public Institutions, Trade, Revenue, Population &c.*, which appeared in 1825. Fisher was born on Staten Island, New York, the son of a Loyalist who served in the New Jersey Volunteers, and came to New Brunswick with his father when he was still an infant. It had been his intention to compile a systematic geographical and statistical account for the province, but when this project was taken over by the New-Brunswick Agricultural and Emigrant Society he gave up the idea and presented the material he had already collected with the hope that "these Sketches . . . may serve to give a faint knowledge of the Country, till a more perfect Work is prepared." The title indicates the subject-matter and organization of the book, in which he includes a description, largely geographical, of each county in the province. Fisher was the first to admit that his information was partial and possibly inaccurate; but his *Sketches* are very attractively written. The book was published in Saint John, New

Brunswick, under the pseudonym "An Inhabitant," the name Fisher used for his other publications as well. (See also chapter 7, section IV, above.)

In 1832 Joseph Howe published Robert Cooney's *A Compendious History of the Northern Part of the Province of New Brunswick and of the District of Gaspé in Lower Canada*. In his *Autobiography*, Cooney (1800–1870) tells how he "explored" the district of Gaspé and the counties of Northumberland, Kent, and Gloucester, camping out and losing no opportunity to talk to the Indians, the lumberers, or the Acadian habitants. He did his best to achieve accuracy under very difficult circumstances. ". . . I have carefully weighed the authenticity of every statement, determined, that although there be no merit in the composition, there should be truth in the narrative." Cooney possessed a vigorous, even flamboyant, style and an impressive understanding of the relationship between events. In speaking of the French Revolution he states, "What the French King endeavoured to establish in America, that was he destined to endure at home." But this was Cooney's "first and last effort as a historian." While he was in Halifax seeing the book through the press, he was converted to God and putting aside "all secular pursuits" he soon entered the ministry of the Wesleyan Methodist church.

New Brunswick was the subject of two additional *Accounts*. In 1844, a Presbyterian minister, W. Christopher Atkinson, published *A Historical and Statistical Account of New Brunswick, B.N.A. with Advice to Emigrants*. It is in fact an extension of his very interesting *The Emigrant's Guide to New Brunswick* (1842). Atkinson felt that the contemplation of "the progress of man from a state of nature towards civilization" was a worthy subject, but he provides very little information about the process. Of more significance is the long historical introduction to *New Brunswick; with Notes for Emigrants* (1847) compiled by the geologist, Abraham Gesner (1797–1864), the man who later discovered kerosene oil. Gesner complains that the value and resources of the British North American colonies are too little known in England and, like Gourlay, he finds in these colonies the answer to the problem of the "redundant population and dormant wealth" of the mother country.

In the same period several books of this kind were put together in the mother country. The best of these from a literary point of view is a *Historical Account of Discoveries and Travels in North America . . . with Observations on Emigration* (2 vols., 1829), by that erudite and retiring geographer Hugh Murray (1779–1846). Not only was he a most industrious scholar, but he was aware also of the significance of the expansion of Europe and of the literary possibilities of the phenomenon. He wrote in the advertisement, "The series of bold adventures by which the coasts of North America were discovered and its colonies founded; the daring attempts to find a Northern Passage by its arctic shores; the unparalleled growth and extending power of the United States; with the openings which America affords to our emigrant population,—all these circumstances conspire to render that continent an object of peculiar interest." In 1839 he published *An Historical and Descriptive Account of British America* in three volumes. Done with Murray's usual care, these volumes contain a most impressive and attractive summary of what information was available. Another interesting work of the same kind is John MacGregor's *British America* which appeared in two volumes in 1832. MacGregor (1797–1857) had lived "for several years in America" and travelled extensively in the colonies. Similarly, the third volume of the *History of the British Colonies* (1834–35) by Robert Montgomery Martin (1803?–1868) covers possessions in North America. Just enough historical information is given to make the statistics intelligible. The inscription on the title-page is typical of the spirit of these undertakings, "Far as the breeze can bear—the billows foam— / SURVEY OUR EMPIRE."

II

But not all historical writing in English in the first half of the nineteenth century in British North America was ancillary to statistical accounts and travel books. There are half a dozen other efforts worthy of attention. The authors of these were not much interested in the subtle relationship between events, but rather in recalling the picturesque happening and drawing the appropriate moral conclusions. For them history was very much philosophy teaching by examples. They borrowed freely from their predecessors such as Charlevoix and from one another. They valued fair-mindedness, clarity of expression, and honesty—for these were some of the virtues they were trying to inculcate. "The citizens of Rome," wrote George Warburton (1816–1857) in the introduction to his *Conquest of Canada* (1849), "placed images of their ancestors in the vestibule, to recal the virtues of the dead, and to stimulate the emulation of the living. We also should fix our thoughts upon the examples which history presents, not in a vain spirit of selfish nationality, but in earnest reverence for the great and good of all countries, and a contempt for the false, and mean, and cruel, even of our own."

The first significant historian writing in English on a Canadian subject was George Heriot (1766–1844), the controversial deputy postmaster-general of British North America from 1799 to 1816. In 1804 he published the first volume of *The History of Canada from its First Discovery; Comprehending an Account of the Original Settlement of the Colony of Louisiana*. It is in fact a carefully written condensation of Charlevoix and it stops abruptly without summary or conclusion at 1731, the year in which Charlevoix's connected narrative ends. Heriot's greatest interest was in the manners and customs of the Indians and in the Indian wars. The second volume of his history never appeared but he did publish in 1807 his very valuable *Travels through the Canadas*. It was, in part, an attempt to convey "an idea of some of the picturesque scenery of the Saint Lawrence, at once the largest and most wonderful body of fresh waters on this globe," an enthusiasm not uncommon among Canadian historians.

More important than Heriot's condensation of Charlevoix is William Smith's two-volume compilation, the *History of Canada, from its First Discovery to the Year 1791*, which was printed by John Neilson in 1815 but appeared on the market only in 1826. Son of the historian of New York State and Loyalist Chief Justice of Canada of the same name, Smith (1769–1847) was Clerk of the Legislative Assembly of Lower Canada and later master in Chancery. His *History* is a jumbled and tortuous narrative—Smith admitted that it did not deserve the name of history—but it contains some valuable information. For the period before the Conquest, not covered by Charlevoix and Heriot, and forming one of the more useful sections in the book, Smith copied what he wanted from an unpublished and anonymous manuscript identified only recently as the work of Louis-Léonard Aumasson de Courville. Smith despised the "arbitrary and despotic" government of the *ancien régime* and betrays a particularly low opinion of the political influence of the Roman Catholic clergy among the people. Clearly he considered the introduction of British institutions as providential. Smith put it bluntly; none the less, this was the view which obtained among most English-speaking historians for the remainder of the century.

The War of 1812 was, predictably, the subject of many reminiscences and some significant historical writing. William James (d. 1827), who is best known for his extensive, five-volume *Naval History of Great Britain from the Declaration of War by France in 1793, to the Accession of George IV* (1822–24) had published in 1818 *A Full and Correct Account of the Military Occurrences of the Late War between Great Britain and the United States of America*, in two volumes, which is very largely an attack on the American accounts of the war. James had been an attorney in Jamaica and was for a time a prisoner in the United States during the conflict. As with his other work, his information was impeccable, but he usually managed to show the British cause to advantage. David Thompson (1796?–1868) in his *History of the Late War between Great Britain and the United States of America with a retrospective view of the causes from whence it originated*... (Niagara, 1832) also complained—and it is a very common complaint among Canadian historians during the nineteenth century, which hardened into a prejudice—that American historians of the war did not tell the truth. Thompson's *History* has few pretensions; but it claims to establish the facts so that "generations yet unborn will trace the footsteps of their ancestors in that glorious struggle for the salvation of their country, and emulate their virtuous example...." It was the first important book to be published in Upper Canada and it was a financial failure. Unable to pay the printer's bill, Thompson was sent to gaol for a time as a debtor.

Much the best written of the early histories of the War of 1812 is Major John Richardson's *War of 1812, Containing a Full and Detailed Narrative of the Operations of the Right Division of the Canadian Army* (Brockville, 1842), which appeared first in the columns of his newspaper, *The New Era*. "No compilation could," he stated in the preface, "with greater propriety or consistency, be placed in the hands of Canadian students, than that which records the gallant deeds performed by their fathers, fighting side by side, with the troops of England in defence of their invaded firesides. . . ." The history is an interesting and reliable guide to the events in which the author as a youth had participated. He had been present at the surrender of Detroit and was taken prisoner at the rout of Procter's force on the banks of the Thames in October 1813. But the history did not increase the sales of his newspaper nor could he induce the district councils to recommend its patriotic message for use in the schools. Rather disappointed by the reception of his account of the war on the western frontier, he left the history unfinished.

Among the early histories the best written and the most sophisticated is *The Conquest of Canada* (1849) by "Hochelaga." Like Richardson, the author, George Warburton (1816–1857), was involved in the Carlist War in Spain. From 1844 to 1846 he served with the Royal Artillery in Canada. In 1846 he published in London an account of his extensive travels in North America under the title, *Hochelaga; or, England in the New World*. Of all the early writers, Warburton is the most interested in ideas and in the complicated relationships between events. He was aware of the influence of the Conquest on the development of an independent spirit in the thirteen colonies and of the significance of the success of the American revolution on European development: "their light has served to illumine the political darkness of the European Continent." Warburton believed that the distinctive aspects in the personality of a nation could be told in the development of its colonies. He was a great admirer of what he called "the Anglo-Saxon empire in America." "New France," he said, "was colonised by a government, New England by a people."

III

In spite of an impressive beginning, little historical writing of any significance was attempted in the Atlantic provinces of British North America for a generation following Haliburton; on the other hand, in the province of Canada there was ambitious and significant activity. Although the object of writing remained very much the same, the history reflected the particular preoccupations of the community. It became increasingly, what it was in other parts of the Western world, the study of past politics, and it was infused, in Canada as elsewhere, with the spirit of nationalism. Furthermore, most of the historians writing in the second half of the nineteenth century in Canada, whether serious or popular in their intentions, possessed that attitude to the historical process which is usually described as the Whig interpretation of history. For those of this sensibility, history is the contemplation of freedom broadening down from precedent to precedent towards an agreeable present. They believe in democracy and in social and economic progress. Their history is Protestant in sympathy and secular in application. It divides individuals, institutions, and movements into those that are for and those that are against progress. This approach, as we shall see, frequently results in misplaced emphasis, vast over-simplifications, and superficial judgments.

In the working out of these political and national objectives, most historians emphasized the significance of the individual as a causative factor in the succession of events. The struggle of the settler against the forest primeval and against uncongenial remnants of his heritage—a landed aristocracy and an established church—presented a situation which could readily be described in terms of individual initiative and protest. Most Canadian historians of the period would have subscribed to Carlyle's great-man theory of history.

The year 1855 was a remarkable one in early Canadian scholarship. It saw the completion by Robert Christie (1788–1856) of a six-volume compilation, *A History of the Late Province of Lower Canada*, and the publication of the first reputable survey of Canadian history, John Mercier McMullen's *The History of Canada from its First Discovery to the Present Time*. In the following year, Charles Roger published the first volume of his survey *The Rise of Canada from Barbarism to Wealth and Civilization*.

In 1846, McMullen (1820–1907) had published in London *Camp and Barrack-Room; or, The British Army as it is*, an interesting guide on how to survive and get ahead in the British army. In 1855, although he had "then only resided for a few years in this country" and was "obliged to attend closely to his business of Book-seller and Printer" in Brockville, he published his *History*, the first large-scale general survey of Canadian history in English. The book rings with unqualified enthusiasm for the prospects of the province of Canada. "The present condition of Canada points to a future national greatness of no ordinary magnitude. Her inland seas and noble rivers, have already become the highways of a vast and rapidly increasing commerce. The silent forest of by-gone days has disappeared before the progress of civilization, and the matin voice of a mighty nation resounds over a scene as varied as it is beautiful." McMullen assumed that "wise legislation" and "identity of interests" would overcome the difficulties arising from diversity of race. The Canadian future was better than the American: "With us the sun of fierce party antagonism, there is every reason to hope, has set forever; in the United

States it rapidly ascends towards the meridian of bitterness." While he recognized that separation from Great Britain was very likely, "a result heralded by the very progress of the race itself," he perceived that the imperial connection "is our true line of policy. . . . it secures to us an independent national existence." He possessed most of the prejudices of his adopted community: he was for liberty (he thought Canada should "continue to be a land of genuine freedom, and the 'city of refuge' to the oppressed man of color"), he regretted the "torpid repose" of the French Canadians and he despised the Family Compact.

McMullen knew what he was about. "To infuse a spirit of Canadian nationality into the people generally—to mould the native born citizen, the Scotch, the English, and the Irish emigrant into a compact whole, a purely Canadian literature . . . is a most important element. A popular history of Canada, issued at a price which places it within the reach of every working man, is a step in this direction." His book was carefully worked over and brought up to date in a second edition published in 1868 and again in a two volume edition which appeared in 1891–1892. McMullen did no research himself; but he was a competent journalist. His was the standard guide to Canadian history in the second half of the nineteenth century.

In the following year, Charles Roger of Quebec City (b. 1819) issued the first volume of his survey of Canadian history which he called *The Rise of Canada from Barbarism to Wealth and Civilization*. Like McMullen he was a recent arrival in the country and a journalist by profession. As the florid analogies he constructed between Canadian development and the history of the Jews might suggest, he had for a time studied for the ministry; but this interest did not produce in his case anything like McMullen's very impressive *The Supremacy of the Bible and its Relations to Speculative Science, Remote Ancient History, and the Higher Criticism* (1905). Roger wrote in a vigorous and entertaining style; but he was careless in points of fact and superficial in judgment. The tone of his history is strongly nationalistic and the point of view crudely Whiggish. Only the first volume, which carried the narrative down to the first departure of Lord Dalhousie in 1824, appeared; he later put together several books on local history including various editions of *Quebec: As it was, and As it is* and *Ottawa Past and Present* (1871).

The degree of interest in the War of 1812 is always a fair indication of the intensity of national feeling in Canada at any particular time. In 1855, Gilbert Auchinleck, one of the editors of the *Anglo-American Magazine*, put together the articles on the war which he had written for the *Magazine* and published them as *A History of the War between Great Britain and the United States of America during the Years 1812, 1813, and 1814*. A decade later, in 1864, with the dangers to Canadian interests resulting from the American Civil War very much in mind, a Canadian soldier and civil servant, William F. Coffin

(1808–1878), published *1812; The War, and its Moral: A Canadian Chronicle*. He begins: "1812—like the characters on the labarum of Constantine—is a sign of solemn import to the people of Canada. It carries with it the virtue of an incantation. Like the magic numerals of the Arabian sage, these words, in their utterance, quicken the pulse, and vibrate through the frame, summoning, from the pregnant past, memories of suffering and endurance and of honorable exertion. They are inscribed on the banner and stamped on the hearts of the Canadian people—a watchword, rather than a war-cry." He was determined "to invest the story told, as far as possible, with a Canadian character; to present the war in Canada in a Canadian point of view; and . . . to impart . . . a Canadian individuality to this Canadian Chronicle of the War." Coffin possessed an excellent style. Unfortunately, he was able to produce only one volume which carried the narrative as far as de Salaberry's victory at Châteauguay.

The charismatic event of Confederation and the problems of the early national period produced a succession of patriotic glosses on Canadian development. "Everyone who can write an article in a country newspaper thinks he is competent to give the world a history of our young Dominion in some shape or other," complained John G. Bourinot in *The Intellectual Development of the Canadian People* (1881). One of the more active and most able was H. H. Miles (1818–1895), professor of Mathematics in the University of Bishop's College and, after 1867, secretary of the Council of Public Instruction in the province of Quebec. Shortly after Confederation he produced *A School History of Canada* (1870) and *The Child's History of Canada for the Use of the Elementary Schools and of the Young Reader* (1870). In 1872 he published *The History of Canada under French Regime 1535–1763*, a sober, extensive, and well-written survey of the political and military history of the French period. Miles complained that the treatment of the French régime in English had been too brief and too biased and suggested that something more was necessary in the interests of national objectives.

That most active young journalist Charles R. Tuttle (b. 1848) published in 1877 *An Illustrated History of the Dominion 1535–1876*. It was, he says, in the field of history, "the first popular work illustrated and sold by subscription" in Canada and was written so that Canadians "might be awakened to the inculcation of a higher and nobler sentiment of patriotism,— a greater love for that country which our beloved sovereign has named the 'Dominion of Canada.'" A second volume, *The Comprehensive History of the Dominion of Canada with Art Engravings*, appeared in 1879 and covered the period from Confederation to the close of 1878. In 1878 he published in Boston a *Short History of the Dominion of Canada, from 1500 to 1878; with the contemporaneous history of England and the United States*. But these books were not written solely for the creation of Canadian national feeling; they were the first Canadian histories written expressly for American readers, "to intensify the admiration for Canadian industries and institutions, which the Dominion exhibits at the Centennial Exposition awakened."

Born in Nova Scotia, Tuttle spent most of his adult life in the United States, although he was in Winnipeg long enough to found a conservative newspaper there, the *Times*, in 1879. Of all the popularizers of the period, including J. Castell Hopkins, he was the most prolific. As a young man he embarked on the ambitious project of writing a one-volume history of each of the states of the American union and got half a dozen of these done. His industry was prodigious. By the time he was thirty, he seems to have written at least eleven books of history and two novels. In 1878, on the appointment of the Marquis of Lorne as Governor-General, he wrote *Royalty in Canada; Embracing Sketches of the House of Argyll, The Right Honorable the Marquis of Lorne . . .* , a book of over two hundred pages, in the space of four days. Needless to say Tuttle did no original research. He merely gathered and arranged, copying whole sections from official documents and from other historians. He could, however, write well and his ideas are always interesting. He accompanied the Hudson Bay Expedition of 1884 and wrote it up in *Our North Land* (1885). He was convinced of the "unerring north-westerly trend of human progress" and held that "the highest latitudes produce the greatest men." He found it strange that "the north is always underrated." Like many others, he was convinced that a distinctive French community was destined to disappear in North America: "Anglo-Saxon civilization," he said, "cannot be circumscribed." He was much interested in religion and predicted that the Methodists would form "the future great church of Canada" becoming ultimately the national church. He was a strong promoter of the myth of Canadian educational superiority. He thought that the common school system had reduced the animosity among the sects and it was "so perfect" that Canadians need have no fears about their ability to develop the country.

In the same year that Tuttle's *Short History* appeared, W. H. Withrow (1839–1908), the cultured and industrious editor of the *Canadian Methodist Magazine*, published *A Popular History of the Dominion of Canada from the Discovery of America to the Present Time*. Believing that "the essential prerequisite of a rational patriotism is an intelligent acquaintance with the history of one's country," Withrow put together with great care a compendious survey of the political and military history of Canada. It was well written and, like his many other books of history, biography and fiction, it was marked, as his obituary in the *Proceedings and Transactions of the Royal Society of Canada* indicated, "by high patriotism and intelligent piety."

Another talented author who attempted a general survey of Canadian history was the distinguished Presbyterian clergyman and educator, George Bryce (1844–1931). He had previously, in 1882, published *Manitoba: Its*

Infancy, Growth, and Present Condition to provide information for the immigrant. He admitted that "a description of the country, its resources, and prospects will be found shining through all the discussions." In 1887, *A Short History of the Canadian People* appeared. Clearly Bryce wanted to give rather less space to political and military history and he indicates that, while he sympathized "with movements for wide extension of true freedom," he could appreciate another set of values. His history is better organized and better written than most; but its contents and point of view are decidedly conventional.

In 1897, John G. Bourinot (1837–1902) contributed *Canada* to Putnam's "The Story of the Nations" series. Clerk of the House of Commons of Canada, Bourinot succeeded Alpheus Todd (1821–1884) as an international authority on comparative government and parliamentary procedure. In his short history, space is given to those events which exercised "the most influence on national development." An interesting chapter on French Canada is included. Although Bourinot is the most sober and level-headed of this group of historians, he radiates a real satisfaction with Canadian parliamentary institutions and with Canadian achievements in the arts and in science.

At the turn of the century, a flurry of patriotic histories from the hand of J. Castell Hopkins (1864–1923) appeared from the presses of Canada, the United States, and Great Britain. In 1899, he published *The Story of the Dominion: Four Hundred Years in the Annals of Half a Continent* and in 1900 the *Progress of Canada in the Nineteenth Century*. He took the position that "Canada only needs to be known in order to be great." These histories were prepared at the same time that he was putting together his extensive and very useful *Canada, an Encyclopaedia of the Country* in six volumes. The variety of information which he collected for the *Encylopaedia* made it possible for him to deal more adequately with such topics as the development of transportation, education, and religion. Hopkins was the biographer of Sir John Thompson (1895) and was frequently an apologist for the Conservative party; none the less, his work represents the first serious attempt to revise the conventional interpretation of the Family Compact.

The list of patriotic surveys would not be complete without the mention of *A History of Canada* by Charles G. D. Roberts (1860–1943) which was published by Morang in 1902. The book was prepared for use in the secondary schools at the instigation of the Dominion Educational Association and submitted in what was called the Dominion History Competition. The sum of two thousand dollars in prizes was contributed by the various provincial governments and by the time the competition closed in 1895 fifteen manuscripts had been received. Roberts did not receive the prize; nor did George Bryce, who also entered the competition. It went to Judge W. H. P. Clement

(1858–1922) for an incredibly dull and fact-ridden volume which was published in 1897 and authorized for use in six provinces and the territories. When Roberts' *History* appeared, the august *Review of Historical Publications Relating to Canada* conceded that it was "from a literary standpoint the most attractive history of Canada which has yet appeared." But the reviewer noted an unseemly patriotism which reminded him of the "prejudiced, boastful spirit, quite in the vein of some of the jingo school-books of the United States." Roberts' book was certainly the most readable general survey of Canadian history produced in the whole period under discussion and it reflects the general tone of these books clearly. It reflects not only the Whig interpretation of Canadian history but suggests the Whig interpretation of Canadian literature: "The real beginnings of a literary spirit in Canada may be said to date from the triumph of Responsible Government. That struggle had broadened men's minds and taught them to think for themselves."

IV

The more serious and specialized historical writing in the second half of the nineteenth century was less obviously nationalistic. The research was done both more intensively and more carefully. Nevertheless, it possesses the same general set of values which are apparent in the more popular and general treatments. History is essentially political history and most of the emphasis is on the extension and development of British parliamentary institutions in the various provinces of British North America or of the Dominion.

Perhaps the earliest of these more specialized political histories and certainly one of the most important is the extensive six-volume *History of the late Province of Lower Canada* of Robert Christie (1788–1856) which appeared between 1848 and 1855. These volumes incorporate most of Christie's earlier writings which are, in themselves, significant: *Memoirs of the Administration of the Colonial Government of Lower Canada by Sir James Henry Craig and Sir George Prevost; From the Year 1807 until the Year 1815, Comprehending the Military and Naval Operations in the Canadas during the Late War with the United States of America* (1818), *Memoirs of the Administration of the Government of Lower Canada by Sir Gordon Drummond, Sir John Coape Sherbrooke, the late Duke of Richmond, James Monk, Esquire, and Sir Peregrine Maitland* (1820) and *Memoirs of the Administration of Lower Canada by the Right Honourable the Earl of Dalhousie* (1829). *A History of the Late Province of Lower Canada* is an attempt to explain why the constitution of 1791 "modelled upon that of Great Britain, as far as circumstances admitted ... proved a failure...."

Christie possessed an intimate knowledge of the political situation in

Lower Canada. In 1827 he was elected member of the Legislative Assembly for the County of Gaspé, which has been described as in those days "the nearest thing to a pocket borough in Lower Canada." As chairman of the quarter sessions of the District of Quebec, he complied with the wishes of the Governor and revised the list of magistrates to exclude those who had led the opposition in the Assembly. For this, he was repeatedly expelled from the Assembly. "He was yet a simple and single minded man," wrote a reviewer in the Montreal *Gazette*, "with almost no guile, at times exhibiting that particular kind of courage which led him to butt his head against the stone wall of a superior power. He dressed quaintly—in the style of a former generation; and as in his dress, so in his manners, he never adapted himself to the times."

Christie had few literary pretensions. He confessed in the preface to the fourth volume that readers must find his books "dry and heavy, if not absolutely a penance." His purpose was simply "to record, for future information, the various and important sayings and doings, parliamentary and political, that have taken place in Lower Canada. . . ." Following these objectives at such length, he produced a work of lasting value. It is not surprising that he possessed little sympathy for the reform party; but he tried throughout to let the facts speak for themselves.

A similar kind of book, although much better organized and much better written, is *The History of Newfoundland from the Earliest Times to the Year 1860* (1863) by a minister of the Congregational church, Charles Pedley (1821–1872). It is essentially a political history culminating in the achievement of responsible government in the colony in 1855. In the same tradition is the voluminous and encyclopaedic *A History of Newfoundland from the English, Colonial, and Foreign Records* by Judge D. W. Prowse (1834–1914), published in London in 1895. Prowse's passion for the history of Newfoundland developed from his interest in the North Atlantic fisheries. "The great English historians," he complained, "ignore altogether the part Newfoundland played in the making of England . . . the daring of West Country traders and cod fishers, who began the conquest and colonisation of a greater England in the new world. . . ." And he bitterly protested British policy: "Our treatment by the British Government has been so stupid, cruel, and barbarous that it requires the actual perusal of the State Papers to convince us that such a policy was ever carried out."

A writer who frankly admired Christie and who worked in the same manner, was Beamish Murdoch (1800–1876) for a time the editor of the *Acadian Recorder*. He was, too, an active politician and a distinguished lawyer. In 1832–33, he published an *Epitome of the Laws of Nova Scotia* in four volumes. In his retirement, he compiled *A History of Nova Scotia or Acadia* which appeared in three vast volumes between 1865 and 1867. Like Christie, he faced a real problem in abridgement, for he was determined to "preserve everything of genuine interest." He loved Nova Scotia, "a happy, free and intelligent province, progressive and prosperous," and felt that its history, "the courage, the endurance and generosity that are the attributes of the early adventurers and settlers" possessed a moral relevance for his own day. He wanted to "transport the reader . . . back to the actuality of past times" and he thought that this could best be done "in its own forms and colors and language." For Murdoch as for Christie, this meant the inclusion of numerous documents within the body of the narrative and the compilation of endless appendices. Writing in the 1860's, he felt that it was necessary to point out the permanent value of colonies. He insisted on the loyalty of the province to the mother country and suggested that the skills of the population might be very useful to the Royal Navy in times of danger.

Murdoch's great volumes on Nova Scotia were followed shortly by one by Duncan Campbell (1819?–1886), *Nova Scotia, in its Historical, Mercantile and Industrial Relations*. Murdoch's *History* closes with the year 1827. Very conscious of this, Campbell gives about half his space to the period between 1827 and the death of Joseph Howe in 1873. Although he had come from Scotland as recently as 1860, he achieved an impressive knowledge of the history of his adopted province. Clearly, he wanted to broaden the content of his history; but, in spite of the title, it is essentially a political narrative. Campbell valued style—"readableness" he called it—much more than Murdoch. The book was handsomely printed and published by John Lovell of Montreal in 1873. In 1875, Campbell produced a *History of Prince Edward Island* which, he hoped, "might claim some degree of merit as to conciseness, accuracy, and impartiality." It covers, in some two hundred pages, the period from the Peace of Paris to the entry of the Province into Confederation and, like his history of Nova Scotia, it is attractively written.

What Murdoch and Campbell had done for historical studies in the other maritime provinces, James Hannay (1842–1910), lawyer and journalist, did for the province of New Brunswick. His first important book was *The History of Acadia, from its First Discovery to its Surrender to England by the Treaty of Paris*, which appeared in 1879. Hannay acknowledged his debt to the "industry and research" of Murdoch, but he felt that there was a place for a "consistent narrative." In 1897 he published *The Life and Times of Sir Leonard Tilley, being a political history of New Brunswick for the past seventy years*. In 1909, his magnum opus, a large two-volume *History of New Brunswick*, appeared. His aim was simply "to trace the development of the constitution, and the growth of the laws of New Brunswick from the foundation of the Province down to the present time." The work terminates with chapters on the churches and education; but these are really appendices to an essentially political narrative. Hannay also published, in 1901, a *History of the War of 1812 between Great Britain and the United States of America*, which was published in England under the title—should that audience miss the point—of *How Canada was Held for the Empire: The Story of the War of 1812*. Like Hannay's other books, it is well written, but unfortunately it is frequently inaccurate and is intensely biased. Very little can be said for the Americans: they ". . . invaded our country, burnt our towns, ravaged our fields, slaughtered our people and tried to place us under a foreign flag." Hannay was also the biographer of *Wilmot and Tilley* (1907) in the "Makers of Canada" series.

The Northwest was also the subject of some good history written in the style of Christie and Murdoch. The most impressive early historian of that vast region was Alexander Begg (1839–1897). In 1867 he introduced the Red River settlement to goods manufactured in Canada and for a number of years he was a leading merchant in Winnipeg. He was a witness to the Red River Resistance of 1869–1870 and from his very valuable daily journal he compiled *The Creation of Manitoba; or, A History of the Red River Troubles*, which appeared in 1871. Years later, when he was living in Victoria, he put together his *History of the North-West* in three volumes, published in 1894 and 1895. His subject is really "the march of civilization in the North-West," which was no longer "a vast hunting ground" but the "home of thousands of thrifty settlers." Not only was the Northwest "one of the brightest jewels in the British Crown," but it was, also, a region of great strategic significance, "one of the most important links in the chain of Imperial unity." The book is written in an effective style and was handsomely produced by the Hunter, Rose Company of Toronto. It contains a mass of information, including many documents, and remains a valuable source of information.

By an extraordinary and confusing coincidence, the best early history of the province of British Columbia was written by a different man with the same name—Alexander Begg (1825–1905). Born in Scotland, he taught public school in Ontario. For a number of years, he was employed by the Department of Internal Revenue in Ottawa and was, for a time, Emigration Commissioner in Scotland for the Province of Ontario. He was the editor of several newspapers in small places in Ontario and publisher of the *Canadian Lumberman*. In 1887, he arrived in Victoria where he was appointed Emigration Commissioner by the Province to investigate the possibility of settling Scottish crofters on Vancouver Island. The idea was abandoned; but Begg appended the initials C.C. (Crofter Commissioner) to his name to distinguish himself from the historian of the Northwest. In 1894 he published his *History of British Columbia from Its Earliest Discovery to the Present Time*. The style is undistinguished and the organization primitive. Like Christie and Murdoch, he attempts to "gather and compile . . . as full and complete a record as possible. . . ." This he did successfully.

As might be predicted, the Northwest inspired many less systematic and more popular histories. One of the best was *From Savagery to Civilization; The Canadian Northwest: Its History and Its Troubles, from the Early Furtrade to the Era of the Railway and the Settler* . . . by Graeme Mercer Adam (1839–1912) which appeared in 1885. It is really "the narrative of three insurrections," the Selkirk massacre and the two Riel Rebellions. From 1860 to 1892 Adam was connected with a succession of distinguished Canadian journals beginning with the *British American Magazine.* He founded the *Canadian Monthly and National Review* (1872–78) and was business manager of *The Bystander* (1880–81, 1883). (See also chapter 11, above.) His history of the Northwest is vigorously written. Even here his Whiggish values did not fail him for he states in the preface that "these revolts, in some degree at least, are the legacy of the days of monopoly and privilege."

The Northwest was also the subject of most of the important work of Agnes C. Laut (1871–1936) and Lawrence J. Burpee (1873–1946). Agnes Laut was a most prolific and energetic writer. Although most of her active life was spent as a journalist in the United States, she never tired of Canadian subjects. In addition to several volumes in the "Chronicles of Canada" series, she wrote a very popular *Pathfinders of the West: Being the Thrilling Story of the Adventures of the Men Who Discovered the Great Northwest: Radisson, La Vérendrye, Lewis and Clark* (1904) and *The Conquest of the Great Northwest* . . . , a large history of the Hudson's Bay Company which appeared in two volumes in 1908. At the time, she was the only person who had access to the Company's archives and she consulted them with great industry. In 1909, she published *Canada, the Empire of the North: Being the Romantic Story of the New Dominion's Growth from Colony to Kingdom* written in what the *Review of Historical Publications Relating to Canada* called "her own vivid and picturesque way." She was sometimes careless about points of fact and intolerant of the conclusions of other scholars; but she was always good reading, for she possessed real gifts of imagination and a vivacious style. If anything, her books are over-written.

Lawrence J. Burpee was a distinguished civil servant and an active writer in such fields as history, geography, and bibliography. He brought these varied interests together in his impressive and scholarly *The Search for the Western Sea: The Story of the Exploration of North-western America* which appeared in 1908. Among other books, he wrote a biography, *Sandford Fleming, Empire Builder* (1915) and contributed to the "Chronicles of Canada" series a popular volume based on his extensive researches, *Pathfinders of the Great Plains: A Chronicle of La Vérendrye and his Sons* (1915). He later edited *Journals and Letters of Pierre Gaultier de Varennes de la Vérendrye and His Sons* . . . for the Champlain Society (1937).

V

But it was the western half of the old province of Canada, later the province of Ontario, that saw the greatest achievements of the Whig school of Canadian historians. There, because of the personalities involved and because of the lively memories of '37, the interpretations were frequently partisan, sometimes resembling extensive political tracts. However undesirable this tendency might be from a scientific point of view, it frequently produced good literature.

One of the most important books produced by this group was by Charles Lindsey (1820–1908), *The Life and Times of Wm. Lyon Mackenzie, with an account of the Canadian Rebellion of 1837, and the subsequent frontier disturbances, chiefly from unpublished documents*, which appeared, in two volumes, in 1862. Born in England, Lindsey came to Canada in 1841. He was an editor of the *Examiner*, a reform newspaper founded by Francis Hincks in 1838, and later was editor-in-chief of the conservative Toronto *Leader*. In 1852, the same year in which the *Leader* was established, he married a daughter of William Lyon Mackenzie and was confronted with the "vast mass" of the reformer's papers. Lindsey got to know Mackenzie well; he admired his energy, courage, and fierce honesty. But he felt that the rebellion was a mistake, "unfortunate and ill-advised." He perceived that "the amelioration which the political institutions of Canada have undergone would probably have come in time," but he argued that change "would not have come so soon" nor would the province "yet have reached its present stage of advancement." The book is as exciting as the events which it describes, although the language is curiously florid. As was the fashion, it contains extended footnotes and the inevitable appendices. Always a strong supporter of the voluntary principle, Lindsey was the author of *The Clergy Reserves— their History and Present Position* ... (1851). In 1877, he published *Rome in Canada: The Ultramontane Struggle for Supremacy over the Civil Power*, a book of almost 400 pages given to an examination of what Lindsey thought was a papal and Jesuit conspiracy against the institutions of a liberal and democratic society.

Of all the Whig historians, the most controversial and the greatest stylist was John Charles Dent (1841–1888). Although he was born in England, he was educated in Canada. He was called to the bar of Upper Canada in 1865, but earned his living as a journalist in London, England, and in Toronto where he was on the editorial staff of the *Globe*. In 1880–81 he published, in four volumes, *The Canadian Portrait Gallery* and in 1881 a political history in two volumes, *The Last Forty Years: Canada since the Union of 1841*, written from the point of view of the Reform party. In 1885 *The Story of the*

Upper Canadian Rebellion, two volumes, appeared. It began with a discussion of the "slow crucifixion" of Gourlay and is throughout a sustained diatribe against the Family Compact. For Dent, the rebellion was "the fitting sequel to a long course of oligarchical tyranny and oppression," the natural result of "a succession of military lieutenant-governors who had no knowledge of or sympathy with our local institutions" and of the interference of a colonial minister "thousands of miles away." With this interpretation many would agree. But he created a furor in his determination to exalt the character and accomplishments of Dr. John Rolph and denigrate the memory of William Lyon Mackenzie. To Dent's way of thinking, Rolph was "unquestionably one of the most extraordinary persons who have ever figured in the annals of Upper Canada"; while Mackenzie was "a creature of circumstances" driven by an "itch for notoriety."

"*The Story of the Upper Canadian Rebellion*," the *Dominion Annual Register* stated soberly for the record, "called forth more favourable and more adverse comments than any Canadian history, excepting, perhaps, Mr. B. Sulte's *Histoire des Canadiens-français*" (8 vols., 1882–84). The father of W. L. Mackenzie King, John King (1843–1916), quickly compiled *The Other Side of the "Story"* (1886), a collection of unfavourable reviews of the first volume and of damaging documents. Most writers agreed with the reviewer in the Toronto *Daily Mail* who suggested that Dent had attempted to make "a hero out of the most unpromising material, the most unheroic of men." The *Story* appeared in two handsome red volumes bearing quantities of gilt. Like *The Last Forty Years*, it is elegantly and lucidly written in a style which the writer in *Canada and its Provinces* compared, not unfavourably, with that of the great Macaulay.

The most prolific of this group of historians was William Kingsford (1819–1898). Born and educated in England, he came to Canada with his regiment in 1837. He remained and qualified as a civil engineer. Outspoken and hot-tempered, he had an uneven career as an engineer. In 1873 he was appointed engineer in charge of the harbours on the Great Lakes and the St. Lawrence, a post from which he was suddenly dismissed by Sir Hector Langevin in 1879. At this point, at the age of sixty, he began his serious historical studies and writing. In 1886 he published *Canadian Archaeology, an Essay*, which is, in spite of its title, "a history of the first printed books in the provinces of Quebec and Ontario." It also contains titles of early newspapers and a survey of manuscript collections in the various archives and libraries. This was followed, in 1892, by *The Early Bibliography of the Province of Ontario* . . . the first careful and critical, but by no means definitive, list of publications on the early history of Ontario.

Between 1887 and 1898, Kingsford published *The History of Canada* in ten large volumes running in all well over five thousand pages. It is the most extensive general history of Canada ever attempted by a single author and it was thought at the time to achieve in the English language what Garneau had done earlier in French. But Kingsford was no artist and his volumes were written in haste, almost at the rate of one a year. He could not match Garneau as a stylist, and his sentences are long, involved, and infelicitous. Nevertheless, his *History* represents a remarkable achievement especially for a man of his years.

The purpose of Kingsford's great study was "to trace the history of British rule in Canada since its Conquest from the French, and to relate . . . the series of events which have led to the present Constitution under which the Dominion is governed." After giving four volumes to the old régime by way of introduction, he proceeded with a most detailed constitutional and political history of Canada in which colonial liberty and imperial authority were ultimately reconciled by the device of responsible government. He was determined that his *History* "should not fail from any insufficiency of fact." But there is little else and the range of interest is very limited. The *Review of Historical Publications Relating to Canada* complained that "There is scarcely an allusion to the social or industrial life of the people, the condition of agriculture, the increase of commerce, or the development of the fur trade. The tide of immigration that set in from and ultimately flowed back to the United States is unnoticed." Kingsford insisted that he never strained the evidence. But that is not the impression most readers have received. A startling example is his determination to prove that the first and perhaps greatest hero of the narrative, Champlain, was a Protestant. But, whatever its defects, his work does represent a summary of the Whig position and a source of information and inspiration for other works with that point of view.

The greatest achievement of this school of historians was the "Makers of Canada" series. With the possible exception of the historical articles in J. Castell Hopkins' *Canada: An Encyclopaedia of the Country* (6 vols., Toronto, 1897–1900), it was the first co-operative venture in Canadian historical writing. "Each of the great figures in our history will be dealt with in a single volume," J. Castell Hopkins wrote to Sir John Willison (1856–1927), editor of the *Globe*, on the subject of the "Makers," "and each will be treated by a writer who is best fitted, by study and taste and eminence, to discuss the particular topic. Some of the writers already arranged with are N. E. Dionne, . . . Principal Grant, . . . Rt. Hon. Sir Wilfrid Laurier. . . ." Principal George Monro Grant (1835–1902) did not live to expand his excellent essays on Joseph Howe and Laurier could not find time to write a biography of A. A. Dorion; but the list indicates the level at which the work was conceived.

The publisher was George N. Morang (1866–1937) of Toronto who used to refer to the "Makers" as "my great enterprise." "The printing, paper and binding . . . ," proclaimed the *Review of Historical Publications Relating to*

Canada, "are beyond praise." The books were sold in sets by subscription; Morang agreed with Mark Twain that selling "through the trade" was like "printing for private circulation only." It was his sales experience with this series which attracted Robert Glasgow to a career of similar publishing. By 1910, Morang had already sold 3,500 sets and the series was still going at the rate of 40 sets a week. At this point, he brought out two less expensive editions (the eleven-volume two-volume-in-one editions) with the hope of selling 10,000 more sets. These are remarkable figures for the period when it is considered that a most significant and well-advertised biography, the *Memoirs of the Right Honourable Sir John Alexander Macdonald* by Sir Joseph Pope (1854–1926) (2 vols., 1894), had over several years sold less than 600 copies.

The original edition was published in twenty volumes between 1903 and 1908. The editors were the poet, Duncan Campbell Scott (1862–1947), and Professor O. Pelham Edgar (1871–1948) of Victoria College. Later William Dawson LeSueur (1840–1917) was added and he did most of the serious and constructive editing. The series comprised biographies of *Lord Elgin* (J. G. Bourinot), *Egerton Ryerson* (Nathanael Burwash, 1839–1918), *Sir Frederick Haldimand* (Jean Newton McIlwraith, 1859–1938), *Papineau, Cartier* (A. D. DeCelles, 1843–1925), *Joseph Howe* (J. W. Longley, 1849–1922), *General Brock* (Lady Edgar, 1844–1910), *Wolfe and Montcalm* (Abbé H. R. Casgrain, 1831–1904), *Mackenzie, Selkirk, Simpson* (George Bryce), *John Graves Simcoe* (Duncan Campbell Scott), *Bishop Laval* (A. Leblond de Brumath, 1854–1939), *Count Frontenac* (W. D. LeSueur), Champlain (N. E. Dionne, 1848–1917), *George Brown* (John Lewis, 1858–1935), *Wilmot and Tilley* (James Hannay), *Lord Dorchester* (A. G. Bradley), *Baldwin, Lafontaine, Hincks* (Stephen Leacock, 1869–1944), *Lord Sydenham* (Adam Shortt, 1859–1931), *William Lyon Mackenzie* (Charles and G. G. S. Lindsey), *Sir John A. Macdonald* (George R. Parkin, 1846–1922), *Sir James Douglas* (Robert Hamilton Coats, 1874–1960, and R. E. Gosnell, 1860–1931). An index volume was added in 1911 and a supplementary volume on *Sir Charles Tupper* in 1916 by J. W. Longley who had already done the volume on *Joseph Howe*.

Although the workmanship was always impressive, the quality of writing varied considerably. The best books in the series were *Lord Sydenham* by Professor Adam Shortt and Jean Newton McIlwraith's *Sir Frederick Haldimand*. In both cases, the authors were able to draw upon extensive collections of documents which had recently been made available by the Public Archives of Canada.

In 1926, a new edition of the "Makers" with extensive alterations was brought out by the Oxford University Press with W. L. Grant (1872–1935), the principal of Upper Canada College, as editor. Lindsey's *William Lyon*

Mackenzie was dropped. A new life of *Bishop Laval* by the Abbé H. A. Scott (1858–1931) replaced the one by A. Leblond de Brumath and J. G. Bourinot's *Lord Elgin* was removed in favour of a new treatment by Professor W. P. M. Kennedy (1880–1963). There were several additions to the original selection. A much-admired book, Sir John Willison's *Sir Wilfrid Laurier and the Liberal Party: A Political History*, which was originally published by Morang in two volumes in 1903, was included. It was described in 1926 by the editor of the *Canadian Historical Review*, W. S. Wallace (b. 1884), "as perhaps the most distinguished example of political biography in Canadian literature. . . ." Also added were *The Life and Work of Sir William Van Horne* by Walter Vaughan (1865–1922) which had first appeared in 1920 and a new life of *Lord Strathcona* by Professor John Macnaughton (1858–1943).

It is not surprising that Morang's "great enterprise" was conceived as a series of biographies. As William Buckingham (1832–1915) and George W. Ross (1841–1914) put it in the first sentence of *The Hon. Alexander Mackenzie His Life and Times* (1892): "The history of an individual is often the history of a nation." The influence of Carlyle was pervasive and to the heady nationalism of the turn of the century the physical environment suggested opportunities not limitations, a challenge to human ingenuity and moral purpose not a range of restricted possibilities. Doubtless because of the achievements of the period, biography has persisted as an unusually popular and successful form of expression for Canadian historians. Although less critical and analytical than the monograph, it possesses great literary possibilities and is probably the most accessible form of history from the point of view of the general reader.

The point of view of the writers was consciously Whiggish. This can be seen in the very selection of the "Makers." Egerton Ryerson is included, but not Bishop Strachan; William Lyon Mackenzie, but not John Beverley Robinson. The politics of the editor is abundantly demonstrated in the long altercation in the courts over the volume on William Lyon Mackenzie. The author was one of the editors, W. D. LeSueur, who had already written a very readable biography of Frontenac for the series. This choice was most offensive to William Lyon Mackenzie King and LeSueur wrote to Sir John Willison that Rodolphe Lemieux, who was successively solicitor-general and postmaster general in Laurier's government, "warned me that I had better take care how I wrote it." None the less, LeSueur received permission from Charles Lindsey, the previous biographer, to use the Mackenzie papers which were in the possession of the family and for five months in 1906 LeSueur lived in Lindsey's house where the papers were kept.

The biography was written with unusual care. Robert Glasgow (1875–1922), who knew a good book when he saw one, insisted as late as 1914 that it was "the best book of history yet done by any Canadian writer." It is clear that LeSueur had wanted for some time to revise the traditional evaluation of Mackenzie. Later, he wrote to John Willison, "I will never ask you to expend much admiration on the so-called 'family compact,' but don't you think it probable that, if a thing has been steadily abused for a couple of generations, the condemnation might have cumulatively become too strong. I suppose that, theoretically, you might paint a fence till there was less fence than paint." LeSueur, whose interests and sympathies were unusually catholic, treated Mackenzie with respect and affection; but he took the position that Mackenzie had a "retardatory" influence on Canadian political development. "Others emerge from my pages in a guise which will disappoint many," he wrote to John Lewis, author of *George Brown* in the same series. "Colonial secretaries, lieutenant-governors, judges, office holders under the old system have been ruthlessly robbed by me of those repulsive features under which an enlightened posterity has loved to contemplate them. They were all, or nearly all, decent old-fashioned folk doing their duty in the several stations to which they had been called in an honest old-fashioned way—not entirely unsuited to the comparatively undeveloped situation of the country. Morang no doubt rolled up his eyes to heaven and held up his hands in horror as he dictated to his type-writer the words (addressed to me): 'You have defended the Family Compact!' "

Morang refused to publish the book and LeSueur was prevented from publishing it elsewhere by an injunction obtained in the courts by the Lindsey family. In 1914, Robert Glasgow offered to publish it under the title, *William Lyon Mackenzie and the "Family Compact": A Political History*, provided the author could remove all the information obtained directly from the Lindsey collection. But G. G. S. Lindsey (1860–1920) argued in a letter to LeSueur that "It is now impossible for you to write a *Life of Mackenzie*, after five months continuous research among his private papers, and after many more brooding over them, without tincturing your manuscript throughout with color thrown into it by material from these sources." This position was upheld by the courts and LeSueur's best book was never published. Its place was taken in the series by a hasty abridgment by G. G. S. Lindsey of his father's two volume biography of the reformer.

The achievements of this group of historians are obvious; but some of the large deficiencies of the Whig point of view, as they apply to Canadian history, should be discussed more fully. In the first place, the Whig interpretation resulted in a vast over-simplification of Canadian development. This came in part from a preoccupation with two particular periods, the conquest of New France and the struggle for responsible government, almost to the exclusion of other vital and interesting areas. One of the signally neglected subjects was the movement for the union of British North America. This is indeed curious in the light of the rampant nationalism of the period. But it seems clear that the Whig sensibility looked upon the confederation movement as a corollary to responsible government, a natural outcome of the achievement of internal colonial liberty which barely needed explanation.

But after all one subject is as legitimate as another. The real criticism of the Whig historians is that they failed to understand adequately even those periods to which they gave so much attention. The fact is that these writers were not really interested in writing about what happened; but rather in demonstrating the truths of their political and social philosophy as they worked themselves out in congenial periods of the country's history. In the French period, they were so anxious to tell the story of the triumph of English over French imperialism, of Protestantism over Roman Catholicism, of liberty over authority, of enterprise over paternalism that they took little note of the complexities of the colony's development and society. For the purposes of their system, a caricature was more manageable than the real thing. And Francis Parkman (1823-1893), in *The Old Régime in Canada* (1874), for all his artistry and meticulous attention to detail, was probably the greatest offender.

Nor did the Whig fixation with the struggle for responsible government result in real understanding. In the first place, thinking of the political transition of the 1830's and 1840's as a struggle misrepresents those complex and vastly creative decades. It confuses the true relationship between the mother country and the colonies and takes little notice of the fact that British political institutions were also in a state of violent flux. To the Whigs everything was simple. "The rebellion, then," wrote John Charles Dent, "though it failed in the field, was very far from being an utter failure. It accelerated the just and moderate constitutional changes for which the Reform party had for years contended, and which, but for the Rebellion, would have been long delayed. It led to Lord Durham's mission, which brought everything else in its train. From Lord Durham's mission sprang the union; from the union sprang the concession of Responsible Government, the end of the Family Compact domination, the establishment of municipal institutions, reform in all the departments of state."

It is astonishing that most of these historians did not seem to know when responsible government actually came into existence. Kingsford seems to have thought that it was achieved with the Act of Union in 1841. In 1907, Stephen Leacock, who had just been through the documents for his book *Baldwin, Lafontaine, Hincks* in the "Makers," felt that it was necessary to point out in an article which he wrote for the first volume of the *American Political Science Review*, that "the interpretation of the principle of responsible government now prevailing was not present in the minds of imperial statesmen at the time of the adoption of the Act of Union of 1840, commonly assigned as the date of the inception of self-government." Nor did these writers understand how responsible government worked. Not until Shortt's *Sydenham* were they aware of Sydenham's administrative reforms and the significance of these changes usually escaped them. They showed little comprehension of the nature of political parties in the 1840's and the process by which responsible government was worked out and put into practice.

Furthermore, the rigidities of the Whig point of view made the evaluation of the individual in the historical process very difficult. There were "good guys" and "bad guys" and there was no difficulty in telling the one from the other. There were those who were for the extension of colonial liberty and those who were against it; there were those who wanted a liberal, rational, democratic, and secular society and those who for one reason or another were wedded to an unenlightened traditional position. This kind of history possesses all the moral subtlety of a cowboy and Indian movie. It is not surprising then that some very significant names just will not fit conveniently into the usual Whig categories. Egerton Ryerson is an example. His ideas on education were, from the Whig point of view, sound; but his support of the reform movement was uneven. So it was largely as an educational reformer that he was included in the "Makers" in the biography by Nathanael Burwash, the president and chancellor of Victoria College. The perplexities of the Whig position are well illustrated just at the end of the first volume of Dent's *The Last Forty Years* where he attempts an evaluation of the work and personality of Sir John A. Macdonald. And Sir George Parkin is really no more successful in the volume he did on Macdonald for the "Makers" series.

VI

The deficiencies of the Whig point of view were in no way corrected by the influence of the two most distinguished foreign historians ever to give their attention to Canadian studies: Francis Parkman and Goldwin Smith (1823–1910). The seven epic volumes of Parkman's *France and England in North America* (1865–92) completely dominated the interpretation of the old régime, especially among English-speaking Canadians, throughout the period under discussion and for a long time afterwards. Parkman laboured under almost incredible physical and mental handicaps, but his research was most carefully done and his volumes were beautifully written in an elaborate and heroic style. He proved definitively that Canadian history need be neither provincial nor dull. It is possible even that the erudition and elegance of the great Bostonian discouraged some able Canadian scholars from working in an area where their efforts might be compared or might seem redundant; but he was a boon to the journalists and popular historians who plundered his magnificent volumes without restraint.

Yet the interpretation was strictly Whiggish. To Parkman, the machinations of rival imperialisms represented simply the struggle between "Anglo-Saxon Protestant liberty—which was the hallmark of Progress—and French Roman Catholic absolutism." As he put it in the final volume of the series: "This war was the strife of a united and concentrated few against a divided and discordant many. It was the strife, too, of the past against the future; of the old against the new; of moral and intellectual torpor against moral and intellectual life; of barren absolutism against a liberty, crude, incoherent, and chaotic, yet full of prolific vitality." Within this frame of reference, as Professor Eccles has pointed out, "Parkman regarded the final war not as a war of conquest, but as a war of liberation. The Canadians were not conquered, they were finally liberated from Absolutism." "A happier calamity never befell a people," wrote Parkman in the concluding paragraph of *The Old Régime in Canada*, "than the conquest of Canada by the British arms."

To this general interpretation of Canadian history, Goldwin Smith also lent his extraordinary talents and international reputation. From 1858 to 1866 he had been Regius Professor of Modern History at Oxford and in 1868 he crossed the Atlantic to become Professor of English History at Cornell. In 1871 he settled in Toronto where he took a lively interest in Canadian political and intellectual life. He had no higher opinion than Parkman of the Indians, the French Canadians, Roman Catholics or the old régime and to this considerable catalogue he added a very real prejudice against the Irish.

But from this distance, Goldwin Smith is most interesting because of his ideas on, to use the title of one of his famous papers, "The Political Destiny of Canada." In a series of lectures and periodical articles, he took the view that Canada was merely "a political expression," "that the movement in favour of Canadian nationality had only political motives on its side." "The Union of the Canadian Provinces resembles, as a wit said in the [Confederation] debate," he stated in his *Reminiscences* (1911), "not that of a bundle of rods, gaining strength by their union, to which a confederationist had complacently compared it, but that of seven fishing-rods tied together by the ends." It was impossible to write even a decent history of the country, he wrote to Professor George MacKinnon Wrong (1860–1948), because of "the difficulty of running the histories of several Provinces abreast and imparting anything like unity to the whole." For reasons "geographical, racial, social, and commercial," he became convinced of Canada's "continental" destiny much to the annoyance of the Canadian nationalists and to the abhorrence of those infected with the enthusiasm for Imperial Federation. He felt Canada had nothing to fear from the United States. As he argued in an important essay, "The Schism in the Anglo-Saxon Race" (1887), "If political union ever takes place between the United States and Canada, it will not be because the people of the United States are disposed to aggression upon Canadian independence, of which there is no thought in any American breast, nor because the impediments to commercial intercourse and to the free interchange of commercial services will have been removed, but because in blood and character, language, religion, institutions, laws and interests, the two portions of the Anglo-Saxon race on this continent are one people."

In 1891, with the question of unrestricted reciprocity before the electorate, Goldwin Smith summarized his position in *Canada and the Canadian Question*. Opinionated and brilliantly written, it is very probably the most exciting interpretative treatment of Canadian development ever written. Although he recognized the operation of other factors, *Canada and the Canadian Question* was the first extensive environmentalist interpretation of Canadian development by a historian.

It should be pointed out, however, that Alexander Monro (1813–1896) had reached the same position in *The United States and the Dominion of Canada: Their Future* which had appeared in 1879. Like Smith, Monro was born in Britain; but he came to New Brunswick as a youth. He was a surveyor and an amateur statistician, and his approach was statistical rather than developmental. Earlier he had published *New Brunswick; with a Brief Outline of Nova Scotia, and Prince Edward Island: Their History, Civil Divisions, Geography, and Productions* (1855), *Statistics of British North America* (1862), and *History, Geography and Statistics of British North America* (1864). These books have more affinities with the old statistical accounts than with history as it was being written at the time. But, on the basis of this information, and having seen a good deal of the country as a land surveyor, he decided that Canada did not possess an independent national destiny. It was his opinion "that the United States and Dominion of Canada belong as it were to each other—that they are the geographical and commercial complement of each other. . . ." He thought that it was "necessary that the branches of the Anglo Saxon and other families in North America, should unite with each other. . . ."

VII

Fashions in history do not change overnight. But by the first decade of the twentieth century, the history which had been written for the preceding half-century seemed to many people inadequate. It was the kind of history which had taken shape with Christie, McMullen, and Murdoch and had culminated in the achievements of Dent, Kingsford and "The Makers of Canada" series. The change which now took place was not so much one of basic values, but rather one of technique. The writing of history became less the hobby of journalists and lawyers and increasingly the province of professional historians, scholars trained in the graduate schools of the United States or Europe and employed as teachers—at one level or another—or as archivists. Although many wrote history who were not professionally trained, they were influenced by the standards and techniques which were being introduced and against which their own efforts were judged.

There were notable changes in emphasis. In the first place, the professional historians insisted on greater accuracy. In the first volume of the *Review of Historical Publications Relating to Canada* (1897), covering publications for 1895 and 1896, E. A. Cruikshank (1853–1939) tore into the seventh volume of Kingsford's *History*, complaining particularly of the "many errors and inaccuracies" and pointing them out much to the annoyance of the historian's friends and admirers. Secondly, they deprecated what the English historian J. R. Green had called "drum and trumpet history" and insisted that history must describe more accurately the development of the total experience of the community. "In my opinion," wrote Robert Glasgow to Professor Adam Shortt, "there should be a severe penalty imposed upon any writer in this day, who would begin his history of Canada with a mention of Columbus or the Northwest passage." "It never occurred to me before," wrote Laurier's future biographer, O. D. Skelton (1878–1941), to Professor Shortt, "how completely and absolutely & inexcusably wanting all the histories of Canada are on the side of trade & commerce & industrial life generally." Professor Shortt suggested to the Canadian Education Association "the desirability of simplifying the treatment and broadening the scope and subject matter of elementary histories, thus getting into touch with primary elements in the life and growth of our social and economic life, from the first breaking into the wilderness to the present day structure of our cities. This involves tracing the gradual stages in linking up the life and interests of the people throughout the Dominion. Such a field of treatment and line of approach would put the facts of history in touch with the life of the children in any part of the Dominion, and prepare their minds for a more intelligent study of constitutional issues on these primary foundations."

In the attempt to find out what actually happened in so many areas of human development and under pressure resulting from the conviction that history, particularly Canadian history, was an essential subject in the educational programme of a democratic society, some historians were quite prepared to surrender any claims which history might possess to be considered as a branch of *belles-lettres*. Professor W. F. Ganong (1864–1941), who was a biologist as well as a historian, told the Royal Society of Canada in his paper "A Plan for a General History of the Province of New Brunswick," read in 1895: "Every man tends to write that kind of book which he likes best to read. A history of mine would be coldly scientific, precise, classified, complete; but it would lack the life and form and colour which should distinguish a history for the people." But most historians were reluctant to abandon the ancient claims of their craft. Some of the professional historians such as Professor G. M. Wrong in his *A Canadian Manor and Its Seigneurs:*

The Story of A Hundred Years, 1761–1861 (1908), *The Rise and Fall of New France* (2 vols., 1928), and *Canada and the American Revolution: The Disruption of the First British Empire* (1935), combined the highest professional standards with literary excellence.

In any case, the collection of books and documents made research very much easier and a good deal more productive. It is easy to forget the difficulties under which the earlier historians laboured. When Charles Lindsey reviewed Kingsford's *Bibliography* in *The Week* (December 9, 1892), he was able to add "several" titles to the list from his own library. In 1851, the government of the Province of Canada sent G. B. Faribault (1789–1866) to France to obtain copies of documents relating to the old régime. In 1857, T. B. Akins (1809–1891), who had helped Murdoch with his *History*, was appointed Commissioner of Public Records by the Province of Nova Scotia and in 1865 the government provided money for the publication of a volume of documents of "moderate size."

But the great break-through came with the systematic organization of a federal collection which was begun in 1872. Under the direction of Douglas Brymner (1823–1902) and his very able successor Arthur Doughty (1860–1936), a most extensive collection of invaluable documents was acquired and put in order, an undertaking which Professor Chester Martin (1882–1958) described as "perhaps the most impressive achievement for historical scholarship in this country." Beginning in 1872, as supplements to the reports of the Minister of Agriculture, the Archives Branch issued an annual *Report* (1872–1905), which summarized sections of the growing collection. Under Doughty's direction, the Archives ceased, for a time, to issue calendars and began, in 1907, to issue documents starting with Shortt and Doughty's *Documents Relating to the Constitutional History of Canada*. In 1917 the federal Government set up the Historical Documents Publication Board which was soon known as the Board of Historical Publications. ". . . the object aimed at by the Board," Adam Shortt wrote to Sir Robert Borden, "is to put at the immediate and convenient service of all persons in any way interested in Canadian History, the most essential documents bearing on the development of the vital interest of the Canadian people."

In 1903 the Province of Ontario established a Bureau of Archives and from the beginning issued an annual *Report* (1903–1933) in which a great number of documents were printed. In 1908 the Province of British Columbia appointed a historian, R. E. Gosnell, as archivist. He was joint author, with R. H. Coats, of *Sir James Douglas* (1908) for "The Makers of Canada" series and wrote, with his successor E. O. S. Scholefield (1875–1919), *A History of British Columbia* (2 parts, 1913).

In the dissemination of documents several provincial and local historical societies did excellent work. From time to time, the venerable Quebec Literary and Historical Society, founded by Lord Dalhousie in 1824, had published important documents. Both papers and documents were printed in the *Collections of the Nova Scotia Historical Society* which started to appear in 1878. In 1899, the Ontario Historical Society, previously known as the Pioneer and Historical Association, began to issue its valuable *Papers and Records* (1899–1946). Some of the local historical societies published important holdings. Under the direction of the Lundy's Lane Historical Society, Lieutenant-Colonel E. A. Cruikshank edited *The Documentary History of the Campaigns upon the Niagara Frontier* (1896–1908), a collection of documents relating to the War of 1812, which ran to nine volumes. The London and Middlesex Historical Society made the best of the William Proudfoot papers available.

Of all the societies dedicated to the publication of documents, the most distinguished was the Champlain Society. It was organized on May 17, 1905, in the board room of the Canadian Bank of Commerce in Toronto. The moving spirit and first president of the Society was Byron Edmund Walker (1848–1924), general manager of the Bank. James Bain (1842–1908), librarian of the Toronto Public Library and indefatigable collector of Canadiana, was the treasurer. The secretaries were Professor G. M. Wrong of the University of Toronto and Professor Charles William Colby (1867–1955) of McGill University. "In the past, while much has been done by local societies for local history," said a letter announcing the existence of the Society, "there has been no society on the lines of such organizations as the Surtees Society, the Hakluyt Society, the Prince Society, etc., which has devoted itself to the task of publishing or republishing important material relating to Canada's history as a whole. The consequence has been that this material has received more attention in the United States than in Canada." "The Society was not to be conducted for profit," wrote W. S. Wallace in 1937 (he was then an honorary secretary), "but was to undertake the publication of rare books or unpublished materials relating to Canada that the ordinary commercial publisher would not accept for publication; and it was understood that its volumes would be published in a form attractive to book-lovers and would be edited by competent scholars, with the necessary critical apparatus." "The books . . . are splendid examples of book making and the historical criticism is the best Canada can afford," Walker wrote to Lord Beaverbrook. They were printed in the United Kingdom and bound in red buckram which was thought more durable than leather. "It will not do to have the Ballantyne name on the title page," wrote Professor Wrong to W. L. Grant. "We shall possibly get into trouble anyhow for having the volumes printed in Edinburgh rather than in Canada, and we do not wish to obtrude our iniquity upon the public gaze."

At first, membership in the Society was limited to 250 persons, who paid a sustaining fee of $10.00 a year. Later, the membership was extended to 500 and 250 memberships were offered to libraries. It was decided to issue two volumes a year. Considering the fee and the fact that each edition was a limited edition, a membership was thought to be an excellent investment— "very valuable from a mere money point of view," as the president put it to an official of the National Trust Company.

As a beginning, the Society brought out the edition (3 vols., 1907–14) of Lescarbot's *History of New France* under the direction of W. L. Grant and H. P. Biggar (1872–1938) and W. F. Ganong's edition of Nicolas Denys's *The Description and Natural History of the Coasts of North America* (1908). In 1908, the Society decided to bring out a definitive edition of *The Works of Samuel de Champlain*, which ran to six volumes (1922–36) and was edited by H. P. Biggar. Other early volumes were: W. B. Munro (1875–1957), *Documents Relating to the Seigniorial Tenure in Canada, 1598–1854* (1908); Lieutenant-Colonel William C. H. Wood (1864–1947), *The Logs of the Conquest of Canada* (1909); and J. B. Tyrrell (1858–1957), an edition of Samuel Hearne's *A Journey from Prince of Wales's Fort, in Hudson's Bay, to the Northern Ocean* (1911). In 1916, Tyrrell edited David Thompson's very valuable and very scarce *Narrative of his Explorations in Western North America 1784–1812* (1916).

In the same years, other important documents were made available. In a magnificent effort, of which the founders of the Champlain Society were all too aware, R. G. Thwaites (1853–1913), secretary of the State Historical Society of Wisconsin, issued a scholarly edition of *The Jesuit Relations and Allied Documents 1610–1791* in 73 volumes (1896–1901). Both the original documents and an English translation were printed. Also significant were the collections compiled by J. G. Hodgins (1821–1912), Deputy Minister of Education for Ontario, 1876 to 1889, and "historiographer" to the department until his death. He published a *Documentary History of Education in Upper Canada from the Passing of the Constitutional Act of 1791 to the Close of the Reverend Doctor Ryerson's Administration of the Education Department in 1876* (28 vols., 1894–1910); *Historical and Other Papers and Documents Illustrative of the Educational System of Ontario 1792–1853* (5 vols., 1911–12) and *The Establishment of Schools and Colleges in Ontario 1792–1910* (3 vols., 1910).

Another phenomenon which greatly assisted the professional historians was the proliferation of local histories in the period following Confederation. Indeed, in 1929, Dr. A. R. M. Lower (b. 1889) complained that local histories "are as the sand on the sea shore." This was the golden age of local history in Canada. The community was young enough to remember its early experiences with some precision and old enough to contemplate them with a certain nostalgia. It is true that the local historians seldom possessed the larger picture; but they were generally accurate. They knew what they were writing about and they preserved a vast amount of information which otherwise would most certainly have been lost. In fact, at this distance, their work is frequently more useful than that of their more ambitious and theoretical contemporaries. It is impossible to mention all the good and useful work done. Only a few books, typical of the better efforts, can be listed.

One of the more important of the earlier writers was James MacPherson Le Moine (1825–1912). Antiquarian, sportsman, ornithologist, he wrote, in both French and English, a series of books and papers mostly about the St. Lawrence River and Quebec City. Alexander Ross (1783–1856), fur-trader and adventurer, produced a valuable history of *The Red River Settlement* (1856). Edward Ermatinger (1797–1876) wrote a *Life of Colonel Talbot, and the Talbot Settlement* (1859) and those remarkable sisters Kathleen (d. 1931) and Robina (d. 1918) Lizars put down the legend of "Tiger" Dunlop in *In the Days of the Canada Company* (1896). Every county had to have its history written up. Good ones include the Reverend James Croil (1821–1916), *Dundas; or, A Sketch of Canadian History, and More Particularly of the County of Dundas* (1861); the Reverend George Patterson (1824–1897), *A History of the County of Pictou* (1877); Robert Sellar (1841–1919), *The History of the County of Huntingdon and of the Seigniories of Chateaugay and Beauharnois* (1888), and Norman Robertson (1845–1936), *The History of the County of Bruce and of the Minor Municipalities Therein* (1906), which was issued under the auspices of the Bruce County Historical Society. There were important regional histories such as those by A. G. Morice (1859–1938), *The History of the Northern Interior of British Columbia, Formerly New Caledonia* (1904) and W. G. Gosling (1863–1930), *Labrador: Its Discovery, Exploration, and Development* (1910). Municipal histories flourished. Among the better are books by Dr. Thomas W. Poole (1831?–1905), *A Sketch of the Early Settlement and Subsequent Progress of the Town of Peterborough* (1867); the Reverend Henry Scadding (1813–1901), *Toronto of Old* (1873); T. B. Akins, *History of Halifax City* (1895) and Agnes M. Machar (1837–1927), *The Story of Old Kingston* (1908).

The fact is that this was a period rich in the production of histories of all kinds and on all subjects. William Peter Smith (dates ?) wrote a humorous history of Canada called *The Victoria Diamond Jubilee History of Canada* (Toronto, 1897), which is very good. Among other things, he poked fun at the frantic industry of J. Castell Hopkins and the *Review of Historical Publications Relating to Canada*, assailing its pretensions and pointing out the imprecision of its language. Denominational histories flourished. Probably the best was by the Reverend William Gregg (1817–1909), *History of the Presbyterian Church in the Dominion of Canada from the Earliest Times to 1834* (1885). But it is impossible to leave out the Reverend John Carroll (1809–1884), *Case and His Cotemporaries; or, The Canadian Itinerant's Memorial:*

Consisting of a Biographical History of Methodism in Canada (5 vols., 1867–77). Also impressive is Father A. G. Morice's *History of the Catholic Church in Western Canada from Lake Superior to the Pacific (1659–1895)* (2 vols., 1910).

A related form of writing, which, like local history, was sometimes heavily genealogical, were the ethnic histories which flourished in the same period. They were a reflection, in part, of a consciousness of race—racial origins, differences, potentialities and disasters—a feeling which became increasingly intense towards the end of the century. One of the earliest and best known of these works is *The Irishman in Canada* (1877), by Nicholas Flood Davin (1843–1901). Born in Ireland, he came to Canada in 1872 where he was both a lawyer and a journalist. In 1887 he was elected Conservative member for West Assiniboia in the House of Commons. Davin identified strongly with the national aspirations of his adopted country. His *History* is developmental in approach, indicating at each stage what the Irish contributed to the growth and well-being of the community. He was conscious of the vituperations of Goldwin Smith and wanted to "raise the self-respect of every person of Irish blood in Canada." He was a real stylist and his books are all vigorously written.

The same house, Maclear of Toronto, also published, by William J. Rattray (1835–1883), *The Scot in British North America* in four volumes (1880–84). The work is divided into five sections: The Scot at Home; The Scot across the Sea; The Scot in Public Life; The Scot in Professional Life; and The Scot in the North-West. The tone is intensely nationalistic. Rattray took the position that "attachment to the land from which we or our fathers came is not only compatible with intense devotion to the highest interests of the country where we dwell, but is a necessary condition of its birth, its growth and its fervour. The dutiful son, the affectionate husband and father, will usually be the best and most patriotic subject or citizen; and he will love Canada best who draws his love of country in copious draughts from the old fountain-head across the sea." Rattray was an able journalist, but his books on the Scot were written in a period of declining health. The final volume was completed by "another hand" and was published posthumously. His real interest was in problems of religion and philosophy. His best work is scattered in his regular contributions to the Toronto *Mail*, with which he was connected as an editor, and in his articles published in the *Canadian Monthly* (1872–78).

The best books in this genre are the two volumes of *The Scotsman in Canada* published by Musson in 1911. The volume on eastern Canada was done by the poet W. Wilfred Campbell (1861–1918) and the one on the west by George Bryce. This was Campbell's only significant effort in the field of historical writing. It was "a labour of love" and the research was very carefully done. He begins with a history of the significant Scottish settlements in eastern Canada and then attempts a broad description of the relationship and the contribution of Scottish people to various areas of Canadian life. Dr. Bryce's book is also an interesting and scholarly one. He was able to draw upon his considerable knowledge of the area as already demonstrated in *The Remarkable History of the Hudson's Bay Company* (1900) and *Mackenzie, Selkirk, Simpson* (1905), which he had done for "The Makers of Canada" series.

There were, of course, histories of other groups in the community which did not share a common ethnic background, but rather a particular experience. A whole literature, for example, grew up around the United Empire Loyalists. The historians contributed abundantly to the revival of interest in the Loyalists which marked the last quarter of the century particularly in Ontario. Here the pioneer work, which supplied much of the information, was by William Canniff (1830–1910), the excellent and carefully researched *History of the Settlement of Upper Canada, (Ontario), with special reference to the Bay of Quinté* (1869). The most extensive treatment of the whole subject by a Canadian was in two ponderous volumes by Egerton Ryerson (1803–1882), *The Loyalists of America and Their Times: From 1620 to 1816* (1880). The first volume carries the Thirteen Colonies down to the Declaration of Independence; the second deals with the Revolutionary War, the migration, the settlements, and the problem of claims. The second volume concludes with a blow by blow account of the War of 1812. "The war between Great Britain and the United States, from 1812 to 1815," wrote Ryerson by way of introduction, "furnishes the strongest example of the present century, or of any age or country, of the attachment of a people to their mother country, and of their determination, at whatever sacrifice and against whatever disparity, to maintain the national life of their connection with it. The true spirit of *the Loyalists of America* was never exhibited with greater force and brilliancy than during the war of 1812–1815." Another valuable local history which was inspired by the Loyalist revival and in turn contributed a good deal of information to it, was by Judge J. F. Pringle (1816–1901), *Lunenburgh or the Old Eastern District, its Settlement and Early Progress: With Personal Recollections of the Town of Cornwall*, which appeared in 1890.

Not only was more information available in these years, but there would shortly be more scholars as well. This resulted largely from the recognition of history as a subject of instruction in the Canadian universities and the creation, at a somewhat later date, of chairs and departments of history. In 1895, the chair of history and English literature at the University of Toronto was divided and G. M. Wrong became the first full-time professor of history. In the same year, Dr. C. W. Colby, who had taken his Ph.D. at Harvard (1890), was appointed Kingsford Professor of History in McGill University. Most of these teachers wrote Canadian history, but this does not mean that Canadian history had achieved a place in the curriculum. As Professor Preston has pointed out: "Soon after Wilson began teaching at Toronto in 1853, the Vice-Chancellor called his department 'really ridiculous' because he only taught the history of Egypt to Cleopatra, of Spain to Ferdinand and Isabella, and of England to Henry VII. Ridiculous or not, this was the prevailing pattern of that time." Although J. B. A. Ferland (1805–1865) had been teaching Canadian history at Laval as early as 1854, no lectures were given in Canadian history in an English-speaking Canadian university until the last decade of the nineteenth century. In 1895 Adam Shortt, of the department of political science, gave the first lectures in Canadian history at Queen's University. In 1898, Professor G. M. Wrong indicated that his department would emphasize the history of England, the United States, and Canada. The trend is clear, but, generally speaking, not much Canadian history was taught in the universities in the period under discussion.

Undoubtedly the most important event in the development of the professional study of history in Canada was the appointment of George MacKinnon Wrong. Born in Elgin County, Canada West, he was educated at University College and Wycliffe College in the University of Toronto. In 1883, he was ordained a priest of the Church of England. From 1883 to 1892 he taught at Wycliffe College and from 1892 to 1894 he was lecturer in history at the University of Toronto. Two years after his appointment as professor, in 1897, he brought out, at his own expense, the first volume of the *Review of Historical Publications Relating to Canada* (1897–1919) in which the growing literature on Canadian history was judged by the standards of the emerging profession. Although Wrong was, in the words of Lionel Curtis, "the kindest man I know," the *Review* could be otherwise. "No hesitation has been shown in pointing out defects," wrote the editor in a preface to the first volume. In fact the reviews were sometimes brutal. E. A. Cruikshank largely demolished Kingsford's reputation and J. G. Bourinot wrote of Joseph Pope's *Confederation: Being a Series of Hitherto Unpublished Documents bearing on the British North America Act* (1895): "Out of the three hundred pages of this volume there are not a dozen which can be fairly considered useful or important." Some readers were disturbed at such ungentlemanly candour, but Professor W. J. Ashley (1860–1927), formerly professor of political economy and constitutional history in the University of Toronto, wrote from Harvard: "I am glad you have not shirked your duty to Kingsford. And you have said something that needed saying about Parkman, whom I cannot regard as a great historian. . . . The philosophy in the *Old Régime* has always seemed to me identical with the narrow bourgeois Liberalism of the '60s & '70s."

The contributors to the *Review* were "free to sign their names or not as they prefer" and the reviews were long enough to give an accurate impression of the book and for the reviewer to develop an idea or two of his own. Starting with the second volume (1898), H. H. Langton shared the editorial duties and the *Review* was organized in five sections, which in themselves indicate the more inclusive definition of the subject which now obtained: Canada's Relations to the Empire; The History of Canada; Provincial and Local History; Geography, Economics and Statistics; and Law, Education and Bibliography. Later, an additional section, Archaeology, Ethnology and Folk-Lore, was added. Both books and articles were noticed. In 1920, the *Review* was reconstituted as a quarterly, the *Canadian Historical Review* (1920–   ) containing both scholarly articles and critical reviews.

In his own books, of which *The Crusade of MCCCLXXXIII, known as that of the Bishop of Norwich* (1892) was the first, Wrong combined the highest professional standards with a pleasant narrative style. As in his lectures, his main purpose was to be "interesting." Most of his work, in one way or another, was a contribution to an examination of the Imperial connection. When he sent André Siegfried's *Le Canada: les deux races* (1906) to Professor W. L. Grant for the *Review*, he suggested, "Dwell as much as you can on his view of Canada's relations to Great Britain. I want to keep that subject before the public mind, in view of the coming Colonial Conference. We must, in some way, get control of our foreign affairs—that Alaska business has sunk deep into the hearts of the Canadian people." He regretted that "Canada has the nondescript title of 'Dominion' instead of being a kingdom" as Sir John A. Macdonald had intended. But he was critical of the position taken by J. S. Ewart (1849–1933) in his *The Kingdom of Canada . . . and other Essays* (1908). "With great skill and ingenuity the author works up an elaborate case against Great Britain. She has checked Canada unduly in the past; she is checking her unduly still, and resisting her assertion of the privileges of the grown-up. Canada has a long list of grievances. Mr. Ewart has read widely, not, one fears, so much to see his subject as a whole, but to make points against Great Britain." But much as Wrong loved English values and society, he realized increasingly that Canada was essentially different from the United Kindom. "The Canadians are becoming indeed a people quite different from the English," he wrote in *The Nineteenth Century* (LXVI, 1909). "The saying of Horace, now trite enough, *coelum non animum mutant, qui trans mare currunt*, is, in this relation, profoundly untrue . . . environment counts for something." On the other hand, he felt that "Canada is not becoming Americanized, if this means that she is drawing closer politically to the United States. On the contrary, just because she has a growing confidence in her own self, she is daily growing farther away from any thought of political union with that country."

Year after year, the *Review of Historical Publications Relating to Canada* chronicled and criticized new achievements in the field of Canadian history.

It can only be described as a kind of creative and scholarly explosion and it culminated in two great co-operative undertakings, *The Chronicles of Canada* (32 vols., Toronto 1914–1916), edited by Professor Wrong and H. H. Langton, and *Canada and Its Provinces: A History of the Canadian People and Their Institutions by One Hundred Associates* (23 vols., Toronto, 1914–1917) edited by Adam Shortt and A. G. Doughty. The publisher in both cases was Robert Glasgow and the books were printed by T. and A. Constable at the Edinburgh University Press.

Glasgow had been involved in selling "The Makers of Canada" and he was convinced of the considerable potential of the market. He left "facts and historical accuracy" up to the professional scholars, but "as to the organization or construction of the books," he wrote to Professor Wrong, "I have never found anyone who could handle this as well as I can myself. On nearly every manuscript I request the author to reorganize his work to some extent and as he nearly always agrees with me, I have come to believe that I understand this phase of making a book." He was a remarkable man. "I don't know whether you know anything about Glasgow," wrote Professor Wrong to J. S. Willison. "He is a coming man in the publishing world, with good ideas, and a high integrity that will always make him respected. He knows how to sell books and to make them pay." In the production of these books, *The Chronicles* and *Canada and Its Provinces*, he worked day and night. In 1918, he moved to the United States, where he brought out *The Chronicles of America* series edited by Professor Allen Johnson (1870–1931), (50 vols., New Haven, 1918–1921). About this series he wrote to Professor Wrong, who contributed a volume on *The Conquest of New France* (1918), "We are getting some great books, and everyone says that the series is going to have great value in cementing the entente of the English-speaking peoples. If so, and I think it is so, this will ease my conscience for not doing direct work for the war." In fact, he gave his life in this cause. Exhausted, he died of a heart attack on April 5, 1922, at the age of 47. He was the greatest publisher in the history of historical writing in Canada.

The Chronicles of Canada were written for the general reader; but most of them were written by professional scholars. Professor Stephen Leacock wrote three volumes and O. D. Skelton two. W. S. Wallace did a revisionist volume on *The Family Compact* (1915); he also wrote the one on *The 'Patriotes' of '37* (1916) although it appeared under the signature of A. D. DeCelles. Glasgow did not think the book would sell under the real author's name in the province of Quebec. A. G. Doughty did *The Acadian Exiles* (1916) and Professor W. B. Munro, *The Seigneurs of Old Canada* (1915). Glasgow believed that the "portraits of men" were "the best thing in history" and a number of biographies were included. Professor C. W. Colby did sketches of Champlain (1915) and Frontenac (1915) and W. L. Grant wrote *The*

Tribune of Nova Scotia: A Chronicle of Joseph Howe (1915). William C. H. Wood, author of *The Fight for Canada* (1904), did six volumes of military history. The books were illustrated and most attractively printed and bound.

But the monument to the professional study of history was *Canada and Its Provinces*. It, too, was the product of "Glasgow's fertile brain." The idea was to cover all the country's history—political and constitutional, economic and social, intellectual and ecclesiastical. The project was intimidating in its scope. "I haven't yet made up my mind about that big history plan," wrote Professor O. D. Skelton to Adam Shortt, "it seems over ambitious." But the publisher and the editors brought the combined resources of the profession to bear on the problem. "The range of facts is so wide and the topics so various and complex," explained the editors, "that no one author could possibly compass them. The work, therefore, has been apportioned among many writers each of whom has some special sympathy and aptitude for the topic with which he deals." The approach was developmental, topical, and regional; the subject was divided into twelve "main divisions": I, New France, 1534–1760; II, British Dominion, 1760–1840; III, The United Canada, 1840–1867; IV, The Dominion: Political Evolution; V, The Dominion: Industrial Expansion; VI, The Dominion: Missions, Arts and Letters; VII, The Atlantic Provinces; VIII, The Province of Quebec; IX, The Province of Ontario; X, The Prairie Provinces; XI, The Pacific Province; XII, Documentary Notes, General Index. Behind the careful scholarship stood an insistent patriotism. ". . . a sound knowledge of Canada as a whole, of its history, traditions and standards of life, should be diffused among its citizens, and especially among the immigrants . . . ," wrote the editors in the introduction to the first volume, ". . . mere wealth-making is not the chief essential of citizenship. Good citizenship grows out of a patriotic interest in the institutions of one's country and a sympathy with the people who dwell there."

The real editor of *Canada and Its Provinces* was Adam Shortt. He also wrote more of it than any other contributor. Born near London, Ontario, he was educated at Queen's University and in the universities of Glasgow and Edinburgh. In 1885, he returned to Queen's as an assistant in the department of philosophy and, in 1891, he was appointed Sir John A. Macdonald Professor of Political Science. He was also the University librarian. Although he possessed a rather low opinion of most politicians, he went to Ottawa in 1908 to become Canada's first Civil Service Commissioner. He greatly admired Lord Acton whom he regarded "as having much the truest conception of history among modern writers" and possessed always a profound respect and persistent enthusiasm for original sources. Much of his early work was concerned with the early economic history of the country and with the nature and influence of the frontier, studies which did not escape the notice of Frederick Jackson Turner. Between 1896 and 1906, he published thirty-two articles on the history of Canadian banking in the *Journal of the Canadian Banker's Association,* and in 1898 a series of these papers came out under the title, *The Early History of Canadian Banking.* "I think most of us appreciate the work which you have done for Canadian economics," wrote Harold Adams Innis (1894–1952), "and I have thought at sometime in the near future of writing an appraisal of your position as the founder of the subject."

The professional historians, like their colleagues of the older school, gave what seems like an exorbitant amount of attention to the seventeenth and eighteenth centuries. But, in combination with such American historians as Parkman, H. L. Osgood (1855–1918), R. G. Thwaites, C. M. Andrews (1863–1943) and G. L. Beer (1872–1920), to mention only the most distinguished, they did a good deal to recover the unity of North Atlantic experience and civilization. From the distance of the early twentieth century and fortified, as they were, with a substantial dose of Anglo-Saxon racism, the disruption of the First British Empire seemed to them more like an unfortunate incident than a cataclysmic event. It had been unpleasant but not fatal to British interests, while in the New World it signalled the birth of not one but two communities—the American republic and English-speaking British North America. In this era of good feeling all parties to the imperial altercation of the eighteenth century looked like winners—all, that is, except the French. And even France had her revenge in the Revolutionary War. But not so the French colony on the St. Lawrence. To most English-speaking historians, French Canada was an unfortunate remnant unredeemed by time. Very few could identify with its history or its aspirations. "Of course Parkman has done the early period," wrote A. H. U. Colquhoun (1861–1936) to Professor Wrong, "but we Canadians of the 20th century cannot live on a past that is really not our own. To me there is much to inspire in all the chief episodes of our history since 1759. . . ." The *Review of Historical Publications Relating to Canada* had to remind G. T. Denison that Canadian history did not begin, as he had assumed, with the arrival of the United Empire Loyalists. This is the kind of thing one would expect from Colonel Denison, but it was a notion widely held in the English-speaking community. The Canadian historians writing in English contributed brilliantly to the integration of the North Atlantic community, but they contributed little to the understanding of the internal cultural dilemma.

Although many of these historians deplored what Goldwin Smith called "the schism in the Anglo-Saxon race," they did not possess any simple answers as to how this unfortunate condition might be healed. The professional historians, for the most part, condemned the Imperial Federation movement or any other system for the political or military integration of the Empire. Many were simply expressing what O. D. Skelton called his "incurable Canadianism." But for most their opposition was more profoundly and rationally based. Discussing his work on the American Revolution with Adam Shortt, Professor Wrong wrote: "What I have feared is blaming the people in England. Their benevolent intentions cannot be doubted and they certainly took abundant pains to find the facts. What they lacked was insight. This lack of insight only shows that people on one side of an ocean can't govern, because they can't understand, the people on the other side of the ocean living in a wholly different environment." "If we are true to ourselves in a broad-minded way we shall not injure the Empire," wrote Shortt to J. S. Willison in 1904. But Imperial Federation, he told E. A. Peacock, would be like pasting "millstones to each others necks."

VIII

As was pointed out, in the nineteenth century the nation state or the interaction of nation states was the usual unit of historical study and this was doubly so in Canada. Canadians were preoccupied with building a nation and most Canadian historians felt that they—if anyone—had something to contribute in the quest for a national identity. Very few overcame the national fixation and fewer still contributed anything of much significance to the literature or the knowledge of the larger world.

Probably the most successful of these scholars was Alpheus Todd (1821–1884) and he was more a political scientist than a historian. His career, as the English historian Spencer Walpole intimated in the preface to the third edition of his *Parliamentary Government in England*, was a paradigm of Victorian self-help. Born in England, he came to Canada with his family when yet a boy. He went to work as a librarian to the Legislative Assembly of Upper Canada and developed an "addiction to parliamentary studies." Although self-educated, he produced, at the age of nineteen, *The Practice and Privileges of the Two Houses of Parliament*, a book of over three hundred pages, which he described as "a Manual of Parliamentary Practice for the use of the Legislature." In 1854 he became the librarian of the Legislative Assembly of Canada and in 1870 he took charge of the Parliamentary Library in Ottawa. At the time of Confederation, he published *On Parliamentary Government in England: Its Origin, Development, and Practical Operation* (2 vols., 1867, 1869), an elaborate discussion of the British constitution, a system of government "so often admired, but never successfully imitated." "There is nowhere to be found," he stated in the preface to the first edition, "a practical treatment of the questions involved in the mutual relations between the Crown and Parliament, or any adequate account of the growth, development, and present functions of the Cabinet Council." He felt that "the great and increasing defect in all parliamentary governments, whether provincial or imperial, is the weakness of executive authority" and insisted that a "political system based on the monarchical principle must concede to the chief ruler something more than mere ceremonial functions." In 1880, he published *Parliamentary Government in the British Colonies*. The work, he admitted, dealt "largely with questions that have arisen out of the working of the new constitution conferred upon Canada in the confederation of the various provinces in 1867"; but he hoped the discussion would be relevant to other British colonies as they moved in the direction of political unification and self-government. In 1881, owing to the intervention of the Governor-General, he was made a C.M.G., but many felt that he did not receive sufficient recognition for his contributions to the study of British institutions. It was on the subject of Todd's deserts that Kingsford, who admittedly was irascible, remarked in connection with the American revolution: "The real grievance was not the Stamp Act, and all the misrepresentation which has been written about the tyranny of the home government. It was the misapprehension and the failure to do justice to the colonial intellect which estranged men like Jefferson, Samuel Adams, and Madison, who learned from personal sentiment to entertain an unextinguishable hatred to England."

Another distinguished scholar, who, like Goldwin Smith, did some of his important work in Canada, was Daniel Wilson (1816–1892), professor of history and English literature in University College, Toronto, from 1853 until his death. In addition to a multitude of scholarly papers, he published while in Canada a greatly revised edition of his *Prehistoric Annals of Scotland* (2 vols., 1851), a work of enormous erudition. The book established Wilson as "the pioneer of scientific Scottish archaeology" and was admired so widely that the word "prehistoric," employed for the first time in the edition of 1851, entered the language. It is a curious combination of information and interests —antiquarian and archaeological, historical and anthropological. On coming to Canada, he turned his attention to the North American Indian and in 1862 his *Prehistoric Man, Researches into the Origin of Civilization in the Old and the New World* appeared. Although inferior as a systematic treatise to his *Prehistoric Annals of Scotland*, it, in the words of his biographer H. H. Langton, "laid the foundation of archaeological study in Canada."

There were other important books. Andrew Bell (1838–1866), who translated Garneau into English and took so many liberties with the text that it is very properly known as "Bell's Garneau" (1860), earlier published *Historical Sketches of Feudalism, British and Continental, with Numerous Notices of the Doings of the Feudalry in All Ages and Countries* (1852). Thomas D'Arcy McGee (1825–1868) produced *A Popular History of Ireland: From the Earliest Period to the Emancipation of the Catholics* (2 vols., 1863), which was very well received both in Canada and in the United States. In 1863, the Reverend John McCaul (1807–1886), president of University College, Toronto, published *Britanno-Roman Inscriptions, with Critical Notes,* a book of little literary significance, but a very great scholarly achievement. Also important is the most scholarly of W. H. Withrow's many books, *The Catacombs of Rome and Their Testimony Relative to Primitive Christianity* (1874). Withrow was, in addition to his other talents and achievements, a linguist and he was able to use the results of Continental research. Although scholarly, his book was also polemical. It was written with the conviction that "the testimony of the Catacomb exhibits, more strikingly than any other evidence, the immense contrast between primitive Christianity and modern Romanism. . . ." The work of John Foster Kirk (1824–1904) cannot go unmentioned. Born and educated in the Maritimes, he was for many years private secretary and amanuensis to the great American historian William H. Prescott (1796–1859). At Prescott's suggestion, he undertook a *History of Charles the Bold, Duke of Burgundy* of which two volumes were published in 1864. A third volume appeared in 1872 after he had examined the archives in France and Switzerland and had visited the scene of Charles's defeat. The style is elaborate, even extravagant; but that was the fashion of the day. The *Saturday Review* stated: "Mr. Kirk has produced a work which is quite entitled to take rank with the writings of his two predecessors [Prescott and Motley] with whom he has, both in his merits and his faults, a certain family resemblance."

Books by Canadian historians on non-Canadian subjects did not become much more numerous in the later period under discussion. Colonel George T. Denison (1839–1925), one of the founding members of the Canada First movement, published an impressive *History of Cavalry* (1877), which won a prize offered by the Tsar of Russia. Goldwin Smith wrote three histories of the survey kind: *The United States: An Outline of Political History, 1492–1871* (1893); *The United Kingdom: A Political History* (1899) and *Irish History and the Irish Question* (1905). William Robinson Clark (1829–1912), who was professor of mental and moral philosophy in Trinity College, Toronto, was the author of *Savonarola, His Life and Times* (1890), *The Anglican Reformation* (1897), and *Pascal and the Port Royalists* (1902). James Mavor (1854–1925), Scottish-born professor of political economy in the University of Toronto (1892–1923), published in 1914, *An Economic History of Russia* in two large volumes. "I got the other day a copy of your prodigious work on Russia and was struck with wonder," wrote Sir William Van Horne to the author. "How the devil did you find time to do such a thing?" In fact it was the labour of seventeen years. The first part was based on V. O. Kliuchevski's *History of Russia* and the value of Mavor's work was somewhat reduced by the translation of Kliuchevski's volumes into English (1911–1930). Also important is J. S. Ewart's *The Roots and Causes of the Wars (1914–1918)*, an elaborate revisionist interpretation which appeared in two volumes in 1924.

This has been a chronicle of development and achievement. And yet, in 1932, Professor Chester Martin, writing in *Fifty Years Retrospect*, an anniversary volume put together for the Royal Society of Canada, said "Sir John Bourinot's verdict fifty years ago is still substantially true: 'the history of Canada, as a whole, has yet to be written.' " By this he meant that the ambitions and pretentions of the professional historians had not yet been realized. At the same time, there was a general deterioration in historical writing as literature. In 1926, W. S. Wallace, then editor of the *Canadian Historical Review*, using De Quincey's categories, insisted that the history being written belonged almost exclusively to the "literature of knowledge" rather than to the "literature of power." "One finds it difficult to think of any book published by a graduate student in British, American or Canadian universities," he wrote, which "the world will not willingly let die." This resulted partly from the choice of subject-matter and partly from attitudes of mind. The rigid constitutionalism, the theoretical environmentalism, the touchy nationalism of the inter-war period were not the stuff of which great history is made. It was not until later, until the English-speaking community in Canada felt threatened, that historical writing in English became what it had always been in French, a literature of survival, and history reclaimed its position as an ornament of Canadian literature and culture.

14. The Growth of Canadian English

M. H. SCARGILL

IT IS IN ITS VOCABULARY that Canadian English is most distinctive; and it is in its varied names that Canadian English is most appealing, something which Canadian authors, such as Pratt in poetry and Hutchison in prose, have not been slow to recognize.

> Ottawa, Toronto, Montreal,
> Wetaskiwin, Pembina, Thrums, St. Paul;
> Skookumchuck, Chilcotin, and Heart's Ease,
> Wintering Hills, Swan Hills, Hills of Peace.

This profusion of colourful names, American Indian, French, Scottish, English, was noticed early by travellers. Writing about the Northwest in *Ocean to Ocean* (1873), almost one hundred years ago, G. M. Grant of Nova Scotia commented that "The name of almost every river, creek, mountain, or district is French or Scotch" (p. 183). And he deplored that "custom of discarding musical, expressive Indian names for ridiculously inappropriate European ones" (p. 31).

But it is not names of places alone that the English language in Canada has borrowed and then made its own. Although, as is the case with American English, the greater part of the vocabulary is shared with British English because it is derived from that source, hundreds of words of various origins have made their way into the Canadian language, either directly or through the United States. New names for new conditions of life, for new flora and fauna, for new peoples, new politics, new weather, all have joined the vocabulary of the New World to that of the Old in Canadian English and given it a vitality and variety that few other languages know.

From the French have come such words as *habitant, voyageur, portage, prairie, gopher, cache, snye*. From native languages have come *shaganappi, pemmican, muskeg, igloo, kayak, manitou, tepee, skookum*, and those numerous "translations" such as *pale face, pipe of peace, bury the hatchet*, and *happy hunting grounds*. From Spanish America, through American English, have come *coyote, stampede, corral, ranch, rodeo, bonanza, chaps, mosey along*. From British English, but with new meanings and in new combinations, and from English dialects have come words like *reeve, Outside, Confederation, York boat, by acclamation, concession, warden, Seaway, separate school, tickle, droke.* And from various languages and peoples come such words as *hoodoos, Doukhobor, Nisei, wiener, cookie, bush,* and *chop suey.*

These borrowings, new uses, and, in some cases, outright coinings (*Splake* from *speckled* and *lake* trout) are found in almost every area of the life and thought of English-speaking Canadians, as the following brief sampling will show. (The parentheses enclose the earliest date for a Canadian use of the words.)

ANIMALS: *caribou* (1672), *carcajou* (1760), *buffalo* (1635), *prairie dog* (1823), *ground hog* (1789), *wolverine* (1743), *loup cervier* (1784), *moose* (1744)
BIRDS: *Acadian owl* (1868), *fool hen* (1760), *whisky jack* (1743), *snow bird* (1749).
FISH: *oolican* (1877), *muskellonge* (1825), *inconnu* (1789), *gaspereau* (1760).
GOVERNMENT: *by acclamation* (1827), *fishing admiral* (1620), *fence viewer* (1793), *hog reeve* (1825), *path master* (1822), *improvement district* (1841), *warden* (as presiding officer of a county council, 1842).
INDIAN LIFE: *Algonquin* (1665), *Huron* (1665), *calumet* (1665), *lacrosse* (1760), *Manitou* (1703), *wampum* (1791), *lodge* (1789).
POLITICS: *Anti-Unionist* (1823), *Clear Grit* (1849), *Radical Reformer* (1833), *Durhamite* (1840), *Family Compact* (1849).
GENERAL: *corduroy bridge* (1824), *Métis* (1816), *arpent* (1703), *sault* (1665), *homestead* (1765) *seigniory* (1703), *York currency* (1799), *Brock copper* (1819), *batture* (a gravel flat in a river, 1815).

It was vocabulary that first caught the attention of early commentators on what was to become Canadian English. Heriot, the "Deputy Post Master General of British North America," in his *Travels through the Canadas* (1807) notes *planters* in Newfoundland: "These are not properly seafaring men and are distinguished by the name of *planters*" (p. 10). He gives us an erroneous derivation of *Quebec* as from the French "Quel bec" (p. 27); and he derives *Eskimaux* from the "Abinaquis language" meaning "an eater of raw flesh" (p. 11). Heriot records *habitant, voyageurs, coureurs de bois, watape* (root fibres), *cahots* (ridges in the snow), *carriole,* and the *King's Posts* (settlements on the northern shores of the St. Lawrence). W. S. Moorsom, an observant English officer, in his *Letters from Nova Scotia* (1830), calls attention (wrongly) to the *freshet*: "This is a word peculiar to America and is expressive of the extraordinary rise of rivers and streams, after either thaws or heavy rains" (p. 185). He also notes *aboiteau* as "a term introduced by the Acadian French" (p. 187); the *loup cervier*, "pronounced Lucifee," he says

(p. 125); the frost "coming out, as it is termed" (p. 165); and a few localisms such as "the marsh frog, the Nova Scotia Nightingale as he is sometimes termed" (p. 163); the "Digby chicken" (p. 254); and "a regular Kentycooker . . . a term used to express a native Nova Scotian of the true breed" (p. 317).

An excellent book on Nova Scotia is T. C. Haliburton's *An Historical and Statistical Account of Nova Scotia* (1829). It contains a most interesting list of names of birds, fish, flowers, with such entries as *Whore's egg, Labrador tea, Indian pipe, Old Wife, Boblincon, Whip Poor Will*. He records *moufle* (II, 392) and *intervale* and *cradle* as "a machine of American invention . . . composed of a scythe, and its handle, with the addition of a few light bars of wood . . ." (II, 365). *Intervale*, he says, "is a term peculiar to America and denotes that portion of land which is composed of the alluvial deposit of large brooks and rivers . . ." (II, 362).

A fascinating book, written about the same time as Captain Moorsom's, describes Upper Canada in the early 1800's through the letters of two families of Irish settlers. *Authentic Letters from Upper Canada* (1833) offers correspondence from the Magraths, who settled near York, and the Radcliffs, who settled in Adelaide. They seem to have been very practical persons, with a real appreciation of all things new, particularly those to do with getting a living. There is much ado about the *Bush*, explained as "the wild forest" (p. 12), the *Bush-road*, the *log-house*, the *clearing*, the *Concession line*, the *maskanonge*, *windrow chopping*, and the *shanty*, described as the "first and most contracted habitation a settler forms" (p. 13). These Irish people had a strong sense of humour, and one letter contains an amusing account of the speech of an Irish servant (invented for the purpose, but doubtless typical), who talks of *maypole sugar*, the *squawl* (squaw), *porpus* (papoose), and of *bumpkin pie*.

Mrs. Susanna Moodie, writing in *Roughing It in the Bush* (1854), is a rather different commentator, not at all happy with herself or with her neighbours. She seems to think of the inhabitants of Upper Canada as English (like herself), Yankees (anybody not born in England), and Irish. One gets the impression that what was different she condemned; and she is the first commentator I know of to distinguish (wrongly) a form of speech which she calls "Vulgar Canadian." She describes *pritters* as "Vulgar Canadian for potatoes" (p. 245). "What is a charivari?" asks Mrs. Moodie (p. 288), rather impatiently one gathers. *I guess* and *to hum, fixings* and *sace* (sauce) are "Yankee." It is interesting to note that Mrs. Moodie does not feel it necessary to explain *habitant, corduroy bridge, wigwam, squaw, papoose, wolverine, mocassin, or maskinonge*. But she does give a note on *logging bee, blazing* (trees), and "to make garden, as the Canadians term preparing a few vegetables for the season" (p. 376).

Canadian English has sometimes been unlucky in its commentators. For example, Anna Jameson was in Upper Canada around 1836, when the population was about 375,000. But she was most uninterested in what she saw and heard. "These streams," she writes in *Winter Studies and Summer Rambles in Canada* (1838), "have the names of Thirty Mile Creek, Forty Mile Creek, Twenty Mile Creek, and so on; but wherefore I could not discover" (p. 21). However, she does explain for us *corduroy, cat-a-mountain* (as the "American tiger"), *bush, lumber, cutter, town line, traverse, kinnikinic*, and *wattup* ("split ligaments of the pine-root").

Bonnycastle, in his *Canada and the Canadians in 1846* (1846), notes the Irish influence in pronunciation and gives a number of words which he records as Canadian: "shops or stores as they are universally called in America and Canada" (II, 53); "keeping tavern, as it is called in the backwoods of Canada West" (II, 207); "his lot, for so a property is called in Canada West" (I, 176).

John Bigsby tells his readers in *The Shoe and Canoe* (1850) that "the French Canadian has brought one remarkable custom—the charivari" (I, 34). He defines a *bee* and says that *chop-cabbage* is a "Canadian by-name . . . applied to the peasantry" (I, 176).

By the middle of the nineteenth century, the English language in Canada was so different in vocabulary from British English that a would-be settler, reading the various "immigrant's guides," must have wondered just what kind of country he was going to. If he picked up, as many did, Mrs. Traill's *The Canadian Settlers' Guide* (1855), he would find a bewildering array of new terms, some with an explanation, some without: *the Bush, logging bee, blazed line, ground-hog, chitmunk* (sic), *Indian summer, mowkowks* (birch baskets). And what pictures he must have formed of the *Whisky jack*, the *whip-poor-will*, and the *chickadee*. Mrs. Traill, quoting from her brother, carefully explains *plan-heap, chopper's shanty*, and how to *log* and to *underbrush*. This latter is so vital that it is explained twice. W. Dunlop, in *Statistical Sketches of Upper Canada* (1832), and J. B. Brown, in *Views of Canada and the Colonists* (1846), also writing for settlers, add to the strangeness of the new land with *Indian Reserves, Crown Lands, Huron Tract, bois-brule* (defined as a half-Indian), and *batteau* (or flat-bottomed boat).

In pronunciation, Canadian English has not pursued quite the same line of independent development as it has in vocabulary. In general, it is closer to northern British English than it is to that variety of English cultivated by B.B.C. announcers and called "Received Pronunciation" even though it is received only by a minority. Some of the differences in pronunciation between Canadian English and British Received Pronunciation, such as the Canadian preservation of *r* in words like *card*, the preference for a short vowel in words of the *grass* type, the presence of an almost unrounded vowel in words like *cot*, may be due to the influence of American English. Other differences, or even all, are due to three causes: the fact that many settlers left England for Canada when all dialects of British English were changing and Received Pronunciation had not developed; the presence of many settlers from areas in England where Received Pronunciation is not common; the fact that many settlers brought with them a variety of Irish or Scottish English.

The Irish and Scottish influences on the pronunciation of Canadian English were early noted and often despised, especially the Irish. And such frequent late eighteenth-century and early nineteenth-century English pronunciations as *sarce* (sauce), *darter* (daughter), *deef* (deaf), *arter* (after), *bile* (boil), *git* (get), *wrastle* (wrestle), *critter* (creature), *varmint* (vermin), were often falsely labelled as "Yankee" in origin.

Mrs. Moodie notes as "Irish": "yer too particular intirely; we've no time in the woods to be clane" (p. 402). And Anna Jameson comments on the "Irish" *iligant, nate, clane*. We do not have these ladies' views on Pope's rhyming of *tea* with *obey*. Captain Moorsom, writing of New Glasgow and Arisaig, says, "Gaelic is the language of this part of the country,—I mean it is the tongue which you hear in every cottage" (p. 332). And of Pictou he writes, "Keen-looking fellows . . . discussing in broad Scotch or pure Gaelic the passing topics of the day" (p. 353). *Sarce* or *sace* (sauce) seems to have fascinated all observers, both as a pronunciation and as a dish. In *Authentic Letters from Upper Canada* we read, "*Sace* is everything you could name—potatoes, vegetables, butter, pickles, and sweetmeats—they're all *sace*—only mustard, pepper, and vinegar is not" (p. 135). But pronunciation never attracted from early observers the same amount of attention as did vocabulary.

As population began to spread, thinly it is true, observers seem to have become more and more aware that the English spoken in Canada was by no means identical with that of England and, moreover, that more than one kind of English was spoken in Canada. But it is not until the latter half of the nineteenth century that much attention is paid to regional differences in speech, although the observant Moorsom had noted, in addition to "Gaelic and broad Scotch," instances of distinctive "Lunenburg talk": "Fy don't you make the vimen vork?" (p. 77). And he writes that the "settlers of German extraction throughout Nova Scotia are commonly called *Dutch*, although there are but few to whom that national appelative is strictly appropriate" (p. 306). Much earlier than this, Cartwright's *Labrador Journal* (1792) offers an interesting glossary containing such words as *caplin, flakes* (for drying fish), *loubscouse* (a sea-food dish), *lolly* (soft ice floating in water), *tilt* (a small hut), and *tickle* (a passage between two masses of land).

Students of Canadian English would wish that there had been more observers of the calibre of G. M. Grant, who crossed Canada in 1872 with Sandford Fleming. He had the makings of a true dialect geographer. Writing in *Ocean to Ocean* about the Prairies, he says, "The Saskatoon are [sic] simply what are known in Nova Scotia as Indian pears, and the kinni-kinnick creeper is our squawberry plant" (p. 164). He notes that *scrub pine* is called "cypress" in the West and that in Victoria "the smallest silver piece is what is called a bit" (p. 342). On the Pacific slope, writes Grant, Indians are called *Siwashes* and farms are called *ranches*. An enclosure for cattle is a *corral*. Among what he calls "slang terms of the Pacific," Grant notes *Doc.*, *git*, *Cap.* (captain), and the *Rockies*. "Every adjective and article that could be dispensed with was rejected from their English . . ." (p. 264). And he tells us that *creek* is universally pronounced "crick" in the Northwest. Grant defines for us (wrongly) *Chinook jargon* as "a barbarous lingo of one or two hundred words, first introduced by Hudson's Bay agents" (p. 242). He explains *lobstick* as "the Indian or half-breed monument to a friend or man he delights to honour" (p. 202). The *Red River cart*, says Grant, is "a clumsy-looking but really light box cart with wheels six or seven feet in diameter and not a bit of iron about the whole consern" (p. 129). *Shaganappi* he defines as "raw buffalo hide" (Miss Pauline Johnson in *The Shagganappi* (1912) says that it is really the name of a creamy-brown colour and spells it with two g's); and he gives *spell* as "the length of the journey between meals and stopping places" (p. 126).

Grant also edited a book called *Picturesque Canada* (1882), which is valuable for scholars interested in dialects. The chapters on Quebec record a variety of terms such as *arpent*, *bonne* (a lumberman's boat), *censitaire*, *caleche*, *seigneur*, and *Canadienne*. Among lumbering terms are *head-swamper* (or roadmaker), *bush superintendent*, *slide master*, *river driver*, *on the cruise* (spotting likely trees). Chapters on the Northwest have *bluff of woods*, *Red River cart*, *prairie schooner*, *tump lines*, *North canoe*, *prairie chicken*, *brigade* (or caravan), *York boat*. Ontario offers *tulip-tree*, *Queen City*, *Soo*, and *Six Nations*. From the Maritimes are entered *Blue nose*, *Digby chicken*, *steam drivers*, *intervale*, *gaspereau*.

A. P. Silver, writing about the Maritimes in *Farm-Cottage, Camp, and Canoe in Maritime Canada* (1908), has some interesting words: *ouananiche* [Lake St. John region] (pronounced "wonaneesh," he says); *bog-sucker* (woodcock); *liveyeres* (as settlers on the Labrador coast); *squaw bushes*; *bogan* (or cove). As pronunciations, Silver offers *pizen* (poison); *wexed* (vexed); *sarve* (serve); *kiver* (cover).

Viscount Milton and W. B. Cheadle, in *North-west Passage by Land* (1865), were impressed by some of the terms of the West, particularly by miners' talk; and they record from Lilloet "bully for you," "caved in," "you bet," "pay dirt." Many miners were from California, and from them our two travellers learned that "a grass widow in America is a woman who has separated or been divorced from her husband" (p. 389).

Among other writers who note terms from the Northwest is Charles Mair in *Through the Mackenzie Basin* (1908), his account of a journey into the Athabasca and Peace River areas in 1899. Mair gives such examples as "small barges, called sturgeons and the old York or inland boat" (p. 32); *snies*, described as "tortuous, narrow channels"; *Klondikers*; *umiak*; *babiche*; *old timers*.

An interesting book by J. T. Bealby, *Fruit Ranching in British Columbia* (1909), describes life in the Kootenays around the year 1907. Bealby is a keen observer of language although he is not able to distinguish regionalisms in speech. To him, anything new is simply "Canadian." But he notes several expressions: "a bunch (of cattle), to use a Canadian idiom" (p. 53); "car being Canadian for a passenger carriage or coach" (p. 2); "squatted on the land or, in the Canadian language, staked it" (p. 66); "and, in the Canadian phrase, might be shipped any day" (p. 71); "one of his [the Canadian's] favorite phrases is up against it" (p. 136).

H. J. Parham, author of *A Nature Lover in British Columbia* (1937), was a member of an English family which settled in the Okanagan valley about 1905. A keen naturalist, he records such words as *kokanee, squawfish, skunk cabbage* (wild arum lily), *coho, tyee, cutthroat*.

So far, I have dealt almost entirely with those writers who were observing the English language in Canada rather than using it creatively. What of our creative writers as distinct from travellers and commentators? Are they Canadian in language? Certainly when they are writing of things Canadian, they are distinctively Canadian, although a man like Galt belies this statement. But when Canadians are writing of "universal" matters, then they draw on that vast stock of English which is common to all English-speaking peoples and to which no special label can be attached. But to an Englishman, the works of Pauline Johnson, for example, reveal an entirely new world of language: *Shagganappi, cayuse, tepee, Reserve, gopher, potlatch, ollallies, snow snake, tillicum*. So do the works of R. J. C. Stead: *colonist car, wolf willow, rampike, pea-vine, Chinook arch*. Thomas H. Raddall's Nova Scotian characters are stamped as Nova Scotian by their speech. There may be an objection here that these are regional varieties of Canadian English. But Canadian English includes its regionalisms; and a Canadian author is as free to draw on them as the British writer is free to imitate Cockney or Lancashire speech in his writings.

A novel that exploits speech differences to the full is John Campbell's *Two Knapsacks* (1892), the tale of a summer holiday in Ontario. The publisher's note to the novel praises "its extremely clever dialect, representing Irish, Scotch, English, Canadian, French, Southern, and Negro speech." It is most interesting to see what Campbell considers to be "Canadian speech." His two heroes, one a lawyer and the other a teacher, are simply represented as speaking a form of English devoid of any pronunciations or phraseology which are used in the book to mark the two Englishmen, one uncultivated and the other cultivated, who say such things as "back to Hold Hingland" (uncultivated), "dawg" (cultivated), and "thanks awfully" (cultivated). But Campbell also offers another variety of Canadian speech which he puts in the mouths of lower-class Canadians, and this is quite different from that of his lawyer "of Osgoode Hall." These uneducated speakers come from the neighbourhood of Barrie, Ontario, and offer such statements as these: "thay's a crick away down the track"; "I guess I've pooty nigh paralyzed his laigs"; "the hull consarn."

Such examples are, of course, conscious. But Campbell himself shows his Canadianism in speech by offering without comment or explanation such words as *lot, concession, township, bee, dug-out canoe*. That is, since he is writing about Canada, he has to employ Canadian English. What else?

One of the most amusing of Canadian novelists is Mrs. Everard Cotes, "Canada's Jane Austen." Although a great lover of England, she is well aware that neither her thinking nor her language are British. In *Cousin Cinderella: A Canadian Girl in London* (1908), she concentrates on emphasizing that "We are not Americans: we are Canadians." Unfortunately, in this book, she avoids Canadian speech, having given her comments on this subject in *An American Girl in London* (1891). Here she does note differences between British and American English, well aware that Canadian English shares these differences with American English. Her heroine asks for *crackers,* to be told that "biscuits is what you mean." She is severely criticized for using *rubbers* instead of "goloshes," *bangs* instead of a "fringe" (of hair), *valise* instead of "portmanteau," and *elevator* instead of "lift."

I have called this chapter "The Growth of Canadian English"; but it should really be called "Recognition of the Growth of Canadian English." Canadian English emerged some time ago; and English-speaking Canadians have been using it for many years. But recognition of a language is always long in coming; and, strangely enough, the people who are slowest to recognize a distinctive form of a language are often the ones who use it. It is really only within the past decade or so that much attention has been paid to the recognition of Canadian English by scholars interested in dictionaries, historical surveys, and so on. Indeed, in 1954, when the Canadian Linguistic Association was formed, one of its immediate aims (still being pursued) was to investigate the possibility of a *Dictionary of Canadian English on Historical Principles.*

A historical survey of evidence such as I have given would be incomplete unless brought into the living present; and, to conclude my chapter, I give the views of a distinguished Canadian author on the nature of the language in which he gives expression to his thoughts and feelings. Here is what Earle Birney has written to me:

As a poet, I like to think I am an heir to the total vocabulary of the English-speaking world, but I know that in reality many of the words I think I choose are supplied by complex subconscious processes which are themselves in part determined by my Canadianism. The particular blend in my verse of what I elect to say and what, in a sense, is elected for me, constitutes whatever I have of a "voice," that unique "saying" of a personality which it is a poet's hope to achieve. My deliberate vocabulary ranges from Chaucerian archaisms like "mappe-mounde" to such coastal words as "clambake," and includes words like "coyote" and "chickenhawk" used to symbolize forces of destruction. But someone else has to point out to me that "lassooing," a word so much a part of me I never had to think to write it, must be a provincial distortion since it is unrecorded, in this spelling or pronunciation, in either the Oxford Universal or Webster's.

As a novelist attempting to create contemporary Canadian characters and make them talk, I have naturally tried much more consciously to catch whatever I feel to be essentially Canadian in speech rhythms and locutions. A novelist is not, however, a linguistic geographer, and must contrive to suggest, as by an occasional spelling device, the highly complex variations in speech he could not possibly record without resort to the IPA and consequent loss of all his readers (except perhaps the members of the Canadian Linguistic Association). In *Turvey*, especially, I tried to call up something of the really considerable range in speech levels and the rich variations in slang, localism, jargon and bawdry which swirled together from 1939 to 1945 to create an original stew of language, neither quite British nor quite American, though borrowing blandly and by right from both— the speech of the Canadian Army. But I am aware how far my characters talked short of the reality, and I wait hopefully for the Canadian novelist who will succeed, before it is too late and we are all talking like American radio announcers, in transporting into art the subtle, challenging distinctiveness and variety of our native speech.

15. New Forces: New Fiction
1880-1920

GORDON ROPER

THE CANADIAN FICTION LANDSCAPE was bleak to the Canadians who wrote about it in the early 1880's. Spring and the growing season seemed very slow in coming. In 1884, in *The Week*, J. E. Collins concluded that "in fiction, Canada makes a wretched showing," and many contemporaries would have agreed. Even in 1893, John Bourinot wrote in his *Our Intellectual Strength and Weakness*: "But if Canada can point to some creditable achievement in history, poetry, and essay writing ... there is one respect in which Canadians have never won any marked success, and that is in the novel or romance." But the unfreezing of the imagination had begun as Bourinot wrote. Thomas G. Marquis looked back from 1912 in his essay on "Canadian Literature" in *Canada and Its Provinces* (vol. XII):

A new movement took place in Canadian poetical literature about the year 1880; some ten years after this date Canadian fiction entered upon a new stage of its development. It would be quite within the mark to take the definite year 1890 as the dividing line between the early writers, more or less provincial in their art, and the modern school, influenced by world standards.

After 1890 the number of Canadians who wrote fiction increased rapidly. The number of volumes of new fiction doubled in the eighties and quadrupled in the nineties. Technical competence became common. Subjects, tone, and treatment became more diversified. The work of a number of Canadian writers became well known in the English-speaking world, in American, British, and Canadian editions, and through translation in many other countries. Canadian writers created images of Canadian life that still linger in Canada, and persist even more firmly abroad.

Our knowledge of the fiction of those years has become fragmentary, partly because with the passing of time almost all of it has disappeared from library shelves, and partly because historians of Canadian literature, judging by literary standards current in mid-twentieth century university departments of English, have dismissed all but one or two books as less than first rate. Reading them in the spirit in which they were written, their contemporary readers judged differently. This chapter and the following two do not quarrel with either judgment; their primary aim is descriptive, not judicial. They present information and perspectives which may help us recover our lost knowledge of that fiction and of the Canada in which it was written. This chapter essays a description of the conditions which shaped the writing of fiction from 1880 to 1920. Chapter 16 continues with a panorama of the kinds of fiction written then, and chapter 17 concludes by presenting a small gallery of portraits of the writing careers of the most prominent fiction writers of the period. The generalizations they suggest are tentative, since they are based on a reading of only about two-thirds of the volumes published in those years, all that is at the moment available in Canadian and American libraries.

The remarkable increase in the writing of fiction in Canada during these years can be seen clearly when the figures for publication of fiction in book form up to 1880 are placed against those for the years 1880 to 1920. Up to 1880 about 150 Canadians published over 250 volumes of fiction. Almost two-thirds of these volumes appeared in the sixties and the seventies; about 100 of them were written by five writers: James De Mille, Thomas Chandler Haliburton, Mrs. Agnes Fleming, Mrs. Susanna Moodie, and Mary Anne Sadlier. In contrast, during the years 1880 to 1920, more than 400 Canadians published over 1,400 volumes of fiction. Charles G. D. Roberts, Gilbert Parker, Robert Barr, James Oxley, Theodore Roberts, and Margaret Marshall Saunders together accounted for more than 200 of this total, and fifteen other writers published from nine to twenty volumes each. These bare figures are for fiction published in book form in a day when most fiction saw the light of day first in magazine form, and many stories never reappeared in book form.

One of the reasons for this striking increase in the number of Canadians writing fiction was that in the years after 1890 the North American market for fiction expanded rapidly, and it became more feasible to add substantially to one's income, or even to make a living, by writing fiction. Of the very few who had earned some kind of living from fiction before 1880, the most widely read and most successful Canadians probably were May Agnes Fleming and James De Mille; both died in 1880. Mrs. Moodie had stopped writing fiction earlier. In the earlier eighties the only prolific Canadian writers of fiction were Agnes Machar, Margaret Murray Robertson, Mary Anne Sadlier, and her daughter Anna Teresa Sadlier. The picture began to change radically in the late eighties. From 1888 to the First World War years, about 50 Canadians established themselves as professional or semi-professional writers, and much of their work was fiction. About two-thirds of the fifty were men. A few of the fifty made comfortable livings by their pens; more supplemented incomes from journalism, editorial work, or freelancing by writing fiction; some were ministers who wrote fiction to extend their ministry; some were wives of ministers or professional men; a few were teachers, lawyers, or doctors.

In almost every year from 1888 to 1914, one, two, or three young Canadian writers published his or her first volume of fiction. To list them is to present a roster of the most prolific Canadian writers of the period. In 1888 Roger Pocock and Clive Phillipps-Wolley published their first fictions in book form; Margaret Marshall Saunders, James Oxley, and Emily Weaver followed in 1889; Sara Jeannette Duncan in 1890; Lily Dougall, William McLennan, and Robert Barr in 1891; Gilbert Parker in 1892; Charles G. D. Roberts and Joanna Wood in 1894; Edward William Thomson, Cy Warman, and Jean McIlwraith in 1895; Ralph Connor (the Rev. Charles Gordon) and Ernest Thompson Seton in 1898; William Fraser, Virna Sheard, and Winifred Reeve in 1899; Arthur Stringer and Basil King in 1900; Norman Duncan and Adeline Teskey in 1901; Alice Jones and Ridgwell Cullum in 1903; John Price-Brown, Susan Jones, and Theodore Roberts in 1904; Robert Knowles, Marian Keith (Mrs. Mary Esther MacGregor), Marjorie Pickthall, Harvey O'Higgins, and Peggy Webling in 1905; Archibald McKishnie and Francis Pollock in 1906; Frederick William Wallace in 1907; Lucy Maude Montgomery, Nellie McClung, Frederick Niven, and Bertrand Sinclair in 1908; Stephen Leacock, Samuel Alexander White, and Hiram Cody in 1910; Robert Service and Frank Packard in 1911; Hulbert Footner and Alan Sullivan in 1913; and Robert Stead in 1914.

This list of those who began writing careers in these years represents only about an eighth of the number of Canadians who published volumes of fiction from 1880 to 1920. About 200 of the some 400 who published wrote only one or two volumes. Some of these were men or women in small communities who published one volume at their own expense, and then no more. Many of these solo flights were more earnest or ambitious than skilful, but among them are a few of the more interesting Canadian fictions of the period: Kathleen Blackburn's *The Dagmar Who Loved*, Frances Beynon's *Aleta Dey*, Margaret Brown's *My Lady of the Snows*, Martin Allerdale Graigner's *Woodsmen of the West*, the Lizars sisters' *Committed to His Charge,* Henry Cecil Walsh's *Bonhomme*, and *In the Village of Viger*, the single volume of tales Duncan Campbell Scott published before 1920.

Changing social, economic, and literary circumstances—inside and outside Canada—produced this wave of fiction writers. They differed primarily from the earlier fiction writers in that they were native born and bred. Almost all the earlier writers had been born and had grown up in England, Scotland, or Ireland before they had migrated to British North America. A few, and they were the most prolific, were native: the Nova Scotian Thomas Chandler Haliburton; May Agnes Fleming and James De Mille of New Brunswick; and Agnes Machar of Kingston. Most of those who wrote after 1880 were native born. Of those listed above, William Alexander Fraser, James Oxley, Alice Jones, Susan Jones, and Margaret Marshall Saunders were Nova Scotians. Charles G. D. Roberts, his brother, Theodore, and Hiram Cody were born in New Brunswick. Basil King and Lucy Maude Montgomery were born in Prince Edward Island. Lily Dougall, Anna Teresa Sadlier, William McLennan, Frank Packard, and Alan Sullivan were born in Montreal. Gilbert Parker, Sara Jeannette Duncan, Norman Duncan, Virna Sheard, Jean McIlwraith, Edward William Thomson, Marian Keith, Arthur Stringer, Harvey O'Higgins, Archibald McKishnie, Nellie McClung, Samuel Alexander White, Ralph Connor, Robert Knowles, Adeline Teskey, and Robert Stead were born in southern Ontario. Stephen Leacock, Robert Barr, Joanna Wood, Emily Weaver, Marjorie Pickthall, Bertrand Sinclair, and Ernest Thompson Seton were born in Great Britain, but were brought to Canada by their families while they were young. Among the few who came from Great Britain after schooling were Roger Pocock, Clive Phillipps-Wolley, Peggy Webling, and Robert Service. Cy Warman was born in Illinois, and Frederick Niven in Chile.

The earlier writers had migrated from the Old Country to one of the separate colonies in British North America. The new writers, however, were born in the Canadian provinces just before or after Confederation. The frontier had been pushed back earlier in the localities in which they grew up, and by the turn of the century being a writer in Canada had become, in Henry James's phrase, a much more "complex fate" than being a writer in a colony, or even in the United States. Most of the new writers grew up in a time of talk and writing about the need of a native literature to body forth a new nation. This had its influence on some of them. But from the subjects and values they expressed in their fiction, it appears that much the strongest influence was that of being native to a small town or rural community, in Nova Scotia, or New Brunswick, or Prince Edward Island, or southern Ontario.

The forces at play on a growing boy or girl in these small communities were not simple. There life focussed upon individuals and what they did, said, and felt, and how they did these things. Story telling was a natural way of talking. Homes were peopled not only with the living generations, but also with the forefathers, and strong filaments of feeling ran back to "the Old Country" and often south to "the States." The village yards and street ends ran out into the country or the woods, or down to water, greatly extending the imaginative world.

The young, imaginative individual also was apt to grow up in a world of print. Families in these small towns and on the adjacent farms often subscribed to one or more newspapers, church papers, or American or British magazines. Books were advertised in these periodicals, and were obtainable by mail order or from travelling book agents. George Doran, who left Canada early in these years to become a publisher, recalled in his *Chronicles of Barabbas* that in the eighties "good bookshops were to be found in every town of more than one thousand inhabitants. Toronto with a population of about 150,000 had at least a score of real book-stores owned and operated by highly intelligent booksellers." It has fewer now. He also estimated that in Canada "the book consumption was higher per capita than in any other country of the world with the possible exception of Australia." Moreover, literacy was particularly high in the homes in which Canadian writers grew up. Their fathers were ministers, lawyers, teachers, or doctors; a few were journalists; frequently their mothers had been school-teachers. Characteristically, their environment was one in which the power of the word—spoken and written—was taken for granted.

They grew up in a world of print, and much of that print was fiction. Daily and weekly newspapers, weekly story papers, religious publications, monthly magazines, and books, at all prices from 5 cents to $1.50 and up, provided the Canadian reader with short stories, fictional sketches, romances, and novels. The quality ranged from serious fiction (in hard covers, and paperback editions at 20 cents or less) by writers as different as George Eliot, Henry James, Thomas Hardy, and Zola, through high romance, historical romance, tales of everyday life, local colour stories, domestic sentimental fiction, boys' adventure books, girls' stories, pious moral tales, stories of detection, crime, Indians, and the West and Northwest. What was not sentimental was apt to be sensational, and often fiction was both sentimental and sensational.

The newspapers sometimes printed short stories in their daily editions, and ran serials along with short stories and the news in their weekly editions. They carried the work of well-known American and British writers, for the syndicates, which supplied stereotypes on a subscription basis to newspapers and magazines, often paid writers more for their work than the magazines, which, in turn, often paid more than book publishers.

During the seventies and the eighties, the popularity of the English penny-weekly, and the even more ubiquitous American counterpart, the story weekly, had declined very little. These mass-produced fiction papers were published in newspaper or smaller format, and sold for about 6 cents in Canada. They had been developed to appeal to the great mass audience which had grown steadily throughout the Victorian years. Even in the mid-century, the three English penny-weeklies, the *Family Herald*, the *London*

Journal, and *Reynolds Miscellany* together issued over a million copies a week, and probably were read by some three million people. Hundreds of periodicals imitated them in format and content, ranging in appeal from the pious to the lurid. In the United States, the most successful of the story weeklies was Bonner's *New York Ledger,* and it too had its hundreds of competitors and imitators. These story papers advertised themselves vigorously and they also boasted of how highly they paid their name authors. Their circulation spread throughout the Canadian provinces. The Montreal *Family Herald and Weekly Star,* founded in 1869, and the Toronto *Saturday Night,* founded in 1887, were Canadian versions of these mass-circulation fiction papers. Nellie McClung, in her autobiography *Clearing in the West,* recalled what the *Family Herald and Weekly Star* fiction meant to her and members of her family when she was young on a new Manitoba farm:

But I was telling about our enjoyment of the weekly newspaper. The continued story was really the high point of interest for we had a whole week to speculate on the development of the plot. There was one story that shook our neighbourhood to its foundation. It was called *Saved, or the Bride's Sacrifice,* and concerned two beautiful girls,—Jessie, fair as a lily, and Helen with blue black hair, and lustrous eyes as deep as the night. They each loved Herbert, and Herbert, being an obliging young fellow, not wishing to hurt anyone's feelings, married one secretly and hurriedly by the light of a guttering candle, in a peasant's hut, (Jessie), and one openly with a peal of organ and general high jinks, at her father's baronial castle, (Helen).

This naturally brought on complications. There were storms, shipwrecks, and secret meetings in caves, with the tide rising over the rocks and curlews screaming in the blast, there were plottings and whisperings; a woman with second sight and one with the evil eye. And did we love it?

I can remember staggering along through the snow behind the sleigh reading the story as I walked, and when I drew near home, members of the family would come out to shout at me to hurry.

Most of the fiction in these story paper weeklies was in the great popular tradition of the sentimental romance, laced with sensationalism. The black and white characters, humble or high, pure or villainous; the dying scenes, the orphans, the lost heirs, the seductions, betrayals, the lost wills, the high confrontations, the tears; the elegant language that was spoken only in fiction of this kind or on the mid-century melodramatic stage; the fine moral sentiments—all were designed to produce a series of strong emotional responses in the willing reader. Some of the young Canadians who later wrote fiction themselves learned about life in fiction from these weeklies.

A wide variety of quality monthly magazines also brought the work of skilful and complex fiction writers into Canadian homes. From England came magazines such as *Blackwood's, Chambers's Journal, Cornhill, London Illustrated News* (weekly), *Macmillan's, Temple-Bar, St. James,* or *Belgravia.* And from the United States came, among many others, *Harper's*

Monthly, Atlantic Monthly, the *North American Review, Lippincott's,* the old *Scribner's Monthly,* and the *Century.* The new issues of these monthlies were advertised in Canadian periodicals, and often were reviewed as if they were new books, since much of the finest fiction and non-fiction appeared in their pages before appearing in book form.

Although both British and American magazines circulated in Canada, the American were more to the taste of the Canadian reader. Sara Jeannette Duncan wrote in *The Week* in 1886 that "the British magazines could not compete in numbers, liveliness, variety, and price with the Americans," and another writer in *The Week* asserted that the American magazines outsold the British 100 to 1 in Canada. This preference for the North American way of seeing things and saying things is manifest later in the fiction written by Canadians who were growing up in the seventies and eighties. But the preference for American magazines does not mean that they rarely read the fiction of British writers, for the American magazines published the fiction of all the prominent British writers, frequently simultaneously with its appearance in British magazines. The quality American magazines also were rich in local colour stories and sketches of New England, the Midwest, the South, and the far West, and the obvious popularity of these stories must have encouraged young Canadian writers to use their own native experience in the fiction they submitted to the editors of American magazines. The young Canadian also could have learned from the pages of the quality American magazines of the literary personalities, the literary trends, and the critical battles in the literary centres, for they contained excellent book reviews, news about the literary great, and critical essays about the warfare beween the new Realists and the old Idealists, about the nature of fiction, and about nationalism in literature. Literature mattered in these pages, and in them an author was a man of high consequence.

Although in the seventies and eighties readers read much of their fiction in periodical form, books also were available easily. Few volumes of new fiction came directly from Great Britain, since the British publishers were monopolistic and maintained high prices, and their cheaper reprints were anticipated and undersold in Canada by American reprints. New fiction, including the new work of the popular British writers, was published in the United States at about $1.50, and quickly went into reprints at a dollar and less. Consequently the Canadian provinces were flooded by books from the United States, at prices from $1.50 down to the 5 cents and 10 cents of the Beedle dime novels and their imitators. One of the results was that very few volumes of fiction by Canadians were published first in Canada, other than those published by Lovell in Montreal—except, of course, for those published at the writer's own expense by his local publishers.

The importation of fiction in book form from the United States increased greatly after 1875 when unorthodox new publishers disrupted the American book trade by publishing mass editions of fiction, including the best recent English fiction, at 5 cents, 10 cents, or 20 cents, in paper covers. This publishing revolution was led partly by young men who had come from Canada to the greener fields of the United States: the Belford brothers and James Clarke from Toronto, John W. Lovell from Montreal, and George and Norman Munro from Halifax. Their cut-rate competition caused a rush among established American publishers to build competing ten-cent libraries. The low price of these libraries was made possible by mass printing, by new means of distribution, and by the use of foreign books unprotected by copyright. The established publishers also drew on their backlog of old fiction. When the publishing of foreign books not protected by copyright in the United States was reduced greatly by the Chace Act in 1891, and when the industry over-extended itself, the cheap libraries declined. Meanwhile, in the late seventies and throughout the eighties they placed fiction from the highest to the meanest quality within the price of all readers. Sara Jeannette Duncan once won a school literary prize of ten dollars and spent it all on 10 cent books, and many of the young Canadians who later would write fiction must have spent their money in the same way. This publishing warfare made book publishers most reluctant to risk the work of new writers, unless that work had appeared first in magazines and had received some critical notice. On the other hand, the magazines were on the hunt for manuscripts and paid well for them. So the young writer fashioned his stories primarily for the magazine editors and readers.

This world of print provided the early reading and fictional models of the Canadians who began to write fiction in the late eighties. But their writing also was moulded by their years of schooling and professional training. One of the forces which moved them out from their native communities was the desire for more education. Of the writers before 1880, De Mille and Haliburton were among the few who had university training. But a striking number of the writers from 1880 to 1920 were university graduates. Of the group of some fifty listed early in this chapter, twenty were graduates of universities, mostly of Canadian universities. Four were graduates of Normal School, two of art academies, and six had private school education. It may be that the university years inhibited as much as encouraged them as writers, for the standard Canadian university training then was classical, from alien professors who were steeped in the past of other lands, and usually were above such sub-literary things as romances and novels. The university student often learned more outside a classroom than in it. At least the university years were further years of training in a world where the word, written and spoken, was a natural and powerful instrument.

Their more intensive and practical training in writing came after their formal education. Many of them moved on from the universities into apprentice work on Toronto, Montreal, Halifax, or Detroit newspapers. There they made a mark as they began to freelance, and then they moved on again. Like their contemporaries from the villages and the small towns of upper New York state, Ohio, Indiana, Michigan, Illinois, and the West, they were pulled to the great centres of publishing and writing, New York, Boston, or London, to work on newspapers and magazines as reporters, correspondents, or editors. Most of those who became prolific professional writers migrated: Robert Barr, Norman Duncan, Charles G. D. Roberts, Theodore Roberts, Sara Jeannette Duncan, Gilbert Parker, Arthur Stringer, Harvey O'Higgins, Edward William Thomson, Roger Pocock, Frederick Niven, Agnes Laut. A few, like Lucy Maude Montgomery or Robert Stead, worked only on Canadian papers. Others left the universities for the ministry— Ralph Connor, Hiram Cody, Basil King, and Robert Knowles—and moved about the country widely in their work as missionaries and ministers. Many of those who wrote only two or three books also were journalists, or ministers, or ministers' wives or daughters.

The forces which caused this migration of young Canadians to New York and London were multiple, but probably the most powerful came from the radical changes in the magazine world in the closing years of the century. New editors, Edward Bok, S. S. McClure, Frank Munsey, and George Lorimer in the United States, and George Newnes and William T. Stead in Great Britain, used the invention of photoengraving, the rapid increase in commercial advertising, and mechanical improvements in rapid, cheap printing to develop a new journalism for various segments of the mass audience. They realized that with large circulation they could make more money by selling advertising space than by selling individual copies of the magazine. They launched 15 cent and 10 cent weekly magazines such as the *Ladies' Home Journal, Munsey's, Cosmopolitan, McClure's, Collier's, Scribner's Monthly, Everybody's, Outdoors*, or *Saturday Evening Post*. These new editors broke through the unwritten rules of taste set by the editors of the genteel *Century* or *Atlantic Monthly,* or by the narrowly moral denominational press. They filled their magazines with vigorous action fiction of politics, life in the slums, labour strife, the plains and mountains of the West, high finance, along with muckraking articles exposing the sore places in North American life. They hunted out writers and manuscripts; frequently they commissioned special articles and stories, and they paid excellent prices. In the nineties the competition from the new magazines raised prices for contributions, and increased greatly the number of places where one could place manuscripts. It encouraged a writer's market.

In Great Britain comparable new magazines also invited more worldly and masculine fiction. New magazines such as the *Strand, Windsor, Pall*

Mall, or *The Idler* competed with the established magazines and appealed to wider audiences. The stir in the magazine world was reflected on the Canadian scene by the establishment of somewhat similar (although quieter) magazines, *Dominion* (1888), *Canadian Magazine* (1893), which made it a special policy to publish Canadian writers, *Maclean's* (1896), or *Westminster* (1897), which added a more liberal tone to the denominational press.

Revolution was stirring also in the book world. In Great Britain a demand for the triple-decker at a high price had come from the great circulating libraries, and had led publishers to confine their fiction publishing largely to the work of well-known popular writers favoured by the libraries. They risked publication of an unknown, young writer only if his manuscript seemed to promise exceptional popular success. In 1894 the subscription libraries dropped their demand for the triple-decker, and publishers began to issue new fiction at six shillings, a price stabilized shortly after by the adoption of a net system of pricing. A wave of young publishers appeared on the scene to hunt out and develop new writing talent. In the United States the passage of the Chace Act in 1891, and the decline of the cheap book industry, enabled the American writer to compete equally with British writers. New techniques of production and distribution were adopted, and new life ran through the publishing houses.

Book production increased greatly in these years. Helmutt Lehmann-Haupt in his *The Book in America* states: "There was not too great difference in the total number of titles published in 1869 and, again, in 1880. But by 1890 the annual output was about doubled, and tripled by 1900, statistical proof of the enormous increase in volume which American publishing experienced at the turn of the century." The publishing of fiction in book form increased even more sharply, until in 1901 more fiction in book form was published in the United States than in any one year before—or since: 2,234 titles out of a total of 8,141 titles of all books. Total annual production for all books climbed until 1910, although the percentage of fiction fell off. The war years ended the boom. But throughout the 1890's and the 1900's, publishing was profitable. George Doran estimated that in the mid-nineties "it was possible to publish fiction, pay 10% royalty, and make a little profit on a 1,200 to 1,500 copies sale; at 5,000 the publisher was in clover." Publishers were on the hunt for books to print. In the book world, as in the magazine world, it was a writer's market in these years.

So the ambitious Canadian writer was attracted to the great fiction markets in the United States or Great Britain. The copyright situation after 1891 in those countries made it most advantageous for him to contract either for first publication in the United States or first publication in Great Britain with "simultaneous publication" in the United States. Many of the great Anglo-American publishing houses had offices on both sides of the Atlantic, or had working arrangements with trans-Atlantic firms. With British and American copyright secured, the British or American firms usually arranged for publication in Canada through an agent in Toronto or Montreal, and so also secured Canadian copyright protection.

The pull to New York or London was a strong one; there was little in the Canadian literary or publishing scene to counter it. Big publishers were few in Canada, and they were concentrating in Toronto. They published little fiction on their own initiative; what they did issue often was printed at the writer's expense, just as small local firms in the various provinces usually printed books at the local author's expense. The large Toronto publisher, William Briggs of Toronto, served the Methodist connection well with sermons, lives of the church fathers, travels by missionaries, and non-fiction of more general or technical interest. But up to 1895 it published only about one Canadian novel or romance a year; from 1895 to 1920 it published on the average three or four a year, mostly of a religious or moral tone. Concurrently, however, as the agent of New York or London firms, it imported stereotypes or sheets of Anglo-American successes and issued Canadian editions under the Toronto imprint. From 1896 to 1917, as agents, Briggs, Copp Clark, Morang, and Revell's Toronto branch of their Chicago–New York firm together issued, under their imprints in Toronto, from 250 to 300 volumes of fiction by some fifty of the best-selling British, American, and Canadian writers. Few contemporary fiction writers of any merit or popularity were overlooked. Thus the Canadian editions of the work of the most prolific Canadian fiction writers from 1880 to 1920 usually were reprints of an earlier edition published in New York, Boston, or London. As Robert Barr said in an article "Literature in Canada" in the *Canadian Magazine* (November 1899): "Toronto will recognize the successful Canadian writer when he comes back from New York or London, and will give him a dinner when he doesn't need it."

Canadian firms occasionally did take the initiative in publishing the work of Canadian writers. The Westminster Press of Toronto issued *Black Rock* and *The Sky Pilot* by Ralph Connor, after they had requested him to write the first as a serial for their magazine, to stir up interest in Western missions. After the turn of the century, Canadian firms became more enterprising, especially the new firm of McClelland and Stewart. But the market for book fiction in Canada was not large. The editor of the *Westminster Magazine* in the November 1902 issue wrote:

"Four thousand copies is a good sale for a novel in Canada," said Mr. Copp, "and I gather that the average is quite under two thousand. Of course, there are a few books that have passed the twenty thousand mark. Gilbert Parker's *The Right of Way* in cloth last season and in paper this summer was one; and Ralph Connor's *The Man from Glengarry* in cloth only passed twenty-five thousand in Canada within ten months of its publication. But that is a rare experience with a publisher."

The market for magazine fiction in Canada also was small. Apart from the numerous religious periodicals, the Canadian writer could look only to a few secular Canadian magazines such as the *Canadian Magazine, Maclean's,* or *Saturday Night,* and a few weekly newspapers like the Montreal *Family Herald and Weekly Star.*

The relative smallness of the book and magazine market for Canadian fiction was primarily the result of the size and composition of the Canadian population. In the nineties the population of Canada was approaching the five million mark. But of those five million, about a third were not English-speaking. Of those who were English-speaking, in spite of a relatively high literacy rate, a number were illiterate or barely literate. Many, literate and illiterate, were completely occupied in making their living in a new land. Among the literate, some assumed that any new fiction by a Canadian was apt to be less interesting than one by a New York or London writer. Because of the sectionalism of the new country, many a Nova Scotian reader naturally looked east or south for his reading, not hinterland to Ontario or the West, while the Ontario reader was apt to ignore Nova Scotian writing as he looked east or south.

Moreover, among the Canadian reading public, two influential elements looked down upon fiction with attitudes varying from aloofness to abhorrence. To many of the most highly educated, trained in the classical tradition, fiction at best was merely popular entertainment, or at worst something that debased public taste. In his *Our Intellectual Strength and Weakness* (1893), John Bourinot wrote:

I do not for one depreciate the influence of good fiction on the minds of a reading community like ours; it is inevitable that a busy people, and especially women distracted with household cares, should always find that relief in this branch of literature which no other reading can give them; and if the novel has then become a necessity of the times in which we live, at all events I hope Canadians, who may soon venture into the field, will study the better models, endeavour to infuse some originality into their creations and plots, and not bring the Canadian fiction of the future to that low level to which the school of Realism in France, and in a minor degree in England and the United States, would degrade the novel and story of every-day life.

Bourinot was addressing the Fellows of the Royal Society of Canada and probably few of them would have disagreed with his high view that the end of fiction was to elevate rather to entertain, that a good history was much more valuable than the best of fiction, that no Canadian had written good fiction, that if and when one did he would be an imitator of a great English (or American) writer. They might also have shared his apprehension that a sub-literary jungle of cheap fiction, fertilized by the commercialism of publishers, was growing up around Canadian readers.

These views, however, were more tolerant than those expressed hotly in many evangelical newspapers and magazines, and delivered from pulpits. A fiction was a lie, inspired by the Father of Lies, unless, of course, it was a "parable" or "allegory" to inculcate moral views. Popular fiction was denounced because it made vice attractive, and made violence seem natural. It spread irreligious, free-thinking, or undemocratic (or democratic) sentiments in seductive form. Many lay members of the fundamentalist flock were equally suspicious of fiction. Some would open a new book to the title-page, and if the title included the word "romance" or "novel," would read no further; if the title claimed the book to be a "tale of real life" or of "everyday life" they might venture on. Some parents prohibited the reading of all fiction to their children; some permitted the reading only of what came from church-sponsored presses and libraries. Some permitted it only on weekdays. When the Toronto Public Library opened in 1882, the guardians of public morality and the public purse tried to prevent fiction from being placed on the shelves. They argued that fiction led readers into sloth; it gave them irresponsible notions about life; it sapped the moral fibre. Or they argued that since it was mere entertainment, public money should not be squandered on providing it free for library readers.

From the fervent evangelical, the idealistic, or the intellectual view, there was cause for concern; for fiction had become endemic in the English-reading world. Some of it did express new and disturbing ideas. Some of it was "cheap and nasty." But the soaring production and sale of fiction in North America and in Great Britain make it clear that those who feared fiction were not the majority of the reading public, not even in what H. L. Mencken later called the North American "Bible Belt." The audience for fiction in Canada had been expanding in the years before 1900, and with the influx of some three million immigrants into the country around the turn of the century, with a wave of prosperity and expansion, with the growth of cities, with the greatly increased numbers of Canadians writing about the Canadian scene, the market for fiction in Canada grew rapidly. Fiction was placed on the shelves of the Toronto Public Library, and on the shelves of Canadian town libraries as they opened under the Carnegie sun. Fiction-printing newspapers and magazines increased in numbers and circulation, and the publication of fiction in book form, inside Canada and outside, rose markedly.

The nationalistic mood which led Prime Minister Sir Wilfrid Laurier to predict that the twentieth century would belong to Canada led a number of Canadians to make special demands on Canadian fiction writers. In Canadian periodicals and in public speeches they called for the creation of a unique Canadian literature which would promote a national consciousness.

A few Canadian fiction writers attempted to respond to this patriotic call. But it is one thing to call for the writing of the Great Canadian Novel, and another thing to write it. The patriotic demand for a national literature may also have been influenced by the campaign for a nationalistic American literature in American periodicals earlier in the century. But even at mid-century Hawthorne had pin-pointed the difficulties of North American literary patriotism when he wrote "We have so much country that we have no country," and added that when a writer attempted to make a land with "no limits and no oneness . . . a matter of the heart, everything falls away except one's native State."

By the end of the century, young Canadian writers could have learned from their American contemporaries in American magazines that a literature should be literature first and only then "national" by being at once local and universal. Certainly in this period, for most Canadian writers everything fell away except the different localities in which they had been born and raised; for the limits of their newly formed political union were much less clear, and their confederation had much less "oneness" than the American Union. Moreover, there was no market for "Canadian" nationalism in the great publishing centres in New York or London, although there was a lively market for stories about the past or present in French Canada, maritime Nova Scotia, New Brunswick, domestic Prince Edward Island, rural Ontario, or the various localities of the great West.

Growing up in this complex of international and domestic circumstances, the Canadian fiction writer naturally assumed concepts of the nature of fiction then common in the English-speaking world. Most British and American fiction writers in the later nineteenth century assumed that the first end of fiction was either to entertain or to instruct. If it instructed, it did so most effectively by entertaining, that is, by engaging a reader emotionally. Consequently the writer had to establish and maintain a close relation with his reader. Trollope had said: "It is the first necessity of the novelist's position that he make himself pleasant." Wilkie Collins's precept was: "Make 'em laugh; make 'em cry; make 'em wait." Even a writer as deeply concerned with the fine art of fiction as Henry James felt a primary obligation to be interesting to his reader.

To be entertaining, a fiction above all had to be a "good story." Readers wanted a moving account of "what happens," told in a way that made them feel part of that happening. They liked the "strong situation," and they liked episode after episode of "telling incidents." They wanted characters (their reviewers said) who were "life-like," by which they meant characters who were much larger, simpler, more ideal, than in life—characters with whom they could identify strongly. They wanted a setting which gave them the pleasures of the exotic and unknown, or the pleasures of recognition of the familiar; in either case, the function of setting was to reinforce the emotional effect of the action. They wanted a structure that engaged them fully, that aroused suspense, that had sudden, surprising turns, and an exciting pace. They wanted a conclusion that resolved the conflict and rewarded the good with fortune and happiness, or, occasionally, with the pleasure of renunciation or atonement. They liked a style that brought out their emotional response.

If one can judge from the prefaces of authors and the reviews and the articles on fiction in contemporary magazines, few late nineteenth-century readers were concerned with the art of the fiction they read—nor are most readers today. What they were concerned with was the qualities of the book; the vitality; the morality, especially the "purity"; the nobility and the villainy; the heroic and the pathetic or the comic; the variety, pace, contrast, and intensity. They judged a fiction by how strongly and frequently it moved them; in a word, they liked melodrama—sentimental or sensational, or a fusion of both. When the term "melodrama" is used in this chapter it is not intended to demean but to describe a literary form in which all elements are organized to produce intense emotional effect in the reader. Melodrama was an all-pervasive art form in the nineteenth century. The sub-structure of much of even the most serious fiction was melodramatic. It was a strong element in nineteenth-century painting, music, opera, sculpture, architecture, and the graphic and decorative arts. The views of God, man, and the universe—with emphasis upon sin, guilt, judgment, hell and damnation—which nineteenth-century churchgoers heard from their pulpits were often melodramatic. Political feelings (such as the emotion about "Greater Britain" and "Soldiers of the Queen," or President Roosevelt's "bully little war" with Spain) were apt to be melodramatic. The contemporary battles between rugged individualism and social conscience were expressed in melodramatic form.

Some fictions were simple melodramas, composed of exciting, fast-paced action, performed by black and white characters, each with a limited set of stock feelings, and occurring in front of an appropriate setting. Melodrama also was used to heighten the other basic modes of the fiction of the day, the "romance" and the "novel." The titles of most fictions then were double-barrelled; the second half of the title often told the reader whether he should expect a "romance" or a "novel," or a "tale of everyday life." The term "romance" promised the reader he would get a picture of life unencumbered by the way things occur every day. It presented life as one would like it to be, or as it ought to be—life reconstituted to satisfy one's fantasies. It often was set in the past, or in the future, or in some glamorous level of society or in some far-away land. Its language was more elaborate, more elegant, or more lyrical than everyday speech. Its characters were much larger than life, and its action usually was erotic in that it concentrated on the mating process, opening with the meeting of a young hero and heroine, emoting with them through the difficulties which inevitably separated them, and ending by their union.

The "novel," on the other hand, tried to present a faithful picture of everyday life, of the here and now, to offer a fictional world where places, people, and events were recognizably like the life the writer and reader knew. What the writer thought life really was like, of course, determined the "realism" of his fiction, and many a tale of domestic tribulation, of put-upon piety sentimentally conceived, was labelled and passed with sentimental readers as a "novel." To the more sophisticated writer and reader a novel meant a fiction in which the author analysed human behaviour and its motivations, and discussed the moral and social consequences of such behaviour. Or it might embody some moral or social concept. Usually in a novel the narrator told his story in a quiet, middle style, often with a tone of detachment or even of irony. It usually contained passages of dialogue in which the writer tried to catch the diction and rhythm of actual speech. While the romance usually focussed on a central group of hero, heroine, and villain (or villainess), the novel more often had a wide range of central characters, and although the action often centred on the mating process, it also was apt to concern itself with other human activities—the process of growing up, of making a living, of achieving success; or it portrayed the clash between generations, the iniquity of institutions, or a growth in spiritual awareness. The end of the romance was to entertain, either by superficial excitements or by appeals to the deeper fantasies. The end of the novel was sometimes to please by stirring the sense of recognition; more often it was to instruct, by embodying some religious or ethical truth, or by dramatizing some social evil, or in the hands of writers like George Eliot, Meredith, William Dean Howells, or Henry James by enlarging the reader's awareness and understanding of the complexities of the human condition.

The modes of romance and novel often mingled in one fiction, especially in the work of the unpractised writer and in the work of the sophisticated professional. Romancers dominated the field of Anglo-American fiction, and novelists coloured their views of ordinary life with sentiment or heightened it with melodrama. The prevalence of what George Meredith called the "rose-pink" and the "blood and glory" pictures of life led to the biggest literary battle of the last quarter of the nineteenth century. The opposing forces were the "realists" on one side and on the other the romanticists and several varieties of "idealists," with a few under the banner of "Art for Art's Sake" skirmishing against both sides. Reviews and articles on fiction in the magazines in the late seventies, eighties, and nineties identified William Dean Howells and Henry James as the leaders of the realists among Anglo-American writers. Howells and James both felt that the reading public was being debauched by fiction that collectively could be published under the title *Slop, Silly Slop*. They believed that fiction could and should be one of the high forms of literature. Howells' credo was that fiction ought to picture ordinary life, and that it must picture that life truthfully, without rhetoric, without melodrama, and without preaching. James was in fundamental agreement with his friend, although he had a different feeling for what was "interesting" in life. Both of them had an intensely moral concept of art in that they believed that its end was to heighten the quality of living. Both believed that a writer could be truthful only by writing out of his own experience of the life he had observed. They encouraged young writers to rely on personal experience—local as it might be—by the example of their own stream of fiction and of reviews and articles on fiction. Howells played a vital part in encouraging regional writing in North America by his preference for local colour and realism in the fiction he chose for the *Atlantic Monthly* during his editorship from 1871 to 1880, and by his influence on the editorial taste of *Harper's Magazine* from 1885 to 1920. As the dean of American letters he gave personal encouragement to young realists as diverse as Hamlin Garland, Stephen Crane, Harold Frederick, Frank Norris, and Theodore Dreiser. This campaign for truthfulness in fiction inclined some young Canadian writers to be anti-romantic and more self-reliant. The fiction of Sara Jeannette Duncan in particular, and in varying degrees of Robert Barr, Frances Beynon, Arthur Campbell, Francis Grey, William Fraser, Arthur Stringer, Robert Stead, Harvey O'Higgins, and Bertrand Sinclair was liberated by the work of earlier British and American realists.

The realists were strongly opposed by a large, diverse, and influential force of writers, reviewers, and readers who denounced the view of life presented by the realists as narrow, mean, pessimistic, and degrading. They argued that the realists looked down, not up, that they showed the animal in man rather than the angel. They feared that Howells and James were opening their optimistic, genteel, middle-class, provincial Anglo-Saxon world to a flood of French realism by Balzac, Flaubert, the de Goncourt brothers, De Maupassant, and Zola, with all its "cynicism," "decadence," and "nasty emphasis" upon sex. An unsystematic sampling of the reviews and articles on fiction in Canadian periodicals during these years suggests that the bulk of Canadian opinion was on the side of the conservatives. Canadian writers like Gilbert Parker and the Protestant ministers who wrote fiction championed romanticism and "idealism," as they understood "idealism."

Comprehension of the feelings and concepts expressed in this literary battle is essential to an understanding of what made the Canadian fiction of this period acceptable to its readers. For idealism—the habit of judging things in the light of how they ought to be—was pervasive among writers and most segments of the Anglo–North American audience. It had many forms, not all compatible, ranging from a raw "Boost; Don't Knock" western attitude at one extreme to various codes of Christian perfectibility or Brahmin moral tone at the other. Both Howells and James were realists because they were idealists in the old American grain of tough-minded, pragmatic humanism. They believed in the self-reliance of the individual, but they believed also that the individual achieved stature through his relation with other individuals in a social milieu. Along with their opponents, they assumed that art is communication—a social matter—not self-expression. Civilized men (and the artist to them was the most civilized of men) willingly inhibited their writing to avoid giving needless offence to others. They accepted the fact that the reading audience, especially of the quality magazines in which most of their work first appeared, was home-centred, and therefore in addressing their readers certain decencies were to be observed as one would observe them in a dinner-table or fireside conversation. One limitation that many English and American writers accepted was that of never bringing a blush to the cheek of that finest flower of the genteel tradition, a young lady.

The quality family magazines and the old-established publishing houses in Boston, New York, and London were dominated by editors and publishers of the genteel tradition, who had a paternalistic attitude towards their readers. The denominational presses dominated another large segment of the publishing world, especially in Canada. The inhibitions of publishers added to the personal inhibitions cultivated in the individual writer by his own particular brand of idealistic upbringing, and wove a network of restraint through much of the fiction of the day. The general feeling was that this was the way it should be; for "the more smiling aspects of life"—in expression as well as in material—to most Americans truly represented life in North America, where they believed life goes so much more "unterribly" than it does in the countries of the Old Land. But life in North America and in Great Britain was changing rapidly during this period, and here and there strands of this network loosened as new publishers and new magazines began to compete for the mass markets. More freedom in attitude, theme, and range of expression is evident in the work of Canadian writers after 1900.

These major assumptions about the nature of fiction were the guide-lines within which Canadians wrote. The matter and manner of their fiction were shaped by the kinds of fiction that were prominent, and waxed and waned in popularity, during these years in the Anglo-North American world. Among the books still widely read in their formative years were the various kinds of fictions by Scott, Cooper, Thackeray, Hawthorne, Charlotte Brontë, Dickens, Bulwer-Lytton, Collins, Reade, and George Eliot; for whenever a fiction achieved popularity in the nineteenth century it was read by more than one generation and by more than one segment of the reading public.

Among the ingredients that sustained the popularity of the fiction of these

English and American writers was their sentimental and sensational melodrama. These melodramatic qualities were singled out and amplified in the work of many British and North American writers in the fifties, the sixties and the seventies. Some of the most widely known books of those decades—and they remained in print in cheap editions into the twentieth century—were the sentimental melodramas of the hearth, or the more sensational melodramas of high life. Hundreds of thousands of readers shed tears over the simple pieties of Elizabeth Wetherell's *The Wide, Wide World* and Maria Cummins' *The Lamplighter*, or the more elegant pieties of Augusta Jane Evans's *Beulah* or Elizabeth Phelps's *The Gates Ajar*; and hundreds of thousands thrilled to the feverish passion and sensation in Mrs. Wood's *East Lynne*, Miss Braddon's *Lady Audley's Secret*, Mrs. E.D.E.N. Southworth's *The Fatal Marriage, Ishmael*, and *Self-Raised*, Ouida's *Under Two Flags*, Miss Evans's *St. Elmo*, or E. P. Roe's *Barriers Burned Away*. These domestic sentimental melodramas and the sensational tales of higher society were written largely by women, and read largely—but certainly not only—by women. Their sensationalism contributed to the mistrust of fiction by the more sober-minded, and led religious publishing houses in Great Britain, the United States, and Canada to encourage the writing of pious fiction to jam the inflow of such unnerving romances into the homes of the faithful. By the mid-eighties this sensational kind became embroidered with more sophisticated elements. A number of Canadian women had considerable success with these melodramas—notably May Agnes Fleming, the Sadliers, mother and daughter, and Margaret Murray Robertson. The sensational kind was imitated most by Canadian writers in the seventies and eighties, and faded out in the nineties into other forms; the pious kind in various sublimations goes on forever.

The early sixties also saw the proliferation of simpler action melodramas for the adolescent and older male audience who had learned of the frontier from Cooper and Simms and Davy Crockett, when the new Beedle dime novels included in their earlier numbers Anna Stephen's *Malaeska; or, The Indian Wife of the White Hunter*, and Edward Ellis's *Seth Jones; or, The Captives of the Frontier*. The yellowbacks not only made scouts, redskins, outlaws, and Indian hunters ubiquitous, they also made bandits and detectives popular with the enormous success of their "Old Sleuth," "Old Cap Collier," and "Nick Carter" series. Books like Wilkie Collins's *The Woman in White* or *The Moonstone*, and Dickens's *The Mystery of Edwin Drood* offered more complex mystery stories. The mystery structure probably had become the most common structural pattern for nineteenth-century fiction, serious as well as light. Sinister characters from the mysterious East were frequent. By the eighties the Pinkerton man and the amateur detective often appeared as minor characters. The detective moved into the centre of the stage with the blaze of popularity of Conan Doyle's Sherlock Holmes stories in the late eighties and early nineties. In the late nineties Ernest Hornung's Raffles, the gentleman-cracksman, became a familiar character. The popularity of specialized forms of crime fiction—suspense stories of the underworld, of private detectives, and of international intrigue—increased in the first years of the twentieth century. The Canadians Arthur Stringer, Frank Packard, and William Fraser were major contributors of mystery and crime stories to the popular magazines, and after their stories appeared in book form they were reprinted frequently in Burt or Grosset & Dunlap cheap reprint editions.

The novel of social protest or problem novel was another kind of fiction widely read in the third quarter of the nineteenth century by the more serious-minded, and by many others also, for it was often as melodramatic as a romance of high life or as exciting as a crime story. This fiction, written to trouble the reader's complacency and his conscience, was as various in theme as Disraeli's *Coningsby,* Thackeray's *Vanity Fair,* Newman's *Loss and Gain,* Kingsley's *Alton Locke,* Dickens's *Bleak House* or *Hard Times,* Mrs. Stowe's *Uncle Tom's Cabin,* Mrs. Gaskell's *North and South,* Reade's *It's Never too Late to Mend* or *Hard Cash,* T. S. Arthur's *Ten Nights in a Barroom,* Mark Twain's *The Gilded Age,* or George Eliot's *Middlemarch.* Controversial fiction often went into edition after edition. Probably more than six and a half million copies of *Uncle Tom's Cabin* in book form alone were sold on both sides of the Atlantic and in translations. *Ginx's Baby* (1870), an attack on English complacency about slum conditions by the Canadian born and bred John Edward Jenkins, appeared in more than thirty-six editions.

Fiction with a purpose was more widely written and read in the socially troubled years from 1880 to 1920. One of the most influential books of the late nineteenth century was Henry George's treatise *Progress and Poverty* (1879) on the relation of capital, labour, and production to land, and its arguments were debated in many fictions. Edward Bellamy's *Looking Backward* (1888) was one of the most successful of more than one hundred Utopian fictions. The strikes that erupted in the mounting struggle between capital and labour were dramatized in stories such as John Hay's *The Breadwinners,* or, more effectively, in *The Mutable Many* by the Canadian Robert Barr, or *A Hazard of New Fortunes* by William Dean Howells. Problems of faith became insistent for many under the pressure of social and intellectual changes, and created an appetite for fiction on religious themes. Among the most widely read and imitated of the religious fictions were General Lew Wallace's historical melodrama of Christians and circuses, *Ben Hur* (1880), Mrs. Humphry Ward's much more intellectual study of loss of faith, *Robert Elsmere* (1888), and one of the most popular fictions ever published in the United States, the Reverend Charles M. Sheldon's *In His*

Steps (1897). *In His Steps* was followed in the next year by Ralph Connor's first success, *Black Rock*, and in the year after that by the equally popular *The Sky Pilot*. Connor's stories were only the most popular of many fictions on religious themes by Canadians.

Another area of disturbing social change was that of the status of women and the relation of the sexes. Henry James's young American girl, Daisy Miller, was discussed widely as a disagreeable (or agreeable) new phenomenon in the early eighties. The "New Woman" began to appear in British and American fiction in the late eighties. The appearance of Ibsen's Nora in *A Doll's House* in the early nineties in England and America intensified the discussion. Varieties of the New Woman appeared in Hardy's *Tess of the D'Urbervilles*, Sara Jeannette Duncan's *A Daughter of Today*, more notoriously in *The Woman Who Did* by the Canadian-born Grant Allen, and in Edith Wharton's *The House of Mirth*. One of the most widely read fictions about female emancipation was Sarah Grand's *The Heavenly Twins* (1893).

Even the leaders of the parade of romances, Marie Corelli and Francis Marion Crawford, stirred currently fashionable ideas about women, love, philosophy, religion, and spiritualism into their successes. Interest in psychic phenomena and spiritualism rose in the late eighties and the nineties and was reflected in the popularity of romances by Corelli, of Rider Haggard's *She*, and Robert Louis Stevenson's *Dr. Jekyll and Mr. Hyde*. Henry James's serial for *Collier's Magazine* in 1898, *The Turn of the Screw*, was only one of the most disturbing of hundreds of ghost stories in the periodicals of the nineties.

In the late nineties new magazines in the United States and Great Britain encouraged the writing of "muckraking" fiction to expose particular political, social, and economic evils; a number of these, particularly Winston Churchill's *Coniston* (1906), *Mr. Crewe's Career* (1908), and *A Far Country* (1915), and *The Jungle* (1906) and others by Upton Sinclair, became best-sellers. Fictions written to advance the cause of temperance had been steadily growing even before Arthur's *Ten Nights in a Barroom* (1855). These crusading books increased greatly in numbers in the closing years of the century as the Prohibition movement gathered strength. Many volumes of domestic fiction or of out-of-door adventure had a strand of anti-drink propaganda woven intemperately through them. The denominational presses, Canadian as well as British and American, published most of the temperance fiction.

The international theme of the innocent from the New World in the Old runs like a thread through North American fiction from Cooper to the present. The theme was early treated humorously or satirically in Thomas Chandler Haliburton's *The Attaché; or Sam Slick in England* (1843) and De Mille's *The Dodge Club; or Italy in 1859*. Mark Twain made his first real success with *The Innocents Abroad* in 1869, followed by *A Tramp Abroad* in 1880, both of which were immediately reprinted in pirated editions in Toronto. Henry James's *Daisy Miller* and his *The Portrait of a Lady* (1880) and William Dean Howells's *The Lady of the Aroostook* (1879) took up this theme in a different mood, and were also popular. As tourism increased in the eighties and as more American heiresses married into the Old World aristocracy, more fictions explored the international theme. To it Canadians with transatlantic experience—Sara Jeannette Duncan, Gilbert Parker, Lily Dougall, Alice Jones, and Susan Jones—made a contribution.

Europe also meant to the Anglo-North American reader the liberating world of art and the artist, on which Henri Mürger first had opened a window in his *Bohemians of the Latin Quarter* (1848, 1851). The artist was romanticized in fiction in the late seventies and the eighties, and Bohemianism became a fad in clubs, magazines, and fiction in the late eighties and the nineties. The romance and mystique of art, embodied in a young painter, singer, musician, or sculptor (rarely a writer), appeared in fiction like Henry James's *Roderick Hudson*, Jessie Fothergill's *First Violin*, Ouida's *Tricotrin*, or Francis Marion Crawford's *A Roman Singer*. The more intense interest in Bohemianism came with Marie Corelli's *A Romance of Two Worlds* (1890), Kipling's *The Light that Failed* (1890), and the Trilby craze that followed Du Maurier's story (1894) of the Latin Quarter artists, artists' models, and the hypnotic Svengali. The glamour of the world of the artist in Europe probably was enhanced for some Canadians by the career of Madame Albani, the Quebec girl who became a well-known opera star and friend of Queen Victoria in the 1870's.

One of the most striking phenomena of the literary taste of the period was the upsurge in popularity of historical romance between 1886 and 1904. The peculiar mixture of spirited romance, local colour, history, and idealism in Scott and Cooper had elevated historical romance to a higher level of respectability than most other kinds of fiction. It had risen and fallen in vogue during the century, but books by Bulwer-Lytton, Ainsworth, G. P. R. James, Dumas, Reade, and Dickens's *A Tale of Two Cities* and Hugo's *Les Miserables* were widely read in the formative years of Canadian writers. Interest in new historical fiction rose with the success of Wallace's *Ben Hur* in 1880 and Robert Louis Stevenson's romances in the late eighties. The deluge, however, came in the nineties; the pace-setters were tales like Stanley Wayman's *Under the Red Robe*, Gilbert Parker's *The Seats of the Mighty*, Sienkiewicz's *Quo Vadis*, S. Weir Mitchell's *Hugh Wynne, Free Quaker,* and *The Adventures of François,* Charles Major's *When Knighthood was in Flower*, and Winston Churchill's *Richard Carvel*. After the publication of Mary Johnston's *To Have and To Hold*, Thompson's *Alice of Old Vincennes*, and Hewlett's *Richard Yea-and-Nay* the vogue diminished. The matter of these romances was Rome in the early Christian days, Elizabethan England, the days of Bonnie Prince Charlie and of Louis the Sun King, colonial North America, the American Revolution and the French Revolution. Some, like Mitchell's *Hugh Wynne, Free Quaker*, were more novel than romance; others were rapier and cloak melodramas. The enormous popularity of historical romance led Canadian writers to write of their own local history or of the romantic days of England, France, or the Thirteen Colonies, or of the early Christian era. A variant of historical romance—the romance of the imaginary kingdom—also had its great vogue in the nineties and early 1900's, with Stevenson's *Prince Otto*, Anthony Hope's *Prisoner of Zenda* and *Rupert of Henzau*, and George McCutcheon's *Graustark,* but this form seems to have offered little to Canadian writers.

The other striking phenomenon of the literary taste of the period was the appetite for local colour, or regional fiction. It was the fashion that affected more Canadian writers of this period than any other. The purpose of the local colourist was to capture in a short story or in a book made up of related sketches the particular flavour of his chosen locality. Some tried for the utmost accuracy—like Mrs. Stowe, who said she had attempted to "make her mind as still and passive as a looking-glass" so that she might reflect in her stories "New England life and character." Others, like Bret Harte, heightened their local scenes with humour and pathos. Although they had earlier British counterparts such as John Galt in his *Annals of the Parish* or Mrs. Gaskell in *Cranford*, and the current work of the Kailyard School, Canadian writers were most impressed with the stories of the American writers that filled the family magazines of the day. After magazine publication, stories often were collected in book form—Bret Harte's *The Luck of Roaring Camp* (1870), Mrs. Stowe's *Oldtown Folks* (1869), and work by Rose Terry Cooke, Mary Wilkins Freeman, William Dean Howells, or Sarah Orne Jewett picturing the New England scene. Edward Eggleston's widely read *The Hoosier Schoolmaster* (1871), Mark Twain's *The Adventures of Tom Sawyer* (1876) and *Adventures of Huckleberry Finn* (1884), and Hamlin Garland's *Main Travelled Roads* (1891) showed different aspects of the Midwest, and George Washington Cable's *Old Creole Days* (1879) pictured the South. Local colour was in demand, and Canadian writers were encouraged to write out of their own experience of their own localities.

The popularity of fiction of the out-of-doors and of the frontiers, related in many ways to the popularity of local colour and regionalism, grew rapidly after 1900 as the enormous popularity of historical romance declined. From Cooper's time, one main stream of North American fiction had been that of frontier adventure. Sometimes, as in the dime novels, the setting was used only as a backdrop for adventure; sometimes as in Cooper it was used to communicate the mystical redemptive quality of Nature. John Burroughs expressed in the seventies a widespread feeling that the progress and salvation of New World society depended "upon the great teachers and prophets, poets and mystics who gain their enlightenment ultimately from the Great Out-of-Doors, God's Nature." The opening of the West had become a matter of fiction in the magazines in the closing years of the century; the Gold Rush in the north and President Roosevelt's publicity for the "virile" life dramatized the out-of-doors to a people who, in spite of the growth of big cities, were still close to it themselves in their daily lives. Charles G. D. Roberts, Ernest Thompson Seton, and Ralph Connor published their first out-of-doors books before 1900. The great wave of popularity rose just after 1900, with Jack London's stories, Owen Wister's *The Virginian* (1902), and stories by Stewart Edward White, Rex Beach, James Oliver Curwood, Zane Grey, and many others. Even the popular domestic sentimental fiction moved out-of-doors with Gene Stratton Porter's *Freckles* and *The Girl of the Limberlost*. Out-of-doors fiction became one of the great staples of Canadian writers. Canadians also became pace-setters in creating the popularity of animal stories during these years.

Before concluding this brief sketch of the fiction current in the Anglo–North American world during the years 1880 to 1920, it is necessary to note the striking popularity of the shorter forms of fiction. In North America before 1891, magazine editors bought much more short fiction than long fiction from native writers. With the increased activity in the magazine world at the close of the century, editors demanded more short stories and serials. During these years several hundred volumes of short stories were published in book form, in spite of the publisher's rule of thumb that books of short stories rarely pay their way. Some of the most esteemed writers—Robert Louis Stevenson, Rudyard Kipling, Conan Doyle, Henry James, O. Henry, and Jack London to name only a few—were known as much for their short stories as for their longer work. Most writers, British, American, or Canadian, began their careers by contributing stories to magazines; most of them continued to write short stories or serials while they published book-length fiction. Many of the Canadian writers noted in these pages formed a first book by collecting together the best of previously published short stories. It is not surprising to find that the qualities of the short story form—emphasis upon situation, action, static character, and atmosphere—predominate in much of their long fiction.

16. The Kinds of Fiction
1880-1920

GORDON ROPER, RUPERT SCHIEDER
AND S. ROSS BEHARRIELL

WRITING WITHIN THE SOCIAL AND LITERARY MILIEU described in chapter 15, more than 400 Canadians published over 1,400 volumes of fiction. In their work seven or eight kinds of fiction predominate: the local colour story; the historical romance; the action or adventure story; the animal story; the mystery, detective, or crime story; novels of ideas or of social criticism; and the sensational and sentimental society story. Like their American and British fellow writers, they wrote most of their society stories in the eighties, and most of their local colour fiction in the nineties and 1900's. They wrote historical romances of various kinds in growing numbers in the eighties, in a flood in the nineties, and fewer after 1904. Their writing of action stories increased greatly after 1900. Throughout the period they wrote romances and novels dramatizing the interplay of religious faith and doubt. Their mystery stories increased in numbers after 1900. They wrote a variety of problem novels during these forty years: some deal with the political scene; some with labour strife; some with education. Forty or fifty present aspects of the artist's life, or of "the New Woman." Many moral melodramas depicting the ravages of drink were written by occasional writers.

These were the popular kinds. Along with them a few philosophical novels appear; a half-dozen Utopian romances in the vein of Bellamy or the train of Donnelly; some fantasies in the manner of Jules Verne, H. Rider Haggard, or H. G. Wells. Other fictions picture farm life, lumbering camps, horse-racing, railroading, college life, and even banking. A number deal with missionary life in the Northwest or in the Orient, and the interest in religious fiction led to the writing of more than a dozen biblical or classical historical romances. The highly emotional atmosphere of the Great War appears in the closing pages of several dozen fictions in the last years of the period. A few—surprisingly few —fictions carry on the comic tradition of Sam Slick, although comic minor characters in the Haliburton-Dickens tradition turn up frequently in other kinds of fiction.

Some of this fiction was written obviously for a local audience; much of it was written for the New York-Boston-London publishing world, and the various segments of the Anglo-North American audience it catered to. Probably few of these writers thought of their work as literature in the sense in which that term was used in the universities. They practised a popular art; they addressed the widest audience; they wrote for the here and now, and they expected to have their writing judged in this light.

There is little in the structural patterns of their fiction or in the views of human nature which moulded the characters and situations they created to mark their work off from that of the British and American fiction writers of their day. But when their work as a body is placed against that of their British and American contemporaries, differences are apparent.

What most distinguished the fiction written by Canadian writers from that written by their British and American contemporaries is their writers' experience of place, and, to a lesser degree, their experience of time. The fiction written by Canadians before 1880 presents scenes of Canadian life in only a few isolated spots in an unknown country. One cleared patch lies along the St. Lawrence, centring on a Quebec City and a Montreal of the Old Régime. Another smaller patch includes the Minas Basin of the Evangeline country, and a vaguely adjacent Louisbourg and Halifax. Another small patch is around Saint John; other, unrelated patches are the bush clearings of the Ontario Front. A few English writers, R. M. Ballantyne, Kingston, and Henty, put Hudson's Bay and the wilds of the Northwest on the fictional map. Canadian critics in the 1880's had good reason to feel strongly that Canadians had not awakened to the possibilities of using their own localities in fiction. An editorial in *The Week* for September 29, 1887, reprinted a note from the *Boston Literary World*, entitled "A Field for Romance," which suggested that American writers ought to exploit the Canadian scene, since little use had been made by Canadians of "the abundant and rich material for fiction afforded by the scenery and history of these neighbouring lands."

In the following thirty years, Canadian writers did use the abundant and rich materials of their own land to a remarkable degree. The panorama of their fiction which follows below is representative, not exhaustive. In these years, the fictional map of Canada expanded as quickly as the physical map had in 1867. By the time of the First World War, the whole known area of Canada had been sketched in, and the scarcely knit, pluralistic localness of Canadian life in those years had been mirrored directly or obliquely in hundreds of short stories, romances, and novels.

The most prominent eastern region on the new literary map is the French-Canadian country along the Upper and Lower St. Lawrence, along the Ottawa, in the Eastern Townships, and in the Gaspé. The Maritime part fills out. The Minas Basin country is explored in greater detail; so is the North Shore, Cape

Breton, and land on both sides of the Bay of Fundy, and the New Brunswick woods. Prince Edward Island appears as a large area centring on Green Gables. The southern Ontario part expands greatly; life there is pictured in settled rural areas and villages, along the Ottawa, in Glengarry County, on the Bay of Quinte, around Orillia, in the Grand River and the Thames valleys, and along the north shore of Lake Erie. Some fictions picture college life in Cobourg and in Toronto; a few picture city life in Toronto and Ottawa.

The fictional opening of the West paralleled the physical opening with only a few years' lag. Winnipeg was also a fictional gateway for settlers and adventurers who spread out on to homesteads to the southeast and southwest, and on over the prairies, into the foothills of the Rockies. In the Rockies and along the Coast, writers exploited the discovery of gold, lumber, and salmon fishing. The "Northwest," or "North of 53," was filled by fiction with trappers, Métis, outlaws, mounted police, exiled young English lords, remittance men, squaws, and beautiful half-breeds. The latest fictional discovery was the Yukon country in '98; fiction came out with the gold.

The French-Canadian scene was widely used by Canadian writers—and others—from 1890 to 1915. It provided a setting for more than seventy-five volumes of historical romances, of local colour stories, and of tales and legends published during these years, most of them between the years 1895 and 1902. Many of these fictions first appeared in American, British, or Canadian magazines. The picturesqueness of the scenery and the culture had been well known to American writers, readers, and travellers since the 1840's. This transplanted version of Old Europe on their northern doorstep had attracted Americans to Montreal, Quebec, and the trip down the River. Longfellow's *Evangeline* (1847) was read in innumerable editions in North America and Great Britain. William Dean Howells had presented a charming sketch of the St. Lawrence and the Saguenay trip in his *The Wedding Journey* (1871). The rich past of French Canada had been made widely available by the volumes of Francis Parkman's history of France and England in the New World, beginning with his *Conspiracy of Pontiac* in 1851, and culminating with *The Old Régime* (1874), *Count Frontenac and New France under Louis XIV* (1877), *Montcalm and Wolfe* (1884), and *A Half-Century of Conflict* (1892). These provided a great warehouse of story and fact for the historical romancers at the turn of the century. Concurrently, information and story were provided by the writings of a group of French-Canadian literary men, Garneau, Ferland, Gérin-Lajoie, Casgrain, Taché, and LaRue. Philippe Aubert de Gaspé had preserved his own memories for later writers to borrow—in his *Les Anciens Canadiens* (translated in 1864, as *The Canadians of Old*, and in 1890 by Charles G. D. Roberts; reissued as *Cameron of Lochiel* in 1905). Sir James MacPherson Le Moine had retold legends of the past and provided information about historical scenes and events in his *Quebec Past and Present* (1876),

The Chronicles of the St. Lawrence (1879), and the seven volumes of his *Maple Leaves* (1863–1906). It was from the sketches of "Chateau Bigot" and "The Golden Dog" in *Maple Leaves* (I and IV) that William Kirby laid the groundwork for his Chien d'Or romance, started in 1865 and published in 1877.

When the tide for romantic historical fiction began to flow strongly in the eighties in Great Britain and North America, and reached its height in the nineties, the French-Canadian past was one matter which American, British, and Canadian writers exploited. Some used it merely as backdrop for sensational romances; others used it to celebrate great men and events; some Canadians deliberately wrote to make a heroic past for their new country. William Kirby had worked long on his *The Golden Dog* to stir his fellow countrymen with a sense of their past. William Douw Lighthall's hero in his *The False Chevalier* (1898) comes out of the French-Canadian countryside into the Guard at Versailles and dies a "real" chevalier to demonstrate native nobility. Andrew Macphail's *The Vine of Sibmah* (1906) dramatizes the 1670's in England, Boston, and Quebec with some historical responsibility. William McLennan and Jean McIlwraith's *The Span of Life* (1899) also used the England, New England, Louisbourg, and Quebec scene in those crucial years, with some sense of historical accuracy. Robert Sellar's *Morven: The Highland United Empire Loyalist* (1911) is a faithful chronicle of settlement in the eastern provinces, and his *Hemlock: A Tale of the War of 1812* (1890) is in the Scott and Cooper tradition of verisimilitude to historical event and physical scene. One of the most graphic reconstructions of a historical situation was made also by Sellar in his "Summer of Sorrow" in *Gleaner Tales* (II, 1895) in which he told in journal form of the immigration from Lord Palmerston's Irish estate in 1847, ending in the tragedy of the quarantine sheds at Grosse Ile.

But the writers who attempted deliberately to stimulate the patriotic sense of their countrymen were relatively few. More used the French-Canadian past as backdrop for costume dramas of mystery, chase, sword-play, and crossed loves. Although Gilbert Parker used historical documents in writing his *The Seats of the Mighty* (1896) the book is more high romance than history. A feeling for the actual men and events plays even less part in Mary Alloway's romance, *Crossed Swords: A Canadian-American Tale of Love and Valor* (1912), which purports to deal with the American invasion. Blanche Macdonell's *Diane of Ville-Marie* (1898), is an equally romantic love story of the 1690's, and Mabel Clint's *Under the King's Bastion* (1902?) is less a story of Quebec in the Spanish-American War than a fictionalized guidebook. John Burham's *Marcelle* (1905) is a crude melodrama of Frontenac's time. Jean McIlwraith used Quebec as background for a charming, lively romance in the 1770's (in which the young Nelson figured) in *A Diana of Quebec*

(1912). Thomas G. Marquis wrote a wooden romance of the days of Jacques Cartier in *Marguerite de Roberval* (1899), and William Douw Lighthall went further back to present a romance of the pre-French days of Hiawatha in *The Master of Life: A Romance of the Five Nations* (1908).

Thanks to the great popularity of Longfellow's *Evangeline* (1847), Acadian history offered materials for an easy appeal to the romantic sensibility of readers in these years. Charles G. D. Roberts wrote four very light action romances based on the country he knew around the shores of the Bay of Fundy; the titles tell their tale: *The Raid from Beauséjour* (1894); *The Forge in the Forest, being the Narrative of the Acadian Ranger, Jean de Mer* (1896); *A Sister to Evangeline* (1898), reissued as *Lovers in Acadie* in 1924; and *The Prisoner of Mademoiselle: A Love Story* (1904).

Other writers used local scene and legend for sentimental and melodramatic historical romances: the Reverend Daniel Hickey in *William and Mary: A Tale of the Siege of Louisburg* (1884); Edward Payson Tenny, *Constance of Acadia* (1886); A. J. McLeod in a long short story, *The Notary of Grand Pré* (1901). Alice Jones's spy romance, *The Night Hawk* (1901) is set in Halifax during the American Civil War. Percy W. E. Hart's *Jason—Nova Scotia* (1903) is a melodramatic tale of Annapolis in the time of Bonnie Prince Charlie. Theodore Roberts spun even lighter historical romances than his brother in his *Brothers in Peril* (1905), *Captain Love* (1908), *A Cavalier of Virginia* (1910), *A Captain of Raleigh's* (1911), and others. Amelia Fytche's *The Rival Forts; or, The Velvet Side of Beauséjour* (1907) is a sentimental costume drama. The coming of the Loyalists to Saint John is narrated in a boy's book, *Roger Davis, Loyalist* (1907) by the Reverend Frank Baird. By 1910 the popularity of historical fiction was ebbing in Great Britain and the United States, and the tide of Canadian historical fiction receded with it.

The fictional form that rivalled historical romance in popularity in these years was the local colour story or sketch. Travel sketches of picturesque foreign lands and atmospheric stories of local American communities filled the *Atlantic Monthly* or the *Century*, and, after 1893, their emulator in Canada, the *Canadian Magazine*. Most of these magazine stories were handsomely illustrated with sketches by skilful artists. A similar taste for the local and the everyday was current in the painting of the day, typified by Millet's canvases, or the work of Horatio Walker or Homer Watson. The growing demand by magazine editors in the eighties and nineties for local colour stories encouraged Canadians to write fictional sketches of French-Canadian life. Many of these stories later were collected in book form. William McLennan, a well-known Montreal lawyer, published a group in *As Told to His Grace, and Other Stories* in 1891; some of the stories included in his *In Old France and New* (1899) also picture *habitant* life, and painstakingly reproduce *habitant* dialect. Edward William Thomson's *Old Man Savarin and Other Stories* (1895) contains some lively stories of the Ottawa River French-Canadians. Duncan Campbell Scott published one of the most skilful collections in his *In the Village of Viger* (1896), and in his later collection, *The Witching of Elspie* (1923). Frank Clifford Smith collected a group in *A Lover in Homespun* in 1896; Louis Fréchette translated some of his stories into English in *Christmas in French Canada* in 1900. Henry Cecil Walsh's *Bonhomme: French-Canadian Stories and Sketches* (1899) is less hazed with sentiment than Fréchette's stories, and includes a few character studies of poor French-Canadian city people. Honoré Beaugrand told more fantastic tales in his *La Chasse-Galerie, and Other Canadian Stories* in 1900. George Moore Fairchild's *A Ridiculous Courting, and Other Stories of French Canada* (1900) stands alongside Scott's in sureness of touch and artistic economy. The tales in Annie Jack's *The Little Organist of St. Jerome and Other Stories of Work and Experience* (1902) probably first appeared in Sunday School papers. James Edward LeRossignol, who published his first book *Little Stories of Quebec* in 1908 and his more impressive full-length story *Jean Baptiste* in 1915, became one of the most prolific writers about the French-Canadian scene.

Most of these writers were visitors to the *habitant* scenes they told about. Their tone is bucolic, as if they are remembering with some quiet pleasure the village scene and the people with whom they had spent some pleasant hours while on a vacation. The sentiment is marked, but not usually heavy; the humour and pathos equally light. They show life centring in individual people in their family roles—the father, the mother, the young son and daughter, the curé. The actions are those of growing up, of courting, or rivalry in the field or village, of leaving home and returning. The characters are animated with devotion to the simpler virtues, to piety, fidelity, to the old ways, resistance to the machine and the city. Money is scarce, and is hoarded. Food is plain and not abundant, until the feast days, when community life boils up in *habitant* homes. Most story-tellers did not attempt to reproduce French-Canadian speech directly, but rather tried to catch the flavour of it through cadences and the odd word of French.

The local colour story was content to picture the local scene for the sake of its own interest. Other writers used the French-Canadian village or seigniory as picturesque background to reinforce romantic melodramas. Gilbert Parker placed his historical fantasy, *When Valmond Came to Pontiac* (1895), in an appropriately romantic French-Canadian village scene, and he returned to the Pontiac scene in his *The Lane that Had No Turning and Other Associated Tales Concerning the People of Pontiac* in 1900. The French-Canadian village during the troubles of 1837 is the setting for his *The Pomp of the Lavilettes* (1896), and he created a mythical parish of St. Saviour for his more contemporary romance *The Money Master* (1915). Contemporary Montreal and a near-by imaginary parish of Chaudière provided the background of one of his most popular books, *The Right of Way* (1901). Parker summed up what many of these writers found attractive in the French Canadian when he wrote: "I think the French Canadian one of the most individual, original, and distinctive beings of the modern world. He has kept his place, with his own customs, his own Gallic views of life, and his religious habits, with an assiduity and firmness. . . . He is essentially a man of the home, of the soil, and of the stream; he has by nature instinctive philosophy and temperamental logic."

The French-Canadian background is even more subordinated to sentimental and sensational foreground in Maud Ogilvy's *The Keeper of Bic Light House* (1891) and her *Marie Gourdon* (1890). Susie Frances Harrison did the same in her *The Forest of Bourg-Marie* (1898) and *Ringfield* (1914). Lily Dougall set part of her religious novel *What Necessity Knows* (1893) in the Matapedia valley, with some care for authenticity. Fashionable Murray Bay and the trip up the Saguenay River form part of the setting in Agnes Maule Machar's romance *The Heir of Fairmount Grange* (1895). Frank Clifford Smith's *A Daughter of Patricians* (1901), although romantic and sensational, does centre on some of the social forces in French-Canadian life.

The novel which achieves the greatest success in presenting unromantically and perceptively a study of French-Canadian life is Francis William Grey's *The Curé of St. Philippe: A Story of French-Canadian Politics* (1899).

Maritime writers were more active in writing about the Maritime localities of their own day than of the past. Arthur Wentworth Eaton and C. L. Betts pictured the Halifax scene in their *Tales of a Garrison Town* (1892). Susan Jones's *A Detached Pirate* (1903) shows the gayer side of garrison life. Grace Dean Rogers published her local colour *Stories of the Land of Evangeline* in 1891. Alice Jones set part of her sensational romance *Bubbles We Buy* (1903) in Nova Scotia. Basil King placed *In the Garden of Charity* (1903) along the lower Nova Scotia coast, and took his heroine from a good Halifax family into Boston society in *The High Heart* (1917). Halifax also afforded some of the background for his *The City of Comrades* (1919). John Alexander Cameron set the early part of his *A Colonel from Wyoming* (1907) in Cape Breton, and made a Cape Breton smuggler captain his chief character in *The Woman Hater* (1912). William Albert Hickman wrote a journalistic epic of icebreakers in the Northumberland Strait in his *The Sacrifice of the Shannon* (1903). Frederick McKelvey Bell fictionalized contemporary history in his *A Romance of the Halifax Disaster* (1918). What appears to be the Annapolis valley scene forms the background for Grace Dean Rogers's *Joan at Halfway* (1919). Margaret Marshall Saunders began her *Rose à Charlitte* (1898, also entitled *Rose of Acadie*) with excellent local colour, but like so many other book-length romances in these years, it turned into romantic melodrama. Carrie Jenkins Harris wrote *A*

Modern Evangeline (1896) and several other light romances of the Windsor area. J. M. Oxley set his *Bert Lloyd's Boyhood* (1892) in Nova Scotia. The life of Nova Scotia fishermen was dramatized most effectively by Frederick William Wallace in his *Blue Water* (1907), *The Shack-Locker: Yarns of the Deep Sea Fishing Fleets* (1916) and later volumes.

The Gaspé country appears in *Marcus Holbeach's Daughter* (1912) and *Flame of Frost* (1914) by Alice Jones. The New Brunswick woods and country form the background for Hiram Cody's *The Fourth Watch* (1911), *The Unknown Wrestler* (1918), *The Touch of Abner* (1919) and others. Half of Theodore Roberts's thirty-four books are set in the Maritimes, many of them in the New Brunswick woods. *Tales of the St. John River and Other Stories* (1904) by Ernest Kirkpatrick, the earlier *Charlie Ogilbie: A Romance of Scotland and New Brunswick* (1889) by Leslie Vaughan, and *Marguerite Verne; or, Scenes from Canadian Life* (1886) by Agatha Armour are New Brunswick stories. The coast of Prince Edward Island provides the local colour for Lily Dougall's mixture of ideas and melodrama, *The Mermaid* (1895); the numerous Anne books made Avonlea famous.

One of the few books of Newfoundland local colour is the Reverend John O'Reilly's loosely knit sketches and anecdotes, *The Last Sentinel of Castle Hill* (1916). The Newfoundland and Labrador background also was used by Ralph Graham Taber in his *Northern Lights and Shadows* (1900); by Theodore Roberts, notably, in his *The Harbor Master* (1913); and by Norman Duncan in his *The Way of the Sea* (1903), *Dr. Luke of the Labrador* (1904), *Harbour Tales Down North* (1918), and his Billy Topsail boy's stories. The medical missionary Wilfred Grenfell proselytized for better living conditions for seamen in his *The Harvest of the Sea* (1905), *Off the Rocks* (1906) *Down to the Sea* (1910), *Down North on the Labrador* (1911), and others.

After the turn of the century the Ontario scene became even more prominent on the Canadian literary map than the Quebec scene. The Ontario that emerges from the fiction of these years is predominantly a projection of the countryside in which its writers grew up. It centres in some locality north of Lake Ontario, or Lake Erie, or along the Ottawa, either in a small town, a crossroads village, or on a near-by farm. The tone of many of these fictions is that of the narrator recapturing his or her past, usually with some affection. In the short story this tone provides a unity; in a book-length story, the narrator frequently, after establishing the tone of his scene, felt the need for stronger interest. His patterns of strong action were the popular melodramas of the late nineteenth century—story or stage—and so what promised in the opening chapters to be an authentic local colour story becomes often an action story, a mystery, or a sentimental romance.

The native scene pictured in most of these stories has a close counterpart in the local colour fiction of New England, and an even closer one in the fiction of village and rural life coming out of the American Midwest: Ohio, Indiana, or Michigan. The centre of this fictional world is the individual, in a family, on a farm or in a small town. Home, school, church, the village store are focal points. The conflict is often between the generations, the old values held by those who have brought them from the Old Country, against those of the young who grow up in the local community. The typical actions are those of growing up, of school and play, of leaving the community, and of returning. Few narratives move out with the protagonist into the outer world. Most of them are romances about the finding of love. They contain little sense of old-world caste; what sense of difference between people there is arises from racial or clan background, or from moral or religious difference. Unconsciously values in them are individualistic, and democratic. What binds people together in these communities is first of all a sense of love; what separates is hate, selfishness, isolation, malicious gossip, and un-Christian lack of charity. The doctor, the father, the mother, the minister are strong figures. Society is assumed to be friendly, and Nature is beneficent, and often inspiring. The characters (and the author) respond to the natural beauty of a winter's night, or a June mid-day, or the changing weather of April or mid-October. For the most part, these fictions present a springtime view of their world. Few were written in the vein of what William Dean Howells called "critical realism," or expressed the "revolt from the Village" which began to appear more frequently in American fiction in the first decades of the twentieth century and culminated most strikingly in Sinclair Lewis's *Main Street* in 1920.

Some of the best stories in Edward William Thomson's *Old Man Savarin* (1895; revised, 1917) picture aspects of life in the Scots communities in Glengarry and along the Ottawa, and Ralph Connor called up his own memories of growing up in Glengarry for the earlier part of *The Man from Glengarry* (1901), in *Glengarry School Days* (1902), and in several of his later books. Robert Lorne Richardson's *Colin of the Ninth Concession* (1903) recaptures similar memories in the first half. His later *The Camerons of Bruce* (1906) also opens with a local Scots scene. The English journalist G. B. Burgin wrote three books about the Hawkesbury locale: *The Only World*, *The Dance at Four Corners*, and *The Judge at Four Corners*. In a tone of simple piety, the Reverend Bertal Heeney's *Pickanock* (1912) recalls affectionately early days near Ottawa and in the lumbering country of the Gatineau. Moving westward in southern rural Ontario, Marian Keith (Mary Esther MacGregor) began her pleasant and sometimes charming imaginative reconstructions of the Scots settlement in Oro Township (near Orillia) in *Duncan Polite* (1905), and most of her subsequent thirteen volumes are of Oro. Stephen Leacock recreated Orillia in his *Sunshine Sketches of a Little Town* (1912), with a touch of nostalgia mixed into his human comedy. Village life somewhere north of Lake Erie provides the scene for May Wilson's sensitively remembered story of family feuds, *Carmichael* (1907). Small village characters are sentimentalized in Adeline Teskey's volumes of tales which began with *Where the Sugar Maple Grows* (1901). The Reverend Archibald McKibbin's mildly didactic story *The Old Orchard* (1903) takes place in Middlesex County, and several of the Reverend Robert E. Knowles', from his *St. Cuthbert's* (1905) on, are of the Grand River valley. One of the stories in Alice Maud Ardagh's *Tangled Ends* (1888) tells a tougher-minded story of life on a Grand River farm. Another story about people in the Grand River valley, *The Untempered Wind* (1894) by Joanna Wood, and *The Unexpected Bride* (1895) by "Constance McDonnell" (Mrs. J. B. Hammond) set near Toronto, are candid pictures of rural Ontario life. Eric Bohn (John Price-Brown) set his scene in a western Ontario village in *How Hartman Won* (1903). The curiously powerful psychological drama *The Dagmar Who Loved* (1904) by Kathleen Blackburn also is set in a western Ontario village. Arthur Stringer wrote in *Lonely O'Malley* (1905) a Tom Sawyerish tale from his own boyhood experiences in Chatham; Archibald McKishnie told a more sensational tale in his *Gaff Linkum: A Tale of Talbotville* (1907). E. E. Sheppard used the Ontario rural scene in his *Dolly, the Young Widder up to Felder's* (1886), written for a farm magazine. Sydney Preston's pleasant *The Abandoned Farmer* (1901) and *On Common Ground* (1906) are set near Clarkson. Not all writers recalled growing up in Ontario villages with pleasure; E. E. Sheppard pictured the old deacon father, leading his family at prayers, with a cold fury in the opening chapters of his *Widower Jones* (1888), and much in the rest of the volume fulfils the promise of the sub-title: "A Realistic Story of Rural Life." W. A. Fraser's *The Lone Furrow* (1907), set in a town much like his own Georgetown, presents with some complexity and insight a group of central characters besieged by villagers with little charity and some viciousness. Kathleen and Robina Lizars' *Committed to His Charge* (1900) pictures effectively the gossip and the meanness which oppresses the life of more sensitive characters in a village like Stratford. The excitement of small town political life and of election day are treated lightly in Kate Carr's *Cupid and the Candidate* (1906), and with much more complexity and realism in Sara Jeannette Duncan's *The Imperialist* (1904), which takes place in Elgin (Brantford). The Reverend LeRoy Hooker's *Baldoon* (1899) has a little of Miss Duncan's satirical touch in depicting village life in Lambton County. Henry Mainer's *Nancy McVeigh of the Monk Road* (1908) is a more sentimental story of a local ministering angel, the old widow who keeps a tavern on the Monck Road in Haliburton County.

Almost all of these fictions of small community life in southern Ontario reveal little awareness of the existence of the Ontario cities of Toronto, Hamilton, London, or Ottawa. Rarely does the action of the book follow a village character who "goes away" from his home; and characters who do leave are more apt to go away to a vague area to the south called "the States." The exception to this self-centredness is the departure of the young man or woman to the city for his or her college years. But only a few narratives accompany the character. Ralph Connor showed his Man from Glengarry going to Varsity, and his central characters in his later *The Doctor* and *The Prospector* also are shown at college. The Reverend William Withrow sent his hero to Victoria in Cobourg in *The King's Messenger* (1879). Maud Petitt sent her heroine from a small western Ontario town to Victoria after it had moved to Toronto, in her *Beth Woodburn* (1897). Harvey O'Higgins's realistic *Don-A-Dreams* (1906) presents a fuller picture of Varsity life before his characters leave for New York. A. R. Carman's *The Preparation of Ryerson Embury* (1900) is set in a college town. And Robert Barr used his memories of the Toronto Normal School for his satire on education in the lively *The Measure of the Rule* (1906).

But college life in these books is not city life, for these undergraduates usually have little awareness of the city lying around the campus. The earliest stories of the city scene were by women writing in the sensational society fiction vein of Mrs. Fleming or Mrs. Sadlier. They sketch a fantasy world of "society" in which their characters intrigue and contend. The most gauche of these is *A Heart-Song of Today Disturbed by Fire from the 'Unruly Member'*, by Mrs. Annie Gregg Savigny in 1886. Her earlier book *Lion, the Mastiff* places its Humane Society story in Toronto, and her later *A Romance of Toronto* (1888) is set in Rosedale. However, these fripperies could have been set in any North American city; the mention of Mr. Eaton's store or of Toronto street names seems to be the only local touch.

Some fictions exploited the widespread belief that virtue lived in the village and vice in the city. Toronto, as a big city, where crookedness reigned in high places, is depicted in E. E. Sheppard's sensational *A Bad Man's Sweetheart* (1889), and much more skilfully in the detective thriller with society and psychological overtones, *Geoffrey Hampstead* (1890) by a prominent young Torontonian lawyer, Thomas Stinson Jarvis. John Charles Dent exploited city crime in his semi-fictional *The Gerrard Street Mystery and Other Weird Tales* (1888). Isabel Ecclestone MacKay's view of the city is more sophisticated in her *Mist of Morning* (1919), in which a country boy encounters an aristocratic young city girl. R. S. Jenkins's overloaded mixture of society romance and murder mystery, *The Heir from New York* (1911), is set in Hamilton and the surrounding countryside.

Several women writers in the Fleming and Sadlier vein also used the Ottawa social scene for sensational and sentimental romances; their books are noted below among the fiction about the federal political scene.

In these years Ontario writers also began to create an imaginative past for their communities. George Millner in his *The Sergeant of Fort Toronto*

(1914) set his strong Cooper-like tale around Toronto and Niagara during the mid-eighteenth century. The Reverend William Withrow narrated a fictionalized history of the establishment of Methodism in Ontario in the 1790's in his *Barbara Heck* (1895). In *Neville Trueman, the Pioneer Preacher* (1880) he attached his young minister to the Canadian forces at Queenston, and constructed a fictionalized history of the Niagara campaign in 1812, and the death of Brock. William Wilfred Campbell in his *A Beautiful Rebel* (1909) pictured the crossed loyalties which sprang from a heroine from a rebel family and a hero in the loyal forces. His dramatization of the battle of Queenston Heights is text-bookish. John Price-Brown was more successful in dramatizing his material in *In the Van; or, The Builders* (1906) which describes the heroic march in 1813 of a British regiment from Nova Scotia to Penetang to build a fort. Graeme Mercer Adam and Ethelwyn Wetherald attempted to fuse two love stories set around Lake Simcoe and York in the 1820's in their *An Algonquin Maiden* (1887) but their romance is overladen with genteel sentiment, intricate plotting, and historical essays. Archibald McKishnie dramatized the conflict between the man of the woods and encroaching "civilization," embodied in a Colonel Talbot-like character, in his *Love of the Wild* (1910). Samuel Mathewson Baylis overwhelmed his story with lecturing and stiff dialogue in "Rebel or Patriot: A Story of '37" in *Camp and Lamp* (1897). John Price-Brown evoked forcefully the drama of Mackenzie's flight from Markham in the middle section of his *The Mac's of '37* (1910). May Wilson ("Anison North") presented the Rebellion from the viewpoint of the rebels in the first half of *The Forging of the Pikes* (1920) and from the viewpoint of the loyalists in the second half, but unfortunately she permitted her love story to overshadow her sense of the past. One of the most vigorous, entertaining stories of pioneer Ontario is Percival John Cooney's *Kinsmen: A Story of the Ottawa Valley* (1916). Daniel Clark's *Josiah Garth* (n.d.) also dealt with the Rebellion.

In *Candlelight Days* (1913), Adeline Teskey told gentle, sentimental tales of the time of the building of the Welland Canal. Marjorie Pickthall's semi-juvenile *Dick's Desertion* (1905) pictures a young boy growing up in a bush clearing near Peterborough, before he responds to the mystical pull of the North. Robert Barr wrote a lively comic treatment of the battle of Ridgeway (Fenian Raids) in his *In the Midst of Alarms* (1894). The description of Ridgeway which appears among the simple sketches of early Ontario rural life in *The Dear Old Farm* (1897) by "Malcolm" (Coll MacLean Sinclair) reads like a non-partisan, first-hand account. In *The Old Loyalist* (1908) Allan Ross Davis wrote "a plain, unvarnished tale" to provoke a greater interest in "our grand old Loyalist ancestors." His amateurish melodrama is a family story of from 1865 to 1884 around Adolphustown, in which Sir John A. appears to make Tory speeches. Sir John A. also is a force in R. E. Knowles's picture of new settlers coming to Glen Ridge, north of Hamilton, in *The Handicap* (1910), and plays *deux ex machina* in what is essentially a sentimental romance.

Probably the part of North America that has most stirred the popular imagination in the Western world has been the West. In the United States it has been the West of the mountain men, the Indian, the covered wagon and the Pony Express, the cowboy, and the miner. In Canada it was first the Northwest Territories, or "North of '53." In 1880 the Northwest Territories included the vast stretch of land north of the St. Lawrence River basin and Lake Superior, the land north of the northern Manitoba border of 52.50', and west of Manitoba to the Rockies and the British Columbia border. The adventure stories of R. M. Ballantyne, W. H. G. Kingston, G. A. Henty, and other English writers had established before 1880 the picture of a great lone land, ruled by the Hudson's Bay Company and inhabited by half-breeds, Indians, Scots factors, or farther north, a white land explored adventurously by men like Franklin. In the early nineties, Gilbert Parker and others turned popular notions about the Northwest into material for stories in English and American magazines. Parker's melodramatic northern stories appeared in *The Chief Factor: A Tale of the Hudson's Bay Company* (1892), *Pierre and His People* (1892), *An Adventurer of the North* (1895), *A Romany of the Snows* (1896), and *Northern Lights* (1909). James Macdonald Oxley wrote more than twenty boy's adventure stories of the North in the nineties and early 1900's. John Burnham's juvenile *Jack Ralston* (1901) is set in Ungava. Susan Jones's *A Girl of the North* (1900) is romantic melodrama. W. A. Fraser centred his excellent tale *The Blood Lilies* (1903) in Fort Donaldson. The second half of Robert Lorne Richardson's *The Camerons of Bruce* (1903) moves to a melodramatic West, and Edwyn Sandys' *Trapper Jim* (1903) is similarly melodramatic. Samuel Alexander White published the first of a number of western action stories, *Empery: A Story of Love and Battle in Rupert's Land*, in 1913 (also published as *Law of the North*). George Ray showed a strong feeling for authentic setting (and sensational melodrama) in *Kasba: A Story of Hudson Bay* (1915). Hiram Cody combined the didactic and the Northwest adventure tale in *If Any Man Sin* (1915) and later stories. W. D. Flatt wrote an even more exemplary tale of two boys making good with the Hudson's Bay Company in *The Making of a Man* (1918). Agnes Laut emphasized the epic quality of the days of discovery and exploration in *Lords of the North* (1900) and followed it by the Radisson story in *Heralds of Empire* (1902).

A different and much more varied West began to emerge in the seventies when settlers moved into what became Manitoba. The transcontinental railroad was completed in 1885, and opened the great plains, the foothills of the Rockies, and the river valleys of British Columbia to the flood of migration which poured westward and northward in the closing years of the old century and the opening decade of the new. The old Northwest Territories shrank in 1905 when the provinces of Saskatchewan and Alberta were carved out of it, and the districts around Hudson Bay became parts of Quebec, Ontario, and Manitoba in 1912. The new West offered many themes for fiction— migration, homesteading, farming, ranching, railroading, mining, timbering, the mingling of cultures, acclimatization, the breakdown of Old World patterns and the forging of new. Smuggling and outlawry and policing were natural subjects for theatrical embroidery. Moreover, the opening of the Canadian West coincided with a rapidly expanding market in American and British magazines for red-blooded, outdoor fiction. This outdoors fiction appealed strongly to a generation conscious of the growth of cities and the swelling complexity of urban and national life. Consequently the Canadian western literary map expanded almost as explosively as did the West itself.

The Manitoba scene first appeared in the memoirs and reminiscences of those who participated in the opening of the West. The first fiction, Alexander Begg's "*Dot-It-Down*" (1871) is partly a satire on men involved in the Red River Rebellion ("Dot-it-down" is the note-taking Charles Mair). Christopher Oakes sketched some vivid scenes of Winnipeg in the boom days of 1882 in the first part of his *The Canadian Senator* (1890). Mrs. M. J. Frank ("A.L.O.M.") gave a semi-fictional, sentimental account of early settlement in *The Brock Family* (1890). A most improbable Manitoba forms the background of James Morton's temperance melodrama *Polson's Probation* (1897), but Ridgwell Cullum's *The Hound from the North* (1904) contains, besides its Yukon melodrama, some realistic scenes of farm life in southeastern Manitoba. Probably the first fiction to be really concerned with the relation of the land and the people who come into it is Ralph Connor's *The Foreigner* (1909) which dramatized the problems of immigration. Mrs. Elizabeth Covey's *Comrades Two: A Tale of the Qu'Appelle Valley* (1907) is more idyllic than realistic; Nellie McClung's stories, *Sowing Seeds in Danny* (1908), its sequel *The Second Chance* (1910), and *The Black Creek Stopping-House* (1912) try to present faithfully the everyday life of small town and farm. The Reverend Edward Anthony Gill's *A Manitoba Chore Boy: The Experience of a Young Emigrant Told from his Letters,* and his *Love in Manitoba,* both published in 1912, deal with immigration and homesteading with some realism. In W. H. Jarvis's amusing exemplary *Letters of a Remittance Man to his Mother* (1909?) the young writer discovers in two years in Winnipeg and on nearby farms why the English "remittance man" (who appears in many western fictions) is held in contempt by Canadians and by Englishmen who are making good. Elinor Marsden Eliot's *My Canada* (1915), in diary form, is description and apologia to outsiders. *The Heart of Cherry McBain* (1919) by Douglas Durkin is a romance of love and action, set in a railroad construction camp near the Saskatchewan border, with considerable feeling for the country. Cy Warman included some tales of early railroading days in the Canadian West in his *Frontier Stories* (1898),

Snow on the Headlight (1899), *The White Mail* (1899), and *The Last Spike* (1906). The best novel to come out of the Manitoba scene before 1920 is Frances Beynon's *Aleta Dey* (1919), although its Winnipeg and Brandon backgrounds play little organic part in the story.

The Rebellion troubles are fictionalized in the highly melodramatic *Annette the Metis Spy: A Heroine of the N. W. Rebellion* (1886) by the journalist J. E. Collins. More romantic and less sensational treatments were published by John Mackie in *The Rising of the Red Man* (1902), and by Joseph Kearney Foran in *Tom Ellis: A Story of the North-West Rebellion* (n.d.). F. D. Reville's *Rebellion: A Story of the Red River Uprising* (1912) is an unskilful mixture of fiction with material from a private journal and an eye-witness account of the earlier troubles.

The early stories of the opening of the Plains and the foothill country stress the dangers and the adventure. General William Francis Butler's *Red Cloud: The Solitary Sioux* (or *Red Cloud: A Tale of the Great Prairie*) (1882) is in the Ballantyne-Kingston-Henty manner. Campbell Shaw's *A Romance of the Rockies* (1888) and Roger Pocock's mixture in *Tales of Western Life, Lake Superior, and the Canadian Prairie* (1888) are simple adventure stories. Love and temptation complicate the outdoor adventure in *The Devil's Playground* (1894), *Sinners Twain* (1895), *They That Sit in Darkness* (1897), and *The Prodigal's Brother* (1899) by John Mackie, the popular Scottish romancer who had been a Mounted Policeman in the eighties. Mounted Police had appeared earlier in Pocock's stories, and in the "Pierre" stories by Gilbert Parker. Cowboys and "Sky Pilots" are central characters in the short stories and sketches of John Maclean's *The Warden of the Plains* (1896). The missionary hero became much more widely known through the success of Ralph Connor's *Black Rock* (1898), and the equally successful *The Sky Pilot* (1899). The North West Mounted Policeman became the hero of full-length romances in Connor's didactic *Corporal Cameron of the North West Mounted Police* (1912) and Hiram Cody's *The Long Patrol: A Tale of the Mounted Police*, published in the same year. An inside picture of the Mounted is presented in Ralph Selwood Kendall's *Benton of the Royal Mounted* (1918) and *The Luck of the Mounted* (1920), since Kendall himself had been one of the force. Non-fictional books on the Force, such as Major-General Sir Sam Steele's *Forty Years in Canada* (1914), also were widely read.

A fictional stereotype of the Mountie became one of the standard figures in the wave of western action stories which followed the innovators early in the century—the American writers Jack London, Stewart Edward White, Owen Wister, and the more commercial Rex Beach, Zane Grey, and James Oliver Curwood. Some Canadians were prolific producers of these formula westerns which appeared first in men's magazines, then in book form, then in cheap reprints issued by A. L. Burt and others. Ridgwell Cullum's first western, *The Story of the Foss River Ranch*, appeared in 1903. His *In the Brooding Wild: A Mountain Tragedy* (1905) dramatizes in epic terms the pre-ranching-trapping-and-trading frontier. Samuel Alexander White's first was *The Stampeder* (1910); and Hulbert Footner's first, *Two on a Trail*, was published in the same year. William Amy, writing under the name "Luke Allan," published his first western, *The Blue Wolf: A Tale of the Cyprus Hills*, in 1913. Some of the most skilfully told western tales appeared in William Alexander Fraser's *Bulldog Carney* (1919), a set of stories about a Robin-Hood-like smuggler in the Alberta foothills.

Other Canadians, native to the Western scene, attempted to portray different aspects of Western life with greater fidelity to what they themselves had experienced. Frances Herring's *On the Pathless West* (1904) was an early attempt to picture life on the plains in romance form, and she followed it with *Nan and Other Pioneer Women of the West* (1913). Frank Robinson's *Trail Tales of Western Canada* was published in the following year. Gilbert Parker tried to picture a situation in the big new West "where destiny is being worked out in the making of a nation" in his *You Never Know Your Luck* (1914), *The World for Sale* (1916), and *Wild Youth and Another* (1919). But Parker knew his Saskatchewan towns only from the outside, and what insight he had into the conflict between races in *The World for Sale* was buried under rhetoric and melodrama. Another exotic, Arthur Stringer, had the advantage over Parker of ranching in Alberta. His trilogy, *The Prairie Wife* (1915), *The Prairie Mother* (1920), and *The Prairie Child* (1922) depict with honest realism some aspects of ranch life, but are marred by being mixed with *Saturday Evening Post* journalism. When his work is compared with that of Harold Bindloss, the popular English writer who had spent a few years in the West before beginning his writing career in England, Stringer's unevenness of intention is apparent. In able romances like his *Ranching for Sylvia* (1912) or *The Girl from Keller's* (1917), Bindloss manages to convey a living sense of his farm environment and the moulding effect of that environment on his pleasant but unheroic characters. The native novelist who developed the realistic portrayal of his Alberta country and his people was Robert Stead. His first fiction, *The Bail Jumper* (1914) reveals his effort to portray his material honestly, although frequently his form was borrowed from the action western. In his *The Homesteaders* (1916) his sense of fidelity to his scene is less distorted by melodramatic form. His range and perception increased in *The Cow Puncher* (1918), and reached the peak of effectiveness in *Grain* (1926), set in Manitoba in the nineties—one of the ablest studies of the transition from pioneering life in the West written by a Canadian. Isabel Paterson's first two novels, *The Shadow Riders* (1916) and *The Magpie's Nest* (1917), also are able pictures of Alberta life.

British Columbian fiction, like British Columbia itself, for outsiders, began with the Cariboo gold rush days of the late 1850's and the early sixties. Anecdotes and tales of the early mining days appeared in Campbell Shaw's *A Romance of the Rockies* (1888), and Arthur Hodgkin Scaife's ("Kim Bilir") *Three Letters of Credit and Other Stories* (1894) and *As It was in the Fifties* (1895). Bret Harte, Mark Twain and other American writers and dramatists had provided the popular forms for fiction about miners and mining. Clive Phillipps-Wolley mined this lode in *Snap: A Legend of the Lone Mountain* (1890), and *Gold, Gold, in Cariboo!* (1894). Ralph Connor combined didacticism, sentiment, and melodrama in his tale of later mining life in *Black Rock: A Tale of the Selkirks* (1898), and he followed this success with *The Sky Pilot: A Tale of the Foothills* (1899), *The Prospector: A Tale of the Crow's Nest Pass* (1904), *The Doctor: A Tale of the Rockies* (1906), *The Pilot at Swan Creek* (1905) and others. Francis Pollock's first books were *The Treasure Trail* (1906) and *The Frozen Fortune* (1910); Bertrand Sinclair's first was *Raw Gold* (1908), and Frederick Niven's was *The Lost Cabin Mine* (1908). Roger Pocock published his *Jessie of Cariboo* in 1911. Julia Henshaw's extravagant melodrama, *Why Not, Sweetheart?* (1901) includes mining scenes, and the heroine of Lily Dougall's *The Madonna of a Day* (1895) sleepwalks from a Pullman in the Rockies into a melodrama of action and ideas in a mining camp. R. E. Knowles followed the pattern of his fellow-minister's *The Sky Pilot* in *The Singer of the Kootenay* (1911). Bertrand Sinclair's hero goes gold-prospecting in his *North of Fifty-Three* (1914), but Sinclair was more concerned with the theme of the redemptive qualities of wilderness living than with exciting action.

Most of these fictions of mining life are action stories. But other fictions are more concerned with communicating the excitement of life in the new British Columbia Eden, an open, awesomely beautiful land which promised the good life to the venturesome, the courageous, and the flexible. Here in farming, ranching, lumbering, or fishing—in the river valleys, in the mountains, and along the coast—the individual could free himself from the pressures of life in the East or the Old Country where social conformity, class structure, and the pursuit of money and status confined the human spirit.

Probably the most effective picture of life on the West Coast is the single volume written by Martin Allerdale Grainger, *Woodsmen of the West* (1908). Grainger knew his lumbering community; his characters are complex and obviously drawn from firsthand acquaintance. His book should remain a minor classic of Coast life. Roger Pocock's *Man in the Open* (1912), although less successful as a whole, has scenes which capture vividly the feel of mountain life, and is peopled with characters who often come alive for some pages. Bertrand Sinclair's novel of the lumbering world, *Big Timber* (1916) and his *Poor Man's Rock* (1920) of the salmon fishing industry, are honest pictures of complex characters in locales which Sinclair knew well. Gilbert Parker early in his writing career worked into part of his novel *Mrs. Falchion* (1893) the conflict between salmon fishermen and lumbering men in a British Columbia coastal village, but the locale seems an incongruous part of the book as a whole. Robert Watson in his *My Brave and Gallant Gentleman* (1918) and *The Girl of O. K. Valley* (1919) used the coast and mountain country more effectively. Like Watson's books, Robert Allison Hood's *The Chivalry of Keith Leicester* (1918) is most occupied with the difficulties of courtship of well-born young English people; the actions of his hero and heroine—both Oxford graduates—take place in the Fraser River farm country and Vancouver. Evah McKowan wrote an engaging book in *Janet of Kootenay* (1919) in which, in letter form, a young "new woman" recounts her adventures in setting up a fruit farm in the Okanagan valley. Minnie Smith's *Is It Just?* (1911) is a unhappier tale of a wife who, after she has to follow her husband from her flourishing Manitoba farm to the Okanagan valley, is deserted and suffers from British Columbia law.

The sensation caused by the gold strikes in Alaska and the Yukon in the nineties immediately led to journalism, anecdote, and fiction about the Gold Rush. Three semi-fictions came out in the year 1898: T. M. Ellis's *Tales of the Klondike*, Thaddeus Leavitt's *Kaffir, Kangaroo, Klondyke*, and Edward Roper's *A Claim on the Klondike: A Romance of the Arctic Eldorado*. The real literary Gold Rush, however, followed the success of the Alaska stories of Jack London and other popular American writers, and even though a Canadian writer might have had some experience of the North, his fiction usually copied the formulas of action fiction. Robert Service's well-known *The Trail of '98* (1911) had woven into it his own experience, but his book imitated the crudest action stories in its characterization, situation, and dialogue, touched up with Service's own literary Bohemianism. Hiram Cody's *The Frontiersman* (1910) and *The Chief of the Ranges* (1913) also derived partly from personal experience, but lost any uniqueness they might have gained from this by their use of stereotype characters, situations, and language. The first part of his later *Glen of the High North* (1920), set in the postwar depression years, gains more power from its originality. Ridgwell Cullum's *Way of the Strong* (1913) and *The Triumph of John Karrs* (1917) are effective action tales, with less of the complexity of the human element sometimes found in his other work. William Henry Jarvis's *The Great Gold Rush* (1913) has more authenticity. Although it is a romantic melodrama, one of the most effective pictures of Dawson City life is caught in Madge Macbeth's *Kleath* (1917). But the Canadian "Northwest" familiar to a world-wide audience in the 1910's and the 1920's was not primarily the Yukon, the Rockies, or the Coast; it was the Peace, Athabaska, and the Mackenzie country. Of the Canadians who wrote of this last of the pre-1920 frontiers, the most popular were Hiram Cody, Hulbert Footner, Samuel Alexander White, Arthur Chisholm, and Ridgwell Cullum. Harold Bindloss, who had travelled in the West before returning to England to begin his prolific writing career, set some of his romances there. The most widely read writer about the Northwest, however, was James Oliver Curwood, a Michigan man who spent many seasons in "God's Country." Following the patterns of the red-blooded and the nature fiction writers of the turn of the century, he achieved a large international following by the melodramatic vigour of his work. His thirty-one romances sold well over four million copies in English, and many more copies in translation in eleven other languages; most of his stories also were converted into popular moving pictures.

The fictions listed above were among the primary agents which during these years established in the minds of the Anglo–North American reading public images of life in the different regions which made up the political entity "Canada." Not all of them were concerned directly with creating a sense of a particular locality; many were more concerned with depicting some aspect of the quickening social, political, economic, religious, and ethical conflicts of their times. The 1880's and early 1890's were periods of intense economic depression in various parts of North America; the later 1890's and the first decade of the twentieth century were boom years. They were the years of the rapid growth of the cities, of the movement of millions of people into North America and from one part of North America to another. They were the years of bitter struggle between capital and labour, and the rise of protest parties and dreams of democratic Utopias. Although Canada was still predominantly rural, some Canadian fiction reflected the growth of industrialization and its social impact. Agnes Maule Machar's *Roland Graeme, Knight* (1892), John Galbraith's *In the New Capital* (1897), A. R. Carman's *The Preparation of Ryerson Embury: A Purpose* (1900), H. P. Blanchard's *After the Cataclysm* (1909), and Mabel Burkholder's *The Course of Impatience Carningham* (1911) deal with the various aspects of labour unrest or industrial social injustice. Robert Barr's novel of labour conflict in an English factory, *The Mutable Many* (1896) is the most effective full-length study of labour–capital strife. William Henry Moore's *Polly Masson* (1919) presents in several of its scenes the conflicting interests of Canadian farmers, union leaders, and business men.

Few Canadian writers presented transcendental schemes for social reform in their fiction; their typical position was that of the middleman, discomforted by pressures from the right and left, feeling that if only capital and labour would stop pushing and behave as decent Christian small-town neighbours, social problems might go away. This middle position is expressed by various narrators in some of Stephen Leacock's sketches, although Leacock, an admirer of Veblen, more frequently took as his mark the pretensions of the plutocracy.

The fiction which reflects some picture of Canada as an entity was built on political themes. Some writers like Christopher Oakes in his *The Canadian Senator* (1890) made fun of pomposity and incompetence in high places. Blanchard's *After the Cataclysm* and Galbraith's *In the New Capital* are more sweeping in rejecting the current political ways. Like Galbraith and "Ex-Journalist" in his *They Two: or, Phases of Life in Eastern Canada Fifty Years Ago* (1888), Moore organized his *Polly Masson* in an omnibus fashion so that he could present a wide range of Canadian political topics: the opening of the West; the building of the C.P.R.; the treatment of the Indians; reciprocity; free trade; Roman Catholic–Protestant tensions; Canadian relations with the United States and Canadian feeling for the Mother Country. Sara Jeannette Duncan wrote *The Imperialist* (1904) to show how ordinary Canadians really felt about Imperial relations. Her delightful irony plays around the colonial-minded in *Cousin Cinderella: A Canadian Girl in London* (1908). Three of her Indian books, *His Honour and a Lady* (1896), *Set in Authority* (1906), and *The Burnt Offering* (1909) are concerned with the tragic consequences of political power. Her novel *The Consort* (1912) pictures the struggle for power between a philanthropist wife and her writer-politician husband in England. Other Canadian women used the political scene to embroider their light society romances: Kate Bottomley's *Honor Edgeworth; or, Ottawa's Present Tense* (1882), Helen Bogg's *When the Shadows Flee Away: A Story of Canadian Society* (1891), and Kate Carr's *Cupid and the Candidate* (1906). Apart from Sara Jeannette Duncan, the only other Canadian woman to write a serious novel on political ideas was Margaret Adeline Brown in *My Lady of the Snows* (1908); unfortunately her intellectual idealism exceeded her art.

One of the subjects most prevalent in Canadian fiction in this period is religion. In 1909, in one of a number of conflicting articles in the *Canadian Magazine*, the Reverend John Paterson Smyth, rector of St. George's, Montreal, discussed "the wide influence which novel-reading exerts in our day in the field of morals and theology." Far from protesting against this influence, he contrasted the advantages of the popular novel, whose circulation might reach 1,000,000 copies, with the limitations of the pulpit. In most sections of the country, as in the United States and parts of Great Britain, the church was the centre of community life, and the clergyman often was an arbiter of culture. In Canada in these years, the ministry, along with journalism, provided more fiction writers than any other profession; more than thirty Canadian ministers published fiction. They were encouraged to do so by religious-minded publishers such as Briggs, Westminster, Copp Clark, and Hunter Rose, and by religious societies abroad. A receptive public, predominantly rural or small town, middle-class and church-going, and largely fundamentalist in training, gave religious fiction its share of the great boom in fiction at the turn of the century.

Religion was presented in a wide variety of ways in these fictions. It was used merely as sensationally different plot material in the Reverend Albert de Long's *A Wolf in Sheep's Clothing* (1905); as part of the historical scene in Gilbert Parker's fiction set in Quebec, or in W. W. Campbell's *A Beautiful Rebel* (1909); or as incidental critical comment in *They Two: or, Phases of Life in Eastern Canada Fifty Years Ago* (1888) by "Ex-Journalist" (Richard Lanigan) and *Tales of a Garrison Town* (1892) by A. W. H. Eaton and C. L. Botts. In *Widower Jones: A Faithful History of his "Loss," and Adventures in Search of a Companion* (1888), E. E. Sheppard in an early scene attacked religiosity and hypocrisy; at one critical point in Robert Stead's *The Cow Puncher* (1918) the hero, revolted by cant, walks out of church.

Pietism predominates in much of the domestic sentimental fiction written largely by women. Mrs. M. J. Frank's *The Brock Family* (1890), Mrs. Emma Wells Dickson's *Miss Dexie: A Romance of the Provinces* (1895), and Rosa Portlock's *The Head Keeper* (1898), are representative. They stress Christian virtues and individual morality in the family and among neighbours. Maud Pettit's *Beth Woodburn: A Canadian Tale* (1897) is unusual in treating the problem of the aspiring young artist, but once the heroine's decision to channel her art to the purposes of religion has been made, it conforms to the general pattern. Not all domestic fiction is sentimental; *Committed to His Charge* (1900) by R. and K. M. Lizars presents the human problems of a young Anglican minister in a small Ontario town, with some complexity of tone.

Less sentimental and more active are the stories in a group whose subject is the clergy. Although some of the best were written by clergymen, they are not particularly sectarian. Much of the material is familiar: the evangelical purpose, the old hymns, the plea for temperance, the repetition of the "prodigal son" story. Related to adventure and frontier fiction, set in the outdoors and packed with physical activity, many of them illustrate the personal influence of one strong man, often the oversized muscular Christian, on the fallen and the stragglers. Outstanding examples are Ralph Connor's *Black Rock: A Tale of the Selkirks* (1898) and *The Sky Pilot: A Tale of the Foothills* (1899), Norman Duncan's *The Measure of a Man: A Tale of the Big Woods* (1911), and, from numerous stories of this pattern by the Reverend Hiram Cody, *The Frontiersman: A Tale of the Yukon* (1910), *The Fourth Watch* (1911), and *The Unknown Wrestler* (1918). Ernest Thompson Seton's *The Preacher of Cedar Mountain: A Tale of the Open Country* (1917) presents the conflict in a minister torn between the call of the city and the frontier ministry.

A number of fictions, written chiefly by ministers, attempted to proselytize by portraying life in a specific religious community. They range in form from a simple presentation of faith, through the tract or sermon, to the arena where differing views contend. *Philip Hazelbrook; or, The Junior Curate* (1886) by the Reverend H. F. Darnell was intended "faithfully to portray the Church of England of to-day as she really is"; the contributions of the extremely popular and prolific Basil King present general moral problems within the framework of the Episcopal church. *Duncan Polite: The Watchman of Glenoro* (1905) by Marian Keith and *St. Cuthbert's* (1905) by the Reverend R. E. Knowles centre in the Presbyterian manse and settlement. Although they are not primarily "religious," W. A. Fraser's *The Lone Furrow* (1907) and Sara Jeannette Duncan's *The Imperialist* (1904) dramatize the importance of the church and church-going in sections of Ontario that are predominantly Presbyterian. *The King's Messenger; or, Lawrence Temple's Probation: A Story of Canadian Life* (1879), *Neville Truman, the Pioneer Preacher: A Tale of the War of 1812* (1880), and *Barbara Heck: A Tale of Early Methodism in America* (1895), represent the Reverend W. H. Withrow's devoted contribution to his particular church.

More closely related to English religious fiction, the battleground for rival sects earlier in the century, are attacks or defences of the Roman Catholic cause. Emily Weaver in *Soldiers of Liberty: A Story of Wars in the Netherlands* (1892) recalled the Spanish persecutions to express her fear of Catholicism. Frank Clifford Smith in *A Daughter of Patricians* (1901) attacked the marriage laws of Quebec and the power of the Catholic clergy over their credulous people. The Roman Catholic cause was defended and advocated by W. J. Fischer's *Winona and Other Stories* (1906), Elizabeth Gagnieur's *Back in the Fifties; or, Winnings and Weedings: A Tale of Tractarian Times* (1907), and the Reverend E. J. Devine's *The Training of Silas* (1906). Lily Dougall, always quick to profit from strange materials, portrayed Mormon struggles sympathetically in *The Mormon Prophet* (1899). J. P. Buschlen's Mormon story, *Peter Bosten: A Story about Realities* (1915) is more partisan. The Amish way of life in their central Ontario settlements is described with understanding by Clyde Smith in his *The Amishman* (1912). The most topical and most controversial of these partisan works was *Looking Forward: The Strange Experience of the Rev. Fergus McCheyne* (1913). Here, using the method of Edward Bellamy, the Rev. Hugh Pedley looked forward to the time when Church Union has been achieved, making Canada "better because a little more of heaven has entered into its life."

These works deal with firm convictions and determined positions. There are several, however, that are more closely linked with contemporary religious uncertainty. These, a mere handful in contrast to the large output in Great Britain and the United States, reflect the dissolution of traditional beliefs, the intellectual problems that result from the impact on traditional religion of science and "Higher Criticism" and the growth of scepticism and agnosticism. The emphasis falls on one central character, around whose spiritual biography the plot is built. The novel traces his doubts, loss of faith, and his search for a new religious position, unorthodox and undogmatic, or for some substitute "religion." The chief problems are the inspiration of the Bible, the presence of pain and evil in the universe, and the divinity of Christ; solutions are found in Pantheism, Universalism, and a belief in "Brotherhood," "true Christianity," the "living Jesus of the Gospels."

An incongruous mixture of current ideas and sensation, mystery and sentiment mars Watson Griffin's *Twok: A Novel* (1887), A. E. Greenwood's *The Light and the Lure* (1897), and James Algie's *Houses of Glass: A Philosophical Romance* (1898). Algie's *Bergen Worth* (1901) is more successful, through his realization of two characters that embody his central idea: the superiority of a religion based on the promptings of the individual conscience, expressed in charitable action, over that based on authority. Lily Dougall, strenuously intellectual, and at the same time sensitive to the requirements of the public, included the search for a new, more tolerant faith in *What Necessity Knows* (1893). In *The Zeit-Geist* (1895) she traced the central character's discovery of what he calls "Pantheism," when he finds himself "alone in the world with his new ideas."

Roland Graeme, Knight: A Novel of Our Times (1906) by Agnes Maule Machar and *The Preparation of Ryerson Embury: A Purpose* by A. R. Carman have much in common. Both heroes, brought up by fundamentalist parents, lose their dogmatic faith at college, but through the dual influence of Henry George and a good minister, come to a new faith that solves the problems of labour by the example of the life of Christ. While Agnes Maule Machar placed her emphasis on external events and direct statement, Carman came closer to finding a suitable form, concentrating on the internal struggle of Ryerson Embury. Reading Paley, Paine, Strauss, and Ingersoll, and disturbed by the problems raised by science, he loses his faith. It is Carman's steady focus on Embury's spiritual odyssey through a significant pattern of events, against a solidly realized social background, that makes *The Preparation of Ryerson Embury* stand out among this group of religious novels.

A number of ministers and their parishioners, militant against drink, used fiction to preach cautionary tales. The titles usually tell the story: the Reverend James Seymour's *The Temperance Battlefield and How to Gain the Day: A Book for the Young of All Ages, full of Humorous and Pathetic Stories* (1882); Austin Potter's *From Wealth to Poverty: or, Tricks of the Traffic: A Story of the Drink Curse* (1884); Lance Bilton's *"Guilty": Forgiven—Reclaimed; "Truth is Stranger than Fiction": A Canadian Story from Real Life* (1906) or the two stories in one volume, *A Fragment of*

Ontario's Scott Act: or, A Ruined Life, by "W.C.T.U." (Mrs. DeWolf) and *Lawyer Robert Streighton's Discovery at a Mineral Spring*, by "Carlton" (Mrs. C. A. Baird). Episodes dramatizing the evils of drink, along with little sermons and tableaux, appear in a number of the longer fictions of the day, such as H. A. Cody's *The Frontiersman* (1910) or Stephen Cureton's *Perseverance Wins* (1880). Some of the realistic novels used alcoholism as one of the grimmer facts of everyday life, such as Frances Beynon's *Aleta Dey* (1919). Temperance reformers are derided in a few fictions, such as E. E. Sheppard's *A Bad Man's Sweetheart* (1889). One of the most spectacular scenes involving drink occurs in James Dunlop's melodrama *Forest Lily* (1898) when a drunkard curses and immediately is snatched up.

Missionaries and their wives wrote fiction to attract support for their work in spreading the gospel. Some missionaries wrote of the Far East: Janet McKillican published her *The Tragedy of Paotingfu* in 1902; the Reverend James Gale wrote of Korea in *The Vanguard* (1904); the Reverend William Walker did the same in *Occident and Orient* in 1905; in 1914 the Reverend Thurlow Fraser published his *The Call of the East: A Romance of Far Formosa*. Other missionaries wrote of the home missionary fields; the romances of Ralph Connor, Robert Knowles, Hiram Cody, and Dr. Grenfell have been noted. The Reverend Egerton Ryerson Young directed his missionary story *Oowikapun; or, How the Gospel Reached the Nelson River Indians* (1895) and five others to young, impressionable readers; his son, of the same name, carried on his work. Christian evangelism welled over into missionary endeavour for animals. Margaret Marshall Saunders is said to have given most of what royalties she received for her many animal stories to Humane Societies; her most famous book, *Beautiful Joe* (1894), published originally by the American Baptist Publishing Society, sold over one million copies in fourteen languages. Miss Saunders' story is not as sentimental as the many animal tales by other Canadian women writers. The men who wrote animal stories—Roberts, Seton, Fraser, and McKishnie—wrote in a different vein; their work is considered elsewhere.

The demand for historical romance led some Canadian writers to write of the past of lands other than their own. Elizabethan and Jacobean England seems to have attracted the more sentimental romancers, such as Emily Weaver in *My Lady Nell* (1889) and *Prince Rupert's Namesake* (1893), Virna Sheard in *Trevelyan's Little Daughters* (1898), *A Maid of Many Moods* (1902) and *By the Queen's Grace* (1904), and Marjorie Pickthall in the more private *Little Hearts* (1915). John A. Copland's *A Meteor King* (1899) is of Richard III. The Spanish Catholic suppression of religious liberty in the Netherlands was used for propaganda by Elizabeth Walshe in *Within Sea Walls; or, How the Dutch Kept the Faith* (1881) and in Emily Weaver's *Soldiers of Liberty* (1892). William McLennan told swashbuckling tales in his *Spanish John* (1898) and *In Old France and New* (1899). Gilbert Parker's romance of the Jersey Islands, *The Battle of the Strong* (1898), was considered by many readers his best historical romance.

Historical romances of biblical, Greek, and Roman times enjoyed a steady success in the nineteenth century. In 1882 the Reverend William Withrow constructed a romantic story *Valeria: A Tale of Early Christian Life in Rome* out of his earlier history of the Catacombs. The Reverend P. J. Harold wrote another romance of female Christian martyrdom in his *Irene of Corinth: A Historical Romance of the First Century* (1884). The journalist and actor William Thorold told a story of Nazareth and Rome in his *Zerola of Nazareth* (1895); the Reverend LeRoy Hooker published *Enoch, the Philistine: A Traditional Romance of Philistia, Egypt, and the Great Pyramid* in 1898. Emily Weaver's *The Rabbi's Sons: A Story of the Days of St. Paul* appeared in 1891. L. O. Loomer used the Amos story in his *The Prophet: A Story of the Two Kingdoms of Ancient Palestine* in 1911. Edgar Maurice Smith exploited the violence and rapine of Hannibal crossing the Alps in *Aneroestes the Gaul* (1898). James Miller Grant's *The Mother of St. Nicholas (Santa Claus): A Story of Duty and Peril* (1899) is a melodrama of lions, Christians, and coliseums in the third century in Asia Minor.

The religiosity of some found outlet in pseudo-spiritual fiction. Canadian versions of the popular kinds of psychic fiction appear in Julia Henshaw's *Hypnotized; or, The Experiment of Sir Hugh Galbraith* (1898), Ida May Ferguson's *Tisab Ting; or, The Electric Kiss* (1896), Flora Macdonald's *Mary Melville, the Psychic* (1900), Benjamin Fish Austin's *The Mystery of Ashton Hall* (1910), and "Q, A Psychic Pstory of the Psupernatural!" in Stephen Leacock's *Nonsense Novels* (1911).

A characteristic part of the experience of a number of Canadian writers during these years was that of "going away" from their small, native communities to alien lands. The three broad movements were westward to the plains, foothills, and the Coast (manifest in the fiction listed above in the description of the literary map of Canada); southward to large American cities, particularly New York or Boston; and eastward across the Atlantic to London or the Continent. Those who used their encounter with the Old World in their fiction possibly followed the success of earlier Canadian writers who had pictured provincials abroad—Thomas Chandler Haliburton in his *The Letter Bag of the Great Western* (1840), his *The Attaché; or, Sam Slick in England* (1843), or De Mille's *The Dodge Club; or, Italy in 1859* (1868–1869), or they followed the success of American books about innocents abroad, passionate pilgrims, and other international themes. Mrs. Carrie Jenkins Harris pursued the comic vein of her Maritime predecessors in her lamer *Mr. Perkins of Nova Scotia* (1891). Sara Jeannette Duncan was much more successful in her spirited social comedies of international manners, *An American Girl in London* (1891), and its sequel *A Voyage of Consolation* (1898). Her central character, Lorne Murchison, in *The Imperialist* (1904) is affected strongly by the vision of imperialism during his visit to England, and one part of the book deals with the political and social consequences of this vision. In Miss Duncan's fullest canvas of the Canadian in England, *Cousin Cinderella* (1908), the young narrator and her brother, sent to England as cultural ambassadors, are conscious of being colonials no longer; "home" is not London but the small Ontario town and countryside. In *Those Delightful Americans* (1902), Miss Duncan pictured the innocent young Englishwoman's encounter with American culture. L. S. Huntington similarly brought a group of English people to America in his *Professor Conant: A Story of English and American Social and Political Life* (1884), with less acuteness than Miss Duncan.

The innocent Canadians abroad in Alice Jones's *Gabriel Praed's Castle* (1904), *Marcus Holbeach's Daughter* (1912), and *Flame of Frost* (1914) are beset by the corrupt forces of the Old World. Miss Duncan had followed faithfully her mentors Howells and James in trying to present the truth as she saw it; Alice Jones highlighted the aspects of the Old World which brought out her romance and melodrama. Susan Jones did the same in *A Girl from the North* (1900); in *A Detached Pirate* (1903) she brought her gay young divorcée from London to Halifax, and narrated through letters her romantic adventures in the garrison set. The spirit and the form make it an amusing contrast to that first of Canadian fictions, Frances Brooke's *The History of Emily Montague*, published 134 years before.

Gilbert Parker (later Sir Gilbert, and a London spokesman for Imperialism) used the theme of the young person from the province in "At the Sign of the Eagle," *The Translation of a Savage* (1893), and *The Trespasser* (1893), some of his earliest work while he himself was assaulting the London literary world. His stories of the people from the periphery in England are of struggle for power, and recognition. Beverley Baxter's *The Parts Men Play* (1920) is the story of an American idealist in wartime England, and suggests a bright young writer's strenuous effort to conceal the fact that he is a Canadian.

Canadian writers had one more dimension to their international experience than their American contemporaries, for they could go south or east. The move to Boston is central to Basil King's *The High Heart* (1917) and *The City of Comrades* (1919), and appears incidentally in some of his other books. Arthur Stringer's ambitious first novel, *The Silver Poppy* (1903), is about a young literary graduate from Oxford who moves to New York to write his great novel. Thomas Stinson Jarvis's *She Lived in New York* (1894) deals in part with New York Bohemia, as his earlier *Dr. Perdue* (1892) had dealt in part with an international smart set. The second half of Harvey

O'Higgins' *Don-A-Dreams* (1906) brings three young Canadian undergraduates to New York to storm the heights. These fictions were written from first-hand experience of the American cities; the second half of Robert Lorne Richardson's *Colin of the Ninth Concession* (1903) was derived apparently from Horatio Alger's stories of the country boy who comes to the big city and achieves financial success by pluck and luck. Susan Frances Harrison's *The Forest of Bourg-Marie* (1898) contrasts the ways of life in provincial Quebec and in a godless American city (Milwaukee).

Although the central character in stories of young Canadians in New York may aspire to be a writer, the great good place for young Canadians with raw talent in the arts was Europe. Jane Conger's *A Daughter of St. Peters* (1889) is the story of young artists in Rome. In Maud Ogilvy's *Marie Gourdon* (1890) a Canadian girl becomes a famous singer, and a boy an artist. In Thaddeus Leavitt's *The Witch of Plum Hollow* (1892) a young Canadian girl becomes a famous artist. Sara Jeannette Duncan sent her "new woman" from Illinois to study painting in the Latin Quarter in *A Daughter of Today* (1894), and after failure in Paris, to free-lance in London. Amelia Fytche's *Kerchiefs to Hunt Souls* (1895) is a melodrama of a young woman who goes to Paris to paint, marries a Frenchman, and is deserted by him. Joanna Wood's heroine in *Judith Moore; or, Fashioning a Pipe* (1898) flees from a great singing career in the outside world to the Ontario village of Ovid, where she finds love. The power of music plays a major part in the romances by Clifford Smith, *A Daughter of Patricians* (1901) and Lilla Nease, *In Music's Thrall* (1903). The title of Albert Richardson Carman's book tells enough of its tale: *The Pensionnaires: The Story of an American Girl who Took a Voice to Europe and Found—Many Things* (1903). Europe as an art world is the background for Alice Jones's *Gabriel Praed's Castle* (1904). The ineffectual heroine in Harvey O'Higgins' *Don-A-Dreams* (1906) fails to achieve a musical career in Europe. Robert Service's *The Pretender* (1914) is a romance of bohemian life in the Latin Quarter. Winifred Reeve's *Marion* (1916) is the story of an artists' model. The hero of John Murray Gibbons's *Hearts and Faces* (1916) moves from Aberdeen, through Soho in London, to Paris in search of his creative soul. Gibbons's *Drums Afar* (1918) also is concerned, in part, with artists. Very few Canadian fictions pictured the writer or artist as indigenous; in W. A. Fraser's anti-romantic *The Lone Furrow* (1907) the narrator is a novelist; in Susie Frances Harrison's *Ringfield* (1914), the heroine acts in a small Montreal theatre. The young heroine in Maud Petitt's *Beth Woodburn* (1897), living in a small western Ontario community, has the ambition to become a novelist, but sacrifices it to become a missionary; Miss Petitt's book is a rare example of the mingling of the worlds of art and religion; in most of the books noted here the world of art is indifferent, or hostile, to the world of religion.

In the last few years of this period, the First World War, chiefly in its domestic aspects, appeared in some Canadian fiction. A few writers wrote as did Nellie McClung in her semi-fictional *The Next of Kin* (1917) to make the home fires burn brighter. Others wrote to capitalize on or commemorate aspects of the war, as Frederick Bell did in *A Romance of the Halifax Disaster* (1918), or Gertrude Arnold in *Sister Anne! Sister Anne!* (1920), or Captain S. N. Dancey in *The Faith of a Belgian: A Romance of the Great War* (1916). Some sentimentalized the home front, as Jean Blewett did in *Heart Stories* (1919).

Other writers used the War as a force to help them express certain themes in their novels. Robert Stead in *The Cow Puncher* (1918) closed his story of his hero's search for identity by having him die at the Front and thus become initiated into the "Order of Suffering." Basil King used the tensions created by Canada's entering the War earlier and for different reasons than the United States in his *The High Heart* (1917) and *The City of Comrades* (1919). Beverley Baxter in *The Blower of Bubbles* (1919) depicted the conflicts in an idealistic pacifist in wartime England and New York, who eventually joins the American army and finds his problems resolved in action at the Front. In the closing section of Frances Beynon's *Aleta Dey* (1919) the heroine loses her man to the War and campaigns for the pacific cause in Winnipeg, is arrested, and dies with a noble pronouncement. Bertrand Sinclair in his equally anti-romantic *Burned Bridges* (1919) made the personal choice of enlistment one of the bridges his hero must burn behind him. The heroine of Evah McKowan's *Janet of Kootenay* (1919) finally joins her fortunes with those of a wounded returned officer. The disenchanted returned man in John Murray Gibbons's *The Conquering Hero* (1920) takes to the woods as a guide. Ralph Connor's *The Major* (1917) is a sentimental romance, set in a small Alberta community, as the world moves into war. His *The Sky Pilot in No Man's Land* (1919) takes a young Alberta chaplain to active service at the Front and to a sacrificial death. It is the epitome of a prevalent Anglo-Saxon Canadian view of the War—idealistic, Protestant evangelical, and British tribal—and probably more prevalent among non-combatants and officers than among Other Ranks.

One other major kind of fiction written by Canadians between 1880 and 1920 is that of mystery and crime melodrama. Many of the books noted above, although not mystery or crime melodramas, open with some mystery —the problem of unknown parents, hidden relationships, inscrutable motives, lost wills, inexplicable disappearances, or the arrival of unknown strangers; and many of them conclude with the solution of the initial mystery and the heroine in the hero's arms. But more than fifty fictions during these years are mystery or crime stories in the stricter sense. Some of them are semi-fictitious accounts of actual happenings, such as the highly melodramatic *The Four*

Canadian Highwaymen; or, The Robbers of Markham Swamp (1886) by Joseph Collins, or John Charles Dent's *The Gerrard Street Mystery and Other Weird Tales* (1888). Some play with supernatural or psychical elements: Thaddeus Leavitt's *The Witch of Plum Hollow* (1892), James Algie's *Bergen Worth* (1901), or Benjamin Austin's *The Mystery of Ashton Hall* (1910). Others mix mystery or crime with local colour, humour, and sentiment, as does E. E. Sheppard's *A Bad Man's Sweetheart* (1889) or the second half of his *Dolly: The Young Widder up to Felder's* (1886), or Isadore Asher's *An Odd Man's Story* (1889). After the turn of the century the fashion changed to the mystery or suspense story of the underworld or of international intrigue. The typical hero became the master-mind, either within or outside the law. One of the pacesetters of the new fashion was Arthur Stringer in his *The Wire Tappers* (1906), *Phantom Wires* (1907), *The Gun Runners* (1909), *The Shadow* (1913), and *The House of Intrigue* (1918). Some of the earliest stories in Frank Packard's long and prolific career are suspense stories of moral and sentimental dilemmas, *Greater Love Hath No Man* (1913), *The Miracle Man* (1914), and *The Beloved Traitor* (1915). Packard produced the first of his widely popular master-mind mysteries in *The Adventures of Jimmy Dale, Detective* in 1917. Harvey O'Higgins published his *The Adventures of Detective Barney* in book form in 1915. Guy Morton's *The Enemy Within* (1918) is the first of his ten mystery stories. Hulbert Footner and W. L. Amy interspersed mystery fiction in the publication of their steady streams of western action tales.

Between 1880 and 1920 few Canadian fiction writers revealed in their work any awareness of the various kinds of "new fiction" which appeared in Great Britain and in the United States as these years rolled by, from writers as diverse as James, Conrad, Crane, Norris, Dreiser, Wells, Forster, Ford, Mackenzie, Lawrence, Joyce, Anderson, Virginia Woolf, and Willa Cather. Often experimental in form, the "new fiction" frequently explored the darker side of human experience. Usually it was written to express the writer's private vision, not to please the tastes of the comon reader. Canadian writers, however, like most of their British and American contemporaries, lived and worked on another floor in the house of fiction. As this panorama of roughly two-thirds of the Canadian fiction published during these years has shown, they wrote in the varieties of fiction read by the great middle band in the spectrum of the reading public. Panoramas of their values, their forms, their characters, and their fictional techniques would show similar community. What did distinguish their work, as a body, was the remarkable extent to which they used their own native grounds as material in their stories.

17. Writers of Fiction
1880-1920

GORDON ROPER, S. ROSS BEHARRIELL
AND RUPERT SCHIEDER

ANOTHER PERSPECTIVE of the contours of Canadian fiction between 1880 and 1920 can be obtained by placing, side by side, sketches of the fiction-writing careers of the more skilful Canadian writers of these years, in order of their first appearance in book form.

John Bourinot's opinion of the barrenness of the Canadian fiction field, quoted at the beginning of chapter 15, was also held by other Canadian commentators on the arts in Canada. In his essay, however, Bourinot did express some hope that the first books recently published by the young Gilbert Parker, Sara Jeannette Duncan, and Lily Dougall marked the end of the barren period. That he did not name two other writers of Canadian background, Grant Allen and Robert Barr, who already had made places for themselves on the London literary scene, suggests that Bourinot shared the uncertainty of other Canadians in the early nineties about who and what was a "Canadian" writer.

Grant Allen (1848-1899) was Canadian in the sense that he had been born near Kingston, Ontario, and had spent his first thirteen years there before his Irish clergyman father moved the family to Connecticut, then to France, and finally to England. Allen graduated from Oxford in 1871 with a keen interest in science. He threw himself into a writing career in London to support his scientific studies and to advance his ideas. Out of a stream of magazine writing on evolution, biology, botany, religion, and human relations, he published some seventy books, including over forty fictions. His fiction often dramatizes new scientific and social ideas; he had a vigorous imagination; his work was controversial, and it was widely read in England and in North America. His fiction includes *Philistia* (1884) which satirized fuzzy Utopianism; the sensational *The Devil's Die* (1888), and the more notorious *The Woman Who Did* (1895) which embodies his ideas about the value of sexual freedom.

Grant Allen's fiction contains little that reflects his Canadian birth and early education. His books were discussed in Canadian journals, but few Canadians, for whatever reasons, thought of him as "one of ours."

More readers thought of Robert Barr as a Canadian writer. Barr (1850-1912) was born in Glasgow, Scotland, but had been brought to Canada by his family when he was five. He grew up on a farm near Wallacetown, Ontario, and after a year at the Toronto Normal School taught near Windsor. He began his professional writing career on the *Detroit Free Press*, and moved permanently to England in 1881 when he was thirty-one. In London he became one of the more successful of those who wrote for the English and American magazines; he also was co-founder with Jerome K. Jerome and editor of the *Idler Magazine* in 1892. Among his many literary and journalistic friends he numbered Stephen Crane, with whom he collaborated in writing a picaresque tale, *The O'Ruddy* (1903). His more than thirty volumes of fiction include examples of almost every kind of fiction popular in the Anglo-American literary world at the turn of the century: adventure romances in the Richard Harding Davis vein; costume dramas and historical romances in somewhat imaginary kingdoms; detective tales; tales of the supernatural; and "muckraking" novels of political, social, and labour strife.

Unlike Grant Allen, Robert Barr drew on his Canadian experience in some of his short stories and longer fiction. *The Woman Intervenes* (1895) has an Ottawa interlude, and his study of political corruption in New York, *The Victor* (1901), has a Montreal episode. Much more fully Canadian was one of his first books, *In the Midst of Alarms* (1894), whose central action is a comic treatment of the battle of Ridgeway during the Fenian Raids. In one of his last books, *The Measure of the Rule* (1906) Barr used still-vivid memories of his Toronto Normal School experience to attack the stuffiness of Ontario life, and, in particular, the Ontario educational establishment, subjects which he must have known would not command universal international attention.

It is understandable that Grant Allen, concerned primarily with the discovery and propagation of new truths, found little or nothing in his Canadian past of use in his writings. Nor is it surprising that Robert Barr, concerned primarily as he was with entertaining the sophisticated Anglo-American reading public, drew little on his Canadian experience. What is odd is that he did write two books so largely concerned with particulars of the Canadian scene.

Like Allen and Barr, Sara Jeannette Duncan (1861-1922) was attracted to literary London, made her début there in book form, achieved an international literary popularity, and never returned to live in her native country. But unlike Allen and Barr who assimilated themselves abroad, Sara Jeannette Duncan made much of her work out of her acute sense of the distinctions between Canadians, Americans, and the English. Even her novels of British India have an angle of vision that is non-English and anti-colonial. Miss Duncan was born and grew up in Brantford, Ontario, and, after a little teaching, sailed into a remarkably successful journalistic career with the Washington *Post*, the Toronto *Globe*, and Goldwin Smith's *The Week*, as correspondent and columnist. Her first book, dedicated to Mrs. Grundy, was published in London in 1890, as *A Social Departure: How Orthodocia and I Went Round the World by Ourselves*. British, American, and Canadian reviewers welcomed it for its freshness and cleverness. She capitalized on this success by writing the first of a number of international comedies, *An American Girl in London* (1891) in which Mamie Wick, a lighter-hearted Daisy Miller from Chicago breezily comments on her English social experiences. This Jamesian heiress of all the ages tells of her later matrimonial and travel adventures on the Continent in *A Voyage of Consolation* (1898). The device is reversed in *Those Delightful Americans* (1902), in which a young English married woman makes her first trip to America. The device was varied again in 1908 in *Cousin Cinderella: A Canadian Girl in London*, where Mary Trent, a young Canadian, narrates her story of a visit to England with her brother as cultural ambassadors for their senator father. Mary is a more natural and more complex character than Mamie Wick; her brother, Graham, has an idealism about Empire similar to Lorne Murchison's in the earlier *The Imperialist*, and the book, for all its comedy, touches serious chords of thought and feeling. The last book in the international vein, *His Royal Happiness* (1914), is a romantic fantasy, expressing a dream of stronger British-American unity.

Meanwhile in 1891 Miss Duncan married Everard Cotes, whom she had met in India, and much of the rest of her life was spent there. Her early experience had given her the materials for her international comedies; her Indian life gave her the experience for nine more books. Her first Indian book was *The Simple Adventures of a Memsahib* (1893), a quiet, charming comedy of a young English girl who goes out to India to marry, and of her day-by-day experiences in adapting herself to her exotic circumstances—a man, an Indian life. Mrs. Cotes used the migrant pattern in a broader vein in *Vernon's Aunt: Being the Oriental Experiences of Miss Lavinia Moffat* (1894). In the same year she published a juvenile, *The Story of Sonny Sahib*.

In 1894 Mrs. Cotes also opened the more serious vein she was to pursue in her later Indian books and in *The Imperialist*, with *A Daughter of Today*, the story of Elfrida Bell, an independent young woman from Sparta, Illinois, who goes to the Left Bank to express her soul. There she finds her talent inadequate, and she moves to a bachelor flat in Kensington to earn a living by journalism and to storm the heights of the literary world. Mrs. Cotes dissects the egotism of this "New Woman" with cool and sustained analysis. No Canadian had ever written a book like this in subject or in tone.

Two years later she pursued this darker vein in one of her finest books, *His Honour and a Lady*, a novel of the English ruling classes in India. It is a tragedy of misplaced love and betrayal, presented in dramatic scenes, with much less author-analysis. *The Path of a Star* (*Hilda*, in the American edition) followed in 1899. This story of two parallel and tangled love affairs, involving a very independent young actress with an Anglican missionary, and a young Englishman with a fanatical Salvation Army girl, was granted "the reality and the force" the critics had found in Mrs. Cotes's earlier work, but some complained of her growing love for tortured metaphor, an element which declined in her later work.

Her interest in the rising controversy over the possibility of a "Greater Britain" led her to write her next serious novel, *The Imperialist* (1904). This is her one novel set in an Ontario town, Elgin (Brantford), with a full cast of hometown people. She wrote it to correct the impression about Canadian enthusiasm for Imperialism spread in England by over-heated oratory at Toronto banquets, by showing how the issue appeared to "the average Canadian of the average small town . . . whose views in the end count for more" than those of banquet speakers. The book reflects her strong feeling for the various aspects of southern Ontario town life, and is touched with humour and indulgent irony.

In 1906 she published *Set in Authority,* a tense drama caused by the zeal of an Indian governor who, with stern idealism, tries to enforce equality of justice to Indian and Englishman alike, and brings tragedy to those close to him. The uglier realities of Anglo-Indian relations underlie the story, and the tone is darker than in the earlier Indian novels. Even closer to immediate unrest in India is *The Burnt Offering* (1909), in which a zealous, idealistic socialist M.P. comes from England to see the social wrongs that are leading Indians to open revolt. With him comes his suffragette daughter; she marries an Indian who has, unknown to her, dedicated himself to the assassination of the Viceroy. This is the most quietly violent of Mrs. Cotes's books; it ends with an unspoken curse on both houses.

Politics also forms the background of Mrs. Cotes's next, and in some ways, most interesting novel, *The Consort* (1912). But the foreground of the book is the moral drama of Mary Pargeter, an assured woman of immense inherited wealth who lives for its stewardship. She has been married by an ambitious literary man who finds himself smothered by his wife's high sense of duty, and by her money. The book is written with power and clarity, and has moments of deep insight.

Mrs. Cotes's last two books are much lighter in weight. *Title-Clear* was published just before her death in 1922 in Surrey, England, and *The Gold-*

Cure (unfinished) was published two years later. She also published earlier in her career four novelettes under the title *The Pool in the Desert* (1903), of which the second "A Mother in India," shows her at her cleverest.

Sara Jeannette Duncan Cotes is of the small company of Canadian writers who, like Leacock and Haliburton, had a sharp eye for the human comedy, but who also, like Henry James and George Meredith, were concerned with what underlay the comedy. Canadian fiction had before her no woman writer of such literary skill and range, and has had only two or perhaps three since.

Horatio Gilbert Parker (1860–1932), like Sara Jeannette Duncan, achieved a career as a popular writer after leaving Canada. About half of his thirty-six romances and novels are set in a Canadian scene, but, unlike Sara Jeanette Duncan, he used his scene as romantic atmosphere to enhance melodramatic action. Gilbert Parker was born in Camden East, a crossroads village northeast of Napanee, Ontario; he was educated locally and at Ottawa Normal School, studied theology at Trinity College where he gave instruction in elocution, and, later, also at Queen's University. After serving as a deacon in Trenton, he set off for the South Seas and Australia. Four successful years of newspaper work and writing plays allowed him to establish himself in London as a writer of short stories about the South Seas and the Canadian Northwest. His first book, *Pierre and His People* (1892), collected seventeen Pretty Pierre stories, and twenty-two more were published in book form as *An Adventurer of the North* (1895 in England, and as *An Adventurer of the North* and *A Romany of the Snows* in the United States). These and the first five tales collected in *Northern Lights* (1909) present a theatrical picture of the Northwest before the railroad came, and, as he said, are full of "poignant mystery, solitude, and big primitive incident." Parker later claimed that they opened up a new field of fiction, but the milieu was hardly new to those who had read Ballantyne, Kingston, or Henty, while the manner seems a mixture of Bret Harte, R. L. Stevenson, and Parker's own strong melodramatic flair and elocutionary rhetoric. Some Canadian readers resented the tales as misrepresentation of the Canadian Northwest.

The other twelve stories collected in *Northern Lights* deal with the changing Northwest as the railroads opened up the country in the eighties. In three later books, *You Never Know Your Luck* (1914), *The World for Sale* (1916), and *Wild Youth and Another* (1919), Parker wrote stories of Saskatchewan town life in the early years of the twentieth century, based on some first-hand knowledge of the scene but more impressive for their action than their fidelity to the local scene or people.

Parker had not seen the Northwest when he wrote his Pierre tales, but had visited French Canada, and his romantic imagination responded to what he felt to be its picturesqueness, and its hierarchical traditional quality. He used French Canada, past and present, for the background of eight of his books before 1920: *The Trail of the Sword* (1894); *When Valmond Came to Pontiac* (1895); *The Pomp of the Lavilettes* (1896); *The Seats of the Mighty* (1896); *Born with a Golden Spoon* (1899); *The Lane That Had No Turning* (1900); *The Right of Way* (1901); and *The Money Master* (1915). His "story of a lost Napoleon," *When Valmond Came to Pontiac*, dramatizes the "pathetic—unutterably pathetic—incident of a man driven by the truth in his blood to impersonate himself," and he looked back upon this as his finest work. This historical fantasy has a unity of tone, action, and character that his better-known *The Seats of the Mighty* lacks, and it has a *panache* that his other work does not have in so sustained a fashion. In *The Seats of the Mighty* he used the fall of Quebec as background for a costume drama that fails to catch the flavour of the times as Kirby had done in the first half of his *The Golden Dog* (1877), or as Francis Parkman had in the historical narratives which Parker used for source materials. The French-Canadian countryside of his own day served Parker much more effectively as atmosphere for his best-selling *The Right of Way*, the mystery of the dipsomaniac Charley Steele who lost his memory and assumed another personality.

Parker once wrote: "Whatever may be thought of my books, they represent nothing but the bent of my own mind, my own wilful expression of myself, and the setting forth of that which seized my imagination." Although he tended to romanticize himself as a writer, the French-Canadian stories probably throw light on Parker's own temperament. Two other early stories, *The Translation of a Savage* (1893) and especially *The Trespasser* (1893), throw a stronger light on their author. Both books have the theme of the impact of an unsophisticated young person from the wilds of Canada upon the "complicated orderly life of England." Unlike Henry James's "passionate pilgrim," Parker's avenging son in *The Trespasser* wills to become a power in the Old Land. In other guises in Parker's stories, this Young Man from the Provinces is a dynamic force, and suggests a self-projection of the writer. For Parker himself moved on from his early writing success to marry a New York heiress, to become a member of the British parliament, and a figure in Imperial affairs in England. He moved in court and upper social circles, was knighted in 1902, made a baronet in 1915, and a member of the Privy Council. During the First World War he was in charge of British propaganda for North America. It was a long way from Camden East.

As he became more involved in the English and Imperial scene, he found new matter for his romances. One of his strongest historical romances, *The Battle of the Strong* (1898), is set in the Jersey Islands during the Napoleonic Wars. *Donovan Pasha* (1902) was a study for a longer Anglo-Egyptian political drama, *The Weavers* (1907). His concern for South African affairs resulted in *The Judgment House* (1913); his political interest in land settlement is reflected in the Saskatchewan stories *You Never Know Your Luck,* and *The World for Sale*. His best work, with the possible exception of *Tarboe* (1927), was done before 1920.

In 1912 his collected work began to appear in the Imperial Edition (1912–1923, 23 volumes), published by Scribner's in a format similar to that of their handsome editions of Dickens, Turgeniev, Meredith, Kipling, and Henry James. Like Henry James, Parker wrote a preface to each volume. James's prefaces were searching explorations of the art of fiction; Parker's prefaces seem more concerned with self-justification and self-enhancement. Against the charge that his work lacked vital relation to life, he stated that he cared more "for truth and beauty than he did for fact," and that an "inner vision permitted him to see life as it really was." Replying to the criticism that his work was badly structured, he claimed that he worked instinctively, not methodically, and that many of his books seemed to write themselves as he worked in a continuous trance-like state. Countering the stricture that he saw character only as a series of melodramatic gestures, he asserted that "in my mind the episode was always the consequence of character." And against the criticism that his attitudes and his style were over-inflated, he answered that he "feared being led into mere rhetoric," and had to curb "a natural yet rather dangerous eloquence." Perhaps he was most just to himself when he wrote "I was a born dramatist." For, in spite of his aggrandizement of his work, he was a successful writer of fiction of strong effect. His strength lay in his power of creating spirited action, and enhancing it with romantic atmosphere.

When *Beggars All*, the first of eleven novels by Lily Dougall (1858–1923), appeared in 1891 it was warmly praised for its success in combining an entertaining story for the ordinary reader and metaphysical discussion for the thoughtful reader. A native of Montreal, and a graduate of classes for women at Edinburgh University, an LL.A. from St. Andrews, and the first editor of *The World Wide*, Lily Dougall lived most of her life in England. Fiction was for her a medium for conveying ideas, and one which she abandoned after 1908 for religion and philosophy. Although often obscured by other elements, the centre of her characteristic novel is religious and philosophical discussion. Her action presents a struggle to overcome doubts, or a conflict between two codes of ethics, or a search for the ideal life, and contains discussions of such subjects as individual responsibility, the Mormon and Adventist religions, and mesmerism. She was against the intolerance and persecution that spring from narrow sectarianism, and she advocated faith in "an eternal and beneficent purpose," tolerance, and Love. To present these ideas she adopted the framework of the mystery novel, with plots overladen with melodramatic incident, coincidences, disguises, hidden pasts, and endings in which threads are pulled together conveniently and miraculously, and good triumphs over evil.

At her best, she could tell a lively story with well-defined plain characters in a graphically described setting—the Rockies in *The Madonna of a Day* (1895), the coast of Prince Edward Island in *The Mermaid* (1895), the lonely backwoods region south of the Ottawa valley in *The Zeit-Geist* (1895) or the isolated farms of the Matapedia valley in *What Necessity Knows* (1893). But by adopting the formulas of sensational fiction, by disconcertingly sudden shifts from the world of realism to a world of sensationalism, and by employing a highly "literary" style, her fiction often fails to be as impressive as it obviously was intended to be.

London had been the great literary magnet in the eighties and the early nineties for ambitious young Canadian writers. The force of the American centres—Boston, Philadelphia, and especially New York—was stronger for the young Canadians who began writing in the mid-nineties. Some moved to New York or Boston as journalists and then became free-lance writers; others remained in their native localities. The alignment with the American centres was less alienating for most than the alignment with London. In the American centres they were accepted as natives, or near-natives, while in London, as Sara Jeannette Duncan pointed out, they often were half-accepted as colonials. The American publishers were nearer, easier of access, and more numerous than the British. American publications had a much greater market in Canada than had British publications. The American publisher was apt to regard fiction about the Canadian scene as an extension of American local colour writing or of American historical romance, and both were extremely popular in the nineties. The British publisher, on the other hand, was apt to find more saleable the exotic and wild aspects of the Canadian scene.

But not all Canadian writers were émigrés. Just before Sara Jeannette Duncan, Gilbert Parker, and Lily Dougall published their first books, two Canadian writers who remained within their native Canada began prolific, semi-professional careers. Margaret Marshall Saunders (1861–1947), author of one of the most widely read books written by a Canadian, *Beautiful Joe*, was born in Milton, Nova Scotia, and educated in Edinburgh and in Orléans, France. She began her career with a pleasant romance *My Spanish Sailor* (1889; enlarged and republished as *Her Sailor* in 1900). Her great success came when she visited some friends in Meaford, Ontario, saw Joe, and wrote his story. *Beautiful Joe* (1894) eventually sold over one million copies in English and in translation in numerous languages. Miss Saunders hoped to do for dogs what *Black Beauty* had done for horses. She shrewdly allowed Joe to tell his own story in a relatively unsentimental way, and Joe told the story well. Most of her twenty-six books are about animals, and follow the didactic pattern and sentiments of her great success. A few, such as *Rose à Charlitte: An Acadian Romance* (1898), reveal in their unencumbered storytelling and feeling for character (at least in the opening pages before the story becomes melodramatic) the qualities which made her animal stories so appealing to millions of young and old.

James Macdonald Oxley (1855–1907) became one of the most popular of the Canadian writers of boy's adventure stories. He was born in Halifax, and educated in the Maritimes and at Harvard. Apart from his literary activities, he had a distinguished legal and business career. He began writing while still in the Maritimes, contributing articles and stories with Canadian themes and settings to a great number of American periodicals. After moving to Ottawa, he turned almost exclusively to juvenile stories. In the twenty years after 1885, he published more than two dozen books. A few of his works are historical novels, usually with a teen-age hero; a few are set in the Maritimes; most of his books are stories of adventure in the remote and more romantic parts of Canada. His books were popular in England and the United States, and undoubtedly spread or reinforced the widespread notion of Canada as a land of simple-minded, exciting adventure.

There was little of the juvenile in the work of Thomas Stinson Jarvis (1854–1926), a member of a prominent Toronto family, who established an international reputation as a criminal lawyer, travelled widely, and distinguished himself as an international yachtsman. In 1890, Jarvis published *Geoffrey Hampstead*; set in Toronto, it is a study in criminal psychology in the form of a detective thriller which makes use of the author's knowledge of economics, criminal law, science, yachting, and upper class "society." The popularity of the book in the United States led him to a new career in letters. Moving to New York, Jarvis became a professional novelist, editor, and dramatic critic.

His second novel, *Dr. Perdue* (1892) is a sequel to *Geoffrey Hampstead*, picking up the criminal's career several years later, after his prison term, and after he has become a famous surgeon. The setting is Paris and England; the characters include both Canadians in Europe and the international yachting set.

The psychology of love is the central theme in Jarvis's final novel, *She Lived in New York* (1894). Daring, but delicately done, the book contains many pictures of the gay life in New York's high society, as well as some realistic description of its bohemia and less attractive *demi-monde*. Liberal and anti-puritan in its view, the novel has a journalistic, sometimes almost documentary flavour; the frankness with which it discusses love and sex is unusual for its time.

Jarvis's novels reflect the wide experience and the wide range of his interests; his urbane style, and his use of the novel as a vehicle for ideas, mark him as one of Canada's more sophisticated authors in the early 1890's.

Charles G. D. Roberts (1860–1943) wrote about fifty volumes of fiction during an unusually prolific writing career. All but a few of his fictions are animal stories, and are discussed elsewhere in this volume. His domestic romance, *The Heart That Knows* (1906) is largely biographical of his own family. His historical romances, *The Raid from Beauséjour* (1894), *The Forge in the Forest* (1896), *A Sister to Evangeline* (1898), and *The Prisoner of Mademoiselle* (1904) are of the *Ancien Régime*, and are located in or near the countryside he knew. *Barbara Ladd* (1902) is a historical romance of New England during the Revolution. *By the Marshes of Minas* (1900) collected a number of Acadian stories. Roberts's writing probably is at its weakest in these historical romances. The actions are episodic and repetitious; the emotional atmosphere is that of the light historical romance so popular in the nineties. The animal characters in his woods stories are more human than the puppets in these costume dramas. The freshest elements in such bread-and-margarine books are the passages describing the Bay of Fundy settings which Roberts obviously recalled with affection.

Edward William Thomson (1849–1924) was one of the most skilful story-tellers of the Canadian writers of his day, and it is a distinct loss that he published so few stories for adults. He was born in Peel County, Ontario, educated at Trinity College School, and, after volunteer experience in the American Civil War and the Fenian Raids, became an editorial writer on the Toronto *Globe* (1879–91), and then editor of the famous *Youth's Companion* in Boston (1891–1901). His first collection of short stories was published as *Old Man Savarin, and Other Stories* (1895). It contains tales, humorous and grave, of French Canadians and of Scotch settlements along the Ottawa, of war experiences and of U.E. Loyalists. "The Privilege of the Limit" has been a favourite of Canadian anthologists. The Canadian tales in this volume were reprinted, with new ones, in his expanded edition *Old Man Savarin Stories: Tales of Canada and Canadians* (1917). These tales are vigorous, dramatic, unsentimental, and economical in style. His other books, *Walter Gibbs, The Young Boss, and Other Stories* (1896), *Between Earth and Sky and Other Strange Stories of Deliverance* (1897), and *Smoky Days* (1901), were for a juvenile audience.

The sudden success of Ralph Connor (Rev. Charles William Gordon, 1860–1937) was phenomenal. His first book *Black Rock* (1898) was a collection of sketches which the young Presbyterian minister had written for his church magazine, to help raise funds for the church's missions in western Canada. *Black Rock* and its sequel *The Sky Pilot*, published the following year, captured the imagination of a vast reading public in Canada, the United States, and England which liked vigorous religion dramatized in story form. *The Man from Glengarry* (1901) sold almost as well. Within a few years the combined sales of his first three books were well over five million. Ralph Connor had become the most widely read Canadian writer, a distinction he was to enjoy for the next twenty years.

In all, Connor wrote more than a score of novels, as well as another half-dozen religious, biographical and autobiographical books. All of his fictions deal with Canada; most are tales of the ranges and timberlands and frontier settlements of the West. In addition to *Black Rock* and *The Sky Pilot*, the western books include *The Sky Pilot at Swan Creek* (1905), a collection of short stories; *Corporal Cameron* (1912) and *The Patrol of the Sun Dance Trail* (1914), North West Mounted Police stories; *The Gaspards of Pinecroft* (1923), a British Columbia romance. *The Prospector* (1904) and *The Doctor* (1906) both start in Ontario, but the stories move to the western frontiers. Early immigration in Winnipeg and the pioneer settlements provide the background for *The Foreigner* (1909); post-war labour problems in Winnipeg provide the theme of *To Him That Hath* (1921). Most of these western stories, particularly the early ones, capitalize on the romance, adventure, and physical beauty of the early West. Connor was writing here about his own experience. "I knew the country," he later wrote. "I had ridden the ranges. I had pushed through the mountain passes. I had swum my bronco across its rivers."

Connor was most at home, however, in his books which dealt with another, earlier aspect of the Canadian scene, the Ontario which he had known in the sixties. The two Glengarry books, *The Man from Glengarry* and *Glengarry Schooldays* (1902), both record Connor's boyhood experiences of pioneer life, as do the opening sections of *The Prospector, The Doctor,* and *Corporal Cameron*. It was in these books that Connor did much of his most effective writing; here are to be found his fine descriptions of many varied phases of the life of the early settlers, ranging from the logging bee to the wake, from the barn-raising to the revival meeting, from the bear hunt to the Dominion Day games. In the tradition of the local colourist, Connor portrayed the manner of life and the characters of an earlier age; in this type of writing, he displayed a skill and an artistry that he was not able to sustain through the larger narrative unit of the novel. Two of the later novels return to this same period, *Torches through the Bush* (1934), and *The Girl from Glengarry* (1933); but only the former succeeds in a limited way in catching the spirit of the earlier works.

The two wartime books, *The Major* and *The Sky Pilot in No Man's Land*, revived Connor's slightly waning popularity. After the war he wrote little that can compare with his earlier work: three historical novels, and three modern romances of the Maritimes and Ontario complete the canon.

Ralph Connor's melodramatic parables are shaped to make the reader identify strongly with the Good, usually simple-hearted Christians, relentlessly oppressed by scoffers and non-believers. After much violence, physical and emotional, Good redeems all. The world he created in these books is a projection of the emotional world of crisis, suffering, and overcoming of an evangelical Protestant minister. He wrote for, and helped to create, an audience that wanted fictionalized morality, and did not care much about artistic standards so long as the morality was pure and simple, the spiritual issues clear and strong, and the action exciting. However, his otherwise undistinguished romances contain many forceful passages. For Ralph Connor could be very effective when he wrote as a local colourist recording life in the early West and in pioneer Ontario.

The thirty or so books by Ernest Thompson Seton (1860–1946) are almost entirely about animals or woodcraft, and are discussed elsewhere in this volume. His books made Seton famous as a story-teller, illustrator, and naturalist. His rare excursion into fiction about adults, *The Preacher of Cedar Mountain: A Tale of the Open Country* (1917), is, in the vein of Ralph Connor, about a young man who goes to divinity school and becomes a minister in a new western town. But Seton's world is more complex than Ralph Connor's. His young minister is pulled from one side by a mystique about Nature, and from the other by his sense of duty to his townsmen. This conflict is complicated when he responds to a call of the city, and goes to South Chicago to start an undenominational worker's club. In the end the Nature mystique proves stronger, and he turns west again to God's country.

William Alexander Fraser (1859–1933) also established his early reputation as a teller of animal stories, *Mooswa and Others of the Boundaries* (1900), *The Outcasts* (1901), and *The Sa'-Zada Tales* (1905). What he called the first, a "simple romance of a simple people, the furred dwellers of the Northern Forests," is true of all three, for the animals speak as humans and take on human traits, good and bad. He also spun tales of Crees, Blackfeet, and white settlers in three tales in his first book, *The Eye of a God and Other Tales of East and West* (1899), and in *The Blood Lilies* (1903). Burma and India provide the setting for the other mystery stories in *The Eye of a God, Thirteen Men* (1906), and *The Three Sapphires* (1918). These incident-packed tales supply excitement through the devices of stolen jewels, spies, spells, drugged wine and opium, and murder, but they are told with a humorous touch that makes the scarcely hidden clues and the far-fetched improbabilities acceptable. He is most successful in his more sophisticated mystery and adventure tales about horse-racing, *Thoroughbreds* (1902), *Brave Hearts* (1904), and *Deliah Plays the Ponies* (1927), where thefts, disguises, crooked trainers and jockeys, doped horses, are ancillary to the effective races. One of his most amusing and exciting racing stories is included in *Bulldog Carney* (1919), a thoroughly entertaining collection of tales about a Robin Hood of the Rockies, who gambles, smuggles, bootlegs, and races, and has a big heart of gold.

The wide variety of people and scene in his stories came from Fraser's varied experience. He was born in Pictou County, Nova Scotia, educated in Boston, New York, and India, and worked in India, Burma, and the Canadian Northwest. He settled in Georgetown, Ontario, and it provided him with the background for the most serious of his fourteen books, *The Lone Furrow* (1907). Setting out to teach the importance of love and tolerance, he traces the career of a minister and his wife in Iona, a small Scottish settlement in Ontario. The frame and some of the materials are melodramatic. The enduring parts of the novel are those in which Iona is evoked: the community gatherings, the vicious local gossip, the religious bigotry, the interior of the houses, and the complex emotions of the central characters.

Fraser was one of the more effective magazine story-writers of his day, and generally he succeeded in doing what he set out to do, to entertain by a lively story, with a number of sharply realized characters, accurate dialect economically handled, and a lack of sentimentality.

Probably most fully professional of all the Canadian writers of the period was Arthur Stringer (1874–1950). In volume of publication, variety, and popularity of appeal, he ranked with Charles G. D. Roberts and Gilbert Parker. All three addressed most of their work first to magazine audiences. Stringer's magazine work reappeared in book form in over forty volumes of fiction, fifteen volumes of poetry, and three plays. He also wrote several biographies, a study of Shakespeare's *King Lear,* and plays and moving-picture scripts (including "The Perils of Pauline"). He was born in Chatham, and educated in London, Ontario. He contributed to Canadian and English magazines while he was at the University of Toronto and at Oxford, and gained his first popular success while working as a journalist for a large New York syndicate. His first volume, *The Loom of Destiny* (1899), had appeared originally in a New York periodical as a series of sketches of boy life in New York's East Side. His first novel, and in some ways one of his most interesting, was *The Silver Poppy* (1903), an ambitious study of a young man, fresh from Oxford, aspiring in New York's Bohemia to express life in a novel. *Lonely O'Malley* (1905) is a lively story of an orphan boy growing up in a Chatham-like town; it is a Canadian *Tom Sawyer*, without Mark Twain's anti-romantic undertone or his fine ear for speech.

Dividing his time between a southern Ontario fruit farm, New York, and travelling on the Continent, Stringer produced a long line of thrillers. The first of these, for which he carefully gathered facts, was *The Wire Tappers* (1906), followed by *Phantom Wires* (1907), *The Under Groove* (1908), and *The Gun Runner* (1909). These underworld adventures were interspersed by volumes of poetry, which he regarded as his serious literary work.

After 1914 he took up ranching in Alberta, and out of his western experiences came *The Prairie Wife* (1915). He achieved immediacy and vitality in this novel by having his gay-spirited, highly educated young New England girl tell in diary form of her arrival at an Alberta ranch as a young bride. In spite of some embarrassingly intimate slang, and some smart *Saturday Evening Post* situations, the underlying anti-romantic tone of the story often is convincing. The prairie wife continues her diary in *The Prairie Mother* (1920), and gives a wry account of the break-up of her marriage in *The Prairie Child* (1922). Stringer moved to New Jersey in 1919, and there wrote more ambitious novels, *The Wine of Life* (1921), *Power* (1925), and *The Mud Lark* (1932), in between new thrillers and stories of adventurous romance in the Canadian Northwest.

Stringer was one of the most competent and popular magazine writers of his day; he wrote a story that was fresh-spirited, fast-paced, dramatically told, with a sophisticated tone. His success in the popular field may have choked out the talent for more serious work that he revealed occasionally in a few of his books.

In contrast to the stream of fiction from Arthur Stringer, Francis William Grey (1860–1939) wrote only one novel, *The Curé of St. Philippe: A Story of French-Canadian Politics* (1899); its quality makes it regrettable that he wrote no more. Grey was English-born and educated, taught English at the University of Ottawa, and later worked in the Archives Bureau. He was a poet, playwright, and a contributor to Canadian periodicals. In his novel, Grey presented current native political and religious issues in the manner of the most finished Victorian novelists. His Trollopian narrator, the most interesting voice in the book, relates a plain narrative of facts about the new parish of St. Philippe des Bois in the Richelieu county. Undramatically and unromantically, he reflects the local elections, the intrigue for political rewards, the creation of the new parish, the building of the church, the business dealings, the social relations of the older generation and the love affairs of the younger. Grey's intelligence and his craftsmanship enabled him to depict the appearance and the forces shaping the appearance of the political, religious, and racial problems of this part of French Canada in the last years of the nineteenth century.

One of the more sophisticated popular novelists of his day, the Reverend William Benjamin (Basil) King was born in Charlottetown, Prince Edward Island, and educated at King's College, Windsor, Nova Scotia. After some years at St. Luke's, Halifax, he became rector of Christ Church, Cambridge, Massachussetts. Forced to retire in 1890 because of ill health, he turned to the writing of fiction; in the next twenty-eight years, he published two dozen novels and several other books. From the beginning, he was competent and successful. His *The Inner Shrine* was first on the American best-selling list in 1909, and his next two books, *The Wild Olive* (1910) and *The Street Called Straight* (1912), also became best-sellers.

Many of King's novels are international in the Jamesian tradition, exploring moral problems, such as divorce or family honour, in the light of the differing cultural conventions of France, England and the United States. But in most of his books he used American themes, settings, and characters.

In the Garden of Charity (1903), one of his earlier works, is wholly Canadian, and although it lacks the polish of his later novels, it is one of his most interesting. It is a story of love, loneliness, and charity in an isolated section along the lower Nova Scotia coast, worked out against a fully realized setting, and through local characters who are sensitively interpreted.

In two of King's later novels, Canadian characters play leading roles. Frank Melbury, in *The City of Comrades* (1919), is a young Canadian architect who dreams of developing a distinctively Canadian architectural style. Although the action takes place largely in the United States, Melbury goes to war for his native country, and the author's strong patriotic feeling is apparent. King's patriotism is as strong in *The High Heart* (1917), but his treatment of Canadian-American relations is more comprehensive. Alexandra Adare, a Halifax girl from a good family, finds that she is not accepted by Boston society because she is Canadian and thus of a lesser breed. In telling the story of her conquest of her suitor's Boston family, King presents one of the few detailed studies of Canadian and American attitudes written in this period.

Although he was a deeply moral and religious man, Basil King avoided the heavy didacticism and sentimentality common in much of the fiction of the day. Unlike many of his contemporaries, he was more concerned with tracing the complex relations between human beings than he was with providing exciting entertainment. In addition, he was a disciplined craftsman, well aware of the structural possibilities of the novel, and at his best, he achieved a high level of technical competence.

Another Canadian who placed Canadian characters under international pressures was Alice Jones (1853–1933). The daughter of a wealthy Halifax business man (later lieutenant-governor of Nova Scotia), she was educated in Europe and knew a more cosmopolitan society than most Canadian novelists of her time. She published short stories and three novels before settling in Mendone, France, in 1905, where she wrote two more novels.

Her first novel, *The Night Hawk* (1901), is a conventional historical romance of the adventures of a Southern girl who becomes a Confederate agent in Halifax during the American Civil War. *Bubbles We Buy* (1903), a thriller set in Nova Scotia and Europe, makes use of her knowledge of the international set. Her most forceful book is *Gabriel Praed's Castle* (1904). The action is melodramatic; Gabriel Praed, a Montreal business man who is purchasing paintings for a new Gothic castle in Montreal, is duped by a villainous Parisian art dealer, but Praed's unsophisticated young daughter, aided by American friends, saves her father. The treatment of the action, and the depiction of the characters, however, are somewhat reminiscent of the early manner of Henry James.

In *Marcus Holbeach's Daughter* (1912) the chief contrast is between a young girl reared in the wilds of the Gaspé and the corrupt aristocratic English society into which she is introduced. *Flame of Frost* (1914) deals with a similar contrast: the unspoiled girl from the woods is moved into corrupt European society.

Alice Jones's work is uneven, and has elements of sensationalism, but her fiction does have an awareness of the complexities of international experience.

Although Norman Duncan (1871–1916) produced such successful books for children as *The Adventures of Billy Topsail* (1906) and its several sequels, and some fifteen other fictions, it is only in a handful of short stories, particularly "The Chase of the Tide," "The Strength of a Man," "The Raging of the Sea," and "The Fruits of Toil," included in *The Way of the Sea* (1903), that he reached a high level of story-telling. In these he limited himself to a representation of the lives of fishermen and seal-hunters of the bleak shores of Newfoundland and Labrador in their fight with the merciless forces of nature.

When he was at his best, Duncan set the scene with precision and economy, and with a vividness of general impression. He allowed his people to demonstrate their qualities by their own actions, and in their own dialect stories. At his best he was an effective regional writer. But even within these particular short stories, he failed to maintain objectivity. His admiration for the prototypes of his characters led him to idealization and platitudinous interruption that recalls the work of Bret Harte rather than that of the serious regional writers. He often forsook the directness and biblical simplicity of the best portions of "The Fruits of Toil" for rhetoric loaded with apostrophe and grandiose generalization.

His few years of experience with Newfoundland and Labrador life provided him with feeling and material which brought out his best writing. Born in Brantford, and a graduate of the University of Toronto, he had become a journalist in New York, in the course of which he had been sent to write about Newfoundland. He returned to further journalism in the United States, and later to college teaching. His American journalism unfortunately seemed to encourage the sentimental and the didactic in his work, especially when he dealt with "mother love" and family relations in *The Mother* (1905), *The Suitable Child* (1909), *Finding His Soul* (1913), and *The Bird Store Man* (1914), or when he dealt with the strong and flawless missionary in *The Measure of a Man* (1911).

Norman Duncan found he had to warn readers of later editions of *Dr.*

Luke of The Labrador (1904) that he had not modelled his hero on Dr. Wilfred Thomason Grenfell (1865–1940) of the Royal National Mission to Deep-Sea Fishermen. Dr. Grenfell wrote his fiction to proselytize. *The Harvest of the Sea* (1905) came from his own medical missionary work aboard the fishing boats, and dramatizes the appalling conditions of that life, and the improvements which could be brought about by the United Fisherman's Christian Association. In *Down to the Sea in Ships* (1910) and *Tales of the Labrador* (1916) his "parables" are straightforward sermons. His writing is similar to Duncan's in its direct didacticism, its black and white characters, the familiar rhetorical adjectives and author's comment, and the episodic and melodramatic structure. His writing differs from Duncan's in its driving Christian and humanitarian evangelism.

Theodore Goodridge Roberts (1877–1953) was a more prolific popular journalist than his elder brother Charles G. D. Roberts. After his education in New Brunswick, he did editorial work on a New York newspaper, acted as a war correspondent during the Spanish-American War, and edited a magazine in Newfoundland before returning to Fredericton to pursue free-lance fiction-writing. His historical romances, adventure stories in the New Brunswick woods and on the Atlantic Coast, and his juveniles appeared first in the magazines; many of them appeared later in book form, starting with *Hemming, the Adventurer* in 1904. His romances reached a total of some twenty-four before he went overseas in 1914 with the Canadian army. After the war another ten appeared in book form. His fiction is largely light and fast-moving action, peopled with conventionally romantic characters, and with only occasionally a glimpse of setting which conveys some of the felt truth of good local colour.

The seven novels of R. E. Knowles (1868–1946), published between 1905 and 1911, are didactic and moralistic. Knowles, a Presbyterian minister, wrote largely about life in a small Ontario town. His first and best book, *St. Cuthbert's* (1905), is the story of a young Presbyterian minister who takes over a new parish. The plot is sentimental, melodramatic, and ragged. But the author has a pleasing prose style, a quiet sense of humour, and an insight into many facets of human nature. The book presents an interesting if prosaic picture of church-centred life in a small Scottish community. *The Undertow* (1906) and *The Attic Guest* (1909) also use a Presbyterian minister as a central figure, the latter novel extending his service to the southern United States, where he takes a stand on the race problem. In *The Handicap* (1910) Knowles turned to pioneer Ontario, and to an even more melodramatic plot. *The Web of Time* (1908) follows Presbyterian morality into the big city; *The Singer of the Kootenay* (1911) uses British Columbia for a sentimental and moralizing tale in the *Black Rock* manner. *The Dawn at Shanty Bay* (1907) is a slight, sentimental

Christmas story set in a northern Ontario lumber camp. Only occasionally do any of these later books come close to the style or the quiet effect of *St. Cuthbert's*.

Knowles's purpose was didactic; he is always the cleric; the artist seldom emerges. But though he never succeeded in creating a coherent narrative structure, he, like Ralph Connor, could be quite effective in short descriptive and non-dramatic passages. His otherwise conventional novels are relieved by some scenes of mild humour and faithful local colour.

The early novels of Marian Keith (Mrs. Mary Esther MacGregor, 1876–1961) are records of life in a small Ontario community. Her writing was heavily influenced by her Presbyterian background, and many of her stories are about ministers and churches; all have a moral appended. Her plots were derived from Victorian melodramatic and sentimental fiction; she had little sense of structure; her characters, except for some fine minor vignettes, were thinly developed and unconvincing. But she wrote about a subject which she knew well: the Scottish settlements of central Ontario in the late nineteenth century. In her books *Duncan Polite* (1905), *The Silver Maple* (1906), *Treasure Valley* (1908), *'Lizabeth of the Dale* (1910), she sketched an authentic and charming picture of rural Canadian life. Some of her scenes are reminiscent of Ralph Connor's kind of Ontario local colour: village life with its Dominion Day picnics, its general store, its church socials, its inter-church and Scotch-Irish rivalries, is all here.

Marian Keith was at her best when dealing with humorous anecdotal material. For example in *The Silver Maple* she related skilfully an incident in which the Glencoe MacDonalds decide to compete with the Orangemen's parade. They stage a "walk" of their own; led by a Highland piper they arrive at the village's only hotel just ahead of the Irishmen; they commandeer all the refreshments, and provide an unexpected anticlimax to the Orange celebrations. In her early works, there are many similar charming, unexaggerated incidents which are typical of the times and the people. These, along with her quieter pictures of family and manse life, enliven her otherwise conventional stories, and lend them an importance and an interest which far exceeds their literary merit. In spite of her shortcomings as a novelist, Marian Keith was an able chronicler of life in rural Ontario.

One of the first writers to make use of the western prairie scene was Nellie McClung (1873–1951), who, although she had been born on an Ontario farm, grew up on a Manitoba homestead. Her first book, *Sowing Seeds in Danny* (1908), tells of everyday life in a small town in southern Manitoba. It is made up of a series of short stories and sketches about Pearlie Watson, a twelve-year-old daughter of a section-hand, who goes into domestic service to help pay off the family debts. Pearl's story is continued in *The Second Chance* (1910), as the family moves out to a homesteading farm a few miles from town. Nellie McClung had resolved from the first to write about life as she saw it around her. She saw life directly, but her crusading spirit led her often to present what she saw in the forms of the Methodist and temperance literature of the day. But her books contain many excellent pictures of the drab and frustrating life of homestead days, relieved by happier scenes of communal gaiety at parties, picnics, or lacrosse games. Here and there in her third book, *The Black Creek Stopping-House* (1912), stories of early life on the Prairies are presented with a clarity and a penetrating understanding of human nature, and also with a charming sense of humour. Her writing was directed by a necessity for telling the truth, by a moral zeal, and by a strong Christian purpose; she had little use for any other artistic standards. However, many of her pictures of the early settlements of the West are deeply felt and effectively drawn.

Lucy Maude Montgomery (1874-1942) was born and raised in Prince Edward Island. She attended various Maritime colleges, and after graduation worked as a reporter and columnist for the Halifax *Echo*. She gave up a promising career to return to Cavendish, Prince Edward Island, to care for her aging and ailing grandmother. Living here under trying conditions, she began writing poetry and short stories for American and Canadian periodicals. In 1906, she began working on her first novel, expanding a short story which had originally been designed for a Sunday School weekly. She described it as "merely a juvenilish story, ostensibly for girls"; accepted by an American publisher, the story *Anne of Green Gables* (1908), turned out to have an appeal far beyond the local and juvenile level. At the request of her publishers, she wrote a sequel the next year, and then continued the story through a series of six Anne books; eventually she carried the story on into another generation. Most of the later books are less successful than the original; for as Anne grew up, she lost many of the charms of childhood and adolescence which had endeared her to the hearts of millions. In 1911 Miss Montgomery married a minister, and moved to southern Ontario, where she spent the rest of her life. She continued writing fiction, usually with a Prince Edward Island setting; but turning for the most part to adult fiction where her talents did not lie, she never came close to the standard or the popularity of the early Anne books. Miss Montgomery's letters reveal an intellectual depth and a speculative mind which is seldom evidenced in her fiction, where her successes are largely to be found in her description of the Prince Edward Island scene, and in her sensitive creation of an imaginative little girl, Anne of Green Gables.

One of the most original stories of the period is *Woodsmen of the West* (1908) by Martin Allerdale Grainger (1874-1941). It is not surprising that it is his only full-length work, for Grainger, born in England, spent a full life on the West Coast: as placer miner and logger; in the service of the province as Chief Forester; and in private business. What is surprising is his high level of technical proficiency. Every element of the narrative serves Grainger's purpose: a factual depiction of the life of the West Coast logger. The events are few and simple, but through Grainger's narrative art the reader is directly plunged into them: the hardships of logging, the trips up and down the Inlet, battling the waves and the weather, and above all, the central dramatic tension between Carter and Mart, the narrator. Mart, built upon Grainger himself, is skilfully and economically presented as the sensitive, perceptive amateur woodsman. But Grainger's finest achievement is the complex character of Carter, the logging boss. Although morbidly vain, pig-headed, maliciously egotistical, with a lust for power over men, Carter assumes heroic proportions in the narrator's eyes. "For among the clinkers and base alloys that made up much of Carter's soul there is a piece of purest metal, of true human greatness." Beside him and the rest of the characters, the loggers of Gilbert Parker, Hiram Alfred Cody, and Ralph Connor stand like stereotypes of fiction transferred to the backwoods or coast. Figures like Carter could only survive such a romantic treatment when placed against a solid background of materials obviously gathered from actual experience, and narrated in an appropriately varied style. With his sense of proportion, his feeling for appropriate pace, Grainger found a unified and flexible structure admirably suited to his own needs. He combined an accurate, detailed factual picture of the woodsmen of the West with a close analysis of complex men to produce, in a gripping narrative, one of the finest pieces of local and psychological realism in Canadian writing.

Although he was less grasping in imagination and often handicapped by undistinguished style, the writer who most closely approached Grainger's success in transmuting West Coast life into fiction was Bertrand William Sinclair (b. 1878). Sinclair was born in Edinburgh, Scotland, but grew up in the eastern foothills of the Rockies and developed a love of the western out-of-doors which later led him to travel extensively out from his home in Vancouver through the mountain and coast country from California to the Arctic Circle. His first books, *Raw Gold* (1908) and *The Land of Frozen Suns* (1910), although "Western" and "Northern" action stories, foreshadow his later emphasis upon the relation of character to environment. *North of Fifty-Three* (1914) dramatizes the corruptive force of Eastern city life, and the redemptive power of love in the British Columbia mountain country. Evidently set in the Harrison Lake area in British Columbia, Sinclair's *Big Timber* (1916) centres on the conflict between big timber interests, run by men in a hurry and careless of employees and nature, and small timber men of integrity and with a deep affinity with their woods. In his next novel, *Burned Bridges* (1919), he structured his work by facing his hero with a series of moral dilemmas and choices. The unconventional Wesley Thompson first fails as a missionary to the Crees, backtrails to the cities, looking for a job and for his identity; works his way to success in the motor industry in California; establishes himself in Vancouver at the head of a sales agency; confronts the personal moral dilemma of enlistment in the First World War, and finally finds himself and his love. Sinclair changed his locale and his focus of interest in *Poor Man's Rock* (1920) which depicts from the inside the fight for supremacy in the fishing industry in Puget Sound. Here, as also in *The Hidden Places* (1922) and *The Inverted Pyramid* (1924), he made effective use of his first-hand knowledge of the localities and the conditions he chooses to write about. *The Inverted Pyramid*, based on the Dominion Trust failure in Vancouver, and probably Sinclair's most ambitious novel, is a narrative of how the fifth generation of an influential British Columbia family meet their responsibilities when the oldest son brings financial and moral disaster upon them. Sinclair returned to the Vancouver scene in a story of rum-running days, *Down the Dark Alley* (1936).

Hiram Alfred Cody (1872–1948), like Ralph Connor, used the matter and manner of popular action fiction to achieve his primary aim of teaching Christian principles. He himself had been a missionary in the Yukon and a rector in New Brunswick parishes; each of his early novels is dominated by a Christian hero who also is either a missionary in the North or a minister in New Brunswick. Keith Stedman, the medical missionary hero of Cody's first romance, *The Frontiersman* (1910), is the traditional noble, lone traveller, the fearless fighter, and the chaste lover. The action is set in the Yukon, and is a series of attacks by wolves, gold thefts, floods, accidents, and coincidences. One of the early tasks of the hero is to overcome the vicious, cowardly villain who is corrupting the Indians by drink. *The Fourth Watch* (1911) presents another commanding figure in Parson John Westmore—somewhat older than Stedman, and under suspicion of theft for most of the story—who demonstrates Christian love in action among the loggers of the St. John River. *If Any Man Sin* (1915) offers both the young medical missionary and the older disgraced clergyman who has fled to the Mackenzie River to escape the church and religion. His faith finally is restored. The hero of *The Unknown Wrestler* (1918) is a farmhand, oversized and powerful, who represents "the spirit of adventure." He not only runs, wrestles, plays the violin, but also reveals himself at the end of the story as the new rector.

The R.C.M.P. officer who is the hero of *The Long Patrol* (1912), the newspaper reporter of *Glen of the High North* (1920), and the central figures of the later historical romances stand and fight for the same Christian principles, and are marked by the same characteristics as the heroes of the early stories. It is only in the titular hero of *The Touch of Abner* (1919), a shrewd local wag, and the townspeople of *The Fourth Watch* that Cody attempted any sharp individualization. Nor did Cody depart from the action tradition in his use of setting or of style. In spite of his first-hand knowledge of the North and his native province, he was content to use the standard idealized mountains, forests, waterfalls, log cabins, or farms merely as a background for his dramatic events. The conventionality is increased by his unnatural diction, by frequent rhetorical questions, and the repetition of stock adjectives and epithets. Cody and his readers, however, were not concerned with originality in these matters. His strength lay in his story-telling drive, and the appeal of his simple, strong-hearted, evangelical heroes.

The writer who was the most skilful humorist of his day and who also embodied in his writing most fully a spirit critical of his place and times was Stephen Leacock (1869–1944). In his attitude towards himself as a Canadian writer he also is representative of a significant difference between the earlier and the later writers of this period. As he wrote in his article "Exporting Humour to England," "I am a Canadian, but for the lack of any other word to indicate collectively those who live between the Rio Grande and the North Pole, I have to use 'American.' If the Canadians and the Eskimos and the Flathead Indians are not Americans, what are they?"

Leacock was born in England, and, after his family migrated to Canada when he was six, grew up on a farm near Lake Simcoe, in Ontario. He was educated locally, at Upper Canada College, and at the University of Toronto. He gave up school-teaching to study at the University of Chicago where Thorstein Veblen was lecturing. With his doctorate from Chicago, he joined the McGill University staff as a full-time lecturer in political science. His career as humorist was achieved concurrently with a distinguished academic career at McGill, during which he published almost one hundred scholarly articles in his own and allied fields and more than two dozen serious books on political science, economics, history, literature, and a variety of other subjects.

But it is as a humorist that Leacock became widely known in the English-speaking world. In 1894, when humour was one of the most popular kinds of writing in North America, he began his career as humorist by contributing sketches to American and Canadian magazines. He collected a number of his early pieces in his first book, *Literary Lapses* (1910), published privately in Montreal, republished in the same year in New York and London, and subsequently reprinted in some twenty editions. From 1910 until after his death in 1944, Leacock's new humorous volumes appeared year by year with almost unbroken regularity: *Nonsense Novels* (1911); *Sunshine Sketches of a Little Town* (1912); *Behind the Beyond* (1913); *Arcadian Adventures with the Idle Rich* (1914); *Moonbeams from the Larger Lunacy* (1915); *Further Foolishness* (1916); *Frenzied Fiction* (1918); *The Hohenzollerns in America* (1919); and *Winsome Winnie* in

1920. Eight more collections of sketches, burlesques, parodies, and stories followed in the twenties, eleven or so more in the thirties, and five in the forties. He not only maintained this steady stream of book publication, but also theorized about humour and anthologized it. His fullest examination of the art appeared in *Humour: Its Theory and Technique* in 1935, and in *Humour and Humanity: An Introduction to the Study of Humour* in 1937. In the thirties he published personal appreciations of his two favourite humorists, Charles Dickens and Mark Twain. Of them he wrote: "Charles Dickens stands at least as eminent as a humorist, if not higher. But Mark Twain was beyond anybody else in the world a technical humorist. He combined the basis of the matter—the inspiration—with the mechanism of it."

Leacock's own art was patterned after the traditions of North American humour which Mark Twain had brought to full flower. The early "Down Easterners," Haliburton and Seba Smith, had derived much of their humour from a hoss-sense view of human nature, expressed by shrewd native characters like Sam Slick or Major Jack Downing. Later the professional "funny men" of the post–Civil War years—Artemus Ward, Josh Billings, Bill Nye, Mark Twain, and others—had developed the verbal arts of humour, in print and on the lecture platform, to the delight of an ever expanding North American and British audience. They made their living (some of them very handsome livings) by making people laugh.

Like them, Leacock often spun nonsense; frequently his nonsense was interspersed with epigrams or afterthoughts which flicked the pretensions of the sophisticated or of the plutocracy. As they did, he used a multiplicity of forms: the dialogue, the memoir, the letter, the travel sketch, the tall tale, the anecdote, the literary burlesque and parody. He had the same bag of highly developed tricks as they had: the pun, chop-logic, the sudden juxtaposition of levels of speech, the mixed metaphor, the absurd coupling of words, the malapropisms, and the apparently witless flow of free association. He did not indulge in the wild spellings which some of them used; his taste for sudden violence was not as over-developed as it was in some of them; but like the best of them he was a master of lean, fresh native speech, and seemed to talk—whether he spoke from the lecture platform or the printed page. Like Mark Twain particularly, Leacock often adopted the persona of an innocent, either a native lunkhead, or a simple outsider (like Twain's Westerner), who with an irreverent spirit and hoss-sense observed the strange world of the city, with its acquisitiveness, its political struggle, its boarding houses, its millionaire clubs, its churches, or the even stranger world of England and the Continent.

Only a few of Leacock's thirty or so humorous books have an over-all unity. *Sunshine Sketches of a Little Town* (1912) and *Arcadian Adventures with the Idle Rich* (1914) are portraits, respectively, of a small Ontario town and of life in the big city. Each is made up of independent sketches, held together only by a common locale and some interlocking characters; neither makes pretensions of having a central plot or structure. The portraits emerge from a series of vignettes, rather than as a single canvas. A few other books have a unity of theme: *My Discovery of England* (1922) and *College Days* (1923) deal with one subject; *Nonsense Novels* (1911) is a collection of literary burlesques.

But these are exceptions; most of Leacock's books are collections of separate, brief comic writings on a variety of topics. *Literary Lapses* (1910), his first and still one of his most popular books, is a good example of the form and subject-matter of all his work. It contains forty-two unrelated sketches, essays, burlesques, parodies, letters, monologues, dialogues, and stories. Leacock himself referred to his writings as "pieces," which is perhaps the only term inclusive enough to describe the many similar but distinct forms in which he cast his comic treatment of a great variety of topics, ranging from economics to barbers, from education to Chinese laundries, from the financial affairs of the Doogalville parish church to the deliberations of the House of Lords.

Literary Lapses, which includes pieces published in magazines as many as sixteen years before, clearly shows that Leacock was already master of the comic craft. It contains examples of every comic technique he would use in his later books. His comic spirit, although still youthful, was already at its height, and was not to grow or decline significantly in the next thirty-four years. Already his sense of the incongruous could evoke laughter through irony or pathos, exaggeration or satire, nostalgia or verbal fun—or sometimes through an undefinable but distinctly Leacockian amalgam of sheer nonsense and deep wisdom.

This is not to suggest that his work is uniformly good. In his off moments, he could try much too hard to play the funny man. Leacock was not a good judge of his own work; as J. B. Priestley has pointed out, Leacock was better in practice than in theory, for Leacock's two books and many articles on humour do not add much to our understanding of his own craft. There is some strained, mechanical material in the canon; but considering that he turned out almost a book a year for thirty-four years, it is remarkable that there is not more.

Leacock has been regarded as a displaced eighteenth-century squire viewing the maddening scene of modern science and industrial organization with a benign eye from his country estate outside of Orillia. He also has been seen as an irascible, embittered, witty satirist with many double-edged axes to grind. Both views have some truth in them; there are, perhaps, two Leacocks.

One could be sharp and cutting; he was against shams and pretensions of all kinds, and he tried to destroy them by making fun of them. He lashed out, sometimes without mercy, against all forms of hypocrisy; spiritualists, doctors, lawyers, utopias, efficiency experts, statisticians, and faddists of all kinds were his special targets. He opposed socialism, prohibition, enforced retirement, misuse of language, and pretentiousness in any form, particularly in writing. When he went after this kind of opponent, he could be bitter, sharp, and satirical. He was bitterest when he attacked a Kaiser or a Hitler or a Mussolini, or anyone who threatened his own Canada or his own Empire. Most often, however, he used his sharpest literary pen against anyone or anything which threatened his sense of human dignity. There are enough pieces with a bitter flavour to suggest that Leacock was not always without malice. And yet it was usually a kindly malice, with the deep recognition of common human failings, and it was usually expressed without any sense of superiority. It is here than Leacock's great charm lies. He never set himself up as an authority on anything. He appears rather as the unspecialized, the unpredictable, the irrational average man whom modern society, modern science, and modern education are attempting to specialize, to predict, to rationalize. From his core, Leacock opposed this dehumanization, and the bitterness which appears in his writing stems from his central view that mankind, imperfect as he may be, is important.

But it is the other, the more purely comic Leacock that is better known. In his lighter moods, he produced his most characteristic and most enduring work. His spontaneous sense of incongruity, touched occasionally with tints of nostalgia, comes from a mellowed vision of human nature, and is combined with a profound human sympathy and understanding. Above all, Leacock's best work is funny; it evokes real laughter.

Leacock and these other twenty-seven writers are only a handful of the Canadians who wrote fiction between 1880 and 1920. But they may be taken as a group large and diversified enough to be representative of the Canadian fiction writers of the day. (The group is unrepresentative quantitatively in that it is made up largely of the more prolific writers of the time. The few more prolific writers not included are Harvey O'Higgins, Archibald McKishnie, and Frederick Niven, who published their first books between 1905 and 1910, and Samuel Alexander White, Frank Packard, Hulbert Footner, William Amy, and Robert Stead, who published their first books between 1910 and 1915. It does not include many of the some four hundred Canadians who published one, two, or a few more volumes of fiction during these years.) Different as were the twenty-eight we have discussed in place of birth, in nurture, in temperament, and in experience, they did hold in common certain assumptions about the writing of fiction, about the reading public, about the nature of fiction, and about their relation to their local Canadian scene.

For the writers in this group, fiction-writing was an occupation; part-time for most, full time for a few. It was not a way of life. Most of them wrote to gain an income or to supplement an income; but while they wrote for money, some also wrote for the pleasure of entertaining their readers, and more wrote to edify their readers and to support them in certain views of life. They assumed that their reading public was local and international, not national. They addressed their fiction to various segments of the wide, middle range of the reading public, not, on the one side, to "the saving remnant," or, on the other, to the readers of cheap pulp magazines. Most of them scored their first success with magazine stories, then with the publication of a first or an early book. Their later books often were variations on the themes and patterns of their first successes. They wrote in a variety of conventional forms, using conventional techniques, often with considerable skill. Their fiction was not personal, subjective, or inward searching; it was communal, written for an audience for whom fiction essentially was "story," and "story" told within a framework of unexamined, idealistic values.

Most of them placed their work with magazine editors and book publishers in New York and London. But although they often published in markets outside Canada, most of them wrote about the local Canadian scene which they knew, or had known, from first-hand experience. Some spun historical pasts for their localities; some told stories of the opening West and North; some told of Canadians abroad. Some tried to record in fiction the communities in which they lived; some built their fictions out of pleasant memories of the small communities in which they had grown up.

However they pictured life in the outside world, when writing of local Canadian scenes these Canadian writers rarely saw their society as institutional. In their fiction the world centred in the individual and in his relations with a few other individuals. The mainsprings of action were the good and bad in human beings, not in social forces. They pictured a self-contained, fluid world, still close to open country. Characters naturally moved out of their local worlds, sometimes south to the city, more often west or north to unsettled country; when they moved they rarely became deeply involved in their new societies. The dream of success common to most of these central characters is primarily emotional, not social or economic, and almost always the dream is fulfilled in the closing pages of these books. Few of these characters had any quarrel with their world; few felt alienated from it. The feeling expressed with such fine modulation in "L'Envoi: The Train to Mariposa," at the close of Stephen Leacock's *Sunshine Sketches of a Little Town*, is much more prevalent than is the feeling "You can't go home again."

Most of these books are now out of print, and are no longer read by the reading public. They are not regarded as serious literature by the literary critics of our day; the pictures of Canadian life they present have been overlooked by the cultural historians. Yet the Canadian fiction-writers between 1880 and 1920 were read more widely by their contemporaries, inside and outside Canada, than have been the Canadian fiction-writers—collectively—since. Because they wrote in the grain of the dominant feeling of their Anglo-North American world, their fiction had a significant reciprocal relation with their times. It reflects, through direct presentation or through fantasy, many aspects of the pluralistic life in Canada between 1880 and 1920; it also provided images of Canadian life which formed a definition of Canadian identity, at home and abroad.

18. Essays and Travel Books

I. Essays 1880–1920

BRANDON CONRON*

THE ESSAY IN CANADA developed slowly from early collections of speeches, magazine articles, sketches, and newspaper columns, all of which resemble the established form of the essay in relative brevity and discursiveness, but differ from it in purpose. The primary intention of the writer of such pieces was usually either hortatory or descriptive; his central interest lay in his subject, or, if he were in public life, in his opinions, but attention to the theme, a principal mark of the essay, was largely coincidental.

The fact that Joseph Howe (1804–1873) is sometimes considered the first Canadian essayist indicates one source of the tradition in Canada. For although the elaborate oratorical flourishes in his *Poems and Essays* (1874) have little more than historical interest, nevertheless, the political speeches and formal orations included were designated as "essays" and were looked to as stylistic models. This concept of the genre accounts in part for the necessity of considering as essayists later in this survey such figures as Osler, Falconer, and Massey.

The greatest single source of the essay in Canada, however, lies in journalism. The columns of *The Week*, "An Independent Journal of Literature, Politics and Criticism" (Toronto, 1883–96), saw the first appearance of many articles which were later collected as "essays." Though differing widely in interests and style, the writers of these pieces had one quality in common: the assumption, whether tacit or expressed, that their work had literary value, even when their purposes were dictated by politics or religion, and their methods by the editorial, the feature article, or the regular column. This assumption was due in part to the policy of *The Week* itself. In an early issue the first editor, Charles G. D. Roberts, made it clear that the journal was a forum for the expression of individual opinion by requiring every writer to sign his name to his contribution. The paper, though founded by Goldwin Smith, had no specific platform or purpose other than that of most Victorian

*Assisted by **Donald Hair**.

journals: "stimulating our national sentiment, guarding our national morality, and strengthening our national growth." Its articles discussing questions of the day and its descriptive sketches are the forerunners of the essay in Canada, though they themselves can scarcely be considered as literature. A typical contributor to *The Week* was the Reverend George Jacobs Low (1836–1906), who discussed current issues and described his own life in "Parson's Ponderings" with genial disregard for form and style.

The articles of Goldwin Smith (1823–1910) are far more polished in style than those of Low, but similarly fall short of being essays. Undoubtedly Smith felt that his discussions of current political questions were, like his earlier *Lectures and Essays* (1881), "contributions to Canadian literature," but his opinions on the Canadian constitution, and his methods as a writer, are of far more interest to the historiographer than they are to the student of literature. Similarly, the articles of Sir James Le Moine (1825–1912), some of which were included in the *Maple Leaves* series (1863–1906), are a storehouse of information for the antiquarian, although they have little literary interest.

The numerous contributions of Sara Jeannette Duncan (1861–1922) to the journal may be divided roughly into two groups: feature articles discussing questions of the day, such as "American Influence on Canadian Thought" (IV, 518), or "Our Latent Loyalty" (IV, 418); and more informal pieces which she called "Saunterings," reminiscent in method, intimate in tone, and unpretentious in style. Though journalistic, these pieces stand closer to the essay tradition than do those of the private secretary to Goldwin Smith, Theodore A. Haultain (1857–1941). Of his few articles, most are, like those of his employer, comments on current political questions. One or two of his descriptive pieces, however, foreshadow his later interest in nature (*Two Country Walks in Canada*, 1903; *Of Walks and Walking Tours*, 1914), and hint at his constant theme—the unity of nature and man. Haultain attempted to compensate for the tenuousness of his "speculations, semi-mystical, semi-intelligible" by paying careful attention to his mode of expression, but the result, except in his witty collection of aphorisms *Hints for Lovers* (1909), is often a stilted self-consciousness.

Of all the contributors to *The Week*, only Archibald MacMechan (1862–1933) deserves the title of essayist. Although born in Ontario, he adopted Nova Scotia, the Ultima Thule of his later descriptive books, as his native province. Its scenery and history are the materials out of which MacMechan shaped the essays of *The Porter of Bagdad and Other Fantasies* (1901) and of *The Life of a Little College* (1914). Fantasy, as the title indicates, is the key. Like the Victorian writers in whom MacMechan took more than the scholarly interest demanded by his position at Dalhousie University, he was the heir of the Romantics. The Dreamer, the agent of MacMechan's fancy, transforms purely descriptive pieces into whimsical reveries celebrating the fresh innocent beauty of nature, art, and woman. MacMechan's romanticism, however, is never escapism. Words order and control his experience, and create a formal if fanciful pattern to fix "golden days in memory for the enrichment of less happier times to come" ("Afoot in Ultima Thule"). The simplicity and restraint of the style, on the one hand, and the luxuriousness of the subject-matter, on the other, combine best in pieces like "Ghosts," "The Fence-Corner," and "My Own Country," where a fresh and distinctive lyricism reveals an imaginative but not unreal world of infinite delights for the thoughtful observer.

The decade in which MacMechan's collected essays first appeared may be taken as the period during which the essay emerged as a literary form in Canada. Its late appearance is not surprising. The essay always exalts being over doing, enjoyment over practicality. It demands leisure and meditation and some degree of detachment in order to realize its primary purpose of communicating to the reader a single and distinctive mode of thought, so as to evoke in him a sense of the essayist as an individual with a distinct personality and a distinct vision. This purpose was realized in different ways by Osler's *Aequanimitas* (1904), Carman's *Kinship of Nature* (1904), and Macphail's *Essays in Puritanism* (1905), three books which set a new if not always adequate standard for the essay in Canada. None of these writers was particularly interested in the easy formality and personal intimacy possible in the essay form; each chose the form because it emphasized the theme and was therefore the best vehicle for his own insights. And while these insights were primarily an illumination of life in general, they frequently had a utilitarian relationship with the writer's vocation, a relationship rather different from the *fin de siècle* tradition in England of essay writing as a leisurely activity pursued in retirement from practical life.

Typical are the essays of Sir William Osler (1849–1919), whose achievements in medicine and in medical education were for many years the principal basis of his fame. As a member of the medical faculty at McGill (1874–1884), Johns Hopkins (1889–1905), and Oxford (1905–19), Osler was often called upon to deliver the addresses upon which his reputation now rests. The address from which the title of his earliest volume *Aequanimitas* was taken introduced the theme that occurred again and again in Osler's works. He warned the graduating students that, should they become engrossed in professional cares, they would soon find no place "for those gentler influences which make life worth living." The gentler influences in Osler's own life came from two ministers, his father, and the Reverend W. A. Johnson, headmaster of Trinity College School, the man who first introduced Osler to

Sir Thomas Browne. Like Browne, Osler tried to strike a balance between the rational and the emotional. This "most serious difficulty of the intellectual life" Osler overcame by harmonizing the two conflicting elements of his nature. Of his vocation he wrote: "The practice of medicine is an art, based on science" ("Teacher and Student"); about the "unhappy divorce" between the humanities and the sciences he said: "Humanists have not enough Science, and Science sadly lacks the Humanities" ("The Old Humanities and the New Science"). The vital synthesis that Osler strove to maintain in everyday life had a firm basis in his religious beliefs, which were quiet but pervasive. He would "rather be mistaken with Plato than be in the right with those who deny altogether the life after death" ("Science and Immortality"). The equanimity of Osler's own mind is reflected in his style. Although his earliest addresses retain a good many oratorical flourishes and rely to a considerable extent on the elaborated aphorism, his later pieces capture the clarity and polish of the best English prose without sacrificing the pithiness of the wise saying. To the best of his essays (and especially to "The Student Life," a model of the form) may be applied what he himself said of Browne: "How pleasant it is to follow his thought, rippling like a burn, not the stilted formality of the technical artist in words, the cadences of whose precise and mechanical expressions pall on the ear."

The claim of Bliss Carman (1861–1929) to the title of essayist is a tenuous one, principally because his constant theme of personal harmonizing exhibits a growing tendency towards didacticism, a tendency that Carman himself was fully aware of when, in his *Talks on Poetry and Life* (1926), he added by way of apology that "one is sometimes betrayed into preaching." His first book, *The Kinship of Nature* (1904), remains his best, though many of the pieces in it are vitiated by the constant concern with self-betterment. Simplicity, grace, and subtle rhythmic patterns enhance the lyrical qualities of his style, but are not sufficient to redeem his prose from a disadvantageous comparison with his poetry. Carman's limitations as a prose writer are painfully evident when one compares his various pieces on spring ("At the Coming of Spring," "The Vernal Ides," "April in Town") with his better-known "Spring Song." The poem renders the emotion, but the prose never does more than talk about "these rare instants of existence."

Like Osler, Sir Andrew Macphail (1864–1938) was a physician but his literary interests were of a more professional nature. In 1907, while teaching medicine at McGill, he became editor of the *University Magazine*, and remained so until 1920. Macphail's concept of the essay tended towards straight discursive writing, as the titles of his books indicate: *Essays in Puritanism* (1905); *Essays in Politics* (1909); *Essays in Fallacy* (1910). In each of the *Essays in Puritanism*, for instance, the biography of a prominent writer or theologian forms the subject-matter, but it is Macphail's own appreciation of the Puritan spirit, with its emphasis on individualism, progress, and independence of all but God, that forms the theme and makes the pieces essays. Where the reader finds the ideas uncongenial, he is likely to be carried along by the genial vigour of the style. Macphail is a master of the clipped phrase, the pungent statement, the epigram. The compression and frequent distortion involved in such a style, however, may alienate the reader. The *Essays in Politics* fail to keep the balance of the *Essays in Puritanism*, partly because of the nature of the subject (Canada's relation to England), partly because Macphail's interests were turning more and more towards criticism and biography, and away from the essay as a literary form.

Neither Osler, Carman, nor Macphail consciously set about making contributions to literature. Thomas O'Hagan (1855-1939) did. A journalist and a teacher, he failed to distinguish the essay from literary criticism, historical writing, and travel literature. All of his pieces are didactic in intent, superficial in approach, and cursory in treatment, nor does his style ever rise above the journalistic hodge-podge of *Chats by the Fireside* (1911), a collection of his articles from the *Catholic Register*. The fact that O'Hagan's tacit assumption that his journalistic background was the proper one for writing essays went unchallenged is indicative of the particular nature of the Canadian essay.

The fame of Peter McArthur (1866-1924) rests upon his column of farm life which for many years appeared twice weekly in the Toronto *Globe*. The articles, re-arranged and to some extent revised, were collected into several books, beginning with *In Pastures Green* (1915) and ending with *Around Home* (1925). McArthur made his reputation as a humorist and sage; he was also peculiarly suited to be a Canadian essayist of the first importance. After a career as a journalist and editor in New York and England, he retired to his rural Ontario farm, like Montaigne to his tower, to take stock of his experience. But McArthur was too carefree and perhaps too careless to reflect on life either at length or in depth, and consequently his best pieces are only sketches that approach the essay. He believed his pieces had a cathartic effect but no literary value: "No particular merit attaches to writing a book." Yet McArthur's humble lack of pretensions should not blind the critic to his merits. His point of view— perhaps the only genuinely pastoral one in Canadian literature—was by nature contemplative, serious, and contented. It yielded the humble chronicles of farm life that we now most typically associate with McArthur. His humour was a pleasant quality of his point of view; his satirical vein was often an unpleasant point of attack. Of a stray calf he writes bluntly: "After the chores were done I took a pail that was as empty as a political platform and she followed me right back into the pen just like an intelligent voter" (*The Red Cow and her Friends*, 1919). McArthur's pastoral point of view, with all the virtues of simplicity and brotherhood implicit in it, served him best when he came to write on the subject that has plagued most Canadian essayists—Canada's international relations. *The Affable Stranger* (1920) is a fresh approach to the plea for better understanding between Canada and the United States. McArthur's more typical concern, however, was his farm. His themes may be summed up in one quotation from "The Return of Spring": "To me all Nature is as much alive as I am myself and flushed with the same life force. Only man with his egotistic self-consciousness misses its reviving touch." The relation of the character sketch to the essay is often ignored, a fact which may account for the sparse attention that seems to have been paid to *The Red Cow and her Friends* (1919), a collection of sketches of farm animals which is in many ways more satisfying than other more generalized pieces. McArthur's greatest deficiency is his style. At all times rambling, loose, and colloquial, it often lapses into sheer carelessness which cannot even be excused as "homely charm." When his theme is not nature, he reverts to the popular phrase, a practice particularly evident in some of the least successful efforts in *The Affable Stranger*. At his best McArthur is genial and easy, at his worst hackneyed and slipshod. But throughout his writing there is the same unassuming note of *In Pastures Green*: "I like to keep my feet on the earth—in good Canadian mud. . . ."

Very different in style and intent are the essays of William Hume Blake (1861–1924). Laurentian fishing trips provided the experiences out of which the Toronto lawyer produced three books in the Waltonian tradition—*Brown Waters* (1915), *In a Fishing Country* (1922), and *A Fisherman's Creed* (1923). Like Walton, Blake juxtaposes the complex world of "politics, stock-markets, courts, theatres, clubs" and the simple natural world where "the evening and the morning are the first and every following day." Simplicity is the mark of Blake's quiet intellectual approach to the world of nature, an approach complemented by the virtues he admires: appreciation of natural beauty, skill in fishing, the courage of the trout, the hospitality and shrewdness of the French guide. In fact, the reader soon discovers that angling is for Blake, as it was for Walton and later would be for Haig-Brown, one of those activities that epitomizes the good life. Fishing in Canada (and particularly in Quebec) has, moreover, its peculiar virtues, not the least of which is the fostering of mutual comprehension between French- and English-speaking Canadians ("Le Long du Sentier"). Closer to Walton is the gentle statement of faith that appears in *A Fisherman's Creed*—the belief in a divine design which each individual is continually furthering or thwarting. In this design the moral struggle is particularly important: "Salvation and damnation are habits of the soul, slowly acquired by the inner self, becoming inveterate in the passage of time." Choice is the mode of the struggle; for Blake himself fishing is undoubtedly a symbol of the continuing choice of good. Blake's style complements his creed. The careful shape of his sentences, the gentle ebb and flow of the rhythm, the unpretentious yet solid structure of his paragraphs, all are marks of the good workmanship which Blake admired so much in every walk of life.

The title Stephen Leacock (1869–1944) gave to his *Essays and Literary Studies* (1916) is an unusually serious one for a humorist, and suggests a gravity of purpose that is soon dispelled by the robust humour of the essays themselves. Nevertheless, the serious note is important because it marks the difference between those pieces in which humour is used as a structural principle, and those which exist solely for the sake of the humour. The former are essays; the latter are not. "The Devil and the Deep Sea: A Discussion of Modern Morality" is a good illustration of Leacock's contribution to the essay form. Simple in structure, it is basically a series of humorous paragraphs, "the cross sections of the moral tendencies of our time," all of which develop the theme: "The devil is passing out of fashion." Leacock's humour is so boisterous, however, that it often overwhelms the theme, so that even he himself in a serious moment must warn his readers "that though they may be conscientiously unable to digest all that I have told them . . . I shall nevertheless be amply satisfied if they will believe the half of it." The point is, of course, that Leacock's primary interest lies in humour, and not in essay writing; and humour works in a very different way from that literary form of the essay which Lorne Pierce has defined as "an epistle to the world of kindred spirits at large."

The development of the essay in Canada between the years 1880 and 1920 is by no means as steady as the literary historian might wish, but nevertheless some general trends are evident. The early essays spring directly from the writers' vocations, and are consequently didactic in intent and serious in tone. Yet this didacticism is subsumed by writers like Osler and Macphail into an attempt to express the eternal verities of human wisdom, and to express them in a distinctive and individual manner. Other writers mitigated the basic seriousness of their approach with humour, fantasy, lyrical description, reminiscence, and wit. Few had models. Whether their purposes were literary or not, these writers strove honestly and independently to express their own insights, and, with the exception of several contributors to *The Week*, left posterity to judge their literary value. Consequently as the essay emerged from its many related forms, it was characterized by a heterogeneous but vigorous individualism that combined the traditional ideals of civilization with the peculiar reactions to a distinctive physical environment and the peculiar problems of a new nation.

II. Travel Books 1880–1920

ELIZABETH WATERSTON

"AND I SUPPOSE when you get home you'll be writing a book?" The question might be asked of the traveller through Canada with sympathy or with sardonic hostility; the answer was usually "yes." Some travellers came with the intention of writing a report. Others, often at the urging of friends, belatedly scrambled journals, letters-home, or random notes into a holiday record. Most travellers packed some literary preconceptions along with their portmanteaux: phrases from *Evangeline* and Tom Moore's "Boat Song," from Dickens and Howells and Mark Twain; and later from Pauline Johnson and W. H. Drummond and Ralph Connor. All sifted what they saw through their own interests and needs, social and economic, personal and national. (A Scottish farmer saw Montreal as "the finest city in Canada" because "The farmers realize £10 per acre for their potatoes there." An ailing lady timidly noted the location and condition of the cemetery in each Canadian town. The first automobilist dismissed Quebec as "a city unfit . . . for a self-respecting touring-car.") The books they produced ranged from slim sketches to ponderous tomes, but there never was a break in the flow of books by travellers who had "done" Canada and were prepared to tell the world what they had found. Peak years in the production of such books occurred in 1885, 1895, and 1911.

Of the hundreds of travel books on Canada published between 1880 and 1920, most were read by a very small audience—the clergyman's flock, the delegate's sponsors, the fellow-suffragists—but a few were very widely read, by both sophisticated and unsophisticated readers: the memoirs of Lady Dufferin and descriptive sketches by Kipling and by Lord Lorne, the Duke of Argyll. These helped fix the picture of Canada for the next generation. Canadian readers probably formed the largest part of this audience, showing early and always an anxiety to know how their country had affected her visitors. Canadian writers also helped supply the demand for books on this country, and in particular exploited the continuing market for books of regional travel and description, mostly panegyric.

Canada challenged her visitors with the unexpected: scenes unimaginably rugged in the early years of railroad travel, a society unimaginably hostile to upper-class Englishmen in succeeding years, and a golden prairie unimaginably cruel still later. The traveller who responded to this challenge by reporting details sharply and by fusing them into a lively yet logical pattern could produce a noteworthy addition to the world's travel literature.

No single book of travel to Canada is as entertaining as Dickens's *American Notes*, or as deeply analytical as Emerson's *English Traits*, but Sandford Fleming's *England and Canada*, Douglas Sladen's *On the Cars and Off*, Walt Whitman's *Diary in Canada*, and Rupert Brooke's *Letters from America* approach the greatest travel books in liveliness and force. Because spaces in Canada were so great, actualities of travel are more emphasized than in books on England or Europe; and in the simpler national texture the rare quaintness of French Canada, of the Indians, of the western homesteader inevitably focuses attention. Compared to books on the United States, these Canadian travel accounts offer less variety in order and organization. In the 1880's, for instance, there was one route only—the Canadian Pacific Railway, and one direction—East to West or, in rare relief, West to East, never such zig-zag itinerary as lured Britons touring the United States. Chapter headings unroll inevitably: "Trip Across," "Maritimes," "Quebec and Saguenay," "Montreal and Ottawa," "The Railway," "Toronto," "Niagara Falls," "The Great Lake Steamers," "Winnipeg and the Prairies," "The Farther West," and "Homeward Bound." Differences in proportion, in accent, in angle of narration, become significant in such a set scheme.

The 1880's

First travel-books of the 1880's were unassuming and informative. Delegations of English and Scottish tenant farmers dutifully published their views on Canada as a field for settlement, beginning a deluge of "Emigrant Guide" books. The range in background of writers of guide books shows how widespread was the interest in Canada as a haven. Thomas Moore, editor of the *Irish Farmer*, offered *A Tour through Canada in 1879* (1880). Hugh Fraser, farmer of Inverness, wrote *A Trip to the Dominion of Canada* (1883). J. E. Ritchie, a journalist, in *To Canada with Emigrants* (1886) reported on politics as well as colonizing. J. G. Holyoake, organizer of the Co-operative movement in England, described his work in *Travels in Search of a Settler's Guide Book* (1884). "S. Scrivener," Secretary of the "Self-Help Emigrant Society," wrote *Off to Canada* (1888) and *With the Self-Help Emigrants* (1888). Tenant farmers published *Reports . . . on the Dominion of Canada as a Field for Settlement* (1880). Henry Tanner, Senior Member of the Royal Agricultural Society, wrote *A Report upon Canada* (1883). All these writers included descriptions of their own travel experiences, as did Peter Mitchell, a Canadian cabinet minister, in *The West and North-West* (1880), "Anglo-Canadian" in *Canada* (1882), "A Retired Officer" in *A Year in Manitoba* (1883), and "Family Man," a British university graduate, now a professional man with a family of sons, who asked *Shall We Emigrate?* (1885). Of all these travel books published in hope of helping would-be emigrants, the most attractive are two ingenuous reports by young men—boys really—who experienced the life of emigrant labourers: J. S. Cockburn's jaunty *Canada for Gentlemen* (1885) and A. J. Church's *Making a Start in Canada* (1889), a cheery account consisting of letters by the sons of a professor of Latin (who solemnly lists his own publications at the end of the book—*Roman Life in the Days of Cicero,* etc.) The boys finally built their own hut out west, "rather like a pig-sty," put up bookshelves and photos, bats, "rackets" and guns, and pronounced the effect "quite jolly." Much more dignified, and more influential, were the volumes produced by the conscientious Marquis of Lorne, *Canadian Pictures* (1884). The Marquis of Lorne incorporated advice to emigrants in his *Canadian Life and Scenery* (1886) along with his account of travels as Governor-General and as holidaying sportsman. The artistic Lorne in his romantic sketches of the wilderness beauty of the West set a visual image often reproduced in later books. His was the most important book of the decade in terms of numbers of readers.

Among "holiday travellers" the range of personalities, professions, and intentions was again wide—much wider than at any time before or after the 1880's. "A. S." wrote *A Summer Trip to Canada* (1885) to induce other ladies to make similar trips; Charles Elliott, F.S.I., Devonshire gentleman and horse-breeder dedicated *A Trip to Canada and the Far North-West* (1886) to Lord Lorne, the Governor-General. Dr. George Bryce bowled along in *Holiday Rambles between Winnipeg and Victoria* (1888) in a "prose idyll," designed to thrill others at the sights he saw: "The Fraser River is not only wonderful, IT IS TERRIFIC in its grandeur." A. S. Hill, D.C.L., Q.C., M.P., self-important partner of the Earl of Latham, described his "autumn wanderings in the North-West" in *From Home to Home* (1885). Few "holiday trippers" could outdo the satisfaction of Hugh Bryce, business man of Paisley, who in *Narrative of a Trip to Canada* (1881) presented "statistics" on wages and prices of haircuts, grapes and the "self-feeding parlour stove"; described the nuns "in a monastery" in Quebec, the churches and schools in Hamilton, the Canadian "language"; and ended "with the gratifying reflection that I had spent no more money during my trip than I had calculated upon."

It is interesting to note how many Englishmen assumed they could "do" Canada and the United States in one holiday trip. Some representative titles strike the jaunty note: M. Jackson's *To America and Back, a Holiday Run* (1886); C. B. Berry's *The Other Side; How It Struck Us* (1880), John Strathesk's *Bits about America* (1887), Rev. John Kirkwood's *An Autumn*

Holiday in the U.S. and Canada (1887). Some cut a still wider swath: J. J. Aubertin's *A Fight with Distances, the States, the Hawaiian Islands, Canada, British Columbia, Cuba, the Bahamas* (1888); Mrs. E. H. Carbutt's *Five Months' Fine Weather in Canada, Western U.S. and Mexico* (1889). Brevity is flaunted in T. P. Powell's *A Trip beyond the Rockies, 8000 miles in Eight Weeks* (1887); Thomas Greenwood's *A Tour in the States and Canada; Out and Home in 6 weeks* (1883); Sir Henry Edwards' *A Two Months' Tour in Canada and the United States* (1889).

All these "rapid tours" are open to criticism for glibness and rapid generalization. E. Catherine Bates, speaking of Canada in chapter One of *A Year in the Great Republic* (1887), reports that she spoke to two immigrants and found both discontented. Of this group three hold considerable interest: Joseph Hatton, whose *Today in America* (1881) gives sensitive political and social analysis of "Canada and the Union"; Emily Faithful, who in *Three Visits to America* (1884) includes a study of the position of Canadian women; and Thomas R. Rickman, a querulous architect, whose *Notes of a Short Visit to Canada and the States* (1885) takes a sour look at Canadian arts. America, the ladies, and the arts—three topics to remain controversial.

The Americans, for their part, produced a variety of travel books, emphasizing social differences from the United States, as in C. D. Warner's serious *Studies in the South and West with Comments on Canada* (1889), or in "Captain Mac's" humorous *Canada* (1882); colourful scenes for children as in H. Butterworth's *Zig-Zag Journeys in Acadia* and *New France* (1885) and in C. A. Stephens's adventures of *6 Young Men in the Wilds of Maine and Canada* (1885); and sports as in J. A. Knox's *A Devil of a Trip* (1888), on a yachting tour up Lake Champlain via the St. Lawrence to Nova Scotia, and in B. Watson's *The Sportsman's Paradise* (1888).

To this last group, the "sportsmen's guides," we may add three British books: J. J. Rowan's *The Emigrant and Sportsman in Canada* (1881), mostly on New Brunswick, and remarkably readable on both society and sport; G. H. Wyatt's *The Traveller's and Sportsman's Guide* (1880), a brief and practical book; and J. A. Lees and W. J. Clutterbuck, *B.C. 1887* (1888), regional in title, but introduced by a continental travel sequence. In or out of western territory, this book is one of the gayest and most vigorous of all Canadian travel books.

Another kind of traveller is the specialist who comes to a convention, then "at the urging of friends or family" re-works his travel diary into a book. In the 1880's, British scientists who had been treated to a trip along the C.P.R. as a climax to the first Canadian session of the British Association added reports on Canada "as seen from the cars." An anonymous writer in the *Canadian Gazette* prepared the way with *A Tour through Canada* (1884).

Commissioner J. G. Colmer followed with *The Dominion of Canada as it will appear to Members of the British Association* (1884); Rev. Harry Jones, chaplain to the Association, wrote *Railway Notes in the North-West* (1884), Gen. Sir J. H. Lefroy wrote *The British Association in Canada* (1885), and Clara Lady Rayleigh, mother of the professor of experimental physics at Cambridge, added *The British Association's Visit to Montreal* (1885). This redoubtable lady outdid the official delegates in vigour and interest.

As well as the emigrant guides, the holiday accounts, the sportsman's digests, and the scientists' memoirs, Canadian travel books in the eighties included some very competent journalists' analyses. Prior to the opening of the C.P.R., Fraser Rae of the London *Times* had "done Canada" very well in *Newfoundland to Manitoba* (1881).

The opening of the transcontinental line of the C.P.R. brought journalists intent on "copy" and C.P.R. publicists into the travel book business. Mrs. Spragge of Toronto rode the first train *From Ontario to the Pacific* and produced a competent little report (1887). *The Times* sent out another special correspondent in 1886 for *A Canadian Tour* (1886). Stuart Cumberland, an Australian reporter, wrote the biggest and liveliest report, a canny, spirited account of the first West-to-East trip on the C.P.R.: *The Queen's Highway* (1887).

Even the Anglican dean of Montreal, Dean Carmichael, in *A Holiday Trip* (1888), produced something suspiciously like a railroad brochure. The Reverend D. V. Lucas got into the act with *All about Canada* (1883) a pocket reference, also heavily featuring the C.P.R. Sandford Fleming's stirring *England to Canada* (1884) is a railway book in a different sense. The great engineer, returning to the Rockies, retraced the steps of locating the last link of the railway through the Illecillewaet gorge. His report, like that of Lees and Clutterbuck, is on a life of action and courage, a Hemingway world of "camping-out." His was the Canada which would appeal more and more strongly to Europe in the years just before the First World War, and again in the distraught 1930's. In organization, Fleming's work is an unusual blend of travel report and memoir. It fuses the account of a routine trip with memories of the dangerous, challenging past. Many later writers would try to enlarge the time-scope of a day-by-day trip, but none have handled the problem of time in a travel book more effectively than Sandford Fleming.

All travellers to Canada in the eighties felt impelled to "do" certain set scenes. There were Montmorency Falls, the Ice Palace in Montreal, the Parliamentary Library in Ottawa, and the University at Toronto. There was Niagara Falls ("The indescribably superb, gigantic, towering flow of the glorious Canadian rapids! Nearer and nearer the billows roll . . . and then the Fall! . . . And this goes on forever!"). There was Winnipeg, a touchstone for the tourist of the eighties, with its astonishing growth from the hamlet in the mud of the previous decade. Then came the prairies, the Rockies, and Vancouver and Victoria, already contrasted.

All tourists commented on the differences between old and new Canada. Farms stood for sale in New Brunswick, and French Quebec dozed in picturesque backwardness. But fabulous harvests in the West brought hope even to the newcomers, the old-country settlers, both the well-born and the ex-waifs, and even to the odd ethnic groups in communal settlements of Mennonites and Icelanders. Beyond this farm world lay the frontier, rough and bare, bringing American visitors a sense of "the ecstasy of freedom," but filling Englishmen with less enthusiasm. Out at the far end of the railway was an odd and colourful world of improvisation and frontier equalitarianism. "When people wants their boots cleaned," said the hotel proprietor at Fort Moody, "they generally in these parts cleans 'em theirselves; but most of 'em don't want 'em cleaned at all."

Everywhere, Canadians seemed to the British "fluent and friendly," democratic ("Zeke eats with the family"), and busy. Politics attracted the best class (in the United States "the best class holds aloof"). Englishmen were bombarded with complaints against British superciliousness and indifference to Canadian trade. On the other hand, American visitors mocked Canadian social pretensions and the apeing of English customs. "Captain Mac" has an amusing chapter on "The Knighting of J. Muggins Jones in Ottawa." Differences between Canada and the United States were constantly explored. "The further West, the more American do the cities become." Yet the frontier was distinctly different from the American West—"no shooting, no frontier lawyers." The Northwest Mounted Police clanked through the trains, visible symbols of law and order, keeping a particularly benevolent eye on the rather shiftless Indians, and maintaining the liquor laws. (They might even be observed sniffing at bottles marked "lavender water," drawn from old ladies' reticules.)

Sport called out most social gatherings: curling, tennis, football, sleighing ("simply splendid"), skating by torchlight, trotting, ice-boat sailing, hunting the wild ram, the bear, the grouse, the snowshoe rabbit, fishing (including tommy-cod fishing through the ice), hockey, "trabogoening" ("which has its literal drawbacks"). There was less activity in the arts: collections at Laval and in Sir Donald Smith's Montreal home; a few artists at the "scenic spots" (Mr. Lucius O'Brien, President of the R.C.A., was observed at Glacier, painting "in raptures" but rather bothered by bears). Theatre was rarely enjoyed, though a few travelling troupes and private theatricals supplemented the Theatre Royal in Montreal. Book pedlars plied their wares on the trains, and in Toronto a tribe of writers turned out "cheap moral literature" exploiting a demand. The greatest cultural medium was the newspaper, proliferating in small towns, great centres, new villages, even in a frontier shanty where "a village might be expected later." (Of course the great number of journalists among the travellers of the eighties in part explains the constant emphasis on newspaper workers.) Other Canadians accessible to tourists included politicians, business magnates, and a mixed bag of celebrities (Hanlan the great oarsman, Janet Hanning the sister of Carlyle, and Jefferson Davis, "vivacious, fragile, erect," self-exiled leader of the Southern Confederacy).

But most writers of the eighties were less concerned with people, or the arts, more concerned with scenery, with the winter ("Here they measure milk by the yard") and with the facts of emigrant life.

The 1890's

Some of the "news value" of a Canadian tour had vanished by 1890. Indeed, this next decade produced about half as many books of travel as had appeared in the previous ten years. Many Canadians proudly wrote in this decade their own version of their country's charms, her power, her claims to attention. G. R. Parkin's *The Great Dominion* (1895) was very widely read, to judge by references to it in later travel accounts. It was equalled in ponderous pride by J. D. Edgar's *Canada and its Capital* (1898) and in J. L. Wood's *Canada from Ocean to Ocean* (1899). These are all less books of travel than glorified guide books, as is G. M. Grant's handsome volume designed for American readers, *Our Picturesque Northern Neighbour* (1899). Such publicizing efforts by prominent Canadians outnumbered the travel books by visiting tourists.

The visitors were lighter in touch. The impression of sprightliness in this decade perhaps reflects the fact that so many of the travel-writers were ladies. Sketch-pad in hand, lady's maid (unwillingly) in tow, a succession of English gentlewomen brightly surveyed the Canadian scene. Greatest of these ladies, both socially and aesthetically, was Lady Dufferin. *My Canadian Journal* (1891) is probably little altered from the informal letters-home written by Lady Dufferin during her years as wife of the Governor-General. Her energy and her enthusiasm for Canadian sports, for theatre, for balls and receptions and camping-trips give this book rare charm. But as a report on Canada it presents a puzzling study in influence. The actual scenes described were those of the seventies but the book was printed twenty years after her experiences in Canada. Because of her prestige and position, it was very widely read. But *My Canadian Journal* fixed in its readers' minds the picture of a life already vanished. Another much read and still readable account of vice-regal life is Lady Aberdeen's self-styled "taffy for the Dominion," *Through Canada with a Kodak* (1893).

Most of the ladies' books sport "Kodak" shots, or drawings by the authors, reproduced in sepia tones; the books are bound in artistic shades of mauve or mustard, ornamented with gold line drawings of flowers and leaves.

Botanizing Lady Theodora Guest in *A Round Trip in North America* (1895) and Lady H. J. Jephson in *A Canadian Scrap-Book* (1897) include "illustrations from the author's sketches." Winnifred, Lady Howard of Glossop, adds to the ladies' books a *Journal of a Tour in the U.S., Canada and Mexico* (1897) and Mrs. Howard Vincent a more serious report, *Newfoundland to Cochin China* (1892).

Gentleman travellers usually rely on photographs for illustration. Holiday "shots" enliven William Smith's *A Yorkshireman's Trip to the United States and Canada* (1892) and A. Giles's *Across Western Waves and Home* (1898). Among other holiday travellers Robert Shields, "the Horatio Alger of Toronto," described *My Travels* (1900); J. G. Colmer wrote *Across the Canadian Prairies* (1895), Hugh Bryce, a delegate to a Christian Endeavour convention in San Francisco, wrote *Across the American Continent* (1898), and W. S. Webb, a businessman travelling by "special private train" contributed *California and Alaska and over the Canadian Pacific Railway* (1891).

Many holiday trips still fitted Canada into an American tour: Rudyard Home's *Columbian and Canadian Sketches* (1895) emphasizes Irish contributions to the New World; W. T. Crosweller reports *Our Visit to Toronto, Niagara Falls and the United States of America* (1898); Alexander Craib in *America and the Americans* (1892) focuses on "home life" and pious Protestant groups like the Y.M.C.A.; Archibald Porteous, *A Scamper through Some Cities of America* (1890), a Scottish business man's account, allots three chapters out of seventeen to Canada, covering Niagara to Hamilton, Ottawa and Montreal. J. Bond's *A Fortnight in America* (1891) reaches the extreme in time limit. Thomas Hughes, popular author of *Tom Brown's Schooldays*, issues his *Vacation Rambles* in 1895 in a late reprinting of travel letters from 1870, perhaps with something of the same effect as Lady Dufferin's delayed report.

Two Australians add records of leisurely trips: J. F. Hogan, *The Sister Dominions* (1896), and J. W. C. Haldane, *3800 Miles across Canada* (1900). Three Americans report: Julian Ralph in *On Canada's Frontier*, gives sketches of sport and adventure in "Nepigon," Hudson Bay, and the "Eldorado" of the new Northwest (1892); H. M. Field, in *Our Western Archipelago*, offers effective analysis by an established author of travel books (1895); and R. H. Davis views *The West from a Car Window* (1892).

Dr. P. E. Doolittle supplements the "railroad" books by an account of Canadian sights of interest to high-perched "wheelmen," *Wheel Outings in Canada* (1895).

Less jaunty are the accounts of immigrant life. These books usually begin with a travel account, then expand the description of life in the new settlements. The best are Wm. Elkington's *Five Years in Canada* (1895), a day-by-day account of farming near Strathclair and later at Qu'appelle; A. A. Boddy's *By Ocean Prairie and Peak*, "some gleanings from an Emigrant chaplain's log" (1896); C. C. Johnstone's *Winter and Summer Excursions in Canada* (1892), case histories of successes and failures designed to offset the over-optimism of official pamphlets; Thomas Moore's *Canada Revisited, 1879-1893* (1893); P. R. Ritchie's *Manitoba and the North-West Territories* (1892), a young farmer's account of travels in search of a new home; and finally a collection of reports on *The Visit of the Tenant-Farmer Delegates to Canada in 1890* (1891). This last is produced in the old small print of the "emigrant guides" of the previous decade.

But the look of most of the travel books in the nineties is impressive. Solid books, in clear big print on glossy paper, most of them were obviously not designed for potential emigrant-farmers. Careful style and structure reflect a changed conception of the aesthetic sophistication of the audience.

In Douglas Sladen's *On the Cars and Off* (1895) and Edward Roper's *By Track and Trail* (1891), the travel book reaches a modest but satisfying height. Both books are energized by the excitement of railway travel (which provides both a literal and a literary dynamic). Both create attractive *personae* as observers, and both add a second dynamic in the interaction between the observer and his companions. Edward Roper focuses his whimsical story of settlers' travels through the eyes of "Miss Maud and Miss Maggie," the two pretty English girls who accompany him west; Douglas Sladen unifies *On the Cars and Off* by a similar use of "The Pretty Girl" and "The Matter-of-Fact Woman." Travel is subtilized, humanized, given artistic unity and structure by these devices. The travel book seems almost to emerge as a literary genre here.

Kipling's *From Sea to Sea* (1899), while even livelier in treatment of scenes on the West Coast, seems fragmentary by contrast. It is good Kipling, but not a great travel book. His tone and themes were already established, and Canada could not effect a change in his palette.

Egerton Ryerson Young's books for boys, such as *Winter Adventures of Three Boys* (1899), not strictly travel books, fixed the image of the "great lone land" in the minds of British schoolboys.

For most tourists of the 1890's people mattered more than in the 1880's. They recorded meetings with Van Horne, with Laurier, with Dunsmuir in British Columbia, with Goldwin Smith in Toronto, with Father Lacombe out west. Scenery mattered less. A sense of re-doing over-worked scenes inhibited the new observers of Quebec, Montreal, the prairies, the Rockies. They strained for subtler effects, as when the Saguenay becomes a "sophisticated dream of death." For Niagara, few raptures: "I duly did the Falls," said one writer. The iridescent arch seemed "no longer what it was"; the scandal of control by speculators and the "cockney treatment" of the surroundings appalled. "No fine scenery, no fine weather—and no fine flowers." At Ottawa there was "no good *coup d'œil*"; in Quebec, city of romance, there was a sense of the real world passing by; in Montreal, a charming view from the Mountain, "but oh! the roads, the horrid, rutty, dirty, muddy, dusty roads!" Disenchantment extended to the hotels. The opulent city establishments like the Windsor (much praised in previous years) now seemed outbalanced by the cheerless bush hotels where half-breeds lingered in an airless kitchen. No blind, no glass, no service in Quebec; no taste, no comfort in Nipissing; no charm anywhere.

These sophisticated travellers found much to interest them in Canadian character. It was bustling, a little priggish, resentful of British criticism, very loyal to Queen Victoria, but hostile to the dissipated British lordlings now on drunken display in western saloons. Yet Canadians bristled against being called "American," and had a laughing rejoinder to annexation talk, "Let them jine us!" There were new concerns too, with "perfidious Russia," and with the new Japan.

The new Canadian gospel was "work." Few festivals broke the year; tales were heard of young men marrying widows to get their children as labourers, and there was little sense of a cultural growth to compensate for this grim practicality. Churches flourished, but in mutual antagonism. The new universities, though blessedly open to all, focused on agricultural science. Teetotalism was militant. (The director of the Canadian National Exhibition invited one visitor into his broom closet for a drink.) Women married too early, lost their freshness. Canadian children, boys as well as girls, did domestic chores, but were hard to manage in school. "All speak with a twang unequalled in ugliness."

Yet most of these details were reported with interest rather than disdain.

The 1900's

As Canada moved into the twentieth century, the vision of a "vast reserve of Empire" continued to inflame British imagination, but enthusiasm was checked by Canadian arrogance. Admiration and irritation alternate in most travel books of the decade. The ladies were silent; in their place came a succession of serious, statistic-minded males. R. J. Barrett, editor of the *Financier and Bullionist*, produces *Canada's Century: Progress and Resources of the Great Dominion* in 1907, a confident report, with economic conclusions firmly set in black-face at the end of each chapter. J. A. Hobson, author of *The Evolution of Modern Capitalism and Imperialism*, sets forth *Canada Today* (1906) in similar analytic vein. H. R. Whates, London journalist from the *Standard,* includes excellent chapters on fiscal policy and national sentiment in *Canada, the New Nation* (1906) but contrasts life in exile, on the prairies, with the luxuries of home, friends, theatre, thoroughfares. Less pretentious accounts come from George Bain, *A Run through Canada* (1905); George Briggs, *Recollections of a Visit to Canada: Experiences of a Member of the Corporation of London* (1907); and Herbert Grange, *An English Farmer in Canada and a Visit to the States* (1904), but these pedestrian books sometimes offer rewarding details: a glimpse of a St.-Jean-Baptiste parade in Montreal, ugly telephone wires, Orange Day in the West, Indian schools, a Chinook in the foothills. Other travel accounts lighter in tone include Fr. E. J. Devine's *Across Wildest America* (1905), about a remembered train ride to a far western mission; Harry Brittain's *Canada There and Back* (1908), an uncritical attempt to persuade friends to try a similar tour through "magnificent country"; and Joseph Adams's *Ten Thousand Miles through Canada* (1909), a vigorous narrative of shipboard and train-ride, emphasizing always the links between old country and new—the Boy Scouts on board ship, the suffragist orators bound for new audiences in Ontario, the prairie-bound brides.

J. W. C. Haldane, in *3800 Miles across Canada* (1900), attempted to solve the technical problem of travel narration by giving himself a "split personality"—and referring to himself alternately as the sharp-eyed "Chiel" and the affable "Happy Traveller." But most travel books of the decade differed only in their geographical pattern of organization from the weighty books of general analysis and description in which the period abounds—books not properly travel accounts but rather panegyrics: A. G. Bradley's *Canada in the 20th Century* (1903), F. A. Wrightman's *Our Canadian Heritage* (1908) and W. W. Campbell's *Canada* (1907), H. J. Morgan and L. J. Burpee, *Canadian Life in Town and Country* (1905). All are heavily partisan, handsomely printed; in numbers they equal the travel accounts by British and American visitors of the decade.

Even books designed for English children, such as J. T. Bealby's *Canada* (1909), though lively in spots, were ponderously informative in others, presenting awed summaries of the outputs of mines, of lumber-yards, of wheat fields. Equally solemn, though less complete in coverage, were the books endemic in this period, by "one-track travellers"—the men who came obsessed by a single idea. Kipling, in *Letters to the Family* (1908), pounded imperialism readably, but still obsessively. C. J. Farncombe, Nonconformist preacher, in *My Visit to Canada* (1907), Sir Frederick Young, in *A Pioneer of Imperial Federation in Canada* (1902), J. C. Smith, of the "Soul-Winning and Prayer Union," in *Holidays for Jesus* (1901), and Bailie D. Wilcox, in *With the British Bowlers in Canada* (1906)—each reports only what relates to his obsession. Joseph Pope's *Tour of Their Royal Highnesses the Duke and Duchess of Cornwall and York* (1901) belongs in this obsessed group, as all royal tours must. The Canadian background fades behind the royal couple, their doings, sayings, and posings for photographers. The Duke of Argyll's Canadian scenes continued to be reprinted, always with new pleas appended for Imperial solidarity and for the use of Canadian spaces as receiving ground for the overcrowded British labouring classes.

Very few travellers attempted to describe the panorama of the whole nation in this decade. Walt Whitman's haunting *Diary in Canada*, the account of his trip from London to the Saguenay (1904), is the best of the regional studies. Paul Fountain writes of *The Great North-West* (1904), James Outram of *The Heart of the Canadian Rockies* (1905), F. G. Pauli of *Chibogamoo* (1907), Major Durham of *A Trip from Buffalo to Chicoutimi* (1901), Andrew Iredale of Niagara and the Thousand Islands in *An Autumn Tour* (1901), John A. Walker of the eastern provinces in *Canada: Or the Western Land of Promise* (1902), St. Michael Podmore of Lake Abitibi in *A Sporting Paradise* (1909), F. E. Herring of the West in a series of books, *Canadian Camp Life* (1900), *B.C.* (1903), and *In the Pathless West* (1904).

The author of a regional sketch straining for unity, might organize it by reference to rivers, as in L. J. Burpee's *By Canadian Streams* (1909), or to seasons, as in Arnold Haultain's delightful *Two Country Walks in Canada* (1903), or to scriptural passages, as in D. W. Lucas's *Canaan and Canada* (1904). (Haultain's book is of interest also for its tone of mildly satiric realism, anticipating Leacock's method and range.) Of all regional studies the most important deal with the crucial Midwest. Brian McEvoy's rapid, colourful *From the Great Lakes to the Wide West* (1902) blends flair for anecdote with patriotic response to the "Boom." James Lumsden, another journalist, in his *Through Canada in Harvest Time* (1903) promises comfort and independence in the golden West. H. A. Kennedy dedicates *New Canada and New Canadians* (1907) to "all who love their country and whose country is the British Empire." All emphasize economic facts rather than moral or social ones: themes of moral disintegration or regeneration by the prairie, and themes of social difficulties in assimilation (valuable to Ralph Connor and other novelists of the period) are unexplored. Two bitter footnotes to the optimism of earlier emigrant guides appear in the works of "Homesteader," *Canadian Life as I Found It* (1908), and of Basil Stewart, *The Land of the Maple Leaf* (1908). Next year Stewart excerpted and reprinted the angriest parts of his report in *No English Need Apply* (1909), a belligerent protest against Canadian boosters, American immigrants, and British emigration pamphleteers.

Inevitably, the more kindly disposed books of this period of "boosting" and independence are Amercan. "There's only one West left, and . . . Young Canada has got that," cried Anson Gard, in a last twist of the old American frontier-worship. Gard, tossing off a series of bright little books, brassy but readable, *The Wandering Yankee* (1902), *The New Canada* (1903), *The Last West* (1906), is an odd partner for the majestic Walt Whitman. Whitman dreamily mused on the Canadian current of life, so strangely separated from "the glorious mid-artery of the great free Pluribus Unum of America," as he dreamily watched Canadian life in a hayfield and on a lake boat. But Whitman united with Gard in sympathy for the new Canada.

All travellers reported now on the new Montreal, of St. James Street, Victoria Bridge, river front, tenement houses, and "foreign Jewry." Toronto was a puzzle of self-conscious culture, of "small-calibred people," of money values, and mealy-mouthed piety. A new Ontario of mines, of the "Soo," and Port Arthur, was emerging. In Winnipeg, the "Canadian Chicago," this raw new world was focused in its shoddiness, its energy, and its anti-British sentiment. The "Great Clay Belt" held promise, and the Far West, exploiting natural resources, "hustled." Everywhere there were comforts, pavements, electricity, telephones, tram-cars. In hotels, a "roughish element" afflicted with superfluous saliva held stations in the uncurtained ground-floor saloons. Rural festivals consisted of Orangemen and lemonade and abuse of the late John A. Macdonald. There were few sports now—baseball, "dreariest and most negative of games," while "cricket flickers but feebly." Football players appeared more warlike than in England, padded and encased.

In contrast with this hustling world of energy and materialism, the natural landscape was filmed over in vapid sentimentalism. Like the pale water-colour illustrations in Campbell's *Canada*, Whitman's descriptions typify this genteel prettiness: Montmorency Falls are "like strings of snowy-spiritual, beautiful tresses."

Englishmen, irritated by the sentimental façade, annoyed by Canadian brashness, disturbed by car-loads of "Galicians"—Russians, Poles, Hungarians—disillusioned by the continuing deterioration of whiskey-laden Indians, uneasy at the "dirty" farming out west and the utilitarian grinding life of wheat-growing, were puzzled and not attracted by twentieth-century Canada. To Kipling, Canada was like the Canadian lady, "powerful, comprehending, vital." Kipling didn't like Canadian ladies.

1910–1920

The great triangle of British-American-Canadian sentiment shifted again in the years around the war. Canadian bragging, intolerable in the raw opening years of the new century, seemed justifiable now that the prairies and the western valleys had been brought to spectacular harvest, not to mention the human harvest of heroism produced by this raw society when war came.

The free new life offered fewer cultural opportunities and no guaranteed reward in wealth, but the sensitive Englishman—Rupert Brooke, for instance —on the eve of European war, was too confused by European troubles to be able to reject the Canadian way as confidently as his predecessors had done. And the survivors of that wave of public school boys, younger sons, remittance men, who had caused so much hostility in the previous decade, were now obviously giving a quality to western Canada very different from the alleged degradation of the American West. British travellers, naturally meeting ex-schoolmates, gained a general impression of the dignity, at least in desire, of the Canadian.

On the other hand, abuse of the Englishman, a staple of conversation in 1910–13, simmered down by the end of the war, doused in part by the war records of the upper-class British soldiers.

Englishmen contributed the majority of the travel accounts of this period. The total number of travel books was growing again. In 1911 the greatest number ever published in a single year appeared, and of these all but four were by Englishmen. In contrast to the previous decade, Canadians now produced about one-fifth of the total number of descriptive accounts. American reports had dwindled to one-tenth of the total.

American influences in Canadian life continued to grow, as every traveller noted. But Americans were no longer completely enamoured with Canada. "America last century—Canada this!" was a phrase often repeated, not designed to win American hearts. Americans in Canada were less likely to be workaday immigrants, more likely to be power figures: wealthy and arrogant tourists, trade union officials, newly nationalized magnates like Van Horne and Charles Hays. The Canadian manner, "semi-tense but friendly," seemed to English visitors an American manner. The new school system in the West with its emphasis on agriculture, the lionizing of scientists like Saunders and Rutherford, all seemed American.

There were still some markedly *Canadian* features, and English and American travellers agreed in enjoying the French-Canadian community (though there was an increasing unease at the extent of Roman Catholic domination evidenced in the Eucharistic Congress of 1910) and the Mounties, "those thousand soldier-dandies, half cowboy, half-dragoon," and the thrill of the far West, Edmonton, Peace River, Athabaska, Okanagon valley—new names for Eldorado. But no longer could the visitors see the great ice palaces (except as a shabby backdrop in a cheap theatre) nor would one hear the old rhapsodies on the railroad. One traveller recounted the legend of a farmer hacking at its rails as at octopus tentacles; and now that the Grand Trunk and the Great Northern rivalled the C.P.R. the romance of that single thread across the great spaces was lessened. There was still the paradox of vast empty spaces plus lack of privacy, in homes, hotels, offices, and stores.

Both English and American visitors recognized in the Canadian woman qualities alien to their own countrywomen: to the American she seemed English in her dress, her colouring, her outdoor life. To the Englishman she appeared American, "bargain-counter haunting, street-car patronizing, hurrying, non-sentimentalizing . . . not a creature of fine bouquet." She antagonized her visitors, but the Canadian woman also aroused admiration and, particularly out west, sympathy.

Similarly, one might be "almost oppressed by the optimism of Canada," the gracelessness, the discourtesy, the "push-pump mentality" of her sections. One might dream of a new-style emigrant poster, reading:

> WANTED for CANADA!
> 300 brainy authors!
> 150 philosophers!
> First-class passage and a good living guaranteed.
> To the right man!
> Also new ideas, plots, scenes, quiet surroundings
> With unlimited nature!

But one recognized the eager support for public libraries, the growth of art galleries and museums, the presence even in rough farm houses of "Scott, Omar, Schopenhauer, Dickens, de Maupassant," and the rise of Toronto as "fourth among large cities on the continent as a music centre."

All of which balancing of culture and anarchy may be the result of another change in the travellers. In the years just before the war, the ladies returned. Not the aristocrats this time, the specially privileged; instead earnest women with a variety of causes: midwives for the midwest, free land for lady homesteaders, suffrage for all. Mrs. George Cran wrote *A Woman in Canada* (1910), Mrs. B. Pullen-Burry *From Halifax to Vancouver* (1912), Georgina Binnie-Clark *A Summer on the Canadian Prairie* (1910) and *Wheat and Woman* (1914). All are effective writers, competent at anecdote, sprightly in style, and close to fictional technique. Miss Binnie-Clark, for instance, uses the Canadian trip as a background for her own story—a shipboard near-romance, a visit with sister Hilaria to their amiable inefficient brother "batching it" on a homestead, a decision to enter farm management. Mrs. Cran provides "a series of [literary] snapshots, offered with ragged edges," but they are competently finished and communicate a strong sense of her personality. Mrs. Pullen-Burry, interested in politics and especially in the suffragette movement, presents information on Canadian attitudes and problems in eminently readable dialogue. Even the less charming accounts offer welcome relief from the heavy solemnity of turn-of-the-century statisticians. E. C. Sykes's *A Home Help in Canada* (1912), Mary J. Sansom's *A Holiday Trip to Canada* (1916), *Our Lady of Sunshine* edited by the Countess of Aberdeen (1910), and Elizabeth Keith Morris's *An Englishwoman in the Canadian West* (1913) are all attractively written, and present individual Canadian lives in convincing reality.

The ladies react against old-style travel books, "neat, dowdy things they are, full of facts and figures, written by people with tidy minds, and packed with information." They make a claim for their own impressionism: "The man who rushes out and back has . . . no affections, no prejudices."

Male visitors report their travel findings in livelier fashion too in these pre-war years. Friendly, good-humoured, with an eye to pathos and whimsy, Copping, Yeigh, and Vernède prepared a trio of books attractively illustrated in clear bright colours and printed on thick matt paper, books obviously designed for a reading mood of friendly relaxed interest: A. E. Copping, *The Golden Land of Canada Today and Tomorrow* (1911), Frank Yeigh, *Through the Heart of Canada* (1911), and P. E. Vernède, *The Fair Dominion* (1911). Less lively but similar in pattern are E. W. Elkington's *Canada, the Land of Hope* (1910) and W. E. Curtis's *Letters on Canada* (1911).

Less pretentious travel diaries in the old style include H. P. Scott's *Seeing Canada and the South* (1911), E. G. Busbridge's *Canada, Impressions of a Tour* (1912). J. B. Bickersteth's *The Land of Open Doors* (1914) consists of the vivid and thoughtful letters of a lay missionary at Edmonton. Frank Carrel in *Canada West and Farther West* (1911) reports a one-month journey, from Quebec to Victoria. Some of these old-style travel books reflect colourful personalities: C. J. Sparling, sharp-eyed, opinionated farm hand, author of *The Irish-Canuck-Yankee* (1910), E. G. F. Walker, zestful "Zummerset" farmer, author of *Canadian Trails* (1911), and N. P. R. Noel, likable young job-hunter, author of *Blanket-Stiff* (1911).

Again there are fragmentary regional sketches, most significantly of the new world of big game and adventure North and West. Readers devoted to Jack London and Robert Service were fed Nicholas Everitt's *Round the World in Strange Company* (1915), F. C. Cooper's *In the Canadian Bush* (1914), F. N. Alfalo's *A Fisherman's Summer in Canada* (1911), Grant Hamil's *Two Sides of the Atlantic* (1917), and the Earl of Dunraven's *Canadian Nights* (1914). These idylls of camp life fixed the image of Canada as refuge, as wilderness haven, towards which so many nerve-shocked Europeans would turn in the 1920's.

Emigrant guides of the pre-war years differ from these cavalier hunting-tales, but differ also from the pedestrian accounts of the nineteenth century. Descriptive books, hotly focused on economic conditions, on new exploitations of resources, on analysis of fiscal policies and trade, they seem designed to attract the small capitalist rather than the tenant farmer. F. A. Talbot in *Making Good in Canada* (1912) emphasizes the opportunities. Basil Sewart in *Canada as it is* (1910) repeats his tale of disillusionment. F. W. Freier in *Canada, the Land of Opportunities* (1919) gives practical hints and a businesslike analysis of openings for "colonizers." H. H. Fyfe, lightly, in *Shall I Go to Canada?* (1912), E. P. Weaver, heavily, in *Canada and the British Immigrant* (1914) and *Canadian Pictures* (1912), H. J. Boam, fulsomely, in *20th Century Impressions of Canada* (1914), J. F. Fraser, analytically, in *Canada as it is* (1911) add to the survey. In all these, the travel element is subordinated to argument. William Maxwell's *Canada of To-day* (1910) and W. L. Griffith's *The Dominion of Canada* (1911) emerge as social studies rather than travel accounts. One little book is titled to show a typical blend of travel with Imperial thesis: P. Machel's *What is My Country? My Country is the Empire, Canada is my Home* (n.d.).

Finally, three books indicate changes of fact, of taste, of theme. T. W. Wilby, in *A Motor Tour through Canada* (1914) triumphantly tallies history: "The canoe, the steamship, the railroad, and now the touring car." And the car, with its "single centre lever control for the gears, pedals for both brakes, two speedometers, a horn worked by foot . . ." provides high drama when the speedometers read 30 mph and local dogs go crazy. The book, and the car, introduce a new route through Canada.

A Canadian writes the second of the trio. B. B. Cooke's *The First Traveler* (1911) gives nine swift, strong sketches of life along the rail line, deepened into the symbolic level by a vision of the transcontinental railway as "the alternating pulse of the nation." This book is linked with emerging energy in another art form, for it is illustrated by the young J. E. H. Macdonald.

Finally, Rupert Brooke, in *Letters from America* (1916), seals the old range of topics with a fine review of the traditional tour: Quebec and the Saguenay, Montreal and Ottawa, Toronto and the Falls, the Prairies, and "outside"—the sportsmen's wilderness. Here he at last finds value in this "country without a soul":

It awaits the sun, the end for which Heaven made it, the blessing of civilization. Someday it will be sold in large portions, and the timber cut down and made into paper, on which shall be printed praise of prosperity; and the land itself shall be divided into town-lots and sold, and sub-divided and sold again, and boomed and re-sold, and boosted and distributed to fishy young men . . . and given in exchange for great sums of money to old ladies in the quieter part of England. . . . And . . . churches, hotels, and a great many ugly skyscrapers [shall] be built, and hovels for the poor, and houses for the rich, none beautiful, and there shall ugly objects be manufactured, rather hurriedly, and sold to the people at more than they are worth, because similar and cheaper objects made in other countries are kept out by a tariff. . . .
But at present there are only the wrinkled, grey-blue lake, sliding ever sideways, and the grey rocks, and the cliffs and hills, covered with birch-trees, and the fresh wind among the birches, and quiet, and that unseizable virginity.

Brooke's report is the best of that legion of books on tours of the United States in which a swing through Canada is included. Here the Canadian note is carefully sounded, for accent, for contrast, and for the intrinsic interest in the theme of the "Northern Neighbour."

19. Nature Writers and the Animal Story

ALEC LUCAS

NATURE WRITING is a comparatively recent literary development. Yet its roots lie deep in folklore, the Bible, and the myths, fables, and pastorals of Ancient Greece, for man has always been concerned with his relationship to the natural world. For the Jew of the Old Testament it manifested the power of the Deity and revealed His purpose. For the Greek it stimulated the mind and fed a love of beauty. The growth of the Christian Church, however, set man at odds with nature, which, as the medieval writers saw it, was distinct from and inferior to man, a *massa perditionis* unworthy of his study. The proper study of mankind was God. Even St. Francis loved birds and animals from a sense of love of God, not from one of companionship with them. He had no desire to learn from and to study them for their own sakes, an attitude which, generally speaking, characterizes modern nature writing. As for the natural historians (except Frederick II, Roger Bacon, and Albert of Cologne), they, too, made little effort to observe for themselves and looked on nature as a way of teaching the good life. Depending on classical authority, especially Pliny, for their facts, their books (bestiaries) are marked by the moralizing allegory and unnatural natural history of this description:

> The elephant is so constructed that he has no joints in his knees, which makes it impossible for him to rise if he falls. Because of this he sleeps leaning against the bole of a large tree. . . . In order to catch the elephant, the hunter saws the tree halfway through. When the elephant comes to sleep he falls with the tree to the ground. If other elephants hear the fallen one trumpeting for help, they come and try to raise him, but without success. Finally a small elephant comes and lifts up the fallen one, in the same way that Christ in lowly human form came to save man from the Devil and raise him up again.

Beast fables, a genre exemplified in Chaucer's "The Nun's Priest's Tale," were another of the popular forms of medieval nature writing. They were, however, like *Aesop's Fables*, their model, a commentary on man rather than nature, for the birds and animals that formed their subjects talked and acted as people. Unlike the bestiary, the beast fable has never died out, and as late as 1947 Philip Grove adopted it in *Consider Her Ways*, satirizing human society in the guise of the ant world. Furthermore, the fable would seem to have fathered the highly anthropomorphic children's animal story of the nineteenth and twentieth centuries.

The sportsman's or outdoors book also began in medieval times with Piers Fulham's discussion of fishing (Ms. 1420, Trinity College, Cambridge) and Dame Juliana Berners's *Treatyse of Fishinge with an Angle* (1496), but not until Izaak Walton's *The Compleat Angler* (1653) did the genre of the sportsman book and the form of *belles-lettres* nature writing become established. Although frequently marked by close observation of nature and an appreciation of its therapeutic value, the outdoors book usually centres in personal experience and presents the hunter, not the hunted, as protagonist. Behind this writing is an acceptance of man's dominion over nature—God's never ending bounty for man's benefit, a concept that accounts in part for the descriptions of the merciless slaughter of wildlife that fill early Canadian sportsman's books.

The rise of humanism during the Renaissance marked a change in man's understanding of nature. Although Petrarch complained that it was of no advantage to be familiar with the nature of beasts, birds, and fish, some thinkers disagreed. On the one hand, Montaigne cited examples of the moral and rational in the animal world which denied man his unique and superior place in the chain of being. On the other, Sir Francis Bacon called for the examination of all nature. If man was to advance, he needed to study his environment, not in terms of classical authority and morality but in the light of his own reason.

Under the stimulus of such thinking, expressed most concisely in Descartes' mathematical logic, men sought to discover a rational proof of an ordered universe, and finally in Newton's work saw it set forth, as they thought, in definitive form. The world was ordered, and all things were part of a vast unity. Men could not overlook the relationships of plants and animals in a kinship based on universal reason. For all the impetus that science thus gave to the study of the natural world, there were those, however, and especially churchmen like the influential John Ray, who believed that plants and animals had been placed on earth for their own sakes, not simply as objects for man's use or as cogs in a machine. Thus religion reconciled a feeling for nature with the predominant rationalism of the day and fostered an appreciation of living things in a mechanistic universe, an appreciation that Gilbert White expressed in *The Natural History of Selborne* (1789). This famous book, characterized by accurate observations and a kindly interest in birds and animals, established the scientific-literary essay as a genre that has since become one of the most popular forms of nature writing.

In the eighteenth century, however, forces were acting to produce an attitude toward nature different from White's. Locke's philosophy stressed the importance of environment and Shaftesbury's, that of feeling. Enclosure and the rise of the industrialized city revivified the old dream of a golden age when man supposedly lived in harmony with nature, for as man extended his control over his world, his interest in and longing for the untamed in contrast to the tamed increased correspondingly. To the formal beauty of the garden and the well-kept country seat he now opposed the sublimity of the "horrid" mountain and the grandeur of the wilderness, and to civilization an Arcadian primitivism.

From these influences in large part came the romantic movement of the early nineteenth century. Now man went to nature not to wonder at evidences of rational order. He went, like Bewick, to observe and to draw pictures from nature or, like Gilpin, to enjoy the picturesque. Under the guidance of Rousseau and Wordsworth, the high priests of a new form of natural religion, he might learn also how to dream and so feel the eternal Presence in all things. If the seventeenth and eighteenth centuries had found God through nature, the early romantics found Him in it, and for them it became a source of inspiration, consolation, and moral guidance. As a result, much romantic writing is highly subjective, since even the intimate details of the natural world tend to lose themselves in this same awe, for, if a sunset could become the source of "elevated thoughts: a sense sublime," so, too, could a mouse become "miracle enough to stagger sextillions of infidels."

Related to the romantic is the humanitarian, who preached the rights of animals *vis-à-vis* the rights of man. He recognized man's dominion, but sought to express it through pity and understanding. Writers of this kind at first selected tame rather than wild animals as subjects, treating them often as if they were members of that favourite Victorian group, "the deserving poor." Ouida's *A Dog of Flanders* and Anna Sewell's *Black Beauty* set the fashion, which, in our literature, is best exemplified by Marshall Saunders's work.

By the mid-nineteenth century man's interest in nature took a new turn, for the publication of Darwin's *The Origin of Species* (1859) and *The Descent of Man* (1871) re-affirmed rationally the relationship between man and nature, but re-focused man's attention on it for itself and not as a path into an ideal world which it symbolized. Many tended to conclude that if man were a superior animal and not a fallen angel, he ought to study nature for what it could reveal about himself. The proper study of mankind was not God, nor man, but animal. Man and animal, as the romantic held, did differ only in degree; but the link was now not Creator but ancestor. Yet if the romantic had raised the natural up and the Darwinian had brought the human down, many nature writers tried to restore the balance by preaching the merits of animals.

Although science spoke out about man, it remained silent about God. He was again an outsider as He had been for the eighteenth-century rationalists. In their mechanistic universe, nevertheless, He had at least created its parts and established the laws by which it operated. Now the parts were self-explanatory and the system self-contained. Whether God was in His heaven was beside the point. For the naturalist, as for the rationalist, and the pantheist, fact was important; not, however, as evidence of order or of the mystery of being, but as the record of an earthly evolution in which Nature, "red in tooth and claw," recognized survival as the only value.

Aside from this intellectual background of Canadian nature writing, there is the matter of physical foreground, since the greatest single fact of the new country was nature—and a most unWordsworthian nature. Explorers marvelled at the great rivers, forests, and mountains; travellers thrilled to the sublime (the awful Niagara Falls) and the picturesque. Their books, however, lie outside this chapter since it includes only those in which the writers have made nature a central interest and whose approaches to it are not purely factual.

One must turn to the early settlers for our first nature writers. They had to live close to nature, whether or not they wished to. Most did not wish to and saw nature as an obstacle on the road to civilization. The grandeur of lake and river was lost in a concern over floods, portages, sawmills, and steamboats. The sublimity of the forests disappeared in counting the chopping days needed to level them. Man's kinship with the wild creatures was usually expressed with rod and gun. Yet some settlers laid these and the axe aside for their quills. Back home the folks wanted to know what life was like "over there." Was it true that flights of pigeons darkened the sky, that there were snowbanks even in the summer? In response, the pioneers often became amateur field-naturalists and in their writing about land grants, "bees," and crops included observations on the world of tree and beast that obtruded dramatically into all their activities. The same general influence has been responsible for the annual crop of books the Arctic now produces. The frontier has simply shifted back a thousand miles and ahead a hundred years.

The best-known pioneer nature writers belong to the Otonabee School—Major Strickland, Thomas Need, the Langtons, Mrs. Frances Stewart, Mrs. Susanna Moodie, and Mrs. Catharine Parr Traill. Although all wrote of nature, only Mrs. Traill (1802-1899) made it the subject of more than incidental commentary. When she came to Canada, she was thirty and had already written about nature, and in her first Canadian book, *The Backwoods of Canada* (1836), she turned to it again, including among many general comments a full chapter on native flowers. Later she expanded it into *Canadian Wild Flowers* (1869), the first book of the kind in our literature, and *Studies of Plant Life* (1885), with the hope that it might "become a household book, as Gilbert White's *Natural History of Selborne* is to this day among English readers." Mrs. Traill kept a nature diary and from it in her old age drew her last book, *Pearls and Pebbles* (1894), another series of literary-scientific essays, but in this case on the commoner birds and animals.

Mrs. Traill was a fairly accurate observer, but, influenced by the romantics, tended to sentimentalize and moralize her natural history. Disliking "anything ugly or disgusting" such as reptiles and spiders, she looked to nature as a source of inspiration and morality. "We stand," she writes, "beneath the pines and enter the grand pillared aisles with a feeling of mute reverence; these stately trunks bearing their plumed heads so high above us seem a meet roofing for His temple who reared them to His praise. . . . And hark! . . . There are melodies in ocean, earth and air . . . heard by unseen spirits in their ministrations of love fulfilling the will of our Father." (*Pearls and Pebbles*, p. 134.)

When Mrs. Traill moved from contemplation of God's grandeur to observation of the details of His world, she sometimes found in them also a way "to refine and purify the mind," to climb "a ladder to heaven." (For all this, however, she can call some of God's handiwork "wicked" and "horrid," when it is a polecat in her henhouse.) Generally, however, her descriptions reveal a genuine liking for nature and much of her writing is characterized by the intimacy of this little sketch:

> Listen to that soft whispering sound. It cannot be called a song it is so soft and monotonous. It is the note of a tiny brown bird that flits among the pine cones, one of the little tree-creepers, a Sitta or Certhia, gentle birds small as the tiniest of our wrens.
>
> They live among the cone-bearing evergreens, gleaning their daily meal from between the chinks of the rugged bark where they find the larvae upon which they feed.
>
> As they flit to and fro they utter this little call-note to their companions, so soft that it would pass unnoticed but for the silence. . . . (*Pearls and Pebbles*, p. 135.)

Since the publication of *The Backwoods of Canada*, the nature essay has grown vigorously. The number of writers in the genre has increased greatly, especially during this century, and includes some of our best-known authors —Peter McArthur (1866–1924), Frederick Philip Grove (1872–1942), Grey Owl (1888–1938), and Roderick Haig-Brown (b. 1908). Over the years, too, its subject has become almost all nature—the general, the specific, the animate, the inanimate. William Lett (1819–1892) describes the deer of the Ottawa valley in *The Antlered Kings* (1884). Samuel Thomas Wood (1886–1917) draws on his field trips in *Rambles of a Canadian Naturalist* (1916), and Stuart Thompson (1886–1961) on his for *Outdoor Rambles* (1958). Egbert Allen (b. 1882) generalizes about nature in *The Out-of-Doors* (1932) and *Our Northern Year* (1937). Hugh Halliday casts his net wide in *Wildlife Friends* (1954), *Wildlife Trails* (1956), and *Adventures among Animals* (1960). Dan McCowan (1882–1956), a regionalist except for *A Naturalist in Canada* (1941), centres, like H. J. Parham in *A Nature Lover in British*

Columbia (1937), on western Canada with *The Animals of the Canadian Rockies* (1935), *From Tidewater to Timberline* (1951), and *Upland Trails* (1955). Lorus and Margery Milne assume an unusual perspective with *The World of Night* (1948). Franklin Russell examines the aquatic world minutely in *Watchers at the Pond* (1961) and M. B. Williams and E. Newton-White turn to problems of conservation in their books.

As for the essay itself its prose style has varied from the lyrical, purple passages of Duncan Armbrest's *The Beech Woods* (1916) to the journalistic of Bruce Wright's *Wildlife Sketches* (1962). The form has ranged from the chatty anecdotal vignettes of Ernest Thompson Seton's *Wild Animals at Home* (1913) and Hubert Evans's *Forest Friends* (1926) to the formal discussions of J. W. Winson's work, especially *Wildwood Trails* (1946); from Richard Saunders's nature diary *Flashing Wings* (1947) and his journal of a birding expedition, *Carolina Quest* (1951) to Kerry Wood's guide books, *Birds and Animals of the Rockies* (1946) and *A Nature Guide for Farmers* (1947). The writers' moods have ranged from the high seriousness of Theodore Haultain's cosmological speculations in *Of Walks and Walking Tours* (1914), the boisterous high spirits of Kerry Wood's *Three Mile Bend* (1945), to the reminiscences of Sherwood Fox's *The Bruce Beckons* (1952). Again, there is on the one hand the naturalism of Grant Allen's series of books that began with *Vignettes of Nature* (1881) and ended, after six more studies of evolution, with *In Nature's Workshop* (1901), and also of Robert McLeod's *In the Acadian Land* (1899) and *Further Studies of Nature* (1910); on the other hand there is the idealism of Bliss Carman's *The Kinship of Nature* (1903) or the whimsical sentimentality of Ernest Fewster's *My Garden Dreams* (1926).

Largely twentieth-century writers, these, for the most part, look on nature neither as evidence of God's law nor as a source of morality, but as a unity in which man is simply another creature. They do not seek "the bird behind the bird." Nature is as it is, and they try to let it be its own commentator, centring their interest in their relationships with the living things of wood and field. Their essays are never quite the depersonalized writing of science. Whether descriptive—even in the expository natural history essay—or narrative and dramatic, their work reveals a human sympathy with the whole natural world.

As an example of descriptive writing, Samuel Wood's *Rambles of a Canadian Naturalist* is excellent, for Wood is a well-informed and enthusiastic field-naturalist and an essayist of literary ability. Like John Burroughs, he is, too, a "natural philosopher" as this characteristic passage (pp. 66–67) illustrates.

> The Night-hawk never takes up the white man's burden. He is a missionary from the great outer world—in the city, but not of it. His name is as ill-applied as it is ill-omened, for he is not connected with the Hawks by consanguinity, sympathy, or unity of purpose. He has a grace of flight peculiarly his own, turning,

wheeling, and darting hither and thither without apparent effort, or circling on easily extended pinions. The conspicuous white spot under each wing looks like a hole, and may have suggested the modern idea of ventilating yacht sails. Nature paints with a careful touch, and the great spots, bands, and patches carelessly displayed by birds in white, black, or colour are laid on the exposed webs or tips, one feather at a time, so that a plucked quill would be as irregular and meaningless as a fragment from a mosaic.

Among the writers who stress the narrative and dramatic Frederick Philip Grove holds a high position, his reputation resting on *Over Prairie Trails* (1922) and *The Turn of the Year* (1923). The first of these books, a collection of seven essays on trips Grove took through western Manitoba, tries to catch something of his total impression of that vast area. A keen observer, with an almost scientific bent, his attention focuses on the phenomena of land formations and the weather. As Malcolm Ross writes, "Every twist and scar of the land is known and wondered at and claimed. Every freak of fog and drift and frost is a mighty event, to be known . . . to be felt, to be re-created and re-set in the 'interior landscape' of the self." Although descriptive of the same austere land, Grove's second book, *The Turn of the Year*, is written with more feeling and from a greater sense of intimacy. Grove turns from inanimate nature to its living things, frequently also dramatizing rather than discussing his experiences with them. Set against the passage cited from Wood, the following (p. 46) reveals sharply the differences between the two methods.

I go east, along the grade, perchance, to where, a mile from my house, the woods recede on the southside, opening up into a meadow which is fenced for a pasture. The bush to both sides is noisily vocal, of course, with the cawing of crows; and perhaps I now hear quite distinctly and unmistakably the quacking of ducks from the sloughs to the north. But when I reach that meadow, unexpectedly, from quite close by, like a great overwhelming joy, I hear the familiar, cheerfully whistling flute-note of the meadow-lark. I jerk my head about; and truly, there he sits on a low charred stump, right next to the road, or perhaps on a fence-post; and his breast is the brightest of all bright yellows; and like black velvet the crescent lifts itself off from the throat.

Grove goes to nature obviously as neither natural historian nor natural philosopher. He seeks no moral law. He wishes only to enjoy the dynamic force of nature. He manages, also, by arranging the essays in seasonal sequence, a fairly common practice, to catch something of its life-and-death rhythm.

As the writers have adopted various attitudes and methods, so, too, have they addressed themselves to several different classes of readers. Some have published nature essays for children, a type which began with Mrs. Traill's *Afar in the Forest* (1850) and has continued to the present with Mrs. Berrill's *Wonders of the Arctic* (1959) and Paul May's *A Book of Canadian Animals* (1962). The genre has not been very popular, most authors preferring to combine natural history with fiction in the bedtime animal story.

Some, aside from Richard Saunders, who was mentioned earlier, have written for (and as) birdwatchers—the voluminous Sir James MacPherson Le Moine (*Maple Leaves*, 1863–1906), the oologist Walter Raine (*Bird-nesting in North-West Canada*, 1892), Hamilton Laing (*Out with the Birds*, 1913), Louise Marsh (*Birds of Peasemarsh*, 1919, and *With the Birds*, 1935), and Hugh Halliday (*Adventures among Birds*, 1959). Some have written books for (and as) fishermen and hunters in the sportsman's or outdoors book, and some, for (and as) "escapists" in the "back-to-nature" book.

Essentially the sportsman's or outdoors book is "escapist" too and frequently reveals the influence of romanticism as obviously as that which advocates a return to nature. In the old tradition the sportsman's book is implicit about man's dominion over nature, whereby one can simultaneously preach the beauty of nature and assume the right to destroy it. In the romantic tradition the book is often explicit about the therapeutic values of the woods and streams, where, far from that villain, the city, man can find peace and self-fulfillment.

The genre began with the letter-writers and itinerant Englishmen of pioneer days and has been popular ever since, soon becoming a favourite with "Residents." Thomas McGrath described his field sports in *Authentic Letters from Upper Canada* (1833). Frederick Tolfrey, if he can be called Canadian because of five years spent with rod and gun slaughtering the wildlife of Quebec, published *The Sportsman in Canada* (1845). Campbell Hardy recounted his experiences in *Sporting Adventures in the New World* (1855); the Reverend Agar Adamson tried to imitate Walton with *Salmon-Fishing in Canada* (1860); the Reverend Joshua Fraser drew on the events of a hunt for *Three Months among the Moose* (1881); and Arthur Silver described his adventures as sportsman in *Through Miramichi with Rod and Rifle* (1890). Seton (1860–1946) and Sir Charles G. D. Roberts (1860–1943) began their literary careers in sportsmen's and outdoors magazines, a fact that the latter's collection of tales and anecdotes in *Around the Campfire* (1896) evidences. ("Bear vs. Birch-Bark," 1886, which appeared in *Around the Campfire*, was the first story by Roberts to be published in a book—entitled *In Peril: True Stories of Adventure*, 1887.) Since the late nineteenth century, the genre has more than held its own in both book and periodical and has gained considerable importance as Canadiana and as history, for the older books are records, available nowhere else, of one phase of pioneer life.

The subject-matter of the outdoors book varies widely within the limits of the type. Seton's *The Birch-Bark Roll* (1902) and *The Book of Woodcraft* (1912), Paul Provencher's *I Live in the Woods* (1953) and Keith Barnes's *Wilderness Camping and How to Enjoy It* (1956) are little more than manuals. Related to these are books which use anecdote to leaven information about the where and how to fish and hunt and the gear required. Edwyn Sandys's *Upland Game Birds* (1902), David Reddick's *Fishing is a*

Cinch (1950), and F. H. Woodling's *The Angler's Book of Canadian Fishes* (1959), for example, comment on each species and then add an essay on an appropriate experience. Some books in this group, like *Trapper Jim* (1903) and *Sportsman Joe* (1924), emphasize narrative. In these two, Sandys tries to vitalize his programme of studies for the successful sportsman by setting himself up as guide to a boy tenderfoot on innumerable field-trips, a method which in general characterizes Arthur Heming's two books (both grim and unimaginative) about life with Indian trappers in northern Canada, *The Living Forest* (1925) and *The Drama of the Forests* (1947). Here, too, belong "Jack" Hambleton's boisterous *Fisherman's Paradise* (1946) and *Hunter's Holidays* (1947).

Generally, however, books of this kind simply try to communicate the pleasures of good fellowship and life in the open air and the thrill (not the technique) of catching fish and bringing down a creature of the chase. In them the reader can vicariously hunt and fish with Arthur Silver (*Farm-Cottage, Camp and Canoe in Maritime Canada*, 1908), accompany Bryan Williams (*On Game Trails in British Columbia*, 1926), follow Nevill Armstrong (*After Big Game in the Upper Yukon*, 1937), or enjoy killing salmon with George F. Clarke (*Six Salmon Rivers and Another*, 1960). Frequently, the subject-matter is less interesting than the writer's personality, a fact that accounts largely for the attractiveness of Richard Pattillo's *Moose Hunting, Salmon Fishing and Other Sketches of Sport* (1902) and Napoleon Comeau's *Life and Sport on the North Shore* (1909). Usually the books are a medley of tales, tall or otherwise, reminiscences, character sketches of guides and companions (even dogs), and casual comments on natural history, "a collection of incidents and observations," like Austen Peters's *Feathers Preferred* (1951), in which the essay tends to become the article. Although man-centred, like all outdoors books, they usually show some interest in and "sympathy" for (but little empathy with) wildlife, especially game birds and animals *vis-à-vis* predators. Yet their authors can argue (probably as pseudo-Darwinians) that hunting "makes for the preservation and increase of the species" (Sandys, *Sportsman Joe*, p. 156). Again they almost always allude to nature's healing powers—usually in terms of the recreational or entertaining. Although normally not solemn books, only in John Robins's *Incomplete Anglers* (1943) and Sherwood Fox's *Silken Lines and Silver Hooks* (1954), however, does their humour rise consistently above the funny story or farcical event. Outdoors books are relatively numerous and, aside from those discussed, there are the ubiquitous Le Moine's *Maple Leaves*, Sidney Kendall's *Among the Laurentians* (1885), Samuel Baylis's *Camp and Lamp* (1897), Sandys's *Sporting Sketches* (1905), Philip Moore's *With Rod and Gun in Canada* (1922) and *The Castle Buck* (1945), Kerry Wood's *Three Mile Bend*, Clint Fleming's *When the Fish are Rising* (1947), Pete McGillen's *Outdoors with*

Pete McGillen (1955), and Phillip Keller's *Wild Glory* (1961), a book which complements McCowan's *Outdoors with a Camera in Canada* (1945), for Keller also hunted with a camera.

McGillen's book is typical. A collection of forty-two essays, it has something for almost everyone interested in nature—for the fisherman, "Muskie Madness"; the hunter, "Blue Geese at James Bay"; the conservationist, "Wildlife Management" and "A Pox on Gang Hunters"; and for those without special interest in either game or fish, there are "Bells for House Cats," "Winter on the Farm," and "Bird-Watching—a Hobby." McGillen writes in a popular manner, enthusiastically and sometimes humorously in chatty English. He says little of the meaning of what he describes. The outdoors is largely a place of legal sizes and bag limits, where one delights in "God's open air" by means of gun and rod. Controversial subjects such as bounties and predators are discussed but superficially. Snapping turtles are "ugly, vicious predators." Duck hunters are warned that "crows, pike, muskrats, skunks, raccoons, and snakes, not to mention the foxes and the hawks" are "whittling the duck population." McGillen has observed the habits of both fish and fisherman, hunted and hunter with some care, and he knows farm life. His writing is that blend of "human interest" and natural fact which characterizes so many books of the kind.

In the outdoors school, William H. Blake (1861–1924) and Roderick Haig-Brown, the Izaak Walton and the Charles Cotton of our literature, rank among the best. Of the two, Haig-Brown is the more prolific with his series *A River Never Sleeps* (1946), *Fisherman's Spring* (1951), *Fisherman's Winter* (1954), and *Fisherman's Summer* (1959). Haig-Brown lives on Vancouver Island, and his books, except the third listed, which describes a South American fishing trip, relate his experiences on West Coast rivers and lakes. Blake left only two books of the kind, *Brown Waters* (1915) and *In a Fishing Country* (1922), and these are set in Quebec. Moreover several of his essays are given over to people and places rather than sport. Again Haig-Brown is the better-informed ichthyologist, and his book *The Western Angler* (1947) is a recognized authority on Pacific Coast fish. Yet Blake was a keenly observant man and, within the limits he set himself, an excellent naturalist. Haig-Brown is the more meticulously detailed, and his books contain many exact descriptions of taking fish. Nevertheless, at his best, he, no more than Blake, lets fact and theory override him. He does not invest his material with overtones in Blake's manner, being less subjective and less the natural philosopher, but rather develops thoughts that grow out of the experience he relates. If the chief concern of both writers is not so much nature but the sport it affords, their subject is not simply the thrill (or the science) but the art of fishing and the world of lake, river, and forest in which they practise it.

More than subject or attitude, however, their prose style differentiates their work from that of other authors. Both avoid the journalistic. Their diction is neither trite nor unduly technical. Their sentences are rhythmical and varied. Sampling them almost anywhere, one finds writing like this from Blake's *Brown Waters* (pp. 67–68):

> For many a year of free and strenuous life his swiftness and dexterity in stemming rapid streams, in pursuing prey, in avoiding the attacks of enemies had been things that counted, and in this, his final struggle, he used the arts which had availed him. After what seemed to be a very long time, but was not and could not be measured by the watch, the rushes became shorter, and we caught a glimpse of a side glorious with red and orange; then did we first know, of a surety, that here at last was the fish worth toiling and waiting for,—the fish of dreams. Fighting to the end, under the utmost pressure of tackle, he came slowly to the bank where Mesgil performed to admiration the task of netting. One breathless moment there was when it seemed that the capacious landing net would not receive him, but his day had come, the last impulse of his powerful tail sent him home and in he swung to meet the *coup de grâce*.

Related to the outdoors books are those that extol the pleasures of a return to nature—to a nook in the country or the wilderness—not for sport but for freedom from the tensions of city living. Many pioneers of the nineteenth century in southern Canada and of the twentieth in the West and North have described lives spent in such surroundings but not as a voluntary return to nature. They are the Crusoes not the Rousseaus of our literature.

The back-to-nature book developed late and only after the rise of the large city, when nature acquired something of the romance of the unknown or the nostalgic. It owes much to the pastoral tradition and may reveal something of man's longing for his lost Eden. Some books are largely reminiscences— A. C. Wood's *Old Days on the Farm* (1918), Sherwood Fox's *'T Ain't Runnin' No More* (1946), a discussion and history of the Aux Sables River, and Kenneth C. Cragg's *Father on the Farm* (1947), a rural version of life with father. More frequently the writers try to capture something of the immediacy and contentment of living in the country. Haig-Brown's *Measure of the Year* (1950) examines the ways of a farming community. Clark Lock's *Country Hours* (1959) describes the creatures of the woods and fields about his home. McArthur and Kenneth Wells (b. 1905) strike a balance between the two. Their subject is the farm—its "breachy" cattle and pugnacious goats, its friendly woodchucks and springtime crows, its seasonal activities of wood cutting, sugaring-off, sowing, harvesting, and apple-picking. (Here we should mention Orlando John Stevenson, 1869–1950, who edited *Country Life Reader*, 1916, a book of essays and poems on farm life.)

McArthur's books, comprising selections from the columns that he published for years in the Toronto *Globe*, are strong pleas for a way of life, not a way of making a living. McArthur feared that mechanization and "the cash crop" would eventually bring to the farm many of the stresses of the city, where man's life and work are things apart. A rural philosopher, he strove from his first book of the genre, *In Pastures Green* (1915), to his last, *Friendly Acres* (1927), to illustrate and preach the virtues and values of country living and to reveal the forces that threaten to depersonalize it. Now didactic and expository, now humorously dramatic (especially in *The Red Cow and her Friends*, 1919, a series of character sketches of a cow, "Fence-viewer," and other farm animals), now wittily aphoristic or satirical, but always genial, these and McArthur's other books, *Around Home* (1925) and *Familiar Fields* (1925), evoke the feeling of living close to the soil. Sensitive to nature and aware of a fellowship with it, he does not unduly humanize and idealize his subject in order to achieve effect. He writes merely as a man who, living at a leisurely pace, has had time to look about him. He enjoys the countryside, and it is the strength of his essays that they convince one of this fact.

When the quail came right up to the door I might have known that something good was going to happen. It was during the cold spell—the lion spell—in the beginning of March. Everything was buried under the snow and at seven o'clock in the morning the thermometer had touched ten degrees below zero.

I was doing the chores at the stable when I heard the quail whistling in the orchard and fully intended going to have a look at them, to see how they were wintering. I had not set out feed for them for, alas, there are enough weeds on the place and in the neighbourhood to feed them fat. But to resume. When I had finished the chores and was starting towards the house I struck the tracks of the quail, looking like a picture of loosely strung barbed wire on the snow. To my surprise I found that they were headed straight for the house. In growing amazement I followed them until they passed around the corner of the house and then I saw the marks of their wings on the snow where they had taken flight, within ten feet of the front door.

I felt really disappointed when I found that they had paid me a visit and I had not been at home. I do not know of many from whom I would have so thoroughly enjoyed a little call. No one in the house had noticed them, but judging from the excitement of Sheppy, the dog, he must have seen them and perhaps had something to do with their flight. He kept running about nosing their tracks and barking. It made me feel that I am being accepted in the country, now that the quail are so friendly. They are very careful about their neighbours and it is not every one they are willing to chum with. (*In Pastures Green*, p. 66.)

The most recent and, aside from McArthur, the most prolific writer of the rustic school is Wells, whose popular *Owl Pen* (1947) set the stage for *By Moonstone Creek* (1949), *Up Medonte Way* (1951), and *By Jumping Cat Bridge* (1956), all books about the author's little place in the country. Although Wells went to school to McArthur, he lacks the insight, sincerity, and style of his master. Entertaining and informative about country life and appreciative of the natural world, his books are marred by superficiality. They leave the impression that Wells is playing at farming. Too frequently the butt of his own jokes, he is the greenhorn who seems almost to pride himself on being one in his misadventures with his goats, ducks, and chickens. He is irritatingly anthropomorphic. McArthur's animals remain animals; Wells's rarely do. Chickens with names, a drake that becomes a "dapper gentleman," and ducklings, "web-footed babes," that stare with "bulging eyes and gaping bills" when they first see water and "talk" when they dive into it all reveal how far Wells fails to depict rural life. His fault is not, however, that he wishes to idealize it, but that in trying to he only makes it cute and sentimental.

Several writers have recounted the pleasures of a return, not to the humanized nature of the farm but to the nature of forest and river. John Rowland's *Cache Lake Country* (1947) dramatizes his experiences and observations as woodsman-naturalist in the Lake of the Woods area. In the manner of Thoreau's *Walden*, Grant Madison's *River for a Sidewalk* (1953) describes his life as a solitary in the mountain fastness of British Columbia. Setting up the old contrast of city and country, Madison plumps for the latter, since there, freed from all the gadgets that get between life and living, he found himself —building his cabin, making a garden, gathering mushrooms, hiking through the wilderness. Although *River for a Sidewalk* is by no means a *Walden*, it does attempt to examine the deeper significance of the man-nature relationship, and it does have a warm sympathy for the world of bird and beast. (Several other books—Martin Hunter's *Canadian Wilds*, 1907, Harry Macfie's *Wasa-Wasa*, 1953, and Eric Munsterhjelm's *The Wind and the Caribou*, 1953, describe life in the woods, but their authors are trappers and hunters. There are also several "back-to-nature" books by Americans who lived in the Canadian wilderness for a time.)

No other Canadian writer had a greater reputation in the 1930's, both at home and abroad, than Grey Owl, another member of this school. Many knew of his pet beavers, Rawhide and Jelly Roll, the stars of several films. Many knew also of Grey Owl the naturalist and conservationist through his autobiography *Pilgrims of the Wild* (1935), his children's book *The Adventures of Sajo and Her Beaver People* (1935), and his essays, *Tales of an Empty Cabin* (1936). But all knew, if they knew nothing else, that he was an Indian. Here was the romantic's noble savage, the natural man who could depict the natural world with an insight denied other authors. So went the thinking, but it was ill founded. Born in England and christened Archibald Stansfeld Belaney, Grey Owl (Wa-Sha-Quon-Asin) was a hoax. As a young man, he had drifted into northern Ontario, where he had lived as hunter, trapper, and guide (a life he recounts nostalgically in *The Men of the Last Frontier*, 1931) before becoming author and conservationist. If he played Indian all his life, he played his part well, and, even if adopted, the hinterland was his true home; moreover, whether Indian, Métis, or white man, he was a gifted writer and naturalist.

In prose now eloquent, now lucidly precise Grey Owl celebrates "the wonders of the wilderness." The forested solitudes, his "Temple of Nature," have a "sanctity" that makes "not a few theosophies seem weak and tawdry." Yet he does not decry their harshness as Thoreau did when he left his rustic haunts in Concord to visit northern Maine. The wilderness is for Grey Owl both "a land of wild, romantic beauty" and "an austere and savage region," for his imagination is such that he can blend these views and see into the very core of his world, as this passage illustrates.

And as the last dying echo fades to nothing, the silence settles down layer by layer, pouring across the vast deserted auditorium in billow after billow, until all sound is completely choked beyond apparent possibility of repetition. And the wolves move on . . . and the frozen wastes resume their endless waiting; the Deadmen dance their grisly dance on high, and the glittering spruce stand silently and watch. (*The Men of the Last Frontier*, p. 44.)

If Grey Owl preached the grandeur of the wilderness, he was no less enthusiastic over its minutiae. A reformed trapper, he writes of the birds and animals as a convincingly sincere humanitarian, and his books are an impassioned plea for a sympathetic appreciation of wildlife. Despite this attitude, Grey Owl is no sentimentalist. He tries to make his case by recounting his personal experiences and presenting accurately intimate details of the ways of his beaver and the other wild creatures that lived about his lodge. As a result his essays focus on both what he learns about the wild creatures and what he learns from them, and are typified by a passage like this.

The two original whiskey-jacks who were attached to this spot when first I came here, have called in off the endless, empty streets of the forest, all of their kin who resided within a reasonable distance, say about five miles, judging by the number of them. This assembly of mendicants follows me around closely on my frequent tours of inspection, wholly, I fear, on account of what there is in it for them, and my exit from the cabin with something in my hands, supposing it is only an axe or an empty pot, anything at all, is the signal for piercing outcries from watchful sentinels who have been waiting patiently for hours for my appearance. . . . They will go to almost any lengths to gain their ends, and I once saw one of them, dislodged from a frozen meat-bone by a woodpecker (a far stronger bird), waiting with commendable patience until the red-head should be through. However, the woodpecker was far from expert, and using the same tactics on the bone that he would have employed on a tree, he pecked away with great gusto, throwing little chips of meat in all directions, thinking them to be wood, only to find, when he got to the heart of the matter, that he was the possesser [sic] of a clean, well-burnished, uneatable bone. This pleased the whiskey-jack mightily, for at once appreciating his opportunities, he hopped around among the flying scraps of meat and had a very good lunch, while the unfortunate woodpecker, who had done all the work, got nothing. (*Tales of an Empty Cabin*, pp. 283, 284.)

As popular as the genres mentioned have been, several other kinds of writing about the animal world have been part of our literature for many years. These are the legend, the nature novel, and the animal story in its various forms of children's story, animal biography, and short story. With the exception of some animal biographies, all are fiction. Paradoxical as it may seem, however, many of their authors, no less than the essayists, pride themselves on the merits of their work as natural history. Yet their method can be explained simply. They select details that are correct and arrange them to suit their purpose and thus seek to have the best of both the naturalist's and the artist's world.

As nature writing, the legend is bound up with folklore, both Indian and Eskimo, and is simply a recording of traditional tales which these people have invented. Sometimes they relate to the mountains, rivers, and lakes as in Pauline Johnson's *Legends of Vancouver* (1911). Sometimes they are accounts of the magical qualities of birds and animals like those retold in Robert Ayre's *Sketco the Raven* (1961). There have been many collections and retellings of legends—Mabel Burkholder's, Charles Clay's, Cyrus MacMillan's, Silas Rand's, and Marius Barbeau's to mention but a few—but only two nature writers have used legends as subjects. Seton, who invented some of his own, published *Woodmyth and Fable* (1905), *Woodland Tales* (1927), and a catch-all collection, *Ernest Thompson Seton's Trail and Camp-fire Stories* (1940). These, however, differ significantly from the native folk tales, for on the one hand they are highly moralistic and on the other they are based on scientifically accurate explanations of natural phenomena. The other author, Haig-Brown, has made the legend a means of organizing his material and presenting natural history. Yet his novel, *Pool and Rapid: The Story of a River* (1932), succeeds in fusing the two without sacrificing the characteristic supernaturalism of Indian lore. His river, the Tasish, is more than a river. It becomes a motif, a way of uniting present and past in his story of lumberman and settlers, a living and constant reminder of the myths and legends by which the Indians explained its existence and the presence of the salmon that ran in multitudes up its waters and the wildlife that dwelt in its forested valley.

The nature novel, the second fictional genre listed earlier, is not simply one with an outdoors setting. A product of both the romantic and the pastoral traditions, it is an amalgam of natural history and a story in which heroes and heroines are veritable children of the wild. Books of the kind are few; it is apparently difficult to turn our rugged hinterlands into Arcadia. An early book, *Panthea, the Spirit of Nature* (1849), by Robert Hunt (1807–1887), author of *The Poetry of Science* (1854), turns Panthea into a Spirit-scientist who warns the hero against the "False" view of nature, in which it becomes "seductive by its poetic associations." The genre really developed from John Murdoch's *In the Woods and on the Waters* (1896), although Joseph Hilts had already introduced natural history into his novel *Among the Forest Trees* (1888). He did so, however, largely through essay-like discussions, whereas

Murdoch makes an organic unity of his story and his knowledge and appreciation of nature. His method is simple. He selects as hero a hunter who spends much time either praising the beauty and bounty of the forest or berating the "falsehood, treachery, and dishonesty" of the city.

As for the other authors of nature novels, Roberts is the most famous but not the most successful. That honour belongs not to his *The Heart of the Ancient Wood* (1902) but to Fred Bodsworth's *The Strange One* (1959). Roberts's book relates the experiences of a young woman—Miranda—a kind of princess-naturalist who becomes a friend of the forest animals and the beloved of a stalwart woodsman. Idyllic and sentimental, its treatment of wild creatures is even less satisfactory than that of its protagonists. With Bodsworth's work, it is otherwise. A study of the habits and life-history of a barnacle goose that in migration has strayed to the Canadian Arctic from Europe, and a story of Kanina, an Indian girl, and Rory Macdonald, a biologist working in the north, *The Strange One* integrates both study and story without injustice to either. If Bodsworth tells two stories, one is always a comment on the other. The hardships that beset the barnacle goose parallel those of the protagonists; in its struggles it becomes for them a symbol of their own aspirations. Yet Bodsworth does not lose the goose in the symbolic—although he may somewhat in the romantic—and surpasses all other writers of the nature novel in combining natural history with fiction.

Between the dates of Roberts's and Bodsworth's books, a few others of the genre appeared—*Willow, the Wisp* (1918), by Archibald P. McKishnie (1875–1946), the eulogy of a heroine (an almost exact duplicate of Roberts's Miranda) who lives on a game preserve in northern Ontario; the same author's *A Son of Courage* (1920), in which the hero seems a Tom Sawyer turned nature student; and John Mantley's *The Snow Birch* (1958), a story of a boy's life among the animals and woodsmen in the far North. These are more melodramatic than Roberts's book, and were it not for their emphasis on nature as foreground would belong with frontier and regional novels like McKishnie's *Love of the Wild* (1910) and Hulbert Footner's *A Backwoods Princess* (1926) in both of which the wilderness is merely a setting for romance and adventure.

The same cannot be said of Haig-Brown's *On the Highest Hill* (1949), although in it, too, nature is largely background. Yet it is always the dominant influence on Colin Ensley's life, conditioning him when as a boy and a youth he roams the forested mountains and luring him back to them after the war. The book is based on the old antithesis of town and country, but Haig-Brown's is not the romantic solution of Murdoch's *In the Woods and on the Waters* and Madison's *River for a Sidewalk*. The hero of *On the Highest Hill* has no place to hide. His valleys have been devastated by lumber companies or closed to him by the government, and when, a fugitive, he falls to his death, he becomes the author's final comment on civilization's ever increasing encroachment on the natural world and its suppression of man's freedom of spirit.

Of the three kinds of animal story in literature, the children's appeared first. Mrs. Traill introduced it with *Afar in the Forest* (1850), which, like her pre-Canadian books, contained several stories of this type since they humanize nature (the animals frequently speak) and aim at teaching natural history and sometimes morals. The children's animal story did not become established until the late nineteenth century, but since then it has been popular and has taken several different forms.

Mrs. Traill published more fable-like tales in *Cot and Cradle Stories* (1895). Seton wrote *The Wild Animal Play for Children* (1900). William A. Fraser (1859–1933) tried his hand at North American Jungle Books in *Mooswa and Others of the Boundaries* (1900) and *The Outcasts* (1901) before submitting even more to Kipling's dominance with *The Sa'-Zada Tales* (1905) about animals of India. Carol Cassidy Cole's *Downy Wings and Sharp Eyes* (1923) and her three similar books of children's adventures with animals, Ralph Sherman's *Mother Nature Stories* (1924), McKishnie's *Dwellers of the Marshlands* (1937), and Edith Tyrrell's *Furry and Fluffy* (1946) are bedtime stories that hint strongly the influence of Thornton W. Burgess. Harper Cory, an Englishman who lived for some years in Canada, also wrote children's books—for example *Wild Life Ways* (1936)—with Canadian settings. Louise de Kiriline's *The Loghouse Nest* (1945), the life of a chickadee, and Mel Thistle's *Peter the Sea Trout* (1954) adapt the full-length animal biography to the children's book. Elizabeth Sanderson's *The Circle of the Year* (1904), James Grant's *On Golden Wings through Wonderland* (1927), and Frances Lloyd-Owen's *The Gnome's Kitchen* (1937) fuse the nature and the fairy story. The genre has also branched off into the boy's book by combining nature study (without cute talking animals) with adventure—as in Seton's semi-autobiographical *Two Little Savages* (1903) and his much less successful *Rolf in the Woods* (1911). (Kerry Wood's *Wild Winter*, 1954, describes the author's life as a boy-naturalist, but is autobiography not an adventure story.) In this category belong also McKishnie's *Openway* (1922), Haig-Brown's *Ki-Yu, a Story of Panthers* (1934), and Muriel Miller's textbookish *Peter's Adventures in the Out-of-Doors* (1940). Books of the kind are not numerous; many that would seem similar, to cite Lloyd-Owen's *The Call of the Cougar* (1941) and "Jack" Hambleton's *Wolverine* (1954) as illustrations, are largely adventure stories with outdoors settings.

The animal biography began as a story of domesticated animals and is exemplified early in English Canadian literature by Mrs. Moodie's *The Little Black Pony and Other Stories* (1850). It was, however, Marshall Saunders's autobiography of a dog, *Beautiful Joe* (1894), the first of her fourteen books about dogs, cats, monkeys, pigeons, canaries, and other pets that gave the animal biography the impetus it has retained to the present; Sheila Burnford's *Incredible Journey* (1961), an account of two dogs and a cat wayfaring in the wilderness, and Carol Pearson's *Brown Paws and Green Thumbs* (1961), a collection of stories about pets (including camels and crocodiles), are only two in a long list of similar books—some by well-known authors—of varying aims, attitudes, and techniques. Mrs. Annie Savigny at once imitated *Beautiful Joe* with a mixture of pity and propaganda in *Lion the Mastiff* (1895). Mazo de la Roche (1885–1961), who also wrote children's animal stories, paid tribute to her Scotch terrier in a memorial, *Portrait of a Dog* (1930), following it with *The Sacred Bullock and Other Stories* (1939), a book of short stories characterized by a similar sensitive insight into the world of man and his pets. Farley Mowat's *The Dog Who Wouldn't Be* (1957) and *Owls in the Family* (1961) belong in the boy-and-his-pet convention of Louise Rorke's *Lefty* (1931) and *Black Vic, the Story of a Boy and his Pony* (1949), but Mowat's books are far less sober-sided and sentimental. Barbara May's *The Five Circles* (1958) adopts the old technique of Saunders (and Sewell) by having a horse tell its story.

Running counter to these "humane" biographies, which praise the gentle, are those that celebrate the heroic. Typical are Fraser's stories of race horses in *Brave Hearts* (1904), Seton's *Santana, the Hero Dog of France* (1945), and the "lives" of tough alley cats and valiant camp dogs scattered throughout his work. Here, too, belong Roberts's "thriller," *Jim, the Story of a Backwoods Police Dog* (1924), which might well have been the model for Hubert Evans's four books about Derry, a courageous and sagacious Airedale, and those stories that recount the lives of feral animals. Although the latter type is fairly common—Roberts and Seton wrote several biographies of the kind—only Francis Dickie's *Hunters of the Wild* (1937), a story, in the Jack London tradition, of a dog that lives as a wolf, is a full-length book.

Many other writers published books about their pets—F. W. Andrew, Russell Cockburn, Kenneth Conibear, Elizabeth Guelton, Edward Sprang, Major Benson Walker, and the Reverend Egerton Young. Yet only Andrew in *Klinker* (1948) analyses animal behaviour. The rest are content to describe it in terms of actions and anecdotes that win sympathy, or in those of adventures and noble exploits that stir admiration.

Stories about wild animals, like those about tame, may be either biographical tales, which present some episode or life history in simple narrative form, or short stories, and all may be either "true" or fictitious. Yet they differ, for the story about the wild animal has a greater scientific bent. It tries to avoid humanizing tendencies, to "convey an accurate idea of the animal's life and behaviour [and] its mental processes" from "the animal's viewpoint" (Seton,

Famous Animal Stories, p. iv). Man may enter, but only as "accessory or villain." The animal must remain central, for the authors stress and pride themselves on the truthfulness of their animal psychology (Roberts, "The Animal Story," *The Kindred of the Wild* (1902), pp. 15-29). Yet for all that John Burroughs labelled them nature-fakirs, an accusation that may seem justified by Seton's attempt to prove in *The Natural History of the Ten Commandments* (1907) that animals are nomistic.

The genre had a twofold beginning in Seton's "The Life of a Prairie Chicken" (*Canadian Journal*, February 1883) and Roberts's "Do Seek Their Meat from God" (*Harper's*, December 1892), the first of many such stories that they and their imitators were subsequently to write. Although both men used the two forms—the biography and the short story—Seton preferred the former, and Roberts, the latter, and between them they have made the history of the wild animal story almost entirely the history of their work in it.

Although Seton published a typical biography in 1883, he did not make his name until 1898, when *Wild Animals I Have Known* appeared. Seton was no arm-chair naturalist, as his two-volume *Life-Histories of Northern Animals* (1909), *The Arctic Prairies* (1911), and his eight-volume *Lives of Game Animals* (1925-27) prove, and his stories of wild animals he had known—"Lobo," "Silverspot," and other wild creatures—written, like all his work, out of experience, combine narrative and natural history admirably. He repeated the success of *Wild Animals I Have Known* with a similar book, *Lives of the Hunted* (1901). (Seton selected stories from both the *Lives* and his earlier book and published them under the following titles: *Lobo, Rag, and Vixen*, 1899; *Redruff, Raggylug*, and *Vixen*, each in a braille edition, 1900; *Krag and Johnny Bear*, 1902; *Johnny Bear, Lobo, and Other Stories*, 1935; *Johnny Bear and other Stories*, n.d.) He followed his two early successes with the similar *Animal Heroes* (1905), *Wild Animal Ways* (1916), and *Mainly about Wolves* (1937), a mixture of fact and fancy in a compendium of "true" accounts of "historic wolves." Interspersed among these works were *The Trail of the Sandhill Stag* (1899) and five later book-length animal stories. In the first of these, Seton as Yan, who was soon to become the hero of *Two Little Savages*, recounts his experiences while hunting a great buck in the Carberry hills. Although an animal biography only in part, *The Trail of the Sandhill Stag* became the forerunner of five stories true to type: *The Biography of a Grizzly* (1900), *Monarch, the Big Bear of Tallac* (1904), *The Biography of a Silver Fox* (1909), *Bannertail* (1922), the life of a grey squirrel, and *The Biography of an Arctic Fox* (1937). Seton also published two books of animal portraits: *Pictures of Wild Animals* (1901), and *Bird Portraits* (1901).

As a writer-naturalist, Seton is much less interested in the art of fiction than in telling a true tale (although "Krag" is a fine short story) and imparting knowledge of the outdoors. His usual method is to stress narrative and events. Yet he does tell good stories, for he never lets his natural history override his narrative, and his events are interesting in themselves. Moreover his success depends, too, on the way in which he appeals to his reader for sympathy with the animal world. It was this trait that brought charges of "nature-fakir," for despite all his claims of literal truthfulness his animals, "brave little souls," sometimes "lonely and sad," "stop to think things over." Much less aware than Roberts of the wider implications of events in nature, Seton seldom reveals anything of the cosmological, of the tragic irony, or of the paradox of nature's changing changelessness. Even his long animal biographies are animal adventure stories, unified by having the same creature participate in all events. If there are unifying overtones they are emotional, for Seton writes much as Saunders wrote of Beautiful Joe, as humanitarian and propagandist, "an animal evangelical." Here as an example is the conclusion of "Redruff":

> Have the wild things no moral or legal rights? What right has man to inflict such long and fearful agony on a fellow-creature, simply because that creature does not speak his language? All that day, with growing, racking pains, poor Redruff hung and beat his great, strong wings in helpless struggles to be free. All day, all night, with growing torture, until he only longed for death. But no one came. The morning broke, the day wore on, and still he hung there, slowly dying; his very strength a curse. The second night crawled slowly down, and when, in the dawdling hours of darkness, a great Horned Owl, drawn by the feeble flutter of a dying wing, cut short the pain, the deed was wholly kind.
> The wind blew down the valley from the north. The snow-horses went racing over the wrinkled ice, over the Don Flats, and over the marsh toward the lake, white, for they were driven snow, but on them, scattered dark, were riding plumy fragments of partridge ruffs—the famous rainbow ruffs. And they rode on the winter wind that night, away and away to the south, over the dark and boisterous lake, as they rode in the gloom of his Mad Moon flight, riding and riding on till they were engulfed, the last trace of the last of the Don Valley race.

Typical of the endings of many of Seton's stories, this passage reveals the cast and limits of their overtones. Or are compassion and kindness such basic truths that Seton can say no more? His animal psychology may be pure surmise, but can we know anything except in our own terms, or express identity with nature in any other way?

Roberts originated the animal short story with "Do Seek their Meat from God" (1892), a "sketch," as he called it, which, with two like it, he published among the fifteen stories of *Earth's Enigmas* (1895). He then dropped the genre. After the success of *Wild Animals I Have Known*, however, he returned to it enthusiastically with *The Kindred of the Wild* (1902), *The Watchers of the Trails* (1904) and went on and on until *Further Animal Stories* (1936) to a total of nineteen volumes. This number does not include nine books, each of a single story selected from the books referred to. He also wrote one magnificent book-length animal biography, *Red Fox* (1905), and a chapter on pre-historic wildlife in a "pre-historic historical romance," *In the Morning of Time* (1919).

The background of Roberts's new genre includes both literature and science. Roberts had already written articles for *Forest and Stream* (in the 1880's) before "Do Seek their Meat from God" appeared. Moreover, the short story was a prominent form at the time, and Roberts simply adapted it to a whole new subject. As for the influence of science, the spread of Darwinism, positing man's evolution from animals, and the increasing number of books on the subject, refocused man's mind on the interrelationship of man and nature.

Roberts's life was also influential on his work. Like Seton, who spent his boyhood, much as Yan had, roaming the countryside near Lindsay and Toronto, Roberts owed his interest in nature to his childhood "passed in the backwoods" in New Brunswick. He was not, however, a naturalist of Seton's stature—was, in fact, not a naturalist but a casual observer. Despite his realism, he did not write his "true" stories like Seton out of his experiences but, in large part, from hearsay and his reading. Consequently, his two hundred or so stories on almost every living creature are often inaccurate and lack something of the attractive intimacy of Seton's. No salmon parr ever matured as rapidly as the one in "The Last Barrier" (*The Haunters of the Silences*, 1907), and no mallard ever flew so fast as the one in "The Nest of the Mallard" (*The Backwoodsmen*, 1909). Yet if he is guilty of misrepresenting facts he is not of misinterpreting them in the wider orientation of the "laws" of nature.

Although free from Seton's practice of upstage comment and generally less subjective, Roberts can be excessively anthropomorphic. In the name of animal "personality," a fox may "fling dignity to the winds," a moose "look with longing eyes," a rabbit "wave long ears of admiration" at a "comely" mate. Again he may present an animal hero almost allegorically as in *Wisdom of the Wilderness* (1922), when "The Little Homeless One" lays down his life during a "moonlit revel" to save the other rabbits. Normally, however, he lets nature speak dramatically through the interplay of protagonist and incident.

Roberts's stories fall into three groups—the animal biography, the story of action, and the "sketch." The first of these, as Roberts handled it, uses event less to present animal habits than to examine animal "conduct." "The Keeper of the Water Gate" in *The Watchers of the Trails* is typical in its stress on the motives and reactions of its muskrat protagonists. The second kind of story subordinates animal personality and natural history to incident and plot as in "The White-slashed Bull" (*The House in the Water*, 1908), an episode in which a moose escapes death through a hunter's mercy. Men almost always appear in these stories, as participants or as choric observers. The third type, the graphic sketch-like story, isolates and dramatizes a single episode that suggests an elemental force governing the natural world from without, rather than within, or "Fate," as Roberts calls it in "The Iron Edge of Winter" (*The Backwoodsmen*). Here a weasel, about to seize a squirrel, is itself seized and carried off by a hawk. Stories of this kind often read as if Chance were a whimsical god playing jokes on his children of the wild, or having a game in which the rule of "survival of the fittest" no longer holds. The "sketch" Roberts wrote less and less frequently and in his later books not at all.

As an artist Roberts has many merits. He writes a fluent prose. He knows how to create suspense by hinting, withholding information, and working toward a major climax—techniques that "The Haunter of the Pine Gloom" (*The Kindred of the Wild*) admirably demonstrates. He gives individuality to essentially type characters by selecting the fleetest, strongest, and wisest as heroes—the "kings" of the species. Unfortunately this practice tends to turn his protagonists into noble savages, thus detracting from his work as natural history. He knows, also, how to unify his stories, opening and closing them with descriptions as if they were the curtains of a play. Yet the descriptions are not separate from the narrative. They are not simply realistic settings, the curtains of a play, or prose lyrics framing a story. They are his way of disclosing, within the transitory, something of the permanence of the natural world. Or again he begins *in medias res* and ends with a denouement that brings the narrative full circle. Even the longer animal biographies he can keep from sprawling by shaping them around some centre as in "The Last Barrier" (*Haunters of the Silences*). This starts and finishes at a falls that a salmon parr descends on his way to the sea and to which he returns years later.

Whatever the story, it also has a unifying theme: the amorality of nature, the struggle for survival, the cyclical aspect of time. This is as true of the longer as of the shorter stories. "The King of Mamozekel" and "The Lord of the Air" (*The Kindred of the Wild*) both depend greatly on narrative and on the facts of life history for their interest, but neither is unified solely as biography. In the one a moose reveals the power of the instinct for the preservation of species; in the other an eagle becomes the embodiment of nature's freedom of spirit forever reasserting itself in defiance of man's attempts to destroy it.

Roberts's adherence to the concept of the animal hero and of nature as conflict frequently leads to the sensational and spectacular. His stories abound in "desperate encounters" (or duels) of courageous beasts, like epic heroes, battling to the death. At times, however, he resolves plot conflict in a conclusion that has wider and subtler implications.

Just about this time a visitor from the hills had come shambling down to the river's edge—one of the great black bears of the Quahdavic valley. Sitting contemplatively on her haunches, her little, cunning eyes had watched the vain leaps of the salmon. She knew a good deal about salmon and her watching was not mere curiosity. As the efforts of the brave fish grew feebler and feebler she drew down closer and closer to the edge of the water, till it frothed about her feet. When, at last, the salmon came blindly into the eddy and turned upon his side, the bear was but a few feet distant. She crept forward like a cat, crouched,—and a great black paw shot around with a clutching sweep. Gasping and quivering, the salmon was thrown upon the rocks. Then white teeth, savage but merciful, bit through the back of his neck; and unstruggling he was carried to a thicket above the Falls. ("The Last Barriers," *The Haunters of the Silences*, pp. 68–69.)

This has some of the pathos so typical of Seton's endings, but it has more than pathos. It contains Roberts's comment on the grim irony and amorality of life in the world of nature.

As Roberts continued to add more and more animals to his "ark" with *Kings in Exile* (1909), *Neighbours Unknown* (1911), *More Kindred of the Wild* (1911), *The Feet of the Furtive* (1912), *Hoof and Claw* (1913), *Children of the Wild* (1913), *Secret Trails* (1916), *They Who Walk in the Wild* (1924), to list some not already mentioned, he tended, in the cause of entertainment, to resort to more derring-do and far-fetched incident and to reduce his stories to formula. This latter development was almost inevitable since there is a sameness about the situations and themes available to him. His grumpy bears and wary foxes and other animals, despite their personalities, of necessity become types—within a species one creature's habits scarcely differ from another's. Consequently many later stories become monotonous variations in terms of species or situation on his fresh and original early work. Yet at their best, whenever written, they are an impressive fusion of art, fiction, and natural history.

The history of the book-length animal biography after Roberts and Seton concerns the writing of only five men. The versatile and talented Haig-Brown has turned to it twice with *Silver: The Life of an Atlantic Salmon* (1931) and the much longer *Return to the River* (1941), the biography of a Columbia River Chinook. Both are excellent as narratives and natural history, but differ from Seton's and Roberts's biographies, for Haig-Brown writes more obviously as scientist than field-naturalist and stresses biology rather than conjectural animal psychology. His first book, *Silver* (which has a British not a Canadian setting) reads, however, as if he were a kindly angler addressing a child, and occasionally stopping to wag a finger about the conservation practices of the "Good Fisherman." *Return to the River* is concerned with similar questions, but is an adult's book, a fictionalized documentary that takes up the broader issue of the wastage of natural resources and man's inhumanity to nature. (Haig-Brown's *The Living Land* (1961) discusses very fully the use and conservation of the natural resources of British Columbia.)

Another book in this category, Gray McClintock's *Itinerants of the Timberlands* (1934), the life story of two Western Canadian wolves, Radus and Lemus, reverts to type. Anecdotal and sensational, like the stories and essays in McClintock's earlier *The Wolves of Cooking Lake* (1932), it manages to incorporate enough heroics and perils to turn it into an animal adventure story.

Shortly after McClintock's book appeared, Kenneth Conibear (b. 1907) published *Northland Footprints* (1936), a trapper's tale about a tame muskrat and a whiskey Jack that saves the life of its snow-blind "master." Conibear writes imaginatively and affectionately of the wild things, and his observations have the authority that comes from his many years in the North. Frank Conibear, like Kenneth, with whom he wrote a dog story, *Husky* (1940), also turned his experiences as a trapper to account (with the help of J. L. Blundell) in *Water Trio* (1948). A biography of a beaver family, it would seem to reveal Grey Owl's influence in the detailed and kindly manner with which it presents their story. That Conibear sets up a plot by introducing Indian trappers adds little to its interest as narrative, but fortunately detracts nothing from its interest as a study of wildlife.

The latest of the animal biographers is Fred Bodsworth, who in 1955 published the *Last of the Curlews*, a book which assuredly begot his later *The Strange One*, for each celebrates the heroic animal in Seton-like fashion —emotionally and admiringly. The *Last of the Curlews* (there have been sight records since 1955) gives exact scientific data, but combines them with a story of interest and poignancy based on the old motifs of the search and the hero's plight as the last of a vanishing race, a victim of man's greed and insensitivity.

Animal stories like Roberts's and Seton's have not been especially numerous. The Reverend Egerton Young's *My Dogs of the Northland* (1902), Fraser's *Thirteen Men* (1906), Alan Sullivan's *The Passing of Oul-I-But* (1913) and *The Cycle of the North* (1938), and Kerry Wood's *Willowdale* (1956) have included some of the kind. Only a few books have been solely collections of animal stories. William MacMillan's *Northland Stories: Tales of Trapping Life in the Canadian Wilderness* (1922) has as its subjects foxes, moose, otters, and a wolverine, a beast that seems to fascinate nature writers with its "villainy." McKishnie's *Mates of the Tangle* (1924) is misnamed; it might better be entitled *Perils of the Tangle*, since the conventional struggle of beast against beast or man is its central theme. Dickie's *Umingmuk of the Barrens* (1927) eulogizes several dogs, but does include a long biography of a musk-ox, which is largely a story of action. *The Silent Call* (1930), by Evans, contains fifteen stories about wildlife (mainly fish) and Indians on the West Coast. Of these only "The

Spark of Life," a dramatic illustration of man's destructiveness, and "Morsels of Chance," a story of a man's defeat in a grim battle with nature, revolve around anything beyond the usual demonstrations of animal courage, loyalty, and shrewdness. Zella Manning's *Lords of the Wilderness* (1933), an anthology of animal stories, contains several by Canadians. Gillese's *Kirby's Gander* (1957), the latest book of the kind, is largely romantic in outlook. Aside from "A Fox is where you find him," a straight forward biography, it is somewhat contrived, highly subjective, and concerned much with crises.

Nature writing, particularly the animal story, had its hey-dey in the late nineteenth and early twentieth centuries. It has long passed. Perhaps the literary vein has been worked out. Perhaps people tired of learning that animals and men are alike and learned from two world wars that they are too much alike. Perhaps urban people, now removed three or four generations from their country forebears, have lost touch with nature almost completely. Unquestionably the biological sciences have been replaced in public imagination by the physical. What might once have been a nature story is now science fiction. Although man has again turned his face to the stars, he may discover once more, however, that a mouse is "miracle enough to stagger sextillions of infidels."

20. Lampman and Roberts

ROY DANIELLS

IT IS CUSTOMARY, in calling the roll of Confederation poets, to commence with Roberts, as the oldest and as the author of *Orion and Other Poems* (1880) which is a landmark in this country's literary history. The other three members of the principal group were, however, all born within the next year or two and the importance of *Orion* is simply that it demonstrated that poetry could be written and published in Canada. It is possible therefore to begin with Lampman and gain the advantage of encountering at the outset the best corpus of poetry, the most attractive of the four personalities, and the most typical critical problem.

Lampman's brief career—he was born in 1861 at Morpeth, in western Ontario, and died in Ottawa in 1899—is all of a piece and the reverse of episodic. The writing of poetry dominated his life and, like his life, his poetry exhibits a consistent wholeness which makes a chronological arrangement of his poems of little importance. The heart of Lampman's poetic achievement, which in turn is the dominant fact and central achievement of his life, consists of a small group of nature poems, the product of his excursions, at all seasons of the year, into the Ontario woods and fields. His first collection, *Among the Millet*, was published in Ottawa in 1888, the second, *Lyrics of Earth*, in Boston in 1893. A collected *Poems* was issued in 1900, just after his death.

The first thing that will strike anyone coming fresh to Lampman is his loving indebtedness to Wordsworth, Shelley, Arnold, Tennyson and Keats. He writes of Keats, "I have an idea that he has found a sort of faint reincarnation in me." At the beginning of his poetic career the influence of Keats was, indeed, predominant. His poem "April" begins,

> Pale season, watcher in unvexed suspense,
> Still priestess of the patient middle day....

Elsewhere we have re-creations of the poetic world of Arnold. In "Between the Rapids" a scene of bygone affections is revisited—

> Aye there they are, nor have they changed their cheer,
>   The fields, the hut, the leafy mountain brows;
> Across the lonely dusk again I hear
>   The loitering bells, the lowing of the cows,

> The bleat of many sheep, the stilly rush
> Of the low whispering river, and through all,
> Soft human tongues that break the deepening hush
> With faint-heard song or desultory call. . . .

In an occasional poem such as "Drought" he borrows from Coleridge: "men /Dropped dead beneath the moon," and then

> Into the mocking sky uprist,
> Like phantoms from the burning west
> Dim clouds that brought no rain

and so on until "Down came the rushing rain."

Innumerable passages of this kind attest Lampman's willing dependence on the Romantics and the Victorians for the tools of his trade and many of the materials of his craft. And it is also clear that in a large overriding sense he is consistently Wordsworthian; he finds his consolation, his sense of the divine, his daily sensuous delights, all in the countryside, the world of farm and forest, lake and rock and stream.

It is easy, if one approaches Lampman from the direction of the great nineteenth-century English poets, to write him off as no more than their pale imitator and ineffectual disciple. It is only in a Canadian context that this judgment can be seen for what it is, somewhat less than a half-truth. Lampman has in fact erected, though on narrow foundations, a small poetic edifice securely his own and the excellence of his best work is conditional upon its not attempting anything beyond these narrow limits. "Winter Uplands," written just before his death, illustrates his strength within these self-imposed bounds:

> The frost that stings like fire upon my cheek,
> The loneliness of this forsaken ground,
> The long white drift upon whose powdered peak
> I sit in the great silence as one bound;
> The rippled sheet of snow where the wind blew
> Across the open fields for miles ahead;
> The far-off city towered and roofed in blue
> A tender line upon the western red;
> The stars that singly, then in flocks appear,
> Like jets of silver from the violet dome,
> So wonderful, so many and so near,
> And then the golden moon to light me home—
> The crunching snowshoes and the stinging air,
> And silence, frost and beauty everywhere.

That the bounds were self imposed and to some degree consciously so is apparent from the last two lines of this sonnet which in first draft ran thus:

> Though the heart plays us false and life lies bare
> The truth of Beauty haunts us everywhere.

Philosophic generalization, that stock-in-trade of the Victorians, was never Lampman's forte.

In the small central core of his poems, which alone entitles him to our present consideration, Lampman makes to the Ontario landscape a characteristic response, to which we must apply the word of his own choice—dream. In the early poem "April" he is "Dreaming of Summer and fruit-laden mirth." In "The Frogs" he is "content to dream" with them.

> That change and pain are shadows faint and fleet,
> And dreams are real, and life is only sweet.

The impressions in his well-known poem "Heat" are "in intervals of dreams." In "Among the Timothy" he finds it sweet to lie in the field, "Nor think but only dream." At the conclusion of the Wordsworthian "Winter Hues Recalled" he wakes "As from a dream." In "Song of the Stream-Drops" the waters move on "dreaming and dreaming" of their mother, the sheltering sea. The lesson of "What do Poets want with Gold" is that they should "Ever dream, but never know." In "Athenian Reverie," the dream wish is made more explicit:

> Happy is he,
> Who, as a watcher, stands apart from life
> From all life and his own, and thus from all,
> Each thought, each deed, and each hour's brief event,
> Draws the full beauty, sucks its meaning dry.
> For him this life shall be a tranquil joy.
> He shall be quiet and free. To him shall come
> No gnawing hunger for the coarser touch,
> No mad ambition with its fateful grasp;
> Sorrow itself shall sway him like a dream.

That his dream is a protection from actualities is hinted in "The City" which, characteristically, he finds beautiful at a distance:

> I see with dreaming eyes
> Even as a dream out of a dream, arise
> The bell-tongued city with its glorious towers.

In "Comfort of the Fields" he desires, when stricken with grief and weariness, to wander

> Where the long daylight dreams, unpierced, unstirred,
> And only the rich-throated thrush is heard.

"At the Ferry" concludes with his characteristic stance:

> Beyond the tumult of the mills,
>   And all the city's sound and strife,
> Beyond the waste, beyond the hills,
>   I look far out and dream of life.

Lampman's ideal natural man, in "The Woodcutter's Hut" endures the long hours of blizzards in his refuge "Without thought or remembrance, hardly awake, and waits for the storm to tire." How closely the idea of this beneficent, salutary dream is associated with Lampman's whole realization of life appears once more in "By the Sea":

> I walk as in a dream 'twixt sea and land—
> The meadows of wise thought, the sea of strife—
> And sounds and happy scents from either hand
> Come with vast gleams that spread and softly shine,
> The joy of life, the energy divine.

The verse echoes Arnold but with none of Arnold's commitment to social struggle.

All of Lampman is summed up and contained in this dream, this moment of trance, of conscious but unspecific self-realization. It is close to the familiar Wordsworthian experience of being "laid asleep in body" to "become a living soul"

> Till with an eye made quiet by the power
> Of harmony and the deep power of joy
> We see into the life of things.

Several concomitants, however, save Lampman from the charge of being Wordsworth's pale imitator. The experience is clearly his own, slowly and often after pain and grief realized, occasion by occasion, in the minutely felt and specifically realized contacts with a local and un-English landscape. Lampman's pervasive, unconscious, and complete honesty, moreover, keeps his poems from the least taint of the facile, of easy rhetoric, of inflation or pretence. In his best poems he says least about the subject of his dreams; they seem to partake of sensations, of an expansive feeling of peace and the resolution of all difficulties, but not to provide him with Shelleyan vision, Wordsworthian philosophy, or Arnoldian didacticism. The conclusion of "Heat"

> In the full furnace of this hour
> My thoughts grow keen and clear

gives not the least clue as to what these thoughts are, though from the imagery of the poem we may be certain that a sense of the goodness of life, the reconciliation of opposites, and the beauty of the earth and seasons pervades them. But it is notable that Lampman refuses to give specific content to his dream or to allow his dreaming to lead him towards philosophic or theological concepts or to make of his dreams any incitement or prelude to action. It follows that as we move outward from this dream, this centre of his poetic experience, we move into spheres which are less and less relevant to his vision. It is nature, and we may say with some confidence only nature, that induces in him the trance of insight into the life of things.

That his brief trances of delight in the experience of natural beauty gave scale and shape to his best poems Lampman himself realizes. In "Ambition" he characterizes his own poetic gift:

> From other lips let stormy numbers flow:
> By others let great epics be compiled;
> For me, the dreamer, 'tis enough to know
> The lyric stress, the fervour sweet and wild:
> I sit me in the windy grass and grow
> As wise as age, as joyous as a child.

In "The Minstrel," another self-characterization, he escapes from the city and its demands upon his song, to the fields and hillsides under a night sky, to sing once more only from the depth of his own spirit.

If we take the normal critical course of inquiring into the influences that shaped Lampman's mind during his formative years, we shall not in fact find anything contrary to what has just been said. He was something of a classical scholar, he lived in a nominally Christian community, he could scarcely avoid the climate of wistfully idealistic and utopian sentiment that pervaded his Victorian world, he could not escape some contact with current Canadian affairs, he assuaged his melancholy and even hypochondriac moments by retreating to his woods and streams and meadows, where his idealism became a dream of perfection.

Well grounded in the classics at school and later in Trinity College, he was enthusiastic about the value of Greek. We find him writing to a friend in 1894, "There never was and never will be another language like the Greek. It is worth while giving two or three years of one's life even to get a moderate knowledge of it." And a few weeks before his death he writes, "I have revived my knowledge of Greek a good deal in the past year or two and read a little every day. I have got so that I can manage a page or two of Homer in a few minutes before breakfast—a good deal easier than Browning." His classicism appears to have made him a careful and sensitive versifier. He writes to a friend, "I send you a little poem written in the strophe that Sappho used to use. I rather like it. Most men who have attempted to write sapphics in English have misused the metre horribly . . . but I flatter myself that these are real sapphics and the proof of it is that the movement is musical." And from his classical reading he derived an ideal of life, in the forms provided by the ancient Greek cities. Like Keats, he finds in Greece an unchanging perfection.

> I remember how of old
> I saw the ruddy race of men,
> Through the glittering world outrolled,
> A gay-smiling multitude,
> All immortal, all divine,
> Treading in a wreathèd line
> By a pathway through a wood.

His long poem "The Land of Pallas" merely amplifies this vision. The story of Sostratus fills him with delight:

> Yet like a gleam out of primitive shadow revealing
> Worlds of old joy and wonder of living and effort
> Named in the book of Herodotus still shall you find him.

It is of interest to see that this delight in the crystallized, unchanging beauty of Hellas, so like Keats's, is all of a piece with his dream of beauty and wonder and that neither the one nor the other is associated with any kind of concrete political or social reform. In spite of many resemblances between Lampman's vocabulary and versification and the techniques of Arnold, Lampman is in temperament far closer to Keats and even to Wordsworth.

Lampman's connection with the Christian tradition is of the most exiguous and awkward kind, and here again we find him in company with many of the English Romantics. His feeble attempts to realize Christian themes in his poems are better evidence, in this context, than any proof that he disliked churchgoing. In his "New Year's Eve" the

> White-haloed groups that sought perpetually
> The figure of one crowned and sacrificed

are totally unconvincing. In "Easter Eve" we have another vision of Christ poetically feeble and psychologically disquieting. The authentic voice of Lampman is heard rather in "A Prayer":

> O Earth, O mighty mother, breathe on us.
> O mother, who wast long before our day,
>   And after us full many an age shalt be,
> Careworn and blind, we wander from thy way:
>   Born of thy strength, yet weak and halt are we;
> Grant us O mother, therefore, us who pray,
>   Some little of thy light and majesty.

As we consider Lampman's relation to contemporary issues and current ideas, we must be prepared to distinguish, all along the line, between Lampman the man and Lampman the poet. The former was interested in reform measures, was said to be a Fabian, and certainly believed in a socialist programme of government. The city and its social inequalities, based on wealth, repelled him. Much of his mildly utopian thinking was identical with the sentiments of *News from Nowhere*. But none of these considerations leads us towards the centre of Lampman's creativity. Like Keats, who influenced him more than any other of the great Romantics and Victorians, his was primarily a life of sensation.

It will be asked, then, why he was not a love poet and the answer illuminates both the man and his situation. His small sonnet sequence "The Growth of Love" was inspired by Maud Playter, whom he married when she was eighteen. The story goes that he pinned together those pages in his manuscript book containing the dozen sonnets of "The Growth of Love," requesting his friends to respect the concealment as they went through the book. It is easy to guess why. The passionate simplicity, purity, and intensity of Lampman's love make of these sonnets a personal rather than a poetic revelation. "With this key" Lampman unlocked his heart, the worse poet he. Few of the great poets who influenced him wrote as well of love as they did of nature. Love as a theme is infinitely complex; some elaborate convention, whether learned as in Dante or popular as in Burns, seems essential to the success of love poetry. Lampman put his emotions directly into simple sonnet form and the results do no more than fill us with sympathy and affection for Lampman the man.

> For like a saint's her yellow hair doth shine
> Most lovely when the soft locks fall amiss,
> And I would call her mouth one perfect bliss
> Of glimmering dimple and pale laughter-line,
> Enough to make a man's heart faint and pine
> To take them all up with one blinding kiss.

One work of Lampman's which deserves special attention is "At the Long Sault: May, 1660," a poem just short of a hundred lines, which was first published in 1943 with an introduction by E. K. Brown. It recounts the historic heroism of Adam Daulac and his band who fought to the death to save their countrymen from massacre by the Iroquois. The best passages, the memorable ones, are the introduction, the conclusion, and the fine simile of the bull-moose fighting a pack of wolves. The opening lines are Lampman at his best:

> Under the day-long sun there is life and mirth
>   In the working earth,
> And the wonderful moon shines bright
>   Through the soft spring night,
> The innocent flowers in the limitless woods are springing
>   Far and away
> With the sound and the perfume of May,
> And ever up from the south the happy birds are winging,
>   The waters glitter and leap and play
>   While the grey hawk soars.

The moose, fighting for life, is realized briefly and with great force,

> Till, driven, and ever to and fro
> Harried, wounded and weary grown,
> His mighty strength gives way
> And all together they fasten upon him and drag him down.

The poem ends:

> But afar in the ring of the forest,
>   Where the air is so tender with May
> And the waters are wild in the moonlight,
>   They lie in their silence of clay.
>
> The numberless stars out of heaven
>   Look down with a pitiful glance;
> And the lilies asleep in the forest
>   Are closed like the lilies of France.

Repeated readings confirm the impression that this poem, like Wordsworth's "Hart-Leap Well," is an account of violence in a context of the serenity and beneficence of nature and yet Lampman goes on to insist, in his evocation of the magnificent bull-moose, that nature itself is productive of cruelty and violence. The elements of the poem are not fully resolved; it is fittingly, as published in 1943, an addendum to Lampman's major work; it is not an entrance into some region of more complex and mature sensibility than we find in the earlier nature poetry.

It is to this nature poetry that the appreciative reader of Lampman must continually return. His vague Victorian forays into the Viking world ("Ingvi and Alf"), Tennysonian idyll ("The Story of an Affinity"), Old Testament history ("David and Abigail"), or idealized classicism ("The Land of Pallas") are all of some interest as they reveal Lampman's character and temperament but were they the substance of his achievement we should not now be considering him.

The craftsmanship of his nature poetry is of a high order. He was rightly pleased with his "Sapphics," a real test of skill surmounted without apparent effort:

> Brief the span is, counting the years of mortals,
> Strange and sad; it passes, and then the bright earth,
> Careless mother, gleaming with gold and azure,
>   Lovely with blossoms—
> Shining white anemones, mixed with roses,
> Daisies mild-eyed, grasses and honeyed clover—
> You and me, and all of us, met and equal
>   Softly shall cover.

But under the smooth recording of the natural scene, there is frequently an identifiable tension of opposites, a need for resolution. It has been well said that the poem "Heat" provides oppositions between movement and stillness, coolness and warmth, sound and silence, darkness and light. The fundamental pulse in Lampman is between apprehensive weariness on the one hand and the reassurance of renewed strength on the other. It has been noted that he comes to nature from something other and often opposite. He walks, typically, from the city into the "comfort of the fields."

> To roam in idleness and sober mirth,
> Through summer airs and summer lands, and drain
> The comfort of wide fields unto tired eyes.

Without this tension of opposites, it is questionable whether Lampman's work could have had any meaning. It is a fair inference that when most desirous of retiring into rural seclusion to write he was still completely dependent for his best poetic effects upon the dichotomy of his experiences.

In this connection it is worth looking rather closely at "The Woodcutter's Hut," one of his best and most original poems.

> The hut of the lonely woodcutter stands, a few rough beams that show
> A blunted peak and a low black line, from the glittering waste of snow.

The woodcutter, even when most isolated and inarticulate, when stormbound "he lies through the leaguering hours in his bunk / Like a winter-hidden beast," awakens the poet's admiration. He is "The animal man in his warmth and vigour, sound, and hard, and complete." Yet when spring comes, with its sunshine and flowers, its gushing streams and liberation from winter's bondage, the woodcutter is gone. "He is gone where the gathering of valley men another labour yields"; he is in fact one of the habitants gone back to the farm after a winter of woodcutting. And the end of the poem is fruitfully ambiguous; the hut stands buried in triumphant forest vegetation,

> And he who finds it suddenly there, as he wanders far and alone,
> Is touched with a sweet and beautiful sense of something tender and gone,
> The sense of a struggling life in the waste, and the mark of a soul's command,
> The going and coming of vanished feet, the touch of a human hand.

In the woodcutter Lampman palpably recognizes his own alter ego, the man to whom total dreaming commitment in natural surroundings is a supreme good, without an articulate philosophy of life but with a vigorous full realization of life, yet this same man committed to another world of activity, an organized community, to explore which is no part of Lampman's poetic intention, and yet without which the refuge in the woods would have no meaning, would not even be possible.

It is worth noting that, like Wordsworth in the early scenes of *The Prelude*, Lampman has a double experience of natural surroundings. There is the harvest of the quiet eye, the reward of solitary excursions into the Ottawa countryside, and there is active participation in snow-shoeing and canoeing, in which we know (with all the regret of hindsight for the harm it must have done to his damaged heart) Lampman took the greatest delight.

An element of unnecessary controversy has entered into the appreciation of Lampman. A dichotomy has been evoked between the enchained and resentful civil servant and the wanderer among woods and meadows and some confusion has arisen between the young man keenly interested in contemporary ideas and the poet whose best work is virtually innocent of ideas. But that Lampman was in any real sense a divided personality seems very unlikely. If we bring into touch the various sides of his character they take their places as facets of a mind of singular purity and simplicity—if it is any longer possible to use these words in their traditional sense. At the centre of his being there burned a small clear flame.

Toward this centre the reader of Lampman is continually drawn. Thoroughly representative of the liberal tradition of his time and place and one of a group of friends to whom a classical education on a British model was the natural road to a career of teaching and writing, Lampman is nevertheless unique in that, like Cézanne, he has his own little sensation in the face of nature which, without alienating him from his surroundings, lifts him into another sphere. This private sensation is not incompatible with what has been well characterized as picturesque realism, "the fusion of a large, general effect with sharply observed detail," but grows directly out of it. The marked quality and indeed the saving grace of Lampman's sensation when confronted by the face of nature is that it does not issue in ideas. It is, as he fully realized, in the whole *ordonnance* of the poem; it is not stated and elaborated. Some lucky inner check in Lampman saved him, when at his best, from going on into the moralized path beaten by Wordsworth and Arnold. What wakes in his blood at the moment of revelation is "A pleasure secret and austere," communicating itself to the reader by a simple shock of recognition for which the tactical dispositions of the poem have already prepared him. This poetry of a secret sensation shared by the prepared and now perceptive reader is all of Lampman that we shall not willingly let die. And it suffices.

It is impossible, however, to leave Lampman without some expression of the affection every reader of his life and works must feel for him. He is not a tragic figure but his struggles, his poverty, his early death throw into relief his eagerness and gaiety which perpetually contended with his frustrations and spells of melancholy and hypochrondria. As he modestly realized, he is much like Keats. He has moreover the innocence and idealism of the Victorians without the least touch of hypocrisy or sentimentality. His outlook on life was classical rather than Christian. He believed in natural happiness, in the capacity of the natural man for insight and for creative effort.

Of less significance than Lampman as a poet, but of more importance as an influence on Canadian writing, is Charles G. D. Roberts (1860–1943). He superficially resembles Lampman in occupying himself, when at his best, with the Canadian landscape, within a framework of late Romantic convention, heavily influenced by the tradition that runs through English poetry from Wordsworth to Tennyson. Like Lampman, he arrives at his most personal utterance by developing the debate between optimism and melancholy in a context of symbols provided by observed nature. "The Solitary Woodsman," one of his few poems without formal flaw, is in subject and treatment closely parallel to "The Woodcutter's Hut" of Lampman. Where the two men differ is in their power to achieve poetic form organized from within. The most commonplace of Lampman's poems bears the marks of growing from a single impulse while even the best of Roberts's pieces reads as though constructed to fit a theme. It is too facile to regard Lampman as an integrated and Roberts as a dishevelled personality but it is fair to point out that Lampmans' life was centripetal upon his creative work and that Roberts's was a life "without a centre."

It has been pointed out that the friends and critics of Roberts who urged him to write on patriotic and philosophical themes were among the worst enemies of his present reputation and the same may be said for the editors who published the love poems later collected as *New York Nocturnes* (1898). Roberts has been rightly praised as a patriot but his verses in praise of his country make painful and embarrassed reading:

> O strong hearts of the North
> Let flame your loyalty forth,
> And put the craven and base to an open shame,
> Till earth shall know the Child of Nations by her name!

Or, regarding Riel's rebellion,

> Saskatchewan, whose virgin sod
> So late Canadian blood made sweet.

It is unfortunate that Roberts shows little if any development of ideas and techniques which permit the reader to pass over early inadequacies with the assurance of better things to come. The love poems written at the turn of the century are frankly appalling whereas *Orion* in 1880 had brought a letter of encouragement from the pen of Matthew Arnold. Not even in his appreciation of a cosmic spirit in nature does his poetry show any advance; he records the healing power of nature as clearly in the poems written before 1880 as in anything later and with more hope and freshness of spirit, and confidence of comforting mankind:

> Yet would I cheer them, sharing in their ills,
> Weaving them dreams of waves, and skies, and hills;
> Yet would I sing of Peace, and Hope, and Truth,
> Till softly o'er my song should beam the youth,—

> The morning of the world. Ah, yes, there hath
> The goal been planted all along that path;
> And as the swallow were my heart as free
> Might I but hope that path belonged to me.

The realization of this dream was too often to dwindle into vague and ill-expressed commonplaces:

> Little brothers of the clod,
> Soul of fire and seed of sod,
>   We must fare into the silence
> At the knees of God.

The best of Roberts is to be found in his descriptions of Canadian landscape. In these he is capable of recording impressions with the fidelity of a genuine devotion, of evoking the *genius loci* of the Fundy shore, of catching the turn of a Canadian season. In a small handful of such descriptive pieces he achieves memorableness. Among them are a group of sonnets on a Sower, an Old Barn, Salt Flats, Pea-Fields, the Potato Harvest, the Mowing. Here the vague moralizing of his weaker poems is absent, his unsureness of diction is reduced to a minimum, and the conventions of the sonnet form supply some firmness of structure.

> Tons upon tons the brown-green fragrant hay
>   O'erbrims the mows beyond the time-warped eaves,
>   Up to the rafters where the spider weaves,
> Though few flies wander his secluded way.
> Through a high chink one lonely golden ray,
>   Wherein the dust is dancing, slants unstirred.
>   In the dry hush some rustlings light are heard,
> Of winter-hidden mice at furtive play.
>
> Far down, the cattle in their shadowed stalls,
>   Nose-deep in clover fodder's meadowy scent,
>   Forget the snows that whelm their pasture streams,
> The frost that bites the world beyond their walls.
>   Warm housed, they dream of summer, well content
> In day-long contemplation of their dreams.

It is possible that Roberts, had he regarded poetry as his sole vocation, might have found in the Romantic tradition a form which carried its own built-in disciplines and might thus have circumvented his own unsureness of phrasing, rhythm, and structure. Some support for this suggestion is found within one group of poems that recount Greek myths in Tennysonian form. The best of these is "Marsyas":

> Then to the goat-feet comes the wide-eyed fawn
> Hearkening; the rabbits fringe the glade, and lay
> Their long ears to the sound;
> In the pale boughs the partridge gather round,

> And quaint hern from the sea-green river reeds;
> The wild ram halts upon a rocky horn
> O'erhanging; and, unmindful of his prey,
> The leopard steals with narrowed lids to lay
> His spotted length along the ground.
> The thin airs wash, the thin clouds wander by,
> And those hushed listeners move not. All the morn
> He pipes, soft-swaying, and with half-shut eye,
> In rapt content of utterance,—
>   nor heeds
> The young God standing in his branchy place,
> The languor on his lips, and in his face,
> Divinely inaccessible, the scorn.

Part of the success of this poem may arise from the poet's identification of himself with the subject.

The poems marked by a personal tone and some distinctiveness of utterance are nearly all reminiscences of what could be seen from the bedroom window of his boyhood home, the vista across the marshes of Tantramar and the waters of the Bay of Fundy to the Minudie Hills. *In Divers Tones* (1886), his second collection, contains "Tantramar Revisited" in which is developed a theme and an attitude to which he was often to return but never with such fullness and conviction.

> Here where the road that has climbed from the inland valleys and
>   woodlands,
> Dips from the hill-tops down, straight to the base of the hills,—
> Here, from my vantage-ground, I can see the scattering houses,
> Stained with time, set warm in orchards, meadows and wheat....
> Yonder, toward the left, lie broad the Westmoreland marshes,—
> Miles on miles they extend, level, and grassy, and dim,
> Clear from the long red sweep of flats to the sky in the distance,
> Save for the outlying heights, green-rampired Cumberland Point;
> Miles on miles outrolled, and the river-channels divide them,—
> Miles on miles of green, barred by the hurtling gusts.

As the description proceeds, some unexplained accession of poetic tact prevents the intrusion of patriotism, philosophy, love, and religion; we have nothing but the evocation of past happiness by a distant scene. It is enough.

> Ah, the old-time stir, how once it stung me with rapture,—
> Old-time sweetness, the winds freighted with honey and salt!
> Yet will I stay my steps and not go down to the marsh-land,—
> Muse and recall far off, rather remember than see,—
> Lest on too close sight I miss the darling illusion,
> Spy at their task even here the hands of chance and change.

Another poem which strengthens the conviction that Roberts would have done well to stay with his early impressions and to cultivate the virtues of provincialism is "The Solitary Woodsman," already mentioned. Like Lampman, Roberts shows an inexplicit recognition of the woodcutter as an alter ego, one who, in close and solitary fellowship with nature, labours actively without philosophizing.

> Green spruce branches for his head,
> Here he makes his simple bed,
>   Couching with the sun, and rising
> When the dawn is frosty red.
>
> All day long he wanders wide
> With the grey moss for his guide
>   And his lonely axe-stroke startles
> The expectant forest-side.
>
> Toward the quiet close of day
> Back to camp he takes his way,
>   And about his sober footsteps
> Unafraid the squirrels play. . . .
>
> And the wind about his eaves
> Through the chilly night-wet grieves,
>   And the earth's dumb patience fills him,
> Fellow to the falling leaves.

It is possible and, indeed, at some point essential to see Roberts and his friends from the stance of the English reviewer, who noted that "Charles G. D. Roberts is still read by schoolboys, for his animal stories," and that "Carman and Lampman have written a few good lyrics." It is quite necessary to see Roberts, in some context, as a restless and unstable wanderer, with a limited capacity for intellectual experience and an emotional life impoverished by wilful separation from his family. It is certainly not possible now to believe that Roberts's prose possesses even the limited aesthetic value of his poetry. The stilted Romanticism of his fiction, its factitious plots, puppet characters, and wooden dialogue have no longer any but an historic interest. His animal stories have had the longest popularity but even they exist in the uncomfortable limbo between deliberate fable and true understanding of animal psychology.

All this, however, would be to ignore the fact that Roberts is nevertheless, to our tradition, "ancestral, important, haunting." His influence on others was widespread and enduring. He early became, and long remained, a symbol. And the achievements which led to this symbolic status are by no means factitious.

All readers of Lampman know the story of his first looking into Roberts's *Orion*, how the recognition that these verses, with their classical background and their Tennysonian manner, "written by a Canadian, by a young man, one of ourselves," "was like a voice from some new paradise of art, calling to us to be up and doing." All the elements of Roberts's influence on Canadian letters are present in this initial and symbolic episode. Early in the bare field, he became the first Canadian man of letters whom his own countrymen and the world at large could recognize. He accepted the editorship of *The Week* in 1880, was elected a fellow of the Royal Society of Canada in 1890 and of the Royal Society of Literature in 1892. In 1893 we find him writing to a friend, "I am sure there are many who would consider that either Carman or Lampman take precedence of me. I am always more than content to be counted the equal of those two. And as for the others,—Campbell and the two Scotts,—they certainly show great possibilities, and any one of them may yet turn out to be the Captain of the whole crowd of us."

It is easy to underestimate *Orion* by basing one's estimate on a wrong premiss. The story begins in a Romantic version of classical landscape:

> Where the slow swirls were swallowed in the tide,
> Some stone-throws from the stream's mouth, there the sward
> Stretched thick and starry from the ridge's foot
> Down to the waves' wet limits, scattering off
> Across the red sand-level stunted tufts
> Of yellow beach-grass, whose brown panicles
> Wore garlands of blown foam. Amidst the slope
> Three sacred laurels drooped their dark-green boughs
> About a high-piled altar.

And as the classic story draws to conclusion,

> Out of their deep green caves the Nereids came
> Again to do him honour; shining limbs
> And shining bosoms, cleaving, waked the main
> All into sapphire ripples, each where crowned
> With yellow tresses streaming. Triton came
> And all his goodly company, with shells
> Pink-whorled and purple, many-formed, and made
> Tumultuous music.

The contemporary reader feels these cadences, this language and sentiment, as Tennysonian and so clearly derivative as to awaken no interest. But to its first readers, especially those in Canada, it was a demonstration that the high style as the Victorians understood it could be achieved by a Canadian. Even from outside there came recognition which to our contemporary uncorrected view seems extravagant. Matthew Arnold, on receipt of *Orion*, wrote a "very kind and helpful letter of three pages" and Oliver Wendell Holmes a long letter "of hearty commendation." Kipling, on receiving a copy of Francis Sherman's *Matins* (1896) from Roberts, wrote that he seemed to see in the giver "a man with a broom sweeping clear the tired literatures, and making way for the fresh, young, sincere work which you Canadian fellows are doing."

Roberts's sense of identity with the whole group of Canadian writers meant that all were heartened by the recognition he received. He was an indisputable Man of Letters. Everything that it lay within his powers to do for literature in Canada, either by intention or by happy accident, he accomplished. The affectionate encouragement he gave to his friends was an extension of the pride and pleasure he took in the literary efforts of his own family. Arthur Stringer recorded in 1904 the general gratitude and esteem: "No man better deserves to be designated as the father of his country's poetry than does Professor Roberts, maintaining, as his poetry does, those traditions of form and phrase-making toward the most perfected expression of man's emotions and aspirations, and yet naturally and harmoniously introducing that newer local note which we now pride ourselves on as distinctively Canadian . . . still again must we call Professor Charles G. D. Roberts *The Father of Canadian Poetry*." Though this and other tributes preserved in the pages of the Pomeroy biography of Roberts are all too reminiscent of Sarah Binks, we may give both Roberts and Stringer credit for complete sincerity. It was possible before 1914 to wave a flag or loudly praise a friend for loyal service to the nation without today's hesitant reservations.

Stringer is right in saying that Roberts combined tradition and innovation. His history of Canada, his excursions into travel guides, his translations of French-Canadian fiction and verse, his regional tales of adventure, his animal stories, all these amounted to a demonstration that Canadian history and landscape and the Canadian sensibility could be projected into literate forms which the English-speaking world was happy to read. The patriotic endeavour was explicit:

> And so I end my random song, returning
> To that which makes perchance its only worth,—
> The patriot warmth within my bosom burning
> Through all my wanderings o'er the curious earth.

Roberts's part in making Confederation a spiritual as well as a political act is not to be passed over. In 1886, he writes, apropos of the literary future of Nova Scotia, "We must forget to ask of a work whether it is Nova Scotian or British Columbian, of Ontario or of New Brunswick, until we have inquired if it be broadly and truly Canadian." He refuses to regard the inhabitants of Upper Canada from the old viewpoint of Howe who thought them "an inland population, frozen up nearly half the year."

Roberts early perceived that the terrain of Canada, as it conditions Canadian life, was the primary subject-matter for Canadian poetry. To extend the vocabulary of the English Romantics to cover the Canadian scene was not easy and many awkwardnesses of style even in his best poems are traceable to this inherent difficulty of adaptation.

> Black on the ridge, against that lonely flush,
> A cart, and stoop-necked oxen; ranged beside,
> Some barrels; and the day-worn harvest-folk,
> Here, emptying their baskets, jar the hush
> With hollow thunders.

Here the fusion of the two levels of diction is incomplete but the intention is patent.

By being recognized, by being prolific in a variety of forms, and by acquiring a public outside Canada, Roberts demonstrated that Canadian literature was a going concern. By working hard and writing voluminously he was an object lesson to all Canadian writers, too many of whom to this day are authors of one book, or specialists in unrealized potentiality. The bald fact that Roberts made his living as a writer becomes a mark to shoot at. His novel *Barbara Ladd* (1902) sold 80,000 copies in the United States and was published in England by Constable, to whom Meredith recommended it. That no one wishes to read *Barbara Ladd* now is in this context irrelevant.

Less and less, as time goes on, do we recover aesthetic satisfactions or imaginative stimulus from Roberts's poems. But his symbolic stature increases. His true role can now be appreciated and a genuine admiration can be achieved for the spirit in which he conceived and carried it out. He was quite literally Canada's first man of letters and the knighthood he received in 1935 was not an inappropriate honour. He had done something for the concept of the Dominion.

21. Crawford, Carman, and D. C. Scott

ROY DANIELLS

ISABELLA VALANCY CRAWFORD (hereinafter referred to as Crawford because Miss Crawford will not do, any more than Miss Bronte would do for the author of *Wuthering Heights*) was born in Dublin in 1850 and came with her family to Ontario as a small child. She was nine years older than Roberts and her life was briefer even than Lampman's (she died in Toronto in 1887) but she is part and parcel of the post-Confederation group we are considering. Indeed, the familiar pattern of indebtedness to English Romantics and Victorians, concern with Canadian landscape, knowledge of classical literature, possession by powerful but vague idealism—all this is immediately apparent to any reader. Her major work appeared in Toronto in 1884, *Old Spookses' Pass, Malcolm's Katie, and Other Poems*, and a *Collected Poems* in 1905.

What distinguishes Crawford from the others is, biographically, her consistent ill fortune which only her indomitable spirit saves from the aspect of tragedy, and, poetically, her endowment of inner, creative intensity, which none of the men can match. This peculiar gift is more difficult to identify or illustrate than the corresponding "dream" of Lampman; his uniqueness is concentrated in a few unflawed poems whereas Crawford's vision flashes unexpected, anywhere in her work. If one poem must be cited, it should probably be "Said the Canoe."

As night falls, two hunters lay their birch canoe on a soft bed of pine and cedar and cover it with fur robes:

> "Now she shall lay her polished sides
> As queens do rest, or dainty brides,
> Our slender lady of the tides!"

This slightly overwrought image, in which the simple element of a camp by a lakeside becomes elegant and erotic, sets the key of the ensuing description. The fire, called simply the "camp-soul," is lit, and animates in the most literal sense this dark site in the bush. Light clings to the trunks of surrounding trees,

> Like a shy child that would bedeck
> With its soft clasp a Brave's red neck,
> Yet sees the rough shield on his breast,
> The awful plumes shake on his crest,
> And, fearful, drops his timid face,
> Nor dares complete the sweet embrace.

Once more, the unexpectedness of the image, its intensity beyond the needs of the situation, stir the reader into a realization that "more is meant than meets the ear." How completely the normal Canadian locale is becoming a secret landscape of the sensibilities reveals itself as the description progresses:

> Into the hollow hearts of brakes—
> Yet warm from sides of does and stags
> Passed to the crisp, dark river-flags—
> Sinuous, red as copper-snakes,
> Sharp-headed serpents, made of light,
> Glided and hid themselves in night.

And from this loving interplay of bright and dark there develops a piercing image of death, unique and unforgettable:

> My masters twain the slaughtered deer
> Hung on forked boughs with thongs of leather:
> Bound were his stiff, slim feet together,
> His eyes like dead stars cold and drear.
> The wandering firelight drew near
> And laid its wide palm, red and anxious,
> On the sharp splendour of his branches,
> On the white foam grown hard and sere
>   On flank and shoulder.
> Death—hard as breast of granite boulder—
>   Under his lashes
> Peered thro' his eyes at his life's grey ashes.

The next stage in this extraordinary pastoral is a delicate, light song of love, the pursuit of flowers, stars, and jewels. Then back to death.

> They hung the slaughtered fish like swords
>   On saplings slender; like scimitars,
>   Bright, and ruddied from new-dead wars,
> Blazed in the light the scaly hordes.

Then round this simple Canadian scene, so suddenly disclosed as full of love and light and life, yet replete with images of the hunter and the hunted and the presence of death, night closes in.

> The darkness built its wigwam walls
>   Close round the camp, and at its curtain
>   Pressed shapes, thin, woven and uncertain
> As white locks of tall waterfalls.

It has been worth our while to look at this poem in detail because it succinctly and clearly embodies the elements of Crawford's originality as a poet. The Canadian landscape, the landscape of a pioneer country, is grasped objectively; yet it is at once and completely infused with intensely subjective realizations of love and struggle and death. James Reaney has remarked (in *Our Living Tradition*, III) that "Crawford sees the Canadian landscape as half-human—as potentially under human imaginative control" and that "she was one of the first to translate our still mysterious melancholy dominion into the releasing potentially apocalyptic dominion of poetry."

This capacity for an intense projection into her poems of her feelings about love and struggle and death separates her from the other post-Confederation poets; she is in the line of Emily Bronte rather than Wordsworth or Tennyson. It also differentiates her poems from the general run in her generation, in that they tend to invite two readings—a straightforward and an esoteric—with very different results. *Malcolm's Katie*, her longest and best known piece, is on the face of it a preposterously romantic love story on a Tennysonian model in which a wildly creaking plot finally delivers true love safe and triumphant. To add that there are some nice pictures of the struggles and satisfactions of clearing the land and building homes in the wilderness is not to add much. What makes this poem also "ancestral, important, haunting" is its ability to pull the raw landscape into an interior world of living passion and fulfilment. Katie's lover, Max, achieves this movement of absorption in a superb passage, central to the poem. It follows an objective description of felling and burning trees.

> And Max cared little for the blotted sun,
> And nothing for the startled, outshone stars;
> For love, once set within a lover's breast,
> Has its own sun, its own peculiar sky,
> All one great daffodil, on which do lie
> The sun, the moon, the stars, all seen at once
> And never setting, but all shining straight
> Into the faces of the trinity—
> The one beloved, the lover, and sweet love.

As we should expect, these images are counterpointed by others, of utter insensibility and the threat of death by water.

> O you shall slumber soundly, tho' the white,
> Wild waters pluck the crocus of your hair,
> And scaly spies stare with round, lightless eyes
> At your small face laid on my stony breast!

In contrast to Lampman, who like Wordsworth knew very well how to induce in himself a state of "dream" by wise passiveness in the presence of nature, Crawford achieves her fusion of inner and outer worlds as if by accident. "Old Spookses' Pass" begins as a shapeless tale of cattle-driving by an illiterate cowboy with a turn for moralizing, but before the poem ends we have experienced the authentic shudder of a haunted mountain defile, of a stampede in darkness and the crash of thunder. The landscape imposes its inner presence unmistakably, though the poem seems to have few formal merits. Elsewhere—notably in such pieces as "The Mother's Soul" and "Said the Skylark"—we find standard Victorian diction, versification, and sentiment emitting an unexpected intensity and sincerity of emotion and the occasion is always the same, an escape of the soul into a natural universe filled with love. The child's soul springs into the arms of its dead mother under the kind light of moon and stars. Or to the caged bird comes the cloud from the open sky,

> And murmuring to him said:
> "O Love, I come! O Love, I come to cheer thee!
> Love, to be near thee!"

It has been often remarked that Crawford is unusual among Canadian poets by her strong mythopoeic feeling for nature. Yet the passages where this faculty is most apparent may be read simply as her habitual infusion of external landscape with her passionate apprehension of love, of struggle, of death. Thus the dark Stag of Night is hunted by the Sun:

> His antlers fall; once more he spurns
>   The hoarse hounds of the day;
> His blood upon the crisp blue burns,
>   Reddens the mounting spray;
> His branches smite the wave—with cries
>   The loud winds pause and flag—
> He sinks in space—red glow the skies,
> The brown earth crimsons as he dies,
>   The strong and dusky stag.

Comparisons between Crawford and the great Victorians and parallels between her and other post-Confederation poets can be multiplied. She has the same range of subjects as, say, Longfellow, the spectrum that runs from an immediate sensuous knowledge of woods and fields to a scholarly and poetic feeling for Rome and Greece. Her poems bring us medieval lovers, the helot of Sparta, Margaton by the stream, classical shepherds, Vikings of the sagas, Indians of legend or real life, biblical figures, and poor exiles from Erin. Patriotism, faith and hope and charity, the round of the seasons, farewells and welcomes: the standard items of Victorian sensibility are present, down to dialect stories of simple countryfolk.

Ideal love is her dominant theme and best expressed obliquely, as we have seen, through some description of nature. Her overt love poems, like Lampman's, lack proper psychic distance, are too immediate, too revealing.

> A golden heart graved with my name alone . . .
> "A golden prophet of eternal truth,"
> I said, and kissed the roses of her palms,
> And then the shy, bright roses of her lips;
> And all the jealous jewels shone forgot
> In necklace and tiara as I clasped
> The gold heart and its shamrocks round her neck.
> My fair, pure soul! My noble Irish love!

Her true and characteristic inner intensity is better revealed in such a poem as "The Lily Bed":

> His cedar paddle, scented, red,
> He thrust down through the lily bed;
>
> Cloaked in a golden pause he lay
> Locked in the arms of the placid bay. . . .
>
> All lily-locked, all lily-locked,
> His light bark in the blossoms rocked.
>
> Their cool lips round the sharp prow sang,
> Their soft clasp to the frail sides sprang. . . .

There are many passages, especially in "Malcolm's Katie," where the dogged, hopeful spirit of pioneer settlers is expressed and this has some interest of an historical and sociological kind. But the conquest of our terrain in which she played her real part was the assimilation of Canadian landscape into the realm of the imagination, or, conversely, the infusion of passionate love, love strong enough to overcome death, into the substance of the simple Canadian scene. This is her triumph, her spiritual victory, her legacy to our uncertain age.

There are a few poets in every generation—and Isabella Crawford is one of them—whose personality shines through their achievement. She had a year less of life than Lampman and her brief history is one of unremitting courage, dignity, and hopefulness in the face of ever recurring calamity. She had all the virtues of romanticism—and predominantly a sense of the power and pre-eminence of the human spirit. From the typical weaknesses and disabilities of romanticism she seems to have been quite immune. She deserves to be remembered, and even longer for her life than for her work.

Bliss Carman (1861-1929) was a product of the same social and educational background as his cousin, Charles Roberts. Both fell under the influence of George Parkin, headmaster of Fredericton's collegiate school, in a classroom where "the *Aeneid* was often interrupted by the *Idylls of the King* or *The Blessed Damozel,* and William Morris or Arnold or Mr. Swinburne's latest lyric came to us between the lines of Horace." Like Roberts, Carman hesitated over embarking on an academic career and was finally unwilling to stay in New Brunswick. Like Roberts he was misdirected by his friends.

After 1886 most of his time was spent in New England, though his restless and indecisive spirit kept him on the move. During his brief career as a student at Harvard, he fell under the influence of Josiah Royce and, less definitely, Francis Child. From Royce's lectures on monism and on Spinoza Carman without doubt derived a large part of the philosophy of life which diffuses itself through his poems. While at Harvard he made the acquaintance of Richard Hovey; the "Vagabondia" which they collaborated in creating remains an essential and extensive part of Carman's poetic landscape. In 1897 he met Mary Perry King, the wife of a New England doctor, and to the Kings he owed a measure of security and stability, which lasted for the rest of his life. Beginning with *Low Tide on Grand Pré* (Toronto, 1893), a series of volumes appeared in the nineties and after the turn of the century in the United States and England, including the five volumes of the *Pipes of Pan* (1902–5).

The significant elements in Carman's poetry are not hard to single out. He is a poet of one mood, an accession of power and insight, in the presence of nature, which fills him with realizations of love and of death. What gives his poems their value, however, is less their ostensible or direct theme than their lyric cry, the cadence of which is the hallmark of his achievement.

> There is something in the autumn that is native to my blood—
> Touch of manner, hint of mood;
> And my heart is like a rhyme,
> With the yellow and the purple and the crimson keeping time.
>
> The scarlet of the maples can choke me like a cry
> Of bugles going by.
> And my lonely spirit thrills
> To see the frosty asters like a smoke upon the hills.
>
> There is something in October sets the gypsy blood astir;
> We must rise and follow her,
> When from every hill of flame
> She calls and calls each vagabond by name.

In this world of brightened colours, of enlarged and simplified symbols, of vague but saturating emotion, a continuous plangent rhythm becomes the principle of unity. Carman's landscapes dissolve as he leaves them. They have nothing of the large objectivity of landscape in Wordworth or Keats. They are the creations of an inner rhythm of the poet, like the scenes that Morris or Swinburne can create. It follows that what matters in Carman's world is not the actuality of love or death but the experience of nature which provides vague but powerful images for lost love or death impending. There is no dialectic, no progression of thought, no resolution or conclusion. There is the simple image of nature which evokes the single, undeviating lyric cry. All the poems of Carman that can be re-read with pleasure are of this kind.

It is paradoxical that Carman's deficiencies were the source of his uniqueness as a poet of the Canadian landscape. He had none of Roberts's practical and prompt character. He shows nothing of the instinct for perfection or the close scrutiny of natural scenes so characteristic of Lampman. Yet his very indiscipline and dishevelment kept him in more senses than one a vagabond, and elicited from him the cheeful songs of morning and the open road or the laments that came with darkening night and thoughts of lost years and lost loves. Vague and imprecise to his unfocusing gaze, nature nevertheless impressed him with her magnified and splendid image, her whispers of immortality, her spectral and haunting presence. "Low Tide on Grand Pré," probably the best known of his poems, is characteristically composed of the *disjecta membra* of romantic inner landscapes, and, although set among the same sea-marshes as delighted Roberts, has none of Roberts's ordered observation and precision of detail.

> So all desire and all regret,
>   And fear and memory, were naught;
> One to remember or forget
>   The keen delight our hands had caught;
> Morrow and yesterday were naught.
>
> The night has fallen and the tide ...
>   Now and again comes drifting home,
> Across these aching barrens wide,
>   A sigh like driven wind or foam:
> In grief the flood is bursting home.

In this world of nature's changing face there is sorrow but no tragedy, hope but no urgency, happiness but no resolved fulfilment. Even death is subdued to the beauty of the world:

> With looming willows and gray dusk
>   The open hillward road is pale,
> And the great stars are white and few
>   Above the lonely Ardise trail.
>
> And with no haste nor any fear,
>   We are as children going home
> Along the marshes where the wind
>   Sleeps in the cradle of the foam.

That Carman consciously committed himself to the expression of undirected aspiration and imprecise emotion is clear from his own pages:

> Right were you to follow fancy, give the vaguer instinct room
> In a heaven of clear color, where the spirit might assume
> All her elemental beauty, past the fact of sky or bloom.

> Paint the vision, not the view,—the touch that bids the sense good-bye,
> Lifting spirit at a bound beyond the frontiers of the eye,
> To superb unguessed dominions of the soul's credulity.

The nearest Carman comes to a statement of faith is in such poems as "The Winter Scene," where the splendour of Orion and Sirius reassures him that

> There are no hurts that beauty cannot ease,
> No ills that love cannot at last repair
> In the victorious progress of the soul.

It is only fair to add that such dilute Wordsworthian pantheism was in fashion at the time and that the Emersonian transcendentalism into which he plunged carried him into the same stream of sensibility.

How much Carman owes to the diffused transcendentalism derived from Harvard and his long residence in New England may be seen in his prose works. These are calculated to induce a gentle moral uplift and are filled with overtones of Emerson, Whitman, Lanier. The sweetness of tone, the purity of language, the total lack of urgency, all reveal Carman the man and the writer. At times it is as though we are listening to Ruskin at a distance which reduces each admonition to a whisper. He considers, for instance, the old dichotomy of the active and the contemplative life:

> In that great pageant of the seasons which passes by our door year after year, in the myriad changes of the wonderful spectacle of this greening and blanching orb, in all the processes of that apparition we call Nature, do I not see both strife and calm exemplified? . . . It may very well happen that circumstances have placed you in the forefront of the fight, where all your splendid life long you shall have never a minute to call your own, where you shall never once be able to rest or meditate or sun your spirit in a basking hour of leisure. Complain not. . . . It may be, on the other hand, that inactive doubt and timorous incertitude beset me, and that I am becoming stale for lack of use. Never mind, the hour will one day strike, and the lethargic torpor of temperamental incapacity will be broken up, and I shall be remoulded into something more trenchant and available for the forwarding of beneficent designs.

It was Carman's extreme misfortune to find himself in a society where neither poets nor moralists nor purveyors of culture were required to deal with any kind of dialectic or to master any body of knowledge. This relaxed intellectual environment, joined to a haphazard way of life and a congenital indecisiveness, robbed his poetry of substance and vitiated its form. Few of his poems take the reader, either intellectually or emotionally, from one point to another and the reader who tries the small trick of transposing stanzas will find it seldom matters much in what order they come. It is necessary to make these apparently disabling admissions if we are to come to the real nature of Carman's achievement. He was widely read on both sides of the Atlantic and remains among the "ancestral, important, haunting" voices of the elder Canadian world.

He is first of all, in spite of the diffuseness of his imagery, a definably regional poet. He belongs to the geographical continuum of the Canadian Maritime provinces and the New England states, where winter and spring signify emphatic change, where deciduous forests, indented hills, and quick rivers running into arms of the Atlantic combine to provide a familiar set of variations within the compass of a day's walk. This is the background of Vagabondia, the ideal country which is less of an affectation than it appears. Here, let us admit, is Carman's habitat, if not home. Here he lives and moves and has his being.

He provides, and this is the secret of his early popularity, a pattern of response to nature which almost any reader can at once in some degree experience. The vagueness itself is in this context a positive advantage. The canoe trip, the walk along a quiet woodland road, the night spent in some cabin under a great maple: these experiences bring physical health, mental calm, and spiritual insight, without definable proportions or progressions. To step into Carman's world is to move from ordinary self to best self in one easy motion. Simple expansive feelings about love and death come so inevitably out of the forms of nature that questions of subjective and objective never arise.

> What is it to remember?
> How white the moonlight poured into the room,
> That summer long ago!
> How still it was
> In that great solemn midnight of the North
> A century ago!
> And how I wakened trembling
> At soft love-whispers warm against my cheek,
> And laughed it was no dream?
> Then far away
> The troubled, refluent murmur of the sea,
> A sigh within a dream!

But Carman, like other good popular poets, not only provides a form for what everyone is willing to feel; he gives this feeling what seems, if only for a moment, to be its ultimate expression.

> Lord of my heart's elation,
> Spirit of things unseen,
> Be thou my aspiration
> Consuming and serene!
>
> Bear up, bear out, bear onward
> This mortal soul alone,
> To selfhood or oblivion,
> Incredibly thine own,—

> As the foamheads are loosened
> And blown along the sea,
> Or sink and merge forever
> In that which bids them be.

Like Swinburne, Carman is up to a point easy to parody and even given to self-parody, but, again like Swinburne, he rises to an authentic and unmistakably personal note in a few of the best of his poems. In these there is a splendid and genuine largeness of utterance sustained by some simple, gorgeous, and quite adequate image.

> All night long my cabin roof resounded
> With the mighty murmur of the rain;
> All night long I heard the silver cohorts
> Tramping down the valley to the plain.

Or this:

> Come, for the night is cold,
>   The ghostly moonlight fills
> Hollow and rift and fold
>   Of the eerie Ardise hills!
> The windows of my room
>   Are dark with bitter frost,
> The stillness aches with doom
>   Of something loved and lost.

To be shown that an individual and unforced response to nature brings health, peace of mind, and spiritual insight was of real benefit to the Canadian reader of Carman's generation. Not only was it being established that poetry could be written in Canada; it was also being demonstrated that the simple surrounding landscape, if poetically apprehended, could provide "all ye need to know." Such a sufficiency within the visible natural world could only be plausible in a new country where the terrain carried few memories or associations, where no standing stones witnessed to the past, where no gods inhabited the mountains. Here the poet's eye could preserve an innocence and immediacy impossible to any other Canadian generation. It was still feasible to avert one's gaze from the visible evidences of industrialism; the acceleration of technology which has proved to be the distinguishing mark of the twentieth century was not yet evident. Mass media, global involvement, mechanized culture: all these were outside Carman's range. But he perfectly expressed the latent feelings of his contemporaries and satisfied their need for a simple, local, accessible, native ethos. That his popularity has steeply declined does not detract from his significance. He is read in the schools where the pure in heart may still be found, and there are few Canadians who would willingly let die the few score lines of verse in which Carman voices our instinctive and traditional response to the Canadian seasons.

> Now is the time of year
> When all the flutes begin,—
> The redwing bold and clear,
> The rainbird far and thin. . . .
>
> How every voice alive
> By rocky wood and stream
> Is lifted to revive
> The ecstasy, the dream. . . .

The most obvious characteristic of Duncan Campbell Scott (1862–1947) is that neither as man nor as poet is he so immediately apprehensible as the other members of his group. A tendency towards shyness and withdrawal and an innate intellectual austerity combined to inhibit the growth of any personal legend, and the technique of his verse, more astringent and more uncertain than that of his contemporaries, delayed recognition of his achievement. He was a friend of Lampman, who indeed first encouraged him to write, and he was well enough known to be included in Lighthall's *Songs of the Great Dominion* (1889), and yet to this day anyone commenting on Canadian poetry, regardless of how he permutes the names of the four men under discussion, will invariably put the name of Scott last on the list. His first collection, *The Magic House and Other Poems*, was published in 1893, when he was thirty, and Carman's first collection also appeared. Further volumes came out in 1898, 1905, 1906, 1916, 1921, 1935 reflecting a long span of writing, and there were collections in 1926 and 1951.

It is useful to think of Scott against the same general background as Lampman's. Both were civil servants in Ottawa and Scott's long and beautifully appreciative preface to the volume of Lampman's collected poems (1900) reveals how similar their responses were to the natural and intellectual climates in which they lived. It is also useful to remember the large resemblances between Scott and the two New Brunswick poets. All were concerned with Romantic subjects, attitudes, and techniques. Scott's address to "the November pansy" is the epitome of his Romantic aspiration.

> And far above this tragic world of ours
>   There is a world of a diviner fashion;
>   A mystic world, a world of dreams and passion
> That each aspiring thing creates and dowers
>   With its own light;
> Where even the frail spirits of trees and flowers
>   Pause, and reach out, and pass from height to height.
>
> Here will we claim for thee another fief,
>   An upland where a glamour haunts the meadows,
>   Snow peaks arise enrobed in rosy shadows,
> Fairer the under slopes with vine and sheaf
>   And shimmering lea;
> The paradise of a simple old belief,
>   That flourished in the Islands of the Sea.

This world of dreams and passions accounts for the poet's vague personal sadness, his search for an "inappellable" secret, his excursions into fantasy as a means of objectifying dream, and the irresolution of his best and best-known poems of the wilderness.

Scott shares with the others a moralizing tendency associated with an evolutionary view of life and an unfocused Christian outlook. The imprecision of his views is in part the result of having nothing specific to oppose. Emerson, Thoreau, Byron, Shelley, and Arnold were all able in their different ways to identify the enemy, but Scott could feel only the irremediable hardship of the northern wilderness, the unavoidable increase of urban industrialism, and the mysterious sorrow of individual lives. Very occasionally, as in his poem "The Harvest," he has a vision of social revolution but it is contradictory and obscure:

> Then when they see them—
> The miles of the harvest
> White in the sunshine,
> Rushing and stumbling,
> With the mighty and clamorous
> Cry of the people
> Starved from creation,
> Hurl themselves onward,
> Deep in the wheat-fields,
> Weeping like children,
> After ages and ages,
> Back at the breasts
> Of their mother the earth.

Even more tenuous is his residual Christian aspiration:

> Shall we not search the heart of God and find
>   That law empearled,
> Until all things that are in matter and mind
>   Throb with the secret that began the world?

It is not surprising that neither a transcendental realization of life nor a tragic view of man's fate is possible in the context of this vague idealism, and certainly Scott fails to move towards either of these poles. He stays with the central perception that nature is on the whole good, if not always beneficent, and he holds to the hope that man's future is one of ceaseless evolution towards better things, however repellent some stages of the journey may prove to be.

In the midst of this general resemblance to his fellow poets, Scott nevertheless stands out quite distinctly, not only by the slower growth of critical recognition but by the greater variety in his tone and technique, which, because it produced a less clear image of the poet for the reader, was itself a contributing cause of delayed recognition. His reading of late Victorians induced in him a current of fantasy which remained intermittent and unsatisfying to the end. Even the often quoted "Piper of Arll" is lacking the compulsion of true magic and such poems as "The Music House" and "In the House of Dreams" reveal only the fascination exercised upon a Canadian mind by the last enchantments of the age of Tennyson. If this predilection of Scott's for "mementoes of destroyed desire" had resulted only in a succession of weak poems, it would be of little account. There was another and more serious effect, however. His diction, phrasing, and cadence remained uncertain and unstable to the end. In a poem of close observation entitled "Leaves," we pass from the firmness of "berries in dense clusters of dark coral / Which the pine grosbeaks share" to the inanity of, "while we muse, there falls a fairy jar / That subtly tells us where we really are."

Unlike Carman and Lampman, Scott had little natural gift for melody; he needed exemplars and models which could have taught him to "build the lofty rhyme" and these he never found. The result is that a number of his longer poems reveal in the clearest way a gap between personal sincerity and poetic sincerity. In this category are memorial poems to Edmund Morris and William Maclennan, "The Dame Regnant," "Spring on Mattagami," and a long set of variations on a passage from Henry Vaughan. Of these it is perhaps "Spring on Mattagami" that reveals most clearly the problem of relating a vaguely apprehended European Romanticism to a deeply felt experience of the Canadian landscape. This poem begins in the northern wilderness:

> Through the lake furrow between the gloom and bright'ning
> Firm runs our long canoe with a whistling rush,
> While Potàn the wise and the cunning Silver Lightning
> Break with their slender blades the long clear hush.

Night falls on the camp in the forest and the poet dreams of Venice and the ideal woman he loved and lost there.

> Once when the tide came straining from the Lido,
> In a sea of flame our gondola flickered like a sword,
> Venice lay abroad builded like beauty's credo,
> Smouldering like a gorget on the breast of the Lord.

Were this pale, proud woman with him in the pure, elemental world of the northern forest, she would be his, "for ever and for ever." But, "vain is the dream" and the reason is not hard to discover: nothing will bring these two worlds together either in real life or in any realm of the imagination to which Scott has access. His final stanza moves towards an attempted resolution in the ultimate depths of nature but a resolution without context of any kind.

> Venus sinks first lost in ruby splendour,
> Stars like wood-daffodils grow golden in the night,
> Far, far above, in a space entranced and tender,
> Floats the growing moon pale with virgin light.

> Vaster than the world or life or death my trust is
> Based in the unseen and towering far above;
> Hold me, O Law, that deeper lies than Justice,
> Guide me, O Light, that stronger burns than Love.

It seems probable that Scott never resolved or passed beyond these problems of style and of subject-matter. But he had a capacity for edging his way out of them, from time to time, into areas controlled by a simpler form of sensibility. To this ability of his we owe the small group of poems on which his reputation ultimately rests. The best of these is probably "Night-Hymns on Lake Nipigon."

We should remind ourselves, before considering this poem, how deeply Scott was committed by profession and by temperament to the Canadian northern wilderness. He was head of the Department of Indian Affairs when he retired in 1932, after more than fifty years of service in the Department. His concern with Indians as wards of the Canadian government was sincere and deep; within the somewhat narrow limits set by official policy he laboured unceasingly for them. All the poems for which he is likely to be remembered are concerned with the northern wilderness, Canada's Indian territory.

The poem opens in an atmosphere of impending gloom and tempest:

> Here in the midnight, where the dark mainland and island
> Shadows mingle in shadow deeper, profounder,
> Sing we the hymns of the churches, while the dead water
>   Whispers before us.
>
> Thunder is travelling slow on the path of the lightning;
> One after one the stars and the beaming planets
> Look serene in the lake from the edge of the storm-cloud,
>   Then have they vanished.
>
> While our canoe, that floats dumb in the bursting thunder,
> Gathers her voice in the quiet and thrills and whispers,
> Presses her prow in the star-gleam, and all her ripple
>   Lapses in blackness.

Then, prepared for by the classical cadence of these unrhymed stanzas, the Christian theme is introduced, for once perfectly harmonized to the wild Canadian landscape through the irony and pathos of the Adeste Fideles chanted by those who have no future:

> Sing we the sacred ancient hymns of the churches,
> Chanted first in old-world nooks of the desert,
> While in the wild, pellucid Nipigon reaches
>   Hunted the savage.
>
> Now have the ages met in the Northern midnight,
> And on the lonely, loon-haunted Nipigon reaches
> Rises the hymn of triumph and courage and comfort,
>   Adeste Fideles.

> Tones that were fashioned when the faith brooded in darkness,
> Joined with sonorous vowels in the noble Latin,
> Now are married with the long-drawn Ojibwa,
>   Uncouth and mournful.

Nowhere do we see more clearly the dominant role which wild nature plays in Scott's imagination and what might be called its power of absorption. The irony of his Indians, whose way of life is doomed, being nevertheless in some sense joyful and triumphant—this irony is not expanded. Nor is the resolution of conflicting emotions ever made explicit. Instead we have the storm itself, by its own return to peace and calm, providing a conclusion. This envelopment of the subject by the surrounding scene is a recurring and deeply significant feature of Scott's best works. Nowhere do we see it more beautifully handled than in this poem.

> Soft with the silver drip of the regular paddles
> Falling rhythm, timed with the liquid, plangent
> Sounds from the blades where the whirlpools break and are carried
>   Down into darkness;
>
> Each long cadence, flying like a dove from her shelter
> Deep in the shadow, wheels for a throbbing moment,
> Poises in utterance, returning in circles of silver
>   To nest in the silence.
>
> All wild nature stirs with the infinite, tender
> Plaint of a bygone age whose soul is eternal,
> Bound in the lonely phrases that thrill and falter
>   Back into quiet.
>
> Back they falter as the deep storm overtakes them,
> Whelms them in splendid hollows of booming thunder,
> Wraps them in rain, that, sweeping, breaks and onrushes
>   Ringing like cymbals.

In most of Scott's wilderness pieces violence of emotion matches the rigour of the land itself. Besides "Night-Hymns" the principal poems in this group are "On the Way to the Mission," "The Forsaken," "The Half-Breed Girl," and "Powassan's Drum." Two other poems, "At the Cedars" and "Night Burial in the Forest," show how easily poems dealing with trappers or lumberjacks associate with the specifically Indian or Métis pieces. It should be added that these themes and settings reappear in the best of Scott's short stories.

It is easy to regard these poems as studies of life in the wilds or manifestations of their author's deep sympathy with the lot of the northern Indians. This is to miss their ultimate meaning, which is the resolution of violence either into the calm of nature or into nature's own impersonal fury of stormy wind and rushing water. If the half-breed girl seems an exception, it is because the adulteration of her true heritage of blood has made her unable to hear when "A voice calls from the rapids, / Deep, careless and free."

We must concede that only nature, and preferably nature in her most primitive and untamed aspect, is capable of releasing Scott's powers as a poet, by providing him with some counterpart or correlative to his own emotions. As we have shown, this correlation is not argued out nor is the transition from human terror or violence to the peace or power of nature logically achieved. Whereas Lampman takes us easily from urban frustration to rural release, Scott transports us to his wild northland, without centre or circumference, by the compulsion of an inner necessity. Unlike those English Romantics who moved into the wilder hills along avenues of pastoral tradition or cheerful pantheism, Scott has trouble in interpenetrating nature with human life. At one moment he is the educated, non-participating observer of a scene of violence or distress; the next instant he has been carried into a commitment to an absolute in nature. Even in the occasional poem such as "The Height of Land" where he appears to employ some apparatus of argument, the conclusion is a movement into the mystery of nature and of life. We feel

> The long light flow, the long wind pause, the deep
> Influx of spirit, of which no man may tell
> The Secret. . . .

This perception, deep and vague, corresponds so well to the permanent needs and possibilities of the Canadian mind that Scott is everywhere felt to belong among the little group of ancestral voices, indispensable to our tradition, haunting to the imagination. In this context the fact that his patriotic poems appear stilted, his love poems conventional, and his odes to Debussy and Keats formless is totally unimportant. And the careful reader who moves among even his least inspired pages will find the occasional line or stanza open like a window upon the natural world of Scott's Ontario. He will see "The wan grey under light of the willow leaves" or watch where "Pallid saffron glows the broken stubble."

For this revelation of Canada's wildness and beauty, of peacefulness or rushing fury in nature as counterparts to our own feelings, Scott will deserve the gratitude of succeeding generations of readers, however urbanized or mechanized their lives may become.

22. Minor Poets
1880-1920

ROY DANIELLS

AMONG MINOR POETS of the period 1880–1920 a half-dozen call for individual attention. William Henry Drummond (1854–1907) was born in Ireland and came to Canada as a small boy. At the age of thirty he achieved a medical degree and, after several years as a country doctor, established a practice in Montreal. Cheerful and kindly, a devotee of winter sports, a good after-dinner speaker, he was everywhere popular. His poems of *habitant* life, the first volume of which in 1897 contained a sympathetic introduction by Louis Fréchette, and which appeared also in four other volumes between 1898 and 1907, were widely read and have never lost their appeal. The picture of *habitant* life is superficial, comedy and pathos are precariously related, the presentation of "un pauvre illettré" (in Fréchette's phrase) as a national type is itself hazardous. But Drummond's transparent goodwill and the sincerity of his regard for his characters serve to overcome his limitations. Behind the clown's mask and the broken English interlarded with French we cannot fail to see "un personnage bon, doux, aimable, honnête, intelligent et droit, l'esprit en éveil, le cœur plein d'une poésie native stimulant son patriotisme, jetant un rayon lumineux dans son modeste intérieur, berçant ses heures rêveuses de souvenirs lointains et mélancoliques." So few Canadian poets induce their characters and readers to join in cheerful and kindly laughter that Drummond has the advantage of being almost unique. Unique also is the illusion he gives of an easy and amiable interchange between the two cultures, French- and English-speaking. The complexities of the actual situation have proved less tractable.

The life of Wilfred Campbell (1861?–1918) conforms fairly well to the standard biographical pattern for Canadian poets of his generation. His father, a clergyman, saw that he was given a classical education. He took holy orders but school teaching and preaching were succeeded by a literary career sustained by grudging appointments in the civil service. He lived for five years in the United States, was influenced by transcendentalism, made repeated visits to Britain, became an Imperialist. Possessing three English great-grandfathers, he regarded himself as a Scottish clansman; he was important as an index to Canadian thought and taste; he will be remembered for half-a-dozen poems, all written early and all concerned with the Canadian landscape. There were volumes published in 1889, 1893, 1899, collections in 1905 and 1923, war poems during the First World War.

His theory of composition was of the simplest. "Poetry is first and last a high emotion"; "the highest class of poetry . . . is that dealing with the eternal tragedy of life in the universe." The reader of poetry "needs no subtle insight into the intricacies of language and the laws of prosody." Campbell read and admired many poets—Homer and Virgil; Shakespeare, Gray, Scott, Byron, Coleridge, Tennyson, Thomas Campbell, Hood, Swinburne; among Americans, Emerson, Poe, Longfellow, Bryant, Whittier. He was atypical in not being attracted to Wordsworth and Arnold. His relations with other Canadian poets were exiguous. He collaborated with Scott and Lampman in the famous "Mermaid Inn" newspaper column but his violent independence of spirit made him a difficult associate.

Campbell's feeling for poetic style was never reliable. There is something wilful about his deliberate infelicity of phrase, insensitive rhythm, obliviousness to requirements of structure and delight in clichés. He attempted a defence of his practice: "The uneven poem may be as necessary to the line or stanza of beauty therein as is the wood or heaven to the flower or star." Or, more emphatically,

> 'Tis the dream, and not the deed
> That doth, eternal, endure;
> The spirit, and not the form,
> That makes earth's literature.

His variant of "true British idealism" enabled him to combine a devotion to tradition with an Emersonian self-reliance, a consciously Scottish independence, and Canadian forthrightness of expression. How well he caught public sentiment at the turn of the century may be judged from the five hundred copies of his *Collected Poems* ordered by Andrew Carnegie for the Carnegie libraries, and from the honorary degree he received in 1906 at Aberdeen University, at which time he was presented to Their Majesties. Regarding himself as a citizen of "vaster Britain," he endeavoured to be a poet of the people in the service of the highest national ideals. In the years preceding his death on January 1, 1918, he threw himself energetically into the Canadian war effort.

It is not for his "Sagas of Vaster Britain" or for his plays in Romantic Shakespearean manner that Campbell will be remembered. Rather for "An

August Reverie," where the common ground that he shared with Lampman is evident, or for "How One Winter Came in the Lake Region":

> That night I felt the winter in my veins,
> A joyous tremor of the icy glow;
> And woke to hear the north's wild vibrant strains,
> While far and wide, by withered woods and plains,
> Fast fell the driving snow.

The Bruce Peninsula, lying between Lake Huron and the Georgian Bay, had in the event an intimate claim on Wilfred Campbell that no vaster region, even among regions of the mind, could match.

Robert Service (1874–1958) was born in England and came to Canada at the age of twenty. His wanderings on the West Coast took him up to the Yukon where he worked for eight years in Whitehorse and Dawson, as an employee of the Bank of Commerce. Though the peak of the gold rush was past, the independent miner was still predominant and Service found ready to hand the materials for such pieces as "The Law of the Yukon," "The Shooting of Dan McGrew," and "The Cremation of Sam McGee." Service's ballads, full of Kipling's earlier devices and thick with melodramatic pathos and humour, were immediately and enormously successful. From 1907 with *Songs of a Sourdough* volumes continued. Poems such as those mentioned gave the illusion of realism, they were exotic in their locale, and their driving rhythms and clanging rhymes invited public recitation. These verses, for which he himself claimed little in the way of poetic merit, are nevertheless an ineradicable part of Canadian tradition and in their stereotype they keep the image of the frozen north, the trail of '98, the half-mythical mining towns. Their hallmark is an enormous expansiveness which still appeals because it has a certain real counterpart in Canadian life of the upper latitudes:

> The strong life that never knows harness;
> The wilds where the caribou call;
> The freshness, the freedom, the farness—
> O God! how I'm stuck on it all.

No case can be made for Service as a poet, yet no history of Canadian letters could fail to find him a place. Like the unknown miner in the ballad of Dan McGrew, he achieves effects outside the ordinary canons of performance:

> The rag-time kid was having a drink; there was no one else on the stool,
> So the stranger stumbles across the room, and flops down there like a fool
> In a buckskin shirt that was glazed with dirt he sat, and I saw him sway;
> Then he clutched the keys with his talon hands—my God! but that man
> could play.

Marjorie Pickthall (1883-1922) came from England to Toronto as a child. She lived in England again from 1913 to 1920, engaging in the war effort, and returned to the far West of Canada, to die in Vancouver. Her first volume was published in 1913, with others in 1915, 1916, 1922 and 1925 and a *Complete Poems* in 1925. She was the antithesis of Campbell and Service in that she worked within narrow limits with great technical proficiency and a very delicate sensibility. While some of her poems deal with Canadian subjects, they are Pre-Raphaelite in tone and overcast with Celtic twilight. Every subject becomes small and delicate; every mood is suffused with love and weariness in the presence of beauty. Père Lalemant in the remote wilderness dreams of the missions founded by his order,

> There where we built St. Ignace for our needs,
> Shaped the rough roof tree, turned the first sweet sod,
> St. Ignace and St. Louis, little beads
> On the rosary of God.

The literary historian, moving from the poets born twenty years earlier to consider Marjorie Pickthall, will emphasize, with regret, the loss of momentum, weakening of grasp, reduction of resonance. She is at too many removes from the original sources of strength. If we think of her, however, as a disciple of Christina Rossetti, it is possible, as in the poem "Resurgam," to find a true poignancy behind her controlled phrasing:

> I shall say, Lord, "We will laugh again to-morrow,
> Now we'll be still a little, friend with friend.
> Death was the gate and the long way was sorrow.
> Love is the end."

The reputation of Pauline Johnson (1862-1913) is at once surprising and significant. Her collected poems, *Flint and Feather* (1912), have been in demand for fifty years. "The Song My Paddle Sings" every schoolchild knows. She was the daughter of an Indian chief and born on the Six Nations Indian Reserve; her mother was an Englishwoman. Her first public reading in Toronto in 1892 was followed, over a period of sixteen years, by hundreds of recitals of her poems in Canada, England, and the United States. She was consciously Indian in her outlook. "My aim, my joy, my pride is to sing the glories of my own people." Her concern with Indian history and legend extended to the ultimate West and a memorial in Stanley Park marks her grave. Such biographical and symbolic elements make up the substance of her reputation. It is somehow fitting that part of her small estate was used towards the purchase of a machine gun which was named after her and "did great service" on the Western front.

What value her poems will have when the memory of her vigorous personality has faded it is difficult to say. In "The Corn Husker" and one or two other descriptive lyrics there appears the pathos of Indian wrongs or the intimacy between Indian life and western landscape. But it is not by such residual pieces that her popularity has over half a century been maintained. It is rather that Pauline Johnson is still what she was at the very beginning, a symbol which satisfies a felt need. Like Service and Campbell, she associates a broadly Romantic view of life with the elements of the vast natural landscape. This need to realize topography in terms of life is, of course, the fundamental fact of Canadian experience.

There is more, however, than Canadian sensibility. Theodore Watts-Dunton, reviewing Lighthall's *Songs of the Great Dominion* in 1889 for the London *Athenaeum,* quoted Pauline Johnson's lyric "In the Shadows," which he regarded as "a new note—the note of the Red Man's Canada." The poem haunted him. He was delighted to find that its author belonged to the Mohawks of Brantford, "that splendid race to whose unswerving loyalty during two centuries not only Canada, but the entire British Empire owes a debt that can never be repaid." Neither "In the Shadows" nor "At the Ferry," her only other contribution to Lighthall's volume, will strike the modern reader as more than pleasant renderings of standard Romantic landscape,

> When the river mists are rising,
> All the foliage baptizing
> With their spray;
> There the sun gleams far and faintly,
> With a shadow soft and saintly
> In its ray.

Pauline Johnson's reputation would appear to be securely based, not on her poetry as such but on the need, felt in England at the turn of the century, for fresh contact with primitive and unspoiled life, and on the continuing secret desire of all Canadians to reach back into an innocent and heroic world of wild woods and waters before the white man came and the guilt of conquests, whether French or English, was incurred.

Francis Sherman (1871–1926) brought out four books of verse at the turn of the century and aptly illustrates the plight of the Canadian poet at that time. Like Marjorie Pickthall, he was induced by the taste of his generation to follow masters and models too far removed from the primal source of Romanticism, and he was at the same time too early for post-war developments in poetry to be of any use. His feeling for landscape and his sense of personal tragedy in life are embodied in the verse conventions of William Morris; the metrical facility is there but not Morris's power to suffuse a landscape, and all these poems of love and death in a context of natural beauty lead simply to the regret that so admirable a man should have been so badly supplied with the tools of the poetic craft. On the rare occasions that he fuses his excellent sense of verse rhythm with the New Brunswick landscape and his own inner emotional struggle, we get a sense of what he might have become had he lived in another poetic environment:

> And yet, should I go down beside the swollen river
> Where the vagrant timber hurries to the wide untrammelled sea,
> With the mind and the will to cross the new-born waters
> And to let the yellow hillside share its peace with me,
>
> —I know, then, that surely would come the old spring-fever
> And touch my sluggish blood with its old eternal fire;
> Till for me, too, the love of peace were over and forgotten,
> And the freedom of the logs had become my soul's desire.

Other minor poets between 1880 and 1920 may be usefully considered as a chorus to the tragi-comedy of Canadian cultural decline, a chorus which "did nothing in particular and did it very well." It is convenient to think of two roughly equal periods: 1871–1896, 1896–1921. During the first of these a community of aims among the poets is easy to discover. They work within the conventions of the English poetic tradition; if they borrow ideas or devices from Emerson or Longfellow it is because these do not deflect them from the path of discipleship to the great Romantics and Victorians. The high colonialism of the Golden Age does not call for any revolt from tradition or for obtrusive originality. A. W. Eaton (1849–1937) in one of his many volumes, apostrophizes L'Isle Ste. Croix,

> Sing on, wild sea, your sad refrain
> For all the gallant sons of France,
> Whose songs and sufferings enhance
> The romance of the western main.
>
> Sing requiem to these tangled woods,
> With ruined forts and hidden graves;
> Your mournful music history craves
> For many of her noblest moods.

If this reminds the reader of *In Memoriam,* we may be certain it was intended to.

It follows from the self-consciousness of high colonial culture that we should expect certain models to be held in general high regard. And such is the case. The *Canadian Monthly*, in three articles on Matthew Arnold, numerous reviews and several discussions of poetry as an art, rehearses the desiderata of good poetry. LeSueur, for example, praises Arnold as a worthy son of Thomas Arnold, having the same honesty, open-heartedness, amiability, firmness, and sagacity, and, in addition, a delicate sensibility and intellectual alertness all his own. "Kensington Gardens" shows that, without pretentions to Wordsworth's mystical insight, Arnold can faithfully render the beauties of nature in everyday language, adding an "earnestness of aspiration which seems to give strength to the will." He has a breadth and calmness of manner which distinguishes the great minds of Greek antiquity; he speaks in "noble accents"; "his influence as a writer tends constantly to the refining of our taste and the ennobling of our moral sense."

In one form or another, all the critics agree with LeSueur. Some make the moral function of ideal poetry more specifically Christian—there is a sharp rejection (1878) of Arnold's scepticism. Some lay more stress on the decorum of verse: "a graceful command of expression and of literary form is spreading among a wide circle" or, more naively,

> Only the same old thoughts
> Clothed with a sweeter sound:
> And lo! a poet's brow
> With laurel leaves is crowned.

With such criteria at hand, there is appreciative reading of the American poets. Longfellow is praised for "his clearness of thought and expression," for "earnest moral purpose," for the humanity which makes him popular.

If to the above considerations we add the predominance, already discussed, of the Canadian terrain as a subject for Canadian poetry the consistency of performance among the minor poets will cause no surprise. What is surprising, and agreeably so, is the frequency with which, in this chorus to the historical drama of high colonialism, the slight poetic mask fails to conceal an honest and charming personality behind it. The inextinguishable "Fidelis" combines a real feeling for the Canadian scene and its seasons with idealist aspiration and Christian hope in dozens of poems for the periodicals. Helena Coleman (1860–1953) contributed many poems of precise form and clear sentiment. George Frederick Cameron (1854–1885) embodied his enthusiasms for political freedom in verses with subjects ranging from Cuba to Ireland and Russia. Mrs. Sarah Anne Curzon (1833–1898) came to Canada in 1862. She had contributed in England to *The Leisure Hour*. She became a journalist and identified herself with the cause of women's suffrage. In 1887 she published *Laura Secord, the Heroine of 1812: A Drama, and Other Poems*. Sir James Edgar (1841–1899), Speaker of the House of Commons, is remembered for "The Canadian Song Sparrow." Mrs. J. F. Harrison (1859–1935), better known as "Seranus," contributed to periodicals, edited an anthology of Canadian poetry in 1887, and published collections of her own, of which the best known is *Pine, Rose and Fleur-de-lis* (1891). Nicholas Flood Davin (1843–1901), came to Canada in 1872 and achieved a career as a lawyer, journalist, and politician. His Irish eloquence flowers in "Eos—an Epic of the Dawn" where Canada is seen to possess "large promise of the mightier day." Edward Hartley Dewart (1828–1903) is remembered not only for his own poems but also as editor of *Selections from Canadian Poets* (1864). His introductory remarks are sometimes applicable to the whole history of Canadian poetry: "Many writers of undoubted genius have been deficient in that thorough literary culture essential to high artistic excellence. But in many instances this want of finish may be traced to want of application, resulting from a low estimate of poetry as an art." Lieutenant-Colonel John Hunter-Duvar (1830–1899) belongs to an older tradition than other post-Confederation poets. Two verse dramas were followed by *Annals of the Court of Oberon* (1895); here romantic fancy and exact observation are embodied in crisp, confident stanzas. John E. Logan (1852–1915) wrote some vigorous descriptions of the Northwest under the pseudonym "Barry Dane" and was sufficiently popular to get liberal representation in *Songs of the Great Dominion*. John McCrae (1872–1918), a medical officer with Canadian forces in the First World War, wrote the best known of all Canadian poems, "In Flanders Fields." It is a restrained, formal, flawless expression of Canadian feeling in 1915. Thomas O'Hagan (1855–1939) is the perfect exemplar of minor poetry of the Golden Age. *In Dreamland and Other Poems* was reviewed (1893) as a "charming volume of poems, each one a tacit protest against worldliness." Theodore Harding Rand (1835–1900) edited *A Treasury of Canadian Verse* (1900); as a poet he is chiefly memorable for his association with the New Brunswick scene; the first edition of *At Minas Basin* appeared in 1897. John Reade (1837–1919) is mainly remembered as a journalist but *The Prophecy of Merlin and Other Poems* (1870) brought him a considerable reputation, Lighthall regarding him as "one of the chief figures in Canadian literature, and probably the sweetest poet," "the *doyen* of English poetic literature in the Province of Quebec." Theodore Goodridge Roberts (1877–1953), a younger brother of Charles G. D. Roberts, shows considerable formal skill in such a poem as "The Blue Heron," where exact description of the details of a natural scene fixes its mood. His themes are contained within a romantic view of life and he records with fidelity the visual effect of exotic places. Carroll Ryan (1839–1910), who is best thought of as a journalist, a Christian Zionist, and a crusader against injustice, published several volumes of poetry, which are marginal to his active public life. Marginal also to a devoted life are the poems of Frederick George Scott (1861–1944). They reflect his love of the Laurentian landscape and the faith and courage which won him wide regard during his service as an army chaplain in the First World War. John Talon-Lesperance (1838–1891) writes with conviction of love and loss, of Canada and its changing seasons; he was "known for his strongly individual style, his learning and his kindliness, all over the

Dominion." Agnes Ethelwyn Wetherald (1857–1940) was a prolific writer whose feeling for Nature is thoroughly representative of the age of Lampman:

> When spring unbound comes o'er us like a flood
>   My spirit slips its bars,
> And thrills to see the trees break into bud
>   As skies break into stars. . . .
>
> And feels its sordid work, its empty plan,
>   Its failures and its stains
> Dissolved in blossom dew, and washed away
>   In delicate spring rains.

By 1920 the chorus of minor Canadian poets was seriously diminished and the survivors of the group under discussion, together with Roberts, Carman, and Scott, were of an average age of well over fifty. In a wider and looser Canadian community new lines of thought, sceptical, divergent, and centrifugal were now appearing; the centralizing impulse of Confederation had spent its force.

23. Philosophical Literature
to 1910

JOHN A. IRVING, ADAPTED BY A. H. JOHNSON*

THE LITERATURE OF PHILOSOPHY frequently has been produced by men whose interests, training, and professional appointments were not confined to philosophy. In some cases, the amount of their philosophical writing was not great. However, these men helped to establish an environment in which later generations of professional philosophers could flourish. This was very evident in the early period of Canadian philosophical literature. A prime example is provided by Thomas McCulloch who came from the old Scotland to the new and exerted a profound influence on the intellectual and social life of Nova Scotia.

An understanding of McCulloch's achievement requires some knowledge of his career as a religious and educational leader.† He was born in 1776 at Fereneze in the parish of Neilston, Renfrewshire, Scotland. Owing to his extreme reticence, nothing is known of his early life and education in his native parish school. At the University of Glasgow, where he studied both Arts and Medicine, he was such an excellent student of Oriental languages that, at the age of twenty, he was conducting a private tutorial class in Hebrew. Although he seems to have completed the course requirements, he never proceeded to the degree of Doctor of Medicine.

---

*Professor Irving was unfortunately seriously ill while this book was in progress and Professor Johnson kindly undertook to prepare a revision of writing previously published by Professor Irving on this subject. In this chapter he has used material in *The Stepsure Letters* (edited by Malcolm Ross, the New Canadian Library, McClelland and Stewart, Toronto 1961) under the heading of "The Achievement of Thomas McCulloch" by John A. Irving; and other material previously published by Professor Irving in the *Canadian Historical Review*, XXXI (Sept., 1950), 252–87; *University of Toronto Quarterly*, XX (Jan., 1951), 107–123; *Philosophy and Phenomenological Research*, XII (Dec., 1951), 224–45; *Philosophy in Canada: A Symposium* (Toronto: University of Toronto Press, 1952); and *The Culture of Contemporary Canada*, edited by Julian Park (Ithaca, N.Y.: Cornell University Press, 1957), 243–73.

†The subsequent discussion of McCulloch is a revision of "The Achievement of Thomas McCulloch" by John A. Irving in *The Stepsure Letters* (New Canadian Library, Toronto: McClelland and Stewart). A.H.J.

In 1799, after the usual period of study at the Secession Divinity Hall at Whitburn, McCulloch was licensed to preach by the Presbytery of Kilmarnock. He was ordained in the Secession Church at Stewarton. Following a successful ministry of four years there, he volunteered for colonial missionary service and was designated by the General Associate Synod to Prince Edward Island. On arriving in Nova Scotia, late in 1803, he was persuaded to take a temporary appointment as minister at Pictou until the spring, a decision which was to keep him there for nearly thirty-five years.

In a short time McCulloch's learning, medical knowledge, and powerful preaching made him one of the best known personalities of his time in Nova Scotia. Despite success and fame he was unhappy, for he had become profoundly concerned with the religious exclusiveness of the two existing institutions of higher education: King's College and Academy at Windsor and the Halifax Grammar School. Finally, in 1816, his dream of a different type of college was realized by the foundation of Pictou Academy. During the next twenty-two years McCulloch's heroic work as principal and teacher raised this institution to the unique place it occupies in the educational history of Nova Scotia.

McCulloch taught logic, moral philosophy, science, Hebrew, and theology. If not quite the first, he was certainly the second teacher of modern philosophy to appear in what is now English Canada. From the beginning he tried to develop a library, to obtain laboratory apparatus, and to build up museum collections. The quality of teaching at Pictou Academy under his *régime* was recognized very early by the University of Glasgow, which conferred the degree of M.A., after the usual examinations, on three of its first graduates. Although McCulloch was perennially thwarted by vested religious interests in his efforts to secure degree-granting powers in Arts for Pictou Academy, he did realize a second great educational ambition—the training of a native ministry.

Towards the end of his life, in a totally unexpected manner, McCulloch finally achieved his ambition of presiding over a degree-granting institution. In 1838 he was appointed the first principal of Dalhousie College, twenty years after its foundation by the Earl whose name it bears. Here as professor of philosophy and political economy, he imbued the students of a pioneer community with a lasting respect for the scholarly and scientific heritage of Western civilization. He worked tirelessly, as at Pictou, to develop a library, to acquire scientific apparatus, and to build up museum collections as aids to the study of the humanities and the natural sciences. When he died in 1843, Nova Scotia had lost its ablest and most persistent champion of liberal education.

McCulloch's educational ideals had been powerfully expressed a quarter of a century before his death in a remarkable address, *The Nature and*

Uses of a Liberal Education Illustrated, delivered at the opening of Pictou Academy in 1818, and published at Halifax in 1819. As a philosopher, he begins with a discussion of human nature and society. An adequate idea of man, he argues, must consider what is innate or natural in the human constitution and what is due to its physical and social environment. Without becoming involved in current controversies, he notes that the mind of man seems to possess an infinite capacity to respond to the challenge of its environment.

It is this flexibility of the mind that underlies McCulloch's optimistic philosophy of education. After a digression into genetic psychology and a discussion of the educational methods of primitive and modern societies, he insists that the ideal of a practical education limited to the three R's must be replaced by the ideal of a liberal education. A liberal education, he declares, strives for "the improvement of man in intelligence and moral principle, as the basis of his subsequent duty and happiness." The fulfilment of this ideal requires that man must be considered "as he exists in society, having property, social relations, and an interest in the general prosperity." Further, society itself must be envisaged "merely as a link in the chain of existence, and equally connected with the past and future ages." A liberal education is therefore essential not only for the members of such learned professions as law, medicine, and theology, but for everybody engaged in the world's work. Each individual, no matter what his occupation may be, must live in organized society and therefore needs to understand the principles of his art or trade and the spirit of his culture. While making it clear that he had no quarrel with the conventional classical curriculum of his time, McCulloch boldly advocated the claims of philosophy, mathematics, and the natural sciences as subjects that would best enable the student to understand nature, man, and society.

McCulloch's strong concern for the Protestant approach to religion led him to write three major volumes in the field of theology. One of these, *Calvinism* (published posthumously in 1849) provides further evidence of his philosophical insight and skill.

II

During the period from 1880 to 1910 the religious and educational life of the Maritimes derived great enrichment from the university careers of a number of clergymen (and a few non-clergymen) who like McCulloch manifest obvious philosophical interests and abilities. Because Thomas McCulloch (in this survey) serves as an outstanding example of this type of person, only very brief reference will be made to the individual members of this group. At Dalhousie, instruction in logic, ethics, and political economy was provided by one of McCulloch's most impressive students, the Reverend James Ross who was the second president of the College (1863–85). James

De Mille, Professor of English and History, also lectured in logic during much of this period. In 1884, Dalhousie's great benefactor, George Munro, established a chair of Metaphysics and assigned to it Dr. Jacob Gould Schurman.

Acadia University appointed in 1838 the Reverend Edward A. Crawley to a professorship of logic, mental philosophy, rhetoric, and mathematics. He also served briefly as president (1853–55). From 1851 to 1869, the Reverend John A. Cramp was Professor of Mental and Moral Philosophy and Theology. He was succeeded by the Reverend A. Wayne Sawyer (1869–96) who also served as President (1869–88). During part of this period, from 1882 to 1905, the Reverend E. Miles Keirstead was Professor of English Literature and Logic.

Three presidents of Mount Allison (all clergymen) taught philosophy in the early days of this institution: Humphrey Pickard, James Inch, and David Allison. Their work in moral philosophy was continued by two other clergymen, Charles Stewart and William Watson.

At the University of New Brunswick,* Dr. Charles Harrison of Trinity College, Dublin, had been for fifteen years Professor of English and Philosophy when, in 1885, he was appointed President and Professor of Mathematics. He remained in this capacity until 1906. John Davidson (M.A., Edinburgh), Professor of Philosophy and Political Science from 1892 to 1902, was the author of numerous volumes in the field of economics. In his courses in philosophy, he stressed the great Greeks, Spinoza, Kant, Mill, and Green. His most impressive student was W. C. Keirstead who taught at the University of New Brunswick from 1906 until 1945. (Chronologically Keirstead belongs in a later period, but for the purposes of this survey it is more appropriate to refer to him at this point.) He was an ardent admirer of John Dewey. Following the example of Davidson and after similar influences at Chicago, Keirstead found it impossible to restrict his energies to the narrow scope of traditional academic philosophy. Lecturing on economics, political science, education, and psychology as well as philosophy, he influenced his students in an unusually profound fashion.

The official histories of the Maritime universities mentioned indicate that these men did not publish books or monographs in the field of philosophy, but rather built up a tradition of philosophical inquiry through their teaching. The situation was otherwise in the case of clerical and non-clerical professors of philosophy in central Canada. They did publish books and monographs which made contributions to Canadian philosophical literature.

*The University of New Brunswick, established in 1859, is the lineal descendant of the College of New Brunswick (1785–1829) which was replaced by King's College (1829–1859). In his address to the graduating class of the College in 1828, the Reverend Dr. James Somerville referred to their instruction in logic and moral science. It is also recorded that Principal Edwin Jacob of King's College was a lecturer in logic and the Reverend George McCawley, a member of the staff from 1829 to 1836 (he was a graduate of King's College, Windsor, Nova Scotia), taught metaphysics.

III

In the last half of the nineteenth century, there were professorships in philosophy at the University of Toronto, Queen's, and McGill. The outstanding authors in philosophy were John Watson of Queen's and John Clark Murray of McGill. Others produced books and monographs, but no one equalled these two men in the quality and quantity of philosophical publication. James Beaven and George Plaxton Young of Toronto were dedicated teachers, who participated actively in the life of their universities and communities. They wrote in other fields. But although they did not engage in extensive philosophical publication, they, like Thomas McCulloch in earlier days, helped to establish the intellectual and social climate in which men of later generations were stimulated to produce the considerable flowering of philosophical literature which took place in Canadian universities in the twentieth century. Their contributions must, of course, be kept in proper perspective. In all these activities, as in the production of the literature of philosophy, Watson and Murray were also the dominant figures.*

At Harvard University the first official appointment specifically in philosophy was made as late as 1766, and the first Harvard professorship of philosophy dates only from 1810. The distinction of being the first academic philosopher in central Canada belongs to James Beaven. He was born in 1801 in Wiltshire and educated at St. Edmund's Hall, Oxford, where he obtained his B.A. in 1824 and his M.A. in 1827. On going down from Oxford, where he had devoted himself mainly to classics and theology, he took holy orders and spent fifteen years in clerical and educational activities. In 1841 he published, in London, *An Account of the Life and Writings of St. Irenaeus*, for which Oxford awarded him the degree of Doctor of Divinity. His book evidently attracted some attention, for the year following its publication saw his appointment as Professor of Divinity in King's College, Toronto. In 1850 he became Professor of Metaphysics and Ethics in the newly reconstituted University of Toronto, a chair he held until his resignation in 1871, when he accepted the position of rector of the Church of England at Whitby, where he died in 1875. In addition to his book on St. Irenaeus, Beaven published through Rivingtons of London two other scholarly works, *Elements of Natural Theology*, in 1850, and an edition of Cicero's *De Finibus* in 1853.

When Beaven, at long last, resigned his professorship in 1871, the appointment of his successor immediately aroused enthusiastic and universal approval. George Plaxton Young had already lived in Ontario for twenty-four years, and his extraordinary abilities and scholarship had won him a great influence

---

*The subsequent discussion of Canadian philosophical literature is a revision of John A. Irving's "The Development of Philosophy in Central Canada from 1850 to 1900," *Canadian Historical Review*, vol. XXXI, no. 3 (Sept., 1950), 252–287. An epilogue has been added. A.H.J.

in religious and educational circles. Born in 1818, in the manse at Berwick-on-Tweed, Young was educated at both the high school and the University of Edinburgh. During his university course he was a distinguished student in his favourite subjects of mathematics and philosophy. On taking the degree of M.A., he taught mathematics at Dollar Academy for a number of years. Then came the great disruption of the Church of Scotland, and Young was so attracted by Chalmers's liberal cause that he entered the Free Church Theological Hall, was subsequently ordained, and given a call to the Martyrs' Church, Paisley. But after a few months he emigrated to Canada. Three years later, in 1850, he became minister of Knox Church in the rising city of Hamilton. In 1853, he was appointed Professor of Mental and Moral Philosophy at Knox's College (as it was then called), where, during the next eleven years, he exhibited his great versatility by filling various chairs in succession: it is said that he lectured in almost every department of the College.

Young's contemporaries were astonished by his phenomenal range of scholarship; they believed that he could have taught Oriental languages, classics, or mathematics as effectively as he taught theology and philosophy. Certainly his contributions to mathematics suggest that he may have missed his calling. He published no less than ten important mathematical papers, six of them in the *American Journal of Mathematics*, mainly in the theory of quintic equations. His colleague in Natural Philosophy, J. B. Cherriman, considered that Young was the most remarkable mathematician of that generation. That his mathematical researches were not entirely unrelated to his philosophy is evident from a paper entitled "Boole's Mathematical Theory of the Laws of Thought" which appeared in the *Canadian Journal* of 1865.

Young published little in philosophy (in the narrowest sense of the term) except several monographs. One entitled *Freedom and Necessity* appeared at the urgent request of the students of Knox College to whom he had delivered a lecture on this topic in the spring of 1870. Henry Calderwood in the *Knox College Monthly* of 1889 characterized this lecture, in which the theories of Edwards, Locke, and J. S. Mill are discussed and the "Liberty of Indifference" attacked, as "a fine example of clear definition, critical acumen, and true appreciation of the difficulties besetting the problem." During his student days at Edinburgh Young had come under the powerful influence of Sir William Hamilton and the philosophy of Common Sense. In an elaborate essay on *The Philosophical Principles of Natural Religion*, which was published in 1862, he explicitly rejected, "root and branch," the doctrines of this school. He then transferred his allegiance to Idealism as expounded by John Watson and T. H. Green.

IV

Queen's University was established in 1841, but it was not until the appointment of James George to a chair of Logic and of Mental and Moral

Philosophy in 1853 that philosophy was specifically recognized as distinct from theology. Queen's first philosopher was not a newcomer: in 1846 he had been appointed Professor of Systematic Theology. After a colourful, if somewhat controversial, nine years in philosophy he returned to a pastoral charge at Stratford, Ontario, where he died in 1870. At least seven of his monographs have survived, including two addresses delivered in his capacity as vice-chancellor (1853–57) at the opening of the fourteenth and fifteenth sessions of Queen's; an address to the Senate and students of Queen's on the occasion of the first conferring of the degree of M.D.; and two public lectures entitled *The Poetic Element in the Scottish Mind*, and *What is Civilization?* His style was characterized by a luxuriant imagination and a certain splendour of illustration which invested the most familiar subject with charm and freshness.

In his address to the first medical graduates of Queen's he naturally warned the new doctors to be on their guard against the materialism of the eighteenth century, which he characterized as "a mass of gratuitous assumptions, supported by such childish and superficial arguments, as to make all men of sense and learning thoroughly ashamed of it." At the same time, he had come to realize, as a result of his pastoral experience, that the connection between mind and body is so subtle and so constant that the role of mental factors in many bodily diseases cannot be denied. The physician who would attain "solid distinction" in the art of healing must, therefore, go through a severe course of training in mental philosophy.

The range of George's reading and sympathies is perhaps best illustrated in his monograph, *What is Civilization?* Civilization, the philosopher affirmed, does not consist in the accumulation of wealth among a people, or in the achievement of splendour, elegance, and excellence in the arts, or in the attainment of polished manners, or even in the creation of literature of a sort. Civilization consists essentially "in the conscience and intellect of a people thoroughly cultivated, and the intellect in all cases acting under the direction of an enlightened conscience." In George's opinion four factors were responsible for the current decay of civilization: insubordination to law and government; dishonest dealings in the ordinary transactions of life; the growing practice on this continent of assassination; and the prevalence of atheism. These dissolving factors were more than counter-balanced, however, by the operation of constructive forces: the triumphs of physical science; the development of world-wide communications; and the extension of Christianity.

v

Born in Glasgow in 1847, John Watson received his early education at the Free Church School, Kilmarnock. He then spent six years at the University of Glasgow where he distinguished himself in philosophy, classics, and English, and from which he received the degree of M.A. in 1872. A few months after graduation he was appointed, on Edward Caird's recommendation, to the chair of Logic, Metaphysics, and Ethics at Queen's. Here he taught philosophy with great learning, rare wisdom, and high authority for the next fifty-two years, and from 1901 to 1924 was Vice-Principal of the University. He survived retirement for fifteen years, dying in 1939 within a month of his ninety-second birthday after having lived in Kingston for sixty-seven years. He was the first, and, up to the present, the only Canadian to receive the high honour of an invitation to give the Gifford Lectures. One of the great teachers of philosophy in Canada during the last hundred years, Watson was the first philosopher in this country to achieve an international reputation through his writings. British and American historians of philosophy always list him as one of the leading representatives of the idealistic movement in the Anglo-Saxon world.

It is difficult to understand Watson's philosophy and influence without some appreciation of the role of Edward Caird in his intellectual development. As a student, and later as a fellow, at Oxford, in the early 1860's, Caird was associated with his tutor, Benjamin Jowett, and his friend, Thomas Hill Green, in the early development of that great philosophical movement known as British Idealism. Green assumed the role of critical analyst of systems opposed to Hegel's, while Caird expounded and examined the critical philosophy of Kant with the object of showing that this philosophy, if interpreted rationally and consistently, led to the absolute idealism of Hegel.

As the new idealism developed, it gradually became apparent that a more rational and more liberal interpretation of Christianity than had hitherto existed was possible. Confronted with the advance of science, the theory of evolution, the new biblical criticism, and an aggressive enlightenment, Edward Caird and his elder brother John Caird, who became Professor of Divinity at Glasgow in 1862, sought to show that absolute idealism preserved the essence of traditional religion while giving to it a more rational and enlightened form.

In 1866, when the young Watson entered the University of Glasgow with the intention of studying for the ministry, Edward Caird had just been appointed Professor of Moral Philosophy. Caird's inaugural lecture made a profound impression upon the new student. Over forty years later Watson remembered the "curious way" in which Caird had linked Socrates and Christianity, Aristotle and St. Paul. He had been accustomed to regard Christianity in a strict Calvinistic fashion, but he now received from Caird a new insight into the kinship of Greek philosophy and the Christian religion. Later, as a student of Caird's for three years, he saw exhibited the process by which Greek philosophy gave rise to the categories by means of which Christian experience was gradually developed into a theology that enabled it to conquer the world.

Watson, aged 25, had barely arrived at Queen's when, on October 16, 1872, he charted his future course in an inaugural lecture, published a year later as a monograph, *The Relation of Philosophy to Science*. It was by any standard a remarkable performance for a man of his years. In it, Watson surveyed incisively and maturely the spheres and limits of philosophy, science, and religion. The presuppositions and weaknesses of T. H. Huxley's scientific materialism, Herbert Spencer's evolutionary naturalism, and J. S. Mill's empiricism were pointed out with devastating accuracy; and the claims of religion were vindicated by an appeal to the Kantian critical philosophy, to which were added the overtones of Caird's idealism. Watson concluded:

> Philosophy elevates itself above all mere opinions, above all untested assumptions, above all caprice and impulse—in short, above all that is peculiar to this or that individual—and lives and moves in the realm of necessary truth. . . . All men, consciously or unconsciously, participate in universal truth, and thus there is a universal consciousness, given *through* the consciousness of the individual, but in no way *dependent* upon it. In thus revealing necessary truth, Philosophy at the same time reveals Him who is Truth itself . . . the assurance which Religion gives to the individual man of the existence of a Supreme Being whom he must reverence and love, Philosophy endorses and supports. The fundamental notions with which it is the office of Logic to deal may not inappropriately be termed the plan of the universe as it existed in the Divine mind before the creation of the world; the long but sure path, by which Metaphysic ascends from the inorganic world to the world of living beings, and thence to the realm first of individual consciousness, and next of universal thought, at last terminates and loses itself in the all-embracing glory of God; and the highest lesson that Ethics has to teach is that only by unity with the divine nature, only by the elevation of his individual will to the high standard of duty, can man enter into the glorious liberty wherewith the truth makes free.

Such was the conception of philosophy that was destined to remain dominant in Canada for the next half-century.

Perhaps the most astonishing aspect of Watson's career is the sheer volume of his publications, amounting to fifteen large books, over sixty major articles, and uncounted book reviews. He contributed to both technical and popular journals in Britain, Germany, the United States, and Canada; and there was scarcely a current philosophical controversy in which he did not engage. Shortly after coming to Canada he identified himself with the St. Louis Hegelians (a remarkable group of enthusiasts for classical German philosophy which had been organized by H. C. Brokmeyer and W. T. Harris), and contributed various articles to their *Journal of Speculative Philosophy*. When the *Philosophical Review* was established in 1892, Watson was the honoured author of its second article on "The Critical Philosophy and Idealism." Such semi-popular magazines as *Canadian Monthly*, Rose-Belford's *Canadian Monthly*, *New World*, and the *Queen's Quarterly* (of which he was one of the mainstays for over thirty years) carried numerous articles from his pen. He was constantly on the war-path against Tyndall, Neitzsche, Spencer, and the American pragmatists; but he was also constantly building up constructive approaches to Kant, Hegel, and his contemporaries in the idealistic movement.

Philo and the New Testament, Gnostic theology, Dante and medieval thought, Leibniz and Protestantism, Lessing and art criticism, the poetry of Browning— all were grist for his mill, and the mill was continually turning out a product of the highest quality.

Watson's books fall into four main groups, according as they are concerned with (1) classical German philosophy, (2) hedonism, positivism, and empiricism, (3) the philosophy of religion, or (4) political philosophy. While it is not within the scope of the present survey to present a technical analysis and evaluation of these varied contributions, nevertheless certain brief comments may enable the reader to appreciate the nature of their author's international reputation. On German philosophy, Watson wrote such authoritative books as *Kant and His English Critics* (1881), *The Philosophy of Kant Explained* (1908), and *Schelling's Transcendental Idealism* (1882). German scholars regarded him as one of the foremost authorities on Kant in the nineteenth century, and Hans Vaihinger invited him to contribute articles to *Kantstudien*, a highly technical journal. In addition to these expository and critical works, he edited and translated *Selections from Kant*, a book which was revised and reprinted eleven times between 1882 and 1934. This project grew out of a deep-seated belief that if students of philosophy were to pass from a lower to a higher plane of thought they must read the classical texts for themselves. He would set his own class of more advanced students at work upon extracts from the philosophy of Kant, watch them as they struggled with its perplexities, and give helpful instruction only when it was needed. This method was adopted at Harvard and spread thence to many other leading American universities. It is no exaggeration to say that Watson did more to promote the study of Kant on this continent than any other North American philosopher.

In 1891 Watson performed a similar service for the empirical school with the publication of *The Philosophy of John Stuart Mill*, a book of extracts. This was followed in 1895 by *Comte, Mill, and Spencer*, ostensibly a critical exposition of nineteenth-century positivism, empiricism, and evolutionism, but actually a constructive introduction to philosophy in general. In 1898 an elaborate addendum, *Notes, Historical and Critical, to Comte, Mill and Spencer*, appeared, and later that year the two volumes were fused and published under a new title, *Outline of Philosophy*. During the next twenty-five years this book ran through half a dozen editions, and formed the basis of the introductory course in philosophy in many American and Canadian universities. Its wide acceptability in that period was guaranteed, of course, by Watson's statement of his position in the preface: "The philosophical creed which commends itself to my mind is what in the text I have called Speculative Idealism, by which I mean the doctrine that we are capable of knowing Reality as it actually is, and that Reality when so known is absolutely rational." The criticism of the empirical tradition in philosophy was supplemented in 1895 with *Hedonistic Theories from Aristippus to Spencer*, an uncompromising demonstration of the view that no hedonistic theory can plausibly explain morality without assuming ideas inconsistent with its asserted principle.

In the popular consciousness Watson is usually associated with the provision of more adequate philosophical foundations for Christian theology. The popular view is, on the whole, correct, but it should be emphasized that he preferred to regard Christianity as an ideal of conduct rather than a historical theology. This approach was developed in a series of lectures given before the Philosophical Union of the University of California and published in 1897 as *Christianity and Idealism*. Here Watson argued that Christianity and idealism, when each is understood, lend each other mutual support. Each proved the other true; each is seen to be but a different expression of the same indivisibly threefold fact—God, freedom, and immortality. Idealism is the principle of morality and the principle of advancing history. Christianity is the germ of which idealism is the full issue. This conception of the relationship between idealism and Christianity was developed further in 1907 in *The Philosophical Basis of Religion*, a series of essays in the reconstruction and history of religious belief which had been delivered before the Brooklyn Institute of Arts and Sciences. Watson's mature philosophy of religion found expression, of course, in the Gifford Lectures which he delivered in the Union of Glasgow during the years 1910 to 1912, and which were published in two massive volumes as *The Interpretation of Religious Experience* (1912). This work, the crowning achievement of his philosophical career, concludes with a passionate plea for a faith which has a rational basis—in idealism:

> ... the religious interests of man can be preserved only by a theology which affirms that all forms of being are manifestations of a single spiritual principle in identification with which the true life of man consists. Living in this faith the future of the race is assured. Religion is the spirit which must more and more subdue all things to itself, informing science and art, and realizing itself in the higher organization of the family, the civic community, the state, and ultimately the world, and gradually filling the mind and heart of every individual with the love of God and the enthusiasm of humanity.

The First World War drove Watson to a deeper consideration of the problems of political philosophy which he, unlike most of the British idealists, had hitherto largely neglected. Two articles in the *Queen's Quarterly* on "German Philosophy and Politics" (1915) and "German Philosophy and the War" (1916) heralded the publication in 1919 of his last book, *The State in Peace and War*. Notable for its detachment, this book contains a survey of the evolution of political ideas from the origin of the city-state to the rise of the modern nation-state, an analysis of the latter in terms of its great associations and institutions, and a lengthy discussion of international relations in peace and war. At the age of seventy-two the sage of Kingston prophesied that the treatment of the defeated Central Powers, as well as the structure of the League of

Nations, would lead to a renewed war. He died seven months before this dire prediction was realized. Even a brief sketch of his writings must indicate that if any Canadian philosopher of the nineteenth century is remembered in future ages it will surely be John Watson.

VI

John Clark Murray was the son of David Murray, Provost of Paisley, Scotland, and his wife, Elizabeth Clark. Born in 1836, he was educated at the Paisley Grammar School and at the universities of Glasgow and Edinburgh, obtaining the degree of M.A. from the latter. From Edinburgh he went to Heidelberg and thence to Göttingen. During Murray's student days in Scotland the reigning philosopher was Sir William Hamilton; and it was to the Scottish Common Sense school of Thomas Reid, Dugald Stewart, and Hamilton that he ultimately belonged. But his studies on the Continent convinced him that the work of this school had to be supplemented by ancient, as well as by modern French and German, philosophy. A student should be presented with the points of view of representative classical systems.

At the age of twenty-six he was already so thoroughly trained and so well known that he was called to the chair of Mental and Moral Philosophy at Queen's University where he remained for ten years, serving as secretary to the Senate during part of this period. Murray then accepted the chair of Mental and Moral Philosophy at McGill, and his life was identified with this university for the next forty-five years.*

While teaching at McGill, Murray became more and more interested in the moral and ethical values of the great speculative systems of the past. Such an emphasis led certain of his students during the last decade of the nineteenth century to suppose that he must be a member of the idealistic school. They were perhaps influenced in this direction by his conception of philosophy as "the key which would unlock the secret of life's divine significance." He overrated Berkeley; and his distaste for empiricism, coupled with the influence of nineteenth-century Hegelian historians of philosophy, caused him to underestimate Locke and Hume. It is difficult to classify Murray in terms of the conventional schools. He had been trained in theology; and it would seem that he never achieved an entirely satisfactory synthesis of Calvinism, Scottish common sense, and German idealism. His final philosophical position is

---

*McGill University was the earliest of the central Canadian foundations, but philosophy seems not to have been recognized as a subject distinct from theology until 1853. In that year William Turnbull Leach (M.A. Edinburgh 1827, ordained by the Church of Scotland 1931 and later as an Anglican priest) was tranferred from the chair of Classical Literature, which he had accepted on the advice and request of Bishop Mountain in 1846, to a professorship of Logic, Rhetoric, and Moral Philosophy. From 1846 he served as Vice-Principal of the University, and from 1853 as Dean of the Faculty of Arts. In 1881 he resigned the Molson chair of English Literature (which he had held since 1858), but retained the administrative positions until his death in 1886.

perhaps best described as eclectic idealism. But Sir William Hamilton was never far beneath the surface.

For a philosopher Murray's scientific knowledge was exceptional. His Scottish training had included a thorough grounding in physics, which had been supplemented by further scientific study in Germany. Throughout his life, he kept up with the latest developments in physics and physiology, and this knowledge gave to his teaching of psychology and metaphysics a refreshing concreteness that was lacking in his philosophical contemporaries in central Canada. At Göttingen and Heidelberg he was also strongly influenced by the new biblical criticism, an influence which confirmed the insight, derived from Spinoza and Kant, that all religious values must be freely examined. Extensive work in psychology enabled him to appreciate also the significance of anthropology and comparative mythology for the study of religious origins.

Although he toiled single-handed in his teaching activities at Queen's and McGill for over forty years, Murray published nine books, some forty articles, a large number of reviews, and occasional verse. Of his nine books, one is concerned with Sir William Hamilton; two deal with ethics, two with psychology, and four with literary themes. His *Outline of Sir William Hamilton's Philosophy*, published at Boston in 1870, is the first technical philosophical book written in Canada. It had been preceded by a series of four articles on Hamilton in the *Canadian Journal* during the years 1866 and 1867. The *Outline* itself was introduced and highly recommended by James McCosh, President of Princeton and leading exponent of the Scottish philosophy in the United States. McCosh and Murray both believed that Hamilton was the great metaphysician of his age and that his writings would be studied by all thinking people in future centuries. It was imperative, therefore, that Hamilton's philosophy should be presented in systematic form, and this was the task Murray had set himself. In view of the diffuse, often chaotic, character of Hamilton's writings it is surprising that Murray should have succeeded in presenting such a tightly articulated, and altogether fair, exposition of his system. In 1870 he was still too much under the influence of Hamilton to venture any criticism of the latter's doctrines, but this defect only enhanced the value and influence of the *Outline* in circles where the Scottish philosophy was still generally accepted, and more especially in the United States.

In his *Introduction to Ethics* (1891), Murray's style is seen at its best, clear, vigorous, thought-compelling, on occasion even passionate. At the time of its pubication this book was noteworthy in that it was not confined to the exposition of ethical concepts in their abstract generality but considered also the concrete application of moral concepts to the principal spheres of human duty. Its method throughout was strongly influenced by the new historical or evolutionary approach; and the conditions under which the principal moral ideals of humanity had been developed were given extended treatment. "The requirements of the moral ideal in any age," wrote Murray, "can be definitely comprehended only when we come to know how it has been formed, just as the precise meaning of a word is often to be reached only by tracing its history; and even if the obligations of the moral life demand an elevation or modification of the existing ideal, the proposed moral advance can itself be understood only when it is viewed as a continuation of the process through which that ideal was attained." The *Introduction* was translated into several languages, including Russian. Several years after his retirement, Murray published *A Handbook of Christian Ethics* (1908) in which the principles developed in his earlier ethical studies were applied to an exposition and philosophical interpretation of Christian ethical ideals. Like Young and Watson, Murray was unalterably opposed to hedonism and utilitarianism, yet he always succeeded in presenting theories with which he differed clearly and honestly.

It was taken for granted until long after Murray's retirement that psychology was a branch of philosophy, and he gave regular lectures in this field during his entire period at McGill. These lectures formed the basis of *A Handbook of Psychology* (1885) and *An Introduction to Psychology* (1904). Both texts were widely used in the United States, the former running through at least five editions in fifteen years. They were eventually displaced, of course, by the writings of William James and his disciples who emphasized a much more physiological and experimental, and a less exclusively analytical, approach to psychology. It is not surprising that Murray's treatment of psychology was not yet freed from epistemological and metaphysical intrusions. But it is remarkable that he should have been so receptive to the scientific material that had become available as an aftermath of the Darwinian biology. His psychology is an interesting blend of Sir William Hamilton and Wilhelm Wundt, the "founder" of experimental psychology. In the later volume the German influence became predominant, and the science of psychology was defined in terms of the conceptual framework laid down by Wundt. Much more extensive use was also made of anthropological material. But to the end the persistent influence of the Scottish School prevented Murray from reaping the fullest harvest of his remarkable alertness to late nineteenth-century movements of thought in science and philosophy.

VII

It is evident that the philosophical literature of nineteenth-century Canada was almost exclusively characterized by a positive religious orientation and devotion to Scottish Common Sense philosophy or some variety of Idealism. Murray was a partial exception. In his case there was a serious interest in natural science and a tendency to break away from the major philosophical emphases and heroes of his contemporaries. To this extent he was a "transition man" who pointed unmistakably towards the more heterogeneous world of twentieth century Canadian philosophical literature.

24. Scientific Writings

A. VIBERT DOUGLAS

THE SUBJECT-MATTER of his choice is not the determining factor as to whether a scholar's writing will or will not have literary merit, perhaps even literary excellence. The useful classification of knowledge into divisions and subdivisions has been done by erecting arbitrary walls where no intrinsic boundaries exist. All branches of knowledge interpenetrate one another, hence to affirm the oneness of all knowledge is no meaningless assertion. It was therefore essential to include a chapter on the literature of science in the present volume. To have done otherwise would have been to neglect a rich field of Canadian scholarship, a field which for more than a century can claim among its expositors men who have handled the English language with distinction and discrimination.

"We approach Nature in the same spirit as we are bidden to approach the Kingdom of Heaven, that is, as little children, and patiently strive by observation and experiment to find out what she is" . . . "the scientific idea of truth is a principle which brings order and harmony into phenomena . . . not arrived at by any mechanical stringing together of facts but by a flash of insight which may be compared to inspiration": so wrote Professor E. W. McBride in the *McGill University Magazine* in 1908 in an essay "The Criterion of Truth." The words "not arrived at by any mechanical stringing together of facts" deserve to be repeated with emphasis since many scholars trained too exclusively in the classical, literary, and social studies fall into the grievous error of imagining that science is in fact no more than just that. "The dramatic fancy which creates myths," wrote Dean W. R. Inge with an all too rare insight, "is the raw material of both poetry and science."

Unavoidable curtailment of space allotted to this chapter necessitated drastic and arbitrary limitation of the scope and depth of the survey and of the interpretation of the phrase "literature of science." The survey is restricted to books and articles of literary merit which are designed to expound and interpret science to the general reader. This rules out all technical papers and reports, and the many catalogues of fish, birds, animals, plants, and rocks, no matter how important these have been in the history of scientific achievement. Hence the names of most of Canada's outstanding scientists do not appear in the pages that follow.

References will be found to astronomy and physics, chemistry and geology, the biological, medical, and applied sciences; but no attempt has been made to cover agricultural science (with the exception of reference to one famous book) or anything pertaining to the Arctic regions. Where there are hundreds of books and essays to be considered, the selection of a few is obviously a very personal choice. In the bibliographies from 1751 to 1867 alone, some 108 authors are listed. After this date, the volume of scientific writing increases, and with striking acceleration in this century. The attempt is here made to select some typical and some of the most outstanding contributions made by native Canadians and by residents of Canada, whether their stay in this country was of long or short duration.

I

Prior to 1800 very little if any literature of science seems to have appeared in Canada. One finds references to almanacs and to practical instructions relating to husbandry, health, the practice of dentistry, and so forth. As R. O. Earl has pointed out in *The Culture of Contemporary Canada* (1957) "the early days of pioneer settlement were not appropriate for the development of scientists nor were scientists likely to come to a country in this stage."

But by the nineteenth century many well-educated professional men were coming out as officers in the army, as surveyors, teachers, medical men, or ministers of religion. In the old Scottish universities, particularly, many of them had acquired considerable knowledge of geology and natural history and they were keenly observant of nature. Scholarly articles and a few books on scientific topics began to be written in Canada.

In Nova Scotia, as early as 1818, the "Letters of Agricola" appeared weekly in the Halifax *Recorder*. Their author, John Young (1773–1837), not only stimulated farmers of the Maritimes to improve their methods and to form groups for the discussion of general and local problems, but he gave them food for thought in a variety of ways. Good examples are Letters 6 and 7 on climate, and Letters 27–32 on manures. In this latter category he included lime. The discursive nature of his writing is illustrated by his digression to recall a visit to the last resting place of Burns where an old gardener talked with him about the poet and then remarked upon the greatly increased fertility of Ayrshire since the poet's day, ascribing this to the application of lime to the fields. Young then advocated this treatment and described the various types of occurrence of lime in Nova Scotia and how best to prepare it for spreading. So highly were these letters regarded and so great was their influence that they were published as a book under the same title in Halifax in 1822.

In 1847 Abraham Gesner, M.D. (1797–1864), who became a surveyor in New Brunswick, geologist, investigator of fisheries, pioneer in extracting kerosene and oils from bituminous substances, published in London *New Brunswick; with Notes for Emigrants*, a book which contains chapters on natural history, climate, soils, and wild life.

One manifestation of growing intellectual activity was the formation by groups of inquiring spirits in Montreal, Quebec, and the Maritimes of natural history societies or literary and scientific societies. The Montreal Natural History Society was founded in 1827, shortly after the Literary and Historical Society of Quebec; a museum was established and the papers read at its meetings were published subsequently in the *Canadian Naturalist*. This magazine undoubtedly helped to form the intellectual atmosphere of those early years.

In Upper Canada a similar function was performed by the *Canadian Journal*, organ of the Royal Canadian Institute which was established in Toronto in 1849. Through its public lectures, its *Journal* (1852–78), and its subsequent *Proceedings* and *Transactions*, the Institute has richly contributed to the intellectual growth of this country. In its Centennial Volume (1949) are found ten essays on "One Hundred Years of Science in Canada."

The Nova Scotia Literary and Scientific Society was established in January 1859 "for the reading and discussion of original communications . . . in Literature, Science, Political Economy, Commerce, Statistics and the Arts . . . to foster a spirit of enquiry and enterprise and generally promote the advancement of science, learning and the useful arts." Many of the papers are of high quality, couched in the dignified, often somewhat ponderous style of the period. In one of the first papers read before the Society, on the "Fossiliferous Rocks of Arisaig," the Rev. David Honeyman wrote: "we see nature, by chemical constituents of these rocks, often times embalming their entombed inhabitants as no Egyptian physician could embalm, not to present, after a few thousand years, a dry and withered mummy, but, after years whose numbers we cannot imagine, to present them almost, if not altogether, as lovely as when they were first entombed."

This somewhat too all-embracive society was modified in 1863 when the Institute of Natural Science was founded and began publication in its *Transactions* of the papers read at its meetings. The seventh paper for that year was by R. G. Haliburton, F.S.A. (1831–1901) (son of Judge Haliburton, satirist), on "The Festival of the Dead," afterwards published in Halifax as the first part of his book *New Materials for the History of Man* (1863). In this he showed that ancient and more recent inhabitants of four continents regulated their Festival of the Dead and their date of the beginning of the new year from the heliacal rising or the midnight culmination of the Pleiades. Haliburton communicated these ideas to Professor Piazzi Smith, and they led the latter to base one of his dates for the construction of the Great Pyramid on the present altitude of the Pleiades at culmination relative to the inclination of a passage to the south face, up which, because of the procession of the equinoxes, the Pleiades could have been seen in 2170 B.C.

In the previous year, 1862, the Principal of Queen's University, Rev. Dr. William Leitch (1814–1864), published in London a little book which gave a good account of the astronomical knowledge of the day with reproductions of the Earl of Rosse's drawings of galactic, elliptical, and spiral nebulae. The tone of the book is set by its title, *God's Glory in the Heavens*. Published also in New York, it ran to a third edition in 1866.

H. Beaumont Small (1832–1919) was the author of *The Animals of North America* (Montreal, 1864), illustrated with many attractive woodcuts and written to meet "a growing desire for further acquaintance with . . . the pleasing study of Natural History . . . felt among a large and increasing class of intelligent readers." Of this little book the Montreal *Gazette* wrote "we can almost imagine 'old Isaak' recommending it to his pupil Venator," and the *Athenaeum* praised it as "well worth perusal, written in a style seldom met with in a concise handbook."

II

A striking feature in our development is the early interest in Canada in the repercussions of advancing scientific knowledge upon religious beliefs. One evidence of this is a work by Henry Taylor (fl. 1819–1860) which seems to have had considerable influence in Great Britain. Published by Coates in Toronto in 1836, it bears the title *An Attempt to Form a System of the Creation of our Globe, of the Planets, and the Sun of our System*. It is founded on the first chapter of Genesis, on the geology of the earth, and "on the modern discoveries in that science and the known operations of the laws of Nature, as evinced by the discoveries of Lavoisier and others in pneumatic chemistry." The author set out "to reconcile the present Geological appearances of our Earth with the Mosaic account of creation" by taking literally "the waters" of the second, sixth, and seventh verses of Genesis and explaining them in the light of "the wonderful discoveries in pneumatic chemistry, of the gaseous bodies and . . . the component principles of water." Out of this "Universal ocean" sun, moon, planets are born, the "days of creation" being successive cycles of time. His manuscript, composed between 1819 and 1825, was shown to Archdeacon Mountain, and to the Bishop of Quebec, who encouraged him to take it to England where he gave a copy to the Lord Bishop of London, to a theologian named Fairholme, and in 1833 to the Royal Institution in London. When he learned in 1836 that Professor Buckland and the theologians Pusey, Chalmers, and Gleig were advocating these very ideas, he hastened to publish his work, fully believing that he was the originator of the ideas. It went through nine editions between 1836 and 1854.

The same serious motive led Thomas Trotter (1853–1918), minister of the Presbyterian Church of Antigonish, to publish in 1845 in Pictou his *Treatise on Geology*, "in which the discoveries of that science are reconciled with the Scriptures, and ancient revolutions of the earth are shown to be of benefit to man." This book was written in the belief that "a comprehensive, connected and scientific view of these events would render an important service to Religion by silencing many of the cavils of the infidel, and solving some of the greatest difficulties which perplex the mind of the inquisitive Christian."

"It is utterly unworthy of the cause of our holy religion, which professes to rest on truth . . . to shrink from confronting any of the established truths of science," wrote Rev. Moses Harvey of St. John's, Newfoundland (1820–1901), and with eloquence and many poetic references he reviewed current advances in geology and astronomy in *The Harmony of Science and Revelation* (Halifax and St. John's, 1856). In this book he upheld the speculative musings of Sir David Brewster on the plurality of inhabited planets in the universe. A different treatment of this theme was T. W. Goldie's *Mosaic Account of Creation of the World and the Noachian Deluge Geologically Explained*, which ran to two editions in Quebec in 1856.

Thoughtful and scholarly men in Canada viewed with the same deep interest and grave concern the great wave of new biological knowledge and speculation which swirled around the words Evolution and Natural Selection throughout the latter half of the nineteenth century and far into the twentieth. The names of Lyell, Darwin, Lamarck, Spencer, Huxley, Haeckel, produced feelings of hopeful exhilaration or of dismay according to the reader's knowledge and temperament. The concern was of two kinds: unreasoned opposition to the new knowledge on the assumption that it was undermining spiritual faith; and honest acceptance leading to earnest and often ingenious efforts to reconcile new scientific knowledge with biblical cosmology. In 1859, the same year in which *The Origin of Species* appeared in London, Dr. James Bovell, M.D. (1817–1880), published in Toronto *Outlines of Natural Theology* of which Professor Chapman wrote in the *Canadian Journal*, "It deserves the attention of all interested in the progress of Canadian Literature." In this book the author, who believed "that a Being exists, who through his works reveals himself, as an author in his volume," proceeded to outline the current state of knowledge in geology, zoology, physiology, quoting numerous authorities such as Lyell, Humboldt, Darwin, Murchison, Huxley, Solly, and Agassiz, stating unequivocally where he agreed or differed with their metaphysical or theological deductions. The influence of

Dr. Bovell on the thinking and activities of the youthful William Osler (afterwards Sir William Osler, M.D.) was a potent one and continued to be a factor throughout Osler's life.

In the opposite camp was a Nova Scotian author, Hon. John G. Marshall (1786–1880), whose letters published in 1863 in the *Christian World* (London) opposed Sir Charles Lyell's views as to the age of the earth, transmutation of species, and gradual development in the natural world. Also among the reactionaries was a schoolmaster, Ezekiel S. Wiggins (1839–1910), whose book published in Montreal in 1864 carried the title and explanation, *The Architecture of the Heavens*, "containing a new theory of the Universe, the extent of the Deluge, the testimony of the Bible and Geology in opposition to the views of Dr. Colenso." Dr. Colenso, it will be recalled, was an Anglican ecclesiastic and mathematician, a pioneer in the Higher Criticism, who became Bishop of Natal but was excommunicated for his liberal views by the Bishop of Capetown.

The proponents of a reconciliation of science and religion had an eloquent champion in that distinguished and prolific Canadian scholar, Sir John William Dawson (1820–1899). Only five of his books will be mentioned here. His classic *Acadian Geology* (Edinburgh and London, 1855), of whose "high scientific merit, very considerable literary merit" Hugh Miller wrote in the *Edinburgh Witness*, is far from being in the category of an ordinary textbook, *vide* his beautiful and dramatic description of the incoming tide in the Cobequid and Chignecto bays and his pages on the history of the name Acadia. Dawson's *Archaia; or, Studies of the Cosmogony and Natural History of the Hebrew Scriptures* (Montreal and London, 1860), was so widely read and valued that he revised it in 1877 and it reappeared under the title *The Origin of the World according to Revelation and Science*. His prestige both in Canada and in Great Britain is further indicated by the reception accorded to two later books. *The Chain of Life in Geological Time* was published in London in 1880, with a second edition in 1885, and a third in 1888. From this little book is taken a passage in the final chapter:

What general conclusions can we reach as to this long and strange history of the progress of life on our planet? Perhaps the most comprehensive of these is that the links in the chain of life or rather its many chains are not scattered and disunited things but members of a great and complex plan. . . . It must also appear that the original plan of nature both in the animal and vegetable worlds, was too vast to be realized at one time on a globe as limited as ours, but had to be distributed in time as well as in space . . . successive aeons in which, one after the other, the work of creation could rise to successive stages of perfection and completeness till it culminated in man.

Dawson's *Modern Ideas of Evolution as related to Revelation and Science* (London, 1890) provided, amongst other topics, a critical examination of the views of Haeckel and Huxley. A tenth impression appeared in 1910.

III

During the latter half of the last century, the scientific magazines like the *Canadian Naturalist*, the *Canadian Journal*, the *Anglo-American Magazine* were providing well-written articles on a wide range of scientific topics: T. Sterry Hunt on lithology, good writing and imaginative thinking; John Matthew Jones, F.L.S., on ocean drifts and currents; Sir William Dawson's presidential address, 1864, to the Natural History Society, in light whimsical vein, and his tribute to Sir William Logan's *Report of the Geological Survey*; Sir Sandford Fleming's tribute to Logan, 1856; Rev. A. De Sola's address in 1868 when he said, "Possibly Robinson Crusoe himself was not so much astonished at the footprints on the sands of his desolate island as the naturalist who first saw the footmark of birds on a slab of sandstone which was turned up by the plow . . . in 1802 at South Hadley in the valley of the Connecticut River"; papers on the great Niagara suspension bridge (1853), on the wave principle in marine architecture (1852), on dew (1853), on the Victoria Bridge (1855); John Langton, Auditor-General and Vice-Chancellor of the University of Toronto, on the age of timber trees (1862) and ethnological investigations (1866).

The *British American Journal* (Montreal, 1845, with a new series beginning in 1860) contained articles and reviews on medical subjects both general and specific. The report on "Quackery, Imposition and Deception" by Dr. William Marsden (1860) reads like a chapter from a modern detective tale.

The growth of productive scholarship in Canada was greatly stimulated by the increase in the number of universities across the country in the latter part of the nineteenth century. These, with their faculties of letters, social, and scientific studies, attracted and encouraged able, ambitious scholars. To provide new outlets for the publication of their ideas, the *Queen's Quarterly* [*Q*] was founded in 1893, *McGill University Magazine* [*M*] in 1901 and *Dalhousie Review* [*Dal*] and *University of Toronto Quarterly* [*T*] twenty years later, as well as the *Canadian Forum* [*F*]. True, high-quality journals like the *Atlantic Monthly* [*A*] (1857) from the United States and the *Hibbert Journal* [*H*] (1902) and *Discovery* [*Disc*] (1920) from Great Britain had found some devoted readers among thoughtful Canadians, but very few Canadian scientists had published in their pages. Canadian periodicals were therefore very necessary and in them much excellent writing is to be found including expositions of scientific ideas and achievements designed for the enlightenment of general readers, articles on the overlapping fields of science, philosophy, and religion, and a large number of able reviews of scientific books. That even the *Canadian Forum* should carry so many such reviews is convincing evidence of the widespread interest in science during the last forty years.

The following names recur time and again in one or in several of these periodicals; by the initials following each name, identification of the periodicals to which each contributed may be made: Frank Allen (T), W. C. Baker (Q), S. Basterfield (T,F), N. J. Berrill (A), G. S. Brett (T,F), N. R. Carmichael (Q), A. L. Clark (Q), C. K. Clarke (Q), A. P. Coleman (T,F), A. V. Douglas $(Q,T,H,A,Disc)$, N. F. Dupuis (Q), R. O. Earl (Q), Sandford Fleming (Q), W. L. Goodwin (Q), D. Fraser Harris (Dal,H), A. P. Knight (Q), A. Macphail (U,Q), W. T. McClement (Q), E. W. McBride (U,H), J. Markowitz (F), R. E. K. Pemberton (F), J. K. Robertson (Q).

With the increasing emphasis on scientific research since the close of the First World War, university research laboratories and federal, provincial, and industrial laboratories have proliferated, one result being an ever increasing flow of published papers, reports, and surveys. While one does not turn to such sources primarily for the delight of finding literary quality, such writing is not absent. It is important to note that the Society of Technical Writers and Publishers is actively promoting higher standards for their work. Many of these writers realize that scientific accuracy, clarity, and succinctness are not incompatible with a good style of expression and a discriminating choice of words.

Some seventy-five Canadian scientific journals and publications are listed in *The Culture of Contemporary Canada* (pp. 327–66). Mention will only be made here of the annual *Proceedings and Transactions* of the Royal Society of Canada, and attention is drawn to some of the presidential addresses delivered to the Society or to one of the science sections. It may appear invidious to single out a few from so many, nevertheless mention may be made of "The Progress of Biology," R. Ramsay Wright, 1911; "The National Domain in Canada and its Proper Conservation," Frank D. Adams, 1914; "The 'Miraculous' Micro-organism," F. C. Harrison, 1924 (Section V); "Time and Life," W. A. Parks, 1926; "Continuity and Discontinuity," J. K. Robertson, 1945; "Mutations," W. P. Thompson, 1948; "Microbes and Men," G. B. Reid, 1953; "Micheli and the Discovery of Fungi," A. H. Reginald Buller, 1915 (Section V), and by the same author as President of the Society in 1928, "The Plants of Canada Past and Present," from which address three passages follow: "Among the great generalizations of science not one seems more secure than that of organic evolution." . . . "What are the first traces of plant life within the boundaries of this broad Dominion? For an answer to this question we must go with the palaeontologist to the oldest rocks of our country and with hammer and chisel extract from them their fossil remains. 'In the never-idle workshop of nature,' as Matthew Arnold has called it, many strange plants have been woven on the looms of time and have left the traceries of their stems and leaves and the beautiful hexagonal pattern of their internal tissues in the sedimentary rocks, but the first products of the loom were doubtless too delicate and too frail for proper preservation." . . . "It is possible that *Eozoon* [J. W. Dawson's discovery in the Precambrian] is one of the rocks that owe their origin to the activity of Blue-green Algae."

IV

When we come to consider the books written at the close of the last century and during six decades of this century, we note the wide range of subject-matter, the almost complete absence of sermonizing, the rarity of adventure into metaphysical regions, the rich sense of history, and an evident pride in solid scientific achievement by men, many of whom have been inspiring teachers and citizens as well as able researchers.

In the broad field of natural science the books of Ernest Thompson Seton have been very widely read by three generations. Seton's keen observation of wild life in Ontario and Manitoba between the ages of four and twenty-four provided the material for his life stories of foxes, rabbits, wolves, grouse, prairie chicken, etc., published in the *Canadian Journal, St. Nicholas, Scribner's* and other magazines. Later sojourns in New York, London, Paris, and eventually New Mexico, added their quota. His books began with *Wild Animals I Have Known* (1898), and include in rapid succession *Lives of the Hunted, Biography of a Grizzly, Animal Heroes, The Trail of the Sandhill Stag, Monarch: The Big Bear of Tallac*. Later came his *Life-Histories of Northern Animals* in two volumes, *Lives of Game Animals* in four volumes, and at the age of 80 in 1940 the charming autobiography *Trail of an Artist-Naturalist*. These works are discussed more fully in chapter 19 on nature writers.

A Canadian-born naturalist whose life was lived chiefly in England and Europe was Grant Allen (1848–1899). Some ten books became well known in the last two decades of the century. *The Story of Plants* (1895) was reprinted in London in 1927. His observations and conclusions as a field botanist won praise from Darwin and Spencer, while T. H. Huxley complimented him on his ability to achieve in his writings "precision with popularity." He termed himself "a scientific middle-man," but he was much more.

A friend of Seton's, William Perkins Bull (1870–1948), wrote the beautifully produced books *From Humming Bird to Eagle* (1936) and *From Amphibians to Reptiles* (1937), and *From Medicine Man to Medical Man* (1934) in which he traced "the efforts of men of science through the past century and a half, not only to increase the pleasure of living, but also to lengthen the span of human life." Sir W. Arbuthnot Lane considered the latter "an important contribution to the literature of public health, particularly for the closely defined area of one Canadian County [Peel Co.]."

From the prolific pen of a contemporary zoologist, N. J. Berrill, have come a series of books for the lay reader: *The Living Tide* (1951), *Journey into Wonder* (1952), *Sex and the Nature of Things* (1954), *The Origin of Vertebrates* (1956), *You and the Universe* (1958), *Man's Emerging Mind* (1961).

To A. G. Huntsman we owe *Life and the Universe* (1959), a veteran biologist's examination of thought, science, will, faith, and purpose. A question of perennial importance is ably discussed by Robert McRae, philosopher, in *The Problem of the Unity of the Sciences* (1961).

Textbooks are not often remarkable for their literary value, but in the eyes of his contemporaries those of Dr. William Clauser Boyd are in this category: *Surgical Pathology* (1925), with a sixth edition in 1947 and a *Text-Book of Pathology* (1933) with a sixth edition in 1953; *An Introduction to Medical Science* (1937); *Fundamentals of Immunology* (1943) with a third edition in 1956; *Pathology for the Physician* (1958).

The history of science has claimed the interest of not a few Canadian scientists, among whom are F. D. Adams, whose erudite *Birth and Development of the Geological Sciences* (1938) is a classic; Sir William Osler in his learned and wholly delightful *Evolution of Modern Medicine* (1921) and *Incunabula Medica, 1467–1480* (1922); Walter Libby, *A History of Medicine in its Salient Features* (1921); Maude E. Abbott, *History of Medicine in the Province of Quebec* (1931); J. J. Heagerty, *Four Centuries of Medical History in Canada and Newfoundland* (1928) and *The Romance of Medicine in Canada* (1940); Frank Allen, *The Universe, from Crystal Spheres to Relativity* (1931); Lloyd G. Stevenson, *The Meaning of Poison* (1959); C. J. S. Warrington and R. V. V. Nicholls, *A History of Chemistry in Canada* (1949), which opens thus: "A thread of metal runs through the whole fabric of Canadian history. The period spans the epoch between the last years of alchemy and the beginning of the atomic era."

Some biographies of men of science are enriched by informative accounts of scientific work and discoveries: *Loring Woart Bailey* by Joseph Whitman Bailey (1925) containing many quotations from L. W. Bailey's notes, letters and his *Reminiscences*; *Thomas Sterry Hunt* by F. D. Adams (1933); *The Life of Sir Thomas Roddick* (1938) and *Maude Abbott: A Memoir* (1941) by H. E. MacDermot; *Sir Frederick Banting* by Lloyd Stevenson (1946); *Arthur Stanley Eddington* by A. Vibert Douglas (1956); *Sir William Osler*, a memorial volume of 119 articles edited by Maude E. Abbott (1920) whose expressed aim was to supply "the unsmelted ore from which the future historian may extract that firsthand evidence which may enable him rightly to estimate the service which William Osler rendered to his day and generation . . ."; *Young Endeavour* (1958) by William C. Gibson, summarizing the "contributions to science by medical students of the Past Four Centuries";

Medicine in the Making (1960) by Gordon Murray and *Amid Masters of Twentieth Century Medicine* (1958) by Leonard G. Rowntree, both containing vivid descriptions of the fight against disease and of the developments in surgical practice made by these masters and their medical contemporaries. *The Chord of Steel* by Thomas B. Costain (1960) portrays the early years of Alexander Graham Bell and his discoveries culminating in the telephone. Leopold Infeld, for many years a professor in Toronto, wrote an inspiring biography, *Albert Einstein: His Work and its Influence on our World* (1950), and an autobiography, *Quest* (1941), recounting not only his life in Europe and America but his intellectual quest in the realm of mathematical physics wherein we read: "The transition from particle physics to field physics is undoubtedly one of the greatest, and as Einstein believes, *the* greatest step accomplished in the history of human thought. Great courage and imagination were needed to shift the responsibility for physical phenomena from particles into the previously empty space and to formulate mathematical equations describing the changes in space and time." Thanks to the Engineering Institute of Canada some important books have been produced. One entitled *Daylight through the Mountain: The Letters and Labours of Civil Engineers Walter and Francis Shanly* (1957) is edited by Frank Norman Walker. Another is the life of one of the founders of the Institute, *Sir Casimir Stanislaus Gzowski* (1959) by Ludwik Rabcewicz-Zubkovski and William Edward Greening.

In the field of applied science R. F. Legget's *The Rideau Waterway* (1955) recounts a great achievement of historic significance to Canada, and his *Geology and Engineering* (1939) is a stimulating book. So too is *Modern Railroad Structures* (1949) by C. P. Disney and R. F. Legget. D. M. LeBourdais in his *Sudbury Basin: The Story of Nickel* (1953) and G. B. Langford in *Out of the Earth: The Mineral Industry in Canada* (1954) have produced books of extreme interest about mineral deposits in Canada and the problems and achievements of mining engineers.

The year 1960 saw the publication of three books on evolution, *Evolution: Its Science and Doctrine*, edited by T. W. M. Cameron, *Darwin in Retrospect*, edited by H. H. J. Nesbitt, and *The Ascent of Life* by T. A. Goudge, indicating the widened scientific, philosophical, and social significance of the theory a century after Darwin's *Origin of the Species*. Goudge has contributed essays in this field to various journals including *Mind* (1954) and *British Journal for the Philosophy of Science* (1955, 1958–59).

Special mention should be made of J. Tuzo Wilson's *I.G.Y., the Year of the New Moons* (1961) where chapters on his journeys and observations from Arctic to Antarctic and to every continent are interspersed with clear informative chapters on the discoveries and new problems confronting science as a result of researches in which men of 67 nations cooperated.

Bare mention of many books of high quality could run to an undue length for this limited chapter; hence only a few more are selected for inclusion. *Nerves and Personal Power* (1922) by Dougall MacDougall King (brother of W. L. Mackenzie King), is an eloquent book by a physician who knew his days were few; *On Understanding Physics* (1938) by W. H. Watson, one of the few philosophical books written by a physicist in Canada; *Our Mobile Earth* (1926) by Reginald A. Daly; *Ice Ages, Recent and Ancient* (1926) and *The Last Million Years* (1941) by Arthur P. Coleman; *Our Wonderful Universe* (1928) by C. A. Chant; *The Stress of Life* (1956) by Hans Selye; *Memory, Learning and Language: The Physical Basis of Mind* (1960) edited by William Feindel with contributions by A. Hoffer, J. W. T. Spinks, Arthur Porter, and Wilder Penfield, O.M., and his own chapter on "The Brain considered as a Thinking Machine," containing the following paragraph:

Each of us has in his possession the most remarkable of galaxies—twelve billion nerve cells with their myriads of subconstellations in the compact universe of the brain. It is this inner space of the mind which surely, of all our natural resources, offers the most exciting potentialities. Consideration makes us realize that we are far from exploiting this thinking machine as efficiently as we might in the broad field of creative learning. To paraphrase Cassius, "The fault, dear Brutus, lies not in our brains, but in ourselves, that we are underlings."

The concluding word must be an exhortation to scientists to take time to interpret science to non-scientists, to bridge the chasm which too often exists between the disciplines. Men with a flair for literary expression, whose interests embrace the exposition of scientific ideas and achievements, are needed in our country. When their "apples" of pure scientific "gold" are given to a hungry reading public in "baskets" of literary "silver" these writers are making an important contribution to the literary history of Canada.

25. Literature of Protest

F. W. WATT

IT HAS LONG BEEN RECOGNIZED that the creation of the Dominion of Canada in 1867 was primarily a conservative act—conservative in the sense of attempting to preserve in the new political entity the character, traditions, and advantages of its colonial components, and to avoid a revolutionary rupture with the circumstances of the past. But from the very beginning Canadians found their energies drawn into a difficult and paradoxical endeavour. They had to devise unique political and economic strategies (and the vocabulary and imagery in which to shape them) in order to project the past into the future along a path never travelled before. This chapter does not concern itself, however, with the conservative tradition which is mainly responsible for the building of the nation of Canada as it is today, but rather with the spirit of protest and dissent which, sometimes deliberately, resisted the main current, and which as a consequence of the necessities of nation-building was almost, but never entirely, stifled.

In the half-century following Confederation most Canadians came to share the social ideals of the nation-builders: religious, political, and racial harmony; rapid commercial and industrial growth; high immigration; continental expansion from sea to sea. Their desire for unanimity produced a national temper or ethos which offered no adequate outlet (except emigration) for those who had criticisms, reservations, or competing ideals. In Victorian Canadian society controversial issues were habitually played down, and conciliation became the national virtue. The major political divisions ceased to reflect any fundamental differences in principles. In the lower orders of society, however, a movement impelled by other motives and opposed or indifferent to the ideals of the conservative tradition appeared and continued to grow during the first fifty years of Confederation, though not until the 1920's did it emerge as a factor of major importance for all levels of society.

The conservative tradition found its first practical form and its symbol in the National Policy of 1879, a programme of economic nationalism. By its chief strategy, the raising of tariff barriers against imported manufactured goods, the N.P. stimulated home industries, linked commercial and manufacturing interests with national existence and material progress, and committed the country to industrial urban expansion as rapidly as world economic conditions would allow. In 1867 the grimmer realities of industrial urbanism, which had long ago loomed large in the lives and minds of Englishmen, and which were rapidly appearing in the United States, had as yet little meaning in the Canadian economic environment, but this situation was soon to change. Growing hints of the future were there for those who had eyes to see them, and radical ideas and protest movements active in Europe and the United States were beginning to receive some attention in the Canadian press by the 1870's. Radicalism such as that which inspired the notorious International Workingmen's Association and Karl Marx, the founder of modern communism, at first seemed not so much repulsive as utterly meaningless and unrelated to the Canadian situation, as early allusions (for instance in the *Canadian Monthly and National Review*) indicate. By the 1880's and early 1890's journalists and men of letters were showing more familiarity with and understanding of Marxian and other serious ideological critiques of capitalist free enterprise and its weaknesses. Governmental concern was growing too. In 1889, ten years after the adoption of the Tory National Policy, the *Report of the Royal Commission on the Relations of Labor and Capital* was submitted, which gave credit to the N.P. for the rapid industrialization of Canada during the previous decade, but which officially recognized the existence of industrial evils—sweated labour, children and women working long hours, unsanitary factory conditions and slum dwellings —and which advocated Parliament's "paternal care" as a necessity for labour as well as for capital. The industrial revolution and all its consequences had reached Canada. By 1894 a social observer in the highly respectable *Canadian Magazine* was able to advance a criticism of the contemporary social order in the manner of the middle-class American "progressives." The essay "Canadian Democracy and Socialism" by John A. Cooper points out the existence of varieties of socialism, from its mildest, comprising such generally accepted social features as the public school system, to more extreme forms, that of Karl Marx, whose *Das Kapital* "has now great influence in the United States and Canada," and that of the extremist Bakounin:

His Second International has caused no end of trouble to the governments of Europe, and there is little doubt that it has many members in the United States and a few in Canada. Its aim is destruction, and its means are the knife and the bomb. Such is the extreme socialism that may some day in the near future force itself into Canada. Among the laborers of this country who have felt the bitter stings of poverty, it smoulders.

"Great soulless corporations" and the unequal distribution of wealth were a good deal to blame; if moderate reforms were adopted now, "extreme socialism would cease to be a menace and anarchism cease to be a nightmare."

But attacks on corporations and trusts, on bigness in business, were rare. More often Canadians, partly because they were accustomed to the large-scale development of resources by government-supported operations, were ready to accept the presence of large and semi-monopolistic enterprises as natural and desirable—an "inevitable stage in the evolution of society," as another witness to these developments expressed it in 1898 (E. R. Peacock in the *Queen's Quarterly*, VI). Threats of monopolistic domination and other abuses, the growth of trade unionism and labour unrest, the increase in complexity and interdependency in industrial urban conditions, the rise of unemployment and slumdom, were features in the "collectivism" of the late nineteenth century which largely came about or were prepared for in the short space of a quarter of a century. Something of a "great social revolution" (see Henry Stephens, *Canadian Monthly*, I, 1872) was indeed taking place, and elsewhere in the world its issues formed the substance of public controversy and political battles. In nineteenth-century Canada the conservative temper and the exigencies of nation-building remained so dominant that it never became a central preoccupation, the issues involved were rarely seriously brought into the arena of public debate and were never sharply drawn, despite the efforts of a militant minority.

As one would expect, the men of letters of Victorian Canada were on the whole no more preoccupied with radical ideologies and the social evils which gave them encouragement than were the politicians and the social and economic theorists. The eminent Torontonian and sometime Oxford Professor of History, Goldwin Smith, was a distinguished exception. He took an intelligent interest in aspects of the "social revolution" at an early stage when Canadians of his class seemed scarcely aware of its significance. In the early 1870's he was drawing attention to the growing power of the working classes whose rallying cry "Union is Strength" was beginning to be taken up by the small Canadian labour force. In the 1880's he frequently pointed out the internationalist implications of the growth of unionism, particularly the rise of the Knights of Labor just then entering Ontario: the movement was towards a "denationalized" working class. Also in the 1880's Smith was among those few Canadians concerned over symptoms of the encroachments of the darker side of industrial urbanism in North America, tramps and paupers and the like: "We admit it with reluctance, but we are everywhere looking forward to the necessity of a public provision for the poor." Though an ardent individualist, Smith was typically prepared to give the devil his due, and so we find him studying extreme varieties of late nineteenth century social panaceas largely shunned by respectable Canadian writers. In 1872 he offered a lengthy and careful review of J. H. Noyes's classic *History of American Socialism*; in the 1880's he repeatedly drew attention to the implications of Henry George's land nationalization schemes; in 1893 he subjected Edward Bellamy's social utopia *Looking Backward* to a detailed analysis. Opposed to state control in any form and holding to his conception of "natural" economic laws, Smith could throw down a challenge to Single Taxer, Socialist, or any other advocate of governmental control alike: "let him ask himself whether his government, or his group of governments, is likely to do better than *nature*" (my italics).

In short, Goldwin Smith was curiously both radical and reactionary. A "liberal of the old school," he felt compelled to examine freely and without prejudice any institution, belief, or theory, but he was passionately committed at the same time to his primary assumption: the right, duty, and ability of each individual to fend for himself. The modern world was producing certain changing conditions which were making it increasingly difficult for the unorganized and independent individual to exist, in actuality or in social theory. Having formed leading ideas of liberalism in the England of the 1840's and 1850's, which he determinedly expounded in North America in the 1880's and 1890's, Goldwin Smith was a man between two worlds, at home in neither.

Another well-known controversialist, though not of Smith's international stature, W. D. LeSueur, was theoretically much more unorthodox and radical in his views. He was, in fact, that almost unique phenomenon of nineteenth-century Canada, a disciple of Auguste Comte. LeSueur fully and explicitly endorsed the "positivist ideal" with its religious scepticism and its faith in science, reason, and progress. "Scepticism," he brashly argued in the 1870's, "occupies somewhat the same position at present that Christianity held before its official recognition as the religion of the Roman Empire." The potential achievements of emancipated reason are great: "faith in reason and faith in progress are sentiments so closely allied they are seldom seen apart. . . . If . . . there are no assignable limits to the conquests of the human mind, there can be none to the progress of society." The religion of the future should take the form of "an earnest study of the laws of life and of morality, personal and social" and its end will be to "transfigure society." These heretical doctrines, so antithetical to the accepted pieties of Canadian Victorians, and revealing that unholy fusion of secularism, science, and social discontent which conservatism thoroughly feared and condemned, remained at the level of the most abstract theory, and LeSueur though criticized was never obliged to forfeit his seat among the respectable.

LeSueur's disinterestedness was the kind Matthew Arnold preached— aloofness from action and immediate practice; and Canadian social and literary critics alike tended to accept this doctrine. A too-active social conscience was looked upon as unhealthy and out of place in the Canadian scene. Writers were praised for their idealism, their respect for the conventional virtues, and their sense of decorum, and by and large they were careful to merit such praise. The case of Agnes Maule Machar's social criticism is instructive. The hero of her *Roland Graeme, Knight: A Novel of Our Times* (1892) reads Henry George along with the Higher Criticism, becomes in effect a Christian socialist, edits a radical newspaper, and throws in his lot with the working class under the inspiration of a "vision of a fair Utopia which might become the noble aim of a modern crusade." His kind of vague socialist idealism, secular in theology but Christian in ethics, was finding its outlet in the rapid spread of the Knights of Labor movement in Canada in the 1880's and 1890's. Miss Machar's novel, however, is set in the United States. And though protesting the selfishness and ignorance of the wealthier classes of society and exhibiting in a relatively favourable light radical and unconventional ideas, it is still basically in the genteel tradition. For all the weight it gives political and economic issues and for all its sympathy for the lower classes, it is essentially a romantic story of high society, and it preaches not social or political revolution but *noblesse oblige*.

Two poetasters, John Henry Brown (b. 1859) and Walter Ratcliffe (b. 1860), flouted decorum to give less inhibited support to the cause of social revolution. Brown's *Poems: Lyrical and Dramatic* (1892) presents the flamboyant person of an atheistical and free-thinking rebel. Politically he proclaims his faith in democracy, is repulsed by the squalor of modern industrial civilization, and propagandizes for a planned society (of the Comtean sort) where scientists replace priests and freedom and social justice prevail. To the poet who looks at the contemporary scene, Brown observes, "Life is barren and grey, Life is gross and vulgar and dull." Two responses are possible; the first, escapism, romantic nostalgia, or "looking backward," Brown emphatically rejects. The other response, which the poet elects in what amounts to a conversion, brings him to the position of the proletariat, and as poet, to a proletarian aesthetic: "I looked on the world and accepted it. . . . Henceforth, I said, the function of the poet is changed. . . ." The poet vows to "accept no good that is not the right of every man."

Walter Ratcliffe's less melodramatic *Morning Songs in the Night: Poems* (1897)—the title alludes to the poet's blindness—contains verse which is more sombre, direct, and earnest. The poet's protests against the vices of capitalistic oppression and social inequalities are strong, however, and, as W. D. Lighthall points out in the Preface, "socialistic." Poems like "Looking Backward" and "The Land Monopolist" indicate by their content as well as their titles the influence of Bellamy and Henry George on Ratcliffe's thinking; and his verse is motivated by the same fervour of sympathy and indignation exhibited by these reformers. "To Canada," a variation on the well-established Confederation ode, explicitly takes issue with the traditional ideals of the nation-builders:

> ... Love thee? Ay, love thee and mourn
> That the crown of thy glory is dross.
> Tinsel and bunting and smoke
> Are not of greatness the pledge.

Among those late Victorian poets whose work retains most literary value, Archibald Lampman and D. C. Scott were almost alone in demonstrating social and ideological concerns of an unorthodox nature. Both reputedly took part in Fabian discussion groups in Ottawa; both wrote poems of revolutionary or utopian inspiration. The title of Scott's second book of verse, *Labor and the Angel* (1896), is a sign of his temper and interest at this period: his sympathy with the underprivileged and dismay and indignation at social squalor and injustice were evidently strong; but after 1900 Scott turned away almost entirely in his verse from social preoccupations. Lampman is a more complex case, for throughout his briefer poetic career he vacillated between the claims of a mild, retiring, sensitive nature-loving temperament and a socially oriented, ambitious, puritanical will—between the idealized rural landscape and the mechanized and vulgarized city, between romantic reverie and social protest. "The City of the End of Things" is a nightmare projection of contemporary industrial civilization; "The Land of Pallas" offers the alternative vision: a utopian society based on idealistic communism. In between nightmare and dream are such direct daylight attacks on the perversions of modern commercial society as "To a Millionaire" and "Epitaph on a Rich Man." Because he is known by his best work, his meditative nature poetry, Lampman has been condemned for turning his back on the contemporary scene, a curious fate for the poet probably most inclined of any of the Group of the Sixties to social analysis, commentary, and protest.

As we have seen, most of the cultivated writers in the years following Confederation accepted and did not seriously explore the social implications of the National Policy and the nation-building programme. In the same period, however, a radical critique of it began to emerge, paradoxically, from that group whose strength and size seemed especially to depend on its success: the working class. The working class had appeared for the first time as a significant national force in the Nine Hour Movement in 1872, finding its voice in the weekly newspaper, the *Ontario Workman*. From then on a proletarian spirit can be seen evolving in the small radical labour press which struggled to support the interests of that class. First there was a simple desire for higher wages and shorter hours (the Nine Hour Movement); then there was the phase of growing class consciousness and eclectic interest in such social theories as those of Henry George, the Knights of Labor, and Edward Bellamy; and later came more dogmatic and exclusive ideologies based on communist and socialist principles. The proletarian spirit from the 1870's to the 1890's manifested itself in disillusion with and radical criticism of the programme of nation-building, and in an inclination to associate the patriotic forces which supported the National Policy with the motives and methods of capitalist exploitation. "Patriotism indeed!" cried the editor of the *Palladium of Labor* (Hamilton) in 1883:

It is all very well for the millionaire, for the Government pensioner, for the oil-tongued politician, and the full-paunched bourgeois to be patriotic. They have reason to—the country has filled their pockets. Its laws are made in their interests. Its institutions permit them to plunder the poor with impunity. Let them throw off their hats and cheer for the Queen or Canadian independence as they prefer; but as for the mass of humanity, they have little to care the toss of a copper what form the Government assumes, or whether we are ruled from Ottawa, Downing Street, or Washington. (Dec. 1, 1883)

Simultaneously there was a growing realization, manifested in savage criticism of the "literary hacks" of "bourgeois" culture (among them "Goldwin Smith, that notorious corrupter of public opinion" *Labor Union*, Sept. 1, 1883), that culture was no mere veneer to grace the lives of the upper classes, but a potent force active in moulding and preserving the social structure. A writer in the *Palladium of Labor* had this realization in mind when he expressed the hope that "the literature of the future will be the powerful ally of Democracy and Labor Reform, instead of the prop and buttress of every form of legalized wrong and injustice" (Aug. 29, 1885). And the editor of the *Labor Union* saw the labour press as a propaganda agent for the insurgent working class: "They should be led to see that the ultimate object in view is not merely to tinker and patch a rotten and corrupt social system, but to replace it by a better and juster one" (March 3, 1883).

The enemies against which the labour press particularly fought were the class interests implied in the National Policy's protective tariff ("Protection for Labor as well as for Capital" was the worker's cry); snobbery; that callous indifference to the underprivileged which was masked by the doctrine of *laissez-faire* individualism; and the harnessing of evolutionary science and capitalistic social philosophy in what has since been called Social Darwinism: the theory that beneficent effects result from competition and the survival of the fittest in human society. The editor of the *Labor Union* did his best to demolish this last pernicious theory: "To accept the doctrines of the survival of the fittest as applied to present industrial conditions is simply to put a premium upon greed, cunning, injustice and dishonesty—and to stamp the virtues and graces which alone make life endurable as so many hinderances to advancement." Against the tenacious doctrines of *laissez-faire*, the labour press opposed evidence of growing "collectivism" in society and the idealistic communal theories of the Knights of Labor and Henry George. Against the indifference of the haves to the have-nots, they opposed the Christian socialist vision: "a religious society recognizing the Fatherhood of God and the Brotherhood of Man, and insisting justice to the Toiler be the outcome" *Labor Union*, Oct. 27, 1883). The radicals of the eighties recognized fully how remote they were from any of the political platforms of the day, but their strength lay in their faith that "the 'Utopian visions' of today are the established facts of tomorrow" (*Palladium of Labor*, April 25, 1885).

The *Labor Advocate* of the 1890's was the vehicle for a less utopian idealism. Its readers were brought in touch with radical movements elsewhere in the world by weekly "Socialist Notes," along with accounts of Edward Bellamy's "Nationalism" propounded in *Looking Backward* (1888) and in other works, of the limitations of Henry George's theories, and of the ideas of the newly emerging Fabian society. T. Phillips Thompson (1843–1933), editor and most eloquent polemicist of the *Labor Advocate*, propagandized for a radical solution to economic evils: "no permanent or satisfying solution is possible which does not change the underlying conditions of industrial servitude, by an entire reorganization of the system of distribution." Elsewhere, in his book *The Politics of Labor* (1887), Thompson had already launched a vigorous attack on the exploiting capitalist class and in particular on the attitudes embodied in the culture and traditions which support it—"the bitter hostility of the supercilious and cynical 'culture' which apes European models and cultivates undemocratic habits of thought, from the ranks of which capitalism recruits its host of literary hirelings and professional henchmen" (p. 143). His main target, however, was the doctrine of Social Darwinism and all it entailed, and Thompson subjected the conclusions of Herbert Spencer, leading spokesman of those who applied evolutionary determinism to man's social life, to a destructive analysis, using Spencer's own ideas to arrive at opposite conclusions. With the uninhibited and vehement protests of such writers as Thompson, it is obvious that the developments of a quarter of a century since the *Ontario Workman* of 1875 had carried proletarian ideology a long way.

During these early stages of Canadian radicalism, the potential power of literature was gradually realized. Seeds of the understanding were already present in the *Ontario Workman*. For despite the editorial view that creative writing was mere entertainment and diversion from the troubles of daily life ("In these columns we will be invited now and then to turn aside from the turmoil and strife of the world, and find peaceful enjoyment"), the newspaper published a good deal of didactic and hortatory doggerel in favour of the workingman's cause, and, beginning on June 27, 1872, one lengthy and notable piece of fiction, the serialized economic novel, *The Other Side*, by a trade unionist and leader in the Canadian Nine Hour Movement, M. A. Foran. A melodramatic tale of factory life, trade unionism, and the eventual triumph of the labour movement over the tyrannical oppression of the capitalist class, it is noteworthy as an early fictional critique of industrial urban society, its class divisions and its economic basis, though it never escapes the limitations of the "bourgeois" novel and its aesthetic qualities are modest to say the least. In the 1880's the pages of the *Labor Union* and the *Palladium of Labor* are adorned with a variety of revolutionary verse, from imported traditional gleanings like Shelley's "Men of Labour" and the Chartist poems of Vincent, Jones, and Massey, to contemporary and local pieces, many written especially for these labour journals: utopian idealism, chiliastic vision, indignation at social injustice, exhortations of general and specific kinds, most of them betraying their semi-literate origins all too clearly. The *Labor Advocate* in the 1890's cast a wider net for English and American literature, and included Chartist verse, selected poems by sympathetic writers like Whitman and William Morris, an economic novel by Ignatius Donnelly printed serially, excerpts from Edward Bellamy. Its editor, Phillips Thompson, was himself a poet of sorts: "The Political Economist and the Tramp" is a facetious exposure of the Social Darwinist fallacy; "Always with You" is a bitter attack on the church's support of the economic *status quo* ("the poor shall always be with you"); and *The Labor Reform Songster* (1892) is a collection of Knights of Labor chants and battle hymns. Worthy of notice too is the *Palladium* series "Our Social Club," in which the anonymous author sets out to provide a Spectator Club for Canadian workers, to entertain his readers with fictional meetings involving a range of typical workers, while at the same time exploring and propagating radical social and political doctrines.

Both in theory and in practice proletarian literature grew in complexity through the 1870's, 1880's, and 1890's. In quality it rarely rose above the level of the crude, naive, sentimental, or melodramatic. But its existence is worth recording because it remained alive to a range of ideals and social experiences largely ignored by the respectable Canadian tradition of the period, and awareness of it places that main tradition in a truer perspective.

II

The causes and nature of Canada's spectacular "boom" beginning about 1896 and lasting with varying intensity for two decades are now generally understood. International and domestic circumstances combined to send a wave of immigration breaking over the empty western prairies, and eastern industries strained and expanded to meet the new demands. It was a time of immense enthusiasm and optimism, succeeding the discouragements of the post-Confederation era. "As the 19th century was that of the United States,"

Wilfrid Laurier proclaimed, "so I think the 20th century shall be filled by Canada." Big business enthusiasts, noting happily the rise of great trusts and corporate enterprises, praised the workings of social evolution in which this process appeared to be a late stage. "If we except a certain class of American politician," wrote a contributor to the *Canadian Magazine* in 1900 (XIV, 243 ff.), "we shall be able to find few persons who are unwilling to believe that trusts are a natural growth, and are the result of a process of evolution." The expansive spirit of the times was caught by poets and novelists like Service, Stead, MacInnes, and Stringer, who were undismayed by the moral and social upheavals of rapid material and population growth. "Sweet is the breath of the prairie," Stead chanted, "where peace and prosperity reign, / And joyous the song of the city, where all is expansion and gain."

Not everyone was so enthusiastic, however. At another extreme the agrarian evangelist Peter McArthur bitterly attacked big business in all its aspects, condemned the growth of mechanistic urban society, and sang the praises of the fast disappearing rural Eden where individualism flourished and farming was a way of life, not a commercial enterprise. A less utopian writer, Stephen Leacock, stood as firmly as McArthur for the cause of individualism and the quietness and simplicity of life being devoured and destroyed by rampant commercial and industrial expansion. The crudeness and stupidities of the new plutocracy are pilloried unmercifully in *Arcadian Adventures with the Idle Rich* (1914), and in *Sunshine Sketches of a Little Town* the virtues of Mariposa are opposed, albeit with whimsy and satire as well as nostalgia, to the corruptions of the big city which it so foolishly tries to imitate. Still others, like the poetess Marjorie Pickthall, shut out the turmoil and noise of contemporary reality altogether to create a fairer dream-world, or like D. C. Scott in "Ode for the Keats Centenary" lamented the flight of "Beauty" from the modern world, "that grew too loud and wounding."

The working classes reached out for their share in the new material prosperity. Trade unions rapidly increased in size and numbers. Internecine battles and ideological disagreements were numerous, but for the most part Canadian unions travelled the path of "business unionism" rather than of political action, that is, the American rather than the British path. But radical workers' parties also sprang up in the era of the boom, and new radical newspapers appeared to give them voice across the country. Though now largely forgotten, sects and schisms in confusing numbers propagandized vigorously in their journals and in public meetings, spreading, for the most part on still barren soil, the doctrines of socialism and communism. In general, despite the extreme dissidence of these dissenters among themselves, it can be said that they looked upon their beliefs as "hard" socialism rather than "soft"— that is, they aimed to be practical in their political and industrial warfare, not utopian dreamers as they saw their predecessors. Second, they were for the most part infected by the evolutionary optimism of "Canada's century," so that they believed in an inevitable movement towards socialism, however unsympathetic the immediate climate—in other words they were proletarian Social Darwinists. "Today," J. Connell argued in "Socialism and the Survival of the Fittest" in the *Western Clarion* in April 1913, "capitalist individualism seems firmly rooted and strongly knit, but the laws of nature are fighting on our side. . . . The time is coming when the waves of the evolutionary tide will break and roar far, very far above it."

The "scientific" or "hard" socialist was interested in the works of Marx, Engels, Sidney Webb, the Fabian Shaw, but was less sympathetic to imaginative literature than his more utopian predecessors. "The Scientific Socialist," wrote one of the Canadian radicals in *The Lance* (Oct. 9, 1909), "unlike his utopian brothers, is not an artist." And the editor of the *Western Clarion* grumbled, "we have no particular desire to pick any quarrel with working-class poets, but we think that straight plain prose is about the best form in which our views can be presented to the proletaire" (Feb. 14, 1914). Nevertheless, in the area of the shorter lyric a large number of proletarian poetasters were active, including at least two whose main work for the radical cause was as party organizers and lecturers: Alfred Budden and Wilfred Gribble. The career of the latter apparently ended in 1916 when he was arrested on charges of sedition while speaking for socialism in the streets of Saint John, New Brunswick.

It will be recognized that political radicalism in Canada has a history going back well before the Russian Revolution, which in 1917 inevitably established itself as the centre of attraction or repulsion for all revolutionary theory and practice in modern times. Between Confederation and the First World War the processes of nation-building were occupying the energies and idealism of the majority of Canadians largely to the exclusion of questions of equality, social justice, and welfare, and only in the small radical press do we find vigorous and uninhibited criticism of the social, political, and economic patterns being laid down. By the end of World War I, however, most of the goals of the National Policy were within reach or attained—the East-West communications had been developed, the West was populated through soaring immigration, home industries had flourished to make Canada, by 1920, a predominantly urban country. Radical criticism of its nature could now be entertained without endangering national existence, and for the first time a critique emerged not merely from the dissident minority among the working classes, but from the respectable middle class intellectuals who had earlier remained aloof.

The optimistic and jingoistic spirit of "Canada's century" which characterized the early 1900's and the World War I period continued into the 1920's. But though the commercial nationalism of the Canadian Manufacturers Association (Buy Canadian Goods) and of the Canadian Authors Association (Buy Canadian Books) was typical, there was also a new and more demanding patriotism, where concern with country was coupled with an earnest desire to see and remedy shortcomings. It is this kind of patriotism which provided the adjective for the titles of such new intellectual journals as the *Canadian Forum* (1920–) and the *Canadian Mercury* (1928–29). The older attitudes found their home in journals like *Willison's Monthly*, also born in the 1920's, which was devoted to the "upbuilding of Canada" through such traditional means as higher tariff protection, buying Canadian goods, and lower taxes on capital. This journal deplored the rise of aggressive democracy, Bolshevism, and the "Jazz psychology" of modern writing. "Repose, conservatism, and stability" are what the world desires, wrote the editor in 1925; and the journal found these ideals in contemplation of the real or imagined nineteenth-century past and in the literary and social amenities of the genteel tradition.

The vital spirit of the 1920's, however, was not retrospective and nostalgic but critical. *The Rebel*, the University of Toronto magazine appearing in 1917, had as its purpose "an honest criticism of things as they are" (I, Feb.). It matured into the *Canadian Forum*, of which the chief aim was "to secure a freer and more informed discussion of public questions" (Oct., 1920). The social philosophy of the *Canadian Forum*'s editorial board was acknowledged to be "progressive," and in general the journal became a focus for those who welcomed or were sympathetic towards the new in art, social attitudes, and politics. In each area it published sufficient articles of a vigorous, witty, caustic, or iconoclastic order to justify the belief that there was indeed in progress a "revolt of the 1920's." By the late 1920's a new journal, the *Canadian Mercury*, announced an even more emancipated critical spirit. Its chief objects of attack were the inhibitions and narrowness of "respectable" Canadian social life and of the Maple Leaf School of writers; its aim was "the emancipation of Canadian literature from the state of amiable mediocrity and insipidity in which it now languishes" (Dec., 1928).

The post-World War I mood of disillusion was an international phenomenon; but local reasons for the growth of a critical spirit among Canadian intellectuals in the 1920's are not far to seek. The Royal Commission on Industrial Relations which published its report on Canada's miniature Russian Revolution, the Winnipeg Strike of 1919 (see the *Canadian Annual Review*) listed at length social evils which were only added to in the 1920's and 1930's, and which were sure signs not only of the impact of the war, but that all the problems of a contemporary industrial urban civilization had arrived in Canada as part of her nationhood. The 1920's were indeed a decade of ferment. The failure of the Winnipeg Strike split the radicals into revolutionary and evolutionary camps, the former eventually leading into Tim

Buck's communism, the latter into Woodsworth's socialism, the Cooperative Commonwealth Federation, and the League for Social Reconstruction of the 1930's. Out of the same ferment the western farmers made their powerful but short-lived protest against eastern big-business ascendancy with the Progressive party. Though in the 1920's the intellectuals continued to remain aloof from political commitments of a radical kind, it is not surprising to find a writer advertising in an article in the *Canadian Mercury* in March of 1928, "Wanted—a Gospel," and lamenting that everywhere Canadians "are searching and wavering, losing one ideal after another, waiting vainly for the stimulus which would be provided by initiation into some combination of writers, poets, and all people with the vision of a socially progressive Canada." A gospel was indeed soon to be found (though, incidentally, not to that same writer's liking) when the calamity of the Great Depression abruptly descended on the land. The aesthetic and moral revolt of certain intellectuals of the 1920's became, in the dark years of the 1930's, aggressively political. The critical tools of Marxism were discovered and seized upon as answering a great need, and economic and political theories once only of interest to a small minority of the lower orders of society became palatable and even desirable to large numbers in every walk of life. The first socially committed organization of radical intellectuals, the League for Social Reconstruction, set to work to articulate a radical social philosophy to meet the challenges of the Depression, and it had an important contribution to make to that fusing of proletarian, agrarian, and old-time socialist rebels in the C.C.F. party in 1933. In the 1930's what had been an insignificant proletarian minority swelled in numbers and power and became, for the first time, of major literary and cultural significance.

The *Canadian Forum* reported the activities of the new left wing with sympathy, and indeed for a short period fell under the sway of the L.S.R., but generally it lived up to its name and provided a forum in which critical discussion could take place. From the pens of left-of-centre intellectuals, especially from that witty, vital, and provocative professor of history, F. H. Underhill, came a critical commentary on Canadian society and politics which had vigour and acuteness rarely achieved before. But angrier and more aggressive periodicals emerged in the 1930's to satisfy the needs of extremists. For two years (1932–34) *Masses* acted as a spokesman for the revolutionary proletariat, preaching Marxist doctrine with considerable violence and lashing its enemies to the right without restraint. *New Frontier* (begun in 1936) was more temperate and literate, but equally distinguishable from the *Canadian Forum*, as its attack on that journal's middle-left affiliation made clear enough: "the depression-born Canadian social democratic party with its professorial brain-trusters is a rather genteel sprig clipped from the suburban hedge of British Fabianism" (April, 1936). Unlike the *Canadian Forum*,

New Frontier purported to be fully engaged in the contemporary political scene. Typically, in December 1936, it published a special issue on Spain, which included the replies of a number of well-known Canadians to the problem, "Where I stand on Spain." The answers, which ranged from W. A. Deacon's "we should cut clear of the Empire and the whole continent of Europe" to E. J. Pratt's "My sympathies in the Spanish situation are wholly with the Popular Front," give a lively indication of the extent to which Canadian society was divided by the international and ideological debate between left- and right-wing ideas and attitudes.

The collapse of the Spanish Loyalists, the triumph of European fascism, and the non-aggression pact between Soviet Russia and Germany in 1939 were blows felt alike by moderate and extreme social revolutionaries in Canada. But soon the *deus ex machina* of global war appeared to close the dying action of this era, and to unravel in its own effective way those tangled social problems of the country which the dialectic of ideas had left unsolved. A remarkable change had taken place, however, in the temper of Canadian thought from the years following Confederation to the years of the Great Depression. In those earlier days any serious social concerns of the intellectual were likely to be associated with or conditioned by nationalism in one of its possible forms. Differences in social ideals were slight, or if they were not, the pressures were all towards making them appear decorously so. Conciliation and compromise were the key notes of public discussion, and basic principles tended to be assumed rather than considered. But in the 1920's and 1930's a range and violence of opinion not imagined before appeared to be possible and indeed to be demanded. Conflicting theories of art and social life were thrust forward with urgency and vehemence, while both domestic and international social realities became inescapable.

Already in the twenties there had been a critical reaction against the poetry of romantic sensibility in favour of the literature of ideas, social realism, and even naturalism. When in the 1930's the break with the nineteenth century tradition was intensified, debate raged as to the nature and validity of Marxist theories of art. Interpretations of proletarian aesthetics were numerous and subtle enough to constitute a new scholasticism, but it is true that many of the better Canadian writers of the time were in agreement at least to the extent of endorsing the literature of social conscience. Few revolutionaries or fellow travellers went so far as Earle Birney who argued in the *Canadian Forum* that art must temporarily cease until revolutionary action had built a new society where true creativity was possible, but just as few writers remained at the opposite pole with Robert Finch, whose verse exhibited a controlled aestheticism and formalism justifying his manifesto: "Beauty my fond fine care." By the middle thirties Canadian literary theory had swung away from "escapist" or "pure" subjective art towards a conception of art as propagandizing for or at least symptomatic of social revolution. The Victorian Canadian assumption that art was the product and ornament of a social and cultural élite had found its antithesis in the belief that the only vital art was derived from the insurgent lower orders of society. Upper- and middle-class culture had met its opposite, proletarian culture.

From the mid-twenties the gulf between proletarian ideals and aspirations and the sympathy of men and women of culture and talent can be seen closing. By the latter part of the decade poems and stories began to appear in the journals of the intellectuals which reflect an increased concern for the condition of the lower orders of society, farmers and labourers and their way of life. The new "angry" note ("sharp shame and dim anger, / Anger at civilization," as B. H. Chambers in "Nocturne" put it in the *Canadian Forum*, XII, 1931–32), is sounded frequently in the *Forum* and consistently in the *Canadian Mercury*, both in poetry and in the stories, where the marks of psychological and sociological realism and a willingness to see things as they are, however unpleasant, appear as never before. With Vernal House's "Eternity goes down the sewer" (*Masses*, I, 1932) and Leo Kennedy's "Life's like a garbage can" (*Canadian Mercury*, June 1928) the alleged complacencies of the Victorian era received their quietus.

As the events of the 1930's proceeded to channel this critical reaction along ideological lines, the impact on both poetry and prose was marked. There appeared numerous examples of "reportage," a new prose form defined in the popular American anthology, *Proletarian Literature* (1935) in this way:

> Reportage is three-dimensional reporting. The writer not only condenses reality; he must get his readers to see and feel the facts. The best writers of reportage do their editorializing via their artistry. . . . Reportage . . . requires delineation of character, of locale, of atmosphere. (P. 211.)

Dorothy Livesay was one of the best practitioners of this genre, as her intense sketch "Corbin—A Company Town Fights for its Life" in *New Frontier* (April 1936) illustrates, but it was a much used form. It required a certain discipline: a balance between editorializing and artistry, an eye for vivid and telling detail, powers of concentration. Its significance was not so much in itself, however, as in the movement which it symptomized and encouraged: the movement towards contemporaneity and realism in fiction. The result was the early domination of fiction, for the first time in Canadian literary history, by contemporary themes. The Depression short story, dealing with unemployment, its causes and consequences, flourished in the early thirties, to such an extent that readers of the *Canadian Forum*, *Masses*, and *New Frontier* became sated and bored. Most writers of the day tried their hand at the form, among them F. P. Grove, A. M. Klein, Morley Callaghan, M. Q. Innis, L. B. Creighton. Grove and Callaghan showed even more vividly in their novels the impact of the Depression and its ideological debates.

Grove's *Master of the Mill*, with its symbolic exploration of the chief contemporary "isms," is in certain respects the most penetrating ideological analysis to come out of the writing of the thirties. Callaghan, from the shabby urban naturalism of *Strange Fugitive* (1928) to the troubled dialectics of *They Shall Inherit the Earth* (1935), took his settings, actions, and themes from the contemporary Canadian scene. Grove and Callaghan both strove for artistic detachment in their works, but the result is a searing protest against the rottenness of the social and political structure of the day. Fictional exploitation of this period is likely to continue as its significance becomes easier to hold in perspective. The direct and savagely indignant protests of Irene Baird's *Waste Heritage* (1939) have no doubt permanently given way to the subtler and more profound probings and ironies of works like Gabrielle Roy's *The Tin Flute* and Hugh MacLennan's *Watch That Ends the Night*, but recent novelists (Ethel Wilson, John Marlyn, Earle Birney, Roger Lemelin) have drawn attention to rather than exhausted the richness of the material.

The leftward swing of the 1930's produced no more permanently valuable poetry than prose, but here the impact is easier to trace, and in many respects is more striking, for the Depression era was like an intense magnetic field that deflected the courses of all the poets who went through it. (That poet laureate of communism, J. S. Wallace, had already set his course long before the Great Depression.) A few like Dorothy Livesay, Leo Kennedy, and Abraham Klein underwent a sudden and dramatic veering. Dorothy Livesay, seeking to "see with the sun's bright honesty," accepted almost overnight the Marxian answer to the current social chaos, and dedicated her art to the revolutionary cause. Like her, Kennedy and Klein turned their backs on "pure poetry" to write hortatory chants and indignant diatribes for the insurgent proletariat. These two, along with F. R. Scott, whose socialism and social satire pre-date the Depression era, justify the symbolical title of the mid-thirties anthology, *New Provinces*, in which they appeared, in company with Finch, A. J. M. Smith, and E. J. Pratt. Even the last two of these more conservative poets showed clearly in their verse the pressure of the Depression ethos. Social injustice and disorder; poverty and suffering among the underprivileged; greed and complacency in high places; the concepts and theories of reform and revolution: these had become the dominant subject-matter of Canadian literature.

In the early 1920's A. J. M. Smith and others were deploring the Canadian writer's inhibitions, his lack of freedom in the choice and treatment of subjects, and the reluctance of Canadian readers, critics, and authors alike to accept the elements of realism and satire in literature. But in the 1930's the realistic mode, the cynical pose, and the weapons of satire were exploited to their fullest. For many the immediate result was a new ideological enslavement. Much of the literature of the Hungry Thirties has little purely aesthetic value and therefore it has understandably been forgotten by its original readers, perhaps even by its writers. But to ignore it is to ignore work which, for some of the chief writers of the present day, "has significance for the authors in the evolution of their own understanding"—to adopt a phrase from the introduction to *New Provinces*. After the 1930's a wide range and freedom were seen to have been won. The old debate about the degree to which a writer should be personally involved in society and committed to an ideology was not over, yet demands upon the artist to be socially committed were not likely to be so naive again nor attacks on "aestheticism" so crude. Taboos with respect to subjects and themes and modes still remained, but the potential range of art in matter and in manner was immeasurably increased. The "new provinces" of radicalism brought disillusion, but their exploration was a cathartic experience for Canadian writers. The conservative culture of nation-building met in full dialectical play the art and politics of protest and rebellion, and each was transformed by the collision. "A culture is not a flow, nor even a confluence," Lionel Trilling has argued in *The Liberal Imagination*; "the form of its existence is struggle, or at least debate—it is nothing if not a dialectic." If this is true, the late emergence of a vigorous literature of protest heralded the emancipation and the maturity of Canadian culture.

PART IV

The Realization of a Tradition

26. The Writer and his Public
1920-1960

DESMOND PACEY

THE FIRST WORLD WAR effectually obliterated in Canada whatever traces of "high colonialism" had survived the boom of the first decade of the twentieth century and the bitter debates over Reciprocity with the United States and the Navy Bill for Empire defence. The War shattered the core of common beliefs and attitudes suggested by the adjective "high": the mood of Canada in 1918 and 1919 was angry, sceptical, and restless. And if Canadians were not yet sure what role they wished their country to play in the world, they were virtually all agreed that it should not be that of a colony.

Change was everywhere. The Easter riots of 1918 in Quebec over conscription, the angry demonstrations of the United Farmers of Ontario in May 1918, the break of western labour with the Trades and Labour Congress and the formation of the radical One Big Union, the Winnipeg Strike in 1919, the victory of the United Farmers of Ontario in the provincial election of October 1919, the formation of the left-wing National Progressive party under Thomas A. Crerar in January 1920, the death of Sir Wilfrid Laurier and the retirement of Sir Robert Borden: these events combined to transform the traditional image of Canadian society beyond recognition. The new Canada had new leaders—William Lyon Mackenzie King of the Liberals, Arthur Meighen of the Conservatives, T. A. Crerar and J. S. Woodsworth of the Progressives—and there was general hopefulness that they might find new solutions to the old problems. For the old problems did remain: the problems of the relations between French and English Canada, between the provinces and the federal government, between Canada and the British Empire.

In spite of the new mood and the new leaders, progress in solving the first two of these problems was disappointingly slow. Mackenzie King, the Liberal prime minister who was to dominate the political life of Canada for almost thirty years, proved an adept at palliating the real or imagined grievances of French Canada, but he never really faced the full implications of the problem—with the unfortunate result that it is even more acute in the 1960's than it was in the 1920's. Not until 1937, with the appointment of the Royal Commission on Dominion-Provincial Relations, was a determined effort made to solve the federal-provincial problem—with the unfortunate consequence that Canada had to meet the crisis of the Great Depression of the 1930's with divided and confused areas of jurisdiction.

But the third problem, that of Canada's status within the British Empire, could be tackled more energetically because there was general agreement as to what that status must be. The war, for all the strains that it had put upon the Confederation, had had the very positive effect of proving Canada's strength both as a military and as an industrial power. A country which had made such a distinct contribution to the Allied war effort was no longer willing to be treated as a "child of nations"—her limbs were altogether too giant-sized for that. Canada demanded and obtained a separate seat at the Peace Conference in 1919, became an independent member of the new League of Nations, balked when Great Britain seemed to take her complaisance for granted during the Chanak Incident of 1922, and in the series of Imperial Conferences held during the 1920's led the struggle for recognition of the British Dominions as equal and autonomous nations within the Commonwealth. The Statute of Westminster in 1931 was only formal recognition of Canada's national status; she had already begun to sign her own treaties and appoint her own ambassadors.

The new spirit of self-confidence engendered by the war was confirmed by Canada's economic progress in the 1920's. It was a decade of unprecedented expansion. The new era of oil and electricity, mining and metallurgy, automobiles and aeroplanes was congenial to Canada's resources. In the age of high speed transportation, Canada's vast distances were no longer a serious obstacle to progress, and her remote districts—northern Ontario, northern Quebec, the Northwest Territories, the hinterland of British Columbia—proved to be rich in minerals, forest products, oil, and water systems suitable for producing hydro-electric power. These new sources of wealth, combined with such traditional Canadian commodities as the wheat of the prairies and the fruit, cattle, timber and fish of the eastern provinces, gave the Canadian economy in the 1920's a buoyancy it had never known before.

It is sometimes difficult to establish direct relations between political and economic developments and literary and cultural ones, but in these years there is no doubt that the general air of change, excitement, and confidence did affect the development of Canadian literature. Just as in the decades immediately following Confederation there had been a conscious effort to create a literature worthy of the new confederacy, so now there was a conscious, at times a self-conscious, determination to create a literature commensurate with Canada's new status as an independent nation. As in the

1870's, magazines were founded to serve as vehicles for the new literature, organizations were formed to protect and promote it, and anthologies and historical surveys were printed to publicize it at home and abroad.

The four magazines which were founded immediately after the war clearly illustrate the main trends. These magazines were the *Canadian Bookman* (1919–39), the *Canadian Forum* (1920–   ), the *Canadian Historical Review* (1920–   ) and the *Dalhousie Review* (1921–   ).

The *Canadian Bookman* at once became the organ of the new spirit of uncritical self-confidence and "boosterism." To the editors of this magazine, a Canadian book was *ipso facto* a good book. The extremes to which it carried literary nationalism were almost incredible. Even such an austere person as D. C. Scott, when he reviewed L. Adams Beck's *The Ninth Vibration* for the *Bookman*, was capable of writing: "As if to emphasize the fact that the book is a product of Canada, the author has added to his signature . . . the word Canada. . . . We would commend this course to our writers as it nationalizes our production and puts the word Canada where it ought to be more frequently, on works of art and literature." But what really delighted the hearts of the editors of the *Bookman* was to be able to write such reports as this: "Dr. Silcox, principal of the Ottawa Normal School, in an address on Canadian Literature last month, comparing Canadian literature with that of the United States, said that much of our literature was superior to anything produced by any other country in any century of our era. He then gave a detailed description of the different classes of Canadian literature, along with brief sketches of some of our outstanding writers. Among others he spoke of Robert Norwood, L. M. Montgomery, Basil King, C. G. D. Roberts, Stephen Leacock, Gilbert Parker, Agnes Laut, Ralph Connor, Pauline Johnson, and L. Adams Beck." That report appeared in November 1926; a month later the *Bookman* proudly noted that "The Native Sons of Canada are sending speakers out to fill engagements in the smaller towns of the West dealing with the need for greater recognition of Canadian literature. The speakers trace the growth of prose and poetry from the earliest productions." This sort of thing was too much even for some of the contributors to the *Bookman*, and in June 1927, in an article entitled "What is Criticism?" Thomas O'Hagan wrote, "As regards Canadian literary criticism, it is woefully lacking in scholarship, poise and judicial discrimination. All our goslings are swans."

This more critical spirit found consistent expression in the *Canadian Forum*. The *Forum* was as concerned for Canadian independence and cultural development as the *Canadian Bookman*, but it wanted the development to be of truly high standard and to be responsive to new ideas whether at home or abroad. Anyone who wants to see the new Canadian spirit at its best should read the whole of the *Forum*'s first editorial (October 1920).

Here are a few key sentences from it: "With interests as fresh and wide as her national responsibilities, Canada refuses instinctively to bind herself with formulae. Too often our convictions are borrowed from London, Paris, or New York. Real independence is not the product of tariff or treaties. It is a spiritual thing. No country has reached its full stature, which makes its goods at home, but not its faith and its philosophy. . . . The *Canadian Forum* had its origin in a desire to secure a freer and more informed discussion of public questions and, behind the strife of parties, to trace and value those developments of art and letters which are distinctly Canadian." The *Forum* proceeded to practise what it had preached: it printed the early poems of E. J. Pratt, Robert Finch, Dorothy Livesay, Raymond Knister, A. J. M. Smith, F. R. Scott, A. M. Klein, and Leo Kennedy, the short stories of Raymond Knister, J. D. Robins, Mary Quayle Innis, Gilbert Norwood, C. F. Lloyd, and Jean Burton, articles on the developing little theatre movement in Canada and on the paintings of the Group of Seven, and balanced, intelligent reviews of all the best Canadian books. From the first it was critical of the boosting tendencies of the *Canadian Bookman* and the Canadian Authors' Association, and the climax came in December 1926 when it printed an article, "Making Literature Hum," by Douglas Bush. "It would seem incredible," Bush wrote, "that intelligent persons who were abreast of the contemporary movement could hold the opinions which most of our 'literati' exuberantly express about their own work and their friends. Every year one hopes to hear the last of our windy tributes to our Shakespeares and Miltons, and every year the Hallelujah Chorus seems to grow in volume and confidence. . . . Inflated rhetoric used to be left to the politicians, its rightful exponents, for use on the first of July; during the last few years it has become the language of literature, and one learns on all sides that Canada is taking its permanent seat in the literary league of nations." Bush went on to tell a few home truths about the books being boosted, and can scarcely have been surprised when his article provoked anguished replies in the succeeding few issues of the magazine.

While the *Canadian Forum* was doing its best to stir up enlightened critical discussion of Canadian writing, the *Canadian Historical Review* was quietly promoting research into the source-material of Canadian history. The *Review* had its antecedent in the *Review of Historical Publications Relating to Canada*, which had been initiated at the University of Toronto in 1896 as part of the programme of that pioneer of Canadian historical scholarship, Professor George M. Wrong. The new *Review* provided a vehicle for the young historians to express their ideas about the Canadian past, and was in considerable measure responsible for the new erudition and critical insights which soon became apparent in the book-length, specialist studies which in this era replaced the more popular historical surveys of the previous period. Instead of being content with a recital of colourful events, the new historians sought for the deeper forces in Canadian historical development, and set out to define the exact nature of the Canadian constitution by subjecting it to close analysis and comparative study. The basis was being laid for a really informed sense of national identity to replace merely sentimental patriotism.

An allied development may be associated with the foundation of the *Dalhousie Review* in 1921. It would be hard to over-estimate the influence of the university quarterlies upon Canadian cultural development. Lacking the weekly journals of opinion which have played such a part in English intellectual life,* Canada has relied upon the quarterlies to provide informed discussion of public affairs, reasoned reviews of current books, and general essays upon literature, art, and social movements. *Queen's Quarterly* had been founded as early as 1893, but remained substantially a magazine of alumni news until the 1920's; the *University Magazine* emanated from McGill between 1901 and 1920; the *University of Toronto Quarterly* was not to be established until 1931. Professor H. L. Stewart, the first editor of the *Dalhousie Review*, summed up the basic aim of all the university quarterlies in his "Salutation": "What we have in mind is the need of that public, concerned about the things of the intellect and spirit, which desires to be addressed on problems of general import and in a style that can be generally understood. . . . We shall always welcome papers that embody historical investigation into our country's records. Thus the outlook of the *Review* is primarily Canadian. . . . In this sense we avow a nationalism that is not prejudice and a provincialism that is not narrowness."

The four magazines which we have just discussed were briefly augmented during the latter half of the 1920's by two little magazines in Montreal, the *McGill Fortnightly Review* (1925–27) and the *Canadian Mercury* (1928–29). Dominated by the young poets who were to be known as the Montreal Group—A. J. M. Smith, F. R. Scott, Leo Kennedy, and A. M. Klein—these magazines sought to introduce to Canada the new, modernist verse and prose of writers such as Eliot, Pound, Edith Sitwell, and James Joyce. The editors and contributors affected to be scornful of literary nationalism and preached the virtues of cosmopolitanism and of a contemporary sensibility. At every opportunity they ridiculed the boosterism of the *Canadian Bookman* and the Canadian Authors' Association. For all this, their activities can be claimed to form a part of the new literary nationalism. Some of their poems —A. J. M. Smith's "Lonely Land," for example—were deliberate efforts

---

*A partial exception to this statement is *Saturday Night* (1887–), which has at some times in its long history, and especially under the editorship of B. K. Sandwell from 1932 to 1951 and the recent editorship of Arnold Edinborough, provided responsible and informed comment on Canadian affairs.

to match in verse the distinctively Canadian features of the paintings of the Group of Seven, and behind all their efforts lay a determination to create a Canadian literature worthy of comparison with the new literature emanating from abroad. Whereas the editors of the *Bookman* said, in effect, that Canadian writing was already as good as any in the world, the editors of the *Fortnightly* and the *Mercury* said that what we had was mediocre and we had better make haste to bring it up to world standards.

The new nationalism which produced these magazines also led to the organization of the Canadian Authors' Association in 1921. At a founding dinner held in Montreal, Bliss Carman was hailed as Canada's unofficial poet laureate and symbolically crowned with laurel. The immediate objective of the association was to secure the passage of a Canadian Copyright Act which would give proper protection to the rights of Canadian authors, but it soon launched an ambitious programme of literary nationalism. In co-operation with the *Canadian Bookman*, which became the official organ of the association, it initiated a series of Canadian Book Weeks designed to publicize and sell the native literary product. Posters such as the following were designed and distributed to all Canadian bookstores:

> 700
> Canadian Authors
> in   our
> Wonderful Canada
> Have you read their books?

As might have been expected, the *Canadian Forum* objected to such high-pressure salesmanship—"shock tactics do not in the long run serve the best interests of literature. There may be immediate and tangible results during the week in question, but, the week after, the old condition will be back again and Canadian literature will stand just where it did two years before"— but the book weeks survived for over a quarter of a century. (Indeed the institution still survives in 1964 in a modified form: it is now called "Young Canada's Book Week" and is confined to books written, not necessarily by native authors, for juveniles.)

Another activity of the Authors' Association was a series of summer schools of Canadian literature. The first such school was thus announced in the *Bookman* of June 1926:

From July 5 to 11 the first Summer School of Canadian literature will be opened at Muskoka Assembly, the literary summer capital of Canada. Classes will be held out-of-doors, in the "Little Theatre in the Woods" at 11 a.m. and 4 p.m., and will be conducted by three outstanding literary men: Charles G. D. Roberts, Wilson MacDonald and John W. Garvin. Dr. Roberts' subject will be "The Method and Technique of Prose and Poetry." Mr. MacDonald will deal with "The Development of Canadian Poetry—Early Canadian Poetry; the Group of the Early 60's;

Canadian Women Poets; The Twentieth Century Group." Mr. Garvin's subject will be "Canadian Prose—Travel and Adventures of the Explorers; Fiction: Richardson, Haliburton, DeMille; Fiction: Kirby, Parker, Lighthall, Duncan; Two Canadian Diaries: Paul Kane, George Monro Grant."

During the remaining hours of this pleasure-plus-profit holiday, the "students" may make themselves at home in the delightful Epworth Inn, overlooking Lake Rosseau, or they may scatter themselves about in boats, or on the tennis courts and bowling green, or in the woods.

Truth is indeed stranger than fiction: Leacock's satires never equal such a passage as this.

The *Bookman* reported that between twenty and thirty students, six of them university graduates, attended that first summer school. Ways obviously had to be found to reach greater numbers. One way was to get Canadian literature accepted as a legitimate subject of study in the universities, as Canadian history had been accepted a generation earlier through the efforts of George M. Wrong. In 1923 the *Bookman* made a survey of the teaching of Canadian literature in the universities, but found the results (as reported in the January 1924 issue) disappointing. The University of British Columbia reported no study at all of the subject, Manitoba one hour a week in the fourth year, U.N.B. had no course currently in operation but had had courses in the past, Toronto included a few Canadian poems in the text-book *Representative Poetry*, Western Ontario studied a little Canadian poetry in the fourth year. Only Acadia, which had a full-term course, Dalhousie, which reported a course on "Literary Movements in Canada," Ottawa, Laval, and McGill, which reported that it "has for the last twenty years given courses in Canadian literature, and is developing the department," gave the subject the attention which the *Bookman* felt it warranted. Indeed it was not until the 1940's and 1950's that Canadian literature became the focus of significant academic scrutiny in Canada. The boosterism of the *Bookman* and the Authors' Association offended the academic mind, and delayed rather than hastened the scholarly study of Canadian literature.

Lecture tours by writers were another way of reaching large audiences, and proved easier to promote. Bliss Carman, Charles G. D. Roberts, and Wilson MacDonald all made triumphant tours of Canada in the mid-twenties. In February 1927 the *Bookman* was able to report as follows:

Not exactly like the troubadours of old, but with perhaps even more beneficial results in a community sense, several of Canada's poets are on tour east and west. Bliss Carman has been giving another series of addresses on poetry to university students in the west. The Roberts—Charles G.D. and Lloyd—have been filling engagements in far western cities, while from the Maritimes come reports of enthusiastic receptions to Wilson MacDonald on his tour of those provinces.

Lorne Pierce was another lecturer who made extensive tours in the twenties, and even the austere Frederick Philip Grove was persuaded to engage in one such venture: he travelled across Canada in 1928 lecturing to members of the Canadian Clubs.

The establishment of literary prizes, the award of which could be announced with a great fanfare of publicity, was another device favoured by the *Bookman* and the Authors' Association for "making literature hum." The *Bookman* triumphantly hailed the establishment in 1922 by the government of the Province of Quebec of a $5,000 annual fund for literary prizes for the best books in English and French, and the Authors' Association at once sought to have the Province of Ontario establish a similar fund. In May 1925 the *Bookman* wryly noted that the Ontario request "got short shrift at the hands of Premier Ferguson on the plea of economy, and the authors are trying to harmonize this with the substantial increases in the salaries of the ministers and in the sessional allowances of the members." The association had better luck a decade later, when it managed to persuade Lord Tweedsmuir to establish the annual Governor-General's Literary Awards. In the meantime, the proponent of literary awards could salute the initiation of the Lorne Pierce Gold Medal of the Royal Society of Canada. This medal, donated by the energetic young editor of the Ryerson Press, was to be awarded not for a specific book, but for a distinguished and sustained contribution to Canadian letters: its first recipient, in 1926, was Charles G. D. Roberts.

The relative paucity of domestic literary prizes in this decade was to some extent compensated by the award to Canadians of valuable foreign prizes. The boosters' claim that Canadians were now making contributions to the literature of the world seemed to receive confirmation from the award of the Dodd-Mead prize to Martha Ostenso's *Wild Geese* in 1925 and of the Atlantic Monthly Prize to Mazo de la Roche's *Jalna* in 1927. These awards, naturally, were announced triumphantly and at length in the pages of the *Bookman* and also, with a rare show of unanimity, in the pages of the *Canadian Forum*.

The final proof of the spirit of literary nationalism and optimism which was characteristic of the 1920's was the proliferation of histories, anthologies, and "master works" of Canadian literature. No less than six histories of Canadian literature were published in the decade: R. P. Baker's *English-Canadian Literature to the Confederation* (1920), J. D. Logan's and D. G. French's *Highways of Canadian Literature* (1924), Archibald MacMechan's *Headwaters of Canadian Literature* (1924), Lionel Stevenson's *Appraisals of Canadian Literature* (1926), Lorne Pierce's *Outline of Canadian Literature* (1927) and V. B. Rhodenizer's *Handbook of Canadian Literature* (1930). The anthologies of the decade included E. K. and E. H. Broadus's *Book of Canadian Prose and Verse* (1923), A. M. Stephen's *The Golden Treasury of Canadian Verse* (1928), and Raymond Knister's *Canadian Short Stories*

(1928), in addition to revised editions of earlier anthologies by Wilfred Campbell and John W. Garvin. The spirit animating these anthologies was perhaps best expressed in Raymond Knister's introduction to his book of short stories. "Literature as a whole is changing," he wrote, "new fields are being broken, new crops are being raised in them, and the changes apparent in other countries show counterparts in our development. . . . Literature in the United States is only lately emerging from the imitative stage, and there are signs that it is doing the same thing here. . . . There is such a thing as a Canadian spirit, and perhaps in no other department of literature is it so vivid and indubitable."

A similar conviction led Lorne Pierce to launch in 1923 the ambitious "Makers of Canadian Literature" series, which was originally intended to include four introductory volumes of literary background, seven volumes in French, and twenty volumes in English. Each of these latter volumes was to be devoted to a single author, and to include a biography, critical assessment, and a sampling of the author's work. The series was too elaborate an undertaking, and petered out after half a dozen volumes, but its very conception indicates the temper of the period. A similarly ambitious series was "Master Works of Canadian Authors," announced in 1925 by the Radisson Society as a deluxe twenty-five volume series priced at $100 per volume: it too, even more predictably, lapsed after two or three volumes had appeared. Many less ambitious reprints also appeared: new editions of almost all Canadian "classics" such as Richardson's *Wacousta*, Moodie's *Roughing It in the Bush*, and Kirby's *Golden Dog*. Monographs on the leading Canadian writers were also published: V. L. O. Chittick's *Thomas Chandler Haliburton* in 1924, Odell Shepard's *Bliss Carman* in the same year, Carl Y. Connor's *Archibald Lampman* in 1929.

All this buoyant optimism received a rude shock when the stock market crashed in 1929 and the Great Depression began. In his budget speech of 1927, the Minister of Finance, J. A. Robb, had been able to report proudly that "The Dominion enters its Diamond Jubilee with a happy outlook. Our farmers have in general enjoyed a bountiful harvest, our industries are active and working well up to capacity. Many, indeed, are working overtime. Employment is on a high level. Our transportation companies report a large volume of business. The retail trade is brisk. Money is plentiful and a buoyant spirit prevails." Three years later Robb was out of office and the new Conservative prime minister, R. B. Bennett, had to call an emergency session of parliament to deal with the grave unemployment situation.

The chief effects of the Depression on Canadian literature were to slow down its production and to turn the writers' attention towards problems of social and economic injustice. The Canadian publishing industry had scarcely existed before 1920—only 26 Canadian books were published in 1917, 43 in

1918, and 70 in 1919—but during the 1920's it had grown with almost incredible rapidity. Now retrenchment was the order of the day. Several firms, and notably one of the most ambitious and experimental, Graphic Press of Ottawa, went bankrupt early in the 1930's; others cut back their lists and survived only by acting as agents for foreign houses. Even established Canadian writers such as Morley Callaghan and Frederick Philip Grove found it increasingly hard to get their books published, and new writers could scarcely get a hearing at all. For example, the young Montreal poets who had made their *débuts* in the magazines in the 1920's should have been publishing their first books in the 1930's, whereas in fact it was not until the 1940's that their first books appeared.

Magazines were similarly hampered by the Depression. The only new literary magazines to appear in the decade were sponsored publications which did not have to make ends meet: the *University of Toronto Quarterly*, initiated by the University in 1931, and the *Canadian Poetry Magazine*, founded by the Canadian Authors' Association in 1936. One or two left-wing magazines made brief appearances—*Masses* (1932–34) and *New Frontier* (1936–37)—but in spite of their proletarian sympathies they could only survive for a few issues. Even the *Canadian Forum* encountered a series of financial crises, and at one point survived only by virtue of handing itself over to the sponsorship of the publishing house of J. M. Dent and Sons.

The literary nationalism of the twenties began to evaporate in the dry atmosphere of the thirties. C. S. Ritchie, in a 1932 article in the *Forum* entitled "On Coming Home," noted the changes five years had wrought: "The tempo of Canadian life and thought has changed. . . . When I left Canada the country was flushed with prosperity. Today . . . the national mood is one of disillusionment . . . an increasing indifference to the old form of flag-waving nationalism." The disillusionment was particularly acute in relation to our literature. The social and economic crisis of the early thirties suddenly made people realize that our much-vaunted literature had virtually nothing to say on social and economic questions. Reviewing V. L. Parrington's *Main Currents of American Thought* in the July 1931 issue of the *Forum*, F. H. Underhill wrote: "The reading of a book such as this is a depressing experience for a Canadian. It makes him realize the awful intellectual and emotional poverty of our Canadian civilization. A country's literature should make it conscious of the social forces which determine its destiny. But our literature since 1867 displays only a Boeotian placidity. We shall never produce a Parrington because we have not produced the literature for him to interpret."

The record of the thirties bore out Underhill's pessimistic prediction. No histories of Canadian literature were published in the decade, there were almost no reprints of Canadian classics, and the only monograph on a

Canadian writer was James Cappon's *Bliss Carman* (1930), which was really a relic of the twenties. Only a few anthologies appeared to sustain the taste for Canadian writing: Nathaniel A. Benson's *Modern Canadian Poetry* (1930), Bliss Carman's and Lorne Pierce's *Our Canadian Literature* (1935), *New Provinces: Poems of Several Authors* (1936), Ethel Hume Bennett's *New Harvesting* (1938), and Alan Creighton's and Hilda M. Ridley's *A New Canadian Anthology* (1938). Perhaps the most significant of these anthologies was *New Provinces*: edited by F. R. Scott and A. J. M. Smith, it brought together for the first time the work of the best of the new Canadian poets, Pratt, Finch, Smith, Scott, and Klein.

The publication of these anthologies, however, makes apparent the persistence of literary nationalism in spite of all the obstacles which now lay in its path. There were other indications that the trend might be slowed down but not halted. The best sustained piece of Canadian literary criticism to appear up to its time was W. E. Collin's brilliant group of essays on Canadian poetry, *The White Savannahs* (1936). In the same year the *University of Toronto Quarterly* began its series of annual reviews of Canadian literature, "Letters in Canada," providing for the first time a systematic, intelligent appraisal of Canadian books of all types. The introduction to the first issue of this survey noted that "there is no annual publication devoted to the cultural and literary life of the Dominion; no bibliography of books and articles on this subject, and no account done in Canada in a given year, in the different departments of writing, creative and critical. This twofold need the *Quarterly* seeks to supply." It then made a statement which marked an important breakthrough in the campaign to make Canadian literature academically respectable: "It will not be denied that letters in Canada is a legitimate and important subject of inquiry, and one in which many Canadian readers, and some outside Canada, are interested."

The year 1936 also saw the institution of the Governor-General's Literary Awards, which provided medals for the best book each year in each of several categories. Another positive development was the establishment of a national broadcasting system in 1932: it was not long before the C.B.C. was sponsoring lectures on Canadian literature (*Canadian Literature Today*, edited by E. K. Brown, 1938) and broadcasting Canadian poems and short stories.

Canadian literature, then, survived the Depression, if only on a modest scale in comparison with the lavish expansiveness of the twenties. But the Depression changed its direction as well as its scale. Poets and prose writers alike turned away from the technical experimentation of the twenties towards the exploration of social and economic themes. The consciousness of the need for new directions is clearly apparent in the apologetic preface to *New Provinces*: "... by the end of the last decade the modernist movement was frustrated for want of direction. In this, poetry was reflecting the aimlessness of its social environment. In confronting the world with the need to restore order out of social chaos, the economic depression has released human energies by giving them positive direction. . . . The poems in this collection were written for the most part when new techniques were on trial and when the need for a new direction was more apparent than what that direction would be." The bread lines, the work camps, the growing threat of a second world war—these things could be ignored by writers for the popular magazines, perhaps, but not by anyone of genuine sensibility. E. J. Pratt turned from his narratives of heroism at sea to the ironies of warfare in *A Fable of the Goats* (1937); F. R. Scott, A. M. Klein, Leo Kennedy, and even the relatively non-political A. J. M. Smith began to write poems attacking the injustices of the capitalist system and promoting socialist ideals; Dorothy Livesay deserted her early imagism for bitter portrayals of the plight of the workers; Anne Marriott, in *The Wind Our Enemy* (1939), depicted the sufferings of the prairie farmers whose economic troubles had been compounded by the dust storms of the mid-thirties. The novelists, strangely enough, were slower to react to the new conditions, but the economic conditions of the time figured prominently in Claudius Gregory's *Forgotten Men* (1933), Morley Callaghan's *They Shall Inherit the Earth* (1935), and Irene Baird's *Waste Heritage* (1939).

The Second World War had much the same effect on Canada as had the First: it accelerated Canadian industrial development, produced a ferment of new ideas, and strengthened Canada's confidence in herself. The return of prosperity made possible the publication of many more books, and poets such as Klein, Smith, and Scott, and a large group of new poets and novelists, soon saw their work in print. There was a renewed sense of national purpose resulting from the virtual unanimity with which Canadians opposed Hitlerism and supported the joint efforts of Churchill, Roosevelt, and Stalin. The war quickened the process of social change: the Rowell-Sirois Report on Dominion-Provincial Relations, published in 1941, finally clarified the role of the federal authority in matters of social security; the Beveridge Report in Britain strengthened Canadian determination to establish the welfare state; there was much debate concerning the type of world organization which must follow the war and seek to preclude its repetition. There was a general shift to the left in Canadian political thinking, an almost general acceptance of some form of collectivism. And once again the massive Canadian contribution to the Allied war effort made Canadians determined to play a strong and independent part in the peace. This time, however, the threat to Canada's independence came not from Britain, but from the United States. It was not a political but an economic and cultural dependence that was threatened, and the effort to escape this dependence was to be a major preoccupation of Canada throughout the forties, fifties and sixties.

Again the general excitement fostered the development of new magazines, and the new magazines welcomed new writers. In far-off British Columbia, Alan Crawley in 1941 established the poetry magazine *Contemporary Verse*, thus initiating a trend which was soon to become significant: the decentralization of Canadian letters. Throughout the first three decades of the century, Toronto had remained the centre of literary activity in Canada, with Montreal as its only rival. In the forties and fifties, however, Toronto's dominance was challenged, in spite of the continued presence there of the *Canadian Forum* and most of the publishing houses. The most lively magazines of the war and post-war years were published in Montreal: *Preview* and *First Statement*, both of which were issued there between 1942 and 1945, and *Northern Review*, their joint successor, which was published there from 1945 to 1955. (*Northern Review*'s last few issues were published in Toronto, where its editor, John Sutherland, became a student at St. Michael's College.)

To re-read *Preview* and *First Statement* is to recapture something of the excitement of those war years in Canadian literary circles. *Preview* began in March 1942 as a mimeographed bulletin issued by five writers who had "formed themselves into a group for the purpose of critical discussion and criticism": F. R. Scott, Margaret Day, Bruce Ruddick, Patrick Anderson, and Neufville Shaw. Militant engagement was the keynote of their opening editorial: "All anti-fascists, we feel that the existence of a war between democratic culture and the paralysing forces of dictatorship only intensifies the writer's obligation to work. Now, more than ever, creative and experimental writing must be kept alive and there must be no retreat from the intellectual frontier. . . . The poets among us look forward, perhaps optimistically, to a possible fusion between the lyric and didactic elements in modern verse, a combination of vivid, arresting imagery and the capacity to sing with social content and criticism." P. K. Page and A. M. Klein were soon added to the group, but the dominant influence from first to last was Patrick Anderson, whose arrival in Montreal in 1940 from England via New York was precisely the catalyst needed to revive the literary activity which had begun so promisingly in the twenties but gradually slowed down in the thirties. The new movement carried on the cosmopolitan interests of the original Montreal Group, but added a new element of socialist commitment.

It was the cosmopolitanism of the *Preview* group which irked the founders of *First Statement*: John Sutherland, Irving Layton, and Louis Dudek. Sutherland, who was as dominant in this group as was Anderson in the other, argued that *Preview*'s alleged cosmopolitanism was just another name for colonialism: "a poet preaching politics in the guise of Auden may be just as colonial as a member of the C.A.A. praising Britain in the metres of Tennyson." What Sutherland wanted was "a poetry that has stopped being a parasite on other literatures and has had the courage to decide its own problems in its own way." The poems and stories that Sutherland published in *First Statement* were less metaphysical and difficult in style than those selected by Anderson for *Preview*, were more direct reflections of the immediate Canadian scene, spoke a plainer and more colloquial language.

The two groups temporarily merged to form the editorial board of *Northern Review* in 1945, but the alliance was short-lived. A bitter review of Robert Finch's poems by Sutherland led most of the *Preview* groups to resign. Sutherland carried his second magazine on for over a decade, but he gradually shifted its emphasis away from social realism towards Catholic apologetics. His own dogmatic but stimulating editorials, aggressively Marxist in the early years and aggressively Catholic in the later years, did more than anything else to make *Northern Review* the most provocative Canadian magazine of its period.

There were other magazines, however, which played a significant part in these years. A group of poets and critics at the University of New Brunswick in Fredericton sought to keep alive the literary tradition established there by Bliss Carman and Charles G. D. Roberts by founding *The Fiddlehead* in 1945. Like *Preview* and *First Statement*, it began as a mimeographed bulletin of the group, but gradually expanded its operations. The first step was to accept outside contributions; it then adopted a printed format; and eventually it began to print short stories and book reviews as well as poems. It has survived now for almost two decades, maintaining in its editorial policy the eclectic point of view with which it began.

A much more ambitious but short-lived foundation was *Here and Now*, which was published in Toronto from 1947 to 1949. Its first editorial was another expression of Canadian literary nationalism: "For too long our artists and writers have been forced either to emigrate or to have their work produced elsewhere. Every country takes the greatest pains to prevent its money from going abroad, but too little care is taken in Canada to keep our brains and our writing at home." *Here and Now* appeared in a handsome format and was a fine example of layout and typography, but it had no clear editorial policy and, unlike the Montreal magazines and *The Fiddlehead*, was not the nucleus of a group of young writers. Its early demise, then, was not surprising.

As in the twenties, there were also signs of literary awakening in the anthologies and literary histories that appeared in the forties. The two most influential books in these categories appeared almost simultaneously in 1943: A. J. M. Smith's *Book of Canadian Poetry* and E. K. Brown's *On Canadian Poetry*. The joint appearance of these books, produced by Canadians who were both to hold important chairs of English literature in the United States, was the final event in the long-drawn-out campaign to make Canadian literature academically respectable. They were distinct improvements over their analogues in the twenties: Smith's anthology was discriminating in its selections and scholarly in its introductions and annotations, and Brown's critical history substituted something of Arnold's detachment for the perfervid patriotism of books such as *Highways of Canadian Literature*. And both Smith and Brown had a definite point of view which stimulated debate: Smith's obvious preference for metaphysical verse and for the cosmopolitan tradition provoked John Sutherland to edit *Other Canadians* (1947), and Irving Layton and Louis Dudek to produce *Canadian Poems 1850-1952* (1952), while Brown's high estimate of Lampman and Duncan Campbell Scott and virtual dismissal of Carman and Roberts initiated a whole series of critical re-appraisals of these poets of the Confederation group. Smith's anthology also had the effect of suggesting Desmond Pacey's *Book of Canadian Stories* (1947), in which he sought to do for Canadian short fiction what Smith had done for Canadian poetry.

Other important anthologies of this period were Ralph Gustafson's *Anthology of Canadian Poetry* (Pelican 1942) and *Canadian Accent* (1947), a book of Canadian prose, and Ronald Hambleton's *Unit of Five* (1944), which provided the first substantial sampling of the poetry of P. K. Page, Louis Dudek, James Wreford, Raymond Souster, and Ronald Hambleton. The period also saw a revival of interest in monographs on Canadian writers: Carl F. Klinck's *Wilfred Campbell* appeared in 1942, Elsie Pomeroy's *Sir Charles G. D. Roberts* in 1943, Desmond Pacey's *Frederick Philip Grove* in 1945. This was also a period of intense activity in the writing of Canadian political and social history. Morden H. Long's *History of the Canadian People* appeared in 1943, Donald G. Creighton's *Dominion of the North* in 1944, and A. R. M. Lower's *From Colony to Nation* in 1946, and these were only the three most striking books of the many that were published in the decade.

The novel, as usual, lagged behind. Callaghan produced only one weak novel in the forties, Grove died in 1948, and Mazo de la Roche had settled down to the endless multiplication of the "Jalna" series. Hugh MacLennan was the only new novelist to produce a significant volume of work in the decade, and the nationalistic emphasis of his novels was the most interesting expression in fiction of the prevailing spirit of the period. First novels by Sinclair Ross, W. O. Mitchell, Hugh Garner, Earle Birney, Joyce Marshall, Henry Kreisel, Malcolm Lowry, and Ethel Wilson provided evidence, however, that even in fiction a new era of creativity was beginning.

Canadian drama, which had shown a few stirrings of life in the twenties and then relapsed into inactivity, also showed renewed signs of life in the forties. Gwen Pharis Ringwood wrote her plays of prairie life, and a whole school of radio dramatists came into existence as the result of the challenge offered by Andrew Allan's C.B.C. "Stage" series.

The C.B.C., indeed, was playing an increasingly important part in the cultural life of the nation. So too was another public enterprise, the National Film Board, established under the dynamic leadership of John Grierson in 1939. But the most ambitious and conscious effort to foster Canadian culture by a public agency was the establishment in 1949 of the Royal Commission on National Development in the Arts, Letters and Sciences. The establishment of this commission was the most tangible evidence of Canada's determination to resist the cultural domination of the United States and to develop an indigenous art and literature. The Order-in-Council stated:

> That it is desirable that the Canadian people should know as much as possible about their country, its history and traditions, and about their national life and common achievements;
> That it is in the national interest to give encouragement to institutions which express national feeling, promote common understanding and add to the variety and richness of Canadian life, rural as well as urban;
> That there exist already certain Federal agencies and activities which contribute to these ends . . . and
> That it is desirable that an examination be conducted into such agencies and activities, with a view to recommending their most effective conduct in the national interest. . . .

In most other countries of the Western world, such an Order-in-Council would have been commonplace; but in Canada, where, except for the Province of Quebec, an attitude of public *laissez-faire* in relation to the arts was long established, it was revolutionary in its implications. For the first time there was open, legal recognition of the necessity of a Canadian culture.

For two years the Commission, under the able chairmanship of Vincent Massey, held hearings throughout Canada. Never before had the arts in Canada been the subject of such animated and sustained debate. And when the Report of the Commission appeared in 1951 it provided a testament of faith in Canada's independent cultural destiny:

> American influences on Canadian life to say the least are impressive. There should be no thought of interfering with the liberty of all Canadians to enjoy them. Cultural exchanges are excellent in themselves. . . . It cannot be denied, however, that a vast and disproportionate amount of material coming from a single alien source may stifle rather than stimulate our own creative effort; and, passively accepted without any standard of comparison, thus may weaken critical faculties. We are now spending millions to maintain a national independence which would be nothing but an empty shell without a vigorous and distinctive cultural life. . . .

If we have properly understood what we have been told, the Canadian writer suffers from the fact that he is not sufficiently recognized in our national life, that his work is not considered necessary to the life of his country; and it is this isolation which prevents his making his full contribution. It seems, therefore, to be necessary to find some way of helping our Canadian writers to become an integral part of their environment and, at the same time, to give them a sense of their importance in this environment. . . .

The work with which we have been entrusted is concerned with nothing less than the spiritual foundations of our national life. Canadian achievement in every field depends mainly on the quality of the Canadian mind and spirit. This quality is determined by what Canadians think, and think about; by the books they read, the pictures they see and the programmes they hear. These things, whether we call them arts and letters or use other words to describe them, we believe to lie at the roots of our life as a nation. . . .

Our military defences must be made secure; but our cultural defences equally demand national attention; the two cannot be separated.

The Report went on to recommend the immediate establishment of a National Library and of "the Canada Council for the Encouragement of the Arts, Letters, Humanities and Social Sciences to stimulate and to help voluntary organizations within these fields, to foster Canada's cultural relations abroad, to perform the functions of a national commission for UNESCO, and to devise and administer a system of scholarships."

The Report of the Massey Commission was in large measure the culmination of the cultural nationalism of the forties, but the fact that its recommendations were implemented well on in the fifties—the National Library was instituted in 1953, the Canada Council in 1957—reminds us that there was no sharp break between the two decades. If the renaissance of the forties had followed the pattern of the other two previous Canadian awakenings—those of the 1890's and the 1920's—it would have slowed down in the fifties. The encouraging thing was that it did not: new magazines, new writers, and new literary movements appeared as frequently in the new decade as in the old.

The events of the fifties at home and abroad, however, did have something of the same chastening effect on Canadian enthusiasm as had the Depression and threat of war in the thirties. The outbreak of the Korean War, the continuation of the Cold War with Russia, the spread of McCarthy's witch-hunt in the United States, the constant threat of annihilation in an atomic war, growing tension between the provincial and federal governments in Canada and between the English and French language groups: all these developments made Canadians uneasy and apprehensive throughout the decade. But beneath all the surface disturbances, the ground-swell of cultural nationalism continued to roll.

Never before had there been so many outlets for Canadian writers. The *Canadian Forum*, the *Fiddlehead*, and the three great university quarterlies continued and indeed strengthened their positions; *Contact* was established in 1952 in Toronto, *Civ/n* in 1953 in Montreal, *Tamarack Review* in 1956 in Toronto, *Delta* in 1957 in Montreal, *Waterloo Review* in Waterloo, Ontario, in 1958 and *Prism* in 1959 in Vancouver. Some of these magazines were short-lived, but as they died others sprang up to take their places. *Alphabet* began publication in London and *Cataract* in Montreal in 1960, *Evidence* in Toronto and *Tish* in Vancouver in 1961, *Edge* in Edmonton in 1963 and *Catapult* in Montreal in 1964. The existence of these magazines was often made possible by grants from the Canada Council; their subscription lists usually ran in the hundreds rather than the thousands; but they provided invaluable opportunities for young writers to try their wings.

The new writers were not slow in appearing. Poets especially appeared in almost uncountable numbers: James Reaney and Jay Macpherson, Eli Mandel and Wilfred Watson, Daryl Hine and Leonard Cohen, Fred Cogswell, Elizabeth Brewster and Alden Nowlan, Margaret Avison and Anne Wilkinson, Alfred Purdy and Milton Acorn, Ronald Bates and D. G. Jones, Henry Moscovitch and George Ellenbogan, Phyllis Webb and Sylvia Bernard, George Bowering and Frank Davey. All of these poets, and a number of others who might be mentioned, published at least one volume of good or promising poetry in the decade, and when their books were added to those of the holdovers from the previous decades—E. J. Pratt, F. R. Scott, A. J. M. Smith, P. K. Page, Irving Layton, Louis Dudek, Raymond Souster, Roy Daniells, Robert Finch, Dorothy Livesay, Earle Birney, and A. G. Bailey— the total volume of production was astonishingly large. The new novelists and short-story writers were less numerous, but there was a new sophistication both of style and subject-matter in the fiction of Ethel Wilson, Robertson Davies, David Walker, Brian Moore, Mordecai Richler, Ernest Buckler, Adele Wiseman, John Marlyn, Sheila Watson, Charles E. Israel, Norman Levine, Jack Ludwig, and Hugh Hood. History and biography also continued to flourish, such distinguished writers as Creighton and Lower being joined by W. L. Morton, R. M. Dawson, William Kilbourn, G. F. G. Stanley, C. P. Stacey, J. M. S. Careless, and F. H. Underhill.

The academic study of Canadian literature also continued in the fifties and sixties. The establishment of the quarterly magazine, *Canadian Literature*, at the University of British Columbia in 1959 was proof of the vitality of this new academic discipline: sceptics who wondered how long such a venture could survive have been confounded by the succession of interesting issues which its editor, George Woodcock, produces year after year. A. J. M. Smith's *Book of Canadian Poetry* went into its third edition in 1957, and Pacey's *Book of Canadian Stories* into its fourth edition in 1961. Other successful anthologies in the decade were Earle Birney's *Twentieth Century Canadian Poetry* (1953), Malcolm Ross's *Our Sense of Identity* (1954) and C. F. Klinck's and R. E. Watters' *Canadian Anthology* (1955). Several books appeared which sought to appraise the developments of the arts in general or of literature in particular: Pacey's *Creative Writing in Canada* (1952) and *Ten Canadian Poets* (1958), Julian Park's *The Culture of Contemporary Canada* (1957), and Malcolm Ross's *The Arts in Canada* (1958).

Had the struggle to create a national literature in Canada finally been won? Much had been accomplished in the forty years since 1920, but much still remained to do. On the positive side, a group of magazines had been established which for the first time offered the Canadian writer a wide choice of outlets for his wares; a reading public had finally been built up large enough to warrant the publication of a Canadian book for the domestic market; by the Report of the Massey Commission and the establishment of the Canada Council the federal government had formally recognized the importance of a national culture; a network of national associations and organizations—the National Library, the Canadian Broadcasting Corporation, the National Film Board, the Canadian Library Association, to name but a few—had been flung across the provinces to bind them into a nation; Canadian literature had established itself as a respectable academic discipline; a body of critics had been assembled who were ready and able to appraise Canadian writing by responsible and informed standards; literary activity in all the major forms except drama was intense and of a worthy standard. Above all, there was no doubt that the nation now did have at least a dawning sense of identity: the inhabitant of Fredericton, New Brunswick, felt closer to the inhabitant of far-off Vancouver, British Columbia, than to the inhabitant of nearby Augusta, Maine.

But all was not well. Just as in the political sphere Canadian problems of the twenties remained problems in the sixties—the problems of federal-provincial relations, French-English relations, and of Canada's dependence on an external power—so did the problems remain in the cultural sphere. Canada still had no writer of the first rank by world standards, was still unsure whether her writers should seek to be cosmopolitan or to develop an indigenous tradition, was still prone either to under-rate Canadian books because they were not reviewed in the fashionable English or American periodicals or to over-rate them because they were our own, still alternated between truculent cultural self-assertion and whining cultural self-pity. The chapters which follow should do something to check this manic-depressive cycle, for they seek neither to boost nor to bust but merely and calmly to record and appraise. For, in the words of St. Augustine quoted as epigraph to the Massey Report, "a nation is an association of reasonable beings united in a peaceful sharing of the things they cherish; therefore, to determine the quality of a nation, you must consider what those things are."

27. Canadian History and Social Sciences
after 1920

I. The Writing of Canadian History

WILLIAM KILBOURN

Canadian historians have not been overly concerned with the art of history. In the period since 1920 they have been more interested in the content than in the form and expression of their work. The best of them have been more successful at analysis and synthesis than narrative, and in the study of determining forces and general trends than in the evocation of particular times and places and men. They have been primarily engaged in the enormous task of searching out and exploring vast reaches of source material, in order to make a usable map of Canadian history. In the universities their natural working partners and allies have been political scientists and economic historians and sociologists rather than students of language and literature. As a result, over the past two generations, an impressive body of periodical literature, monographs, and general histories has accumulated. In spite of the large areas still to be charted and the lack of many significant contributions outside the Canadian field, the work of Canadian historians has been comparable in professional competence with the best history written elsewhere.

Like most contemporary history writing, however, it has left a good deal to be desired as literature. It has prompted one observer to comment that most Canadian histories are two or three drafts from completion, and another to remark that we have had too much accurate Canadian history and too little accurate Canadian imagination. There have been only a handful of historians, most notably Frank Underhill and Arthur Lower, whose incisive wit and trenchant powers of analysis have given their work a polish and readability that might justify their inclusion in a list of the best prose writers of their times. There has been only one Canadian historian, Donald Creighton, whose conscious literary craftsmanship, thorough scholarship, and passionate commitment to a few great themes, have produced work approaching the nobility and the grandeur of a Parkman or a Macaulay.

Historians of the first rank, like Wagnerian tenors or concert cellists, are rare—rarer at any rate than great novelists or lyric poets. The technical requirements, the sheer quantity of fact to be surveyed and sifted, are apt to turn creative writers to other forms of art than history. Most history if it is to get done accurately at all is not in the twentieth century likely to be great literature.

The scarcity of literary craftsmen among Canadian historians, however, must not obscure the central significance of their work for the literature of ideas. The contribution of historians to the understanding of modern Canada and the shaping of a Canadian consciousness is a major one.

In the first place, their subject is perhaps the last of the amateur disciplines in the universities, and the only one whose practice is presided over by a muse. Most of their writing has been free of technical language, and accessible to the public in a way that the work of economists and scientists, philosophers and literary critics, has not. Canadian historians have always enjoyed a small but significant educated audience of public servants and leaders in the professional and business communities. It is no accident that many of Canada's diplomats have also been historians. Her first native governor-general and her only prime minister well known abroad began their careers teaching history at the University of Toronto. One historian, Frank Underhill, was a founding father of a national political party, and the concept of NATO emerged from the work of another, J. B. Brebner (1895–1957) *North Atlantic Triangle: The Interplay of Canada, the United States and Great Britain* (1945).

Since 1945 a minor boom in the publishing industry has brought forth a harvest of history books written for a wider public, as publishers competed to head their trade lists every year with several new items of Canadiana. Such has been the preoccupation with the question of Canada itself and with a search for a national identity in a nation where it does not exist in as palpable and obvious a way as in Europe and the United States that one is sometimes left with the odd sensation that Canada is nothing but a figment of the historical imagination, a concept nurtured in the minds of a small minority of Canadian leaders in each generation, aided and abetted by a few historians.

In the years immediately after the First World War, Canada acquired the last major attributes of nationhood. She sent her first diplomatic representatives abroad. She gained control of her own foreign policy. As a result of Canadian initiative, dominion status was formally defined at the Imperial Conference of 1926 and confirmed in the Statute of Westminster in 1931. She had entered the war as a self-governing colony; she emerged, in self-regard at least, a nation.

Most of the historians who began their careers during the decade after the war were preoccupied with the development and meaning of Canada's new constitutional position. Unlike their more colonially minded predecessors, they were not content to see Canada's history as merely part of the expansion of England, the story of a frontier and the Empire's rivalry with the United States for the control of North America. But they were thoroughly British rather than American in their assumptions and approach. Their attitude was a little like Canada's position at Versailles, where she was present and voting both by herself and as part of the British Empire delegation.

Notable members of this group of historians were the constitutional lawyer, W. P. M. Kennedy (1879–1963), the historian of Confederation Reginald Trotter (1888–1951), and O. D. Skelton (1878–1941), later to be Under Secretary of State for External Affairs and the biographer in 1921 of Sir Wilfrid Laurier, the prime minister who had set Canada's course in the direction of dominion status. Their work was solid, useful, and uninspiring. Perhaps the books of greatest literary interest from among this group are Chester New's definitive biography of Lord Durham (1929) and the lively sketches by William Smith (1859–1932) of *The Political Leaders of Upper Canada* (1931). Another important historian of the same generation is W. Stewart Wallace. Librarian and editor, collector of Canadiana and author of a dictionary of Canadian biography, his writing on a wide variety of local and national subjects spans half a century. His article of 1920 in the first volume of the *Canadian Historical Review*, of which he was original editor, was a sign of a new nationalism in Canadian historiography.

The most original of the political nationalists, however, as well as the most inspired and the most extreme, was Chester Martin (1882–1958), a scholar from Manitoba who moved east in 1929 to be head of the University of Toronto's History Department until his retirement over twenty years later. Although the synthesis of his life's work, *The Foundations of Canadian Nationhood*, did not appear until 1954, it was the expression of attitudes formed in the twenties, when he had already begun to publish the earliest of his articles and books about British North America. Martin wrote with an unsophisticated elegance that reminds one strongly of the acute but courtly country manner of his character and presence. His writing is suffused with the aroma of freshly harvested source material: he was in the habit of strewing his work with bits and pieces of old despatches and excerpts from letters and papers ("Shirley's Great Plan"; "the sheet anchor of my policy"; "the last best West"), some of which keep recurring with the frequency and insistency of *leit-motivs*. None of his work makes easy reading. But Martin's deep piety towards his subject-matter, grounded on intimate knowledge and strong conviction, ultimately compels the persevering reader to respect and fascination.

From first to last Martin's over-arching vision was one of Empire. Through the history of British North America in the mid-eighteenth century down to the settlement of the Canadian West in the early twentieth, he pursued and marked out the origins of the process by which the world's greatest empire transformed itself into a community of self-governing nations. It was the most successful peaceful solution to the problem of local freedom and imperial authority that the world had seen, and in its achievement Canada played a leading role. As in the late Roman Empire, apotheosized splendidly in the silver poetry of Spanish Prudentius and Egyptian Claudian, it was often provincials who loved and understood the Empire best. A few British North American colonial leaders, guiding and working with a rare group of enlightened and concerned British governors and politicians from the age of Murray and Burke to that of Durham and Elgin and Grey, were the true prophets, the men who saw within the British parliamentry tradition the essential secret of what was to become the Commonwealth. Like his heroes Howe and Lafontaine, old Dr. Baldwin and his son Robert, with whose innermost political passions he identified so completely, Martin was impatient with Tories and Republicans alike, and hence with the majority of Britons and North Americans who disliked or did not understand British political traditions or care enough about them to apply them to the Empire. Martin's attack on the British Conservative historian Sir Reginald Coupland who had somewhat glibly described the Quebec Act as a great act of statesmanship, reminds one of a nineteenth century Canadian politician doggedly explaining to some unenlightened governor or colonial secretary the essence of parliamentary government and the need to practise it in Canada. But Martin's deepest aversion was from those who saw an answer in violence and revolution. He was dedicated to a position of moderation with the single-mindedness though not the unbalance of a fanatic. There is a stubborn and passionate pride in the opening assertion of his master work: "The political traditions culminating in Canadian nationhood are now the oldest in the American hemisphere—the only political traditions unbroken by a revolution or civil war."

Martin, however, was not writing a chapter in some smoothly developing success story. He was not indulging in any smug Whiggish justification of the *status quo*. His work was very much an account of loss and defeat, the greatest at the beginning; it was a cry for what might have been. He was never quite reconciled to the loss of the thirteen colonies. He harked back with "a melancholy interest" and longing to the undivided North America of the mid-eighteenth century, when Benjamin Franklin called the British Empire the greatest political structure that human wisdom and freedom had ever yet erected, and dared to predict "that the foundations of [its] future grandeur and stability . . . lie in America."

When the men of moderation were defeated and the British and American extremists won the day, it was left to the small and far from brilliant northern provinces to perpetuate parliamentary traditions and evolve a new type of nationhood in America. Through the long struggle of the next century and a half there was for them no easy success and usually repeated failure.

Canadian history . . . has been a tough and intractable business. Little of it falls into neat patterns against the background of the universe. Much of it has been a stolid and phlegmatic struggle against heavy odds. Denied the assurance of a "manifest destiny"... [Canadians] were almost invariably competing with superior resources. They dealt, as a rule, with forces beyond their control, in many cases the by-products of other lands. "Courage in adversity," the motto of the old Nor'Westers, remained a stark national necessity for the Canadian brigades that shot the rapids and toiled across the portages of their stormy history. ... Few of the makers of Canada lived to see what they had helped to make. ... A "goodly company" of them, whatever their achievement for posterity, never emerged from the dust and heat of conflict. (P. 514)

As with the rest of his generation of historians, Martin's interests, even when he was writing of commerce or settlement, were overwhelmingly political. He was concerned with men's conscious purposes, with a bending of will and intellect to "prodigies of statesmanship" in the face of chance and circumstances, rather than with the determining forces that might shape both man and circumstance. In his last work he went so far as to dismiss economic factors such as "Western oil, Quebec iron, the St. Lawrence seaway, prolific industrial expansion," as "the more specious aspects of nationhood." Canada itself he saw less as a pattern of trade routes and communities and cultures than as "a giant's causeway of provinces" whose "organization" completed the basic structure of nationhood.

Before Martin and the political nationalists had reached the peak of their influence between the two world wars, other historians appeared whose premises and interests were radically different. Without rejecting the nationalists' findings, which proved to be of permanent value so far as they went, these historians simply turned away from the study of the formal development of institutions and the achievement of self-government to other questions. That study had been inspired in part by optimistic Victorian beliefs about human nature in politics which the younger generation of historians did not accept. They were more impressed with Charles Beard's economic interpretation of the American Constitution than the political nationalists had been. They were sympathetic to the approach of such new disciplines as anthropology and the sociology of ideas. They were generally influenced more by American than by British scholars. They were impelled by the same concern to study the whole of the human past, the details of everyday life of all classes of men, which had led John Dewey's colleague, James Harvey Robinson, to proclaim the gospel of the new history which won such widespread allegiance in the American graduate schools. If any further influence was needed to move Canadian historiography towards an examination of the social and economic basis of politics and ideas, the great depression supplied it.

The new historians in Canada have been called the Environmentalists. The name rightly suggests that the landscape played an even greater part in their work, just as in Canadian painting of the period, than it did in that of their American contemporaries. Since the 1930's, geographical determinants have been central to two prevailing interpretations of Canadian history.

The first interpretation emphasized the vertical connections north and south between different Canadian regions and their American counterparts just across the border. This interpretation was applied and used more thoroughly during the 1930's than it was later. But it did establish once and for all that in the matter of class distinction and in much of the spirit and practice of political democracy, religion, and education, Canadian history has shown the development not of a British but of a North American society. This North American historical view tended to minimize the differences between Canada and the United States. Its proponents studied the migrations of people and customs and ideas back and forth across the unobstructed border. Their sympathies lay with the popular movements of social protest generated near the frontiers of settlement and directed against the remnants of imperial rule embodied in chateau clique, family compact, or mercantile aristocracy. They owed much to the American historian Frederick Jackson Turner's thesis that the vital elements of American society came from the forests and fields of the frontier. Turner's influence was reflected in two large sets of studies—one of Canadian frontiers of settlement and the other of Canadian-American relations —begun during the 1930's by scholars on both sides of the border with American foundation support. Canadian members of this North American school of interpretation have included A. S. Morton (1870–1945) and Fred Landon, and more recently the sociologist S. D. Clark. Gerald Craig's post-war work on early Upper Canada as an extension of the American frontier has shown how valid that approach can continue to be. Several leading historians who were attracted to the frontier approach during the 1930's, however, soon tempered or combined it with another interpretation of Canadian history. Without denying their frontier and democratic sympathies, Frank Underhill, Arthur Lower, and A. L. Burt explored in their work the power and influence of metropolitan centres in the development of Canada.

The other Environmentalist view of Canadian history was intimately related but not limited to the idea of metropolitan influence. This view stems primarily from the work of Harold Innis (1894–1952), particularly his study of *The Fur Trade in Canada* published in 1930, and from Innis's younger colleague and biographer, Donald Creighton, whose first major work, *The Commercial Empire of the St. Lawrence*, was published in 1937. These two men, sometimes named Laurentians after the continental shield and the great river they celebrated in their writing, offered a distinctively Canadian interpretation of their nation's history.

For them, the North American frontier approach left too much of Canada's peculiar development unexplained. It made of Canadian history a pale and laggardly imitation of American history. They believed that Canada was more than the artificial product of imperial policy and political circumstance. The acts of will and imagination which created and sustained the dominion were working with a transcontinental pattern inherent in the North American environment. Canada existed not in spite of geography but because of it. Canada was a creature of the early trade routes running east and west from the metropolitan centres of Europe and eastern Canada and along the great river systems of the St. Lawrence, the Saskatchewan, and the Mackenzie. After Confederation, the Canadian Pacific Railway recaptured through a new medium of transport the older Canadian economic unity of the fur trade. It was a unity which Canadians projected into the twentieth century by many new links of transport and communication, of which perhaps the most important was the Canadian Broadcasting Corporation.

According to this interpretation, for the first three centuries and more Canada's history was largely the story of a hinterland exploited for a succession of staple products—fish, fur, timber, and wheat. In return, from the centres of cultivation in Europe and the few densely peopled river valleys of southern Canada came the ideas and the organizing power, the capital and the culture, that the hinterland needed in order to survive. Canada's extreme climate, difficult topography, and sparse settlement made her extraordinarily dependent on her own metropolitan centres and those of Europe for the necessities as well as the amenities of civilized life. This fact alone has made her radically different from the United States. It helps explain the conservatism and lack of a revolutionary tradition in Canada. In adopting the Laurentian view, historians have contrasted the American wild west with the Canadian frontiers that have been successfully planned and ordered by government and large private corporations in advance of settlement. Since the mid-nineteenth century Western Canada has been the domain of priest and mounted policeman, railway agent and branch bank manager, rather than that of sheriff's posse and desperado and lonely pioneer. From the founding of the Hudson's Bay Company in 1670 to that of the dozens of great crown corporations of twentieth-century Canada, the large-scale and carefully planned enterprise, dominating its field and aided by government regulation and support, has been typical of Canadian development.

To the outlying regions, this domination by central Canada has often made Confederation seem an instrument of injustice. No historian has expressed that view more eloquently than William Morton, a Western conservative whose first book *The Progressive Party in Canada* (1950) was a sympathetic study of a protest movement. Even so, Morton in his own way accepted the Laurentian viewpoint, and has gone even further than Innis and Creighton in asserting the uniqueness of Canada as a northern land, and in demonstrating a particular kind of conservatism inherent in its traditions. In *The Canadian Identity* (1961) and *The Kingdom of Canada* (1963), Morton has pointed out that Canada in contrast to the United States is a monarchy founded on the principle of allegiance rather than social contract and on the organic growth of tradition rather than by an explicit act of reason or assertion of revolutionary will. The British North America Act sets up the objectives of peace, order, and good government rather than those of life, liberty, and the pursuit of happiness. One of the most fundamental but least obvious differences between Canada and the United States is that for Canadians the fact and the principle of authority have been established prior to the fact and principle of freedom. In a country of "economic hazard, external dependence and plural culture," Morton concludes, government has needed to possess an objective life of its own (*The Canadian Identity*, p. 111).

While not all Canadian historians would necessarily accept Morton's development of it in the 1960's, the Laurentian thesis was certainly dominant during the forties and fifties. No thoroughly worked out alternative to it emerged as a serious rival. A brilliant definitive article by J. M. S. Careless, "Frontierism, Metropolitanism, and Canadian History" (*Canadian Historical Review*, March, 1954) clearly established that the idea of Canada as the creature of metropolitan planning and control, a society whose development was radically different from that of the United States, has been central to his generation's understanding of Canadian history. The climate of opinion in the country from 1940 to 1955 was peculiarly attuned to this point of view. Canada's early and heavy involvement in the Second World War and her renewed concern for transatlantic ties with Britain and Europe brought her out of her North American isolation of the inter-war period. Until the revival of the major European nations and the emergence of powerful nations in Asia during the 1950's, this country of sixteen million people was the world's fourth- or fifth-ranking power and even for a time after that she played a role in the United Nations out of keeping with her size. The great expansion of Canadian industrial capacity, the huge increase in the powers of the federal government, and the habit, at least among English-speaking Canadians, of thinking of their country as a single national entity, were all congenial to the transcontinental outlook of the Laurentian view of Canadian history.

Further developments took place, however, which were not so easily accommodated to that point of view, and which for many Canadians appeared to call into question the very nature and future viability of the nation itself. It became clearer than ever during the 1950's that the major external metropolitan influence on Canada had become not London but Washington and New York. The Canadian economy and Canadian defence and foreign policy were being more closely integrated with those of the United States, and there was a growing similarity between the two affluent societies. The forces of regionalism and provincial autonomy and the old north-south sectional pull, which had always been a factor in Canadian history, were now balanced by no counterweight other than forces within the nation itself and a determination on the part of Canadians to remain the independent people that history had made of them.

In spite of these developments, the historical writing of the 1940's and 1950's, unprecedented in quantity and often high in quality, was not directed to the discovery or definition of any new theory of Canadian history or even to a major revision of the view expressed by Careless in his 1954 article. It was chiefly involved in two other tasks: first, the work of synthesis and re-presentation in narrative form of recent research, and, secondly, the exploration of topics either entirely untouched before or unreviewed for two or three generations.

The first resulted in the appearance of many one-volume histories of Canada, an almost non-existent species during the previous generation. The liveliest and most provocative of these was probably *Colony to Nation* (1946) by a pioneer of economic and social history in Canada, Arthur Lower. Full of colourful detail, strong opinion, and a caustic wit, its most recurring theme was the confrontation in Canadian history between the predominantly static, catholic, and rural French-speaking community and the predominantly dynamic, Calvinist, and commercial English-speaking community. In contrast to the informality of Lower's prose were the Gibbonian cadences, abstract language, and scrupulous generalization of *Canada: A Social and Political History* (1947) by a historian of international relations, Edgar McInnis, the most complete and balanced of all the one-volume histories. Perhaps closer than either to being a recreation of the past by the art of narrative and the skilful use of source material was Donald Creighton's *Dominion of the North* (1944). All three of these very different works represented a substantial contribution to Canadian literature. Along with J. M. S. Careless's shorter history, they have been the best known of the one volume works, and in their original and revised versions they have sold widely in Canada and abroad ever since they were first published.

Most historical writing of the fifties, however, consisted not of general histories but of the exploration of small specific themes in depth and with a new subtlety. While much of this exploration meant monographs of only marginal relevance to a literary history, the emphasis on small manageable segments of the past, the study of a particular event, place, person, or period of time did make it possible for the historian, if he chose, to re-discover his *métier* as an artist. It was possible to imitate the dramatist's attempt to realize one or all of the unities of time, place, and action, and each abstract thesis or general trend could be given a local habitation and a name.

In no field was there a more obvious need for the practice of the art of history than in that of political biography. In 1948, before a decade of great change, Donald Creighton commented caustically on the state of Canadian writing in this field:

Canadian biographies have a formal, official air, as if they had been written out of the materials of a newspaper morgue, or from the resources of a library largely composed of Blue Books and Sessional Papers. In all too many cases, the subject remains an important Public Personage . . . dwarfed by the circumstances of his "Times," which are portrayed in great chunks of descriptive material, pitilessly detailed, and among which he drags out an embarrassed and attenuated documentary existence like an insubstantial *papier mâché* figure made up of old dispatches and newspaper files. It seems difficult for us even to make our characters recognizably different; and as one reads through a small shelf-full of Canadian biographies, one is aware of a growing and uncomfortable sensation that one is reading about one and the same man. Is it possible that, even in Canada, people can actually be so indistinguishably alike? Is there really only one Canadian statesman, whose metamorphoses have merely involved a change of name? Or are all Canadian statesmen simply members of the same family, a spiritual family at any rate, with certain persistent and unchangeable family characteristics, and a distinguished hyphenated surname? Are there really biographies of [Robert] Baldwin, [Sir Francis] Hincks, and [Sir Wilfrid] Laurier, or are these merely lives of Robert Responsible-Government and Francis Responsible-Government, and Wilfrid Responsible-Government? ("Sir John A. Macdonald and Canadian Historians," *Canadian Historical Review*, XXIX, 4.)

The most substantial response to such criticism was Creighton's own two-volume biography of Sir John A. Macdonald (*The Young Politician* (1952) and *The Old Chieftain* (1955)), which is discussed below. Although this work had no rival as a literary masterpiece it was accompanied and followed by a great number of historical biographies that changed the picture described in 1948 decisively for the better. Of these there was perhaps only one, J. M. S. Careless's two-volume portrait of George Brown, the great newspaper editor and Liberal politician, which equalled Creighton's work in weight and significance. The book not only illustrated Careless's views about the contribution of British ideas to Canadian liberalism and about the growing influence of Toronto over its metropolitan hinterlands, it also presented the best balanced and most complete study of mid-nineteenth century Canadian politics yet written. Although the political narrative is very detailed and densely structured it is enlivened by many finely drawn sketches of persons and places, by a sustaining though not intruding point of view throughout and by the easy good-natured informality of Careless's prose style.

Among other recent biographical studies of nineteenth-century Canadian politicians were those of two of the more important British governors: Donald Kerr's *Sir Edmund Head* (1954) and W. S. MacNutt's *Days of Lorne* (1955); Elisabeth Wallace's study of the great publicist and intellectual, Goldwin Smith (1957); Dale Thomson's biography of Canada's second prime minister, Alexander Mackenzie (1960); and G. F. G. Stanley's impartial, thorough, and definitive study of Louis Riel (1963). Two of the most interesting major biographies have been William Eccles' *Frontenac: The Courtier Governor* (1959), a cool and dispassionate piece of demythologizing of accepted scripture about one of the most colourful figures of the French *régime,* and *A Prophet in Politics* (1959), the life of the saintly founder of Canada's socialist party, J. S. Woodsworth, whose author, Kenneth McNaught, was passionately committed in the best sense and in the most illuminating way to his subject. Still to be completed are the last parts of multi-volume biographies of two twentieth-century prime ministers, the arch-rivals William Lyon Mackenzie King and Arthur Meighen. As high-principled and unsuccessful in his own way as Woodsworth, the unrepentant and unrevised Conservative Meighen also aroused a strong feeling of commitment in his biographer, Roger Graham, along with a cordial dislike for the man who frustrated both Meighen and Woodsworth by occupying the dead centre of Canadian politics for nearly thirty years.

Mackenzie King's official biographers, the late Robert MacGregor Dawson and his successor, H. Blair Neatby, have maintained a much greater distance from their subject and Neatby in particular shows a certain ironic detachment as well as a deep sympathetic understanding of his subject. If the King biographies present a more interesting, complete, and intimate portrait than those of any of the other modern Canadian figures, it is in no small measure due to their authors' access to the unusually full and self-revealing diary of a complex, lonely, and often pathetic man, a mystic who understood more about political power than he did about himself and his motives in achieving it.

The Mackenzie King Record: 1939–44 (vol. I, 1960) by J. W. Pickersgill, a close associate of the prime minister, relies even more heavily on King's diary and is deliberately intended to be more of an edited autobiography than an historical biography. Another work on King, by a newspaperman who knew him well, was Bruce Hutchison's *The Incredible Canadian* (1953). While it was done without access to King's papers and diary, it did offer many fascinating personal insights, and it remains a highly entertaining book. It may be grouped with a number of other recent histories and biographies, usually not written by academic historians, whose chief value lies not so much in any definitive judgment upon their subjects, or even in important new presentations of fact or interpretation based upon unworked source material, but rather in their concern to practise the art of narrative and to hold the attention of the reader. Besides Hutchison's *The Incredible Canadian*, Pierre Berton's lively, informative, and very personal history of the Yukon gold rush, *Klondike* (1958), and a number of other works by first-rate journalists, one might mention in this category Josephine Phelan's *The Ardent Exile* (1951), a biography of the great orator of Confederation, D'Arcy McGee, W. H. Graham's biography of Tiger Dunlop (1962), John Morgan Gray's *Lord Selkirk of Red River* (1963), and William Kilbourn's *The Firebrand* (1956), the story of the 1837 rebellion and its chief instigator William Lyon Mackenzie.

The author of this type of book often used techniques borrowed from the novel, the short story, and journalism. Some of them had clearly learned, either directly or by osmosis, a good deal from Lytton Strachey, whose occasional freedom with fact and unfairness to his subjects led academic historians to reject too readily the virtues of the revolutionary new approach he brought to the writing of non-fiction in the twentieth century.

The Firebrand also made use of an approach somewhat similar to that of the film scenario, or it was, at least, strongly visual in character. As a means of evoking time and place and persons, particularly in the narrative of the 1837 rebellion itself, it presented a structure of action shots and stills, panorama and close-up, often drastically cut or deliberately enlarged, and related as closely as possible to the central action and character. In the use of language it tried to avoid naming things by their too familiar names and to let them be seen as if for the first time. *The Elements Combined*, a more ambitious work by the same author, employed similar approaches to attack a more diffuse topic, the biography of a business, and the problem of making a history rather than a monograph out of research in an unworked field. By using some of the patterns of myth and imagery inherent in the working of a steel mill and in the fierce games of high finance, management, and labour, it attempted to bring another dimension of dramatic meaning and order to the common experience and concerns of men living in an industrial society.

Other company histories of general interest have included Marjorie Campbell's *The North West Company* (1957), G. R. Stevens's *Canadian National Railways* (2 vols., 1960 and 1962), and Merrill Denison's *The Barley and the Stream* (1955), which affords a colourful view of the history of Montreal since the Conquest as seen in the lives and work of the Molson family dynasty. One might well argue, however, that by far the best business history yet written is E. J. Pratt's narrative poem on the building of the Canadian Pacific Railway, *Towards the Last Spike* (1952). It has a grandeur and a precision of language and structure that are missing from most contemporary historical writing, both academic and popular, and as with Parkman's work, it depends on the author's painstaking research and something like a direct experience of its subject-matter. The supreme modern myth of man and industry, as well as one of the best factual studies of a particular industry, is of course Melville's *Moby Dick*.

With the exception of a few books by practising economic historians, such as Hugh Aitken's *The Welland Canal Company* (1954), and from an earlier period, Harold Innis's *History of the Canadian Pacific Railway* (1923), most of the company histories must be judged for the intrinsic interest of the narrative itself and for the reflection of Canadian life and society found in them, rather than as contributions to the interpretation of Canadian economic history, which still awaits precise economic analysis of most major industries. Economic history as such is best discussed as part of the literature of the social sciences, but the appearance of the first important synthesis of the subject, *Canadian Economic History* (1956), by W. T. Easterbrook and

Hugh Aitken, should at least be recorded here. This work, like Easterbrook's thorough bibliographical essay "Recent Contributions to Economic History: Canada" (*Journal of Economic History*, vol. 19, no. 1, March, 1959), a useful companion piece to Careless's article mentioned above, tended to reinforce rather than revise Innis's staple theory and hence fitted well with the Laurentian view of Canadian history.

The first comprehensive social history of Canada, Arthur Lower's *Canadians in the Making*, appeared in 1958, written in a style that is conversational in tone yet spare, well wrought, sometimes even epigrammatic. Lower's anecdotes and quotations help the book evoke the spirit of Canadian life as well as any history ever written. While several guidelines are used throughout—religious, racial, and cultural division; the conflicts between urban and rural values, and between old and new Canadians—Lower adopts as his chief theme the evolution of a society through the stages of trading post to colony to province and, where it has happened, to the maturity of nationhood.

The liveliest history of any of the visual arts in Canada to date, Alan Gowans' *Looking at Architecture in Canada* (1958), which should be read in conjunction with R. H. Hubbard's *The Development of Canadian Art* (1963), is also, in miniature, a revealing sketch of the development of Canadian society. For other significant contributions to Canadian social history one must look chiefly to the work of Canadian sociologists, particularly S. D. Clark, and the wide-ranging series of volumes on western Canada (with the slightly misleading title of "Social Credit in Alberta") of which he was the editor.

Clark's *Church and Sect in Canada* (1948) is also one of the few major contributions to the field of religious history in Canada. Other historians who have done useful work in this field recently include G. S. French, John Moir, T. R. Millman, and H. H. Walsh. The greatest single achievement remains, however, C. B. Sissons's definitive two-volume *Life and Letters of Egerton Ryerson* (1937, 1947). Ryerson's work as journalist, politician, educator, and Methodist minister made him chief guardian of the Ontario conscience and one of the most formidable figures in nineteenth-century Canada. The most important work of George W. Brown was also in the field of religious history, although his unique and invaluable contribution to Canadian historiography lay in the great scope of his influence as an editor, of the *Canadian Historical Review* among other things and most recently of the projected multi-volume dictionary of Canadian biography whose foundations he laid before his death in 1963.

The publication in 1963 of G. Ramsay Cook's *The Politics of John W. Dafoe and the Free Press* was a hopeful sign that that most neglected of all fields, Canadian intellectual history, might soon receive greater attention. Until now, however, the liveliest and most illuminating discussion of political ideas in Canada, that by Cook and by Frank Underhill, for example, has taken place in short occasional pieces, essays, and reviews, often published in non-academic journals such as the *Canadian Forum*.

Some of the best historical writing by Canadians has been regional or local in character. Among the interesting works of this sort have been the story of Halifax by the novelist Thomas Raddall, two histories of Montreal by J. I. Cooper and Stephen Leacock, W. S. MacNutt's history of pre-Confederation New Brunswick, Gordon Rothney's shorter studies in Newfoundland history, the work of L. H. Thomas and Morris Zaslow on the history of the Northwest Territories, Edwin Guillet's richly detailed descriptions of early Upper Canada, and the work of a group of writers in western Ontario, notably Fred Landon, W. Sherwood Fox, James Talman, F. C. Hamil, and Charles Johnston who have done much to keep alive the colour of their region. The two most successful provincial histories are *British Columbia* (1959), a large and beautifully written volume by Margaret Ormsby, and *Manitoba* (1957), the finest of William Morton's works. Perhaps more than any other major Canadian historian Morton has been consciously concerned to define and practise the art of history, just as he has aimed deliberately and precisely at working out an explicit interpretation of the Canadian experience. Always a highly disciplined writer of expository prose, he has not often achieved or tried for the lyric and dramatic qualities in his narrative writing which he admires in the greatest historians. However in the vivid accounts of his province's beginnings, of the life of the Métis and their buffalo hunt, in the stories of Selkirk and Riel, Morton has written a moving tribute to "those who by endurance in loyalty to older values than prosperity, had learned to wrest a living from the prairie's brief summer and the harsh rocks and wild waters of the north." (P. 473.)

The fields of imperial and military history have been better served than most in Canadian historical writing, which is fitting enough in a country whose history has until recently been part of a larger struggle for empire, and whose virtues seemed to be more evident in periods of war than in peace. The standard military history is *Canada's Soldiers* (1954) by G. F. G. Stanley and Harold Jackson. Charles Stacey, an exacting research historian with a crackling style and keen critical mind, was in charge of the official history of the Canadian Army during World War II (three volumes have appeared at time of writing). His most recent book *Quebec, 1759* is an entertaining piece of detective work, at the expense of the reputation of General Wolfe, to celebrate the bicentenary of the capture of Quebec. Stacey's first book, *Canada and the British Army 1846–71* (1938 reissued 1963), was a contribution to the study of British colonial policy, as was David Farr's *The Colonial Office and Canada, 1867–87* (1955). Among many earlier works in the field of imperial history were those by A. L. Burt and Hilda Neatby on the old province of Quebec, and those of W. B. Kerr and J. B. Brebner on the Maritime provinces. Gerald Graham, a Canadian who became Rhodes Professor of Imperial History at the University of London, has written a series of works on empire and sea power in the struggle for North America. Like these, his general history of Canada was designed to approach the subject "from the outside rather than from within North America" and "to give as much weight to European as to indigenous influences," but even so he acknowledged that "the presence of the United States on the border of Canada was still the basic fact of Canadian history."

The theme of Canadian-American relations was a central one in the history of Canada's foreign policy, a field well served by the Canadian Institute of International Affairs in its continuing series of volumes on "Canada and World Affairs," and by historians of the calibre of F. H. Soward, George Glazebrook, Harold Nelson, Robert Spencer and Edgar McInnis, the Institute's President for some years and author of several books, including a six-volume account of the Second World War and the general history discussed above. The most prolific writer on Canada's external relations in the 1960's has been the political scientist James Eayrs. His *Northern Approaches* (1961) and *The Art of the Possible* (1961) are particularly worth reading for their elegantly written and perceptive observations on modern Canada, quite apart from their contribution to the study of international relations.

In recent writing on the evolution of Canadian government, as in the field of international relations, political scientists and historians have been doing essentially the same kind of work. This can be seen, for example, in the "Canadian Government" series, begun in 1946 and first edited by R. MacGregor Dawson (1895–1958), the father of Canadian political science. While the whole series sets a high standard, two books in particular, the political scientist J. E. Hodgetts' nineteenth-century administrative history, *Pioneer Public Service* (1955), and the historian J. T. Saywell's *The Office of Lieutenant-Governor* (1957), are examples of clear vigorous academic prose at its best. By scrutinizing closely a limited and neglected field of study, they each opened up new perspectives on the whole of Canadian political history. Saywell has also been responsible for re-founding and editing, since 1960, the *Canadian Annual Review*, an essential record of contemporary Canadian history, and for writing its political narrative. As a director of research, and as co-author (with Blair Neatby) of a seminal article on the Quebec Conservative party (*Canadian Historical Review* vol. 37, no. 1), he did much to initiate during the later fifties a new and more systematic study of the political history of French Canada since Confederation. It is too soon to say, however, what effects new interpretations of post-Conquest Quebec by French Canadian historians such as Michel Brunet and Fernand Ouellet will have on English Canadians' interpretation of their history, let alone the ways in which the great Quebec social revolution of the 1960's might influence English Canadian historical writing.

While the 1950's saw a great increase in the sheer quantity of Canadian history being published, the record of the sixties appeared likely to surpass them. In addition to many projected new works, two paperback series, published by the University of Toronto Press and by McClelland and Stewart in the Carleton Library, made readily available many standard works, some of which like George Glazebrook's *History of Transportation in Canada* and D. C. Masters's *The Reciprocity Treaty of 1854*, had been long out of print. Essential source materials—collections of speeches, letters and debates; diaries and early narratives—introduced by an appropriate interpretative essay, have also been published in the Carleton Library and in Macmillan of Canada's Pioneer Books, two of which fittingly enough were edited by the Dominion Archivist, W. Kaye Lamb, whose vast knowledge, sound advice, and good planning underlay much of the post-war renaissance in Canadian historical study.

Works appropriate for the celebration of Canada's centenary in 1967 began to appear some years before. P. B. Waite's colourful book on *The Life and Times of Confederation, 1864–1867* was published in 1962. Most ambitious of all is the projected seventeen-volume history of Canada edited by William Morton. One of these, *Upper Canada: The Formative Years, 1784–1841*, a penetrating, finely balanced study by Gerald Craig, had already been published in 1963. By that date all but the last part of a six-volume popular history of Canada edited by Thomas Costain had appeared and was selling widely in the United States and Canada. Although none of it was particularly distinguished as literature and some of it was of doubtful academic validity, the best writing in this series at least passed muster as attractive prose narrative and managed to make Canadian history interesting to a large public, something that few academic historians have achieved or even attempted.

There was, however, one Canadian historian who had accomplished that task, and without any sacrifice of the highest standards of scholarship or literary art. "The phrase 'literary historian' . . . does not mean a historian with a talent for turning an occasional pleasing trope to decorate the collected facts" but rather "the historian who saw the body of his subject while still it lay scattered in unorganized source materials; who re-created the body by re-animating the form it required." In these words, from *The American Adam*, R. W. B. Lewis might easily have been describing Donald Creighton. In his three most important works, *The Commercial Empire of the St. Lawrence* (1937), *Dominion of the North* (1944), and his two-volume biography of Sir John A. Macdonald (1952, 1955), Creighton's subject forms itself around the central image of the river—the river of Canada—and the hero who grasped its meaning and embarked upon the immense journey to possess and subdue the inland kingdom to which the river was the key.

It was the one great river which led from the eastern shore into the heart of the continent. It possessed a geographical monopoly; and it shouted its uniqueness to adventurers. The river meant mobility and distance; it invited journeyings; it promised immense expanses, unfolding, flowing away into remote and changing horizons. The whole west, with all its riches, was the dominion of the river. To the unfettered and ambitious, it offered a pathway to the central mysteries of the continent . . . from the river there rose, like an exhalation, the dream of western commercial empire. . . . The dream . . . runs like an obsession through the whole of Canadian history; and men followed each other through life, planning and toiling to achieve it. The river was not only a great actuality: it was the central truth of a religion. Men lived by it, at once consoled and inspired by its promises, its whispered suggestions, and its shouted commands; and it was a force in history, not merely because of its accomplishments, but because of its shining, ever-receding possibilities. (*The Commercial Empire of the St. Lawrence*)

Whether the hero's name was Cartier or Mackenzie, Champlain or Simon McTavish, some half-remembered merchant or nameless *coureur de bois*, whether his journey and his mastery were mainly one of stout limb and heart or one of the willing imagination, it mattered little; in the hero's act of penetration and possession of the land of the St. Lawrence there lay the central secret of Canadian history.

The first Canadian statesman to be caught in the Laurentian spell was the great seventeenth-century Intendant of New France, Jean Talon.

Talon began it. No doubt he had gone out to Canada with his head full of neat, orderly Colbertian asumptions about the future of New France. His first term was almost exemplary. He planned some model villages at Charlesbourg. He built a brewery. He was busy encouraging shipbuilding, hemp production, and manufacture. And yet, almost from the beginning, something began to happen to him. He started writing the oddest letters back to Colbert. He dilated upon the vast extent of the country. He urged the capture of New York. He assured the King that "nothing can prevent us from carrying the name and arms of his Majesty as far as Florida. . . ." These curious effusions, with their hints of suppressed excitement and their sudden vistas of gigantic empires, surprised and perplexed the minister at home. . . . Colbert made the prudent comment "Wait" on the margin of one of Talon's most intemperate suggestions. . . . Talon ought to have been impressed by it, but he was scarcely aware of the rebuke. He had suddenly become conscious of the river and of the enormous continent into which it led. He had yielded to that instinct for grandeur, that vertigo of ambition, that was part of the enchantment of the St. Lawrence. (*Dominion of the North*, pp. 68–9.)

The St. Lawrence had a rival, however, and in the end it did not bring its heroes the possession of the entire continent. "Something stood between the design and its fulfilment." "Two worlds lay over against each other in North America. . . . Of their essence, the St. Lawrence and the seaboard denied each other. Riverways against seaways, rock against farm land, trading posts against ports and towns and cities, *habitants* against farmers and fur traders against frontiersmen—they combined, geography and humanity, in one prime contradiction." Creighton's first book was the story of the frustration of the original grand design. By his choice of a beginning and end date for his subject (one of the few choices that the historian as artist possesses), Creighton managed to suggest the pattern of tragedy in the story of the empire of the St. Lawrence between the Conquest and the end of the Second British Empire in 1850. His *Dominion of the North* told in longer perspective of the three centuries of rivalry between the rich seaboard colonies, who rebelled and made a nation of the southern temperate zone of the continent, and the proud Judah of the north, which stubbornly held to its original Laurentian and imperial destiny. Creighton's masterpiece, the biography of Sir John A. Macdonald, celebrated the greatest but also the most practical of the Laurentian heroes, the statesman who gave to the northern kingdom the political frame which its nature and economy and history had so long demanded.

Creighton's was a tale of vast dimensions, and he did not shrink from telling it in the grand manner. But rarely after his first book was there the least sign of rhetorical overwriting. He had the natural gifts of the story-teller. He could change the pace and mood of his narrative without losing any of its power. He deliberately prepared his climaxes, and he made it a rule never to cast ahead in analysing the aspects of a given moment in time and so lose both the suspense of the story and the feel of the actual historical moment. He had a poignant sense of the place and an ability to describe in loving sensual detail the homely pastoral landscape of picnic and country fair or the most formal of state occasions. Rarely, but with telling effect, would he break away from the quiet clear development of the details of a political story to illuminate it with some stark dramatic juxtaposition of natural to human catastrophe: "On a night in early September, 1883, a black and killing frost descended out of a still, autumnal sky on the wheat crop of the north-west . . . before the autumn was out, the depression, like a sinister grey familiar, returned to haunt the Dominion." (*The Story of Canada*, p. 173.)

Creighton varied with great care the construction and length of sentences and paragraphs. He was particularly fond of the spare simple sentence at the beginning of a chapter ("In those days they came usually by boat." "It was his day if it was anybody's"), followed by a longer sentence describing, explaining, carrying forward the narrative. These openings always made some precise historical point, but, more important, they were his own unmistakable way of casting a spell, his manner of saying "Once upon a time."

Creighton's brief history *The Story of Canada* (1959) is a fine example of his narrative style. Cartier's departure from St. Malo, Champlain's first encounter with the Iroquois, the capture of Quebec, the rebellions of Mackenzie and Riel are all succinctly and dramatically recreated. The book is a gallery of character sketches, a *commedia* of persons captured in the description of a telling gesture or feature. One powerful sentence brings together two of the central actions of modern Canadian history, and evokes the whole struggle of a dominion linking two oceans and encompassing two cultures in its farflung diversity:

On November 7th [1885], far out in the mountains, at a spot which Stephen determined must be called Craigellachie in memory of his clan's meeting-place and battle slogan, the bearded Donald Smith drove home the last spike in the railway's transcontinental line; and nine days later, on November 16th, while the autumnal sun rose late over plains which were white with hoar frost, the sprung trap in the Regina prison gave and Riel dropped to his extinction. (P. 180.)

In spite of his achievement, there is a sense in which Creighton has appeared somewhat isolated from his contemporaries and from the life of contemporary Canada. Even his narratives tend to grey and sadden a little as they approach the present. On occasions he has wrapped himself in the mantle of Don Quixote to go tilting at Americans, Establishment Liberals, and the Fabians he took for something far worse. In the face of a philistine world of journalist-historians, and the confident, successful, efficient professionals of the learned societies and graduate schools, he has sometimes responded with Eeyore's gloom and baleful eye.

Yet if anyone has reshaped the tradition of Canadian historical writing it has been Donald Creighton. It is difficult to think of a narrative on a nineteenth-century subject by any of his younger contemporaries in the past decade whose style or structure does not owe him some debt. There are times when one could wish it otherwise. One tires of rather patronizing gestures of consideration for the general reader, of earnest and embarrassing attempts at poetic prose, and of clumsy, inappropriate insertions of little Creightonesque tableaux in the midst of dry recitals of facts. None of Creighton's followers, even at their best, quite show his ability to make use of a broad general culture in their writing. But it is a revealing measure of a writer's true stature if the only major fault to be found in him is that he has too many disciples.

In a sense, it is difficult to conceive of a man whose thinking and writing, whose life style and very being, would stand in sharper contrast to Donald Creighton than Canada's other pre-eminent historian of the mid-twentieth century, Frank Underhill. Born in 1889, thirteen years before Creighton, a Clear Grit from that North York farm country beyond the ridges which supplied the Mackenzie rebellion with its best recruits, he has been for almost forty years the chief gadfly of the Family Compact's spiritual descendants and of any and all Canadian Establishments, including that liberal-intellectual one which has embraced but never quite smothered or tamed him with its honours and applause. Where Creighton was a scholar and an artist, the bardic singer celebrating and creating a nation by giving it a past, Underhill was an intellectual, a Socratic teacher, and a Shavian wit. Creighton's chief medium has been the prose narrative of epic dimensions, Underhill's the lecture and the informal essay or review; Underhill has never written a book although his work has been collected in books. Creighton uses several different modes of expression, from that of the ruminative academic to the incantation and the lyric. Underhill's voice never strays far from that of conversation, of clear, simple, brilliant talk.

Creighton's sympathies have been not so much conservative as with the living past itself, and with those great scholars like Harold Innis whom he admired for their refusal to be caught up in intellectual fashions of the day or to turn their history into present politics. Underhill on the other hand attacked the majority of his Canadian academic colleagues "who lived blameless intellectual lives, cultivated the golden mean and never stuck their necks out." His historical writing is alive with insights which might never have been gained but for his involvement in the present.

Trained as a classicist at the University of Toronto, a Victorian liberal turned Fabian by three years of pre-war Oxford and the acquaintance of A. D. Lindsay and G. D. H. Cole, Underhill was caught up during the 1920's in the excitement of prairie politics in the halcyon days of the Progressive movement and of his two Canadian heroes, J. S. Woodsworth and John W. Dafoe. In 1933 he became the author of the founding manifesto of Canada's first social democratic party. By the 1950's, while still a sympathetic if pointed critic of the democratic left in Canada, he was "less interested in the fortunes of political parties as such and more concerned with the climate of opinion . . . which determines to a great extent what parties accomplish or try to accomplish." He became more and more sceptical of doctrinal political solutions. He wished, a little sadly, that he "could be as sure about anything as some people I know are about everything." He compared himself to Huckleberry Finn at the end of his adventures, someone with no political home to go to and needing to light out for the Territory. Certainly much of Underhill's great power as a teacher and a historian came from qualities of candour and humility, gentleness and human sympathy very like those of Huckleberry Finn. But he also had a little of Mark Twain's showman about him. Like George Bernard Shaw he sometimes could be too easily typecast and dismissed as a brilliant clown by the dominions and powers he made fun of. He once compared himself, not altogether inaccurately, to the man who applied to John Morley for a job on the *Pall Mall Gazette* but denied special knowledge of any of a dozen fields Morley named, and when pressed said "My specialty is general invective."

A good deal of Underhill's important historical writing, along with some samples of his invective, has been collected in *In Search of Canadian Liberal-*

ism (1960) to which is appended a representative list of some seventy of his other works, ranging from a book of lectures (*The British Commonwealth*, 1956) to several of his elegant brief book reviews. Among the pieces still uncollected are six articles on the career of the Liberal leader Edward Blake, and two long essays in intellectual history, "The Political Ideas of J. S. Ewart" (*Canadian Historical Association Report*, 1933) and "The Revival of Conservatism in North America" (*Transactions of the Royal Society of Canada*, 1958).

A useful summary of Underhill's approach to his central theme, the history of party politics, is to be found in his pamphlet *Canadian Political Parties* (1957). Taking the American political tradition for his point of reference as he did so often, Underhill states that the main agent in the making of Confederation and in Canadian political history since has been a kind of Hamiltonian federalist party. This party has been a coalition of diverse sectional, racial, and religious interests whose chief dynamic has been supplied by the transcontinental drive for power and profit of the big business interests of Toronto and Montreal. For thirty years Macdonald's Conservative party played this role, until it was displaced after 1896 by Laurier's Liberals during the great period of western settlement. A third "governmental" party forged by Mackenzie King has held power with only two major interruptions from 1921 down to the present day, although in this period the business interests were more divided and more sophisticated than in the era of the Great Barbecue, and the party leadership was no longer so bold and exciting. Underhill recognized a kind of historical necessity in the existence of the first two parties, if the nation was to be built at all. For the last, however, King's party "of the extreme centre," which effectively dulled the edge of intelligent political debate that made American and British politics so lively, Underhill reserved some of his bitterest attacks. Nevertheless Mackenzie King's very skill in hanging on to power, and his ability to find policies to keep both French and English Canadians together in the same party, in the end won his grudging admiration.

> The essential task of Canadian statesmanship is to discover the terms on which as many as possible of the significant interest-groups of our country can be induced to work together in a common policy. . . . Mr. King has been the only political leader of the last generation who has understood [this]. . . . His statesmanship has been a more subtly accurate, a more flexibly adjustable Gallup poll of Canadian public opinion than statisticians will ever be able to devise. He has been the representative Canadian, the typical Canadian, the essential Canadian, the ideal Canadian, the Canadian as he exists in the mind of God.

> . . . Mr. King . . . was not the traditional kind of parliamentary leader that you read about in the textbooks. . . . He obviously disliked Parliament. The representative side of democracy he did not find congenial, and he worked out a much

more direct but also much more indefinable relationship between himself and the Canadian people. . . . And without any of the apparatus of mass hypnosis and police coercion to which vulgar practitioners of the art like Hitler and Mussolini had to have recourse, he succeeded with hardly a mistake for twenty-five years in giving expression, by way of that curious cloudy rhetoric of his, to what lay in the Canadian sub-conscious mind.

The commonest criticism of Mr. King was that he never gave a definite lead in any direction or committed himself in advance to anything concrete and tangible. . . . But there was one field in which he did . . . —external affairs. And it is in this field that we can now see most clearly that intuitive quality of Mr. King's mind. . . . He grasped what Canadians wanted better than they did themselves, and he was very clear-headed and persistent in moving towards a goal which he saw from the start. . . . He was primarily a North American. He resisted all attempts to make a political or economic or military unit out of the British Commonwealth. . . . Even in the emotional atmosphere of the war he declined all Churchillian invitations into an Imperial War Cabinet. Instead, he was vigorous both in peace and war in strengthening our American ties. . . . He never consulted parliament or people about these steps; he simply kept us informed. (Quotations are from the chapter "W. L. Mackenzie King," in *In Search of Canadian Liberalism*)

Like King, Underhill was "primarily a North American." Yet to develop and maintain the best of the North American democratic tradition in Canada has not been easy; liberalism and the political left have never flourished here. In Underhill's view the oldest and strongest of Canadian traditions from the "great refusal of 1776" to the Reciprocity issue of 1911 and to the Diefenbaker era, has been "our determination not to become Americans." "We were born saying 'No' " to the Enlightenment and the American Revolution, and for a century and a half we have regularly indulged in outbursts of anti-American feeling and rejected the best that American thought and society has had to offer us. "But if we allow ourselves to be obsessed by the danger of American cultural annexation, so that the thought preys on us day and night, we shall only become a slightly bigger Ulster. The idea that by taking thought, and with the help of some government subventions, we can become another England—which, one suspects, is Mr. [Vincent] Massey's ultimate idea—is purely fantastic."

In his 1946 presidential address to the Canadian Historical Association, Underhill made a plea for two kinds of history little studied in Canada. He asked first for more Canadian intellectual history—political ideas, religion, and education—as a means of correcting and supplementing the Environmentalist emphasis on geographical determinants and abstract forces which often made Canadian history appear to be "a ghostly ballet of bloodless economic categories." Secondly, he noted with regret that Canadian historians concentrated so much on the writing of their own parochial national history and that *Christianity and Classical Culture* (1940) by C. N. Cochrane (1889–1945) was one of the few important books on world history written by a

Canadian. He looked forward to the time when "we have asserted our full partnership in the civilization of our day by Canadian writing on the great subjects of permanent and universal interest."

Since 1946 there has been very little writing of major importance that could be considered an adequate response to Underhill's first request. In the second area, however, a significant beginning has been made. It will be impossible to do justice here to the variety and scope of recent writing in a wide variety of fields by Canadian scholars, but some slight idea of its quality and extent may be given by naming a few of the historians who have published significant work. In ancient history these have included E. T. Salmon, Gilbert Bagnani, Mary White, Malcolm McGregor and F. M. Heichelheim; in medieval history, Bertie Wilkinson, Karl Helleiner, C. C. Bayley, T. J. Oleson, and M. R. Powicke; in European history since the Renaissance, Wallace Ferguson, E. R. Adair, R. M. Saunders, Ralph Flenley, and John Cairns; in British and imperial history, W. S. Reid, Chester New (1882–1960), John Norris, D. J. McDougall, W. W. Piepenburg, John J. Conway, A. P. Thornton, J. B. Conacher, and J. H. S. Reid (1909–1963); in American colonial history, R. A. Preston; in Japanese history, Herbert Norman (1909–1957); in Russian history, Robert McNeal; in the history of art, Peter Brieger, Jean Boggs, and Stephen Vickers; and in American business history, Richard Overton.

Looking back to the 1920's, the most important of the founders of business history as a field of study was Norman S. B. Gras, a Canadian who occupied the first chair in the subject at Harvard University. Gras also developed the idea of studying the metropolis and the pattern of metropolitan growth as a general approach to the history of modern society, an approach used in such books as D. C. Masters' *The Rise of Toronto* (1947).

However it has been the literary scholar, Marshall McLuhan, who, by developing an approach to the study of technology and communications first tentatively explored in the later work of Harold Innis, has made the most original Canadian contribution to the interpretation of the history of civilization. When some Canadian historians take McLuhan's *The Gutenberg Galaxy* (1962) seriously enough to try to grapple with its explosive, jargon-proud, joke-filled, non-linear prose, and to let its insights or its errors act as a stimulus to the examination of their own canons of interpretation, their writing might well reach that level of maturity and excitement to which Frank Underhill looked forward a generation ago. As one of the most perceptive contemporary critics, Frank Kermode, has said of *The Gutenberg Galaxy*, "In a truly literate society this book would start a long debate."

*   *   *

The last best word on the subject of the historian and literature (and the sharpest comment on what Canadian historical writing most often neglects) is still that of the young Thomas Macaulay: "Our historians neglect the art of narration, the art of interesting the affections and presenting pictures to the imagination. . . . The perfect historian gives to truth those attractions which have been usurped by fiction. In his narrative a due subordination is observed: some transactions are prominent; others retire. But the scale on which he represents them is increased or diminished according to the degree in which they elucidate the condition of society and the nature of man. . . . A history which in every particular incident may be true, may, on the whole, be false." William Morton has shrewdly remarked that the first and perhaps the only major choice made by the historian as artist is the choice of his subject-matter, the act of seeing the whole form of his narrative, its beginning, its middle and its end. However, within the strict and difficult limits of what can be known about what actually happened, the historian does have a kind of freedom not easily achieved by the novelist. He need not strain for plausibility or limit his plot to what merely might have been. He need not use elaborate devices to establish the credibility of the narrative voice. He is free, by the very nature of his art, his discipline, and his subject, to explore and show forth in all its variety and complexity and strangeness the incredible truth.

II. Writing in the Social Sciences

HENRY B. MAYO

In speaking of the literature of the social sciences in Canada, we use the word "literature" loosely, without any overtones of elegant style. The phrase simply means scholarly books, thus excluding on one side the mass of government publications and on the other the mass of journalism, monographs, and periodical articles. The affinities of social science scholarship are more with history, psychology, and geography than with literature in the narrow sense. This is not to assert that social science writings have no good literary qualities: in social science as in history, one occasionally finds books that are of some value as literature.

For several reasons, we should expect the literature of the social sciences to be meagre. Until very recent times, Canada could be regarded as "underdeveloped." Its small and scattered population has been preoccupied with the economic tasks of settlement and building, and with political survival and expansion. The country is divided into two language groups, and both peoples have been able to borrow freely from abroad. The universities have been small—scarcely more than arts colleges with a few professional schools. It is from the universities, as they expanded and improved, that writing in the social sciences might be expected and has indeed largely come.

All of which is to say that a certain maturity of economic development, a settled cultural environment, cities, a reading public, educated if not leisure classes—these and perhaps other conditions are prerequisites for the substantial growth of social sciences. The study of society requires the accumulation of data for descriptive accounts, it requires a curiosity as to how the social system works, it requires a certain detachment—or at any rate self-consciousness. Only then can social analysis be undertaken, and an explanatory and theoretical set of social science disciplines be developed. There is also the point that the social sciences are in an intimate reciprocal relation to the society which they study. They reflect the society and yet they alter it, by the very fact of analysing, explaining, criticizing, publishing. In a very real sense one may say that a society which has been exposed to the social sciences is never the same again. No doubt literature also has great effects, yet it is the social sciences which document and validate the impressions and intuitions of a society as reflected in its literature.

Before the First World War, social science writing in Canada was neither abundant nor for the most part of high quality. Nor was it possible to see in the better writing anything especially Canadian about either the men or their methods; both were imported. One thinks of the eccentric Robert Gourlay (1778–1863) and of Edward Gibbon Wakefield (1796–1862), with their nineteenth-century studies of land settlement, as well as of John Rae, an original economic theorist who was (perhaps characteristically) not read in Canada although he became famous abroad (his important writings, along with a biography, will re-appear in 1964). One thinks, in a somewhat later period, of W. J. Ashley (1860–1927)—called the founder of the "Toronto School" of economic history—of John Davidson (1869–1905) and his work on labour economics, and of James Mavor (1854–1925), another economic historian. Adam Shortt (1859–1931), who set the long-lasting trend to applied Canadian economics at Queen's University, is the only Canadian who can compare with the immigrant scholars from Britain.

After the First World War, the picture changed quickly. By the twenties and thirties social scientists, chiefly in the universities, began to be plainly noticeable, and it was possible to get over the feeling of surprise that good books on Canada should be written by Canadians. As Canadian society became more self-conscious, more of the prerequisites for social science were present. When the flow of books and other studies started, the preoccupation naturally enough was with the unique Canadian scene—with its economy, politics, and social structure—and above all with interpreting the history of Canada. The efforts of authors were directed much less to testing and modifying social theory than to practical ends, including in these the broad purpose of the preservation and expansion of a nation. Some of the best social science analysis has, in fact, been cast in historical form—alike in economics, politics, and sociology.

Economics

Of the social sciences proper, perhaps economics has developed furthest. From one point of view, economic analysis could be done only when the Canadian material—statistical and other—was available; at the same time part of the inquiry itself was to unearth the data. Economic studies could presumably be made either for theoretical or for practical policy purposes, but, on the whole, the main emphasis has been on the latter. Canada is a country where economic forces and political events have been closely intertwined—as in the nineteenth-century National Policies, the continuing Dominion-Provincial disputes within the federal system, and the development of resources. The political authorities have felt responsible for economic policy and development, so that determination by economic factors has seldom been pushed far in interpreting Canadian history.

The economic history of Harold A. Innis (treated elsewhere in this book) concentrated on staple production, a method which gave his early work a unifying theme: the intimate connection of politics and economics. His *Political Economy in the Modern State* (1946), which dealt with contemporary problems, especially those arising from the combination of economic and political power, shows the theme somewhat played down. He came to emphasize technology more, and in his *Empire and Communications* (1950), to centre upon communication and its techniques, and how these might be causally related to empires and civilizations. The modern world was in danger, he believed, from the "monopoly" of communication—a theme which he pursued still further in *The Bias of Communication* (1951) and *Changing Concepts of Time* (1952). These books also reflected his increasing consciousness of the need for Canada to resist United States encroachment in many fields. Few, if any economists today have the broad historical sweep of Innis, and none has followed him in using historical studies of Canada as a take-off into wider speculative theory about the future of man.

The historical approach to the study of the Canadian economy has, of course, continued. There are, for instance, the nine volumes of *Canadian Frontiers of Settlement*, edited by W. A. Mackintosh and W. L. G. Joerg in the 1930's and 1940's. The historical, combined with more economic theory, is typical of later works, for example of commercial and fiscal policy by O. J. McDiarmid and J. H. Perry, of banking by R. Craig McIvor, of labour by Stuart Jamieson and of growth theory by O. J. Firestone.

For the most part, applied economics has been the dominant strain, with the "Queen's School" of applied studies being the most outstanding representative. W. A. Mackintosh, whose first works were on the prairie economy, including *Economic Problems of the Prairie Provinces* (1935), moved on to the wider study *The Economic Background of Dominion-Provincial Relations* (1939). O. D. Skelton (1878–1941), W. C. Clark (1889–1952), C. A. Curtis, F. A. Knox and K. W. Taylor are the best known of this school which has always associated economics with government and public service.

The impact of the Great Depression and the Second World War again concentrated much of the work of Canadian social scientists upon institutions and policy, while at the same time the Keynesian revolution in economic theory encouraged a more sophisticated economic analysis. Out of the depression came, for instance, the scholarly *Report of the Royal Commission on Dominion-Provincial Relations* (1940) and the many special studies made for the Commission. These deal with a range of the social sciences—economics, political science, constitutional law, and sociology—and with their subdivisions and interconnections so far as they relate to public policy. The Gordon Commission, *Report of the Royal Commission on Canada's Economic Prospects* (1957), although less historical and more limited in scope, also drew heavily upon university talent. Out of the hundreds of Royal Commissions it is fair to say that these, and a few others (on broadcasting, arts and letters, medical services, etc.) have been an important means of encouraging much first-rate scholarship in the social sciences: directly in so far as special studies have been commissioned; indirectly by the stimulus to research in general. The important factor is that some commissions contract for research, and are not content to hold hearings and collect opinions from interested parties. Governments have found social scientists useful, and have, in turn, provided the money for research.

Specialized economic studies have been numerous. In agricultural economics there is G. E. Britnell (1903–1961), *The Wheat Economy* (1939), and V. C. Fowke, *The National Policy and the Wheat Economy* (1957). Of more general scope is A. E. Safarian's *The Canadian Economy in the Great Depression* (1959); Irving Brecher has written a theoretical work on Canadian monetary policy (1953). Other studies, too numerous to mention, have been conducted on banking, corporation finance, farm credit, trade unionism, certain manufacturing and other industries, transportation, war economics, national income, welfare economics, foreign trade, capital formation, balance of payments, etc. At the risk of being invidious one might suggest that the chief writers have been D. A. MacGibbon, H. A. Logan, W. T. Easterbrook, V. W. Bladen, D. C. MacGregor, J. Douglas Gibson, A. F. W. Plumptre, and Stuart Jamieson. Apart from these, others have written on population and economic geography, among them Mabel Timlin, Griffith Taylor, and A. W. Currie. Still another field of distinguished work has been that of public finance, in which W. A. Mackintosh, John Deutsch, J. A. Maxwell, J. H. Perry, Eric Hanson and Robert M. Clark are prominent.

It is in fact now possible to publish good anthologies of readings in Canadian economics, and there is moreover a market for them inside the country. With increasing industrialization and a more complex economy it is not possible, however, for authors to give the same kind of over-view, or integrated interpretation, that was provided by the "staples" or export commodities approach, taken in an earlier period.

A few books have combined a treatment of general economic principles and Canadian data, for instance H. A. Logan's and M. K. Inman's *A Social Approach to Economics* (1939) and V. W. Bladen's *An Introduction to Political Economy* (1941). The former was succeeded by M. K. Inman's *Economics in a Canadian Setting* (1959). Later works of a similar kind have been produced by R. C. Bellan, and by Helen and Kenneth Buckley. Craufurd D. W. Goodwin has written an historical account of *Canadian Economic Thought* (1961).

Economic theory of an advanced and systematic kind, not particularly linked to Canadian data, has been less well represented by original works, exceptions being D. B. Marsh on international trade theory, and B. S. Keirstead with *The Theory of Economic Change* (1948) and *Capital, Interest and Profits* (1959). Wm C. Hood has edited *Studies in Econometric Method* (1953), a field which E. F. Beach has also cultivated. No one can deny that the technical level of competence of economic analysis in Canada is now high especially among younger men such as Harry G. Johnson, H. Scott Gordon, Anthony Scott, Clarence Barber, and William Mackenzie. It remains true perhaps that only a few works may be said to have added to the international body of economic theory or "science."

Political Science

The study of politics and government in Canada has lagged behind the study of the economy. Political science, in any technical sense, was a late starter and even now economists vastly outnumber political scientists. The early writings on politics tended to be either historical or constitutional, a natural development given the larger number of historians and the fact that constitutional law and judicial interpretation have a whole profession devoted to them.

When political science addressed itself to the realities of the political system a number of studies of institutions began to appear, including *The Principle of Official Independence* of R. MacG. Dawson (1895–1958) and R. A. MacKay's *The Unreformed Senate of Canada* (1926, new edition 1964). The institutional emphasis predominates even in Alexander Brady's *Canada* (1932), and the institutional and historical approaches are united in Dawson's *Constitutional Issues in Canada, 1900–31* (1933), and *The Development of Dominion Status, 1900–1936* (1937).

With the expansion and changing nature of the universities, the stimulation of certain Royal Commissions, and the flow of research funds (chiefly from the United States), the number of institutional studies has immensely increased in the last two decades. The federal government, as might be expected, has been studied most. Some of the studies commissioned for the Rowell-Sirois Commission were highly competent political-cum-constitutional works, and there are also Eugene Forsey's *The Royal Power of Dissolution of Parliament in the British Commonwealth* (1943), and Paul Gérin-Lajoie's *Constitutional Amendment in Canada* (1950). Norman Ward's works on the House of Commons (1950, 1962) are outstanding in their field, and are informed by a keen analysis of principles.

Public administration, again mostly at the national level, is represented chiefly by R. MacG. Dawson's *The Civil Service of Canada* (1929), by J. E. Hodgetts' *Pioneer Public Service* (1955), by Taylor Cole's *The Canadian Bureaucracy* (1949), and by an anthology edited by J. E. Hodgetts and D. C. Corbett (1960).

Provincial governments have been less studied, the chief impetus here having come from the "Canadian Government" series. An institution common to all provinces has been analysed in John T. Saywell's *The Office of Lieutenant-Governor* (1957). The provinces for which general accounts of their governments have appeared are Prince Edward Island (by Frank MacKinnon, 1951), Nova Scotia (by J. Murray Beck, 1957), New Brunswick (by Hugh G. Thorburn, 1961) and Manitoba (by Murray S. Donnelly, 1962).

The municipal level of government has drawn even less attention, the chief works being the general surveys by Kenneth G. Crawford, *Canadian Municipal Government* (1954) and D. C. Rowat's *Your Local Government* (1955). There is, however, a ferment in local government today. As urbanization proceeds, the financial and other pressures upon the inherited framework and theory of local government continue to mount. Signs are apparent that this level of government will be the subject of vastly increasing research in the near future. Unfortunately, however, the number of men in Canada interested in and qualified to undertake such research is likely to be a severely limiting factor.

The yield of studies in constitutional law and judicial interpretation is broad in scope and high in quality, the chief legal writers being W. P. M. Kennedy, F. R. Scott, Bora Laskin, V. C. McDonald, and Edward McWhinney. Political scientists—notably Eugene Forsey, J. R. Mallory, and Paul Gérin-Lajoie—have also made substantial contributions to constitutional studies.

Systematic analyses of the Canadian political system as a whole could hardly appear until the spadework of initial particular studies had been done. These initial studies appeared not only in the works mentioned, but also as articles in the *Canadian Journal of Economics and Political Science*, founded in 1935. The first comprehensive work was that of H. McD. Clokie, *Canadian Government and Politics* (1944) followed by Dawson's *The Government of Canada* (1947). Somewhat more theoretically weighted were the comparative study by J. A. Corry, *Democratic Government and Politics* (1946) and Brady's *Democracy in the Dominions* (1947).

It is now possible to see where the gaps lie in our knowledge of Canadian politics and government. These are most conspicuous for the political process, i.e., in the fields of parties, pressure groups, voting behaviour, electoral systems, public opinion, propaganda, etc. Nor is there any book on the Cabinet or the prime ministership. In spite of preliminary forays into these territories here and there since the 1940's, much is still unexplored and certainly under-cultivated. The gaps have been partly filled, to date, by political biographies, by monograph literature in the journals, and by studies of the minor political parties.

On voting behaviour and electoral studies there is John Meisel's *The Canadian General Election of 1957* (1962), and the statistical account by Howard A. Scarrow, *Canada Votes* (1962).

On political parties, much of the work has been by American scholars— on the national C.C.F. party by Dean E. McHenry (1950) and on the C.C.F. in Saskatchewan, a sociologically oriented book by S. M. Lipset (1950), and on the Conservative party by J. R. Williams (1956). The latter book came from the Duke University series, which has sponsored some excellent books by Canadians about Canada, among them A. R. M. Lower, F. R. Scott, *et al.*, *Evolving Canadian Federalism* (1958).

The massive series on "Social Credit in Alberta" covers this Canadian phenomenon from the viewpoint of a number of disciplines. The political and constitutional aspects have received full-scale treatment by C. B. Macpherson, *Democracy in Alberta* (1953) and J. R. Mallory, *Social Credit and the Federal Power in Canada* (1954). The Progressive party in Canada, the Liberal party in Alberta, the Union Nationale in Quebec, have all been the subject of competent studies, historically oriented. The great national parties, Liberal and Conservative, still await both the historian and the political scientist. Meantime we make do with biographies, autobiographies, anthologies of articles from the periodicals, and journalism. It is a curious fact that we know much more about the smaller parties which have never held national office than about the parties which have actually governed. This is the sort of pattern that justifies a common criticism of the social sciences: what they study may not be important, but at least it will be well documented.

Canadian scholars have not followed the American example in developing an empirical or non-normative general theory of the political process. Neither has there been much scholarly writing that could be called political philosophy. The nearest we come to it are the writings of party apologists (and this is not very near), the incidental ideological analysis found in books on parties, and a rare volume of essays like that of F. H. Underhill, *In Search of Canadian Liberalism* (1960) or the book by W. L. Morton, *The Canadian Identity* (1961), or that edited by Michael Oliver, *Social Purpose for Canada* (1961). It may be possible to write a book of sorts on the history of Canadian political thought—though it has not yet been done—but it would be a bold man who dignified it with the title of Canadian political philosophy.

As in economics, little political theory of a general nature, not tied to the Canadian scene, has appeared. Early exceptions to this generalization were Stephen Leacock's *Elements of Political Science* (1906) and R. M. McIver's *The Modern State* (1926). In more recent years there are H. B. Mayo's *Democracy and Marxism* (1955) and *Introduction to Democratic Theory* (1960); C. B. Macpherson's *The Political Theory of Possessive Individualism* (1962), and Terence H. Qualter, *Propaganda and Psychological Warfare* (1962).

Canadian external relations have been studied by both the historians and the political scientists, though rather less by the latter. Historical works by G. P. de T. Glazebrook, W. A. Riddell (1881–1963), F. H. Soward, Gordon Skilling, H. A. Angus and others can only be mentioned here. The curious love-hate relationships with Britain and the Commonwealth on one side, and with the United States on the other, have frequently been prominent elements in political life, and hitherto the dominant themes in scholarship. The enormous set of volumes on "Canadian-American Relations" testifies to one part of this preoccupation.

Foreign policy is of course played on a wider stage today, more particularly since the founding of the U.N., and being adrift in a more dangerous world, Canada and its scholars have tried to work out a suitable role for the country. Among the earlier works are Robert A. MacKay, *Canada Looks Abroad* (1938), and F. H. Soward and Edgar McInnis, *Canada and the United Nations* (1956). Representative of the recent literature are James Eayrs's *The Art of the Possible: Government and Foreign Policy in Canada* (1961), Peyton V. Lyon, *The Policy Question* (1963), and a series of volumes sponsored by the Canadian Institute of International Affairs.

At home, Canada is in the midst of re-defining the terms of its federal system. There may be subsidiary reasons for this, but the most obvious is that the French-speaking people of Quebec, aware of their changing society, are not only conducting a quiet revolution in their own house but are seeking a re-definition of their place in Canada. This exciting phenomenon is having a large impact on the political life of Canada—on parties, public finance, the constitution, etc.—and the present may be one of the nodal points in Canadian history. Already there has been a renaissance of studies inside Quebec, and one may expect this fertilizing stream of thought to lead to new political analyses and theoretical constructions outside that province, particularly in relation to federalism, the parliamentary system, and democracy itself.

Sociology and Anthropology, etc.

Political science is under-developed compared with economics; the other social sciences lag far in the rear. Many universities are even yet scarcely aware that there are such disciplines as sociology, anthropology, and criminology.

In anthropology, some work has been done on the Eskimo, but far more on the native Indians. Most characteristic perhaps of the earlier work is that of Diamond Jenness and Marius Barbeau. The best contemporary work is that of T. F. McIlwraith (1899–1964), *The Bella Coola Indians* (1948) and the volume by Harry B. Hawthorne, Cyril Belshaw, and Stuart Jamieson, *The Indians of British Columbia* (1958).

Other ethnic groups, particularly in the Western provinces, have usually been studied by a broad, interdisciplinary approach, for example, *The Doukhobors of British Columbia* (1955), edited by Harry B. Hawthorn; F. E. LaViolette, *The Canadian Japanese and World War II* (1948); John Cosa, *Land of Choice: The Hungarians in Canada* (1957).

General interpretations of Canada may perhaps be brought under the umbrella of sociology, however impressionistic and lacking in rigour some of them may be. One thinks of J. W. Dafoe, *Canada, An American Nation* (1935), Julian Park (ed.), *The Culture of Contemporary Canada* (1954), Miriam Chapin, *Contemporary Canada* (1959), and A. R. M. Lower, *Canadians in the Making* (1960).

Of more technical sociological writings, usually on an historical basis, the best known are of S. D. Clark, *Movements of Political Protest in Canada, 1640–1840* (1959), *The Social Development of Canada* (1942), which emphasized the frontier influence, *Church and Sect in Canada* (1948), and *The Developing Canadian Community* (1962). The emphasis has been rather more on economic history with C. A. Dawson's *The Settlement of the Peace River Country* (1934), though less so in his *Group Settlement* (1936).

Several volumes in the "Social Credit" series also have social-psychological and sociological orientation, namely those by John A. Irving, *The Social Credit Movement in Alberta* (1959), by Jean Burnet, *Next Year Country* (1951), and W. E. Mann, *Sect, Cult, and Church in Alberta* (1955).

The impact of industrialization and urbanization is becoming of increasing interest. Everett C. Hughes's *French Canada in Transition* (1943) examines these forces in relation to Quebec's traditional culture, a theme of absorbing interest alike to both French- and English-speaking social scientists nowadays. It may well be true that the unique Canadian situation which arises from the French-English speaking symbiosis has so far been most perceptively treated by outsiders. This is certainly borne out by André Siegfried in *Canada* (1937) and by Mason Wade in *The French Canadian Outlook* (1946) and, as editor, *Canadian Dualism* (1960).

On the impact of urbanism in general there is the composite work edited by S. D. Clark, *Urbanism and the Changing Canadian Society* (1961). Of special studies, the best known is J. R. Seeley, R. A. Sim, and Elizabeth Loosley, *Crestwood Heights* (1956), a study of a Toronto suburb.

To judge only by the number of books mentioned in sociology and kindred disciplines would give a misleading underestimate of the actual scholarship. Professional attention has been directed, in depth, to an ever increasing range of social phenomena: to immigration, marriage and the family, religion, the professions, the military, delinquency, social stratification, the power élite, and so forth. A substantial anthology of recent work has already appeared, edited by R. B. Blishen, F. E. Jones, Kaspar Naegele, and John Porter, *Canadian Society: Sociological Perspectives* (1961).

Canadian universities are experiencing a phenomenal rate of growth. It is safe to predict that, as the scholars increase rapidly in numbers, sociology, like all social sciences, will vastly expand its output of scholarly writing.

28. Literary Scholarship

MILLAR MacLURE

I

LITERARY SCHOLARSHIP has no roots in this country; what has been written in this way, and it is very impressive—"the one kind of writing in which Canadians have won really wide international recognition" (F. E. L. Priestley)— has been grafted onto the universities, those colonial plantations set in piety, expediency, or simply under pressure of population upon a landscape alien to the leisured disciplines. Of late years an indigenous scholarship, occasionally parochial and esoteric but with an interesting Commonwealth connection, has grown upon "creative writing in Canada," but it is still true that most of the valuable monuments have only a Canadian address. He that seeketh his "identity" shall lose it. Scholarship has always been international in any case, from the neoplatonic glosses on Homer to the recent Japanese book on Milton, yet in deeper rooted cultures differences of emphasis appear: the footnote-draped Germanic disintegrators used to be opposed by the urbane English with their strong sense of unity of text and liberty of interpretation; now the American "new critics" have combined the meticulousness of the one with the "style" (sometimes very self-conscious) of the other to create a scholasticism which dominates, almost politically, the Western academy. George Woodcock, one of the very few free-wheeling men of letters working in this country (he has written books on Peter Kropotkin, Aphra Behn, Oscar Wilde, Proudhon, and Godwin, as well as books of travel and occasional pieces), once called for a *Canadian* criticism, but that remains "the shape yet undefined" (Roy Daniells' phrase), for this country is unhappily not an organism but an agglomeration. We are still in migration: we move like the Canada goose and the white-throated sparrow, and make as diverse sounds.

*I am indebted for assistance and advice in the preparation of this survey to G. W. Field, D. M. Hayne, C. D. Rouillard, F. W. Watt, and Mary E. White. H. Pietersma assisted me in preparing the basic file of authors from which I worked. All errors of omission and commission and all opinions expressed are my own. This survey, with some minor exceptions, comes down to 1960. A census of scholarly production in Canada since that date would require another chapter.

Northrop Frye, whose name will inevitably appear in more than one context of this short view of part of the Canadian academy, in one of his many animadversions upon the state of our intellectual life, has observed that there has been of late "a vast increase in the systematizing of scholarship," and has referred, not without some politic ambiguity, to the current "cult of productivity." The dilettante, or the man who, in the old Oxbridge tradition, simply *was* his subject, has been replaced by the "producing scholar," and the publication curve has shot up like a rocket at the right side of our time-graph. This is, of course, owing in part to simple increase of numbers, and F. E. L. Priestley, himself a prominent scholar-editor and adjutant of the academic brigade for the Humanities Research Council, once noted that "pressure to publish, to produce in God's name the infinitesimal product is (or has been) less heavy in most Canadian universities than it is popularly reputed to be south of the border." The qualifying parenthesis has, I think, considerable weight at present.

It was not always so, and complaints of inadequate scholarly activity in the Canadian intellectual community are easy to collect, though naturally they multiply toward the end of our period. J. E. Wells (1836–1898), writing in the *Canadian Monthly* (1875), felt that Canada's intellectual growth was not keeping pace with her commercial progress, and that there were no pecuniary conditions for scholarship. In his retrospective address on the fiftieth anniversary of the Royal Society of Canada (1931), Sir Robert Falconer (1867–1943) recalled the situation in 1881: "The universities had no contact with one another. Most of them had been conceived, born, and nourished for sectarian purposes, and all were very poor. . . . Professors were badly paid, libraries were meagre." In 1893, and again in 1902, members of the Royal Society were reminded that the prospects for scholarship were very poor, and that organized research in the humanities did not exist in Canadian universities. The doyen of French studies in this country, A. F. B. Clark, in a thumping article in the *Canadian Forum* (1930), claimed that "as a recognized and organized force, literary scholarship simply does not exist in our universities," condemned the pedantry of the Ph.D. (as Frye does in the lecture referred to above), and spoke pretty sharply about academic laziness (golf and the summer cottage, etc.), an accusation repeated in considered terms by A. S. P. Woodhouse and Watson Kirkconnell in their survey *The Humanities in Canada* (1947). In 1943, Desmond Pacey, writing in *Queen's Quarterly*, found Canadian scholarly "output" in languages and literatures, as contrasted with history and the social sciences, "deplorably low." Woodhouse and Kirkconnell reminded their readers that "Canadian universities are primarily undergraduate teaching institutions," that facilities for scholarship (e.g., microfilm, travel grants, a national census of library holdings, etc.) were undeveloped or unenthusiastically employed, and that the Canadian scholarly community had suffered much from the long exodus of native sons to the United States: "It is doubtful if any other nation in history has lost so large a part of its most valuable human resources with such apparent unconcern." The "Massey Report" (1951)—an important landmark, for it recommended the formation of the Canada Council, which one young scholar has called "that warm featherbed for talent"—while it incidentally noted that there was "no vigorous intellectual life in Canada outside the universities," a remark retrospectively unfair to the CBC, the theatre, and even the coffee clubs, still recorded that "apart from the work of a few brilliant persons, there is a general impression that Canadian scholarly work in the humanities and social sciences is slight in quantity and uneven in quality."

I have assembled these sombre observations partly by way of contrast to the achievements noted below—though many of those achievements owe their successful completion to action initiated by these and other complaints—and partly to illustrate an activity which seems to me one of the few recognizably "Canadian" aspects of our culture: Canadians of an intellectual cast are given to constant stock-taking; even our poets and painters assemble frequently to see how things are going. Also we love to run ourselves down; urbane foreigners profess to find in this dour Northern habit a national characteristic of understatement.

Apart from such qualities of industry, intelligence, and taste as he may possess or acquire, the "producing" scholar needs four conditions to flourish: a first-class library, or access by way of travel, film, photostat or facsimile to the holdings of other libraries; a learned community, or "institute," in which to associate with his fellows; recess from full-time undergraduate teaching; and means of publication. All these cost money. To trace how these facilities have been made more available to Canadian scholars, and how they have multiplied during the last decade, would be to write a chapter in the history of higher education in this country; here I only call attention to two or three significant developments.

The strictures of J. B. Brebner (1895–1957) in 1943 upon the meetings and proceedings of the Royal Society of Canada ("drowsy gatherings . . . the transactions slumber undisturbed," etc.) may have been deserved, but it was on instruction from Section II that the Humanities Research Council was organized in 1943, and a study of its Reports is sufficient to indicate the variety of ways in which it has promoted literary scholarship in this country, by way of investigation, fund-raising and distribution of grants, aids to publication, and not least perhaps in creating an atmosphere of competition for its benefits. The theory of the Honours course is too deeply seated in Canadian universities to be abandoned in favour of a set of elegant or vulgar gymnasia with transferable credits for undergraduates, set apart from highly integrated schools or institutes for specialized study at the graduate level; but institutes are essential, and the model for such development in Canada is of course the Pontifical Institute of Mediaeval Studies in Toronto, founded in 1929, on the suggestion of Etienne Gilson. E. J. McCorkell, in his brief history of the Institute (*Varsity Graduate*, July 1956), points out how from the beginning the advantages of association with the graduate school of the University were taken into account; here we have an example of how an institute international in its connections and highly specialized in its disciplines (the first class in Latin palaeography in Canada was started by J. T. Muckle in 1929), can at once add lustre to and derive part of its strength from association with a larger centre of learning. Other interdisciplinary institutes may be expected to develop; the Institute of Canadian Studies at Carleton University, established in 1957, directed by R. L. McDougall and productive of four (to date) volumes of the interesting series *Our Living Tradition*, is a parallel with a difference. Departments of comparative literature have not taken root in our universities, though monographs written by Canadian scholars in the European tradition, some of which will be mentioned below, come into this category, but the fact that English has in effect replaced Classics as the operative centre of the humanist disciplines (English literature being "foreign" to high-school graduates who no longer read the Bible and who have learned little or no classical mythology) helps to create the condition without the name, for the modern scholar-critic in English often takes all humanist knowledge as his province. (G. W. Field, a specialist in Thomas Mann and Hermann Hesse, finding in the *Germanic Review* for February 1960 what seemed to him a most illuminating article on Mann as the "last Wagnerite," wrote a note of congratulation to the author, c/o Department of German, University of Saskatchewan. The author is William Blissett, a professor of English with a long bibliography of articles on Renaissance subjects.) The local facilities for publication have also increased: the expanded scholarly publication programme of the University of Toronto Press, the recent founding of the McGill University Press, with the extension and inauguration of university "series," point in this direction.

II

One of the most distinguished Canadian scholars of the middle generation recently said to the editor of the *University of Toronto Quarterly* that he was publishing too many footnotes. He did not mean it so, but he was pointing to a shift in form and intent, foreshadowed in what we might call the Johns Hopkins influence in Canadian scholarship (see *Proceedings of the Royal Society of Canada*, Third Series, vol. XXIV, Section II, p. 33), which I can best summarize by giving another turn to what I wrote on this subject in 1957 (in *The Culture of Contemporary Canada*, p. 223): "The old imperial tradition, which 'colonized' the greater universities from Oxford, Cambridge,

Edinburgh and Dublin . . . has been transformed into a wholesome exchange of talent and opinion. But the intimate association of Canadian scholars with their fellows in the United States, through the MLA, in the great research libraries, in the forum of the learned journals, and in other less formal but equally productive relationships, while it has gained for many Canadian scholars a large following and influence in the world of American scholarship, has inevitably drawn Canadian scholarship firmly into the larger orbit of American scholarly and critical activity." One paradigm of this shift may be found in classical studies: from Gilbert Norwood (1880–1954) and E. T. Owen (1882–1948)—of whose *The Story of the Iliad as Told in the Iliad* (1946) Norwood observed that 'sweeping aside that notorious and many-headed bogey, the Homeric Question, with a few politely devastating words . . . [he] lighted up the whole poem for every student"—to the emphasis among the present generation on what the editor of the *Phoenix* terms "professional scholarship," source-study, epigraphy, numismatics, archaeology, text-criticism. In a complementary context, Frye has noted that "the advance of critical techniques seems to be increasing the professionalizing of literary study, and thereby widening the gap between the critic and the plain reader." It is relevant to recall that the *UTQ*, in its first avatar (1895–96), was a collection of lectures before university and other societies, e.g. the Modern Language Club or the Philosophical Society, with the qualities and form incident to that kind of presentation.

When we turn to some typical productions of the late nineteenth and early twentieth centuries we find well established the tradition of what one might call the "extension" lecture, and a recognition of what Mudie Macara, in "A Prize Essay, in the form of an Address to the Members of the Mercantile Library Association of Hamilton" (1855), referred to as "the advantages, intellectual and social, of associate institutions for literary objects." The genre may be illustrated by an address of the Rev. Henry Scadding (1813–1901) on *Shakespeare the Seer*, given to the St. George's Society of Toronto on April 23, 1864, a properly florid effort, considering the occasion; by S. E. Dawson (1833–1916) with *A Study with Critical and Explanatory Notes of Lord Tennyson's Poem, The Princess* (1884), which arose from a paper prepared for "a small semi-social, semi-literary society," which went to two editions, and for which the author received a letter of commendation from the Laureate himself; or by the Rev. John King (1829–1899) in his *Critical Study of In Memoriam* (1898), which had its origin in "a course of lectures delivered to ladies in Manitoba College." (This is, however, a more "scholarly" effort.) These excellent men anticipated a function which Woodhouse has attributed to much of the writing of Maurice Hutton (1856–1940), the founder of the Honours course in Toronto and author of *The Greek Point of View* (1925): he was "a missioner of culture to the Province." There were giants in the land in those days, but they were primarily great teachers; their bibliographies are short, but the memory of them is long. Such were W. J. Alexander (1855–1944) of Toronto, whose only important published work is *An Introduction to the Poetry of Robert Browning* (1889), Archibald MacMechan (1862–1933) of Dalhousie, and John MacNaughton (1858–1943) of Queen's, of whom W. D. Woodhead observed (in *Queen's Quarterly*, 1943) that he was "always somewhat indifferent to Research with a capital R," and that "he remained throughout his life a personality rather than a writer." There was a continuity, it appears, through the lecture to undergraduates, the "missionary" address, and the published essay. The loving exposition of familiar monuments, clear of technical clutter and informed by personality and prejudice: that is the form. From W. F. Osborne (1873–1950), Professor of English at Wesley College in Winnipeg, we have *The Genius of Shakespeare and Other Essays* (1908); the other essays are on *In Memoriam* and the *Idylls of the King*. (Here a certain crankiness appears: Shakespeare had "his full share of the pensiveness of the Teutonic race," which is superior to "the southern or Latin peoples.") A. W. Crawford (1866–1933), also of Manitoba, published, in 1916, *Hamlet, an Ideal Prince*. Such were the contents, too, of the *University Magazine* (1901–20)—it died as the *Canadian Forum* was being born—edited after 1907 by Sir Andrew Macphail (1864–1938), a journal of general culture; such is the tradition of *Queen's Quarterly* (begun 1893), early contributors to which included MacNaughton on the presentation of drama in ancient Greece, and T. R. Glover, who came to Queen's in 1896.

The list of editors on the title-page of a forgotten student anthology, *Great English Poets* (1929), indicates a bridge between two worlds; the names are A. W. Crawford, Aaron J. Perry, and A. S. P. Woodhouse. Or one might cite the succession in the English department at University College, Toronto: Alexander, Malcolm Wallace, Woodhouse. I remember Wallace (1873–1960), the biographer of Sir Philip Sidney, himself a meticulous researcher with a strong ethical and political sense, saying to me, very kindly but firmly, after I had read a rather esoteric paper on *Hamlet*, that he thought I was off the main track of literary study. (Of Woodhouse I shall have more to say below.) Or, finally, there is the remark of G. S. Brett (1879–1944), in a paper read before the English Association of Toronto in 1918, and published in the *University Magazine*: he *feared* that a book on the "philosophy" of Conrad would appear sooner or later.

But the kind of writing just characterized does not exhaust the scholarly production of the first era after the establishment of the Canadian universities. It is true that a run through Morgan's invaluable *Bibliotheca Canadensis* (1867) gives the impression that most of the intellectual energy of the provincials was expended in arguing the merits of infant baptism and of the prohibition of alcoholic beverages, and in studying the geology of the country, and a nice essay could be written on the avocations of nineteenth-century clergyman-educators. Rev. William Cochrane (1745-1833), for example, Professor of Languages, Logic and Rhetoric in King's College, Windsor, N.S., a Trinity College Dublin man, published "A Fast Sermon," and kept a journal of the barometric readings at Windsor. Archdeacon W. T. Leach (1805-1886), Professor of Logic and Moral Philosophy and Molson Professor of English Literature at McGill, has left us "A Discourse on the Nature and Duties of the Military Profession" (1840), "Observations on the Hypothesis of the former existence of a great Fresh Water Inland Sea within the Continent of America" (1845), *On the Uses and Abuses of Phrenology* (1846), *An Advent Sermon* (1851), and—a timeless touch—*A Lecture on Education* (1864). Two conspicuous figures, both classical scholars, dominate the field of more conventional and specialized scholarship. The first is John McCaul (1807-1886), President of University College, Toronto, also a TCD man, who published before he came to this country studies in Terence and Horace, but whose chief work was his *Britanno-Roman Inscriptions* (1863), of which an English reviewer observed: "It could scarcely have been expected in the old world, that in the remote capital of Western Canada, a scholar would devote his time to correcting by accurate knowledge and acute reasoning the errors of those who would seem to have much better means of examining the particulars . . . than himself." The second is Sir William Peterson (1856-1921), Principal of McGill from 1895-1919, who was an editor of Latin texts; see his *M. Tulli Ciceronis Pro A. Cluentio Oratio* (1899), etc.

III

The beginnings, development, and flowering of studies in Canadian literature fall, for the most part, into the obvious pattern I have already employed: complaint leading to accomplishment and systematization; *belles-lettres* and general surveys supplanted by specialization and the search for the mythos of Canadian culture. We may begin with a perceptive remark by Wilfred Campbell, whom Carl Klinck has studied in his proper context as a "provincial Victorian": "The grave weakness of our literary life is the same as that at the bottom of our national existence. Sad to say, we are less a people with one aim and sympathy than we are a bundle of cliques, each determined to get what it calls its rights and caring little for matters outside its own interests" (Toronto *Globe*, Dec. 10, 1892). True then and true now. In the *Dalhousie Review* article referred to above, George Woodcock condensed the pseudo-problem which has haunted the literary life of this country in recent times: "Of criticism which, in the full sense, seeks to evaluate Canadian writings in a creative manner and to relate it, not only to creative experience, but also to a universal criterion, there is almost none. Reviewers exist in plenty, making *ad hoc* judgments . . . which are rarely more than superficial." (For the moment he had forgotten *UTQ*'s "Letters in Canada," which since 1936 has provided, in the words of its first editor, "material for a conspectus, not merely of literature in the narrow sense, but of that culture of which it forms a part.") Woodcock goes on to desiderate a journal devoted to such criticism; this hope has been realized in *Canadian Literature* (begun 1959), the beautifully produced magazine he edits at Vancouver. More practical, less pontifical, is Desmond Pacey's plea (in the Royal Society's *Studia Varia*, 1957): "There has been some improvement in the quantity and quality of Canadian criticism, especially since about 1925 when the first handbooks began to appear, but much remains to be done. Really informed and intelligent criticism, such as that of the late E. K. Brown . . . of W. E. Collin . . . or of . . . "Letters in Canada," is precisely what a nascent literature such as ours most requires." (Note the assumption in the last sentence: that our literature, in 1957, is still "nascent.") Pacey goes on to note the wholesome influence in this respect of *The Week* (1883-96)—studied by Claude Bissell in the *Canadian Historical Review* (Sept. 1950)—the *Canadian Forum*, and *Northern Review* (1946-55), the only Canadian literary magazine which has achieved, by the virtue, intelligence, and evil fortune of one man, a tragic moment, when John Sutherland (1919-1956), from his Stryker frame, finished his testament, a significant study of E. J. Pratt, *The Poetry of E. J. Pratt* (1956).

Pacey's view of criticism, it appears, is progressive, industrial; he believes in symposia, in periodic assessment of "the progress of Canadian letters." In this he carries on, with some sophistication, the pious and patriotic intentions of his predecessors, the anthologists, the writers of handbooks, and the contributors to the "Makers of Canadian Literature" series, from the Rev. E. W. Dewart (1828-1903) *Selections from Canadian Poets* (1864), through Archibald MacMurchy (1832-1912) *Handbook of Canadian Literature* (1906), J. W. Garvin (1859-1935) *Canadian Poets* (1916, 1926), R. P. Baker's *History of English-Canadian Literature to the Confederation* (1920), a work not superseded until the present volume, *Our Canadian Literature* (1922), edited by A. D. Watson (1859-1926) and Lorne Pierce (1890-1963), whose services to Canadian literature as publisher (Ryerson), editor, bibliographer, and publicist are outstanding, *Highways of Canadian Literature* (1924), by J. D. Logan (1869-1929) and D. G. French (1873-1945), to Lionel Stevenson's *Appraisals of Canadian Literature* (1926). Compare Logan and French with Stevenson, and you will find a significant change in critical method. Logan (according to Garvin, he delivered the first series of lectures on Canadian literature in a Canadian university, at Acadia in 1915-16), a victim, says Pacey, of "classifying mania," collects on four astonishing pages the critics of Canadian letters up to his time, leader-writers, dilettantes, professors—there are twenty potential M.A. dissertations in Can. Lit. in those pages, and, for all I know, most of them have already been written—and classifies them in three "schools": the Pioneer or Traditional, the Academic or Dilettante, the Pragmatic or Pedagogic. Stevenson, on the other hand, anticipates Frye in his perceptive observations on the Canadian literary scene—and this, we should remember, was before the best of Pratt. "Canadian poetry," he writes, "is equally [with painting] concerned with the apocalyptic. . . . In Canada the modern mind is placed in circumstances approximately those of the primitive myth-makers. . . . The Canadian poet is instinctively a romantic." Frye has, in his series of "Letters in Canada" reviews, in his "Preface to an Uncollected Anthology" (*Studia Varia*, 1957), in his review of A. J. M. Smith's *Book of Canadian Poetry* in the *Forum* (1943), and elsewhere, "re-written the history of Canadian poetry, adjusting it to the focus of his mythopoetic lens" (Eli Mandel), which is a-historical, and invites us to take our ancestors on our own terms. He has been followed by James Reaney in his attempt to "find out painfully what symbolic language expresses the feelings [the poet] has about living in this country" through meditations on Isabella Valancy Crawford (who was edited by Garvin) and E. J. Pratt; (see also his "The Canadian Poet's Predicament," *UTQ*, April, 1957). But the traditional approach continues, in Pacey's standard work, *Creative Writing in Canada* (1952, 1961), with its indispensable bibliography, and its rather tiring succession of writers who either fulfil or do not fulfil (usually not) their "early promise," and, in another way, in such enterprises as the New Canadian Library, general editor Malcolm Ross, an admirable series of reprints introduced by a variety of editors, which illustrate generally the high degree of organization in Can. Lit., the occasional superiority of the critic to his material, and in one case at least, a curious lapse of judgment, when *The Stepsure Letters*, the lucubrations of that tedious old pharisee Thomas McCulloch (1777–1843), first President of Dalhousie, were exhumed by an elaborate apparatus from their decent grave in *The Acadian Recorder*.

"It is not a nation but an environment that makes an impact on poets," Frye observes. James Cappon (1854–1939), whose studies of Roberts (*Roberts and the Influences of His Time*, 1905) and Carman (*Bliss Carman and the Literary Currents and Influences of His Time*, 1930), are classics of Canadian literary history, would have subscribed to this; the study of Carman especially conveys his fine sense of a poet's context—Carman had some very odd contexts. But Cappon is, of course, by current critical standards as dated as the "conservative and correct" Archibald MacMechan (1862–1933) in his *Headwaters of Canadian Literature* (1924); a student contribution to *The Rebel* noted in a report of Cappon's address to the Toronto English Association (1917), that "the test which Professor Cappon applies to poetry as a working criterion is 'Has it a rationalized concept?' Yeats he found lacking in clarity of thought." And he was capable of attributing to Carman, Roberts, and Whitman alike something that he called "the cosmic touch." Looking through the admirable books on Canadian poetry published since 1930, from W. E. Collin's over-written but influential *The White Savannahs* to R. E. Rashley's *Poetry in Canada: The First Three Stages* (1958), one finds parochial hyperbole giving way to thoughtful analysis, supported more and more by scholarly revaluation of minor figures. To this task E. K. Brown (1905–1951) in his *On Canadian Poetry* (1943) brought a patient and open-minded lucidity, and A. J. M. Smith the resources of a born anthologist, a taste at once catholic and refined, and a nice sense of historical development. *The Book of Canadian Poetry* (1943, 1948) has been for long our guide, and now the *Oxford Book of Canadian Verse* (1960) will be our breviary.

The ground, then, has been mapped, inventories and assessments continue, but now there is less danger than a half-century ago of mistaking archaeology for criticism, and subsuming both under a doctrine of inevitable development. This happy situation is a by-product of the remarkable proliferation of scholarly activity in Canadian universities over the last quarter-century, but it is also owing to the breadth of view and range of interests of some of the main contributors to this kind of research and criticism. Frye and Ross and Brown I shall mention again; to these we should add Milton Wilson, a student and critic of the Romantics, and probably the most influential reviewer (in *Canadian Forum* and *UTQ*) of Canadian poetry now writing.

IV

The categories, making for convenience if not for wisdom, so far employed in this survey, fail when we turn to the scholarly and critical writing which has been produced of late in this country in the disciplines of Classics and Modern Languages. Nor is a simple chronological approach useful, partly because of that explosion of publication which I have noted above, chiefly because of the prominence of certain individuals rather than of "schools"— and indeed of some individuals who deserve not a sentence but a chapter each. I take as examples two men who between them span two generations of Canadian scholarship, one a Cambridge man transplanted, the other a Canadian who studied at Harvard in the days of Babbitt and Kittredge: Gilbert Norwood and A. S. P. Woodhouse.

Norwood was at home wherever there are scholars to disagree about Euripides (see his posthumously published *Essays on Euripidean Drama* [1954], recently attacked in Durham University *Journal*, 1959), urbane, witty, the delight of many a common room. As he went on writing, he went deeper and deeper; there is a vast difference between the intent and style of his *Greek Tragedy* (first published 1920) and his elegant but by no means definitive *Pindar* (1945): both insist on the necessity of seeing the work in terms of its form, but in the second the interpretation less conventionally flowers out from the discovery of the symbolic centre of each ode. Norwood always kept his imagination fixed upon the immediate experience of literature, "appreciation" he would have called it; he was always the tutor, ready with the happy penetrating gloss—a centripetal man, who found it easy to live in the world on account of that centre. Woodhouse turned early to the history of ideas and to an almost reverent sense of their power to create patterns in both literature and life. His astonishing 100-page introduction to the Army Debates (*Puritanism and Liberty* (1938, 1950) remains the definitive analysis of the Puritan ethos; his occasional articles on Spenser and Milton (e.g., "Nature and Grace in *The Faerie Queene*," *ELH*, 1949; "The Argument of Milton's *Comus*," *UTQ*, 1941) have become the periods from which following critics have commenced their highly documented sentences. A quarter-century of graduate students, bemused by end-of-term marathon seminar sessions, have often confused him with Milton, but in spite of his editorial and critical labours on Milton he is not just a Miltonist. He is a humanist, committed to power as well as knowledge (hence centrifugal), and a great deal of his intellectual energy has been devoted influentially to advancing the cause of the humanities in Canada, and to shaping the careers of a generation of proconsuls who have carried his principles through most Canadian, and some American universities.

Neither a horizontal order (by type of scholarship) nor a vertical order (by "field") will do to describe the synthetic man, who lives and works on the diagonal, whether it be a man like G. G. Sedgewick (1882–1949), a teacher (at British Columbia) of legendary histrionics, whose *Of Irony, Especially in Drama* (1935, 1948) is as much the expression of a personality as the development of a theme; or F. M. Salter (1895–1962), whose authoritative—yet curiously sentimental—*Medieval Drama in Chester* (1955) exhibits his meticulousness and his pugnacity; or Watson Kirkconnell, whose extraordinary linguistic accomplishments, range and mass of publication (the *Acadia Bulletin* for January 1961 has published a "selective" list of 370 books, pamphlets and contributions to periodicals), and intransigence in opinion make him unique among Canadian scholars—only he could have produced *The Celestial Cycle* (1952), a collection of the major analogues to the *Paradise Lost* theme; or, again, Barker Fairley, whose *Study of Goethe* (1947), in which the stages on Goethe's way become acts in the drama of the creative spirit and a demonstration of the subtle relations between life and art, has an intention parallel to his experiments in portrait painting, while the enthusiastic humanism which informs his championshp of F. H. Varley against the Shield-to-abstraction movement in Canadian painting (*Our Living Tradition*,

2nd & 3rd Series, 1959) directs him also to persuasive interpretations of such neglected or misunderstood writers as C. M. Doughty (1927) or Wilhelm Raabe (1961). Or Northrop Frye.

Frye has written many things, besides those already noticed and others appearing as I write: to say nothing of his early contributions to the *Canadian Forum*, he has written introductions to selections from Milton and Byron, to the *Collected Poems of E. J. Pratt* (2nd ed., 1958), and to *The Tempest* (*Pelican Shakespeare*); to the *Hudson Review* he has contributed the only short views which make sense of Wallace Stevens, C. J. Jung, and Samuel Beckett. But there is no journalistic diffusion in these enterprises—his world is architectonic. One characteristic mark of his style, otherwise proceeding, though witty in the seventeenth-century sense, *en clair*, the "natural" similes, in which giraffes and the Milky Way appear in the midst of abstract categories, is the sign of unity: he finds types in stones and forms in everything. Beginning with Blake—in the Moncton Public Library, of all places in the world—he developed (*Fearful Symmetry*, 1947) a critical grammar based on the traditional typological interpretation of the Bible and on a demonstration of the unity of myth; this he has since (*Anatomy of Criticism*, 1957) worked into a synthesis of critical theory, controversial, of immense influence (especially in the graduate schools of this continent), Spenglerian in its cyclical complications, overpowering in its range of reference, and depending polemically on such first principles as: "Criticism can talk, and all the arts are dumb"; "literature is not a subject of study, but an object of study"; "the study of literature can never be founded on value-judgments"; "the symbol neither is nor is not the reality which it manifests"; "the mathematical and the verbal universes are doubtless ways of conceiving the same universe." We are too close to Frye to assess his ultimate influence on the intellectual life of the Western academy; his work as scholar-administrator and lecturer-at-large in the cause of the humanities is spread very widely at present, and demonstrates one continuity in Canadian intellectual life, for it significantly recalls, with necessary differences, the careers of those missionaries of culture (noticed above) who created the constituencies of the Canadian universities. The "minister's study" (Frye, though many forget it, is a clergyman too) is still a powerhouse.

This "cabinet of characters" illustrates, among other things, the traditional non-specialist aspect of Canadian academic achievement. Other examples may be cited as well, beginning with Sir Daniel Wilson (1816–1892), who is perhaps best remembered—apart from his importance in the history of the University of Toronto—as the author of *Caliban, the Missing Link* (1873), a real period piece, but who also produced such diverse studies as a biography of Chatterton (1869) and sundry anthropological papers, including *The Lost Atlantis* (1892). G. H. Needler (1866–1961), soldier and grammarian, devoted his retirement to "a new career of research in his favorite English writers, always with some German or Canadian connection," e.g., Scott (*Goethe and Scott*, 1950). In the next generation we have Marshall McLuhan, who did his M.A. thesis on Meredith and his doctor's dissertation on Thomas Nashe, has written most ably on Tennyson and other literary subjects, and has become an internationally known expert and publicist in the field of "communications," beginning with *The Mechanical Bride: Folklore of Industrial Man* (1951), a very comical and profound collage, and continuing in the journal *Explorations* (1953–57), in *The Gutenberg Galaxy* (1962) and elsewhere; my favorite McLuhan title is "Sign, Sound and Fury" (in *Mass Culture*, Glencoe, Ill., 1957). In this group we should notice first those at home in most quarters of the English-speaking literatures, such as Pelham Edgar (1871–1948), the first Canadian Jamesian (*Henry James, Man and Author* [1927]), whose posthumously published sketches for an autobiography, *Across My Path* (1952) will provide the reader with a good deal of the human interest lacking in this survey; E. K. Brown, who, in addition to his essay on Canadian poetry, made influential contributions to the study of Matthew Arnold (*Matthew Arnold: A Study in Conflict*, 1948), of E. M. Forster (*Rhythm in the Novel*, 1950) and Willa Cather (*Willa Cather: A Critical Biography* (1953); or Malcolm Ross, whose contributions to Canadian letters are overshadowed, in the present writer's view, by his *Milton's Royalism* (1943), a study of conflict between symbol and idea in Milton's creative activity, and his *Poetry and Dogma* (1954), a Laudian antidote to the Grand Whiggery of scholarship in seventeenth-century poetry. Then there are those who have established themselves as mediators between disciplines, for example F. E. L. Priestley, between literature and science (e.g., "Science and the Poet," *Dalhousie Review*, 1958), or Reid MacCallum (1897–1949), between literary criticism and aesthetics by way of the philosophy and sacramental order of religion. His posthumously published *Imitation and Design* (ed. William Blissett, 1953), in appearance a collection of essays, is actually the vehicle for an austere and firmly outlined *via media* between those heretical dualisms of art and religion, the tyranny of the abstract and the tyranny of the concrete. The temper and intelligence of the work remind one, not altogether inappropriately, of Pascal.

Here, before I turn to the specialists, is the place to notice Charles Cochrane (1889–1945) and his *Christianity and Classical Culture* (1940), which H. A. Innis called "the first major Canadian contribution to the intellectual history of the West." In Cochrane's choice of subject ("heroic" in the Miltonic sense) and in his understanding of the tension between classical naturalism and Augustinian eschatology, we can follow with elevated pleasure the transformation of scholarship into art, the end of art being, as Horace and Sidney said, to teach and delight.

I have before me at this point a bibliography of studies in Classics, English and the Romance languages, produced by scholars working in Canadian universities since about 1920, which runs to roughly 150 items, in addition to those mentioned above—and it is highly selective and incomplete, even for books. Nor does this include, of course, publications in disciplines of ever growing importance and interest: in the Scandinavian languages and literatures, e.g., A. Anstensen's *The Proverb in Ibsen* (1936); or in Slavic studies, e.g., the numerous publications of G. Luckyj, the first editor of the *Canadian Slavonic Papers*; or in East Asiatic studies, e.g., W. A. C. H. Dobson's *Late Archaic Chinese: A Grammatical Study* (1959); or scholarship in the literatures, ancient and modern, of the Near East, e.g., the publications of G. M. Wickens on modern Persian literature, two of which have appeared in *UTQ* (Jan. 1959; Jan. 1960), or the ancient Near Eastern specialists, whose philological and archaeological studies move toward biblical theology, e.g., T. J. Meek, whose *Hebrew Origins* (1936, 1950, 1960) is one of the most meticulous and influential products of a strong school of Semitics at Toronto ("The book is fully documented with references, as I feel all books should be"), or the historians of the ancient Mediterranean world, e.g., E. T. Salmon, *A History of the Roman World from 30 B.C. to A.D. 138* (1944).

But my list does include publications which have an important place in the history of scholarship in their fields, and some recent contributions which testify to the range and power of the "establishment" in *litterae humaniores*.

Apart from the invaluable bibliographical contributions to Canadian studies, by E. Goggio *et al.*, R. Tanghe, R. Watters, etc., which are noticed elsewhere in this volume, the work of M. A. Buchanan (1878–1952), once termed "Canada's only Hispanist with an international reputation," in modern language methodology and Spanish literary chronology, the contributions of J. H. Parker to current Spanish and Portuguese bibliography (in *Bulletin of the Comediantes*, *SP*, etc.), and J. R. MacGillivray's *Bibliography and Reference Guide* to Keats (1949), there is a not unsurprising dearth of bibliographical studies. There are some conspicuous contributions to philology, linguistics, and of late to lexicography. To begin with, one must mention R. A. Wilson's (1874–1949) *The Miraculous Birth of Language* (1937, four editions since), with its preface by Bernard Shaw, in which he noted that "provincial Canada had with this volume drawn easily ahead of Pasteurized Pavloffed Freudized Europe"; another monument, also *sui generis*, Andrew Bell's (1856–1932) *The Latin Dual and Poetic Diction* (1923), a work of specialized and rigorous opacity; W. L. Graff's *Language and Languages* (1932), "a general introduction to the science of language"; the guide to Canadian and United States spoken English, *Pronunciation* (1930), by Thorleif Larsen and F. C. Walker—Thorleif Larsen is better known as an authority on the dramatist George Peele, and his unpublished papers have been used in preparing the new Yale edition of Peele. A more important contribution to Canadian linguistics was made during his years at Queen's by Henry Alexander, not only in his popular textbook *The Story of Our Language* (1940), but in his studies for the linguistic atlas for the United States and Canada and as one of the "founders" of *The Canadian Dictionary*, a large co-operative project, at this writing just published. Works in specialized lexicography include J. F. Madden and F. P. Magoun, *A Grouped Frequency Word-List of Anglo-Saxon Poetry* (1957), and J. B. Bessinger's *Short Dictionary of Anglo-Saxon Poetry* (1960), which "presents for the first time a complete glossary of Old-English poetry in normalized early West-Saxon orthography," and pioneers new fields in Old-English lexicography. This description is taken from a review by L. K. Shook, the President of the Pontifical Institute, who has published several important studies in the field, including interpretations of the Old English Riddles.

This is the era of the editors. Almost every university of note seems to have a big project in hand and "teams" at work; Yale is of course conspicuous in this respect, with More, Milton, Boswell, etc., but nearer home we have an example in the University of Toronto Press's preparations for a complete J. S. Mill, with F. E. L. Priestley as General Editor and J. M. Robson as Associate Editor. Then we go down the scale from the original edition from MSS through the special-purpose editions of major authors to the "case-books" and anthologies required for mass teaching in the universities. But even with all this going on, the reader may well share my initial surprise in finding how numerous, varied, and important have been the contributions of Canadian scholars to this department of learning.

There is of course a tradition from the editing of classical texts: I have mentioned Sir William Peterson, and may now add a later example in W. H. Alexander (1878–1962), with numerous editorial publications in Seneca (e.g., *Seneca's Dialogi*, 3 vols., 1943–45). Besides the editing of specific texts, we have the findings of the epigraphers and numismatists, such as M. F. MacGregor, one of the authors of *The Athenian Tribute Lists* (1938–53), or W. P. Wallace, *The Euboian League and its Coinage* (1956), and other publications directed to the documentation of ancient history, as are the very numerous contributions of F. M. Heichelheim to the study of papyri and the economic history of the ancient world. From such achievements in the collation of and inference from *fragmenta*, we pass to the embarrassing riches of English literature. Here probably the most outstanding enterprise is Kathleen Coburn's edition of the Coleridge notebooks, of which two double-volumes have at this writing appeared (1959–   ). This is a prolonged and thorough resurrection of a "little world of man," travel, language and code, poem, criticism and philosophy, scandal and aside, metabolism and katabolism of the imagination—everything. Miss Coburn, also the general editor of the projected

Complete Coleridge, is at once captain of academic industry and curious polymath; her earlier essays in Coleridgean editing include the *Philosophical Lectures* (1949) and the *Letters of Sara Hutchinson* (1954). The chief of her (Canadian) associates has been George Whalley, who has to his credit a highly Coleridgean work of speculative aesthetics (*Poetic Process*, 1953), and perhaps should have been included in my earlier collection of "non-specialists," since he has contributed to the *CBEL* Supplement, to Allan Wade's Yeats bibliography, to the Charles Lamb Society *Bulletin*, and to the legends of the Canadian North (in *Tamarack Review*, V); in this context we have *Coleridge and Sara Hutchinson and the Asra Poems* (1955). Earlier large editing enterprises include Burns Martin's edition of the *Works of Allan Ramsay* (1953) for the Scottish Text Society and Priestley's edition of Godwin's *Political Justice* (1946); before that, there were several editions in the "Philology and Literature" series of the University of Toronto; of late years, Douglas Grant, during his productive and influential years at Toronto, brought out his Oxford edition of the *Poetical Works of Charles Churchill* (1956), with necessarily copious annotation, Ernest Sirluck has edited the second volume of the Yale edition of the *Complete Prose Works of John Milton* (1959), and G. M. Story, with Helen Gardner, has rescued the *Sonnets of William Alabaster* (1959) from obscurity; these are devotional exercises by one of the most unsettled in conscience of all Tudor and Stuart divines. The University of Western Ontario's series "Studies in the Humanities" has been inaugurated competently by Herbert Berry with an edition of *Sir John Suckling's Poems & Letters from Manuscript* (1960), containing six poems and fourteen letters with full critical apparatus. Nor should we forget the right copious and happy industry of Joyce Hemlow among the huge masses of the Burney papers, in the New York Public Library, in the British Museum and elsewhere, the first-fruits of which are to be found in her pleasantly discursive *History of Fanny Burney* (1958).

It is not a long step from Coleridge to Friedrich Schlegel, whose *Literary Notebooks, 1797–1801* (1957) have been edited by Hans Eichner; something of what is said of him in the introduction to this intimately documented set of fragments might apply to STC as well: ". . . most of his countless projects never progressed beyond tentative beginnings . . . he was always teeming with ideas . . . the constant flux of his thought. . . ." A less tendentious connection with English literature is apparent in Beatrice Corrigan's *Curious Annals* (1956), where the editor translates some newly discovered documents relating to the *cause célèbre* which inspired Browning's *The Ring and the Book*; Miss Corrigan is an authority on Italian Renaissance drama (see *Studies in the Renaissance*, V, 1958 and her *Catalogue of Italian Plays, 1500–1700, in the Library of the University of Toronto*, 1961). In French studies, the most important editing, on the whole, has been done with medieval texts, beginning with A. J. Denomy's (1904–1957) *Old French Lives of St. Agnes* (1938)—Father Denomy is better known for his *The Heresy of Courtly Love* (1947), a much-cited treatment of the relation between *amour courtois* and the neo-Manicheanism of Provence—and C. M. Jones's edition of the *Chronique du Pseudo-Turpin* (1936), and continuing with Bernadine Bujila's *La vie de sainte Marie l'Egyptienne* (1949) and W. H. Trethewey's *French Text of the Ancrene riwle* (1958). To these must be added a most elegant set of texts in Renaissance literature, the edition in six volumes in the "Textes littéraires français" series of the works of Desportes, with the commentary of Malherbe, by Victor E. Graham, four of which are published (1958–   ).

The range and quality of contemporary scholarship in Classics may be studied in *Phoenix* (from 1946), the journal of the Canadian Classical Association. The scholars of this generation, whose work is from time to time represented there (as elsewhere in their professional journals), are carrying on the various traditions of their field, literary criticism (e.g., D. J. Conacher on Euripides; W. J. N. Rudd on Horace and Juvenal), ancient history (e.g., S. E. Smethurst on Cicero and his times; C. W. J. Eliot on the demes of Attica), archaeology, influenced here by Homer Thompson (e.g., J. W. Graham on the Cretan palaces). Here one might mention especially, as extensions of the field, D. F. S. Thomson's studies in Renaissance Latin, and E. G. Berry's *Emerson's Plutarch* (1961), a book "really about Emerson" (H. L. Tracy), of which perhaps the most interesting part is the account of the idea of "Hellenism" in the Romantics and post-Romantics.

(Here, as elsewhere in these necessarily abbreviated notices, I call attention to a few items either of special interest or obviously representative.)

The immediate tradition behind these scholars may be indicated by reference to the productions of O. J. Todd (1884–1957), author of the *Index Aristophaneus*, translator of Xenophon's *Banquet* in the Loeb series; of W. Sherwood Fox, whose curious productions in Classics and Semitics include such items as "Lucian in the Grave-scene of *Hamlet*," and "The Origin of the Conical Cap of Cyprian Aphrodite Worship"; of W. D. Woodhead (1885–1957), *Etymologizing in Greek Literature* (1928)—hardly representative of his capacities; of Skuli Johnson (1888–1955), who was as at home among the Icelandic sagas as with his Horace (see his *Selected Odes of Horace*, 1952). The tradition has always had, however, its centre in knowledgeable piety before texts (see my reference to Norwood, above), and in this respect as in others G. M. A. Grube has been an influential figure. His earlier *Drama of Euripides* (1941), in which a thorough discussion of the dramatic devices of the Greek stage precedes an analysis of each play seen in the context of its times, has been succeeded by *Sophocles the Playwright* (1957), of S. M. Adams (1891–1960) which has much the same attention to text in context of religious belief and dramatic convention; Grube's latest book, *A Greek Critic: Demetrius on*

Style (1961), preceded by other investigations in Greek literary criticism (e.g., in *AJP*, 1957; *Trans. RSC*, 1956), displays another aspect of his interests: he gives a fresh translation of the document, so difficult to reproduce that there has to be a good deal of Greek in the footnotes, places it in the context of ancient writing on rhetoric, and argues at length for a date *c.* 270 B.C. This is technical and debatable, but the treatise itself is of interest to any student of rhetorical figures, and even the layman may amuse himself with the illustrations. His *Plato's Thought* (1935) is also of interest apart from its merits, still conspicuous among the constant re-interpretations of Plato, for it adumbrates another aspect of classical studies, more recently exemplified by M. D. C. Tait (1896–1958) (e.g. "Plato's Use of Myth," *UTQ*, 1957) and L. E. Woodberry on Parmenides and other studies. Gilbert Bagnani's *Arbiter of Elegance* (1954), like its subject, Petronius, makes the best of two worlds, in this case the intricate problem of the date and authorship of the *Satyricon*, and the delightful if conjectural reconstruction of the life of its author. If E. T. Owen (see above) set aside the "Homeric question," L. A. MacKay in *The Wrath of Homer* (1948) approaches it by arguing that "Homer" used the story of the wrath of Achilles to organize two cycles, one dealing with Agamemnon's expedition, the other with the revenge of Achilles. I do not know how this stands with the experts, Denys Page *et al.*, but it is a vivid scholarly demonstration.

As I have implied above, A. S. P. Woodhouse has exerted a strong influence on English studies, whether specifically in the development of an approach to Milton—as in A. E. Barker's *Milton and the Puritan Dilemma* (1942), a now standard work, which analyses Milton's thought in relation to the Puritan ideal of the "holy community," and follows its transformations through the alchemy of political controversy—more generally in his sympathy to such studies in the history of ideas as William Robbins' *The Ethical Idealism of Matthew Arnold* (1959), started under the direction of E. K. Brown; or in political and social history, e.g., my *The Paul's Cross Sermons, 1534–1642* (1958); or in the adoption of his categories for seventeenth-century ethical and religious experience. H. S. Wilson (1904–1959), for example, turned Woodhouse's formulation of the nature-grace dichotomy to a study of Shakespeare's tragedies (*On the Design of Shakespearean Tragedy*, 1957), not altogether persuasively, though the book remains valuable for its incidental insights and subtle analyses of dramatic action; and A. C. Hamilton, in his recent *The Structure of Allegory in the Faerie Queene* (1961), an asymmetrical but always interesting book, professes more debt to Woodhouse's discussion of the poem than he demonstrates. In Renaissance studies, the students of the Toronto "school" have also been deeply influenced by Wilson himself and by N. J. Endicott, the scope of whose researches in Sir Thomas Browne is suggested in *UTQ*, January 1961. I have mentioned William

Blissett in another connection: he has also two important articles on Elizabethan "Caesarism" (*SP*, 1956; *JHI*, 1957); other contemporary representatives of these influences are H. N. Maclean (on Fulke Greville, in *HLQ*, 1953, 1958), and A. E. Malloch, who has written on Donne's paradoxes and their tradition (*SP*, 1956), and on the Renaissance casuists (*SEL*, 1962). Roy Daniells' contributions to scholarship in this period range from his edition of Traherne's *Serious and Pathetic Contemplation* (1941) to more recent studies in the Baroque. The most outstanding contributions to this field from outside this group have been made by John Peter, in his *Complaint and Satire in Early English Literature* (1956), most valuable in its discussion of the rediscovery of Latin satire in the 1590's and its effects, and his *A Critique of Paradise Lost* (1960). Among contemporary Shakespeareans we should notice Marion B. Smith, who has also published on Marlowe's imagery (1940), and F. D. Hoeniger, a frequent contributor to the *Shakespeare Quarterly* and the editor of *Pericles* in the New Arden series. J. K. Johnstone's *The Bloomsbury Group* (1954) is an important contribution to twentieth-century literary history.

Some contributions to Old and Middle English scholarship have been noted above; to these should be added R. K. Gordon's translation *Anglo-Saxon Poetry* (1927) and his *The Story of Troilus* (1934), both of which, and especially the former, have been extraordinarily useful to literary students. A few monuments in scholarship and criticism of eighteenth- and nineteenth-century English literature must serve to conclude this section. W. O. Raymond's *The Infinite Moment* (1950 and expanded 1964), a collection of essays on Browning written over a considerable period, remains a useful part of any Browning library; W. L. MacDonald in *Pope and His Critics* (1951), investigates how far "personalities" entered into contemporary views of Pope, but the result is more an essay in biography than in the history of criticism. Clarence Tracy's biography of Richard Savage, *The Artificial Bastard* (1953), opens up accurately for the first time a fascinating chapter in the social and literary life of the eighteenth century, and R. M. Wiles, in his *Serial Publication in England, before 1750* (1956), provides an account, among other things, of the early publication of abridged versions of *Robinson Crusoe, Pamela*, and *Joseph Andrews*. Kenneth MacLean's *John Locke and English Literature of the Eighteenth Century* (1936) is a standard work on the influence of Locke's theories of mind on the eighteenth-century imagination, and is especially useful for Sterne; his *Agrarian Age: A Background for Wordsworth* (1950), a study of "agrarian sentiment" in the period, is touched by its author's sensitive, often eccentric (in the best sense) insights: e.g., "Wordsworth [in the French Revolutionary period] was the perfect young intellectual: his dress was rather loud. . . ." The most recent book of importance in this general category is *The Valley of Vision* (1961), a study of

Blake's revolutionary dialectic in the context of the Age of Enlightenment, by Peter F. Fisher (1918–1958). Fisher, though he wrote articles on *Beowulf*, Scott, Milton, and Shakespeare, had primarily a philosophic mind, and this book demands much of its readers, who are rewarded by association with what Frye, editing this posthumous volume, calls "a critical mind of singular erudition and power."

Surprisingly, not much has been done in the way of interpretations of American literature. It is a long step from Pelham Edgar's *Henry James* of 1927 to Peter Buitenhuis, who has edited *Henry James, French Writers and American Women* (1961), and contributed to a special group of James articles in *UTQ*, January 1962. Gordon Roper, whose "Mark Twain and his Canadian Publishers" (*American Book Collector*, 1960) is of more than bibliographical interest, has an edition of Hawthorne's *The Scarlet Letter* (1949), and Hugo McPherson has published a number of articles on Hawthorne (e.g., in *American Literature*, 1958; *UTQ*, 1959) and on other American authors.

In Germanic scholarship and criticism the figures are more isolated, there is less question of influence or schools; there is an interesting concentration of late years upon modern German literature, not true generally of the publications of Heinrich Henel, which range indeed from an edition of *Aelfric's De Temporibus Anni* (1942) through articles on Goethe, Hebbel and a study of the nineteenth-century Swiss poet C. F. Mayer (1954); but H. Steinhauer, who has published anthologies of German novelle (1936) and drama (1938) of the nineteenth and twentieth centuries, has written much on Hauptmann. The most recent work on Hauptmann is by Margaret Sinden, a study of his realistic prose plays (1957) which by extensive analysis introduces these dramas to English readers. Also in the modern field is W. L. Graff's *Rainer Maria Rilke: Creative Anguish of a Modern Poet* (1957), which is most convincing when it expounds the significance of certain recurring symbols in Rilke, "angels," "transformations."

Hermann Boeschenstein, who succeeded Barker Fairley at University College, Toronto, is representative of a different academic background and scholarly interests which coincide chiefly in the German novel—he has translated Fairley's *Raabe*. I am incompetent to assess his total contribution to date to studies of modern German culture, except to observe that the common reader may learn more about the contemporary German imagination and its implication for modern Europe from his *Der Neue Mensch: Die Biographie im deutschen Nachkriegsroman* (1958) or from such an unobtrusive but penetrating article as "The Germans Look at the Atomic Age" (*UTQ*, 1959), with its account of the intellectuals' distrust of the technology for which their compatriots are universally praised, than from any amount of popular interpretations of the German soul. His "report" (as he calls it) on

German fiction during World War II, *The German Novel 1939-1944* (1949) examines with tolerance and care the persistence of traditional themes in the genre, and the devices of indirection and irony which helped to preserve these themes and values under National Socialism.

That gap in our scholarly concerns, the neglect of the American tradition, which I noted in the context of English studies, is not so glaring in the publications of the Italianists and Hispanists: E. Goggio, for example, from his *Italians in Early American History* (1930), through a whole series of publications on the relations of Irving, Longfellow, Cooper, and Emerson to Italian literature and culture, has domiciled comparative studies of this kind in Canada; a younger contributor to the study of Western hemisphere is Kurt L. Levy, with a thoroughly documented book on Thomas Carrasquilla, a Toronto doctoral thesis, published in Spanish in Colombia (1958). Carrasquilla was "a pioneer of Spanish-American regionalism." In the European tradition, we have Ulrich Leo's *Torquato Tasso* (pub. Bern in German, 1951), a study of Tasso's tormented sensibility and its results for his style, and J. E. Shaw's (1876-1962) *Guido Cavalcanti's Theory of Love* (1948), an elucidation of the *Canzone d'Amore*; "the poem," said E. H. Wilkins, "has waited for 650 years to receive a duly satisfying interpretation, and it has found that interpretation not in its native Tuscany, but in Ontario."

This whole matter of inter-cultural relations, in the context of comparative literature, is especially illuminated by a series of investigations by scholars in the field of French studies. Here are some representative titles: Harry Ashton, *Du Bartas en Angleterre* (1908); Margaret Cameron, *L'influence des saisons de Thomson sur la poésie descriptive en France, 1759-1810* (1927); E. A. Joliat, *Smollett et la France* (1935); C. D. Rouillard, *The Turk in French History, Thought and Literature, 1520-1660* (1940); E. J. H. Greene, *T. S. Eliot et la France* (1951). These adventures across linguistic boundaries make a good deal of Eng. Lit. thesis production look rather parochial, especially when, in the present political and cultural context, we add to these not only W. E. Collin's surveys of French-Canadian literature in "Letters in Canada," and D. M. Hayne's bibliography in progress of the French-Canadian novel, but such studies as M. B. Ellis's *De Saint-Denys Garneau* (1949) or G. A. Klinck's edition of the *Mémoires intimes* of Louis Fréchette (1961).

In the main tradition of the major study of the major writer, there is A. F. B. Clark's *Racine* (1939), which sets the dramas conventionally in the context of the age, the biography, and the conventions of French classical tragedy. French studies at British Columbia in the twenties and thirties have left us besides Ashton's *Madame de la Fayette* (1922) and his *Molière* (1930). In the eighteenth-century field, we have C. W. Hendel's two-volume *Jean-Jacques Rousseau, Moralist* (1934), which traces the evolution of Rousseau's thought in terms of occasions and inward development, with much massive exposition of texts and little epigrammatic force. M. B. Ellis's *Julie; or, La Nouvelle Héloise* (1949) demonstrates the consistency between the moral philosophy of the work and the moral theory in Rousseau's earlier writings. These volumes are representative of the history of ideas; the various publications of D. O. Evans on the drama and novel in the Romantic period, and his *Social Romanticism in France, 1830–1848* (1951), are concerned with literature in its social relations—see the pages on Hugo in the industrial hell of Lille, in this book, which contains a bibliography of French socialism from Saint-Simon to Proudhon.

V

There, then, are the pigeonholes, and from each peeps the spine of a book or the curling edge of an offprint, bent with its freight of footnotes. The various "genres" of literary scholarship are all there and all represented. What does this kind of summary prove?

It proves the vitality of research and teaching—for many of these works started in classroom notes—in the humanities in Canada, or one branch of the humanities, and provides a happy ending to the dark surveys and forecasts with which I decorated the first pages of this essay. It proves that the antiquary is as creative as the astronomer, and his enterprise as much a challenge to the active intellect. The spaces between dates—and between words—are psychologically as great as the spaces between stars, and have the same masterful irrelevance to natural resources and political programmes.

So far as the Canadian ethos is concerned, it proves very little. For many of the persons noted above, a Canadian university was or is a pause in passage and no continuing city; for most of them, too, inclusion in a survey like this is accidental, for each belongs with his fellows in his "field" (a good word, field, you use a hoe in a field, not a placard), and only there is the real association. Such a generalization is not altogether right for those whose achievements have made them prestigious symbols for their universities, or those who have helped to create the conditions under which literary research has flourished and by their teaching and example have raised the standards of the profession. To them I have tried to give the prominence they deserve.

But all these writers have in common an adherence to the disinterested use of words; this is the dominant element in an otherwise complex tradition, and they maintain it in the age of the electronically disseminated corruption of the word. There is an academic jargon too, but at least its aim is usually definition, not sedation. And this is very valuable, especially in a country with four languages (French, English, TV, and "joual"), but essential at all times and in all places to the creation of civility.

29. Literature of Religion and Theology

VERY REV. JAMES S. THOMSON

IN AN ARTICLE contributed to the first number of the newly founded *Canadian Journal of Theology* in April 1955, G. R. Cragg remarked that "prominent among the forces" shaping Canadian theology "has been a kind of theological 'colonialism'—a dependent spirit which persistently looked elsewhere for leadership. . . . It was tacitly assumed that no good thing could come out of a Nazareth as remote as ours from the fountainheads of truth." This judgment is supported by the first theological work in English to appear on Canadian soil. It came from the pen of the celebrated Henry Alline in 1781 with the quaint title *Two Mites on some of the most important and much disputed points of Divinity*. Despite the modest insinuation of the title, it ran to 342 pages and was printed by A. Henry in Halifax. The author was born at Newport, R.I., in 1748 and came to Nova Scotia in 1760; after some twenty years he returned to the States and died in New Hampshire in 1784. He had undergone a remarkable spiritual experience recounted in *The Life and Journals of the Rev. Henry Alline* published in Boston in 1806, a volume which so attracted the attention of William James as to be noted in his celebrated *Varieties of Religious Experience*. Henry Alline was profoundly influenced by the New Light movement in New England and, following his conversion, he became an itinerant preacher. From his work sprang the Baptist Church in Nova Scotia. Concerning the far-reaching effects of his work, H. H. Walsh writes in *The Christian Church in Canada* (1956), "The mystical religion which he preached with such vehemence did not long survive his death, but his demand to bring religion to the test of feeling and experience was taken up by other sects and became a determining influence in the social and political development of Canada." (See also chapter 5.)

Alline's work provoked a challenging response from Jonathan Scott (1744–1819) on behalf of the more orderly Congregational churches which were rent asunder by the evangelical zeal of the New Light preacher. This appeared as *A Brief View of the Religious Tenets and Sentiments . . . in . . . Two Mites* in 1784 and, like the volume against which it was directed, hardly supported the suggestion of the title, for its brevity extended to 334 pages.

Also to be noted in addition to his published sermons is Alline's other work *The Anti-Traditionalist* (1783).

The claim of *Two Mites* to temporal priority in English theology might be disputed by *An Essay on Infant Baptism* by Charles Inglis (1734–1816), first Anglican bishop of Nova Scotia, but for the fact that it was published in New York in 1768 before the author came to Canada in 1787.

Controversial theological writing was not confined to the Puritan divines. Its prevalence among the Presbyterians is witnessed by the publication in Edinburgh (1808) of a work by T. McCulloch (1776–1843), afterwards the first President of Dalhousie University, entitled *Popery Condemned by Scripture and the Fathers*. A massive reply came from the pen of E. Burke (1753–1820), the Roman Catholic bishop of Halifax, extending to 403 pages in *Remarks on a Pamphlet entitled Popery Condemned by Scripture and the Fathers* (1809). The same writer published *A Treatise on the First Principles of Christianity* in two volumes (1808–10). McCulloch returned to the charge in *Popery Again Condemned* lengthened out to 429 pages. A less controversial work appeared in 1849, *Calvinism, the Doctrine of the Scriptures* by the same author.

The question of baptism continued to provoke controversial writing. In 1835, E. A. Crawley (1799–1888) of Acadia University required 119 pages for his *Treatise on Baptism* in reply to a work written by William Elder (1784–1848) on *Infant Sprinkling* (1823) and James Robertson (1801?–1878) joined the fray in 1836 with *A Treatise on Infant Baptism*. J. M. Cramp (1796–1881), President of Acadia, began a long career of publication in 1831 with *A Textbook of Popery* (439 pp.), which ran to three editions, followed, among many lesser works, by *The Reformation in Europe* (1844), a monumental *Baptist History* (1868), *The Lamb of God* (1871), and *Paul and Christ* (1873).

The Anglicans also made their contributions to both expository and controversial theology. Daniel Falloon (d. 1862) published *An Historical View of the Church of England* (2 vols., 1830), followed by *Dialogues on the Apostolic Church* (1837). T. W. D. Gray wrote *A Brief View of the Scriptural Authority and Historical Evidence for Infant Baptism* (1837).

The Methodists were represented among other writers by the dynamic A. Egerton Ryerson (1803–1882) who was destined to play such a determinative part in the political and social development of Canadian life. As early as 1828, he wrote *Claims of the Churchmen and Dissenters of Upper Canada* to be followed by *The Clergy Reserve Question* (1839), *Scriptural Rights of the Members of Christ's Visible Church* (1854) and *Canadian Methodism* (1882) as well as a number of more journalistic and incidental writings. A. W. McLeod wrote other works of Methodist persuasion: *Universalism in its Modern and Ancient Form* (1837), *The Methodist Ministry Defended* (1839) and *Methodist Ministry Further Defended* (1840).

While there was a prevailing note of denominational controversy in the earliest theological writing, other themes also made their appearance in various works. Among them G. J. Mountain (1789–1863), Anglican Bishop of Montreal, produced *The Foundation and Constitution of the Christian Ministry* (1826). S. T. Thompson published *Scripture Sketches* (1829). W. T. Wishart (d. 1853) should be noted as among the first of the more systematic theologians in Canada with his series of works: *A System of Temporal Retribution* (1841), *The Decalogue* (1842), *A Series of Outlines; or, Theological Essays* . . . (1846) and *Six Disquisitions on Doctrinal and Practical Theology* (1853). John Roaf (1801–1862) published his *Lectures on the Millennium* in 1844.

At the close of the eighteenth and during the first half of the nineteenth centuries, writing on religious subjects was concerned mainly with the rival claims of denominations. The Baptist question was a symbol of conflicts that penetrated to the remotest settlements where life was still at a pioneer stage. Religious traditions gained strength through being transplanted to new soils where they were valued as sources of spiritual security in arduous conditions. On the other hand, there was also a pervading sense of new freedom that found expression in evangelistic zeal and ecclesiastical novelty, not to speak of the sheer excitement of religious controversy. Closely allied were questions pertaining to efforts for Church Establishment and the creation of educational systems, including the setting up of universities and colleges on rival religious foundations.

By mid-century, questions no less controversial were projected from movements of thought in the wider world. The scientific spirit, engaging itself with the rationalism of German philosophy, began to affect theology at its central point—the nature of revelation in the Bible. This new spirit came from two directions which were closely related in their impact. On the one hand there was Darwin's theory of evolution and on the other, there was the higher criticism of the scriptures. They combined to cast doubt on the historical veracity of the creation narratives in *Genesis*, and by inference, it appeared, on the nature of all scriptural authority. In the very year (1859) of Darwin's *Origin of Species*, J. Bovell (1817–1880) published a large volume entitled *Outlines of Natural Theology for the Use of the Canadian Student* in which he cited biological and anatomical evidence for theistic belief along the lines of Paley's celebrated work on the same subject half a century before. This was followed by *Passing Thoughts on Man's Relation to God and God's Relation to Man* in 1862. However, it was Sir J. W. Dawson (1820–1899), Principal of McGill University, who entered with apologetic and expository zeal on a long series of writings calculated to reconcile natural science with biblical revelation. These were mostly considerable works, one of which, *Modern Ideas of Evolution as related to Revelation and Science* (1890) ran to six editions. He was much earlier taken up with what appears to have been his accepted vocation by the publication of *Archaia* (1860) a work designed to relate cosmogony to the Hebrew scriptures. Others of his writings concerned with such relationships were *Nature and the Bible* (1875), *The Origin of the World* (1877), *Modern Science in Bible Lands* (1888), *The Meeting Place of Geology and History* (1895), and *Eden Lost and Won* (1895).

The traditional view of the scriptures was defended by Charles Freshman (1819–1875) in *The Pentateuch* (1864), followed by *The Jews and the Israelites* (1870). J. M. Hirschfelder (1819–1902) wrote *The Scriptures Defended* (1863) which he continued with two lectures on *The Creation* (1874) and later two large volumes entitled *Biblical Expositor* (1882–85) mainly dealing with the nature of Hebrew literature and, in particular, the Book of Genesis.

The full impact of biblical criticism was not felt in Canada until nearer the end of the century in a storm of controversy that gathered around the figure of George Workman (1848–1936), who was dismissed from his teaching appointment in Victoria University, Toronto, because of his views on the nature of biblical inspiration. Workman was an able scholar and a prolific writer whose aim was to reconcile the new views of the scriptures with their essential value as divine revelation. This was emphasized in his earliest work, *The Old Testament Vindicated* (1897) followed by such other writings as *Messianic Prophecy Vindicated* (1899), *The Atonement* (1911), and *Jesus the Man and Christ the Spirit* (1928). His principal opponent was Albert Carman (1833–1917), General Superintendent of the Methodist Church, himself the author of *The Guiding Eye* (1889), a study of the doctrine of the Holy Spirit. The temper of this dispute is indicated by the *Sabre Thrusts at Free-Thought* (1898) of W. W. Walker (1858–1946), and, even more, by a publication in Peterborough (1891) of John Carlisle described as *An Exposé of and a Red Hot Protest against a Damnable Heresy smuggled into Methodism and taught by Professor Workman of Victoria University*.

The conflict that culminated in the dismissal of Professor Workman is indicative of the two major movements of thought in Canada during the second half of the nineteenth century. On the one hand, there was the influence of tradition grounded in the strict authority of the holy scripture. On the other hand, there was the impact of more liberal attitudes deriving mostly from European sources. Expositors of the more conservative views were thrown into an attitude of defence. Typical of such writings were *The Exclusive Claims of David's Psalms* (1855) by William Sommerville (1800–1878) and *The Architecture of the Heavens* with the sub-title *In Opposition to the Views of Dr. Colenso* (1867) and *Universalism Unfounded* (1867) both by E. S. Wiggins (1839–1910). John G. Marshall (1786–1880), a judge in Cape Breton, was a prolific Methodist pamphleteer. Among his many publications we note *Answers to "Essays and Reviews"* (1862) and *Scriptural Testimonies to the Doctrines and Duties of Christianity* (1873). The Rev. W. Cochrane (1831–1898) wrote a large volume on *Future Punishment* (1886) and J. S. Evans produced two notable volumes, *The One Mediator* (1884) and *Christian Rewards* (1880). The same eschatological interest is exemplified by *Immortality versus Annihilation* by William Jackson (1872).

R. C. Horner (1854–1921) was typical of a persistent element in Canadian religious life. Along with a strongly traditionalist influence that gained emphasis from the spiritual security it afforded while institutions were still at the formative stage, there have been movements that express an equally powerful feeling of religious liberty that develops into libertarianism. For the most part, they are of the prophetic, enthusiastic type and have resulted in a constant appearance of sectarian denominations. Their sociological and political influence has been rather far-reaching in Canadian life. Horner was something of a Henry Alline *redivivus*. He created quite a stir particularly among the Methodists in Ontario. With their evangelistic zeal, the Methodists provided a hospitable soil for the germination of such movements. Horner was instrumental in setting up a Holiness Movement church which persisted well into the following century. Two of his more influential works were *Original and Inbred Sin* (1896) and *Pentecost* (1891).

The more liberal trend in theology took two directions. The first was one which has continued to hold a considerable place in Canadian thought—the philosophical approach to religious truth. Robert Shaw published a large work on *Existence and Diety* (1872) and W. J. Penton wrote *The Riddle of the Universe Solved* (1890). In the same vein, James Tait (1829–1899) produced a short but valuable work, *Mind in Matter* (1884). The most notable exponent of the philosophy of religion was John Watson (1847–1939) of Queen's University whose writing attracted attention far beyond the Canadian scene. Watson came from Scotland and he represented the prevailing school of Idealism. His influence was profound and through his work the intellectual life of Canada took a forward leap. He was a voluminous writer on general philosophy but his main contributions to religious thought were *Christianity and Idealism* (1897) and, much later, his Gifford Lectures on *The Interpretation of Religious Experience* (1912) (see also chapter 23). The other trend was also represented at Queen's University in the work of its Principal, G. M. Grant (1835–1902). It took the form of a comparative study of religion as is witnessed by his work on *The Religions of the World* (1894). Also to be noted as an evidence of the same movement of thought and of Canada's growing influence beyond its own borders is a series of lectures delivered in

Japan by C. S. Eby (1845–1925), a Methodist missionary of outstanding ability. These were published under the title of *Christianity and Humanity* (1883).

The beginning of the present century saw the publication of a large two-volume work by Nathanael Burwash (1839–1918) of Victoria College, Toronto, bearing the title *Manual of Christian Theology on the Inductive Method* (1900). It was indicative of a new stature in Canadian theology and inaugurated a sustained contribution of scholarly work that has since continued. Much of it has been undertaken by teachers who have come from overseas to spend a relatively short period in Canada—such as George Jackson, J. E. Macfadyen, T. R. Glover, E. F. Scott, A. R. Gordon and John Baillie. These and other expatriates gained their first foothold on the ladder to subsequent fame while here in Canada. However, Canadian soil was not simply a jumping-off point into the wider world of scholarship. They remained long enough to make an enduring impression on Canadian thought and to have a determinative effect on the life of the Canadian churches. Some like John Watson and, later, T. B. Kilpatrick, Robert Law, and W. Morgan made Canada their adopted home and established its fame abroad by the distinguished quality of their writing. Not of least importance was their seminal influence in raising a crop of native scholars and teachers. This, however, took time to develop and still awaits the fulfilment of its promise.

By the present century, Canadian writing had reached sufficient importance to warrant one of the leading theological publishing houses in London in projecting "The Canadian Library of Religious Literature." One of this series, *Redemption* (1822) by J. Dick Fleming, was notable not only because of its enduring worth as a contribution to the doctrine of the Atonement but for the fact that it was written in Winnipeg—indicating that the theological interest which had hitherto been confined mostly to the Maritime Provinces, Quebec, and Ontario had now moved out to the rapidly expanding west. Other contributors to this Library series were R. E. Walsh with his *Classics of the Soul's Quest* and A. R. Gordon with his *Prophets of the Old Testament* (1919). Both of these writers worked at the newly established project for joint theological teaching in Montreal which was later to develop into the Faculty of Divinity in McGill University. Gordon also wrote on *The Poets of the Old Testament* (1919) in a British series of studies in the literature of the Old Testament. He later returned to St. Andrews in Scotland.

Gordon's work was characteristic of the new kind of biblical scholarship that now began to leave the older type far behind. It silenced the voice of controversy by the positive enlightenment of the contributors who were able to give convincing demonstration that the critical view of the scriptures could actually contribute to their spiritual meaning. This achievement imparted a notable element to Canadian religious life. It meant that after the first bitter clashes between exponents of the older and the newer points of view the Canadian churches were spared the excesses of theological acrimony and ecclesiastical turmoil which afflicted church life south of the border during the earliest years of this century. Here and there strident voices were raised in protest against what was considered the apostasy of the critical scholars; but this opposition came from only the periphery of the main teaching of the churches, which were profoundly influenced by the presence in their theological colleges of able and enlightened professors who combined the new learning with fidelity to the essentials of the Christian faith. J. E. Macfadyen, who later returned to his native Scotland, wrote a typical work on *Old Testament Criticism and the Christian Church* (1903). Others of equal note were George Jackson with his *Studies in the Old Testament* (1909) and *The Preacher and the Modern Mind* (1912), also G. H. Porter with his *Reality of the Divine Movement in Israel* (1911). The most distinguished and permanently influential of this school of thought was W. G. Jordan (1852–1939) of Queen's University, a fine scholar and a prolific writer. He entered the field with *Prophetic Ideas and Ideals* (1902) to be followed, among many other works, by *Biblical Criticism and Modern Thought* (1909), *Commentary on . . . Deuteronomy* (1911), *History and Revelation* (1926). He set the tone for Canadian study of the Old Testament, continued by such scholars as E. W. Pilcher of Wycliffe College, Toronto, with *Hosea, Joel and Amos* (1929) and, later, R. B. Y. Scott of Montreal with *The Relevance of the Prophets* (1944).

New Testament scholarship was not less significant. The main centre of influence was in Toronto where Robert Law (1860–1919) published a notable study of the First Epistle of St. John under the title *The Tests of Life* (1909), which is still highly regarded as a worthy example of expository writing. The same author gave us *The Emotions of Jesus* (1915). T. B. Kilpatrick (1858–1930) wrote on *New Testament Evangelism* (1911) and later, *The Redemption of Man* (1920). The two brothers Falconer were fine New Testament scholars who established a wide repute for their works. James W. Falconer (1868–1956) in Halifax wrote an early work on the Church in the New Testament age bearing the title *From Apostle to Priest* (1900), followed by *The Three Crosses* (1907) and, much later, *The Passion according to St. John* (1944). His brother Sir Robert Falconer (1867–1943) was a shining example of what has been a repetitive feature in Canadian religious thought. Some of its most outstanding expositors have combined their interest in theological learning with academic leadership. Amidst his many labours as the first president of the University of Toronto, Sir Robert found time to publish, among other lesser works, *The Pastoral Epistles: Introduction, Translation and Notes* (1937), which still holds a secure place in the significant literature of New Testament scholarship. The

Rev. W. Patrick (1852-1911) wrote an important work on *James, the Lord's Brother* (1906). W. Morgan of Queen's University broke new ground in Pauline studies with his book on *The Religion and Theology of St. Paul* (1918). This was a major work which interpreted the apostle in terms of his contemporary environment and used the knowledge of the mystery religions to illuminate the New Testament. J. T. L. Maggs wrote on *The Spiritual Experience of St. Paul* (1901) and it is interesting to note that E. J. Pratt (1883-1964), who was later to gain fame as a leading Canadian poet, presented a thesis to the University of Toronto for which he was awarded the Ph.D. degree and which was published under the title *Studies in Pauline Eschatology* (1917). Rev. William Caven (1830-1904) of Knox College, Toronto, wrote on *Christ's Teaching concerning the Last Things* (1908). These writers on the New Testament accomplished the same effect as their colleagues achieved for the Old Testament. While there was nothing uniquely original about their approach to biblical studies, they were the means of bringing into Canadian religious thought the influences of the wider world of scholarship. And the contributions which they were able to make to that same world were by no means negligible.

The philosophy and psychology of religion was also represented in Canadian writing, notably by G. J. Blewett (1873-1912) of Victoria College, Toronto, who was invited to deliver the Nathaniel Taylor Lectures at Yale University, which he later published under the title *The Christian View of the World* (1912). An earlier work by the same author was *The Study of Nature and the Vision of God* (1907). G. B. Cutten, President of Acadia University, was a pioneer in the new territories of religious psychology with his *Psychological Phenomena of Christianity* (1908), followed by *Three Thousand Years of Mental Healing* (1910), *Mind, its Origin and Goal* (1927), and *Instincts and Religion* (1940). W. Morgan showed his diversity of interest and scholarship along the same new line of interest in *The Nature and Right of Religion* (1926). George Jackson, who was prominent in the fight for the newer theology, gave convincing proof that he could combine liberal scholarship with evangelical zeal in his book on *The Fact of Conversion* (1908). J. Clark Murray (1836-1917), Professor of Philosophy in McGill University, produced a *Handbook of Christian Ethics* (1908). J. Paterson Smyth (1852-1932) may be justly regarded as the most popular of all Canadian writers on theology. The only rivals are Charles W. Gordon (Ralph Connor) and Lloyd Douglas who both achieved widespread acclaim as novelists with works that were more religious than doctrinal. Paterson Smyth was a prolific writer with an engaging and attractive style which gave his works a remarkably wide circulation. He combined genuine scholarship with a gift for popular appeal. Before coming to Canada, he had held a professorial appointment in the University of Dublin but his main place of industry was in Montreal where he contrived to combine a career of literary work with the duties of rector in the large city parish church of St. George's. One of his earliest works, *The Old Documents and the New Bible* (1890), indicates the prevailing interest of his mind. His accepted vocation was to interpret the results of biblical scholarship for the general reader, and in this enterprise he achieved remarkable success. An earlier work on the same line was *How we got our Bible* (1885) and it ran to twenty editions. His book on *The Gospel of the Hereafter* (1910) was in the nature of a theological *tour de force* which achieved a circulation of 70,000 and was translated into several languages. *A People's Life of Christ* (1920) fully deserved its title. It appeared just after the First World War when there was something of a literary vogue in which a wide variety of writers (mostly lay) such as Middleton Murry, Papini, G. K. Chesterton, and T. R. Glover attempted to present a fresh non-dogmatic portrait of Jesus. This they undertook despite the negative admonitions which had marked the conclusion of Schweitzer's *Quest of the Historical Jesus* to the effect that a hundred years of biblical research had failed to yield any indisputable reconstruction of the gospel story. Among these works (with the exception of T. R. Glover's *Jesus of History*), Paterson Smyth's rendering is still widely accepted as the most successful—and in many ways, his account of Jesus was much less subjective in its interpretation than Glover's. He followed with *The Story of St. Paul's Life and Letters* (1924). Glover, who was Smyth's only rival in popularity, spent some time on the staff of Queen's University, Kingston, and during his later career as Fellow of St. John's College and Public Orator at Cambridge, he was a frequent visiting lecturer at universities in Canada.

The same interest that provided the stimulus for the writing of Paterson Smyth was further represented by Trevor Davies of Toronto, who was also a preacher, in his study of the gospel record entitled *The Inner Circle* (1924). Davies was a writer with a singular spiritual sensitivity which he was able to communicate to his literary expression. Also, at a later date, there was a similar contribution by Charles W. Gordon (1860–1937) who had achieved such fame with his Glengarry novels (see chapter 17). However, he was not quite so successful with his expository work as with his fictional creations, although a late work entitled *He Dwelt among Us: A Study of the Life of Jesus* (1936) deserves notice for its own sake and because it continues a prevailing *motif* in religious writing even beyond its first dominant vogue. Also worthy of note, still in the same vein, is *The Man Who Dared to be God* (1929) by Robert Norwood (1874–1932). Like Paterson Smyth he was a popular Anglican preacher with the gift of reaching the popular mind. Dr. W. T. Grenfell (1865–1940) also joined the ranks of interpreters for the person of Christ. He gained fame by his medical work on the Labrador coasts and he made no secret of the source of inspiration for his life of devoted service. He was a deeply religious man who accepted himself as much as an evangelist as a doctor. The accounts of his work in literary form achieved a wide popularity. Amidst his many labours he found time to produce a series of books expounding his philosophy of life in such form as *The Adventure of Life* (1912). His contribution to the study of the life of Jesus was a personal confession *What Christ Means to Me* (1927). Much more theological than any of these other treatments of the person of Christ was one of the earlier works of John Baillie (1886–1963) while he was on the staff of Emmanuel College, Toronto. His stay in Canada was shorter than that of most of the young British scholars who have developed their academic legs on our soil only to march off to greener fields in the United States or the home land; Baillie became one of the most influential theologians of his time. He remained long enough in Canada to attract first notice of his work by *The Place of Jesus Christ in Modern Theology* (1929). Also while in Toronto he produced one of his earlier works, *The Interpretation of Religion* (1929), an extended study in the philosophy of religion.

Bishop Alexander MacDonald (1858–1941) created quite a stir in Roman Catholic circles and projected discussion that reverberated beyond Canada by his work on *The Sacrifice of the Mass* (1905). As the title suggests, it was concerned with the central act of worship in the Catholic Church. The author's thesis was that the Mass is a continuation in history of the event that happened at Calvary, rather than the more accepted view that it is a representation of the death of Christ. The same view was accepted by Delataille, a French theologian, in his well-known work *Mysterium Fidei*. Delataille had an interesting incidental connection with Canada in acting for a time as a chaplain to Canadian troops on the battlefield in France. Bishop MacDonald was a prolific writer who was nothing if not original in his ideas. His other work of some importance is *The Symbol of the Apostles* (1903) in which he contended for the somewhat unique view that the Apostles' Creed is literally what the name suggests, i.e., that it was actually the creed of the apostles rather than a formulation that derives from post-apostolic times. His other writings were published sermons, mostly doctrinal in character.

The formation of the United Church of Canada in 1925 produced a considerable volume of literary work both before and after the event. Some of it was polemical in character but, for the most part, the writing was expository with the contenders for union endeavouring to defend the theological basis of the new ecclesiastical alignment. Considering the foremost place the Canadian union has occupied in the widespread ecumenical movement of modern church life, these discussions have attracted widespread attention. The United Church of Canada has been cited as an outstanding example of how diverse doctrinal traditions can be reconciled.

The urge to union sprang from different sources. Already before the union, the churches involved (Presbyterian, Methodist, and Congregational) had brought together the diverse elements within their own denominations. This had been accomplished largely under the constraint of a sense that Canada had become a distinctive nation and that the divisions within communions were really a colonial heritage without any continuing relevance. Even more, the churches had on hand the practical engagement of meeting the spiritual needs of an expanding country. Competition within churches was a hindrance rather than a help particularly when the causes of separation belonged to a fast receding epoch in Canadian history. Also, Christian unity had begun to be a question under general discussion in many parts of the world and the shaping forces that have now converged in the contemporary ecumenical movement were emerging in the life of all the churches. There was a widespread conviction that the time had come for all Christian people to consider how far age-long separation should continue to keep them apart; in the words of a well-known collect, church people felt that they should "seriously lay to heart the great danger we are in by our unhappy divisions." Added to this, the early part of the twentieth century was a time of rapid new settlement, particularly in the Canadian west. Already the churches were co-operating in an endeavour to cope with the problems of ministering to the frontier communities and, even before 1925, these same communities had begun to take matters in their own hands by the establishment of "united" churches.

The best accounts of the union movement are to be found in *Church Union in Canada: Its History, Motives, Doctrine and Government* (1923) by E. L. Morrow and (also bearing the same title) *Church Union in Canada* (1933) by C. E. Silcox. The former work was written prior to the union and, although it purported to deal with the subject objectively, the author admitted that he betrayed his own prejudices which were very much on the union side. The work by Silcox was an abler study undertaken for the Institute of Social and Religous Research and it is rightly regarded as of fundamental importance both for the ability of the writer and for the adequacy of his work. It has become a classic work in modern ecclesiology. There was a considerable minority of the Presbyterian Church who finally refused to enter the union and insisted on continuing the old allegiance. Their strongest champion was Ephraim Scott (1845–1931) and he gave his account of the union under the title *"Church Union" and the Presbyterian Church of Canada* (1928). S. D. Chown (1853–1933), a leading figure in the Methodist Church, followed with *The Story of Church Union in Canada* (1930). Much later, George C. Pidgeon, first Moderator of the United Church, who had played a large part in its formation, wrote *The United Church of Canada* (1950).

Prior to the union there was considerable writing on the questions of church polity and doctrine. One of the earliest works was by Arthur Morton (1870–1945) who later became a distinguished historian of the Canadian West. He approached the matter from the historical point of view in *The Way to Union* (1912). A rather contrary presentation was given by Robert Campbell (1835–1921) in *The Relations of the Christian Churches* (1913). A, literally, novel contribution was made by Hugh Pedley (1852–1923) of Montreal in his book, *Looking Forward* (1913) which was an imaginative account of what was described as *The Strange Experience of the Rev. Fergus McCheyne*. The "experience" was a vision in which the clergyman had a "preview" of spiritual union realised.

The union itself was productive of a series of works mainly designed to expound the doctrinal position of the new church, notably *The Doctrinal Basis of Union and its Relation to the Historic Creeds* (1926) by Alfred Gandier (1861–1932), Principal of Emmanuel College in Toronto, and a collaboration by T. B. Kilpatrick (1858–1930) and K. H. Cousland, both of Toronto, entitled *Our Common Faith* (1928). Much later, John Dow (1885–1964), a fine scholar who came to Toronto from Edinburgh and who had attracted attention by his work entitled *Jesus and the Human Conflict* (1928), followed with a semi-official publication that attained a wide circulation *This is our Faith* (1943). Later still, R. C. Chalmers of Halifax, who has become one of our most vigorous theologians, expounded the doctrine of the United Church in *See the Christ Stand* (1945).

The ablest theologian among the continuing Presbyterians was W. W. Bryden (1883–1952), Principal of Knox College, Toronto. He stated his position in *Why I am a Presbyterian* (1934) but his more considerable contribution was *The Christian's Knowledge of God* (1940). An earlier work was entitled *The Spirit of Jesus in St. Paul* (1924). Bryden was the foremost exponent in Canada of what is generally described as the neo-orthodox point of view in theology. This was a movement that appeared particularly in Germany after the First World War and was associated with the names of Karl Barth and Emil Brunner through whom and other writers of the school it has had an immense influence on general theological thought. It is a radical criticism of the modern liberal position that had prevailed during the previous century. A still later work by Bryden was *Separated to the Gospel* (1956). John Macnab, editor of the *Presbyterian Witness* and a Moderator of the Church, was a strong contender for the Presbyterian cause in *Our Heritage and our Faith* (1956) and, the following year, he edited a volume *What Presbyterians Believe* (1957).

Discussion of church order and doctrine was not confined to the uniting churches. As early as 1897, W. R. Clark (1829–1912) published *The Anglican Reformation* in addition to other theological works. Canon W. B. Heeney (1873–1955) of Ottawa combined a strong loyalty to the Anglican Church with a spirit of fraternal regard for other communions. Along with others, he published *What Our Church Stands for* (1932) and, later, he edited a collection of essays by writers of different churches entitled *Essential Unity* (1953). Canon C. W. Vernon (1871–1934) published *The Old Church in the New Dominion* (1929) being the story of the Anglican Church in Canada. G. T. Daly discussed *Catholic Problems in Western Canada* (1921). W. J. Armitage (1860–1929) wrote *The Story of the Canadian Revision of the Prayer Book* (1922) and F. W. Vroom (1856–1944) published *An Introduction to the Prayer Book* (1930). J. R. P. Sclater (1876–1949) a distinguished minister from Scotland who became a Moderator of the United Church, produced two books contributing to the general interest in doctrine and order: *Modern Fundamentalism* (1927) and *The Public Worship of God* (1927). Alexander MacMillan (1864–1961) was a devoted student of hymnology and became our chief Canadian authority on the subject. He published *Hymns of the Church* (1935). H. L. Stewart (1882–1953), who occupied the chair of philosophy in Dalhousie University, matched his wide range of interest and learning with an urbanity of style in his writing. He adhered to the continuing Presbyterian Church but his studies in the history of religious thought had a much broader outlook than the local scene in Canada. Among other works of a philosophical and literary interest he published *A Century of Anglo-Catholicism* (1929) and *Modernism, Past and Present* (1932).

A movement known as "The Social Gospel" was a religious reflection of the widespread interest in social action during the early part of the twentieth century. In Canada it had an anticipatory expression as early as 1882 in *The Need of the World* by S. G. Phillips (1831–1892) who gave us what he described as "a contemporary study of applied Christianity." J. S. Woodsworth (1874–1942), who was destined to be a potent figure in Canadian political life as leader of the C.C.F. party in parliament, wrote *My Neighbour* (1911), largely on the basis of his experience as a minister working among immigrants in Winnipeg. Salem G. Bland (1859–1950) was an able exponent of the social gospel in *The New Christianity; or, The Religion of a New Age* (1920). A collection of essays edited and partly written by R. B. Y. Scott of Montreal and Gregory Vlastos of Kingston, Ontario, appeared in the midst of the great economic depression of the thirties bearing the title *Towards the Christian Revolution* (1936). This was a forceful expression of a widespread sentiment for economic and social reform that animated the church life of the period. E. H. Oliver (1882–1935), the Principal of St. Andrew's College in Saskatchewan, published a series of writings dealing with the place of the Church in the development of Canadian social life which are still regarded as important contributions to Canadian sociology, notably, *The Social Achievements of the Christian Church* (1930), *The Winning of the Frontier* (1930), *His Dominion of Canada* (1932) and *Tracts for Difficult Times* (1932).

In 1936, a group of prominent ministers published their concern for international peace in a volume entitled *The Church and War*. S. H. Prince, an

Anglican professor at King's College, Halifax, was a leader in expressing the need for the Church to accept a social application of its teachings. He produced an important study on *Society and the Housing Crisis* (1936). In the United Church, Ernest Thomas (1865–1940) had something like a roving commission across Canada to advocate the social and ethical implications of the Gospel. He expressed his views in *The Message of Jesus for the Life of To-day* (1932). J. Wesley Bready (1887–1953) made his contribution to the same cause in a series of historical studies designed to portray the moral impact of Christian personalities on social life—notably *Lord Shaftesbury* (1926), *Doctor Barnado* (1931) and his major work, *England before and after Wesley* (1939). A still later work was *This Freedom Whence?* (1943). Much later, *This Most Famous Stream* (1954) by the historian A. R. M. Lower, should be included as a rather distinctive contribution to the sociological and cultural effects of Christianity on national life. It should also be remarked that there has been a very definite religious influence at work in the Social Credit movement, particularly in Alberta under the leadership of William Aberhart and, later, of his successor E. Manning. They both took a rather literalistic view of the scriptures which they applied to social and political problems.

In 1924, the literary discussion of theology achieved a new self-consciousness in the appearance of the *Canadian Journal of Religious Thought*. This periodical was well edited and most of the leading Protestant writers on religion in Canada contributed articles which covered a wide range of interest. The *Journal* was also of sufficient merit to attract contributions from prominent theologians in Great Britain and the United States. Its pages afford an indication of the trends of religious interest during the second half of the 1920s. Broadly speaking, the prevailing outlook could be described as liberal. The present phase of biblical and dogmatic theology had not yet arrived on the Canadian scene. The title of the journal as one devoted to *Religion* rather than *Theology* is significant of the emphasis in its pages. The writers were largely concerned with the relation of religion to life. The discussion of religion was mainly philosophical and psychological. There were some fine articles on the spiritual interpretation of general literature. At the same time the *Journal* revealed a continuing work of exact biblical scholarship. The main publications in the contemporary literature of theology were well reviewed. The *Journal* attained a high standard of scholarly activity with an adequate literary expression and is indicative of a worthy interest in its subject during the relatively short period of the publication. It was an early casualty in the depressed economic conditions of the 1930s, and in 1932 had to abandon its work.

From the large number of articles in the *Canadian Journal of Religious Thought* it is hardly possible to single out any for special mention in this review. However, many of the writers also produced work of more permanent importance and a study of the *Journal* serves to bring them before us as well as others of the same period. Nobody was more active than Richard Roberts (1874–1945) who was an able preacher with a fine style and a ready pen. He was particularly concerned to translate the Christian message into the contemporary idiom of thought. A long list of books stands to his credit. Even before he came to Canada from England, he had published *The Renascence of Faith* (1912). This title was emblematic of his sense of literary and expository vocation. Later came *The High Road to Christ* (1914) followed by *The Untried Door* (1921), *The New Man and the Divine Society* (1926), *The Christian God* (1929), *The Spirit of God and the Faith of Today* (1930), *The Strange Man upon His Cross* (1934), and *The Contemporary Christ* (1938). John M. Shaw had also begun his long and distinguished career of theological writing before he came from Scotland to be a professor, first at Pine Hill, Halifax, and, later, after a brief stay in the United States, at Queen's University. His earliest work was *Christianity as Religion and Life* (1914). Thereafter he wrote *The Resurrection of Christ* (1920), *The Christian Gospel of the Fatherhood of God* (1924), *Essentials and Non-Essentials of the Christian Faith* (1928), and *Life after Death* (1941). Shaw has been an able and scholarly theologian who crowned his life work in a volume entitled simply *Christian Doctrine* (1953), which has been highly acclaimed as one of the best contemporary textbooks on the subject. In response to a widespread entreaty he gave us a more popular version of his larger work in *The Wonder of the Christian Gospel* (1959). John Line of Toronto had begun his theological work with *Inspiration and Modern Criticism* (1925) and *The Doctrine of Christ in History* (1926). N. Micklem, who came from England to spend some years at Queen's University, had already contributed a study of the historical Jesus in a highly popular book entitled *The Galilean* (1920). Later he wrote *Prophecy and Eschatology* (1926) and *God's Freeman* (1933). Subsequently he returned to Oxford where he has continued his career of writing. Sir Robert Falconer also contributed in this field, with his Ingersoll Lecture on *The Idea of Immortality and Western Civilization* (1930). R. M. Pounder made an interesting and highly original contribution to the philosophy of religion under the title *Artist, Thinker, and Saint* (1936), indicating three phases or stages of spiritual expression.

Biblical scholarship was represented by J. Hugh Michael of Emmanuel College, Toronto, with his commentary on *Philippians* (1928) in the Moffatt series of expositions. William Manson, who spent some years at Knox College, Toronto, before returning to Edinburgh to continue a distinguished career as a writer on the New Testament, also contributed to the same series of commentaries with his volume on *The Gospel of St. Luke* (1930). H. L. MacNeill of Brandon College, Manitoba, wrote on *The Christology of the Epistle to the Hebrews* (1928). W. C. Graham (1887–1955), first at Montreal, later at

Chicago, and finally at Winnipeg, wrote *The Meaning of the Cross* (1923) and *The Prophets and Israel's Culture* (1934). R. B. Y. Scott, perhaps the most active of Canadian Old Testament scholars, had begun his writing career with *The Original Language of the Apocalypse* (1928). While at Montreal he produced his book on *The Relevance of the Prophets* (1944) in which he displayed not only his scholarly knowledge but also his keen sense of the social application of religious teaching. Philip Carrington, who was later to become Anglican Archbishop of Quebec, contributed to biblical commentary by his works on *The Meaning of the Revelation* (1931) and *The Road to Jerusalem* (1933). Already he had given proof of his interest in the early period of church history by his book on *Christian Apologetics of the Second Century* (1921) which had gained the Hulsean Prize. Still later, he made a characteristically original contribution to New Testament study in two volumes entitled *The Primitive Christian Catechism* (1940). and *The Primitive Christian Calendar—related to Mark* (1952). In the latter work he endeavoured to trace an early connection between the observance of the Christian Year and the Gospel of Mark and maintained that this gave a clue to the composition of that gospel. Further still he exhibited his continuing interest in the same gospel by *A Running Commentary on the Gospel of Mark* (1960). Also worthy of note is *Icelandic Meditations on the Passion* (1930) by G. V. Picher, an able Old Testament scholar of Wycliffe College, Toronto.

In 1929, the Pontifical Institute of Mediaeval Studies was established at the University of Toronto. This was a project of the Basilian Fathers who have been closely associated with Canadian university life. The Institute was fortunate in attracting the eminent French philosopher Etienne Gilson to take part in its work. Among his writings are *Reason and Revelation in the Middle Ages* (1938), *God and Philosophy* (1941), *The Christian Philosophy of St. Thomas Aquinas* (1956), and *Elements of Christian Philosophy* (1960). G. B. Phelan was one of the first writers connected with the Institute with his *Study of Jacques Maritain* (1937), followed by *St. Thomas and Analogy* (1941) and *The Wisdom of St. Anselm* (1961). As might be expected, the work of the Institute has been mainly concerned with translating, editing, and expounding the teachings of the mediaeval scholastic philosophers. J. T. Muckle has published two translations: *Abelard* (1949) and *The Metaphysics of Algazel* (1951), J. R. O'Donnell has edited a collection of texts under the title *Nine Mediaeval Thinkers* (1955). Joseph Owens has produced a large work on *The Doctrine of Being in the Aristotelian Metaphysics* (1950). J. A. Raftis has made a valuable contribution to the study of monastic organization under the title of *The Estates of Ramsey Abbey*, J. J. Ryan has written a study of *St. Peter Damiani and his Canonical Sources* (1954), and T. P. McLaughlin has edited *Summa Parisiensis on the Decretum Gratiani* (1952). There is also a series translating some works of St. Thomas Aquinas by A. A. Maurer and G. B. Phelan. The work of the Institute has been a unique and distinguished contribution from Canada to the study of philosophical theology.

Two Anglican scholars have contributed to the study of the mediaeval period. E. G. Jay, who is Principal of the Montreal Diocesan College and also Dean of the Faculty of Divinity at McGill University, wrote on *The Existence of God* (1946) as a commentary on St. Thomas's five ways of demonstrating the existence of God. As a contribution to the study of the patristic period, the same writer translated *Origen's Treatise on Prayer* (1954) with a valuable commentary and a study of prayer in the early church. Eugene Fairweather of Trinity College, Toronto, contributed a volume to the "Library of Christian Classics" under the title *A Scholastic Miscellany —Anselm to Ockham* with translation and notes (1956). Also in the realm of translation, Waldo Smith of Queen's University rendered a translation of an important work in Italian by the Waldensian scholar Giovanni Miegge on *The Virgin Mary* (1955), this being a rather remarkable treatment of the subject of the place of the Virgin in Christian thought and devotion from the Protestant point of view.

The contemporary period of religious thought is generally recognized as a time of theological revival. There has been not only a quickening of interest, but something of a sea-change in the movement. Sometimes it is described as a Copernican revolution. The revival is directed largely by an attempt to relate theology to the crisis in contemporary civilization. The events of two world wars and the impending threat of a third have compelled a drastic review of human nature. These conflicts are deemed to be symptoms of a profound malaise in our modern world and constitute a radical critique of the spirit of humanistic optimism that pervaded the opening period of the twentieth century. The theologians contend for the need to recover older traditions of Christian teaching about the nature of human depravity and, above all, about the essential relation of man to God.

Theology had been deeply affected by the idealistic and humanistic thought of the earlier period. The scriptures and the historical origins of the Christian faith had been brought under such critical review that a re-statement of their authority became a necessity. Revelation was regarded as a human approach to God rather than a divine initiative towards us. The new movement in contemporary thought has been an attempt to reinstate the theological dimension of life not so much as an extension of human existence but as essentially prior. This, it is contended, is the forgotten or neglected factor in our contemporary culture and theologians are now engaged in a sustained endeavour to provide an interpretation on nothing less than a cosmic scale.

An appropriate estimate of the impact of this contemporary movement on Canadian writing is provided by a review of the articles in the *Canadian*

Journal of Theology. The appearance of this publication in 1955 is itself an indication of the revival of interest in theological thought. In this review, it would be difficult to select particular articles for special mention but their general character may provide an index to the prevailing interests which are even more fully revealed by the acceleration of publication in theological books. The contents of the new periodical provoke comparison with the former *Canadian Journal of Religious Thought* which came to its untimely end in 1932. The earlier publication had been concerned with religious thought on a broad liberal scale. The new periodical (as is indicated by the significant change of title) is avowedly theological in a much stricter sense. Biblical scholarship prevails but, while there is a new positive note, there is no return to any literalistic fundamentalism. The continuing debate on the problems of church unity within the ecumenical movement is fully reflected. The Church itself is regarded with a new emphasis on its essential character. There is a fresh interest in history and the force of tradition as factors within the meaning of Christianity. The prevailing philosophy is existential rather than idealistic. There is an expressed urgency about the whole work of the Church in the modern world and its relation to contemporary culture.

The period of the war retarded the stream of publication, but it had quickened by 1945 and soon after it became something in the nature of a flood. As has been indicated, the nature of the Church has provided a theme for varied writing. In 1946, W. A. Gifford (1877–1960) of Montreal published a one-volume history under the title *The Story of the Faith*. This is a work of outstanding distinction and it has now passed into ten editions. It was written by an able scholar in fine literary style and indicates the new approach to church history as more than the record of an institution. The subject is really the movement of the Christian faith in relation to the successive cultures in which it has developed. *Christianity and Classical Culture* (1940) by C. N. Cochrane (1889–1945) of Toronto has now attained universal acclaim as a work of major importance. The same year (1940), H. W. Vaughan, now of Toronto, was contributing editor to a collection of essays entitled *The Living Church*. Philip Carrington followed his earlier handbook *A Church History for Canadians* (1946) with two massive volumes, most handsomely produced, on *The Early Christian Church* (1957). George Johnston, who is now at McGill University after a period in Toronto, went back to origins with his work on *The Church in the New Testament* (1943). A later work by the same author was *The Secrets of The Kingdom* (1954). Before he returned to Oxford, G. B. Caird, also of McGill, published an authoritative work on *The Apostolic Age* (1958). His previous writings had been a handbook entitled *The Truth of the Gospel* (1950) and *Principalities and Powers* (1956), a study in Pauline thought.

Discussion of ecumenical problems is represented by Eugene Fairweather, in a volume in which he collaborated with R. F. Hettlinger entitled *Episcopacy and Reunion* (1952). Later, along with E. R. Hardy, he wrote on *The Ecumenical Council* (1961). J. W. Grant, now of Emmanuel College, made two contributions: *World Church: Achievement or Hope* (1956) and *The Ship under the Cross* (1958). I. Beaubien S.J. of Montreal wrote *Towards Christian Unity in Canada: A Catholic Approach* (1956). John Line of Toronto employed some of his time in semi-retirement to produce a relevant study on *The Doctrine of the Christian Ministry* (1959).

The practical work of the Church has also come under review. J. D. Smart, who has now gone to the United States, has written on *The Rebirth of Ministry* (1960) and J. Stanley Glen, Principal of Knox College, Toronto, on *The Recovery of the Teaching Ministry* (1961). Donald Macleod, a Canadian now at Princeton, has discussed worship in *Word and Sacrament* (1960) and Victor Fiddes has made a useful contribution in *The Architectural Requirements of Christian Worship* (1958).

The sociological and cultural relations of Christianity have been represented by a number of works of historical and contemporary interest. G. R. Cragg, until recently of Montreal, has attracted deserved notice by a series of scholarly works on the seventeenth and eighteenth centuries in English church history: *Puritanism in the Period of the Great Persecution, 1660–1688* (1957), *From Purantism to the Age of Reason* (1958), and *The Church and the Age of Reason, 1648–1789* (1960). E. M. Howse of Toronto has written *Saints in Politics: The Clapham Sect* (1952). The proliferation of sects and their relation to Canadian life is the subject of a major work by S. D. Clark entitled *Church and Sect in Canada* (1948). In the same field of interest, W. E. Mann has written *Sect, Cult and Church in Alberta* (1955). John S. Moir discusses a particular phase in *Church and State in Canada, 1841–1867* (1959) and in the same year an important work by C. B. Sissons of Toronto was entitled *Church and State in Canadian Education*. A most notable event was the appearance of the first complete church history of Canada covering the entire field by H. H. Walsh of McGill University with the title *The Christian Church in Canada* (1956). His earlier work had been *The Concordat of 1801: A Study of the Problem of Nationalism in the Relations of Church and State* (1933).

A feature of the theological revival has been a return to historical origins and an emphasis on the witness of particular confessions. The important work of the Institute of Mediaeval Studies in Toronto has already been noted in this regard. The voice of Protestantism has not been silent. R. C. Chalmers of Halifax has been one of the most vigorous writers. *The Protestant Spirit* appeared in 1955 in succession to his earlier works, *See the Christ Stand* (1945) and *The Pure Celestial Flame* (1948). The same author has collaborated with J. A. Irving of Toronto to edit two volumes of essays by various writers entitled *The Light and the Flame* (1956) and *Challenge and Response* (1959). W. Hordern wrote a *Layman's Guide to Protestant Theology* (1955). K. Hamilton, now of Winnipeg, gave us *The Protestant Way* (1956) and E. Cragg of Toronto, *Protestant Faith and Life* (1958). J. C. McLelland of McGill University wrote *The Reformation: Its Significance Today* (1961). His earlier work had dealt with the same period in a more particular study entitled *The Visible Words of God: An Exposition of the Sacramental Theology of Peter Martyr Vermigli* (1957), also a smaller book on *The Seventh Day* (1959) dealing with the practical implications of Christianity in social life.

Biblical scholarship continued to be represented by such works as *The Meaning of Christ for Paul* by E. Andrews of Queen's University (1949), *No Graven Images* by C. W. Leslie of Toronto (1954), *The Gospel Jesus Preached* (1957) by S. M. Gilmour also of Queen's, *The Life, The Question and the Answer* (1956) by A. J. Ebbutt of Mount Allison University and, by the same author, *The Bible and Christian Education* (1959). E. M. Howse wrote on *Our Prophetic Heritage* (1945), later on *Spiritual Values in Shakespeare* (1955). The tradition of theological writing by heads of Canadian universities has been maintained by G. P. Gilmour of McMaster in *A Handbook of the Gospels* (1956) and *The Memoirs called Gospels* (1959), also by A. E. Kerr of Dalhousie in *The Ten Words* (1960). S. B. Frost, Dean of Graduate Studies at McGill, wrote a study of the Book of Genesis in *The Beginning of the Promise* (1960); an earlier work by the same author was *Old Testament and Apocalypse* (1952). J. D. Smart produced *The Interpretation of the Bible* (1961). N. W. DeWitt of Victoria College, Toronto, wrote an interesting work on *St. Paul and Epicurus* (1954). F. W. Beare of Trinity College, Toronto, was in the forefront of exact expository scholarship in his two commentaries, *The First Epistle of Peter* (1946, 2nd ed., 1958) and his *Commentary on Philippians* (1959). A more popular work by A. L. Griffith of Ottawa was *The Roman Letter for Today* (1959). C. E. Silcox wrote a devotional commentary entitled *They Met at Philippi* (1958) on the epistle addressed to that city. On the more general theme of the bible, J. Jocz of Wycliffe, Toronto, published *The Spiritual History of Israel* (1961), J. S. Thomson, former Dean at McGill, published a short series of biblical studies under the title *The Word of God* (1959). D. Mathers of Queen's began a new series of textbooks in his volume on *The Word and the Way* (1962). The veteran scholar-preacher of Toronto, G. C. Pidgeon, deserves mention for his devotional volume *The Vicarious Life* (1946).

Canadian scholarship was well represented in an imposing project of biblical exposition and commentary which resulted in a series of volumes covering the entire range of the scriptures. This was known as *The Interpreter's Bible*, designed in relation to the new Revised Standard Version of the bible which appeared in 1952. W. R. Taylor wrote the volume on *The Psalms*. R. B. Y. Scott collaborated with G. G. D. Kilpatrick on *Isaiah*. G. B. Caird dealt with *I and II Samuel*. S. M. Gilmour wrote on *Luke*, G. R. Cragg on *Romans*, G. P. Macleod on *Colossians* and F. W. Beare added to his exposition of the New Testament by his work on *Ephesians*.

In the more general field of philosophical theology, E. Andrews of Queen's wrote on *Modern Humanism and Christian Theism* (1939). D. R. G. Owen, now Provost of Trinity College, Toronto, discussed an important contemporary topic in two works, *Scientism, Man and Religion* (1952), followed by *Body and Soul* (1956). J. S. Thomson combined the biblical with the theological approach to contemporary thought in *The Hope of the Gospel* (1955). A volume edited by A. G. Reynolds on *Life and Death* (1956) also attracted widespread attention.

In the earlier period, the general study of religion was most notably represented by S. A. B. Mercer, Dean of Trinity College, Toronto, in his two related works entitled *The Growth of Religious and Moral Ideas in Egypt* (1927) and *Etudes sur les origines de la religion d'Egypt* (1929). J. L. Stewart of Saskatoon wrote on *Chinese Culture and Christianity* (1925). R. H. L. Slater while at McGill University produced a study of Buddhism entitled *Paradox and Nirvana* (1951). His earlier works were *God of the Living* (1939) and *God and Human Suffering* (1941). W. A. Gifford of Montreal discussed the universal aspects of religious aspiration in *The Seekers* (1957).

The establishment of the Institute of Islamic Studies at McGill University in 1952 introduced a new element into Canadian religious thought. The first Director of the Institute, W. C. Smith, was a distinguished Canadian scholar who has become a leading authority on Islam. While still a missionary, he wrote *Modern Islam in India* (1946) and during his time at McGill he published *Islam in Modern History* (1957) now reprinted in a cheaper popular edition. As at the Institute of Mediaeval Studies at Toronto, much of the work at McGill has appeared in articles contributed to journals. Here it is possible to mention only some of the books that have been written by the members. Fazu-r-Rehman wrote on *Prophecy in Islam* (1958) and *Avicenna's De Anima* (1959). D. Rahbar published *God of Justice* (1960). In the same year Thomas Hodkin produced *Nigerian Perspectives: An Anthology*. N. Berkes translated *Turkish Nationalism and Western Civilization* (1959) while S. A. Kamali gave us an English translation of al-Ghazali's work on *The Incoherence of the Philosophers*. Other work of translation has been done by A. Howard Reid and the director W. C. Smith.

Canadian church history is too extensive and localized to permit reference except to the most important works of general interest. Mention has already been made of the single-volume history of the entire church in Canada by

H. H. Walsh. There have been numerous accounts of individual congregations and parishes which afford much information about church life. Here, it is possible only to cite some of the more significant denominational histories. Of the early period, there are two small but important publications: *Settlements and Churches in Nova Scotia, 1749-1776* (1930) by I. K. Mackinnon and *The Great Awakening in Nova Scotia* (1948) by M. W. Armstrong. W. S. Reid (1913-1963) gave an account of the attempt to establish the Presbyterian Church in *The Church of Scotland in Lower Canada* (1936). The Baptists and the Methodists have been especially interested in their history, particularly in the Maritime Provinces. The *History of the Baptists of the Maritime Provinces* (1902) by E. M. Saunders (1829-1916) and later *The Baptists of the Maritime Provinces, 1753-1946* (1946) by G. E. Levy are specially important. A more general account is furnished by E. R. Fitch (1878-1935) in *The Baptists of Canada* (1911). Accounts of the Methodist Church are more voluminous. Five great volumes on *Case and His Cotemporaries* by J. Carroll (1809-1884) appeared as early as 1867. Subsequent histories are a two-volume work by T. W. Smith (1836-1902), *History of the Methodist Church [in Canada]* (1890), *The First Century of Methodism in Canada* (1910, also two volumes) by J. E. Sanderson (1830-1913), and *Methodism in the Middle West* (1946) by J. H. Riddell (1863-1952). These are in addition to a considerable number of histories dealing with aspects of the Methodist expansion. The most important work on the Presbyterians is by the distinguished historian J. T. McNeill, who, prior to his departure for Chicago, held the chair of Church History at Knox College, Toronto. It is entitled *The Presbyterian Church in Canada, 1875-1925* (1925). An earlier work was *A Short History of the Presbyterian Church in the Dominion of Canada* (1892) by W. Gregg (1817-1909).

For the Anglicans there are many historical records of dioceses and provinces. The main works are *The Church of England in Canada, 1759-1793* (1893) by H. C. Stuart (1844-1909), *The Rise and Progress of the Church of England in the British North American Provinces* (1849) by T. B. Akins (1809-1891), *From Strachan to Owen: How the Church of England was Planted and Tended in British North America* (1938), by W. Perkins Bull (1870-1948), *History of the Church in Eastern Canada and Newfoundland* (1892), by J. Langley and *The Anglican Episcopate of Canada and Newfoundland* (1928) by O. R. Rowley (1868-1949). *The Anglican Episcopate of Canada* (1928, two volumes) by A. R. Kelly and D. B. Rogers is a useful reference work. Philip Carrington's *Church History for Canadians* (1946) (already mentioned under more general history) is also largely an Anglican record.

Accounts of the Roman Catholic Church are to be found in *The Jesuit Missions* (1910) by T. G. Marquis (1864-1936) and two publications by

A. G. Morice (1859-1938): *History of the Catholic Church in Western Canada* (1910, two vols.) and *The Catholic Church in the Canadian Northwest* (1936). There is also a discussion by G. T. Dely entitled *Catholic Problems in Western Canada* (1921). *The Catholic Church in Canada* appeared in 1956.

A record of the Lutherans is given by V. G. Eylands, entitled simply *The Lutherans in Canada* (1945). A. G. Dorland wrote *A History of the Society of Friends . . . in Canada* (1927). *A Brief History of the Mennonites in Ontario* (1935) by L. J. Burkholder extended to 358 pages. J. F. Galbraith wrote about *The Mennonites in Manitoba, 1875–1900* (1900). R. Butchart has published *The Disciples of Christ in Canada since 1830* (1949). The Pentecostalists gave an account of themselves in a composite volume entitled *What God Hath Wrought* (1958) by G. G. Kulbeik. There is an interesting account of the Doukhobors in *The Doukhobors at War* (1952) by J. P. Zubek and P. A. Solberg.

Canadian missionary interest has had a large and varied literary expression. The Canadian churches were themselves the fruit of missionary endeavour and they, in turn, have been much occupied with the formidable missionary task of advancing with the expanding frontiers of settlement, and also with ministering to the aboriginal peoples of the land. At the same time, missions to foreign lands have made a constant appeal to the Canadian spirit of adventure. Much of this interest has been reflected in a continuous stream of publication which is far too extensive to permit adequate mention in this survey. Only some of the more significant publications, and these more general in character, can be noted. As early as 1824, John West (1775?–1845) published in London *The Substance of a Journal during a Residence at the Red River Colony*. Still earlier, in 1816, Joshua Marsden (1777–1837) wrote a *Narrative of a Mission to Nova Scotia*. A small but important publication in the history of overseas missions was a sermon by John Geddie (1815–1872) of Prince Edward Island entitled *The Universal Difference of the Everlasting Gospel* (1846). He and his wife supported the plea of his discourse by going to the New Hebrides as missionaries. John Ryerson (1800–1878) gave an account of a missionary tour in *Hudson's Bay* territory (1855). John Coil wrote a history of Protestant missions under the title *The Missionary Problem* in 1883, and the following year George Patterson (1824–1897) was awarded a prize for an essay on *The Heathen World*. John Maclean (1851–1928) gave an interesting account of the remarkable work of James Evans, who with resourceful skill invented a syllabic system for the Cree language, and with even greater ingenuity made it legible by melting old tea chests into lead for type and making printing ink from soot and sturgeon oil. The book is entitled *James Evans, Inventor of the Syllabic System of the Cree Language* (1890). An account of a great *Canadian Missionary Congress* appeared in 1909. A. J. Brown wrote on *The Why and How of Foreign Missions* in 1913. W. S. Harrington published *Martyrs of New France* in 1909. S. Gould described the Church of England missions to the Indians and the Esquimaux in a book entitled *Inasmuch* (1917). In the same year W. T. Gunn (1867–1930) published *His Dominion*. Mrs. F. G. Stephenson wrote *One Hundred Years of Methodist Missions, 1824–1924* (1924) and later collaborated with Sara Vance in *That They May be One* (1929). R. W. Harris published *The Cross Bearers of the Saguenay* (1930).

Sir W. T. Grenfell wrote a series of books about his work in Labrador among which are *Forty Years for Labrador* (1933), *The Romance of Labrador* (1934), and *A Labrador Logbook* (1938). J. F. McFadyen of Queen's University, who had been a missionary in India, wrote on *The Missionary Idea in Life and Religion* (1928). An important study of missionary endeavour was written by L. M. Outerbridge (1900–1960) entitled *The Lost Churches of China* (1952). He had been a missionary in that land until the last expulsion of foreigners. J. S. Thomson expounded the modern view of missions in *The Divine Mission* (1958). J. W. Grant wrote about *God's People in India* (1959). E. C. Woodley gave an account of the work of the Bible Society in *The Bible in Canada* (1953). An earlier work by the same author was *Introducing the Bible* (1944).

Most of the Canadian churches have compiled hymnals and a number of native authors have contributed their work. Reference has already been made to A. MacMillan's book on hymnology entitled *Hymns of the Church* (1935). A Canadian *motif* has inspired some of the hymns. There is, of course, "O Canada, our Home and Native Land" which has assumed the character of a national anthem; it is Dr. Stanley Weir's free translation of a French song by Judge A. B. Routhier (1880) for music by Calixa Lavallée. Robert Murray wrote two Canadian hymns "From Ocean unto Ocean" (1880) and "Sow the Seed beside All Waters" (1897). On the same theme are "Lord of the Lands, beneath Thy Bending Skies" (1917) by A. D. Watson, "God of the Nations of the Earth" (1927) by Mary S. Edgar, "O'er the Trackless Ocean Guided" (1930) by W. H. Adams, and "God of the Prairies" (1938) by C. C. Richardson. A version of the 121st psalm "Unto the Hills Around" (1872) by the Marquis of Lorne while he was Governor-General of Canada has attained wide use and favour.

W. Bullock, who also compiled *Songs of the Church* (1854), was one of the earliest Canadian hymn-writers with a composition that has achieved a world-wide acceptance, "We Love the Place, O God" (1854). J. S. Cook wrote a beautiful Christmas carol "Gentle Mary Laid Her Child" for which the distinguished Canadian musician Sir Ernest MacMillan (son of the above-named A. MacMillan) arranged a musical setting. Archdeacon F. G. Scott, a well-known Canadian poet, wrote among a number of hymns "We Hail Thee

Now, O Jesu" (1886) and "Cast Thy Care on Jesus" (1894). Other Canadian hymns are "Lamb of God to Thee We Raise" (1908) and "King of Saints" (1908) by W. E. Eman, "Temple of God's Holy Spirit" (1908) by R. M. Millman. "God Who Touchest Earth with Beauty (1925) is a favourite hymn for the open air at camps and is often sung at vesper services. A. Whitehead wrote words and music for a Christmas carol, "Come in, dear Angels" (1938). "As Comes the Breath of Spring" (1929) by D. L. Ritchie is an appropriate hymn for that season of the year. Kathryn Munro was up to date with her hymn for travellers by air "O Thou within Whose Sure Control" (1928) which was an adaptation of the familiar hymn "Eternal Father Strong to Save."

30. Philosophical Literature
1910-1964

I. The Achievement of G. S. Brett

JOHN A. IRVING, ADAPTED BY A. H. JOHNSON*

THE PHILOSOPHICAL LITERATURE produced in Canada during the period from 1800 to 1910 was chiefly the work of two men: John Watson of Queen's and John Clark Murray of McGill. The twentieth century has been more richly endowed. George Sidney Brett (University of Toronto), Etienne Gilson (Pontifical Institute of Mediaeval Studies, Toronto), Rupert Carleton Lodge (University of Manitoba), and Herbert Leslie Stewart (Dalhousie) made very great contributions to Canadian philosophical literature. One of the most striking features of this period is the fact that two of these men, Brett and Gilson, inspired students and colleagues to participate in an impressive expansion in this field of literature.

There is considerable similarity between Brett and the great philosophers of the preceding century. He combined impressive literary ability with consummate skill as a teacher and extensive participation in the affairs of his university and the community in general. Murray of McGill was a "transition" man, embodying the best of nineteenth century philosophy but "pointing beyond." Brett achieved the transition and exerted a decisive influence in making and shaping Canadian philosophical literature in the twentieth century.

The fact that the following detailed examination of his life and work is not repeated in the cases of Gilson, Lodge, and Stewart is not to be interpreted as indicating lack of appreciation of their greatness. Rather it is a tribute to Brett's uniqueness.

George Sidney Brett was born in Briton Ferry, South Wales, in 1879. His parents were English, his father was a Methodist clergyman. While at Kingswood School, Brett felt the lures of science and of classics. He contemplated a career in medicine. These early interests remained with him all through his life. In 1898 he won an Open Exhibition in classics at Christ Church, Oxford.

*Because of Professor Irving's illness, Professor Johnson has prepared this essay based on material previously published in *University of Toronto Quarterly*, XIV (July 1945), 329–65, and *Psychological Review*, LV (January 1947), 52–58. See also note, p. 431.

Here he met two great scholars who exerted a profound influence on him: J. A. Stewart, author of *The Myths of Plato* and a two-volume commentary on Aristotle's *Ethics*, and J. H. Blunt whose interests were in the field of German philosophy. Blunt in particular encouraged the development of traits which were dominant characteristics of G. S. Brett, tolerance and exactness. In 1904 Brett went to Lahore in the Punjab as Professor of Philosophy in the government college. The four years which he spent in this environment were stimulating and informative ones. New vistas opened before him. He acquired a knowledge of Hindustani, Sanscrit, and Arabic. He grappled with the problem of the relations between Indian and Western culture. Yet even in the midst of a busy academic, social, and athletic life in India, Brett was at work laying the foundations of his literary reputation. In 1908, the year he left India and came to Trinity College, Toronto, his book *The Philosophy of Gassendi* had just been completed. He was working on a monumental treatment of some aspects of the history and philosophy of science, with full regard for related metaphysical and epistemological issues.

Brett's official appointment at Trinity College in Toronto was Lecturer in Classics and Librarian.* He was appointed Professor of Ethics and Ancient Philosophy the following year, and continued his connection with Trinity until 1921. Shortly after coming to Trinity he also began lecturing in the University of Toronto. He was made Acting Head of the Department of Philosophy in 1926, Head in 1927, and Professor of Ethics in University College in 1932.

Brett seemed to be above the conflicts of less profound thinkers, and his vision was distant enough to see that apparently contradictory philosophies usually became synthesized in the mould of time. He strenuously rejected subjective idealism, varieties of realism which interpose ideas or essences between the subject and the object (both were regarded as confessions of agnosticism), and pragmatic or activistic points of view. He did not think that philosophy should be overweighted with logical positivism or symbolic logic: the psychological, historical, and social contexts were more suitable and significant. It is fair to say that he was a realist—but a realist whom it is difficult to place within the conventional schools, either ancient or modern. A wide and vivid appreciation of all things in the world around him seems to have been the motive of his realism. Things in their pressing and significant reality are apprehended, and the concepts or categories of thought can be evident only within such a matrix. But the nature of this kind of experience, in relation to what have commonly been known as *sensa*, was not made clear in his

---

*The subsequent discussion of G. S. Brett's contributions to Canadian philosophical literature is a revision of John A. Irving's "The Achievement of George Sidney Brett," *University of Toronto Quarterly*, XIV (July 1945), pp. 329–65. For a complete bibliography of Brett's writings see pages 361–65 of this article. (A.H.J.)

teaching; nor did he seem to have a conclusive doctrine of precisely what we are dealing with when we talk about concepts, forms, subsistences.

Influenced unquestionably by long research on Gassendi and by careful studies of Leibniz and Lotze, Brett's metaphysical position was a form of dynamic pluralism. Significant and intelligible action is the key to explanation; action manifests itself at different levels, the inorganic, the organic, the rational, etc. There are two forms of pluralism, one metaphysical, the other methodological. Existent objects are individuals, and the individual is not to be interpreted (as by the Aristotelians) within the species. To admit the teleology which raises the species above the individual is to bring back the old essence under another guise and to substitute an abstraction for an existent entity. Methodological pluralism emphasizes categorical areas; each specific science has its categories, which in each case constitute an inter-definitive system. As objects become more and more complex, more and more systems of categories are involved in explanation and classification. Brett believed that no scheme has been devised as yet in which the different systems of categories, such as those of physics and psychology, are unified within more inclusive categories. Metaphysics is not, therefore, the ultimate general science holding within its framework the more restricted sciences.

The great Oxford idealists, Green, Bradley, and Bosanquet, exerted over Brett a perennial fascination. He realized that they had tried strenuously to reconcile presuppositions not peculiar to themselves with experience as a "given," and to do it on a grand scale. In their thinking, no matter how intellectual reality might be *as a system*, its other characteristics as a *realm of values* arose from the fact that the full nature of the given was their real concern.

While a student at Oxford, Brett had attended Thomas Case's lectures on Aristotle's psychology, in which topics such as sensation, memory, habit, and intellect were discussed from the point of view of the old "mental philosophy." But, owing no doubt to the scientific interest stimulated during the Kingswood days, he seems to have remained restless and dissatisfied with this arid approach. Then he read James's *Principles of Psychology*. It is perhaps not merely a coincidence that his last considerable contribution to scholarship was a chapter entitled, "The Psychology of William James in Relation to Philosophy," which appeared in a co-operative volume published in 1942 to commemorate the hundredth anniversary of James's birth. Under the spell of the greatest of American psychologists Brett began to realize, somewhat dimly at first but very clearly in 1908, that philosophical thought could be studied anew in terms of the expansion of the idea of mind and body. As James emphasized again and again the interaction of philosophy and science through the ages, it gradually became more and more obvious to Brett that the locus or middle ground of this intellectual interaction lay between the fields of logic and physiology, that is, in psychology. Henceforth he was interested in the problem of the emergence of psychology from an undifferentiated mass of literature on human nature and social behaviour. A re-reading of the great philosophers convinced him that many of their most valuable insights into human nature had been neglected owing to a theological or metaphysical emphasis. As these investigations progressed, he realized also the importance of studying more practical subjects like rhetoric, education, ethics, politics, and theology. The outcome of this vast research was his own monumental history of psychology.

Brett's three-volume *History of Psychology* (1912–1921) is his most outstanding and permanent contribution to scholarship. The term "psychology" is here used in a very broad sense. This study is, in effect, an exercise in the history and philosophy of science with extensive reference to epistemological and metaphysical problems.

This impressive treatise was the supreme intellectual adventure of his life, but at the same time it would be unsound to assume that Brett was not interested primarily in philosophy. In a new approach to the history of psychology, it would seem that he had found a field in which could be established, from the first and throughout his life, a fruitful synthesis of interests in philosophy, psychology, medicine, science, and, to a lesser extent, religion. In Brett's life work we have perhaps as complete a synthesis of these varied approaches as it is possible for a human being to attain in the twentieth century.

In the selection of material and the grouping of data, Brett regarded the nature of man as forming the centre of three great lines of interest: "the study of human activities as the psychologist sees them, the study of human life as the doctor looks at it, and the growth of systematic beliefs as reflected in philosophy and religion." An autobiography of the human mind would be given through a union of these in their historical development. It was admitted at the outset that such a history would be extremely complicated and almost inextricably entangled with the history of the natural sciences, not to mention all manner of metaphysical and theological speculations.

With these criteria and considerations before him, Brett undertook the fourfold task of giving for each historical period an account of the state of the sciences which influenced psychology, the state of psychology itself, the influence of psychology upon other sciences, and its general applications. It was clear from the beginning that the history of psychology must be interpreted as a part of the larger history of science. In magnificent prose he has set forth his conception of the permanent educational significance of the whole enterprise:

> A history of science is a unique species of history. For the content of the science the student may go to the last textbook, where he may learn the established truths without any reference to their genesis or to the men who established them. For those who require no more a history is superfluous: it can add nothing to that knowledge

and may be wholly disregarded. But there is another and a different object for which it has a specific function. If the student is not to be left with the idea that knowledge is a fixed quantity of indisputable facts, if on the contrary he is to acquire a real understanding of the process by which knowledge is continually made and remade, he must learn to look at the movement of ideas without prejudice as a separate fact with its own significance and its own meaning for humanity. To despise forgotten theories because they no longer hold good, and refuse on that account to look backward, is in the end to forget that man's highest ambition is to make progress possible, to make the truth of today into the error of yesterday—in short, to make history. (II, 6–7)

Within the scope of the present chapter it would be impossible to convey an adequate impression of the rich contents of Brett's *History*, but perhaps one may refer briefly to a few of its more salient features. The first volume opens with an account of the characteristics of primitive thought and a discussion of the relation between scientific views and religious beliefs. A consideration of the early Greek philosophers and medical schools is followed by a careful and lengthy analysis in seven chapters of the psychological theories of Plato and Aristotle. Brief descriptions of the Indian, Egyptian, Persian, and Hebrew standpoints precede a fascinating comparison of Hebrew and Hellenic schools of thought, after which the Pauline psychology, the Alexandrian school, Origen, the Pneumatists, the Neo-Platonists, Gregory of Nyasa, and Augustine receive detailed treatment. One is impressed throughout by the author's careful statement of his sources and authorities, his sound scientific sense of his responsibilities, his freedom from predilections, and his powerful synoptic faculty. The differences between ancient and modern belief and opinion are appreciated, but at the same time one is made profoundly conscious of the indebtedness of modern thought to the psychological and ethical speculations of the ancients. The treatment of Plotinus is especially illuminating; it is maintained that in his writings, "for the first time in its history, psychology becomes the science of the phenomena of consciousness, conceived as self-consciousness." Brett's compact style is an unusual combination of sanity, objectivity, distinction, and clearness. The calm beauty of its unhurried cadences may perhaps be illustrated best by references to his sympathetic evaluation of the psychological doctrine of Augustine's *Confessions*. "Here we have clearly a state of feeling, the awakening of thoughts that lie too deep for words, vivid realisation of limitless possibilities, and a condition charged with greater power than is found in the detached thinking of daily life" (II, 347–48).

The second volume of the *History* deals with the background of mediaeval thought, the development of psychology from the ninth to the end of the sixteenth century, and the rise of the modern temper in the seventeenth and eighteenth centuries. The chapters on the Arabian teachers and the ground work of mediaeval thought are especially illuminating. Brett maintains that Europe owes the Arabs a debt of gratitude not only for their preservation of ancient documents but also for their development of the idea of experience, or the reflective study of the inner life, in such a way that new ideas might later emerge. He also emphasizes the gradual restoration of Aristotelian doctrine, modified so as to conform to theology, in the work of men like Albertus Magnus and Thomas Aquinas. The sixteenth century is pictured primarily as an age of destruction, with the result that in the seventeenth there was a desire not necessarily to create new systems but to think systematically under the new conditions. In dealing with psychology in the eighteenth century the author evidently found that he could not strictly adhere to the chronological method, and a new order, partly national, partly topical, replaced the original plan. The last part of the volume contains chapters on British psychology, Continental empiricism, the beginnings of German psychology, and the influence and applications of psychology in the eighteenth century.

The third volume is concerned mainly with the nineteenth century, but it refers also to certain men whom we ordinarily think of as twentieth-century figures. Three chapters on the transition to the modern point of view in Britain, France, and Germany are followed by a consideration of modern psychology which occupies three-quarters of the volume. Early in his treatment of this period Brett raises the important question as to whether scientific psychology can dispense with metaphysics. A reading of the history of psychology leaves little doubt that the views held by psychologists about such problems as the nature and structure of the mind, or its relation to the brain, have been influenced, even in the nineteenth and twentieth centuries, by their philosophy. In discussing Lotze, Brett puts this question very forcefully: "It is an open question whether a psychologist can be an idealist or a realist. He should perhaps be simply a psychologist. But apart from collectors of detail and writers of monographs, history has failed to produce a psychologist who was not a philosopher of some kind; and it is notorious that a rejection of all metaphysics is the most metaphysical of all positions" (III, 147–48).

The most common charge against Brett, especially in the United States, is that he devotes too much space to a discussion of purely epistemological and metaphysical problems. This criticism reflects, of course, the highly self-conscious and almost desperate attempts that American psychologists have made in our time to emancipate their science from epistemology and metaphysics. So far it would seem that their efforts, and those of their allies the logical positivists, have failed; the desired "standpointlessness" has *not* been achieved. At the same time one must in all fairness admit that Brett's treatment of modern psychologists does tend to be unduly philosophical. His interest in medicine enabled him to appreciate the physiological approach to mind, and his Oxford training made him alive to the cultural and social backgrounds of psychology. But he seems to have had only a flickering interest in the laboratory and statistical techniques that have been developed during the last hundred years. In his treatment of nineteenth-century psychologists he is excessively partial to Lotze, Ward, and Stout; it would appear that his own philosophical problems and ideals were satisfied by the work of such men. It is true that the founders of laboratory psychology, men like Fechner, Wundt, Ebbinghaus, and various members of the "Würzburg" school are considered, but here again Brett is inclined to deal almost entirely with their attitudes towards essentially philosophical questions rather than to inform us regarding their experimental methods and their detailed results.

In the perspective provided by more recent studies what is the contemporary estimate of Brett's achievement? Perhaps no living psychologist is better qualified to give an appraisal than Gardner Murphy: "In an era in which experimental psychologists tended to repudiate the past, it was Brett first and Brett chiefly, who made available to English-speaking psychologists the historical context and meaning of their subject."

Because of his world pre-eminence as an historian of psychology Brett was honoured with invitations to contribute the article in this field to the fourteenth edition of the *Encyclopædia Britannica* and to participate in international symposia entitled *Feelings and Emotions* (1928) and *Psychologies of 1930*.

The Hegelian-Darwinian theory of "development" has led to an increasing emphasis on the importance of the historical approach to the problems of philosophy. As a result of this interest, European and American scholars have carried out a vast amount of research not only on the general history of philosophy but also on special periods and individual thinkers. Brett's earliest publication, the monograph on Pierre Gassendi, indicates that the historical approach to philosophy had profoundly influenced him. In writing this book he was not merely concerned to fill in a hiatus in the history of philosophy; he wished also to correct two common misconceptions, based largely on ignorance, which identified Gassendi's name merely with opposition to Descartes in both physics and philosophy and with the advocacy of a sort of patched-up Epicurean materialism.

Gassendi, who was actually the first modern philosopher to attempt a systematic reconstruction of atomism, wrote a *Syntagma Philosophicum* which is characterized by "prolixity of statement," "prodigality of learning," and "display of erudition," and which runs to six volumes folio, with a total of 4,095 double-columned pages. Holding the view that a proper appreciation of Gassendi's importance depends upon a knowledge of the *Syntagma* (which has never been translated from the Latin into English), Brett devoted a large part of the monograph to a summary of it. In accordance with this design, an introductory chapter on the historical development of the atomistic type of thought is followed by a lengthy but compact account of Gassendi's views on logic, physics, ethics, and the nature of God. Throughout this exposition, which displays an admirable union of enthusiastic interest and temperate judgment, Brett tries to confine himself, as far as possible, to an objective account of Gassendi's text and to leave an evaluation to a concluding general review. Nevertheless, long before the final interpretive chapters are reached, one feels that the author has made out his case, if not for the originality, at any rate for the importance, of the long-neglected seventeenth-century French philosopher. For Brett makes it clear that Gassendi's work must be considered an integral part of philosophy conceived as a moving body of ideas: "He has tried to unite the results, not only of philosophy in the narrower sense, but of all previous and contemporary thought, into one whole, as consistent as he thought it could be." Gassendi sought to establish a synthetic philosophy for the seventeenth century; his aims may be compared with those of Herbert Spencer in the nineteenth century: "The difference of their material is a significant comment on what has been done; and their similarity an equally significant comment on what has not been achieved."

One sometimes hears it said that Brett's concluding chapter, which is mainly concerned with a discussion of the epistemological and metaphysical theories of Leibniz and Lotze, is irrelevant in the sense that it hardly contributes to a further understanding of Gassendi himself. It must be admitted that this criticism is very largely justified. Further, neither Leibniz nor Lotze was influenced by Gassendi's views. Why, then, were their epistemological and metaphysical theories discussed at considerable length? The answer to this question involves another, "What had attracted Brett to Gassendi in the first place?" The clue to the answer to this latter question consists in the realization that, during the years he was working on Gassendi, Brett was struggling to develop for himself satisfactory positions in epistemology and metaphysics, and the seemingly irrelevant concluding chapter of the *Philosophy of Gassendi* is a piece of intellectual autobiography, thinly disguised, in which this inner conflict is recorded. One hears, as it were, the young Brett thinking aloud about the merits of monism and pluralism, idealism and realism, with Gassendi, Leibniz, and Lotze standing by to supply him with arguments in favour of pluralism and realism. Nowhere else in his published writings, as far as one can discover, has Brett given as much insight into his own positions in epistemology and metaphysics as in this concluding chapter.

During the years after the completion of his book on Gassendi, Brett contributed numerous articles and reviews to journals of philosophy, psychology, science, and religion. As a reviewer of philosophical and psychological works of wide range (from A. E. Taylor's *Varia Socratica* to J. R. Kantor's *Social Psychology*), he sought always to give the reader as adequate an idea as possible of the actual contents of the book, and any comments on its value were free from the unkind criticisms of the controversial schools. Some twenty of his articles fall within the field of the history of philosophy broadly interpreted to include certain aspects of the history of science and the history of literature. Five of them are concerned with the lives and times of Maimonides, Berkeley, James, Santayana, and Paul Elmer More. Here the dominant problem is the influence of personal and social factors in the determination of the structure of philosophical systems (but not at all in Lenin's sense). One derives from these studies a deeper knowledge of the "psychology of philosophers" without at the same time becoming sceptical regarding the referential aspects of conflicting systems.

No one could have argued more vigorously than Brett for the importance of science; at the same time no one could have protested more vigorously than he against the superstition that "Science is All." (See his article "The Limits of Science.") For he realized too well that science has not inevitably been the benefactor of society, rescuing it from political strife or religious mania; nor has science been entirely free from bigotry and narrow-mindedness. It would be good for scientists to know that they are not independent of social forces; the history of science would give them an essential insight into their failures as well as their successes: "The object of a history of science is not to produce scientific discoveries so much as to create the right attitude toward science, and to make people realise that the spirit of discovery is only a species of curiosity which is innate in most minds, and with proper encouragement can survive the monotony of routine." His technical contributions to this field (such as the papers on "Astronomical Symbolism" and "The Effect of the Discovery of the Barometer on Contemporary Thought") are rich illustrations of the power of the philosophic intelligence to illuminate that type of cultural environment which sustains and fosters the growth of the scientific outlook.

While in India, Brett edited, for the use of Indian students, a volume of representative English poems, in the introduction to which he exhibits a keen awareness of the inter-relations between philosophy and literature. Ten years afterwards this theme was developed more fully in a paper on "Parallel Paths in Philosophy and Literature," and later still essays on "Aristotle's Theory of Tragedy" and on "Shelley's Relation to Berkeley and Drummond" were contributed to memorial or co-operative volumes. He refused to separate rigidly philosophy and science; he was equally unaware of any gulf between philosophy and literature. In fact he believed that Greek and Roman literature and philosophy could be made a single comprehensive topic if properly treated (see his article "Parallel Paths in Philosophy and Literature"). Nor can one conceive of the existence of modern literature without postulating a system of social relations in which one finds some degree of science and philosophy as well as fiction or poetry—there is a common foundation for all.

Although Brett held professorships of ethics at both Trinity and University Colleges, he published nothing (apart from book reviews) which could be considered as technical contributions to this subject. One received the impression that he found it difficult, if not impossible, to think in terms of the traditional academic ethics, and that he considered courses which consisted mainly of refutations of the fallacies of hedonism to be a waste of time. From his point of view, ethics and social and political philosophy are inseparable; and this union is emphasized even in his paper on "The Problem of Freedom after Aristotle," which is otherwise mainly an historical survey. In his encyclopædia article on "Thomas Hill Green" he maintains that "the moral philosopher is most severely tested at the point where the individual and the common good come into consideration, for he has then to choose the way in which he will formulate their relation and maintain their agreement or their incompatibility." In the same year that these words were written, Brett published *The Government of Man*, which was described as an introduction to ethics and politics.

This book represented almost a new venture in both ethics and political science, for it was an attempt to interpret ethical and political theories in terms of their social and historical setting. Brett believed that it is possible to write on logic, ethics, or metaphysics without being truly philosophic, but it is not possible to be truly philosophic without coming to terms with the daily life of common people. Ethical and political speculations have been controlled by the intellectual climate of their time. Accordingly, in selecting the material for *The Government of Man* he emphasized the economic, political, social, and religious conditions which have characterized each period in the development of Western civilization from early times to the nineteenth century. The contents of this book cannot be described in detail here, but in an age in which people are so universally disorganized that terms like "schizophrenia" and "maladjustment" have become commonplace, it is perhaps well to direct attention to Brett's conception of the organized life:

> There are, of course, many different types of organisation: in some cases a high degree of concentration upon a single idea or purpose will produce an adjustment of every other part of the person's life to this one end; and this may occur very early in life. Still, in reference to the average man, it is true that life exhibits a process towards unity of system, and we may accept the formula that life begins in action and ends in conduct. Conduct, in this terminology, signifies action brought under a rule, and corresponds therefore to what we mean by moral as opposed to non-moral action. In this context moral means simply "regulated by a principle." (Page 1)

Although he begins with a definition of morality, Brett would have been the last to claim that this book was an original contribution to ethics as such. It was conceived, essentially, as a popular and historical introduction to great contemporary problems, among which might be mentioned the future of democracy, the relation of public to private morality, the meaning of religion for the state and for the individual, and the power and the weakness of reason or of feeling. But the student of social and political philosophy may still find that its illuminating generalizations will help him to appreciate more fully the different influences that have joined to create the moral and political outlook of every stage of civilization. The present generation, confronted as it is with ever wilder political prophets, could also learn much from Brett's unfailing sense of proportion and balance, which was reflected in a quiet, dry sense of humour directed against any form of extravagance in thought and expression. For, above all, he sought to inculcate care and soundness of judgment in the discussion of ethics and politics.

Any final estimate of Brett's contribution to philosophy, whether in his teaching or his publications, must necessarily emphasize the unique historical and synoptic method which he employed in the treatment of philosophical problems. But it would be a mistake to assume that, because the historical approach predominated, he did not possess a powerful capacity for philosophical analysis as well. For, when he wished, he could analyse points with all the logical subtlety of Moore or Wittgenstein. But he used the analytic method very rarely in his philosophical publications, and even then it was never freed entirely from the historical context.

II. Other Philosophers*

A. H. JOHNSON

SOME OF Brett's students remained at the University of Toronto to become his colleagues. Two main types of philosophical literature characterize this group. One continues the well-established Canadian tradition of concentration on "great men"; the other is concerned with specific problems.

Three volumes by Fulton H. Anderson belong in the first category. His *The Argument of Plato* (1934) is a vigorous and vivid introduction to the thought of the great Greek, with extensive use of apt quotations. Anderson's approach to Plato is revealed by the following typical comments: "Plato is primarily a dramatist and not an announcer of theories. . . . His dialogues show an extraordinary sympathy for every mood, struggle, and achievement of human nature. . . . They open up a thousand leads which . . . compel attention, but lead to no predetermined haven of conclusion." This book was followed by

---

*The rest of this survey of Canadian philosophical literature will deal only with books. Although the authors mentioned also wrote a number of articles, their books provide an adequate indication of the nature of their work. Only volumes published while their authors were resident in Canada will be noted.

two important studies of Francis Bacon. *The Philosophy of Francis Bacon* (1948) provides a thorough exposition of Bacon's method and theories in the context of comparative reference to earlier and contemporary thinkers. However, no attempt is made to evaluate Bacon's conclusions or the judgments he passes on other philosophers. In *Francis Bacon, His Career and Thought* (1962) Anderson argues (contrary to majority opinion) that Bacon was a thoroughly moral man (possessing both the major Greek virtues, also the theological ones) and a serious, original, systematic philosopher. His apparent political immorality is interpreted as devotion to firm royalist convictions. It is further suggested that Bacon's empirical orientation compares favourably with Renaissance flights of speculative fancy. In addition to these volumes Anderson edited a number of important classical texts: Plato's *Symposium* (1948); Plato's *Meno* (1949); Plato's *Phaedo* (1951); Bacon's *New Organon* (and Related Writings) (1960).

Thomas A. Goudge's *The Thought of C. S. Peirce* (1950) is another example of the Toronto "great man" approach to philosophy. This is a well-documented and comprehensive survey of the complex thought of one of the most influential of recent American philosophers. Goudge contends that Peirce can be best understood as a man whose philosophy issued in two different approaches to the world. The author devotes himself to a detailed exposition of the contrast which he finds between what is termed Peirce's naturalism and Peirce's transcendentalism. Goudge has also edited Bergson's *Introduction to Metaphysics* (1949).

Brett's students who became colleagues also produced books dealing with "specific problems." Among these is Goudge's informative discussion of contemporary evolutionary theory, *The Ascent of Life* (1961). This work, firmly based on the most recent investigations in the field of the biological sciences, considers with judicious care relevant linguistic, logical and metaphysical issues. In 1948 Marcus Long wrote *Introduction to Systematic Philosophy*. His *The Spirit of Philosophy* (1953) provides a useful and sprightly textbook introduction to a number of traditional philosophical problems. A collection of preliminary exploratory essays, entitled *Science and Values* (1952), by John A. Irving indicates his interest in psychology and other social sciences. He examines the status of value judgments in the social sciences and the bearing of social philosophy on practical problems. In 1959 Irving published his perceptive *The Social Credit Movement in Alberta*. He has also engaged in extensive editorial activities, providing introductions and component chapters for numerous volumes. He edited E. J. Urwick's *The Values of Life* (1948). He initiated and contributed a major essay to *Philosophy in Canada* (1952), whose other contributors were Charles W. Hendel (McGill), Allison H. Johnson (Western), Rupert C. Lodge (Manitoba). Similar projects are *Architects of Modern Thought* (originally presented as CBC talks) to which Irving contributed discussions of Russell and Spencer;

and *Mass Media in Canada* (1962). R. C. Chalmers shared editorial responsibility for *The Light and the Flame* (1956) and *Challenge and Response* (1959). Derwyn R. G. Owen's *Scientism, Man and Religion* (1952), based on his Religious Knowledge lectures to students at Trinity College, Toronto, concentrates on psychological, sociological, and political issues. He concludes: "The chief weakness of the 'scientific' tradition and the various forms of scientism is a failure to understand the depths and heights of human nature itself" (p. 173). This discussion was followed in 1956 by a volume entitled *Body and Soul. Metaphysics and Historicity* (1961) by Emil L. Fackenheim is an able but very complex treatment of a vast topic. His concern is with the nature and development of the human self and, in particular, with issues raised by contemporary existentialism. In this context he examines the implications of historicity and rejects them because historicity issues in a metaphysics which denies to man a permanent nature and timeless truths.

Another Brett man, A. H. Johnson, who since graduation from Toronto has been at the University of Western Ontario, published *Whitehead's Theory of Reality* (1952) and *Whitehead's Philosophy of Civilization* (1958). These volumes focus attention on the comprehensive scope of Whitehead's mature philosophy. They attempt to show that he is successful in dealing with all major phases of human experience in terms of a few basic concepts: individuality, creative processes, organic interraction, permanence, value. Johnson has also edited *The Wit and Wisdom of Whitehead* (1947), *Whitehead and the Modern World* (1950), *Whitehead's American Essays in Social Philosophy* (1959), and *Alfred North Whitehead: The Interpretation of Science* (1961). He edited *The Wit and Wisdom of Dewey* (1949).

During his career at the University of New Brunswick, David A. Stewart (also a student of Brett's) wrote *Know Yourself* (1946), a book which draws on recent works in psychology in developing a theory of value. In 1956 he published *Preface to Empathy*.

Among the staff members at the University of Toronto who were Brett's colleagues but not his students, a number of scholars are noteworthy for their literary attainments in the field of philosophy. George M. A. Grube's *Plato's Thought* (1935) discusses the main themes in Plato's philosophy. Well-balanced, perceptive chapters deal with the Ideas, Pleasure, Eros, the Soul, the Gods, Art, Education, Statescraft. In his *John Locke and English Literature of the 18th Century* (1936), Kenneth MacLean demonstrates an accurate understanding of the fundamentals of Locke's philosophy and a keen sense of his profound effect on contemporary and subsequent literature. These insights are effectively documented by quotations. Reid MacCallum's *Imitation and Design*, edited after his death in 1949 by William Blissett (1953), is a group of philosophical and literary essays. The main concern is with a defence of Art, Myth, Philosophy, and Religion against the threats of "scientism." Critical and aesthetic canons of argument are developed and used with skill and elegance. Norman W. De Witt, in *Epicurus and His Philosophy* (1954), provides a detailed account of his subject's life followed by a thorough investigation of his epistemology, physics, and ethics. This discussion is notable in that De Witt rejects the usual interpretations of Epicurus. It is here contended that he is not an empiricist, rather that he accepts the theory of innate ideas; he is not an egoist, rather an altruist. In *St. Paul and Epicurus* (1954), the "transformation" is continued by the suggestion that, far from being an enemy of religion, Epicurus recognized its value; further, his ethical theories were strongly influential in the Pauline epistles.

During the Brett era at Toronto, there was in the University a distinguished social philosopher who was a member of the Department of Political Economy, Edward J. Urwick. Motivated by a profound concern for the well-being of "the common man," and convinced of the primacy of the individual over the state, Urwick developed a vigorous critique of contemporary civilization (with its emphasis on science and material progress) in terms of the ultimate moral and spiritual values which he found in Platonism (and discussed at length in *The Message of Plato*, 1920). While at Toronto, Urwick wrote *The Social Good* (1927). In 1948, his *The Values of Life* (ed. J. A. Irving) was published posthumously.

In the post-Brett era at Toronto, William Dray has published *Laws and Explanation in History* (1960). This perceptive, broadly based study is a spirited refutation of the claim that the logical structure of explanation of historical events in every cause is subsumption under "covering law." Subsequently, he produced an introductory text, *Philosophy of History* (1964). After a lengthy introductory discussion of philosophy and ethics, Francis E. Sparshott's *An Enquiry into Goodness* (1958) offers a definition of good: "To say that X is good, is to say that it is such as to satisfy the wants of the person or persons concerned." It thus becomes evident that, under some conditions, questions about values are actually questions about facts. This volume was followed in 1963 by *The Structure of Aesthetics* in which the main problems and theories of aesthetics are subjected to a careful analysis and evaluated in terms of the criterion of "order." *The Problem of the Unity of the Sciences: Bacon to Kant* (1961) by Robert F. McRae outlines, with a minimum of critical analysis and comment, the views on this topic of Descartes, Leibniz, Diderot, D'Alembert, and Comte, as well as those of Bacon and Kant. Mrs. M. M. Kirkwood's *Santayana: Saint of the Imagination* (1961) makes clear that, for Santayana, imagination is the creator of a rich and complex symbolism and is engaged in the formulation of an ideal vision which makes animal life tolerable. Her view of Santayana is based primarily on his *Life of Reason* series rather than on the later *Realms of Being* volume. Also worthy of note is D. P. Gauthier's *Practical Reasoning* (1963).

Etienne Gilson (b. 1884), one of France's greatest contributions to the cultural life of Canada, came to Toronto in 1928. He was influential in the founding of the Institute of Mediaeval Studies at St. Michael's College in 1929, and was the Director of Studies from the beginning. This institution in 1939 became the Pontifical Institute of Mediaeval Studies. During his Toronto career, this international scholar produced a truly large number of impressive volumes. In *The Spirit of Mediaeval Philosophy* (1936), which he delivered as Gifford Lectures at the University of Aberdeen (1931–32), he proposes to demonstrate the existence of a Christian philosophy. The following statement is typical: "His [the Christian philosopher's] faith provides him with . . . a principle of discernment and selection allowing him to restore rational truth to itself by purging away the errors that encumber it" (pp. 31–2). This is not to deny that there are many philosophical questions which can be appropriately dealt with by reason without the aid of revelation. Gilson notes that there are several systems of Christian philosophy. In this book he concentrates on areas of agreement. There are effective discussions of the being and attributes of God (in particular, God's free creative action) and the relative and dependent being of the world. The nature of man and his status in the universe is also discussed at length. The book provides an admirable introduction to the thought of the great medieval philosophers. Typical of his more restricted and less technical studies is *Reason and Revelation in the Middle Ages* (1938), the Richards Lectures in the University of Virginia. Here he develops a lucid exposition of the main trends in the Middle Ages with reference to this problem. He outlines the differences among men of faith, for example, Tertullian and Augustine, and also the differences among those who, while relying primarily on reason, strike out on diverse paths, for instance, the Latin Averroists in contrast to John of Jandun. Last, and best in Gilson's opinion, is St. Thomas Aquinas who achieved a harmony of faith and reason. Gilson's greatness as a "trail blazer" and inspiration in the world of scholarship is manifest in his *History of Christian Philosophy in the Middle Ages* (1955). This is a masterly guide to the vast amount of philosophical material that the Middle Ages provides, much of which has not been properly edited and is still available only in manuscript form, known for the most part only in part or by indirect references. In addition to these representative works, Gilson published *Saint Thomas Aquinas* (1935), *Mediaeval Universalism and Its Present Value* (1937), *The Unity of Philosophical Experience* (1937), *The Philosophy of Saint Bonaventure* (1938), *God and Philosophy* (1941), *History of Philosophy and Philosophical Education* (1947), *Being and Some Philosophers* (1948), *Dante the Philosopher* (1948), *Wisdom and Love in St. Thomas Aquinas* (1951), *Jean Duns Scot* (1952), *The Christian Philosophy of St. Thomas Aquinas* (1956), *Painting and Reality* (1957), and *The Philosopher and Theology* (1962). Professor Gilson is also General Editor of

A History of Philosophy. He is co-author of the volume (in this series) *Modern Philosophy, Descartes to Kant* (1963).

Like Brett, Gilson attracted students and colleagues who engaged in the expansion of Canadian philosophical literature. The work of this group has taken two forms: exposition and criticism, and the translation and editing of texts.

Professor Gerald Phelan has the distinction of being, with Professor Gilson, one of the founders of the Mediaeval Institute. He is the author of *Feeling-experience and Its Modalities* (1925), *Jacques Maritain* (1937), and *St. Thomas and Analogy* (1941). In the last-mentioned volume, for example, Phelan demonstrates his characteristic incisive skill in clarifying distinctions. He contends that efficiency in metaphysics depends on the clear understanding of analogy. He then proceeds to consider three notions of analogy. Phelan concludes that the use of analogy found in geometrical thinking and the doctrine of Aristotle concerning analogy are not satisfactory. In his judgment, the Thomistic theory is an appropriate basis for metaphysics. The versatility of this scholar is further demonstrated in his brief study entitled *The Wisdom of St. Anselm* (1961). He has also translated Jacques Maritain's *The Degrees of Knowledge* (1959). It is typical of the activities of the Institute of Mediaeval Studies that, in this project, he had the assistance of Ralph MacDonald, Lawrence Lynch, Mrs. Lawrence Lynch, and Mrs. Alfred Byrne. Similarly, his translation of St. Thomas's *On the Governance of Rulers* (1935) has been revised and provided with introduction and notes by I. T. Eschmann.

Another prominent figure at the Institute is Anton C. Pegis. His *St. Thomas and the Problem of the Soul in the Thirteenth Century* (1934) is a thorough exposition of attempts by St. Bonaventure, St. Albert the Great, and St. Thomas to formulate a suitable theory of the nature and being of the soul, and its relation to the body, in the light of conflicting Platonic and Aristotelian doctrines which had an influence in the thirteenth century. This book is not concerned with the function of the soul; that is, it is metaphysics, not psychology. The problem of immortality is of fundamental importance. Like many of his colleagues, Pegis has engaged in extensive editorial activities. Typical of these is *The Wisdom of Catholicism* (1949), a massive volume nearly 1,000 pages in length, which makes readily available a wide selection of representative works. They range from St. Ignatius of Antioch (first century) to Gilson and Maritain. Among the over thirty authors represented are Augustine, Dante, Chaucer, Pascal and Newman. In addition to these representative volumes, one notes with admiration *St. Thomas and the Greeks* (1939), *Essays in Modern Scholasticism* (ed. 1944), *Basic Writings of St. Thomas Aquinas* (ed. and tr. 1945), *On the Origin of the Thomistic Notion of Man* (1963), and *St. Thomas and Philosophy* (1964).

Joseph Owens is another distinguished member of the Institute. *The Doctrine of Being in the Aristotelian Metaphysics* (1951) merits particular attention. This interpretation of Aristotle's doctrine concentrates on his *Metaphysics* rather than extending consideration to his writings in biology and logic. Within these limits, it manifests an impressive grasp of investigations of Aristotle by scholars publishing in all the major languages. Owens argues in favour of an arrangement of the books of the *Metaphysics* which differs from that of Jaeger. Care is taken to show the limitations of Aristotle's analysis of being in comparison with that of St. Thomas. Owens considers that both are concerned with metaphysics as the quest for a divine supersensible being. In addition to this volume, Owens is the author of *St. Thomas and The Future of Metaphysics* (1957), *A History of Ancient Western Philosophy* (1959), and *An Elementary Christian Metaphysics* (1963).

In his discussion of *Christian Philosophy* (1963) (a series of talks given on the CBC), Lawrence E. Lynch, associate of the Institute and head of the Department of Philosophy in St. Michael's College, concentrates on one type of Christian philosophy, that is St. Thomas's. It is interpreted as an attempt to understand God and the world (including man) in terms of a new metaphysics "derived from natural principles found in things but inspired by God's having revealed himself to be 'The Being Who Is' " (p. 23). However, any philosophy, including that of St. Thomas, is a search for the most profound understanding that human powers can produce (see p. 96). Lynch is also the editor of the English translations of Josef Pieper's *Justice* (1955) and Gilson's *Christian Philosophy of Saint Augustine* (1960).

Joseph T. Muckle's *Algazel's Metaphysics* (1933) is worthy of note, as is E. J. McCorkell's *Cardinal Newman and the Christian Philosophic Tradition* (1933).

The high quality of the scholarship of Armand A. Maurer is indicated by his volume *Medieval Philosophy* (1962), a precise introductory survey covering the period from St. Augustine to Francis Suarez. (It specifically does not propose to function on the advanced level of Gilson's *History of Christian Philosophy in the Middle Ages*.) In dealing with any philosopher, Maurer makes extensive comparative references to St. Thomas Aquinas. There are informative sections on logic, physics and "speculative grammar." Excellent bibliographies are included. He has also translated and edited *St. Thomas Aquinas On Being and Essence* (1949) and *On the Division and Methods of the Sciences* (from *De Trinitate* by Boethius) (1953).

This survey of the achievements of the Pontifical Institute of Mediaeval Studies would be incomplete without reference to the following scholars and books: Norah Eveline Michener, *Maritain on the Nature of Man in a Christian Democracy* (1955); Charles J. O'Neil, *An Etienne Gilson Tribute* (1959); J. R. O'Donnell (ed.) *Nine Mediaeval Thinkers* (1955); Eugene R.

Fairweather (ed. and tr.) *A Scholastic Miscellany: Anselm to Ockham* (1956); and Vernon J. Bourke, *Will in Western Thought* (1964).

Mention should also be made of other philosophers, associated with Toronto, whose work has achieved distinction: Bernard J. H. Lonergan, *Insight, A Study of Human Understanding* (1957); and Leslie M. Dewart, *Christianity and World Revolution* (1963).

We now leave the Toronto scene and turn eastward to the province which, as we have seen earlier, owes so much to Thomas McCulloch. It is significant that two of Brett's most outstanding "students who became colleagues," F. H. Anderson and T. A. Goudge, began their study of philosophy at Dalhousie in classes conducted by Professor H. L. Stewart (1882–1953).*

Stewart was educated at Lincoln College, Oxford, and at the Royal University of Ireland. The influence of Bernard Bosanquet at Oxford was a decisive factor in his philosophical development. Before coming to Dalhousie in 1913, he lectured at the university in Belfast for four years. During his career at Dalhousie he excelled in demonstrating the value of the Oxford tutorial method. He required a particularly thorough knowledge of Greek philosophy and of the British empiricists. However, his frequent references to T. H. Green and his use of A. E. Taylor's *Elements of Metaphysics* as a text provided unmistakable evidence of his convictions concerning the superiority of Idealism. As editor of the *Dalhousie Review*, H. L. Stewart rendered service to Canadian Literature. As author of numerous articles and as commentator on the national radio system he was recognized as an influential educator of the Canadian public.

Stewart's main philosophical concern is with the value experience of human beings. While engaging in a careful analysis of value judgments and the standards on which they are based, he is not a narrow or primarily technical "specialist." His outstanding volume, *Anatole France, the Parisian* (1927), is an example of his deep and comprehensive approach to the "theory in practice" of human values. This study of the man and the nation is a perceptive identification of the conflicting ideologies which have brought much misery to French life. Stewart is convinced that the clue to the understanding of men and nations lies in the literature of their culture. This insight and Stewart's general approach to philosophy are clearly illustrated by the titles of his other books: *Questions of the Day in Philosophy and Psychology* (1912); *Nietzsche and the Ideals of Modern Germany* (1915); *A Century of Anglo-Catholicism* (1929); *Modernism Past and Present* (1932); *From a Library Window* (1940); and *Winged Words* (1953).

*The subsequent discussion of Stewart is a revision of part of A. H. Johnson's contribution to *Philosophy in Canada*, pp. 40–41.

From his chair at the University of Manitoba, Professor Rupert Carleton Lodge made outstanding contributions to Canadian philosophical literature. He had two main concerns: the first was Plato, the second was the achieving of a balanced approach to the three basic conflicting "isms" which confronted philosophy in the first part of this century: Idealism, Realism, Pragmatism. Claiming to take his cue from Plato, Lodge appeared to find congenial a type of balance which would have been approved by Bosanquet. A typical statement of Lodge's view of Plato is found in *Plato's Theory of Art* (1953). He states that Plato "compares what his predecessors and his contemporaries profess to believe, and tries to attain to a judicious balance; without any one-sided dogmatism of acceptance or rejection, but with a whole-hearted faith in the gradual evolution of philosophic truth" (p. 7).

Similarly, in his own discussion of Plato's theory of art, Lodge not only states thoroughly Plato's specific points in the total context of his philosophy, but also makes extensive comparative references to the work of other philosophers. Further insight into Lodge's approach to Plato is afforded by his last major work, *The Philosophy of Plato* (1956). In general, Lodge attempts not merely to inform his readers, but primarily to encourage them to achieve a sympathetic identification so that they will think *with* Plato. His cultural background is sketched, his views on ethics, aesthetics, religion, and education are delineated with clarity and vigour. In this presentation, Plato also appears as a devotee of the natural and the social sciences. Reflecting the interest of the time when the book was written, Lodge deals with the charges that Plato had a real kinship with communism and naziism. In addition to these volumes, Lodge produced additional characteristic volumes: *Simple Modes in the Philosophy of John Locke* (1918), *Introduction to Modern Logic* (1920), *Plato's Theory of Ethics* (1928), *Philosophy of Education* (1937, 1947), *The Questioning Mind* (1937, 1947), *Philosophy of Business* (1945), *Plato's Theory of Education* (1947), *The Great Thinkers* (1949), *Applied Philosophy* (1950).

John Macdonald, for many years Professor of Philosophy at the University of Alberta, wrote several books in the area of social philosophy: *The Community* (1938), *The Corner Stone of Democracy* (1939), *The Expanding Community* (1944), and *Mind, School and Civilization* (1952). These volumes reflect Macdonald's conviction that philosophy should be linked with the social sciences and be deeply concerned with social action. More specifically, educational processes must be designed which facilitate more accurate investigations of facts and a clearer and more rational formulation of value ideals and the development of techniques for their application.

It is essential to realize that, in the great universities of "French-speaking Canada" (and in the bilingual University of Ottawa), important contributions are made to the "English language" literature of philosophy. Consider, for example, Charles de Koninck's *The Hollow Universe* (1960), a critique from a (broadly speaking) Aristotelian point of view of the contemporary worship of natural science and, in many quarters, devotion to analytic philosophy. The former focuses attention on the merely quantitative, the latter indulges in verbal manipulations withdrawn from a serious consideration of many traditional philosophical problems. In de Koninck's judgment, these types of abstractions fail to do justice to the concrete complexity of nature, man, and God. The author does not content himself with destructive criticism. He offers an (Aristotelian) alternative. In his Aquinas Lectures, given at Marquette University, *St. Thomas and Epistemology* (1946), Louis-Marie Régis outlines an imaginary philosophical encounter between Descartes, Kant, St. Thomas, and Neo-Thomists. The point at issue is the ability of Thomistic metaphysics to withstand the criticisms of Descartes and Kant. Régis rejects, in varying degrees, all views except that which he attributes to St. Thomas. Régis is also author of *Epistemology* (1948), and *Etienne Gilson's Contributions to the Field of Epistemology* (1948). In addition, this group includes A. Eugene Babin's *The Theory of Opposition in Aristotle* (1940); Joseph Henri Grenier's *Thomistic Philosophy* (1948); and Robert J. Kreyche's *The Critical Realism of Roy Wood Sellars* (1952).

J. C. Murray had laid solid foundations at McGill during the later nineteenth century. In 1913, William Caldwell published *Pragmatism and Idealism*. During his tenure as MacDonald Professor of Moral Philosophy, Charles W. Hendel produced *Jean-Jacques Rousseau, Moralist* (1934), a monumental two-volume work that makes extensive use of important material which is available only in mansucript form. While dealing with Rousseau as a moralist, Hendel provides a broad background sketch of his subject's mental development, thus making available a context in which his published writings may be more fully appreciated. He also edited the letters of Rousseau in 1937 (*Jean-Jacques Rousseau: Citizen of Geneva*). Again at McGill, one observes with admiration the extensive editorial labours of Raymond Klibansky. Since coming to Canada in 1948, he has continued work on the series entitled "Medieval and Renaissance Studies" (with R. W. Hunt). He has also edited Benedetto Croce's *Essays on the Moral and Political Problems of Our Time* (1949), and *New Letters of David Hume* (1954), with D. C. Mossner. In the field of Platonic studies his editorial work, making use of translations by A. E. Taylor, includes *Plato's Philebus and Epinonis*, with G. Calogero (1956) and *Plato, Sophist and Statesman*, with E. Anscombe (1961). Klibansky is also general editor of the "Nelson Philosophical Texts" and the four-volume survey, *Philosophy in the Mid-Century* (1958-9). Editions of "selected" works of Hume were produced at McGill by D. C. Yalden-Thomson (*Theory of Knowledge*, 1951) and Frederick Watkins (*Theory of Politics*, 1951). In 1963

Donald Evans published *The Logic of Self-Involvement*, a discussion of religious concepts which reflects the influence of J. L. Austin. While living in retirement in Montreal, W. D. Woodhead translated and edited *Socratic Dialogues* (1953). In 1959, F. Rahman edited Avicenna's *De Anima* (Arabic text).

The great days of Kantian scholarship at Queen's have been revived by the presence of Alastair R. C. Duncan, author of *Practical Reason and Morality* (1957), in which he defends a new interpretation of the *Foundations of the Metaphysics of Morals*. Contrary to the usually accepted view that Kant's book is an ethical treatise, Duncan, on the basis of thorough examination of the text, argues that it is, as its title indicates, a critique of practical reason.

For many years (1895–1932) James Ten Brooke was an ardent exponent of idealism on the campus of McMaster University. His main interests are reflected in the title of a book published in 1932, *The Moral Life and Religion*. This university now is represented by George P. Grant whose volume *Philosophy and the Mass Age* appeared in 1959, after being read initially as radio talks (CBC). It is a series of "lay sermons" on twentieth-century society, including reference to historical backgrounds, and pointing out the defects of this society, one of which is its capitalistic domination of individual men. The basic defect is lack of absolute moral standards. The solution is a return to respect for natural law.

During his three-year sojourn at the University of Western Ontario, Albert L. Hilliard published *The Forms of Value* (1950), which proposes to accept (not defend) a hedonistic theory of value as an hypothesis, examining its explanatory and unifying powers. He envisages as a practical consequence the placing of aesthetics and ethics under the jurisdiction of empirical science. The University of Waterloo's Leslie Armour is the author of *The Rational and the Real* (1962), an essay in metaphysics outlining the "conditions which must be met by reality" in order to account for experience and our ability to talk sense about it. The problem of the self is discussed at length. His colleague, Zigmund Adamczewski, published in 1963 *The Tragic Protest*, an examination of a number of tragic heroes ranging from Aeschylus' Prometheus to Sartre's Orestes. In each case, attention is focused on a tragic choice which illuminates the man's character and vision of the world.

Free Will and Determinism (1960) by Allan M. Munn, a physicist at Carleton University, deals with the question: does the principle of indeterminancy (uncertainty) in physics have any bearing on the problem of freedom of the human will? There is considerable discussion of physics, ancient and modern. Much recent relevant ethical discussion does not come into focus. Munn's main conclusion seems to be that, while earlier physics ruled out free will, contemporary physics re-opens the question.

Frederick T. Kingston of the University of Windsor's Canterbury College wrote *French Existentialism: A Christian Critique* (1961) in an attempt to portray a conversation between Gilson, Marcel, and Sartre. A number of "supporters" also appear. For the most part, the Thomistic view has the last word. Before his departure from the University of British Columbia, Avrum Stroll published *The Emotive Theory of Ethics* (1954). This small volume restricts itself to the logical aspects of the topic and concentrates on the views of A. J. Ayer and Charles Stevenson. Stroll also wrote two elementary texts, *Philosophy Made Simple* (1956) and *Introduction to Philosophy* (1961).

In the interest of inclusiveness, but at the risk of the accusation of drawing from another field, it is well to note additional books in an area which may be termed political philosophy: William Lyon Mackenzie King's *Industry and Humanity* (1918); Robert W. MacIver's *The Modern State* (1926); and Harold Adams Innis's *Empire and Communications* (1950), *The Bias of Communication* (1951), and *Changing Concepts of Time* (1952). In these last works the late Dean Innis was pursuing interests very different from those of his earlier studies. His concern with communication over time and space and in a number of media has proved to be a great stimulus to later inquirers.

In the mid sixties of the twentieth century, scholars are greatly encouraged by increased support for their research and publication, from their universities, the Canada Council and other bodies. There is promise of an impressive new era in Canadian philosophical literature.

31. Travel Books on Canada
1920-1960

ELIZABETH WATERSTON

"TRAVELS are day-dreams translated into action." In the years after the Great War, the world's dream of Canada was summarized: "a lone figure on the sky-line . . . golden miles of grain fields . . . the Mountie in his scarlet regalia . . . the quaint habitant by his log cabin." Item by item, the dream symbolized individualism, fertility, law, tradition—ideals achingly desired in the faceless, formless, lawless world between wars. Travel books of these times are tense with the recognition that Canadian actuality differed from the dream.

The series starts in gay vein, deepens into disillusionment, bafflement, cynicism.

A post-war restlessness may account for the great popularity of travel books in the 1920's. Certainly the Canadians themselves were ready to move around the country and to record their moves. About one-third of the travel books of this decade were by Canadians. A larger group, however, came from English visitors, including a number of women. The number of Americans, Scots, and Irishmen reporting on Canada decreased noticeably—a trend that continued in the thirties.

The twenties began with "the jolliest Royal Tour on record." W. D. Newton in *Westward with the Prince of Wales* (1920) trailed the popular young prince through a ragtime trip, in high good spirits, noting (for instance) the banners at Cobalt that shouted to H.R.H. "Glad U Come! The town is yours. Paint it Red or any old Colour you like!" Other "tours" produced quieter reports: A. F. Barker, Professor of Textile Industries at the University of Leeds, described *A Summer Tour through the Textile Districts of Canada and the United States* (1920); A. H. Godwin and F. B. Low edited *Teachers' Trails in Canada* (1925), "an illustrated review of the tour of the British Educationists' party"; *A Joyous Adventure* (1928) recounted the experiences of the choirs of Westminster Abbey.

All visitors in the twenties—especially the choir boys—reacted vigorously to the "luscious colour in the store windows," the sky signs, the white clean lunch-rooms, of post-war Canada. Most marvelled at a world of material "comforts": telephones, gramophones, motor-cars, "splendid" picture palaces.

Hostility to Englishmen had lessened in war years. Being an Englishman was now a comic disadvantage, not an insurmountable barrier to friendship. Shared "war yarns" made casual conversation easy. Canadians seemed honest, efficient ("fine staff work" was remembered of the Canadian Expeditionary Force under Sir Arthur Currie). Men had no legendary quality—the "wild and woolly West" was laughingly remembered, while Mounties "rode" for the visitors in their "famed" show. If one were lucky he might see "a cowboy (the real thing)" from the train window.

Once-controversial ethnic groups now roused little interest. Indians seemed comic; we are told of "an old squaw waddling under a wide-brimmed hat . . . built somewhat on the plan of a sea-lion." French Canadians were dismissed with laughing tales about their evasion of conscription. The new Canadians out West, generally lumped together as "Galicians," with their ungrudging, undespairing work, appeared to show "just those qualities which are desirable" on the prairies. For "older Canadians," "clubland" flourished, and most travellers became conscious of the Canadian Club and its many rivals.

Toronto and Edmonton shared the centre of interest. The new terminus in Toronto replaced the domes and fortresses of older views. But even the new cities caught less attention than the hinterland, the immense, sleepy, murmuring prairie, the "lonely land," the backwoods, the new North (not quite yet a major focus in travel accounts). Nature exhilarated; spring brought "champagne-like air," and winter seemed "one of the jolliest seasons."

The culture of the country was modest (one visitor noted that portraits of King George and Queen Mary had been "executed" by local artists out West). But the young people seemed hopeful and energetic. "There is a stretching out in this country." In this "real democracy," university students worked as waiters, farmhands, or street excavators. It was a world different from "Home"; but rigid standards had eased, and differences were usually met with interest or even admiration, rather than with the pre-war arrogant amusement.

The post-war book may be a delayed report on an earlier visit, or an account of a tour "planned in 1912, delayed till 1922." It may be an attempt to jump a band-wagon of "travel-books," to add a new item to a successful series. J. T. Faris adds *Seeing Canada* (1924) to his *Seeing the Middle West, Seeing the Sunny South*, etc. Vernon Quinn adds *Beautiful Canada* (1925) to his *Beautiful America, Beautiful Mexico*, etc. J. E. Ray adds *Things Seen in Canada* (1927) to *Things Seen in Constantinople*. M. I. Newbigin's *Canada, the Great River, the Lands and the Men* (1927) and H. A. Kennedy's *The Book of the West* (1925) are also the work of old hands at the travel-book business. Percy Gomery's lively *A Motor Scamper 'Cross Canada* (1922) marks the substitution of a new mode of travel for the old railroading ways, and is one of a series of "car-centred" books. Most of these works follow a sedate path from east to west, with the still-inevitable lunge off the track to Niagara Falls. The point of view in many is that of the bright, open-minded woman of the post-war decade, adventurous, rather inclined to rosy vision, but bringing neither the gentility of the ladies of the nineties nor the militant energy of the pre-war suffragettes. Yvonne Fitzroy in *A Canadian Panorama* (1929) and Katherine Hale (1878–1956) in *Canadian Cities of Romance* (1928) represent English and Canadian versions of the viewpoint of the new woman. Victoria Hayward's *Romantic Canada* (1922) heralded by its publisher as "the first important book in this category" is indeed the most readable.

Different in tone, as in ordering and intention, are the reports of wanderers in hungry search of work. The titles are suggestive: *Adventures and Misadventures* (1922) by "Lofty"; *Ups and Downs in Canada* (1922) by V. H. Ricci; *Life is a Jest* (1924) by C. W. Thompson (F.R.C.S.). "I challenged Fate and got my whack in reply" is "Lofty's" condensed version of these travel tales. Here is the first sounding of themes dominant in the thirties and forties. One answer to this despair appears in *Across the Prairie* (1922), Miss Hasell's account of the rewarding life on the Sunday School caravans. L. M. Guest's *Canada as a Career* (1927) also represents Western life in a bracing vein, as does J. Peat Young's *A Newcomer in Canada* (1924). All these meander from one topic to another in the random pattern of their restlessness.

Less uneven is the work of the professional journalists who came to report on "Canadian facts." The Imperial Press Conference brought numbers of newsmen to Canada in 1920 and their reports dutifully appeared. P. Donald's is the official account; J. C. Glendinning (representative of the Irish Newspaper Society) in *Oh! Canada* (1921), and E. W. Watt (a Scottish newsman) in *A Canadian Tour* (1921) present livelier personal versions. Later Eldred Walker, West of England journalist, in *Canadian Trails Revisited* (1926) commented on changes in farming and social life since 1914. Canada still "baint Zummerset," as another West-Country journalist agreed—F. J. Cox in *A Holiday in Canada* (1924).

An odd and interesting associated report comes from T. E. Naylor, a delegate to the Imperial Press Conference representing the mechanical side of newspaper production. *A Compositor in Canada* (1921) probes into union meetings, into labour halls loaded with unhappy memories of the Winnipeg riots of 1919, into workers' homes, into a socialist open-air rally, which approved the Labour Irish policy and condemned British intervention in Russia. It is a sociological reminder that several "Canadas" were emerging, and that a traveller would be hard put to see them all.

Besides the clear representatives of the travel-book genre, books of the period include many related publications: memoirs, publicists' brochures, hand-books, guide-books, historical accounts, some including descriptive and travel passages such as enliven D. H. McCormick's *Lloydminster, or 5000 Miles with the Barr Colonists* (1929).

Finally, analysis, description, and travel story blend in two unusual books: Sarah MacNaughton's *My Canadian Memories* (1920), disorganized perhaps because of its posthumous publication but particularly interesting on Canadian people, groups and individuals; and Peggy Webling's *Peggy* (1924), a back-stage version of the life of a touring group, with sharp-biting accounts of the hotels, the concert halls, the louts, the pianos, the foods, and the enthusiasm that greeted this energetic actress.

Peggy and "Lofty" produce the youngest, jauntiest, and therefore the most representative travel books of the decade. Their perspective is always cheerful, even if their prospect is not. But no really interesting example of a handling of the travel book as genre emerges from the twenties.

If the twenties brought a high point in *camaraderie* between travellers and their Canadian hosts, the thirties witnessed a reverse into disdain, resentment, or hostility.

The number of travel books increased, to a level just below the never-equalled eighties, but the tone is radically different from the confidence of those earlier times. Now depression days brought emigrants to the disillusionment of a "Land of Bull and Bale-Wire"—*anglice*, of boasting and "making do." Travellers met compatriots who were bitter, homesick, "bushed." Hire-purchases kept up appearances, for Canada was slow to admit she was hard up. But the soldier-settlement scheme now appeared "a disastrous failure."

A new land had its tyrannies, its hardships for body and spirit. Droughts, wire screens, storm windows, over-heating, snow-boots, chewing-gum, radio talk about laxatives, soft drinks, "Ritz-Carlton red hots," all-day suckers: the minutiae irritated visitors as much as Canadian egotism, chauvinism, philistinism ("Young Canadians think that literature and art constitute the realm of women and of teachers"—"merchant venturers are their heroes"). Work was a fetish, and in dull rural areas the second generation walked with the "tread of an Indian, tread of a bear." A yearning to be together trapped all. A craze for education, mostly "on the practical side," made hardship for families (though most university students still paid their own way). Oddities in the educational scene—the school train, the fraternity house, the Junior Red Cross concert, the oral language teaching—caught the traveller's attention. So of course did bootlegging.

There was promise of growth in art. One heard of Tom Thomson, of "old masters" in Montreal, of the Little Theatre movement, of theatre at Hart

House, in Winnipeg, in Vancouver. "The whole country's tired of American films."

Indeed the "American Invasion" of "souse-hunting" Yankees, the closed American border of 1924 which had dumped labour into Canada, the shift of American tourists from Canada to Europe, all brought sour comment from Canadians. Englishmen were regarded with no greater affection. British capital was popular because of the collapse of the dollar, but a public school voice or an Oxford accent still posed a problem. Canadians assumed the Englishman incompetent. "He may be able to preach a sermon or write a book or give a lecture, but is not expected to be able to stoke a furnace, cook a chop, wield an axe, or hammer a nail straight into a piece of wood."

Visitors returned the scorn: Canadian society seemed selfish in its security, filled with "the sound of many dollars."

The French Canadian now came back into the spotlight. Much discussed in the thirties were his character, his traditions, his religion, his gaiety or graciousness, the barrier he raised against Americanization. Indians also regained their pathos. "How little interest the average Canadian takes in the only really romantic people in their midst!" The facts of immigration forced also a focus on the new Canadians, no longer quietly assimilating, but "tough-looking," ever present in the West—"Bohunks," Poles, 'Slovaks, Ukrainians, Germans, Finns, Hutterites, Mormons, "Douks," and "Dagoes" in Toronto road work —not pleasant in themselves and all increasing the danger of secession to the United States. Out on the coast was talk of "J.C.," the new province— "Japanese Columbia."

It is people who fill the pages of the travel books of the thirties, easing out both descriptions of cities and rhapsodies over nature. "High and clear the call of the North": but except for that call, Canada's voice is the voice of the Bohunk and the hobo; the housewife "slamming the door" on a salesman; the minister urging all to sing together "action songs of the nursery" or "Alouette"; the demagogues—Houde and Aberhart, Tim Buck. (Hepburn and Bennett and Mackenzie King, Miss Hasell and Cora Hind get passing mention too.)

In that distressed epoch, the most interesting travel accounts are written by tension-ridden travellers, themselves under stress. The complacent, value-assured observer found nothing in Canada to stir him or satisfy him. But someone like Kathryn Trevelyan, the nervous and arrogant daughter of the British Minister of Education, flinging aside her débutante dilettante life in London to hitch-hike across Canada, found here new pressures and new values, even though most of the trip rubbed sensibilities raw. Her *Unharboured Heaths* (1930), like the best books of the twenties, is more rewarding to the psychologist or sociologist than to the literary critic. More polished in presentation, but still provocative in content is *England's French Dominion*

(1932) written by a young politician, William Teeling, in an interval between "nursing his constituency."

We find, of course, a few trailing survivors of the old-style travel book, the east-to-west, day-by-day account of a holiday trip or a business tour. Only one is memorable, and that mostly for its title: *Hell! I'm British* (1938) by affable A. C. Elliott. There is the old familiar baggage of special interests, as in *Canadian Journey* (1939) by H. P. Thompson, editorial secretary of the Society for the Propagation of the Gospel; *Going Places* (1939) by Colin Hood, a Glasgow businessman; *Lodging for a Night* (1939) by gourmet Duncan Hines.

One group of regional studies adds to the old emphasis on the West: M. Harrison's *Go West—Go Wise!* (1930), Stephen Leacock's *My Discovery of the West* (1937), Frederick Niven's *Canada West* (1930), A. Kriztjansson's *In the West* (1935). Another, larger, group focuses on the new North: E. A. Powell's *Marches of the North* (1931); and the strong series of Greenland sketches by Vihjalmur Stefansson (1879–1962). Memoirs consolidate the image of the old wilderness places. Most interesting, and including most of traditional travel material—trip out, etc., is Roger Vardon's *English Bloods* (1930).

A much more important group in the thirties return to the "bitter land" theme. Bleaker aspects of travel, hobo style, saddening views of farm land and city, appear in G. H. Westbury's *Misadventure of a Working Hobo in Canada* (1930), J. H. Hooker's *The Heart of an Immigrant; or, "Just Life" in Canada* (1931), E. F. G. Fripp's *The Outcasts of Canada: Why Settlements Fail* (1932), J. H. Walker's *A Scotsman in Canada* (1935), Harold Baldwin's *A Farm for Two Pounds* (1935), James Kinniburgh's *Sidelights on Canada* (1936), W. G. Carr's *High and Dry* (1938). Tales of hard times, of depression, of strikes, of harvesting abuses, of the narrow life in rural areas, laziness, intolerance, snobbery—these sourly realistic books are of great importance for their reversal of the old image of peace and plenty, happiness, freedom and prosperity. In form Fripp is most interesting, for he copes with the bulk of his experiences by dividing the book in two, the first half a unified narrative of the struggles of a soldier-settler and his "plucky" English wife to "make land" in the West; the second half is a series of tales of his own troubles in Canadian cities, trying to "make a go" of selling vacuum cleaners, brushes—anything the depression-weary Canadian housewife might be charmed into buying by the once-despised "English accent."

For pleasant fare, but always with a wry recognition of depression realities, we might turn to *The First Winter* (1935) by H. Herklots, canon of St. John's Cathedral in Winnipeg, and professor at St. John's College there. This little book, "published to save fellow Englishmen from having to write letters home," ranks among the most attractive of all visitors' accounts. Other amiable descriptions appear in books for children, publicists' work (like that of Murray Gibbon) and hand-book writers. Canadian writers skim regional life for local colour. The "search for identity" has hardly affected this kind of writing as yet; deeper probing must wait till the forties.

Meantime, the thirties brought the inevitable "Royal Tour" books. Boorman's *Merry America* (1939), and C. K. Carnegie's *And the People Cheered* (1940) are standard reports. There is another of those car-centred efforts; this one is M. L. O'Hara's *Coast to Coast in a Puddle-Jumper* (1930). (Sample this to see how awful a travel book can be!) Probably the last of the "lady travellers" was Lady Kitty Vincent (Ritson) whose *Two on a Trip* (1930) gaily chit-chats about discomfort and fun in the backwoods. A less pretentious lady, also the last of a long line, is Miss Hilda S. Primrose. *North American Summer* (1939) is one of those gentle genteel holiday accounts devoted to a tour of the United States plus a brief swing over the border (53 pages out of 355). Her one claim to fame among her peers is that she "left Niagara unvisited."

In the 1940's, "missing Niagara" symbolizes the fashion. The old high spots are by-passed now, in favour of by-ways. Ile d'Orléans, not Quebec City; Prescott, not Toronto; Saanich, not Victoria—the substitutions are Bruce Hutchison's, but they are typical.

For the first time, Americans equal British travellers in number of books published. More significant still, both are outnumbered (also for the first time) by Canadian reporters. The total number of travel books is down, largely because of the war, but partly also because the complexity of the country now awed most "holiday-trippers."

This is a heavier time. Instead of glimpses of farm life we hear abstractly of "forces of agrarian unrest." The geographers see the land in terms of vast "wedges," "bolts," "channels." Probably the air age produced this new perspective, just as it produced for most travellers a new route and a new time sense and a modified reaction to those two old horrors, the winter and the vastness. Mode of travel has always provided the dynamic in travel books, the base line of their composition. A new mode brings fresh vigour in organization.

The Canadian character emerged in a better light as always in wartime: arrogance justified by effort, "making-do" justified by world necessity. Canada's resentment of world ignorance of her strength was acceptable now to most tourists, impressed by her war effort. The big gray shapes of warships haunting the coastline made national limits seem clearer to both English and American visitors. A British lecturer, after a wartime lecture tour in the States, revived in Vancouver before "a 100 percent friendly audience." Stations of the Commonwealth Air Training Scheme, toured by most "official" visitors, stirred with the paradox of Canada's integration with the far-away war effort. American visitors might acknowledge their ignorance, their anticipation of seeing "the Canadian shore lined with Mounted Police, little Dionnes, or French Habitants," but they were ready for romantic, half-rueful admiration of the war-time seriousness of their northern neighbours.

French Canadians were again a focus of conversation for both American and British visitors. Now in uneasy urgency one heard of their "exploitation by the Axis," their political corruptions, their religious separatism. Louisa M. Peat, in *Canada: New World Power* (1945) marks the changing focus on Canada, with her emphasis on racial animosities, the "Zombies," the air force, and her anecdotes of wartime life, "the Drama of the Doukhobor," old and new Canadians, and so on. This book is an interesting distance-marker of the times, over-wrought in style, chaotic in order, but sounding the themes of the amazing period. Most visitors were anxious—over-anxious—to "understand" Canada, rather than to describe her; but Canada was becoming too mobile, too closed and secret in her complexities, too confusing for clear impact. The number of visitors bold enough to attempt a coast-to-coast report dwindled.

Larry Nixon in *See Canada Next* (1940), follow-up to *See America First!* presents a vision of a luxurious vacation land, "where you get $21 change from a $20 bill." Mary Bosanquet in *Saddlebags for Suitcases* (1942), reprinted in England as *Canada Ride* (1944), recounts an "economy holiday" across the country with two spunky little horses. William R. Watson adds *And All Your Beauty* (1948) to the heap of method-of-travel books, this one featuring a trailer.

Most of the travel books of the forties are selective, the specialist's affair. *Canada: A Study of Cool Continental Environments* (1947) by Griffith Taylor (1880–1963) illustrates the limit of specialized description. J. H. Stembridge, geographer of the Oxford University Press, humanizes the "geographic angle" in a humorous account of a brief wartime tour, *A Portrait of Canada* (1943). Basil Newman's *American Journey* (1943) tucks five chapters on Canada into a sound report on wartime moods, from a broadcaster's point of view. Regional studies continue, particularly of the barren lands, and there are books for children: Lilian H. Strack's *Crossing Canada* (1940) (with John and Judy) and Frances Carpenter's *Canada and her Northern Neighbors* (1946) (with "our friend the pilot" and "Miss Bobby, the airline hostess"). Lady Tweedsmuir's *Canada* (1941) is a sadly thin entry in the list of vice-regal accounts.

Two American women contribute animated studies: Frances Arleen Ross, *The Land and People of Canada* (1947) and Dorothy Duncan, *Here's to Canada!* (1941). The latter is a moving account of the author's "conversion to Canada." When this gifted writer faced the formal problems of the travel book, however, she was obviously baffled. Her chapters, strung along the old east-to-west line, are anecdotal, deftly handled. But they are interlarded with guidebook statistics, set in italics, and they end with summaries of "What to Buy," "Approaches by Road," etc. Uncertainty regarding the functions of the travel book—aesthetic or practical—reaches its sad climax here.

The uncertainty is firmly solved by Bruce Hutchison. In *The Unknown Country* (1942) he evolves a new form. On a surface order of east-to-west he builds a surface pattern of essays of regional analysis handled through anecdotes of travel and of talk by the way. He adds poetic inter-chapters, blending memory, drifts of phrase and of legend, with his present perspective as Westerner, married man, journalist—all the personal attitudes which furnish a point of reference. Thus a cross-cut in time is achieved, and a unity built of refrain and the recurrence of the personal perspective. It is a technical *tour de force*. Precious? Perhaps. Certainly there is no concealed art here.

The elaborated technique seems finally to corrupt the vision: clichés appear, effectively worded and dextrously placed, but still clichés—ideas about French Canadians, for instance, which can be maintained if one looks closely at the Ile d'Orléans and one's own memories, not if one looks objectively at Montreal. All is coloured by Hutchison's impassioned "Canadianism" (according to his own definition).

After Hutchison's careful subtleties, would any traveller dare revert to the old thinness of "We embarked . . . French Canada is . . . Niagara next . . . and then the prairies . . . and so, homeward bound?" Would any outside observers, skimming the surface, dare report their findings, after all this probing in by-ways of time and place? Yes, indeed they would, and did in the fifties, in the same old ways.

The 1950's produced many regional studies such as Clifford Wilson's *North of 55 Degrees* (1954) and Pierre Berton's *The Mysterious North* (1956). Some are theses rather than descriptions: LeBourdais' *Canada's Century* (1951), Leslie Roberts' *Canada, the Golden Hinge* (1952), E. Westropp's *Canada, Land of Opportunities* (1959). There were also glossy pictorial works with a tiny text; B. K. Sandwell's *Cities of Canada*, in paintings (1951), and Jean Bruchési's *Canada*, in photographs (1952), Wilfred Eggleston's *Image of Canada*, essays and photographs (1953). There are slick books angled at tourists, like M. Chapin's *Contemporary Canada* (1959) and brochures like S. S. Ericsson's *Are Canadians Really?* (published by a committee of the U.S. Chamber of Commerce, 1954). The children's books continue and there is a trickle of old-style "holiday tour" accounts, including Australian Frank Clune's *Hands across the Pacific* (1951), Ray Dorien (author of *Venturing to New Zealand, Venturing to Australia*), *Venturing* (what else?) *to Canada* (1955) and Nicholas Monsarrat's *Canada, Coast to Coast* (1955), disappointingly thin. The decade ends with Gordon and Elspeth Winter's *Ourselves in Canada* (1960), regional (mostly in Toronto, Montreal and Ottawa), limited to treatment of daily life in the suburbs, "the Canadian way of life as lived by ordinary people." The modest hey-day of the travel book on Canada is over. Never a year without its "Summer Tour" but never a year with the bumper crops of those good old years, 1885, 1911, 1930.

In many of the books of the fifties, Newfoundland receives heavy emphasis, because of its recent entry into Confederation, and because of a continuing emphasis on raw resources and on the places that produce them. Ungava, Noranda, Rouyn, Chicoutimi, Kapuskasing, Churchill, Norman Wells, Port Nelson, Kitimat, Prince Rupert: this is the new roll-call of names mingling with the old list of city centres. (One nice variation on an old theme—"Victoria plays Lady Nelson to Vancouver's Lady Hamilton.") The old sights still pulled: the Rockies, Quebec City; and Niagara wielded its old sledgehammer effect on prose. "Gosh, I had to turn away, couldn't bear it so suddenly. Stupendous!" (Then a cryptic postscript—"Oh well . . .")

The sense of distances and of rawness was restored by the new routes of air travel, and the new emphasis on the North revived the old themes of cold and snow and frozen emptiness.

In society the women seemed "formidable beyond measure"; the homes, kitchens, gardens, shops, and clothes burdened the country with post-war efficiency and utilitarianism. But here European culture could regenerate itself in a country opening still, among Canadians, more cautious than the Americans, but intelligent and without illusions.

At the end of the period 1920–1960, two books appeared, in fantastic opposition. One is Bruce Hutchison's vision, *Canada, Tomorrow's Giant* (1957). It repeats the pattern of inter-chapters set in italics, repeats the east-west progression, repeats the emphasis on side-roads and casual chat, repeats the optimism and the stress on personal perspective.

Beside this, place Norman Levine's *Canada Made Me* (1958). Canada, says this bitter revenant, is "a dream, an experiment that could not come off." Remembering his share of the dream and the experiment as a child in Ottawa, a youth at McGill, a young man out West, he returns to the present reality. In Halifax, after a fantastic trip out, he meets a burlesque reception: rudeness in customs, official boredom and petty corruption, and a hearty reception only from a Kellogg's representative, passing out boxes of Corn Flakes "from the Canadian wheat field . . . and cheap too." "I am a Zero," he concludes, and perhaps his native land, "recognized" (as his epigraph from Camus suggests) "at the moment of losing it," is a Zero too. Certainly the Canada he travels is vulgar and careless, a shoddy world of dingy restaurants filled with blank-eyed girls and leather-jacketed youths. Blobs of chewing-gum stuck underneath the table signal the return to Canadian life.

In Levine's treatment of Ottawa and Montreal, his receptivity plays against the remembered resentments to create a curious tension. His technical power in anecdote usually controls the obsessed quality, but the total effect of the book is that of a nightmare, where brilliant particles of realistic reporting whirl into a grotesque reprise. *Canada Made Me* is a memorable book. Like the best of the travel books on Canada, it reflects the shock, stimulus, elation, and despair roused in a sensitive observer by this nation.

In the best travel accounts, Canada is preconceived as having unity, is perceived in sharp and fresh detail, and is presented through the personal fusion of dextrous composition and style in a tone uncorrupted by the temptations of the travel genre.

32. Essays and Autobiography

I. Essays 1920−1960
BRANDON CONRON*

THE JOURNALISTIC SLANT of the Canadian essay became more pronounced after 1920. Essays were still being published in scholarly periodicals such as the *Queen's Quarterly* and the *Dalhousie Review*, but it was the critical spirit of the new journals such as *Canadian Forum* and *Canadian Mercury* that did most in directing the genre towards the "preaching, expostulation and tub-thumping" that Lorne Pierce deplored in 1932. What appeared to be exhortation was really a restless questioning of the Canadian way of life, for few writers had a platform, and the editors of the *Forum* itself failed to agree on a political and social philosophy.

Most eloquent among the new voices in the *Forum* was Douglas Bush, whose scholarly training in English literature produced a genial irreverence for the introspective and moral seriousness of both Canadian literature and the Canadian character. W. D. Woodhead (1885–1957) had much in common with Bush, but made more use of humour. The essay on Prohibition ("If Winter Comes"), in which Woodhead joked about "the unnatural dryness of the moral atmosphere," belongs with Bush's "Plea for Original Sin" and Pratt's *Witches' Brew*. Other contributors to the *Forum* were too opinionated to be skilful essayists. John MacNaughton (1858–1943) was often belligerent in defence of the humanities. A. J. M. Smith's plea for Canadian criticism was taken up by Frederick Philip Grove (1871–1948) and expanded into a survey of the needs of Canadian art (*It Needs to be Said*, 1929). In other issues, E. K. Broadus (1876–1936) attacked contemporary poetry, and B. K. Sandwell (1876–1954) contributed a discussion on education. In his incisive and critical scrutiny of Canada and her political relationships, Frank Underhill gave a broad and highly personal interpretation of his subject. Even such whimsically humorous pieces as "Exposed the Golfic Mysteries" of John D. Robins (1884–1952) did not avoid the thrust of satire.

Underlying the restlessness of the twenties and thirties was the attempt to define Canadianism. Many of those who contributed to the *Forum* had an academic background, and stood therefore in a tradition of free inquiry, a

*Assisted by Donald Hair.

tradition which enjoined a sympathetic consideration of all points of view. And while these writers strove for a specific ideology, it was their heritage, the critical spirit itself, that came to be identified with Canadianism. As the uncertainty of the twenties and thirties gave way to the struggle of the forties and the optimism of the fifties, this spirit grew. Its adolescent intensity still permeated the radio scripts of John Fisher, an impassioned critic of those who apologized for, or refused to support, things Canadian. Mature expression came with the speeches and articles of Vincent Massey, whose quiet prudence seemed to be the essence of Canada. The Canadian character has been, and probably will be, a perennial theme for the essayist. It is significant that when Malcolm Ross set about making an anthology of Canadian essays, he produced a book called *Our Sense of Identity* (1954).

For the essayist, who needs some degree of detachment and quiet contemplation, the critical temper of the twenties was not always a congenial one. To attack, to criticize, involved venturing from the tower to the marketplace, and, once there, the temptation to stay was strong. The forays of William Arthur Deacon were typical in that they led him away from the essay entirely. Unpredictable, often belligerent, rarely dull, Deacon characterized himself as a "literary adventurer," a pirate, one of "those irresponsible but picturesque seamen of old who went on erratic journeys to bring back treasure. . . ." Deacon's earliest journeys were the most successful, partly because of the vigour of his approach, partly because he thought of himself as an essayist and therefore tried for a clear muscular prose style. The treasure of *Pens and Pirates* (1923) is typically diversified, ranging as it does from barbering to the "national character," from whimsy to stern humour. The pace is so brisk that the reader often forgets the erratic organization. Much smoother in rhythm is *Poteen* (1926), "A Pot-Pourri of Canadian Essays." Deacon's real interest lay in defying "the conservatism of the Canadian Mind." In 1931 he was joint editor of *Open House*, a collection of articles representing "a free flow of frank and fearless opinion on many subjects." With *My Vision of Canada* (1933) the critical temper took over completely, and Deacon disregarded the demands of form and style in the passionate hope that he might thereby speak more openly and frankly about Canada's needs.

While many of their academic colleagues found much to attack and little to defend, a group of classics professors at the University of Toronto was quietly fostering traditional humanist ideals. The scholarly essays of Maurice Hutton (1865–1940) are largely revised public lectures on people, books, and ideas. Hutton's approach is thoughtful and leisurely, and combines the best of the two great classical cultures. The spontaneity of the Greek spirit appears in his robust sense of humour, the conservatism of the Roman mind in his intelligent consideration of ancient virtues. The lucidity and balance of Hutton's style are reflected in the polished phrases of one of his students, John Charles

Robertson (1864–1956). Like his master, Robertson treats "various matters of perennial interest in which the ancient and the modern world throw light each upon the other." Gilbert Norwood (1880–1954) stands apart from his colleagues, partly because a good deal of his professional life was spent in England, partly because he is lively and outspoken while Hutton and Robertson are restrained and poised.

The essay in Canada has always had some of the timeliness usually associated with journalism. Newspaper articles, on the other hand, sometimes approach the timelessness that traditionally characterizes the essay. Hence we must consider a number of books containing collections of newspaper columns, published by their authors with the not entirely misplaced hope that they had some literary value. A columnist like Pierre Berton, whose interest lies in people, events, and issues, or a journalist like H. W. Charlesworth (1872–1945), who chronicles the social and political currents of his time, does not make contributions to literature. "The best columns," Pierre Berton has said, are the "most topical, written in the heat of the moment and in prose that is something less than imperishable." Once the columnist begins avoiding the "heat of the moment," however, he approaches the essay. His style, it is true, may betray the effects of an imminent deadline, but his methods and materials are similar to those of the essayist. Description, anecdote, reminiscence, and humour form his stock-in-trade. His appeal lies in an entertaining display of his personality and tastes. One of the best of these peripheral literary figures was T. B. Roberton (1879–1936), whose articles in the *Winnipeg Free Press* were sufficiently polished to warrant two posthumous collections. From the *Winnipeg Tribune* came C. B. Pyper's *One Thing after Another* (1948) and *This For Remembrance* (1949), by W. T. Allison (1874–1941). Bruce West's *A Change of Pace* (1956), reprinted from the Toronto *Globe and Mail*, has little literary value. More skilful is Jack Scott's *From Our Town* (1959), a selection of articles from the *Vancouver Sun*.

Of all the columnists, the humorists were most widely read and best loved. Peter Donovan's *Imperfectly Proper* (1920), a collection of his sketches from the Toronto *Saturday Night*, set the pace. Newton McTavish (1877–1941), editor of the *Canadian Magazine*, followed with *Thrown in* (1923), reminiscences of a rural childhood. Gregory Clark collected his humorous anecdotes in several volumes. His finest pieces appeared in the *Weekend Magazine*, and were gathered together in *The Best of Gregory Clark* (1959). Like the other humorists, Eric Nicol relied on anecdotes of personal experiences. His social satire, however, was often distinctive and refreshing.

The bogey of every journalist is the "average reader." This mythical but all-powerful creature not only dictates what he likes to read, but how he likes it written. The humorists (with the possible exception of Nicol) managed to please because each cultivated an "average man" attitude and an idiomatic style. Donovan was perhaps typical. His pieces, the "random impressions of an Earnest Soul," were dedicated to "Constant Reader" and "Old Subscriber." He liked the good old days, sports (usually fishing), and "getting away from it all"; he disliked silly women, affectation, and social teas. Common sense, tolerance, and amusement marked his approach to life.

Though the "average reader" was no obstacle to the humorists, he posed a real dilemma for the serious essayist. Most essays in Canada are published in journals and magazines commanding a fairly wide audience. Few readers are interested in literary value. As Gregory Clark wrote bluntly in the preface to *Which We Did* (1936), "nobody but invalids and retired clergymen read essays any more." In spite of this bleak situation, most essayists found a solution. Some, like Hugh MacLennan, contributed principally to sophisticated journals like the *Montrealer*. Others, like B. K. Sandwell, editor of *Saturday Night*, tried to correct the "average reader." Robertson Davies ignored him: "I do not believe in wasting good talk on people who are plainly unable to appreciate it."

The essays of Hugh MacLennan will probably always take second place to his fiction, especially since many of the pieces are used to formulate definitions and to work out ideas later incorporated into the novels. Yet these pieces are by no means alien to the essay tradition in Canada. In the preface to *Thirty and Three* (1954) MacLennan sounds the note of virtually every Canadian essayist after 1920. Discarding the traditional concept of the essayist as a "man who lives a life of quiet but surprisingly cheerful desperation, reconciled to the facts of existence," MacLennan writes: "I am still unreconciled to the kind of world I live in and I view many things with alarm besides myself, including most politicians and a good many voters." He speaks of the period in which he lives as "transitional," and his search after definitions is largely an attempt to understand the nature of the transition. The Canadian character is the principal subject of *Cross-Country* (1949), while *Scotchman's Return* (1960) ranges more widely. MacLennan tends to make his definitions statements of general truths (a practice which may irritate the reader who does not share his opinions), when they are in fact themes, "a mood or a cluster of ideas which somehow has emerged," MacLennan himself says, from the writer as an individual. This tendency is only partially offset by his practice of so loading the essays with reminiscences and personal revelations that they might almost be chapters in an autobiography. Personal likes and dislikes provide the basis on which MacLennan works out his definitions, but when he goes astray and comes to the wrong conclusions, he fails to charm as the essayist should. This failure is mitigated in part by a style in which his craftsmanship is never obtrusive, and even when the content falters its touch is strong and sure.

As editor of a weekly journal, Bernard Keble Sandwell (1876–1954) shared in the prevailing critical spirit, but his temper was highly individual. "I am not a leader of society. I am a follower of it. I follow it at a respectful distance, near enough to permit me to study its many interesting qualities, but far enough away to make it clear that I do not belong to it." The Swiftian overtones of this statement are strengthened by the title of the volume from which it is taken, *The Privacity Agent and Other Modest Proposals* (1928). Irony is the mark of many of the essays, but while Swift's irony is often savage, Sandwell's is mocking and witty, or, to use his own word, "skittish." A polished style, characterized by short thrusting phrases, gives this irony a cutting edge that resembles that of satire. The parallel is intentional, for Sandwell's purpose was to improve the Canadian social and political world. His norm was the "good old days," his own role that of *laudator temporis acti*. Sandwell's ideal is not to be found in any one era, however; it is rather that utopia where reason, common sense, and justice prevail. It is an ideal implied rather than described, and it lurks behind his every incisive criticism of twentieth century life. Typical of his provocative wit is the following statement from "The Hispano-Suiza Aristocracy": "I have, I must say, a great deal of sympathy with superior persons. Their path in life, in this age of the triumph of the inferior, is terribly hard. It is becoming so difficult for them to convince the inferior persons of their inferiority." With such material, readers both common and uncommon may be shocked into that one activity that Sandwell desires, but most shun: "thinking solemnly about solemn things."

The "average reader," that creature of "Drabbery and Squirtdom," is completely ignored by Robertson Davies, in spite of the fact that this versatile writer was literary editor of *Saturday Night*, and subsequently editor of the Peterborough *Examiner*. For his audience he looks to the "clerisy," those few "who read for pleasure and with some pretension to taste." One of the most prominent members of this clerisy is his dyspeptic Samuel Marchbanks, whose *Diary* (1947) and *Table Talk* (1949) make use of forms which, like the letter, are traditionally related to the essay. A compound of shrewd observation, razor-edge comments, playful sallies, evaporations of wit, and exuberant humour, these pieces make up an anatomy of the tastes and opinions of a fictional character whose ultimate purpose is the frank and often critical illumination of the Canadian way of life. The "national passion for dowdy utility," the prevalence of "boobs, yahoos and ninnies," is more than offset by Marchbanks himself who, like Dr. Johnson, "loved tea, conversation and pretty women, and had not much patience with fools." Davies admires intelligence, not the dull pedantic kind, but that lively appreciation of life that is the natural concomitant of the well-stocked cultivated mind. Just as angling was for W. H. Blake the central activity of the good life, so reading is for Davies the principal pursuit of the intelligent individual. "Reading is my theme," he announces at the beginning of *A Voice from the Attic* (1960), "and reading is a private, interpretative art." "Private" is a key word. Like Sandwell, Davies places his hope for the future on the capacities of the individual: "Only individuals think; gangs merely throb."

The gangs of "average readers" not infrequently so alienated a journalist that he fled from the city and sought out a country home. One of the unusual and perhaps most significant themes arising out of the journalistic world was this return to nature, in part a retreat, in part a resurgence of the pioneering spirit. The pattern was set in an academic fashion by E. K. Broadus (1876–1936), whose *Saturday and Sunday* (1935) records impressions of an odyssey from Harvard to Edmonton to set up the University of Alberta. But while Broadus was an educational pioneer, the journalists had more in common with Thoreau. Frederick Philip Grove summed up their purposes when in commenting on *Friendship* (1943) he said of its author, H. L. Symons: "What he wanted was a piece of land which would help him to grow, to live himself into the soil and to come out of it a completer man."

Both Symons and John D. Robins (1884–1952) often vitiate their theme with humorous clichés. Kenneth McNeill Wells is more successful. A long series of articles in the Toronto *Telegram*, later gathered together in four books, chronicled life at the Owl Pen, the author's farm "up Medonte way." Like Peter McArthur, Wells was a world-weary writer who turned to "that which is eternally and datelessly of the farmstead and concession line, that which is evergreen." A much more careful writer than McArthur, Wells was accurate but not lyrical in his descriptions. His penchant was to story-telling, not to humour, and he was particularly skilful in transcribing the idiom of the Ontario farmer.

Nature remained an important topic for the Canadian essayist. Some writers, like Ernest Fewster (1868–1947) and W. S. Johnson, attempted unsuccessfully to reproduce the descriptive fantasies of Archibald MacMechan. *Sunlight and Shadow* (1928) by Cecil Francis Lloyd (1884–1938) has some value, however, principally because Lloyd has a flair for finding the right descriptive word. His *Malvern Essays* (1930) are modelled on Montaigne, and, like his master, he derives "a mild and chequered enjoyment from being alive." His attitude is ambivalent, recognizing as it does the permanent and the fleeting, the beautiful and the homely, life and death. As he tells us in "The Burden of Existence," he takes life as it is, but his acceptance is wistful and weary. Lloyd's style has individual faults, but in general it is easy and graceful, and faithfully portrays a sensitive, rather sad personality.

Far different from the approach of Archibald MacMechan is that of Frederick Philip Grove (1871–1948), who described nature in a detailed, almost scientific fashion. When the reader is informed that a cloud "covers the sky in the northwest to an angular height of thirty degrees," he may wonder if the description is literary at all, but he soon discovers that such details fit together in an infinitely suggestive whole. Grove himself wrote: "While I am trying to set down facts, I am also trying to render moods and images begot by them. . . ." It is, in fact, only such careful accuracy that enables him to describe in *Over Prairie Trails* (1922) seven trips over the same Manitoba road, and to differentiate the mood and emotion of each journey. More important, such detail somehow brings the reader closer to the mystery of existence. "I wanted the simpler, the more elemental things," writes Grove, "things cosmic in their associations, nearer to the beginning or end of creation." In spite of Grove's personal love for such forbidding country, these cosmic associations keep obtruding. *The Turn of the Year* (1923), a description of the passing of the seasons on the prairie, has a certain harsh largeness of vision not quite suited to the personal scope of the essay. In the introduction to the original edition, Arthur Phelps spoke of the "epic comment" which seemed to characterize the book. The sketches of the settlers, of the Sower and the Reaper, are dwarfed by the total design. The documentary of the passing seasons seems as determined and inexorable as nature herself. The strong forward stride of Grove's prose rhythms complements the descriptions of nature's power.

While Grove described nature with cosmic implications, Roderick Langmere Haig-Brown dwells upon its value for the individual. The difference is one of tradition. Grove was a novelist whose realism did not always avoid the determinism of the naturalist school. Haig-Brown, on the other hand, is a fisherman in the Waltonian tradition, a tradition naturalized in Canada by W. H. Blake. Consequently, fishing is never a utilitarian skill, but an "art, ephemeral, graceful, complicated, full of tradition yet never static." Haig-Brown is often as technical and scientific as Grove, but the technicalities subserve his primary purpose of entertaining, "in its highest sense of providing sustenance for the mind." Fishing is not, as some of Haig-Brown's critics have suggested, his way of life; rather, it is both an adjunct to, and a symbol of, life as Haig-Brown believes it should be—the pleasurable experience of an intelligent individual. This thought, expressed in *A River Never Sleeps* (1946), is one of Haig-Brown's earliest answers to the question "Why Fish?" In *Measure of the Year* (1950) his pleasure in fishing is extended to all the experiences of life in the country. From *Fisherman's Spring* (1951), *Fisherman's Winter* (1954) and *Fisherman's Summer* (1959) emerges, for the writer, a pattern of civilized life, for the reader, "thoughts and ideas that might otherwise have remained idle and forgotten in the back of the mind." Haig-Brown's style is as quiet and thoughtful as his approach to life. Rarely lyrical or humorous, sometimes flat and heavy, it is regularly polished and eloquent.

The essays of Arctic explorer Vilhjalmur Stefansson (1879–1962) stand somewhat apart from the development traced in this section. The pieces that make up *Adventures in Error* (1936) are complex structures where irony and sly humour lurk under an approach that seems as orderly and systematic as a philosophical treatise. Even the title is ironical, for Stefansson is in search of truth. Stefansson's approach would lead one to believe that truth lies in empirical fact, and error in man's wilful disregard of such facts. But the "errors" of the human imagination are empirical facts and, in that sense, true. Human desires, moreover, are significant even when self-deceptive. The reader is soon forced to acknowledge that man's mental processes have a validity of their own, and that the "standardization of error" is desirable. Logical organization and a clear impersonal style aid Stefansson's multiple irony.

Speeches were relatively unimportant in the development of the essay during the period from 1920 to 1960, principally because writers no longer looked to oratorical eloquence as a stylistic model. Orators themselves were using a simpler, more direct style. The addresses of Sir Robert Falconer (1867–1943), published as *Idealism in National Character* (1920), are vigorous, idiomatic, and forceful. Vincent Massey's speeches are unobtrusively eloquent.

Journalism was primarily responsible for the general change in style which marked the development of the essay from 1880 to 1960. Utilitarian clarity and conciseness are the marks of journalistic prose, and lend themselves well to the kind of writing where content is more important than style. To the critical temper of the 1920's, a merely ornamental style was anathema. In contrast, the essay writer usually prides himself on a distinctive style which not only reflects his character and tastes, but is largely responsible for communicating the mood or emotion of his chosen subject. For the essayist, style is never purely ornamental. Some of the contributors to *The Week* scorned attention to style, but most were as careful in cultivating an individual mode of writing as were the essayists who followed them. With the advent of the 1920's, however, prose became a vehicle for attack and criticism. Form and content became distinguishable as they never had been before. Later essayists adapted the directness and force of the journalistic tradition into their own styles, and found that the vigour of the modern idiom was by no means alien to the carefully integrated and unobtrusively artful style of the essay.

II. Autobiography

JAY MACPHERSON

CANADIAN AUTOBIOGRAPHIES generally offer more of historical or social than of literary interest. With many, title or sub-title offers a fair idea of the content: *Arctic Bride, Artist at War, Memoirs of a Canadian Merchant, Soldiering in Canada, We Keep a Light, When the Steel Went Through.* With others the author's name suffices: Mrs. George Black, C. T. Currelly, Lady Eaton, Madge Macbeth, Egerton Ryerson, Goldwin Smith, A Staff Surgeon (Walter Henry). The interest of such extroverted books is mainly in a locality or a subject-matter. This chapter will discuss, not a cross-section of these, but a selection of the autobiographies of writers and painters, which, while they display much variety of outward circumstance, may be expected to dwell more on the inner life. However, while the artist appears in Goldsmith as government official, in Major John Richardson as defender of calumniated honour, in others as crusader, adventurer, journalist, invalid, and in Norman Levine as parasite, only in a few autobiographies is the artist as such very conspicuously present.

John Galt (1779–1839) published his two-volume *Autobiography* six years before his death. In an uncommon phrase he describes his state at the time of writing: "Infirm and ailing as I am, deprecating death with art." Art is less in evidence than the effort to direct belated attention to his earlier works and to justify his conduct on certain past occasions. Nearly a third of the book concerns the founding and operations of the Canada Company, as whose agent Galt spent three years in Upper Canada, returning home ruined in fortune and reputation. One of the few happy moments described is the founding of Guelph: yet "from the day that I announced the founding of this metropolis to the directors of the Canada Company, my troubles and vexations began, and were accumulated on my unsheltered head till they could be no longer endured." His account is detailed and involved, and his legal training causes him to bring forward numerous documents in his defence against misunderstandings and false imputations. After his return he devotes himself full time to his old avocation of literature, having earlier produced plays, poems, and works of travel and biography: now come his two novels of Scottish settler life in Canada, *Lawrie Todd* and *Bogle Corbet*. The *Autobiography* deals with Galt's public rather than with his domestic life: he says of his marriage only that it took place on a Tuesday, and we know that he had three sons—who all later settled in Canada—because he mentions his arrest for failure to pay their school fees.

Oliver Goldsmith (1794–1861) spent his life as a conscientious official of the army commissariat, occupying posts in Halifax, Saint John, Hong Kong, St. John's, and Corfu, from which last ill health forced him to retire in 1855. Settled with a sister in Liverpool, where he was to spend his remaining years, Goldsmith outlined his life in a notebook, "with the view of recording circumstances with their dates when they occurred, before time may have erased them altogether from my Memory." It was interest in the author of *The Rising Village* that caused publication of the *Autobiography* in 1943, but Goldsmith himself took his literary career very lightly. Looking back after thirty years, he says: "It was very fortunate for me that [the poem] was the occupation of leisure Hours. My living did not depend on my poetical talent, lucky fellow, and in this respect I had the advantage of the immortal Poet. After this essay, I abandoned the Muses, and I have not had the pleasure of any further intercourse with the lovely ladies." In the manner of the day, Goldsmith ornaments his rather plain prose with literary allusions: however, to him writing, like reading, is one among the diversions of a modest and accomplished bachelor. Others include playing Tony Lumpkin in amateur theatricals, participating in Masonic and Mechanics' Institute activities, gardening—"my Strawberries and Celery were superior"—and undertaking a pious journey to Lissoy in Ireland, the Goldsmith family home. Here his pride in "the immortal Poet," his great-uncle, lends glory to the scene. Perhaps it is evident too in a Saint John reminiscence of him skating, quoted in the editor's notes: "The skill with which, by sweeping clean-cut curves upon the hard glassy ice, he used to write, in large yet elegant letters, the words 'Oliver Goldsmith,' it was worth going a long way to see."

The autobiographical works of Susanna Moodie (1803–1885) were written mainly to earn money, and also intended to instruct. *Roughing It in the Bush* (1852) is a personal narrative in which she is deliberately using the history of her family's struggles in the deep woods near Peterborough as an object-lesson to prospective settlers. This is one of the best known, and among the most impressive, of Canadian books. In *Life in the Clearings* (1853), a leisurely account of reasonably civilized life in Belleville, a well-bred reserve replaces the earlier self-revelation. That during these years a fire destroyed house and possessions, a son was drowned, and Mrs. Moodie became seriously ill, we are told only because she wants to record the kindness of a Catholic priest, the force of Belleville's river Moira, and the occasion for her undertaking the trip to Niagara that is the book's main event. Humour and a balanced outlook are among her assets as a writer. John Galt sent his servant to report on Niagara Falls, a hundred yards away: for Mrs. Moodie the sight of them is one of life's great climaxes, but she nevertheless includes in her book, as part of an excellent anonymous sketch, the lines:

> My thoughts are strange, magnificent, and deep,
> When I look down on thee;
> Oh, what a glorious place for washing sheep
> Niagara would be!

She shows more lightness in *Life in the Clearings* than earlier, because her personal battle with Canada is over; but her concerns never become trivial. While carefully and objectively describing natural detail and social customs, notably camp-meeting and mourning ones, like Galt she has a visionary enthusiasm for the future that Canada will build up on the labour of those to whom she offers dignity and independence. Comparable narratives of pioneer life were written by Mrs. Moodie's brother Samuel Strickland and her sister Catharine Parr Traill.

Mrs. Moodie thinks of literature largely as an instrument of social improvement, citing *Oliver Twist* and "The Song of the Shirt": so do the Manitoba novelists Rev. Charles W. Gordon (1860–1937, "Ralph Connor"), who wrote at first to win support for Presbyterian missionary work in the West, and Nellie McClung (1873–1951), inspired in youth by Dickens. Both were personally engaged, sometimes together, in the same causes, fights against the liquor interests and for women's suffrage and better factory conditions. Both, visiting the League of Nations at Geneva, see a kind of culmination of their own labours, though Mrs. McClung goes on to record its failure. Gordon's *Postscript to Adventure* (1938), lively and far from solemn, is full of youthful muscle-building, heroic men and women, dramatic confrontations, and its author's innocently prideful view of himself as a small but honest cog that has turned some big wheels: "'Excellent! What was Sir Wilfrid's reply?' asked [Mr Asquith] eagerly." Mrs. McClung's *Clearing in the West* (1935) and *The Stream Runs Fast* (1945) convey a practical intelligence, warm feeling, and an unerring inaccuracy about books: "I knew every word of *In Tune with the Indefinite*." Also unerring is her eye for characters and anecdotes (a Brandon landlady: "I like to charge my boarders plenty and then I won't be begrudgin' them"); her use of a notebook for such observations gives life and thickness to her novels. "The people of this neighbourhood drew a sharp line between summer and winter drinkers." Drinking in harvest-time is like eating one's seed-corn, an act of despair. From Mrs. Moodie to Stephen Leacock we are shown that, in the former's words, "Drinking is the curse of Canada." Many staples of Connor and McClung fiction—the picnic spoiled by whisky, the drunken husband who fails to bring the doctor, the petted girl unfit to be a settler's wife—have their originals in their authors' life-stories, though one searches in vain for the reformed saloon-keeper. On the whole these autobiographies record more convincingly than the novels the unsocial setting in which the W.C.T.U. was a liberal movement of its time and it was no longer mainly the Indians for whom the churches needed missionaries.

R. W. Service (1874–1958) has two autobiographical books: *Ploughman of the Moon: An Adventure into Memory* (1945) describes his early life in Scotland and his North American wanderings, while *Harper of Heaven: A Record of Radiant Living* (1948) covers his later life in France and California. His contact with persons and places seems callously superficial, while his treatment of experience is sensational and highly coloured. Service's literary career grew out of a talent for public declamation and a knack of producing verse to formula: "attack, build-up and pay-off"; "What about the old triangle. . . ? Sure fire stuff. . . . Give it a setting in a Yukon saloon and make the two guys shoot it out. . . ." However, he fancies the role of inspired poet, and gives us hints of creative frenzies, with comments like, "I have ever been a minion of the moon. . . ." The original Endymion went through life with his eyes shut; and the titles of Service's books do not begin to convey his jaunty, vulgar style, his preening, and his contempt for literature. Ernest Thompson Seton (1860–1946) shares with Service a fuzzy natural religion, a cult of wholesome living, and a sense that the true America is California. *Trail of an Artist-Naturalist* (1940) is best in its depiction of the perilous excitements of a backwoods farm and the acquisition, mainly in Ontario and Manitoba, of Thompson Seton's unsurpassed knowledge of wild life.

A third Scotsman, Frederick Niven (1878–1944), published *Coloured Spectacles* in 1938. The art of this book is so self-effacing, and the impact of reality so direct, that the title slightly misleads. "Memory winnows," he says, impressionistically recreating with lights and colours and smells a boyhood oriented geographically between Valparaiso and Glasgow, and imaginatively between Andrew Lang and Deadwood Dick. The chapters were at first essays separately published, but are drawn together by our recognition of a real person's modesty and skill and the sustained search for unity in diversity, the contemplative threads that connect the here and there, the then and now. Whatever he talks about he gives us the feel of, developing, for example, a Canadian wilderness scene out of the thin smoke of a campfire. His theme is perhaps the search for home, or the way memory makes identity. His thoughtfulness continually orders and relates, rather than dwelling like Service on petty irony and contrast. He makes an unusual conquest of distance: such a mind carries its treasures with it, and he not only finds Scotland in Canada, but sees how Scotland has prepared him for Canada. Sitting with an Indian friend on the prairie, he thinks "of the days . . . when as a small boy I visited the camps of the Blackfeet—invisible to all but me—in Scotland, and smoked the pipe of peace with a viewless, imagined Crowfoot. The sound of the Bow River below us, flowing shallow through the Blackfoot Reservation in Alberta was, for a few minutes, the sound of Gryffe, in Renfrewshire, rippling over its stones." Unexpected versions of such identity also occur: an Indian devoted to the ways of his people, learning that his interviewer is a Scotsman, returns "Me too!"; and a fanatical Scot encountered in Nelson, B.C., at last declares, " 'Leave Scotland, is't? Never been in Scotland! I come frae Glengarry County, Ontario.' He repeated it with sonorous articulation like that of Alan Breck announcing that he bore a king's name: '*Glengarry County, Ontario.*' " The technique of the book is subjective without egotism: the impression of human and literary maturity comes in part from Niven's not finding it necessary to arrange his record around social movements or even crucial events in his own life, but rather letting his casually gathered material take its life from him, in the imaginative force with which memory has endowed it: hence the book strikes us as a real creation and its author as an adult.

The most deliberate effort to portray the artist as such is made by Frederick Philip Grove (1872-1948) in *In Search of Myself* (1946). The dominating intention causes him to mingle fact and (apparently) fiction, realism and symbolism, to make his hero carry out the fate foreshadowed in the highly self-conscious epigraph, *Ça vous amuse, la vie?* From the beginning this hero is one set apart for a special destiny, even foredoomed. He plays out for us Grove's favourite drama, that of the strong man with a wound that will take his whole lifetime to kill him. Peculiar ironies surround him; and as fate bludgeons him with them, so he bludgeons the reader, most severely in the Prologue. His romantic Titanism is at once both imposing and absurd: "like the face of Europe my memory is a palimpsest. . . ." "The ultimate working out of what was in me: a sort of reaction to the universe in which man was trapped, defending himself on all fronts against a cosmic attack," is perhaps most completely achieved in his life rather than in his work, whose failure as a totality is what *In Search of Myself* sets out to explain. A comparison he suggests between Siberia and the intellectual life of western Canada is not meant to be ironic, but the inherent reality is so: the wilderness is to Grove both nourishing and destroying, and this is true also of solitude and conversely of human ties. The strength which he phenomenally displays can in other lights look like wilfulness and weakness: in his writing it is hard to distinguish between bang and whimper. This book seems less admirable than *A Search for America* in that it presents a thinner and more confined reality: social milieu is perfunctorily given and other people appear as objects, even ultimately as obstacles.

Stephen Leacock (1869-1944) in *The Boy I Left Behind Me* (1946) shows a reticence like Galt's about his personal life. In these rambling pieces he feels safest with topics of mild general interest, but enough of his circumstances becomes clear to enlighten the reader about the attitudes he displays elsewhere. His father was a spineless English gentleman packed off by his family to a bush farm near Lake Simcoe, where he took to drink and at length wandered off altogether. Looking back, while still humorously nostalgic about his British origins, Leacock seems glad to have left behind a land where some people were "born to be poor" for one where the family servant "in whose old-fashioned Yorkshire mind wages due from the aristocracy were like shares in the National Debt" is an anachronism.

Confessions of an Immigrant's Daughter (1939), by Laura Goodman Salverson, is one of the most rounded, intelligent, and attractive of Canadian life-stories. Her Icelandic family and its community provide some wonderful characters—Aunt Haldora the midwife, Great Uncle Jonathan with tales of his seafaring youth, Great Aunt Steinun who dragged her injured husband in winter from Gimli to Winnipeg on a wood-sledge, Indians inscrutable but good-hearted—and illuminate the qualities of independence and imagination developing in the sickly little girl. Many of the events are common to several of the writers' backgrounds: the westward migration in search of fortune, the struggles with poverty and illness, the yearly arrival of babies too feeble to live but whose lives must still be fought for, the effort while still very young to become a teacher, which was Mrs. Salverson's great but hopeless desire. For Mrs. Salverson the determination to be a writer comes with the first visit to a library, where the world of books opens before her. We might compare, for its characteristic difference, Norman Levine's account in *Canada Made Me* (1958) of first entering a library and being handed a book by the librarian: "I wanted to do things to her, but I was too young": clearly, life is what you make it. Humour, sympathy, and a sense of proportion carry Mrs. Salverson through grim experiences as a working girl in Duluth on starvation wages, and the book concludes in the happier days that followed her marriage.

A Painter's Country (1958) by A. Y. Jackson and the autobiographical books of Emily Carr (1871-1945), while written late in life by painters who respect each other's work, have nothing else in common. Dr. Jackson's is a very external account, generally impersonal, in which he is anxious carefully to outline the constitution and history of the Group of Seven of which he was so important a member, and to do exact justice both to it and to its detractors. For his own work he leaves the excellent reproductions to speak. Emily Carr, who on the whole liked animals better than people, writes of her battle to be herself and do her own work, from the first without family support or communication with other Canadian artists, and always subject to periodic physical collapses: when these at length put an end to her painting, she began seriously to write. *Klee Wyck* (1941) describes her painting trips to Indian villages on the northern British Columbia coast, *The Book of Small* (1942) her Victoria childhood, *The House of All Sorts* (1944) her career as a Victoria dog-breeder and landlady, *Pause* (1953) her stay in an English sanatorium, and *Heart of a Peacock* (1953) some animal friends. *Growing Pains* (1946) is her autobiography, presented characteristically in a series of quick sketches. She tells her story with force, often with malicious comedy, but this book unlike the others offers as much embarrassment as pleasure. She arranges her scenes much as Dr. Gordon does his, if less crudely: both have a natural arrogance that must snatch the last word, even when unspoken. Her diction, though expressive, teeters between innocence and affectation, at worst developing a squirming coyness that fits ill with either the forthrightness of her painting or the brooding and sibylline Miss Carr of a late photograph. Nevertheless, it is a heroic record.

Canadian autobiographies notably reflect a practical grasp of outward reality rather than any inward illumination: the bulk of those not discussed here are naïvely external narratives, shaped at the least by mere chronology, at the most by the fortunes of some cause, movement, or institution with which the writer identifies his own. As a group the women autobiographers perhaps present themselves better than the men: whether by nature or by training, they seem less self-absorbed and more actively interested in the people around them, and so able to give a fuller sense of life. Besides the hard physical struggle to keep going, Mrs. McClung, Mrs. Salverson and Emily Carr had in addition to cope with the gradual and difficult realization of what society expected of women, and none of them was content with the role laid down for her. Clearly, they often caused grief to those closest to them, and they did well if they escaped becoming unduly vulnerable or defensive.

Most of the books on this list are less vivid in their later parts, whether because the child's point of view embraces a more manageable cosmos, or because as they go on the writers lose the sense that it rests with them to show us a vanished way of life, and therefore in the later, more familiar settings allow their accounts to become fragmentary.

In the Canadian scene, where literature presses less heavily on experience than in Europe, we can note some curious effects of the working of literary convention on life. Mrs. Moodie includes in *Life in the Clearings* the stories of "Michael Macbride" and "Jeanie Burns," both declared to be absolutely true, and both obviously either modelled on or influenced by sentimental domestic romance of the most standard kind: they stick out from the rest of the book in much the same way as Mrs. Moodie's verse does from her prose. Similarly extraneous in *Clearing in the West* are the stories of Bertha and Mrs. Thorne: the youthful mind into which these items fell must have been well schooled in temperance tracts before it turned them out again as exempla. At an opposite extreme is the all but obsessively conscious case of Grove. In the first chapter of *Walden*, a book which Grove apparently admired and knew well long before settling in Canada, Thoreau says: "The cost of a thing is the amount of what I will call life which is required to be exchanged for it, immediately or in the long run." Grove's entire career as related in *In Search of Myself* is an illustration of this saying, which he restates at the end of his book as his discovery. Has he ordered the pattern of his life so as to demonstrate an already accepted truth? Or, making like a Grove hero a choice both necessary and fatal, did he choose the life that would prove it? Where the artless writer gives his own history as a somewhat random record but shapes extra matters like conventional fiction, the over-conscious writer, aware of nothing but himself, shapes such a pattern of fatality as to make us feel we have read one more of his novels. The soundest ground is the middle area occupied by writers who, whether solid like Mrs. Salverson or slight like Niven, are just artistic enough to give their record of life both its pattern and its freedom.

33. Children's Books

MARJORIE McDOWELL

THE FIRST RESIDENT of Canada to write for children was Mrs. H. Bayley, the wife of a British army officer living at Isle aux Noix, Lower Canada. Her *Improvement; or, a Visit to Grandmama* (1833) was praised by an English reviewer as "A sweet little book for children . . . it abounds in pious feelings and moral lessons, combined with general and useful information." Three years later, turning to a theme of travel and adventure which has proved popular ever since, she produced *Henry; or, The Juvenile Traveller, a faithful delineation of a voyage across the Atlantic in a New York packet; a description of a part of the United States . . . a journey to Canada*. The merit of being first in the field belongs to *Improvement*; it is *Henry*, however, which introduced an original and persisting theme. We learn what it is like to travel to and in Canada and how Canadian people and Canadian animals live. It requires no great effort at identifying archetypal imagery to see that Canadian rivers and lakes, mountains, forests and prairies, filled with wolves and bears, deer and buffalo, salmon and eagles, with which travellers and settlers contend, will evoke instant response from a young imagination. If children's books from Canada have enjoyed an international vogue beyond their strictly literary deserts, it is because the Canadian terrain has spread itself so enticingly behind a child's dream.

Forests, wilderness, and wild mountains are a natural setting for the struggle to survive. An early Canadian contribution to the Robinson-Crusoe-*cum*-Swiss-Family-Robinson theme appears in *Canadian Crusoes* (1852) by Catharine Parr Traill (1802–1899). Later issued as *Lost in the Backwoods*, this story follows the adventures of three boys, one a French Canadian, lost for several years in the woods and sustaining themselves by evolving a campcraft which ensures their survival among many hazards. The theme persists more mildly in Mrs. Traill's *Stories of the Canadian Forest* (1857) in which a child of English background by questioning her Canadian nurse learns about the Canadian wilderness and Canadian Indians. *Cot and Cradle Stories* (1895), written towards the end of her life, scale down Mrs. Traill's world of wild life for the very young, who can hear happily of the animals God "cares for so wisely and well."

CHILDREN'S BOOKS

To this Canadian world of Indians and settlers, animals wild and domestic, backwoods and clearings, R. M. Ballantyne (1825-1894) added a northern dimension, an emphasis on adventure, and a consistently romantic atmosphere. These components came naturally to a young Scotsman whose postings in the service of the Hudson's Bay Company had taken him to York Factory, Norway House, and Fort Garry in the old West and to Tadoussac and Seven Islands in the Gulf of St. Lawrence region. *Hudson's Bay* (1848), in fact, incorporates material from letters and diaries and reflects his detailed observation of people and things. *The Young Fur-Traders* (1856) merely extends these into fiction. The romance and adventure are authentic; the humour, sensibility, and courage are Ballantyne's own qualities; even what may appear Victorian prudishness is relieved by his genuine feeling for religion. Stevenson and Henty owe him something, as in a different way do Roberts and Seton.

Mrs. Bayley, Mrs. Traill, and Ballantyne exemplified the responses of British sensibility to the Canadian scene. It was now the task of native Canadian writers to amplify and extend this response out of their more intimate knowledge of Canadian situations. Three who succeeded to the point of establishing a collective tradition were Charles G. D. Roberts (1860-1943), Ernest Thompson Seton (1860-1946) and Lucy M. Montgomery (1874-1942).

Roberts's somewhat factitious historical stories such as *The Raid from Beauséjour* (1894) at least encouraged the background use of Canadian history. His animal stories, beginning with *Around the Campfire* (1896), have outlasted his other prose work and they have done so through the persistence of their appeal to children. Representative of his large output are *The Kindred of the Wild* (1902), *More Kindred of the Wild* (1911), *Babes of the Wild* (1912, republished the next year as *Children of the Wild*), *Hoof and Claw* (1914), *Some Animal Stories* (1921), *They that Walk in the Wild* (1924).

The first twenty-three years of Roberts's life were spent in New Brunswick and he made many subsequent visits to its woods. He was devoted to canoeing trips which involved fishing, camping, and wide observation of wild life. It is probable, moreover, that his schoolmaster George Parkin, who accompanied him on some of these expeditions, imparted to Roberts the habit of associating careful observation with careful description, as part of an English literary tradition he so deeply admired. Roberts's best stories are the product of direct knowledge of animal life in the temperate North American region, though he sometimes ventures into Arctic or tropical scenes. The human actors are characteristically lumberjacks, trappers, and farmers, who shared their environment with animals.

Roberts is still read by children because his tales are filled with action and with facts of animal existence. Though somewhat impeded by descriptive passages, his plots are clear, his movement fast, and his effects always dramatic. It is doubtful whether his juvenile readers notice his occasional imputation of human motives to his animal characters or his underlying assumption that survival in the wilds depends on the elimination of the weak. More apparent is his repeated assertion that freedom in the midst of hazards is better than the safety of a captive condition.

Ernest Thompson Seton, who may reasonably be classified as a Canadian writer, was brought from England to Canada before the age of six. He grew up in Ontario and later homesteaded in Manitoba. He styled himself an artist-naturalist and his books bear the double impression. His own photographs, diagrams, line-drawings, and silhouettes are scattered thickly throughout his text. His stories of animals are based on close and protracted observation and informed by a feeling of kinship which only rarely falls into sentimentality. The naturalist in Seton desires to protect and conserve animal life and this feeling is reinforced by a sense of identity which nevertheless does not betray him into anthropomorphism. *Wild Animals I Have Known* (1898) strikes at the beginning of his literary career the characteristic Seton note: "I hope some will herein find emphasized a moral as old as scripture—we and the beasts are kin. Man has nothing that the animals have not at least a vestige of, the animals have nothing that man does not in some degree share. Since, then, the animals are creatures with wants and feelings differing in degree only from our own, they surely have their rights. . . ." In the same book Seton says summarily, "The life of a wild animal always has a tragic end." He accepts the fact as part of the price of Darwinian survival but his humanity rebels against man's interfering cruelty in killing or capturing needlessly. Representative of Seton's large output are *The Trail of the Sandhill Stag* (1899), *Lives of the Hunted* (1901), *Wild Animals at Home* (1913), *Manual of Woodcraft Indians* (1915), and *Famous Animal Stories* (1932).

In the midst of a long series of books about animals, Seton wrote *Two Little Savages* (1903), for which generations of children have been grateful. It is a compound of autobiography, adventure, and, above all, woodcraft. Adventure is kept within the bounds of plausibility, humour grows out of boyish efforts to experience and learn, camping skills are effortlessly imparted. Seton's lighthearted illustrations keep pace with the reader, in the margins.

The highest survival value, among books of this period, is probably possessed by the "Anne" and "Emily" stories of Lucy Maud Montgomery. From her recollections of childhood in Cavendish, on the shores of Prince Edward Island, came *Anne of Green Gables* (1908), followed by *Anne of Avonlea* (1909). Intensely regional, her stories manoeuvre their episodes on a flowing tide of description. Idiosyncratic characters are rendered in loving detail; Scottish tradition, Calvinistic influence, and rural habits of individualism all play their parts. Domestic incident, handled with whimsical humour and gentle idealism, holds the reader's attention. Above all, the natural charm of the island province, its trees and blossoms and overhanging stars, felt in changing days and seasons: this suffuses the style and turns the setting into a true Arcadia. The moral tone is in keeping. God is in all nature and the father of men; delight in living is held in balance by altruistic idealism and inward conscience. Defects of sentimentality and over-optimism pass unnoticed in the powerful unity of mood, an outcome of the author's personal and artistic sincerity. Young readers, moreover, falling under the spell of the early books, read on into later, weaker variants of this theme of girlhood growing into womanhood, without losing their affection for this lovely world. All told, the corpus of L. M. Montgomery's work represents a real, if modest, triumph in the history of Canadian letters and her place in the record is assured.

The work of Roberts, Seton, and Montgomery sets up certain expectations which time has now confirmed. Predominant in children's books is the Canadian terrain itself, with its variants of arctic wilderness, plains and forests, mountains and prairies. Traversed by rivers, studded with lakes, and bordered by oceans, these great landscapes support an abundant wild life, produce the environment of pioneers and, in the settled communities, give rise to pastoral life filled with rural beauty. It follows that early stories of wild adventure and fierce conflict will gradually take on more regional characteristics, that human society will receive increasing emphasis. It is possible that, in the same way that the immigrant settler has mixed with the Indian, the policeman, and the pioneer, and peaceful life in farm and village has rendered up its own materials for plot and characterization, so stories for young Canadians in the near future will commence to centre on urban life as the concentration of people in the cities continues. Children may at some future time be presented with stories of city life on an international plan, the specifically Canadian element reduced to a minimum. It seems improbable, however, that Canada's inheritance of magnificently varied terrain, still fabulous in its extent and still largely unassimilated, will ever fail to stir youthful imaginations.

It goes without saying that attempted classifications of children's books will overlap. The animal story, the adventure story, the story of Indians or Eskimos, the regional story: these lead by easy access into one another. Even the historical and biographical accounts tend to involve themselves with adventures of exploration or military action. It is nevertheless useful to suggest these and other categories, so long as they are recognized as tentative.

The first animal story written by a Canadian which reached an international audience was *Beautiful Joe* (1894), by Marshall Saunders (1861-1947), describing the unhappy life of a dog. This won a contest which the American Humane Society sponsored in an effort to match Anna Sewell's *Black Beauty*

(1877) with an American story. *Beautiful Joe* was an immediate success and the author continued, through a long series of stories, to put forward the claim of birds and animals to a share of human compassion.

Variants of the animal story appear in *Mooswa and Others of the Boundaries* (1900) and *The Outcasts* (1901) by W. A. Fraser (1859-1933); in these tales the animals resemble human types and the problems are essentially human ones. Olaf Baker's *Shasta of the Wolves* (1919) is in the manner of Kipling's Jungle Stories. Carol C. Cole wrote stories such as *Velvet Paws and Shiny Eyes* (1922) for very young children, in the tradition of Beatrix Potter. "Grey Owl" (1888-1938), an English trapper who lived in Canada like an Indian, achieved a wide audience with his interpretation of animal ways in *Men of the Last Frontier* (1931), *Pilgrims of the Wild* (1935) and *The Adventures of Sajo and her Beaver People* (1935). J. W. Lippincott wrote of the life of wolves in *Wolf King* (1933) and *Wilderness Champion* (1944), Mel Thistle of the life of a fish in *Peter the Sea Trout* (1954). *The Incredible Journey* (1960) of Sheila Burnford has become widely known through its filmed version. Almost any writer on Canadian subjects is liable to the impulse to write an animal story, from Mazo de la Roche who in 1955 wrote a fantasy about a domestic lamb, *The Story of Lambert*, to Farley Mowat, whose *Owls in the Family* (1961) is a boy's account of the impact of a pet owl upon his family and their neighbours in Saskatoon.

The problem of the inadequate portrayal of Indians and Eskimos in Canadian writing is beyond the scope of this sketch. Writers for children have, on the whole, been fairly responsive to their subjects in this field. Indians are treated with comprehension and respect by Theodore Goodridge Roberts (1877-1953) in *Red Feathers* (1907); in Charles Clay's *Young Voyageur* (1938) and its sequel *Fur Trade Apprentice* (1940) which tell of a boy's adventures in the fur trade and the founding of the North West Company; and in George F. Clarke's *The Adventures of Jimmy Why* (1953). Similar attention is focussed on the Eskimos in Violet M. Irwin's *Kak, the Copper Eskimo* (1924) which she wrote with Vilhjálmur Stefansson, in W. G. Crisp's *Ook-pik* (1952) and in Alma Houston's *Nuki* (1953). *At the Dark of the Moon* (1956), by M. T. Good, is a deeply satisfying story of life on an Indian reservation. John Craig's *The Long Return* (1959) handles convincingly the Indian captivity theme.

Folklore as material for children's stories has been derived not only from Indian and Eskimo tradition but also from folk customs of settlers from Europe including those of the original French Canadians. Numerous writers have presented the mystery and humour of these variously derived tales in forms acceptable to children. Cyrus Macmillan made an early and successful attempt to interpret Indian legends in two books, *Canadian Wonder Tales* (1918) and *Canadian Fairy Tales* (1922), republished together as *Glooskap's Country* in 1955. Pauline Johnson recorded Indian folklore in *Legends of*

Vancouver (1911). Noteworthy among many subsequent collections are: *Legends of French Canada* (1931) by E. C. Woodley, *Thunder in the Mountains* (1947) by Hilda M. Hooke, Jack Tremblay's *Ten Canadian Legends* (1955) and Marius Barbeau's *The Golden Phoenix, and Other French-Canadian Fairy Tales* (1958). A successful attempt to combine Western regional mythology with present-day adventure has been made by Catherine A. Clark in *The Golden Pine Cone* (1950), *The Sun Horse* (1951), *The One-Winged Dragon* (1951) and *The Silver Man* (1958). The success of these books depends on their author's ability to create an imaginative world in which the fantasy is solidly based on reality. They are set in the Kootenays and embody authentic and typical Canadian characters; legend, myth, and fantasy combine in a synthesis of European and Indian elements in which the Indian contribution plays the largest part.

History, either presented as fact or woven into fiction, has never ceased to provide a staple for children's entertainment. Although Roberts's interpretations of history are inferior to his animal tales, they were in their own time exemplary and therefore important. At the same time Agnes Maule Machar (1837–1927) was pursuing a parallel path; *For King and Country* (1874) was a romantic novel about the War of 1812 dedicated to "young Canadians." She went on to write stories of New France, of Old Kingston and of the Empire at large. After the turn of the century many historically based books appeared. *The Curious Career of Roderick Campbell* (1901), *A Diana of Quebec* (1912), and *The Little Admiral* (1924), by Jean Newton McIlwraith (1859–1938), were filled with a sense of joyful adventure and helped to popularize the historical form. A similar service was performed by the works of Thomas G. Marquis (1864–1936). Culminating in *Brock* (1912), his books reveal a flair for period atmosphere and heroic, though partisan, biography. Regions west of the Great Lakes were employed as background by Agnes C. Laut (1871–1936). In *Lords of the North* (1900), *Heralds of Empire* (1902), and *The Story of the Trapper* (1902) she shows an intimate knowledge of the Hudson's Bay Company, the Red River Settlement, and the history of the fur trade. Notable books in more recent years are *Drums in the Forest* (1936), a story of French Canada in 1686, by Allan Dwight; *The Champlain Road* (1939), Franklin D. McDowell's story of the Jesuits' work in Huronia; *Rebel on the Trail* (1953) by Lyn Cook; *The Boy Who Ran Away* (1954), Josephine Phelan's story of Hudson's Bay territory; *The Young Surveyor* (1956) in which Olive E. Knox tells of the building of the Canadian Pacific Railway; C. A. M. Edwards's *Son of the Mohawk* (1954), a well-written account of Radisson, and *Brook Watson of Beauséjour* (1957) an essay in fictional biography. J. F. Swayze deals with La Salle's expeditions in *Tonty of the Iron Hand* (1957); Edith L. Sharp's *Nkwala* (1958) enters into the life of a Salish boy; Wilma P. Hay's *Drummer Boy for Montcalm*

(1959) is an example of the well-integrated historical novel. In *Treason at York* (1949), *A Land Divided* (1951), dealing with the Acadian expulsion, and *Rebels Ride at Night* (1953), a story of the rebellion of 1837, John F. Hayes uses formula plots but achieves a genuine sense of the course of Canadian history and its effect upon individuals.

In the field of history and biography, Macmillan of Canada have performed a valuable service by instituting the "Great Stories of Canada" series, in which the claim is fulfilled that "each volume is written by a popular Canadian writer who has the ability to infuse long-dead stories and characters with the excitement, the personality and the immediacy of contemporary events." By 1963 the series comprised twenty-eight titles by such writers as Orlo Miller, Marjorie W. Campbell, Pierre Berton, Edward A. McCourt, Kerry Wood, Josephine Phelan, R. S. Lambert, Joseph Schull, Thomas Raddall, and Roderick Haig-Brown. Another series, "Canadian Portraits" put out by Clarke Irwin, helpfully groups its subjects, for example *Famous Doctors* (1956) by Viola W. Pratt. Noteworthy among further biographies are *Champlain Northwest Voyager* (1944) by Louise H. Tharp, Ronald Syme's story of Radisson, *Bay of the North* (1950), and his *Champlain of the St. Lawrence* (1952).

A single romantic theme, with an historical basis, may attract a number of writers. Stories of the Royal North-West Mounted Police (now the R.C.M.P.) are, as one would expect, fairly abundant. Muriel Denison's *Susannah: A Little Girl with the Mounties* (1936), which gained an international audience, has been followed by Harwood Steele's *To Effect an Arrest* (1947) and *The Marching Call* (1956), by T. M. Longstreth's *Mounty in a Jeep* (1949) and by John F. Hayes's *Bugles in the Hills* (1955), among others. Roderick Haig-Brown's *Mounted Police Patrol* (1954) is a factual analysis of R.C.M.P. organization.

A single writer may pass easily across related kinds of Canadian juvenile fiction. James M. Oxley (1855–1907) produced tales of sport and adventure, *My Strange Rescue and Other Stories* (1903); episodic travel stories, such as *The Boy Tramps; or, Across Canada* (1896); period stories such as *Fergus MacTavish* (1893); and examples of the historical novel in the manner of Henty, such as *North Overland with Franklin* (1901). Oxley is uneven and is seldom strong in plot construction, but he has a place in the tradition of Stevenson and Henty and he nicely exemplifies Canadian juvenile tastes of his period.

Regional stories are of many kinds: the historical account may include a descriptive realization of terrain; animal plots often lay stress on regional environment; an Eskimo or Indian tale may lean heavily on locality. The regional element in Canadian juvenile writing is, however, becoming of increasing importance in its own right; the vogue for high adventure with stereotyped setting and characters gives way to a desire for realistic rendering of everyday, localized experience. Mention has already been made of the "Anne" and "Emily" stories of L. M. Montgomery and other similar early examples of the regional story. To these should be added *Three Boys in the Wild North Land, Summer* (1896) by E. R. Young (1840–1909) and Newfoundland stories by Norman Duncan (1871–1916), *The Adventures of Billy Topsail* (1906) and *Billy Topsail and Co.* (1910). Alan Sullivan's *Brother Eskimo* (1921) tells of a struggle for survival in the North; his *Brother Blackfoot* (1937) is a story of adventure in the foothills of the Rockies. *Jory's Cove* (1941), by Clare Bice, depicts the life of a Nova Scotia fishing village; in *The Great Island* (1954) his subject is Newfoundland. In *Starbuck Valley Winter* (1943) and *Saltwater Summer* (1948) intensely personal observation and a distinguished prose style give permanence to Roderick Haig-Brown's descriptions of the wild life, landscape, and seascape of British Columbia. Mabel Dunham's *Kristli's Trees* (1948) deals with the life and problems of a Mennonite boy on an Ontario farm. Jack Hambleton's *Forest Ranger* (1948) tells of a boy's work for the Department of Lands and Forests in the northern Ontario bush. Lyn Cook has written three exceptionally good stories: *The Bells on Finland Street* (1950), the story of a girl from Finland living in Sudbury; *Judy and the General* (1955), set on a Niagara fruit farm; and *Pegeen and the Pilgrim* (1957), a story of the Stratford drama festival. In 1956 Farley Mowat renewed the practice of using the Northland as a setting with his prize-winning *Lost in the Barrens*, later published as *Two against the North*. Kerry Wood's *Wild Winter* (1954) is a character study worked out in a context of prairie isolation. R. H. Protheroe's *Little Chief of the Gaspé* (1955) and Stella F. Rapaport's *A Whittle too Much* (1955), which also centres in the Gaspé peninsula, combine with *Alphonse, the Bearded One* (1954) and *Sashes Red and Blue* (1956), Natalie S. Carlson's collections of French-Canadian tall tales, to give yet another regional emphasis.

Canadian children's writing has a strong basis of actuality and not many covers open to reveal a Wonderland. Among authors who have succeeded with fantasy is Mary Grannan, whose *Just Mary* (1941) was the first of a series of successful radio broadcasts, subsequently published. To anthropomorphic animals more life was given by radio voices than is suggested in print. In Louise Riley's *Train for Tiger Lily* (1954) fantasy is made completely plausible by logical connections with actuality; from the transcontinental train we step confidently into a magic circle. Pierre Berton's *The Secret World of Og* (1963), having recourse to some well-tried formulae, projects order, logic, and consistency of character into an imaginary world. In *Return of the Viking* (1955) by Eva-Lis Wuorio, fantasy is combined with historical tradition.

The number of memorable poems for children written in Canada is not large. In 1918 appeared *Shining Ship*, a collection of delicate lyric verse by Isabel E. Mackay (1875–1928). The tradition of Stevenson and Milne has been carried on in Desmond Pacey's *Hippity Hobo and the Bee* (1952) and *The Cow with the Musical Moo* (1952); unforced humour, freshness of rhyme pattern, and consistent gaiety of tone lift these books to a high level. It should be noted that, although the group of post-Confederation poets wrote few pieces specifically for children, many of their nature poems appear in school texts and are appreciatively read. Carman's rhythm and bold imagery, for example, appeal to a wide range of sensibility.

Canadian children's books which have achieved popularity outside Canada have generally been written in series, in the manner of G. A. Henty in England or S. G. Goodrich and Jacob Abbott in the United States. Notable among early writers who once possessed such popularity is James De Mille (1834–1880) of Saint John, N.B., whose "Brethren of the White Cross" series, begun in 1869, was filled with the natural history and regional geography of Canada's southeast coasts. Equally informative and didactic was De Mille's "Young Dodge Club" series, which conducted its readers through Italy. A number of popular novels originally intended for adults have later been appropriated by children, among them *The Seats of the Mighty* (1896) by Gilbert Parker, *The Golden Dog* (1897) by William Kirby, and *Glengarry Schooldays* (1902) by Ralph Connor. At the present time it is Mazo de la Roche's Jalna series which exerts the strongest attraction for young readers, always excepting the Montgomery books, whose appeal is timeless. *Anne of Green Gables* has given rise to several films; many volumes of the "Anne" and "Emily" series have been widely translated: like the more famous works of Louisa M. Alcott, these books project an idealized and ever pleasing image of life.

The best general discussion of Canadian books for children appears in *The Unreluctant Years* (1953) by Lillian Smith, whose object is to provide standards by which parents may judge the available work.

When one takes into consideration the fact that Canadian books for children have existed for little more than a century and that they have been written by a handful of authors, one may safely conclude that they compare favourably with the books of other nations. In animal stories, in historical fiction and biography, and in Indian legend, a distinctively Canadian contribution has been made. Seizing the opportunities presented by a romantic environment and an adventurous population, such authors as Charles G. D. Roberts, Ernest Thompson Seton, L. M. Montgomery, Roderick Haig-Brown, and Farley Mowat have achieved unique success in creating, at home and abroad, a favourable image of this country.

34. Drama and Theatre

MICHAEL TAIT

I. DRAMA, 1920–1960

MANY REASONS have been advanced to explain the lack in Canada of a dramatic literature of any real distinction. In this area of the arts more than in any other, critics protest, this country has been in the disadvantageous position of a cultural colony. Canada has so much in common with both America and England that their playwrights easily provide immediately entertaining fare for Canadian audiences. When the distinctive qualities of one group of dramatists begins to pall, a second is available. There is also, the argument continues, the thorny problem of geography. How is it possible to conceive of a national drama in a country comprised of two main races and so many regions separated by such great distances? What has a play about commercial Toronto to say to a rancher in Alberta or one about the strength of English traditions in Victoria to a *habitant* in Quebec? This difficulty exists of course for the poet and the novelist as well, but not in so acute a form. Either may reach a widely dispersed, if select, audience with comparative ease. Theatre depends upon concentrated support in each community and to be truly national, drama must be meaningful to a cross-section of the total population. Moreover, it is often claimed that theatre can only flourish at the centre of a society, at a focal point where social cross-currents meet and clash, in an atmosphere of intense feeling and lively intellectual debate. Although the cultural climate of certain cities, Toronto and Montreal in particular, is becoming increasingly cosmopolitan, no such centre exists as yet in Canada.

The comparative feebleness of Canada's dramatic output has been attributed to a variety of other interrelated factors. The amorphous nature of Canadian society, its lack of distinctive features which may be readily exploited on the stage, have added to the playwright's difficulties. In addition, the traditionally conventional, somewhat staid habits of mind that characterize Anglo-Saxon Canada are not easily converted into exciting theatre. In so far as such capacious generalizations are possible, English Canadians with their high regard for reticence and propriety have perhaps little national affinity for the theatre, that most extravagantly exhibitionistic of the arts. Certainly their inhibited modes of speech make them awkward propositions on stage.

However, some assert, it is not simply a matter of manners but also of morals. The twofold Puritan heritage of Scotland and New England has perpetuated a view of the theatre as an expendable commodity to be tolerated perhaps so long as it never presumes to explore themes offensive to respectable persons. Merrill Denison, writing in the *Year Book for the Arts in Canada* (1929), stated pessimistically: "The two or three indubitably Canadian plays that might be written would never find a welcome in a Canadian theatre, even if there was one" (p. 55). This supports the view put forward by Professor Arthur Phelps that Canadians have an innate distaste for the kind of spiritual self-discovery serious drama affords. The rise of the cinema before a native drama could take hold has consolidated this general indifference towards the stage and hence the work of Canadian playwrights. But in the absence of audiences and governmental subsidy there has been no money to build throughout the country the playhouses and to develop the sort of companies which enable the young playwright to acquaint himself with the potentialities and limitations of his medium. At the same time, the dearth of proper facilities has been a further reason for the public's refusal to support the theatre. One particularly damaging consequence of the lack of large and knowledgeable audiences has been the absence of severe critical standards which compel the playwright to aim high or risk ridicule.

Of course no one of these factors or all of them together necessarily preclude the appearance of a major dramatist. For such a figure adverse circumstances would simply be grist to the mill. Continual developments in the Canadian theatrical world would make such an advent, if by no means inevitable, at least a possibility.

It should be noted before we begin to record actual accomplishments that in a survey of this kind the emphasis necessarily falls upon published material. It should also be noticed, however, that the publication of plays in this country is a very haphazard process. Merit is not by any means always the criterion. Lister Sinclair, Len Petersen, Joseph Schull, Ted Allan, Harry Boyle, Morley Callaghan, Stanley Mann, Andrew Allan, Mavor Moore, Patricia Joudry, Donald Jack, John Gray, and Jack Winter among others have written plays of considerable interest which have received performance but have not found a publisher.

The first Canadian playwright of any stature whatever is Merrill Denison, whose appearance coincided with the quickening of the Little Theatre movement in this country. He was closely associated with Hart House Theatre in the active years immediately following its foundation in 1919. Although early in his career he departed for lucrative opportunities in the United States, he left behind him several slight but interesting plays. These include *Balm*, which appears in volume I of *Plays from Hart House Theatre* (1926), *The Prizewinner* (1928), and a volume entitled *The Unheroic North* containing four pieces, *Brothers in Arms, From Their Own Place, The Weather Breeder*, and *Marsh Hay*. In every respect these little plays offer a vivid contrast with the sort of thing which had preceded them: Marjorie Pickthall's *The Woodcarver's Wife* (1922) or the interminable poetic closet dramas of the nineteenth century. They are short (most of them one act), realistic in manner, display a nice command of dialogue, and are eminently suitable for performance. Their content is in the main satirical; their mood is in harmony with the critical temper of the twenties. Denison's technique is to strike out in as many directions as possible, debunking whatever seems to him pretentious or absurd in Canadian attitudes of mind. The title, *The Unheroic North*, gives the clue to one such attitude. This is the notion (common among Canadian writers of the last century but entertained perhaps by many city dwellers before and since) of the Northland as an environment conducive to moral uplift, inhabited by figures ten feet tall who live a life of virtuous simplicity as a result of their close contact with the soil. In *The Unheroic North* we are rapidly disabused of this view. For example, in *Brothers in Arms* Dorothea, seeking "romance in the land of Robert Service and Ralph Connor," is confronted by the backwoodsman Syd, who is transfigured in her eyes but is in fact lazy, obtuse, and probably dishonest like his counterparts in *From Their Own Place*. But Denison's satire has many dimensions. The figure of Syd is played off against the third character, a pompous business man, and before the play is done, the army, patriotism, social standing, and such ideals as thrift and industry, the shibboleths of the city in effect, have been held up to derision. The characters of course are blatant types, and as in all of Denison there is a hint of the wrong kind of artificiality here and there. *Brothers in Arms* is nevertheless an enjoyable play. *The Weather Breeder, From Their Own Place*, and *The Prizewinner* also illustrate with a variety of comic flourishes the benighted quality of life in the Ontario backwoods. (*Balm* stands a little apart, being set in the city. This entertaining trifle concerns a frigid social worker who scotches an attempt by two old maids to adopt a child. Its theme, the conflict between the repressive forces of society and the creative, often feckless exuberance of the individual, is one which is treated repeatedly by Canadian playwrights.) Mr. Denison has carefully observed the community he depicts and his portrayal suggests an understanding of its dark as well as its comic aspects. At moments in certain of these satirical farces one has the sense that the laughter proceeds partially from a recognition by author and audience of a submerged level of violence and terror. (This alarming facet of rural life provides the basis for *The Killdeer* by the contemporary poet James Reaney, a play set in a land equally unheroic and distinctly macabre.) For example, in *The Prizewinner* one member of a dubious road show on tour in the backwoods advises the impresario not to arouse the critical wrath of the community and remarks, "Back here they can't even write. . . . Say it with canthooks is their motto." An exaggeration no doubt, but comic in part because of an unnerving truth somewhere offstage.

It is not strange, then, that Denison's most ambitious and interesting play is not a comedy. In *Marsh Hay*, his only full-length published drama, he delineates directly the sombre, often desperate existence of a northern family. The underlying theme is a strong one, the crippling effect morally, intellectually, and emotionally, of the backwoods environment, particularly on those who must attempt to wring a living from the worthless land. By and large Denison avoids passing judgment. The squalor and the attempts to escape through sexual promiscuity, the bigoted and perverse mores of the little community, the utter breakdown of human relations in the family, these are circumstances for which no one in particular is to blame, and for which no solution is offered. The play has a number of flaws: one or two episodes are naïve and improbable, certain themes such as the indifference of governments to the plight of the region are not sufficiently integrated into the action, the dialogue is somewhat repetitive, the ending strikes one as rather too remorselessly pat. Nevertheless *Marsh Hay* is a creditable achievement that almost stands comparison, in its intensity of mood at least, with O'Neill's *Desire under the Elms*. It is without question the best Canadian play of the decade. But while *Brothers in Arms* has been performed many times there is no record to date of a production of *Marsh Hay*. Denison also produced a volume of six radio plays based on the exploits of figures in Canadian history. They are competently done, but the author does not seem altogether at ease, either with the medium or the limitations imposed by his subject-matter.

Apart from Merrill Denison, no playwright of proven merit emerged during the 1920's. However, the rise of the little theatre prompted the composition of numerous plays. Optimism and confidence were in the air. On every hand there were hopes for and predictions of a Canadian dramatic renaissance reminiscent perhaps of developments in Ireland. Quite suddenly the need for theatrical expression seemed urgent. Would-be dramatists throughout the country essayed a wide variety of genres—fantasy, farce, melodrama, grand guignol, plays exploiting the romance of Canadian, British, or Ancient Egyptian history, plays based on Indian themes, or depicting Ontario's rural society, or England's high society, plays incorporating expressionistic devices, and so forth. Regrettably, the great mass of this writing is quite without merit. Everywhere originality, intensity, technique are lacking. However a few collections and single plays may be noted. Two volumes of *Plays from Hart House Theatre* appeared successively in 1926 and 1927, introduced by Vincent Massey. Volume I, besides three pieces by Denison, and a few negligible items, contains *Pierre* by Duncan Campbell Scott (1862–1947) and Britton

Cook's *The Translation of John Snaith*. *Pierre* is a domestic tragedy set in rural Quebec. Its plot is over-familiar, the return after many years of the ne'er-do-well son, and the dialogue is written in the specious idiom English Canadians always seem to attribute to the French. The play, however, has dignity and there is genuine pathos in the last scene as Madame Durocher, the universal mother, speaks of the happy future in store for her son, unaware that Pierre has departed again having stolen the meagre savings of the family. *The Translation of John Snaith* is a more complex and interesting work. It is set in a northern Ontario town during World War I and presents us with a number of themes: the spiritual sterility of the region, the hunger of its inhabitants for some intimation of beauty and joy, the attitude of certain Englishmen who view Canada as incorrigibly barren, fit only for commercial exploitation, the destruction of a vital Indian culture by the barbaric white man who can replace it with nothing, and finally the urgent need for local heroes or myths that will serve to unify and inspire the life of the community. As is so often the case with Canadian plays, the ideas are stronger than their dramatic realization. The characterization is unsubtle, and the melodramatic ending fails to convince. But in the early death of Britton Cook Canada lost a playwright of promise.

Volume II of *Plays from Hart House Theatre* contains three full-length pieces. Leslie Ried's *Trespassers* has nothing to recommend it. *The Freedom of Jean Guichet* by L. A. MacKay displays a certain originality but is defeated by its incongruous mixture of farce and melodrama. *God of Gods*, by Carroll Aikins, first produced by the Birmingham Repertory Theatre in 1919, sets forth in an Indian setting the conflict between the vital individual vision of the poet and the tyrannical and superstitious prejudices of the tribe. There are a few theatrically effective moments here and some acceptable comedy. Mr. Aikins's main problem, and that of all who attempt to put the Canadian Indian on stage, is one of diction. Anything but the most rudimentary language rings somehow false, but then how is one to make a play out of monosyllables? The choice (a dilemma which confronts many modern playwrights, unconcerned with Indians, who accept the restrictions of realism) seems to be between an inexpressive verisimilitude and fraudulent eloquence. Mr. Aikins chooses the latter, a precarious poetical prose which is prone to alarming descents into bathos. (AMBURI *harshly*: "Since when has the God's Priestess had a mate?".)

Another volume to appear during the twenties was *One Third of a Bill*, six one-act plays by Fred Jacob (1882–1926). Most of these are mildly amusing and depict, when they reflect the Canadian scene at all, the foibles of an Ontario urban bourgeoisie. Mr. Jacob by and large derives his plots from the battle of the sexes, or, once again, from the triumph of the energetic individual in his encounter with a conformist society. These little plays are competently put together but somewhat pale. Only one of them, *The Basket*, promises greater distinction. Its setting is rural Ontario in the 1880's and its theme, the plight of a Mediterranean man in an alien northern culture, has possibilities. Unfortunately these are dissipated and confused amid melodramatic hocus-pocus.

Another collection of some interest is *Six Canadian Plays* edited by Herman Voaden and published in 1930. This volume is the result of a competition in which the contestants were enjoined to attempt explicitly nationalistic drama set in a northern landscape and capturing, if possible, the mood of the painters in the Group of Seven. It is indicative of the rearguard position occupied by the drama in this country that at a time when the revolt of the twenties was no longer in the least revolutionary and the leading poets were increasingly occupying themselves with urban subjects, Canadian dramatists should be seeking inspiration in the great outdoors. The plays themselves, though disappointing, illustrate the earnest search for dramatically viable Canadian themes. *The Bone Spoon* by Betti Sandiford is an attempt, as the editor puts it, "to work over the rich materials of our adventurous past." The figure of Prudence, who clearly has the author's unaffected sympathy, speaks of "these glorious old rocks" and of her desire "to write something great and romantic and brave like the country." Prudence we have seen before from a somewhat different perspective in the satires of Merrill Denison. *Mother Lode* by Archibald Key concerns an idealistic prospector and his search for the good life close to nature, a life threatened by the expansion of a corrupt civilization. This too, of course, is a common *motif* in nineteenth-century Canadian literature. The influence of expressionism is apparent in T. M. Morrow's *Manitou Portage* which in atmosphere, plot, and stage effects suggests O'Neill's *The Emperor Jones*. *Lake Dore* by J. E. Middleton (1872–1960), incorporating Franz Johnston's picture "The Deserted Cabin" as a backdrop, offers little. C. E. Carruthers' *God Forsaken* is a sardonic comment in the style of Denison on back-country mores and *Winds of Life* by Dora Smith Conover written around the auspicious theme of an Englishman's inability to cope with a harsh Canadian environment is nullified by absurdly sententious dialogue. In general this volume illustrates the danger of trying to produce a Canadian drama through self-conscious determination.

One further collection remains. *One Act Plays by Canadian Authors* is a book compiled in 1926 by the drama group of the Canadian Authors Association. These short plays were selected primarily "for productions by Little Theatres, Community Players, amateur dramatic societies." Almost all are very bad indeed. T. M. Morrow's *The Blue Pitcher* with its cluttered interior, wan farm woman, and distraught atmosphere is a paradigm for the many inferior imitations of *Marsh Hay* which comprise the Canadian stove-pipe school. One charming little play in this primitive anthology is *The Death *of Pierrot* by H. Green. There is delicately mordant satire in Mrs. Solomon Grundy's indignation that Pierrot and Columbine should live together "in a decent city." She immediately pins a black skirt on Columbine. "Oh hideous hideous," grieves Pierrot. "It can't be hideous," comes the retort, "it's the fashion." The volume also contains two plays *Low Life* and *Come True* by Mazo de la Roche (1885-1961). Although the action in both cases is trivial, the dialogue is deft. Another of her one-act plays (not in this collection), *The Return of the Immigrant*, generates a complex mood but is flawed by its stage Irish idiom. The prolific Miss de la Roche is also the author of a three-act play *Whiteoaks* that enjoyed an extremely long run in London's West End, and of which Bernard Shaw was heard to remark: "Amazing! There has been nothing like it in London since Henry Irving in *The Bells*."

In the early years of the thirties, Canadian plays continued to appear in profusion, although as the depression wore on their numbers diminished. The Dominion Drama Festival, organized in 1932, included among its awards the Sir Barry Jackson Trophy for the best performance of a native play. Samuel French Limited instituted a Canadian Playwright Series for the purpose of publishing whatever Canadian drama seemed to have merit and promise profit. Various associations and little theatres continued to encourage writers through competitions and prizes. Martha Allan, L. Bullock-Webster, Raymond Card, Mary Farquharson, Elsie Gowan, Madge Macbeth, Isabel MacKay, Janet McPhee, George Palmer, Marjorie Price, W. S. Milne, Lois Reynolds, Lillian Thomas are a few of the authors who grappled with the medium.

One figure who stands somewhat apart is Gwen Pharis Ringwood. Unquestionably she is the most capable playwright of this period. Miss Pharis wrote about ten plays in all, a number of them in connection with the Alberta Folk Lore project. *Stampede*, for example, has to do with the break-up of the old West and increasing commercialism of the annual festivities at Calgary. Only three, *Still Stands the House*, *The Courting of Marie Jenvrin* and *Dark Harvest*, are readily available. The action of *Still Stands the House* takes place in a farm house in southern Alberta, a region that Miss Pharis knows intimately, during the droughts of the depression. The farm is unproductive and a buyer has offered a good price for it. The conflict arises with inevitability out of the relation of the three main characters: the man torn between a desire to appease his wife and to hold on to the barren soil, the gentle city-born wife who finds the place intolerable, and a crazed love-starved sister (rather overdrawn) for whom the dead father's farmhouse is a sacred thing. Gwen Pharis creates the atmosphere of despair very well indeed and Bruce Warren's anguished identification with his bitter Alberta prairie lingers in the mind as a symbol for all human attachments of this kind. The dialogue is entirely natural without seeming flat. Miss Pharis's infrequent images ("Wheat like gold on the hills," "hair—black as a furrow turned in spring") are always in context and lend an unobtrusive expressiveness to the speech of her characters. The main defect of this, as of so many short plays in English, is a surfeit of well-made plot which tries to go too far, too fast. *The Courting of Marie Jenvrin* tells of a French-Canadian girl and her suitors in the Northwest Territories. It is an unremarkable but well-executed comedy. In *Dark Harvest*, an ambitious three-act drama, Miss Pharis explores again the evil consequence of her protagonist's fanatical devotion to the land. In spite of serious flaws—a gratuitously sensational ending and a style which lacks the necessary vigour to prevent the tragic mood from degenerating into dreariness—the play is powerfully conceived.

Further west, A. M. D. Fairbairn is the author of four *Plays from the Pacific Coast* (1935). All are concerned with the unhappy relations between the white man and the Haida Indians of British Columbia. *Ebb Tide* and *A Pacific Coast Tragedy* depict the insidious influence of the wretched remnant of the tribe upon those who live too long with it, whereas *The Tragedy of Tanoo* and *The Wardrums of the Skedans* are concerned with the moral damage done to the Indians by the whites. The red man is a notoriously opaque and difficult subject for any drama but his own; consequently the first two plays of this list are the more successful. *Ebb Tide* evokes something of the squalor of certain remote Indian communities. Once again it is an unlikely plot and unpalatable characterization (the heroine Ann, whatever the author's intentions, sounds like a race supremicist) that negate the play. The most absorbing piece is *A Pacific Coast Tragedy*. It portrays an English missionary who had come to the area twenty-five years before zealously determined to cure the diseased bodies and superstitious souls of the native inhabitants. In his desire to reach these people he had married an Indian wife. When the play begins a visitor from England finds him completely stalemated by the environment. He has made no impact whatever on the community, his wife is a vast, repellent squaw, and his son a criminal. In the course of the play Hopwood, the protagonist, discovers that his youngest daughter is to have an illegitimate child and his son has been arrested, charged with murder. At the end he takes his life, leaving an impression halfway between that of Job and the protagonist of Somerset Maugham's *Rain*. In spite of stiff dialogue and a dramatically incredible accumulation of disasters, the play has its effective moments: Hopwood's introduction of his squaw, for example, to the fastidious advocate from London, or a local Indian lad's description of how he is in the habit of sawing up his tribe's ancient totems for firewood.

A more accomplished dramatist of the thirties (one who is still actively engaged in his craft) is John Coulter. His plays include *Oblomoff*, a dramatization of Gontcharev's novel, *The Drums are out*, an Irish Civil War piece, a libretto for an opera *Dierdre of the Sorrows, The House in the Quiet Glen, The Family Portrait, Sleep My Pretty One, Holy Manhattan*, and *Riel*. Several of Mr. Coulter's plays are set in his native Ireland and show clearly the influence of Ireland's celebrated group of dramatists, Lady Gregory in particular, Synge less often. Coulter understands the value of economy in dialogue and his best plays—*The House in the Quiet Glen* is an example—reveal both inner vitality and careful construction. Too often in Canadian drama the one or the other is absent. To those detractors who might deny the value of writing Irish plays in Canada, Mr. Coulter in a preface to his libretto for *Deirdre* has this to say: "The art of a Canadian remains with but little differentiation the art of the country of his forebears and the old world heritage of myth and legend remain his heritage to be used for suitable ends though the desk on which he writes be Canadian."

A considerable number of dramas which appeared during the thirties and for which there are no counterparts before or since were inspired by the Great Depression. They have for the most part sociological interest only, but the pity and just anger they reflect, rare emotions in Canadian drama, are often curiously impressive. M. E. Bicknell's *Relief* is an earnest portrayal of the effects of drought on a Saskatchewan homestead. *Twenty-Five Cents* by Eric Harris is concerned with the calamities, material and psychological, which befall a family when the father who is a skilled machinist loses his job. *Such Harmony* by the same author depicts, to quote the preface, "The possible beginnings of authoritative control of freedom of speech, the vague influences which if given free play might usher in Fascism even in a country like Canada." The chief drawback of almost all these depression plays is a confusion in their authors' minds between the impact of emotion recollected in excitement and the effects of art.

The Second World War interrupted many of the country's dramatic activities and after it far fewer plays appear, in published form at least. It is as if the first optimistic experiments have been tried and it is now discouragingly clear to all that play-making is a craft long to learn, especially for Canadians. In addition, developments in the field of radio had the effect of diverting the energies of potential playwrights towards this remunerative and, at the time, exciting medium. However, during the forties, Canada's most prolific dramatist to date made his appearance.

Robertson Davies has written a good deal for the stage. He has produced, besides "King Phoenix" and "Hunting Stuart," two unpublished works, a volume of one-act plays, *Eros at Breakfast* (1949), *Fortune My Foe* (1949), *At My Heart's Core* (1950), *A Masque of Aesop* (1952), and *A Jig for the Gypsy* (1954). These pieces display a large measure of theatrical inventiveness, satiric flair, and refreshingly literate dialogue. Certain familiar themes reappear: the widespread philistinism, narrowness, and prudery of life in

Canada, the collision between the many who would confine the human spirit and the few who would liberate it, the fate of the creative imagination in an inhospitable climate which is home and hence inescapable. What distinguishes Davies from his predecessors is the greater insight, force, and variety with which he explores his subject. *Eros at Breakfast*, the title play of its volume, is described by the author as a "psychosomatic interlude." It is a clever fantasy in which each character represents one of the internal organs of a Canadian youth whose regimen has been disturbed by the onset of romantic impulses. None of the characters, of course, can agree on the proper attitude towards this development, thus opening the way for satiric thrusts at Canadian manners and a common human predicament. *The Voice of the People* is a more conventionally conducted attack on the fatuous complacence of the common man. The banning of Molière's *Tartuffe* in Quebec in 1693 provides the basis for *Hope Deferred*. This play touches on a number of the author's deepest concerns: the low estate of theatre in Canada, the wholesale departure of artists to more civilized countries, and the alarming power of unenlightened virtue. The effect of this bitter little comedy is heightened by particularly trenchant dialogue. *At the Gates of the Righteous* is weak, but *Overlaid* is perhaps the most entertaining short play ever written in this country. The setting is Merrill Denison's rural wasteland, and although the plot which hinges on a financial windfall is commonplace, the characters are intensely alive. The surrender of Pop, with his immortal longings for the high life, to his daughter Ethel whose dream is a granite headstone for the family plot, is both hilarious and poignant. But there is subtlety in the portrait of Ethel, who is obscurely sympathetic and in Pop's defeat which is not unqualified. This is the only play about the backwoods to contain so great a measure of exuberance and truth.

Fortune My Foe, Mr. Davies' first three-act drama, is less satisfactory. The author's dialogue is, as always, lively and precise; his themes, the purblind philistinism of the Canadian public and the improvidence of a society which continually loses its talented citizens through its indifference to them, lend an angry energy to many scenes. However the crucial distance between the author and his work seems unstable. One feels that the dramatist's emphatic opinions periodically overcome him and disturb the play's equilibrium. The result is that the central characters, though animated, lack genuine vitality. The good ones, those who subscribe to a creed of sweetness and light, tend to be sentimentalized while the bad ones who oppose or misunderstand them emerge as creatures of spleen rather than imagination.

At My Heart's Core, Mr. Davies' next full-length play, is a stronger work. Once again the theme he chooses is the fate of the civilized minority in a culturally barren Canadian environment. In this instance, however, the dramatist has greater control of his material. By setting the action of the play in Upper

Canada in 1837, he more easily presents the issues which concern him with the necessary degree of detachment. The period setting, too, enables the author (who is not entirely at ease with the amorphous idiom of modern urban speech) to exploit without incongruous effects his gift for precise rhetoric. The main plot of *At My Heart's Core* concerns the attempt by Cantwell, a mysterious and baleful figure, to undermine the composure of three women: the two Strickland sisters and one Mrs. Stewart, a lady of aristocratic antecedents, whose husbands have gone to York to fight the rebels. Cantwell's strategy is to persuade each in turn that the development of her particular talents or qualities is totally thwarted by the social and domestic wasteland that surrounds her. All three repudiate him, cleave to their husbands, and remain in Canada. The ending, however, like that of *Fortune My Foe*, is ambiguous. In both plays Davies seems at the same time to assert that faith in Canada's cultural future is an admirable thing, and to question whether such faith is worth the sacrifice of the rich possibilities life offers elsewhere.

A Masque of Aesop which was originally written for a cast of boy actors is Davies' most successful work for the stage. Like *At My Heart's Core*, it is not a direct portrayal of the contemporary scene and again one has the sense that the highly conventional masque form has provided the dramatist with a maximum of freedom for his satiric sallies against bigotry, complacence, and insensitivity, enduring qualities in human nature generally, but which for Davies inform so distressingly the Canadian scene in particular. In *A Masque of Aesop* there is none of the unassimilated residue of rancour that mars *Fortune My Foe*. The satire has both charm and bite; wit, gravity, and absurdity combine to make each point with maximum effect.

Mr. Davies' last published play to date is *A Jig for the Gypsy*. The action is set in Wales in 1885 at the time of a national election and revolves around the attempt by a group of Radical politicians to enlist the aid of Benoni Richards, a gypsy with mysterious powers of divination. When she permits herself to be drawn into the political hurly-burly, the results are disastrous. Both the Radical and Conservative factions eventually turn upon her and in anger she returns to her traditional way of life outside the framework of ordinary society. The play in essence illustrates the conflict of two worlds. Benoni's richly imaginative and intuitive style of life is contrasted with the doctrinaire rationalism of Jebson, the Radical candidate, who is dedicated to a vulgar ideal of public success. Davies, like Matthew Arnold's Oxford scholar, seems to regard the gypsies as possessors of an ancient, esoteric power and wisdom which modern society ignores or ridicules, but which in its deprived condition it can ill afford to do without. The play's conclusion, a ritual dance in which Benoni is joined by Conjuror Jones, a fellow magician, communicates a mood of optimism missing from *Fortune My Foe* or *At My*

Heart's Core. Benoni's jig seems to affirm the essential invulnerability of the life of the imagination, even in the most unpropitious circumstances, even, one is left to deduce, in Canada.

Norman Williams is one of the most promising playwrights to appear in the fifties. He has published one volume of six short plays *Worlds Apart* (1956) and has written a full-length work "To Ride a Tiger" which was performed in 1957 but is not as yet available in print.

Mr. Williams's range in his choice of subjects and forms is considerable. Although not given to radical experiment, in *A Battle of Wits* and *Protest* he manipulates the non-illusionistic devices of the Chinese theatre with ease and originality. Elsewhere, in *Dreams* for example, he does not hesitate to disturb the conventions of realism to make his point. Even such modest departures from the realistic mode are rare in Canadian drama and lend particular interest to Mr. Williams's work. His themes are diverse. The most persistent is the conflict between inherited conventions or loyalties and private impulse, the refusal of the individual to accommodate himself to traditional values and attitudes. This conflict is present in some form in *The King Decides* and the two Chinese plays of *Worlds Apart*, where Mr. Williams demonstrates both the comedy and the pathos which proceed from it. But this volume also contains plays which centre around the plight of a negro mother, the death of a movie star, and the assassination of Philip of Macedonia. Although the political and moral ideas in *The King Decides* or *The Mountain* lack incisiveness, Williams's dialogue is always both neat and fluent and (with the possible exception of *The Mountain*) all his plays build to excellent climaxes.

Certain other pieces published in recent years deserve some comment. One work that has attracted attention and a degree of commercial success is Patricia Joudrey's *Teach Me How to Cry* (1955). It received its first performance in Toronto and was subsequently produced in both New York and London.

In Miss Joudrey's words the play "concerns the manner in which human beings shape one another, and tells the story of a troubled teen-age girl who is steered away from a hazardous life of escapism by the love of a boy who has himself learned to face reality." The prevailing mood of delicate pathos is reminiscent of *The Glass Menagerie* by Tennessee Williams which in perhaps too many respects this play resembles. However it is written with sincerity and considerable technical skill. Miss Joudrey plots each crisis with careful economy and achieves a good balance between her characters, all of whom are conceived in terms of the central theme: the perils of illusion, the salvation in an acceptance of reality. The play is designed for a multiple set that facilitates a quick succession of short scenes. This arrangement best serves the action of the piece which, as the author observes, "is essentially emotional rather than physical."

It is unfortunate that the real merits of *Teach Me How to Cry* are largely nullified by its shortcomings. In the first place, the appeal of the two young people at the centre of the play is too calculated. Their value as protagonists is radically reduced by the lack of any suggestion of pimples, of the grotesquerie of adolescence, of the crassness of immaturity. They emerge inevitably as bloodless imitations of their counterparts in life. A comparable pallor afflicts most of the other characters who are sketched with the same kind of life-destroying compassion. The play as a result lacks verve and excitement, qualities that no degree of gentle, rueful perception can replace. Similarly, the poetical "atmosphere" of the drama cannot compensate for the poverty of the dialogue.

Teach Me How to Cry illustrates the dangers and difficulties which confront the Canadian playwright who attempts to treat a popular theme in an established idiom. The tribulation of the sensitive small-town adolescent who struggles to realize himself in the face of an inadequate older generation is, of course, a commonplace of the contemporary American stage. The theme, though overworked, is valid enough, but if the Canadian dramatist chooses to deal with it he must find his own voice and style.

A more imposing work is Lister Sinclair's *Socrates* (1957) which was first performed in 1952 at the Museum theatre in Toronto. As the title suggests it is an ambitious play. Sinclair undertakes to present the issues which culminated in the arrest of Socrates, the trial itself, and in the last scene, the philosopher's celebrated death. The author exploits dramatic licence to the full in assembling and deploying a large cast drawn in the main from Plato's dialogues. At the same time he contrives to adapt and incorporate into his play some of the most notable passages from the *Symposium*, the *Apology*, the *Crito*, and the *Phaedo*.

However, in spite of a nicely calculated structure, precise characterization, and an easy command of dialogue which ranges from colloquial prose to a stately verse measure, the play lacks power. At the root of the difficulty is the playwright's attitude toward the central figure. Sinclair has been unable to resist his admiration for his hero. Socrates is portrayed as an immaculate idealist destroyed by a purblind or corrupt gang of worldly sceptics. This is certainly the popular view but it is too simple-minded a conception to build a satisfactory play upon. One looks in vain for an astringent touch of Ibsenesque ambivalence. To the extent that Socrates is sentimentalized, his stature is diminished and the impact of the play as a whole is weakened. This central flaw has unfortunate ramifications. The trial scene, for example, fails because Socrates' opponents are characterized almost without exception as fools or knaves. There is a strong case, if not an ultimately convincing one, to be made against Socrates. His accusers are not permitted to make it. (Unhappily this scene invites comparison with the trial in *Saint Joan* which gains so much from Shaw's scrupulous portrait of Cauchon and the Inquisitor.) Moreover, in his anxiety to recommend his hero to the spectator, Sinclair has been careful to sidestep all the aspects of Socrates' life and thought, as Plato transmits them, which might disturb a modern audience: the banishment of the poet from the ideal state; the profoundly undemocratic view of human nature; the homosexual love which is the unspoken assumption of the *Symposium*; the disdain for political democracy. This is not to suggest that the inclusion of any of these issues might necessarily have improved the play. It is simply that the removal of any serious challenge to the hero of the piece precludes the possibility of significant conflict and vitiates this attempt to dramatize an exceptionally dramatic historical episode.

A Beach of Strangers: An Excursion (1961) by John Reeves which won an international award in 1959 has been widely translated and performed. Although it was written in the first place as a radio drama, it has been successfully staged. In this respect as in others the work recalls its prototype, *Under Milk Wood*. The action of the play takes place within an explicitly allegorical framework. On a holiday beach by the sea a variety of figures frolic, despair, love, and are estranged from one another. The characters represent a cross-section of mankind, and the sea, "man's first womb," laps on a beach emblematic of the context of all human life. The play's three-part structure is determined by the actions and fantasies of three sets of interrelated characters during the single day which is the fictional time span of the drama.

A Beach of Strangers is in essence a set of variations upon the theme of human solitude and the poignancy of the precarious reprieve from isolation which love in its several forms accomplishes. Like most good themes this one is entirely familiar, but in the play's best scenes it is handled with the authority of fresh insight. The strength of the theme, however, is somewhat undermined by stylistic uncertainties. Although Reeves writes with energy and invention his idiom is disconcertingly eclectic. Auden, Eliot, and others are discernible behind the verse interludes, while Dylan Thomas is overwhelmingly present in the sections of prose dialogue. Reeves has not yet assimilated these disparate influences to the point where they serve a style of his own. One evidence of this is an occasional incongruity between matter and manner. For example, the surface of certain ruminative passages in verse is altogether too oblique and complicated for the substance of the author's thought.

Another kind of problem is posed by the method of characterization. The audience's response to the people in the drama is rigorously controlled by means of ironic commentary. This commentary is delivered not only by a detached narrator but in many instances by a character who himself reflects in the third person upon his own nature. The device is theatrically successful but it tends ultimately to produce the effect of caricature. The characters too often appear deprived of the possibilities of freedom and hence of their human stature. In so far as they are reduced to the level of determined objects, they seem simply ludicrous or pitiful.

Nevertheless in its technical assurance and its often moving treatment of a large theme, *A Beach of Strangers* is a considerable achievement.

Important episodes from Canadian history have always appealed to native playwrights concerned to promote directly a sense of cultural identity. Mr. Coulter's *Riel* (1962) is the most recent instance of this kind of drama. (Charles Mair's *Tecumseh* is a notable early example.) Coulter's play is in two parts which trace the major phases of the Northwest Rebellion. The protagonist's trial and execution constitute the play's climactic concluding scenes.

There is much in *Riel* to praise. The play is designed for production on a bare stage with a minimum of properties. This allows the dramatist maximum freedom for presenting events which historically are separated widely in space and time. Moreover in the absence of any fixed set, one brief scene follows another with a rapidity which generates excitement and holds one's interest. Although the panoramic technique entails in some instances a certain sacrifice of character to external action, Coulter's portrait of Riel himself is complex and powerful. He emerges as an enigmatic but entirely convincing blend of simplicity, ruthlessness, piety, fanaticism, and nobility; in short, as a theatrically fascinating figure.

The play has weaknesses. Too many of the Englishmen, particularly the officers and men of the British army, are caricatured in the standard, tedious manner. Moreover, it is doubtful whether the scenes which require crowds and spectacle could be made quite credible in any medium except film. More serious is the playwright's failure to suggest successfully the wider implications of the action. Much of the excitement of *Riel* results from a skilful dramatization of historical events which, in outline at least, are familiar to any informed audience. What is lacking is a sense that these events have been sufficiently disciplined and exploited to serve some insight into Canadian society or some more general view of human experience. To an extent, especially in the trial scene, this transfiguration of an historical record into a significant dramatic fiction has taken place. Unfortunately, a good deal of the play gives the impression that the author has capitulated too readily to his somewhat intransigent source material.

When all criticisms have been made, however, *Riel* remains much the best play of its type to be written in Canada since Confederation.

Without much question, the most arrestingly individual voice among contemporary Canadian playwrights belongs to James Reaney whose *The Killdeer and Other Plays* appeared in 1962. This volume contains, in addition to the title work, a brief masque for one performer, the libretto of an opera, *Night Blooming Cereus* (for which John Beckwith has composed music), and one other play, *The Sun and the Moon*. Another early piece, *The Easter Egg*, is not included in this collection.

Reaney's genre is pastoral comedy but his buoyant, wayward drama eludes categories. The geographical context, like that of much of Reaney's best verse, is small town Ontario, but in these plays both landscape and character are strangely transfigured. As one might expect, there are obvious stylistic and thematic parallels between Reaney's lyric poetry and his works for the stage. Predictably also, both the strengths and the limitations of the plays proceed from the fact that he is in the first place an eloquent and original poet, still, as yet, experimenting with dramatic modes. It is unrewarding and somewhat inappropriate therefore to dissect these plays too precisely into the traditional components of plot, character, theme, and so forth. The force of much of Reaney's best drama springs from patterns of imagery and the moods these generate. This is particularly true of *The Killdeer*, Reaney's most ambitious play, in which themes are projected and conflicting characters define themselves through sets of images expressive of such large antitheses as innocence and experience, eternity and time, fertility and death.

The tangled wealth of character and incident in *The Killdeer* defies summary. In so far as it is legitimate to isolate a single theme, the action concerns the quest for maturity, or more exactly the movement from a vulnerable and imperfect innocence to experiential wisdom, first by Harry, the mother-ridden adolescent, and then by Eli, a youth who has retreated to infantilism under the impact of traumatic shock. A corollary theme, the initiation of the tender consciousness into the repellent mysteries of the fallen world (a central motif in *The Red Heart*, Reaney's first book of verse), appears in *The Easter Egg* and, less prominently, in *The Sun and the Moon*.

James Reaney's qualities as a poet are rare; his faults as a dramatist commonplace. The necessity for a tolerably unified action sometimes escapes him. In the exuberance of his invention, for example, two or three separate plays jostle and compete within the loose structural confines of *The Killdeer*. He has not, moreover, mastered the technique of artful exposition and too frequently he dissipates the effect of potentially powerful scenes in superfluous or unstageworthy dialogue. More seriously, the various levels, symbolic, fantastic, naturalistic, on which certain of his characters are conceived (Madame Fay in *The Killdeer*, or Kenneth in *The Easter Egg*) fail to coincide, and as a result their effectiveness on any level diminishes. Finally, although Reaney is adept at farce and scenes of poignant charm, he has shown little capacity to project strong emotion. This would not necessarily be a matter for criticism except that such plays as *The Killdeer* and *The Easter Egg*, in spite of their comic framework, revolve about acts of great violence and horror. The imaginative perspective, however, from which these pieces are written tends to deny the reality of these acts and hence to nullify the sympathetic response of the audience towards the characters who are menaced by them.

Nevertheless, amid (for the most part) the grey wastes of Canadian drama, Reaney's plays shine with a peculiar brilliance. Not the least of his achievements is to have made, in a variety of dramatic forms, imaginative sense out of one geographical area of Ontario.

At present, it is hard to discern any significant continuity or developing pattern in the course of Canadian drama since 1920. There are, it is true, tenuous points of contact between such figures as Denison and Davies, and certain themes appear and reappear in the drama of this period. For example, as we have noticed, many of the plays set in a rural context have at their centre the struggle of the protagonists with an intimidating natural environment, while several of those set in the city present in some form the struggle between the exuberant, creative individual and a censorious life-denying society. In both cases, it is the precise quality of the conflict which gives these plays, the better ones at least, their "distinctively Canadian" character. However, the overriding impression one receives from the last four decades of drama in Canada is of a group of playwrights, some with considerable gifts, separated primarily not by space and time but by the absence of a common dramatic tradition, a tradition that may be accepted or challenged, but within which action produces reaction. In an important sense, the playwright in this country has hardly anything either to follow or to repudiate. He must begin each time to build from the bottom and in such circumstances it takes a dramatist of formidable energy and skill to build very high.

This problem is related to a wider and more profound one. Francis Fergusson has pointed out in his *Idea of a Theater* that what characterizes modern drama in general is the bewildering variety of partial perspectives on the human situation it affords. The modern theatre, unlike that of Sophocles, Shakespeare, or Racine, for a great number of complex reasons can no longer provide a comprehensive and coherent image of the age. Because Canada shares as deeply as any nation in the break-up of the kind of metaphysical, moral, and social order which formed the matrix for these older modes of theatre, the demand for a dramatist whose work will present a total and decisive revelation of life in this country will not readily be satisfied.

Any final evaluation of the significance and stature of Canadian drama will necessarily depend on the criteria one chooses to employ. Judged by national standards the accomplishment of Canadian playwrights is not inconsiderable. Canadian novelists taken as a group have done better; Canadian poets much better; but it may be argued that the dramatists constitute a respectable third. Certainly drama in Canada compares favourably with that of other Commonwealth nations. Judged however by an undiluted, international standard—a level of dramatic excellence set and intermittently sustained by countries with a flourishing national theatre and secure dramatic tradition, the achievement of Canadian playwrights is distinctly unimpressive. Some explanations have been offered in the foregoing account. Behind all these reasons is simply a perplexing failure of the imagination; a failure to capture in the art of the theatre the complicated intensities of human experience as it is subtly or strikingly coloured in the context of this dominion. Dr. Claude Bissell has observed that by and large Canadian novelists have had difficulty in seeing Canada as a human society. A comparable incapacity in even greater measure has afflicted the dramatists. In the absence of this vision, our drama (with isolated exceptions), assessed against the highest standard, has been imitative and curiously irrelevant. It is in the theatre therefore that the long deferred promise of cultural maturity is awaited with keenest anxiety and expectation.

The future of the theatre will of course be influenced by developments in the mass media. C.B.C. radio has had a distinguished record in the field of drama. Andrew Allan's "Stage" series, for instance, maintained a consistently high standard and did much to foster public interest in good plays. The theatre may continue to benefit from scripts written in the first place for radio (Len Petersen's *Burlap Bags* is an example) which are then revised for stage production. It is not yet clear whether television will have equally desirable repercussions. There are some, no doubt, who would concur with Paddy Chayevsky's remarkable opinion that television will emerge as the basic theatre of the twentieth century. However, such volumes as Arthur Hailey's *Close Up: On Writing for Television* only prove that Canadian playwrights have yet to investigate the potentialities of the new medium.

But it is impossible to predict the ultimate quality and influence of television drama. If dramatists emerge who prove capable of meeting the challenge it presents, changes may occur. The vast audience reached today only by television may in such circumstances have its collective taste shaped and sharpened to the point where it will seek once again the experience of theatre in its traditional form.

II. THEATRE, 1920–1960

The Background: Commercial Theatre from Abroad

In one sense Canadian theatre, that most insecure of the arts in this country, flourished with greatest vigour during the later nineteenth century and in the years prior to World War I. This was the era of the celebrated stars, American and British, who toured the extent of Canada supported either by their own companies or else relying on local talent in each town or city to provide a supporting cast. Edmund Kean, Charles Macready, Edwin Booth, Henry Irving, Sara Bernhardt, James O'Neill, Ellen Terry, Johnston Forbes-Robertson, Robert B. Mantell, Cyril Maude, John Martin-Harvey, George Arliss, Minnie Fiske, Seymour Hicks, John Barrymore, and other illustrious performers of the period visited Canada, some many times. It was during these years, moreover, that theatres sprang up all over the country to accomodate the touring groups. Only the larger centres like Toronto, Montreal, or Winnipeg could afford to build elaborate opera houses, but every community of any size whatever had some sort of structure, almost invariably grand in name if not design. These theatres dispensed an extraordinarily democratic sort of entertainment. The appeal was to every age group, economic bracket, and social level, and there was a generous disregard by public and often by actor of the distinction between varieties of amusement. For example, Sir John Martin-Harvey relates without comment how in Vancouver he played *Hamlet* and *A Cigarette Maker's Romance* (a romantic melodrama adapted from a novel by Marion Crawford) on successive nights, both to overflowing houses. From roughly 1870 to 1914 then, theatre in Canada was in a way more robust and much more an integral part of social life than at any subsequent period.

From another standpoint, of course, these years are of negligible significance. Apart from the physical fact of the playhouses, there was virtually no theatrical activity which bore any organic relation to the Canadian environment. Almost all plays and actors were foreign imports. The few local troupes devoted themselves in the main to a kind of rootless slapstick, although the Marks Brothers also presented melodramas and the wartime Dumbells on occasion included some topical satire in their act. No doubt the example of the visiting stars did something to encourage native Canadians who later gained fame on the stage, but with success such performers as Mary Pickford, Margaret Anglin, Walter Huston, and Raymond Massey left Canada permanently to become citizens of New York or London. Because of lack of opportunity at home, until quite recently this departure of the talented and ambitious has been the rule. The absence, moreover, in many regions of any native company of even modest pretentions made the aspiring playwright's job next to impossible. There was no way he could learn the vital practical aspects of his craft by working in the theatre and seeing his plays performed. Although the considerable upsurge of nationalistic sentiment generated first by Confederation and then World War I resulted in a number of dramas, most were written only for the study, and none was really adequate for the stage.

The years following World War I marked the breakdown of the touring system. Vastly increased travelling expenses and the advent of the talking pictures which offered the mass audience greater sensationalism at less cost, are two important causes among many which led to the collapse of "the

Road." During the twenties when visits from stars and touring companies were becoming less and less frequent, an attempt was made by certain repertory companies, mainly English, to supply the market. They too eventually fell on evil days but for a while they endeavoured to give the public the best of those modern plays which had proved successful in New York or London. Of these companies Vaughan Glaser's established itself most firmly, playing six years in Toronto, from 1921 to 1926. Other resident repertory groups that achieved some measure of success included Cameron Matthews English Players, Charles Hampden's British Players, the English Repertory Company, and the New Empire Company. (These were reassuring names to those Canadian theatre-goers who welcomed the invasion of the commercial British theatre as protection from what they regarded as the less palatable vulgarities of the American.) However, by the late 1920's the prospects for the professional stage in Canada were very unpromising indeed. The films had changed decisively the entertainment routine of the nation which, lacking a native theatre, had no secure tradition of theatre attendance. Many of the old playhouses were converted into cinemas and the new managers were naturally reluctant to rent their premises to competition. Others were torn down to provide space for offices and car parks or were destroyed by fire or time. Only the Royal Alexandra in Toronto and Her Majesty's in Montreal survive to this day, fulfilling by and large their original function as touring houses.

Amateur Theatre: The Dominion Drama Festival

Simultaneous with the decline in the number of companies from abroad was the quickening of an unpretentious native theatre. Amateur play acting has a long history in Canada dating back to the Garrick Club of Hamilton founded in 1862, to theatricals put on by garrison officers of the British Army posted in Halifax, and even further to a performance of a play by Marc Lescarbot presented in 1606 in honour of Sieur de Poutrincourt. Three hundred years later in 1907 the Governor-General instituted the Earl Grey Music and Dramatic Trophy Competition "for the encouragement of dramatic arts throughout the dominion." This competition persisted for five years until the departure of Earl Grey. After 1918, the Little Theatre movement, as it came to be called, gained great momentum. The reasons are not far to seek. The nationalistic impulses reinforced by Canada's role in the Great War intensified the desire for some form of national self-expression in this as in the other arts. Moreover, to concerned minorities everywhere it was becoming apparent that if they were to have any legitimate theatre at all, they must fend for themselves. The movement in Canada, too, was influenced by the growth of the Little Theatre in America and expressed the same protest against the stultifying impact of routine films and the chronic surrender of art to commerce on Broadway.

Drama groups proliferated everywhere. The Ottawa Drama League was formed in 1913 and had seventeen hundred members by 1928. The Arts and Letters Players Club of Toronto, which had been active since 1905, provided some of the impetus which led to the founding of Hart House Theatre in 1919 under the aegis of Vincent Massey. This admirably equipped stage on the campus of the University of Toronto immediately became a focal point for the creative energies of such figures as Roy Mitchell, its first director, Arthur Lismer, Lawren Harris, and Merrill Denison. Their work was continued under a series of able directors including Bertram Forsythe, Carroll Aikins, Edgar Stone, and Nancy Pyper. Carroll Aikins himself had previously established the Home Theatre on his farm in British Columbia's Okanagan Valley and was the first to organize a group of actors called the Canadian Players which toured the neighbouring villages. Other community theatres appeared in rapid succession. By 1930 the Montreal Repertory Theatre was active under the exceptionally able direction of Martha Allan, and Vancouver, Edmonton, Calgary, Regina, Winnipeg, and many smaller centres had flourishing drama societies. One of the most notable was formed in London in 1934 when four separate groups amalgamated and later acquired the Grand Theatre, a playhouse built in the hey-day of the touring companies. In recent times a number of foreign stars, including John Gielgud and Michael Redgrave, have chosen this theatre as a starting point for their tours of North America.

Inevitably the kind of plays produced, the seriousness of purpose, and the standard of achievement varied, and continues to vary, greatly from group to group. But quite often in the best little theatres dedication and talent had rewarding results. Moreover, because the people involved were in it for the love of the thing, the plays presented covered a much wider range than was common or possible on the professional stage. A list of representative productions during the 1920's includes such authors as Pirandello, Schnitzler, Capek, Claudel, Molière, Ben Jonson, Goethe, Maeterlinck, Rice, Yeats, and Synge, with Shaw, Ibsen and Shakespeare as hardy perennials. For the first time, too, the Canadian playwright had an opportunity to see his work performed and was encouraged by competitions sponsored by such organizations as the Canadian Authors Association and the I.O.D.E., as well as the little theatres themselves. For example, it was the policy of Hart House Theatre to stage at least one Canadian play each year.

During the thirties in spite of the depression which gave the *coup de grâce* to the touring professionals, amateur theatre continued to thrive. If anything it grew for a few years in richness and variety. In Toronto, for instance, the Playwrights' Studio Group devoted itself to the development of native dramatists, Herman Voaden's Theatre Studio Group experimented with techniques of expressionism, while a plea for an ideologically committed drama came from the Theatre of Action, whose spokesmen, vehement Marxists all, denounced the existing Little Theatre as an enfeebled expression of a moribund society.

In 1932 this diverse theatrical activity was further stimulated and to an extent co-ordinated through the establishment of a kind of national theatre. Local and provincial competitions had been in effect for some time, but in the autumn of 1932 the Earl of Bessborough called a meeting of representatives from drama groups across the land and the Dominion Drama Festival was launched. The country was divided into regions and in each of these preliminary competitions were held in the spring. The first finals took place at Ottawa in May 1933. Except for an interruption during the war, the Festival has been an annual event ever since, expanding and consolidating itself through the years, and has served a number of important purposes. It has created a kind of tenuous theatrical tradition in a country extremely poor in this respect. It has helped to stimulate all aspects of Canadian theatre and maintain standards of performance most notably during the long period when the professional stage was almost non-existent. To some extent, difficult to calculate, it has served as a unifying cultural force enabling widely different groups to meet each year in a common endeavour. It has provided, moreover, a valuable opportunity to young designers, actors, and directors, amateur and professional, to gain knowledge and experience. The Festival, however, has had to contend with certain disadvantages. The level of production, although high as a rule, has inevitably been influenced by the fact that the majority of participants are amateurs, dedicated perhaps, but unable to devote full time and energy to the arts of the theatre. Also as the site of the Festival changes each year every group but the local one must accommodate its production to an unfamiliar, sometimes unsuitable, stage with a minimum of rehearsal time. Most seriously perhaps the personnel of the competing groups is in continual flux from year to year, an unavoidable circumstance that has militated against the type of ideal performance only approached by an able company working together over a long period.

Nevertheless, the D.D.F. with its verve and atmosphere of excitement has been a significant phenomenon. It has offered in the past incentive to amateur groups everywhere, and has provided in part a groundwork for the development of professional theatre.

Professional Theatre

Except for the extraordinary phenomenon of Stratford, indigenous professional theatre has had an uncertain and somewhat dispiriting history. Although such companies as the John Holden Players (now defunct) and the Brae Manor Theatre at Knowlton, Quebec, which closed in 1956 were active as early as the mid-thirties, professional theatre emerged in the main after the Second World War. Its growth offers a parallel to the rise of the Little

Theatre after the First. The centres of professionalism have been chiefly the larger cities—Vancouver, Montreal, Ottawa, and Toronto. However, the failure record of the various enterprises is a melancholy index of the indifference with which the mass of Canadians regard the legitimate stage. In British Columbia Sidney Risk's Everyman Theatre, founded in 1946 with the intention of building up a repertory of Canadian plays, is no longer operating. The Totem Theatre in Vancouver lasted two seasons. The most permanent venture in the West has been Theatre under the Stars which is subsidized by the city of Vancouver. At Ottawa, the Canadian Repertory Theatre, an outgrowth of the Stage Society, collapsed in 1956 after five years. Toronto, the most active centre of English-speaking theatre, has had the highest mortality rate. The Earle Grey Players (whose annual Shakespearean Festival pre-dated Stratford by five years) have now departed. The Avenue, the Lansdowne, and, most recently, the Civic Square are some of the theatres which have been compelled to close.

However, there have been real achievements. Of particular interest was the founding of the New Play Society in Toronto in 1947 by Dora Mavor Moore and her son Mavor. Their purpose was to develop "a living Canadian Theatre on a permanent but non-profit basis" and for a few years the N.P.S. was very active indeed. It used as a nucleus C.B.C. radio actors, supplementing this group with amateurs from Hart House Theatre and elsewhere. The facilities available to the N.P.S.—the little Museum theatre—were very inadequate, but its productions displayed singular energy and conviction. One especially admirable feature of the N.P.S. was its willingness to gamble on Canadian plays. Morley Callaghan's "Going Home," Harry Boyle's "The Inheritance," John Coulter's *Riel*, Mavor Moore's "Who's Who," "Narrow Passage" by Andrew Allan and later Donald Harron's adaptation of Earle Birney's novel *Turvey* all received their first (and in most cases their last) performance by the N.P.S. The Society's audience, though loyal, was never large and in latter years its activities have been restricted to a drama school and an annual review, *Spring Thaw*, which has regularly proven enormously popular and profitable. *Spring Thaw* continues now independently under the direction of Mavor Moore.

At first glance it is perhaps surprising that audiences which by and large shy away from the conventional traffic of the stage should find the satirical revue, a relatively sophisticated kind of theatre, so suited to their taste. Much of the reason is the refreshing irreverence of satire in a nation which has tended to solemnity. These revues, moreover, have provided an astringent commentary on Canadian life which is not to be found in imported theatrical fare.

The years after the war saw the appearance of numerous summer stock companies across the country: the Kingston International Players (who first produced Robertson Davies' *Fortune My Foe*), the Mountain Playhouse in

Montreal, the Red Barn at Lake Simcoe, several in the Niagara peninsula, one at Peterborough, and others in the Maritimes and the West. While providing an excellent training ground for actors they too have had a precarious existence and many have either changed hands repeatedly or disappeared altogether. One of the most durable has been the Straw Hat Players, formed in 1948 by the Davis brothers. In 1953, with the aim of making their venture a year-long project, the Davises took over a Toronto movie house and established the Crest Theatre. In spite of a good percentage of fine productions it too has had great difficulty in finding consistent audiences. So much so that the Davises have found it necessary to transform it into a non-profit foundation, thus making it eligible for Canada Council support. Another promising development in Toronto has been the emergence of George Luscombe's Theatre Workshop founded on the principles of group theatre associated with Joan Littlewood. In the prairie provinces the most successful professional venture has been the Manitoba Theatre Centre under the direction of John Hirsch.

One of the factors that has assisted the professional theatre in Canada, particularly the actor, has been the C.B.C. Any competition the C.B.C. may have offered the legitimate stage has been outweighed by the opportunities it has provided, especially through television. It has enabled an increasing number of actors to earn a living, meagre for most, abundant for a few, at their profession the year around. Thus they have been free to accept less lucrative engagements in the theatre proper. Moreover television, penetrating into houses everywhere, has exposed a number of actors consistently enough that a few have something of the status of national stars, and the public will more readily turn out when these figures appear on the stage. Work, money, and a measure of prestige: these three essentials the C.B.C. is capable of affording the Canadian actor. There are, of course, certain drawbacks. Television, which most of the time demands a muted, casual, ultra-realistic acting style is of only limited value to the actor primarily interested in the stage.

Stratford

Undoubtedly, the most spectacular and significant event in the history of Canadian professional theatre was the launching of the Festival at Stratford, Ontario, in July 1953. The danger, of course, was that such a festival would emerge as a pale imitation of the famous English original. That it has not done so is owing in particular to the highly independent talents of Sir Tyrone Guthrie and Miss Tanya Moiseiwitsch who together designed the superb stage, and in general to the feeling of all concerned that imitation was as impossible as it was pointless. Although the policy has been to import one or two widely acclaimed actors from abroad each season, the bulk of the company has been Canadian and something like a native Shakespearian style is in the process of developing. The verse is spoken with a conversational vitality which at its most successful avoids both the operatic excesses of English delivery and the harshness of American. The nature of the stage, too, has tested the ingenuity of the directors and prompted them to experiment in deploying their actors. There are, naturally, criticisms to be made. Sir Tyrone's presence has been of incomparable value, but some of his more flamboyant mannerisms have tended to haunt subsequent productions. The subtler values of the text have too often been sacrificed to speed and spectacle. However these are faults which may well be corrected as the Festival matures artistically. Certainly Stratford at its best is very good indeed. Such productions as *All's Well That Ends Well*, *The Merchant of Venice* and *Twelfth Night* have worked a unique magic, enriching incalculably the Canadian cultural scene.

From the first it has been recognized that if Stratford is to approximate a national theatre it must be more than just an elegant stage devoted to Shakespeare. Clearly other playwrights, including whenever possible Canadians, must be represented. A move towards widening the scope of the Festival was made in 1955 with an impressive presentation of *Oedipus Rex* which was taken the following year to the Edinburgh Festival. On this occasion *Oedipus* was accompanied by a production of *Henry V* starring Christopher Plummer, probably the first unambiguously Canadian actor of international repute. Another offshoot of Stratford was the Canadian Players, a two-unit company which tours America and Canada in the winter months bringing theatre, necessarily in a somewhat austere form, to outlying communities across the country. One of the motives behind the formation of the Canadian company was the desire to offset in some small way the cultural isolation of the various regions of this country. Stratford, too, is a product in part of an increasingly vigorous nationalism in the arts. In the past America, England, and Europe have too frequently been accepted by Canadians as the exclusive sources for standards of dramatic excellence. Behind the foundation of the Festival Theatre is the impulse to establish such standards within the borders of Canada.

Stratford has its imperfections and it certainly will not alter overnight the unsatisfactory character of the total theatrical situation. It is however an auspicious development which has materially hastened the day when drama and the theatre will be at least on a par with the other arts in Canada. Most important, the prestige attendant upon the production of an original play at Stratford, particularly if it meets the challenge of the Festival's arena stage, may stimulate native dramatists to new endeavour, which may in turn do something to rectify perhaps the most depressing feature of theatre in Canada: the lack of any vital and continuing relation between theatrical activity and the work of the Canadian playwright.

35. Fiction
1920-1940

DESMOND PACEY

LOOKING BACK from the vantage point of the mid-century, we are apt to see Canadian fiction of the twenty years between the two World Wars as a barren area peopled only by Frederick Philip Grove, Morley Callaghan, and Mazo de la Roche, with perhaps a few small figures of historical romancers such as Frederick Niven and Laura Goodman Salverson grouped around them. A more detailed scrutiny, however, now for the first time made feasible by the publication of R. E. Watters' *Check List of Canadian Literature* (1959), reveals that the novels and novelists were surprisingly numerous. In these twenty years, some seven hundred novels were published by Canadians, and to the readers of that time many of them appeared as important as, if not more important than, the few novelists whose reputations have survived.

In spite of this great bulk of fiction, however, it is still true to say that Grove, Callaghan, and to a lesser extent Mazo de la Roche were the most significant writers, and that their joint achievement is almost equivalent to the total achievement of the period. One reads on and on through the hundreds of novels, hoping against hope that some forgotten masterpiece will reveal itself. The revelation never comes. A few forgotten novels have virtues that lift them above the level of mediocrity, and elicit their meed of praise, but even the best of them fall short of the level of Grove and Callaghan.

What was the achievement of the fiction of this period? It was certainly not to leave behind a legacy of imperishable work, novels which caught forever the very note and trick of Canadian life in the period. In view of the virtual monopoly of romanticism in Canadian fiction of the nineteenth and early twentieth centuries, this would have been to expect too much. All that the best novelists of this period were able to do was to begin the process of turning the eyes of readers and fellow-writers from a fabled past or a romanticized present towards the actual conditions of Canadian life. If this period deserves remembering at all, it is as the time when a few novelists first seriously tried to come to terms with their Canadian environment, and to find a suitable style in which to seal the bargain.

By far the great majority of the novelists of these twenty years, however, made no such effort. Most of them conceived the novel and the short story merely as media of light entertainment, and contented themselves with providing some form of romantic escape.

There were many forms of this escapism. Some of them had no connection with Canada, but were merely re-tracings of escape routes that had been well mapped by writers elsewhere. Novels about the mysterious Orient, for example, were produced in quantity. The prolific Lily Adams Beck (d. 1931) wrote a number of novels with Oriental settings (*The Key of Dreams*, 1922; *The Treasure of Ho*, 1924; *The Garden of Vision*, 1929; etc.), as did James Livingstone Stewart (*The Laughing Buddha*, 1925, etc.), Harold Kingsley (*Kong*, 1927), and Florence Ayscough (*A Chinese Mirror*, 1925, etc.).

Another standard escape route, that into the realm of crime, detection, and mystery, was also followed assiduously by Canadian writers of this time. "Luke Allan" (William Lacey Amy) was perhaps the most prolific Canadian producer in this genre, publishing well over a score of novels with such titles as *The Ghost Murder* and *Black Opal*. Other mystery writers with long lists were Frank L. Packard (1877–1942) (*The Devil's Mantle*, 1927; *Shanghai Jim*, 1928; etc.), Guy E. Morton (1884–1948) (*Black Gold*, 1924; *Ashes of Murder*, 1935; etc.), Hopkins Moorhouse (*The Golden Scarab*, 1926; etc.), Maurice B. Dix (b. 1889) (*The Dartmoor Mystery*, 1935; etc.), Pearl Foley (d. 1953) (*The Grome Mine Mystery*, 1933; etc.), and Hulburt Footner (*Antennae*, 1926; etc.).

Rather similar to these novels of crime and detection were those dealing with amorous intrigue and high adventure. Novels of this sort, the staples of the lending library trade, were written in quantity by Elizabeth Sprigge (*Faint Amorist*, 1927; *Castle in Andalusia*, 1935; etc.), John Murray Gibbon (1875–1952) (*Pagan Love*, 1922; *Eyes of a Gipsy*, 1926; etc.), Percy Gomery (1881–1960) (*Curve, Go Slow: A Romance of the Pacific Coast*, 1927; etc.), F. W. Wallace (1886–1958) (*Captain Salvation*, 1925; etc.), Grace Murray Atkin (*That Which is Passed*, 1923; etc.), Virna Sheard (d. 1943) (*Fortune Turns Her Wheel*, 1929; etc.), Robert Watson (1882–1948) (*The Spoilers of the Valley*, 1921; etc.), Madge Macbeth (*The Patterson Limit*, 1923; etc.), Douglas Leader Durkin (*The Lobstick Trail*, 1921; etc.), and Robert Allison Hood (*The Quest of Alistair*, 1921; etc.).

More specifically Canadian in inspiration were the escape novels of another variety: those treating of life in the Far North, and especially of the lives of the Eskimos. Here indeed was an opportunity to deal realistically with a way of life unfamiliar to writers of other countries, and something really compelling might have been made out of the strange terrain, the long dark winters and short vivid summers, the small tenacious inhabitants of the North. In fact, however, with the partial exception of some of the short stories of Alan

Sullivan (1868-1947), the opportunity was completely missed. Frank J. Tate (*Red Wilderness*, 1938), Robert Watson (1882-1948) (*High Hazard*, 1928), Kenneth Conibear (*Northland Footprints*, 1936), and Samuel Alexander White (*Ambush*, 1920; *Code of the Northwest*, 1940; etc.) saw only material for melodrama in the life of this region. Even Alan Sullivan packed most of his many novels with melodramatic incidents, but in some of the short stories in *The Passing of Oul-I-But* (1913) and *Under the Northern Lights* (1926) he did capture something of the authentic atmosphere and spirit of the North.

Closely allied to novels of the North, and indeed sometimes overlapping with them, were romantic novels of the West, usually known as "westerns." Although the Canadian West was never "wild" in the sense that many parts of the western United States were, this did not deter a few writers from trying to invest it with glamour and excitement. "Luke Allan," whom we have already encountered as a writer of mysteries, also wrote such "westerns" as *Blue Pete: Half Breed* (1921), and A. M. Chisholm (1872-1960) made a career of doing so, producing between 1911 and 1929 a dozen novels including *The Boss of Wind River* (1911), *Prospectin' Fools* (1927), and *Red Bill* (1929). As we might expect, the Mounted Police were the focus for many of these Canadian "westerns." Harwood Steele (*Spirit of Iron*, 1923; *The Ninth Circle*, 1928; etc.) specialized in stories of the Mounties, and there were many Canadian novels with such titles as *The Case of Constable Shields*, *The Luck of the Mounted*, and *Campbell of the Mounties*.

By far the most popular types of escape literature, however, were the two that have become traditional in Canadian fiction: the historical romance, and the regional idyll.

Historical Romances

Historical romances dealing with almost every phase of human history were produced in Canada during these decades. British, French, biblical, Scottish, and Roman history all found their exponents. The most popular Canadian historical subjects were the French régime in Quebec, and the early history of the West. The history of Ontario and the Maritimes was not entirely overlooked, but it was given relatively little attention.

The most prolific purveyor of historical romances during the period was "E. Barrington," whom we have met as a writer about the Orient under her real name of Lily Adams Beck. Mrs. Beck, indeed, had two pseudonyms: not only was she "E. Barrington," she was also, in her novels dealing with the Mediterranean area, "Louise Moresby." Her total output of novels, under her three names, was in the vicinity of thirty. A resident of Victoria, B.C., she first won fame under the name of "E. Barrington" with her historical romance *The Divine Lady* (1924). She was obviously a woman of wide geographical and historical knowledge, for she wrote novels with equal success about England and Egypt, France and China, Anne Boleyn and Lord Byron, Mary Queen of Scots and the Empress Josephine. But her work, so apparently disparate, had one unifying thread: the bright thread of love. *The Divine Lady* has as its theme the love of Lord Nelson for Lady Hamilton; *Glorious Apollo* (1925) deals with the love life of Lord Byron; *The Exquisite Perdita* (1926) chronicles the loves of the notorious Perdita Robinson; *The Thunderer* (1927) lays bare the love life of Napoleon and Josephine; *The Empress of Hearts* (1928) provides intimate glimpses of the affairs of Marie Antoinette; and the whole series reached its inevitable climax in *The Laughing Queen* (1929), a record of the delightful amours of that queen of lovers, Cleopatra of Egypt!

It may seem absurd to give so much space to the forgotten author of amorous pot-boilers. Her career, however, might legitimately be claimed to be part of the literary history of Canada as an example of how readily the Canadian literary public of the twenties could mistake grandiosity for greatness. For the astonishing fact is that "E. Barrington" was taken seriously by her contemporaries. Duncan Campbell Scott, then President of the Royal Society of Canada, reviewed her 1922 collection of Oriental tales, *The Ninth Vibration*, and praised it highly: "We know it to be a competent and beautiful book and we are neither glad nor sorry that there is nothing specially Canadian about it. We know that it is a real addition to our literature and that is all we are concerned with." The *Canadian Bookman* declared of *The Divine Lady*: "At last a Canadian . . . has written a novel of distinction destined for a high place among those which endure." The *Canadian Annual Review* of 1924–25 called the same novel "the book of the year from every point of view." The Byron novel, *Glorious Apollo*, was given for review to Frederick Philip Grove, and even he, while expressing scepticism about historical novels generally and urging Mrs. Beck to write about the present, opined that "this book has great merits." In March 1927 the editors of the *Canadian Bookman* were able to report proudly that "Mrs. L. Adams Beck, who has been spending some time in London, is receiving great recognition. She is the centre of attraction in the literary world there." It was left for the *Canadian Forum*, in March 1930, to prick this bubble of over-estimation and reduce Mrs. L. Adams Beck, alias E. Barrington, alias Louise Moresby, to her proper size. Reviewing *The Laughing Queen*, the *Forum* said sensibly, "It is primarily a popular novel. . . . The style is smooth and easy, and on the whole it is a readable, amusing and interesting book with enough in it to hold one's interest for a few hours."

Other historical romancers of this period who dealt with extra-Canadian subjects included H. J. O. Bedford-Jones (1887–1949), whose specialty was French history (*D'Artagnan*, 1928; *Rodomont: A Romance of Mont St.*

Michel in the Days of Louis XIV, 1926; etc.), W. G. Hardy, a professor of classics and ancient history who chose either classical or biblical themes, and Isabel M. Paterson, who in *The Singing Season* (1924) and other novels dealt with the history of Old Spain. The only one of these who deserves somewhat more extended notice is W. G. Hardy. His first novel, *Father Abraham* (1935), is the story of Abraham's life from boyhood to old age, and stresses especially his love for Sarai and Hagar and his search for the true God, Yahweh. The latter purports to be the main theme, but the major emphasis actually falls on Abraham's amorous adventures. The novel is replete with lively action and vigorous characters, but there is little depth of thought and scarcely any grace of style. In his foreword, Hardy says, "Time makes characters and events legendary. Under its alchemy Sarai and Abraham have become figures of such heroic proportions and of such far-off majesty that they have lost their reality. We have forgotten that they were people like ourselves. But they, too, must have known hunger and simple joys and satisfactions and all the thousand and one monotonies and trivialities of which the sum total is everyday life. . . ." The trouble is that Hardy makes them all too human. It is hard to believe that such a legend of spiritual greatness would have sprung up around as ordinarily sensual a figure as Abraham appears here.

For his second novel, *Turn Back the River* (1938), Hardy chose ancient Rome in the days of Catiline and Clodia. Here his preoccupation with physical love continued, and led one critic to describe him as "the bold champion of a fleshly school of Canadian fiction." The novel attempts to defend Catiline, to uphold him as an intelligent aristocrat dedicated to defending the republican ideal, and to vilify Cicero as the spokesman of tyrannical reaction and economic royalism. This more serious theme, however, is greatly obscured by the vast amount of amorous intrigue and dalliance. Hardy seemed unable to decide whether he was writing a serious historical novel or a pot-boiler for the drug store trade.

This dichotomy of intention has continued to weaken Hardy's later novels, *All the Trumpets Sounded* (1942), which deals with the life and loves of Moses, *The Unfulfilled* (1952), his only venture into the study of contemporary Canadian life, and *City of Libertines* (1958), another attempt to portray Roman civilization in its decadence. It is in his short stories that Hardy's more restrained and sensitive responses find expression; his novels have vigour and crude energy, but they are too often coarse and flamboyant.

The great bulk of Canadian historical fiction, in this and indeed in all periods, dealt not with ancient Rome but with New France. Why the French régime in Canada has continued to cast such a spell over Canadian writers and readers is a most interesting question. From the days of Mrs. Leprohon in the mid-nineteenth century, through Gilbert Parker in the late nineteenth century, and up to the present, it has remained the favourite hunting-ground for seekers after romance. Perhaps English-Canadians are haunted by a sense of guilt over the Conquest; perhaps they are conscious of the relative drabness of English-Canadian society and yearn for the colour and gaiety which they can imagine to have characterized *l'ancien régime*; perhaps this quest for the French past is an indirect protest against the materialism and money-grubbing of the Anglo-Saxon present. Whatever the reason, the fact remains.

Novelists who produced historical romances of the French régime between the wars included Leslie Gordon Barnard (1890–1961), who was perhaps best known for the sensitive short stories contained in *One Generation Away* (1931) and *So Near is Grandeur* (1945) but whose novel *Jancis* (1935) is a romantic study of life in old Quebec; Philip Child, author of *The Village of Souls* (1933) and of several later novels on contemporary themes; Joseph P. Choquet, author of *Under Canadian Skies* (1922), sub-titled *A French-Canadian Historical Romance*; the prolific Louis Arthur Cunningham (1900–1954), who wrote romances of many times and places but whose *The King's Fool* (1931) is set in the Quebec of Louis XV; Annie Ermatinger Fraser (d. 1930), author of *The Drum of Lanoraye* (1932); Gordon Hill Graham, author of *The Bond Triumphant* (1923); L. C. Servos, author of *Frontenac and the Maid of the Mist* (1927); Alan Sullivan, who in 1941 deserted his Northland specialty to write the very popular French-Canadian romance, *Three Came to Ville Marie*, and Franklin Davey McDowell, who published *The Champlain Road* in 1939. None of these novels deserves separate, detailed treatment. Two or three of them—*The Village of Souls, Three Came to Ville Marie*, and *The Champlain Road*—are more memorable than the others, but they all had their reward in contemporary popularity and few of them are likely to be of permanent interest. It is a mark of the improvement that has subsequently taken place in the quality of Canadian fiction that in the early years of World War II *The Champlain Road* and *Three Came to Ville Marie* were adjudged worthy of the Governor-General's Award, as the best Canadian novels of their respective years.

Rather strangely, in view of their relative youth, the runners-up to French Canada as the most popular venue for historical romances were the Canadian prairies. The Red River settlement, near what is now the city of Winnipeg, was especially popular with novelists. John Herries McCulloch, who was later to write quite a realistic novel entitled *Dark Acres* (1935), began his career in fiction with two such historical romances: *The Men of Kildonan* (1926) and *The Splendid Renegade* (1928). James McGillivray, in *The Frontier Riders* (1925), and B. A. McKelvie (1889–1960) in *Huldowget* (1926), *The Black Canyon* (1927), and *Pelts and Powder* (1929), dealt with the romantic period of early exploration and settlement of the West. Alexander Maitland Stephen (1882–1942), in *The Kingdom of the Sun* (1927), spun a very romantic tale of the early days in British Columbia. But the three writers who were regarded as the leading exponents of this kind of western historical romance were Frederick Niven (1878–1944), "Jane Rolyat" (E. Jean McDougall) and Laura Goodman Salverson (b. 1890).

Many of Frederick Niven's almost two score novels were published prior to 1920 and belong to an earlier section of this history; several of his novels of this inter-war period are set in Scotland and do not belong in the present context; but he does belong here by virtue of his trilogy of novels tracing the historical development of the Canadian prairies: *The Flying Years* (1935), *Mine Inheritance* (1940), and *The Transplanted* (1944). Based on a great amount of detailed historical research, these three novels are attempts to show the processes by which the inhabitants of the West developed from the primitive nomadic life of the Indians to the civilized and settled society of the early twentieth century. They are thus a most ambitious undertaking, and although they fail fully to realize their author's somewhat grandiose intentions they are probably the best historical novels yet produced of and in this area. Their strengths are their documentary accuracy, their liveliness, and their descriptive power: Niven has studied the sources, knows how to tell an anecdote, and has great skill in capturing the appearance and atmosphere of the prairie landscape. But Niven's thematic and documentary approach often gets in the way of his characterization: the characters frequently serve merely as pegs on which historical or thematic material is hung. And his novels are too loosely episodic: he is so anxious to work in all the incidents that his historical research has uncovered that he ignores the novelist's task of selection, arrangement, and development. For all this, his work stands well above the average level of Canadian historical romance: there is in his books a serious attempt to deal with things as they actually were and are, and some sense of style and form.

Frederick Niven's name is still remembered, but that of "Jane Rolyat" (E. Jean McDougall) seems to have been completely forgotten. It is a legitimate piece of Canadian literary history, however, to record that in the early 1930's she was regarded as the chief hope of Canadian fiction. Her first novel, *The Lily of Fort Garry* (1930), was advertised by J. M. Dent and Sons as *The Canadian Novel* in the September 1930 issue of the *Canadian Forum*, and the London reader's enthusiastic assessment of the manuscript was printed in full. The concluding paragraph of the assessment ran as follows: "The book has genuine beauty and charm. . . . Miss Rolyat may easily develop into an accomplished writer of English prose. There is every possibility that she may become the first Canadian novelist of importance." The October issue of the *Forum* quoted S. Morgan Powell of the Montreal *Daily Star* as saying of the novel: "It would be difficult to pick out any emphatic indication that this is a first novel. Its literary quality rather stamps it as a work of one who is at any rate mistress of the art of writing. Its poetic qualities are an integral part of its appeal, and the sheer lyric beauty of much of the writing in no wise detracts from its power as a study of a historic period, as well as of the emotional reactions characteristic of that period."

In June of 1933, Dent took a full-page advertisement in the *Forum* to announce Miss Rolyat's second novel, *Wilderness Walls* (1933). *Wilderness Walls* was announced as the first of a trilogy, in which Miss Rolyat had captured "the stillness and beauty of our own north country"; and excerpts were quoted from enthusiastic reviews in English newspapers. Canadian reviewers of this book were a little more cautious, but it had been given such a build-up that they did not dare to dismiss it outright. E. C. K(yte?) in *Queen's Quarterly* wrote that "The great Canadian novel is yet to be written. Until it arrives we can be glad if there are published no worse tales than *Wilderness Walls*. . . . As a contribution to Canadian fiction the book is noteworthy." Burns Martin, writing in the *Dalhousie Review*, found fault with the style of the novel but concluded warily that "if Miss Rolyat is a good critic of her own work, and is not afraid of labour, the next two volumes may be significant in Canadian fiction." L. A. MacKay, in the *Forum*, had much the same approach: "It is too much to ask that this book be re-written in a less flashy, inaccurate and fatiguing idiom; but one may hope in the remaining books of the trilogy to find a purer style that will give her real qualities freer play." The remaining books of the trilogy, incidentally, seem never to have appeared.

The contemporary reader who, in the light of these assessments, goes back to *The Lily of Fort Garry* and *Wilderness Walls* hoping to discover forgotten masterpieces will be gravely disappointed. The first is not without merit. An historical romance of the Red River Settlement in the mid-nineteenth century, its basic stuff is a reasonably convincing account of the day-to-day life of the settlers. But this basic material is overlaid with two very romantic plots. The heroine, Margaret Moore, called the lily of Fort Garry because of her blonde beauty, has a father who is forever disappearing on mysterious journeys, and it transpires that he is looking for a long-lost brother who is reputed to have acquired great wealth; and the heroine falls in love with a handsome and arrogant half-breed, Roger MacLachlin, with whom she eventually goes off to live in the wilds. The novel does have some documentary value, and some passages of good description, but it fails to fuse realism and romance in its matter, and it fails to be consistent in its style. Miss Rolyat is far too prone to lapse into flowery phrases such as "a wild vanity palpitated through her."

The overly romantic elements present to some degree in *The Lily of Fort Garry* are much more prominent in *Wilderness Walls*. This novel deals with the life of a Hudson's Bay Company post on the shores of Lake Huron in the 1860's. The hero, Vincent Reid, comes out from Montreal as a young apprentice-clerk, to discover that the chief factor is half-mad from grief for his dead wife and that his own predecessor as junior clerk, one McIvor, has given up his job because he is reputed to have inherited great wealth. Out in the nearby woods one day Reid confronts and is attacked by a wild man dressed in Indian fashion, and he eventually finds that this supposed savage is McIvor, who has murdered the child he has fathered by a local Indian girl and "gone native." This is the romantic overlay: underneath, it is only fair to say, there is a fairly solid account of Reid's routine work as a clerk, credible conversations and arguments about the future of Canada, and some exact description of the wilderness scenery. Again the failures are glaring inconsistencies in both matter and style.

The astonishing thing about these books, as about those by Lily Adams Beck, is that reputable Canadian critics once took them seriously. Canadians in the twenties and thirties were so anxious to discover the great Canadian novel that they saw it in books which had no claim whatever to genuine literary distinction. At the same time they came very close to ignoring the few books, such as the novels of Grove and Callaghan, that did at least come within striking distance of greatness.

The third historical novelist of the West worthy of separate mention, Laura Goodman Salverson, has specialized on one aspect of that area: its settlement by pioneers of Scandinavian, and especially Icelandic, stock. Her first novel, *The Viking Heart* (1923), should perhaps not be described as historical, since its action ends in World War I, shortly before the novel was written. There is a sense in which *The Viking Heart* might be considered as a realistic study of western life, and be grouped with the novels of Stead, Ostenso, and Grove. It deals in a realistic way with the hardships of the Icelandic pioneers; but, as Professor E. A. McCourt has convincingly argued, it is basically romantic in tone and outlook. Whereas in the novels of Grove there is a pervasive sense of doom, there is in Mrs. Salverson's novel, as McCourt puts it, "the comfortable assurance that everything is going to turn out all right in the end." McCourt's summary is a just one: "Although *The Viking Heart* is not, as has so often been claimed, a serious realistic treatment of Icelandic settlement in Manitoba, it is a fine romantic tale, written with much sympathy and tenderness and understanding."

Mrs. Salverson's later novels did not live up to the promise of *The Viking Heart*. *When Sparrows Fall* (1925) is on a similar theme of pioneer hardships, set in the northern United States, but has little of the charm of its predecessor. In *Lord of the Silver Dragon* (1927) she went back to the days of Leif Ericson in an effort "to interpret the little known and greatly misunderstood character of the Norsemen," but the book is little more than an historical costume melodrama. *Johann Lind* (1928) is a third attempt to depict the lives of Scandinavian settlers, this time in the province of Saskatchewan, but it lacks clarity and unity. *The Dove* (1933) is an historical romance based on a seventeenth-century Icelandic saga which tells of a raid of Barbary corsairs on the south coast of the island, and of the captivity of the Icelanders in

Algiers. The central character is a beautiful woman known as the dove because of her charity; she acts as a ministering angel to her fellow-slaves, but is so beautiful that a prince falls in love with her. The novel, in short, is a romance of the type beloved by the women's magazines. *The Dark Weaver* (1937) reverts to her favourite theme of Scandinavian settlement of the West and is on a much higher level of achievement, but Mrs. Salverson attempts to deal with too many characters and too many episodes, and the result is rather confusing. *Black Lace* (1938) is a mere pot-boiler about Louis XIV, his mistress and some pirates, but *Confessions of an Immigrant's Daughter* (1939), Mrs. Salverson's autobiography, is an authentic record of her own development and perhaps her finest single achievement apart from *The Viking Heart*.

Historical romances dealing with areas of Canada other than Quebec and the prairies are rare, and not usually of much significance. Louis Arthur Cunningham wrote a few novels, including his first, *Yvon Tremblay* (1927), about the Acadian period of the Maritime provinces; John M. Elson's *The Scarlet Sash* (1925) is a romance of the old Niagara frontier district; and Miss C. H. MacGillivray (d. 1949) wrote in *The Shadow of Tradition* (1927) a story of early days in Ontario's Glengarry County. The only writers in this group worthy of slightly more extensive notice are Mabel Dunham (1881–1957) and Else Porter Reed. Miss Dunham chose to write of the early nineteenth-century emigrations of the Dutch Mennonites from Pennsylvania to Waterloo County in Ontario. Her four novels, beginning with *The Trail of the Conestoga* in 1924 and including *Towards Sodom* (1927), *The Trail of the King's Men* (1931), and *Kristli's Trees* (1948), are based on extensive research and thus have some documentary value, but they are deficient in plot, form, and style. When Miss Dunham deserts historical fact for imaginative fiction, she frequently lapses into sentimentality. Mrs. Reed wrote only one novel, *A Man Forbid* (1935), but it is a quite powerful study of the effects on a small Nova Scotian community in the mid-nineteenth century of the arrival there of a mysterious negro sailor.

Regional Idylls

In quantity, though certainly not in quality, historical romances continued to dominate Canadian fiction during this twenty-year period; their nearest rivals in popularity were regional idylls, or novels of local colour and sentiment. I think that the term regional idyll is the most fitting phrase to apply to these novels, for they aim at portraying the life of a small area of Canada, usually of a rural or semi-rural area, in a way which stresses its beauty, its peculiar customs, its traditions and its aspirations. The emphasis is always on domesticity, the little events of everyday life, and the tone is predominantly optimistic. Trials and hardships are not completely ignored, but they are overcome or circumvented, and we are asked to believe that the world is essentially a good place in which such qualities as thrift, industry, and integrity will always, in the long run, triumph.

The regional idyll had established itself in Canada well before World War I, and it steadily declined in importance during the period at present under review. A few of its survivors are, however, worthy of brief notice, and one of them, Mazo de la Roche, brought the form to its climax of popular fame and made her romantic version of life in rural Ontario current throughout much of the world.

Between them, these regional idyllists covered most of Canada. Edith J. Archibald (1854–1934), in *The Token* (1930), sought to capture the quality of Cape Breton life in the late nineteenth century, stressing its Scottish customs and its religious devotion; Frank Parker Day (1881–1950), in *Rockbound* (1928) and *John Paul's Rock* (1932), produced two vigorous stories of the harsh lives of fishermen off the Nova Scotia coast; J. F. Herbin (1860–1923), in *Jen of the Marshes* (1921), attempted to portray the farm life and scenery of the Grand Pré district of Nova Scotia; and John Freeman, in *This My Son* (1923), and George Frederick Clarke in *Chris in Canada* (1925), *The Magic Road* (1925), and *The Best One Thing* (1926), gave us idealized pictures of life in rural New Brunswick. Rural Quebec provided the setting for Maurice B. Caron's *The Curé of St. Michel* (1925), Angus A. Graham's *Napoleon Tremblay* (1939), Vivian Parsons's *Lucien* (1938) and "V. V. Vinton" 's (Mrs. R. J. Dale's) *To the Greater Glory* (1939).

The middle and far West of Canada, probably because of their recent settlement, received little attention from the writers of regional idylls. Ethel Chapman attempted a romance of Saskatchewan in *The Homesteaders* (1936), and Frank Parker Day produced a somewhat more realistic story of life in northern Manitoba in his *River of Strangers* (1926)—but it is worth noting that neither of these authors was a resident of the West. The only western native to produce novels of this type was Ethel Kirk Grayson, author of *Willow Smoke* (1928), a romance set in a small Saskatchewan town, *Apples of the Moon* (1933), a university story, and *Fires in the Vine* (1942), a family novel set in Ontario. The typical product of the Western imagination was either something much more adventurous than the idyll, or something much more sombrely realistic.

The largest group of regional idylls came, as we might expect, from the populous province of Ontario. Apart from the novels of Mazo de la Roche, there were in this period Clara Rothwell Anderson's *John Matheson* (1923), Jessie L. Beattie's *Hill Top* (1935) and *Three Measures* (1938), Ethel Chapman's *God's Green Country* (1922) and *With Flame of Freedom* (1938), Fred Jacob's *The Day before Yesterday* (1925), Alexander Knox's *Bride of Quietness* (1933); also *Savour of Salt* (1927) by Florence Randal Livesay (1874–1953), and *The Yellow Briar* (1933) and *Robert Harding*

(1938) by "Patrick Slater" (John Mitchell, 1882–1951). This group is not only the largest, it is probably also the best of the regional genre. Jessie L. Beattie's stories are honest, unpretentious, and accurate evocations of Ontario farm life; Fred Jacob (1882–1926) works into his study of an Ontario small town in the late years of the nineteenth century a good deal of the wit and satire which was to enliven his later *Peevee* (1928); Alexander Knox's novel has some excellent passages descriptive of the hills and streams of the upper Ottawa valley and a refreshingly simple and delicate love story. Perhaps best of all is Slater's *Yellow Briar*, a delightfully informal, semi-documentary and autobiographical story of Toronto and rural Ontario from roughly 1836 to 1865. It is a book replete with Irish humour and sentiment, accounts of pioneer social gatherings, and descriptions of the Ontario landscape: a rustic idyll without pretensions of any sort and thoroughly delightful.

But the novelist of rural Ontario who by both the quality and the quantity of her production deserves pride of place is Mazo de la Roche (1885–1961). Some critics might question the wisdom of including her in this category, since there are elements in her work which suggest that she had a more ambitious intention than that of writing romantic idylls of rural life. But to attempt to discuss Mazo de la Roche as in any sense a social realist is to misconceive the whole temper of her work. Judged as a realist, she is almost pitifully vulnerable: of course rural Ontario life is not typically as she describes it in the Jalna series, nor in the early novels which preceded *Jalna* (1927). Miss de la Roche was from the outset a romantic writer who set out to communicate an imaginary world of her own creation, and who had the skill and patience to make the real world share her vision. This limits her achievement certainly, but it also defines it, as that of one of the leading popular novelists of her time.

The romantic bent of Miss de la Roche's imagination was apparent from the very beginning of her career. Her first short story, published in the *Atlantic Monthly* in August 1915, was entitled "Buried Treasure" and is an amusing tale of three boys and an eccentric archaeologist who pretends to be a pirate and as such leads the boys to buried treasure in their own backyard. One of the old man's speeches might serve as the motto for almost all of Mazo de la Roche's writing: "We do what we can to keep a little glamour and gaiety in the world. Some folk would like to discipline it all away." Her first book, *Explorers of the Dawn* (1922), was a highly imaginative recreation of the lives of three children, whom she saw as living in a perpetual state of innocent wonder and freedom. Thus early was established her ruling idea: that of the superiority of the primitive and the instinctive over the civilized and conventional. Her heroes, whether they be children, adolescents, or old men and women, are those who have managed to retain a fresh, instinctive, passionate response towards life.

The romantic emphasis was continued in Miss de la Roche's early novels, *Possession* (1923) and *Delight* (1926). *Possession* is the story of Derek Vale's passionate involvement with an Indian girl in the fruit belt of Ontario, and it romanticizes sex as a force which is irresistible and transforms the rather prosaic southern Ontario landscape into a kind of primitive paradise. *Delight* has as its theme the impingement of instinctive freedom and sensuousness upon a conventional society. The heroine, Delight Mainprize, is described as "a creature of instincts, emotions, not much more developed intellectually than the soft-eyed Jersey in the byre, nor the wood-pigeon that called upon the cedars." And it is this creature of instinct whom her creator allows to triumph, after the grim moral matrons of the small Ontario town have done their best to destroy her.

Delight, in fact, illustrates most of the qualities, good and bad, that were to mark all of Mazo de la Roche's work as a novelist. It is packed with varied, interesting, and passionate characters, characters who are a little larger than life and are the products of romantic exaggeration rather than realistic observation. It is a succession of exciting, unexpected episodes which seem to follow one another haphazardly but actually are grouped around three major crises to form a pattern of development. The novel is given additional continuity by the employment of thematic symbols, the chief of which are the crows, symbolizing the free life and mockery of conventional values which Delight herself stands for. Birds, and other wild creatures, play a large part in this novel: Miss de la Roche takes pleasure in describing them, and almost all her similes and metaphors relate to them. But *Delight*, for all its liveliness, has many deficiencies: it has little psychological depth; its philosophy of primitivism is not deeply considered; it has no claim to social realism; its style is frequently coy and artificial. It is, in short, a romantic tale whose chief value is as entertainment for an idle afternoon. But to provide entertainment for millions, as Miss de la Roche has done, is no mean achievement.

One of the most dramatic events in the literary history of Canada between the wars was the 1927 award of the *Atlantic Monthly*'s $10,000 prize to Miss de la Roche's *Jalna* as the best novel submitted for its contest. Toronto, which has always yearned to be the literary centre of Canada, for once had some basis for the claim, and proceeded to make the most of it. The following account of the civic celebrations, taken entire from the *Canadian Bookman* of May 1927, is offered as a document in Canadian literary history:

> On the occasion of the complimentary banquet presentation to Mazo de la Roche, Toronto, in the civic sense, justified itself besides honoring a clever daughter, for the city demonstrated that laurels won in the mental arena were deemed not less worthy of recognition than those concerned with physical prowess.
> There have been a series of events in which Toronto organizations have paid tribute to the talented author upon her winning of the "Atlantic Monthly's"

$10,000 prize with her novel "Jalna," the latest being the dinner at the Arts and Letters Club of Toronto on May 14th, but the most significant and most elaborate was at the Queen's Hotel, Toronto, on Saturday, May 7th, under the auspices of the Toronto Branch of the Canadian Authors Association.

In proposing the toast, "Our Guest of Honor," Dr. Charles G. D. Roberts spoke of the honor which the gifted young author had brought not only to her native city but to all Canadian writers.

Miss de la Roche's simple response delighted everyone. She recalled that it was at the Queen's Hotel that she had eaten her first hotel dinner at the tender age of six. On that occasion she had been so awed and charmed by the splendid gentleman in evening dress, who pulled out her chair and showered attentions upon her throughout the meal, that, when leaving, she had seized him by the hand and thanked him. Miss de la Roche said she found that winning a prize was a very wonderful experience, but one that required perfect mental balance.

When his Worship, Mayor Thomas Foster, had presented her with a handsome silver tea service, Miss de la Roche's words were few because, she said, her heart was very full.

In proposing the toast to "The Arts in Education," Sir Robert Falconer, President of the University of Toronto, said that he had been struck by the simplicity and sincerity of Miss de la Roche's words on this occasion, and that he had noticed these same qualities in the first instalment of "Jalna"; they were the two essential qualities of all great art. The speaker drew attention to Canada's geographical position in the very centre of the civilized world, and pointed out that this author's achievement was all the more impressive because she had been measured with the best of other countries. Speaking of universities, he said that these institutions were not only producing a creative class but another very necessary class of appreciative readers and critics.

In his reply, Premier Ferguson outlined what had been done to raise the general standard of school pupils in Ontario. He also appealed to Canadian authors to contribute stories woven around Canada and things Canadian in this Jubilee year.

Professor Pelham Edgar, proposing a toast to "Canadian Authors," expressed the opinion that Canada was on the verge of great intellectual prosperity.

Mrs. John Garvin (Katherine Hale), Miss Marshall Saunders and Hon. Mr. Justice W. R. Riddell replied. Mrs. Garvin recalled her schoolgirl friendship with Mazo de la Roche and the latter's early literary successes, while Miss Saunders made witty remarks about many of those present. Hon. Mr. Justice Riddell warmly congratulated Miss de la Roche and concluded by saying that as 1837 had laid the foundation of the present "Commonwealth of Nations," it was up to the Canadian authors to lay the foundation for the greater development of a literature Canadian in subject and sentiment.

In addition to the tea service from the City, Miss de la Roche received a beautiful basket of flowers from the Canadian Literature Club of Toronto.

During the evening music was provided by Cassar George Finn, pianist, and Mrs. Fenton Box, soloist, accompanied by Mr. D'Alton McLaughlin.

Among the distinguished guests was Bliss Carman, who, when his presence was made known, received a flattering welcome.

Jalna is by now so well known that it would be redundant to attempt a full-scale analysis of it. It is far from being a great novel, in the strict sense of that phrase, but it is still a very entertaining one. What impresses us most about it is its liveliness, especially the liveliness of its characters. Miss de la Roche had learnt from Dickens how to fix a character in our minds by attaching to it a few strong identifying gestures, mannerisms, or habits of speech. Almost equally impressive is the way in which the old house which gives the book its name, and the luxuriant gardens and fields and woods which surround the house, are made so real a presence. The plot is ingenious and continuously exciting, and the style, if a little too precious for our austere modern taste, is fresh and beguiling. Miss de la Roche is prodigal with metaphors: a bird fills the air with its rich throaty notes, "tossing them on to the bright sunshine like ringing coins"; and young trees stand in snowy rows "like expectant young girls awaiting their first communion." Writing of this sort is apt to sound offensive to contemporary ears, but if the style of *Jalna* has tarnished, its chief glory—the character of Grandmother Whiteoak— remains. Blunt, coarse, greedy, rude, extravagant, sensual and selfish, she dominates the family and earns the reader's grudging affection by her immense vitality, her insatiable appetite for experience.

Jalna, of course, was so popular that its author had no choice but to write its sequel: *The Whiteoaks of Jalna* (1929). And having written one successful sequel, more and still more were demanded of her, until there were eventually sixteen novels in the series. But the indefatigable Mazo de la Roche found time to write a dozen books outside the series: her love of animals found expression in *Portrait of a Dog* (1930) and in the short stories collected in *The Sacred Bullock* (1939); her fondness for children led her to write the juveniles *Lark Ascending* (1932), *Beside a Norman Tower* (1934), *The Very House* (1937), and *The Story of Lambert* (1955); and in *Growth of a Man* (1938), *The Two Saplings* (1942) and *A Boy in the House* (1952) she produced novels of Ontario rural life outside the Jalna setting. She also wrote some one-act plays, some historical studies, and her autobiography, *Ringing the Changes* (1957). All in all, it was a remarkably productive career, and marked the apogee in the history of the regional idyll in Canadian fiction.

Some Minor Forms

Before turning from romance to the beginnings of realistic Canadian fiction in this inter-war period, we should glance at the development of three minor categories of fiction: stories for younger readers, humorous novels, and the short story.

Juvenile literature in Canada had had a great deal of success in the first two decades of the twentieth century, especially in the work of Ralph Connor, L. M. Montgomery, and Marshall Saunders. The period 1920 to 1940, however, was relatively barren in this respect. The Reverend Frank Baird (1870– 1951) wrote two quite good adventure stories for boys: *Rob McNabb* (1923) and *Parson John of the Labrador* (1924). Similar tales of outdoor adventure were written by Cameron Blake (*Set Stormy*, 1931, and *Only Men on Board*, 1933) and Charles Clay (*Young Voyageur*, 1938, and *Muskrat Man*, 1946). Adventure stories for girls were attempted by Muriel Denison (*Susannah, a Little Girl with the Mounties*, 1936 and *Susannah of the Yukon*, 1937) and Grace Leonard (*The Canadian Family Robinson*, 1935.) Perhaps the most successful writer for girls in the period, apart from Mazo de la Roche, was Marjorie MacMurchy (d. 1938), whose *The Child's House* (1923) and *The Longest Way Round* (1937) are sensitive evocations of the moods and fancies of small children, written in a clear and simple style.

There was no humorous writer who even approached the achievement of Stephen Leacock in the preceding period. The chief of the small and mediocre group was Madge Macbeth, who wrote two satirical novels about Ottawa and the Canadian Parliament under the pseudonym of "Gilbert Knox." Her *The Land of Afternoon* (1924) and *The Kinder Bees* (1935) both occasionally land telling blows on the targets of our social pretensions and hypocrisies, our political compromises and corruptions, but they both frequently veer off into farce on the one hand or melodrama on the other. They lack the clearly articulated positive values which must underlie first-rate satire, and they exaggerate the vices they attack to the point of incredibility. A similar inconsistency and uncertainty bedevils the two comic novels by J. E. Middleton (1872–1960), *Green Plush* (1932) and *The Clever Ones* (1936). Both purport to be satires on Toronto business methods, but their author seems unable to decide whether he really approves or disapproves of the respectable, acquisitive life of that city.

Other satires on Toronto (an obvious butt) were Fred Jacob's *Peevee* (1928), Leslie Bishop's *The Paper Kingdom* (1936) and Francis Pollock's *Jupiter Eight* (1936). The central character of *Peevee* is Pierre Vincent Macready, a budding Canadian writer who is diverted into journalism and politics and dies without fulfilling his early promise. The satire at the expense of Canadian literary self-consciousness, social hypocrisy, religious insincerity, and political corruption is often quite shrewd, but its effect is blurred by the multiplicity of characters and sub-plots. The novel is best in its early pages: as it proceeds it grows increasingly diffuse and directionless. *The Paper Kingdom* deals with an immigrant Irishman's attempt to establish a monthly literary magazine, *The New Conquest*, in Toronto. This theme might have formed the basis for a strong satirical or realistic novel, but Bishop's effort is merely farcical. There is a little incidental satire at the expense of Toronto's materialism and pretentiousness, but its edge is blunted by the incredibility of almost all the events and characters. *Jupiter Eight* is the best satire of the group. Francis Pollock, an Ontario bee-keeper, had published in 1935 an unusually sophisticated version of the regional idyll in *Bitter Honey*, a curious book in which the parts descriptive of the Ontario countryside and of the routine of bee-keeping are very well done but in which the characters are stereotyped and the plot is overly involved. *Jupiter Eight* is a good if a trifle indeterminate satirical novel about the artistic pretensions of Toronto residents. The tone throughout is that of light raillery, and it is well sustained. The title refers to a sports car, the symbol of the aggressive, materialistic, death-dealing society which Pollock conceives Toronto really to be.

The last satire worth noting was set in British Columbia: Magnus Pyke's *Go West, Young Man, Go West* (1930). The story of a young English immigrant, it begins as a fairly realistic, sceptical study of Canadian society, but deteriorates into inconsequential farce.

The short story fared much better than humour in this period, but here as in the novel the great bulk of the production was romantic in tone and emphasis. Some good short stories of contemporary life appeared in the pages of the *Canadian Forum*, especially by J. D. Robins, Raymond Knister, J. R. Fisher, Mary Quayle Innis, and Luella Bruce; when *Queen's Quarterly* began to print short stories in 1931 it secured some excellent ones from Frederick Philip Grove, Leslie Gordon Barnard and, above all, from Sinclair Ross; and during the depression of the thirties there were some powerful if too obviously propagandist stories in such left-wing magazines as the *New Frontier* and *Masses*. The great bulk of magazine stories, however, as printed in quantity during these two decades in *Maclean's* and the *Canadian Magazine*, were purely escapist efforts about the Far North, true love and domestic bliss.

Books of short stories were rare in the period and, with a few conspicuous exceptions, of low quality. Their generally escapist quality is suggested by the popularity of stories about the old days in rural Quebec: of some twenty-five books of stories published between 1920 and 1940, at least six were collections of legends of French Canada: James E. Le Rossignol's *The Beauport Road* (1928), *The Flying Canoe* (1929) and *The Habitant-Merchant* (1939); Duncan Campbell Scott's *The Witching of Elspie* (1923), P. A. W. Wallace's *Baptiste Larocque* (1923), and *Legends of French Canada* (1931) by the Reverend E. C. Woodley (1878–1955). Closely allied to these stories were nostalgic tales of the Maritime Provinces, as in *Old Province Tales* (1924) of Archibald MacMechan (1862–1933) and *Stories of the Land of Evangeline* (1923) by Grace McLeod Rogers (1865–1958). Even when the writers chose contemporary life as their subject, they usually turned it into sentimentality, farce, or melodrama. These three elements are the chief ingredients, for example, in P. A. W. Wallace's *The Twist and Other Stories* (1923) and M. Eugenie Perry's *The Girl in the Silk Dress and Other Stories* (1931).

There were only about five reputable books of short stories produced in Canada in this period: Morley Callaghan's *A Native Argosy* (1929) and *Now That April's Here* (1936), Jessie G. Sime's *Sister Woman* (1920),

Leslie Gordon Barnard's *One Generation Away* (1931) and Mazo de la Roche's *The Sacred Bullock* (1939). Perhaps we should add to this list Raymond Knister's anthology, *Canadian Short Stories* (1928), which gathered together some of the best stories which had appeared in the magazines up to that time.

The stories of Morley Callaghan (b. 1903) are by far the best of the group. Profiting from the example of three writers who were transforming the short story in English while he was a student at Toronto—Sherwood Anderson, Katherine Mansfield, and Ernest Hemingway—Callaghan looked closely at the people about him, and in a simple, stripped, suggestive prose style recorded the small triumphs and tragedies of their ordinary lives. As Callaghan himself has put it, "I try to be honest, to give an insight or illumination of the character, to place the character in life, to give a higher kind of truth to it [the story] in terms of my own emotion for the character." This emotion is seldom a merely simple or straightforward one: Callaghan's stories usually intrigue us by their subtle combination of tenderness and irony, faith and scepticism. His stories are good by any standards, but by comparison with most of the romantic tales being spun in Canada in the twenties they stand out like pyramids in the desert.

Leslie Gordon Barnard's stories have not the astringency of Callaghan's, nor their compressed style, but they are characteristically gentle, quiet, and restrained, fragments of remembered experience held up, in Conrad's phrase, "in the light of a sincere mood." Only very occasionally does the author's detached objectivity give way to sentimentality. The same flaw weakens some of the stories in *Sister Woman* by Jessie G. Sime (b. 1880). This is a book of short stories about women, mostly working-class immigrants to Canada, and their relations with their lovers and husbands. The stories all seem to be modelled on Flaubert's "Un Cœur Simple"—they are tender, wistful, and ironic. The point of view is that of "the new woman," wanting to be free by virtue of earning her own living, but also wanting a man to love and be loved by. Many of the sexual relationships described are unconventional, but Miss Sime is careful not to condemn them. She does not, however, consistently maintain Flaubert's objectivity or irony. Furthermore, the stories are all so similar that, read consecutively in book form, they grow monotonous.

Miss Sime, a Scotswoman who settled in Montreal during World War I and lived there until 1945, was also one of the pioneers in introducing the realistic novel to Canada. Her *Our Little Life* (1921) was the first novel to deal fully and accurately with the contemporary life of a Canadian city. This novel, set in Montreal during the latter years of World War I, applies the rather grey, drab photographic realism of George Gissing's *Demos* or Arnold Bennett's *Old Wives' Tale* to the lower middle class life of Montreal. The main characters are a middle-aged seamstress, Katie McGee, and a young English immigrant and would-be writer, Robert Fulton. This queerly assorted pair live in the same run-down apartment house, and a great friendship, with curious sexual undertones, develops between them. Fulton is working as a clerk in a store and writing a book on Canada which he reads to Miss McGee in the evenings. They occasionally go out to a concert or a lecture, but most of the time their life is a boring routine enlivened only by their evenings together. At the end of the book, Fulton completes his book and dies in the 'flu epidemic of 1918. The novel combines drab urban realism with the immigrant theme which was to become so popular in Canadian novels of the twenties and thirties: Fulton's book is a study of the immigrant and of the effect of Canada upon him. *Our Little Life* strikes one as a terribly honest book, but it is too long and uneventful, the main characters are a little too sweet to be wholesome, and the whole story has a tone of patient wistfulness which eventually becomes cloying. But the historical importance of the novel, as the first sustained effort at urban realism in Canadian fiction, cannot be denied.

Realistic Fiction

Realism, and especially urban realism, was a very unusual commodity in Canadian fiction between the wars. Such realism as there was developed almost exclusively on the prairies, where there was a distinctive pattern of life which could be clearly differentiated from that of Europe and even from that of the United States, and where the conditions of pioneer life were so forbidding that it was almost impossible to idyllicize them. It was prairie writers such as Robert J. C. Stead (1880–1959), Martha Ostenso (b. 1900), and above all Frederick Philip Grove (1871–1948) who began the systematic transformation of Canadian fiction from romance to realism.

R. J. C. Stead had begun his career as a novelist during World War I, but it was with *Neighbours* (1922), *The Smoking Flax* (1924), and especially *Grain* (1926) that he really established his claim to be the pioneer realist of Canadian rural life.

Neighbours is perhaps closer to being a regional idyll of the West than a truly realistic novel, although even in it there are detailed descriptions of actual pioneer processes and hardships which give it more substance than we usually find in the idyll. It is a pleasant, humorous novel about two young men and their sisters who move out from a small Ontario village to neighbouring homesteads on the prairie near Regina. Jack Lane and his sister Jean form one household, Frank Hall and his sister Marjorie the other, but Jack is in love with Marjorie and Frank with Jean, and the romantic side of the plot is provided by the vicissitudes of these love affairs and the eventual marriages of the two couples. Forming the backdrop for this romantic action, however, is the arduous business of finding desirable land and establishing a homestead upon it, and of breaking the soil and raising the first crops. The prairie landscape is described accurately if a trifle romantically, and the few settlers on adjoining properties are characterized distinctly and wittily. As in almost all Canadian novels of this period, there is some discussion of Canada's search for identity, of its desire to distinguish itself from the United Kingdom on the one hand and from the United States on the other. On the whole, the novel is unpretentious and charming.

The Smoking Flax (1924) introduces us to the Stake family, who were also to appear in *Grain*. Cal Beach, a young eastern university graduate, goes out West in search of improved health, taking with him his small nephew, Reed, the illegitimate son of his deceased sister. He finds work on the Stake farm, and falls in love with the daughter of his employer, Minnie Stake. By a glaring coincidence, the eldest Stake son, Jackson, turns out to be the father of Reed, and causes a good deal of trouble until he is killed by a fall from a train. The novel ends happily with the marriage of Cal and Minnie. Thus baldly summarized, the novel sounds like a romantic melodrama. The fact is, however, that for all its conventionality of plot the novel is convincing. Like *Neighbours* it gives us many descriptions of farming operations, makes credible most of its rural characters, and provides documentation of the early social life of the West.

Grain, however, is a much more consistently realistic novel than either *Neighbours* or *The Smoking Flax*. Its central character was a minor character in the latter novel—Gander Stake, the villainous Jackson's younger and more dependable brother. The plot of *Grain* traverses some of the same ground covered in *The Smoking Flax*—the marriage of Cal and Minnie occurs near the end of *Grain*—but it goes farther back, to the birth of Gander in 1896. The early part of the novel is written in the light, chatty, humorous style of *Neighbours*, and deals in an interesting and lively way with the ordinary incidents of a boy's life on the prairie: his early experiences as a schoolboy, hunter, harvester, and farm hand, and the first stirrings of sex. When war breaks out in 1914, however, the tone of the book grows much more serious. Gander is shy, and the thought of being herded together with scores of other men in barracks terrifies him. He determines to evade military service, and tries to find refuge in heavy work, but he is ill at ease and draws more and more into himself. This part of the novel, carefully analysing Gander's motives and state of mind, is extremely well written. The last section of the novel, however, dealing with the early post-war years, is less satisfactory: the plot concerning Jackson Stake, Cal and Reed Beach, and Minnie Stake, intrudes on Gander's story, and makes the last chapters unnecessarily difficult to follow.

Each of these novels by Stead has obvious faults, but together they do give us a basically accurate picture of prairie life in the first two decades of the twentieth century. In some ways the picture is more accurate than that which emerges from Grove's novels: Stead deals with the lighter moments of prairie life, such as hunting, dancing, and baseball playing, which Grove almost totally ignores. Grove's novels, however, have a power and consistency which Stead's lack.

With Martha Ostenso we encounter an example of that problem which so often confronts the Canadian literary historian: is the author properly considered a Canadian? For Martha Ostenso was born in Norway, grew up in Minnesota and North Dakota, and lived in Manitoba only from 1915 to 1921, when she left for permanent residence in the United States. The answer is, I think, that Martha Ostenso is an American novelist, but that her first novel, *Wild Geese*, set in Manitoba and the product of her Manitoba experiences, is a Canadian novel.

Wild Geese, which its author originally entitled "The Passionate Flight," received the prize of $13,500 offered by the *Pictorial Review*, the Famous Players–Lasky Corporation, and Dodd, Mead and Company, for the best first novel by a North American author; 1,389 novels were reported to have been submitted for the competition. The novel is set in a remote pioneer district of Manitoba. The new young schoolmistress, Lind Archer, arrives in the spring and becomes a boarder with the family of Caleb Gore, a flax farmer. The family consists of Caleb and his wife Amelia, their two daughters Judith and Ellen, and their two sons Charlie and Martin. Caleb is a tyrannical husband and father, who keeps his wife in subjection by threatening to reveal "a dreadful secret" about her former life: the fact that she had an illegitimate son, Mark Jordan. Various neighbours play minor roles in the story, but the main lines of the plot follow the relationship between Lind Archer and Mark Jordan, Judith and Sven Sandbo, and Caleb and Amelia. At the end of the novel, Amelia is released from Caleb's tyranny when he dies fighting a fire in his flax crop, and the two young couples are married. Although the novel thus has a modified happy ending, its prevailing tone is sombre in the extreme. The primitive characters and their primitive setting are described powerfully and vividly, and the atmosphere is one of relentless tragic pressure. The unities of time, place, and action are scrupulously observed: the time is a single summer season, between the arrival and departure of the wild geese; the setting is confined to the flax farm and its immediate environment; and the action concerns almost exclusively the members of a single family. The physical appearance of the characters, the farmhouse, and the landscape are described in great detail, and the three elements are fused into a single amalgam of harsh power.

Martha Ostenso's later novels—*The Dark Dawn* (1926), *The Mad Carews* (1927), *The Stone Field* (1937) and many others—were almost all set in the northern United States, and were more or less unsuccessful attempts to repeat her own achievement in *Wild Geese*. But *Wild Geese* itself is the single most consistent piece of western realism to appear before the novels of Frederick Philip Grove, and has a niche of its own in the history of this phase of our literary development.

Frederick Philip Grove

Frederick Philip Grove would have been the first in time as well as the first in quality among the prairie realists if his first novels had been published when they were written. He would, indeed, have been the pioneer realist in North America, pre-dating Theodore Dreiser whom he in many ways resembles. For Grove tells us in his autobiography, *In Search of Myself* (1946), that he wrote his first novels in the 1890's, that between 1892 and 1912 he had written no less than twelve of them, but that they were all consistently rejected by publishers until the publication of *Settlers of the Marsh* in 1925. As the novels were, in their original manuscript versions, very long, and written in longhand on both sides of the paper, it is not surprising that they were rejected.

Grove was born in eastern Europe, near the Russo-Polish border, and spent his early boyhood on his father's estate in Sweden. Much of his adolescence was occupied in travelling about Europe with his mother, and he had spent terms at the universities of Paris, Rome and Munich when he came to North America as a tourist in 1892. Stranded in Toronto in August of that year—his father had died suddenly, leaving nothing but debts—Grove turned to a variety of menial occupations and within a few months settled into the life of a hobo or itinerant farm-hand in the American and Canadian Midwest. From 1912 to 1929 he lived in Manitoba, as a schoolteacher in small towns, and from 1929 to 1948 lived in Ontario, where he owned a small farm near Simcoe. Grove was thus almost ideally equipped to become the chronicler of prairie settlement. Unlike Stead and Ostenso, both of whom had grown up in the Midwest, Grove knew something of other places, and so was able to see prairie life in perspective; as a young man in Europe he had read widely and had met many of the European writers of the late nineteenth century; his university training, which was mainly in the field of archaeology, provided him with scientific and historical background and enabled him to consider the processes of pioneer life in the context of world history and prehistory; and his many years of experience as a farm-hand and small-town schoolteacher gave him the necessary personal knowledge of midwestern society.

Grove's writing career, as we have seen, extended over half a century, but his books were published in the last twenty-five years of his life. Between 1922 and 1947 he published twelve books, including the three volumes of essays *Over Prairie Trails* (1922), *The Turn of the Year* (1923), and *It Needs to be Said* (1929), his autobiography *In Search of Myself*, and eight novels: *Settlers of the Marsh* (1925), *A Search for America* (1927), *Our*

Daily Bread (1928), *The Yoke of Life* (1930), *Fruits of the Earth* (1933), *Two Generations* (1939), *The Master of the Mill* (1944), *and Consider Her Ways* (1947). In addition, he published half a dozen short stories, mainly in *Queen's Quarterly*, three poems in the *Canadian Forum*, several autobiographical essays, and a number of articles on literature and on education.

Some critics would give pride of place among Grove's productions to his essays, especially to those contained in *Over Prairie Trails* and *The Turn of the Year*. The primary interest of these books lies in Grove's effort to capture the spirit of the northwestern climate and landscape, and to record with accurate detail and in exact tone the varied manifestations of nature's activity. His success in catching this spirit, its curious combination of hostility and friendliness, of starkness and fragile beauty, is remarkable. There is no doubt that he was thoroughly at home in this kind of writing, perhaps more at home than he was in the novel. The style of the essays has fewer lapses into pomposity, the manner is easier and more assured, the load of philosophical commentary is carried more lightly. The passages of pure description contained in these essays are the finest writing Grove ever produced, packed as they are with exactly observed details and with phrases and images that are tremendously evocative. But on the whole, for all the merits of these essays, I should rank them below Grove's prairie novels. The novels may not achieve their aim so completely, but their aim is considerably higher.

Grove's autobiography, *In Search of Myself*, is also a fine book that may outlast his novels. Uncompromising in his determination to record the truth as he sees it, Grove here sets down the record of his strange and often tragic career with great candour. He spares neither himself nor his fellows; the result is that he and they emerge from the page as living human beings, compounds of good and evil, wisdom and weakness. His candour may have offended some, but his honesty must impress all. *In Search of Myself* is in many ways a painful book, but it will survive as a record of unusual but credible personal adventures, as a document shedding light upon the development of North American society, as a detailed and convincing account of the special difficulties which beset the artist in a pioneer community.

It is by his novels, however, and especially by his five prairie novels, that Grove's status will probably be judged. The three non-prairie novels—*Two Generations*, which is a chronicle of Ontario farm life in the early decades of this century, *The Master of the Mill*, which traces the fortune of a flour-mill and its owners from the 1890's to the 1930's, and *Consider Her Ways*, a satirical fantasy in which comments are made on North American society by means of the behaviour and discoveries of an invading colony of South American ants—each has its merits, but they do not have the sustained power of the prairie group. *Two Generations* is the most successful attempt yet made in fiction to capture the apparently elusive nature of Ontario rural life, it embodies one of Grove's favourite themes of the necessary antagonism between fathers and sons, and it is satisfying in structure and style, but it strikes us as the novel of an outsider whereas the prairie novels are unmistakably the products of an insider. *The Master of the Mill* is technically the most ambitious of Grove's novels, making use of temporal discontinuity, multiple points of view, and a technique closely resembling stream of consciousness; it is also his most thorough-going attempt at political and sociological analysis and commentary, concerning itself with the problems of labour and management and with the effect of the machine upon human society; but the characters are often obscure, the plot is marred by touches of melodrama, and the total effect is one of some confusion. *Consider Her Ways* is a clever and disturbing book. In the ants' secure conviction that they are the very apex of creation, Grove mocks at human pride in making the same assumption; the account of a slave-holding tribe of ants is used to satirize capitalism and its by-products, imperialism and war; another tribe has a peculiar caste of creatures which have obvious, and unflattering, resemblances to authors and critics; and masses of ants die in their frantic efforts to acquire "the scent of royal favour." All this is clever; the book is also erudite, full of scientific information about ants, their species, and their ways. But this clever satire, on one reader at least, has the opposite effect of that intended: it makes me rally to man's defence against the cold, superior, all-wise probing of the ants' sharp poisonous gasters.

The five prairie novels are more fully satisfying than any of these. *Settlers of the Marsh,* the first to be published but not the first to be written, suffers somewhat from the fact that it is, in Grove's phrase, "a garbled extract" from a much longer work projected in three volumes under the general title of "Pioneers." Especially in the first half of the book there are many scenes and sentences which trail off into a row of dots, presumably indicating ruthless abridgement. A few of the episodes, moreover, hover on the verge of melodrama, and there are some improbabilities in the relations of the three main characters, the shy young farmer Niels Lindstedt, the neurotically virginal Ellen, and the exuberantly lusty Clara. But the processes of homesteading in the bush country of northern Manitoba, and the landscape of that region, are described with brilliant fidelity, and in general the psychological analysis of Niels's motives is acute and profound. Over the whole novel broods Grove's conception of tragic inevitability, of human behaviour controlled by forces which man himself cannot comprehend; Niels is "a leaf borne along in the wind . . . a fragment swept away by torrents." This was the first novel to introduce into Canada the naturalism which, finding its chief source in Emile Zola, spread over the whole Western world in the late decades of the nineteenth century and the early decades of the twentieth.

A Search for America is a semi-autobiographical novel which records in slightly fictionalized form Grove's own efforts to come to terms with North American civilization. In its early pages, Grove describes the Toronto restaurant in which he obtained his first job, his activities as an itinerant book salesman in the eastern United States, and his short-lived period of employment in a midwestern furniture factory; but the bulk of the book is concerned with his experiences as a hobo in the Midwest. He has many perceptive comments on the plight of the immigrant, and on the nature of American society. The novel is in the picaresque tradition, and is thus a succession of lively episodes, unified to some extent by the omnipresence of its hero, Phil Branden, and by Grove's deterministic philosophy of life. Its chief strength, however, is in the vivid details of its descriptions of persons, places, and things: its panoramic sweep is frequently interrupted by close-up shots of an old man's face, the interior of a restaurant kitchen, the buildings of a prairie farm. *A Search for America* was Grove's most popular novel, but it lacks the concentration of his best.

The choice of his best novel must rest among the three remaining items in the prairie series: *Our Daily Bread*, *The Yoke of Life*, and *Fruits of the Earth*. These three novels, all set wholly in the rural West and each concentrating on a small group of characters in a restricted area of time and space, admirably complement one another. *Our Daily Bread* is primarily the story of an old man who, having built up his farm and established his family, sees them both gradually disintegrate; *The Yoke of Life* is the story of a youth who struggles futilely to establish himself and dies before he has accomplished anything; and *Fruits of the Earth* is the story of a man's middle years, when he is establishing himself but is beginning to see that his establishment cannot long endure. All of the novels have weaknesses, especially a certain cumbersomeness of style and structure, but they all have great strengths: characters who are strong-willed and yet who cannot withstand the corrosive acid of time and the bleak indifference of nature; plots which confine themselves almost exclusively to events which are representative of the processes of life in a pioneer community; and settings which are at once true to the realities of the western landscape and symbolic of Grove's conception of nature's indifference to human aspirations.

Frederick Philip Grove, vulnerable as he is to certain sophisticated types of criticism, is the one novelist of this period in Canada who has a thoroughly worked out and consistent philosophy and a technique which is fully adapted to his intentions. In a passage of his autobiography describing the effect upon him of a song heard from the lips of some Kirghiz herdsmen, Grove wrote: "It was a vast, melancholy utterance, cadenced within a few octaves of the bass register, as if the landscape as such had assumed a voice: full of an almost inarticulate realization of man's forlorn position in the face of a hostile barrenness of nature, and yet full, also, of a stubborn, if perhaps only inchoate assertion of man's dignity below his gods." This is an apt description of Grove's own prairie novels. They portray man in conflict with a forbidding land and a forbidding climate, in conflict with his own inchoate impulses and with the often contrary impulses of his fellows, and in conflict always with time which quickly eats away that which he builds; and yet man retains his dignity even in defeat. Technically, Grove's novels embody the strengths and the weaknesses of that school of naturalists who dominated the European and American novel from roughly 1880 to 1914. Like the novels of Zola and Dreiser and Hamsun, Grove's have strength and solidity, present masses of accurate sociological detail, and embody in plain prose a deterministic view of human character; but like those novels, too, they are somewhat deficient in flexibility and subtlety, in grace and wit. They are perhaps rough hewn, but they are hewn from granite.

Some Minor Realists

By the time of the publication of *Fruits of the Earth* in 1933, the school of prairie realism had largely lost its momentum. Stead had given up writing to confine his attention to his duties in the civil service, Martha Ostenso had moved to the United States, and Grove had moved to Ontario. Occasional realistic novels have since appeared from the prairie region—one thinks, for example, of the sombre and strange *Think of the Earth* (1936) by Bertram Brooker (1888-1955), John Herries McCulloch's *Dark Acres* (1935), a rather odd combination of realism and romance concerning English immigrants on an Alberta farm in the early thirties, and Wilfred Eggleston's *The High Plains* (1938), which similarly combines authentic documentary material with a somewhat melodramatic plot—but no other novelist has sought in any systematic way to chronicle the prairie way of life. Perhaps this is because by 1930 the pioneer process had virtually ended, and the life of the prairie farmer and small town resident had settled into a routine which was not markedly different from that in other parts of Canada and the United States.

This group of prairie realists, however, did while it lasted constitute something more nearly approaching a school than did any other Canadian novelists of this period. Realistic accounts of rural and urban life in other parts of Canada were sporadic and intermittent. The Maritime Provinces, perhaps because their culture is so nostalgic, produced almost nothing except historical romances and regional idylls. The only partial exception was "Pierre Coalfleet" (Frank C. Davison, 1893-1944?), a native of Hantsport, N.S., a graduate of McGill and Harvard, and a journalist and international civil servant who is believed to have been killed during World War II while working for the French resistance movement. Davison published four novels under his pseudonym of Pierre Coalfleet: *Sidonie* (1921), *Solo* (1924), *The Hare and the Tortoise* (1926) and *Meanwhile* (1927). The only one of these that is really significant is *Solo*. *Sidonie* is set in London, and is the story of a woman of many lovers: it is a modern *Moll Flanders* prettified for the circulating library trade. *The Hare and the Tortoise* is a novel of Alberta farm life written in a totally inappropriate style, making a western ranch sound like a large English country estate. *Meanwhile* is better than either of these, though it too suffers from some superficiality. Probably autobiographical in basis, it is the story of a young Harvard-trained dilettante who dreams of becoming a great painter or writer but ultimately decides that his talent is only sufficient for the role of an advertising illustrator. *Solo* is also presumably autobiographical, and is more consistent in its realism. The first part of the novel, dealing with the hero's boyhood in a small Nova Scotia village, is detailed and convincing; the latter part, dealing with the young man's adventures as a sailor, his refusal to enlist in World War I, and his years of poverty and illness in Paris as a struggling young pianist, often becomes either melodramatic or sentimental.

Apart from Jessie G. Sime's *Our Little Life*, there were no realistic novels set in the province of Quebec during this period. The poetic movement which developed in Montreal in the twenties had, rather curiously, no counterpart in fiction. It was not until the 1950's in the later novels of Callaghan, the novels of Mordecai Richler and Brian Moore's *The Luck of Ginger Coffey* that Montreal became the setting of credible stories of Canadian life.

Ontario did produce a few realistic novels during this period, but even its fiction continued to be dominated by the historical romance and the regional idyll. There was, of course, Morley Callaghan; but before we look at his work we should glance at that of some minor writers.

Hansen: A Novel of Canadianization by Augustus Bridle (1869–1952), elicited a good deal of approving comment when it appeared in 1924. It is the long and involved story of Olaf Hansen, a young Norwegian immigrant who acquires an education in a small Ontario town, graduates from the University of Toronto, becomes a reform-minded newspaperman, goes out West where he disgustedly views the land speculation in Edmonton, and is eventually elected as an Independent Liberal in the new Alberta legislature in 1905. Interwoven with all this are Hansen's love affairs with three women, one of whom he eventually marries. The theme of the novel, as its sub-title suggests, is the emergence of a distinctive Canadian national type, and some of its social and political comments are shrewd. It is not successful as a novel, however: it attempts to cover too much space and time, it has too many characters, and it is too jerky in style. It is an honest book, but it is not sufficiently integrated to be a real work of art.

The two novels by Beaumont S. Cornell (b. 1892), *Renaissance* (1922) and *Lantern Marsh* (1923), also received much praise from Canadian reviewers in the early twenties. *Renaissance* does not repay re-reading today —it is a political melodrama involving a mysterious Russian musician who is promoting a communist revolution in Britain—but *Lantern Marsh* is still of some interest. The novel is biographical, telling the story of a young man's upbringing on an Ontario farm, his education at the University of Toronto, and his disillusioning experiences as a teacher in a small Ontario city. Like Coalfleet's *Solo,* however, its early chapters are much stronger than its later ones, which frequently indulge in melodrama.

Both *Solo* and *Lantern Marsh* give us fairly authentic pictures of Ontario rural life at this period, but the best attempt at this subject, with the possible exception of Grove's *Two Generations,* was *White Narcissus* (1929) by Raymond Knister (1900–1932). Knister was born and brought up on an Ontario farm, graduated from the universities of Toronto and Iowa State, and was for a brief period an editor of the midwestern American literary monthly, *The Midland.* His death by drowning in 1932 cut short a most promising career: he was the author of some experimental short stories of Ontario rural life, of some strikingly straightforward poems on the same subject, and of two novels, *White Narcissus* and *My Star Predominant* (1934). The latter novel won for Knister, ironically enough after his death, a valuable prize offered by Ottawa's Graphic Press, but it is not the equal of his first novel. *My Star Predominant* is a biographical novel about John Keats, and is a quite successful effort to recreate a past time and place by the use of contemporary documents. There is nothing forced or romantic about it—this is an historical novel, not an historical romance—but its weakness is its rather cluttered episodic structure. There are too many minor characters, too many briefly sketched events: the novel needed shaping and moulding. *White Narcissus* is also far from perfect, but its treatment of Ontario farm life, and especially its capacity to recreate the atmosphere of the Ontario rural landscape, makes it more memorable. The plot is involved and sometimes incredible, the characters are weird but powerful, and the style is a curious combination of simple directness and pretentious double-talk. We feel in this novel as in Knister's short stories that he is wrestling with language, trying to put it into the posture which will be suitable for his own purposes. He can, at his best, write as directly and simply as this: "He went with swinging steps and one arm held out, toward the pig-pen, a swill-pail brushing his bulky, stiffened overalls at every step." On the other hand, Knister can be guilty of such over writing as this: "His rather bashful smile was not belied by the freshet of reminiscential inquiry with which such meetings are accompanied"; or this: "Richard Milne had never ceased to admire the peripety of life, its myriad fugaceous shadings like lake tints which become more intricate to the sight with care in scrutinizing them." Knister, in short, resembled Keats in his uncertainty of taste, but unlike Keats he never achieved true greatness. His early death was a heavy loss, for there were few other writers to take up the task he had laid down, that of describing honestly the Ontario rural scene.

One writer who attempted the task with some success was Angus Mowat (b. 1892). His two novels *Then I'll Look Up* (1938) and *Carrying Place*

(1944) are both largely set in islands in the Great Lakes. Mowat has considerable descriptive power, and is able to build up powerful suspense, but he is too imitative of previous writers to be taken in full seriousness. *Then I'll Look Up* borrows very heavily from Conrad's *Lord Jim* in both theme and technique, and *Carrying Place* mingles the technique of Conrad with a theme very reminiscent of *Wuthering Heights*. There are some good passages in both novels, but one wishes that Mowat had had the courage to undertake Knister's independent struggle with language. Mowat's books are too slick to be convincing.

Philip Child (b. 1898) also made an early attempt at the task of describing the Ontario rural scene in the opening chapters of his *God's Sparrows* (1936), but the bulk even of that novel is set elsewhere—in France during World War I—and his later novels are set in the city rather than in the country. *Day of Wrath* (1945) has its setting in Nazi Germany, and is the moving story of a little man's attempt to preserve integrity, dignity, and love in the midst of Hitler's barbaric régime; and *Mr. Ames against Time* (1949) describes the efforts of a rather similar hero to preserve some modicum of decency in the Toronto underworld. In his concern with the preservation of human values in a decadent society, Child is somewhat like Morley Callaghan in outlook, although he writes in a more formal and more explicit style. Child is a Christian humanist who believes—as the title *God's Sparrows* would suggest—that every individual is supremely important in the eyes of God; his novels are rich in compassion and in a sense of the necessity of human brotherhood and love. He has himself stated the theme of all his work in this sentence from his early historical novel, *The Village of Souls*: "Only in the consummation of love can a man share his loneliness with another and make for himself a dust-speck world within the infinite wilderness, forgetting for a little its pressure which never entirely ceases upon a man's spirit." There can be no quarrel with Child's ideas, but his skill as a novelist is not quite commensurate with the splendour of his ideals. A professor of English at Trinity College, Toronto, Dr. Child tends to be too didactic in his fiction, to be unwilling to rely upon indirection and implication and to preach his Christian humanism too obviously.

A much more glaring example of excessive didacticism, however, but still interesting because of its unusualness in the context of Canadian fiction of this period, is the work of Claudius Gregory (1889-1944). Gregory was born in England, came to Canada at the age of seventeen, and lived in Toronto and Hamilton. He was the author of three novels: *Forgotten Men* (1933), *Valerie Hathaway* (1933), and *Solomon Levi* (1935). All of these novels are much too long—by judicious pruning they could have been cut down at least by half—and much too obviously propagandist. They are, however, among the few items of Canadian fiction which attempt to deal seriously with the social problems of the depressed era of the 1930's. In *Forgotten Men*,

Christopher Watt, the twenty-eight-year-old son of a Hamilton steel magnate, gives up his leisurely life to devote himself to the cause of the unemployed. A Christ-like figure, he founds the Society of Forgotten Men, has twelve disciples who meet in an upper room, is arrested for sedition when betrayed by Jude Braithwaite, and dies of pneumonia resulting from prolonged imprisonment. A kind of Christian socialism is the doctrine preached, but it is preached too often and is made to appear too easy. The allegory is too transparent, and the characters are not developed in any depth. However, beside the mass of romances being turned out in Canada at this time, the novel is an interesting experiment. *Valerie Hathaway* is even more repetitive and didactic, and deals with a less manageable subject: the survival of the spirit after death, and the possibility of establishing a contemplative, Brook Farm type of community as an escape from contemporary materialism. But *Solomon Levi*, although it too is often redundant, is almost as interesting as *Forgotten Men*: the careful, well-documented study of the boyhood, youth, and manhood of an American Jew, it becomes an impassioned plea for racial tolerance and an attack on the policies of Hitler's Germany.

Gregory's propagandist novels were clearly the products of the social and economic disorder of the 1930's, and we might have expected these conditions to provoke a large number of novels of social protest. Canadian poets had reacted quickly to these conditions, and such verse writers as F. R. Scott, A. M. Klein, Leo Kennedy, and Dorothy Livesay produced many poems of social protest in the period. Novels of this kind, however, were rare and of low quality. An early example was Douglas Leader Durkin's *The Magpie* (1923), which is set in a western city (Winnipeg?) at the end of World War I and is a bitter commentary on the failure of the post-war society to realize the ideals for which the war had been fought. Strongly pro-communist in its sympathies, *The Magpie* is a fairly good picture of social upheaval, but its propaganda is too explicit and its characters are stereotyped.

Another early novel of this type was *The Gleaming Archway* (1929) by Alexander Maitland Stephen (1882–1942), who also wrote poetry, plays, and the historical romance of early British Columbia, *The Kingdom of the Sun* (1927). *The Gleaming Archway* is the story of a Vancouver newspaper man who becomes interested in the labour movement, joins a radical paper, and eventually uncovers a government spy in the labour ranks. The reporter stands for evolution rather than revolution, and he comes to the conclusion that it is by changing individuals rather than by mass action that society must be reformed. The story is written in a romantic style, the plot is melodramatic in the extreme, and the characters are caricatures. The novel is really only topical journalism, tricked out with a lot of over-rich description and pseudo-profound philosophizing.

The only other novels of social propaganda came near the end of our period: Ted Allan's *This Time a Better Earth* (1939) and Irene Baird's

Waste Heritage (1939). The former is one of the most readable novels of this period: brisk, clear-cut, a succession of closely observed and exactly described scenes. A realistic novel of the Spanish Civil War, it incorporates a leftist point of view but not in an obtrusive way: it is mainly a close description of air-raids, skirmishes, and of intrigues behind the lines. Ted Allan (pseudonym for Alan Herman) (b. 1916) has since become a playwright of some distinction, but has unfortunately not written any more novels. Irene Baird had written *John* (1937) two years before she produced *Waste Heritage*, and she published a third novel, *He Rides The Sky*, in 1941. Neither of these books, however, is the equal of *Waste Heritage*. *John* is a domestic romance set on Vancouver Island, and is chiefly distinguished by its charming descriptions of the British Columbia landscape; *He Rides The Sky* is an epistolary novel in which a young Canadian airman writes home his impressions of life in the Royal Air Force immediately before, and in the early stages of, World War II. Both these novels were marked chiefly by tenderness; *Waste Heritage* is much tougher and more substantial. Its focal point is the violence that broke out in Hastings Street, Vancouver, in 1938, during a sit-down protest by the unemployed, and it succeeds very well in evoking the mass fury which resulted from long years of unemployment and frustration. The novel suffers somewhat, however, from its imitativeness: the two main characters, Matt Striker and his timid friend Eddy, are reminiscent of the two friends in John Steinbeck's *Of Mice and Men*, and other parts of the novel strongly resemble *The Grapes of Wrath*. The minor characters are lacking in clarity, and the style is rather repetitive and hackneyed. But the novel does give us a clear picture of conditions in Vancouver and Victoria at that terrible time, it does enable us to share the frustration and sense of alienation of the unemployed, and it is often acutely ironic in its treatment of the public attitude to the strikers.

There were then, in the period between the wars, a few examples of realism in Canadian fiction apart from the prairie realists such as Stead and Grove. The record would be a very weak one, however, if it were not for the contribution of Toronto's Morley Callaghan (b. 1903), whose work is in many ways the urban counterpart of Grove's rural realism and who was the only real rival to Grove's pre-eminence in Canadian fiction in this era.

Morley Callaghan

Morley Callaghan is in some senses a bridge between this era in our fiction and the one that followed it. In an obvious sense he is such a bridge, since his career as a novelist began in the twenties and has continued into the sixties. But he is also a bridge in a more subtle sense: he began his career as a fairly straightforward realist or naturalist, and has steadily progressed to a more complex and symbolical way of writing.

Callaghan was born in Toronto, educated there at St. Michael's College and the Osgoode Hall Law School, and has spent most of his life in that city. The only significant interval in his Toronto residence was a few months spent in Paris in the late twenties, when he associated with such expatriate writers as James Joyce, Ernest Hemingway, and Scott Fitzgerald. His association with Hemingway, which had begun in Toronto when the American writer was temporarily on the staff of the *Daily Star*, was particularly influential: his early stories and novels are very similar to those of Hemingway, both in style and in subject-matter. In style, he began by appropriating Hemingway's spare manner of understatement and simplification; and in matter he wrote, especially in his first novel *Strange Fugitive*, of "tough guys," loose women, and violent action. Another important early influence was that of Sherwood Anderson, whose bewildered, pathetic, "I want to know why" characters often crop up in Callaghan's stories. A later and more permanently decisive influence was that of Jacques Maritain, the French Catholic philosopher, whom Callaghan came to know well in Toronto in the winter of 1933 and from whom he may have derived the philosophy of Christian humanism or personalism which dominates his later fiction.

Callaghan has so far published eleven novels (including *Luke Baldwin's Vow*, 1948, for juvenile readers), a privately printed novella, *No Man's Meat* (1931), three collections of short stories, and an autobiographical reminiscence of his early career, *That Summer in Paris* (1963). The short stories contained in *A Native Argosy* (1929), *No Man's Meat* (1931), *Now That April's Here* (1936) and *Morley Callaghan's Stories* (1959) have already been briefly described: they are admittedly fine examples of that genre, and easily the best short stories to be written by a Canadian in the first half of this century. Although his stories have their limitations, they are almost perfect within those limits: there is no doubt that in the short story Callaghan is quite at home, and that he is in at least a minor degree a member of the great modern short story tradition which includes Flaubert, Maupassant, Chekhov, Mansfield, Anderson, and Hemingway. There is far less unanimity about Callaghan's stature as a novelist. Each of his novels has had a mixed reception from the critics, and recent attempts to sum up his work have ranged from Edmund Wilson's dicta that he is "the most unjustly neglected novelist in the English-speaking world" and "a writer whose work may be mentioned without absurdity in association with Chekhov's and Turgenev's," to descriptions of him as "an outstandingly dull writer" whose books are "oddly leaden." His ideas have been praised as profound expressions of Christian thought and damned as confused sentimentality, and his style has been described as beautifully simple and clear on the one hand and as indistinguishable from that of the *Ladies' Home Journal* on the other.

There is no doubt that there was a certain degree of confusion in Callaghan's early novels. His Catholic education had impressed on him the idea that man was a morally responsible, freely choosing son of God; his reading of and association with naturalist writers had suggested to him the idea that man was a rigidly determined creature of heredity and environment; the social disorder of the late twenties and early thirties brought him into contact with the Marxist thesis that man is the product of his economic environment but that that environment can be changed by social revolution; and either through his reading or through conversations with such writers as Joyce, Callaghan became aware of the Freudian interpretation of man as to a large extent the product of childhood traumas and the prey of irrational desires. The early novels reveal Callaghan trying to find a *modus vivendi* among these four irreconcilable philosophies, tending on balance to accept the naturalistic thesis but not finally rejecting any of the alternatives.

In *Strange Fugitive* (1928), the somewhat melodramatic account of the descent of an ordinary lumber-yard worker into bootlegging and other forms of crime, the naturalistic element is certainly uppermost: there is much stress on the weakness of Harry Trotter's heredity and on the barrenness of his environment. At the same time there are a number of references to the Catholic Church, and one critic has even suggested that Trotter's wife Vera, whom he deserts, is a symbol of Christian truth and love. A bow is made towards the Marxist interpretation when Trotter goes to the Labor Temple and is "interested in the lively way speakers talked of direct action, solidarity, mass action." The Freudian influence has its play when we learn that Trotter slept with his mother until he was nine, and is accused by a friend of still being in love with her. In theme, then, this first book is confused, and it is only by its crisp style, its brisk clear-cut descriptions of the Toronto scene, and its patently honest groping after truth that it makes a claim on our admiration.

It's Never Over (1930) and *A Broken Journey* (1932) are similarly melodramatic in plot and indecisive in thought. In the former novel, the story is of the effect upon a man's family and friends of his being involved in a murder. The very title of the novel suggests that here too the naturalistic hypothesis is dominant: it suggests the uninterrupted chain of cause and effect which is "never over." The killer's sister, Isabella, feels the inevitability of her degradation, and she drags her former lover and his new mistress down with her. Unfortunately, Callaghan does not succeed in convincing us of the inevitability of the successive steps downward: we derive rather the impression of weak characters who make circumstances the scapegoats of their own vacillation. *A Broken Journey*, the story of an unusual love triangle involving the joint love of a mother and daughter for the same man, is only slightly clearer and more consistent in thought. The general tone, as in the first two novels, is of bewildered compassion for the inevitability of human suffering, and the naturalistic hypothesis is apparent in the stress that is laid on the daughter's inheritance of her mother's weakness of character. The characters are all seeking a faith to live by but none of their alternatives seem very satisfactory: Catholicism is the mother's chief solace, but its representatives, Father Sullivan and a young Anglo-Catholic parson, are hardly such as to give us much confidence in it; humanism is suggested, but in a half-hearted way, when Marion Gibbons says "Yes, you've got to admire loyalty, and believe that it's in people, or nobility, or courage, even when you wonder whether such virtues touch your life at all." We are left with an impression of human futility, to which the only reliable response is pity: almost every character in the story expresses pity for the other characters at some stage. Peter Gould's feelings for his mistress Patricia are representative: "But now, as he glanced at her, he was full of sympathy, for the uneasiness that was so deep in her life and in her soul seemed but a part of the vast discontent and unrest in his own soul, and on this afternoon at least it was as though they were being drawn closer together by the force of the agitation that was all around and within them too."

A clarification of Callaghan's thinking resulted from his long conversations with Jacques Maritain at the Institute of Mediaeval Studies—a fact which Callaghan acknowledged by dedicating his fourth novel *Such is My Beloved* (1934) in these words: "To those times with M. in the winter of 1933." From this time forward, Callaghan gave up the negative futility which had marked the early novels, made a clear but not simple choice of the Christian rather than the naturalistic, Marxist, or Freudian interpretations of experience, and concentrated upon the spiritual lives of his characters rather than upon their physical appetites. His philosophy becomes that of Christian humanism or personalism: probably in his case Christian personalism would be the more accurate phrase, since humanism puts much stress on reason and moral discipline, whereas Callaghan's stress is rather on intuition and moral freedom. His Christian personalism amounts to this: the supremely important thing on earth is the human person, and the supremely important thing in the person is his soul or spirit; the soul finds its fullest earthly development in self-sacrificial love, through the exercising of which it plays its proper role in God's design; playing the proper role in this divine scheme of things may, and usually will, involve collisions with such earthly schemes as the state, society, and even the church in its earthly establishment; hence the individual soul will frequently be defeated, derided, or destroyed on earth, but will have a triumph which is not of this world. The true destiny of the individual, in other words, will be sainthood; and the saint will often seem uncommonly like a sinner and will always be something of a puzzle and an embarrassment from any merely logical or human point of view. This is the conception of man, the outlines of which will be found in Jacques Maritain's *The Rights of Man and Natural Law* (1945), which dominates all of Callaghan's later novels.

Certainly this is the conception which dominates *Such is My Beloved*, perhaps the most fully satisfying of all of Callaghan's novels. In Father Dowling's attempts to save the souls of the prostitutes, Callaghan found an ideal objective correlative for his theme of self-sacrificial love. The priest's attempts bring him into conflict with society and the hierarchy of his own Church, and are in earthly terms a failure since the girls are driven from the city by the police and Father Dowling himself is temporarily housed in a mental asylum. But at the end of the novel the priest has a moment of illumination in which he realizes the eternal rightness of his actions no matter what the temporary effects may be: "There was a peace within him as he watched the calm, eternal water swelling darkly against the one faint streak of light, the cold night light on the skyline. High in the sky three stars were out. His love seemed suddenly to be as steadfast as those stars, as wide as the water, and still blowing within him like the cold smooth waves still rolling on the shore." The symbolism of this passage is not unique: the whole novel, as Malcolm Ross has cleverly demonstrated in his recent introduction to the New Canadian Library edition of the book, has an elaborate (but not obtrusive) symbolic framework, relating Father Dowling's experiences to those of Christ on earth.

The novels which followed *Such is My Beloved*, with the exception of *The Varsity Story* (1949), a rather slight book in which Callaghan seeks to find the "soul" of the University of Toronto, have all been efforts to find equally persuasive objective correlatives for Callaghan's Christian personalist theme. In *They Shall Inherit the Earth*, Michael Aikenhead has his moment of illumination when he realizes that the true way of life is not that of self-realization and the cherishing of personal ambition but that of meek self-surrender, the way of his sweetheart Anna: "She went on from day to day, living and loving and exposing the fullness and wholeness of herself to the life around her. If to be poor in spirit meant to be without false pride, to be humble enough to forget oneself, then she was poor in spirit, for she gave herself to everything that touched her, she let herself be, she lost herself in the fullness of the world, and in losing herself she found the world, and she possessed her own soul. People like her could have everything. They could inherit the earth." In *More Joy in Heaven* (1937) the closeness of the saint to the sinner is emphasized: the hero is the reformed bank robber, Kip Caley, who on his release from jail is at first worshipped as a hero and then destroyed by a society which cannot really believe in his reformation. To the Church hierarchy, Caley is a sinner, whose remains the bishop orders to be buried in unconsecrated ground; but to Callaghan, it is clear, he is something of a saint, for he has exercised charity, has given to others in a spirit of self-sacrificial love.

Callaghan's three most recent novels—*The Loved and the Lost* (1951), *The Many Colored Coat* (1960), and *A Passion in Rome* (1961)—all give us variants of this same theme, but the theme is embodied in a more complicated plot and expressed by means of a more complex technique. There was a certain amount of symbolism and allegory in Callaghan's earlier novels, but in these later ones these elements are much more prominent and much more carefully worked out. *The Loved and the Lost*, for example, uses as thematic motifs a toy leopard (symbolic of violence and terror), a tiny church (symbolic of purity and reverence), falling snow (the white world of death and evil), and a white horse (symbolizing material prestige and possessions), and weaves them into a complex pattern of meaning. *The Many Colored Coat* has a number of analogies with the biblical story of Joseph and his brethren, and *A Passion in Rome* works out its plot against the elaborate symbolic and ritualistic background of the election and installation of a new pope. I am not sure that this elaboration of structure, challenging as it is for those critics who delight in symbol-hunting, is a gain in Callaghan's fiction: his characters tend to be ambiguous and multifaceted in any case, his plots are always intricate, and his ideas are subtle, and when to these is added a deliberate multiplication of symbolic motifs the result is often baffling.

The record of Callaghan's development thus far has been one of a gradual clarification of theme and complication of technique. In my view he most fully succeeded when these two elements were in equilibrium, in the three novels of the mid-thirties. His early novels were too confused in thought, and his later novels have been too consciously complex in technique. But it would be false to exaggerate the change in his work: from the first he has retained certain constant qualities. His chief strengths have always been his capacity for concrete, exact description of persons and places, his generally restrained and controlled style, and his abundant sympathy for suffering human beings. His chief faults are tendencies to indulge in a kind of misty mysticism, a vague all-forgiving tolerance which blurs essential ethical distinctions, and to attempt to suggest a profundity of meaning which he cannot fully contain in the fictional situations he devises. But he is by far the most complex and challenging novelist of his Canadian generation.

36. Fiction
1940-1960

HUGO McPHERSON*

IN THE YEARS since 1940 Canadian fiction has shown a vitality which Canada-in-excelsis patriots too frequently describe as "a coming of age"; but that analogy must be resisted, for it leads directly to another biological (or mythological) misunderstanding of the "Child of Nations, giant-limbed" variety. The prosaic facts are that the great majority of Canada's novelists have reached no sudden metaphorical maturity; they still dream of Green Gables, northern adventures, rustic or suburban triangles, and the thrust and rut of historical romance. And though such writers now deck themselves in the mail-order finery of book club or Good Housekeeping patterns, they are yet more vapid than their predecessors; escapist romance and innocent self-celebration may have been the normal fictional expression of a pioneer community, for the pioneer needs diversion and reassurance rather than criticism; but in a complex and self-conscious society the artist must reassume his traditional roles of critic or visionary. What "maturity" there may be in recent Canadian fiction belongs to a very few writers who, flying the nets of nostalgia, parochialism, and naïve nationalism that fetter the imagination, have confronted their experience with critical independence and have recorded their insights with a new subtlety and technical power. Following upon the stuttering promise of Grove and the April glories of the early Callaghan, these few persuade us that the Canadian novel has begun to find its tongue; has begun, indeed, to "create" Canada in the way that Hawthorne, a century earlier, helped to create New England.

Underlying the new independence and articulateness of such writers as MacLennan and Richler, Davies and Wilson, is a larger phenomenon, the most important psycho-social event of Canada's history: bruised by the mischances of economic depression and war, and brought face to face with the world by space-destroying advances in communications, Canada in the forties began to find its identity—not the extravagant *pro patria* maple-leaf-waving

*Assisted by Douglas Spettigue of Queen's University, Kingston, and Miss Miriam Leranbaum.

of the twenties, but an objective awareness of its name and nature. However inchoate and amorphous the national mind appeared, there could no longer be any doubt that Canada had acquired a distinct consciousness that could be felt in the street, could be documented and described by statisticians and analysts in government, industry, and higher education. For the perceptive writer, this *Gestalt* in the nation's development proved infinitely liberating: freed simultaneously from the demands of an artificial Canadianism and the equally artificial notion that he should somehow duplicate the achievements of Dickens, Faulkner, or Joyce, he could begin to be simply himself. Canadian identity was not a matter of patriotism but a fact of geography and experience; and whether the writer mocked his country, praised it, analysed it or ignored it, he recognized that his prime concern—using whatever materials he could command—was to be a good writer. "The centre of reality," as Northrop Frye has said, "is wherever one happens to be, and its circumference is whatever one's imagination can make sense of." This is the intuition which has informed the best fiction of the recent period.

I

Before turning to the articulate few whose imagination is thus expanding Canadian consciousness, we must notice the verbose and deciduous many whose leaves are swept together by the social and literary historian if not by the critic. First, a summary of the total production for the period. In the twenty-one years from 1940 to 1960, 350 writers produced 800 volumes of fiction and *belles-lettres* (not to mention an uncounted number of children's books and their authors). Of these, approximately 75 per cent were novels, 15 per cent *belles-lettres* (a term which in Canada refers principally to the reminiscences of journalists, clergymen, and professors) and 10 per cent short stories and humorous pieces. These figures contain no surprises. After nonfiction, which in Canada as elsewhere has now become the principal means of social documentation, the novel reigns supreme. The economics of publishing and the simpler economics of the writer's bread and butter discourage essayists and short story writers alike, but the novel maintains its prestige as "major" work, and entices the would-be writer with extravagant dreams of fame and fortune. Moreover, the pressures of the market account in part for the dominance of stereotyped forms among the 570-odd novels published. In this group, 15 per cent were detective novels or thrillers, written to formula for a mass audience and published more often than not in the United States; 20 per cent were historical romances or frontier adventures (three-quarters of which used North American settings); and the remaining 65 per cent were contemporary narratives ranging in setting from Bombay and Accra to Montreal and Penticton, and in manner from pseudo-Shaw through Sherwood

Anderson to any of the American ladies with three names. Though this large group contains almost all of the significant novels of the period, its bulk consists of domestic romances, often honest or earnest in intention, but abjectly imitative of the stereotypes of magazine fiction. J. R. MacGillivray's summation of the year's work in "Letters in Canada: 1940" could be applied without qualification to over 80 per cent of the fiction of the next two decades:

> There has been, with only trifling exception, no imaginative study of our Canadian life and society, no looking out upon the world, no interest in fiction as a fine art, no apparent awareness of ideas and events, but a perfect isolation from place and time. . . . Where else is there the equal to that ivory tower, soundproof, windowless, air-conditioned, and bombproof, in which these novelists tap at their typewriters undisturbed by the falling heavens?

For such writers, the only exit from the ivory tower was a door hopefully opening on the market-place.

Of the patent forms which make up the bulk of recent fiction, the historical romance has had the greatest vogue with both writers and public. Evelyn Eaton, Thomas B. Costain, W. R. Bird, and Thomas Raddall have each published a half dozen or more works in the genre (Costain's total for the period is eleven), and a score of others have explored subjects as diverse as Genghis Khan and General Wolfe, Hippocrates and William Lyon Mackenzie. Not unexpectedly, a number of writers return to the period of Christ or to Old Testament materials, and another group recall with equal piety the events of various Jacobite risings; but the subjects which outdistance all others are the history of Acadia and New France (Nova Scotia and Quebec), the saga of the United Empire Loyalists, and the rebellion of 1837. Yet despite this natural preference for materials which are close to their traditions or to Canada's history, and despite the painstaking research which their work often displays, these historical novelists have contributed very little to literature. Deceived by the apparent simplicity of a form which requires a high degree of skill and control, they have regularly stumbled into one or other of the traps of historical distortion, mechanical characterization, or wildly improbable plotting. Even more important, they have not clearly understood whether their aim was simple entertainment as in Stevenson, historical reconstruction as in Robert Graves, or historical-philosophical analysis as in Hawthorne. In the face of such divided purposes, Kirby's *chien d'or* dozes on in comfortable security.

Several writers, however, deserve mention for particular qualities in their work, and one, Thomas Raddall, transcends the preceding generalizations. Thomas H. Raddall (b. 1903), born in England and raised in Nova Scotia, is the best of the numerous Maritime novelists who have made Canadian history their garden. Rooted in a community where tradition is long by North American standards, and the urban tangles of Montreal and Toronto remote, he has absorbed the history, landscape, manners, and accent of his region with a completeness that amounts to possession. In addition, he has an unusual ability to recreate moments of dramatic action, and a vigorous, fluent, highly sensory style. After publishing a collection of stories which attracted the attention of John Buchan, *The Pied Piper of Dipper Creek* (1939), he produced in 1942 the best historical novel of the period, *His Majesty's Yankees*, the story of David Strange, a revolutionary agent and soldier in the turbulent days of 1774 when Nova Scotia had to choose between the dubious alternatives of Boston Whiggery and London Toryism. Crammed with the excitement of intrigue, imprisonment, escape, battle on land and sea, and amorous involvement, the action mounts to a rousing picture of the attack on Fort Cumberland; and though the pace slackens in the final section, the author's control does not falter. In subsequent works, *Roger Sudden* (1944), *Pride's Fancy* (1946), etc., the formula of historical romance diminishes the reality of the illusion; but Raddall's power remains unimpaired in two further volumes of tales, *Tambour* (1945) and *The Wedding Gift* (1947). In *The Nymph and the Lamp* (1950), a tale of life at a wireless station on Sable Island, and *Warden of the North* (1949), a history of Halifax, he shows himself to be at ease in two new areas. Raddall's principal weakness, one realizes, is his inability to penetrate deeply into the psychology of his characters, but since action, the vivid recreation of personality, and the memorable use of landscape are central to his work, the reader does not demand more. For Raddall, above all, is a gifted entertainer; and when he evades the stereotypes which mar the average narrative of derring-do, he is superbly satisfying.

Equally prolific but less accomplished than Raddall is Will R. Bird (b. 1891), chronicler of the eighteenth-century Yorkshiremen who emigrated to Nova Scotia. Evelyn Eaton (b. 1902) and Thomas B. Costain (b. 1885), both living in the United States, have had wide popular success, Mrs. Eaton with stories of Acadia, and Costain with tales of Christ, Attila the Hun, Napoleon, and the rulers of New France, which have gained him an international reputation as a manufacturer of literary placebos. Two other strains in the historical novel, though not yet strongly developed, offer hopeful alternatives to the standard formula. Grace Campbell (1895–1963) in *Thorn Apple Tree* (1942) and *The Higher Hill* (1944), recreates the pioneer experience of Glengarry Township, Ontario, with a loving attention to details of daily life, and a generally disarming unpretentiousness. This approach to history, rejecting with tranquil firmness both the sentimental excesses of a Ralph Connor and the romantic absurdities of a Major Richardson, is akin to the low-keyed beauty of such American regional writers as Sarah Orne Jewett and Willa Cather. In another direction, Louis Vaczek's *River and Empty Sea* (1950)—a chronicle of the voyage of two Jesuit fathers to Hudson's Bay in 1672—charges a scrupulously recorded historical event with the significance of parable. Vaczek is the only historical novelist of the period who has seen in the genre the possibilities of meaning which E. J. Pratt realized so powerfully in his historical poems. Unfortunately Vaczek has not followed up this initial success.

Analogous to the historical romance in both impulse and conventional artifice are contemporary stories of adventure (5 per cent of the period's production) and detective stories or thrillers (15 per cent). Given the new ubiquity of the aeroplane, the adventure writers take us to such exotic or barren places as Malaya, the Labrador coast, the West Indies, and the Yukon, and they introduce us to the standard cast of prospectors, fatal ladies, police, Indians, Esquimaux, sky-pilots, and rogues. But without exception their work is inferior to the non-fiction "I-was-there" adventures of documentary writers and foreign correspondents. A remark made in the *Times Literary Supplement* about one of Nicholas Monsarrat's many stories applies to the semi- or sub-literary nature of all this work: "If he would write with greater care, his nonsense would be greater fun." The detective story, by sticking closer to its recipe of suspense, violence, and narrative ingenuity, spiced with sex or recondite information à la *Time* magazine, is generally less offensive. Frances Shelley Wees and Margaret Millar, who now lives in California, are competent professionals in the field, and such writers as Brian Moore, Louis Vaczek, and Douglas Sanderson have produced thrillers for the paperback trade. Arthur Hailey, a literary business man who began by writing simple stories of suspense—aeroplane crews afflicted by food poisoning, etc.—has become wizard-king of the pops by transforming one narrative from TV play to radio play to film script to novel. Of such, for the average Canadian author, is the kingdom of heaven. The market, however, is not Hailey's exclusive interest; with each new novel he shows an increased awareness of fiction as an art.

In contrast to the clear formulae of these works, the final group of patent narratives—the contemporary romances—present a problem of definition. And since they constitute more than half of the fiction produced since 1940, one must press beyond the wondering awe and the ennui which they inspire in an attempt to lay bare their corporate heart. In "Letters in Canada: 1959," C. T. Bissell distinguished such works sharply from the American romances of Hawthorne and Melville which, in Richard Chase's phrase, possess "a certain intrepid and penetrating dialectic of action and meaning, a radical skepticism about ultimate questions." The typical Canadian romance, far from this radical and inquiring exploration of experience, clings to familiar people and situations, finds moral edification in the workings of adversity, and reconciliation in the rituals of courtship and marriage. The writer of this kind of novel, Dr. Bissell concludes, can have no genuine theme: "He is not analysing experience; he is sentimentalizing it. Instead of a theme, instead of a passionate apprehension of experience, a reader gets at the best a moralistic reflection." These works, in short, belong in the ivory tower described by J. R. MacGillivray, that chamber from which there is no genuine "looking out upon the world," no real "interest in fiction as a fine art, [and] no apparent awareness of ideas and events." The heart of the Canadian romance is, in fact, a folk-story or fairy-tale, deeply coloured by the Sunday-school pieties of Protestant morality, and resolutely anti-intellectual. And though it has documented the experience of Canadians in every province and in every walk of life from the Cabinet to the callhouse, it has rarely brought action and setting into living relation with meaning. In fairy-tale the "they" who oppose the hero (whether trolls, ogres, or nasty stepmothers) need not be analysed, but when the novelist enters the contemporary world and makes a "they" of employers, stuffy parents, unions, bureaucrats, or crass business men, he cannot allow his hero to transform or escape *that* world with one flourish of a magic wand.

The romance pattern itself, of course, is not suspect; we see it shaping the conflict of such varied works as *Wuthering Heights* and Conrad's *Victory*. But the writer must be faithful to the manner which he adopts, whether it be unflinching realism, or the spice and sentiment of Arcadia. Hence and not unexpectedly, the most successful practitioners of the romance form have been Mazo de la Roche at one extreme, and Hugh MacLennan and Mordecai Richler at the other. Mazo de la Roche, by refusing to heed even the detonation of Hiroshima, preserved her world of Jalna as a country of the heart. (The information that in 1960 she was, with A. J. Cronin, the favourite author of French school children, is recent evidence of her peculiar appeal.) On the other hand, Hugh MacLennan, as we shall see below, has made the romance an instrument of social analysis, and Mordecai Richler has given it ironic bite by allowing both the friends and the enemies of the hero an ambivalent value. Between these poles stretches a long file of naïve romancers who, in this study at least, must remain anonymous. For many of them, perhaps, the novel is primarily an instrument of rationalization, for they raise ugly realities and subdue them with implausible ease. In homage to Grace Metalious, one might best describe their work, for all its variety in setting— as patent people in patent places.

II

The stereotyped forms noticed above reveal the opposing pulls of the market and the private dream on the average Canadian novelist; the sections which follow will study that small group of writers who in various ways have expanded the Canadian consciousness of the self, and its relation to ideas, imagination, and events. Since there is nothing in this body of work that can be described as a "school" or "movement" in the sense that applies to a more substantial and mature literature, and little that can be classified usefully by such labels as "realism" or "social consciousness," the discussion will avoid the conventional groupings of literary criticism and consider the themes which have preoccupied the novelist, and the technical means which he has found to express them. Such subjects as national identity, the quest of the imagination, the discovery of self, the meaning of war and social change, and the impact of other cultures, will thus shape this chapter as they have shaped the best fiction of the recent period.

Roy Daniells, in his outline of Canadian literature in *The Culture of Contemporary Canada* (Julian Park, ed., 1957), sees Hugh MacLennan (b. 1907) as the representative novelist of the contemporary period, and though criticism has not judged any one of his novels an unqualified success, this claim for his centrality has not been effectively challenged. On the debit side MacLennan has been charged with a habit of allegorizing and theorizing which at once over-simplifies the social and psychological issues that he explores, and deprives his characters of independent life. On the credit side, however, he has been commended for his breadth of vision, his vitality in narrative writing, and his urbane style. But whatever the final artistic verdict, he stands out in historical terms as the first novelist to subject the Canadian mind to a searching and informed scrutiny.

MacLennan's background and training gave him unusual qualifications for the pioneer task of exploring the *terrain inconnu* of the Canadian consciousness. Born in Cape Breton Island, he was a Rhodes scholar at Oxford, took a Ph.D. in Classics at Princeton, and travelled widely before embarking on a teaching career. Wearied of the unreality of Canadian fiction, just as Hawthorne had wearied of the "damned scribbling women" of his day, he adopted the popular romance form and, like Hawthorne, transformed it into an instrument of social analysis and criticism. *Barometer Rising* (1941) is the key work for an understanding of his purposes and method. Unlike romances which use reality as a backdrop for daydream, this work fuses a superbly realized account of the Halifax explosion of December, 1917, with a classic plot reminiscent of the Perseus legend. Neil MacRae, a falsely discredited army officer, returns to Halifax to accomplish two things: vengeance upon his Anglophile uncle, Colonel Wain, the author of his disgrace; and reunion with the Colonel's daughter Penny, who has borne him a child. At the moment when Neil's vengeance becomes possible, the city is blasted by the explosion of a munitions ship. In the nightmare of rescue work which follows, Neil realizes that he "has changed too much to care for . . . [the revenge] he had a right to enjoy." Freed of the tyranny of the older generation, he and his Penelope, with the child who now bears their name, are ready to begin a new life. As the well-ordered time sequence of these events unrolls, MacLennan keeps the image of the city so carefully in focus that we finally see it in the relation of macrocosm to the microcosm of Colonel Wain and his circle:

both typify the decadent colonial society whose callous self-seeking has betrayed an innocent generation into the pain and horror of war. And both, having sown the seeds of sin, reap the wild wind of death and disaster. In Hugh MacLennan's hands, then, the Halifax explosion becomes a parable of Canadian history: it marks the end of the colonial era and heralds the beginning of a Canadian nation.

As this brief summary may suggest, the task which Hugh MacLennan set himself was to write not a fairy-tale but a critique of Canadian society. In doing so he was forced more than once to sacrifice both plausibility and fullness of characterization to the demands of theme; and his subsequent work reveals his search for new means of reconciling the opposed elements of realism and symbolic statement. *Two Solitudes* (1945) studies a major social problem, the distrust and animosity that separate different racial groups within the community—in this instance the French-English conflict in Quebec. Again, the characters and the settings take on symbolic weight, but Part I of the novel—the account of Athanase Tallard and Captain Yardley, the elderly men of good will, who fail equally in their attempt to heal the schism in Canadian life—is so fully and richly executed that the symbolic and realistic elements sound in resonant harmony. (This section, indeed, is one of the best things in Canadian fiction.) Unfortunately the final sections, which chronicle the problems of the younger generation, and end in a French-English "marriage," are threadbare and theoretical, though carefully designed.

In *The Precipice* (1948), a study of Puritanism and its effects on Canadians and Americans, MacLennan's symbolic method breaks down, for psychic states resist the kind of personification which makes possible the dramatization of *social* forces. In *Each Man's Son* (1951), however, MacLennan pursued the same theme with more success. Here, within the circumscribed life of a Cape Breton mining village, he was able to explore the traumas of Puritanism in depth, and to find for his hero, Dr. Ainslie, and the "son" whom he inherits, a promise of release. Still dissatisfied with what he calls the "clinical" method, however, MacLennan turned in *The Watch That Ends the Night* (1959) to a first-person narrator, George Stewart, whose reflections and analyses at once lay bare his inmost heart and give the action a new immediacy. Stewart is a political commentator and professor whose frail wife Catherine has suffered since childhood from heart disease (someone remarks that she is a symbol of "our sick civilization"). Catherine's first husband was an idealistic doctor who, after a childhood of violence and a youth of Christian piety, embraced in manhood political causes which took him progressively to Spain, Germany, Russia, and China. In the decade of "the bomb" this almost mythical figure returns to Canada, maimed and broken, but glowing with an existential knowledge which he believes can end the gloom of the long night watch—the darkness of self, or of history (again the microcosm-macrocosm pattern is implied). "Life is a gift," he affirms, and man, faced with the ultimate disaster (whether Catherine's death or the holocaust of the bomb), must cherish it in wonder and in love. This simple but difficult intuition floods the darkness of the self with light—with a new and tranquil assurance. Armed with this credo for an atomic age, George Stewart, the doubter and worrier, can now live fully in the present.

The broadly religious implications of this theme make *The Watch That Ends the Night* the most ambitious of Hugh MacLennan's novels, and the new narrative method makes it his most finished work, but at the same time its freight of didactic commentary is unnecessarily bulky; one feels, indeed, that the essayist at this point is crowding out the novelist—that MacLennan is ultimately more comfortable with discursive statement than with dramatic rendering. And this speculation is in large degree confirmed by his three volumes of essays, *Cross Country* (1949), *Thirty and Three* (1954), and *Scotchman's Return* (1960). In these urbane and often warmly personal discussions of subjects as varied as the St. Lawrence River, Ernest Hemingway, and student life at Oxford, we find narrative serving as the handmaiden of thought, and feel that this paternal relation is perhaps the truest image of Hugh MacLennan's gifts. He has endeavoured, above all, to see the shape and meaning of Canadian experience, and if other writers have now gone beyond his position, his trail-blazing has helped them—whether positively or negatively—to find their direction.

III

Hugh MacLennan's work is typical of the main development in recent Canadian fiction, but it does not dominate. If other novelists share with him the major themes of the self, the nature of Canadian society, and the religio-philosophical question of "how to live," as well as the technique of combining social documentation with symbolic patterning, they nevertheless speak with great individuality. Morley Callaghan, Gabrielle Roy, Robertson Davies, Ethel Wilson, Mordecai Richler, and Brian Moore have all mapped out important areas of the Canadian *terrain inconnu*, and a dozen other figures have contributed individual works of interest. The majority of these authors have been concerned with what is best described as "the discovery of self," a theme which will be treated in the next section; proceeding from Hugh MacLennan, however, we must now consider a number of writers whose approach to society ranges from a quest for ultimate value to highly specific analysis and criticism.

The most prolific and technically gifted of these writers, Morley Callaghan (see chapter 35 for a full discussion of his work), though related in style to Sherwood Anderson and the American group of the twenties, is fundamentally a religious novelist whose study of the contradictions between temporal and eternal values brought him in *The Loved and the Lost* (1951)—and again in *The Many Colored Coat* (1960)—to the perplexing question of the fate of the innocent in the conventional world of a modern city. In earlier novels Callaghan had used Canadian settings as unobtrusive backgrounds to his spiritual quest, but in *The Loved and the Lost* he portrayed Montreal as a fully articulated community which (like Alexandria or Paris or London) epitomizes mankind's spiritual dilemmas. In this tangled urban setting—with its unyielding black mountain, home of the rich whites, opposed to the fluid, snow-covered whiteness of the lower town, home of negroes and paupers—in this ambiguous world he placed Peggy Sanderson, a wilful innocent who refused to recognize colour bars of any kind; and in her painful history he revealed dramatically how temporal institutions, white, black, or grey, finally crush the individual who flouts their rules. The novel is not without flaws in both style and structure, but it stands as a landmark in Canadian writing. In *The Many Colored Coat*, Montreal is again the background of a parable on the nature of innocence; but though its angry, idealistic hero, Harry Lane, is a memorable creation, the story lacks the warmth of the earlier work. Free of the somewhat theoretical tone of *The Many Colored Coat*, and of the discursive commentary which diminished the power of MacLennan's *Two Solitudes*, *The Loved and the Lost* had the double gifts of a vivid sense of place and an action which speaks to all men.

Because she writes in French, Gabrielle Roy (b. 1909) might appear to be even farther than Callaghan from the provincial Canadian heart, but her work, in translation, has been so influential that it cannot be ignored. In Miss Roy's vision, the growth of Canada from a pastoral, if austere, childhood to the anguish of the urban present, is associated with the progress of the race and the individual from innocence to experience. Thus in *Bonheur d'occasion* (*The Tin Flute*, 1947) she studies with excruciating immediacy the career of a Montreal slum family, the La Casse brood—the "boxed" ones. For such as these, the terrible meek, there is no escape from the pain of experience: one cannot retreat to the sugar-maple grove of youth, or to a nunnery, or to the bogus glory of the army; and riches, imaged in the exclusive steel fences of Westmount gardens, are equally delusive—another trap. There is, indeed, only one solution—love, the humane devotion of a Gandhi who, in a later novel, becomes the idol of Miss Roy's caged hero, the bank teller Alexandre Chenevert (*The Cashier*, 1955).

Gabrielle Roy's style, an uneasy combination of Victorian descriptive techniques and a colloquialism which catches the last syllable of the market vendor's cry and the vagrant's tragic rhetoric, is far removed from the echoes of Donne, George Eliot, and Galsworthy which ring through Hugh MacLennan's work, and the calculated flatness which is Callaghan's triumph and cross. But all three writers, while unmistakably viewing experience from a northern perspective, come close to the springs of human action and feeling that flow through literature everywhere. Two very different writers—Robertson Davies and Sinclair Ross—look at society with a similar clarity and intensity, and offer fresh evidence of stylistic eclecticism: Davies leans heavily on such wits as Swift and Dr. Johnson, Shaw and Samuel Butler, and even on Mencken and Sinclair Lewis; and Ross gives us something of the clenched power of D. H. Lawrence and Thomas Wolfe. But these two writers introduce a theme new to Canadian fiction, though central in our poetry—the absorbing problem of the imagination, of the artist.

Robertson Davies (b. 1913), raised in Ontarian comfort and educated in Canada and England, came to the novel with wide experience in journalism and the theatre (see chapter 34), and with a background of reading which included both the monuments and a good deal of the curiosa of Western literature. In *The Diary of Samuel Marchbanks* (1947) and *The Table Talk of Samuel Marchbanks*—both based on columns published in the Peterborough *Examiner*—he created an irascible character who attacked Canadian and American provinciality in all its manifestations; no one, from the brigadier's spinster daughter to the solicitor's clerk or the chocolate-stuffed child, escaped his lash. Marchbanks was a caustic Johnsonian eccentric who would neither permit the folkways of his community to infringe on his privacy, nor forgive their public gaucherie. But though Davies continued this energetic whacking of the nation's backside in his fiction, he also formulated, in action rather than talk, some positive solutions to the problem posed.

Tempest-Tost (1951), the first of three novels dealing with the historic town of Salterton (or Kingston), Ontario, exposes mercilessly the ignorance, pretentiousness, and materialism which pass for "love of the arts" in old Ontario. Davies' satirical device is to cast a Little Theatre production of *The Tempest* with the best equivalents to Shakespeare's characters that Salterton can offer. In the travesty that results, Prince Ferdinand becomes a lustful young officer from the Royal Military College who is intent on seducing Ariel, the gilt-edged heiress of a local manufacturer; the wise councillor Gonzalo is a tongue-tied Presbyterian schoolteacher; Caliban is an irresponsible employee of the government liquor commission; and Prospero, the great intellectual, is a pedantic classics professor whose glum and repressed daughter Pearl is the unloved Canadian Miranda. In this dismal affair, the producer of the play, Valentine Rich (recalled from the United States as a professional expert) is finally driven from the field. Salterton is clearly more interested in a military ball, with its storm of uniforms, decorations, dowagers, and dignitaries, than in Shakespeare's *Tempest* and its sweet affirmation of the power of imagination.

But if the imagination is routed in *Tempest-Tost*, it gains a partial victory over the forces of convention and genteel taste in *Leaven of Malice* (1954). In this ingeniously plotted satirical romance, Davies looks with deadly candour at the pomposities of old families, academics, journalists, lawyers, and culture-loving ladies; but the book ends in a marriage between Pearl Vambrace, Salterton's neglected Miranda, and Solly Bridgetower, a young English professor who yearns to create a Canadian literature rather than study the fossils of such too-well-named writers as Heavysege. The malice of the Victorian "old guard" against this couple, and against Gloster Ridley, the editor of the local newspaper, paradoxically enables all three to escape the "Dead Hand" of the provincial past. The native imagination may yet come into its own.

In *A Mixture of Frailties* (1958) Davies attacks the same theme from a new angle, and finds new technical means to express it. In the first novels, despite their wealth of comic invention, wit, and satiric observation, the characters do not come fully to life; they are caricatures whom the omniscient narrator mocks so effectively that his deeper purpose is obscured. *A Mixture of Frailties*, by contrast, gives us a fully developed heroine, Monica Gall, a naïve member of Salterton's Heart and Hope Gospel Quartet, who is sent to England to train as a concert singer; all the satiric elements of the previous books are still present, but they now take on new meaning, for they reveal dramatically, existentially, what Monica *is*. Thus Monica's mother comes to represent the spoiled and soured imagination, the artist *manqué*; the British voice-coach Murtagh Molloy, who attempts to seduce Monica, and the composer Giles Revelstoke who makes her his mistress, suggest the opposing claims of technical virtuosity and inspiration on the young artist. And since music, for Davies, is regularly associated with the imagination, the completion of Monica's training and her happy return visit to Salterton suggest that her community has at last found its voice. Davies' technical control in this novel is still too uncertain to save him from implausible moments of melodrama or farce, but his copiousness, his new psychological focus and his imaginative insight into the problems and prospects of his culture, make the book his most important achievement.

In setting, tone, and method, the work of Sinclair Ross (b. 1908) is totally unlike that of Davies: where the latter, shy of inner probings, attempts to spank his smug Ontario neighbours into self-awareness, Ross plunges straight to the parched and anguished heart of his prairie community. But like Davies—and like Ernest Buckler, who will be treated in a different context—Ross's central theme is the imagination and its failure in Canada. Born in Saskatchewan, Ross published a number of distinguished short stories before the appearance of his first novel, *As for Me and My House* (1941). Written in diary form, this work records the experience of the Reverend Philip Bentley and his wife in the desolate town of Horizon, one of the many wasteland parishes in which they have struggled during the twelve years of their marriage. The narrative, as told in Mrs. Bentley's compressed, elegiac style, is a relentless record of frustration, spiritual atrophy, and desperate hope which charts the very pulse and temperature of the prairies during the depression years, and endows the entire action with the richness of parable. Thus Horizon, a dot on an apparently endless railway line, becomes finally a timeless image of spiritual travail. Here the Bentleys are assailed by the scourges of wind and dust, suffocating heat and piercing cold; they are bruised by the sadism or the indifference of small-town minds and hearts, and inwardly tormented by the spectres of a religion which they practise without belief. In this barren setting, music, painting, literature, and thought all wither or freeze; Mrs. Bentley's hands stiffen and her piano takes on a honky-tonk tone; and Philip sits in his study drawing faceless people and bleak sketches of the false store-fronts that line the main street. But the twelve-year ordeal ends in a springtime of qualified hope. The Bentleys adopt a child and prepare to move to a small university town where Philip will open a bookstore; the journey from emptiness and pain to a somewhat more humane society is beginning, but there is no suggestion that the goal is at hand.

The rigidly limited point of view and the rhythmic use of repetition in *As for Me and My House* support the meaning and mood of the novel admirably; Ross does not always escape the trap of a reiteration which is merely reflex, yet in technique his book remains one of the most finished works that Canada has produced. Regrettably, Ross's production diminished after 1941. Short stories of great merit continued to appear occasionally, but a second novel, *The Well* (1958), concerned with a young criminal's development towards moral awareness, failed to match the intensity and resonance of the Bentleys' odyssey.

The Well brings us again to the central theme of recent Canadian writing— the discovery of self, but several other works which deal with specific social problems should first be mentioned. Perhaps the most professional of these is Gwethalyn Graham's *Earth and High Heaven* (1944), a study of anti-semitism in Montreal. Alert, fluent, ironic, this story contrasts social hatred and its vocabulary of jargon and cliché, with true love and its passionate search for communication. Although Miss Graham's very articulate lovers quote poetry instead of living it, her rendering of their problem is clear-sighted, and that in itself is an achievement. Similarly competent and forceful is Selwyn Dewdney's *Wind without Rain* (1946), an attack, with Orwellian overtones, on modern education. When teachers deliberately adopt the tactics of business men's service clubs and value massed choral recitations of "Mary Had a Little Lamb" above more orthodox literary studies, education is subverted; and when a principal instals a two-way public address system which enables him to spy on teachers and interrupt classes, the advent of Big Brother is at hand. John Cornish's *The Provincials* (1951) satirizes Vancouver's culture-buying élite in a style more notable for exuberance than control, and Hugh Garner's *Cabbagetown* (1951) records with naturalistic energy the case histories of residents in Toronto's worst slum. Three other novels record with some success the stories of embattled individuals caught up by social or political situations beyond their control: radio and TV playwright Len Petersen's *Chipmunk* (1949) chronicles bleakly the experience of a Toronto bakery worker in his regimented, spiritless world; Don MacMillan's *Rink Rat* (1949) follows the career of a professional hockey-player; and poet Earle Birney's *Down the Long Table* (1955) recalls, with the hindsight of the post-McCarthy era, the left-wing political struggles of the thirties in Ontario. Snatching up more bombastic weapons, Ralph Allen's *The Chartered Libertine* (1954) brings into range such targets as Canadian politicians, broadcasters, censors, and do-gooders; his *Peace River Country* (1958) records the semi-picaresque journey of a mother and her two children across the prairie provinces. However, this latter work, though it looks with genial sharpness at such phenomena as the country fair, the small-town baseball hero, and the Moose Jaw boarding house, is finally concerned with the individual's search for equilibrium and meaning. Here as elsewhere in Canadian fiction, the railway line is an image of the inward journey; but Allen, unlike the popular romancers, knows that the episodes of the journey are more important than the idyllic goal; that the Peace River country, indeed, may never be reached: as a C.P.R. conductor assures the travellers, "It's further than anybody thinks."

IV

The regional nature of the bulk of Canadian fiction is rather a fact to be observed than a useful basis for critical classification. Unlike nineteenth-century America, in which genuinely regional idioms did develop, twentieth-century Canada is too close to articulate neighbours and too urgently pressed by international responsibilities to enjoy either the leisure or the isolation which produces distinct regional movements. Even such unmistakably regional novels as *Tamarac* (1957), Margaret Hutchison's romance of British Columbia, suggest an expansive impulse—a need to establish an active rather than passive identity. And "identity," however much it may upset our fashionable critics, is the right word, for the plain fact is that Canada's most gifted writers are in the throes of self-discovery; their struggle (whether in Davies, Ross, Wilson, or Richler) has been to reject the stolid provincial mask and, in Warren Tallman's phrase, "come into presence." And if this presence is still naïve—still hesitant and awkward—it may finally produce (as R. E.

Watters has argued) not a skilful imitation of other literatures but an original new vision. In any case, this common impulse towards self-discovery now transcends and obviates regional distinctions. Each of the works to be discussed in this section speaks less for a region or group than for individual and communal consciousness. Putting aside, then, such distinctions as geographical and racial background, such labels as "immigrant novel" and "adult western," and such stylistic categories as realism and stream-of-consciousness, we meet a group of writers whose first purpose is to discover the meaning of their own experience, but who—because their centre of consciousness is Canadian—also reveal pattern and shape in the snow-covered expanses of their community. The most serene and mature of these is Ethel Wilson; the most youthful and daring is Mordecai Richler.

Ethel Wilson (b. 1890) has been variously described as the most traditional, experimental, artless, and sophisticated of Canada's novelists, and in a curious way all of these contradictory labels stick. They stick because Mrs. Wilson is an odd mixture of artist and sibyl who tells her tales with delicacy and astringent sympathy; who knows that life is without plot though instinct with meaning; and who believes that the artist must, above all, convey a personal impression of life, whatever the cost to unities and decorums. In short, Mrs. Wilson's art is erratically objective and personal, traditional and adventurous, but the reader is never in doubt that he has met in her pages a person of extraordinary sensibility and wisdom.

Her first novel, *Hetty Dorval* (1947), establishes in epigraph the themes (all from Donne) which dominate her work: "No man is an Iland, intire of it selfe"; ". . . makes one room an everywhere"; "Good is as visible as greene." And from these themes, naturalized in British Columbia, she develops recurring images—birds in flight; flowing, branching streams; the sea; the islanded self (Conrad, too, is a major influence on her thought); and the cycle of time and the seasons. In these terms the circumscribed area of Vancouver and the Fraser River valley is a world in microcosm; and England, a sea-change away, is simply another "part of the maine." In this world of correspondences Hetty Dorval, a coquette whose unvarying variety is known from Hong Kong to London, is a kind of anti-heroine. She becomes the idol of a warm-hearted British Columbia girl, but—luxuriously islanded in self—betrays this last chance for genuine friendship and disappears, golden and blind, into the darkness of Dollfuss's Austria. Extending this theme of human interdependence, *The Innocent Traveller* (1949) covers the century-long life of Topaz Edgeworth from the childish day when she examined Mr. Matthew Arnold's shoes under the family dining-table in England, to her volatile death in Vancouver. Deliberately episodic and unplotted, this work, by telling almost nothing, somehow reveals "the buried life" which the infantine Topaz first encountered in Mr. Arnold's mundane shoes.

The Equations of Love (1952) and *Swamp Angel* (1954) are Ethel Wilson's major works; *Love and Salt Water* (1956) develops the established themes named in its title, but falters in control. In the first of the *Equations of Love* ("Tuesday and Wednesday") we get a centripetal view of the nature of love, fate, and human inadequacy as revealed in a dozen characters; in the second ("Lilly's Story") we get a linear view of the forms which love takes in a single life. These equations certainly do not exhaust the subject, but within their compass they are at once sensitive and profound. Lacking the metaphysical chill of Hardy and the supersensitive *longeur* of Proust, they somehow remind us of both; and they recall at the same time the independence of Gertrude Stein and the decorum of James. *Swamp Angel*, a novel which calmly mixes experiment and tradition (with little regard for consequences), gives us Mrs. Wilson's two best characters: Maggie Lloyd, a thwarted housewife who rejects the sterility of her marriage for a precarious but genuinely engaged life; and Mrs. Severance, a retired and worldly circus queen whose fearless juggling with death (a talismanic "Swamp Angel" revolver) helps her friends to face life. Mrs. Severance, indeed, is an almost mythical figure whose saving power is her knowledge that the virtues and the verities are not identical.

But in all this excellence there is a disturbing flaw; the artist and the sibyl in Ethel Wilson are never quite in harmony, and though both are delightful, their impulses are often in conflict. The artist sketches in delicate details of scene and character—frail, beautiful water-colours—but the sibyl, uncertain of this communication, interrupts parenthetically or cuts the artist off before the rendering is complete. The result is an uncertainty in point of view and an abruptness in narrative method which (though consonant with Mrs. Wilson's vision of the real discontinuity of life) diminish the spell of her art rather than augment it. But the spell is potent nevertheless, for if the image flickers erratically, the light behind it is steady and bright.

In four very different works the quest for the self takes us, as in Mrs. Wilson's novels, across the Atlantic, but the backgrounds here are Continental—Germany, Austria, the Ukraine, and Israel. In each of these works (all are first novels), the hero undergoes an ordeal in isolation; he is cut off from his old culture, yet feels an outsider in the new. Reduced to the poor, forked creature he is, stripped of the garment of his *amour propre*, he ends by discovering his involvement "in mankinde."

It is impossible to escape the sense that the four protagonists are tragic witnesses, that they increase in spiritual stature as they shrink in the realm of worldly prestige. In *The Rich Man* (1948), Henry Kreisel tells the antiheroic story of an immigrant who leaves his factory job in Toronto to visit his family in Vienna, posing as a rich man. His imposture is revealed when he is called upon to help those whom he had wanted only to impress. His two absurd (and symbolic) purchases, a white suit and a livid painting, are soiled or wantonly destroyed as he learns through pain to accept the limitations of the human condition.

The central character of *How Many Angels* (1956) by Charles E. Israel is the doctor in charge of a very small hospital in the Sudetenland in 1943. Middle-aged, meek, his marriage barren, his profession and his adopted daughter his only passions, he is compelled by a humanitarian spirit he has tried to ignore to conceal refugees from the Nazis. His daughter betrays him to her lover, a Nazi informer. Deported from Germany, he is deserted by his wife, who becomes the mistress of a rising socialist leader. Finally, bereft of every personal and social support, he is accidentally reunited with his wife; neither wishes to live, but fate launches them again into the world—a world which may, perhaps, raze some of the domestic, social, and political walls that cut men off from the recognition of their common humanity. This is a nightmarish yet darkly affirmative work. A second novel, *The Mark* (1958), studies the rehabilitation of a sex deviate. Here, Israel displays all the gifts which make him a leading writer of documentary films and socio-historical dramas for radio and television: the social and psychological patterns are sharply drawn; the humane, anti-didactic conclusion is clear. But the Dostoevskian passion and commitment which the subject cries for are missing. Israel, an American citizen who has lived in Toronto since 1953, exhibits a professionalism too seldom seen in Canadian writing. When his imaginative vision takes command of his intelligence and skill, he may produce works of exceptional power.

Adele Wiseman's *The Sacrifice* (1956) records with humour and dramatic power the story of a Jewish-Ukrainian family in Winnipeg. Echoing the biblical story of Abraham and Isaac, the action contrasts the rigorous piety and ambition of immigrant parents with the changing attitudes of their children and grandchildren. Abraham, the father, has in some sense made a human sacrifice of his son Isaac; and then, still failing to understand the parable, he slaughters a ewe-like woman, his image of sterility and despair. Finally, confined in a madhouse, he understands that Life and Love are God's supreme commandments, and transmits this painfully won intuition to his grandson.

The poet Abraham Klein's only novel, *The Second Scroll* (1951), draws near one of the limits of the novel's range in the direction of the "anatomy," and near another in the direction of poetry. It has the rhetorical power, the exuberance in handling words observable in the best of Klein's poems, and it includes sections of poetry in the glosses that make the novel, with its five books from "Genesis" to "Deuteronomy," not only a parallel to the "First Scroll" but also to the sacred commentaries upon it. From the pogroms of 1917 to the State of Israel in 1949, it records the exile, exodus, and return of the chosen people as a young Jewish-Canadian journalist, in search of his multiform and Messianic uncle, Melech Davidson, comes to understand that miracle. Stylistically brilliant, *The Second Scroll* may be, like *Under the Volcano*, an exotic in the Canadian field, though its author is Canadian-born. But here it is worth noting that in one respect Klein is not alone: if we except MacLennan, Callaghan, Davies, Wilson, and Richler (and such transAtlantic imports as Walker and Moore), all the writers to be reviewed at any length in this chapter have produced only one novel of consequence; and many of them have produced one novel only. *The Second Scroll* had its place in the corpus of Klein's poetry, but as a novel it appears as another of those brief and flaring candles which at once inspire hope and reveal with new force the unilluminated reaches of Canadian fiction.

In contrast to the four preceding works, which look towards Europe and towards the past in their search for value, is a group bound closely to the Canadian environment and concerned with recording the equally painful effort of young people to come to terms with, or rise above, the provincial mentality of their families and communities. In *Under the Ribs of Death* (1957) John Marlyn portrays the abortive struggle of a Hungarian immigrant's son in Winnipeg to escape his origins by climbing the slippery ladder of commercial success. The faithful rendering of the boy's growing awareness of his surroundings and of the vulnerability of the young, the poor, and the alien, makes the first half of the book promising indeed; it is the sort of thing—the shrewd and sensitive recasting of what is essentially one's own early emotional experience—that Canadian writers have learned to do well. The second part, showing the collision of his desperate materialistic ambition with the more humane tradition he is trying to deny, becomes increasingly academic. His financial ruin and resultant spiritual rebirth are unconvincing. One sees again the failure of the Canadian writer to integrate the individual experience with the larger pattern.

W. O. Mitchell's *Who Has Seen the Wind* (1947) describes the encounters of a small-town Saskatchewan boy, Brian O'Connal, with "the realities of birth, hunger, satiety, eternity, death." Like Mark Twain looking back on his boyhood in Missouri, Mitchell sees the dark forces of his community as humorous or melodramatic figures; but though Brian's experience is frequently moving, it lacks the satirical bite of *Huckleberry Finn*. There is cruelty in both, but the humour that intensifies the Mississippi setting sugar-coats the actualities of the Saskatchewan town (potentially the grimmer setting of the two), so that Brian never encounters those "realities" in any significant way. He learns less how to face life than to avoid it by making it a fantasy of humour characters. The charm of Mitchell's recreation of boyhood, as well as this inevitable bias of his humour towards formula comedy, account for the popular appeal of his subsequent radio series "Jake and the Kid."

David Caanan, the hero of Ernest Buckler's *The Mountain and the Valley*

(1952), maintains at least a consistent, if terrible, relation to his Nova Scotia environment. A mute artist, hyperconsciously aware of the vividness and multiplicity of experience, David escapes the abrasive rub of ordinary life by retreating to a private world of his own. His sister (his spiritual alter-ego) marries a sailor and commits herself to the world of war and chance. Then, in final anguish, David climbs the mountain, where the colourless all-colour of snow drowns his intensities in its total ubiquity. In style, this novel reflects David's sensibility in an unrelenting search for the exact image to describe a neglected orchard in autumn, or a train streaking through the valley towards Halifax. Never, one feels, has rural Nova Scotia been more vividly recreated. Yet this intensity—like David's inability to risk the travail of either art or life —is at length disconcerting, for it has only one feverish note to sound. Buckler's novel is the cruellest picture of "the buried life" in Canadian fiction.

A continent away, and even more isolated than the valley of Buckler's novel, the British Columbia farming community of Sheila Watson's *The Double Hook* (1959) achieves something of the universality of a Walden or Winesburg, Ohio. Here, in a world which is still shadowed by the tyrannical Indian spirit Coyote, a pioneer family plays out the ageless drama of denial and self-discovery—discovery that darkness and glory, fear and joy, are complementary aspects of the human condition; "that when you fish for the glory you catch the darkness too." This is the double hook. James Potter, after seducing a neighbour's daughter and striking down his mother, flees in fear to the nearest village; but the spectacle of deceit and perversity which he encounters there leads him to return to his valley and embrace the fear and the glory which are man's destiny. This story, as simple as a medieval folk ballad, is told with a poetic compression and allusiveness, and a vividness of imagery that make its regional setting both a sharply realized *here* and "an everywhere." Repeatedly the style kindles echoes from Eliot and Faulkner, Job and the *New Testament*, and Anglo-Saxon poetry, but Mrs. Watson is so fully in control that idiom and action never gape apart as they sometimes do in Ethel Wilson's work. *The Double Hook*, indeed, is the most literary, and probably the most sophisticated novel of the period.

Two other writers who have taken up this search for individual or communal identity deserve mention; they are Roderick Haig-Brown, the Vancouver Island nature writer (*The Highest Hill*, 1949) and Saskatchewan English professor Edward McCourt (*Music at the Close*, 1947, *Home is the Stranger*, 1950, and *Walk through the Valley*, 1958). The writer who stands farthest from Ethel Wilson's quiet affirmation, however, is Mordecai Richler. His brash rejection of Canada's imported and inherited pieties brings to a close one phase of the Canadian quest for self, and in a flurry of fireworks launches another.

The uniqueness of Mordecai Richler (b. 1931) is easy to explain. Like Thoreau, who decided that Harvard taught all the branches of knowledge but none of the roots, Richler wants to get at the prime meanings of experience—to drive life into a corner and see whether it is a good thing or bad. But Richler does not live at Walden; his reality lies somewhere beneath the encrusted hypocrisies and orthodoxies of urban culture; and though in burrowing towards this reality he is often naïve, cranky, and even short-sighted, he is determined (in the words of his best critic, Peter Scott) "to keep to the experience at hand and to the truth which is available." Far from the reflective or analytical mood that has been characteristic of Canadian fiction, Richler's spirit resembles that of the "angry" young Englishman and the "beat" writers of "the great American night"; but though, like them, he strips away the world's pretences, he does not end as an outsider, in alienated or intoxicated freedom. Richler belongs (as Brian Moore does) in society, and he has enough verve to refuse alienation. If orthodox frauds reject him, he will simply bypass them and create his own order—a crude one, perhaps, but bracing in its directness, and electric with energy.

Since 1954, when he was twenty-two, Richler has produced a tide of film and television scripts, short stories, articles for British, American, and Canadian journals, and four novels which, though flawed individually, constitute in sum the most promising *œuvre* of the recent period. *The Acrobats* (1954) and *Son of a Smaller Hero* (1955) might both be described as "first novels"; both deal with a hero obsessed by self and in reckless opposition to a world which is stifling, corrupt, and Protean in its deceit. *The Acrobats* recounts the spiritual agony and eventual death of André Bennett, a young Canadian painter in Spain—the symbolic arena of shattered ideals, lost causes, and vain hopes. In this shadowy post-war limbo, Richler's hero learns two truths: "that the poor should have more because they were human and no human should be ugly"; and that the individual must act on what he knows, for "not to act would mean nonliving." Yet when André does act—striking out drunkenly against the ugliness of a former Nazi officer—he is destroyed. He succumbs because of his inexperience, but he does act; and the novel ends in a symbolic birth. André's mistress bears a child (fathered by the Nazi) whom she names André; then, counselled by a sage and benevolent restaurateur, Chaim, she embarks for a new life in America. As Chaim, the humanitarian whose passport is revoked by state after state, affirms: "there is always hope.... There has to be."

The forced symbolism of this ending is only one of *The Acrobats'* shortcomings: the festival of San José glitters like the fireworks which conclude it, but falls short of the structural significance which similar rites achieve in Hemingway or Mann; the narrative method flickers uncertainly because the narrator is not sufficiently distinct from his hero; and the echoes of Hemingway, Sartre, and others are more often reflexes than conscious devices. But though the book is not, as one critic claims, "a guide to intelligent, contemporary pastiche," it has a nervous, exploratory power.

Son of a Smaller Hero (1955) is in effect an earlier chapter in fictional autobiography. But if Richler is on firmer ground in the Jewish community of Montreal than he was in Spain, he is still uncomfortably close to his hero's anger and confusion; the family and community described come magnificently to life, but the hero, Noah Adler, is such an unreliable guide to his own experience that the closing ambiguity of the novel appears inadvertent rather than deliberate. The step from this to *A Choice of Enemies* (1957) and *The Apprenticeship of Duddy Kravitz* (1959) is the enormous stride from denial to assertion, from rejection to deliberate choice. As in battle, the technical units lag behind the attack forces in both of these works, but the objectives are taken and held. In *A Choice of Enemies*, the hero is a left-wing expatriate, Norman Price, who has sought refuge in London's Hampstead bohemia, only to discover that his friends, Fifth Amendment heroes (mostly writers and film-makers) are no less ignoble than their bourgeois enemies, and perhaps even more exclusive in their group orthodoxy. As in *The Acrobats*, the central problem concerns a Nazi (this time a refugee from East Germany). In the course of defending this young man's right to strip off the labels with which society has marked him, Norman clashes with his friends and is himself stripped of every mark of prestige which he had enjoyed as an insider. In the nuclear age, Norman realizes, the real enemies are not communism, fascism, or capitalism but the ancient scourges of pride, covetousness, and the lust for power. Finally, after an attack of amnesia (the symbol is awkward) Norman "dies into life"; he chooses to marry a very ordinary English girl and to return to disinterested scholarship; to live not for prestige or power but for unheroic, humane values. Then, sensing perhaps a hint of complacency in this easy-difficult choice, Richler gives the reader a final jab: Norman's "ordinary" wife, it appears, is dazzled by the prestige of his former friends, and begins ingratiating herself with them even before the honeymoon begins.

In *A Choice of Enemies*, Richler the film-writer occasionally interferes with Richler the novelist; suspense is introduced whether meaning requires it or not, and dialogue is often geared to the film editor's cut. In *The Apprenticeship of Duddy Kravitz* the novelist is again in control, but a new problem, the relation between realism and comedy or farce, presents itself. Duddy's apprenticeship—his chequered progress from a Montreal slum to a shaky status as landowner—is a story by turns comic, pathetic, bawdy, and farcical; and though the exuberant reality of Duddy himself is never in doubt, the modulation of other characters from pathos to farce makes the reader's suspension of disbelief something less than willing. But these flaws are principally evidence of the rapidity of Richler's artistic development. The theme of *Duddy Kravitz* extends the quest for value of the earlier books, but this time Richler dares a hero whose background is hard knocks and whose only capital is his ability to charm, twist, dream, calculate, and work. And since Duddy has none of the training or experience of Norman Price, the ironies of his experience are presented without comment; everything is kaleidoscopic, headlong action, and everything is indispensable to the total statement. Hacking his way through the urban jungle of hypocrisy and chicane, Duddy outsmarts enemies and exploits friends, but he finally gets his land, an untouched tract of lake and fields in a high Laurentian valley. In doing so he has sacrificed the respect of his *zeyda* and his sweetheart; both are worthy people, but their codes would bind Duddy permanently in the nightmare of modern urban life. Thus the conclusion of Duddy's ascent is a beginning rather than an end; unlike Nick Carraway of *The Great Gatsby*, however, he possesses not a corrupt Long Island but a virgin tract of Canada from which he raucously dismisses his deformed and vicious rival, Dingleman. Richler does not pose a final question, but one hangs in the air: Will Duddy reproduce on his own land the nightmare which he has escaped?

Mordecai Richler has asked piercing questions on issues which involve the self, the nation, and mankind, and he has dismissed the stock replies that religion, politics, and the polite social sciences and humanities customarily offer. His exuberant style and intellectual toughness make him the most exciting and promising of Canada's younger novelists.

V

There can be no question that Canadian fiction has profited immensely since 1940 from the experience of writers who have gone abroad, and from the fresh vision of writers who have come to live in Canada. Service in World War II and subsequent duties as occupation units and in international organizations have taken unprecedented numbers of Canadians abroad in this period; prosperity, mass air travel, and the communications systems of the "jet age" have made the outside world immediate to most Canadians; immigration has not only brought colour and variety to Canada's urban centres but has made the encounter with other languages and other customs part of the day-to-day experience of most of our people. Inevitably the provincial Canadian has resisted the change, but inevitably, too, a cultural expansion has occurred. As a result, the discovery of Canada now demands of the artist a discovery of the wider world, and such writers as Margaret Laurence (her *This Side Jordan*, 1960, is a distinguished story of life in Ghana), Mavis Gallant, Graham McInnes, and others, are documenting that discovery with skill and insight.

Fiction based on the experience of World War II, however, reveals that this expansion of consciousness is still embryonic. Writers who attempted to deal with the major issues of the war and the peace had not done enough homework in history and philosophy, and writers who made the conflict an occasion for personal exploration, lacked the power to get outside their own experience. The best works, not unexpectedly, were those which recreated the soldier's experience graphically, without indulging in summit generalizations or muddy introspection.

In these terms, *Storm Below* (1944) by Hugh Garner, is the most impressive Canadian novel of World War II. Less committed and more colloquial than Conrad as an observer of life at sea, Garner brings the world of a corvette on the North Atlantic convoy route into mundane yet mysterious life. Nature and fate and man himself, as Garner sees them, are inscrutable, but man develops curious loyalties and animosities in the process of adapting to life, even if his adaptation is no more than a tropism. *Storm Below* is thus an unheroic but oddly warming record of an encounter of nature, fate, and man during six days at sea in 1943. The corvette's crew does not choose to go to sea, but when storms without and storms below-deck face them, "they'll be there, and they know what to do." *Execution* (1958) by Colin McDougall matches Hugh Garner's realism and occasionally rises to poetry, but the philosophical truth which the author attempts to rescue from his war experience in Sicily and Italy sinks finally, if melodiously, to muddy death. In various ways McDougall's protagonists learn that war, execution, and sadism are one extremity of a spectrum which terminates in friendship, sympathy, and love. But the brutal facts of execution weigh so heavily that McDougall's spiritual intuitions appear as gossamer theory. He understands the love–pain paradox of *Billy Budd* but lacks the passion which invests Melville's work with its authority. Three novels by Lionel Shapiro (1908–1958), *The Sealed Verdict* (1947), *Torch for a Dark Journey* (1950), and *The Sixth of June* (1955), deal skilfully and at times movingly with the Allied occupation of Germany, the ideological dilemma of a Czeck scientist in post-war France, and the great offensive that ended the war; but though Shapiro's concern over the moral and intellectual issues which he raises is genuine, his work is closer to expert journalism and scenario-writing than to the autonymous patterns of art. Ralph Allen's *Home Made Banners* (1946) lacks the patina of Shapiro's work but is somehow truer. His criticism of the recruiting system and of military training rests on sharp observation, and his distinction between propaganda and personal or "home made" banners raises a major issue; the title, however, promises more than Allen delivers. Earle Birney's "military picaresque," *Turvey* (1949) laughs with uneasy heartiness at the dilemmas of man regimented, but misses the universality at which it aims; and Norman Levine's *The Angled Road* (1952) is an erratic and groping account of an airman's search for value.

Complementing the fiction produced by Canadians abroad, the work of immigrant writers—some of them, like Malcolm Lowry, long-term residents who came, conquered, and departed—has further extended the circumference of Canadian reality. A writer like Brian Moore, for example, is closer to Joyce's *Dubliners* and to the vigorous young Englishmen of the so-called "angry" group than to any Canadian pattern, but the fact that Moore is here rather than in Belfast gives him a special importance for Canadian readers and writers alike. The vision that talented young novelists bring to Canada, indeed, may affect the whole development of Canadian writing.

Malcolm Lowry (1909–1957), who lived intermittently in British Columbia from 1939 to 1954, is the richest and most exotic novelist who has associated himself with Canada. Born in England and educated at Cambridge, he found in Canada a world as yet unspoiled by the delirium that had overtaken Europe; and it was here that he wrote *Under the Volcano* (1947) and a matchless collection of short stories of British Columbia life which his executors have prepared for publication under the title *Hear Us O Lord from Heaven Thy Dwelling Place*. In effect, *Under the Volcano* is a twentieth-century *Inferno*, compounded of images from Joyce and Mann, Dante and *The Cabbala*, and from Lowry's own *saisons en enfer*. Its protagonist, Geoffrey Firmin (the infirm one) is a British consul in Mexico who plays out in a symbolic landscape the last agonies of an individual (and a civilization) that has abused its magic powers. Firmin drinks *mescal*, not for its vision-inducing properties but as an escape from the demands and pressures of modern life. Unfortunately the "linked analogies" which universalize Firmin's experience proliferate in such dizzying circles that the complex structure of the work is obscured. Like Melville, Lowry is a "possessed" writer; the range and intensity of his imagination are extraordinary, and the simultaneous vividness and allusiveness of his style make every page a prose poem. He lacks the control which would complete these gifts, however, and though he avoids the excesses of a *Mardi*, he does not achieve the synthesis which makes *Moby Dick* a masterpiece.

A native of Belfast who now lives in Montreal and New York, Brian Moore (b. 1921) sounds a note new to Canadian fiction. Combining high humour with shrewd social observation, authentic dialogue with fluent narrative, and moral toughness with real tenderness, his work at once recalls the bitter-sweet atmosphere of Joyce's "Clay" and the moral agony (minus the literary décor) of Eliot's "Prufrock." Each of his three novels is a variation on a single theme—the struggle of the individual to commit himself to life, to abandon protective disguises or self-deceptions and, like "a drop of water joining an ocean," embrace his humanity. Moore's triumph is to give both his protagonists and the world in which they exist a palpable reality. Thus in *The Lonely Passion of Judith Hearne* (1955) we enter the world of an aging Belfast spinster who drowns the knowledge of her aloneness in alcohol, and ends in a hospital for indigents where her unassailably lifeless realities are a photograph of her dead aunt and a chromo of her dead God. This bleak but moving work was followed in 1947 by *The Feast of Lupercal*, the history of Diarmuid Devine, a Belfast schoolmaster whose fear of giving offence to anyone causes him to betray the one woman (Una) who might have released him from spiritual and physical barrenness. In style this work is an advance on *Judith Hearne*, where effects borrowed from Joyce and Eliot are not fully assimilated; but though its dramatic scenes are superb, its use of repetitive devices is somewhat obvious. In overcoming these difficulties, *The Luck of Ginger Coffey* (1960) adopts a manner almost too relaxed, too chary of images which might thicken the surface texture; but it is an excellent novel nevertheless. Ginger Coffey, a self-deluding Irishman who has followed a dream of success and prestige to Montreal, is gradually stripped of every one of his illusions, but unlike Judith Hearne and Devine, Coffey—after hilarious and humiliating experiences as diaper deliveryman, proofreader, and prisoner at the bar of a Montreal court ("a fait pisser juste dans la grande porte du Royal Family Hotel")—Coffey finally recognizes that he may "die in humble circs: it did not matter." And with this recognition he is suddenly free to embrace life for what it is. Because Moore's central theme is a timeless ethical problem, the sea-change from Ulster to Canada has been easy for him. His response to Canada, seen through the rueful eyes of Ginger Coffey, is at once exuberant and sharply in focus. One hopes that some of his freshness may be communicated to more solemn Canadian writers.

David Walker, born in Scotland in 1911, served a term in Canada as aide to the then Governor-General, Lord Tweedsmuir, waited out most of World War II in a German prison camp, and spent some time in India before settling in Canada in 1947 to write. Since then he has published six novels revealing not only his wide travels and varied experiences but also his easy exploiting of the popular types of fiction. *The Storm and the Silence* (1949) describes a manhunt in Scotland; *Harry Black* (1956) a tiger-hunt in India. *Geordie* (1950—Walker's most popular work) and *Digby* (1953) combine "escapist romance . . . sprightly comedy, and . . . moral tale." In *The Pillar* (1952) Walker draws on his own POW experience for a highly dramatic and suspenseful tale of self-discovery according to the *Stalag 17* formula. Walker's only novel having a Canadian setting is *Where the High Winds Blow* (1960), a combination of northern adventure, domestic romance, and a rugged-enterprise thesis which again illustrates both Mr. Walker's competence in fiction and his reluctance to risk that competence on less popular themes.

Perhaps it is enough to be grateful for, that there has been, in recent Canadian fiction, the leaven of professional "know-how" from visiting and immigrant novelists. This, of course, takes us back to the beginnings of our literature, to *Emily Montague* and *Roughing It in the Bush*; but with all the difference that comes of there being, now, a native lump to leaven.

VI

What remains to be noticed—short stories, works of humour, and *belles-lettres*—is such a spindly harvest that one is more inclined to ponder the reasons for its failure than to study individual straws. Canada's cultural climate in the post-war period is certainly responsible in part for this failure, but the brutal realities of the market bulk even larger; and the two factors, climate and market, usually appear in combination. *Belles-lettres*, for example, demands a soil rich in ideas and a bracing air of controversy, but Canada, even in the fifties, shunned controversy, and regarded ideas as a disease of professors and eccentrics. At the same time, there is still no daily press and no substantial periodical press which provides a forum for expert and literate opinion. In this situation, academics devote themselves, for intellectual and economic reasons, to scholarship, and publish as often in British and American learned journals as in Canada; journalists, dependent on what press there is, almost inevitably descend to well-worn formulas of wit or impudence, to the superficial glance at issues and events, or to controversy for its own sake. And between these extremes of the academy and the press-club there is almost nothing of interest. Superannuated clergymen and professors collect their reminiscences and scattered "thoughts"; newspapermen select—but never strictly enough—their best columns; and poets, novelists, and after-dinner speakers publish occasional essays. *Belles-lettres*, in short, does not flourish in Canada. There are signs, however, that the unique combination of grace, wit, and humane learning which characterizes the literary essay is known and valued by a few writers. Such varied works as Emily Carr's reminiscences of sketching trips in British Columbia, *Klee Wyck* (1941), Pierre Berton's informal history, *Klondike* (1958), and the best essays of MacLennan and Davies point in the right direction. Periodical articles by Millar MacLure, John W. Graham, Peter Scott, and Kildare Dobbs —to name only four of a growing number—achieve that happy balance of wit and erudition, vigour and grace, which is one of our greatest unclaimed legacies from English literature. And finally, George Woodcock's editorial activities, and his numerous books and articles on travel, literature, and social criticism demonstrate that the man of humane letters, if not yet an indigenous figure, can at least survive in contemporary Canada.

Apart from Robertson Davies, the record of humorous writers is much less encouraging—so unpromising, indeed, that the prematurely established Stephen Leacock Medal for humour is at present an annual embarrassment. As we have seen above, one vein of Leacock's genius—the gently sardonic observation of society—has developed into full-scale satire in Davies' work. Another—the spectacle of the "little man" torn between necessity and desire, real and ideal—has been reduced by Eric Nicol and others to a pale shadow of Thurber's Walter Mitty; and the plain style appropriate to this figure has been abandoned for chattering wisecracks *à la* Bob Hope. Apart from these directions, W. O. Mitchell has developed a superior formula for "Western" humour in his tales of Jake and the Kid; Robert Fontaine's *The Happy Time* (1945) turns the experience of his Ottawa childhood into formula comedy of the "family entertainment" variety familiar on radio and television; and Paul Hiebert's *Sarah Binks* (1947) satirizes Canada's literary nationalism and academic criticism with such weightiness that the author himself barely escapes the baleful eye of travesty.

Compared with *belles-lettres* and humour, the record of the short story is good, but its importance in Canadian expression is declining. Since 1940 more than fifty volumes of short stories by individual authors have been published, as well as such anthologies as *A Book of Canadian Stories* (Desmond Pacey, ed., in four editions since 1947), *Canadian Short Stories* (Robert Weaver, ed., 1960), and *Klanak Islands* (Henry Kreisel, *et al.*, 1959). The volumes by individual writers include many of the established novelists—Callaghan, Wilson, de la Roche, Raddall, Bird, Garner—and such younger writers as Mavis Gallant who is most widely known for her contributions to the *New Yorker*. Canadian stories, moreover, appear occasionally in such journals as the *Atlantic Monthly* and in Martha Foley's annual anthology of the best short stories of the year. Yet despite this record, and despite the continuing interest in the form exhibited by Richler, Reaney, Alice Munro and others, the short story has lost much of its prestige; a generation ago it was the recognized proving-ground for aspiring novelists, and many writers returned to it intermittently throughout their careers; in 1960 it still flourishes in small reviews and student literary magazines, but the majority of young writers abandon it after their apprentice years. This decline in the prestige of the short story is so marked, in fact, that it must be recognized as symptomatic of a radically changed literary situation.

What should be recognized first in assessing this change is that until the advent of television and the concomitant upsurge in film-making in Montreal and Toronto, a great deal of Canadian writing has been "amateur," the work of Sunday writers—professors, part-time journalists or broadcasters, and housewives. And for these writers (there are still many of them), the short story, the essay, and the radio talk have been popular forms. The short story, moreover, carried with it a prestige established by such writers as Poe, Chekov, James, Conrad, Joyce and Faulkner. It was a major form, and a form particularly suited to the needs of writers who could not find time for the extended effort demanded by the novel. Moreover, the short story led into broader avenues; success in this genre ended in offers from publishers, offers which might usher the part-time writer into a full-time literary career.

But with the arrival of television (an event which coincided with a great increase in Canada's population), the old order changed. The mass media (film, television, and radio) clearly required the services of full-time writers; and in response to this demand a gifted group of professional writers has developed. But at the same time, in Canada as elsewhere, magazines recognized that they could not compete with the "instant" short fiction of television drama, and turned almost exclusively to educational or documentary essays. A few small reviews continue to publish short stories, and the C.B.C. will still broadcast them, but these outlets have become blind alleys for writers who wish to reach a mass audience.

Thus in a period of about ten years the "amateur" status of the Canadian short story writer has been seriously shaken. The choices which now present themselves to him are these: he can use the mass media rather than the short story as a stepping-stone to the novel (a form which is now finding its epic shape in the *roman fleuve*); he can adapt his art to the needs of the mass media and identify himself with them; or he can stick with the short story as a special, if currently neglected, genre. Special pleas for the short-story writer would be futile at this date. As Robert Weaver has suggested, the artist who genuinely wants to write short fiction is now forced to compete in the international market. There is still a devoted international audience for this form; and at this date that is where the Canadian short-story writer probably should be competing.

In this difficult, exacting, and now declining genre, Morley Callaghan is still the acknowledged Canadian master. Others have used the form with considerable skill, but only a handful have managed to sustain their quality through a complete volume, and none of these—unless it be, fitfully, Ethel Wilson—approaches the authority of a Eudora Welty or Frank O'Connor. Raddall's quality, as suggested above, combines the excitement of adventure with robust characterization and the authentic recreation of a regional scene. Hugh Garner's *The Yellow Sweater and Other Stories* (1952) probes calmly, almost sadistically, beneath the frailties and hypocrisies of ordinary people, and in pieces like "One, Two, Three Little Indians" lays bare the monstrousness of our polite humanitarianism. In *The Other Paris* (1956), Mavis Gallant isolates with great delicacy and subtlety the threads of apparently trivial words and events which lead to the deepest reaches of the human heart. In these structures, the past flows freely into the present; the personality is seen to consist, as existentialists express it, of "areas of care." Just as Dos Passos and O'Hara are clearly in the background of Garner's writing, Henry James sounds distantly in Mavis Gallant's work. The world she creates is small, but within its bounds she is "one of those upon whom nothing is lost."

What has been said of Ethel Wilson's novels applies also to her short stories, with the difference that the uncontrolled element—the province of the sybil—is not obtrusive in the best of them. Set in Vancouver or London or Munich or on the banks of the Nile, they are more cosmopolitan than Callaghan's, while the contrast between the first and last stories in *Mrs.*

Golightly and Other Stories (1961) suggests a wider range of mood than even Callaghan commands. Although "Mrs. Golightly and the Convention" is the most frequently reproduced of Ethel Wilson's stories, "The Window" is perhaps more representative. Its title image, the window framing by day the empty scene and mirroring by night the sterile life of the protagonist, is central not only to hers but to much modern Canadian fiction. This seems to be the vision of contemporary life which our fiction is now recording, and it is not impossible that both Morley Callaghan and Ethel Wilson will be judged finally to have recorded it as convincingly in their short stories as in their novels.

A number of other writers in this genre deserve mention. Sinclair Ross's lyric, elegiac tales of prairie life have been noticed above. James Reaney, Alice Munro, and Douglas Spettigue have been more successful than most novelists in capturing the flavour and mood of rural Ontario (in Reaney and Munro this region takes on something of the macabre atmosphere that we associate with Truman Capote and Carson McCullers). And a half dozen others, of whom Jack Ludwig is the most accomplished, are documenting urban life with a zest that dispels the faint melancholy which has pervaded the bulk of our short fiction.

In looking at the transcontinental sweep of Canadian fiction, critics from Northrop Frye to Warren Tallman have seen its development as a struggle against the violence, or the snowy indifference of nature—as an effort to humanize and give articulate shape to this vast landscape; to encompass it in imaginative terms, and in so doing, to discover the self. In these terms, the fiction of the recent period reveals that the process is still far from complete. The majority of writers still inhabit romantic worlds which have very little to do with the realities of Canadian life in the post-war period, while others, conscious of the limitations of their community, seek to escape it by becoming American or British or something else that seems to them to be superior. Ironically, this attempt at escape cannot succeed, but the stretching of the imagination which it entails is the best thing that can happen to Canadian writing, for what the writer who goes abroad learns is that he cannot simply slough off his Canadian experience. By establishing a relation with other cultures he may gain a great deal that is valuable; but even more important, he will learn something of his Canadian uniqueness. As both Emerson and James recognized in the last century, the passion for foreign experience proved, finally, to be a potent "Americanizing" force. Unquestionably, Canadian fiction is now in a similar expanding phase. It is not too extravagant to imagine that in the period upon which it now enters it will truly establish "an original relation to the universe."

37. Poetry
1920-1935

MUNRO BEATTIE

I

THROUGH THE FIRST THREE DECADES of this century the impulses that had animated Canadian poets in the eighties and nineties slackened and deteriorated. By 1920 the romantic-Victorian tradition was at its last gasp. Yet, during the 1920's, its conventions persisted in thousands of mediocre lines published annually in Canadian magazines, on the home-makers' and book-editors' pages of Canadian newspapers, and in the flimsy volumes issued by Briggs or Musson or other Toronto presses. This was a body of verse that, almost without exception, modelled itself upon the lesser works of the nineteenth-century masters of English poetry and upon such minor Americans as Lanier, Riley, Whittier, Cawein, and Bayard Taylor. In the years following World War I other voices as well began to echo through Canadian verse: the voices of Symons, Thompson, Housman, Kipling, Rupert Brooke, Masefield, Alfred Noyes, the early Yeats, and the Georgian poets of pre-war England.

This Canadian poetry derived its metaphysics from the eighteenth-century reconciliation of the Newtonian universe with a belief in a Creator, from the nineteenth-century synthesis of evolution and faith, and from the transcendentalism of New England—not so much from the tragic insight of Hawthorne and Melville as from the more optimistic transcendentalism of Emerson, Thoreau, and Whitman. In diction it was unremittingly "poetic." One touch of the colloquial would have been disastrous, for this was writing in a style that, in T. S. Eliot's words, "aspired to the elevation of verse" before having become "assimilated to cultivated contemporary speech." Its prosodic patterns were conventional: sonnet, quatrain, octosyllabics, rhyme royal, the Spenserean stanza in various adaptations and disformations, the "Lady of Shalott" stanza, the "In Memoriam" stanza, and countless variants and repetitions of forms originally signed with the individuality of Keats, Poe, Browning, or Swinburne. In metre it was oppressively and inflexibly iambic; or if trochaic, with cadences straight out of "Locksley Hall"; if anapaestic, with a lilt reminiscent of something by Scott or Moore.

Worst of all, the versifiers of this arid period, having nothing to say, kept up a constant jejune chatter about infinity, licit love, devotion to the Empire, death, Beauty, God, and Nature. Sweet singers of the Canadian out-of-doors, they peered into flowers, reported on the flittings of the birds, discerned mystic voices in the wind, descried elves among the poplars. They insisted upon being seen and overheard in poetic postures: watching for the will-o'-the-wisp, eavesdropping on "the forest streamlet's noonday song," lying like a mermaid on a bed of coral, examining a bird's nest in winter, fluting for the fairies to dance, or "wandering through some silent forest's aisles." John Garvin's anthology, *Canadian Poets* (1916, revised 1926), in which appear most of these instances, abundantly demonstrates that poetry in Canada as the 1920's opened was dying of emotional and intellectual anemia.

By the mid-thirties signs of revitalization—infrequent but unmistakable signs—had appeared. The twenties was a time of fresh beginnings in Canada and of receptivity to stimulus from without. The forces of modernism—the "new poetry" of England and the United states—gradually re-invigorated writers and writing in Canada. Anyone who searches diligently through the 1912–25 files of the Manitoba *Free Press*, the Toronto *Globe, Saturday Night*, the *Canadian Magazine*, the *Canadian Bookman*, and the *Canadian Forum* (founded in 1920, at the right moment to be of service to new attitudes and new methods), will discover evidence that a few Canadians were reading the new poetry and reacting to it. They were coming upon, in the pages of *Poetry: A Magazine of Verse* (Chicago), poems, strange and exciting poems, by Vachel Lindsay, Carl Sandburg, Amy Lowell, Wallace Stevens, Ezra Pound, and T. S. Eliot. They were being exhilarated by books by these poets, and books by Robert Frost, Edgar Lee Masters, E. E. Cummings, Robinson Jeffers, and D. H. Lawrence. They were learning to prefer the successive Imagist anthologies to the volumes of *Georgian Poetry*. They were threshing out in the correspondence columns of "literary" pages such agitating questions as "Is the reign of Tennyson over?" and "Is free verse really only shredded prose?"

The modern movement in poetry was a threefold revolution: first, prosodic experiment—free verse, conformity to none of the conventions of metre, line-length, stanza form; secondly, the use of language and imagery appropriate to a modern sensibility; thirdly, the enlargement of subject-matter to take in areas of behaviour, attitude, and milieu neglected or shunned by most poets of the late nineteenth or early twentieth century. Experimental verse was the aspect easiest to argue about, and to imitate. Free verse became a shibboleth among reviewers and newspaper correspondents. The Canadian Authors' Association (founded in 1921) split nationally and in all its branches, although the first president of the association, John Murray Gibbon, enthusiastically sponsored free verse and wrote for the first issue of the *Canadian Bookman* a sensible and well-informed article about *vers libre*. Canadian readers in general—at least, the minuscule minority who read any poetry at all and who were aware that Canadian poets, a few of them, were poised on the verge of violence—were assured by the *Globe*'s complacent literary editor that, "We usually write in metre and dislike poetical as well as other kinds of Bolshevism."

Several poets, however, were un-Canadian enough to try their hands at experimental verse. The earliest was Arthur Stringer (1874–1950) whose book of poems *Open Water* came out in 1914, when *vers libre*, even in the United States, was still the concern only of a few "little" magazines. Stringer, a prolific and versatile writer of third-rate quality, produced during his career a number of novels and fifteen books of verse that ranged from poetic dramas on classical themes to facile and sentimental "Irish" songs. His preface to *Open Water* was a carefully worked out manifesto: to express the feelings of a new era, the poet must emancipate his writing from stereotyped rhythms and out-moded forms. The sixty poems of *Open Water* go some distance towards justifying the preface and the method. They are almost wholly unmarred by "poetic diction." They display the virtues of economy and directness. Their scope of mood and material is wider than other Canadian books of the period show. But they fail to realize the peculiar kind of impetus and unity that good free verse can attain to. They are mostly gatherings of prose sentences arbitrarily divided into lines of varying length, as illustrated by this example, "One Night in the Northwest":

> When they flagged our train because of a broken rail,
> I stepped down out of the crowded car,
> With its clamour and dust and heat and babel of broken talk.
> I stepped out into the cool, the velvet cool, of the night,
> And felt the balm of the prairie-wind on my face,
> And somewhere I heard the running of water,
> I felt the breathing of grass,
> And I knew, as I saw the great white stars,
> That the world was made for good!

Frank Oliver Call, less competent than Arthur Stringer as a literary journeyman, was equally doctrinaire. "*Vers libre*, like the motor car and aeroplane, has come to stay whether we like it or no." This is the thesis of the foreword to his small volume of verse, *Acanthus and Wild Grape* (1920). The title refers to a double purpose. The acanthus poems illustrate conventional modes, and manage to be as inane and hackneyed as most other Canadian poems of the period. The wild grape poems are intended, on the other hand, to demonstrate the superiority of free verse, but they have only the interest of novelty. Novelty is to be preferred to repetition, but only success justifies prosodic novelty. Not one of these wild grape poems forms a satisfying whole. Four years later, F. O. Call published in *Blue Homespun* a group of pleasant and perceptive sonnets about French Canada. His gift did, after all, belong to the traditional and conventional rather than the experimental.

Among the few Canadians who took note, between 1915 and 1925, of the new English and American poetry no one wrote more sensibly and sympathetically about it than Arthur L. Phelps (b. 1887). As well, he contributed several poems of his own in free verse to the *Canadian Magazine*. Of these the most accomplished was a sequence published as a chapbook in 1919, *Bobcaygeon: A Sketch of a Little Town*. The diction is scrupulously unadorned and the rhythms are matter-of-fact. The short poems of the group project with a fair degree of skill the moods of nostalgia and quiet joy. Like Leacock's "The Train to Mariposa," Phelps's poems develop a double theme: the life of the little town beside the lake and the city-dweller's sense of it as a haven and a home. Phelps had a better understanding than most of his contemporaries of the nature of free verse. He perceived that it must realize a new rhythm and not merely distort old rhythms.

Lawren Harris (b. 1885), whose paintings are an important part of the artistic renaissance of the twenties, ventured into verse in *Contrasts* (1922), a collection of Whitmanesque notations on Canadian life. The poems are insistently "realistic"; that is, they emphasize squalor and mention forms of conduct not discussed by nicely brought up Canadians. Harris's scorn for an industrial and commercial civilization, his scepticism of "bourgeois values," and his indignation over the ugliness of Toronto and environs come through with crude force. As poetry *Contrasts* is undistinguished in diction and awkward in rhythm, but its colloquial directness here and there calls to mind Lawrence's *Nettles* and *Pansies*. Lawren Harris's pictures do a better job of recording his vision of city life in the 1920's.

Other books of free verse were published which, like those already mentioned, are of historical rather than literary interest. Louise Morey Bowman (1882–1944) sounded the more contemplative tones of free verse in two books: *Moonlight and Common Day* (1922) and *Dream Tapestries* (1924). The usefulness of irregular verse for exotic effects was exploited by a Canadian missionary to China, Florence Ayscough, who, in collaboration with Amy Lowell, produced an attractive little book of little poems, *Fir-Flower Tablets* (1922). Considerably more skill and insight appeared in the free-verse adaptations of west coast Indian songs that Constance Lindsay Skinner (1879–1939) had begun publishing in 1913 and 1914 in *Poetry* and the London *Bookman* and which were brought together into the collection entitled *Songs of the Coast Dwellers* (1930). Miss Skinner's irregular cadences splendidly re-create the verbal and emotional effects of primitive poetry. The interest of her poems is literary as well as anthropological.

Careful search discovers a number of mediocre poems in free verse scattered through magazines and newspapers. One virtue sets them off from the conventional poems among which they appeared, the trite sonnets and insipid lyrics: a more direct way of looking at and speaking about reality. They avoided, on the whole, inflated diction, flights into the empyrean, pressure on the picturesque. The practice of free verse helped to clear away some of the literary clutter of the period. Otherwise, this small flurry of free-versifying in the early twenties is of importance only to the literary historian, as symptom and portent. Free verse as a battle cry has never had much meaning for the practising poet, who is not so much interested in freedom as in finding the way to devise lines and patterns that will most effectively compose his perceptions into poems. Even some poets who certainly would have been claimed by the "conservatives" in the debate over the new poetry departed, when it suited their purposes, from conventional metrics and stanza forms. Some of Duncan Campbell Scott's finest poems (for instance "At Gull Lake: August 1810," "The Forsaken," "The Height of Land") were composed in lines that eschewed traditional prosody, though not in a way that would astonish readers of Matthew Arnold. Marjorie Pickthall, too, depended on her excellent ear rather than on a careful count of syllables for the rhythms of "Père Lalement," "The Little Sister of the Prophet," and "The Pool."

Furthermore, a poet whose attitudes and themes were thoroughly "traditional" might discern in free verse the most efficient method of handling his material. Arthur Bourinot (b. 1893) is an example. Early in his career Bourinot discovered that he could best put down his delicate impressions of nature in short irregular lines. In the frequent collections that he has published since *Laurentian Lyrics and Other Poems* (1915), his most successful poems of mood and description have been of this fashion. Such vigour as his narrative poems attain to is worked up by the rapid succession of short strongly accented lines (*Collected Poems*, 1947).

Almost all poetry written in Canada since the 1920's might be called free verse. Each poem takes the shape dictated by the movement of feeling and thought; every poem must appear to be the first of its kind. Even in the "rage for order" that impelled poets following the Second World War to compose strict and sinewy stanzas, the stanzas were new creations in lines of diverse lengths and rhythms, rather than re-creations of traditional forms. Modern poets had learned that the value of free verse does not reside in its superficial novelty and visual stimulus, but in its fidelity to the essential rhythm of the poem.

This was a prosodic wisdom learned by only two of the early writers of modernist verse in Canada, and the best work of both was completed in the twenties: Eustace Ross and Raymond Knister.

W. W. E. Ross (b. 1894) in the title of his 1930 collection, *Laconics,* implied a temperamental aversion from the looseness and garrulity—"all this fiddle," as Marianne Moore, one of his preceptors, put it—of the usual magazine verse of the era. Some few of his own poems betray a tendency to wordiness, poems composed in longish, Whitmanish lines like those of Lawren Harris: "Sunnyside," "Wind Conquest," "Sprightly Young Woman" (a charming poem, however), and "High Park." Ross also made translations from Catullus and Euripides that did not wholly avoid current weaknesses of metre and diction. His *Sonnets* (1932) are intellectually interesting in an angular fashion, but ungainly as verse.

The poems by Ross that count are the free-verse poems in *Laconics,* those that show his characteristic method: to reduce a poem to its essentials, its bare bones, and to give it typographical distinctiveness. Prosodically, this is less audacious than it looks. A rhythmic unit of four lines generally prevails, quatrains from which everything has been eliminated but the minimum words for the statement of a succession of images: "Fish," "The Dawn; the Birds," "A Death," "The Diver." Ross had a gift for looking directly at a place or an object and recognizing the things about it that gave it identity. Since he usually recorded impressions gathered in the Canadian countryside, his best poems—those already cited and others, such as " 'The saws were shrieking,' " "In the Ravine," and "The Walk"—perfectly create the effect that he said he wished to create:

> something "North American"—
> and something of
> the sharper tang of Canada.

Poets of a later generation recognized the merits of W. W. E. Ross's work. *Experiment,* published by the Contact Press in 1956, was both a gathering of the verse he had composed in the twenties and a salute to his integrity and skill as a writer.

Raymond Knister (1900–1932) wrote short stories and novels as well as poems, and it is probable that, if his career had been prolonged, his greatest achievement would have been in fiction. The qualities that mark all his work, however, are precisely those most vividly brought out by free verse: honesty in reporting experience and a flair for the rhythms of speech.

Knister's poems, almost without exception, came out of his years on his father's farm, first in Essex, and later in Kent county in Ontario. The drudgery of farm labour, the counterpoint of the seasons and the chores, the loneliness and silences, the closeness of animal to human life, the sacrifices imposed by the resolve to study and to write—these were the decisive elements in Knister's youthful experience and the subjects of his poems. His *Collected Poems* were published in 1949 with a useful chronology of his writing and a sympathetic memoir and critical study by Dorothy Livesay.

His objective in writing was "to make things real," to present rather than to interpret:

> Birds and flowers and dreams are real as sweating men and swilling pigs. But the feeling about them is not always so real, when it gets into words. Because of that, it would be good just to place them before the reader, just let the reader picture them with the utmost economy and clearness, and let them move him in the measure that he is moved by little things and great.

This is the effect of Knister's best poems, which are direct, short, and in uncomplicated verse and plain diction. Sometimes a poem does no more than round off a succession of details with the intimation of a mood or the hint of an impression. Sometimes the places and activities of the farm provide pretexts for bits of bucolic sagacity that, ingratiatingly, avoid an excess of the cracker-barrel or the homespun.

Knister was well read in contemporary poetry and fiction. Moreover, at certain periods he lived and worked among writers of an *avant-garde* sort. His tone often suggests the poems of William Carlos Williams. "The Plowman" and "Ambition" and "White Cat" have something of the accent of Robert Frost. The portrait gallery of horses in "A Row of Stalls" calls to mind *Spoon River Anthology*. "The Hawk" employs the technique of Imagism, but is more interesting in content than Imagist poems ordinarily are. Knister had his own distinguishing qualities. He had learned—almost alone among Canadian writers of the twenties—the principal requisite of free verse: that cadence and feeling must be thoroughly fused, as, for instance, in "The Colt":

> Through the gate
> The boy leads him,
> Turns him, expectant,
> Around;
> Slips off the halter:
> He whirls, is gone—
> Boy brandishing
> The halter at his going,
> Clapping his hands—
> Unnecessary—
> In long lopes he speeds,
> Rising and dipping,
> Down the rolling lane.
> Such beauty, see,
> Such grace,
> Moving (diversely!)
> Never was. . . .

Although his intentions as a poet were modest, Knister had positive aspirations for the poetry, the literature and culture, of his native country:

... we might feel differently about many ... common things if we saw them clearly enough. In the end we in Canada here might have the courage of our experience and speak according to it only. And if we trust surely, see directly enough, life, ourselves, we may have our own Falstaffs and Shropshire Lads and Anna Kareninas.

During his lifetime Knister's poems did not appear in Canadian magazines, but in *Poetry, Voices, This Quarter,* and especially in *Midland,* a little magazine of some importance published in Iowa. In 1932, about the time of his death, the *Canadian Forum* reprinted a group of these poems accompanied by an article on Knister's life and work by Leo Kennedy. This represented a joining of the forces of modernism. For Kennedy was one of a group of young poets who, while Knister and Ross and a few other Canadian writers were making their experiments, were carrying on an intensive campaign against the forces of conservatism. The scene of their endeavours was Montreal.

II

In the history of twentieth-century Canadian poetry two Montreal publications are documents of peculiar importance. Sixteen issues of the *McGill Fortnightly Review,* a literary supplement of the *McGill Daily,* came out between November 1925 and April 1927. Its successor was the *Canadian Mercury: A Monthly Journal of Literature and Opinion,* which made six appearances through the winter and spring of 1928–29. The aims of the young editors and contributors were both critical and creative. They were bent upon showing up the degenerate poetic tradition, and they were determined to lead the way to better things. They would strive unflaggingly for "the emancipation of Canadian literature from the state of amiable mediocrity and insipidity in which it now languishes." Symbolic of their spirit was the drawing upon the cover of the first issue of the *Canadian Mercury*: a rambunctious godling with his thumb to his nose.

These "restless, dissatisfied, and, on the whole, sceptical young people" (as Leo Kennedy described himself and his fellows) perceived the involvement of Canadian writing with Canadian life. It was not enough to denounce the kinds of poetry currently prevalent ("sired by Decorum out of Claptrap"); they must denounce with equal vigour the forces that were hostile to creative freedom, to spontaneity and joy, forces which they described as Victorianism, puritanism, and colonialism. They disdained the agencies which, by marshalling these forces of reaction, imposed a killing conformity upon society and literature alike: ". . . we have no affiliation whatsoever: we own no allegiance to the Canadian Authors' Association, the Canadian Manufacturers' Association, the Young Communist League of Canada, the I.O.D.E., the Y.M.C.A., the U.F. of A. or C.P.R." More positively, they pointed the way to salvation. Canadian poets must put themselves to school to the new poets of England and the United States: "If a living, native literature is to arise we must discover our own souls, and before that can happen a mass of debris has to be removed. No better helpers in this task can be found than among our contemporaries in England and America." They would be, these young critics and poets of Montreal, the importers of new influences, and they would demonstrate in their own writings how the new influences might reinvigorate Canadian poetry.

In Montreal they inaugurated the second phase of modernism in Canadian poetry. They saw deeper than the free-verse enthusiasts into the true inwardness of modernism: that to be modern, poets should aim not only at simplification but even more at concentration and evocation. They understood that the most successful new poetry was strengthened by symbolism, irony, myth. They grasped the central paradox of the modern movement, that twentieth-century sensibility might best find the way to express itself by studying certain poets of nineteenth-century France and of seventeenth-century England.

In these matters the clearest sighted and most articulate of the Montreal poets was A. J. M. Smith (b. 1902). When the *McGill Fortnightly Review* began publication, Smith was already well acquainted with what had been going on in contemporary poetry. He completed in 1926 a Master's essay on the poetry of W. B. Yeats; during his doctoral studies at the University of Edinburgh his special interest was metaphysical poetry. Smith has over the years done much service to Canadian letters as one of the first exponents of modernism and as editor of two of our most discriminating and comprehensive anthologies. He has practised as well as expounded the art of poetry and has published three volumes of his own verse: *News of the Phoenix* (1943), *A Sort of Ecstasy* (1954), and *Collected Poems* (1962).

In three articles in the *McGill Fortnightly Review*, Smith acknowledges gratefully the pre-war English and American poets whose achievement was "to bring the subject-matter of poetry out of the library and the afternoon-tea salon into the open air, dealing in the language of present-day speech with subjects of living interest." But his affinities were patently with three strains of modernist poetry: the symbolist ("the use of a conscious technique based on evocation and suggestion, and the deliberate determination not to tell all"); the metaphysical, which stretched from Donne to T. S. Eliot; and the work of such poets as Edith Sitwell and Wallace Stevens, who "have constructed their own artificial, beautiful and cubist world." Year in and year out, Smith admonished the Canadian poets of his generation and the next to be fastidious:

> Set higher standards for yourself than the organized mediocrity of the authors' associations dares to impose. Be traditional, catholic, and alive. . . . Remember that poetry does not permit the rejection of every aspect of the personality except intuition and sensibility. . . . It is an intelligent activity. (*University of Toronto Quarterly*, January 1939)

Practice supported precept. Clearly Smith has refined and polished his own poems with unremitting care. His subtle imagination and skilful craftsmanship most strikingly display themselves in the poems ("Shadows There are," "Ode: The Eumenides," "The Bridegroom," "News of the Phoenix," "Like an Old Proud King in a Parable," and "The Plot against Proteus") which most clearly derive from the poetic strategy learned, through Eliot, Stevens, Edith Sitwell, and the later Yeats, from the *Symbolistes*. If a few of these poems produce an effect of airlessness, that may be because they seem to have been composed on the same principle as some of Mallarmé's sonnets: imagery, rhythm, and incident evoke the emotional quality of an experience without defining it. A small narrative is stated or implied in words and images which contrive to be at once precise and mysterious— "an artificial, beautiful, and cubist world."

In a few slightly later poems, particularly in several contributions to *New Verse* in the early thirties ("Noctambule," "Poor Innocent"), he pushes his imagery in the direction of fantasy, achieving an effectively surrealistic quality. Other and more impressive poems, on the whole—such as "Son-and-Heir," "The Common Man," "The Face," and "Far West"—comment cryptically and ironically on some twentieth-century perils and aberrations. His finest symbolist poem is his "Ode: On the Death of William Butler Yeats."

One manner he essayed in his earliest years as a poet he has not, unfortunately, returned to. This is the descriptive-evocative landscape poem in short, sensitive free-verse lines. "Sea Cliff," "The Creek," "Swift Current," and "The Lonely Land," poems which are technically akin to W. W. E. Ross's, are all admirable. "The Lonely Land" in its first appearance, in the *McGill Fortnightly Review*, January 1926, carried a sub-title "Group of Seven," which interestingly spoke of a meeting between the new Canadian poetry of the 1920's and the new Canadian painting.

A less genial meeting, between the new poetry and the conventional kind, provided the inspiration for "The Canadian Authors Meet" by F. R. Scott, a poem which also first appeared in the *McGill Fortnightly Review* (April 1927). Frank Scott, born in Quebec City in 1899, the son of Archdeacon Frederick George Scott, is now professor of constitutional law at McGill University. A long, thorough, and critical acquaintance with Canadian affairs, a leading part in the creation of the Co-operative Commonwealth Federation, and a period as a United Nations representative in Burma have qualified him for incisive and authoritative comment on contemporary problems. Better still, the informed mind has been perfectly co-ordinated with the civilized heart. His finest poems proceed from a whole personality, which makes itself heard with clarity and force in their cadences. His style is almost always colloquial in its diction and conversational in its rhythms.

From the beginning, at McGill, Scott's poems have been as direct and "public" as Smith's have been complex and hieratic. The works of the two writers typify the double development of poetry in Canada during the past four decades: on the one side, the lineage of symbolism, the "metaphysicals," Yeats, Eliot, and Stevens; on the other, the verse of spoken commentary, its antecedents Whitman and Pound (with some hints from Samuel Butler), and such contemporaries as William Carlos Williams and Kenneth Fearing. Two collections—*Overture* (1945) and *Events and Signals* (1954)—contain the body of Scott's work, the best of which has been reprinted in *The Eye of the Needle: Satires, Sorties, Sundries* (1957). As this sub-title indicates, Scott is a satirist and social critic whose tone ranges from amusement through scorn to cold rage. His career as a poet does not show development so much as an increase and diversification of targets. Wherever his eye has lighted upon an injustice or a folly he has struck hard. He has the knack of saying precisely enough and no more and with the most telling use of quotation, illustrative anecdote, and rhythmic mockery. Even when the events commented on have become part of the past, the poems retain most of their vitality; some ultimate loss of relevance is the penalty the satirist pays for immediate local impact. Canadian conditions, however, will have to have altered inconceivably before Scott's most pungent satires and sorties become entirely outdated.

Time, certainly, has taken something away from his best-known poem, "The Canadian Authors Meet," but not its essence. It is the indispensable defiance, in satirical terms, of the literary "establishment" as it struck a rebellious generation in 1927; hence its persisting vitality derives less from its literary qualities—not that they are to be disdained—than from its impudent wholeness as a symbolic action. Scott's poetry as a whole has kept alive— and been kept alive by—a splendidly undergraduate forthrightness of opinion, combined with the restraint and wisdom of the experienced man. He has remained faithful to the undergraduate's certainty that a never-ending conspiracy among the rich and powerful is the explanation for the injustice he sees in society, the undergraduate's confidence that the good life can be brought to pass in this world by the benign co-operation of natural and social scientists. This is the significance of the poem to which he chose to give the climactic final place in *Events and Signals*: "Eden." This is the source of his indignation against stupid or opportunist politicians (both Mr. Bennett and Mr. King, for instance), greedy entrepreneurs and landlords, misuse of public resources, and inequity in the legal system—an indignation which, fortunately, he has always been able to turn to satire and to poetic form.

From the time of the *Fortnightly Review* and the *Mercury* F. R. Scott has written poems in other modes than the satirical. In his McGill days these poems, sometimes signed "Bernard March," were little more than the kind of literary doodlings of which we have seen too many in our time: tiny nature sketches after the model of the Imagist, fragments of Eliotic wistfulness, the verse of a sensitive young man with an eye on the seasons and a tendency to come a cropper in love. But this side of Scott's talent has also produced some fine poems, especially when the emotions of deprivation could be fused with a sense of a larger loss than the merely personal ("A Grain of Rice," "On the Death of Gandhi"), or with the feeling that society in general has been diminished by the loss ("For Bryan Priestman," "For Pegi Nicol"). To feel with the intensity that makes a poem memorable, F. R. Scott, it would appear, must be engaged intellectually as well as emotionally in his theme. "Last Rites," which beautifully achieves this equipoise, is possibly his best poem.

The third of the "Montreal group" was Leo Kennedy, born in England in 1907, educated in Montreal, apostate from Roman Catholicism, author of short stories as well as poems, now resident in the United States. As an editor, and as a contributor to the two McGill periodicals and later to the *Canadian Forum*, Kennedy was considerably more pugnacious than his colleagues—gave promise, indeed, of becoming Canada's own Mencken— but less talented as a poet. The verse which he contributed to the magazines was more obviously "poetic" than Smith's or Scott's, showing large indebtedness to Emily Dickinson, the gloomier side of Pre-Raphaelitism and the Decadence, to Housman, Yeats, Edna St. Vincent Millay, Elinor Wylie, and, most of all, T. S. Eliot (Eliot, of course, stamped all that generation, Scott in his "Burlap" poems, Smith pervasively). Kennedy's numerous mortuary pieces, abounding in images of death, burial, decay, and resurrection, are mostly composed in well-knit stanzas. In the year that his one volume of verse was published—*The Shrouding* (1935)—he served as inspiration for an essay by W. E. Collin, "Leo Kennedy and the Resurrection of Canadian Poetry" (*Canadian Forum*, October 1935). Collin celebrated Kennedy as the discoverer of something Canadian poets had always been in want of, something such poets as Lampman would have been immeasurably improved by: a myth.

Kennedy's emotions, according to Collin, had been "permeated" by the Myth of the Cycle, Life-Death-Life, and so he had found the word to suit the Myth; thus had been "engendered all his poems; which are the living figures of his unified sensibility." In Canada, where nature must be of dominating interest to poets, the most compelling nature poetry will be, or so it seemed to Collin, that which, like Leo Kennedy's, deepens and enriches the poet's treatment of nature by the integration of phenomena and timelessness. "A new Myth had to blow over our frost-bound Canadian fields that a new Poet might marvel at the miracle of 'water slurring underground' and chant the unfailing quickness of Beauty and Love."

This would be enlightening if Kennedy's poems had any discernible relation to Canadian nature. But his tansy sprouts out of, his moles burrow through, his bulbs split their caskets in, a plot of cemetery already staked out by John Webster and Elinor Wylie. The landscape over which his Myth blows is the landscape of the international wasteland of the twenties; and the Myth is no more than enfeebled whispers of immortality. Now and again Kennedy strikes out a memorable image or sequence of images. A few of his poems show competence in handling forms and rhythms that would not have abashed Bliss Carman. He had much less to contribute to the modern movement as a poet than as a journalist.

By far the most gifted of the Montreal poets, and one of Canada's four or five finest, is Abraham Moses Klein. Montreal, where he was born in 1909, has been his home all his life. There he has practised as a barrister and occasionally lectured at McGill University. A. M. Klein came into his strength as a poet at the opening of the thirties. His first considerable poems came out in the *Canadian Forum*, three especially: "Out of the Pulver and the Polished Lens" (September 1931), "The Diary of Abraham Segal, Poet" (May 1932), and "The Soirée of Velvel Kleinburger" (August 1932). Klein's persona in at least two of these poems was a young Prufrock of the Montreal wasteland. The rhythms and images of Eliot's usage served to create a mood of disgust over the banalities and sordidness of the modern city. *Hamlet, The Canterbury Tales*, Shakespeare's Sonnet XXIX and "Hark, Hark, the Lark," and Marlowe's "Passionate Shepherd" provided quotations for ironic counterpoints to the urban awfulness of the poem. The Beatitudes, the Psalms, and the *Book of Common Prayer* comment indirectly on the commercial horrors of twentieth-century Montreal.

But Klein is utterly unlike Eliot and comes out of a different tradition. His mind is stored with Jewish lore, his temperament has been formed and stimulated by life in a Jewish family in a Jewish community. His lovely poem "Autobiographical" celebrates his "nonage days," recalling the "Torah-escorting band," the "synagogal hum," the "rabbi patting a coming scholar-head," his father's "tall tales about the Baal Shem Tov," the "Torah-dance on Sinchas-Torah night," the "kindergarten home . . . full—Saturday night—with kin and compatriot." His studies for the rabbinate, a vocation which he did not fulfil, sent him journeying into the rich and exotic countries of the *Talmud* and the *Cabbala*. The particular timbre of such poems as "Autobiographical" and "Heirloom" is unique. Other Canadian-Jewish writers do not sound these almost Wordsworthian notes of piety and remembered bliss.

As the 1930's passed into the 1940's, Klein engaged with a monstrous theme. Several of the poems in his first collection, *Hath Not a Jew . . .* (1940), as well as the longer poem published separately as *The Hitleriad* (1944), respond, in satire or in lament, to the iniquities of anti-Semitism. The second collection of his shorter poems, the *Poems* of 1944, contains such stern pieces as "*In Re* Solomon Warshawer," and Psalm VI of "The Psalter of Aram Haktani" ("A psalm of Abraham, concerning that which he beheld upon the heavenly scarp"). In these poems he is more convincing than in the poems of social protest he wrote during the Depression for the *Canadian Forum* and *New Frontier* ("Barricade Smith" and "Of Daumiers a Portfolio"). Since the Second World War, Klein's devotion to Jewish history and to the welfare of contemporary Jews—a devotion which has had extra-literary aspects as well—has expressed itself in *The Second Scroll* (1951), an eloquent and ingeniously composed novel, the narrative of a quest for a Jewish messiah and a homeland.

A. M. Klein's post-war poetry has come out of his own Canadian time and place. *The Rocking Chair and Other Poems* (1948—Governor-General's Award) contains his best work. A clear-eyed and patient observer, Klein has caught the look and feel of Quebec, the province and the state of mind, in such poems as "The Snowshoers," "The Sugaring," "Indian Reservation: Caughnawaga," "The Break-Up," "The Notary," and "The Spinning Wheel." These are not loose clusters of impressions but exquisitely wrought structures in which rhythm, tone, and image both embody and interpret a broad vision of a way of life. The rocking-chair symbolizes this ancient way of life: static, secure, traditional, grounded in authority. But Klein also perceives that this agricultural, home-centred, river-orientated folk has been industrialized, urbanized. The rocking chair has yielded to the filling-station, the spinning-wheel to the power mill. The descendants of the habitant have been learning to be factory-workers, office-workers, entrepreneurs, investors, suburbanites. Several of the poems, most notably "Filling Station," express the theme of change. Klein is aware, too, that the province must cease, and is ceasing, to be a geographical outpost, a historical backwater. In its six deft lines, "Air-Map" places Quebec right where the routes of aerial travel and warfare criss-cross.

The Rocking Chair poems are liveliest and tenderest when they find their material in that enchanting metropolis, Montreal, city of two traditions and two sets of attitudes. Klein's difference from either enables him to participate in the life of the city and yet observe it without restriction, maintaining a point of view apart from it and distinctly his own. He can, for example, respect a kind of religion sharply unlike that in which he was instructed; as in the moving little poem admiringly and affectionately addressed to the nuns who serve as nurses in a great Montreal hospital: "For the Sisters of the Hotel Dieu." He can understand the faith which impels thousands of cripples to the renowned oratory and up the many stairs to the shrine where miraculous cures have happened and may happen again. But the most memorable of the Montreal poems are those in which the poet looks on at the doings of ordinary French-speaking Montrealers. Benignly, for example, he watches the horse-play of the jaunty young law-students ("Université de Montréal") and reflects on how their youthful exuberance portends the banked fires of middle age, when they will have settled down to being men with offices, large responsibilities, and large families. He is amused by the enterprising M. Laberge ("Annual Banquet: Chambre de Commerce") who combines business with fidelity to the old French-Canadian way of fathering numerous sons and daughters: "O love which moves the stars and factories. . . ." He sketches, without sentimentalizing, the plight of the "Filles Majeures," who, lacking a vocation, are condemned to loneliness. He re-creates the excitement of the political meeting and the sinister power of the speaker who can sum up in his person as in his words the resentment of his compatriots: "The whole street wears one face." He powerfully suggests ("Monsieur Gaston") the odour of municipal corruption. Gaston, engaging *vaurien* turned racketeer, represents one pole of Klein's range of feeling about the city. At the other is the sense of beauty, dignity, and mystery with which he evokes the city, in the poems about Mount Royal and in that linguistic tour de force, "Montreal":

> O city metropole, isle riverain!
> Your ancient pavages and sainted routes
> Traverse my spirit's conjured avenues! . . .

The society which the poems present, a society in many ways despicable, is not despised by the poet. When in the role of poet he transcends his society ("Portrait of the Poet as Landscape") it is precisely so that, from above, he may take another and different look at it. Much modern poetry voices a feeling of deprivation, the loss of faith or the withering of traditional assumptions. Klein's writing about Quebec never for long tends towards the elegiac. To be sure, his account of his world is at times mordant or melancholy, but irony and amusement keep breaking in. The Jewish vision of life and history provides a salutary perspective. Those qualities which might be thought of as peculiarly Jewish—a sombre sort of wit, a mellowed scepticism, a resignation that is never flaccid—are just the qualities that have best served A. M. Klein in his dealing with the world of his poems, even where his subjects have been least Jewish.

III

Creativity was not confined to Montreal. In Toronto during the 1920's several poets began careers that have been among the most important of the modern period: Robert Finch, Dorothy Livesay, and, most impressive of all, E. J. Pratt.

From the beginning the poems of Robert Finch (b. 1900) have implied a modern sensibility. They are the creations of a subtle wit, a flair for style, and an alertness to psychological insights. They show a fresh handling of standard metres and verse forms. The poems of Finch's that count begin with "Egg and Dart," published in the April 1929 issue of the *Canadian Forum*. Here, as in his other most characteristic poems (not gathered together until *Poems* of 1946), Finch deploys a technique novel to Canadian verse-making: the interweaving of word, image, and rhythm into a texture so intricate as to become at times almost riddling, suggestive a little of certain poems by William Empson. Like Empson—and his followers of the "Movement" in British poetry of the 1950's—Finch uses a conversational, low-pitched but intense tone, shaded by irony, in a diction stripped of all ornament, and a kind of versification that seems quite unexperimental but on closer examination shows itself to be exceedingly crafty and ingenious. "Over" and "Egg and Dart" both display these traits, and both show how efficiently his technique sets forth as much as he wishes to reveal of the poet's somewhat disenchanted and self-mocking view of life.

The dynamism of the earlier poems is a zest for patterns and similitudes. The patterning is both verbal and visual. Hence the poet's devotion to symmetrical forms, the quatrain and the sonnet in particular, which emphasize balance and antithesis, and to such devices as internal rhymes, repetitions, and echoes. There is almost no free verse in Finch's earlier collections. He abounds in puns, another kind of verbal patterning, and in interlocking syntax. His nature poems especially display his delight in design. Sometimes the pattern is within the landscape, waiting for the poet to identify its outline. In "Window-Piece," for instance,

> The hedge, the driveway, mock in counterpoint
> The inverted canon of the winding creek . . .

and in "Etobicoke, Thanksgiving,"

> The scarecrow
> Shanks in snow
> Is parody to the bridge's skeleton
> Whose iron legs quiver in the whitewashed stone.

Sometimes the pattern is in the events that constitute the little "plot" of such a poem as "The Statue" or "The Sisters" or "The Lost Tribe." But, almost as often, the pattern exists first in the poet's perception and he transforms nature to match the inner geometry. Like Wallace Stevens, Finch composes poems of metamorphosis. "Train Window," one of his most successful poems, is a succession of metamorphoses. Many of the poems are presentations of scenes looked at from a human or humane *locus*, a window particularly; in this they are unlike Lampman's poems of nature description, for instance, which profess to have been written on the spot, in the woods or on the water. In bringing about his transformations Finch employs probably more synaesthetic metaphor than any other poet. It is hard to understand why his poems should have been described (by A. J. M. Smith) as "sensuous"; the interplay of sense impressions is so complicated, and exhilarating, that the reader receives no sense impression at all. Frequently also images drawn from the life of reading and writing are fused with images of nature:

> The round pond is the fiction of a lake . . .
>
> A jay to prove this silver silence true
> Startles the marvel with a word of blue . . .
>
> During a snow the page has been erased . . .
>
> The ironic incense of the bonfire smoke
> Describes upon a wall of air like ice
> The victory of an old conservative . . .
>
> The white rope net of the rails
> fences this gouache geometry
> ship-shape, straight as a string,
> clean tilted through a plane of sun
> on a table of green glass, toward a blue paper
> thumbtacked with a moon.

Sometimes an entire poem, or most of it, consists of an extended metaphor or conceit:

> The lake has drawn a counterpane of glass
> On her rock limbs up to her island pillows
> And under netting woven by the swallows
> Sleeps in a dream and is a dream. . . .

Snow especially provokes Finch's virtuosity as an analogist. One poem about snow is entitled "Similes" and is composed of one simile after another. If snow can be likened to a host of other things, the device can be reversed, as it amusingly is in "Teacher":

> Examinations snow
> between our meeting:
> my burning pencil
> melts the white hindrance.

Finch's most valuable work appears in his first two collections: *Poems* (1946) and *The Strength of the Hills* (1948). The poems of two later books, *Dover Beach Revisited* and *Acis at Oxford* (both 1961) have been praised by reviewers, and the latter volume received a Governor-General's award (as had *Poems* in 1946). These contain poems that are the work of a mature and perceptive artist. As occasional pieces, reflective and descriptive, some of them have an almost eighteenth-century "Georgian" charm. The Dover Beach suite adds a few novelistic *aperçus* to Arnold's famous poem. Nine pieces under the heading "The Place Revisited" graphically describe the invasion operations out of Dover against Dunkirk in late May and early June of 1940; detail and diction combine to bring about a documentary plainness and authenticity of effect.

But a pervasive relaxation of tensions, both in feeling and in rhythm—reflected in the looser verse forms—marks most of these later poems. To some of his admirers Robert Finch's most durable work will continue to seem those poems which reminded readers in the twenties and thirties that poetry need not be the enemy of wit and elegance.

Dorothy Livesay's first success came early. This was "City Wife," for which, during her second year as a student at the University of Toronto, she was awarded the Jardine Memorial Prize. In 1928, when she was nineteen, Macmillan published a small collection of her poems, *Green Pitcher*; four years later, in 1932, appeared *Sign Post*. These poems give testimony that Dorothy Livesay belonged to the new dispensation. She had felt the effects of the free-verse movement and of the work of several American poetesses. Affinities of attitude rather than imitation explain the echoes of Elinor Wylie, Edna St. Vincent Millay, Dorothy Parker, and Emily Dickinson. (This is made clear in Alan Crawley's informative essay in *Leading Canadian Poets*, 1948.) Later, in her postgraduate years at the Sorbonne, Miss Livesay deepened her understanding of the French symbolist poets and their influence on twentieth-century writers. Probably, in first working out her own way of writing, she had no conscious intention more deliberate than to be unlike the Canadian poetesses of her mother's generation.

This required, for one thing, complete avoidance of facile metrical effects. Dorothy Livesay never indulged in the glib appeal of lilting stanza or coy anapaest. She learned early to use muted rhymes, broken rhythms, tentative stanza forms; all these expressed a particular temperament and vision of life, but they were signs, as well, that she shared the determination of the other new poets to deny to their writings the mannerisms of an outworn tradition. No Canadian poet of the past four decades has been more consistently loyal to the principle of organic form. The other main quality of her work, from the beginning, has been her devotion to actuality. Her first considerable piece of writing, "City Wife," shows that she was learning to be modern in the fashion of Robert Frost or Edward Thomas, by precisely rendering a group of realistic details in the tones of the speaking rather than the singing voice. Other small achievements in that vein were "Prince

Edward Island," "Old Man," and "Vandal." Less successful poems—"Sonnet for Ontario," "September Morning"—draw what strength they have from this same commitment to honesty of observation and statement. The reader of *Sign Post* readily understands her sympathy with the work as well as the personality of Raymond Knister.

Day and Night (1944) took its title from the poem which established Dorothy Livesay's reputation when it first appeared in the opening issue of *Canadian Poetry Magazine* in January 1936. "Day and Night" was a product of the most hateful decade of modern times and of Dorothy Livesay's rage and grief over what she saw in the world about her. Her opportunities for observation were ample. She studied at the School of Social Work in Toronto, served in the Family Welfare Agency in Montreal and in a relief office in New Jersey, participated in conferences of angry young men and women, witnesses to and victims of the misery brought about by wide-scale unemployment. In the same years she was responding to the poems of W. H. Auden, Stephen Spender, and C. Day Lewis, to their message as to their manner. Like them she became a poet of protest and revolution. But she shared also their limitations. The poet of social protest cannot bear to write as an outsider. He must become the chum as well as the spokesman of the worker, a role which class, education, and sensibility make implausible. At the emotional centre of "Day and Night" there speaks a gentle suffering spirit which is clearly the poet's and not the factory-worker's. But the poem powerfully evokes the violence and oppressiveness of industrial labour; anguish and aspiration are expressed in two-stress lines in quatrain, strain in passages in free pentameter. This effective alternation of rhythms and tones is the structural principle of other poems in the 1944 collection: "Prelude for Spring," "Serenade for Strings" (later re-titled "Nativity"), and "Lorca." This last poem most convincingly combines the rage with the grief.

Fortunately, in the books that followed the sensitive reverberator has prevailed over the agitator. The most rewarding way for the expression of her talents is illustrated by "Fantasia" (in *Day and Night*): the communication of private sensations in precise images and delicately shifting cadences. This is the way that has made for success in the best poems of her later volumes: *Poems for People* (1947), *Call My People Home* (1950), and *New Poems* (1957). The *Selected Poems* (1957) displays chronologically the evidence of a widening and deepening sensibility with which her powers of expression have admirably kept pace. Poems which most clearly show her sensitivity and craftsmanship are "London Revisited," "Page One," "Lament," "Bartok and the Geranium." For two of her books Dorothy Livesay has received Governor-General's Awards and for her services to Canadian letters, creative and critical, she was awarded in 1947 the Lorne Pierce Medal.

38. E. J. Pratt

MUNRO BEATTIE

EDWIN JOHN PRATT was born in Newfoundland—at Western Bay on February 4, 1883—and there he lived his first twenty-four years. In Toronto and at Victoria College, where in 1920 he began a notable career as a teacher of English, his life and work found a propitious centre. The city and the college provided unlimited opportunities for congenial and stimulating encounters with all sorts of people. They helped to focus and release a creative power unmatched in the whole range of Canadian letters. By 1953, when he retired from teaching, E. J. Pratt had brought out eighteen books of poetry.

Newfoundland Verse was published by the Ryerson Press in 1923. On many of its pages the virtues that were to distinguish Pratt's writing over the following three decades were muffled by the idiom and metrics of the early 1920's. He had simply taken over the modes available: lyrics in the late-romantic fashion, nondescript blank verse, meditative and descriptive pieces in random rhyme-schemes and line lengths, *vers libre* in the manner of Sandburg, Masters, and the Imagists—the kinds of verse it might almost have been said that the Canadian Authors' Association had been founded to perpetuate. Nevertheless, the virtues shone through magnificently. Reviewers were properly enthusiastic. "Such maturity and strength and beauty are in these poems," exclaimed William Arthur Deacon (*Saturday Night*, April 21, 1923), "that the day of their publication is a date to be remembered in the annals of Canadian literature."

High among the new poet's virtues stood accuracy of observation and representation. Nothing in the book better displayed this than "The Shark," a poem in free verse that adds detail to detail at precisely the rate of perception and from a point of view that shifts revealingly; rhythm and line-divisions are flawlessly matched to the movement of the shark:

> His fin,
> Like a piece of sheet-iron,
> Three-cornered,
> And with knife-edge,
> Stirred not a bubble
> As it moved
> With its base-line on the water.
> . . . .

> And as he passed the wharf
> He turned,
> And snapped at a flat-fish
> That was dead and floating.
> And I saw the flash of a white throat,
> And a double row of white teeth,
> And eyes of metallic grey,
> Hard and narrow and slit.
>
> . . . .
>
> That strange fish,
> Tubular, tapered, smoke-blue,
> Part vulture, part wolf,
> Part neither—for his blood was cold.

A kind of magnanimity and robustness that succeeding books were to reconfirm showed up in *Newfoundland Verse* in the jovial and colloquial poems of the section headed "Monologues and Dialogues." The best of these, "Carlo," whimsically eulogizes, in easy octosyllabics, an heroic dog in whose line somewhere "a dam / Formed for the job by God's own hand, / Had littered with a Newfoundland." The rescue that inspired "Carlo" prefigured the situation of a later poem, *The Roosevelt and the Antinoe*. The dog illustrated the view of heroism that pervades all Pratt's poems: heroic action derives not only from knowing what must be done but, even more important, from knowing how it can be done.

The verve and energy of the poet were most manifest in *Newfoundland Verse*—as through all his career—when he had a story to tell. "The great things are the narratives," wrote R. S. Knox in a review (*Canadian Forum*, June 1923) more measured than Deacon's but every bit as laudatory; and he singled out a poem that most of Pratt's admirers still count among his masterpieces, "The Ice-Floes." The impetus of events in this narrative combines with exactitude of detail to produce a poem that is extraordinarily moving, graphic, and believable. The rhythm draws its power from four-beat lines along which anapests and spondees are cunningly distributed. The chief source of strength, however, is the poet's masterful grasp of his subject. He thoroughly knew the life and work of the seal-hunters. He was expert in the jargon of their calling. He had learned as a boy and a young man what life was like in Newfoundland. Above all, his youthful sensibility had been shaped by the sea—by the way it incessantly and uncaringly invaded the lives of men. The best poems in this first collection—"The Ice-Floes," "The Ground Swell," "Overheard in a Cove," "Sea Variations," and "Newfoundland"—drew their rhythms from the movements of the sea and their most memorable images from the life of sea-farers: reef, breaker, cape, gale, fog, jetsam, grapnel hook, the pounding and booming of the surf, the scream and howl of the nor'-easter, the foghorn, the warning bell on the buoy, the low and insistent note of the ground-swell.

The decorations for *Newfoundland Verse* were designed by Frederick Varley, a reminder that since 1910 painters had been endeavouring to do justice on canvas to what was rugged and violent in the beauty of Canada. Pratt in poetry likewise expressed a new vision. It was not in technique or form that Pratt made his contribution to the modern movement. For the most part, he has done his work in conventional and traditional modes, always refashioned for his peculiar purposes. His was the break-through in tone and subject-matter. He extended our knowledge and understanding, made us see new faces of Canada, hear new voices. The dominant voice was the sound of the sea.

The action of *The Witches' Brew* (1925) takes place in and under the sea. This extravaganza relates how three witches, perched on a submarine volcano peak, concoct a gargantuan cocktail to make all the fishes drunk. An amphibious Cretan blacksmith of the line of Vulcan fashions for them a copper punch-bowl capacious for gallons upon gallons of food and drink. To a stock of liquor the witches add sea-foods and delicacies traditionally necromantic. The stench resuscitates the inhabitants of Hades and troubles St. Peter at his postern wicket. In motley procession all follow their noses, but are prohibited from sharing the brew intended for the finny tribe. The cauldron is patrolled by Tom, a monstrous cat from Zanzibar, who, after he has been ladled enough of the potent mixture, makes onslaught on his kin and kindred. Tom is seen as the story ends bound at meteoric speed, his tail electro-tipped, for the Irish Sea.

The poet has spun this fantastic yarn with untiring vivacity in rapid and witty octosyllabics. (His wife has recalled how when he was composing it— for a wedding anniversary—he would chuckle and laugh aloud.) Can *The Witches' Brew* be interpreted allegorically, as a Rabelaisean protest against anti-drink laws in Canada during the thirsty twenties? Not likely. The hell broth of the three witches is strikingly unfit for consumption, human, piscine, or feline. The poet, with a resonance almost Miltonic, rehearses the names of renowned brewers and distillers. Schlitz, Seagram, and Gordon are all very fine, but what have they to do together in a punch-bowl? (Similarly, a later and shorter poem, "The Depression Ends," describes an apocalyptic dinner, not one plateful of which would tempt the palates of the guests, "the shabby ones of earth's despite"—

> . . . all the gaunt, the cavern-cheeked,
> The waifs whose tightened belts declare
> The thinness of their daily fare;
> The ill-starred from their natal days,
> The gaffers and the stowaways,
> The road-tramps and the alley-bred
> Who leap to scraps that others fling,
> With luck less than the Tishbite's, fed
> On manna from the raven's wing.)

Seeing social justice established or routing the forces of prohibition would seem to Pratt second, by a long way, to the demands of a lively story. Exultation over the exorbitant was always more likely to animate his writings than concern for the thirsty or the hungry.

Titans (1926) brought together two longish narratives of the sea. "The Cachalot" was the first of his poems to receive the kind of acclaim that was to make Pratt the most popular of Canadian poets. The November 1925 issue of the *Canadian Forum*, in which it first appeared, was sold out with unprecedented rapidity, and hundreds of requests for copies had to be denied. It is one of Pratt's most consummate works, again in the octosyllabics that he handled so skilfully and distinctively. The management of the enjambment is masterly, the momentum of the rhythm springing forward irresistibly from line to line. The initial action is a mammoth conflict between the cachalot and a kraken—cetacean against cephalopod. The story is lucid and vigorous, the subject-matter gruesome. The main incident is the battle between the cachalot and a Nantucket whaling barque, the *Albatross*. In the concluding sequence of images Pratt shows his power of evoking transcendent terror begotten by the mystery of the deeps:

> In a white cloud of mist emerged—
> Terror of head and hump and brawn,
> Silent and sinister and gray,
> As in a lifting fog at dawn
> Gibraltar rises from its bay.

"The Great Feud," which is the companion poem, is sub-titled "A Dream of a Pleiocene Armageddon." It recounts the waging of battle between the denizens of the ocean and the hordes and flocks of the land, where the Australasian shore sloped into the sea. The poem, repellent in its details, is a work of breath-taking virtuosity, most of all in its cataloguing of creatures terrene and aquatic. Out of the vast and varied carnage emerge representatives of the three cardinal and enduring principles of life as Pratt sees it. Sheer animal size and strength are embodied in the gigantic lizard, Tyrannosaurus Rex. The great volcano, whose eruption marks the climax of the narrative, stands for the unpredictable and non-partisan violence of nature. Intelligence—memory, cogitation, anticipation—shows itself in the female anthropoidal ape who musters the forces of the land and with whose crooning and breast-beating the poem concludes.

The action of *The Roosevelt and the Antinoe* (1930) is modern and the actors are human. This is a stirring account of how a ship of the Hoboken line rescued the crew of the British freighter *Antinoe*, battered into helplessness by the fierce North Atlantic storm of January 1926. Pratt tells the story with untiring competence. There is no sag, no drift, in the narrative. The passage of time, the ordering of events, the data of seamanship, weather, and mood—all are managed with complete effectiveness. The measure is iambic pentameter in ever varying arrangements of rhyme. Most impressive is the thoroughness of the poet's research. He is entirely at home with the incidents of the sea-rescue. Unmistakable is his zest for the way things work, the marvels of science, the resourcefulness of man. (When he was a college student in Newfoundland, in 1901, Pratt was among the onlookers at Signal Hill when Marconi received the first wireless message from across the ocean—the most dramatic day in the poet's memories of his life.) The means and methods of communication had a fascination for him, peculiarly relevant to a poet in a country so situated as Canada. Yet the crucial incidents in *The Roosevelt and the Antinoe* depict sailors in open boats barehandedly pitting against the sea their strength and perseverance.

The most affecting moment of the poem occurs when a Roman Catholic priest, pronouncing final absolution for two drowned seamen of the *Roosevelt*, confronts the tumult of the sea:

> But no Gennesaret of Galilee
> Conjured to its level by the sway
> Of a hand or a word's magic was this sea,
> Contesting with its iron-alien mood,
> Its pagan face, its own primordial way,
> The pale heroic suasion of a rood.

Climactic moments in Pratt's writings, however, declare his faith in the rood as a source of strength for man in his never ending struggle against the mechanical hostility or indifference of the universe. In "The Truant," man fiercely cries out against the demiurge, the Lord of Hosts as distinct from the Lord of Love ("Cycles"):

> "We who have met
> With stubborn calm the dawn's hot fusillades;
> Who have seen the forehead sweat
> Under the tug of the pulleys on the joints,
> Under the liquidating tally
> Of the cat-and-truncheon bastinades;
> Who have taught our souls to rally
> To mountain horns and the sea's rockets
> When the needle ran demented through the points;
> We who have learned to clench
> Our fists and raise our lightless sockets
> To morning skies after the midnight raids,
> Yet cocked our ears to bugles on the barricades,
> And in cathedral rubble found a way to quench
> A dying thirst within a Galilean valley—
> No! by the Rood, we will not join your ballet."

Enactments of this philosophy of human defiance were the themes of Pratt's next two major poems.

The Titanic (1935) far surpassed the narratives that preceded it. Its superiority is not due to the story only, a story that has cast a spell over men's imaginations for five decades. It draws upon a deeper source of tension than the earlier narratives: from the sharply defined conflict between human values and the blind menace of the sea. The iceberg more imposingly embodies man's eternal foe than either the cachalot or the North Atlantic storm. His students at Victoria College remember with what relish Professor Pratt used to read them Hardy's poem "The Convergence of the Twain: Lines on the Loss of the *Titanic*." Pratt's poem, though it at no single point has the shocking impact of Hardy's, is more terrifying in its detail, more agonizing in its specification of disaster. One of his aims, perhaps the foremost, was to show the many ironies interwoven with the events of the disaster—"as if some power with intelligence and resource had organized and directed a conspiracy" (notes to *Ten Selected Poems*, 1947), a conspiracy against the pride of man manifested in the unsinkable ship.

The reader is bound to marvel at the exhaustiveness of Pratt's documentation, the creative skill with which he has made use of detail, particularly the dramatic snatches of dialogue, the variations of pace and pitch, the complete accommodation of the verse to the demands of the story. For many readers it is likely to stand as one of his three or four supreme achievements. For many readers—among them thousands of school children—it must count as the most engrossing poem written by a Canadian.

By the end of the 1930's no one doubted that E. J. Pratt was the greatest of living Canadian poets. His almost laureate position is exemplified by the longer poems that he wrote during the Second World War: *Dunkirk* (1941), *They are Returning* (1945), and *Behind the Log* (1947). Of these the last is the best. *Behind the Log* is a verse documentary—not unlike similar projects by the National Film Board—of the perils and triumphs of a North Atlantic convoy shepherded by four ships of the Canadian navy, a destroyer and three corvettes. Once more, the research was impeccable. The poet brought complete understanding to the treatment of every aspect of the subject. As in his earlier narratives of the sea, human courage and skill have clearly inspired the story-teller; even more, the resourcefulness of man in devices of communication. Here the scientific wonder is *asdic*: anti-submarine detection.

All these poems of the thirties and forties, except possibly *The Titanic*, are overshadowed by *Brébeuf and His Brethren*, published and widely acclaimed in 1940. Much study and contemplation went to the making of this poem, much reading in the *Jesuit Relations*, much talk with historians and theologians. The poet visited Midland and its environs, the scene of Father Brébeuf's martyrdom in 1649. The poem aspires to an amplitude of theme and organization far beyond anything attained in the narratives that preceded it. By means of a prelude ("The winds of God were blowing over France . . . ") and an epilogue ("Three hundred years have passed, and the winds of God / Which blew over France are blowing once more . . ."), the poet has not only given his story an aesthetic framework, but has also enhanced its significance. The missionary ardours of the Old World find fulfilment in the New; the past makes a splendid claim upon the understanding and gratefulness of the present. The plan of *Brébeuf* is large-scaled. The main line of narrative, which recounts the adventures of Brébeuf from his novitiate in Bayeux to his terrible death at the mission of St. Ignace, is interspersed with episodes—for instance, the appalling story of Father Jogues —that extend and illuminate the central story. To re-tell these glorious and heart-rending deeds of faith was an heroic undertaking for which Pratt was, by training and by temperament, uniquely qualified. Certainly, no other writer of our times could have so unmistakably perceived, and so stirringly proclaimed, the ultimate source of Brébeuf's power:

> In the bunch of his shoulders which often had carried a load
> Extorting the envy of guides at an Ottawa portage?
> The heat of the hatchets was finding a path to that source.
> In the thews of his thighs which had mastered the trails of the Neutrals?
> They would gash and beribbon those muscles. Was it the blood?
> They would draw it fresh from its fountain. Was it the heart?
> They dug for it, fought for the scraps in the way of the wolves.
> But not in these was the valour or stamina lodged;
> Nor in the symbol of Richelieu's robes or the seals
> Of Mazarin's charters, nor in the stir of the *lilies*
> Upon the Imperial folds; nor yet in the words
> Loyola wrote on a table of lava-stone
> In the cave of Manresa—not in these the source—
> But in the sound of invisible trumpets blowing
> Around two slabs of board, right-angled, hammered
> By Roman nails and hung on a Jewish hill.

There is nothing existential in Pratt's conception of human behaviour. His characters are always men committed to a course of action: the code of the sea or the drive of Christian faith or the determination (voiced in "The Truant") to explore and exploit the whole range of human experience.

Towards the Last Spike (1952) is the third of Pratt's long poems inspired by man's struggle against those inveterate opponents, time and space. Here the challenge is issued by the rugged breadth of a continent; the poem is subtitled a "Panorama" of the building of the first transcontinental railway. It is the sort of anomaly that sometimes comes late in a long career, a narrative poem that dispenses with the two chief virtues of the earlier narratives: a closely knit continuum of motive and action, and a systematic exposition of the process by which a task is carried out. The narrative, indeed, is curiously fragmented; the story gets told in discrete episodes and scenes. Did the subject—the political, financial, geological, and technological difficulties in the struggle to build the first Canadian transcontinental railway—resist organization into a coherent and unified story? Did the poet, rather, decide to subordinate—by a principle almost Jamesian—the orderly unfolding of events to an arrangement that would confer special effects of emphasis, point of view, climax, and dispersal of centres of interest? The poem will have baffled many readers, and by some of them will have been judged a failure. Yet every reader must have recognized in *Towards the Last Spike* some of Pratt's most sinewy and weighty blank verse. His myth-making powers never more strikingly exhibited themselves than in the vision of the mammoth lizard of the North Shore. In no other poem had Pratt shown such vigour and insight in his presentation of human personality as here in his portraits of Macdonald and Van Horne.

In *The Titanic* man's ingenuity and audacity had been frustrated by the inscrutable forces pent up in the inanimate world. That poem fades out on one of the most terrifying images in modern poetry:

> And out there in the starlight, with no trace
> Upon it of its deed but the last wave
> From the *Titanic* fretting at its base,
> Silent, composed, ringed by its icy broods,
> The gray shape with the palaeolithic face
> Was still the master of the longitudes.

But in the concluding lines of *Towards the Last Spike* man—having more wisely taken the measure of his opponent—has been the conqueror:

> And somewhere in the middle of the line
> Of steel, even the lizard heard the stroke.
> The breed had triumphed after all. To drown
> The traffic chorus, she must blend the sound
> With those inaugural, narcotic notes
> Of storm and thunder which would send her back
> Deeper than ever in Laurentian sleep.

Understanding of Pratt's philosophy of life and recognition of his technical range cannot be achieved without careful reading of many of his shorter poems. These have been brought out in *Newfoundland Verse* (1923), *Many Moods* (1932), *The Fable of the Goats and Other Poems* (1937), *Still Life and Other Verse* (1943), and the *Collected Poems* (the second edition, 1958, includes both the long and the short poems, and an introduction by Northrop Frye that is the best short study ever made of Pratt and his writings).

Several of the poems display, on a smaller scale, his gifts for story-telling and myth-making: especially "The Submarine," "The 6000," and "The Dying Eagle." These poems work by analogy between natural creatures and man-made instruments of motion—the submarine and the shark, the locomotive engine and the fabulous bull, the eagle and the aeroplane. Others of the shorter poems reflect Pratt's obsession with language and distance, and the means of communication: "The Baritone" and "The Radio in the Ivory Tower." Still others, a most significant group, evoke the terror of an atavistic swing from the primitive to the modern or from the present to the primordial: "The Prize Cat," "From Stone to Steel," "Father Time," "Cycles," and "Come Away Death." Except by indirection, Pratt has not often written of twentieth-century fears and dilemmas. But his system of values gives special force to such poems as "Still Life," "The Old Organon" and "The New," "Autopsy on a Sadist," "Myth and Fact," and that poem towards which all his work points and which sheds light on all his poems, "The Truant." In a class by itself, and surely one of the most memorable poems of the century, is "Silences."

In Canadian literature the poems of E. J. Pratt are an isolated splendour. Neither in theory nor in practice has Pratt declared himself part of the modernist movement. Yet in the revitalization of Canadian poetry in the decades since 1920, Pratt's work has counted for more than any other man's—counted by virtue of its craftsmanship, its breadth of subject-matter, its competence in dealing with the devices and phenomena that engage the interest of twentieth-century men and women, its uninhibited and exhilarating vision of life.

39. Poetry
1935-1950

MUNRO BEATTIE

BY THE MID-THIRTIES the new poetry was well established in Canada. This was confirmed by the *Canadian Forum* in an ingenious bit of editorial strategy. Through the monthly issues of two years, from February 1930 to December 1931, the *Forum* ran a series of articles under the heading, "The New Writers": articles about D. H. Lawrence, Virginia Woolf, James Joyce, T. S. Eliot, and others. The issues of 1932 put forward, in even ampler essays, a series called "The New Writers of Canada." Then, having identified and bestowed its approval upon the Canadian writers of the new era, the *Forum*, during 1933, craftily surveyed, and cut down to size, the "Canadian Writers of the Past."

Dorothy Livesay was the first of the new Canadian poets in the 1932 series. W. E. Collin's essay was devoted chiefly to making clear her kinship with the most recent literary movements in England and the United States. He explained why her poetry ought to be called "metaphysical" rather than "romantic." He traced the parts played by T. E. Hulme and T. S. Eliot in the "revolt against the romantic spirit in literature." Dorothy Livesay's "way of feeling" Collin likened to H. D.'s; her manner he described, not altogether accurately, as imagist. "She abhors words which are supposedly poetic."

Leon Edel in his essay on A. M. Klein (May 1932) undertook to define the "exotic rich note among the younger Canadian poets of his time" which Klein had derived from his profound studies in the Bible and the Talmud. Edel's essay made plain the connection between the new poetry and the "Montreal group" (of whom Edel himself had been one). He pointed out that Klein's "individual" poems bore "the imprint of that arch-realist Eliot," that they "verge[d] at moments on the metaphysical," and that, above all, Klein had shown himself "well-equipped to give us some real Canadian poetry—whatever that may be."

L. A. MacKay, in discussing the work of Audrey Alexandra Brown for the June 1932 issue, was dealing with a young poetess (b. 1904) who had recently been praised for her Keatsian diction and prosody in *The Dryad of*

Nanaimo (1931). Her technique and choice of theme, however skilfully handled, were sharply at variance with the mood of the anti-romantic critics of MacKay's generation, and with his own sophisticated, frequently sardonic verse. He admitted to admiration for her work but stressed its difference from the kind of poetry being written by those "most promising younger poets" who, as he put it, "are being irrigated with very invigorating results by the more extreme and emphatic revolutionaries among contemporary English and American poets." Miss Brown's talent for adapting various nineteenth-century influences in vocabulary and metrics he could concede, but he made plain his preference for the poets of other affiliations.

Canadian recognition came at last to Raymond Knister in the study of his work contributed by Leo Kennedy to the September 1932 number of the *Forum*. Kennedy recognized in Knister a poet of the new order, one who had broken with the post-romantic native tradition and who, as a consequence, had not been acceptable for publication in Canada. Knister's poems had anticipated, so it seemed to Kennedy, the movement to free Canadian poetry from a sterile confinement to a particular range of themes and effects. In the same issue of the *Forum* appeared nine poems by Raymond Knister which well exemplified his virtues and the virtues of the new poetry.

The *Canadian Forum* articles of the following year, "Canadian Writers of the Past," were probably what E. K. Brown had in mind when ten years later he wrote in *On Canadian Poetry*: "Against the elder poets the sad young men rose in angry revolt." These young men were not, however, sad; they gaily charged into battle. It is true that the essay by E. J. Pratt on the poetry of Marjorie Pickthall was neither angry nor destructive. He recognized the distinction of her writing, however much it owed to the examples of Swinburne and the earlier Yeats. But he could not deny that her limitations, as they now appeared to be, alienated the new poets:

> Her expressed dislike of Ibsen and his school, the absence of any analysis of life on the side of its civilized contradictions, her complete immunity to cynical and satirical moods, reveal a temperament which, common enough twenty-five years ago, seems . . . far removed from contemporary psychology.

More trenchant by far was Robert Ayre's essay on Pauline Johnson. "A pretty legend," he termed the Indian poetess and elocutionist, "nothing more nor less than a very genteel lady in a bustle who had nice thoughts about Nature and the proper sentiments toward love and yearning, motherhood, and the manly virtues."

In February 1932, L. A. MacKay happily assailed Bliss Carman. The bardic role had seduced Carman into the peculiar failings of that role: flabbiness, repetition, glibness. It was significant that MacKay's obliteration of Carman—whom, just a few years before, the Canadian Authors' Association had crowned as Canada's unofficial laureate—was undertaken in accordance with the criteria of modernism and by comparison of Carman, to his great disadvantage, with three of the new poets: E. J. Pratt, Dorothy Livesay, and A. M. Klein. In November, MacKay turned with equal zest upon W. W. Campbell, labelled him "minor," condemned his prestige as an important Canadian poet, and pointed out his dependence for manner, theme, and vocabulary upon the romantic poets. "The great names seduced him from the literary cultivation of the senses to the literary cult of the soul. If he had paid less attention to his soul and more to his senses, he would have written better verse."

What was left standing of the romantic tradition by the late spring of 1933 was demolished and swept off into limbo by Leo Kennedy in his *Forum* article on Archibald Lampman. Kennedy's aim was to discredit the kind of Canadian poet that Lampman's admirers, according to Kennedy, had erected as the ideal: " . . . the conventional poet of the last century, a hater of cities, crowds, etc., a worshipper of nature, an advocate of extremely simple and very high ideals, a solitary dreamer of dreams which are never defined or described." Lampman's admirers had encouraged Lampman to be insular, to write without ever displaying interest in contemporary activity and developments, without ever reflecting "Canadian politics of the 90's." Now, in the thirties, Lampman must be shelved and Canadian readers must learn to respect other poetic modes and later poets:

> The current generation of Canadian poets, of whom I am a hobbling member, has chucked him out, neck, crop, and rhyming dictionary. Our quarrel is, perhaps, not so much with Lampman as with his time and poetic tradition. The pot-bellied serene Protestantism of Victorian England which . . . underlay Lampman's spiritual make-up causes us to chafe. We are impatient of reading into the face of nature the conservative policies of an Anglican omnipotence. We are principally concerned with the poetry of ideas and emotional conflicts. . . . We reject Lampman and his fellows as exponents of a second-hand inheritance which does not stand the harsh light of our day.

Crammed as it was with misinformation and misunderstanding, Kennedy's study of Lampman was less a piece of criticism than a manifesto on behalf of the new generation of poets. Their cause was better served in the early thirties by the frequent appearance of their own poems. In making that possible the *Canadian Forum* did more for native literature than by its succession of funeral services over Canadian poets of the past.

Even more significant as a literary milestone was the publication in 1936 of *New Provinces*, a small anthology organized by F. R. Scott and containing poems by six writers: Finch, Kennedy, Klein, Pratt, Scott, and Smith. *New Provinces* marked a turning point, "the emergence," as E. K. Brown recognized (*University of Toronto Quarterly*, April 1937), "of a group of poets who may well have as vivifying an effect on Canadian poetry as the Group of Seven had on Canadian painting."

The slim anthology celebrated and exemplified the two main achievements of the new poetry: "a development of new technique and a widening of poetic interest beyond the narrow range of the late Romantic and early Georgian poets." But it was intended to be something more than a literary signpost. For, as the preface went on to declare, "the search for content was less successful than had been the search for new techniques, and by the end of the [twenties] the modernist movement was frustrated for want of direction." In short, the preface repudiated the poems it was meant to introduce, and summoned Canadian poets to serious labours. The methods of modernism—the straightforward diction, the colloquial rhythm, the imagery drawn from contemporary life—must be applied to the social and international issues of a troubled decade.

These were years of profound concern to Canadian intellectuals. In Europe, in Africa, and in Asia, outrages had been committed against civilization and worse threatened. Civil liberties in Canada, especially in Quebec and on the prairies, had been violated. The sufferings of the Depression had thrown into harsh relief the economic inequities of Canadian society. It was plain, moreover, that the new poetry was splendidly equipped to deal with the actualities of the contemporary world. In 1936—the year of *New Provinces*—Leo Kennedy in a vehement article in *New Frontier* called upon Canadian poets to recognize "immediates" and serve the social good with their pens. The response was curiously sparse (all round, in fact, the thirties was the most barren period in the history of modern Canadian poetry): apart from F. R. Scott's short satirical pieces, Dorothy Livesay's "Day and Night," *The Wind our Enemy* by Anne Marriott, A. M. Klein's small sketches in verse for the *Canadian Forum* and *New Frontier*, and a sixteen-line poem by Frederick E. Laight entitled "Soliloquy" (quoted in full, and with strong approval, in the *University of Toronto Quarterly*'s annual review of letters in 1937)—apart from these, nothing that deserves disinterment. Even E. J. Pratt's "The Depression Ends" is not an indictment of an age or a social system but an account of the apocalyptic dinner that the poet would serve to all those who had for a decade been wearing their belts too tight. Canadian poetry of social protest was written after the depression was over, by the young poets of the next generation.

The most diverting poetic souvenirs of the thirties are some of the poems of L. A. MacKay (b. 1901), who under the pseudonym "John Smalacombe" published a Ryerson chapbook winningly entitled *Viper's Bugloss* (1938); some of its contents with additional poems made up *The Ill-Tempered Lover and Other Poems* (1948). That title well indicates MacKay's temperamental range. The collection opens with poems addressed to a beloved woman (or to several beloved women) which pass from adoration through disillusionment to bitterness and regret. These are unabashedly romantic in their ardour but couched in stanzas and language that impose a firm classical control, not surprising in a poet who was also a professor of classics. Classical too are the poems of satire that follow the love poems, though in the neo-classical manner of Pope, most of them, rather than the Roman style. MacKay is not altogether plausible as a satirist, for all his incisiveness, which at times achieves the epigrammatic. He too obviously enjoys laying about him in fiercely rhythmic couplets. Nostalgia is the mood most likely to be evoked by a backward look at the scoldings he delivered in the thirties, by three poems particularly: "And Spoil the Child" (1931), which energetically parades before the reader representatives of the major faults in Canadian poetry of that period; "Fidelia Vulnera Amici" (1931), a lecture to Canadians on such fatuities as nationalist aspirations, preferential tariffs, the unguarded frontier, and economic mismanagement that brought unemployment and depression; and "Prelude and Ballade: For the Dissolution of the Canadian Forum Committee, April 1934." Generously, the poet concludes the first two poems with prescriptions for reform. "Frankie Went Down to the Corner" is a glancing blow at the shabby gentility of Ontario's beverage rooms. Several of L. A. MacKay's excellent shorter poems will survive as long as anthologies of Canadian poetry are compiled: "Admonition for Spring," "Hylas," and "Battle Hymn of the Spanish Rebellion."

II

Modernism came also to the Maritimes, even there where the themes and vocabulary of Carman and Roberts might have lingered on most obsessively. Three writers in particular began their work as poets under the influence of those themes and that vocabulary, but completed, each in his own fashion, the passage from convention to individuality.

Kenneth Leslie (b. 1902) has published four books of verse: *Windward Rock* (1934), *Such a Din* and *Lowlands Low* (1935), and *By Stubborn Stars and Other Poems* (1938—Governor-General's Award). Leslie is a minor writer who now and again surpassed himself. His successes are the poems in which, by instinct or a more than usual artistic austerity, he has put away the trappings of poetic soulfulness in favour of more colloquial rhythms and words. He perceived, evidently, that the kind of poem he could best do would be built out of specific feelings and details. Above all, he saw through the heresy that, since the turn of the century or longer, had hampered Canadian poets: that when a poet took up his pen he must anaesthetize his intellect. As well, he learned a good deal from his reading of post-war American poetry, especially the poems of Edwin Arlington

Robinson, Robert Frost, and Edna St. Vincent Millay. But what counted most, as far as the reader can surmise, was that Kenneth Leslie's emotional life supplied him with some highly usable data at a time when his skill and intelligence were capable of coping with it.

These opportunities and qualities brought into being his half-dozen most interesting poems. "The Shenachie Man" is an insubstantial and slightly facile piece, but it creates some musical and mysterious effects by fairly traditional means. "Lowlands Low" illustrates his way of handling free verse, and shows how he could make a feeling statement without slipping into bathos. His wit and mental dexterity best display themselves in a remarkable piece called "Cobweb College." Leslie's highest level of achievement is a group of twenty-six sonnets, "By Stubborn Stars." The sequence, reminiscent of "Modern Love," somewhat obscurely tells a story of triangular passion; both substance and treatment are entirely novel in Canadian literature. Two or three of these sonnets (the typography is novel, too, the lines beginning in lower case except where they coincide with sentence beginnings), those in which feeling and imagery and rhythm are perfectly composed, are certainly Leslie's most enduring work, notably "The chart is doubtful for the course I take," "The waters of my life, lying so still," and "The silver herring throbbed thick in my seine."

Charles Bruce (b. 1906) first published a book of poems in 1927—*Wild Apples*; then came *Tomorrow's Tide* (1932). In the pages of these first two books may be glimpsed occasionally what was to be the most praiseworthy quality of his later collections, *Personal Note* (1941), *Grey Ship Moving* (1945), *The Flowing Summer* (1947) and *The Mulgrave Road* (1951—Governor-General's Award). This quality is a sober and straightforward way of recording his observations of, and affection for, the sea and the coastlands of Nova Scotia. His manner, at its best, is perfectly in keeping with the subdued colouring of Guysborough County and with the quiet nostalgia which, evidently, it inspires in the Nova Scotian who, for the sake of money or career, is compelled to spend most of his adult life in Toronto, Ottawa, or Montreal.

Bruce is most successful in short descriptive poems that present a landscape, a personality, or an impression, especially in several of the poems that make up the first section of *The Mulgrave Road* ("Biography," "Coast Farm," "Eastern Shore," and "Back Road Farm"). These lines from "Nova Scotia Fish Hut" exemplify the sureness of detail and control of tone that mark these poems:

> Bare as the bare stone of this open shore,
> This building grey as stone. The filtered sun
> Leaks cold and quiet through it. And the rain,
> The wind, the whispering sand, return to finger
> Its creaking wall, and creak its thuttering door.

> Old as the shore is. But they use the place.
> Wait if you like: someone will come to find
> A handline or a gutting-knife, or stow
> A coiled net in the loft. Or just to smoke
> And loaf; and swap tomorrow in slow talk;
> And knock his pipe out on a killick-rock
> Someone left lying sixty years ago.

The same kind of Maritimes material is similarly handled in the longer pieces. Since Bruce is a poet of low temperature, he often makes his impression gradually, through the clustering of numerous small details of place and feeling. *The Flowing Summer* is an account, in iambic pentameter, of a Toronto boy's vacation visit to his grandfather's sea-side farm. The narrative substance is almost too tenuous and the style almost too prosaic, but they both come across with a restrained agreeableness and even combine, by the end of the narrative, to enforce a moral. "Words are Never Enough" is an expository poem, an apologia for the lives, the labours, and the feelings of fishermen; with considerable effectiveness, Bruce employs the resources of the realistic method—concrete and colloquial diction, well supplied with technical terms and the jargon of jobs, specific place-names and names of people, sympathetic insight into the thoughts and emotions of men who do not naturally put these into fluent words, and concern for the hardships of the workers and wrath for the exploiters. The risk in such writing is that the line may be crossed from poetry to propaganda. Several of his poems, indeed, remind us that Charles Bruce has been an eminent Canadian journalist. In the title poem of *Grey Ship Moving* the scene is a transport ship crossing the Atlantic eastward during the Second World War. The emotional centres of the situation are four Canadians, from Toronto, the Okanagan Valley, the Eastern Townships, and Saskatchewan. The poem provides a guide to the Canadian temperament under stress, the kind of project undertaken by the CBC during and just after the war years. The documentary details are well handled and the involvements of the chief characters are treated convincingly; the sense of wartime shipboard life is well communicated; but the "sociological" intent has called forth a script rather than a poem. Now and again, however, responding with greater intensity to a "current event," Charles Bruce has struck out a real poem of social significance: "Words are Never Enough," of course, and "Immediates," a poem inspired by a controversy of the angry thirties.

Of the Maritime poets, Alfred Goldsworthy Bailey (b. 1905) has made the longest journey, in technique and sensibility, from his first two collections, *Songs of the Saguenay and Other Poems* (1927) and *Tâo* (1930), to *Border River* (1952). Like Leslie's and Bruce's, Bailey's early poems manifested the Carman syndrome. They showed a preference for firmly patterned quatrains, an addiction to raptures about Love, Nature, and Beauty, and a predilection for "poetic" diction. In a few of these early poems, although the gamut of feeling and language is still pretty conventional, the versification shows a pull towards something new: the chances for expressiveness that might be opened up by breaking down the standard metrical patterns and creating lines and stanzas in which the rhythm would grow out of a system of dispersed stresses rather than from a regular alternation of stressed and unstressed syllables. As well, Bailey began to show a strong attraction to the single-line cadence (a few of the *Border River* poems eschew enjambment almost entirely). These tendencies make for discomfort in stanzas with decisive rhythmic patterns. The result in these early poems is unattractive but suggestive (for example, "*Urbs Antiqua Fuit*"). What would have been metrical audacity—and something to be commended—if it had been sustained by intellectual and verbal force, sounds like prosodic uncouthness.

The prosody in *Border River* is not uncouth, but it is gnarled and stubborn, with an effect admirably in keeping with the idiom and the play of fancy. Discarding completely the metrical and thematic paraphernalia of his earlier poems, Bailey emerged in the 1940's as one of the most individual of Canadian poets. His method is audacious and sometimes misses the target. A few of the poems in *Border River* are signally bad, but bad according to an interesting principle. His poems make a kind of assault upon their subjects and upon the reader's imagination and intelligence. The meaning issues gradually, if at all, out of a wrestle with a complication of images crowded along a tortuous line of narrative, as in the opening stanza of "The Unreturning":

> Blue is my sky peter
> and white my frayed gull.
> We had begun to sail
> into the milky magma,
> the gull's cry
> and the moon's tail
> beyond the glassy ports and the squeaking cordage
> where the long waves leap
> and the crests of wind reform their ragged continents.

This stanza, and the poem as a whole, might be contrasted with several of the *Saguenay* poems ("Night on Ile des Alouettes," "Trinity Bay," "Child of the Waves," and "Night") which were composed out of somewhat similar descriptive and emotional material. It is a difference not of prosody only but even more of perception. The later poems—"Miramichi Lightning," for example—deal less with appearances and events than with their power to produce a subtle and sometimes exciting interplay among the various elements of subject and feeling.

Such poems ask for alert reading, and their riddling method does not always escape obscurity. The reward for the effort is a considerable amount of wit and insight. The method has produced a number of excellent poems, Canadian in grain though cosmopolitan in technique. These might be thought of in three groups. First, the poems of sophisticated play: for example, "Variations on a Theme," which takes off from a line of T. S. Eliot's. Second, the poems in which the poet seems to be cerebrating on philosophical and social matters: "Shrouds and Away," "Regression of the Pelasgians," and "Whistles and Wheels." The third and most important group includes "Border River," "Colonial Set," "Hochelaga," and "Algonkian Burial." These make use of Canadian material, but in ways never beheld before. As an historian Dr. Bailey understands that some subjects yield their chief significance only through a shifting of times and tones. His Canadian places are made present to our imaginations chronologically and historically rather than, as with most other Canadian "historical" poems, geographically or scenically. He manages in these poems—above all, in that admirable composition, "Border River"—to achieve an effect of double vision: what the past was like when it was past, and what it means to someone contemplating it from the present.

III

Far off on the other side of the country, Floris Clarke McLaren (b. 1904) also was learning through the thirties how to give poetic life to her vision of familiar and beloved scenes—for her, Alaska and British Columbia. In 1937 she published a collection of thirty poems in a volume entitled *Frozen Fire*. The collection possesses more unity than slim volumes of verse usually have. Almost every poem is devoted to an impression of the West Coast mountain country or the Pacific. In general, Mrs. McLaren, like her contemporaries in the Maritimes, recognized that the most direct and memorable way of re-creating a landscape is to make it present through a few vivid essential details. To many of her poems, furthermore, she added force by dramatizing rather than merely presenting her material. A variety of persons utter, in a variety of tones, reactions to the mountain country: longing ("The Northerner," "Exile"); resistance ("Transplanted," "Mountain Dread," "Gene's Bride"); disenchantment ("The Reflexions of Constable Peters," "Stampede Bill"). Although it is a country that demands fortitude and patience, most of the speakers—and this includes the poetess herself—admit, half grudgingly, half ecstatically, that this country must always be their hearts' home ("Hill Water," "Shadow of Mountains," "Bits of the Pattern"). "Frozen Fire," the title poem, the most powerful in the book both in feeling and in versification, communicates that dual sense of dread and delight that has been the matrix of much Canadian poetry.

Apart from the title poem, *Frozen Fire* is not a greatly accomplished book, but it is a quietly satisfying collection. Its author was to continue to develop in skill and in the power to find words and images for her own way of feeling and observing. During the forties and fifties, Floris Clarke McLaren published further poems in several periodicals (including *Contemporary Verse*, which she devotedly served as business manager). These later pieces are unquestionably more subtle in rhythm, more sophisticated and "cosmopolitan" in the handling of language and imagery than the poems of *Frozen Fire*. Especially attractive are "Visit by Water," "Crusoe," and "No More the Slow Stream." In these poems she continued to make effective use of mountain and wildwood material, and thus was able to resist the drift towards allegory that is the bane of several of her other later poems.

The first book by Anne Marriott (b. 1913) has remained her best. This is the Ryerson chapbook, *The Wind Our Enemy*, published in 1939. A sequence of ten short poems inspired by the prairie drought, unemployment, and misery of the 1930's, this work shows that no poet has better understood how to make the methods of modernism yield full value. The verse is free: that is, its lines follow the rhythms of speech and feeling rather than a repeated design. The language is appropriate to the subject and the speakers, with scarcely a literary or "romantic" touch. Carefully chosen details are preferred to extensive passages of description. Feelings are dramatized, projected through a little cast of characters rather than as proceeding from the author. What has counted most, however, has been the poet's intense concern over the land and the people.

Miss Marriott could hardly hope to find another *donnée* so compelling. The Governor-General's Award was conferred upon her second chapbook, *Calling Adventurers* (1941), which consists of the choruses from *Payload*, a radio documentary. A crisp and graphic use of details is its most commendable quality. For its medium it is effective in rhythm and diction. But *Calling Adventurers* has neither the impetus nor the poignancy of the earlier sequence. In Anne Marriott's two succeeding chapbooks—*Salt Marsh* (1942) and *Sandstone and Other Poems* (1945)—a few poems draw their strength from her principal virtue as a writer: to find images and epithets for her careful observations of objects and places. A few of these poems carry intimations that make the details coherent and significant. This is true of "Woodyards in the Rain," "Business Man, War Year," "Portrait," and, most of all, "Prairie Graveyard," which begins thus:

> Wind mutters thinly on the sagging wire
> binding the graveyard from the gouged dirt road,
> bends thick-bristled Russian thistle,
> sifts listless dust
> into cracks in hard grey ground.

> Empty prairie slides away
> on all sides, rushes toward a wide
> expressionless horizon, joined
> to a vast blank sky.

Roy Daniells (b. 1902) included in his collection of poems, *Deeper into the Forest* (1948), a meditation in rhymed and assonanted elegiac quatrains entitled "Farewell to Winnipeg." This poem movingly evokes not only the feeling of the place but something of its historic associations. The poem derives its memorable quality from the finely handled fusion of mood and weather, and the skilful use of Riel and his rebellion as a point of reference from which the poet's intensely wrought musings expand into a larger consideration of Canada and the world in the present era. The poem recalls, without echoing, both Coleridge's "Dejection" and Yeats's "Coole and Ballylee," and is none the worse for that.

Daniells is not, however, primarily a regionalist. The poems of his which most readers are likely to remember with affection are several of the sonnets which make up the sequences entitled "Deeper into the Forest" and "Anthony," especially the former in which narrative, mostly derived from myth or fairy-tale, combines with imagery to produce delicate and haunting effects of enchantment, happiness, and terror. These are charming slight things that contain a thousand subleties of prosody, even though they lack the substance and power of "Farewell to Winnipeg."

Earle Birney (b. 1904) is a western poet, too, by birth and by residence for the greatest part of his life. But his experiences have related him to many parts of Canada as well as to Europe, Mexico, and Japan; and he has derived his data not only from British Columbia but from the world at large and from the problems and aspirations of modern international man. Yet, the most cosmopolitan of our poets in ideology and experience, he is in several senses the most Canadian of them all. In his writings Birney comes back, again and again, to the questions: What is Canadian? What is a Canadian?

Poems by Earle Birney first appeared in various periodicals at the end of the thirties and the beginning of the forties. His first book was *David and Other Poems*, published in 1942 and winner for that year of the Governor-General's Award. It has been followed by four other collections of verse, two novels, and a number of stories, essays, and radio plays. He has edited an anthology, *Twentieth Century Canadian Poetry*. As well, he acted as literary editor of the *Canadian Forum* from 1936 to 1940 and, for two lively years, 1946–48, as editor of the *Canadian Poetry Magazine*. He served with the Canadian Army during the Second World War, was supervisor of European-language broadcasts for CBC's Radio Canada, and since 1946 has taught English literature and creative writing at the University of British Columbia.

"David," the title poem of Earle Birney's first book, has several times been called a minor classic. It is a narrative poem, effectively structured in both incident and symbol, in interlinked quatrains of four or five stress lines subtly assonantal. This interesting verse combines narrative inclusiveness and rhythmic impetus. The story of the mountain climb and its consequences is supremely well told; moreover, it conveys significance that goes beyond the narrative. The poet skilfully builds his story to a climax that drives the narrator into an extremity of dread and decision; he has entered upon a new phase of his emotional and narrative life:

> I said that he fell straight to the ice where they found him
> And none but the sun and incurious clouds have lingered
> Around the marks of that day on the ledge of the Finger,
> That day, the last of my youth, on the last of our mountains.

The 1942 volume also contained a score of short poems in a variety of forms. The most striking are two that illustrate the poet's eye for details that recreate a scene and a mood ("Dusk on English Bay" and "Hands") and an ingenious adaptation of Old English alliterative verse to modern squalid urban subject-matter ("Anglo-Saxon Street"). His second book, *Now is Time* (1945—also a Governor-General's Award), is organized in three sections: "Tomorrow," "Yesterday," and "Today." The first sub-section of "Yesterday," sub-titled "Canada 1939–1942," reprints five poems from the *David* collection and adds one new poem. The sub-section entitled "Europe 1942–1945" comprises poems about the lives and thoughts of Canadians killed in the war ("Joe Harris," "For Steve") and the reflections of the poet among scenes of war ("Invasion Spring," " 'And the Earth Grow Young Again,' " "D-Day," "This Page My Pigeon," "The Road to Nijmegen," and "VE-Night"). Three of the poems in the collection ("For Steve," "Joe Harris," and "On a Diary") handle narrative material. None of them quite comes off, but all three are interesting both in their methods and in their substance. Birney's determination to understand other people and to express compassion without condescension or sentimentality is one of his most likable traits. All these wartime poems have a documentary as well as an artistic value—"the most powerful expression of a Canadian's reaction to the Second World War" (A. J. M. Smith)—and one of them, "The Road to Nijmegen," is almost wholly excellent. What spoils it is a tendency, manifested in the closing lines, to worry about the world. Such concern is appropriate, of course, and almost inevitable for a poet of Birney's temperament and experience. But he has never quite succeeded in making poetry of it. Anxiety and anger are the emotions also of the other two sections of *Now is Time*: "Tomorrow" and "Today." The main defect of all these poems shows up most clearly in the longest of them, "Man on a Tractor." The intimate and knowledgeable particulars that are the source of Birney's strength here and in other poems, and his accurate sense of spoken language, quarrel with his urge to editorialize. But it is churlish to censure a poet for wishing to place his skill at the disposal of decent aspirations. The collection closes with "World Conference":

> The quiet diesel in the breast
> propels a trusting keel
> whether we swing toward a port
> or crocodiles of steel.
>
> The compassed mind must quiver north
> though every chart defective;
> there is no fog but in the will,
> the iceberg is elective.

Also schematic is the third of Birney's books, *The Strait of Anian* (1948). Part One is headed "One Society"; Part Two, "One World." The second part is almost entirely of poems which appeared in the two earlier books, arranged chronologically and with places of composition indicated, to form a survey of the poet's experiences. Two of the five poems not hitherto published ("Man is a Snow" and " . . . Or a Wind") impressively fuse feeling and rhythm. Part One comprises seventeen poems in a trans-Canada sequence, opening with "Atlantic Door" and closing with "Pacific Door," companion poems with significant differences. The other poems take the reader on a sharp-eyed and sharp-witted tour of key points across the continent. The range of tone is considerable, from the sophisticated ironies of "Montreal" (which should be compared with A. M. Klein's "Montreal") to the crude idiom and objects of "Prairie Counterpoint." For the British Columbia stage of the tour, "David" is once more reprinted, along with "Reverse on the Coast Range," "Slug in Wood" and two new poems. The pathos and tawdriness of the life that has come to Canada with settlement and the spread of population contrast with the natural strength and beauty of the land. The poet makes out a telling case against man and his dwelling-places: in "Montreal" by a constant juxtaposition of magnanimous past and meagre present; in "The Ebb Begins from Dream" by the accumulation of dreary detail in the daily life of Toronto; in "Prairie Counterpoint" by an alternation of lyric-descriptive prairie passages with passages spoken by a disillusioned westerner. The Pacific zone comes more creditably out of the survey, represented by such untainted things as mountain-climbing, trees, driftwood, and again the ingratiating "Slug in Wood." In the pure waters of the Gulf of Georgia, poet, or reader, can wash away entirely the contamination of life in Canada:

> Dive from the shining fluted land
> through the water's mesh
> to the crab's dark flower and the starfish.

> Trail the laggard fins of your flesh
> in the world's lost home
> and wash your mind of its landness.

The title of the fourth book threatens a more stringent treatment of the west coast: *Trial of a City and Other Verse* (1952). "Trial of a City" (originally a radio drama entitled "The Damnation of Vancouver") is a fantasy-drama in mingled verse and prose of both present and future idiom. The situation is a hearing to determine whether Vancouver should be annihilated. Witnesses are materialized from among the dead: Captain George Vancouver, the headman of the Indian nation that formerly occupied the site, Gassy Jack Deighton, and the author of *Piers the Plowman*. Living witnesses are a professor of geology and a Vancouver housewife. There is much excellent fooling, a great deal of good sense, and a thorough treatment of two of Birney's principal themes: the squalor of contemporary urban life and the need for hopeful decisiveness about the next stage of human history. His versatility as a prosodist is strikingly demonstrated. The professor couches his geological erudition in a bleak four-stress rhythm with deep caesuras and emphatic alliteration; the housewife speaks in lyric stanzas; and Langland utters his condemnation in a version of fourteenth-century alliterative poetry. The superb achievement of "Trial of a City" is the sequence of passages spoken by the Salish chief summoned to describe for the officials "a way of life that died for yours to live." These sturdy and shapely lines, abounding in vividly realized details, are as splendid as any of Birney's.

The book contains, besides "Trial of a City," thirteen shorter poems—under the heading "North Star West"—in which once again the poet escorts the reader across the continent, once more in search of the unifying "Canadian" principle. Again, in spite of numerous local insights, it eludes him, and it is only in a geographic sense that he can exult, as the plane puts down at Vancouver:

> Yet for a space we held in our morning's hand
> the welling and wildness of Canada, the fling of a nation.

Once more, the best poems are evoked by the West Coast: "Bushed," "Takkakaw Falls," "Images in Place of Logging," and "Climbers":

> Above the last squeak-squeal of wheels
> stench of the highest backlot
> lithe climbers escape. . . .

This brings us back to the opening of "David":

> We climbed, to get from the ruck of the camp, the surly
> Poker, the wrangling, the snoring under the fetid
> Tents. . . .

The cleansing water of the gulf or the clear air of the mountain peak: these are the ways of escape from Canada, or from Canadians and what they have made of the country.

In his fifth collection of poems, *Ice Cod Bell or Stone* (1962)—a most accomplished, and physically handsome, book that shows in a clear light Earle Birney's great gifts of craftsmanship and understanding—the poet seems to have turned his back upon Canada as a source of subject-matter. The East, Mexico, and the plight of the world in our time offer more incitement to his mind and more scope to his creative powers. The book includes, however, a poem which appears to sum up the deficiencies of Canada as a theme for poetry (as, in an earlier book, "Canada: Case History" had summed up the shortcomings of the country as a setting for a sane adult life):

> Since we had always sky about,
> when we had eagles they flew out
> leaving no shadow bigger than a wren's
> to trouble our most aeromantic hens.
> Too busy bridging loneliness to be alone
> we hacked in trees what Emily had in bone.
> We French, we English, never lost our civil war,
> endure it still, a bloodless civil bore:
> no wounded lying about, no Whitman wanted.
> It's only by our lack of ghosts we're haunted.

The poem is entitled "Can. Lit."

IV

In the nineteen-forties, when the Depression was over and World War II had broken out, modern Canadian poetry came into its full force. The "renaissance" of the forties—and this was not the first "renaissance" in the history of Canadian literature—was the culmination of the modernist movement which had begun shortly after the end of World War I. The inaugurators of that movement—the "elder" poets as they might now be considered—Scott, Smith, Livesay, Klein, and Pratt, not only served as mentors for the new generation but contributed to the creativity of the forties. Not until then, indeed, did most of them attain to publication in book form: Klein's *Hath Not a Jew* (1940), Smith's *News of the Phoenix* (1943), Scott's *Overture* (1945), Finch's *Poems* (1946), Knister's *Collected Poems* (1949). Another sign of achievement was the publication of anthologies that gave full recognition to these and other newer poets: Ralph Gustafson's Penguin collections, *Anthology of Canadian Poetry* (1942) and *Canadian Accent* (1944) and, for New Directions, *Canadian Poets* (1943); A. J. M. Smith's *Book of Canadian Poetry* (1943, revised 1948 and 1957); and several small anthologies in the shape of special Canadian issues published by the American periodicals *Poetry* and *Voices*, and the British *Outposts*.

These books, anthologies, and Canadian issues confirmed what had already been accomplished. The most vital indication of new vigour was the appearance in the early forties of new Canadian periodicals devoted principally to the theory and practice of poetry. An older periodical continued to serve the cause. During the middle years of the thirties, the *Canadian Forum* had seemed relatively indifferent to poetry. Only an occasional poem of note—usually by E. J. Pratt, or A. M. Klein—showed a persisting care for Canadian literature as compared with Canadian social and economic problems. Towards the close of Earle Birney's term as literary editor, however, Canadian writing and criticism of Canadian books again began to receive something like the emphasis of 1928–33. Moreover, most of the poets who were to found their reputations in the forties and fifties made their first, or very early, appearances in the receptive, in the main discriminating, pages of the *Forum,* pages in which, as well, critical standards for Canadian writers were scrupulously maintained—a service rendered also, from 1935 on, by the annual survey of letters in Canada by the *University of Toronto Quarterly*.

The poetic flowering of the forties manifested itself chiefly in several new periodicals. *Contemporary Verse: A Canadian Quarterly*, published in British Columbia, from September 1941 to March 1953, was mainly the creation of a devoted and gifted editor, Alan Crawley, assiduously aided by four poetesses: Dorothy Livesay, Anne Marriott, Doris Ferne, and Floris Clarke McLaren. To read through the files of this small, neat magazine is to feel sustained respect for Mr. Crawley's judgment and catholicity, and astonishment at the number of good Canadian poets who sent him their poems. In these pages we find mature writings from the best of the Canadian poets whose careers began in the 1920's, and we find, as well, some of the earliest (in a few instances, the first) poems in print by writers who were to come into their prime during the decade. Furthermore, a chronological reading of *Contemporary Verse* seems to show a steady increase in poetic craft and power. As an editor, Alan Crawley, although never weakly impersonal, was almost entirely free from bias. His aims consistently were to stimulate the writing and reading of good poems, and to provide a means of publication that would be free from the restrictions of politics, prejudices, and personalities, to keep his pages open to poetry that was "sincere in thought and expression and contemporary in theme, treatment, and technique." When he believed that his job had been completed, Alan Crawley ceased the publication of *Contemporary Verse*, after twelve years of useful life, in 1953.

More local and more doctrinaire were two little magazines issued in Montreal, still headquarters for the modern movement in Canadian poetry:

Preview and *First Statement*. These periodicals came out, not with perfect regularity, between 1942 and 1945, and then were merged with, or absorbed by, *Northern Review*. *Preview* (March 1942–January 1945) professed to be not a magazine but a periodic selection of works in progress by a small group of writers who shared certain literary and political convictions: they were socialist and anti-fascist; they believed in, and practised, creative and experimental writing; they were bent upon achieving a synthesis "between the lyric and didactic elements in modern verse, a combination of vivid, arresting imagery and the capacity to 'sing' with social content and criticism" (March 1942).

A few flimsy sketches in inept prose figured as the chief endeavour towards proletarian realism. The most notable feature of *Preview* was the number of interesting poems it printed, by several poets, who (like the "Montreal Group" of the 1920's) were to be spoken of, for some years to come, as a group, the "*Preview* group." The best poems were those by P. K. Page, Patrick Anderson, and F. R. Scott; an occasional piece of some merit came from Ronald Hambleton, Bruce Ruddick, Neufville Shaw, Miriam Waddington, and Kay Smith. An impulse towards exegesis was evident; from time to time the members of the group commented on one another's poems. The editors of *Preview*, for all their stress on "cosmopolitanism" and scorn for "colonialism," were by no means beyond the fervours of patriotism. During the summer of 1943, in a Victory Broadsheet published as a special supplement, Patrick Anderson devoted four war songs to the cause of the United Nations and Canada, "to bring poetry to the people" and "to stimulate morale by explaining the issues of the war and the problems of the peace in terms of Canadian history and life." At the same time, the editors affirmed their belief in international ideologies and literary standards. "We have lived long enough in Montreal to realize the frustrating effects of isolation." And they had lived long enough in Canada to realize the narrowness of Canadian subject-matter hitherto and, on the whole, the conventionality of Canadian verse.

> To-day the poet is no longer silent. He has yet to come to grips with himself and stop crying "Help" from the prairies and woods and mountains. If instead he will hitch-hike to the towns and identify himself with people, forget for awhile the country of his own head, he may find his age and consequently his belief. (P. K. Page, October 1942)

First Statement: A Magazine for Young Canadian Writers, the first issue of which appeared only six months after the first issue of *Preview*, cared less about cosmopolitanism, more about native achievements and possibilities:

> For a number of generations, Canadians have been writing and expressing themselves in literary forms. In that time they have produced a literature with

enough breadth and scope to be called Canadian. . . . [It is] the business of a Canadian magazine . . . to serve Canadian writers only. . . . Our desire [is] to exhibit . . . the various modes and types of writing as we find them in Canada. We would like to become the mirror of this variety and so provide the Canadian reader with the freedom of choice that he requires. (September 26, 1942)

The three poets principally introduced by *First Statement* were Louis Dudek, Irving Layton, and Raymond Souster.

The most significant fact about *First Statement* is that its editorial board included, and was to be dominated by, John Sutherland. Sutherland, a wretched poet but an excellent editor, was, until his death in 1956, the most stimulating and least inhibited of Canadian editors and critics. His quality made itself manifest in *Northern Review*. Whereas its Montreal predecessors have a merely historical interest, *Northern Review* remains valuable as a repository of poems, fiction, and critical essays. Its poetry is not as uniformly good as the poetry printed in *Contemporary Verse*, but its critical articles make it one of the small number of indispensable literary periodicals published in this country. Sutherland encouraged the unbiased and searching study of Canadian writers of the past as well as the present. He himself acted as arch-critic, taking on all comers zestfully and, most of the time, victoriously. It was nothing for him to collate in one article (October–November 1947) the views of most of the established commentators on Canadian literature—E. K. Brown, Lionel Stevenson, W. E. Collin, Lorne Pierce, Northrop Frye, A. J. M. Smith *et al*.—extract the few notions he was willing to commend, and dismiss the bulk of their opinions as anachronistic: "These critics are on the defensive because they cling to a past world in order to deny the excitement of the present one. Genuinely afraid of science, of socialist experiment, of characteristic tendencies in twentieth-century life. . . ." Sutherland himself was about to become an anachronism. The poetry of social protest was going out of fashion. He might have discerned that the best poetry he was publishing in *Northern Review* did not conform to his prescription. The shift in emphasis is clear in the introduction that Dudek and Layton wrote in 1952 for *Canadian Poems 1850–1952*. Paradoxically, Sutherland's conversion in 1953 to Roman Catholicism, which transformed the magazine, and the critical method he exercised in his book on the poetry of E. J. Pratt, brought Sutherland into sympathy with the younger poets of Canada at a time when he appeared to have lost the desire to publish them. But in its ten years (1946–56) *Northern Review* had thoroughly fulfilled the classic function of the "little magazine," as proclaimed in its first editorial: to publish serious work, to make no concessions, to maintain critical and artistic standards. Those tasks might have been carried out by other agencies—perhaps the universities? No, retorted Sutherland: "Valuable as the universities are in the field of history and scholarship, they have only rarely shown themselves capable of sympathetic and intelligent understanding of the aims and accomplishments of our younger poets and story writers." The literary facts of the 1950's seem to suggest that Sutherland was in error. Here, however, in an elementary and moderate form, is the conflict that Irving Layton a decade or more later was trying to substantiate.

These "little" magazines of the 1940's and early 1950's—and *Direction* and *Contact*, though less important, ought to be mentioned also—exhibited the new vigour of Canadian writing. Books followed to confirm the triumph. In 1944 was published a slight but interesting anthology, *Unit of Five*, which contained poems by Louis Dudek, Ronald Hambleton, P. K. Page, Raymond Souster, and James Wreford. In 1947, John Sutherland published, as the fifth book in the "New Writers" series, *Other Canadians: An Anthology of the New Poetry in Canada 1940-1946*. Sutherland included among his "other" Canadians the poets of *Unit of Five* and added to them Patrick Anderson, Margaret Avison, Irving Layton, James Reaney, Bruce Ruddick, Neufville Shaw, Kay Smith, Miriam Waddington, and a few others. *Other Canadians* came out almost exactly ten years later than *New Provinces*. The two anthologies, in their similarities and their more frequent differences, conveniently display two phases of modernism in Canadian poetry.

Why "other" Canadians? Other, as John Sutherland's polemic introduction makes clear, than the poets represented in A. J. M. Smith's *Book of Canadian Poetry* published in 1943; Smith had failed to do justice to the new poetry of the 1940's. *Other Canadians*, accordingly, would serve as appendix to Smith's book and its introduction as corrective to Smith's criteria of inclusion and classification. Smith, the rebel of the 1920's, now figured as the bishop of tradition. His deficiencies, by Sutherland's count, were three. He insisted on distinguishing in Canadian poetry a double tradition—native and cosmopolitan—that simply was not there. He sponsored and represented the "movements of the twenties and thirties which have either proved abortive or been superseded by something else." He judged by aesthetic and religious rather than social standards; his prestige words were "classical" and "metaphysical." The new poets, on the other hand—"the *Preview* group" and "the *First Statement* writers"—were, according to Sutherland, "concerned with the individual and the individual's reaction to society. . . . If God still talks to these poets, in private, he carries less weight than Karl Marx and Sigmund Freud." Smith made the necessary adjustments for the second edition of his anthology. But by that time the younger poets in Canada bore no resemblance to the group described in the introduction to *Other Canadians*, and John Sutherland himself had begun to be a different person. So rapidly does stage succeed stage in the short crowded history of modern Canadian poetry!

The most highly gifted of the poets who contributed to *Preview* and collaborated in *Unit of Five* was P. K. Page (b. 1917). Miss Page has published a novel, a number of short stories, and two collections of poems: *As Ten As Twenty* (1946) and *The Metal and the Flower* (1954—Governor-General's Award). The poems of the earlier book came in part out of the Auden-Isherwood-Spender era, the period of the Spanish Civil War, the Popular Front, the struggle against fascism, but their author has clearly listened more attentively to Sigmund Freud than to Karl Marx. A few of her earliest poems, several not reprinted in *As Ten As Twenty*, show that her sympathies were not with the Anglo-Canadian "establishment," show it wittily, for example, in "Election Day":

> and in the polling station I shall meet
> the smiling, rather gentle overlords
> propped by their dames and almost twins in tweeds,
> and mark my X against them and observe
> my ballot slip, a bounder, in the box.

But there is nothing in these poems politically more radical than the general desire to do the decent thing as a member of a society, as "A Generation" suggests, and the poem that gives the book its title. On the contrary, P. K. Page's poems are intensely, almost oppressively, private. Her frequent theme is separateness, the incapacity to escape from the self or to communicate with others. The direction in most of the poems is from the outer objective world of typewriters and snowfall to the world of fantasy, nerves, complexes, madness. She takes a virtuoso's delight in delineating a neurosis ("Round Trip," "Magnetic North," "If It Were You," "Only Child"; and, in the second volume of verse, such chillingly precise studies as "Man with One Small Hand," "Portrait of Marina," and "Paranoid"). Even more striking are the poems in which she has composed a montage of imagery to suggest the horror or the mystery that lies behind the phenomena of the commonplace world ("Adolescence," "The Stenographers," "The Bands and the Beautiful Children").

Script-writing for the National Film Board was for a while Miss Page's occupation, and it is easy to recognize in her work a flair for cinematic treatment. Several of her poems might serve as scripts for little experimental films meant for "art" theatres. Action flows into action, image melts, "by a slow dissolve," into image:

> Bell rings and they go and the voice draws their pencil
> like a sled across snow; when its runners are frozen
> rope snaps and the voice then is pulling no burden
> but runs like a dog on the winter of paper. . . .

yet they weep in the vault, they are taut as net curtains
stretched upon frames. In their eyes I have seen
the pin men of madness in marathon trim
race round the track of the stadium pupil.
("The Stenographers")

Sometimes these metamorphoses of imagery are unforgettably effective, as in two fine poems of *The Metal and the Flower*, "T-Bar" and "Photos of a Salt Mine." Occasionally the reader's patience is tried by an excessive, Dylan Thomas kind of clottedness: "bugles of breath," "Niagaras of blood," "the milk of sheets," "the boy-friends of blood." Yet sometimes the grotesquerie has a surrealistic appropriateness:

> She walked forever antlered with migraines
> her pain forever putting forth new shoots
> until her strange unlovely head became
> a kind of candelabra—delicate—
> where all her tears were perilously hung
> and caught the light as waves that catch the sun.
> ("Portrait of Marina")

The poems of the second collection show a remarkable increase in skill and subtlety. Like the earlier poems, they achieve their effects through a series of brief precise statements set down in lines of varying lengths that unite to form stanzas of many shapes. The diction is less extraordinary for its grace or music than for the exactness with which it presents images. These poems are the exquisite patterns of meaning and suggestion composed by a rare and fastidious sensibility that never quite discloses itself or comes too near to the objects of its observation. P. K. Page has somewhat resembled her own "Permanent Tourists," although she has used a cine-camera with lenses of surpassing keenness, slightly out of focus and aimed from odd angles and through glass or water.

Patrick Anderson (b. 1915) was also a leading contributor to *Preview*. Anderson can be counted as only temporarily a native poet. Born in England, he came to Montreal, after a time in New York, in 1940, and by the end of the decade had moved on. In Montreal he was caught up in the lively artistic and intellectual life of the war years, engaged tentatively in the leftist political activities of the time, and wrote a good deal of poetry, collected in two books, *A Tent for April* (1945) and *The White Centre* (1946). A later collection, *The Colour as Naked* (1953), although it reflects also his life in Malaya and in England, derives in large part from his years in Montreal.

"The Dylan Thomas of Canada" was a label that even Anderson himself accepted as apt. He has been described perceptively as "a kind of tea-drinking

Dylan Thomas." He lacks Thomas's fierce imagination and irresistible rhythmic force, but his treatment of words was learned from Thomas and his use of imagery is similar, a technique of multiple, constantly shifting images that pass from sense to sense and from scale to scale of size.

> He unlocked an apple first, then lifted the latch
> of the ancestral tree,
> whistled amongst the tall corn gaily
> like a scythe of birds:
> on the shore the lion waves lay down on their paws
> and above the trodden sand
> a storm of gulls made sadness as white
> as April does: . . .
> He called to the hunting morning then
> to shoot his blood,
> he asked the seamstress of the woods
> to stitch his manhood . . .
> To every spar and nerve he set
> his orchard sails
> and in the fleet of love his eyes
> were sea-blue admirals,
> while at his telescope of brass
> she lulled her palms
> lay level to his pride, lay still
> to his rocked rigging. . . .
> ("Summer's Joe")

These lines show Anderson's principal gift—an extraordinary fluency of image-invention—which is also the source of his principal defect. In some poems he goes on adding image to image with the effect of a tape transmitted by a metaphor-machine into which the poet has fed his raw material.

Although his poetic method resembles that of P. K. Page, his subject-matter is entirely different. He revels in sensuous experience, encounters, people, landscape. The poems that he wrote during his sojourn in Montreal have, for this reason, a documentary value. Coming from another part of the world he looked with fresh acuteness at things and situations that Canadians had seen so often they had stopped seeing them. Such poems as "Winter in Montreal," "The Pines: Christieville," "Brome Lake," and "Ski Train" not only give verbal shape to specific times and places; they betray a rather charming eagerness on the poet's part to become a participant, a Canadian too in his understanding and response. Indeed, Anderson shows almost everywhere a tendency to identify with his material, whether it is landscape ("Camp"), experience ("Sleighride"), or a person ("Summer's Joe," "Portrait"). He discloses particularly an intense awareness of boyhood, the appearance and sensations of teen-aged youths who are less conscious of their budding sexuality than their observer is. While this interest, or obsession, can be troublesome, as in "Boy in a Russian Blouse," it has also been the inspiration of some of his most satisfying poems, especially "Mother's Boy" and "My Bird-Wrung Youth."

Anderson's "Poem on Canada" (*The White Centre*), a long reflective-narrative composition in five sections, is an attempt to define the characteristics and the genesis of the "Canadian experience" by means of a selective historical survey and an analysis of the present feeling about Canada by inhabitants and visitors. Because it has been, of necessity, worked up from books, "Poem on Canada" does not have the authenticity of the Montreal poems, but it communicates several flashes of truth. The most suggestive passages are the account of the arrival of the white men, the diverting vignette of Aunt Hildegard and her Canadian lakes, and several parts of the "Cold Colloquy" of section five, a dialogue between Canada personified and those who would question her identity. At one point Canada replies:

> I am the wind that wants a flag.
> I am the mirror of your picture
> until you make me the marvel of your life.
> Yes, I am one and none, pin and pine, snow and slow,
> America's attic, an empty room,
> a something possible, a chance, a dance
> that is not danced. A cold kingdom.

"A something possible"—one day Patrick Anderson, whose gifts and insight were surely waxing strong when he left Canada, will return to seek further into the meaning of this country.

The Second World War made few appearances in Canadian poetry, the most extensive being in certain poems by Earle Birney, Douglas Le Pan, and Raymond Souster. Patrick Anderson in Montreal wrote a few pieces about the grief and dismay that war causes to civilians ("Railway Station," "The Wives," "Order Medical Examination") and, relying upon his imagination and the war news, several episodes of the war-front ("Bombing Berlin," "The Airmen," "Arnhem"). Closer to the actuality of war came Bertram Warr (1917–1943), a Toronto boy who crossed to London as a stowaway in 1938 and five years later was killed in action in a Royal Air Force engagement over Germany. In 1941 a pamphlet of his poems, *Yet a Little Onward*, was published in London in the "Resurgam Younger Poets" series.

Bertram Warr at his best convincingly communicated the insight and compassion with which he had been observing London life, especially in the poorer quarters of the city. His style is straightforward and thoughtful, frequently conversational, rarely rising above the level of sober fact; his forms are free and various. His kind of writing is at almost the opposite pole to the image-spinning technique of Patrick Anderson and P. K. Page. The chief sources of his poetic strength—and it was considerable, even though he had barely crossed the threshold of a career as a writer—were his desire to be honest and his sense of the poet's vocation. *Contemporary Verse* published, in October 1945, a sympathetic article about the life and work of Bertram Warr, along with a bibliography of his writings.

The first book of poems by Miriam Waddington (b. 1917), an alumna of *Preview* and *First Statement*, was *Green World* (1945). Many of the poems of *Green World* celebrate in sinuous cadences the joyous life of the senses, but the collection closes with a sequence entitled "Morning until Night" that laments the onset of age with its threat to innocence and spontaneity:

> Gradually I enter solitude,
> I open the door and where I thought to see
> Green meadows flowering with my name
> Miriam written in wind, a star on the sea,
> I meet only the broken face of pain
> That dogged me all day and now has found the way
> To my secret self. . . .
> Oh God deliver me from that sad and broken face
> The crippled laugh and slow relinquishing
> Of life, I would be transformed swift
> As lightning, my evil discovered utterly
> And proclaimed in its own season.

The pervasive theme of her next book, *The Second Silence* (1955), is the constriction of adult life. The second silence ("Worlds") is the world of dreams where the grown-up, however hardened or disillusioned, may sometimes recapture the simplicity and completeness of the child's communion with reality. More often, however, the adult is overwhelmed from within by guilt and regret ("Morning until Night," "Night in October"). But *The Second Silence* is not all melancholy. The compensations of maturity are affirmed by several of the poems: the complex satisfactions of adult love ("At Midnight," "Thou Didst Say Me"); the perspective that experience brings ("Interval," "Lovers," "Catalpa Tree"); most of all, the satisfaction of becoming helpfully related to the lives of others. Mrs. Waddington has served a good many years as a social worker in family and children's agencies, in prisons and hospitals. Her poems of work are among the best in *The Second Silence* ("Investigator," "Foundling," "Journey to the Clinic"). Many pages of the book record, too, the quiet pleasure of recognizing, as she moves about her adult world of loss and burden, the scenes and people that await the sympathetic observer. "Music Teachers," although the diction and rhythms are slovenly, illustrates this kind of insight. "Wonderful World," the happiest poem in the book, proclaims that her lyric gift has not been so deeply eroded as she might have feared.

The harvest of mature perception and craftsmanship ought to have come in her third book, *The Season's Lovers* (1958), but it is a blighted harvest. Certainly, her considerable powers of phrasing and shaping stanzas, which sometimes have not been entirely under control, are at their finest in several of the lyric pieces in the fourth and final section of the book ("Exchange," "Song (Paint me a bird upon your wrist)," "In the Sun," "The Season's Lovers," "An Elegy for John Sutherland"). But the poems in the third section, "To Be a Healer"—the products of her encounters as a case-worker and prison visitor—poems potentially of great strength, are aesthetically disappointing. The poetess's own harrowed reactions to the miseries poured into her ears almost drown them out. Moreover, the reader detects, or suspects, a kind of exasperation with the very processes of art (perceptible, also, in "The Exhibition: David Milne"). The poetess can scarcely, one might surmise, endure all the bother of transforming this material, which she finds so compelling in its raw state, into images and lines, stanzas, poems.

She is much more scrupulous about making poems out of her own sardonic view of life and these are the most important in the book. The disenchantment of the middle-aged leftist intellectual speaks out with almost shocking clarity in "When World was Wheelbarrow." This poem, along with the elegy to John Sutherland, puts a period to the political and poetic ferment of Montreal in the forties that gave impetus in the early stages of their careers to this writer and her contemporaries. "The Young Poet and Me" brings together their generation and the next; the poetess finds that she can barely make the effort to communicate, feeling that it is doomed in advance:

> But love must be endured in long experiment;
> until he knows *what makes our love mean hate
> our life be death,* he'll have no proof of it,
> however long he lingers at the gate
>
> Of busy paradise, nor will tears clarify
> this rendered question; he has come too early
> to dine on answers, and I, ill served by fate,
> dug up from scullery, have come too late.

The most memorable poems in *The Season's Lovers* are two, in the first part of the book, in which the centre of consciousness is a woman alone in a city and oppressed by the lonely agonies she feels about her ("The City's Life" and "Poets and Statues"). These two are extraordinary among Canadian poems for their tone, the intensity with which real anguish has found expression.

Two other contributors to *Unit of Five* deserve mention: Ronald Hambleton, who edited it, and James Wreford. A. J. M. Smith has described Ronald Hambleton (b. 1917) as "one of the younger poets who are approaching the proletarian theme from an intellectual and metaphysical standpoint."

Hambleton's work, as a whole, however, has touched only occasionally on proletarian subjects. "Metaphysical" and "intellectual" may be the aptest terms for his method of making poems; this appears to have been an almost perverse insistence on subduing all emotion or lyricism to an arid discourse that comes as close as it can to prose without quite ceasing to be verse. Sometimes he displays surprising skill in making viable stanzas out of such recalcitrant prosodic material. The method goes about as far as it can in such poems as "Letter to Francis" and "A Lover and His Lass"; justifies itself, despite some presumptuous touches, in "Elegy on the Death of Virginia Woolf"; and yields considerable pleasure in a few poems where meaning and feeling break through the verbal and cerebral apparatus, notably in "Her Body is in the Trees" and "Last Night, When Fevered Minutes." The anthologists have decided that his best poem is "Sockeye Salmon." Since the publication of his sole book of verse, *Object and Event* (1953), Ronald Hambleton has become a proficient writer for radio and television, and has published a novel.

When one turns to the poems of James Wreford (b. 1915) one perceives the usefulness of Hambleton's stringency. Several of the poems that Wreford (a Scot temporarily resident in Canada in the 1940's) contributed to *Preview* and to *Unit of Five* have something to say and say it with some strength and technical expertness. But the work collected in *Of Time and the Lover* (1950 —Governor-General's Award) is marked by a sapless grandeur of language and metaphor, a style that takes up where the Georgians left off, but tricked out with "modern" touches of "metaphysical" wit and "contemporary" imagery: "the termite of indifference in the house of passion" . . . "the love which like a blackout screams" . . . "the eugenics of the heart" . . . "Her breasts like towers of Parliament / set on a hill, rise up. / There all my members go to sit." These snags apart, Wreford has devised a verse medium for his musings on love and mutability that has flowed glibly from the pen and slips readily from the reader's mind.

Louis Dudek (b. 1918) was also a contributor to *Unit of Five*. Since 1944 he has written many poems, has co-edited (with Irving Layton) an admirable anthology—*Canadian Poems 1850–1952*—and has worked as diligently as any man on behalf of new Canadian poetry, principally by helping with various little magazines: not only *First Statement* in the early forties, but also, during the fifties, *Contact, CIV/n,* and *Delta*. The first book of poems by Louis Dudek was *East of the City* (1946). In 1952 he joined Irving Layton and Raymond Souster in a happily titled collection, *Cerberus*, designed to refute the rumour that the poetic "renaissance" of the forties had petered out by the end of the decade. In 1952 Dudek put forth, as well, *Twenty-Four Poems* and *The Searching Image*. *Europe*—a sequence of ninety-nine poems provoked by the events and observations of a journey across the Atlantic and through England, France, Italy, Spain, and Greece—was published in 1954. *The Transparent Sea* (1956), *En Mexico* (1958), and *Laughing Stalks* (1958) have brought the total of his books of verse to seven, most of them published by the Contact Press.

Prolific and uneven as a writer, Dudek has probably published too much. In the dedicatory poem of *Laughing Stalks* he half facetiously admits the charge. His career might serve as paradigm of the quandary of the contemporary lyric poet: how to exploit the possibilities of poetry as a craft while remaining faithful to the theory of poetry as the spontaneous announcements of epiphanies? The poem that stands on the first page of *East of the City* describes his mode of operation:

> Hanging over a rail of the harbour bridge,
> knocking mud
> out of the corners and angles of shoes,
> diverting traffic
> I am walking full of poems; I make them
> hitting home runs, taking the sun,
> worrying, looking at people.
> I am breathing under the excitement.
> ("Making Poems")

He functions as a poet by detecting in an object or an episode the particular intensity or beauty or significance that marks it as a piece of experiential poetry. A poem entitled "Woman" begins, "These are poetry which would be sung— / the budding genitals, the fearful phallus. . . ." Charles Chaplin's film *Limelight* inspired a poem that opens, "The poetry in it is what gets me." It is the poetry in things that meet his gaze as he looks around his world that gets Dudek, that prompts him to communicate the perception in terms of the delight it has given him. He has composed a number of poems according to this principle with complete success; they are brief, direct, satisfying in cadence and shape. "Making Poems" well typifies them. But to dozens and scores of such notes in free verse the reader may feel tempted to reply merely "So what?" The method would seem to preclude the building of larger and nobler structures. Simple amplification is ruinous to poetry of this sort. One can fancy the poet endeavouring by various sorts of composition to circumvent the limitations of his poetics.

The problem solves itself when his data offer sufficient substance, especially when the sensuous elements will support a narrative movement or a considerable amount of interfused commentary. Several of Dudek's finest poems combine "body" with insight in this fashion: for instance, in *The Transparent Sea*, "Upstate Tourism," "Coming Suddenly to the Sea," and "The Sea at Monhegan." Similarly the poet may record the train of reflections inspired by his observations. "Meditation over a Wintry City" (*The Trans-*

parent Sea) is more effective than "East of the City" because it derives unity and coherence from the presence of the elaborating intellect as well as the scanning eye; but both poems tend to go on rather than to develop. Stanzaic construction glaringly shows up this kind of weakness. Stanzas must not merely succeed one another but should show an ever shifting tension between the discourse and such constant elements as line-length, rhyme-scheme, and rhythmic pattern. In a poem by Dudek, however, everything happens at once; the stanzas all operate at the same level of intensity; there is no progression ("The Sea" in *Unit of Five*, "Mr. Gromyko" in *East of the City* "Autumn" in *The Transparent Sea*). Occasionally, technical devices, dramatically employed, may create an effect of development ("Garcia Lorca" in *East of the City* and "Midnight" in *Twenty-Four Poems*), but Dudek has never cared to depart for long from the lines of varying length which follow the rise and fall of the speaking voice. Variation of tone would be another means of extending his range. When he tries the "tough-guy" style or sophisticated invective (as in *Laughing Stalks*), he fails to be convincing. He is pretty well restricted to his own voice—sober, civilized, and candid—which is completely suited to the kind of subject he handles most successfully.

So far Dudek's most rewarding way of putting his talents to work on a larger scale has been the sequence or journal poem, which brings together a group of reflections on a related topic or situation. In *The Transparent Sea*, "Keewaydin Poems" and "Provincetown" illustrate this method. The former group, however, produces an involuted effect; the things seen and heard count for less than the strangely congested state of the poet's mind. "Provincetown" more persuasively catches the quality of place, combining observation with comment, although the observation of American life is superficial and the images selected to represent it are too obvious. *Europe* and *En Mexico*, book-length travel-diary sequences, are more ingratiating because of the greater variety of scenes and the broader range of moods and topics. Both demonstrate a workable method of achieving expansion and development within a unifying framework. To a reader who wishes to enjoy Louis Dudek's gifts at their fullest stretch these are the two books, along with *The Transparent Sea*, that should be recommended. In spite of some irksome echoes of Ezra Pound, the tone and the temperament are unmistakably Dudek's. This means that, although the language may sometimes be flat and the ideas banal, we are listening to the voice of a poet who can be depended on to sound always like a decent and honest human being.

Still another poet whose career has grown out from a debut in *Unit of Five* is Raymond Souster (b. 1921). Joining forces with Dudek and Irving Layton in *Cerberus*, he has also been associated with Dudek as editor of the mimeographed magazine *Contact* and in the work of the Contact Press. His own books of verse appeared in steady sequence: *When We are Young*

(1946), *Go to Sleep, World* (1947), *City Hall Street* (1951), *Shake Hands with the Hangman* (1954), *A Dream That is Dying* (1954), *For What Time Slays* (1955), *Walking Death* (1955), *Crêpe-Hanger's Carnival: Selected Poems 1955–58* (1958), and *The Selected Poems,* edited by Louis Dudek in 1956.

The dates of these books, it will be recognized, make Souster as much a poet of the fifties as of the forties, and suggest that sooner or later the historian's arbitrary groupings must break down. At the same time, Souster's work from first to last has maintained a marked consistency of tone and texture. In some of the more recent poems one may discern a tendency to compacter rhythms and even a greater amount of objectivity; more surprisingly still, touches of humour and irony and a touch or two of verbal sportiveness. Such new departures cannot conceal, however, that the voice is, gratifyingly, still the voice of the young poet of *Unit of Five.*

In that period of his life Souster wrote several poems about his wartime experiences and observations. Some are raffish, some elegiac, but most of them utter a longing for a beloved person and for the city that inspires in him a mixture of feelings, something not far from love predominant: the city of Toronto. Souster is much more the poet of Toronto than Dudek or Layton is the poet of Montreal. It is not always the wasteland city. Souster's city people, bound and inarticulate though they are, have it in them to make one more spirited gesture of rage or defiance—even the old men "bumming cigarettes on Queen Street," even the zany prostitute Jeanette. The nightside of Toronto, the derelict quarters of the city, have so often served as settings for Souster's poems that the reader may have failed to notice that the gaiety and vitality of the city, its afternoon and evening charm (perceptible, it may be, only to inveterate Torontonians), its parks and its streets alive with young women, its islands and waterfront, the coarse festivities of Sunnyside—these too have figured prominently in the poet's impressions and memories. For the range of moods in Souster's city poems is considerable. The disenchantment of "Lower Yonge Street" is at a far remove from the quiet exultation of "Sunday Night Walk." The restlessness of "Yonge Street, Saturday Night" contrasts with the wry excitement of "First Spring Day in the Canyons." Certainly, he may reach out in memory and touch some spot of earth or water unsoiled by the city ("Lagoons: Hanlan's Point" and, an especially moving poem, "North of Toronto") as though they were amulets against the destruction of the spirit. Yet the city abounds with joys as well as with sorrows and anger: jazz, people to watch, tavern conviviality, above all love and recollections of love. His poems have plenty of talk about sex, wholehearted and harmonious sex, the best in Canadian literature. When he sounds a censorious note, it is provoked by a frivolous or destructive use of sex ("O Young Men O Young Comrades," "World Traveller at 21," "Ersatz").

The reader may suspect that Souster is less knowledgeable than he would appear; his notion of the lives of "chorus girls" ("Post Mortem" and "Nice People") suggests a naive outsider's view of sophisticated decadence. But he never puts a foot wrong when he is writing about the kind of loving he knows. Love is set off against the city ("The Hated City," "You Do Not Belong Here"); again, the home in the city is often the scene of blissful memories. In the earlier poems there are only a few intimations of mortality ("The Penny Flute," "When I See Old Men," "Not Wholly Lost") but in later collections (even in their titles: *For What Time Slays, Walking Death, Crêpe-Hanger's Carnival*) the cold breath of time can be felt. Even so, life remains good and love bountiful.

Souster would never be guilty of the instant sociology of such a poem as Dudek's "Provincetown." He is aware of the tawdriness and oppressiveness of a good deal of life in our times, particularly in the city, but he never forgets that the people fumbling about in the labyrinth are people, not merely users of canned beer, Kleenex, and Tasti-Freez. His compassion is without condescension, his fidelity to fact without cynicism. This emerges even from so slight a poem as "The Collector":

> What she collects is men
> as a bee honey, leaving out
> the subtlety of that swift winger. There's little
> in the way her eyes look into theirs (O take me),
> her body arches forward (possess me *now*).
>
> At her age (other women say)
> it's ridiculous: but how much envy
> mixes with fact? They will say, none,
> but we know better, watching their faces.
> Still, admit, what she collects finally is pain.

Souster shows special insight and spirit in his pictures of women ("Study: The Bath," "Jeanette," "The Negro Girl"). Perhaps his only false notes are in the poems of protest against "intellectuals."

In form his poems have changed scarcely at all over the years since 1944. And properly so, since Souster early recognized the contours of his own speaking voice and devised the cadences to reproduce them. Critically scrutinized, the style does disclose occasional lapses, especially a sprinkling of cliché. This kind of poetry may, however, make its peculiar effect, since it is so close to ordinary speech, through suitable clichés. The poems as a whole have a hit-and-miss quality that, again, for the purpose, may be indispensable. At any rate, Souster appears to have escaped, most of the time, the particular disability of his sort of versification: disjointedness. He admirably manages to achieve coherence and articulation of rhythm without loss of actuality and immediacy. Not all his poems come off successfully—

far from it—but none of them lacks interest of some sort, and the best of them are as satisfying as any in our literature.

Of all the Canadian poets whose careers began when the thirties were passing into the forties, Irving Layton (b. 1912) possesses the richest talents and the greatest capacity for development. His three principal gifts are a matchless ease and spontaneity of phrasing, an acute ear for line and stanza cadences, and the power to declare himself with indomitable authority on many topics. The authority derives from the most superb self-confidence in Canadian literature and from total faith in a handful of pseudo-ideas adapted from Nietzsche and Lawrence. Most of these views belong to the stock-in-trade of the anti-bourgeois writers from Sherwood Anderson to Alan Ginsberg. From this base Layton has been able to denounce a considerable proportion of his fellow humans as philistines, pharisees, puritans, and pedants.

The denunciatory Layton, bent upon uttering "a loud nix to the forces high-pressuring us into conformity or atomic dispersion" (*Cerberus*, p. 45), emerged in the fifties. His earlier poems—first gathered together in *Here and Now* (1945) and *Now is the Place* (1948) and in the anthologies *Other Canadians* (1946) and *Cerberus* (1952)—are mostly descriptive. Only a few poems (for instance, "The Swimmer," a distinctive and delightful piece) resemble the imagistic writings of P. K. Page and Patrick Anderson. Layton in the forties was satisfied to act as the camera, recording with clarity and force scenes with which he had been familiar from childhood. His relation with this milieu, Montreal and Jewish, is mostly visual. He succeeds by his selection of details in communicating his loathing of economic inequity, racial intolerance, institutional religion, commercialized pleasures, and middle-class *mores* ("DeBullion Street," "Compliments of the Season," "Excursion," "Jewish Main Street").

During the fifties the "indestructible egotist" ("Trumpet Daffodil") took over, convinced that the enemies of creativity, "gentility, propriety, respectability . . . this genteel tradition preserved by clergymen, underdeveloped school-marms, university graduates, and right-thinking social workers," might be routed by the "barbaric yawp" of a Canadian Whitman. Layton's vision of Canadian society, however, had only minimal likeness to reality, as he would have realized if he in the least resembled Whitman in his way of looking at the people around him. Possibly, Layton was working out a strategy. Rather than endlessly adding poem to poem, like Dudek and Souster, he would find a way of integrating the elements of his career. He would devise a myth: the myth of the poet-outsider at odds with his society. On the one side, the poet, unconventional, unacademic, uninhibited, the darling of nature, the favourite son of Eros, one of the fine warty fellows; on the other side, a society mostly middle-class, repressed and repressive, hypocritical, dedicated to profits and status, bulwarked by an unjust economic system and an obsolete educational theory. Such a confrontation was of excellent ancestry; better, it was practicable and fructifying. It has several defects. It leads the poet into repeating stereotypes rather than taking a new look for himself. Even worse, it is an attitude that leads to satire and Layton has little talent as a satirist.

Nevertheless, the poet's admirers did not despair. Even in the little collections that the poet-outsider stance produced—*The Black Huntsmen* (1951), *The Long Pea-Shooter* (1954), *The Blue Propeller* (1955), and *Music on a Kazoo* (1956)—appeared poems of memorable dignity and insight. The day would come when the poet would be overwhelmed by his poems. This hope was encouraged by the publication of *Love the Conqueror Worm* in 1952 and fulfilled by *The Cold Green Element* and *The Bull Calf and Other Poems* in 1956. *The Improved Binoculars: Selected Poems* (1956), a rigorous garnering from ten years and eight books, made clear that at last Layton's evaluation of his poems was beginning to coincide with his critics'. *The Improved Binoculars* contains poems as good as any ever written in this country. The rhetoric had become less obtrusive, the sound of an authentic voice speaking of believable things could be clearly heard. Quite properly, the Governor-General's Award was conferred in 1959 on *A Red Carpet for the Sun*, a more generous selection of the earlier poems and with the addition of pieces from *A Laughter in the Mind* (1958) and seven new poems. *A Red Carpet for the Sun* contained "all the poems I wrote between 1942 and 1958 that I wish to preserve." The foreword went on to announce that the man who had written those poems was now dead. Thus the poet completely submitted to his true genius—a genius not for satire or social criticism but for giving elegant and powerful expression to man's awareness of the intermingled beauty and horror of his condition.

The best poems of Irving Layton encompass many themes and moods. The poet sees the fatal conflict between body and spirit ("Seven O'Clock Lecture"), the terror that haunts the most ordinary existences ("Metzinger: Girl with a Bird," "Summer Idyll"), man's partial or complete complicity in the destruction of life ("Cain," "The Bull Calf," "The Improved Binoculars"), in the thwarting of vitality ("The Puma's Tooth," "Mr. Ther-Apis," "The Paraclete"), and in annihilation of the self ("Letter from a Straw Man," "The Comic Element"). Several of the poems express a large sense of the poet's own being and function as poet: his identity with nature ("The Cold Green Element," "Metamorphosis," "Garter Snake"), his power to transcend reality ("Enemies," "Winter Fantasy," "Paging Mr. Superman," "Venetian Blinds"), his impulse to unify experience ("The Birth of Tragedy," "The Poetic Process"), his readiness to accept the fact of human differences and divisions ("Berry Picking," "Mildred," "Early Morning in

Cote St. Luc"), his proneness to apprehend in the joy and beauty of the moment the threat of time and death ("Boys Bathing"). Even, in a few of the poems, he acknowledges the buffoon side of the poet's nature—particularly in a poem that borrows imagery from three poems by Yeats, "Whatever Else Poetry is Freedom." Yeatsian, also, are the lines, in "Orpheus," that speak of the poet's faculty for reconciling life and death:

> ... the poet's heart
>   Has nowhere counterpart
>
> Which can celebrate
> Love equally with death
> Yet by its pulsing bring
>   A music into everything.

The career of Ralph Gustafson (b. 1909) has traversed the same three phases of development as the careers of other Canadian poets of his generation: infatuation with the mannerisms of late romanticism; response to the possibilities of modernism; and creation of his own style. His first book, *The Golden Chalice* (1935) resolutely embraces the traditional, in Keatsian narrative and in sonnets of the sort transmitted from Shakespeare by Rupert Brooke, John Masefield, and Edna St. Vincent Millay; and spurns modern poetry, as represented by

> Those modern poem-mongers, new, inane—
> To psycho-analytic tags confined,
> To super-clever vagaries inclined,
> Who splutter phrases reasonlessly sane
> Or intricate obscurities. ...

This is not far from the sort of reaction to the new poetry that was represented by the reviewer who dubbed T. S. Eliot "a drunken helot." A longish verse-meditation, "A Poet in Exile," deplores the passing of an age hospitable to "simple loveliness," "noble passion," and "high endeavour," to be replaced by "an age of grovelling cynicism" when "Small praise awaits the poet who believes / That life is not identical with sex / Nor that sincere emotion but relieves / What its neurotic ganglion effects."

Gustafson's next two publications, *Epithalamium in Time of War* (1941) and *Lyrics Unromantic* (1942) persevere in "traditional" postures, although with an access of the sardonic that may have owed something to the background of the Second World War, and with a new audacity of expression that certainly owed a great deal to the influence of Gerard Manley Hopkins. *Lyrics Unromantic* (title inaccurate) exhibits also considerable variety and competence in stanza forms. The contents of these two slim volumes were incorporated with other poems into a sizable collection *Flight into Darkness* (1944). The new poems display unmistakable signs of conversion to modernism. Images from contemporary life appear. An occasional intonation suggests an ironic or an ambiguous intent. Worms, skulls, dust, bones, and graves remind us of the potent spell cast in those years by "Whispers of Immortality" and the revived interest in Webster. "April Eclogue" betrays the impact of *The Waste Land* and *Sweeney Agonistes*. The inflections of Auden and Spender murmur in the background. The most modish of ancient *personae*—Icarus, Theseus, and the Minotaur—re-enact their story ("Mythos"). In several of the poems of the final section, "Of Places and Sarcasm," the poet feels free to juxtapose neologisms, and learned derivatives, and words of lyric connotations. In short, Gustafson had yielded to the seductions of an era of verse-making whose slogan may be said to be "anything goes." His best poems of that period, however, show a well-advised admixture of old and new in their vocabulary and metrics ("On the Struma Massacre," " 'S.S.R., Lost at Sea'—The Times," and "The Fish").

This poet became fully himself only in his most recent collections, *Rocky Mountain Poems* and *Rivers among Rocks* (both 1960). The latter especially, a handsomely mounted collection, shows how astonishing is his range of manners and themes. Indeed, it is easier to enjoy such a book of poems than to summarize it. In spite of some show of organization—the poems are grouped into three divisions each with its motto (two from Job, one from *Romeo and Juliet*)—the system of arrangement is not readily discerned. The reader is best advised to browse, making an entry where he can. Many of these poems are excessively arcane. Gustafson might blush to recall his scolding, a quarter of a century earlier, of modern poets who dealt in "intricate obscurities." His own kind of obscurity is associated with his title. Rivers that force their channels, carrying life through inert and hostile matter, represent the poet's very syntax, which cuts its own exuberant way through the usual conventions of language: ellipses as stunning as Browning's at their boldest; pell-mell succession of sentence elements; brevities that are more cryptic than witty; baffling alternations of concrete and abstract. These, added to mannerisms learned from Hopkins, make for strenuous reading. Usually, the effort is justified, for in many of these poems Gustafson draws on a substantial amount of insight and wisdom as well as an extraordinary command of verbal and prosodic effects.

Three kinds of poems he does particularly well: poems celebrating sexual love or recreating the mood and setting of an act of love—that is, most of the poems in the second section of *Rivers among Rocks*, as well as "Armorial" in the first; poems that vividly present a scene and an action, either actual or subjective ("Legend," "Ophiography," "The Little Elderly Lady Visits the Old Ladies' Home"); poems that capture the sense of place ("Quebec Winterscene," "On the Road to Vicenza," "Quebec, Late Autumn," and most of the contents of *Rocky Mountain Poems*).

40. Poetry
1950-1960

MUNRO BEATTIE

IN THE NINETEEN-FIFTIES Canada had become veritably "a nest of singing birds"—as one of the birds was heard to say. Looking about, indeed, a Canadian concerned about such things might well reflect that this country was, by per capita estimate, as well supplied with proficient poets as any country in the world. Periodicals of poetry were no more numerous or long-lived than in the forties—in fact, with the death of *Northern Review* Canadian poets lost their sole reliable outlet—but the quantity and quality of publishable poetry had never been so high. Moreover, poets could be heard reading their own or their friends' poems in coffee houses, with or without the accompaniment of jazz, in college auditoriums, and over the air on the admirable C.B.C. programme "Anthology."

Most of the poets whose origins went back to the beginning of the modern movement in the 1920's continued in the fifties to be occasionally creative. A. J. M. Smith published *A Sort of Ecstasy* in 1954; F. R. Scott, *Events and Signals* in the same year; Dorothy Livesay her *Selected Poems* in 1957. In 1956 the Contact Press brought out a collection of the 1920's poems of W. W. E. Ross under the title *Experiment*. The most impressive book of the decade was E. J. Pratt's *Towards the Last Spike*, published in 1952. Of the *First Statement* and *Preview* poets of the early forties, James Wreford and Patrick Anderson had departed from Canada. P. K. Page ceased to write verse after the publication of *The Metal and the Flower* in 1954. Other poets of that generation continued to flourish, especially Raymond Souster, Louis Dudek, Miriam Waddington, and Irving Layton. Earle Birney, Charles Bruce, and A. G. Bailey also contributed to the poetic abundance of the 1950's.

What was most gratifying in this decade (or the years, rather, between 1948 and 1960) was the appearance of a greater number of first books by Canadian poets of talent than at any other period in our literary history. Chronologically, to be sure, some of these poets belonged to the same generation as those who first appeared in the Montreal magazines of the early forties; several of them had contributed to these periodicals and to *Contemporary*

Verse. But their first books belong to the fifties and stand with the other books on the small shelf of excellent new Canadian poetry—a shelf of extremely comely books, many of them, for in this decade Canadian publishers of verse took unprecedented pains over the design of books, jackets, and typography.

A summary view of Canadian poets of the 1950's is provided by *Pan-ic: A Selection of Contemporary Canadian Poems* (New York, 1958), edited by Irving Layton, or by a *Queen's Quarterly* pamphlet, edited by Milton Wilson, entitled *Recent Canadian Verse* (1959). These may be compared with collections made in the two preceding decades: *Other Canadians* (1947) and *New Provinces* (1936). If the comparison includes entire books of verse it will strike the reader at once that Canadian poets have been becoming more sophisticated in their prosody, more ingenious in verbal play, more venturesome in choosing themes and techniques. Certainly, poetry as a craft has been taken seriously by more poets than ever before. Also evident is a new kind of intellectual toughness. The lyric impulse has been by no means inhibited. But this new generation of poets has shown a power to think feelingly over a broad range of objects and concepts. They do not fear such epithets as "academic" and "erudite," recognizing that a valid part of a poet's experience, and so a legitimate source of subject-matter, is his encounters with books and ideas. A mingling of sorts of experience has been accompanied by a broadening of usage; the editorial policy of the latest edition of the Webster dictionary would receive ample support from the practice of recent Canadian poets. The fusion of speech-levels sometimes produces a jarring effect, but most of the poets of the fifties have shown great skill in assimilating prose rhythms and colloquial turns of speech into poetic discourse. They have followed a more fruitful method than the poets of the forties who, modelling themselves upon Auden and Spender, often in the end wrote neither prose nor verse.

Few of the poets represented in *Recent Canadian Verse* appear to live in the city. It may be significant that, of the two poems by Raymond Souster in the anthology, one recounts an incident of Toronto in 1885, the other takes as its point of view the thirty-fifth floor of a Toronto skyscraper from which the reader's gaze is led out over the city and beyond to where "A lone Mountie / In his bloodier-than-red jacket / Was chasing three Eskimos and a walrus / Across the frozen ice-cubes / Of Real Gone Valley." The consciousness of Canada as a vastness sparsely settled and only tenuously attached to the world of literature has concerned the critics more than the poets; only a few poets have brought bits and pieces of the vastness into an expressive state. But the city, so compelling a subject or field of observation for the poets of the forties, appears to have lost its appeal. Nor do most of the new poets care about social issues as the preceding generation, for a while at least, did. Such detachment is rather a sign of the times—good times for Canada—than of numbed consciences. If Karl Marx no longer speaks to these poets, neither does Sigmund Freud. The deep pools of imagery are the Bible, Blake, Bulfinch (or Graves), Kafka, and Lewis Carroll. As for objective reality, whether of city or country, place or person, it has never since the twenties come so close to being entirely out of fashion. It may be that metamorphosis and analogy rather than direct transcription are the poet's way of staking out his own realm in an era when the novelist seems dominated by external phenomena.

Canadian poets appear to have been pondering of late upon two problems. One is the problem of "aesthetic distance." The poet of lyric impulse continues to be content to be overheard digesting experience in his own person. But for other poets the indispensable "I" may be an encumbrance. They have shown various shrewd ways of projecting *personae* that speak in voices not necessarily proceeding from the poet himself. The other problem is the creation of larger and more comprehensive poetic unities. The long narrative or narrative-descriptive poem seems unworkable in this age. Only E. J. Pratt, on his own special terms, has succeeded in narrative; Earle Birney (in *David*) and Philip Child (in *The Victorian House*) are the only other poets who have shown narrative competence, and both of them on a more confined scale than Pratt's major poems. Another sort of unity is the assemblage of short poems about a central theme or situation: as in Earle Birney's collections, *Now is Time* and *The Strait of Anian*, and Louis Dudek's *Europe* and *En Mexico*. Several of the most notable books of verse of the fifties have achieved, in diverse ways, integration and articulation of their contents. Some poets, however, remain content with the book of poems on a variety of themes and in a variety of forms and moods among which the reader may, if he wishes, discern patterns of relationship for himself. Margaret Avison, for instance, when she assembled her book *Winter Sun* (1960), "arranged her poems for readers who like to skim through a book when they first take it up"—in this, according to the dust jacket, resembling the author herself, who "approaches a new book of poetry in this way and would rather find her own groupings than have the poems already grouped for her."

The following survey of poetry in the fifties opens with poets who have, on the contrary, been intensely conscious of the value of articulation within a collection of poems.

The first book of poems by James Reaney (b. 1926) was a book for skimming and browsing. The poems gathered together in *The Red Heart* (1949— Governor-General's Award) formed a unity, however, because of the quality of the author's imagination and his feeling for the part of Canada that served as setting for his reminiscences and fancies: Stratford, Ontario, and the adjacent countryside. Such engaging pieces as "The Katzenjammer Kids" and "The School Globe" reproduce with extraordinary clarity the sights and feelings of childhood. "The Chough," "The Plum Tree," "Mrs. Wentworth," "The Gramophone," "Anti-Christ as Child," and the "Great Lakes Suite" manifest Reaney's peculiar angle of vision, his highly personal kind of verbal music, and his skill in blending the actual with the fantastic or the macabre.

For his second book of verse, *A Suit of Nettles* (1958—also winner of a Governor-General's award), Reaney found an enclosing and controlling form in the rare device of a set of twelve eclogues, on the model of Spenser's *Shepheard's Calendar*. The setting is a farm not far from Stratford and the characters are mostly geese. In the bucolic tradition, the sequence includes dialogues, dissertations on love and its hardships, singing competitions, a pastoral funeral, incidental narratives, and a tenuous plot that moves forward or stands still at the author's convenience. The convention is flexible enough to make room for a variety of themes and diversions: a child's picture-book history of Western philosophy, a riddling synopsis of Canadian history, a sermon, and disquisitions on educational methods and literary criticism. These are ingeniously integrated into the total form, but some of them sort oddly with a *dramatis personae* of geese.

Like Spenser, Reaney uses his eclogues as a showcase for his proficiency and versatility as a prosodist. The first three are mainly in stanzas of ten mostly iambic lines, a compendious unit admirably suited to the discursive and descriptive matters these eclogues deal with. A long and entertaining passage in "May" is composed in long doggerel rhythms with almost regular couplet rhymes. Another narrative, in "March," is cast in octosyllabic couplets. Most of "December" is in somewhat haphazard blank verse. Branwell, the principal goose, in "February" sings a sestina. A variety of lyric stanzas appear in the other months: three-lined, quatrain, and in the modes of traditional songs. In spite of considerable waywardness of metre and rhyme (some of which may serve the purposes of imitative harmony), the poet handles these forms with great competence. The satiric intention of the work, announced by an "Invocation to the Muse of Satire," is not so successfully realized. Certainly, the inanities on birth control, on some species of education not identified in the poem, and on the critical methods of Dr. Leavis (or so we are informed by the gloss) do not fulfil any current definition of "satire." Reaney, indeed, would appear to have a mind completely innocent of satiric insight. His more natural gift for capricious whimsy finds plenty of scope throughout the twelve sections.

Jay Macpherson (b. 1931) first published poems in several periodicals and in two charming chapbooks, *Nineteen Poems* (1952) and *O Earth Return* (1954). When she brought out *The Boatman* (1957—Governor-General's Award) it became apparent that these poems and groups of poems belonged to a larger scheme. *The Boatman* is the most intricately unified book in Canadian poetry. It is a collection of lyric poems grouped under six sub-titles. The poems are short, a few of them almost epigrammatic, exquisitely moulded and carefully polished, but without any loss of lyric impetus. The forms are traditional—or suggest traditional measures—and call to mind (without duplicating) such models as popular ballads, carols, Elizabethan songs, nursery rhymes, hymns, and the shorter poems of George Herbert, William Blake, and William Gilbert. The diversity of tones, within so consciously limited a range of metres and stanzas, is astonishing. But the supreme achievement of the book is the enhancement of significance in individual poems by the interplay within a whole network of references and counter-references. The poetess has undeniably made a "Cosmos of a miscellany."

This result is partly brought about by the use of several recurrent and interlinking symbols: phoenix, unicorn, fish; and in part from the development of a group of themes through individual poems and poems in groups. It is clear that for sections two and three ("O Earth Return" and "The Plowman in Darkness") she has taken a hint from Blake's songs of innocence and experience. Most of the poems in these two sections are counterparts whose subjects are certain female figures of crucial significance in the mythic history of man: Eve, Euronyme, the Sibyl of Cumae, and Mary Magdalene. These "fallen women" are presented in two moods and two tones, the tragic and the colloquial. For instance, we hear two voices of Mary. In "Love in Egypt" the voice is solemnly exultant:

> Love, here are thorns, and here's a wilderness
> —And yet you visit me?
> I have a cell, your rod—
> No more to see.
>
> A spring restores these sands,
> Pouring its rocky basin full.
> Love, will you drink from my hands,
> Or rather from my skull.

By contrast the voice of Mary in the corresponding poem of "The Plowman in Darkness" is gay and ribald:

> ... In a far-off former time
> And a green and gentle clime,
> Mamma was a lively lass,
> Liked to watch the tall ships pass,
> Loved to hear the sailors sing
> Of sun and wind and voyaging,
> Felt a wild desire to be
> On the bleak and unplowed sea.
> Mamma was a nice girl, mind,
> Hard up, but a good sport and kind—
> Well, the blessed upshot was,
> Mamma worked her way across
> From Egypt to the Holy Land,
> And here repents, among the sand.

Similarly, the Queen of Sheba in "O Earth Return" represents mystery and grace; in "The Plowman in Darkness" the corresponding poem depicts a Beggars' Opera wedding scene in which a harlot is the central figure.

In the fourth section, "The Sleepers," men of archetypal significance—Adam, Endymion, and the heroes associated with Circe, Psyche, and Helen—provide the *personae*. In the fifth section, "The Boatman," Noah, without a woman but with his ark, moves into the foreground of the anagogic scene and sets in motion the main theme of the final part of the book: the theme of cosmos within cosmos. Section six, "The Fisherman," resolves the various motifs of the preceding sections and concludes with the vision of a fisherman who is several things, one of them the poet as a type of creator. If we compare this fishing figure with the forlorn fellow behind the gashouse in *The Waste Land*, Miss Macpherson's fisherman seems to suggest that, rather than shore up our ruins with fragments of other men's poems, we must make poems of our own—or, better still, accept Miss Macpherson's offer of a *vade-mecum* from our world of delusion and separateness to the poet's world of enlightenment and wholeness.

Anne Wilkinson (1910–1961) writes from a single point of view—her own consciousness looking out upon the natural world and listening to the intimations of her spirit—and, accordingly, in a more consistently personal tone. What she shows in common with Miss Macpherson (and with some other poets) is an absorbing interest in the poet's special way of assimilating and interpreting his experience. One of her central poems is "Lens":

> The poet's daily chore
> Is my long duty;
> To keep and cherish my good lens
> For love and war
> And wasps about the lilies
> And mutiny within....
>
> In my dark room the years
> Lie in solution,
> Develop film by film....

Here are her two themes, as well as their setting and purpose. The poems in Mrs. Wilkinson's two collections—*Counterpoint to Sleep* (1951) and, a strikingly mature book, *The Hangman Ties the Holly* (1955)—are the records of encounters: between the senses and the world of nature ("Winter Sketch, Rockcliffe, Ottawa," "A Poet's Eye View," "In June and Gentle Oven"); between the individual and the diversity of experience ("I was a boy and a maiden . . .," "Easter Sketches, Montreal," "The Red and the Green," "Tigers Know from Birth," "Christmas Eve," "Three Poems about Poets"); between present awareness and intimations from the past ("Summer

Acres," "Once upon a Great Holiday," "Greek Island"); between the transforming imagination and the commonplaces of existence ("After Reading Kafka," "A Child Can Clock," "Items of Chaos"); and, most poignant of all, the conflict between exultant life and prefigured death ("Time is Tiger," "On a Bench in a Park," "Carol"). It will be seen that Anne Wilkinson's subject-matter was the proper and usual stuff of lyric poetry. But her very special powers of perception bestowed on these commonplaces both freshness of handling and novelty of insight. Her rhythms and forms were as individual as her response to experience. In the earlier of her two books she appeared at times to struggle, without complete success, to say what she had to say in the way she had chosen. Most of these problems were solved in her second book, most gratifyingly wherever she yielded to the attraction of traditional patterns, particularly the patterns of nursery rhyme, carol, and popular song. Even when most traditional, however, she followed her own ear for rhythm, her own knack of word-play, and her own imaginative way of looking at things. The unity in her books is the unity of a rare sensibility.

Wilfred Watson (b. 1911) belongs with these three poets, because he shares their liking for traditional forms and their feeling for popular modes. But the poems in his first book, *Friday's Child* (1955—Governor-General's Award), are, unlike Mrs. Wilkinson's, apocalyptic; unlike Miss Macpherson's, expansive in form; and, unlike Reaney's, fervent in tone and frequently incantatory in rhythm. The unifying principle of his collection is dual awareness: of the natural world where beauty and chaos contend and of a world of enlightenment and exaltation. The delusions of the natural world may be cleared away by the will working on behalf of love. Works of art may provide us with instances of the misuse of the will: the shooting of the albatross ("The White Bird"), the rape of Lucrece ("Tarquin"), the instability of Aeneas ("Invocation"), the lover's impulsiveness ("Orpheus and Eurydice"), and the lover's obduracy ("Yeats and Maud Gonne"). But art may, on the contrary, teach wisdom by making clear the disciplinary effects of experience ("Yeats and Maud Gonne," "Of Hendrickje as Bathsheba"). Moreover, art may take as its function the illumination of reality, not so much by vividly representing it as by interpreting it through various kinds of transformation—as, he declares in one of his most exciting poems, Emily Carr did:

> Like Jonah in the green belly of the whale
> Overwhelmed by Leviathan's lights and liver
> Imprisoned and appalled by the belly's wall
> Yet inscribing and scoring the uprush
> Sink vault and arch of that monstrous cathedral,
> Its living bone and its green pulsing flesh—
> Old woman, of your three days' anatomy
> Leviathan sickened and spewed you forth
> In a great vomit on coasts of eternity.

> Then, as for John of Patmos, the river of life
> Burned for you an emerald and jasper smoke
> And down the valley you looked and saw
> All wilderness become transparent vapour,
> A ghostly underneath a fleshly stroke,
> And every bush an apocalypse of leaf.

Works of art do not, after all, furnish the only sources of wisdom. Certain kinds of experience, especially those that demonstrate the power of love—"Friday's child" is, we remember, "loving and giving"—may show us how to redeem our time. For human love is the link between the fallen world and the world of divine presence; Eve and Mary are the polar symbols ("Love Song for Friday's Child"). Wilfred Watson's finest poems, then, are the poems that in simple and ardent diction, frequently of a religious cast, proclaim the dogmas of the wrought-up imagination: that death is a terrible certainty ("In the Cemetery of the Sun," "The Windy Bishop," "For Anne, Who Brought Tulips"); that every human pleasure and consolation is under sentence of death ("Ballad of Mother and Son"—a tremendous achievement in the ballad manner); but that, gloriously, eternity strikes through time not to destroy but to clarify and exalt ("Canticle of Darkness").

Watson treats with considerable power a number of traditional themes and symbols. His professional schooling declares itself, perhaps too conspicuously, through echoes of Hopkins, Yeats, Eliot, and, most obsessively, Dylan Thomas, to whom he dedicates two poems, one an "admiration" and the other a "contempt." Thomas's way with metaphor is almost too plainly Watson's model. But even when he uses the other poet's idiom, Watson usually succeeds in making something of his own, as he has done with the moving "Lines: I Praise God's Mankind in an Old Woman," one of the most memorable pieces in *Friday's Child*. Although Dylan Thomas served as genesis, the revelations are almost wholly Watson's. For sustained power of expression on an intense imaginative level, the poems of Wilfred Watson cannot be matched among Canadian poems of the decade of the fifties.

Phyllis Webb (b. 1927) is yet another of these sensitive explorers of the regions between experience and expression. Her first collection of poems was published under the title "Falling Glass" as one of the three sections of *Trio* (1954). Discarding some of these poems (with commendable self-criticism) and adding others, she put together her first book, *Even Your Right Eye*, in 1956. As the subjective experiences she has drawn upon have been even more private than those of the poets already considered—for she takes no bearings from religion, myth, or folklore—so her forms are more thorough-going in their novelty and individuality. She refers to no conventional patterns, not even the flexible modes of nursery rhymes and popular songs. Every sensation, every perception, is unique and demands a unique form of utterance. This is a risky procedure. Some of her poems do not sufficiently realize the insights that evoked them. But when they do communicate they are capable of producing in the reader a glow of recognition.

If Phyllis Webb's poems seem almost unnecessarily subtle, it is not so much because she has sought to be secretive as that she has assumed the difficult task of bringing into a verbal condition a range of subjective states not rare but rarely communicable: the overlapping of appearance and reality, the minute shifts of comprehension brought about by minute shifts of time or mood, the perceptive elements in the experiencing of loneliness, pain, sexual ardour, and grief. To do poetic justice to her chosen data, the poetess must compel language in various subtle ways (even the syntax carries a burden of implication—study the conjunctions in the refrains of "Sacrament of Spring"). Forms must correspond to the patterns of feeling, even sometimes to the point of typographical expressionism. Her organizations of words work as they should more often than not, and her forms encompass a variety of effects, from the tentative notations of "Fragment" to the bravura of "Standing." Moreover, in spite of so much idiosyncrasy of form she produces a surprising range of tone, from the cerebral playfulness of "Earth Descending" to the quasi-philosophical toying with a group of notions in "Marvell's Garden," "Poetry," and "Double Entendre"—a delectable piece of work. Even if the example of Marianne Moore is the taking-off point for several of these engaging little rambles from object to object and from image to image, the ultimate effect is entirely personal. Illustrative of Miss Webb's mode of operation is "Fantasia on Christian's Diary," which was inspired by the C.B.C. documentary, "Death in the Barren Grounds," but does not undertake to retell the story. "It attempts rather to give a shape to the atmosphere of that story." Similarly, in most of her poems Phyllis Webb is sparing of narrative or connective material, supplying the reader, rather, with the ingredients of a poem that he must co-operate with the author to bring into complete being.

The most striking section of *Trio* is a group of "Minotaur Poems" by Eli Mandel (b. 1922). The protagonist of these haunting narratives is an Icarus-Theseus figure fused with the modern man who speaks in the person of the poet. The same method is at work in most of Mandel's other *Trio* poems, particularly "Orpheus," "Leda and the Swan," "Aspects in a Mirror" (in which Icarus and Theseus again figure, along with Narcissus), "Not Poppy nor Mandragora" (a restatement of Desdemona's undoing in terms of international peace and betrayal), and a poem about the poet's natal town, "Estavan, Saskatchewan," in which mood and locale are given emotional tone by themes from *Hamlet*. The impulse to re-interpret myth in contemporary terms—and, at the same time, to impart to contemporary subject-matter overtones of timelessness and universality—has evoked also the principal poems of Eli Mandel's first book, one of the finest of recent years, *Fuseli Poems* (1960).

Motifs from the work of Fuseli provide imagery and tone for several poems. The subtlest and strongest of these is "Fuseli: Girl Combing her Hair Watched by a Young Man," in which the theme evolves from the image suggested by Fuseli (complicated by suggestions from Keats's *Eve of St. Agnes*), through a moral and metaphysical interpretation, to its bearing upon the condition of the poet—the persona, more properly, of this and several other poems in the collection: "Notes from the Underground," "Biopsy," "Two Part Exercise on a Single Theme," and "The Professor as Bridegroom." This persona, whom it is difficult to resist associating with the poet's own personality and experience, is a diffident and sardonic creature, with a sharply developed sense of the ironic and the grotesque. Parts of him are clearly recognizable in other poems, for example in both the hunchback and the wizard of "A Castle and Two Inhabitants," the quixotic dotard in "Conversation Overheard between a Knight and a Girl," the Old Testament nomad of "Pillar of Fire," and the townsman who incisively and suggestively reports the sinister occurrences of "Prologue" and "Epilogue." All these poems, like the Minotaur suite, owe their distinctive power to the skill with which the poet has combined and counterpointed a rich assortment of elements: the "personal" and the mythic, the melodramatic and the commonplace, the actual and the fantastic. Among contemporary Canadian poets, none is more consummately the "maker" of poems.

As well, he can scarcely be bettered in his command of a middle style of discourse. However phantasmagoric his subject-matter, his choice and order of words are almost unfailingly precise, decorous, civilized, touched with wit, and with a sure feeling for the placing of the single telling word or image. Occasionally, in striking the attitude of the folktale-teller, he slips beyond the colloquial into the slovenly, as in the first two stanzas of "A Castle and Two Inhabitants," or he forsakes his comely syntax to whore after modish perversities, as in the group of "Val Marie" poems in *Trio*, but his writing in general provides again and again the peculiar delight of hearing the elusive thing phrased with grace and clarity. There is, moreover, a special piquancy in the interplay between the Canadian scenes and attitudes of several of his poems and the romantic imagination and "Jewish" humour of the poet.

Gael Turnbull (b. 1928), the third of the *Trio* poets, is the least ambitious in the choice of themes and technique. His field is actuality, his most usable gifts keen observation, a wide range of sympathies, and an engaging resoluteness to make the reader share his visual and emotional perceptions. His descriptive pieces, accordingly, are far more successful than the poems that deal with moral or political problems. His virtues are most plainly to be recognized, among the *Trio* poems, in "Lumber Camp Railway," "Industrial

Valley (Northern England)," and "In a Strange City." His little book *Bjarni* (1956) shows considerable competence in narrative and in the re-creation of medieval heroic episodes and characters, especially in "An Irish Monk on Lindisfarne." The poems in *The Knot in the Wood* (1955) are slight but reveal remarkable power of compression and suggestiveness in the handling of colloquial idiom. Specially worthy of mention are Gael Turnbull's translations in collaboration with Jean Beaupré, of poems by the French-Canadian poets Saint-Denys-Garneau, Paul-Marie Lapointe, Roland Giguère, and Gilles Hénault (published in four mimeographed collections, 1955).

The poetry of Kay Smith (b. 1911) is considerably more declamatory. Her poems were published during the 1940's in *Contemporary Verse*, the *Canadian Forum*, and *Northern Review*: she was well represented in John Sutherland's *Other Canadians* in 1947; and her only book of poems was published in the New Writers Series of the First Statement Press, *Footnote to the Lord's Prayer* (1951). This collection is remarkably consistent in tone and rhythms. The point of view is isolated and subjective, the theme is human existence in its beauty and horror, but the treatment is strangely impersonal—the poetess seems to speak in her own person only once in the entire book. Although it contains eleven short lyric-contemplative poems, each about a page long, three-fifths of its space is occupied by two poems organized on "public" principles. "Conversations with a Mirror" presents successively the soliloquies of a girl, a harlot, a spinster, a wife, a soldier, and Death; each expresses an emotional involvement with war. The poem is one of the few civilian records of the period in Canada of World War II. The other poem is the work that gives a title to the collection, "Footnote to the Lord's Prayer." It takes the form of commentaries in verse on each clause or petition in the prayer, a sequence of improvisations on a set of themes. Because of her power to convey her intense earnestness, her resourcefulness in imagery, and her skill in alternating long and short rhythms, the poetess carries out with fair success her rather daunting assignment.

Almost all the poems in *The Wounded Prince* (1948), the first book brought out by Douglas LePan (b. 1914) are sensitive and accomplished, but in several of them a certain slackness of rhythm and blurriness of imagery betray a lack of central intensity of theme. It is surely not mere chauvinism that singles out as more successful, because more serious, the poems made out of Canadian material: "Coureurs de Bois," "Canoe Trip," and "A Country without a Mythology." This country is the untrammeled and untravelled wilderness of northern Ontario or Quebec. LePan shows considerably more force in making its quality actual to the reader than he does in gathering together his impressions of the landscapes of the mind of other poems in the collections. Moreover, in these three poems, which discourse of the loreless tracts of uninhabited country, the poet joins certain of his compatriots in the co-operative enterprise of bringing Canada, acre by acre, street by street, into the world of poetry. The masterpiece of *The Wounded Prince* is a longish poem called "Image of Silenus." This too may be considered "Canadian," both in its beautiful realization of the blue heron of the first stanza and in its poignant evocation, in its closing passages, of an urban society longing hopelessly for the world of wonder to which the heron flies away, where men may be free to emulate the archetypes contained in the statue of Silenus and splendidly enact "all the other roles that men have pictured for themselves."

In the first book the Canadian landscape contains no Canadians. In Le Pan's second, and greatly superior, book of verse, *The Net and the Sword* (1953—Governor General's Award), Canadians do appear, act, think, and feel—but in a foreign landscape. The poems in this book derive from the author's experiences in the Italian campaign of World War II. Distance in time from the events and the emotions that they contemplate has given these poems a wholeness of vision and the special intensity of focus that memory creates. The title poem suggests the unifying image of the book, an image drawn from gladiatorial contests. The sword is symbol of the Canadian, the North American, consciousness opposed to the net of war, of Europe, of alien experience. Two things the poet manages with particular skill. One is the graphic presentation of an isolated episode and the actor in it ("Persimmons," "An Incident," "One of the Regiment," "The New Vintage"). The poet finds exactly the right tone and the right details for bringing before our mind's eye the young Canadian soldier, disciplined and determined to make the best of an ugly assignment, not essentially a warrior in spite of his well-kept rifle and "bronzed rigidity," ignorant or heedless of the long history of the farms and villas destiny has brought him to, a temporarily displaced person whose senses do not falter in their response to warmth and light and the lusciousness of persimmons, and whose memory dwells upon "the boyhood that he left at home / Skating at Scarborough, summers at the Island," although his intellect only partially understands the larger meaning, if there is one, of the "crusade" in which he is participant.

LePan's other poetic strength lies in the extended contemplation of a situation or a mood ("Tuscan Villa," "Field of Battle," "Elegy in the Romagna"). In such poems he works on an ample scale, composing his impressions, memories, and feelings into full-bodied poems of meditation and recollection. There is some truth in the remark that Irving Layton intended as a quip: "A Lampman on a battlefield" ("Prologue to the Long Pea-Shooter"). Precisely Lampman's kind of sober fidelity and fullness in recording his observations and reactions is what makes LePan's poetic essays satisfying. True, Yeats could have made to them the same objection he made to Wilfred Owen's poems. The suffering *is* futile, the misery without issue—

but how else do justice to the terrible truth? These poems may have a peculiar value because they are among the few poetic records of the Canadian experience in the Second World War.

> Arrange the scene with only a shade of difference
> And he would be a boy in his own native
> And fern-fronded province
> With a map in his hand, searching for a portage
>   overgrown
> With brush. . . .
> Who alone by the worm-holed flower of the rose-pink
>   house
> Bears the weight of this many-ringed, foreign noon,
> Shadowless, vast and pitiless.
> Notched by the wedge of his frown, it takes no notice. . . .
> What is he waiting for
> As he studies a map the colour of his youth? . . .

In the poems of John Glassco (b. 1909) we again confront Canadian scenes, and again the Canadians are missing or almost so. *The Deficit Made Flesh* (1958) draws much of its strength from the author's intimate acquaintance with farm life in the Eastern Townships of Quebec, a milieu and a way of life ("no way of living but a mode of life" the first poem calls it, with bitter realism) that he has observed over many years, and from the special vantage point, during World War II, of the rural mail-carrier. The book's central and recurrent images are decaying farmhouses and jolting roads that lead nowhere. This poet is unstinting in his use of descriptive detail, and his reports on the externals of farm life will carry complete conviction to readers in many parts of Canada, where such an image as "this heaven-riving road thrown / Like a noosed lifeline to five worthless farms" ("The Brill Farm") or such a bucolic vignette as this stanza from "Gentleman's Farm" presents:

> And where the regional serf, time out of mind,
> Morning and evening, blind with sweat and fury,
>   Hollaed his shaggy tyke
> After the peaked-arse cows in the hummocky pasture
> Till they buckjumped to the dislocated barn,
>   Their slack bags black with muck,

will sharply produce the shock of recognition.

John Glassco is not a simple regional realist, but a sophisticated artist. His prosody is skilful and ingenious; he has a special flair for the handling of blank verse and the composition of stanzas both rhymed and unrhymed. His most characteristic effect of style is the long sentence—intricately involved, with many parenthetical elements and wide separations of verbs and subject—that straddles two stanzas and densely interweaves its rhythm with the rhythm of the verse-pattern. Clearly, he is less bent upon accumulating the data of rural sociology than upon communicating a peculiar kind of consciousness. When the reader looks more closely at these poems he discerns in some of them an attitude to life that is both compelling and repulsive. In the constant struggle between the rank and unresting forces of nature and the energies and hopes of men, the speaker in most of these poems has put his money on nature—and with a frightening kind of relish. It is almost indecently inappropriate in speaking of these sardonic elegies to invoke such names as John Clare and Edward Thomas.

"Stud Groom" is addressed to a man who has confined his entire life to his job: the care and training of horses for racing at annual fairs. He has abstained from every sort of profound or permanent human association. This remarkable poem is ambiguous and ironic but its general intent seems congratulatory: this is a smart way of dealing with such frailties as wanting a wife and children who, in any event, would be doomed at birth to the pangs of being human. Where the will is not powerful enough to carry through the process of mutilation, nature will provide the means. In "The White Mansion" the house itself, a handsome burden demanding for its upkeep more than the owner can provide, is the agent of destruction. In this poem the speaker is the mansion itself:

> Two hearts, two bodies clove, knew nothing more.
> Ere I was done I tore them asunder. Singly
> They fled my ruin and the ruin of love.
> I am she who is stronger than love.

"Noyade 1942" is a confession of the unreliability of human fidelity assaulted by the natural appetites of frail flesh. The "natural" ambitions of a hard-working farmer ("The Entailed Farm") have ruined his son—"the bearded man that walked like a bear, / His pair of water-pails slung from a wooden neckyoke, / Slipping in by the woodshed"—and destroyed the farm:

> ... the mute, sealed house,
> Where the spring's tooth, stripping shingles, scaling
> Beam and clapboard, probes for the rot below
> Porch and pediment, and blind bow-window ...
>
> Where the stone wall is a haven for snake and squirrel
> The steepled dovecote for phoebe and willow-wren,
> And the falling field-gates, trigged by an earthen swell,
> Open on a wild where nothing is raised or penned,
> On rusty acres of witch-grass and wild sorrel
> Where the field-birds cry and contend.

Any endeavour to thwart the process of disintegration ("Gentleman's Farm") the poet mordantly attributes to "the structural mania of the heart" and condemns in advance to failure:

> See that the wreck of all things made with hands
> Being fixed and certain, as all flesh is grass,
>   The grandiose design
> Must marry the ragged matter, and of the vision
> Nothing endure that does not gain through ruin
>   The right, the wavering line.

"The right, the wavering line" is celebrated in "Deserted Buildings under Shefford Mountain." In a strain oddly reminiscent of the tone and rhythms of *In Memoriam* the poet discourses of the pleasures to be got from ruins— "Some troubled joy that's half despair." He cannot, or will not, identify this joy; the final stanza fobs us off with the flimsy notion that the ruins prove once more the defeat of "progress and its emmet plan." The true quality of his joy that's half despair comes through clearly enough in the two closing lines:

> Dark houses that are void of man,
> Dull meadows that have gone to seed.

After these poems it comes as no surprise that the poet should in another poem have built an Eastern Townships farmhouse for a perverse Penelope, and that, in an admirable sonnet, he should salute the painter Utrillo for recognizing that the empty streets of his paintings make the same corrosive commentary on human feelings and aspirations.

Pessimism so inordinate is not new, of course, to literature. Some readers will consider it a valid "philosophy of life." Others, however, may regard these poems as splinters from a damaged sensibility. Some of the makeweight poems in the collection—interesting though not wholly worked out ("A Devotion," "Didactic," "Hail and Farewell," "The Whole Hog")— provide a few clues, as do two quite successful but troubling poems: "Villanelle" and "Shake Dancer." So does "The Burden of Junk," read not simply as a parody of the *Evangeline* metre but with attention to what is said—and said, it seems, in total seriousness:

> Mine is a burden of junk that ought to be left with him also:
> This is where it belongs, with the wheels and the beds and
>   the organ,
> With all the personal trash that the spirit acquires and
>   abandons,
> Things that have made the heart warm and bewildered the
>   senses wih beauty
> Long ago,—but that weakened and crumbled away with the passion
> Born of their brightness, the loves that a dreary
>   process of dumping
> Leaves at last on a hillside to rot away with the season.

Elizabeth Brewster (b. 1922) also has a well-developed sense of place—her place being rural New Brunswick—and considerable insight into local folkways. Her poems speak with the authentic voices of the region and its people. Miss Brewster's first collection was *East Coast* (1951), six short poems, the most notable of which is the title piece. Its theme is the isolation —geographical, cultural, and personal—which is reinforced by, and symbolized by, the fierce incessant wind. "River Song" captures the sense of a vitality that has become part of the province's past; and "London Fog" contrasts, through the eyes of the poetess far from home, the bleakness of the great city with the remembered loveliness of her Maritime landscape by starlight.

Lillooet (1954) is the picture of a small New Brunswick town. The touch seems very sure with which the poetess selects the details of place, personality, and idea to recreate the life of the town. She completely individualizes this particular place, Lillooet, yet intimates that in many respects it stands for life in general in rural New Brunswick—or even, in some aspects, small towns everywhere. Spoon River and Winesburg have been suggested as analogues, but Miss Brewster's treatment is less objective than Masters', less subjective than Anderson's; her attitude combines affection, entirely devoid of sentimentality, with amusement entirely without bitterness. Next to the handling of specific detail, the main achievement of the poem is its tone, which seems, interestingly, to represent both the people of Lillooet and their historian. Tone is sustained by style: a competent, seemingly off-hand, kind of doggerel, with many unexpected felicities that distinguish *Lillooet* from other treatments, in verse or prose, of the same kind of material.

Elizabeth Brewster's third chapbook of verse, *Roads and Other Poems* (1957), derives only part of its contents from her New Brunswick insights and observations. Observation and recollection give her the substance of the poems entitled "Roads," "Canon Bradley," "Louise," and "Home for the Aged." These four poems show considerable range in rhythm and feeling; they demonstrate, even more convincingly, that gift for recording actuality that marked the two earlier books. *Roads*, however, includes another kind of poem, represented in *East Coast* by "In the Library," an effective evocation of a moment of doubt about self-identity, and in *Roads* by "Supposition" and "To Hanai." These subjective, non-representational poems suggest that the next phase of Elizabeth Brewster's development may be towards a less local point of view, a tendency to look out over a larger world of people and ideas, or into the even vaster world of the self.

Another poet of New Brunswick is Fred Cogswell (b. 1917), who has published five books of verse: *The Stunted Strong* (1954), *The Haloed Tree* (1956), *The Testament of Cresseid* (1957), *Descent from Eden* (1959) and *Lost Dimension* (1960). Something in this poet's temperament or his breeding inclines him to sententiousness. This has fathered a number of proficient little poems of a satiric and epigrammatic sort, each dexterously scoring a hit on a large thematic target: death, birth, love, bigotry, spiritual nakedness, sexual instability, conventions, racial discrimination in Fredericton. A reader's sensibility may at time be grated by the semantic snip-snap with which an ingenious image or turn of phrase points up a significance. More pleasing, because less emphatic, are two or three ballads and the grim little anecdotes that rehearse the consequences of lust. The poet also realizes with some success certain forms of inner distress and longings ("Death Watch," "The Seed I Sowed, Believing," "Snake Shadow," "Within My Templed Flesh"); and creates analogues for various kind of religious experiences ("A Christmas Carol," "The Idiot Angel," "The Web: For Easter").

Fred Cogswell's most interesting poems, however, are his sonnets about New Brunswick characters. Sixteen of these sonnets make up *The Stunted Strong*, most of which are reprinted in *Descent from Eden*. They are wholly conventional in style and metrics, in a manner that pleasantly recalls Goldsmith, Crabbe, Whittier, and E. A. Robinson, but their subjects are grim: seduced small-town girls, illegitimate babies, feeble-minded aunts, scandalmongers and gossips, drunkards, sadists, runaway farm girls who become burlesque queens. Extra-provincial readers may wonder how statistically sound this sonnet sociology is, but the poet makes most of it seem convincing —mainly by the strategy of placing himself as observer and confidant among the people of his fictional community. Moreover, he does not condemn his compatriots and contemporaries for their frailties. He understands them and recognizes them as the warped products of a stern tradition and a harsh setting, as he shows in "Valley-Folk," "The Jacks of History," and "The Stunted Strong":

> Not soft the soil where we took root together;
> It grew not giants but the stunted strong,
> Toughened by suns and bleak wintry weather
> To grow up slow and to endure for long;
> We have not gained to any breadth or length,
> And all our beauty is our stubborn strength.

Fred Cogswell is completely *au courant* with "modern" poetic modes (he has been co-editor and business manager of that estimable Fredericton magazine of verse, *The Fiddlehead*) and he does not shrink from handling subject-matter that one suspects would horrify conservative New Brunswick readers. Yet he is not as far removed from his provincial progenitors as might be expected. His ballads recall some of the narrative lyrics of Duncan Campbell Scott; his stanzaic poems bear resemblances to Carman's, though his are more precise in diction and audacious in imagery; his "realistic" pen-portraits and bleak bucolics are stylistically akin to some of Roberts's *Songs of the*

Common Day, though shorn of poetic fiddle-faddle and determined, as Roberts's poems never were, to celebrate the fornication, gore, and frustration that have shaped the psyches of New Brunswick.

The first book of poems by Alden Nowlan, born in Nova Scotia in 1933, was *The Rose and the Puritan*, published in 1958 in the *Fiddlehead* Poetry Book series. Some of the poems in this collection would look at home in Cogswell's, notably "The Brothers and the Village," "Hens," "All Down the Morning," and "Child of Tabu"; for these poems take the same mordant view of Maritime life and deal with such phenomena as feeble-mindedness, illegitimacy, farmyard bloodshed, and feminine forwardness. But Alden Nowlan's more memorable poems have their own identifying traits. Chief among these is the tenderness, only slightly tinged with self-pity, that colours the poet's recollections of episodes and persons belonging to his childhood ("Cattle among the Alders," "When Like the Tears of Clowns," and "A Poem to My Mother"). In other poems he shows the power to project, through narrative and imagery, those subjective crises when the self is temporarily aware of its naked weakness and its susceptibility to evil and good ("Two Strangers" and "The Rose and the Puritan"). In the third place, his rhythms show a tendency to slide out of the conventional pattern into new effects in keeping with mood or theme.

Nowlan's subsequent books—*A Darkness in the Earth* (1959), *Under the Ice* and *Wind in a Rocky Country* (both 1961)—repeat and enlarge on these qualities. He has continued to prefer the short poem that decisively delivers a single perception, memory, or scene. His data are supplied by his observations or recollections of small town types in the Maritimes: the escape from the aridity of their lives into the excitements of evangelical religion ("Marian at the Pentecostal Meeting," "Baptism"); the release afforded by fraternal masquerades ("The Lodge," "Our Brother Exalted") or by an interlude of masculine time-wasting ("Homebrew"); tiny vignettes of nature ("Pussy-willows in March," "Summer," "Purple Trilliums"); rueful contemplation of the ways man has contaminated nature and, sometimes, nature's way of revenge ("These are the Men Who Live by Killing Trees," "St. John River," "Abandoned House"); the means by which feelings find outlet in spite of years of repression and discipline ("Poem for the Golden Wedding of My Puritan Grandparents," "The Coat"); the thwarting and warping of ordinary sexual life ("Beginning," "Cousins," "Father," "Rosemary Jensen," "This Woman's Shaped for Love," "Georgie and Fenwick").

To a considerable extent the poems in Alden Nowlan's four books are more successful as sociology than as literature. When they are extremely brief, as many of them are, they frequently lack an ultimate intensification of style. When they venture to a greater length they lack cohesion and impact. A commendable number of them, however, perfectly fuse matter and medium, and a few add a particular touch of magic and energy—for example, "A Letter to My Sister," "A Night Hawk Fell with a Sound like a Shudder," and the unforgettable poem of which the first half goes thus:

> God sour the milk of the knacking wench
> with razor and twine she comes
> to stanchion our blond and bucking bull,
> pluck out his lovely plumbs.

R. G. Everson (b. 1904), a Montreal lawyer and editor who, after twenty-five years' abstention, returned productively to the writing of verse, has published two collections: *Three Dozen Poems* (1957) and *A Lattice for Momos* (1958). These two attractive books consist of short pieces of verse, most of them between six and twelve lines in length, each, elegantly set upon a single page, just the length of an observation or an insight. The great majority of them are composed in the kind of *vers libre* that was in vogue in the 1920's. But, when he wishes to, Everson can deftly turn a stanza or a set of stanzas. "The Abbé Lemaître's Universe" ingeniously pivots its quatrains on three rhymes, and "After Evening Milking" sports dexterously with alternate half-rhymes. Short though they are, few of these little poems are epigrammatic in tone. The effect they are after is not of smartness but of understanding.

This poet revels in the powers of the poet—to recognize significant pattern in the flux of daily existence, to clarify an insight by communicating it through the operative rhythm and phrasing, to perceive metaphor. He particularly revels in the metamorphic work of the imagination:

> Paint me a fallacy: the surf as frieze
> of children at a soda-fountain greeting
> noisily (hands in air and heads gyrating)
> pistachio sundaes of in-coming seas.

So begins "Peggy's Cove," one of his friskier pieces; and a fine parade of images leaps from his pen, as though he were demonstrating to the wielders of cameras and brushes at that noted beauty-spot the superior flexibility of his re-creation of reality. He shows, in more serious poems, a knack for bringing together out of a scene the details that will realize the mood. Frequently the mood is one of well-being ("Elevator Ride," "When I'm Going Well"), for this poet seems to find plenty of causes for contentment even in the wasteland of the modern metropolis, seems aware that the wasteland is only in the imagination of modern man:

> A large wild animal
> prowls outside my office.
> I chant Audograph incantations
> and, bowing, drum the typewriter.

> These hold away the creature,
> but the kind face
> of my old cleaning woman
> is bitten by loneliness.
> The nightwatchman, nomadic,
> wandering barren floors,
> cries out, "Monsieur, bon soir."
> The large wild animal
> prowls at all my doors,
> crowds my empty streets,
> howls across my quiet city.
>
> ("Working Late")

Other poems ("Laprairie Hunger Strike," "One-Night Expensive Hotel") powerfully suggest those nightmare images that rise from the unconscious or hover in the radioactive atmosphere. His chief gift is the perception of analogies. Several of the poems use this method of making a commentary on human nature or behaviour: boys playing in the city streets equated with men in various occupations and conditions (" 'All Wars are Boyish . . .' "); the fishduck and the brilliant actress ("Flying in from Ecuador at Dawn"); the dung beetles strolling under the electrified fence that inhibits the horses ("Letter from Underground").

In this flair for analogy lies Everson's most notable significance as a poet using Canadian material. Nothing about his work is more striking than the way his mind flashes off from an object or an *aperçu* to link up a correspondence in literature, history, or philosophy. Themistocles racked with envy of Miltiades, Landor nobly refraining from strife, and generations of contentious Canadian legislators are all contrasted with the self-completed lovers in the first of the three dozen poems:

> Under the Parliament and medaled only with leaves
> lovers possess the world while overthrown.

Gathering wood for a campfire brings to mind other kinds of blazing-up of energy:

> . . . dazzlements that rear
> Strange as in Lincoln who—middle-aged—awoke,
> Or that one century when Athens blazed,
> Florence but half that long, and in the mind
> Of Keats the one great year when seas would burn. . . .

Watching the moths flying against the lighted window of a friend's studio suggests an image for the terror of creative fury in the experience of a Coleridge or a Van Gogh. Returning to the snow-cumbered streets from a performance of *The Tempest*, he finds his perceptions still alert to mystery:

> The whole town had been silenced. A deep nap
> Of sidewalk plush kept up a whispered count
> Of their footsteps. In a dark house that they passed
> A telephone hunted with magical empty sounds.
> Snow bleached the hung long bones that were the elms.
> Across the frozen quiet, far away
> A motor car was swelling out its chest
> And a tantrum of steam engine started a train.

Marvell suggests a way of responding to the drama of Montmorency Falls. In "To My Father" the Parthenon and the Acropolis on their large scale stand for the intensity with which the poet regards the trivial things that stir his memory. The metaphor of a flashfire for maple-trees in autumn brings in the burning of great ancient cities. Alcibiades is involved with an X-ray examination. The eddies and spray of the French River inspire a corrective memorandum to Heracleitus. A figured pebble spaded up in his garden shares the glamour of the Rosetta stone. A startling historical analogy serves for a solacing toast, "To the Works Superintendent on His Retirement":

> Old Age, like mainland Romans of Venetia
> whom wild Hun years harass
> down from golden villas, may contrive
> great Venice in sea grass.

By means of this kind of analogy he puts contemporary Canada into relation with the past ("Quebec City Real Estate," "Last of the Batoche Métis," "Fall of the City") and brings present time in Canada into relation with cosmic relativity ("Flight 421, over Oshawa," "June 21," "Fish in a Store-window Tank on Rue Ste. Catherine").

George Johnston (b. 1913) is in most respects a more accomplished craftsman in verse than R. G. Everson, but the two poets are alike in their affection for the commonplaces of life and in their power to make poetry out of these realities. George Johnston's first book, *The Cruising Auk* (1959), is a cunningly integrated and unified collection of short poems mostly in formal measures. They are organized into three parts. Part One, "The Pool," and Part Three, "In It," may be called the "personal" parts—made up, that is, of poems in which the speaker seems to be the poet himself. An engaging serenity of tone and the deftness of the workmanship prevent us from realizing, until we are well into the book, how decided a tilt towards melancholy most of the poems take. They tell us, in stanzas of exquisite wit and precision, that the certainties of childhood do not endure, that no man can wholly communicate with another, that a thin partition divides bliss from disaster, that the quest for permanent happiness can never be fulfilled. These topics are voiced again, with variations and resolutions, in Part Three, and provide the thematic framework for the poems of Part Two. As well, a symbolic framework relates part to part and poem to poem by two sequences of imagery: images of water and images of flight. The water images modulate in Part One from pool through river to rain and tears and on to "the everlasting swishing of the whitecaps." The image of flight that appears at the close of Part One is a crow that, aimless and lugubrious bird though it seems to be, the poet yearns to emulate:

> Me too! I would like to fly
> Somewhere else beneath the sky,
> Happy though my choice may be
> Empty tree for empty tree.

Part Two is the triumph of the book. Most of the poems in this part are about other people. Thirty or so are referred to, many of them are named, and several appear frequently and vividly enough to establish identities. The people of the poems constitute a small society, in a run-down quarter of centre-town. They represent what we call the real world, but at random, as individuals and not schematically. Their relation to the real world is about the same as that of the people in Stanley Spencer's paintings: ordinary people, perhaps on the verge of an apocalypse but without knowing it, busy being themselves. They include Mr. Murple, who

> Splendid on skates comes forth to spin the night
> Upon his arms outstretched and whirling eyeballs,

or goes noctambulating with his "dog that's long / And underslung and sort of pointed wrong," or brings his mother a bottle of gin for Mother's Day; and Edward reading detective stories by the trilight until he has scared "his inner workings / Into a fluid state / And his outer same to jerkings"—Edward whose hat, while the poet "looks along the darkening bank," makes on the water towards the sea; and Mrs. Murple with her "nice red rose to show I'm still alive," and Bridget with her bulge, Elaine in her bikini (again, the poet watches "on the bright shore / Waiting for darkness"), Miss Knit with her cutting pliers, Mrs. Beleek, one of the wondrous aunts, baffling the bugs and being baffled by the children round her flower bed.

Certainly these are "characters" and many of the poems are "funny." But there is a steady undermurmur of doom. The birds and squirrels in the poem "Cats" of Part One should have forewarned us:

> Life is exquisite when it's just
> Out of reach by a bound
> Of filigree jaws and delicate paws. . . .

The people of Part Two live in a world that is, on the whole, full of contentment, but they live dangerously—as we all do. Death is ever at hand. Edward actually drowns, leaving behind, besides his hat, a twenty-dollar debt to the poet. From a corner of the kitchen the ghost of Mrs. Belaney's soldier son looks on while his mother and her friends tearfully take their tea and ominously eye "the encroaching fat." Mr. Murple cannot quite put his three questions into word, however much the poet aids him, but they undoubtedly have to do with ultimate things. Mr. Smith, "at the moment of wild escape / In the telephone booth," is poised not simply between "bliss and fear" or "fire and rape," but between this world and the next, as Mrs. McWhurtle also is, and as the aunts are—all of them:

> .. all my aunts, however full in sight,
> However giant-bowelled, -breasted, -sinewed,
> Will founder, as the suns behind the chimneys. . . .

As for Mr. Goom, for whom "Earth fills her lap . . . with gifts":

> Always round the door he knows
> The brink of darkness drops away
> And sure enough the door will close
> After him over it one day.

Though Mr. Goom's "dilettant attention shifts / From time to time to mortal ends," they seem to be in the poet's mind most of the time. Not that the certainty of death is the worst thing he has to contemplate. More appalling is the touch of time and mutability on everything youthful, hopeful, splendid. The poet's contemporaries, as sketched in the middle stanzas of "Music on the Water," demonstrate this dismal truth, and so does the auk itself. The point about the auk is that it *is* extinct. We can never hope to see it again. The sequence of the images of flight closes in Part Three with the image of airborne man, the airman:

> Nightly the lonely diesel that mourns among the fields
> Calls to me in my bedroom till my compassion yields;
> Nightly the wee jet aircraft that search the dreadful sky
> Draw the tears to my pillow that has so long been dry.
>
> My room is floored with pity, my walls are shored with grief,
> My roof is wide to Heaven, my door invites the thief;
> Why am I not then airborne? They mock me, night and day,
> The clock and the blundering diesel and the wee jets far away.
>   ("This Way Down")

These "funny" poems are full of the tears of things. Well may Mrs. McGonigle deliver her maternal little lecture to Mary Anne ("Mrs. McGonigle on Decorum"):

> Carry a little water can
> To catch the quiet tear....
>
> Don't be nervous, Mary Anne,
>   Everyone else, you know,
> Carries a little water can
>   And doesn't let it show.

George Johnston's poems are not only wise and witty but enchanting to read—or to hear, especially if the reader is the poet himself. His technical skill rests firmly on two qualities: a nearly flawless ear for ordinary speech rhythms and an expert control of traditional metres. He is capable of a remarkable variety of verbal effects. By drawing on sub-literary locutions he achieves, when it is appropriate, a cosy smallness of effect, the quiet chuckle in a corner. Also, without sounding in the least pompous or pretentious, he can slip in a Latinate polysyllable—divaricate, lenticulate, inscrutable, incalculable, disconsolate—which, meshing splendidly with the metre, confers both impetus and resonance. His prosody, too, is highly individual within its conventions; by slight pushes of pause or accent in one direction or another he gives the reader's ear a constant succession of delicious little shocks.

Although poems by Margaret Avison (b. 1918) have been appearing in periodicals and anthologies since 1939, her first book came out in 1960. *Winter Sun* (Governor-General's Award) contains some of the most stimulating and endearing poems ever written in this country. The mind of the maker—an energetic, life-loving, boldly ranging mind—vitalizes the poems and informs their imagery and rhythm. Comparisons with other poets suggest themselves. No doubt, the sensibility of Emily Dickinson has been an incitement, and the technique of Marianne Moore has been instructive. A reviewer once spoke of her as a disciple of E. E. Cummings and of W. C. Williams; erroneously, for her way with both words and concepts is more subtle than Cummings', her idiom much less colloquial than Williams'. Margaret Avison is very much her own woman, though it is possible to recognize in her the one true heir, in her generation, of E. J. Pratt. Like Pratt, she loves to grapple with time and space on a heroic scale; she shares his zest for the wonder of things as they are; although, unlike him, she rarely employs regular metre, her handling and selection of words resemble his.

Miss Avison revels in the scrutiny of reality, even more in speculations on the encounter between the individual mind and the phenomena of space and time. "The optic heart," a phrase from a poem entitled "Snow," epitomizes the interplay of cerebration and feeling that carries her from object to object, from hypothesis to hypothesis through the course of a characteristic poem—"Perspective," for example, or "Neverness," two poems not collected in *Winter Sun*. In "Perspective" she debates the difference between the ordinary way of perceiving distance and her way:

> . . .
> But do you miss the impact of that fierce
> Raw boulder five mile off? You are not pierced
> By that great spear of grass on the horizon?
> You are not smitten with the shock
> Of that great thundering sky? . . .

In the end she concedes that her mode of experiencing space, however invigorating it may be, is somehow frightening:

> . . .
> Your fear has me infected, and my eyes
> That were my sport so long, will soon be apt
> Like yours to press out dwindling vistas from
> The massive flux massive Mantegna knew
> And all its sturdy everlasting foregrounds.

In another poem, however, she refuses to acquiesce in the flattening of the landscape that the coming of night seems to effect:

> . . .
> In this clear twilight contour must contain
> Its source, and distances with contour come
> Opening peacock vistas that can no man entomb.
> ("Rigor Viris")

In "Neverness" her mind swings into the remotest reaches of time, back to the present, then on into the conceivable future, in an endeavour to reconcile the concept of time as sequence with the concept of time as plurally scattered among countless worlds. "Prelude" hauntingly considers light as shape occurring at a variety of points in time and place. One of her wittiest poems, "Grammarian on a Lakefront Park Bench," represents her mind as for once quiescent, her consciousness a "gill that sloughs and slumps / in a spent sea." Even on such a holiday from distinction-making and perception-registering, her mind continues to take in large draughts of actuality and to organize them into images and appropriate sounds (notice the superb alliteration).

Such mental travels as these poems report frequently arrive at no destination. The poet betrays, indeed, a dread of finality and fixity:

> . . . the fix, the frill
> precision can effect, brilliant with danger. . . .
> ("Butterfly Bones; or Sonnet against Sonnets")

Ultimate understanding would spoil the fun for a mind so insatiably speculative. The first poem in her book, "The Apex Animal," fancifully nominates as "the ultimate Recipient / of what happens, the One Who is aware" the Head of a Horse. The last poem, "The Agnes Cleves Papers," might be thought of as Miss Avison's "Gerontion," for it organizes its *personae* and incidents as elements catalysed by memory, and evokes the pathos of opportunities missed and meanings perceived too late. It renders the life and temperament of the nostalgic speaker as a series of projections and extensions from her immediate present, into the past and back to the present, between here and elsewhere. The musings are drawn to a close that is not a conclusion at some undefined point between Moscow and Lima, between the images of a yacht putting out to sea and children playing hopscotch. Throughout *Winter Sun* other poems similarly evade finality. "Voluptuaries and Others," for instance, contrasts two kinds of illumination. Unmistakably, the poet's preference is for the "eureka" of Archimedes, which figures as

> ... a particular instance of
> That kind of lighting up of the terrain
> That leaves aside the whole terrain, really,
> But signalizes, and compels, an advance in it.

On the other side, the Russian experiment by which a dog's head was kept alive exemplifies

> ... that other kind of lighting up
> That shows the terrain comprehended, as also its
>   containing space,
> And wipes out adjectives, and all shadows
>   (or, perhaps, all but shadows).

Paradoxically, yet understandably, Margaret Avison's dynamic imagination is touched off, beyond the measure of any other Canadian poet's, by the satisfactions and observations of everyday existence. Their value, doubtlessly, is enhanced by their being interludes in the mind's cosmic forays, and because like all mortal things they are under the threats of transience and destruction. "Chronic," for all its wry comedy, registers the mind's struggle to retain its identity among the shiftings of time. "Intra-Political" and "Our Working Day May be Menaced" also take into account, each in its own delightfully fanciful way, the mystery underlying and surrounding our lives, that now and again makes us wonder, as the poet does in "November 23," why

> Stillness glimmers beyond there—just beyond the senses—
> That makes me sweat with vertigo
> On this peculiar shelf
> Of being?

In spite, however, of these and other poems ("From a Provincial," "The

Swimmer's Moment," "Rondeau Redoublié," "The Mirrored Man," "Identity," "Mordent for a Melody") that diversely allude to the matchwood partition between security and terror, the predominant tone of *Winter Sun* is beatific. The poems celebrate not only the excitement of sharing in the exuberance of the natural world ("Birth Day," "Apocalyptic?" "Far off from University"), but even more the quiet satisfaction of having a room of one's own:

> . . .
> Gentle and just pleasure
> It is, being human, to have won from space
> This unchill, habitable interior
> Which mirrors quietly the light
> Of the snow, and the new year,
> ("New Year's Poem")

of having the help of friends to resolve the suspense between moving and feeling at home in one's rooms ("Hiatus"). She is constantly surprising in the breadth of her sympathies, even for milieus and types that would strike most of her compatriots as beyond the poetic pale. What other contemporary poet would deal so compassionately with the young man in "September Street" who by bettering his business prospects has somehow worsened his human position? Who else, again, would write of suburbia as she has done in "The World Still Needs," giving it a likable genesis and blessing it in the closing stanza with a lovely image? She descends lower in "Apocalyptics," into the world of public rinks and swimming pools, viewing their frequenters with womanly concern, taking over as the poet's field of activity the "jungle jim" of the city. Above all, whatever her doubts about the inflexibilities and inconsistencies of the physical universe, she never ceases to hope for the human future—as in the upbeat conclusion of "Apocalyptics":

> . . .
> Each broods in his own world
> But half believes
> Doctrines that promise to,
> After some few suppressions here and there,
> Orchestrate *for* all worlds; . . . .
>
> In Bowles Lunch, in the passage to
> the washrooms and the alley exit,
> They have an old piano, in case of
> a wedding, or 30-years-medal party for one of the ones
> who lope and sway and pick at things on any of the
> Twenty-four (24) levels above.
> Don't you suppose
> Anything could start it?
>   Music and all?
>   Some time?

If a reader in the 1960's would realize summarily the variety and potentiality of Canadian poetry, let him compare the works of two of the most talented among the younger poets. Daryl Hine (b. 1936) has published four books: *Five Poems* (1954), *The Carnal and the Crane* (1957), *The Devil's Picture Book* (1960), and *Heroics* (1961). Leonard Cohen (b. 1934) has published two: *Let Us Compare Mythologies* (1956) and *The Spice-Box of Earth* (1961). These two writers appear to have nothing at all in common except that both were born and grew up in Canada—Hine in Vancouver, Cohen in Montreal—and that each has had a volume published in the McGill Poetry Series.

In no respect whatever is Daryl Hine's poetry "Canadian." His context is resolutely European, with particular devotion to Augustan Rome, seventeenth-century England in its pastoral-metaphysical phases, and late nineteenth-century France; his principal masters have been Virgil, Donne, Baudelaire, Swinburne, Stevens, and Auden. The reader is likely to be struck first by the remarkable charm of language and cadence that this poet can command. Then by an astonishing lack of "presence" in the poems—either of personality or of location. Nothing is *there* but words seductively put together, images, rhythm. Poetry could scarcely be more "pure." One result of the method (and most of the poems do seem to have been fabricated by a poetic machine of superb delicacy and subtlety, as a master craftsman might produce rolls of exquisite wallpaper or lengths of tapestry) is the intense obscurity of almost all of the *Five Poems* and about the first half of *The Carnal and the Crane*. The reader who patiently resists being irritated by this obscurity, and by a baroque stateliness of utterance, will perceive with some admiration the ingenuity with which the poet has animated and diversified his material. Intricate and ambiguous syntax sets up titillating eddies of doubt and certainty about what the lines literally mean—these lines, for instance, the opening stanza of "In Praise of Music in Time of Pestilence":

> The fall which twisted love to lust,
> unfranchising the physical,
> and made pleasure barren, lost
> innocent magnificence, and all
> things change, man and animal,
> air and countryside, and temporal
> forms change and are lost in flux.

Again, he refracts reality into images seen as in a mirror or reflected on the surface of water or gazed at from its depth:

> ... reversed world where trees fall,
> blue and intricate and classical,
> a glass for mirror and a grave for love. ...
> ("The Boat")

Similarly, the poet subjects traditional themes to new and surprising adaptations—by distributing the matter among several speakers ("A Masque of Kings," "The Year One"), by placing the interpretative emphases at novel points ("At Pompey's Statue," a pentad of well-turned sonnets), by elaborating and distorting familiar stories (observe what becomes of the Owl and the Pussy-cat, of the twa corbies, and of the fox and the crow, in "Four Fabulary Satires"). Several poems (for example, "Lines on a Platonic Friendship," "The Lake," "Poem for Palm Sunday," "Epithalamium") generate a species of cerebral excitement by seeming to discourse of major topics; but they leave in the end the impression of neither caring much nor expecting the reader to care much about their theses. The treatment of sexual subjects and activities is of the same sort. A good deal of erotic behaviour seems to be going on, or to have been going on— satiety and remorse are two discernible moods in a few of the poems—and the words "vice" and "lust" recur as words; but syntax and imagery combine to veil from the reader exactly what is happening. The poet can, however, convey the quality of a tender relationship, as in these haunting lines:

> Remember that you thought me beautiful
> and praised the muscled flesh above the bone,
> the angle of the head, and used to call
> my skill the body's silent falconry
> that could release and call the falcon home.
> I'm hunter, hawk, and hunted, and I shine
> in the apocalyptic landscape as I shone
> amid the simple views of Arcady.
>   ("Cain and Abel and the Armed Head")

The third of Daryl Hine's collections, *The Devil's Picture Book*, is more straightforward in style ("I am more facile and articulate" runs the last line of the first poem), but less impressive as poetry. With decongestion of the medium much of the magic has evaporated. The reader is confronted by a charmless Circe, an enervate Proserpine, a rarefied Sodom. "Osiris Remembered" and "Osiris Dismembered" are returns to the intricate tapestry technique of the previous books, but the effect is superficial. The whole book, indeed, gives off an aroma of the nineties, of the succession of authors, from Baudelaire to Tennessee Williams, who have handled the roses and regrets of evil. "Under the Hill" is a pallid summary of Beardsley's once notorious little work. "The Acclamation" suggests "The Harlot's House." "Nox Nocti Indicat Scientiam" suggests Lionel Johnson. At least one line in "The Destruction of Sodom" might have come from the lips of Lady Bracknell. A sense of self-division (the Jekyll-and-Hyde, the Dorian Grey theme) has begotten at least three of the poems: "The Suitor," "The Devil's Picture Book," and "The Double-Goer." However thin and jaded this pretty little book may be, it everywhere provokes the reader's respect for proficiency in the use of words, the composition of stanzas, the variegation of rhythm.

Leonard Cohen's poems happen in the context of the contemporary world and of Montreal. Like A. M. Klein and Irving Layton, Cohen has drawn upon Jewish-Canadian experience, one of the most fruitful sources in our time for both poetry and fiction. Many of Cohen's poems allude to streets, milieus, attitudes, and moods that belong to Montreal. Many of them are composed in the language of street conversations or of tabloid narratives:

> There are so many cities!
>   so many knew of my lady and her beauty,
> Perhaps he came from Toronto, a half-crazed man
>   looking for some Sunday love;
> or a vicious poet stranded too long in Winnipeg;
> or a Nova Scotian fleeing from the rocks and preachers. . . .
>   ("Ballad")

The cultural blending that has made Cohen alert to the excitements and squalors of the big city has also given him that peculiar mixture of irony, tenderness, and harshness with which the American Jew usually contemplates his life and his past. Cohen's tradition also finds expression in his poems. The first piece in *Let Us Compare Mythologies* makes an obeisance to the other tradition by being about Orpheus. Elsewhere in his two books, however, he derives his narratives, his images, even his rhythms, from the Bible and from the plights and alternatives forced upon the Jew in the twentieth century. "Exodus," "Before the Story" (David, Bathsheba, Absalom), "The Adulterous Wives of Solomon," "Isaiah"—these poems and references in other poems testify to the vitality that the ancient persons and situations retain for the imagination of the poet. Several of the poems take the Crucifixion for their theme ("For Wilf and His House," "Ballad (He pulled a flower)," "Saviors"). In the last of these poems the significance of the Crucifixion as an historical and religious symbol is extended to Jewish heroes:

> Nailed high on a mountain
> Moses stares beyond the Jordan
> beyond the giants and crumbling walls
> and sighs an Egyptian curse
>
> Job hangs in a burnt field
> unable to frighten the crows
> his friends still talking at his feet
> and no whirlwind disturbs the quiet desolation
>
> David swings from his roof
> and the people say that in his mind
> he and his warriors build a great temple
>
> And all the saints and prophets
> are nailed to stakes and desert trees. . . .

Cohen's interest in the stories of his people is neither mythic nor antiquarian. He fiercely fuses past and present, finding in episodes from history analogues or intimations of contemporary anguish ("The Song of the Hellenist," "Credo," "Letter," "Pagans"). This power to relate one era to another, one order of experience to another order, is Cohen's most promising characteristic.

The horrors of the purge and the pogrom may yield an episode of love, as in "Lovers"; and as a tribute to love, the poet offers, in "The Genius," to take on at request all the humiliating and grotesque roles that the Jew has had to assume in the modern world. Sexual passion is the most pervasive of the other themes in Cohen's books. His erotic poems run through a wide range of moods: apprehensiveness in "Song of Patience," arrogance in "Song (The naked weeping girl)," disillusionment in "Folk Song," horror and grief mingled in "Ballad (My lady was found mutilated)," overwhelming delight in "On Certain Incredible Nights," "You Have the Lovers," "When I Uncover Your Body," "Celebration," and "Beneath My Hand," doubts and velleities in "Had We Nothing to Prove" and "Poem (I heard of a man)," renunciation and fatigue in "The Flowers that I Left in the Ground," and bitterness in "The Cuckold's Song" and "The Unicorn Tapestry." These difficult and dangerous subjects Cohen manages almost always to make convincing and appealing. He can venture even into fantasy:

> My lover Peterson
> He named me Goldenmouth
> I changed him to a bird
> And he migrated south
>
> My lover Frederick
> Wrote sonnets to my breast
> I changed him to a horse
> And he galloped west . . .
> ("Song")

or into cosmic certitude:

> With your body and your speaking
> you have spoken for everything,
> robbed me of my strangerhood,
> made me one
> with the root and gull and stone,
> and because I sleep so near to you
> I cannot embrace
> or have my private love with them.
>
> You worry that I will leave you.
> I will not leave you,
> Only strangers travel.
> Owning everything,
> I have nowhere to go.
> ("Owning Everything")

The love poems, intense and intimate, counterpoint the poems evocative of the florid, exotic, and exuberant quality of the Jewish memory. But all the poems of Leonard Cohen seem to occur in the very forefront of experience, with an effect that to some readers will seem almost sensational or brutal. This effect is enhanced by the colloquial emphasis of the diction and the energy of the verse in many of his poems; other poems, however, achieve a quite different effect of quietness and tenderness. Obviously, for all his gifts, Cohen is a poet who has not yet entirely organized his talent.

Poetry continues to be the most flourishing branch of Canadian literature. The creative energy that so notably manifested itself during the 1950's has diminished very little in the 1960's. New books, every one of them abounding in characteristic virtues—with, here and there, characteristic shortcomings—have been brought out by most of the senior or established poets: A. J. M. Smith's *Collected Poems* (1962); *Ice Cod Bell or Stone* by Earle Birney (1962); *The Chequered Shade* by Roy Daniells (1963); *Twelve Letters to a Small Town* by James Reaney (1962); *The Sea is Also a Garden* by Phyllis Webb (1962); from Irving Layton, three collections—*A Red Carpet for the Sun* (1959), *The Swinging Flesh* (1961), and *Balls for a One-Armed Juggler* (1963); from Raymond Souster, two of special note—*A Local Pride* (1962) and *Place of Meeting: Poems 1958–1960* (1962); and a volume which only in part belongs in a record of Canadian literature, *Selected Poems of Malcolm Lowry* (1962).

It is proper to mention also poets of promise rather than clearly defined fulfilment. Several collections of poems published in the late fifties and early sixties suggest that out of their midst may come some of the best things of the decade. Of these the most distinctive are *The Brain's the Target* by Milton Acorn (1960); *Frost on the Sun* (1957) and *The Sun is Axeman* (1961) by D. G. Jones; *The Drunken Clock* (1961) by Gwendolyn MacEwen; *This Citadel in Time* by John Robert Colombo (1958); *The Wandering World* by Ronald Bates (1959); *Within the Zodiac* by Phyllis Gotlieb (1964); *The Crafte So Long to Lerne* by Alfred W. Purdy (1959). The reader who would thoroughly savour the range and copiousness of Canadian poetry at the approach to the centenary of Confederation should augment this list with other names: Dorothy Roberts, Peter Dale Scott, David A. Donnell, Joan Finnigan, Margaret Eleanor Atwood, Heather Spears, Norman Levine, George Walton, Edward Yeomans, Kenneth McRobbie, Douglas Lochead, Fred Swayze, John Paul Harney, Maria Fiamengo.

Such a reader would be well advised to look for these poets, and for others still younger, in the pages of the literary magazines. From year to year the level of accomplishment remains high in the magazines that have always made poetry welcome: the *Canadian Forum, Queen's Quarterly, Fiddlehead,* and *Tamarack Review*. Little magazines, those mayflies of the publishing world, still proliferate in Canada, never more numerously than in the early 1960's; of special interest, for varying reasons, have been *Alphabet, Prism, Tish, Mountain, Evidence,* and *Cataract*. Anthologies provide a measure of achievement. *The Blasted Pine* (1960) adduced evidence that satire has been a fruitful mode among Canadian poets. *Love Where the Nights are Long* (1962) edited by Irving Layton, although it scarcely validates its thesis—that Canadian poets have a peculiar talent for love poetry—brought together an assortment of admirable poems. *A Canadian Anthology: Poems from "The Fiddlehead" 1945-1959,* however uneven the quality of its contents, demonstrated beyond doubt that poetry has been thriving in Canada since the Second World War.

This zealous and indefatigable reader would discern in all these books and magazines various tendencies that he might take for signs of the times; a closer look at some of them, however, would make clear that they were developments out of the forties and the fifties. In one quarter he would be struck by an obsession with mythography, in another by concern about the oppressiveness of "bourgeois" values. On some pages he would find erudite whimsy, on others a colloquialism more determinedly tough than ever before. He would observe a growth in speculative poetry, in typographical peculiarity, in versified exchanges of personalities. He would perceive the influence of the latest American vogues in theme and style, and in the same magazines he would read poems that appear to renounce the modernist movement altogether and to return to standards that are Romantic and even Georgian. In short, the reader of contemporary Canadian poetry would recognize the sort of literary fermentation—exhilarating, exasperating, and diversified—that may promise well for the next "Renaissance."

CONCLUSION

CONCLUSION

Conclusion

NORTHROP FRYE

IT IS NOW SEVERAL YEARS since the group of editors listed on the title-page met, under Carl Klinck's leadership, to draw up the first tentative plans for this book. What we then dreamed of is substantially what we have got, changed very little in essentials. I expressed at the time the hope that such a book would help to broaden the inductive basis on which some writers on Canadian literature were making generalizations that bordered on guesswork. By "some writers" I meant primarily myself. I find, however, that this book tends to confirm me in most of my intuitions on the subject: the advantage for me is that this attempt at conclusion and summary can involve some self-plagiarism.

The book is a tribute to the maturity of Canadian literary scholarship and criticism, whatever one thinks of the literature. Its authors have completely outgrown the view that evaluation is the end of criticism, instead of its incidental by-product. Had evaluation been their guiding principle, this book would, if written at all, have been only a huge debunking project, leaving Canadian literature a poor naked *alouette* plucked of every feather of decency and dignity. True, the book gives evidence, on practically every one of its eight hundred odd pages, that what is really remarkable is not how little but how much good writing has been produced in Canada. But this would not affect the rigorous evaluator. The evaluative view is based on the conception of criticism as concerned mainly to define and canonize the genuine classics of literature. And Canada has produced no author who is a classic in the sense of possessing a vision greater in kind than that of his best readers (Canadians themselves might argue about one or two, but in the perspective of the world at large the statement is true). There is no Canadian writer of whom we can say what we can say of the world's major writers, that their readers can grow up inside their work without ever being aware of a circumference. Thus the metaphor of the critic as "judge" holds for the Canadian critic, who is never dealing with the kind of writer who judges him.

This fact about Canadian literature, so widely deplored by Canadians, has one advantage. It is much easier to see what literature is trying to do when we are studying a literature that has not quite done it. If no Canadian author pulls us away from the Canadian context toward the centre of literary experience itself, then at every point we remain aware of his social and historical setting. The conception of what is literary has to be greatly broadened for such a literature. The literary, in Canada, is often only an incidental quality of writings which, like those of many of the early explorers, are as innocent of literary intention as a mating loon. Even when it is literature in its orthodox genres of poetry and fiction, it is more significantly studied as a part of Canadian life than as a part of an autonomous world of literature.

So far from merely admitting or conceding this, the editors have gone out of their way to emphasize it. We have asked for chapters on political, historical, religious, scholarly, philosophical, scientific, and other non-literary writing, to show how the verbal imagination operates as a ferment in all cultural life. We have included the writings of foreigners, of travellers, of immigrants, of emigrants—even of emigrants whose most articulate literary emotion was their thankfulness at getting the hell out of Canada. The reader of this book, even if he is not Canadian or much interested in Canadian literature as such, may still learn a good deal about the literary imagination as a force and function of life generally. For here another often deplored fact also becomes an advantage: that many Canadian cultural phenomena are not peculiarly Canadian at all, but are typical of their wider North American and Western contexts.

This book is a collection of essays in cultural history, and of the general principles of cultural history we still know relatively little. It is, of course, closely related to political and to economic history, but it is a separate and definable subject in itself. Like other kinds of history, it has its own themes of exploration, settlement, and development, but these themes relate to a social *imagination* that explores and settles and develops, and the imagination has its own rhythms of growth as well as its own modes of expression. It is obvious that Canadian literature, whatever its inherent merits, is an indispensable aid to the knowledge of Canada. It records what the Canadian imagination has reacted to, and it tells us things about this environment that nothing else will tell us. By examining this imagination as the authors of this book have tried to do, as an ingredient in Canadian verbal culture generally, a relatively small and low-lying cultural development is studied in all its dimensions. There is far too much Canadian writing for this book not to become, in places, something of a catalogue; but the outlines of the structure are clear. Fortunately, the bulk of Canadian non-literary writing, even today, has not yet declined into the state of sodden specialization in which the readable has become the impure.

I stress our ignorance of the laws and conditions of cultural history for an obvious reason. The question: why has there been no Canadian writer of classic proportions? may naturally be asked. At any rate it often has been.

Our authors realize that it is better to deal with what is there than to raise speculations about why something else is not there. But it is clear that the question haunts their minds. And we know so little about cultural history that we not only cannot answer such a question, but we do not even know whether or not it is a real question. The notion, doubtless of romantic origin, that "genius" is a certain quantum that an individual is born with, as he might be born with red hair, is still around, but mainly as a folktale motif in fiction, like the story of Finch in the Jalna books. "Genius" is as much, and as essentially, a matter of social context as it is of individual character. We do not know what the social conditions are that produce great literature, or even whether there is any causal relation at all. If there is, there is no reason to suppose that they are good conditions, or conditions that we should try to reproduce. The notion that the literature one admires must have been nourished by something admirable in the social environment is persistent, but has never been justified by evidence. One can still find books on Shakespeare that profess to make his achievement more plausible by talking about a "background" of social euphoria produced by the defeat of the Armada, the discovery of America a century before, and the conviction that Queen Elizabeth was a wonderful woman. There is a general sense of filler about such speculations, and when similar arguments are given in a negative form to explain the absence of a Shakespeare in Canada they are no more convincing. Puritan inhibitions, pioneer life, "an age too late, cold climate, or years"—these may be important as factors or conditions of Canadian culture, helping us to characterize its qualities. To suggest that any of them is a negative cause of its merit is to say much more than anyone knows.

One theme which runs all through this book is the obvious and unquenchable desire of the Canadian cultural public to identify itself through its literature. Canada is not a bad environment for the author, as far as recognition goes: in fact the recognition may even hamper his development by making him prematurely self-conscious. Scholarships, prizes, university posts, await the dedicated writer: there are so many medals offered for literary achievement that a modern Canadian Dryden might well be moved to write a satire on medals, except that if he did he would promptly be awarded the medal for satire and humour. Publishers take an active responsibility for native literature, even poetry; a fair proportion of the books bought by Canadian readers are by Canadian writers; the C.B.C. and other media help to employ some writers and publicize others. The efforts made at intervals to boost or hard-sell Canadian literature, by asserting that it is much better than it actually is, may look silly enough in retrospect, but they were also, in part, efforts to create a cultural community, and the aim deserves more sympathy than the means. Canada has two languages and two literatures, and every statement made in a book like this about "Canadian literature" employs the figure of speech known as synecdoche, putting a part for the whole. Every such statement implies a parallel or contrasting statement about French-Canadian literature. The advantages of having a national culture based on two languages are in some respects very great, but of course they are for the most part potential. The difficulties, if more superficial, are also more actual and more obvious.

Some of the seminal facts about the origins of Canadian culture are set down with great clarity near the beginning of this book. Canada began, says Mr. Galloway, as an obstacle, blocking the way to the treasures of the East, to be explored only in the hope of finding a passage through it. English Canada continued to be that long after what is now the United States had become a defined part of the Western world. One reason for this is obvious from the map. American culture was, down to about 1900, mainly a culture of the Atlantic seaboard, with a western frontier that moved irregularly but steadily back until it reached the other coast. The Revolution did not essentially change the cultural unity of the English-speaking community of the North Atlantic that had London and Edinburgh on one side of it and Boston and Philadelphia on the other. But Canada has, for all practical purposes, no Atlantic seaboard. The traveller from Europe edges into it like a tiny Jonah entering an inconceivably large whale, slipping past the Straits of Belle Isle into the Gulf of St. Lawrence, where five Canadian provinces surround him, for the most part invisible. Then he goes up the St. Lawrence and the inhabited country comes into view, mainly a French-speaking country, with its own cultural traditions. To enter the United States is a matter of crossing an ocean; to enter Canada is a matter of being silently swallowed by an alien continent.

It is an unforgettable and intimidating experience to enter Canada in this way. But the experience initiates one into that gigantic east-to-west thrust which, as Mr. Kilbourn notes, historians regard as the axis of Canadian development, the "Laurentian" movement that makes the growth of Canada geographically credible. This drive to the west has attracted to itself nearly everything that is heroic and romantic in the Canadian tradition. The original impetus begins in Europe, for English Canada in the British Isles, hence though adventurous it is also a conservative force, and naturally tends to preserve its colonial link with its starting-point. Once the Canadian has settled down in the country, however, he then becomes aware of the longitudinal dimension, the southward pull toward the richer and more glamorous American cities, some of which, such as Boston for the Maritimes and Minneapolis for the eastern prairies, are almost Canadian capitals. This is the axis of another kind of Canadian mentality, more critical and analytic, more inclined to see Canada as an unnatural and politically quixotic aggregate of disparate northern extensions of American culture—"seven fishing-rods tied together by the ends," as Goldwin Smith, quoted by Mr. Windsor, puts it. Mr. Kilbourn illustrates the contrast in his account of the styles, attitudes, and literary genres of Creighton and Underhill.

The simultaneous influence of two larger nations speaking the same language has been practically beneficial to English Canada, but theoretically confusing. It is often suggested that Canada's identity is to be found in some *via media*, or *via mediocris*, between the other two. This has the disadvantage that the British and American cultures have to be defined as extremes. Haliburton seems to have believed that the ideal for Nova Scotia would be a combination of American energy and British social structure, but such a chimera, or synthetic monster, is hard to achieve in practice. It is simpler merely to notice the alternating current in the Canadian mind, as reflected in its writing, between two moods, one romantic, traditional and idealistic, the other shrewd, observant and humorous. Canada in its attitude to Britain tends to be more royalist than the Queen, in the sense that it is more attracted to it as a symbol of tradition than as a fellow-nation. The Canadian attitude to the United States is typically that of a smaller country to a much bigger neighbour, sharing in its material civilization but anxious to keep clear of the huge mass movements that drive a great imperial power. The United States, being founded on a revolution and a written constitution, has introduced a deductive or *a priori* pattern into its cultural life that tends to define an American way of life and mark it off from anti-American heresies. Canada, having a seat on the sidelines of the American Revolution, adheres more to the inductive and the expedient. The Canadian genius for compromise is reflected in the existence of Canada itself.

The most obvious tension in the Canadian literary situation is in the use of language. Here, first of all, a traditional standard English collides with the need for a North American vocabulary and phrasing. Mr. Scargill and Mr. Klinck have studied this in the work of Mrs. Moodie and Mrs. Traill. As long as the North American speaker feels that he belongs in a minority, the European speech will impose a standard of correctness. This is to a considerable extent still true of French in Canada, with its campaigns against "joual" and the like. But as Americans began to outnumber the British, Canada tended in practice to fall in with the American developments, though a good deal of Canadian theory is still Anglophile. A much more complicated cultural tension arises from the impact of the sophisticated on the primitive, and vice versa. The most dramatic example, and one I have given elsewhere, is that of Duncan Campbell Scott, working in the Department of Indian Affairs in Ottawa. He writes of a starving squaw baiting a fish-hook with her own flesh, and he writes of the music of Debussy and the poetry of Henry Vaughan. In English literature we have to go back to Anglo-Saxon times to encounter so incongruous a collision of cultures.

Cultural history, we said, has its own rhythms. It is possible that one of these rhythms is very like an organic rhythm: that there must be a period, of a certain magnitude, as Aristotle would say, in which a social imagination can take root and establish a tradition. American literature had this period, in the northeastern part of the country, between the Revolution and the Civil War. Canada has never had it. English Canada was first a part of the wilderness, then a part of North America and the British Empire, then a part of the world. But it has gone through these revolutions too quickly for a tradition of writing to be founded on any one of them. Canadian writers are, even now, still trying to assimilate a Canadian environment at a time when new techniques of communication, many of which, like television, constitute a verbal market, are annihilating the boundaries of that environment. This foreshortening of Canadian history, if it really does have any relevance to Canadian culture, would account for many features of it: its fixation on its own past, its penchant for old-fashioned literary techniques, its preoccupation with the theme of strangled articulateness. It seems to me that Canadian sensibility has been profoundly disturbed, not so much by our famous problem of identity, important as that is, as by a series of paradoxes in what confronts that identity. It is less perplexed by the question "Who am I?" than by some such riddle as "Where is here?"

Mr. Bailey, writing of the early Maritimes, warns us not to read the "mystique of Canadianism" back into the pre-Confederation period. Haliburton, for instance, was a Nova Scotian, a Bluenose: the word "Canadian" to him would have summoned up the figure of someone who spoke mainly French and whose enthusiasm for Haliburton's own political ideals would have been extremely tepid. The mystique of Canadianism was, as several chapters in this book make clear, specifically the cultural accompaniment of Confederation and the imperialistic mood that followed it. But it came so suddenly after the pioneer period that it was still full of wilderness. To feel "Canadian" was to feel part of a no-man's-land with huge rivers, lakes, and islands that very few Canadians had ever seen. "From sea to sea, and from the river unto the ends of the earth"—if Canada is not an island, the phrasing is still in the etymological sense isolating. One wonders if any other national consciousness has had so large an amount of the unknown, the unrealized, the humanly undigested, so built into it. Rupert Brooke, quoted by Mrs. Waterston, speaks of the "unseizable virginity" of the Canadian landscape. What is important here, for our purposes, is the position of the frontier in the Canadian imagination. In the United States one could choose to move out to the frontier or to retreat from it back to the seaboard. The tensions built up by such migrations have fascinated many American novelists and historians. In the Canadas, even in the Maritimes, the frontier was all around one, a part and a condition of one's whole imaginative being. The frontier was primarily what separated the Canadian, physically or mentally, from Great Britain, from the

United States, and, even more important, from other Canadian communities. Such a frontier was the immediate datum of his imagination, the thing that had to be dealt with first.

After the Northwest passage failed to materialize, Canada became a colony in the mercantilist sense, treated by others less like a society than as a place to look for things. French, English, Americans plunged into it to carry off its supplies of furs, minerals, and pulpwood, aware only of their immediate objectives. From time to time recruiting officers searched the farms and villages to carry young men off to death in a European dynastic quarrel. The travellers reviewed by Mrs. Waterston visit Canada much as they would visit a zoo: even when their eyes momentarily focus on the natives they are still thinking primarily of how their own sensibility is going to react to what it sees. Mrs. Waterston speaks of a feature of Canadian life that has been noted by writers from Susanna Moodie onward: "the paradox of vast empty spaces plus lack of privacy," without defences against the prying or avaricious eye. The resentment expressed against this in Canada seems to have taken political rather than literary forms: this may be partly because Canadians have learned from their imaginative experience to look at each other in much the same way: "as objects, even as obstacles," to quote Miss Macpherson on a Canadian autobiography.

It is not much wonder if Canada developed with the bewilderment of a neglected child, preoccupied with trying to define its own identity, alternately bumptious and diffident about its own achievements. Adolescent dreams of glory haunt the Canadian consciousness (and unconsciousness), some naïve and some sophisticated. In the naïve area are the predictions that the twentieth century belongs to Canada, that our cities will become much bigger than they ought to be, or, like Edmonton and Vancouver, "gateways" to somewhere else, reconstructed Northwest passages. The more sophisticated usually take the form of a Messianic complex about Canadian culture, for Canadian culture, no less than Alberta, has always been "next year country." The myth of the hero brought up in the forest retreat, awaiting the moment when his giant strength will be fully grown and he can emerge into the world, informs a good deal of Canadian criticism down to our own time.

Certain features of life in a new country that are bound to handicap its writers are obvious enough. The difficulties of drama, which depends on a theatre and consequently on a highly organized urban life, are set out by Mr. Tait. Here the foreshortening of historical development has been particularly cruel, as drama was strangled by the movie just as it was getting started as a popular medium. Other literary genres have similar difficulties. Culture is born in leisure and an awareness of standards, and pioneer conditions tend to make energetic and uncritical work an end in itself, to preach a gospel of social unconsciousness, which lingers long after the pioneer conditions have disappeared. The impressive achievements of such a society are likely to be technological. It is in the inarticulate part of communication, railways and bridges and canals and highways, that Canada, one of whose symbols is the taciturn beaver, has shown its real strength. Again, Canadian culture, and literature in particular, has felt the force of what may be called Emerson's law. Emerson remarks in his journals that in a provincial society it is extremely easy to reach the highest level of cultivation, extremely difficult to take one step beyond that. In surveying Canadian poetry and fiction, we feel constantly that all the energy has been absorbed in meeting a standard, a self-defeating enterprise because real standards can only be established, not met. Such writing is academic in the pejorative sense of that term, an imitation of a prescribed model, second-rate in conception, not merely in execution. It is natural that academic writing of this kind should develop where literature is a social prestige symbol, as Mr. Cogswell says. However, it is not the handicaps of Canadian writers but the distinctive features that appear in spite of them which are the main concern of this book, and so of its conclusion.

II

The sense of probing into the distance, of fixing the eyes on the skyline, is something that Canadian sensibility has inherited from the *voyageurs*. It comes into Canadian painting a good deal, in Thomson whose focus is so often farthest back in the picture, where a river or a gorge in the hills twists elusively out of sight, in Emily Carr whose vision is always, in the title of a compatriot's book of poems, "deeper into the forest." Even in the Maritimes, where the feeling of linear distance is less urgent, Roberts contemplates the Tantramar marshes in the same way, the refrain of "miles and miles" having clearly some incantatory power for him. It would be interesting to know how many Canadian novels associate nobility of character with a faraway look, or base their perorations on a long-range perspective. This might be only a cliché, except that it is often found in sharply observed and distinctively written books. Here, as a random example, is the last sentence of W. O. Mitchell's *Who Has Seen the Wind*: "The wind turns in silent frenzy upon itself, whirling into a smoking funnel, breathing up top soil and tumbleweed skeletons to carry them on its spinning way over the prairie, out and out to the far line of the sky." Mr. Pacey quotes the similarly long-sighted conclusion of *Such is My Beloved*.

A vast country sparsely inhabited naturally depends on its modes of transportation, whether canoe, railway, or the driving and riding "circuits" of the judge, the Methodist preacher, or the Yankee peddler. The feeling of nomadic movement over great distances persists even into the age of the aeroplane, in a country where writers can hardly meet one other without a social organization that provides travel grants. Pratt's poetry is full of his fascination with means of communication, not simply the physical means of great ships and locomotives, though he is one of the best of all poets on such subjects, but with communication as message, with radar and asdic and wireless signals, and, in his war poems, with the power of rhetoric over fighting men. What is perhaps the most comprehensive structure of ideas yet made by a Canadian thinker, the structure embodied in Innis's *Bias of Communication*, is concerned with the same theme, and a disciple of Innis, Marshall McLuhan, continues to emphasize the unity of communication, as a complex containing both verbal and non-verbal factors, and warns us against making unreal divisions within it. Perhaps it is not too fanciful to see this need for continuity in the Canadian attitude to time as well as space, in its preoccupation with its own history (the motto of the Province of Quebec is *je me souviens*) and its relentless cultural stock-takings and self-inventories. The Burke sense of society as a continuum—consistent with the pragmatic and conservative outlook of Canadians—is strong and begins early. Mr. Irving quotes an expression of it in McCulloch, and another quotation shows that it was one of the most deeply held ideas of Brett. As I write, the centennial of Confederation in 1967 looms up before the country with the moral urgency of a Day of Atonement: I use a Jewish metaphor because there is something Hebraic about the Canadian tendency to read its conquest of a promised land, its Maccabean victories of 1812, its struggle for the central fortress on the hill at Quebec, as oracles of a future. It is doubtless only an accident that the theme of one of the most passionate and intense of all Canadian novels, A. M. Klein's *The Second Scroll*, is Zionism.

Civilization in Canada, as elsewhere, has advanced geometrically across the country, throwing down the long parallel lines of the railways, dividing up the farm lands into chessboards of square-mile sections and concession-line roads. There is little adaptation to nature: in both architecture and arrangement, Canadian cities and villages express rather an arrogant abstraction, the conquest of nature by an intelligence that does not love it. The word conquest suggests something military, as it should—one thinks of General Braddock, preferring to have his army annihilated rather than fight the natural man on his own asymmetrical ground. There are some features of this generally North American phenomenon that have a particular emphasis in Canada. It has been remarked—Mr. Kilbourn quotes Creighton on the subject—that Canadian expansion westward had a tight grip of authority over it that American expansion, with its outlaws and sheriffs and vigilantes and the like, did not have in the same measure. America moved from the back country to the wild west; Canada moved from a New France held down by British military occupation to a northwest patrolled by mounted police. Canada has not had, strictly speaking, an Indian war: there has been much less of the "another redskin bit the dust" feeling in our historical imagination, and only

Riel remains to haunt the later period of it, though he is a formidable figure enough, rather like what a combination of John Brown and Vanzetti would be in the American conscience. Otherwise, the conquest, for the last two centuries, has been mainly of the unconscious forces of nature, personified by the dragon of the Lake Superior rocks in Pratt's *Towards the Last Spike*:

> On the North Shore a reptile lay asleep—
> A hybrid that the myths might have conceived,
> But not delivered.

Yet the conquest of nature has its own perils for the imagination, in a country where the winters are so cold and where conditions of life have so often been bleak and comfortless, where even the mosquitoes have been described, Mr. Klinck tells us, as "mementoes of the fall." I have long been impressed in Canadian poetry by a tone of deep terror in regard to nature, a theme to which we shall return. It is not a terror of the dangers or discomforts or even the mysteries of nature, but a terror of the soul at something that these things manifest. The human mind has nothing but human and moral values to cling to if it is to preserve its integrity or even its sanity, yet the vast unconsciousness of nature in front of it seems an unanswerable denial of those values. I notice that a sharp-witted Methodist preacher quoted by Mr. Cogswell speaks of the "shutting out of the whole moral creation" in the loneliness of the forests.

If we put together a few of these impressions, we may get some approach to characterizing the way in which the Canadian imagination has developed in its literature. Small and isolated communities surrounded with a physical or psychological "frontier," separated from one another and from their American and British cultural sources: communities that provide all that their members have in the way of distinctively human values, and that are compelled to feel a great respect for the law and order that holds them together, yet confronted with a huge, unthinking, menacing, and formidable physical setting—such communities are bound to develop what we may provisionally call a garrison mentality. In the earliest maps of the country the only inhabited centres are forts, and that remains true of the cultural maps for a much later time. Frances Brooke, in her eighteenth-century *Emily Montague*, wrote of what was literally a garrison; novelists of our day studying the impact of Montreal on Westmount write of a psychological one.

A garrison is a closely knit and beleaguered society, and its moral and social values are unquestionable. In a perilous enterprise ones does not discuss causes or motives: one is either a fighter or a deserter. Here again we may turn to Pratt, with his infallible instinct for what is central in the Canadian imagination. The societies in Pratt's poems are always tense and tight groups engaged in war, rescue, martyrdom, or crisis, and the moral values expressed are simply those of that group. In such a society the terror is not for the common enemy, even when the enemy is or seems victorious, as in the extermination of the Jesuit missionaries or the crew of Franklin (a great Canadian theme, well described in this book by Mr. Hopwood, that Pratt pondered but never completed). The real terror comes when the individual feels himself becoming an individual, pulling away from the group, losing the sense of driving power that the group gives him, aware of a conflict within himself far subtler than the struggle of morality against evil. It is much easier to multiply garrisons, and when that happens, something anti-cultural comes into Canadian life, a dominating herd-mind in which nothing original can grow. The intensity of the sectarian divisiveness in Canadian towns, both religious and political, is an example: what such groups represent, of course, vis-à-vis one another, is "two solitudes," the death of communication and dialogue. Separatism, whether English or French, is culturally the most sterile of all creeds. But at present I am concerned rather with a more creative side of the garrison mentality, one that has had positive effects on our intellectual life.

They were so certain of their moral values, says Mr. Cogswell, a little sadly, speaking of the early Maritime writers. Right was white, wrong black, and nothing else counted or even existed. He goes on to point out that such certainty invariably produces a sub-literary rhetoric. Or, as Yeats would say, we make rhetoric out of quarrels with one another, poetry out of the quarrel with ourselves. To use words, for any other purpose than straight description or command, is a form of play, a manifestation of *homo ludens*. But there are two forms of play, the contest and the construct. The editorial writer attacking the Family Compact, the preacher demolishing imaginary atheists with the argument of design, are using words aggressively, in theses that imply antitheses. Ideas are weapons; one seeks the verbal *coup de grâce*, the irrefutable refutation. Such a use of words is congenial enough to the earlier Canadian community: all the evidence, including the evidence of this book, points to a highly articulate and argumentative society in nineteenth-century Canada. Mr. MacLure remarks on the fact that scholarship in Canada has so often been written with more conviction and authority, and has attracted wider recognition, than the literature itself. There are historical reasons for this, apart from the fact, which will become clearer as we go on, that scholarly writing is more easily attached to its central tradition.

Leacock has a story which I often turn to because the particular aspect of Canadian culture it reflects has never been more accurately caught. He tells us of the rivalry in an Ontario town between two preachers, one Anglican and the other Presbyterian. The latter taught ethics in the local college on weekdays—without salary—and preached on Sundays. He gave his students, says Leacock, three parts Hegel and two parts St. Paul, and on Sunday he reversed the dose and gave his parishioners three parts St. Paul and two parts Hegel. Religion has been a major—perhaps the major—cultural force in Canada, at least down to the last generation or two. The names of two Methodist publishers, William Briggs and Lorne Pierce, recur more than once in this book, and illustrate the fact that the churches not only influenced the cultural climate but took an active part in the production of poetry and fiction, as the popularity of Ralph Connor reminds us. But the effective religious factors in Canada were doctrinal and evangelical, those that stressed the arguments of religion at the expense of its imagery.

Such a reliance on the arguing intellect was encouraged by the philosophers, who in the nineteenth century, as Mr. Irving shows, were invariably idealists with a strong religious bias. Mr. Irving quotes George as saying that civilization consists "in the conscience and intellect" of a cultivated people, and Watson as asserting that "we are capable of knowing Reality as it actually is.... Reality when so known is absolutely rational." An even higher point may have been reached by that triumphant theologian cited by Mr. Thomson, whose book I have not read but whose title I greatly admire: *The Riddle of the Universe Solved*. Naturally sophisticated intelligence of this kind was the normal means of contact with literature. Mr. MacLure tells us that James Cappon judged poetry according to whether it had a "rationalized concept" or not—this would have been a very common critical assumption. Sara Jeannette Duncan shows us a clergyman borrowing a copy of Browning's *Sordello*, no easy reading, and returning it with original suggestions for interpretation. Such an interest in ideas is not merely cultivated but exuberant.

But using language as one would use an axe, formulating arguments with sharp cutting edges that will help to clarify one's view of the landscape, remains a rhetorical and not a poetic achievement. To quote Yeats again, one can refute Hegel (perhaps even St. Paul) but not the *Song of Sixpence*. To create a disinterested structure of words, in poetry or in fiction, is a very different achievement, and it is clear that an intelligent and able rhetorician finds it particularly hard to understand how different it is. A rhetorician practising poetry is apt to express himself in spectral arguments, generalizations that escape the feeling of possible refutation only by being vast enough to contain it, or vaporous enough to elude it. The mystique of Canadianism was accompanied by an intellectual tendency of this kind, as Mr. Daniells indicates. World-views that avoided dialectic, of a theosophical or transcendentalist cast, became popular among the Canadian poets of that time, Roberts and Carman particularly, and later among painters, as the reminiscences of the Group of Seven make clear. Bucke's *Cosmic Consciousness*, though not mentioned by any of our authors so far as I remember, is an influential Canadian book in this area. When minor rhetorically-minded poets sought what Samuel

Johnson calls, though in a very different context, the "grandeur of generality," the result is what is so well described by Mr. Beattie as "jejune chatter about infinity," and the like.

Mr. Watt's very important chapter on the literature of protest isolates another rhetorical tradition. In the nineteenth century the common assumption that nature had revealed the truth of progress, and that it was the duty of reason to accommodate that truth to mankind, could be either a conservative or a radical view. But in either case it was a revolutionary doctrine, introducing the conception of change as the key to the social process. In those whom Mr. Watt calls proletarian social Darwinists, and who represented "the unholy fusion of secularism, science and social discontent," there was a strong tendency to regard literature as a product and a symbol of a ruling-class mentality, with, as we have tried to indicate, some justification. Hence radicals tended either to hope that "the literature of the future will be the powerful ally of Democracy and Labour Reform," or to assume that serious thought and action would bypass the creative writer entirely, building a scientific socialism and leaving him to his Utopian dreams.

The radicalism of the period up to the Russian Revolution was, from a later point of view, largely undifferentiated. A labour magazine could regard Ignatius Donnelly, with his anti-Semitic and other crank views, as an advanced thinker equally with William Morris and Edward Bellamy. Similarly, even today, in Western Canadian elections, a protest vote may go Social Credit or NDP without much regard to the difference in political philosophy between these parties. The depression introduced a dialectic into Canadian social thought which profoundly affected its literature. In Mr. Watt's striking phrase, "the Depression was like an intense magnetic field that deflected the courses of all the poets who went through it." In this period there were, of course, the inevitable Marxist manifestos, assuring the writer that only social significance, as understood by Marxism, would bring vitality to his work. The *New Frontier*, a far-left journal of that period referred to several times in this book, shows an uneasy sense on the part of its contributors that this literary elixir of youth might have to be mixed with various other potions, not all favourable to the creative process: attending endless meetings, organizing, agitating, marching, demonstrating, or joining the Spanish Loyalists. It is easy for the critic to point out the fallacy of judging the merit of literature by its subject-matter, but these arguments over the role of "propaganda" were genuine and serious moral conflicts. Besides helping to shape the argument of such novels as Grove's *The Master of the Mill* and Callaghan's *They Shall Inherit the Earth*, they raised the fundamental issue of the role of the creative mind in society, and by doing so helped to give a maturity and depth to Canadian writing which is a permanent part of its heritage.

It is not surprising, given this background, that the belief in the inspiration of literature by social significance continued to be an active force long after it had ceased to be attached to any specifically Marxist or other political programmes. It is still strong in the *Preview* group in the forties, and in their immediate successors, though the best of them have developed in different directions. The theme of social realism is at its most attractive, and least theoretical, in the poetry of Souster. The existentialist movement, with its emphasis on the self-determination of social attitudes, seems to have had very little direct influence in Canada: Mr. Beattie's comment on the absence of the existential in Pratt suggests that this lack of influence may be significant.

During the last decade or so a kind of social Freudianism has been taking shape, mainly in the United States, as a democratic counterpart of Marxism. Here society is seen as controlled by certain anxieties, real or imaginary, which are designed to repress or sublimate human impulses toward a greater freedom. These impulses include the creative and the sexual, which are closely linked. The enemy of the poet is not the capitalist but the "square," or representative of repressive morality. The advantage of this attitude is that it preserves the position of rebellion against society for the poet, without imposing on him any specific social obligations. This movement has had a rather limited development in Canada, somewhat surprisingly considering how easy a target the square is in Canada: it has influenced Layton and many younger Montreal poets, but has not affected fiction to any great degree, though there may be something of it in Richler. It ignores the old political alignments: the Communists are usually regarded as Puritanic and repressive equally with the bourgeoisie, and a recent poem of Layton's contrasts the social hypocrisy in Canada with contemporary Spain. Thus it represents to some extent a return to the undifferentiated radicalism of a century before, though no longer in a political context.

As the centre of Canadian life moves from the fortress to the metropolis, the garrison mentality changes correspondingly. It begins as an expression of the moral values generally accepted in the group as a whole, and then, as society gets more complicated and more in control of its environment, it becomes more of a revolutionary garrison within a metropolitan society. But though it changes from a defence of to an attack on what society accepts as conventional standards, the literature it produces, at every stage, tends to be rhetorical, an illustration or allegory of certain social attitudes. These attitudes help to unify the mind of the writer by externalizing his enemy, the enemy being the anti-creative elements in life as he sees life. To approach these elements in a less rhetorical way would introduce the theme of self-conflict, a more perilous but ultimately more rewarding theme. The conflict involved is between the poetic impulse to construct and the rhetorical impulse to assert, and the victory of the former is the sign of the maturing of the writer.

III

There is of course nothing in all this that differentiates Canadian from other related cultural developments. The nineteenth-century Canadian reliance on the conceptual was not different in kind from that of the Victorian readers described by Douglas Bush, who thought they were reading poetry when they were really only looking for Great Thoughts. But if the tendency was not different in kind, it was more intense in degree. Here we need another seminal fact in this book, one that we have stumbled over already: Mr. Hopwood's remark that the Canadian literary mind, beginning as it did so late in the cultural history of the West, was established on a basis, not of myth, but of history. The conceptual emphasis in Canadian culture we have been speaking of is a consequence, and an essential part, of this historical bias.

Canada, of course, or the place where Canada is, can supply distinctive settings and props to a writer who is looking for local colour. Tourist-writing has its own importance (e.g., *Maria Chapdelaine*), as has the use of Canadian history for purposes of romance, of which more later. But it would be an obvious fallacy to claim that the setting provided anything more than novelty. When Canadian writers are urged to use distinctively Canadian themes, the fallacy is less obvious, but still there. The forms of literature are autonomous: they exist within literature itself, and cannot be derived from any experience outside literature. What the Canadian writer finds in his experience and environment may be new, but it will be new only as content: the form of his expression of it can take shape only from what he has read, not from what he has experienced. The great technical experiments of Joyce and Proust in fiction, of Eliot and Hopkins in poetry, have resulted partly from profound literary scholarship, from seeing the formal possibilities inherent in the literature they have studied. A writer who is or who feels removed from his literary tradition tends rather to take over forms already in existence. We notice how often the surveyors of Canadian fiction in this book have occasion to remark that a novel contains a good deal of sincere feeling and accurate observation, but that it is spoiled by an unconvincing plot, usually one too violent or dependent on coincidence for such material. What has happened is that the author felt he could make a novel out of his knowledge and observation, but had no story in particular to tell. His material did not come to him in the form of a story, but as a consolidated chunk of experience, reflection, and sensibility. He had to invent a plot to put this material in causal shape (for writing, as Kafka says, is an art of causality), to pour the new wine of content into the old bottles of form. Even Grove works in this way, though Grove, by sheer dogged persistence, does get his action powerfully if ponderously moving.

This brings us nearer the centre of Mr. Hopwood's observation. Literature is conscious mythology: as society develops, its mythical stories become structural principles of story-telling, its mythical concepts, sun-gods and the like, become habits of metaphorical thought. In a fully mature literary tradition the writer enters into a structure of traditional stories and images. He often has the feeling, and says so, that he is not actively shaping his material at all, but is rather a place where a verbal structure is taking its own shape. If a novelist, he starts with a story-telling impetus; if a poet, with a metaphor-crystallizing impetus. Down to the beginning of the twentieth century at least, the Canadian who wanted to write started with a feeling of detachment from his literary tradition, which existed for him mainly in his school books. He had probably, as said above, been educated in a way that heavily stressed the conceptual and argumentative use of language. Mrs. Fowke shows us how the Indians began with a mythology which included all the main elements of our own. It was, of course, impossible for Canadians to establish any real continuity with it: Indians, like the rest of the country, were seen as nineteenth-century literary conventions. Certain elements in Canadian culture, too, such as the Protestant revolutionary view of history, may have minimized the importance of the oral tradition in ballad and folk song, which seems to have survived best in Catholic communities. In Canada the mythical was simply the "prehistoric" (this word, we are told, is a Canadian coinage), and the writer had to attach himself to his literary tradition deliberately and voluntarily. And though this may be no longer true or necessary, attitudes surviving from an earlier period of isolation still have their influence.

The separation of subject and object is the primary fact of consciousness, for anyone so situated and so educated. Writing for him does not start with a rhythmical movement, or an impetus caught from or encouraged by a group of contemporaries: it starts with reportage, a single mind reacting to what is set over against it. Such a writer does not naturally think metaphorically but descriptively; it seems obvious to him that writing is a form of self-expression dependent on the gathering of a certain amount of experience, granted some inborn sensitivity toward that experience. We note (as does Mr. McPherson) how many Canadian novelists have written only one novel, or only one good novel, how many Canadian poets have written only one good book of poems, generally their first. Even the dream of "the great Canadian novel," the feeling that somebody some day will write a Canadian fictional classic, assumes that whoever does it will do it only once. This is a characteristic of writers dominated by the conception of writing up experiences or observations: nobody has enough experience to keep on writing about it, unless his writing is an incidental commentary on a non-literary career.

The Canadian writers who have overcome these difficulties and have found their way back to the real headwaters of inspiration are heroic explorers.

There are a good many of them, and the evidence of this book is that the Canadian imagination has passed the stage of exploration and has embarked on that of settlement. But it is of course full of the failures as well as the successes of exploration, imaginative voyages to Golconda that froze in the ice, and we can learn something from them too. Why do Canadians write so many historical romances, of what Mr. McPherson calls the rut and thrust variety? One can understand it in Mr. Roper's period: the tendency to melodrama in romance makes it part of a central convention of that time, as Mr. Roper's discerning paragraph on the subject shows. But romances are still going strong in Mr. Pacey's period, and if anything even stronger in Mr. McPherson's. They get a little sexier and more violent as they go on, but the formula remains much the same: so much love-making, so much "research" about antiquities and costume copied off filing cards, more love-making, more filing cards. There is clearly a steady market for this, but the number of writers engaged in it suggests other answers. There is also a related fact, the unusually large number of Canadian popular best-selling fiction-writers, from Agnes Fleming through Gilbert Parker to Mazo de la Roche.

In Mr. Roper's chronicle not all the fiction is romance, but nearly all of it is formula-writing. In the books he mentions that I have read I remember much honest and competent work. Some of them did a good deal to form my own infantile imagination, and I could well have fared worse. What there is not, of course, is a recreated view of life, or anything to detach the mind from its customary attitudes. In Mr. Pacey's period we begin to notice a more consistent distinction between the romancer, who stays with established values and usually chooses a subject remote in time from himself, and the realist, who deals with contemporary life, and therefore—it appears to be a therefore—is more serious in intention, more concerned to unsettle a stock response. One tendency culminates in Mazo de la Roche, the other in Morley Callaghan, both professional writers and born story-tellers, though of very different kinds. By Mr. McPherson's period the two tendencies have more widely diverged. One is mainly romance dealing with Canada's past, the other is contemporary realism dealing with what is common to Canada and the rest of the world, like antique and modern furniture stores. One can see something similar in the poetry, a contrast between a romantic tradition closely associated with patriotic and idealistic themes, and a more intellectualized one with a more cosmopolitan bias. This contrast is prominently featured in the first edition of A. J. M. Smith's anthology, *A Book of Canadian Poetry* (1943).

This contrast of the romantic and the realistic, the latter having a moral dignity that the former lacks, reflects the social and conceptual approach to literature already mentioned. Here we are looking at the same question from a different point of view. Literature, we said, is conscious mythology: it creates an autonomous world that gives us an imaginative perspective on the actual one. But there is another kind of mythology, one produced by society itself, the object of which is to persuade us to accept existing social values. "Popular" literature, the kind that is read for relaxation and the quieting of the mind, expresses this social mythology. We all feel a general difference between serious and soothing literature, though I know of no critical rule for distinguishing them, nor is there likely to be one. The same work may belong to both mythologies at once, and in fact the separation between them is largely a perspective of our own revolutionary age.

In many popular novels, especially in the nineteenth century, we feel how strong the desire is on the part of the author to work out his situation within a framework of established social values. Mr. Roper notes that in the success-story formula frequent in such fiction the success is usually "emotional," i.e., the individual fulfils himself within his community. There is nothing hypocritical or cynical about this: the author usually believes very deeply in his values. Moral earnestness and the posing of serious problems are by no means excluded from popular literature, any more than serious literature is excused from the necessity of being entertaining. The difference is in the position of the reader's mind at the end, in whether he is being encouraged to remain within his habitual social responses or whether he is being prodded into making the steep and lonely climb into the imaginative world. This distinction in itself is familiar enough, and all I am suggesting here is that what I have called the garrison mentality is highly favourable to the growth of popular literature in this sense. The role of romance and melodrama in consolidating a social mythology is also not hard to see. In romance the characters tend to be psychological projections, heroes, heroines, villains, father-figures, comic-relief caricatures. The popular romance operates on Freudian principles, releasing sexual and power fantasies without disturbing the anxieties of the superego. The language of melodrama, at once violent and morally conventional, is the appropriate language for this. A subliminal sense of the erotic release in romance may have inspired some of the distrust of novels in nineteenth-century pietistic homes. But even those who preferred stories of real life did not want "realism": that, we learn, was denounced on all sides during the nineteenth century as nasty, prurient, morbid, and foreign. The garrison mentality is that of its officers: it can tolerate only the conservative idealism of its ruling class, which for Canada means the moral and propertied middle class.

The total effect of Canadian popular fiction, whatever incidental merits in it there may be, is that of a murmuring and echoing literary collective unconscious, the rippling of a watery Narcissus world reflecting the imaginative patterns above it. Robertson Davies' *Tempest Tost* is a sardonic study of the triumph of a social mythology over the imaginative one symbolized by Shakespeare's play. Maturity and individualization, in such a body of writing, are almost the same process. Occasionally a writer is individualized by accident. Thus Susanna Moodie in the Peterborough bush, surrounded by a half-comic, half-sinister rabble that she thinks of indifferently as Yankee, Irish, native, republican, and lower class, is a British army of occupation in herself, a one-woman garrison. We often find too, as in Leacock, a spirit of criticism, even of satire, that is the complementary half of a strong attachment to the mores that provoke the satire. That is, a good deal of what goes on in Mariposa may look ridiculous, but the norms or standards against which it looks ridiculous are provided by Mariposa itself. In Sara Jeannette Duncan there is something else again, as she watches the garrison parade to church in a small Ontario town: "The repressed magnetic excitement in gatherings of familiar faces, fellow-beings bound by the same convention to the same kind of behaviour, is precious in communities where the human interest is still thin and sparse." Here is a voice of genuine detachment, sympathetic but not defensive either of the group or of herself, concerned primarily to understand and to make the reader see. The social group is becoming external to the writer, but not in a way that isolates her from it.

This razor's edge of detachment is naturally rare in Canadian writing, even in this author, but as the twentieth century advances and Canadian society takes a firmer grip of its environment, it becomes easier to assume the role of an individual separated in standards and attitudes from the community. When this happens, an ironic or realistic literature becomes fully possible. This new kind of detachment of course often means only that the split between subject and object has become identified with a split between the individual and society. This is particularly likely to happen when the separated individual's point of view is also that of the author, as in the stories of misunderstood genius with which many minor authors are fascinated. According to Mr. Tait this convention was frequent in the plays put on in Hart House during the twenties; it certainly was so in fiction. But some of the most powerful of Canadian novels have been those in which this conflict has been portrayed objectively. Buckler's *The Mountain and the Valley* is a Maritime example, and Sinclair Ross's *As for Me and My House* one from the prairies.

Mr. Conron quotes B. K. Sandwell as saying: "I follow it [society] at a respectful distance . . . far enough away to make it clear that I do not belong to it." It is clear that this is not necessarily any advance on the expression of conventional social values in popular romance. The feeling of detachment from society means only that society has become more complex, and inner tensions have developed in it. We have traced this process already. The question that arises is: once society, along with physical nature, becomes external to the writer, what does he then feel a part of? For rhetorical or assertive writers it is generally a smaller society, the group that agrees with them. But the imaginative writer, though he often begins as a member of a school or group, normally pulls away from it as he develops.

If our general line of thought is sound, the imaginative writer is finding his identity within the world of literature itself. He is withdrawing from what Douglas LePan calls a country without a mythology into the country of mythology, ending where the Indians began. Mr. Tait quotes John Coulter's comment on his play, or libretto, *Deirdre of the Sorrows*: "The art of a Canadian remains . . . the art of the country of his forebears and the old world heritage of myth and legend remains his heritage . . . though the desk on which he writes be Canadian." But the progress may not be a simple matter of forsaking the Canadian for the international, the province for the capital. It may be that when the Canadian writer attaches himself to the world of literature, he discovers, or rediscovers, by doing so, something in his Canadian environment which is more vital and articulate than a desk.

IV

At the heart of all social mythology lies what may be called, because it usually is called, a pastoral myth, the vision of a social ideal. The pastoral myth in its most common form is associated with childhood, or with some earlier social condition—pioneer life, the small town, the *habitant* rooted to his land—that can be identified with childhood. The nostalgia for a world of peace and protection, with a spontaneous response to the nature around it, with a leisure and composure not to be found today, is particularly strong in Canada. It is overpowering in our popular literature, from *Anne of Green Gables* to Leacock's Mariposa, and from *Maria Chapdelaine* to *Jake and the Kid*. It is present in all the fiction that deals with small towns as collections of characters in search of an author. Its influence is strong in the most serious writers: one thinks of Gabrielle Roy, following her *Bonheur d'occasion* with *La poule d'eau*. It is the theme of all the essayists who write of fishing and other forms of the simpler life, especially as lived in the past. Mr. Conron quotes MacMechan: "golden days in memory for the enrichment of less happier times to come." It even comes into our official documents—the Massey Report begins, almost as a matter of course, with an idyllic picture of the Canada of fifty years ago, as a point of departure for its investigations. Mr. Bailey speaks of the eighteenth-century Loyalists as looking "to a past that had never existed for comfort and illumination," which suggests that the pastoral myth has been around for some time.

The Indians have not figured so largely in the myth as one might expect, though in some early fiction and drama the noble savage takes the role, as he does to some extent even in the Gothic hero Wacousta. The popularity of Pauline Johnson and Grey Owl, however, shows that the kind of rapport with nature which the Indian symbolizes is central to it. Another form of pastoral myth is the evocation of an earlier period of history which is made romantic by having a more uninhibited expression of passion or virtue or courage attached to it. This of course links the pastoral myth with the vision of vanished grandeur that comes into the novels about the *ancien régime*. In *The Golden Dog* and *The Seats of the Mighty* the forlorn little fortress of seventeenth-century Quebec, sitting in the middle of what Madame de Pompadour called "a few arpents of snow," acquires a theatrical glamour that would do credit to Renaissance Florence. Mr. Klinck gives a most concise summary of the earlier literary romanticizing of this period, and Mr. Pacey studies its later aspects. The two forms of the myth collide on the Plains of Abraham, on the one side a marquis, on the other a Hanoverian commoner tearing himself reluctantly from the pages of Gray's *Elegy*.

Close to the centre of the pastoral myth is the sense of kinship with the animal and vegetable world, which is so prominent a part of the Canadian frontier. I think of an image in Mazo de la Roche's *Delight*, which I am encouraged to revert to because I see that it has also caught Mr. Pacey's eye. Delight Mainprize—I leave it to the connoisseurs of ambiguity to explore the overtones of that name—is said by her creator to be "not much more developed intellectually than the soft-eyed Jersey in the byre." It must be very rarely that a novelist—a wideawake and astute novelist—can call her heroine a cow with such affection, even admiration. But it is consistent with what Mr. Pacey calls her belief in the "superiority of the primitive and the instinctive over the civilized and conventional." The prevalence in Canada of animal stories, in which animals are closely assimilated to human behaviour and emotions, has been noted by Mr. Lucas and Miss McDowell particularly. Conversely, the killing of an animal, as a tragic or ironic symbol, has a peculiar resonance in Canadian poetry, from the moose in Lampman's Long Sault poem to the Christmas slaughter of geese which is the informing theme of James Reaney's *A Suit of Nettles*. More complicated pastoral motifs are conspicuous in Morley Callaghan, who turns continually to the theme of betrayed or victorious innocence—the former in *The Loved and the Lost*, the latter in *Such is My Beloved*. The Peggy of *The Loved and the Lost*, whose spontaneous affection for Negroes is inspired by a childhood experience and symbolized by a child's toy, is particularly close to our theme.

The theme of Grove's *A Search for America* is the narrator's search for a North American pastoral myth in its genuinely imaginative form, as distinct from its sentimental or socially stereotyped form. The narrator, adrift in the New World without means of support, has a few grotesque collisions with the hustling mercantilism of American life—selling encyclopaedias and the like—and gets badly bruised in spirit. He becomes convinced that this America is a false social development which has grown over and concealed the real American social ideal, and tries to grasp the form of this buried society. He wants to become, to reverse Mr. Lucas's clever phrase, a Rousseau and not a Crusoe of his new world. In our terms, he is trying to grasp something of the myth of America, the essential imaginative idea it embodies. He meets, but irritably brushes away, the tawdry and sentimentalized versions of this myth —the cottage away from it all, happy days on the farm, the great open spaces of the west. He goes straight to the really powerful and effective versions: Thoreau's *Walden*, the personality of Lincoln, Huckleberry Finn drifting down the great river. The America that he searches for, he feels, has something to do with these things, though it is not defined much more closely than this.

Grove drops a hint in a footnote near the end that what his narrator is looking for has been abandoned in the United States but perhaps not yet in Canada. This is not our present moral: pastoral myths, even in their genuine forms, do not exist as places. They exist rather in such things as the loving delicacy of perception in Grove's own *Over Prairie Trails* and *The Turn of the Year*. Still, the remark has some importance because it indicates that the conception "Canada" can also become a pastoral myth in certain circumstances. Mr. Daniells, speaking of the nineteenth-century mystique of Canadianism, says: "A world is created, its centre in the Canadian home, its middle distance the loved landscape of Canada, its protecting wall the circle of British institutions . . . a world as centripetal as that of Sherlock Holmes and as little liable to be shaken by irruptions of evil." The myth suggested here is somewhat Virgilian in shape, pastoral serenity serving as a prologue to the swelling act of the imperial theme. Nobody who saw it in that way was a Virgil, however, and it has been of minor literary significance.

We have said that literature creates a detached and autonomous mythology, and that society itself produces a corresponding mythology, to which a good deal of literature belongs. We have found the pastoral myth, in its popular and sentimental social form, to be an idealization of memory, especially childhood memory. But we have also suggested that the same myth exists in a genuinely imaginative form, and have found its influence in some of the best Canadian writers. Our present problem is to see if we can take a step beyond Grove and attempt some characterization of the myth he was looking for, a myth which would naturally have an American context but a particular reference to Canada. The sentimental or nostalgic pastoral myth increases the feeling of separation between subject and object by withdrawing the subject into a fantasy world. The genuine myth, then, would result from reversing this process. Myth starts with the identifying of subject and object, the primary imaginative act of literary creation. It is therefore the most explicitly mythopoeic aspect of Canadian literature that we have to turn to, and we shall find this centred in the poetry rather than the fiction. There are many reasons for this: one is that in poetry there is no mass market to encourage the writer to seek refuge in conventional social formulas.

A striking fact about Canadian poetry is the number of poets who have turned to narrative forms (including closet drama) rather than lyrical ones. The anthologist who confines himself wholly to the lyric will give the impression that Canadian poetry really began with Roberts's *Orion* in 1880. Actually there was a tradition of narrative poetry well established before that (Sangster, Heavysege, Howe, and several others), which continues into the post-Confederation period (Mair, Isabella Crawford, Duvar, besides important narrative works by Lampman and D. C. Scott). It is clear that Pratt's devotion to the narrative represents a deep affinity with the Canadian tradition, although so far as I know (and I think I do know) the affinity was entirely unconscious on his part. I have written about the importance of narrative poetry in Canada elsewhere, and have little new to add here. It has two characteristics that account for its being especially important in Canadian literature. In the first place, it is impersonal. The bald and dry statement is the most effective medium for its treatment of action, and the author, as in the folk song and ballad, is able to keep out of sight or speak as one of a group. In the second place, the natural affinities of poetic narrative are with tragic and ironic themes, not with the more manipulated comic and romantic formulas of prose fiction. Consistently with its impersonal form, tragedy and irony are expressed in the action of the poem rather than in its moods or in the poet's own comment.

We hardly expect the earlier narratives to be successful all through, but if we read them with sympathy and historical imagination, we can see how the Canadian environment has exerted its influence on the poet. The environment, in nineteenth-century Canada, is terrifyingly cold, empty and vast, where the obvious and immediate sense of nature is the late Romantic one, increasingly affected by Darwinism, of nature red in tooth and claw. We notice the recurrence of such episodes as shipwreck, Indian massacres, human sacrifices, lumbermen mangled in log-jams, mountain climbers crippled on glaciers, animals screaming in traps, the agonies of starvation and solitude—in short, the "shutting out of the whole moral creation." Human suffering, in such an environment, is a by-product of a massive indifference which, whatever else it may be, is not morally explicable. What confronts the poet is a moral silence deeper than any physical silence, though the latter frequently symbolizes the former, as in the poem of Pratt that is explicitly called "Silences."

The nineteenth-century Canadian poet can hardly help being preoccupied with physical nature; the nature confronting him presents him with the riddle of unconsciousness, and the riddle of unconsciousness in nature is the riddle of death in man. Hence his central emotional reaction is bound to be elegiac and sombre, full of loneliness and fear, or at least wistful and nostalgic, hugging, like Roberts, a "darling illusion." In Carman, Roberts, and D. C. Scott there is a rhetorical strain that speaks in a confident, radio-announcer's voice about the destiny of Canada, the call of the open road, or the onward and upward march of progress. As none of their memorable poetry was written in this voice, we may suspect that they turned to it partly for reassurance. Mr. Daniells remarks of D. C. Scott: "The imprecision of his views is in part the result of having nothing specific to oppose." The riddle of unconsciousness in nature is one that no moralizing or intellectualizing can answer. More important, it is one that irony cannot answer:

> The gray shape with the paleolithic face
> Was still the master of the longitudes.

The conclusion of Pratt's *Titanic* is almost documentary: it is as stripped of irony as it is of moralizing. The elimination of irony from the poet's view of nature makes that view pastoral—a cold pastoral, but still a pastoral. We have only physical nature and a rudimentary human society, not strong enough yet to impose the human forms of tragedy and irony on experience.

The same elegiac and lonely tone continues to haunt the later poetry. Those who in the twenties showed the influence of the death-and-resurrection myth of Eliot, notably Leo Kennedy and A. J. M. Smith, were also keeping to the centre of a native tradition. The use of the Eliot myth was sometimes regarded as a discovery of myth, as Mr. Beattie notes, but of course the earlier poets had not only used the same myth, but were equally aware of its origins in classical poetry, as Carman's *Sappho* indicates. The riddle of the unconscious may be expressed by a symbol such as the agonies of a dying animal, or it may be treated simply as an irreducible fact of existence. But it meets us everywhere: I pick up Margaret Avison and there it is, in a poem called "Identity":

> But on this sheet of beryl, this high sea,
> Scalded by the white unremembering glaze,
> No wisps disperse. This is the icy pole.
> The presence here is single, worse than soul,
> Pried loose forever out of nights and days
> And birth and death
> And all the covering wings.

In such an environment, we may well wonder how the sentimental pastoral myth ever developed at all. But of course there are the summer months, and a growing settlement of the country that eventually began to absorb at least eastern Canada into the north temperate zone. Pratt's Newfoundland background helped to keep his centre of gravity in the elegiac, but when he began to write the feeling of the mindless hostility of nature had largely retreated to the prairies, where, as Mr. Pacey shows, a fictional realism developed, closely related to this feeling in mood and imagery. The Wordsworthian sense of nature as a teacher is apparent as early as Mrs. Traill, in whom Mr. Lucas notes a somewhat selective approach to the subject reminiscent of Miss Muffet. As the sentimental pastoral myth takes shape, its imaginative counterpart takes shape too, the other, gentler, more idyllic half of the myth that has made the pastoral itself a central literary convention. In this version nature, though still full of awfulness and mystery, is the visible representative of an order that man has violated, a spiritual unity that the intellect murders to dissect. This form of the myth is more characteristic of the second phase of Canadian social development, when the conflict of man and nature is expanding into a triangular conflict of nature, society, and individual. Here the individual tends to ally himself with nature against society. A very direct and haunting statement of this attitude occurs in John Robins's *Incomplete Anglers*: "I can approach a solitary tree with pleasure, a cluster of trees with joy, and a forest with rapture; I must approach a solitary man with caution, a group of men with trepidation, and a nation of men with terror." The same theme also forms part of the final cadences of Hugh MacLennan's *The Watch That Ends the Night*: "In the early October of that year, in the cathedral hush of a Quebec Indian summer with the lake drawing into its mirror the fire of the maples, it came to me that to be able to love the mystery surrounding us is the final and only sanction of human existence."

It is the appearance of this theme in D. C. Scott which moves Mr. Daniells to call Scott one of the "ancestral voices" of the Canadian imagination. It is much stronger and more continuous in Lampman, who talks less than his contemporaries and strives harder for the uniting of subject and object in the imaginative experience. This union takes place in the contact of individual poet and a landscape uninhabited except for Wordsworth's "huge and mighty forms" that are manifested by the union:

> Nay more, I think some blessèd power
> Hath brought me wandering idly here.

Again as in Wordsworth, this uniting of individual mind and nature is an experience from which human society, as such, is excluded. Thus when the poet finds a "blessèd power" in nature it is the society he leaves behind that tends to become the God-forsaken wilderness. Usually this society is merely trivial or boring; once, in the unforgettable "City of the End of Things," it becomes demonic.

The two aspects of the pastoral tradition we have been tracing are not inconsistent with each other; they are rather complementary. At one pole of experience there is a fusion of human life and the life in nature; at the opposite pole is the identity of the sinister and terrible elements in nature with the death-wish in man. In Pratt's "The Truant" the "genus *homo*" confronts the "great Panjandrum" of nature who is also his own death-wish: the great Panjandrum is the destructive force in the Nazis and in the Indians who martyred

Brébeuf, the capacity in man that enables him to be deliberately cruel. Irving Layton shows us not only the cruelty but the vulgarity of the death-wish consciousness: as it has no innocence, it cannot suffer with dignity, as animals can; it loses its own imaginary soul by despising the body:

> Listen: for all his careful fuss,
> Will this cold one ever deceive us?
>   Self-hating, he rivets a glittering wall;
> Impairs it by a single pebble
> And loves himself for that concession.

We spoke earlier of a civilization conquering the landscape and imposing an alien and abstract pattern on it. As this process goes on, the writers, the poets especially, tend increasingly to see much of this process as something that is human but still dehumanized, leaving man's real humanity a part of the nature that he continually violates but is still inviolate.

Reading through any good collection of modern Canadian poems or stories, we find every variety of tone, mood, attitude, technique, and setting. But there is a certain unity of impression one gets from it, an impression of gentleness and reasonableness, seldom difficult or greatly daring in its imaginative flights, the passion, whether of love or anger, held in check by something meditative. It is not easy to put the feeling in words, but if we turn to the issue of the *Tamarack Review* that was devoted to West Indian literature, or to the Hungarian poems translated by Canadians in the collection *The Plough and the Pen*, we can see by contrast something of both the strength and the limitations of the Canadian writers. They too have lived, if not in Arcadia, at any rate in a land where empty space and the pervasiveness of physical nature have impressed a pastoral quality on their minds. From the deer and fish in Isabella Crawford's "The Canoe" to the frogs and toads in Layton, from the white narcissus of Knister to the night-blooming cereus of Reaney, everything that is central in Canadian writing seems to be marked by the imminence of the natural world. The sense of this imminence organizes the mythology of Jay Macpherson; it is the sign in which Canadian soldiers conquer Italy in Douglas LePan's *The Net and the Sword*; it may be in the foreground, as in Alden Nowlan, or in the background, as in Birney; but it is always there.

To go on with this absorbing subject would take us into another book: *A Literary Criticism of Canada*, let us say. Here we can only refer the reader to Mr. Beattie's able guidance and sum up the present argument emblematically, with two famous primitive American paintings. One is "Historical Monument of the American Republic," by Erastus Salisbury Field. Painted in 1876 for the centennial of the Revolution, it is an encyclopaedic portrayal of events in American history, against a background of soaring towers, with clouds around their spires, and connected by railway bridges. It is a prophetic vision of the skyscraper cities of the future, of the tremendous technological will to power of our time and the civilization it has built, a civilization now gradually imposing a uniformity of culture and habits of life all over the globe. Because the United States is the most powerful centre of this civilization, we often say, when referring to its uniformity, that the world is becoming Americanized. But of course America itself is being Americanized in this sense, and the uniformity imposed on New Delhi and Singapore, or on Toronto and Vancouver, is no greater than that imposed on New Orleans or Baltimore. A nation so huge and so productive, however, is deeply committed to this growing technological uniformity, even though many tendencies may pull in other directions. Canada has participated to the full in the wars, economic expansions, technological achievements, and internal stresses of the modern world. Canadians seem well adjusted to the new world of technology and very efficient at handling it. Yet in the Canadian imagination there are deep reservations to this world as an end of life in itself, and the political separation of Canada has helped to emphasize these reservations in its literature.

English Canada began with the influx of defeated Tories after the American Revolution, and so, in its literature, with a strong anti-revolutionary bias. The Canadian radicalism that developed in opposition to Loyalism was not a revival of the American revolutionary spirit, but a quite different movement, which had something in common with the Toryism it opposed: one thinks of the Tory and radical elements in the social vision of William Cobbett, who also finds a place in the Canadian record. A revolutionary tradition is liable to two defects: to an undervaluing of history and an impatience with law, and we have seen how unusually strong the Canadian attachment to law and history has been. The attitude to things American represented by Haliburton is not, on the whole, hostile: it would be better described as non-committal, as when Sam Slick speaks of a Fourth of July as "a splendid spectacle; fifteen millions of freemen and three millions of slaves a-celebratin' the birthday of liberty." The strong romantic tradition in Canadian literature has much to do with its original conservatism. When more radical expressions begin to creep into Canadian writing, as in the poetry of Alexander McLachlan, there is still much less of the assumption that freedom and national independence are the same thing, or that the mercantilist Whiggery which won the American Revolution is necessarily the only emancipating force in the world. In some Canadian writers of our own time—I think particularly of Earle Birney's *Trial of a City* and the poetry of F. R. Scott—there is an opposition, not to the democratic but to the oligarchic tendencies in North American civilization, not to liberal but to laissez-faire political doctrine. Perhaps it is a little easier to see these distinctions from the vantage-point of a smaller country, even one which has, in its material culture, made the "American way of life" its own.

The other painting is the much earlier "The Peaceable Kingdom," by

Edward Hicks, painted around 1830. Here, in the background, is a treaty between the Indians and the Quaker settlers under Penn. In the foreground is a group of animals, lions, tigers, bears, oxen, illustrating the prophecy of Isaiah about the recovery of innocence in nature. Like the animals of the Douanier Rousseau, they stare past us with a serenity that transcends consciousness. It is a pictorial emblem of what Grove's narrator was trying to find under the surface of America: the reconciliation of man with man and of man with nature: the mood of Thoreau's Walden retreat, of Emily Dickinson's garden, of Huckleberry Finn's raft, of the elegies of Whitman, whose reaction to Canada is also recorded in this book. This mood is closer to the haunting vision of a serenity that is both human and natural which we have been struggling to identify in the Canadian tradition. If we had to characterize a distinctive emphasis in that tradition, we might call it a quest for the peaceable kingdom.

The writers of the last decade, at least, have begun to write in a world which is post-Canadian, as it is post-American, post-British, and post everything except the world itself. There are no provinces in the empire of aeroplane and television, and no physical separation from the centres of culture, such as they are. Sensibility is no longer dependent on a specific environment or even on sense experience itself. A remark of Mr. Beattie's about Robert Finch illustrates a tendency which is affecting literature as well as painting: "the interplay of sense impressions is so complicated, and so exhilarating, that the reader receives no sense impression at all." Marshall McLuhan speaks of the world as reduced to a single gigantic primitive village, where everything has the same kind of immediacy. He speaks of the fears that so many intellectuals have of such a world, and remarks amiably: "Terror is the normal state of any oral society, for in it everything affects everything all the time." The Canadian spirit, to personify it as a single being dwelling in the country from the early voyages to the present, might well, reading this sentence, feel that this was where he came in. In other words, new conditions give the old ones a new importance, as what vanishes in one form reappears in another. The moment that the peaceable kingdom has been completely obliterated by its rival is the moment when it comes into the foreground again, as the eternal frontier, the first thing that the writer's imagination must deal with. Pratt's "The Truant," already referred to, foreshadows the poetry of the future, when physical nature has retreated to outer space and only individual and society are left as effective factors in the imagination. But the central conflict, and the moods in which it is fought out, are still unchanged.

One gets very tired, in old-fashioned biographies, of the dubious embryology that examines a poet's ancestry and wonders if a tendency to fantasy in him could be the result of an Irish great-grandmother. A reader may feel the same unreality in efforts to attach Canadian writers to a tradition made up of earlier writers whom they may not have read or greatly admired. I have felt this myself whenever I have written about Canadian literature. Yet I keep coming back to the feeling that there does seem to be such a thing as an imaginative continuum, and that writers are conditioned in their attitudes by their predecessors, or by the cultural climate of their predecessors, whether there is conscious influence or not. Again, nothing can give a writer's experience and sensitivity any form except the study of literature itself. In this study the great classics, "monuments of its own magnificence," and the best contemporaries have an obvious priority. The more such monuments or such contemporaries there are in a writer's particular cultural traditions, the more fortunate he is; but he needs those traditions in any case. He needs them most of all when what faces him seems so new as to threaten his identity. For present and future writers in Canada and their readers, what is important in Canadian literature, beyond the merits of the individual works in it, is the inheritance of the entire enterprise. The writers featured in this book have identified the habits and attitudes of the country, as Fraser and Mackenzie have identified its rivers. They have also left an imaginative legacy of dignity and of high courage.

BIBLIOGRAPHY AND NOTES

CONTRIBUTORS

INDEX

ACKNOWLEDGMENTS

Bibliography and Notes

GENERAL BIBLIOGRAPHY
(Selected Books in print in 1964)

A. BASIC REFERENCE BOOKS

WATTERS, REGINALD EYRE (compiler). *A Check List of Canadian Literature and Background Materials, 1628–1950* [Canadian Literature in English] (compiled for the Humanities Research Council of Canada). Toronto: University of Toronto Press, 1959. (Abbrev. *Watters C. L.*)

WATTERS, REGINALD EYRE, and INGLIS FREEMAN BELL (compilers). *On Canadian Literature, 1806–1960: A Check List of Articles, Books and Theses on English-Canadian Literature, Its Authors, and Language.* (To be published in 1965 by the University of Toronto Press.)

B. BIBLIOGRAPHIES

Amtmann, Bernard, Inc. (booksellers). Catalogues. Montreal: 1948–   See *A Catalogue of the Catalogues Issued since 1948* (1964).

Canadian Historical Review (quarterly). Toronto: University of Toronto Press, 1920–   . Contains (quarterly) a list of "Recent Publications Relating to Canada." (Abbrev. *C.H.R.*)

Canadian Literature (quarterly). Vancouver: University of British Columbia, 1959–   . Contains annual "Check List."

Canadian Periodical Index. Toronto: Toronto Public Libraries, 1929–1932, and 1938–   .

Canadiana: A List of Publications of Canadian Interest. Ottawa: National Library of Canada, 1951–   .

Dominion Drama Festival. *Canadian Full-Length Plays in English: A Preliminary Annotated Catalogue.* Edited by W. S. Milne. Ottawa: The Festival (200 Cooper St.), 1964.

PACEY, DESMOND. *Creative Writing in Canada.* Toronto, Ryerson Press, 1952; revised, 1961. Pp. 283–300.

PRIESTLEY, F. E. L. *The Humanities in Canada.* Toronto: University of Toronto Press, 1964. See "Appendices," pp. 93–246.

SMITH, A. J. M. *The Book of Canadian Poetry.* 3rd edition, revised; Toronto: W. J. Gage, 1957. Pp. 505–21.

STATON, FRANCES M. and MARIE TREMAINE (editors). *A Bibliography of Canadiana.* Toronto: Public Library, 1934. *First Supplement* by GERTRUDE M. BOYLE, assisted by MARJORIE COLBECK, 1959.

TREMAINE, MARIE. *A Bibliography of Canadian Imprints, 1751–1800.* Toronto: University of Toronto Press, 1952.

University of Toronto Quarterly. Toronto: University of Toronto Press, from 1931–   . Contains an annual review of "Letters in Canada" (since the review for the year 1935).

WATTERS, R. E. (compiler). "Bibliography" in C. F. KLINCK and R. E. WATTERS (editors), *Canadian Anthology*. Toronto, W. J. Gage, 1955, 1957; revised for 1965.

C. STUDIES AND BIOGRAPHICAL SKETCHES

Canadian Literature (quarterly). Vancouver, B.C.: University of British Columbia, 1951– . Devoted to critical articles on Canadian literature.

Dictionary of Canadian Biography (Toronto: University of Toronto Press). A series of volumes of which the first, covering the years up to 1700, will be published in 1965.

EGGLESTON, WILFRID. *The Frontier and Canadian Letters*. Toronto: Ryerson, 1957.

Encyclopedia Canadiana. Ottawa: Grolier Society, 1957. 10 vols.

MCDOUGALL, ROBERT L. (editor). *Our Living Tradition*. Carleton University and University of Toronto Press, 1957, 1959, 1962, 1965. (The 1957 volume was edited by CLAUDE T. BISSELL.)

New Canadian Library series. General editor, MALCOLM ROSS. Paperback reprints of Canadian literary works with special introductions for each volume by Canadian scholars. Toronto: McClelland and Stewart.

PACEY, DESMOND, *Creative Writing in Canada*. Toronto: Ryerson, 1961.

────── *Ten Canadian Poets*. Toronto: Ryerson, 1958.

PARK, JULIAN (editor). *The Culture of Contemporary Canada*. Ithaca, N.Y.: Cornell University Press, 1957.

PERCIVAL, WALTER P. (editor). *Leading Canadian Poets*. Toronto: Ryerson, 1948.

RASHLEY, R. E. *Poetry in Canada: The First Three Steps*. Toronto: Ryerson, 1958.

ROSS, MALCOLM (editor). *The Arts in Canada*. Toronto: Macmillan, 1958.

ROYAL SOCIETY OF CANADA. *Proceedings and Transactions*. Contains in each volume "Biographical Sketches of Deceased Members."

SMITH, A. J. M. *The Book of Canadian Poetry*. 3rd edition, revised; Toronto: W. J. Gage, 1957.

SYLVESTRE, GUY, BRANDON CONRON and CARL F. KLINCK. *Canadian Writers/ Ecrivains canadiens*. Toronto: Ryerson, 1964.

University of Toronto Quarterly. Toronto: University of Toronto Press, 1931. "Letters in Canada" (critical articles), annual surveys since the year 1935.

WALLACE, W. STEWART. *The Macmillan Dictionary of Canadian Biography*. 3rd edition; Toronto: Macmillan, 1963.

D. ANTHOLOGIES

BIRNEY, EARLE (editor). *Twentieth Century Canadian Poetry*. Toronto: Ryerson, 1953.

DUDEK, LOUIS and IRVING LAYTON (editors). *Canadian Poems 1850–1952*. 2nd edition; Toronto: Contact Press, 1952.

GUSTAFSON, RALPH (editor). *The Penguin Book of Canadian Verse*. Toronto and New York: Harmondsworth, 1958.

KLINCK, C. F. and R. E. WATTERS (editors). *Canadian Anthology*. Toronto: W. J. Gage, 1955, 1957; revised for 1965.

LAYTON, IRVING (editor). *Love Where the Nights are Long*. Toronto: McClelland and Stewart, 1962.

NELSON, GEORGE E. (editor). *Cavalcade of the North*. New York: Doubleday, 1958.

PACEY, DESMOND (editor). *A Book of Canadian Stories*. Toronto: Ryerson, 1947, revised 1962.
ROSS, MALCOLM (editor). *Our Sense of Identity: A Book of Canadian Essays*. Toronto: Ryerson, 1954.
ROBINS, JOHN D. and MARGARET V. RAY (editors). *A Book of Canadian Humour*. Toronto: Ryerson, 1951.
SMITH, A. J. M. (editor). *The Book of Canadian Poetry*. 3rd edition, revised; Toronto: W. J. Gage, 1957.
SMITH, A. J. M. (editor). *The Oxford Book of Canadian Verse in English and French*. Toronto: Oxford University Press, 1960.
SMITH, A. J. M. and F. R. SCOTT (editors). *The Blasted Pine*. Toronto: Macmillan, 1959.
TOYE, WILLIAM (editor). *A Book of Canada*. Toronto: Collins, 1962.
WEAVER, ROBERT (editor). *Canadian Short Stories*. World's Classics edition. Toronto: Oxford, 1960.
WEAVER, ROBERT (editor). *The First Five Years: A Selection From The Tamarack Review*. Toronto: Oxford, 1962.
WEAVER, ROBERT (editor). *Ten for Wednesday Night*. Toronto: McClelland and Stewart, 1961.
WEAVER, ROBERT and HELEN JAMES. *Canadian Short Stories*. Toronto: Oxford University Press, 1952.

SPECIAL BIBLIOGRAPHIES, BY CHAPTERS

EDITORS' NOTE: As a general rule, footnotes to the chapters were avoided in favour of inclusion in the text of all relevant material and an indication of the sources of most references and quotations. For some chapters, therefore, no additional notes are supplied. For others, the reader will find in this section the contributors' lists of the most useful printed sources which they have consulted, together with their suggestions for further reading.

The appropriate items in Watters' *Check List* and in our "General Bibliography" should be consulted for each chapter of this *Literary History*; abbreviations in the notes (e.g. Staton and Tremaine) refer to such items.

CHAPTER 1. THE VOYAGERS

Many books have been written about the voyages to the New World in the sixteenth and seventeenth centuries, and only a few of them can be mentioned here. Of the numerous bibliographies of early Americana, two that I have found especially useful are: E. G. Cox's *A Reference Guide to the Literature of Travel*, vol. II, *The New World* (Seattle: University of Washington Press, 1938), and Joseph Sabin's *A Dictionary of Books relating to America from its Discovery to the Present Time* (29 vols.; Amsterdam: N. Israel, 1961–62). An excellent guide to manuscript material is *A Guide to Manuscripts Relating to America in Great Britain and Ireland*, edited by B. R. Crick and Miriam Alman (London: British Association for American Studies, 1961). Watters' *Check List* is of little use for sixteenth- and seventeenth-century source material because only one item in it,

Robert Hayman's *Quodlibets* . . . (London, 1628), is dated earlier than the year 1700.

The most valuable collections of voyage literature are, of course, those of Hakluyt and Purchas, both of which have been printed in twentieth-century editions. Richard Hakluyt's *The Principal Navigations, Voyages, Traffiques & Discoveries of the English Nation* was published by Maclehose (12 vols.; Glasgow, 1903–5) and by Dent (London, 1927–28). There is also a cheap Everyman edition. Samuel Purchas's *Hakluytus Posthumous or Purchas His Pilgrimes* was published by Maclehose (20 vols.; Glasgow, 1905–7). The publications of the Hakluyt Society (London, 1849–   ) provide further accounts of the voyages, some of them not in Hakluyt or Purchas. An unpublished doctoral dissertation by William Beckler White, "The Narrative Technique of Elizabethan Voyage and Travel Literature from 1550 to 1603" (Lehigh University, 1955) is useful in its assessment of the literary merits of voyage literature in the second half of the sixteenth century.

Boies Penrose's *Travel and Discovery in the Renaissance, 1420–1620* gives a good survey of two hundred years of travel in different parts of the world, but it is annoying for the serious student to find that Penrose does not give the sources for so much of his information. Of more relevance to students of Canadian history and literature is the sometimes inaccurate and biased, but nevertheless valuable, *A History of Newfoundland* (London: Eyre and Spottiswoode, 1896) by D. W. Prowse, and *A Historical Geography of the British Colonies*, vol. V, Part IV, *Newfoundland* (Oxford: Clarendon Press, 1931), by J. D. Rogers. G. P. Insh's *Scottish Colonial Schemes, 1620–1686* (Glasgow: Maclehose, Jackson & Co., 1922) deals with Scottish settlements in Nova Scotia and in other parts of the New World. Two books by R. R. Cawley, *The Voyagers and Elizabethan Drama* (Boston: Modern Language Association of America, 1938), and *Unpathed Waters: Studies of the Influence of the Voyagers on Elizabethan Literature* (Princeton: Princeton University Press, 1940), deal with the impact of the voyagers on the literature of sixteenth- and seventeenth-century England, and contain useful bibliographies.

The following item came to my notice too late for me to mention it in the text: "Englands Honour Revived. By the valiant exploytes of Captain *Kirke*, and his adherents, who with three Ships, viz. the *Abigaile* Admirall, the *Charitie* vice Admirall, and the *Elizabeth* the reare Admirall: did many admirable exploytes; as is exactly showne in the iusuing [sic] story." This broadside ballad was written by "M[athew] P[arker]" and "Printed for M. Trundle, Widdow" in 1628. It was edited by J. Stevens Cox and re-printed by the Toucan Press, Beaminster, Dorset, England, in 1964. "Here, celebrated in a hundred and thirty two lines of jovial pedestrian verse, is a tribute to the first expedition to Canada of David Kirke and his two brothers who in 1628–29 drove out the French and took possession of the shores of the St. Lawrence and the fortress of Quebec for the English Crown."

NOTES

1 (p. 3). *The First Three English Books on America*, ed. Edward Arber (Birmingham, 1885), 71.

2 (p. 3). *The Plays and Poems of Robert Greene*, ed. J. Churton Collins (Oxford, 1905), I, 224. Edmund Waller, *The Poems*, ed. G. Thorn Drury (London, n.d. [1893]), I, 67.

3 (p. 5). It is unlikely, I think, that more than three or four hundred copies of such large and expensive volumes as *The Principal Navigations* were printed. We know very little about the numbers of individual editions of books printed during the Elizabethan

BIBLIOGRAPHY AND NOTES 857

period, but "of John Dee's *General and Rare Memorials pertaining to the Art of Navigation*, 1577, as we know from a statement in the dedication, only 100 copies were printed." See R. B. McKerrow, *An Introduction to Bibliography* (Oxford, 1951), 131–32.

4 (p. 5). J. Holland Rose, *The Cambridge History of the British Empire* (Cambridge, 1929–   ), I, 96; R. B. Nye and J. E. Morpurgo, *A History of the United States* (Penguin Books, 1955), I, 20.

5 (p. 5). For a brief discussion of the map and globe, see George Bruner Parks, *Richard Hakluyt and the English Voyages* (New York, 1928), 186.

6 (p. 5). The broadside ballads were an ephemeral form of "literature" and the majority of them have probably been lost. It is, also, sometimes difficult to decide whether a ballad is *primarily* or *incidentally* about the New World. By my calculations, however, there were 32 ballads about the Northern Rebellion and 25 about the New World. Hyder E. Rollins, *An Analytical Index to the Ballad Entries (1557–1709) in the Registers of the Company of London* (University of North Carolina Press, 1924), lists 24 ballads on the New World and 27 on the Northern Rebellion. V. de Sola Pinto and A. E. Rodway, *The Common Muse* (London, 1957), write: "no less than a hundred ballads were licensed at Stationers' Hall for publication in 1569–70 alone, and about three-quarters of them dealt with the Northern Rebellion" (p. 17).

7 (p. 6). Rastell's *New Interlude* was edited by W. C. Hazlitt in Dodsley's *Old English Plays* (4th ed.; London, 1874–76), vol. I, and often reprinted.

8 (p. 7). William Beckler White, "The Narrative Technique of Elizabethan Voyage and Travel Literature from 1550 to 1603" (unpub. doct. diss., Lehigh University 1955), finds that 54 out of 176 accounts (some not in Hakluyt) have "significant literary merit."

9 (p. 8). *Ibid.*, 579, 587.

10 (p. 9). Howard Mumford Jones, "The Image of the New World," in *Elizabethan Studies and Other Essays in Honor of George R. Reynolds* (Boulder, Colorado, 1945), 68.

11 (p. 9). *Roxburghe Ballads*, ed. J. W. Ebsworth (London, 1877), VI, 377. Another, and slightly different, version is preserved in Ashmolean MS. 36 in the Bodleian Library. De Sola Pinto and Rodway reprint the MS. version in *The Common Muse*, 39–40.

12 (p. 9). Ashmolean MS. 208; reprinted in *Ballads from Manuscripts*, ed. W. B. Morfill (London, 1873), 282–83. Another poem, "A Commendation of Martin Frobisher," in the same MS., and reprinted in the same volume (pp. 284–85), seems to be of later date.

13 (p. 10). References to Zuniga, Rich, and Price may be found in Alexander Brown, *The Genesis of the United States* (London, 1890), I, 147, 312–16, respectively.

14 (p. 11). Marc Lescarbot, *The History of New France* (3 vols.), English translation by W. L. Grant, introduced by H. P. Biggar (Toronto: Champlain Society, 1907–14). Part of Lescarbot's work was translated into English by P. Erondelle (London, 1609), under the title of *Nova Francia*.

15 (p. 11). *The Works of Samuel de Champlain* (6 vols.), ed. H. P. Biggar *et al.* (Toronto: Champlain Soc., 1922–36).

16 (p. 11). *Travels and Explorations of the Jesuit Missionaries in New France* (73 vols.), ed. R. G. Thwaites (Cleveland, 1896–1901).

17 (p. 11). Mason Wade, *The French Canadians: 1760–1945* (London, 1955), 25.

18 (p. 11). Donald Creighton, *Dominion of the North* (Toronto, 1957), 128.

19 (p. 12). Helmut Kallmann, *A History of Music in Canada, 1534–1914* (University of Toronto Press, 1960), 25.

20 (p. 12). *The Voyages and Colonising Enterprises of Sir Humphrey Gilbert*, ed. D. B. Quinn (London: Hakluyt Soc., 1940), 440.

21 (p. 14). For a brief discussion of the problem as to who wrote the first verse in English in North America, see Richard Beale Davis, *George Sandys: Poet Adventurer* (London, 1955), 225–26. Sandys' *Ovid* was, of course, a translation. Davis considers Vaughan as a candidate, but Mark Eccles, "A Biographical Dictionary of Elizabethan Authors," *H.L.Q.*, V, 286, writes that he "can find no evidence that Vaughan crossed the Atlantic at all."

22 (p. 15). George Pratt Insh, *Scottish Colonial Schemes, 1620–1686* (Glasgow, 1922), p. 43.

23 (p. 16). J. L. Lowes, *The Road to Xanadu* (London, 1930), 337, 133.

24 (p. 17). Bacon and Drummond are quoted by R. R. Cawley, *The Voyagers and Elizabethan Drama* (Boston, 1938), 310n, 352n.

25 (p. 17). Gilbert Chinard, *L'Amérique et le rêve exotique* (Paris, 1934), 169.

26 (p. 18). For a full account of the visit of the Indian Kings see Richmond P. Bond, *Queen Anne's American Kings* (Oxford, 1952).

CHAPTER 2. EXPLORERS BY LAND (TO 1860)

There is almost no literary criticism published on the writings of Canadian explorers. Ray Palmer Baker's *History of Canadian Literature to the Confederation* (1920) contains a brief and sketchy chapter on the subject, as does Thomas Guthrie Marquis's *English-Canadian Literature* (1913), a reprint from *Canada and Its Provinces*. Historical works sometimes give hints in passing about the literary quality of their sources, or show some literary appreciation in their choice of quotations. Such works include Arthur S. Morton's *History of the Canadian West* (1939 and to be reissued), E. E. Rich's *History of the Hudson's Bay Company* (1958–59), John Bartlet Brebner's *The Explorers of North America* (1933), Jeanette Mirsky's *To the Arctic!* (1948) and Leslie H. Neatby's *In Quest of the North West Passage* (1958). Also, editors of particular texts sometimes show appreciation of their character as literature, for instance, Richard Glover in his edition of Hearne's *Journey to the Northern Ocean* (1958). Similarly, some biographical studies such as Grace Lee Nute's *Caesars of the Wilderness* (1943) yield hints.

Among bibliographies Marie Tremaine's *A Bibliography of Canadian Imprints* (1952) and *Arctic Bibliography* (1953–) are very useful, as are also Lorne Pierce's *An Outline of Canadian Literature* (1927) and Watters' *Check List*. However, none of these can be considered as giving a complete list of either primary or secondary works about Canadian exploration. Several studies, such as some mentioned in the first paragraph, or Catherine M. White's *David Thompson's Journals Relating to Montana* (1950) contain useful special or background bibliographies.

In many ways the literature of Canadian exploration is more extensive than the chapters concerned indicate. Many journals and narratives written before 1860 are not referred to, although perhaps they deserve mention. Such omissions may be due to ignorance or oversight, but in many cases I feel that the material is of slight literary interest. Examples are the journals of Philip Turnor and the letters of John Henry Lefroy, although they have some importance in history and geographical science. Also, there may be works with small reference to exploration which should still have been included, such as David Douglas's *Journal 1823–1827* (1914). Douglas is an early figure in a line of scientific travellers and geographers which becomes quite impressive after 1860, including such writers as John Palliser, Henry Youle Hind, George Mercer Dawson, James William Tyrrell, and Frank Russell. I am not saying that any of these are good writers; I am drawing attention to a tradition which is related to my chapter but falls outside it. The tradition may deserve investigation. Another thread that appears towards the end of the period of basic exploration is that of early western settlement. Mark Sweeten Wade's *The Overlanders of '62* is, of course, historical research, but what of the literary value of the journals and letters which are his primary sources? Expeditions to investigate the fate of Franklin's men continued beyond the limits of this chapter, and their stories were published. The Franklin theme, of course, merges into the continuing theme of Arctic exploration and travel.

CHAPTER 3. EXPLORERS BY SEA: THE WEST COAST

In general, the note on chapter 2 applies to the ocean explorers of the West Coast. The best discussion of primary documents is F. W. Howay's 1924 address to the Royal Society of Canada, "The Early Literature of the North-West Coast," printed in the *Proceedings and Transactions of the Royal Society of Canada*, 3rd series, XVIII (1924), Section II, pp. 1–31. Although primarily an historian, Howay is alert to literary quality. Howay's other essays and introductions to editions of various works are also valuable. The most useful history is E. O. S. Scholefield's volume I of Howay and Scholefield's *British Columbia* (1914). It includes a helpful bibliography. Dorothy O. Johansen's *Empire of the Columbia* (1957) is good for background, as is Marius Barbeau's *Pathfinders in the North Pacific* (1958). Some editions of texts have valuable introductions, for example Gordon Grant's edition of *The Life and Adventures of John Nicol, Mariner* (1936).

Some readers may wish to follow up some of the topics touched on during this chapter. The question of apocryphal voyages is well treated by Henry Raup Wagner in his *Apocryphal Voyages to the Northwest Coast of America* (1931) and his *Cartography of the Northwest Coast of America* (1937). Possible early Chinese voyages to America are discussed at length but not very satisfactorily in Edward P. Vining's *An Inglorious Columbus* (1885). W. Kaye Lamb has assembled the facts and documents about Mrs. Barkley's Diary in the *British Columbia Historical Quarterly* for January 1942. The University of British Columbia Library has photostats and microfilms of the unpublished diaries of Captain Vancouver's crews. It also has a typescript translation by William L. Schurz of a copy of Estevan's journal.

Steller's narrative (mentioned on page 42) may be read in English in the second volume of *Bering's Voyages* (1925), edited for the American Geographical Society by F. A. Golder.

CHAPTERS 8 AND 9. LITERARY ACTIVITY IN THE CANADAS, 1812–1841 AND 1841–1880

The most useful general lists are Henry J. Morgan's *Bibliotheca Canadensis* (Ottawa, 1867); Philéas Gagnon's *Essai de bibliographie canadienne* (vol. I, Québec, 1895; vol. II, Montréal, 1913); Staton and Tremaine with Boyle's Supplement; Watters' *Check List*. William Kingsford's *The Early Bibliography of the Province of Ontario* (Toronto, 1892) is interesting, but unreliable. Early writing in the Canadas (now Quebec and Ontario) has been largely neglected by literary historians. Two good surveys should be mentioned: John Reade's "English Literature and Journalism in Quebec," in J. Castell Hopkins, ed., *Canada, an Encyclopedia of the Country* (Toronto, 1899, V, 147–65), and Lawrence M. Lande's *Old Lamps Aglow: An Appreciation of Early Canadian Poetry* (Montreal, 1957), Ray Palmer Baker's *A History of English-Canadian Literature to the Confederation*

(Cambridge, Mass., 1920) was devoted primarily to the Maritime Provinces, but it contains a few pertinent sketches, especially one of Major John Richardson. See also Desmond Pacey's study of Richardson in the journal, *Canadian Literature*, issues 2 and 3 (1959–1960), and his chapter on Sangster in *Ten Canadian Poets* (1958).

Research for these chapters brought out much detailed information about various authors which could not be included in the text. For details the reader may consult articles in *Ontario History* (the publication of the Ontario Historical Society) on Galt, Richardson and Holmes (XLV, 1953, 155–163), on Major Richardson (XLVIII, 1956, 101–7), and on Galt (XLIX, 1957, 187–194). See also articles on Adam Kidd in *Queen's Quarterly* (LXV, 1958, 495–506); on Levi Adams in *Dalhousie Review* (XL, 1960, 34–42. Useful also are introductions to the *New Canadian Library* editions of Frances Brooke's *Emily Montague* and Susanna Moodie's *Roughing It in the Bush*; and the introduction and notes to *The Poems of Adam Hood Burwell* ("University of Western Ontario History Nuggets, no. 30"). See also Carl F. Klinck, *William "Tiger" Dunlop, Blackwoodian Backwoodsman* (Toronto, 1958).

The author is indebted to the work of some postgraduate students of the University of Western Ontario and their M.A. theses: Carl Ballstadt's "The Quest for Canadian Identity in Pre-Confederation English-Canadian Literary Criticism"; Marilyn I. Davis's "*Belinda* and the Sentimental Seduction Tradition" (1963); Kathleen O'Donnell's "Thomas D'Arcy McGee's Irish and Canadian Ballads" (1956); and Mary (Markham) Brown's *Index to the Literary Garland (Montreal 1838–1851)* which was published by the Bibliographical Society of Canada in 1962.

CHAPTER 11. LITERARY PUBLISHING

The history of book publishing in Canada is a virgin field for research. The late Dr. Lorne Pierce was unable to complete the collaborative work on which he was engaged at the time of his death. The present writer has prepared for publication by the Bibliographical Society of Canada a book entitled *Book Publishing and Publishers in Canada before 1900*. A few Canadian publishing and printing firms have issued house histories, e.g. Lorne Pierce, *The Chronicle of a Century, 1829–1929* (Toronto: Ryerson, 1929) and *The House of Ryerson* (Toronto, Ryerson, 1954); *A Canadian Publishing House* [The Macmillan Company of Canada Limited] (Toronto: Macmillan, 1923); *Warwick Bros. & Rutter Limited: The Story of the Business, 1848–1923* (Toronto: Warwick, 1923); Eleanor Harman (editor), *The University as Publisher* (Toronto: University of Toronto Press, 1961).

George H. Doran, *Chronicles of Barabbas, 1884–1934* (New York: Reinhart, 1952), in the opening chapter, deals with publishing in Toronto at the turn of the century. For the earlier period the only first-hand account is Samuel Thompson's *Reminiscences of a Canadian Pioneer for the last Fifty Years: An Autobiography* (Toronto: Hunter, Rose, 1884). Two trade journals are useful, *Canada Bookseller*, 1872, and *Books and Notions*, 1884–85.

For the early press in Canada the standard works are Aegidius Fauteux, *The Introduction of Printing into Canada* (Montreal: Rolland Paper Co., 1930), and Marie Tremaine, *Bibliography of Canadian Imprints, 1751–1800*. See also Miss

Tremaine's article "A Half-Century of Canadian Life and Print" in *Essays Honoring Lawrence C. Wroth* (Portland, Me., 1951), and *The Canadian Book of Printing* (Toronto: Toronto Public Library, 1940). A monograph by the present writer, *Early Printers and Printing in the Canadas*, was published by the Bibliographical Society of Canada (Toronto, 1957).

For the newspaper press there are valuable notes in *Canadian Newspapers on Microfilm: Catalogue* (loose-leaf, mimeographed) issued by the Canadian Library Association (Ottawa, 1959, and continuing); also J. Russell Harper, *Historical Directory of New Brunswick Newspapers and Periodicals* (Fredericton: University of New Brunswick, 1961), and Edith Firth, *Early Toronto Newspapers, 1793–1867* (Toronto Public Library, 1961). The best study of the periodical press in Canada is R. L. McDougall, "A Study of Canadian Periodical Literature of the Nineteenth Century," unpublished Ph.D. thesis, University of Toronto.

CHAPTER 12. CONFEDERATION TO THE FIRST WORLD WAR

See Alfred G. Bailey, "Creative Moments in the Culture of the Maritime Provinces," *Dalhousie Review*, XXIX, 231–44; Claude T. Bissell (ed.), *Our Living Tradition* (University of Toronto Press, 1957); S. D. Clark, *The Social Development of Canada* (University of Toronto Press, 1942); Donald G. Creighton, *Dominion of the North* (Boston: Houghton Mifflin Co., 1944); William Douw Lighthall (ed.), *Songs of the Great Dominion* (London: Walter Scott, 1889) and (Wilfred Chateauclair, pseud.), *The Young Seigneur* (Montreal: Wm. Drysdale and Co., 1888); Robert L. McDougall, "A Study of Canadian Periodical Literature of the Nineteenth Century," unpublished Ph.D. thesis, University of Toronto; Robert L. McDougall (ed.), *Our Living Tradition*, Second and Third, and Fourth Series (University of Toronto Press, 1959 and 1962); W. L. Morton, *The Kingdom of Canada* (Toronto: McClelland and Stewart, 1963); Desmond Pacey, *Creative Writing in Canada* (new edition; Toronto: Ryerson Press, 1961); Elisabeth Wallace, *Goldwin Smith: Victorian Liberal* (University of Toronto Press, 1957); Frank W. Watt, "Radicalism in English-Canadian Literature since Confederation," unpublished Ph.D. thesis, University of Toronto, 1957.

CHAPTER 13. HISTORICAL WRITING IN CANADA TO 1920

In addition to an examination of the books discussed, the private papers of the more important historians were consulted when available. The following list contains the more useful collections. The code number of the Union List of Manuscripts in Canadian Repositories is included in cases where it has been determined. *Thomas Beamish Akins Papers*, Public Archives of Nova Scotia, Halifax, (1–26); the *George Bryce Papers*, Public Archives of Manitoba, Winnipeg, (9–32); *William Wilfred Campbell Papers*, Douglas Library Archives, Queen's University, Kingston; *William Canniff Papers*, Ontario Archives, Toronto, (8–70); *James Henry Coyne Papers*, Lawson Memorial Library, University of Western Ontario, London; *Arthur Doughty Papers*, Public Archives of Canada (hereafter referred to as P.A.C.), Ottawa; *George Taylor Denison Papers*, P.A.C. (7–1111); *John*

Skirving Ewart Papers, Public Archives of Manitoba (9–97); *George Monro Grant Papers, William Lawson Grant Papers,* P.A.C.; *John Castell Hopkins Papers,* P.A.C. (7–758); *Joseph Howe Papers,* P.A.C.; *George Johnson Papers,* P.A.C.; *Stephen Leacock Papers,* Stephen Leacock Memorial Home, Orillia, Ontario (95–1); *William Dawson Le Sueur Papers,* P.A.C.; *Lizars Papers,* Lawson Memorial Library, University of Western Ontario; *Charles Mair Papers,* Douglas Library Archives, Queen's University (75–28); *James Mavor Papers,* University of Toronto Library (16–356); *Henry James Morgan Papers,* P.A.C.; *W. B. Munro Papers,* Huntington Library, San Marino California; *Duncan Campbell Scott Papers,* University of Toronto Library (16–19); *Adam Shortt Papers,* Douglas Library Archives, Queen's University (75–37); *Goldwin Smith Papers,* Mann Library, Cornell University, Ithaca, New York. Some of the Cornell collection is on microfilm in the P.A.C. (7–1639) and copies of the Smith letters in the New York Public Library are on microfilm in the University of Toronto Library (16–256); *Sir Byron Edmund Walker Papers,* University of Toronto Library (16–391); *Sir Daniel Wilson Papers,* Ontario Archives (8–342); *Sir Daniel Wilson Typescripts,* University of Toronto Library (16–283); *G. M. Wrong Papers,* University of Toronto Library. An intensely interesting collection not used in this survey is the *E. B. O'Callaghan Papers,* P.A.C. Irish born, O'Callaghan (1797–1880) was implicated in the rebellion of 1837 in Lower Canada. He became the historian and archivist of New York State and compiled *The Documentary History of the State of New York . . .* (4 vols., 1849–51) and the first 11 volumes of *Documents Relative to the Colonial History of the State of New York . . .* , which appeared between 1853 and 1861. He also wrote a *History of New Netherlands; or, New York under the Dutch* (2 vols., 1846–48).

The ruminations of the presidents of the Canadian Historical Association printed in the annual *Report* (1922–   ) contain many useful suggestions, summaries, and criticisms. For the period under discussion the most useful interpretative article is J. K. McConica, "Kingsford and Whiggery in Canadian History," *Canadian Historical Review,* XL (1959), 108–20. Also very helpful was V. L. O. Chittick, *Thomas Chandler Haliburton ('Sam Slick'): A Study in Provincial Toryism* (New York: Columbia University Press, 1924). On Parkman, particularly useful were William J. Eccles, "The History of New France According to Francis Parkman," *William and Mary Quarterly,* 3rd series, XVIII (1961), 163–75, and G. M. Wrong, "Francis Parkman," *Canadian Historical Review,* IV (1923), 289–303. On Goldwin Smith, see Elisabeth Wallace, *Goldwin Smith: Victorian Liberal* (Toronto: University of Toronto Press, 1957) and, by the same author, "Goldwin Smith on History," *Journal of Modern History,* XXVI (1954), 220–32. On the professional study of history, see Chester Martin, "Fifty Years of Canadian History," *Royal Society of Canada: Fifty Years Retrospect: Anniversary Volume 1882–1932* (n.d., n.p.), 63–69 and "Professor G. M. Wrong and History in Canada," *Essays in Canadian History presented to George MacKinnon Wrong for his Eightieth Birthday* (Toronto: Macmillan, 1939), 1–23. On the development of archives in Canada, see Duncan McArthur, "The Canadian Archives and the Writing of Canadian History," *Canadian Historical Association, Report,* 1935, 5–17. On the teaching of history in Canadian universities, see Richard A. Preston, "Breakers Ahead and a Glance Behind," Presidential Address read before the Canadian Historical Association, June, 1962, printed in the *Canadian Historical Association, Report,* 1962, 1–16. As an example of the development of local history, see Hugh A. Stevenson, "James H. Coyne: An Early Contributor to Canadian Historical Scholarship," *Ontario History,* LIV (1962), 25–42.

CHAPTERS 15, 16, 17. FICTION (1880–1920)

The most comprehensive bibliography of Canadian fiction from 1880 to 1920 is embedded in R. E. Watters' *Check List*, pp. 159–302 and 717–21. The first comprehensive bibliography was by Lewis Emerson Horning and Lawrence J. Burpee, *A Bibliography of Canadian Fiction* (English) (Toronto, 1904).

Large or special collections of Canadian fiction are in the Library of Parliament, Ottawa, the Toronto Public Library, and the libraries of the following institutions: Dalhousie University, Halifax; Massey College, University of Toronto; McGill University, Montreal; Queen's University, Kingston; University of British Columbia, Vancouver; University of New Brunswick, Fredericton; University of Toronto; Victoria University, Toronto; the University of Western Ontario, London; the British Museum; the Library of Congress, Washington; and the University of Texas, Austin, Texas.

Biographical information on some or many of the writers mentioned in these chapters will be found in O. F. Adams, *A Dictionary of American Authors* (5th edition; Boston, 1904); W. J. Burke and Will D. Howe, *American Authors and Books* (New York, 1943); *Encyclopedia Canadiana* (Ottawa, 1957); S. J. Kunitz and H. Haycroft, *American Authors, 1600–1900* (New York, 1928); R. J. Long, *Nova Scotia Authors and their Work* (East Orange, N.J., 1918); W. G. MacFarlane, *New Brunswick Bibliography* (Saint John, 1895); A. N. Marquis, *Who's Who in America*, vol. I (Chicago, 1900); *Who's Who among North American Authors*, vol. I (Los Angeles, 1921); Rev. W. E. McIntyre, *Baptist Authors* (Montreal and Toronto, 1914); H. J. Morgan, *The Canadian Men and Women of the Time* (Toronto, 1898; revised, 1912); Sir C. G. D. Roberts and A. L. Tunnell, *A Standard Dictionary of Canadian Who Was Who* (Toronto, 1934–1938); W. S. Wallace, *The Dictionary of Canadian Biography* (Toronto, 1945); W. S. Wallace, *A Dictionary of North American Authors, deceased before 1950* (Toronto, 1951); W. S. Wallace, *The Encyclopedia of Canada* (Toronto, 1935); W. Stewart Wallace, *The Macmillan Dictionary of Canadian Biography* (Toronto, 1963).

Information on the literary and social milieu is to be found in articles on fiction and book reviews in Canadian magazines and newspapers, especially in Goldwin Smith's *The Week* and in the *Canadian Magazine*. Reviews also are to be found in British and American periodicals. See also the autobiographies by Charles Gordon (Ralph Connor), Nellie McClung, Frederick Niven, Roger Pocock, Robert Service, Ernest Thompson Seton, and Henry Beckles Willson (Watters, pp. 333–429), and the volumes of Hector Charlesworth (Watters, p. 446). For more information on the Anglo–North American literary currents, see James D. Hart, *The Popular Book: A History of America's Literary Taste* (New York, 1950); Frank Luther Mott, *Golden Multitudes: The Story of Best Sellers in the United States* (New York, 1950), and Richard Altick, *The English Common Reader* (Chicago, 1957).

Descriptive and critical studies of Canadian fiction are contained in the histories of Canadian literature by Logan and French, Archibald MacMechan, Archibald MacMurchy, T. G. Marquis, Lorne Pierce, V. B. Rhodenizer, Lionel Stevenson, and O. J. Stevenson (see Watters, pp. 642–73). Special studies have been made by Edward McCourt, *The West in Canadian Fiction* (Toronto, 1949), and Frank William Watt, "Radicalism in English-Canadian Literature," unpublished doctoral dissertation, University of Toronto, 1957.

For studies of the individual writers Sara Jeannette Duncan, Sir Gilbert Parker, Sir Charles G. D. Roberts, and Stephen Leacock, see bibliographies in C. F. Klinck and R. E. Watters, *Canadian Anthology* (Toronto, 1955), pp. 527; 541–42;

545–47; and 535–37. For a biography of Stephen Leacock, see Ralph L. Curry, *Stephen Leacock* (Philadelphia, 1956); see also Joan Walsh, "Stephen Leacock as an American Humorist," unpublished Master's thesis, University of Toronto, 1963. For a critical study of the work of Sara Jeannette Duncan, Sir Gilbert Parker, Robert Barr, and Norman Duncan, see Fred Cogswell, "The Canadian Novel from Confederation to World War I," unpublished Master's thesis, University of New Brunswick, 1950.

CHAPTER 20. LAMPMAN AND ROBERTS

See Claude Bissell, "Literary Taste in Central Canada during the late Nineteenth Century," *Canadian Historical Review*, XXXI (September 1950), 237–51; A. S. Bourinot (editor), *Some Letters of Duncan Campbell Scott, Archibald Lampman and Others* (Rockcliffe, Ottawa: the editor, 1959); E. K. Brown, *On Canadian Poetry* (Toronto: Ryerson, 1943); James Cappon, *Charles G. D. Roberts* (Toronto: Ryerson, n.d.); Archibald Lampman, *Poems* (fourth edition; Toronto: Morang and Co., 1915); John P. Matthews, *Tradition in Exile* (University of Toronto Press, 1962); James Reaney, "The Canadian Poet's Predicament," *University of Toronto Quarterly*, XXXVI, 284–95; Charles G. D. Roberts, *Poems* (Boston: L. C. Page & Co., 1907); Lloyd Roberts, *The Book of Roberts* (Toronto, Ryerson, 1923); E. M. Pomeroy, *Sir Charles G. D. Roberts: A Biography* (Toronto, Ryerson, 1943); Frank W. Watt, "The Masks of Archibald Lampman," *University of Toronto Quarterly*, XXVII, 169–84.

CHAPTER 21. CRAWFORD, CARMAN, AND D. C. SCOTT

See E. K. Brown, *On Canadian Poetry* (Toronto, Ryerson, 1943); James Cappon, *Bliss Carman* (Toronto, Ryerson, 1930); Isabella Valancy Crawford, *Collected Poems* (Toronto, Wm. Briggs, 1905); Katherine Hale, *Isabella Valancy Crawford* (Toronto, Ryerson, 1923); Muriel Miller, *Bliss Carman: A Portrait* (Toronto, Ryerson, 1935).

CHAPTER 22. MINOR POETS (1880–1920)

See Mrs. W. Garland Foster, *The Mohawk Princess* (Vancouver: Lion's Gate Pub. Co., 1931); Carl F. Klinck, *Wilfred Campbell: A Study in Late Provincial Victorianism* (Toronto: Ryerson, 1942); Desmond Pacey, *Creative Writing in Canada* (2nd edition; Toronto: Ryerson, 1961); R. E. Rashley, *Poetry in Canada: The First Three Steps* (Toronto: Ryerson, 1958); A. J. M. Smith (editor), *The Book of Canadian Poetry* (3rd edition; Toronto, W. J. Gage, 1957); A. J. M. Smith (editor), *The Oxford Book of Canadian Verse* (Toronto, Oxford University Press, 1960).

CHAPTER 23. PHILOSOPHICAL LITERATURE (TO 1910)

For pages 435–36, in text above, see a bibliography of Young's mathematical papers in [W. J. Alexander], *The University of Toronto and Its Colleges, 1827–1906*, pp. 253–54. A recent discovery of C. B. Sissons suggests that President S. S. Nelles must have offered Young the chair of Mathematics in Victoria University towards the end of the latter's service with the Department of Education. In Nelles's unpublished diary, under date January 8, 1868, the following entry appears: "Called on Prof. Young. Find he has fully decided not to come as Prof. of Mathematics." For pages 437–42, see a bibliography of Watson's writing between 1872 and 1922 in *Philosophical Essays, Presented to John Watson* (Kingston, Ontario, 1922), pp. 343–46. For pages 442–44, see a bibliography of Murray's writings from 1867 to 1894 in *Proceedings of the Royal Society of Canada*, XII (1894), 61–62.

CHAPTER 25. LITERATURE OF PROTEST

Page 458, above, line 15: *Canadian Monthly and National Review*, I (1872), 93–94. Pp. 459–60: articles by Goldwin Smith in *The Week*, III (1885–86), 75; *Canadian Monthly and National Review*, I (1872), 425 and II (1872), 524; also *CMNR*, VI (1874), 425 ff; *Questions of the Day*, 11 and 50 ff. Pp. 460–61: articles by LeSueur in *The Nation* (Dec. 31, 1874), p. 474; *CMNR*, VII (1875), 322–25; "Mr. Malloch on Optimism," *Popular Science Monthly*, XXXV (1889), 541. P. 461, line 2: for example *CMNR*, VI (1874), 386–88; *The Week*, IX (1892–93), 800–2. P. 462, line 33: see F. W. Watt, "Sir John Macdonald, the Workingman, and Proletarian Ideas in Victorian Canada," *Canadian Historical Review*, XL, no. 1 (March 1959), 1–26, for a more detailed treatment of this subject. P. 467, line 29: see *Western Clarion*, March, 1916. P. 468, line 26: see Elisabeth Wallace, "The Origin of the Social Welfare State in Canada," *Canadian Journal of Economics and Political Science*, XVI (1950), 383–93. P. 468, line 26: this phrase occurs in A. G. Bailey's "Creative Moments in the Culture of the Maritime Provinces," *Dalhousie Review*, XXIX (1949), 231–44. P. 470, line 36: "Proletarian Literature: Theory and Practice," *Canadian Forum*, XVII (1937–38), 58–60.

CHAPTER 27. I, THE WRITING OF CANADIAN HISTORY

A useful general survey is Robin Winks's booklet *Recent Trends and New Literature in Canadian History* (Washington, 1959). It is designed as a bibliographical guide for teachers of Canadian history and while it is by no means exhaustive, it provides a fuller and more comprehensive outline of historical scholarship on Canadian subjects than is attempted in this essay. There is a brief article on the writing of history in Canada, with a list of the best articles on Canadian historiography, by W. L. Morton in the *Encyclopedia Canadiana*. The articles by Careless and Easterbrook cited in the text contain references to all the important books within the scope of their subjects up to the time the articles were published.

For the most complete consideration of Canadian historical writing, one must turn to the *Canadian Historical Review*, which has reviewed all the significant historical works written by Canadians since 1920. There have been many penetrating and brilliant reviews and review articles in *Canadian Forum* (1920–   ), and a number of useful pieces in the *Queen's Quarterly* during the same period. The *Canadian Annual Review* (1960–   ) and the annual review of Canadian literature in English published by the *University of Toronto Quarterly* since 1935 provide useful surveys. The Canadian Historical Association annual reports for the past forty years include several estimates of the state of Canadian historical writing, particularly in a number of the Presidential Addresses.

There is, however, no recent one-volume bibliography of Canadian historical writing comparable to R. G. Trotter's bibliography for an earlier period. Watters' *Check List* does not attempt to cope with several historical fields and also omits many important titles within its scope. F. E. Priestley's *The Humanities in Canada*

(1964) includes the names and publications of many historians; supplements are to follow. The book, however, does not cover historical writing by those who are not now in Canadian universities.

Unfortunately few of the reviewers of Canadian historical writing have shown either a disposition or an ability to subject the works at hand to the serious literary criticism which many of them deserve. The sort of penetrating and brilliant review article "Historians' Viewpoints" undertaken by Margaret Ormsby in *Canadian Literature*, No. 3, Winter, 1960, has been all too rare.

A few other historical reviews of merit are to be found in the *Waterloo Review* (1958–61), and, occasionally, in the book pages of the weekly sections of such newspapers as the *Globe and Mail* and the *Montreal Star*. There is one fine general essay on history as literature, "The Art of Narrative," by W. L. Morton, in the periodical *Culture*, which occasionally uses the style of Canadian historians, notably Creighton, Lower, and McInnis, to illustrate its argument.

* * * * *

The scope of the article in this volume is necessarily limited to published work in English by Canadian writers. The contributions of French Canadian historians (to be discussed in a companion volume) and of the many distinguished non-Canadian historians who have written Canadian history (such as Mason Wade, the Chairman of the Canadian Studies Institute at Rochester University and President of the Canadian Historical Association 1964–65) are not considered except in an occasional reference. Since the emphasis has been upon history writing as a part of Canadian literature, some names and works have been treated more fully than would be the case if this were an article on Canadian historical scholarship for the *Encyclopedia of the Social Sciences* or the *Canadian Historical Review*. Indeed, because of the nature of the article and the limits of space, many of those who have contributed most to historiography in Canada, both as teachers and scholars, have simply not been discussed at all. But anyone interested in pursuing the subject will refer to the work of men and women such as W. N. Sage, J. W. Dafoe, A. G. Dorland, D. C. Harvey, Norman Macdonald, D. A. MacGibbon, Aileen Dunham, J. L. Morrison, M. Long, R. S. Longley; and among those who have begun their writing within the last generation or so, A. G. Bailey, H. P. Gundy, Mary Quayle Innis, Eric Harrison, Lewis G. Thomas, G. N. Tucker, F. J. Boland, G. W. L. Nicholson, C. B. Fergusson, J. S. Conway, H. W. McCready, S. G. Mealing, Paul Cornell, F. W. Gibson, S. F. Wise, F. F. Thompson, E. E. Rose, J. G. Gwynne-Timothy, John Rowe, Joseph Schull, K. A. MacKirdy, Donald Schurman, A. V. Tucker, P. C. White, D. R. H. Macdonald, A. L. Murray, I. M. Lambi, J. H. Trueman, Margaret Banks, D. M. Young, J. K. Chapman, G. A. Wilson, and Margaret Prang.

Since a separate essay is devoted to the literature of the social sciences, only a few of the many political scientists, sociologists, and economic historians who have made substantial contributions to Canadian history are mentioned here. Although his seminal ideas in Canadian economic history are discussed, it has not been possible to do justice to the range and scope of the writing of Harold Innis. Fortunately, the reader can be referred to an excellent short biography by Donald Creighton, *Harold Adams Innis: Portrait of a Scholar*, and for a discussion of Innis's later work, to H. M. McLuhan's article on the subject in the *Queen's Quarterly*, LX (1953), 385–94. Recent brief studies of McLuhan's work include

Frank Kermode's review of *The Gutenberg Galaxy* (*Encounter*, No. 113, Feb. 1963), reviews by John Simon (*New Republic*, Oct. 8, 1962), Raymond Williams (*University of Toronto Quarterly*, April 1964), Robert Fulford (*Maclean's Magazine*, June 20, 1964), and James Reaney's editorial in *Alphabet*, No. 6, June, 1963. There are many good reviews of his latest work *Understanding Media* (1964).

Note to page 502 above: "Since the mid-19th century Western Canada has been the domain of priest and mounted policeman, railway agent and branch bank manager, rather than that of sheriff's posse and desperado and lonely pioneer": see W. Kilbourn, *The Elements Combined* (Toronto, 1960), p. 82 and V. Massey, The Chairman's Address in *Conference across a Continent* (Toronto, 1963), pp. 41–42. The particular phrasing of the idea here owes most to a remark of Merrill Denison's in 1958.

CHAPTER 29. LITERATURE OF RELIGION AND THEOLOGY

The main sources are: Collections of Canadian theological writing at the Archives of Divinity Hall, McGill University, Montreal, and Victoria University, Toronto; also the libraries of theological colleges; *Bibliography of Canadian Imprints* by Marie Tremaine; Watters' *Check List*; H. H. Walsh's *The Christian Church in Canada* (Toronto, 1956), the only single comprehensive history; the main histories of particular churches mentioned in the text; *Canadian Journal of Religious Thought* (1924–32), and *Canadian Journal of Theology* (1954–   ).

CHAPTER 30. PHILOSOPHICAL LITERATURE (1910–1964)

1. *The Achievement of G. S. Brett*

Page 584, lines 10–11: "The Limits of Science," *University of Toronto Monthly*, XIV (1913), 34–38. Page 584, lines 16–20: *Transactions of the Royal Society of Canada*, XIX (1925), Section II, 46. Page 584, line 36: "Parallel Paths in Philosophy and Literature," *University Magazine*, XVIII (1919), 220.

CHAPTER 34. THEATRE AND DRAMA

There is as yet no comprehensive history of Canadian theatre. Useful short articles and studies include: William Angus, "Theatre," in *Encyclopedia Canadiana* (Ottawa: Grolier Society of Canada, 1958) X, 61–67. John Ball, ed., "Theatre in Canada: A Bibliography," *Canadian Literature* No. 14 (Autumn, 1962), 85–100; Nathan Cohen, "Theatre To-day: English Canada," *Tamarack Review*, XIII (Autumn 1959), 24–37; Robertson Davies, on the Stratford Shakespearean Festival: *Renown at Stratford, Twice Have the Trumpets Sounded, Thrice the Brinded Cat Hath Mew'd* (Toronto: Clarke Irwin, 1953, 1954, 1955); W. S. Milne (editor), *Canadian Full-Length Plays in English: A Preliminary Annotated Catalogue* (Ottawa: Dominion Drama Festival, 1964); James Mavor Moore, "The Theatre in English-speaking Canada," in Malcolm Ross (editor), *The Arts in Canada; A Stock Taking at Mid-Century* (Toronto: Macmillan, 1938), 77–82; Herbert Whittaker, "The Theatre," in Julian Park (editor), *The Culture of Contemporary Canada* (Ithaca, N.Y.: Cornell University Press, 1957), 163–180; Herbert Whittaker, "Canada—Theatre," in *Encyclopedia Americana*, Canadian edition (Toronto: Americana Corporation of Canada, 1958), V, 436–40.

Contributors

ALFRED G. BAILEY. Professor and Head of the Department of History and Anthropology, University of New Brunswick, Fredericton, New Brunswick.
    Author of *The Conflict of European and Eastern Algonkian Cultures, 1504–1700* (Saint John, 1937), and of several books of poetry, *Tâo* (Toronto, 1930) and *Border River* (Toronto, 1952); editor of the *New Brunswick Memorial Volume* (Fredericton, 1950); author of many articles on Canadian political, economic and literary history, and on anthropological subjects.

MUNRO BEATTIE. Professor and Head of the Department of English, Carleton University, Ottawa, Ontario.
    Co-author with Elizabeth Waterston of *Composition for Canadian Universities* (Toronto, 1964) and author of an article on Archibald Lampman (in *Our Living Tradition*, 1957) and on Henry James (*Dalhousie Review*, 1959–60).

S. ROSS BEHARRIELL. Associate Professor, Department of English, Royal Military College of Canada, Kingston, Ontario.
    Author of Introductions to Ralph Connor's *The Man from Glengarry* (Toronto, 1960), and Stephen Leacock's *Nonsense Novels* (Toronto, 1963).

CLAUDE T. BISSELL. President, The University of Toronto, Toronto, Ontario.
    Editor of *Our Living Tradition* (Toronto, 1957), Sara Jeannette Duncan's *The Imperialist* (Toronto, 1961) and Ernest Buckler's *The Mountain and the Valley* (Toronto, 1961); author of many articles on nineteenth-century British and Canadian fiction, and on education, and editor of *University College: A Portrait* (1953) and *Canada's Crisis in Higher Education* (1958).

FRED COGSWELL. Professor of English Literature, University of New Brunswick, Fredericton, New Brunswick.
    Editor of *The Fiddlehead*, author of books of poetry, *Descent from Eden, The Stunted Strong, Lost Dimension, The Haloed Tree*, and translator of Robert Henryson's *The Testament of Cresseid*.

BRANDON CONRON. Professor of English, University of Western Ontario, London, Ontario.
    Editor of the Latin pieces in *The Literary Works of Matthew Prior* (Oxford, 1959), and co-author of *Canadian Writers/Ecrivains canadiens* (Toronto, 1964).

ROY DANIELLS. Professor and Head of the Department of English, University of British Columbia, Vancouver, B.C.
    Author of books of poetry, *Deeper into the Forest* (Toronto, 1948) and *The Chequered Shade* (Toronto, 1963), and of a volume of criticism, *Milton,*

CONTRIBUTORS

Mannerism and Baroque (Toronto, 1963); editor of Thomas Traherne's *A Serious and Pathetical Contemplation* (Toronto, 1945); and author of many articles on seventeenth-century literature and on the Canadian literary tradition.

ALICE VIBERT DOUGLAS. Professor of Astronomy (retired), Queen's University, Kingston, Ontario.
   Author of *Arthur Stanley Eddington* (Toronto, 1956), and of articles in the *Hibbert Journal, Atlantic Monthly*, university quarterlies, etc. (1925–1960).

EDITH FULTON FOWKE. Vice-President of the Canadian Folk Music Society and member of the American Folklore Society and International Folk Music Council.
   Author of *Canada's Story in Song* (Toronto, 1960, with Alan Mills and Helmut Blume), *Folk Songs of Canada* (Waterloo, 1954), *Folk Songs of Quebec* (Waterloo, 1957, with Richard Johnston), *Songs of Work and Freedom* (Chicago, 1960, with Joe Glazer), and articles in journals.

NORTHROP FRYE. Principal of Victoria College, University of Toronto, and Professor of English.
   Author of *Fearful Symmetry: A Study of William Blake* (Princeton, 1947) and *Anatomy of Criticism* (Princeton, 1957), *The Well-Tempered Critic* (Bloomington, 1963), *Fables of Identity* (New York, 1963), and of addresses on education notably *The Educated Imagination* (Toronto, 1963). Author also of numerous other books and articles and editor of many volumes of literary criticism.

DAVID GALLOWAY. Professor of English, University of New Brunswick, Fredericton, New Brunswick.
   Author of *Shakespeare: Seven Radio Talks* (Toronto, 1961), of articles on Shakespeare and the Elizabethan period, and of short stories.

HENRY PEARSON GUNDY. University Librarian, Queen's University, Kingston, Ontario.
   Author of *Early Printers and Printing in the Canadas* (Toronto, 1957) and editor of *Historic Kingston* (Transactions of the Kingston Historical Society).

VICTOR GEORGE HOPWOOD. Associate Professor of English, University of British Columbia, Vancouver, British Columbia.
   Author of articles on the theory of literary criticism and on David Thompson, the explorer.

JOHN A. IRVING. Professor and Chairman, Department of Philosophy, Victoria College, University of Toronto, Toronto, Ontario.
   Author of *Science and Values* (Toronto, 1952) and *The Social Credit Movement in Alberta* (Toronto, 1959); editor and co-author of *Challenge and Response* (Toronto, 1959); and author of many articles in books and journals on philosophy and social psychology, and the history of philosophy in Canada.

ALLISON H. JOHNSON. Senior Professor of Philosophy, University of Western Ontario, London, Ontario.
   Author of *Whitehead's Theory of Reality* (Boston, 1952), *Whitehead's*

Philosophy of Civilization (Boston, 1958), and *Whitehead's Interpretation of Science* (Indianapolis, 1961); editor of books of selections from Whitehead's writings; author of many articles, and a contributor to *Philosophy in Canada* (Toronto, 1952).

WILLIAM M. KILBOURN. Professor and Chairman of the Humanities Division, York University, Toronto, Ontario.

Author of *The Firebrand* (Toronto, 1956) and *The Elements Combined* (Toronto, 1960); member of the editorial boards of the *Tamarack Review* and the *Canadian Forum*; and author of reviews in Canadian and British history and Canadian art.

CARL F. KLINCK. Senior Professor of English, Middlesex College, University of Western Ontario, London, Ontario.

Author of *Wilfred Campbell* (Toronto, 1942); co-author with Henry W. Wells of *Edwin J. Pratt* (Toronto, 1947); editor of books by Major John Richardson, William "Tiger" Dunlop, Frances Brooke, and Susanna Moodie; co-editor with R. E. Watters of *Canadian Anthology* (Toronto, 1955) and with Guy Sylvestre and Brandon Conron of *Canadian Writers/Ecrivains canadiens* (Toronto, 1964).

ALEC LUCAS. Associate Professor and Assistant Chairman of the Department of English, McGill University, Montreal, Que.

Associate editor of *Atlantic Anthology* (Toronto, 1961); editor of C. G. D. Roberts' *The Last Barrier and Other Stories* (Toronto, 1958); and author of articles on nature writers.

MARJORIE MCDOWELL. Supervisor of School Library Services, City of Saint John, New Brunswick.

MILLAR MACLURE. Professor of English, Victoria College, University of Toronto, Toronto.

Editor of the *University of Toronto Quarterly* and (with F. W. Watt) of *Essays in English Literature from the Renaissance to the Victorian Age, Presented to A. S. P. Woodhouse 1964* (Toronto, 1964); author of *The Paul's Cross Sermons, 1534–1642* (Toronto, 1958), of a chapter on Literary Scholarship in J. Park (editor), *The Culture of Contemporary Canada* (Ithaca and Toronto, 1957), and of articles in learned journals, chiefly on English Renaissance literature.

JAY MACPHERSON. Assistant Professor of English, Victoria College, University of Toronto, Toronto, Ontario.

Author of books of poetry, *Nineteen Poems* (Majorca, 1952), *O Earth Return* (Toronto, 1954), and *The Boatman* (Toronto, 1957); and of *Four Ages of Man: The Classical Myths* (Toronto, 1962).

HUGO MCPHERSON. Professor of English, University College, University of Toronto, Toronto, Ontario.

Editor of Gabrielle Roy's *The Tin Flute* (Toronto, 1958), Hugh MacLennan's *Barometer Rising* (Toronto, 1959), and Morley Callaghan's *More*

Joy in Heaven (Toronto, 1960); and author of articles on Canadian and American novelists, painters, and sculptors.

HENRY B. MAYO. Senior Professor of Political Science, University of Western Ontario, London, Ontario.

Author of *Democracy and Marxism* (New York, 1955), *Introduction to Marxist Theory* (New York, 1960), *Introduction to Democratic Theory* (New York, 1961), and of articles on contemporary political theory.

DESMOND PACEY. Dean of Graduate Studies and Professor and Head of the Department of English, University of New Brunswick, Fredericton.

Author of *Frederick Philip Grove* (Toronto, 1945), *Creative Writing in Canada* (Toronto, 1952); and *Ten Canadian Poets* (Toronto, 1958); editor of *A Book of Canadian Stories* (Toronto, 1947); and author of numerous articles on Canadian writers.

GORDON ROPER. Professor and Head of the Department of English, Trinity College, University of Toronto, Toronto, Ontario.

Editor of Hawthorne's *The Scarlet Letter and Selected Prose Works* (New York, 1949) and Gabrielle Roy's *Where Nests the Water Hen* (Toronto, 1961), and author of articles on American and Canadian fiction.

MATTHEW HARRY SCARGILL. Assistant to the President, University of Victoria, Victoria, British Columbia.

Author of *Three Icelandic Sagas* (with M. Schlauch; Princeton, 1950), *An English Handbook* (Toronto, 1954), and *Dictionaries of Canadian English* (with W. S. Avis and R. J. Gregg; Toronto, 1962–1964), and of articles on the English language.

RUPERT M. SCHIEDER. Assistant Professor of English Literature, Trinity College, University of Toronto, Toronto, Ontario.

Editor of M. A. Grainger's *Woodsmen of the West* and John Buchan's *Prester John*.

MICHAEL S. TAIT. Formerly member of the Department of English, Ryerson Polytechnical Institute, Toronto, Ontario.

Author of articles on Canadian drama.

JAMES J. TALMAN and RUTH DAVIS TALMAN. James J. Talman is Chief Librarian and Professor of History, University of Western Ontario, London, Ontario.

Co-authors of *Western, 1878–1953* (London, Ont., 1953). James Talman: author of *Huron College, 1863–1963* (London, Ont., 1963); editor of *Loyalist Narratives from Upper Canada* (Toronto, 1946), and *Basic Documents in Canadian History* (Princeton, 1959); and author of numerous articles on Canadian history.

JAMES SUTHERLAND THOMSON. Dean of the Faculty of Divinity and Professor of Philosophy of Religion (retired), and now Lecturer in Philosophy and Divinity, McGill University, Montreal, Que.

Author of *The Hope of the Gospel* (The Alexander Robertson Lectures, University of Glasgow, London, 1955), *The Divine Mission* (Toronto, 1958), *God and His Purpose: The Meaning of Life* (Toronto, 1964).

ELIZABETH HILLMAN WATERSTON. Assistant Professor, Middlesex College, University of Western Ontario, London, Ontario.

Co-author of *Composition for Canadian Universities* (Toronto, 1964) and author of articles on Tennyson, pioneers in agriculture, and travel-books.

FRANK W. WATT. Professor of English, University College, University of Toronto, Toronto, Ontario.

Editor of "Letters in Canada" in the *University of Toronto Quarterly*; author of *Steinbeck* (Edinburgh and London, 1962) and of critical articles on Canadian literature and history.

KENNETH NEVILLE WINDSOR. Junior Fellow of Massey College and Lecturer in History at Trent University.

Author of the articles on "Religion" in the *Canadian Annual Review*.

Acknowledgments

ABELARD-SCHUMAN CANADA LIMITED, Toronto 3, for quotations from Daryl Hine's *The Carnal and the Crane* (1957) and *The Devil's Picture Book* (1960).
GEORGE ALLEN AND UNWIN LTD., London W.C.1, for a quotation from G. S. Brett's *History of Psychology* (1912–21), II, 6–7.
AMERICAN PSYCHOLOGICAL ASSOCIATION, Washington, D.C., for quotations from John A. Irving's "George Sidney Brett 1879–1944" in the *Psychological Review*, LIV (Jan. 1947), 52–58.
MISS MARGARET AVISON, Toronto, for a quotation from "Perspective," (*Poetry*, Chicago; and from *Poetry of Mid-Century 1940/1960*, ed. Milton Wilson, McClelland and Stewart, 1964).
G. BELL & SONS LTD., London W.C.2, for a quotation from G. S. Brett's *The Government of Man* (1913).
ERNEST BENN LIMITED, London E.C.4, for quotations from the *Collected Verse of Robert W. Service* (1930).
Professor EARLE BIRNEY, Vancouver, for quotations from *David and Other Poems* (Ryerson, 1942), *Now is Time* (Ryerson, 1945), *The Strait of Anian* (Ryerson, 1948), *Trial of a City and Other Verse* (Ryerson, 1952), and *Ice Cod Bell or Stone* (McClelland & Stewart, 1962).
THE BODLEY HEAD LTD., London W.C.2, for a quotation from Arthur Stringer's *Open Water* (1914).
Mrs. PAULINE CAMPBELL, London, Ontario, for her service as principal typist and secretary of the project and recorder of items in the Index.
The CANADA COUNCIL, Ottawa, for grants-in-aid of research to Fred Cogswell, David Galloway, F. E. Gattinger (assisting C. F. Klinck), V. G. Hopwood, Alec Lucas, Henry Pietersma (assisting John A. Irving), Gordon Roper, Michael Tait, Hugo McPherson (assisted by Miriam Lerenbaum and Douglas Spettigue), Desmond Pacey (assisted by John Ripley), Ross Beharriell, William M. Kilbourn, Frank Stiling (assisted by Donald Hair and succeeded by Brandon Conron), M. H. Scargill, A. Vibert Douglas, and Elizabeth H. Waterston.
CANADIAN HISTORICAL REVIEW (University of Toronto Press), for quotations from Donald Creighton's "Sir John Macdonald and Canadian Historians," *CHR*, XXIX (March 1948), 1–13; and from John A. Irving's "The Development of Philosophy in Central Canada from 1850 to 1900," *CHR*, XXI (Sept. 1950), 252–287.
CLARKE, IRWIN & COMPANY, Toronto 10, for a quotation from Douglas Le Pan's *The Net and the Sword* (1953).
Mr. LEONARD COHEN, Montreal 6, for quotations from *Let Us Compare Mythologies* (McGill Poetry Series, 1956) and *The Spice-Box of Earth* (McClelland & Stewart, 1961).
CORNELL UNIVERSITY PRESS, Cornell University, Ithaca, N.Y., for quotations from John A. Irving's "Philosophy" in *The Culture of Contemporary Canada* (1957), edited by Julian Park.
PETER DAVIES LTD., London W.C.1, for a quotation from Grey Owl's *Tales of an Empty Cabin* (1936).
J. M. DENT AND SONS (CANADA) LTD., Toronto, for quotations from Peter McArthur's *In Pastures Green* (1915), and from Samuel Wood's *Rambles of a Canadian Naturalist* (1916).
J. M. DENT AND SONS LTD., London W.C.2, for a quotation from Samuel Wood's *Rambles of a Canadian Naturalist* (1916).

ACKNOWLEDGMENTS

DODD, MEAD AND COMPANY, New York 16, for quotations from *The Complete Poems of Robert W. Service* (1940).

Mr. R. G. EVERSON, Montreal, for quotations from *Three Dozen Poems* (Cambridge Press, Montreal, 1957), and *A Lattice for Momos* (Contact Press, Montreal, 1958).

FABER AND FABER LIMITED, London W.C.1, for a quotation from Wilfred Watson's *Friday's Child* (1955).

FARRAR, STRAUS AND GIROUX, New York, for a quotation from Wilfred Watson's *Friday's Child* (1955).

Professor RALPH GUSTAFSON, Lennoxville, for a quotation from *The Golden Chalice* (Nicholson & Watson, London, 1935).

Dr. DONALD HAIR, University of Western Ontario, for research assistance to Brandon Conron.

HUMANITIES RESEARCH COUNCIL OF CANADA, for financial support and encouragement, especially to these officers of the Council: Dr. Roy Daniells, Dr. J. A. Gibson, Dr. J. R. Kidd, Dr. Maurice Lebel, Dr. Francis Leddy, Dr. John E. Robbins, Dr. G. O. Rothney, Dr. R. M. Wiles, the late Dr. A. S. P. Woodhouse.

Mrs. W. A. IRWIN (P. K. PAGE), Victoria, B.C., for quotations from *As Ten as Twenty* (Ryerson, 1946) and *The Metal and the Flower* (McClelland & Stewart, 1954).

CHIEF LIBRARIANS and their assistants in the following Libraries: the Public Archives, Ottawa; the Provincial Archives of British Columbia and Ontario; the Toronto Public Library; the Provincial Libraries of British Columbia and Manitoba; the university libraries of British Columbia, Dalhousie, McGill, New Brunswick (and Bonar Law–Bennett collection), Queen's, St. Michael's, Victoria (Toronto) and Western Ontario; the Glenbow Foundation in Calgary; the Divinity Library, McGill, and the University Library, Cambridge, England; the Hudson's Bay Company (microfilms); the National Library of Scotland; the British Museum.

McCLELLAND AND STEWART LIMITED, Toronto 16, for quotations from Alfred G. Bailey's *Border River* (1952); Earle Birney's *Ice Cod Bell or Stone* (1962); *Bliss Carman's Poems* (1922); Leonard Cohen's *The Spice-Box of Earth* (1961); A. W. Eaton's *Acadian Ballads and Lyrics* (1930); Robert Finch's *The Strength of the Hills* (1948); John Glassco's *The Deficit Made Flesh* (1958); Frederick Philip Grove's *The Turn of the Year* (1923); John A. Irving's "The Achievement of Thomas McCulloch" in *The Stepsure Letters*, New Canadian Library (1961); Irving Layton's *A Red Carpet for the Sun* (1959); P. K. Page's *The Metal and the Flower* (1954); *The Complete Poems of Marjorie Pickthall* (1936); Charles G. D. Roberts's *The Haunters of the Silences* (1905); *Poetry of Mid-Century 1940/1960* (1964), edited by Milton Wilson.

The estate of Mrs. HELEN J. MACKENZIE, Montreal, for a quotation from W. H. Blake's *Brown Waters* (Macmillan, Canada, 1925).

ROBERT MACLEHOSE & Co. Ltd., Glasgow W.3, for a quotation from John Watson's *The Interpretation of Religious Experience* (James Maclehose & Sons, 1912).

Mrs. ANNE MARRIOTT McLELLAN, North Vancouver, B.C., for a quotation from Anne Marriott's *Sandstone and Other Poems* (Ryerson, 1945).

THE MACMILLAN COMPANY OF CANADA LIMITED, Toronto 2, for quotations from Charles Bruce's *The Mulgrave Road* (1951); Donald Creighton's *Dominion of the North* (1944, 1957) and *The Story of Canada* (1959); Grey Owl's *The Men of the Last Frontier* (1932) and *Tales of an Empty Cabin* (1936); *The Collected Poems of E. J. Pratt* (1958); Frank Underhill's *In Search of Canadian Liberalism* (1960); Anne Wilkinson's *The Hangman Ties the Holly* (1955); W. H. Blake's *Brown Waters* (1915).

MIDDLESEX COLLEGE, former Principal Brandon Conron and Principal D. G. G. Kerr, for providing assistance to the General Editor.

THE MUSSON BOOK COMPANY LTD., Toronto 17, for quotations from Pauline Johnson's *Flint and Feather*.

THOMAS NELSON AND SONS (CANADA) LIMITED, Don Mills, Ontario, for a quotation from Ethelwyn Wetherald's *Lyrics and Sonnets* (1931).

Mr. ALDEN NOWLAN, Saint John, N.B., for a quotation from *Under the Ice* (Ryerson, Toronto, 1961).

ACKNOWLEDGMENTS 875

OXFORD UNIVERSITY PRESS, Don Mills, Ontario, for quotations from Robert Finch's *Poems* (1946); George Johnston's *The Cruising Auk* (1959); Jay Macpherson's *The Boatman* (1957).

Mr. RALEIGH PARKIN, for the use of the *William Lawson Grant Papers*.

Philosophy and Phenomenological Research (Professor M. Farber, editor), for quotations from John A. Irving's "Philosophical Trends in Canada between 1850 and 1950," *P & PR*, XII (Dec. 1951), 224–245.

PONTIFICAL INSTITUTE OF MEDIAEVAL STUDIES, Toronto, for information kindly supplied by the Very Rev. L. K. Shook and Professor Armand Maurer, C.S.B., and by Dr. L. E. M. Lynch, Professor of Philosophy, St. Michael's College, Toronto.

E. J. PRATT's estate, for quotations from *The Collected Poems of E. J. Pratt* (Macmillan, 1958).

Dr. JOHN D. RIPLEY, Dalhousie University, for research assistance to Desmond Pacey.

Professor MALCOLM ROSS, Trinity College, Toronto, for quotations from Thomas McCulloch's *The Stepsure Letters* (McClelland & Stewart, New Canadian Library, 1960).

ROUTLEDGE and KEGAN PAUL, Ltd., London E.C.4, for quotations from Margaret Avison's *Winter Sun* (1960).

THE RYERSON PRESS, Toronto 2B, for quotations from Patrick Anderson's *A Tent for April* (1945) and *The White Centre* (1946); Earle Birney's *Trial of a City and Other Verse* (1952); Louis Dudek's *East of the City* (1946); *The Poetical Works of Wilfred Campbell* (1923); Donald Creighton's *The Commercial Empire of the St. Lawrence* (1937); John A. Irving's "Philosophical Trends in Canada" in *Science and Values* (1952); *Selected Poems of Raymond Knister* (1949); *Selected Poems of Archibald Lampman* (1947); *Selected Poems of Sir Charles G. D. Roberts* (1955); *Selected Poems of Duncan Campbell Scott* (1951); *Complete Poems of Robert W. Service* (1940); *Complete Poems of Francis Sherman* (1935); Raymond Souster's *The Colour of the Times* (1964); Miriam Waddington's *The Second Silence* (1955) and *The Season's Lovers* (1958).

CHARLES SCRIBNER'S SONS, New York 17, for quotations from Rupert Brooke's *Letters from America* (1916); Grey Owl's *Tales of an Empty Cabin* (1936); Ernest Thompson Seton's *Wild Animals I Have Known* (1898).

SIDGWICK AND JACKSON LTD., London W.C.1, for a quotation from Rupert Brooke's *Letters from America* (1916).

The J. B. SMALLMAN RESEARCH FUND of the University of Western Ontario for a grant-in-aid of research for chapters 8 and 9, and to Dean Frank Stiling (now retired) for his assistance.

UNIVERSITY OF TORONTO, the President's Committee in Aid of Research, for assistance to Gordon Roper and others writing on "Fiction, 1880–1920."

UNIVERSITY OF TORONTO PRESS, for quotations from Margaret Avison's *Winter Sun* (1960); John A. Irving's *Philosophy in Canada: A Symposium* (1952); Chester Martin's *Foundations of Canadian Nationhood* (1955).

University of Toronto Quarterly (University of Toronto Press), for quotations from John A. Irving's "One Hundred Years of Canadian Philosophy," *UTQ*, XX (Jan. 1951), 107–23; and "The Achievement of George Sidney Brett," *UTQ*, XIV (July 1945), 329–65.

UNIVERSITY OF WESTERN ONTARIO, London, for secretarial assistance.

Sir BYRON EDMUND WALKER's estate, for permission to see his papers.

ANNE WILKINSON's estate, for a quotation from *The Hangman Ties the Holly* (Toronto, Macmillan, 1955).

Index

Abandoned Farmer, The (1901), 293
Abbott, Jacob, 632
Abbott, Joseph, 132
Abbott, Maude E., 454
Abelard, P., 566
Aberdeen, Countess of, 353, 361
Aberhart, William, 564, 602
Abram's Plains (1789), 85
Acadia Bulletin, 539
Acadian Exiles, The (1916), 244
Acadian Geology (1855), 450
Acadian Recorder, 93, 106, 221, 537
Acadiensis, 207
Acanthus and Wild Grape (1920), 725
Account of Six Years Residence in Hudson's Bay, An (1752), 24
Account of the Life and Writings of St. Irenaeus, An (1841), 435
Acis at Oxford (1961), 740
Acorn, Milton, 494, 816
Acrobats, The (1954), 713–14
Across My Path (1952), 541
Across the American Continent (1898), 354
Across the Canadian Prairies (1895), 354
Across the Prairie (1922), 600
Across Western Waves and Home (1898), 354
Across Wildest America (1905), 357
Actress' Daughter, The (1886), 111
Adair, E. R., 518
Adam, Graeme Mercer, 154, 161, 184–6, 194, 197, 202, 204, 206, 224, 295

Adam, Stevenson & Co., 185–6
Adamczewski, Zigmund, 596
Adams, Frank D., 452, 454
Adams, James, 73
Adams, Joseph, 357
Adams, Levi, 126–9, 131, 133, 137
Adams, S. M., 545
Adams, Samuel, 248
Adams, W. H., 574
Adamson, Rev. Agar, 371
Addison, Joseph, 18, 92, 131, 141
Address on the Present Condition . . . of British North America, An (1857), 100
Adrian, Brother (Henry Deneau), 157
Advent Sermon (1851), 535
Adventure of Life, The (1912), 560
Adventure of the North, An (1895), 296, 317
Adventures among Animals (1960), 368
Adventures among Birds (1959), 371
Adventures and Misadventures (1922), 600
Adventures in Error (1936), 615
Adventures of Billy Topsail, The (1906), 328, 631
Adventures of Detective Barney, The (1915), 312
Adventures of François, The (Mitchell), 281
Adventures of Jimmy Dale, Detective, The (1917), 312
Adventures of Jimmy Why, The (1953), 628
Adventures of Sajo and Her Beaver People, The

(1935), 376, 628
Adventures of the First Settlers on the Oregon or Columbia River (1848), 33
Adventures on the Columbia River (1832), 33
Advice to Young Men (1830), 80
Advocate, The (1865), 157
Aelfric, 548
Aeneid, 410
Aequinimitas (1904), 342
Aeschylus, 596
Aesop's Fables, 364
Afar in the Forest (1850), 370, 380
Affable Stranger, The (1920), 345
After Big Game in the Upper Yukon (1937), 372
After the Cataclysm (1909), 302, 303
Agassiz, Alexander, 449
Agnes Mailard (Herbert), 109
Agrarian Age: A Background for Wordsworth (1950), 547
Aikens, Carroll, 637, 653
Ainsworth, W. H., 281
Aitken, Hugh, 508
Akins, T. B., 236, 239, 572
Alabaster, William, 544
Alathea; or, The Roman Exile (1840), 110
Albani, Madame, 281
Albert of Cologne, 364
Albert Einstein (1950), 455
Alberta Folklore Quarterly, 166
Albertus Magnus, 581, 591
Alcott, Louisa M., 632
Aleta Dey (1919), 262, 298, 307, 311
Alexander, Henry, 543

878 INDEX

Alexander, James Lynne, 140
Alexander, W. H., 543
Alexander, W. J., 534
Alexander, Sir William, 15, 17
Alfalo, F. N., 362
Alfred North Whitehead: The Interpretation of Science (1961), 588
Algazel's Metaphysics (1933), 592
Alger, Horatio, 310, 354
Algie, James, 306, 312
al-Ghazali, 571
Algonquin Maiden (1887), 295
Alice of Old Vincennes (Thompson), 281
All about Canada (1883), 351
All the Trumpets Sounded (1942), 662
Allan, Lt. Adam, 80
Allan, Andrew, 491, 634, 650, 655
Allan, Luke; see Amy, William Lacey
Allan, Martha, 639, 653
Allan, Peter John, 109, 114, 122
Allan, Ted; see Herman, Alan
Allan Gray and His Doubts (1881), 116
Allen, Egbert, 368
Allen, Frank, 452, 454
Allen, Grant, 280, 313–14, 369, 453
Allen, John S., 119
Allen, Ralph, 707, 716
Alline, Henry, 59, 68, 73, 74–7, 81, 106, 551, 552, 555
Allison, David, 434
Allison, W. T., 611
Alloway, Mary, 287
All's Well That Ends Well, 657
Alphabet, 494, 817
Alphonse, the Bearded One (1954), 631
Alsop, Richard, 50
Alton Locke, 279
Ambush (1920), 660
America and the Americans (1892), 354

American Adam, The, 511
American Girl in London, An (1891), 309, 315
American Journey (1943), 605
American Notes (Dickens), 348
American War (Cockings), 73
Americans at Home, The; or, Byeways, Backwoods, and Prairies (1854), 101
Amid Masters of Twentieth Century Medicine (1958), 455
Amishman (1912), 305
Among the Forest Trees (1888), 378
Among the Laurentians (1885), 372
Among the Millet (1888), 389
Amusements of a Mission (1818), 82
Amy, William Lacey, 299, 312, 337, 659, 660
Anacreon, 206
Anatole France, the Parisian (1927), 593
Anatomy of Criticism (1957), 540
Anciens Canadiens, Les (de Gaspé), 286
And All Your Beauty (1948), 605
And the People Cheered (1940), 604
Anderson, Clara Rothwell, 668
Anderson, Fulton H., 586–7, 593
Anderson, Patrick, 489, 490, 767, 769, 771–3, 781, 785
Anderson, Sherwood, 312, 675, 689, 695–6, 702, 712, 781, 800
Andrew, F. W., 381
Andrews, C. M., 246
Andrews, E., 570, 571
Aneroestes the Gaul (1898), 308
Angled Road, The (1952), 716
Angler's Book of Canadian Fishes, The (1959), 372
Anglican Episcopate of Canada, The (Kelly and Rogers, 1928), 572
Anglican Episcopate of Canada and Newfoundland, The (Rowley, 1928), 572
Anglican Reformation, The (1897), 249, 562
Anglin, Margaret, 651
Anglo-American Magazine (Toronto), 143, 150, 182–3, 216, 451
"Anglo-Canadian," 348
Anglo-Saxon Poetry (1927), 547
Angus, H. A., 526
Animal Heroes (1905), 382, 453
Animals of North America, The (1864), 448
Animals of the Canadian Rockies, The (1935), 369
Annals of the Court of Oberon (1895), 429
Annals of the Parish (1821), 141, 282
Anne of Avonlea (1909), 626
Anne of Green Gables (1908), 331, 626, 632, 840
Annette the Métis Spy (1886), 298
Anscombe, E., 595
Anspach, Lewis Amadeus, 69–70
Anstensen, A., 542
Answers to "Essays and Reviews" (1862), 555
Antennae (1926), 659
Anthology of Canadian Poetry (Gustafson, 1942), 491, 765
Anti-Traditionalist, The (1783), 552
Antlered Kings, The (1884), 368
Antoinette de Mirecourt (1864), 127, 157–8
Antony and Cleopatra, 8
Apostolic Age (1958), 568
Apples of the Moon (1933), 668
Applied Philosophy (1950), 594
Appraisals of Canadian Literature (1926), 484, 536
Apprenticeship of Duddy Kravitz, The (1959), 714–15

INDEX

Aquinas, St. Thomas, 566, 581, 590–2, 595
Arbiter of Elegance (1954), 546
Arcadian Adventures with the Idle Rich (1914), 334, 335, 466
Archaeology and Prehistoric Annals of Scotland, The (1851), 154, 248
Archaia; or, Studies of the Cosmogony and Natural History of the Hebrew Scriptures (1860), 450, 554
Archibald, Alexander Kent, 106, 117
Archibald, Edith J., 668
Archibald Lampman (1929), 485
Architects of Modern Thought (CBC series), 587
Architectural Requirements of Christian Worship, The (1958), 569
Architecture of the Heavens, The (1864), 450, 554–5
Arctic Bride, 616
Arctic Exploration: The Second Grinnell Expedition (1857), 39
Arctic Prairie (1911), 382
Ardagh, Alice Maud, 293
Ardent Exile (1951), 506
Are Canadians Really? (1954), 606
Argall, Samuel, 57
Argimon; a Legend of the Micmac (1847), 110
Argument of Plato, The (1934), 586
Argyll, Duke of; *see* Lorne, Marquis of
Aristotle, 438, 576, 577, 580, 591, 592, 595
Arliss, George, 651
Armbrest, Duncan, 369
Armitage, W. J., 563
Armour, Agatha, 110, 291
Armour, Leslie, 596
Armour & Ramsay, 180–81
Armstrong, Alexander, 38
Armstrong, M. W., 572
Armstrong, Nevill, 372
Arnold, Gertrude, 311
Arnold, Matthew, 118, **147**, 160, 161, 204, 206, 389, 392, 394, 398, 399, 410, 417, 423, 427, 452, 460, 490, 541, 643, 727, 740
Arnold, Thomas, 427
Around Home (1925), 344, 375
Around the Campfire (1896), 371, 625
Art of the Possible, The: Government and Foreign Policy in Canada (1961), 510, **526**
Arthur, T. S., 279, 280
Arthur Stanley Eddington (1956), 454
Artificial Bastard, The [Richard Savage] (1953), **547**
Artist at War, 616
Artist, Thinker, and Saint (1936), 565
Arts and Letters Club (Toronto), 653, 671
Arts in Canada, The (1958), 495
As for Me and My House (1941), 705–6, 839
As It was in the Fifties (1895), 300
As Ten As Twenty (1946), 770
As Told to His Grace, and Other Stories (1891), 288
Ascent of Life, The (1961), 455, 587
Asher, Isadore, 312
Ashes of Murder (1935), 659
Ashley, W. J., 242, 520
Ashton, Harry, 549
Askin, Col. John, 138
Astor, Jacob, 33, 34
Astoria, 32, 131
At Minas Basin (1897), 429
At My Heart's Core (1950), 641–3
At the Dark of the Moon (1956), 628
At the Gates of the Righteous (1949), 641–2
Athenaeum, 426, 448
Athenaeum Club (Montreal), 157
Athenian Tribute Lists, The (1938–53), 543
Atkin, Grace Murray, 659
Atkinson, W. Christopher, 211
Atlantic Monthly, 266, 268, 276, 288, 451, 484, 669, 670, 720
Atonement, The (1911), 554
Attaché, The; or, Sam Slick in England (1843), 97, 99, 280, 308
Attempt to Form a System of the Creation of our Globe . . . (1836), 448
Attic Guest, The (1909), 329
Aubertin, J. J., 350
Auchinleck, Gilbert, 151, 216
Auden, W. H., 489, 646, 741, 770, 784, 786, 812
Augustine, St., 193, 495, 580, 590–2
Auld Eppie's Tales (McCulloch), 93
Austen, Jane, 258
Austin, Benjamin F., 308, 312
Austin, J. L., 596
Authentic Letters from Upper Canada (1833), 253, 255, 371
Autobiography (Cooney), 211; (Galt), 617
Autumn Holiday in the U.S. and Canada, An (1887), 349–50
Autumn Tour, An (1901), 358
Avicenna, 571, 595
Avicenna's De Anima (1959), 571
Avison, Margaret, 494, 769, 787, 808–11, 844
Avray, Baron d', 205
Ayer, A. J., 597
Ayre, Robert, 378, 752
Ayrshire Legatees, The (Galt), 99, 141
Ayscough, Florence, 659, 726
Aytoun, W. E., 203

Babbitt, Irving, 538
Babes of the Wild (1912), 386, 625
Babin, A. Eugene, 595
Bach, J. S., 206
Back, Capt. George, 37, **167**

880 INDEX

Back in the Fifties: or, Winnings and Weedings (1907), 305
Backslider, The: A Descriptive Moral Poem (1815), 82
Backwoods of Canada, The (1836), 143, 144, 367, 368
Backwoods Princess, A (1926), 379
Backwoodsmen, The (1909), 384, 385
Bacon, Sir Francis, 4, 16, 365, 586–7, 589
Bacon, Roger, 364
Bad Man's Sweetheart, A (1889), 294, 307, 312
Baffin, William, 16
Bagnani, Gilbert, 518, 546
Bail Jumper, The (1914), 299
Bailey, A. G., 204, 494, 757–9, 785, 826, 840
Bailey, Jacob, 60, 78
Bailey, Joseph Whitman, 454
Bailey, L. W., 454
Baillie, John, 556, 560
Bain, George, 357
Bain, James, 237
Baird, Mrs. C. A., 307
Baird, Frank, 288, 672
Baird, Irene, 472, 488, 687–8
Baker, Olaf, 628
Baker, R. P., 484, 536
Baker, W. C., 452
Bakounin (Bakunin), M. A., 458
Baldoon (1899), 293
Baldwin, Augusta, 182
Baldwin, Harold, 603
Baldwin, Robert, 499, 505
Baldwin, Dr. William W., 499
Baldwin, Lafontaine, Hincks (Leacock), 228, 231
Ballad Poetry of Ireland, The (1845), 156
Ballads and Sea Songs of Newfoundland (1933),172
Ballads and Songs (1965), 172
Ballantyne, Robert Michael, 159, 167, 237, 285, 296, 298, 317, 625
Balls for a One-Armed Juggler (1963), 816

Ballstadt, Carl, 133, 149
Balm (1926), 634
Balzac, Honoré de, 276
Banished Briton and Neptunian, The (1843), 140
Bannertail (1922), 382
Baptist History (Cramp, 1868), 552
Baptiste Larocque (1923), 165, 674
Baptists of Canada, The (1911), 572
Baptists of the Maritime Provinces, 1753–1946 (1946), 572
Barbara Heck (1895), 295, 305
Barbara Ladd (1902), 322, 405
Barbeau, Marius, 165–7, 169, 378, 527, 629
Barber, Clarence, 523
Barker, A. E., 546
Barker, A. F., 598
Barkley, Capt. Charles, 47
Barkley, Mrs. Frances Hornby, 47
Barley and the Stream, The (1955), 507
Barnard, Leslie Gordon, 663, 674, 675
Barnes, Keith, 371
Barometer Rising (1941), 700
Barr, Robert, 261–3, 268, 270, 276, 279, 294–5, 302, 313 ,
Barrett, R. J., 356
Barriers Burned Away, 278
Barrington, E., see Beck, L. A.
Barrymore, John, 651
Barth, Karl, 562
Bartlett, William, 78
Basket, The (Jacob), 638
Basterfield, S., 452
Bates, E. Catherine, 350
Bates, Ronald, 494, 816
Bates, Walter, 110
Bathurst Courier, 152
Battle of the Nile, The: A Poem in Four Cantos (1844), 116
Battle of the Strong, The (1898), 308, 318
Battle of Wits, A (1956), 644

Baudelaire, P., 812, 813
Baxter, Beverley, 309, 311
Bay of the North (1950), 630
Bayley, C. C., 518
Bayley, Cornwall, 86
Bayley, Mrs. H., 624–25
Baylis, Samuel Mathewson, 295, 372
B.C. (Herring, 1903), 358
B.C. 1887 (Lees and Clutterbuck, 1888), 350
Beach, E. F., 523
Beach, Rex, 283, 298
Beach of Strangers, A (1961), 646–7
Beaglehole, J. C., 45
Bealby, J. T., 257, 357
Beard, Charles, 500
Beardsley, Aubrey, 813
Beare, F. W., 570, 571
Beattie, Jessie L., 668, 669
Beattie, Munro, 833, 834, 844, 846, 848
Beaubien, I., 569
Beaugrand, Honoré, 289
Beauport Road (1928), 674
Beaupré, Jean, 795
Beautiful Canada (1925), 599
Beautiful Joe (1894), 307, 320, 380, 381, 627, 628
Beautiful Rebel, A (1909), 295, 304
Beaven, James, 435
Beck, J. Murray, 524
Beck, Lily Adams, 479, 659, 660, 661, 666
Beckett, Samuel, 540
Beckwith, John, 648
Beckwith, Julia Catherine; see Hart, Mrs. G. H.
Bedford-Jones, H. J. O., 661
Bee, The (Pictou), 178
Beech Woods, The (1916), 369
Beechey, F. W., 36
Beer, G. L., 246
Begg, Alexander, 223, 297
Beggars All (1891), 319
Beginning of the Promise, The (1960), 570
Behind the Beyond (1913), 334
Behind the Log (1947), 747
Behn, Aphra, 529
Being and Some Philosophers

INDEX 881

(1948), 590
Belaney, Archibald Stansfeld, 368, 376, 377, 628, 840
Belgravia (Magazine), 265
Bell, Alexander Graham, 455
Bell, Andrew, 248, 542
Bell, Frederick McKelvey, 290, 311
Bella Coola Indians, The (1948), 527
Bellamy, Edward, 279, 284, 305, 460–5 *passim*, 833
Belford Brothers (publishers), 267; *see also, Rose-Belford's Canadian Monthly*
Belinda (1843), 150
Bellan, R. C., 523
Bellefeuille, E. L. de, 158
Bells, The (Irving), 639
Bells on Finland Street, The (1950), 631
Bellot, Joseph René, 38–9
Beloved Traitor (1915), 312
Belshaw, Cyril, 527
Ben Hur, 279, 281
Bengough, J. W., 187
Bennett, Arnold, 602, 675
Bennett, Ethel Hume, 487
Bennett, R. B., 485, 734
Benson, Nathaniel A., 487
Bentley, Richard (publisher), 109
Benton of the Royal Mounted (1920), 298
Beppo, 127
Beresford, William, 47
Bergen Worth (1901), 306, 312
Bergson, Henri, 587
Bering, Vitus, 42, 204
Berkeley, George, 442, 584
Berkes, N., 571
Bernadotte, Marshal, 28
Bernard, Sylvia, 494
Berners, Dame Juliana, 365
Bernhardt, Sara, 651
Berrill, N. J., 452, 454
Berrill, Mrs. N. J., 370
Berry, C. B., 349
Berry, E. G., 545
Berry, Herbert, 544
Bert Lloyd's Boyhood (1892), 291
Berton, Pierre, 506, 606, 611, 630, 631, 719

Beside a Norman Tower (1934), 672
Bessborough, Earl of, 654
Bessinger, J. B., 543
Best, George, 7–8
Best of Gregory Clark, The (1959), 611
Best One Thing, The (1926), 668
Beth Woodburn (1897), 294, 304, 310
Betts, C. L., 290, 304
Between Earth and Sky and Other Strange Stories of Deliverance (1897), 322
Beulah (Evans), 278
Bewick, Thomas, 366
Beynon, Frances, 262, 276, 298, 307, 311
Bias of Communication, The (1951), 521, 597, 829
Bible and Christian Education, The (1959), 570
Bible in Canada (1953), 574
Biblical Criticism and Modern Thought (1909), 557
Biblical Expositor (1882–5), 554
Bibliography (Kingsford), 236
Bibliography of Canadian Imprints, 1751–1800 (1952), 175
Bibliotheca Canadensis (1887), 154, 208, 534
Bice, Clare, 631
Bickersteth, J. B., 362
Bicknell, M. E., 641
Bidwell, Barnabas, 87
Big Timber (1916), 300, 332
Biggar, H. P., 238
Bigsby, John J., 31, 167, 254
Bilir, Kim; *see* Scaife, A. H.
Billings, Elkanah, 153
Billings, Josh, 335
Billy Budd, 716
Billy Topsail and Co. (1910), 291, 631
Bilton, Lance, 306
Bindloss, Harold, 299, 302
Binnie-Clark, Georgina, 361
Biography of an Arctic Fox, The (1937), 382
Biography of a Grizzly, The (1900), 382, 453

Biography of a Silver Fox, The (1909), 382
Birch-Bark Roll (1902), 371
Bird, Will R., 696, 697, 720
Bird-Nesting in North-West Canada (1892), 371
Bird Portraits (1901), 382
Bird Store Man, The (1914), 328
Birds and Animals of the Rockies (1946), 369
Birds of Peasemarsh (1919), 371
Birney, Earle, 18, 51, 123, 258, 470, 472, 491, 494, 655, 707, 716, 761–5, 766, 773, 785, 787, 816, 846, 847
Birth and Development of the Geological Sciences (1938), 454
Bishop, Leslie, 673
Bishop Laval (de Brumath), 228, 229
Bissell, Claude, 160, 536, 650, 698
Bits about America (1887), 349
Bitter Honey (1935), 673
Bjarni (1956), 795
Black, Mrs. George, 617
Black, Samuel, 34
Black Beauty, 320, 366, 627–8
Black Canyon, The (1927), 663
Black Creek Stopping-House, The (1912), 297, 331
Black Gold (1924), 659
Black Huntsmen (1951), 782
Black Lace (1938), 667
Black Opal (Amy), 659
Black Rock (1898), 270, 280, 298, 300, 304, 322–3, 329
Black Vic: The Story of a Boy and his Pony (1949), 381
Blackburn, Kathleen, 262, 293
Blackwood (publisher), 46, 93, 180
Blackwood's Edinburgh Magazine, 132, 136, 142, 151, 168, 265
Bladen, V. W., 523

Blake, Cameron, **673**
Blake, Edward, **516**
Blake, William, 149, 540, 548, 787, 789
Blake, William Hume, 345–6, 373–4, 613, 615
Blakes and Flanagans, The (1855), 157
Blanchard, H. P., 302, 303
Bland, Salem G., 563
Blanket-Stiff (1911), 362
Blasted Pine, The (1960), 817
Bleak House, 279
Blennerhasset, Harman, 135
Blennerhasset, Mrs. Margaret, 133, 135
Blessed Damozel, The, 410
Blessington, Lady, 110
Blewett, G. J., **558**
Blewett, Jean, 311
Bligh, Capt., 49
Bliss, William Blowers, 104
Bliss Carman (1924), 485
Bliss Carman and the Literary Currents and Influences of His Time (1930), 487, 537
Blishen, R. B., **528**
Blissett, William, **532, 541, 546–7, 588**
Blood Lilies, The (1903), 296, 324
Bloomfield, L., 164
Bloomsbury Group, The (1954), 547
Blower of Bubbles, The (1919), 311
Blue Homespun (1924), 726
Blue Pete: Half Breed (1921), 660
Blue Pitcher, The (1926), 638
Blue Propeller, The (1955), 782
Blue Water (1907), 291
Blue Wolf, The: A Tale of the Cyprus Hills (1913), 299
Bluenose Ghosts (1957), 166
Blume, Helmut, 172
Blundell, J. L., 387
Blunt, J. H., **577**
Boatman, The (1957), **788**
Boam, H. J., 362
Boaz, Franz, 164
Bobcaygeon: A Sketch of a Little Town (1919), **726**
Boddy, A. A., 355
Bodsworth, Fred, 379, **387**
Body and Soul (1956), **571,** 588
Boeschenstein, Hermann, **548**
Boethius, 592
Bogg, Helen, 303
Boggs, Jean, **518**
Bogle Corbet (1831), 142, 617
Boit, John, 49
Bohemians of the Latin Quarter (1948, 1851), 281
Bohn, Eric; see Price-Brown, John
Bok, Edward, 268
Bolton, H. E., 43
Bonaventure, St., 591
Bond, J., 354
Bond Triumphant, The (1923), 663
Bone Spoon, The (1930), 638
Bonheur d'occasion; see, *Tin Flute, The*
Bonhomme: French-Canadian Stories and Sketches (1899), 262, 289
Bonnycastle, Sir Richard Henry, 70, 254
Book for the Young (1856), 109
Book of Canadian Animals, A (1962), 370
Book of Canadian Poetry (1943, 1948), 6, 490, 494, 537, 538, 765, 769, 837
Book of Canadian Prose and Verse (1923), 484
Book of Canadian Stories (1947), 491, 494, 720
Book of Small (1942), 622
Book of the West (1925), 599
Book of Woodcraft (1912), 371
Bookman (London), 726
Books and Notions, 184, 187
Boorman (travel writer), **604**
Booth, Edwin, 651
Borden, Sir Robert, 236, 477
Border River **(1952), 757, 758**
Born with a Golden Spoon (1899), 318
Bosanquet, Bernard, 578, 593–4
Bosanquet, Mary, 605
Boss of Wind River (1911), 660
Boston Literary World, 285
Boswell, James, 543
Bottomley, Kate, 303
Bouchette, Joseph, 128, 208, 209
Boulton, D'Arcy, 90–1
Bourassa, Henri, 192
Bourgeois de la Compagnie du Nord-Ouest (1889), 29
Bourinot, Arthur, 727
Bourinot, J. G., 196, 217, 219, 228, 242, 250, 260, 271, 313
Bourke, Vernon J., **593**
Bovell, James, 153, 449, 553
B.O.W.C., The: A Book for Boys (1869), 112
Bowering, George, 494
Bowman, Ariel, 135, 176
Bowman, Louise Morey, 726
Boy I Left Behind Me, The (1946), 621
Boy in the House (1952), 672
Boy Tramps, The (1896), 630
Boy Who Ran Away (1954), 629
Boyd, William Clauser, 454
Boyle, Harry, 634, **655**
Boys of Grand Pré School, The (1870), 112
Braddon, Miss, 278
Bradford, William, 55
Bradley, A. G., 228, 357
Bradley, F. H., **578**
Bradley, Mrs. Mary, 74, 81
Brady, Alexander, **524**
Brae Manor Theatre, 654
Brain's the Target, The (1960), 816
Brave Hearts (1904), 324, 381
Breadwinners, The (Hay), 279
Bready, J. Wesley, **564**
Brébeuf, Father Jean de, 21, 168, 747, 846
Brébeuf and His Brethren (1940), 21, 747–8
Brebner, J. B., 26, 61, 497, 510, 531

INDEX

Brecher, Irving, 522
Brendan, Father, 43
Brett, G. S., 452, 534, 576–86, 587–93 *passim*, 829
Brewster, Sir David, 449
Brewster, Elizabeth, 494, 800
Bride of Quietness (1933), 668
Bridle, Augustus, 684
Brief Account, A (Rolph, 1836), 141
Brief History of the Mennonites in Ontario, A (1935), 573
Brief View of the Religious Tenets and Sentiments... in... Two Mites (1784), 551
Brief View of the Scriptural Authority and Historical Evidence for Infant Baptism (1837), 552
Briefe Discourse of the New-found-land (1620), 13, 14
Brieger, Peter, 518
Briggs, George, 357
Briggs, Henry, 16
Briggs, William (publisher), 186–7, 188, 270, 303, 723, 832
Britannia, a Poem, 131
Britanno-Roman Inscriptions (1863), 248, 535
British America (1832), 212
British American Journal, 150, 451
British American Magazine, 154, 224
British American Review, 185
British Association in Canada, The (1885), 351
British Association's Visit to Montreal, The (1885), 351
British Canadian Review, 185
British Columbia (1959), 509
British Columbia Archives, 49
British Commonwealth, The (1956), 516
British Dominions in North America, The (1831), 209

Britnell, G. E., 522
Brittain, Harry, 357
Broadus, E. H., 484
Broadus, E. K., 484, 609, 614
Brock, General Isaac, 137, 138, 170, 196
Brock (1912), 629
Brock Family, The (1890), 297, 304
Broken Journey, A (1932), 690
Brontë, Charlotte, 277
Brontë, Emily, 406, 408
Brook Watson of Beauséjour (1957), 629
Brooke, Frances, 64, 84–5, 126, 131, 150, 157, 309, 830
Brooke, James Ten, 596
Brooke, Rev. John, 84
Brooke, Rupert, 348, 359, 363, 723, 783, 826
Brooker, Bertram, 683
Brother Blackfoot (1937), 631
Brother Eskimo (1921), 631
Brothers in Arms (Denison), 635, 636
Brothers in Peril (1905), 288
Brown, A. J., 573
Brown, Audrey Alexandra, 751–2
Brown, E. K., 395, 490, 491, 536, 538, 541, 546, 752, 753, 768
Brown, George, 153, 505
Brown, George W., 508
Brown, J. B., 254
Brown, John Henry, 461
Brown, Margaret, 262, 303
Brown of the Globe (Careless), 152, 505
Brown Paws and Green Thumbs (1961), 381
Brown Waters (1915), 345, 373, 374
Browne, Sir Thomas, 342, 343, 546
Browning, Robert, 204, 206, 393, 440, 544, 547, 723, 784, 832
Bruce, Charles, 756, 757, 785
Bruce, Luella, 674
Bruce Beckons, The (1952), 369

Bruce County Historical Society, 239
Bruchési, Jean, 606
Brumath, Leblond de, 228
Brunet, Michel, 510
Brunner, Emil, 562
Bryant, William Cullen, 129, 206, 423
Bryce, George, 218–19, 228, 240–41, 349
Bryce, Hugh, 349, 354
Bryden, W. W., 562
Brymner, Douglas, 236
Bubbles from the Deep (1873), 119
Bubbles of Canada, The (1839), 100
Bubbles We Buy (1903), 290, 327
Buchan, John, 696
Buchanan, M. A., 542
Buck, Tim, 468–9, 602
Bucke, R. Maurice, 832
Buckingham, William, 229
Buckler, Ernest, 494, 705, 711–12, 839
Buckley, Helen, 523
Buckley, Kenneth, 523
Budden, Alfred, 467
Bugles in the Hills (1955), 630
Buitenhuis, Peter, 548
Bujila, Bernadine, 545
Bulfinch, Thomas, 787
Bulkeley, Peter, 55
Bull, William Perkins, 453, 572
Bull Calf and Other Poems, The (1956), 782
Bulldog Carney (1919), 299, 324
Buller, A. H. Reginald, 452
Bullock, W., 574
Bullock-Webster, L., 639
Bulwer-Lytton, E. G. E., 277, 281
Bureau of Archives (Ont.), 236
Burgess, Thornton W., 380
Burgin, G. B., 292
Burham, John, 287
Burke, Edmund, 95, 71, 156, 499, 552, 829
Burkholder, L. J., 573
Burkholder, Mabel, 302, 378
Burlap Bags (Peterson), 650
Burned Bridges (1919), 311, 332

Burnet, Jean, 528
Burney, Fanny, 544
Burnford, Sheila, 381, 628
Burnham, John, 296
Burns, Robert, 98, 107, 117, 118, 151, 156, 395, 446
Burnt Offering, The (1909), 303, 316
Burpee, Lawrence J., 224, 357, 358
Burr, Aaron, 135
Burrell, Sergeant, 59
Burroughs, John, 283, 369 382
Burt, A. L., 298, 501, 509
Burton, Jean, 480
Burwash, Nathanael, 228, 232, 556
Burwell, Adam Hood, 132, 136, 139
Burwell, Mahlon, 139
Busbridge, E. G., 362
Buschlen, J. P., 305
Bush, Douglas, 480, 609, 835
Butchart, R., 573
Butler, Gen. William Francis, 298
Butler, Samuel, 704, 733
Butterfield, Herbert, 4
Butterworth, H., 350
Button, Sir Thomas, 16
By Canadian Streams (1909), 358
By Jumping Cat Bridge (1956), 375
By Moonstone Creek (1949), 375
By Ocean Prairie and Peak (1896), 355
By Stubborn Stars and Other Poems (1938), 755
By the Marshes of Minas (1900), 322
By the Queen's Grace (1904), 307
By Track and Trail (1891), 355
Byles, Mather, Jr., 78
Bylot, Robert, 16
Byrne, Mrs. Alfred, 591
Byron, Lord, 107, 108, 117, 122, 124–32 *passim*, 137, 148, 417, 423, 540
Bystander, The, 162, 207, 224

C., W.P., 149–50
Cabbagetown (1951), 707
Cabbala, The, 717, 736
Cable, George Washington, 282
Cabot, John, 5, 6, 10, 19
Cabot, S., 5, 6
Cache Lake Country (1947), 376
Caird, Edward, 438
Caird, G. B., 568, 571
Caird, John, 438
Cairns, John, 518
Calderwood, Henry, 436
Caldwell, William, 595
Calgary Eye-Opener, 166
Caliban: The Missing Link (1873), 154, 160, 161, 540
California and Alaska and over the Canadian Pacific Railway (1891), 354
Call, Frank Oliver, 725–6
Call My People Home (1950), 741
Call of the Cougar (1941), 380
Call of the East, A Romance of Far Formosa (1914), 307
Callaghan, Morley, 471, 472, 486, 488, 491, 634, 655, 658, 666, 674, 675, 684, 686, 688–93, 694, 702, 703, 711, 720, 721, 722, 833, 837, 841
Calling Adventurers (1941), 760
Calogero, G., 595
Calvinism: The Doctrine of the Scriptures (1849), 433, 552
Cameron, George Frederick, 428
Cameron, John Alexander, 290
Cameron, Margaret, 549
Cameron, T. W. M., 455
Cameron Matthews English Players, 652
Cameron of Lochiel (1905), 286
Camerons of Bruce, The (1906), 292, 296
Camp and Barrack-Room; or, The British Army as it is (1846), 215

Camp and Lamp (1897), 295, 372
Campbell, Sir Archibald, 114
Campbell, Arthur, 276
Campbell, Duncan, 222
Campbell, Grace, 697
Campbell, James, & Son, 183
Campbell, John, 257–8
Campbell, Marjorie W., 507, 630
Campbell, Robert, 561
Campbell, Wilfred, 67, 130, 131, 139, 158, 160, 161, 240, 295, 304, 357, 359, 422–4, 425, 426, 485, 535, 753
Campbell of the Mounties, 660
Canaan and Canada (1904), 358
Canada: "Anglo-Canadian" (1882), 348; J. T. Bealby (1909), 357; John G. Bourinot (1897), 219; A. Brady (1932), 524; J. Bruchési (1952), 606; Wilfred Campbell (1907), 357, 359; "Captain Mac" (1882), 350; Lady Tweedsmuir (1941), 605; A. Siegfried (1937), 528
Canada: An Encyclopaedia of the Country (1897–1900), 208, 219, 227
Canada, Le: les deux races (1906), 243
Canada: New World Power (1945), 605
Canada: A Social and Political History (McInnis, 1947), 504
Canada: A Study of Cool Continental Environments (1947), 605
Canada: or, The Western Land of Promise (1902), 358
Canada, a Descriptive Poem (1806), 86
Canada, an American Nation (Dafoe, 1935), 527
Canada, Coast to Coast (1955), 606

Canada, Impressions of a Tour (1912), 362
Canada, Land of Opportunities (1959), 606
Canada, the Empire of the North (1909), 224
Canada, the Golden Hinge (1952), 606
Canada, the Great River, the Land and the Men (1927), 599
Canada, the Land of Hope (1910), 362
Canada, the Land of Opportunities (1919), 362
Canada, the New Nation (1906), 357
Canada, Tomorrow's Giant (1957), 607
Canada and Her Northern Neighbours (1946), 605
Canada and its Capital (1898), 353
Canada and its Provinces (1914–17), 226, 244, 245, 260
Canada and the American Revolution (1935), 236
Canada and the British Army 1846–71 (1938), 509
Canada and the British Immigrant (1914), 362
Canada and the Canadian Question (1891), 234
Canada and the Canadians in 1846 (1846), 254
Canada and the United Nations (1956), 526
Canada as a Career (1927), 600
Canada as it is: Stewart (1910), 362; Fraser (1911), 363
Canada Bookseller, 185
Canada Council, 493, 494, 495, 531
Canada First (1890), 160
Canada for Gentlemen (1885), 349
Canada from Ocean to Ocean (1899), 353
Canada in the 20th Century (1903), 357
Canada Looks Abroad (1938), 526

Canada Made Me (1958), 607, 608, 622
Canada of Today (1910), 363
Canada Revisited 1879–1893 (1893), 355
Canada Ride (1944), 605
Canada's Century (1951), 606
Canada's Century: Progress and Resources of the Great Dominion (1907), 356
Canada's Soldiers (1954), 509
Canada's Story in Song (1960), 172
Canada There and Back (1908), 357
Canada Today (1906), 356
Canada Votes (1962), 525
Canada West (1930), 603
Canada West and Farther West (1911), 362
Canada-West Magazine (Winnipeg), 207
Canadian Accent (1947), 491, 765
Canadian Airs, 167
Canadian-American Relations series, 526
Canadian Annual Review: ed. Hopkins, 468, 661; ed. Saywell, 510
Canadian Anthology, ed. Klinck and Watters (1955), 494
Canadian Anthology: Poems from "The Fiddlehead," 817
Canadian Archaeology, an Essay (1886), 226
Canadian Authors' Association, 481, 482, 484, 486, 489, 638, 653, 671, 724, 731, 732–3, 742, 752
Canadian Ballads (1858), 156
Canadian Bookman, The, 479–84, 661, 670, 724, 725
Canadian Broadcasting Corporation, 487, 491, 495, 502, 531, 650, 655, 656, 721, 757, 761, 784
Canadian Brothers, The; or,

The Prophecy Fulfilled (1840), 137, 138, 181
Canadian Bureaucracy, The (1949), 524
Canadian Camp Life (1900), 358
Canadian Cities of Romance (1928), 600
Canadian Crusoes (1852), 624
Canadian Dictionary, The, 543
Canadian Dualism (1960), 528
Canadian Economic History (1956), 507
Canadian Economic Thought (1961), 523
Canadian Economy in the Great Depression, The (1959), 522
Canadian Fairy Tales (1922), 165, 628
Canadian Family Robinson, The (1935), 673
Canadian Folk-Life and Folk-Lore (1897), 165
Canadian Folk Songs Old and New (1928), 169
Canadian Forum, 6, 199, 451, 468, 469, 470, 471, 479–80, 482, 484, 486, 489, 493, 509, 530, 534, 536, 537, 538, 540, 609, 664, 665, 674, 680, 724, 730, 734, 735, 736, 738, 743, 745, 751, 752, 753, 754, 761, 766, 795, 816
Canadian Frontiers of Settlement (9 vols.), 522
Canadian Gazette, 350
Canadian General Election of 1957, The (1962), 525
Canadian Government and Politics (1944), 525
Canadian Government series, 510
Canadian Historical Association, 516, 517, 519
Canadian Historical Review, 140, 229, 243, 250, 479, 480–1, 498, 503, 505, 508, 510, 519, 536
Canadian Homes; or, The Mystery Solved (1858), 182

Canadian Idylls (1881), **158**
Canadian Identity, The (1961), 502, 503, 526
Canadian Institute, 153
Canadian Institute of International Affairs, 510
Canadian Japanese and World War II, The (1948), 527
Canadian Journal, The: A Repertory of Industry, Science and Art (Toronto), 150, 153–4, 382, 436, 443, 447, 449, 451, 453
Canadian Journal of Economics and Political Science, **525**
Canadian Journal of Religious Thought, 564, **568**
Canadian Journal of Theology, 551, 567–8
Canadian Journey (1939), 603
Canadian Life and Scenery (1886), 349
Canadian Life as I Found It (1908), 358
Canadian Life in Town and Country (1905), 357
Canadian Linguistic Association, 258
Canadian Literary Journal (Toronto, 1870–1), 207
Canadian Literary Magazine (York, 1833), 140–1, **179**
Canadian Literature (1959–   ), 494, 536
Canadian Literature Club (Toronto), 671
Canadian Literature Today (1938), 487
Canadian Magazine (Montreal, 1823–5), 127, 132, 133, 176, 177
Canadian Magazine (Toronto, 1893–1939), 77, 194, 197, 201, 204, 269, 270, 271, 288, 303, 458, 466, 611, 674, 724, 726
Canadian Magazine (York, 1833), 140, 179
Canadian Manor and Its Seigneurs, A (1908), 236
Canadian Mercury, 468, 469, 471, 481–2, 609, 730, **734**

Canadian Methodism (1882), 552
Canadian Methodist Magazine, 218
Canadian Missionary Congress (1909), 573
Canadian Monthly and National Review (1872–8), 150, 161, 162, 185, 186, 194–207 passim, 224, 240, 427, 439, 458, 459, 530 (known as *Rose-Belford's Canadian Monthly*, 1878–82)
Canadian Municipal Government (1954), 524
Canadian National Railways (1960, 1962), 507
Canadian Naturalist, 153, 451, 447
Canadian Nights (1914), **362**
Canadian Panorama, A (1929), 600
Canadian Pictures: Lorne (1884), 349; Weaver (1912), 362
Canadian Players, 653, 657
Canadian Playwright series, 639
Canadian Poems 1850–1952 (1952), 768, 776
Canadian Poetry Magazine, 486, 741, 761
Canadian Poets: Garvin (1916, 1926), 536, 724; Gustafson (1943), 765
Canadian Political Parties (1957), 516
Canadian Portrait Gallery, The (1880–1), 225
Canadian Repertory Theatre, 655
Canadian Review (Montreal, 1824–6), 127, 132, 133, 137–8, 139, 177, 178
Canadian Scrap-Book, A (1897), 354
Canadian Scenery (1842), 143
Canadian Senator, The (1890), 297, 303
Canadian Settlers' Guide, The (1855), 254
Canadian Short Stories: Knister (1928), 484–5, 675; Weaver (1960), 720

Canadian Slavonic Papers, 542
Canadian Society: Sociological Perspectives (1961), 528
Canadian Times (Montreal, 1823), 135
Canadian Tour, A (1886), 351; Watt (1921), 600
Canadian Trails (1911), 362
Canadian Trails Revisited (1926), 600
Canadian Wild Flowers (1869), 143, 367
Canadian Wilds (1907), 376
Canadian Wonder Tales (1918), 165, 628
Canadians in the Making (1958), 508, 527
Canadians of Old (1864), 286
Candlelight Days (1913), 295
Canniff, William, 241
Canterbury Tales, The, 735
Canzone d'Amore (Cavalcanti), 549
Capek, K., 653
Capital, Interest and Profits (1959), 523
Capote, Truman, 722
Cappon, James, 487, 537, 832
Captain Love (1908), 288
Captain of Raleigh's, A (1911), 288
Captain Salvation (1925), 659
Captivity of Babylon, The (1840), 116
Carbutt, Mrs. E. H., 350
Card, Raymond, 639
Cardinal Newman and the Christian Philosophic Tradition (1933), 592
Careless, J. M. S., 152–3, 494, 503, 504, 508
Carleton Library, 511
Carlisle, John, 554
Carlson, Natalie S., 631
"Carlton"; see Baird, Mrs. C. A.
Carlyle, Thomas, 118, 206, 229, 353
Carman, A. R., 294, 302, 310, 554
Carman, Bliss, 63, 67, 109,

122, 186, 198, 204, 205, 342, 343, 344, 369, 403, 410–16, 417, 482, 483, 485, 487, 490, 491, 537, 538, 632, 671, 735, 752, 755, 757, 801, 832, 843
Carmichael, Dean, 351
Carmichael, N. R., 452
Carmichael (1907), 293
Carnal and the Crane, The (1957), 812
Carnegie, Andrew, 272, 423
Carnegie, C. K., 604
Carolina Quest (1951), 369
Carols of the Coast (1892), 104, 117
Caron, Maurice B., 668
Carpenter, Frances, 605
Carr, Emily, 622, 623, 719, 791, 828
Carr, Kate, 293, 303
Carr, W. G., 603
Carrasquilla, Tomas, 549
Carrel, Frank, 362
Carrington, Philip, 566, 568, 572
Carroll, Rev. John, 239, 572
Carroll, Lewis, 787
Carruthers, C. E., 638
Carrying Place (1944), 685–6
Cartier, Jacques, 6, 19–20, 288, 512
Cartwright, George, 69, 255
Cary, Thomas, 85–6
Case, Thomas, 578
Case and His Cotemporaries (1867–77), 239–40, 572
Case of Constable Shields, 660
Casgrain, Abbé H. R., 228, 286
Cashier, The (1955), 703
Casselman, A. C., 137
Cassini, Cesar François, 69
Castle Buck, The (1945), 372
Caswell, H. S., 182
Catacombs of Rome and Their Testimony Relative to Primitive Christianity (1847), 249
Catalogue of Italian Plays, 1500–1700 (1961), 544
Catapult (Montreal), 494
Cataract (Montreal), 494, 817

Cather, Willa, 312, 541, 697
Catholic Church in Canada, The (1956), 573
Catholic Church in the Canadian North-West, The (1936), 573
Catholic Problems in Western Canada (1921), 563, 573
Catholic Register, 344
Catullus, 104, 728
Cavalier of Virginia, A (1910), 288
Caven, Rev. William, 558
Cawdell, James Martin, 139, 140
Cawein, Madison, 723
Celestial Cycle (1952), 539
Century (U.S.A.), 266, 268, 288
Century of Anglo-Catholicism, A (1929), 563, 593
Cerberus (1952), 776, 778, 781
Cézanne, Paul, 398
Chain of Life in Geological Time, The (1880 etc.), 450
Challenge and Response (1959), 569, 588
Chalmers, R. C., 562, 569, 588
Chambers, B. H., 471
Chambers's Journal (London), 265
Champlain, Samuel de, 11, 20, 22, 57, 227, 238, 244, 512
Champlain, Northwest Voyager (1944), 630
Champlain of the St. Lawrence (1952), 630
Champlain Road, The (1939), 629, 663
Champlain Society, 31, 224, 237–8
Chandler, Amos Henry, 118
Change of Pace, A (1956), 611
Changing Concepts of Time (1952), 521, 597
Channing, Mrs., 111
Chant, C. A., 456
Chantons un peu (1961), 169
Chapin, G. B., 182
Chapin, Miriam, 527, 606

Chapman, E. J., 153, 154, 449
Chapman, Ethel, 668
Chappell, Lt. Edward, 70
Characteristics of Women (1831), 143
Charivari, The (1824), 126, 131, 133
Charles II, King, 22
Charlesworth, H. W., 611
Charlevoix, Pierre F. X. de, 88, 210, 212
Charlie Ogilbie: A Romance of Scotland and New Brunswick (1889), 291
Chartered Libertine, The (1954), 707
Chase, Richard, 698
Chasse-Galerie, La, and Other Canadian Stories (1900), 289
Chateauclair, Wilfred; *see* Lighthall, William D.
Chats by the Fireside (1911), 344
Chatterton, Thomas, 540
Chaucer, G., 193, 364, 529, 591
Chayefsky, Paddy, 650
Cheadle, Dr. W. B., 35, 256
Check List of Canadian Literature (1959), 542, 658
Chekhov, Anton, 689, 720
Cheney, Harriet V., 146
Chequered Shade, The (1963), 816
Cherriman, J. B., 153, 436
Chesterton, G. K., 559
Chibogamoo (1907), 358
Chicanot, E. L., 171
Chief Factor (1892), 296
Chief of the Rangers, The (1913), 301
Child, Francis James, 169, 411
Child, Philip, 663, 686, 787
Children of the Wild; *see*, *Babes of the Wild*
Child's History of Canada, The (1870), 217
Child's House (1923), 673
Chinese Culture and Christianity (1925), 571
Chinese Mirror (1925), 659
Chipmunk (1949), 707
Chisholm, Arthur M., 302, 660

888 INDEX

Chisholme, David, 127, 132, 133, 134, 176, 177
Chittick, V. L. O., 485
Chivalry of Keith Leicester, The (1918), 301
Choice of Enemies, A (1957), 714
Chord of Steel, The (1960), 455
Choquet, Joseph P., 663
Chown, S. D., 561
Chris in Canada (1925), 668
Christian Apologetics of the Second Century (1921), 566
Christian Church in Canada, The (1956), 551, 569
Christian Doctrine (1953), 565
Christian Examiner (1819–20), 176
Christian God, The (1929), 565
Christian Gospel of the Fatherhood of God, The (1924), 565
Christian Guardian, 140, 180
Christian Philosophy (1963), 592
Christian Philosophy of Saint Augustine, The (1960), 592
Christian Philosophy of St. Thomas Aquinas, The (1956), 566, 590
Christian Rewards (1880), 555
Christian View of the World, The (1912), 558
Christian World (London), 450
Christianity and Classical Culture (1940), 517, 541, 568
Christianity and Humanity (1883), 556
Christianity and Idealism (1897), 441, 555
Christianity and World Revolution (1963), 593
Christianity as Religion and Life (1914), 565
Christian's Knowledge of God, The (1940), 562
Christie, Dr. A. J., 132, 133, 134, 177

Christie, Robert, 128, 215, 220, 221, 222, 223, 234
Christmas in French Canada (1900), 289
Christology of the Epistle to the Hebrews, The (1928), 565
Christ's Teaching concerning the Last Things (1908), 558
Chronicles of America, The, 244
Chronicles of Barabbas, 264
Chronicles of Canada, The (1914–16), 244
Chronicles of the St. Lawrence, The (1879), 287
Chronique du Pseudo-Turpin (ed. 1936), 545
Chubb, Henry, 178
Church, A. J., 349
Church and Sect in Canada (1948), 508, 527, 569
Church and State in Canada, 1841–1867 (1959), 569
Church and State in Canadian Education (1959), 569
Church and the Age of Reason, 1648–1789, The (1960), 569
Church and War, The (1936), 563
Church History for Canadians, A (1946), 568, 572
Church of England in Canada, 1759–1793 (1893), 572
Church of Scotland in Lower Canada, The (1936), 572
Church in the New Testament, The (1943), 568
"Church Union" and the Presbyterian Church in Canada (1928), 561
Church Union in Canada: E. L. Murrow (1923), 561; C. E. Silcox (1933), 561
Churchill, Charles, 544
Churchill, Winston, 280, 281, 488
Cicero, M. Tullius, 435, 535
Cigarette Maker's Romance, A (play), 651
Circle of the Year, The (1904), 380

Cities of Canada (1951), 606
City Hall Street (1951), 779
City of Comrades, The (1919), 290, 309, 311, 327
City of Libertines (1958), 662
Civil Service of Canada, The (1929), 524
Civ/n, 493, 776
Claim on the Klondike, A (1898), 301
Claims of the Churchmen and Dissenters of Upper Canada (1828), 552
Clare, John, 798
Clark, A. F. B., 530, 549
Clark, A. L., 452
Clark, Catherine A., 629
Clark, Daniel, 295
Clark, Ethel May, 165
Clark, Gregory, 611, 612
Clark, Robert M., 523
Clark, S. D., 202, 501, 508, 527, 528, 569
Clark, W. C., 522
Clark, William Robinson, 249, 562
Clarke, C. K., 452
Clarke, George F., 372, 628, 668
Clarke, James, 267
Classics of the Soul's Quest (Walsh), 556
Claudel, Paul, 653
Clay, Charles, 378, 628, 672
Clearing in the West (1935), 265, 619, 623
Clement, W. H. P., 219–20
Clemo, Ebenezer, 182
Clergy Reserve Question, The (1839), 552
Clergy Reserves, The: Their History and Present Position (1851), 225
Cleveland, Benjamin, 77
Clever Ones, The (1936), 673
Clinch, Rev. Joseph, 116
Clint, Mabel, 287
Clockmaker, The (1836 etc.), 92, 94, 95–100, 106, 178, 284
Clokie, H. McD., 525
Close up: On Writing for Television (Hailey), 650
Clune, Frank, 606
Clutterbuck, W. J., 350, 351

INDEX 889

Coalfleet, Pierre; *see* Davison, Frank C.
Coast to Coast in a Puddle-Jumper (1930), 604
Coates (publisher, Toronto), 448
Coats, Robert Hamilton, 228, 236
Cobbett, William, 80, 140, 847
Coburn, Kathleen, 543
Cochrane, Charles N., 517, 541, 567
Cochrane, Rev. W., 555
Cochrane, Rev. William, 535
Cockburn, J. S., 349
Cockburn, Russell, 381
Cocking, Mathew, 27
Cockings, George, 72–73
Cockloft, Jeremy, 131
Cockrel, Richard, 90
Code of the North West (1940), 660
Cody, Hiram, 262, 263, 268, 291, 296, 298, 301, 302, 304, 307, 332, 333, 334
Coffin, Wiliam F., 216–17
Cogswell, Fred, 494, 800, 801, 802, 828, 830, 831
Cohen, Leonard, 494, 812, 814–16
Coil, John, 573
Colburn, Henry (English publisher), 109
Colby, Charles William, 237, 241, 244
Cold Green Element, The (1956), 782
Cole, Carol Cassidy, 380, 628
Cole, G. D. H., 515
Cole, Taylor, 524
Coleman, A. P., 452, 456
Coleman, Helena, 428
Colenso, Dr., 450
Coleridge, Samuel T., 16, 44, 45, 69, 159, 193, 390, 423, 543–4, 761, 804
Coleridge and Sara Hutchinson and the Asra Poems (1955), 544
Colin of the Ninth Concession (1903), 292, 310
Collected Poems: A. Bourinot (1947), 727; I. V. Crawford (1905), 406; R. Knister (1949),

729, 765; E. J. Pratt (540, 769); A. J. M. Smith (1962), 731, 816
Collection of Several Commissions, A (1772), 84
College Days (1923), 336
Collier's Magazine, 268, 280
Collin, W. E., 487, 536, 538, 549, 734, 751, 768
Collins, J. E., 185, 260, 298
Collins, Joseph, 312
Collins, Wilkie, 195, 273, 277, 278
Colmer, J. G., 351, 354
Colombo, John Robert, 816
Colonel from Wyoming, A (1907), 290
Colonial Advocate, 140
Colonial Office and Canada, 1867–87, The (1955), 509
Colonial Pearl (Halifax), 178
Colony to Nation (1946), 504
Colour as Naked, The (1953), 771
Coloured Spectacles (1938), 620
Colquhoun, A. H. U., 246
Columbian and Canadian Sketches (1895), 354
Columbus, Christopher, 3, 5, 204, 206
Combe, William, 29, 47
Come True (1926), 639
Comeau, Napolean, 372
Commentary on Deuteronomy (Jordan, 1911), 557
Commentary on Philippians (Beare, 1959), 570
Commercial Empire of the St. Lawrence, The (1937), 501, 511
Committed to His Charge (1900), 262, 293, 304
Community, The (1938), 594
Compendious History of the Northern Part of the Province of New Brunswick . . . (1832), 211
Complaint and Satire in Early English Literature (1956), 547
Compleat Angler (1653), 365

Complete Poems (Pick & Hall) (1925), 425
Compositor in Canada, A (1921), 600
Comprehensive History of the Dominion of Canada with Art Engravings, (1879), 217
Comrades Two: A Tale of the Qu'Appelle Valley (1907), 297
Comte, Auguste, 460, 461, 589
Comte, Mill, and Spencer (1895), 440
Comus, 539
Conacher, D. J., 545
Conacher, J. B., 518
Concordat of 1801, The (1933), 569
Confederation: Being a Series of Hitherto Unpublished Documents bearing on the British North America Act (1895), 242
Confessions of an Immigrant's Daughter (1939), 621, 667
Conflagration, The (1838), 117
Conger, Jane, 310
Conibear, Kenneth, 381, 387, 660
Coningsby, 279
Coniston (1906), 280
Connell, J., 467
Connor, Carl Y., 485
Connor, Ralph; *see* Gordon, Charles W.
Conover, Dora Smith, 638
Conquering Hero, The (1920), 311
Conquest of Canada (1849), 212, 214
Conquest of New France, The (1918), 244
Conquest of the Great Northwest, The (1908), 224
Conrad, Joseph, 312, 534, 675, 686, 699, 716, 720
Conron, Brandon, 839, 840
Consider Her Ways (1947), 365, 680, 681
Consideration on the Expediency of Procuring an Act of Parliament . . . (1766), 83

890 INDEX

Consort, The (1912), **303**, 316
Conspiracy of Pontiac (1851), 286
Constable (English publisher), 244, 405
Constance of Acadia (1886), 288
Constitutional Amendment in Canada (1950), 524
Constitutional Issues in Canada, 1900–31 (1933), 524
Contact, 493, 769, 776, 778
Contact Press, 728, 777, 778, 785
Contemporary Canada (1959), 527, 606
Contemporary Christ, The (1938), 565
Contemporary Review, 161, 194
Contemporary Verse (1941–53), 489, 760, 766, 768, 774, 785–6, 795
Contrasts (1922), 726
Conway, John J., 518
Cook, Britton, 636–7
Cook, G. Ramsay, 508
Cook, James, 35, 41, 43–6, 47, 48, 49, 51, 58
Cook, Lyn, 629, 631
Cook, J. S., 574
Cooke, B. B., 363
Cooke, Rose Terry, 282
Cooney, Percival John, 295
Cooney, Robert, 211
Cooper, F. C., 362
Cooper, J. I., 509
Cooper, James Fenimore, 138, 277, 278, 280, 281, 282, 287, 295, 549
Cooper, John A., 458
Copland, John A., 307
Copp, Clark Publishing Co., 183, 188, 270, 303
Copping, A. E., 362
Coquette, The (1797), 146
Corbett, D. C., 524
Cord and Creese (1869), 112
Corelli, Marie, 280, 281
Cormack, W. E., 70
Corn Goddess, The, and Other Tales from Indian Canada (1956), 165
Corner Stone of Democracy,

The (1939), 594
Corneille, Pierre, 11
Cornell, Beaumont S., 684
Cornhill (magazine), 265
Cornish, John, 707
Corporal Cameron (1912), 298, 323
Corrigan, Beatrice, 544
Corry, J. A., 525
Cory, Harper, 380
Cosa, John, 527
Cosmic Consciousness (1901), 832
Cosmopolitan (magazine), 268
Costain, Thomas B., 455, 511, 696, 697
Cot and Cradle Stories (1895), 380, 624
Cotes, Everard, 315
Cotes, Mrs. Everard; *see* Duncan, Sara Jeannette
Cotton, Charles, 373
Cotton, John, 55
Coues, Elliott, 31
Coulter, John, 640, 641, 647, 655, 840
Count Filippo (1860), 149
Count Frontenac and New France under Louis XIV (1877), 286
Counterpoint to Sleep (1951), 790
Country Hours (1959), 374
Country Life Reader, 374
Coupland, Sir Reginald, 499
Course of Impatience Carningham, The (1911), **302**
Courting of Marie Jenvrin, The (Pharis), 639–40
Courville, Louis-Léonard Aumasson de, 213
Cousin, Victor, 202
Cousin Cinderella: A Canadian Girl in London (1908), 258, 303, 309, 315
Cousland, K. H., 562
Covey, Mrs. Elizabeth, 297
Cow Puncher, The (1918), 299, 304, 311
Cow with the Musical Moo, The (1952), 632
Cowdell, Thomas Daniel, 80, 176
Cowper, William, 80, 136
Cox, F. J., 600

Coyne, James Henry, 861, 862
Cox, Ross, 33, 34
Crabbe, George, 801
Crafte So Long to Lerne, The (1959), 816
Cragg, E., 570
Cragg, G. R., 551, 569, 571
Cragg, Kenneth C., 374
Craib, Alexander, 354
Craig, Gerald, 501, 511
Craig, John, 628
Cramp, Rev. John A., 434, 552
Cran, Mrs. George, 361
Crane, Stephen, 276, 312, 314
Cranford, 282
Crawford, A. W., 534
Crawford, Francis Marion, 280, 281, 651
Crawford, Isabella V., 158, 160, 161, 198, 406–10, 537, 843, 846
Crawford, Kenneth G., 524
Crawley, Alan, 489, 740, 766
Crawley, Rev. Edward A., 434, 552
Crawley, Edmund, 106
Creation, The (1874), 554
Creation of Manitoba, The (1871), 223
Creative Writing in Canada (1952), 495, 537
Creighton, Alan, 487
Creighton, Donald G., 491, 494, 496, 501, 502, 504, 511–15, 825, 829
Creighton, Helen, 166, 169, 172
Creighton, L. B., 471
Crêpe-Hanger's Carnival: Selected Poems 1955–58 (1958), 779, 780
Crerar, Thomas A., 477
Crespi, Fray Juan, 43
Crest Theatre, 656
Crestwood Heights (1956), 528
Crèvecoeur, Hector St. Jean de, 96
Crisp, W. G., 628
Critical Realism of Roy Wood Sellars, The (1952), 595
Critical Study of In Memorium (1898), 533

INDEX 891

Critique of Paradise Lost, A
 (1960), 547
Croce, Benedetto, 595
Crockett, Davy, 278
Croft, Henry, 153
Croil, Rev. James, 239
Cromwell, Oliver, 17
Cronin, A. J.,699
*Cross Bearers of the Sague-
 nay, The* 1930), 574
Cross-Country (1949), 612,
 702
*Crossed Swords: A Cana-
 dian-American Tale of
 Love and Valor* (1912),
 287
Crossing Canada (1940),
 605
Crosweller, W. T., 354
Crowne, John, 17, 57
Crowne, William, 57
*Cruelty of the Spaniards in
 Peru, The* (1658), 17
Cruikshank, E. A., 235, 237,
 242
Cruising Auk, The (1959),
 805–6
*Crusade of MCCCLXXXIII,
 The, Known as that of the
 Bishop of Norwich*
 (1892), 243
Crusoe, Robinson, 43, 374
Cryptogram, The (1871),
 112
Cullum, Ridgwell, 262, 297,
 298, 301, 302
*Culture of Contemporary
 Canada, The* (1957), 446,
 452, 495, 527, 532, 700
Cumberland, Stuart, 351
Cummings, E. E., 724, 808
Cummins, Maria, 278
Cunningham, H. H., 176,
 177, 181
Cunningham, Louis Arthur,
 663, 667
Cupid and the Candidate
 (1906), 293, 303
Curé of St. Michel, The
 (1925), 668
Curé of St. Philippe, The
 (1899), 290, 326
Cureton, Stephen, 307
Curious Annals [Browning]
 (1956), 544
*Curious Career of Roderick
 Campbell, The* (1901), 629

Currelly, C. T., 617
Currie, A. W., 523
Currie, Sir Arthur, 599
Currie, Margaret Gill, 119
*Cursory Observations Made
 in Quebec* (1811), 131
*Cursory View of the Local,
 Social, Moral and Political
 State of the Colony of
 Lower Canada* (1829),
 129
Curtis, C. A., 522
Curtis, Lionel, 242
Curtis, W. E., 362
*Curve, Go Slow: A Romance
 of the Pacific Coast*
 (1927), 659
Curwen, Samuel, 72, 73
Curwood, James Oliver,
 283, 298, 302
Curzon, Sarah Anne, 428
Cushing, Mrs. Eliza L., 146,
 151, 181
Cutten, G. B., 558
Cycle of the North, The
 (1938), 387

DAFOE, JOHN W., 515, 527
Dagmar Who Loved, The
 (1904), 262, 293
Daily Witness (Montreal),
 148
Daisy Miller, 281
Dale, Mrs. R. J., 668
Dale, Thomas R., 148, 149
D'Alembert, 589
Dalhousie, Countess of, 128
Dalhousie, Earl of, 79, 128,
 132, 153, 162, 176, 209,
 210, 216, 432
Dalhousie Review, 451, 479,
 481, 535, 541, 593, 609,
 665
Daly, G. T., 563
Daly, Reginald A., 456
Dance at Four Corners, The
 (Burgin), 292
Dancey, Capt. S. N., 311
Dane, Barry; see Logan,
 John E.
Daniells, Roy, 494, 529,
 547, 700, 761, 816, 832,
 842, 845
Dante, 193, 395, 440, 591,
 717
Dante the Philosopher
 (1948), 590

Dark Acres (1935), 663,
 683
Dark Dawn, The (1926),
 678
Dark Harvest (Pharis),
 639–40
*Dark Secret, The; or, The
 Mystery of Fontelle Hall*
 (1875), 111
Dark Weaver, The (1937),
 667
Darkness in the Earth, A
 (1959), 802
Darnell, Rev. H. F., 182,
 305
D'Artagnan (1928), 661
Dartmoor Mystery, The
 (1935), 659
Darwin, C., 44, 108, 203,
 366, 372, 384, 449, 453,
 455, 463, 553, 833, 843
Darwin in Retrospect
 (1960), 455
Daughter of Patricians, A
 (1901), 290, 305, 310
Daughter of St. Peters, A
 (1889), 310
Daughter of Today, A
 (1894), 280, 310, 315
D'Avenant, Sir William, 17
Davey, Frank, 494
David and Other Poems
 (1942), 123, 761, 787
Davidson, John, 434, 520
Davies, Robertson, 494, 612,
 613, 614, 641–4, 649, 655,
 694, 702, 704, 705, 707,
 711, 719, 720, 838
Davies, Trevor, 559
Davin, Nicholas Flood, 240,
 428
Davis, Allan Ross, 295
Davis, Donald and Murray,
 656
Davis, Jefferson, 353
Davis, John, 9
Davis, Marilyn, 150
Davis, Richard Harding,
 314, 354
Davis, Thomas, 155, 156
Davison, Frank C., 683–84,
 685
Dawn at Shanty Bay, The
 (1907), 329
Dawson, C. A., 527
Dawson, George Mercer,
 162

Dawson, Sir John William, 153, 449, 451, 553
Dawson, Robert MacGregor, 494, 506, 510, 524, 525
Dawson, S. E., 533
Day, Frank Parker, 668
Day, Margaret, 489
Day and Night (1944), 741
Day before Yesterday, The (1925), 668
Day of Wrath (1945), 686
Daylight through the Mountain: The Letters and Labours of Civil Engineers Walter and Francis Shanly (1957), 455
Days of Lorne (1955), 505
De Fonte, Bartholomew, 42
De Fuca, Juan, 41–2
De Guignes (French sinologist), 42
De la Roche, Mazo, 381, 484, 491, 628, 632, 639, 658, 668–75, 699, 720, 837, 841
De l'Isle (map maker), 42
De Mille, James, 63, 105, 111–14, 182, 261, 263, 267, 280, 308, 433, 483, 632
De Quincey, T., 250
De Roberval (1888), 114–15, 123–4
De Saint-Denys Garneau (1949), 549
De Sola, Rev. A., 451
Deacon, William Arthur, 470, 610, 742, 743
Dear Old Farm, The (1897), 295
Death of Pierrot, The (1926), 638–39
Debussy, Claude, 421, 825
Decalogue, The (1842), 553
DeCelles, A. D., 228, 244
Dee, John, 4
Deeper into the Forest (1948), 761
Deficit Made Flesh, The (1958), 797
Defoe, D., 18, 42, 78, 141
Degrees of Knowledge, The (1959), 591
Deidre of the Sorrows (Coulter), 641, **840**
Delataille, Maurice de, 560

Deliah Plays the Ponies (1927), 324
Delight (1926), 670, 841
"Delta"; *see* Moir, David Macbeth
Delta (Montreal), 494, 776
Dely, G. T., 573
Democracy and Marxism (1955), 526
Democracy in Alberta (1953), 525
Democracy in the Dominions (1947), 525
Democratic Government and Politics (1946), 525
DeMonts, 57
Demos (Gissing), 675
Denison, Col. George T., 159, 246, 249
Denison, Merrill, 507, 634–6, 638, 642, 649, 653
Denison, Muriel, 630, 673
Dennis, John, 17–18
Denomy, A. J., 545
Dent, J. M., and Sons, 486, 664–5
Dent, John Charles, 140, 225, 226, 231, 232, 234, 294, 312
Deny, Nicholas, 238
Des Sauvages (1604), 20
Descartes, 365, 582, 589, 595
Descent from Eden (1959), 800, 801
Descent of Man (1871), 366
Description and Natural History of the Coasts of North America, The (1908), 238
Deserted Village, The (Goldsmith), 85, 120
Desire under the Elms, 636
Desportes, P., 545
D'Estimauville, Chevalier R.-A., 129, 131
Detached Pirate, A (1903), 290, 309
Deutsch, John, 523
Developing Canadian Community, The (1962), 527
Development of Canadian Art, The (1963), 508
Development of Dominion Status, 1900–1936, The (1937), 524

Devil of a Trip, A (1888), 350
Devil's Die, The (1888), 313
Devil's Mantle (1927), 659
Devil's Picture Book, The (1960), 812, 813
Devil's Playground (1894), 298
Devine, Rev. E. J., 305, 357
Devoir, Le (Montreal), 192
Dewart, Edward Hartley, 147, 148, 151, 158, 159, 183, 429, **536**
Dewart, Leslie M., 593
Dewdney, Selwyn, 706
Dewey, John, 434, 500, 588
De Witt, N. W., 570, 589
DeWolf, Mrs., 307
Dialogues on the Apostolic Church (1837), 552
Diana of Quebec, A (1912), 287–8, **629**
Diane of Ville-Marie (1898), 287
Diary (Mrs. Simcoe), 167
Diary in Caanda (1904), 348, 358
Diary of Samuel Marchbanks, The (1947), 613, 704
Dickens, Charles, 26, 101, 112, 141, 151, 203, 206, 277, 278, 279, 281, 284, 319, 335, 347, 361, 619, 672, 695
Dickie, Francis, 381, 387
Dickinson, Emily, 734, 740, 808, 848
Dick's Desertion (1905), 295
Dickson, Mrs. Emma Wells, 304
Dickson, Stephen, 86
Diderot, 203, 589
Diefenbaker, John, 517
Digby (1953), 718
Dionne, N. E., 227
Direction, 769
Disciples of Christ in Canada since 1830, The (1949), 573
Discourse and Discovery of Newfoundland, A (1620), 13
Discovery (periodical), 451
Discovery of the NorthWest Passage (1856), 38

Disney, C. P., 455
Disraeli, B., 279
Divine Lady, The (1924), 660–1
Divine Mission (1958), 574
Dix, Maurice B., 659
Dixon, Frederick Augustus, 108, 114
Dixon, George, 46, 47
Dobbs, Arthur, 24
Dobbs, Kildare, 719
Dobson, W. A. C. H., 542
Doctor, The: A Tale of the Rockies (1906), 294, 300, 323
Doctor Barnardo (1931), 564
Dr. Jekyll and Mr. Hyde, 280
Dr. Luke of the Labrador (1904), 291, 328, 329
Dr. Perdue (1892), 309, 321
Doctrinal Basis of Union and its Relation to the Historic Creeds, The (1926), 562
Doctrine of Being in the Aristotelian Metaphysics, The (1951), 566, 592
Doctrine of Christ in History, The (1926), 565
Doctrine of the Christian Ministry, The (1959), 569
Documentary History of Education in Upper Canada (1894–1010), 238
Documentary History of the Campaigns upon the Niagara Frontier (1896–1908), 237
Documents Relating to the Constitutional History of Canada (1907), 236
Documents Relating to the Seigniorial Tenure in Canada, 1598–1854 (1908), 238
Dodd, Mead and Company, 484, 678
Dodge Club, The (1860), 112, 113, 280, 308
Dog of Flanders, A (Ouida), 366
Dog Who Wouldn't Be, The (1957), 381

Doll's House, A, 280
Dolly, the Young Widder up to Felder's (1886), 293, 312
Domett, Alfred, 141
Dominion Annual Register, 226
Dominion Drama Festival, 639, 654
Dominion Illustrated Monthly, 269
Dominion of Canada, The (1911), 363
Dominion of Canada as it will appear to Members of the British Association (1884), 351
Dominion of the North (1944), 491, 504, 511, 513
Don-A-Dreams (1906), 294, 310
Don Juan, 107, 117
Donald, P., 600
Donne, John, 3, 14, 547, 703, 708, 731, 812
Donnelly, Ignatius, 284, 465, 833
Donnelly, Murray S., 524
Donovan, Peter, 611, 612
Donovan Pasha (1902), 318
Doolittle, P. E., 354
Doran, George, 264, 269
Dorien, Ray, 606
Dorion, A. A., 227
Dorland, A. G., 573
Dos Passos, John, 721
"Dot-It-Down" (1871), 297
Double Hook, The (1959), 712
Dougall, Lily, 262, 263, 281, 290, 291, 300, 305, 306, 313, 319, 320
Doughty, Arthur G., 236, 244
Doughty, C. M., 540
Douglas, A. V., 452, 454
Douglas, Sir Howard, 110
Douglas, John (Bishop), 45
Douglas, Lloyd, 558
Doukhobors at War, The (1952), 573
Doukhobors of British Columbia, The (1955), 527
Dove, The (1933), 666
Dover Beach Revisited

(1961), 740
Dow, John, 562
Down the Long Table (1955), 707
Down North on the Labrador (1911), 291
Down the Dark Alley (1936), 333
Down to the Sea (1919), 291
Down to the Sea in Ships (1910), 329
Downy Wings and Sharp Eyes (1923), 380
Doyle, Conan, 279, 283
Doyle, Gerald S., 172
Drake, Sir Francis, 9, 14, 41, 58
Drama of Euripides (1941), 545
Drama of the Forests, The (1947), 372
Dray, William, 589
Drayton, Michael, 10, 14, 139
Dread Voyage, The (1893), 161
Dream Tapestries (1924), 726
Dream That is Dying, A (1954), 779
Dreamland and Other Poems (1868), 159, 160
Dreams (1956), 644
Dreiser, Theodore, 276, 312, 679, 683
Drum of Lanoraye, The (1932), 663
Drummer Boy for Montcalm (1959), 629–30
Drummond, William, of Hawthornden, 17
Drummond, William Henry, 126, 165, 171, 347, 422, 584
Drums Afar (1918), 310
Drums are Out (Coulter), 640
Drums in the Forest (1936), 629
Drunken Clock, The (1961), 816
Dryad of Nanaimo, The (1931), 751–2
Dryden, John, 17
Du Bartas en Angleterre (1908), 549

Dubliners, 717
Dudek, Louis, 489, 491, 494, 768, 769, 776-8, 779, 781, 785, 787
Dufferin, Countess of, 347, 353, 354
Dufferin, Earl of, 201
Duffy, Charles Gavan, 155, 156
Du Maurier, G., 281
Dumas, A., 158, 281
Duncan, Alastair R. C., 596
Duncan, Dorothy, 605
Duncan, Norman, 262, 263, 268, 291, 304, 328, 329, 483, 631
Duncan, Sara Jeannette, 258, 262, 263, 266, 267, 268, 276, 280, 281, 293, 303, 305, 308-9, 310, 313-17, 320, 341, 832, 839
Duncan Polite: The Watchman of Glenoro (1905), 292, 305, 330
Dundas (1861), 239
Dunham, Mabel, 631, 667
Dunkirk (1941), 747
Dunlop, James, 307
Dunlop, Dr. William, "Tiger," 128, 131, 132, 134, 141, 142, 143, 145, 254, 506
Dunraven, Earl of, 362
Dunsmuir, 355
Dupuis, N. F., 452
Durham, Lord, 128, 231, 498, 499
Durham, Major, 358
Durkin, Douglas Leader, 297, 659, 687
Duvar, John Hunter; see Hunter-Duvar, John
Dwellers of the Marshlands (1937), 380
Dwight, Allan, 629
Dying Indian's Dream, The (1872), 104

Each Man's Son (1951), 701
Earl, R. O., 446, 452
Earle Grey Players, 655
Early Bibliography of the Province of Ontario, The (1892), 226
Early Christian Church, The (1957), 568

Early History of Canadian Banking, The (1898), 246
Earth and High Heaven (1944), 706
Earthly Paradise (Morris), 123
Earth's Enigmas (1895), 383
East Coast (1951), 800
East Lynne, 278
East of the City (1946), 776, 777, 778
Easter Egg (Reaney), 648, 649
Easterbrook, W. T., 507, 508, 523
Eaton, A. W., 290, 304, 427
Eaton, Evelyn, 696, 697
Eaton, Lady, 617
Eayrs, James, 510, 526
Ebb Tide (1935), 640
Ebbutt, A. J., 570
Eby, C. S., 556
Ecarté (1829), 138
Eccles, William, 233, 505
Echo (Halifax), 331
Economic Background of Dominion-Provincial Relations, The (1939), 522
Economic History of Russia, An (1914), 249
Economic Problems of the Prairie Provinces (1935), 522
Economics in a Canadian Setting (1959), 523
Ecumenical Council, The (1961), 569
Edel, Leon, 751
Eden Lost and Won (1895), 554
Edgar, Sir James, 187, 353, 428
Edgar, Mary S., 574
Edgar, Lady Matilda, 91, 228
Edgar, O. Pelham, 228, 541, 548, 671
Edge (Edmonton), 494
Edgeworth, Maria, 141
Edinburgh Philosophical Journal, 70
Edinburgh Review, 29, 132
Edinburgh Witness, 450
Edwards, Bob, 166
Edwards, C. A. M., 629
Edwards, G., 436

Edwards, Sir Henry, 350
Edwards, Jonathan, 59, 74
Egerton Ryerson (Burwash), 228
Eggleston, Edward, 282
Eggleston, Wilfrid, 174, 606, 683
Eichner, Hans, 544
Eight Years in Canada (1847), 138, 181
1812: The War and its Moral: A Canadian Chronicle (1864)
Einstein, Albert, 455
Elder, William, 552
Elegy (Gray), 841
Elementary Christian Metaphysics, An (1963), 592
Elements Combined, The (Kilbourn), 507
Elements of Christian Philosophy (1960), 566
Elements of Natural Theology (1850), 435
Elements of Political Science (1906), 526
Elgin, Lord, 499
Eliot, C. W. J., 545
Eliot, Elinor Marsden, 297
Eliot, George, 147, 202, 264, 277, 279, 703
Eliot, T. S., 41, 481, 549, 646, 712, 717, 718, 723, 724, 731-5 *passim*, 751, 759, 783, 792, 835, 844
Elizabeth I, 9, 12, 823
Elkington, E. W., 355, 362
Ellenbogan, George, 494
Ellice, Edward, 134
Elliott, A. C., 603
Elliott, Charles, 349
Ellis, Edward, 278
Ellis, Henry, 24
Ellis, M. B., 549, 550
Ellis, T. M., 301
Ellis, Thomas, 9
Ellis, William, 45
Elson, John M., 667
Eman, W. E., 574
Emerson, Ralph Waldo, 147, 203, 204, 348, 413, 417, 423, 427, 545, 549, 722, 723, 828
Emerson's Plutarch (1961), 545
Emigrant, The: A Poem (1842), 135, 136

Emigrant, The and Other Poems (1861), 136, 151
Emigrant and Sportsman in Canada, The (1881), 350
Emigrant's Assistant, The (1821), 133
Emigrant's Guide to New Brunswick, The (1842), 211
Emotions of Jesus, The (1915), 557
Emotive Theory of Ethics, The (1954), 597
Emperor Jones, 638
Empery: A Story of Love and Battle in Rupert's Land (1913), 296
Empire and Communications (1950), 521, 597
Empress of Hearts, The (1928), 661
Empson, William, 738
En Mexico (1958), 777, 787
Enamorado, The (1879), 114, 124
Encouragement to Colonies, An (1624), 15
Encouragements for ... undertakers of the New Plantation of Cape Breton (1625), 15
Encyclopaedia Britannica, 200, 582
Endicott, N. J., 546
Enemy Within, The (1918), 312
Engels, F., 467
England and Canada (Sandford Fleming), 348
England before and after Wesley (1939), 564
England to Canada (1884), 351
English and Scottish Popular Ballads (Child), 169
English Association, 534, 537
English Bloods (1930), 603
English-Canadian Literature to the Confederation (1920), 484
English Farmer in Canada, An (1904), 357
English Repertory Company, 652
English Traits (Emerson), 348

English-woman in the Canadian West, An (1913), 361
Enoch, the Philistine (1898), 308
Enquirer (Quebec), 129, 176
Enquiry into Goodness, An (1958), 589
Entertainment of King Charles (1633), 17
Enthusiasm and Other Poems (1831), 146
Epicurus and His Philosophy (1954), 589
Episcopacy and Reunion (1952), 569
Epistemology (1948), 595
Epithalamium in Time of War (1941), 783
Epitome of the Laws of Nova Scotia (1832–3), 221
Equations of Love, The (1952), 709
Ericson, Leif, 666
Ericsson, S. S., 606
Ermatinger, Edward, 139, 167, 239
Ernest Thompson Seton's Trail and Camp-fire Stories (1940), 378
Eros at Breakfast (1949), 641, 642
Eschman, I. T., 591
Espinosa, 48
Essay on Infant Baptism, An (1768), 552
Essays and Literary Studies (Leacock) (1916), 346
Essays in Fallacy (1910), 343
Essays in Modern Scholasticism (1944), 591
Essays in Politics (1909), 343, 344
Essays in Puritanism (1905), 342, 343, 344
Essays on Euripidean Drama (1954), 538
Essays on the Moral and Political Problems of Our Time (1949), 595
Essential Unity (ed. Heeney), 563
Essentials and Non-Essentials of the Christian Faith

(1928), 565
Essentials of Price Theory (1942), 523
Establishment of Schools and Colleges in Ontario 1792–1910 (1910), 238
Estates of Ramsey Abbey, The (Raftis), 566
Estella's Husband: or, Thrice Lost, Thrice Won (1891), 111
Ethical Idealism of Matthew Arnold, The (1959), 546
Etienne Gilson's Contributions to the Field of Epistemology (1948), 595
Etienne Gilson Tribute, An (1959), 592
Etudes sur les origines de la religion d'Egypt (1929), 571
Etymologizing in Greek Literature (1928), 545
Euboian League and its Coinage, The (1956), 543
Euripides, 538, 545, 728
Europe (1954), 776, 787
Evangeline (1847), 95, 286, 288, 347
Evans, Miss, 278
Evans, Augusta Jane, 278
Evans, D. O., 550
Evans, Donald, 596
Evans, Hubert, 369, 381, 387
Evans, J. S., 555
Evans, James, 573
Eve of St. Agnes, 794
Even Your Right Eye (1956), 792
Events and Signals (1954), 733, 785
Everitt, Nicholas, 362
Everson, R. G., 803–5
Everybody's magazine, 268
Everyman Theatre, 655
Evidence (Toronto), 494, 817
Evolution: Its Science and Doctrine (1960), 455
Evolution of Modern Capitalism, The (Hobson), 356
Evolution of Modern Medicine (1921), 454
Evolving Canadian Federalism (1958), 525
Ewart, J. S., 243, 249, 516
Examiner (newspaper), 225

Examiner (Peterborough), 613, 704
Exclusive Claims of David's Psalms, The (1855), 554
Excursions in and about Newfoundland (Jukes), 70
Execution (1958), 716
Existence and Deity (1872), 555
Existence of God, The (1946), 567
"Ex-Journalist," 303, 304
Expanding Community, The (1944), 594
Experiment (1956), 728
Explorations (1953–57), 541
Explorers of the Dawn (1922), 669
Exposé of and a Red Hot Protest against a Damnable Heresy ... by Professor Workman of Victoria University (1891), 554
Exquisite Perdita, The (1926), 661
Eye of a God, The, and other Tales of East and West (1899), 324
Eye of the Needle, The: Satires, Sorties, Sundries (1957), 733
Eyelands, V. G., 573
Eyes of a Gypsy (1926), 659

Fable of the Goats, The, and Other Poems (1937), 488, 749
Fackenheim, Emil L., 588
Facts of Conversion, The (1908), 558
Faerie Queene, 539
Faint Amorist (1927), 659
Fair Dominion, The (1911), 362
Fairbairn, A. M. D., 640
Fairbanks, Cassie, 116
Fairchild, George Moore, 289
Fairley, Barker, 539, 548
Fairley, Margaret, 140
Fairweather, Eugene R., 567, 568, 592–93
Faith of a Belgian, The: A Romance of the Great War (1916), 311
Faithful, Emily, 350
Falcon, Pierre, 168
Falconer, James W., 557
Falconer, Sir Robert, 340, 530, 557, 565, 616, 671
Falloon, D., 552
False Chevalier, The (1898), 287
Familiar Fields (1925), 375
Family Compact, The (1915), 244
Family Herald and Weekly Star, 158, 264, 265, 271
Family Portrait (Coulter), 641
Famous Animal Stories (1932), 382, 626
Famous Doctors (1956), 630
Famous Players–Lasky Corporation, 678
Fanning, Col. David, 77–8
Far Country, A (1915), 280
Faribault, G. B., 236
Faris, J. T., 599
Farm-Cottage, Camp and Canoe in Maritime Canada (1908), 256, 372
Farm for Two Pounds, A (1935), 603
Farncombe, C. J., 357
Farquharson, Mary, 639
Farr, David, 509
Fatal Marriage, The (Southworth), 278
Father Abraham (1935), 662
Father on the Farm (1947), 374
Faulkner, William, 695, 712, 720
Fearful Symmetry (1947), 540
Fearing, Kenneth, 733
Feast of Lupercal (1947), 718
Feast of Saint Anne, The, and Other Poems (1878), 116
Feathers Preferred (1951), 372
Feeling and Emotions (1928), 582
Feeling-experience and Its Modalities (1925), 591
Feet of the Furtive, The (1912), 386
Feindel, William, 456
Fergus MacTavish (1893), 630
Ferguson, G. Howard, 484, 671
Ferguson, Ida May, 308
Ferguson, Samuel, 155
Ferguson, Wallace, 518
Fergusson, Adam, 141
Fergusson, Francis, 649
Ferland, J. B. A., 242, 286
Ferne, Doris, 766
Fewster, Ernest, 369, 614
Fiamengo, Maria, 816
Fiddes, Victor, 569
Fiddlehead, 490, 493, 801, 816
"Fidelis"; *see* Machar, Agnes Maule
Fidler, Isaac, 141
Field, Erastus Salisbury, 846–7
Field, G. W., 531
Field, H. M., 354
Fielding, Henry, 84
Fifty Years Retrospect (Royal Society) (1932), 250
Fight for Canada, The (1904), 245
Fight with Distances: The States, the Hawaian Islands, Canada, British Columbia, Cuba, the Bahamas (1888), 350
Finch, Robert, 470, 472, 480, 487, 490, 494, 738–40, 753, 765, 848
Finding His Soul (1913), 328
Fir-Flower Tablets (1922), 726
Firebrand, The (1956), 506, 507
Fires of the Vine (1942), 668
Firestone, O. J., 522
First Century of Methodism in Canada, The (1910), 572
First Epistle of Peter, The (1946), (1958), 570
First Statement: A Magazine for Young Canadian Writers, 489–90, 767, 768, 769, 774, 776, 785

First Traveler, The (1911), 363
First Violin (Fothergill), 281
First Winter, The (1935), 603
Fischer, W. J., 305
Fisher, J. R., 674
Fisher, John, 610
Fisher, Peter (1782–1848), 104, 106, 116, 120–1, 122, 210
Fisher, Peter F. (1918–1958), 548
Fisherman's Creed, A (1923), 345
Fisherman's Paradise (1946), 372
Fisherman's Spring (1951), 373, 615
Fisherman's Summer (1959), 373, 615
Fisherman's Summer in Canada, A (1911), 362
Fisherman's Winter (1954), 373, 615
Fishing is a Cinch (1950), 371–72
Fiske, John, 161
Fiske, Minnie, 651
Fitch, E. R., 572
Fitzgerald, Scott, 689
Fitzroy, Yvonne, 600
Five Circles, The (1958), 381
Five Months' Fine Weather in Canada, Western U.S. and Mexico (1889), 350
Five Poems (Hine) (1954), 812
5000 Miles with the Barr Colonists (1929), 601
Five Years in Canada (1895), 355
Flame of Frost (1914), 291, 309, 328
Flashing Wings (1947), 369
Flatt, W. D., 296
Flaubert, G., 276, 675, 689
Fleet, William Henry, 149
Fleming, Mrs. Anne Cuthbert, 127
Fleming, Clint, 372
Fleming, James, 127
Fleming, J. Dick, 556
Fleming, John, 127, 209
Fleming, May Agnes, 105, 111, 182, 261, 263, 278, 294, 837

Fleming, Sandford, 255, 348, 351, 451, 452
Flenley, Ralph, 518
Fletcher, Alice, 166
Fletcher, Francis, 41
Fletcher, J. W., 75
Fleurieu, C. P., 46
Flight into Darkness (1944), 783
Flint and Feather (1912), 425
Flowing Summer, The (1947), 756, 757
Flying Canoe, The (1929), 674
Flying Years, The (1935), 664
Foley, Martha, 720
Foley, Pearl, 659
Folk Songs from Newfoundland (1934), 172
Folk Songs of Canada (1954), 172
Folk Songs of French Canada (1928), 169
Folk Songs of Old Quebec (1935), 169
Folk Songs of Quebec (1957), 169
Folk-Tales of Salishan and Sahaptin Tribes (1917), 164
Fontaine, Robert, 720
Footner, Hulbert, 262, 299, 302, 312, 337, 379, 659
Footnote in the Lord's Prayer (1951), 795
For King and Country (1874), 162, 629
For What Time Slays (1955), 779, 780
Foran, Joseph Kearney, 298
Foran, M. A., 465
Forbes-Robertson, Johnston, 651
Ford, F. M., 312
Foreigner, The (1909), 297, 323
Forest and Stream (journal), 384
Forest Friends (1926), 369
Forest Gleanings (Traill), 151
Forest Lily (1898), 307
Forest of Bourg-Marie, The (1898), 290, 310

Forest Ranger (1948), 631
Forest Wreath, The: A Collection of Lyrics (1833), 119
Forge in the Forest, The, being the Narrative of the Acadian Ranger, Jean Le Mer (1896), 288, 322
Forging of the Pikes, The (1920), 295
Forgotten Men (1933), 488, 686, 687
Forms of Value (1950), 596
Forsey, Eugene, 524, 525
Forster, E. M., 312, 541
Forsythe, Bertram, 653
Fortnight in America, A (1891), 354
Fortnightly Review, 161, 482, 734
Fortune my Foe (1949), 641, 642, 643, 655
Fortune Turns Her Wheel (1929), 659
Forty Years for Labrador (1933), 574
Foster, Hannah Webster, 146, 150
Foster, Miss T. D.; *see* Giles, Mrs. Henry
Foster, William A., 159, 160, 191
Fothergill, Charles, 140
Fothergill, Jessie, 281
Foundation and Constitution of the Christian Ministry (1826), 553
Foundations of Canadian Nationhood (1954), 498
Fountain, Paul, 358
Four Canadian Highwaymen (1886), 311–12
Four Centuries of Medical History in Canada and Newfoundland (1928), 454
Fourth Watch, The (1911), 291, 304, 333
Fowke, E., 169, 836
Fowke, V. C., 522
Fox, George, 195
Fox, W. Sherwood, 369, 372, 374, 509, 545
Foxe, Luke, 16
Fragment of Ontario Scott Act, A; or, A Ruined Life (1893), 306–7

France and England in North America (1865–92), 232–3
Franchère, Gabriel, 33, 34
Francis Bacon, His Career and Thought (1962), 587
Frank, Mrs. M. J., 297, 304
Franklin, Benjamin, 79, 121, 499
Franklin, Sir John, 35, 36–37, 38, 39, 40, 133, 296, 831
Fraser, Annie Ermatinger, 663
Fraser, Hugh, 348
Fraser, J. F., 362
Fraser, Rev. Joshua, 371
Fraser, Simon, 29–30, 65, 849
Fraser, Rev. Thurlow, 307
Fraser, William Alexander, 262, 263, 276, 279, 293, 296, 299, 305, 310, 324, 325, 380, 381, 387, 628
Fray Juan Crespi (1927), 43
Frazer, Sir James, 161
Fréchette, Louis 289, 422, 549
Freckles (Stratton-Porter), 283
Frederick, Harold, 276
Frederick Philip Grove (1945), 491
Frederick II, 364
Free Press (Winnipeg), 611, 724
Free Will and Determinism (1960), 596
Freedom and Necessity (1870), 436
Freedom of Jean Guichet, The (1927), 637
Freeman, John, 668
Freeman, Mary Wilkins, 282
Freier, F. W., 362
French, D. G., 484, 536
French, G. S., 508
French, Samuel (publisher), 639
French, Sarah, 109
French Canada in Transition (1943), 528
French Canadian Outlook, The (1946), 528
French Existentialism: A Christian Critique (1961), 597

French Text of the Ancrene Riwle (1958), 545
Frenzied Fiction (1918), 334
Freshman, Charles, 554
Freud, Sigmund, 691, 769, 770, 787, 834
Friday's Child (1955), 791
Friendly Acres (1927), 375
Friendship (1943), 614
Fripp, E. F. G., 603
Frobisher, Martin, 7, 8, 9, 12, 18
From a Library Window (1940), 593
From Amphibians to Reptiles (1937), 453
From Apollyonville to the Holy City: A Poem (1880), 119
From Apostle to Priest (1900), 557
From Colony to Nation (1946), 491
From Halifax to Vancouver (1912), 361
From Home to Home (1885), 349
From Humming Bird to Eagle (1936), 453
From Medicine Man to Medical Man (1934), 453
From Ontario to the Pacific (1887), 351
From Our Town (1959), 611
From Puritanism to the Age of Reason (1958), 569
From Savagery to Civilization: The Canadian Northwest (1885), 224
From Sea to Sea (1899), 355
From Strachan to Owen (1938), 572
From the Great Lakes to the Wide West (1902), 358
From Their Own Place (Denison), 635
From Tidewater to Timberline (1951), 369
From Wealth to Poverty: A Story of the Drink Curse (1884), 306
Frontenac, Count, 22, 244
Frontenac: The Courtier Governor (1959), 505
Frontenac and the Maid of the Mist (1927), 663

Frontier and Canadian Letters, The (1957), 174
Frontier Missionary, The (1853), 78
Frontier Riders (1925), 663
Frontier Stories (1898), 297
Frontiersman, The (1910), 301, 304, 307, 333
Frost, Robert, 724, **729**, 740, 756
Frost, S. B., **570**
Frost on the Sun (**1957**), 816
Froude, J. A., 7
Frozen Fire (1937), **759,** 760
Frozen Fortune (1910), 300
Fruit Ranching in British Columbia (1909), 257
Fruits of the Earth (1933), 680, 682, 683
Frye, Northrop, 6, 530, 533, 537, 538, 540, 548, 695, 722, 749, 768
Fugitives, The (1909), 119
Fugitives, The; or, A Trip to Canada (1830), **132**
Fulham, Piers, 365
Full and Correct Account of the Military Occurrences of the Late War (1818), **213**
Fulton, Robert, 675, 676
Fulton, S. C., 107
Fundamentals of Immunology (1943), **454**
Fur Hunters of the Far West, The (1855), 33
Fur Trade Apprentice (1940), **628**
Fur Trade in Canada, The (1930), **501**
Furry and Fluffy (**1946**), 380
Further Animal Stories (1936), **383**
Further Foolishness (1916), 334
Further Studies of Nature (1910), 369
Fuseli Poems (1960), **794**
Future Punishment (1886), 555
Fyfe, H. H., **362**
Fytche, Amelia, 288, 310

Gabriel Praed's Castle (1904), 309, **310, 327**

INDEX

Gabriel West and Other Poems (1866), 119
Gaff Linkum: A Tale of Talbotville (1907), 293
Gage, W. J., & Co., 188
Gagnieur, Elizabeth, 305
Gagnon, Ernest, 167
Galbraith, John, 302, 303, 573
Gale, Rev. James, 307
Galilean, The (1920), 565
Gallant, Mavis, 715, 720
Galsworthy, John, 703
Galt, John, 99, 131, 141, 142, 144, 168, 257, 282, 617, 618, 621
Gandier, Alfred, 562
Ganong, W. F., 235, 238
Gard, Arson, 358, 359
Gard, Robert, 166
Garden of Vision (1929), 659
Gardner, Helen, 544
Garland, Hamlin, 276, 282
Garneau, François-Xavier, 128, 208, 227, 248, 286
Garneau, Saint-Denys, 549, 795
Garner, Hugh, 491, 707, 716, 720, 721
Garrick, David, 36
Garrick Club (Hamilton), 652
Garvie, Alexander Rae, 115, 116, 122, 123
Garvin, John W., 482, 485, 536, 537, 724
Garvin, Mrs. John W., 600, 671
Gaskell, Mrs., 279, 282
Gaspards of Pinecroft, The (1923), 323
Gaspé, Philippe Aubert de, 286
Gassendi, Pierre, 582, 583
Gates Ajar, The (Phelps), 278
Gauthier, D. P., 589
Gazette (Halifax), 12
Gazette (Montreal), 130, 132, 133, 177, 221, 448
Gazette (Quebec), 126
Geddie, John, 573
Geikie, Rev. A. C., 153
General Brock (Lady Edgar), 228
General Description of Nova Scotia (1823), 95

Genius of Shakespeare, The, and Other Essays (1908), 534
Geoffrey Hampstead (1890), 294, 321
Geographical History of Nova Scotia, A ... (1749), 210
Geographical View of the Province of Upper Canada (1813), 136
Geological Survey of Canada, 451
Geology and Engineering (1939), 455
Geordie (1950), 718
George, Henry, 193, 279, 306, 460, 461, 463, 464
George, James, 436–7, 832
George Brown (Lewis), 228, 230
Gérin-Lajoie, A., 168, 286
Gérin-Lajoie, Paul, 524, 525
German Novel 1939–1944, The (1949), 549
Gerrard Street Mystery, The, and Other Weird Tales (1888), 294, 312
Gesner, Abraham, 211, 447
Ghost Murder, The (Amy) 659
Gibbon, John Murray, 169, 310, 311, 604, 659, 725
Gibson, J. Douglas, 523
Gibson, John, 145, 181
Gibson, William C., 454
Gielgud, John, 653
Gifford, W. A., 568, 571
Giguère, Roland, 795
Gilbert, Sir Humphrey, 7–10, 13, 19
Gilbert, William, 788
Gilded Age (Twain), 279
Giles, A., 354
Giles, Mrs. Henry, 146
Gill, Rev. Edward Anthony, 297
Gillese (nature writer), 388
Gilmour, G. P., 570
Gilmour, S. M., 570, 571
Gilpin, William, 366
Gilson, Etienne, 532, 566, 576, 590, 597
Ginsberg, Alan, 781
Ginx's Baby (1870), 279
Girl from Glengarry, The (1933), 323

Girl from Kellner's, The (1917), 299
Girl in the Silk Dress, The, and Other Stories (1931), 674
Girl of O. K. Valley, The (1919), 301
Girl of the Limberlost, The (Stratton-Porter), 283
Girl of the North, A (1900), 296, 309
Gissing, George, 675
Gladstone, W. E., 95, 194
Glaser, Vaughan, 652
Glasgow, Robert, 228, 229, 230, 235, 244, 245
Glass Menagerie, The (Williams), 644
Glassco, John, 797–99
Glazebrook, G. P. de T., 510, 511, 526
Gleaming Archway (1929), 687
Gleaner Tales (Sellars), 287
Glen, J. Stanley, 569
Glen of the High North (1920), 301, 333
Glendinning, J. C., 600
Glengarry Schooldays (1902), 323, 632
Globe (Toronto), later Globe and Mail, 225, 227, 315, 322, 344, 374, 535, 611, 724, 725
Glooskap's Country (1955), 628
Glorious Apollo (1925), 661
Glossop, Winnifred, Lady Howard of, 354
Glover, R., 26
Glover, T. R., 534, 556, 559
Gnome's Kitchen (1937), 380
Go to Sleep, World (1947), 779
Go West—Go Wise! (1930), 603
Go West, Young Man, Go West (1930), 674
God and Human Suffering (1941), 571
God and Philosophy (1941), 566, 590
God Forsaken (1930), 638
God of Gods (1927), 637
God of Justice (1960), 571

God of the Living (1939), 571
Godey (*Lady's Book*), 145
God's Freeman (1933), 565
God's Glory in the Heavens (1862), 448
God's Green Country (1922), 668
God's People in India (1959), 574
God's Sparrows (1936), 686
Godwin, A. H., 598
Godwin, William, 529, 544
Goethe, 203, 539, 541, 548, 653
Goethe and Scott (1950), 541
Goggio, E., 542, 549
"Going Home" (Callaghan), 655
Going Places (1939), 603
Gold-Cure, The (1924), 316–17
Gold, Gold, in Cariboo! (1894), 300
Golden Bough, The, 161
Golden Chalice, The (1935), 783
Golden Dog, The (1877), 66, 157, 158, 166, 171, 182, 286, 318, 485, 632, 841
Golden Fleece (1626), 13–14
Golden Grove, The (1600), 13
Golden Land of Canada Today and Tomorrow, The (1911), 362
Golden Phoenix, The, and Other French-Canadian Fairy Tales (1958), 165, 629
Golden Pine Cone, The (1950), 629
Golden Scarab, The (1926), 659
Golden Treasury of Canadian Verse, The (1928), 484
Golder, F. A., 42
Goldie, T. W., 449
Goldsmith, Oliver (Canadian poet), 104, 107, 116, 119–20, 121, 122, 127, 139, 178, 617–18, 801
Goldsmith, Oliver (Anglo-Irish poet), 71, 85, 119–20, 136, 139, 158
Goldwin Smith, Victorian Liberal (1957), 161
Gomery, Percy, 599, 659
Concourt brothers, 276
Gontcharev, I. A., 640
Good, M. T., 628
Goodrich, S. G., 632
Goodwin, Crawfurd D. W., 523
Goodwin, W. L., 452
Gordon, A. R., 556
Gordon, Charles W. (Ralph Connor), 262 263, 268, 270, 279, 283, 292, 294, 297, 298, 300, 304, 307, 311, 322–4, 330, 332, 333, 347, 358, 479, 558, 559, 619, 622, 632, 635, 672, 697, 832
Gordon, H. Scott, 523
Gordon, R. K., 547
Gordon, Sir Robert, of Lochinvar, 15
Gore, Francis (Lt. Gov.), 139
Gore Gazette, 140
Gosling, W. G., 239
Gosnell, R. E., 228, 236
Gospel Call to Sinners, A (1797), 76
Gospel Jesus Preached, The (1957), 570
Gospel of St. Luke, The (Moffatt series, 1930), 565
Gospel of the Hereafter, The (1910), 559
Gotlieb, Phyllis, 816
Goudge, T. A., 455, 587, 593
Gould, S., 574
Gourlay, Robert Fleming, 87, 139, 140, 208, 209, 211, 226, 520
Government of Canada, The (1947), 525
Government of Man, The (1920), 585
Governor-General's Awards, 487, 663, 736, 740, 741, 755, 756, 760, 761, 762, 770, 776, 782, 787, 788, 791, 796
Gowan, Elsie P., 639
Gowans, Alan, 508

Grace Displayed (1813), 82
Graff, W. L., 542, 548
Graham, Andrew, 27
Graham, Angus A., 668
Graham, Gerald, 510
Graham, Gordon Hill, 663
Graham, Gwethalyn, 706
Graham, J. W., 545
Graham, John W., 719
Graham, Roger, 506
Graham, Victor E., 545
Graham, W. C., 565
Graham, W. H., 506
Grain (1926), 299, 676, 677
Grainger, Martin Allerdale, 262, 300, 331, 332
Grand, Sarah, 280
Grange, Herbert, 357
Grannan, Mary, 631
Grant, Douglas, 544
Grant, George Monro, 227, 251, 255, 256, 353, 483, 555
Grant, George P., 596
Grant, Mrs. J. P., 118, 182
Grant, J. W., 569, 574
Grant, James Miller, 308, 380
Grant, W. L., 228, 237, 238, 243, 244
Grapes of Wrath (Steinbeck), 688
Graphic Press (Ottawa), 486, 685
Gras, Norman S. B., 518
Graustark (McCutcheon), 282
Graves, Robert, 696, 787
Gray, Archibald, 119
Gray, John (playwright), 634
Gray, John Morgan, 506
Gray, Robert, 49
Gray, T. W. D., 552
Gray, Thomas, 139, 423, 841
Grayson, Ethel Kirk, 668
Great Awakening in Nova Scotia, The (1948), 572
Great Dominion, The (1895), 353
Great English Poets (1929), 534
Great Gatsby, The (Fitzgerald), 715
Great Gold Rush (1913), 301

Great Island, The (1954), 631
Great North-West (1904), 358
"Great Stories of Canada" series, 630
Great Thinkers (1949), 594
Greater Love Hath No Man (1913), 312
Greek Critic, A: Demetrius on Style (1961), 545-6
Greek Point of View, The (1925), 533
Greek Tragedy (1920), 538
Green, H., 639
Green, J. R., 235
Green, T. H., 434, 436, 438, 578, 584
Green Pitcher (1928), 740
Green Plush (1932), 673
Green World (1945), 774
Greene, E. J. H., 549
Greene, Robert, 3
Greening, William Edward, 455
Greenleaf, Elizabeth Bristol, 172
Greenough, W. P., 165
Greenwood, A. E., 306
Greenwood, Thomas, 350
Gregg, Rev. William, 239, 572
Gregory, Lady, 641
Gregory, Claudius, 488, 686, 687
Grenfell, Dr. Wilfred T., 291, 307, 329, 559, 574
Grenier, Joseph Henri, 595
Greville, Fulke, 547
Grey, Earl, 499, 652
Grey, Francis William, 276, 290, 326
Grey, Zane, 283, 298
Grey Owl; *see* Belaney, Archibald Stansfeld
Grey Ship Moving (1945), 756, 757
Gribble, Wilfred, 467
Grierson, John, 492
Griffin, Watson, 306
Griffith, A. L., 570
Griffith, W. L., 363
Grinnell Expedition, The (1854), 39
Grip magazine, 192
Grome Mine Mystery, The (1933), 659

Groseilliers, Médart Chouart des, 22, 23, 57
Group of Seven (painters), 480, 482, 622, 732, 744, 754
Group Settlement (1936), 527
Grouped Frequency Word-List of Anglo-Saxon Poetry, A (1957), 543
Grove, Frederick Philip, 364, 368, 370, 471, 472, 483, 486, 609, 614, 615, 621, 623, 658, 661, 666, 674, 676, 678, 679-83, 684, 685, 694, 833, 836, 841, 842, 848
Growing Pains (1946), 622
Growth of a Man (1938), 672
Growth of Religious and Moral Ideas in Egypt, The (1927), 571
Grube, G. M. A., 545, 588
Guards in Canada, The (1848), 181
Guelton, Elizabeth, 381
Guest, L. M., 600
Guest, Lady Theodora, 354
Guiding Eve, The (1887), 554
Guido Cavalcanti's Theory of Love (1948), 549
Guillet, Edwin C., 509
"Guilty": Forgiven-Reclaimed (1906), 306
Gulliver's Travels, 42, 113
Gun Runners (1909), 312, 325
Gunn, W. T., 574
Gurnett, George, 140-1, 179
Gustafson, Ralph, 491, 765, 783, 784
Gutenberg Galaxy, The (1962), 518, 541
Guthrie, Sir Tyrone, 656
Guy, John, 12-13
Guy Earlscourt's Wife (1872), 111
Gyles, John, 57, 72, 73
Gzowski, Sir Casimir Stanislaus, 455

Habitant-Merchant, The (1939), 674

Haeckel, 449, 450
Hagan, Henry John, 132
Haggard, H. Rider, 113, 280, 284
Haida Myths Illustrated in Argillite Carvings (1953), 165
Haig-Brown, Roderick T., 345, 368, 373, 374, 378, 379, 380, 386, 615, 630, 631, 632, 712
Hailey, Arthur, 650, 698
Hakluyt, Richard, 4-5, 7-9, 12, 16, 19, 41, 55, 72
Hakluyt Society, 45, 237
Haldane, J. W. C., 354, 357
Hale, Katherine: *see* Garvin, Mrs. John W.
Half Century of Conflict, A (1892), 286
Haliburton, Lucy Chandler Grant, 94
Haliburton, R. G., 447
Haliburton, Robert J., 159
Haliburton, Thomas Chandler, 62, 92, 94-101, 105, 106, 108, 113, 166, 175, 178, 205, 209-10, 214, 253, 261, 262, 267, 280, 284, 308, 317, 335, 447, 483, 485, 825, 826, 847
Haliburton, William H. O., 94
Halifax Monthly Magazine, 178
Hall, Capt. Basil, 141
Hall, Charles F., 16
Hall, Charles Windsor, 116
Hall, Christopher, 7
Hall, Lt. Francis, 141
Halliday, Hugh, 368, 371
Haloed Tree, The (1956), 800
Hambleton, Jack, 372, 380, 631
Hambleton, Ronald, 491, 767, 769, 775
Hamil, Fred, 509
Hamil, Grant, 362
Hamilton, A. C., 546
Hamilton, K., 570
Hamilton, Pierce Stevens, 116
Hamilton, Thomas, 141
Hamilton, Sir William, 436, 442, 443, 444

902 INDEX

Hamlet, 11, 534, 545, 650, 793
Hamlet, an Ideal Prince (1916), 534
Hammond, Mrs. J. B., 293
Hampden, Charles, 652
Hamsun, K., 683
Handbook of Canadian Literature: (MacMurchy, 1906), 536; (Rhodenizer, 1930), 484
Handbook of Christian Ethics (1908), 444, 558
Handbook of Psychology (1885), 444
Handbook of the Gospels (1956), 570
Handel, George Frederick, 206
Handicap, The (1910), 296, 329
Hands across the Pacific (1951), 606
Hangman Ties the Holly, The (1955), 790
Hanlan, Ned, 353
Hannay, James, 222, 223, 228
Hanning, Janet, 353
Hansen: A Novel of Canadianization (1924), 684
Hanson, Eric, 523
Happy Time, The (1945), 720
Harbour Master, The (1913), 291
Harbour Tales Down North (1918), 291
Hard Cash (Reade), 279
Hard Times (Dickens), 279
Hardy, Campbell, 371
Hardy, E. R., 569
Hardy, Thomas, 149, 264, 280, 709, 747
Hardy, W. G., 660, 662
Hardscrabble (1850), 138
Hare and the Tortoise, The (1926), 683
Hargrave, Letitia, 35
Harmon, Daniel Williams, 25, 30, 34
Harmony of Science and Revelation, The (1856), 449
Harney, John Paul, 816
Harold, Rev. P. J., 308
Harp, The (Montreal), 207

Harper, John Murdoch, 118
Harper of Heaven: A Record of Radiant Living (1948), 619
Harper's Magazine, 161, 265–6, 276, 382
Harrington, W. S., 574
Harris, Carrie Jenkins, 290, 308
Harris, D. Fraser, 452
Harris, Eric, 641
Harris, Lawren, 653, 726, 728
Harris, R. W., 574
Harrison, Dr. Charles, 434
Harrison, F. C., 452
Harrison, Mrs. J. F., 197, 428
Harrison, M., 603
Harrison, Susie Frances, 290, 310
Harrison, William Henry, 138
Harron, Donald, 655
Harry Black (1956), 718
Hart, Mrs. G. H., 107, 109–10, 133, 140, 176
Hart, Percy W. E., 288
Hart House Theatre, 601, 653, 655, 839
Harte, Bret, 206, 282, 300, 317, 328
Harvest of the Sea, The (1905), 291, 329
Harvey, Moses M., 70, 71, 449
Hasell, Miss, 600, 602
Hath Not a Jew ... (1940), 736, 765
Hatton, Joseph, 71, 350
Haultain, Theodore Arnold, 341, 358, 369
Haunters of the Silences, The (1907), 384, 385, 386
Hauptmann, G., 548
Haverhill; or, Memoirs of an Officer in the Army of Wolfe (1831), 128
Hawkridge (explorer), 16
Hawley, William Fitz, 130, 131
Hawthorn, Harry B., 527
Hawthorne, N., 273, 277, 548, 694, 696, 698, 723
Hay, John, 279
Hay, Wilma P., 629

Haye, Edward, 7, 8
Hayes, John F., 630
Hayman, Robert, 14, 15, 56
Hayne, D. M., 549
Haynes, James, 119
Hays, Charles, 360
Hayward, Victoria, 600
Hazard of New Fortunes, A (Howells), 279
He Dwelt Among Us: A Study of the Life of Jesus (1936), 559
He Rides the Sky (1941), 688
Head, Sir Francis Bond, 141, 149
Head, Sir George, 141
Head Keeper, The (1898), 304
Headwaters of Canadian Literature (1924), 484, 537
Heagerty, J. J., 454
Hear Us O Lord from Heaven Thy Dwelling Place (1961), 717
Hearne, Samuel, 25–7, 28, 34, 58, 238
Heart of a Peacock (1953), 622
Heart of an Immigrant, The (1931), 603
Heart of Cherry McBain, The (1919), 297
Heart of the Ancient Wood, The (1902), 379
Heart of the Canadian Rockies, The (1905), 358
Heart-Song of Today Disturbed by Fire from the 'Unruly Member,' A (1886), 294
Heart Stories (1919), 311
Heart That Knows, The (1906), 322
Hearts and Faces (1916), 310
Heathen World, The (1884), 573
Heavenly Twins, The (1893), 280
Heavysege, Charles, 147, 148–9, 157, 206, 705, 843
Hebbel, C. F., 548
Hebrew Origins (1936, etc.), 542
Hedonistic Theories from

INDEX 903

Aristippus to Spencer (1895), 441
Heeney, W. Bertal, 292, 562
Hegel, G. W. F., 438, 439, 832
Heichelheim, F. M., 518, 543
Heir from New York, The (1911), 294
Heir of Fairmount Grange, The (1895), 290
Helena's Household: A Tale of Rome . . . (1867), 112
Hell! I'm British (1938), 603
Helleiner, Karl, 518
Hemans, Felicia, 71, 136, 145
Heming, Arthur, 372
Hemingway, Ernest, 675, 689, 702, 713–14
Hemlock: A Tale of the War of 1812 (1890), 287
Hemlow, Joyce, 544
Hemming, the Adventurer (1904), 329
Hemsworth, Wade, 171
Hénault, Gilles, 795
Henday, Antony, 24–5, 27, 58
Hendel, Charles W., 549, 587, 595
Henel, Heinrich, 548
Henry, A. (printer), 551
Henry, Alexander, the elder, 23, 25, 27–8, 30, 34, 50, 65, 88
Henry, Alexander, the younger, 30–1
Henry, O., 283
Henry, Walter, 128–9, 142, 617
Henry; or, The Juvenile Traveller (1836), 624
Henry V, 657
Henry James (Edgar, 1927), 548
Henry James, French Writers and American Women (1961), 548
Henry James, Man and Author (1927), 541
Henshaw, Julia, 300, 308
Henty, G. A., 204, 285, 296, 298, 317, 625, 630, 632
Hepburn, Mitchell, 602

Her Sailor (1900), 320
Herald (Montreal), 132, 140
Heralds of Empire (1902), 296, 629
Herbert, George, 788
Herbert, Mary, 109
Herbert, Sarah, 109
Herbin, J. F., 668
Here and Now (1945), 781
Here and Now (journal), 490
Here's to Canada! (1941), 605
Heresy of Courtly Love (1947), 545
Heriot, George, 88, 212–13, 252
Herklots, H., 603
Herman, Alan, 634, 687–8
Heroics (1961), 812
Herring, Frances E., 299, 358
Hesperus (1860), 148
Hesse, Hermann, 532
Hettlinger, R. F., 569
Hetty Dorval (1947), 708
Hewlett, M., 281
Heywood, Thomas, 17
Hiawatha (Longfellow), 161, 164
Hibbert Journal, 451
Hickey, Rev. Daniel, 288
Hickman, William Albert, 290
Hicks, Edward, 848
Hicks, Seymour, 651
Hickscorner (c. 1510), 6
Hidden Places, The (1922), 333
Hiebert, Paul, 720
High and Dry (1938), 603
High Hazard (1928), 660
High Heart, The (1917), 290, 309, 311, 327
High Plains, The (1938), 683
High Road to Christ, The (1914), 565
Higher Hill, The (1944), 697
Highest Hill, The (1949), 712
Highways of Canadian Literature (1924), 484, 491
Hilda; see, Path of a Star, The

Hill, A. S., 349
Hill Top (1935), 668
Hilliard, Albert L., 596
Hilts, Joseph, 378
Hincks, Sir Francis, 225, 505
Hind, Cora, 602
Hind, Henry Youle, 153, 154, 159
Hine, Daryl, 494, 812–14
Hines, Duncan, 603
Hints for Lovers (1909), 341
Hippity Hobo and the Bee (1952), 632
Hirsch, John, 656
Hirschfelder, J. M., 554
His Dominion (1917), 574
His Dominion of Canada (1932), 563
His Honour and a Lady (1896), 303, 316
His Majesty's Yankees (1942), 697
His Royal Happiness (1914), 315
Histoire des Canadiens-Français (1882–84), 226
Historical Account of Discoveries and Travels in North America (1829), 211
Historical and Descriptive Account of British America (1839), 212
Historical and Other Papers and Documents Illustrative of the Educational System of Ontario 1792–1853 (1911–12), 238
Historical and Statistical Account of New Brunswick (1844), 211
Historical and Statistical Account of Nova Scotia (1829), 95, 96, 178, 209, 210, 253
Historical Sketches of Feudalism, British and Continental (1852), 248
Historical View of the Church of England (1830), 552
History and Revelation (1926), 557
History, Geography and Statistics of British North America (1864), 234

History of Acadia, from its First Discovery to its Surrender ... (1879), 222
History of American Socialism (1872), 460
History of Ancient Western Philosophy (1959), 592
History of British Columbia (Gosnell and Scholefield), (1913), 236
History of British Columbia from Its Earliest Discovery to the Present Time (Begg) (1894), 223
History of Canada: Heriot (1804), 88, 212; Kingsford (1887–98), 226, 235; McMullen (1855), 215; Roberts (1902), 219–20; Wm. Smith (1826), 127, 213
History of Canada under French Regime 1535–1763 (1872), 217
History of Cavalry (1877), 249
History of Charles the Bold, Duke of Burgundy (1864), 249
History of Chemistry in Canada (1949), 454
History of Christian Philosophy in the Middle Ages (1955), 590, 592
History of Emily Montague, The (1769), 84–5, 309, 718, 830
History of English-Canadian Literature to the Confederation (1920), 536
History of Fanny Burney (1958), 544
History of Halifax City (1895), 239
History of Medicine in its Salient Features (1921), 454
History of Medicine in the Province of Quebec (1931), 454
History of New Brunswick (1909), 222
History of Newfoundland from the Earliest Times to the Year 1860 (Pedley, 1863), 221

History of Newfoundland from the English, Colonial, and Foreign Records (Prowse, 1895), 221
History of New France (Lescarbot, ed. 1907–14), 238
History of Nova Scotia: Haliburton (1829), 209; Murdoch (1865–7), 80, 221–2, 236
History of Philosophy and Philosophical Education (1947), 590
History of Prince Edward Island (1875), 222
History of Psychology (Brett, 1912–21), 578–82
History of Russia (Kliuchevski, trans. 1911–30), 249
History of the Baptists of the Maritime Provinces (1902), 572
History of the British Colonies (1834–35), 212
History of the Canadian Pacific Railway (1923), 507
History of the Canadian People (1943), 491
History of the Catholic Church in Western Canada from Lake Superior to the Pacific 1659–1895 (1910), 240, 573
History of the Church in Eastern Canada and Newfoundland (1892), 572
History of the County of Bruce and of the Minor Municipalities Therein (1906), 239
History of the County of Huntingdon and of the Seignories of Chateaugay and Beauharnois (1888), 239
History of the County of Pictou (1877), 239
History of the Island of Newfoundland and the Coast of Labrador (Anspach) (1819), 69
History of the Late Province of Lower Canada (1848–55), 215, 220
History of the Late War between Great Britain and the United States of America (1832), 213
History of the Methodist Church [in Canada] (1890), 572
History of the Northern Interior of British Columbia (1904), 239
History of the North-West (Begg, 1894–95), 223
History of the Presbyterian Church in the Dominion of Canada from the Earliest Times to 1834 (1885), 239
History of the Roman World from 30 B.C. to A.D. 138 (1944), 542
History of the Settlement of Upper Canada (Ontario), with special reference to the Bay of Quinté (1869), 241
History of the Society of Friends ... in Canada (1927), 573
History of the War between Great Britain and the United States of America ... 1812, 1813, and 1814 (Auchinleck, 1855), 151, 216
History of the War of 1812 between Great Britain and the United States of America (Hannay, 1901), 222
History of Transportation in Canada (Glazebrook), 511
Hobson, J. A., 356
"Hochelaga"; see Warburton, George
Hochelaga; or, England in the New World (1846), 214
Hodgetts, J. E., 510, 524
Hodgins, J. G., 238
Hodkin, Thomas, 571
Hoeniger, F. D., 547
Hoffer, A., 456
Hogan, J. F., 354
Hogg, James, 104, 119, 132, 178
Hohenzollerns in America, The (1919), 334
Holcroft, Thomas, 129

INDEX 905

Holden, John, 654
Holiday in Canada, A (1924), 600
Holiday Rambles between Winnipeg and Victoria (1888), 349
Holiday Trip, A (1888), 351
Holiday Trip to Canada (1916), 361
Holidays for Jesus (1901), 357
Holiwell, Mrs. M. J. H., 155
Hollow Universe, The (1960), 595
Holmes, Abraham S., 148, 150
Holmes, James, 147
Holmes, O. W., 203, 403
Holmes, Sherlock, 279, 842
Holy Manhattan (Coulter), 641
Holyoake, J. G., 348
Home, Rudyard, 354
Home Help in Canada, A (1912), 361
Home is the Stranger (1950), 712
Home Made Banners (1946), 716
Homer, 194, 206, 393, 423
"Homesteader," 358
Homesteaders, The: Chapman (1936), 668; Stead (1916), 299
Hon. Alexander Mackenzie, His Life and Times (1892), 229
Honeyman, Rev. David, 447
Honor Edgeworth; or, Ottawa's Present Tense (1882), 303
Hood, Colin, 603
Hood, Hugh, 494
Hood, Robert, 37
Hood, Robert Allison, 301, 659
Hood, Thomas, 423
Hood, Wm. C., 523
Hoof and Claw (1913), 386, 625
Hook, Theodore, 98
Hooke, Hilda M., 629
Hooker, J. H., 603
Hooker, Rev. LeRoy, 293, 308
Hoosier Schoolmaster, The (1871), 282

Hope, Anthony, 282
Hope Deferred (1949), 642
Hope of the Gospel, The (1955), 571
Hopkins, Gerard Manley, 783, 784, 792, 835
Hopkins, J. Castell, 208, 218, 219, 227, 239
Hopwood, Victor, 831, 835, 836
Horace, 104, 535, 541, 545
Hordern, W., 570
Horner, R. C., 555
Hornung, Ernest, 279
Hornyansky, Michael, 165
Hosea, Joel and Amos (1929), 557
Hoskins, John, 49
Houde, Camilien, 602
Hound from the North, The (1904), 297
Hours of Childhood and Other Poems (1820), 135, 176
House in the Quiet Glen, The (Coulter), 641
House in the Water, The (1908), 384
House of All Sorts, The (1944), 622
House of Intrigue, The (1918), 312
House of Mirth, The (Wharton), 280
Houses of Glass (1898), 306
House, Vernal, 471
Housman, A. E., 734
Houston, Alma, 628
Hovey, Richard, 411
How Canada Was Held for the Empire: The Story of The War of 1812 (1901), 222-23
How Hartman Won (1903), 293
How I Came to be Governor of the Island of Cacona (1852), 149
How Many Angels (1956), 710
How we got our Bible (1885), 559
Howard, Sir Robert, 17
Howay, F. W., 49, 50
Howe, John, 176
Howe, Joseph, 62, 94, 95, 96, 104, 106, 115-16,

121-22, 175, 178, 182, 205, 209, 210, 211, 222, 227, 340, 499, 843
Howell, John, 46
Howells, William Dean, 146, 203, 275, 276, 277, 279, 280, 282, 286, 292, 309, 347
Howison, John, 133, 141
Howse, E. M., 569, 570
Hubbard, R. H., 508
Huckleberry Finn, 282, 515, 711, 848
Hudson, Henry, 16, 20
Hudson's Bay (Ryerson, 1855), 573
Hudson's Bay; or, Life in the Woods of America (Ballantyne, 1848), 159, 167, 625
Hugh Wynne, Free Quaker (Mitchell), 281, 282
Hughes, Everett C., 528
Hughes, Thomas, 354
Hugo, Victor, 281, 550
Hui Shan, 43
Huldowget (1926), 663
Hulme, T. E., 751
Humanities in Canada, The (1947), 530
Humanities Research Council, 530, 531
Humboldt, A., 449
Hume, 442
Humour: Its Theory and Technique (1935), 335
Humour and Humanity: An Introduction to the Study of Humour (1937), 335
Humphrey Clinker (Smollett), 99
Hunt, R. W., 595
Hunt, T. Sterry, 153, 451
Hunter, Martin, 376
Hunter, Robert, 180
Hunter Rose Publishing Company, 184, 188, 303
Hunter-Duvar, John, 62, 105, 114-15, 123-4, 429, 843
Hunter's Holidays (1947), 372
Hunters of the Wild (1937), 381
"Hunting Stuart" (Davies), 641
Huntingdon, Richard, 105
Huntington, L. S., 309

Huntsman, A. G., 454
Huron Chief, The (1830), 130
Huron Signal, 152
Huron-Wyandot Traditional Narratives in Translations and Native Texts (1960), 165
Husky (1940), 387
Huston, Walter, 651
Hutchison, Bruce, 251, 506, 604, 606, 607
Hutchison, Margaret, 707
Hutton, Maurice, 533, 610
Huxley, T. H., 204, 439, 449, 450, 453
Huyghue, Douglas S., 110
Hymns and Spiritual Songs (Alline, 1802), 76
Hymns of the Church (1935), 563, 574
Hypnotized; or, the Experiment of Sir Hugh Galbraith (1898), 308

I Live in the Woods (1953), 371
Ibsen, Henrik J., 280, 645, 653
Ice Ages, Recent and Ancient (1926), 456
Ice Cod Bell or Stone (1962), 765, 816
Icelandic Meditations on the Passion (1930), 566
Idea of a Theater (Fergusson), 649
Idea of Immortality and Western Civilization, The (1930), 565
Idealism in National Character (1920), 616
Idler, The (Eng. magazine), 269, 314
Idylls of the King, 158, 410, 534
If Any Man Sin (1915), 296, 333
I.G.Y., The Year of the New Moons (1961), 455
Ill-Tempered Lover, The, and Other Poems (1948), 754
Illustrated English Social History (Trevelyan), 4
Illustrated History of the Dominion, 1535-1876 (1877), 217
Image of Canada (1953), 606
Imitation and Design (1953), 541, 588
Immortality versus Annihilation (1872), 555
Imperfectly Proper (1920), 611
Imperialist, The (1904), 293, 303, 305, 309, 315, 316
Improved Binoculars, The: Selected Poems (1956), 782
Improvement; or, A Visit to Grandmama (1833), 624
In a Fishing Country (1922), 345, 373
In Divers Tones (1886), 401
In Dreamland and Other Poems (1893), 429
In His Steps (1897), 279-80
In Music's Thra' (1903), 310
In Memoriam (Tennyson), 427, 534, 799
In Nature's Workshop (1901), 369
In Old France and New (1899), 288, 308
In Pastures Green (1915), 344, 345, 375
In Peril: True Stories of Adventure (1887), 371
In Search of Canadian Liberalism (1960), 515-16, 517, 526
In Search of Myself (1946), 621, 623, 679, 680
In the Acadian Land (1899), 369
In the Brooding Wild (1905), 298-9
In the Canadian Bush (1914), 362
In the Days of the Canada Company (1896), 143, 239
In the Garden of Charity (1903), 290, 327
In the Midst of Alarms (1894), 295, 314
In the Morning of Time (1919), 384
In the New Capital (1897), 302, 303
In the Pathless West (1904), 358
In the Van (1906), 295
In the Village of Viger (1896), 262, 289
In the West (1935), 603
In the Woods and on the Waters (1896), 378, 379
Inasmuch (1917), 574
Inch, James, 434
Incomplete Anglers (1943), 372, 845
Incredible Canadian, The (1953), 506
Incredible Journey, The (1960), 381, 628
Incunabula Medica, 1467-1480 (1922), 454
Index Aristophaneus (O. J. Todd), 545
Indian Legends of Canada (1960), 165
Indian Emperor, The (Dryden), 17
Indian Queen, The (Howard, 1662), 17
Indians of British Columbia, The (1958), 527
Industry and Humanity (1918), 597
Infant Sprinkling (1823), 552
Infeld, Leopold, 455
Infinite Moment, The (1950), 547
Influence des saisons de Thomson sur la poésie déscriptive en France, 1759-1810, L' (1927), 549
Inge, Dean W. R., 445
Ingersoll, Robert, 306
Inglis, Charles, 552
"Inheritance, The" (Harry Boyle), 655
Inman, M. K., 523
Inner Circle, The (1924), 559
Inner Shrine, The (1909), 326
Innis, Harold Adams, 246, 501-2, 507, 508, 515, 518, 521, 541, 597, 829
Innis, Mary Quayle, 471, 480, 674

Innocent Traveller, The (1949), 708
Innocents Abroad (Twain), 112, 281
Insight: A Study of Human Understanding (1957), 593
Inspiration and Modern Criticism (1925), 565
Instincts and Religion (1940), 558
Institute of Canadian Studies, 532
Intellectual Development of the Canadian People, The (1881), 217
Interpretation of Religion, The (1929), 560
Interpretation of Religious Experience, The (1912), 441, 555
Interpretation of the Bible, The (1961), 570
Interpreter's Bible, The, 570–71
Introducing the Bible (1944), 574
Introduction to Democratic Theory (1960), 526
Introduction to Ethics (1891), 443, 444
Introduction to Medical Science, An (1937), 454
Introduction to Metaphysics (1949), 587
Introduction to Modern Logic (1920), 594
Introduction to Philosophy (1961), 597
Introduction to Political Economy, An (1941), 523
Introduction to Psychology, An (1904), 444
Introduction to Systematic Philosophy (1948), 587
Introduction to the Poetry of Robert Browning, An (1889), 534
Introduction to the Prayer Book, An (1930), 563
Inverted Pyramid, The (1924), 333
Iredale, Andrew, 358
Irene of Corinth: A Historical Romance of the First Century (1884), 308

Irish-Canuck-Yankee, The (1910), 362
Irish History and the Irish Question (1905), 249
Irishman in Canada, The (1877), 240
Irving, Rev. G. C., 153
Irving, Henry, 639, 650
Irving, John A., 528, 569, 587, 589, 829, 832
Irving, Washington, 33, 131, 549
Irving, William, 131
Irwin, Violet M., 628
Is It Just? (1911), 301
Isham, James, 27
Isherwood, C., 770
Ishmael (Southworth), 278
Islam in Modern History (1957), 571
Island Minstrel, The (1860, 1867), 117
Israel, Charles E., 494, 710
It Needs to be Said (1929), 609, 679
Italians in Early American History (1930), 549
Itinerants of the Timberlands (1934), 387
It's Never Over (1930), 690
It's Never Too Late to Mend (Reade), 279
Ives, Edward D., 172

JACK, ANNIE, 289
Jack, Donald, 634
Jack Brag in Spain (Richardson), 181
Jack Ralston (1901), 296
Jackson, A. Y., 622
Jackson, Sir Barry, 639
Jackson, George, 556, 557, 558
Jackson, Harold, 509
Jackson, M., 349
Jackson, William, 555
Jacob, Fred, 637, 668, 669, 673
Jake and the Kid (Mitchell), 840
Jalna (1927), 484, 669, 671, 823
James I, King, 15
James, G. P. R., 281
James, Henry, 263, 264, 273–83 *passim,* 309, 312,
315, 317, 318, 319, 326, 327, 541, 548, 709, 720, 721, 722, 749
James, Thomas, 16
James, William, 74, 213, 444, 551, 578
James Evans, Inventor of the Syllabic System of the Cree Language (1890), 573
James, the Lord's Brother (1906), 558
Jameson, Mrs. Anna, 127, 139, 143, 167, 181, 254, 255
Jameson, Robert S., 143
Jamieson, Stuart, 522, 523, 527
Jancis (1935), 663
Janet of Kootenay (1919), 301, 311
Jarvis, Thomas Stinson, 294, 309, 321
Jarvis, William Henry, 297, 301
Jason—Nova Scotia (1903), 288
Jay, E. G., 567
Jean Baptiste (Adams, 1825), 126–7
Jean Baptiste (LeRossignol, 1915), 289
Jean Duns Scot (1952), 590
Jean-Jacques Rousseau: Citizen of Geneva (1937), 595
Jean-Jacques Rousseau, Moralist (1934), 549, 595
Jebb, Dr. John, 129
Jeffers, Robinson, 724
Jefferson, T., 135, 248
Jefferys, Thomas, 42
Jen of the Marshes (1921), 668
Jenkins, John Edward, 279
Jenkins, R. S., 294
Jenness, Diamond D., 165, 527
Jennings, Clotilda, 119
Jephson, Lady H. J., 354
Jephthah's Daughter, 149
Jerome, Jerome K., 314
Jessie of the Cariboo (1911), 300
Jesuit Fathers, 164, 831
Jesuit Missions (1910), 572
Jesuit Relations, The, and

INDEX

Allied Documents 1610–1791 (1896–1901), 11, 20, 21, 164, 177, 238, 747
Jesus and the Human Conflict (1928), 562
Jesus the Man and Christ the Spirit (1928), 554
Jewett, Sarah Orne, 282, 697
Jewitt, John, 23, 48, 50
Jews and the Israelites, The (1870), 554
Jig for the Gypsy, A (1954), 641, 643
Jim, the Story of a Backwoods Police Dog (1924), 381
Joan at Halfway (1919), 290
Jocz, J., 570
Joerg, W. L. G., 522
Jogues, Father, 21, 22, 748
Johann Lind (1928), 666
John (1937), 688
John Graves Simcoe (Scott), 228
John Locke and English Literature of the Eighteenth Century (1936), 547, 588
John Matheson (1923), 668
John Paul's Rock (1932), 668
John Saint John and Anna Gray: A Romance of Old New Brunswick (Currie), 119
John a' Var: His Lays (Hunter-Duvar), 124
Johnny Bear and Other Stories (Seton), 382
Johnny Bear, Lobo, and Other Stories (1935), 382
Johnny Chinook (1954), 166
Johnson, Allen, 244
Johnson, Allison H., 587, 588
Johnson, Frank, 182
Johnson, Harry G., 523
Johnson, Lionel, 813
Johnson, Pauline, 165, 166, 256, 257, 347, 378, 425, 426, 479, 628, 752, 840
Johnson, Col. Richard M., 138
Johnson, Samuel, 613, 704, 833

Johnson, Skuli, 545
Johnson, Rev. W. A., 342
Johnson, W. S., 614
Johnston, Charles, 509
Johnston, Franz, 638
Johnston, George, 568, 805–8
Johnston, Mary, 281
Johnston, R., 169, 172
Johnstone, C. C., 355
Johnstone, J. K., 547
Joliat, E. A., 549
Jones, Alice, 262, 263, 281, 288, 290, 291, 309, 310, 327, 328
Jones, C. M., 545
Jones, D. G., 494, 816
Jones, F. E., 528
Jones, Rev. Harry, 351
Jones, James Athearn, 128
Jones, John Matthew, 451
Jones, Susan, 262, 263, 281, 290, 296, 309
Jongleur Songs of Old Quebec (1962), 169
Jonson, Ben, 14, 653
Jordan, W. J., 557
Jory's Cove (1941), 631
Joseph Andrews (Fielding), 547
Joseph Howe (Longley), 228
Josiah Garth (D. Clark), 295
Joudry, Patricia, 634, 644
Journal (Mountain, 1845), 129
Journal (Witherspoon), 72
Journal and Letters (Curwen, 1864), 72
Journal de M. Miertsching (1857), 38
Journal d'un voyage aux mers polaires (1851), 39
Journal of a Tour in the U.S., Canada and Mexico (1897), 354
Journal of a Voyage for the Discovery of a Northwest Passage . . . 1819–20 (1821), 35–6
Journal of Speculative Philosophy, 439
Journal of Transactions and Events . . . Labrador (Cartwright, 1792), 69
Journal of Voyages and Travels in the Interior of North America (1820), 30
Journals and Letters of Pierre Gaultier de Varennes de la Vérendrye and His Sons . . . (1937), 224
Journey from Prince of Wales's Fort in Hudson's Bay to the Northern Ocean (1795), 25–6, 28, 238
Journey into Wonder (1952), 454
Jowett, Benjamin, 438
Joyce, James, 312, 481, 689, 690, 695, 717, 718, 720, 751, 835
Joyous Adventure, A (1928), 598
Judge at Four Corners, The (Burgin), 292
Judgement House, The (1913), 318
Judith Moore; or, Fashioning a Pipe (1898), 310
Judy and the General (1955), 631
Jukes, Joseph Beete, 70
Julie; or, La Nouvelle Héloïse (1949), 550
Jung, C. J., 540
Jungle, The (1906), 280
Jupiter Eight (1936), 673, 674
Just Mary (1941), 631
Justice (1955), 592
Juvenal, 24, 545

Kaffir, Kangaroo, Klondyke (1898), 301
Kafka, Franz, 787, 836
Kailyard School, 282
Kak, the Copper Eskimo (1924), 628
Kaleidoscope Echoes (1895), 70
Kalm, Peter, 131, 159
Kamali, S. A., 571
Kane, Elisha Kent, 39
Kane, Paul, 35, 153, 159, 483
Kant, Emmanuel, 202, 434, 438, 439, 440, 443, 589, 595, 596

Kant and His English Critics
    (1881), 440
Karpeles, Maud, 172
*Kasba: A Story of Hudson
    Bay* (1915), 296
Kean, Edmund, 651
Keats, John, 63, 147, 159,
    160, 193, 205, 206, 389,
    393, 394, 411, 421, 542,
    685, 723, 751, 783, 794
*Keats: A Bibliography and
    Reference Guide* (1949),
    542
Keeling, Capt. William, 11
*Keeper of Bic Lighthouse,
    The* (1891), 290
    (1895), 310
Keirstead, B. S., 523
Keirstead, E. Miles, 434
Keith, Marian: *see* Mac-
    Gregor, Mrs. Mary Esther
Keller, Phillip, 373
Kelly, A. R., 572
Kelsey, Henry, 24, 57–8
Kendall, Ralph Selwood, 298
Kendall, Sidney, 372
Kennedy, H. A., 358, 599
Kennedy, Leo, 471, 472,
    480, 481, 488, 687, 730,
    734, 735, 752, 753, 754,
    844
Kennedy, W. P. M., 229,
    498, 525
Kensington Gardens in 1830
    (1830), 138
Kent, John, 140–1, 179
Kerchiefs to Hunt Souls
    (1895), 310
Kermode, Frank, 518
Kerr, A. E., 570
Kerr, Donald, 505
Kerr, W. B., 510
Key, Archibald, 638
Key of Dreams, The (1922),
    659
Khan, Genghis, 696
Kidd, Adam, 130–31, 132
Kilbourn, William, 494, 506,
    825, 829
Killdeer, The (1962), 635,
    648–9
Kilpatrick, G. G. D., 571
Kilpatrick, T. B., 556, 557,
    562
Kinder Bees, The (1935),
    673
Kindred of the Wild, The
(1902), 382, 383, 385,
    625
King, Basil: *see* King, Rev.
    William Benjamin
King, Dougall MacDougall,
    456
King, James 45
King, Rev. John (1829–
    1899), 533
King, John (1843–1916),
    226
King, Mary Perry, 411
King, Rev. William Benja-
    min, 262, 263, 268, 290,
    305, 309, 311, 326–27, 479
King, William Lyon Mac-
    kenzie, 192, 226, 456, 477,
    506, 516, 517, 597, 602,
    734
King Decides, The (1956),
    644
King Lear, 325
King Phoenix (Davies), 641
Kingdom of Canada, The
    (Morton, 1963), 502
*Kingdom of Canada, The,
    . . . and Other Essays*
    (Ewart, 1908), 243
Kingdom of the Sun, The
    (1927), 663, 687
King's Fool, The (1931),
    663
Kings in Exile (1909), 386
King's Messenger, The
    (1879), 294, 305
Kingsford, William, 226,
    227, 234, 236, 248
Kingsley, Charles, 204, 279
Kingsley, Harold, 659
Kingston, Frederick, T., 596
Kingston, William H. G.,
    153, 182, 285, 296, 298,
    317
Kingston International Play-
    ers, 655
Kinniburgh, James, 603
Kinship of Nature (1904),
    342, 343, 369
*Kinsmen: A Story of the
    Ottawa Valley* (1916),
    295
Kipling, Rudyard, 281, 283,
    319, 347, 355, 357, 359,
    380, 403, 424, 628, 723
Kirby, William, 66, 136,157,
    158, 162, 166, 171, 174,
    182, 186, 187, 286, 318,
483, 485, 632, 696
Kirby's Gander (1957), 388
Kirk, John Foster, 249
Kirkconnell, Watson, 530,
    539
Kirke, Sir David and Sir
    Lewis, 57
Kirkland, Mrs. Caroline M.,
    150
Kirkpatrick, Ernest, 291
Kirkwood, Rev. John, 349
Kirkwood, Mrs. M. M., 589
Kiriline, Louise de, 380
Kittredge, G. L., 538
Ki-Yu, a Story of Panthers
    (1934), 380
Klanak Islands (1959), 720
Kleath (1917), 301
Klee Wyck (1941), 622, 719
Klein, A. M., 471, 472, 480,
    481, 487, 488, 489, 687,
    710, 735–7, 751, 753, 763,
    765, 766, 814, 829
Klibansky, Raymond, 595
Klinck, Carl F., 491, 494,
    535, 821, 825, 830, 841
Klinck, G. A., 549
Klinker (1948), 381
Kliuchevski, V. O., 249
Klondike (1958), 506, 719
Knight, Anne Cuthbert; *see*
    Fleming, Mrs. Anne
    Cuthbert
Knight, A. P., 452
Knight, Matthew Richey,
    106, 108, 118
Knister, Raymond, 480, 484,
    485, 674, 675, 685, 686,
    728–30, 741, 752, 756,
    846
Knot in the Wood, The
    (1955), 795
Know Yourself (1946),
    588
Knowles, Rev. Robert E.,
    262, 263, 268, 293, 295,
    300, 305, 307, 329, 330
Knox, Alexander, 668, 669
Knox, F. A., 522
Knox, Gilbert; *see* Macbeth,
    Madge
Knox, J. A., 350
Knox, Olive E., 629
Knox, R. S., 743
Knox College Monthly, 436
Kong (1927), 659
Konink, Charles de, 595

Krag and Johnny Bear (1902), 382
Kreisel, Henry, 491, 709, 720
Kreyche, Robert J., 595
Kristli's Trees (1948), 631, 667
Kriztjansson, A., 603
Kropotkin, Peter, 529
Kulbeik, G. G., 573
Kyte, E. C., 665

Labor Advocate (journal), 464, 465
Labor and the Angel (1896), 462
Labor Reform Songster, The (1892), 465
Labor Union (journal), 463, 464, 465
Labrador: A Poetical Epistle (1882), 69
Labrador: Its Discovery, Exploration, and Development (1910), 239
Labrador Journal (1792), 255
Labrador Logbook (1938), 574
Lacombe, Father, 164, 355
Ladies' Home Journal, 268, 689
Ladies Magazine, 151
Lady Audley's Secret (Mrs. Braddon), 278
Lady of Aroostook, The (1879), 281
Lady Rosamond's Secret (1880), 110
Lady's Book (Godey), 145
Lafontaine, H., 499
Lahontan, Baron, 17
Laight, Frederick E., 754
Laing, Hamilton, 371
Lake Dore (1930), 638
Lalemant, Père Gabriel, 21, 425, 727
Lamarck, Jean, 449
Lamb, Charles, 122, 206, 544
Lamb, W. Kaye, 29, 129, 511
Lamb of God, The (1871), 552
Lambert, John, 89–90, 126, 131, 175

Lambert, R. S., 630
Lamplighter, The (Cummins), 278
Lampman, Archibald, 67, 160, 186, 193, 198, 201, 389–400, 402, 406, 409, 416, 418, 421, 423, 430, 462, 491, 739, 753, 796, 841, 843, 845
Lance, The (journal), 467
Land and People of Canada, The (1947), 605
Land Divided, A (1951), 630
Land of Afternoon, The (1924), 673
Land of Choice: The Hungarians in Canada (1957), 527
"Land of Cockayne, The," 3
Land of Frozen Suns, The (1910), 332
Land of Open Doors, The (1914), 362
Land of the Maple Leaf, The (1908), 358
Lande, Lawrence M., 135
Landon, Fred, 501, 509
Landon, Letitia E., 145
Landor, Walter Savage, 118
Lane, Edward, 131–2
Lane, Sir W. Arbuthnot, 453
Lane That Had No Turning, The (1900), 289, 318
Langevin, Sir Hector, 226
Langford, G. B., 455
Langland, William, 764
Langley, J., 572
Langton family, 66, 367
Langton, H. H., 243, 244, 248
Langton, John, 451
Language and Languages (1932), 542
Lanier, Sidney, 413, 723
Lanigan, G. T., 169
Lanigan, Richard, 910
Lantern Marsh (1923), 684, 685
La Pérouse, Jean, 27, 45
Lapointe, Paul-Marie, 795
Lark Ascending (1932), 672
Larry Gorman: The Man that Made the Songs
Larsen, Thorleif, 542 (1964), 172
LaRue, F. A. H., 286

La Salle, R. R. Cavelier, 20, 22, 629
Laskey, John K., 110
Laskin, Bora, 525
Last of the Curlews (1955), 387
Last Forty Years, The: Canada since the Union of 1841 (1881), 225, 226, 232
Last Million Years, The (1941), 456
Last Sentinel of Castle Hill, The (1916), 291
Last Spike, The (1906), 298
Last West, The (1906), 359
Late Archaic Chinese (1959), 542
Laterrière, P. de Sales, 209
Latham, Earl of, 349
Latin Dual and Poetic Diction, The (1923), 542
Lattice for Momos, A (1958), 803
Laughing Buddha, The (1925), 659
Laughing Queen, The (1929), 661
Laughing Stalks (1958), 777, 778
Laughter in the Mind, A (1958), 782
Laura Secord, The Heroine of 1812 (1887), 428
Laurence, Margaret, 715
Laurentian Lyrics and Other Poems (1915), 727
Laurier, Sir Wilfrid, 199, 227, 272, 355, 466, 477, 498, 505, 516
Laut, Agnes C., 224, 268, 296, 479, 629
Lavallée, Calixa, 574
La Vérendrye, François de, 20
LaViolette, F. E., 527
Law, Robert, 556, 557
Law, William, 75
Law of the North (1913), 296
Lawrence, D. H., 312, 704, 724, 726, 751, 781
Lawrie Todd (1830), 142, 144, 617
Laws and Explanation in History (1960), 589
Lawyer Robert Streighton's

INDEX

Discovery at a Mineral Spring (1893), 307
Lay of the Wilderness, The (1833), 106, 116, 121
Layman's Guide to Protestant Theology (1955), 569
Layton, Irving, 489, 491, 494, 768, 769, 776, 778, 779, 781–3, 785, 786, 796, 814, 816, 817, 834, 846
Leach, Dr. MacEdward, 172
Leach, Archdeacon W. T., 535
Leacock, Stephen, 101, 143, 228, 231, 244, 262, 263, 292, 302, 308, 317, 334–7, 338, 346, 358, 466, 479, 483, 509, 526, 603, 619, 621, 673, 719, 726, 831, 839, 840
Leader (Toronto), 225
Leading Canadian Poets (1948), 740
Leaven of Malice (1954), 705
Leaves of Grass (Whitman), 154
Leavis, F. R., 788
Leavitt, Thaddeus, 301, 310, 312
Le Bourdais, D. M., 455, 606
Lecture on Education, A (1864), 535
Lectures and Essays (Goldwin Smith, 1881), 341
Lectures, Literary and Biographical (Harvey, 1864), 71
Lectures on the Millennium (1844), 553
Ledyard, John, 45
Lees, J. A., 350, 351
Lees, John, 88
Lefroy, Sir J. H., 351
Lefty (1931), 381
Legends of French Canada (1931), 629, 674
Legends of the Gulf (1870), 116
Legends of the Micmacs (1894), 164
Legends of the St. Lawrence (1898), 165
Legends of Vancouver (1911), 165, 378, 628–9
Legget, R. F., 455

Leggett, W. M., 104, 119
Lehmann-Haupt, Helmutt, 269
Leibniz, G., 440, 578, 583, 589
Leigh, Charles, 7
Leisure Hour, The (Eng. magazine), 428
Leisure Hours: Poems (1812), 82
Leitch, William, 448
Lemelin, Roger, 126, 472
Lemieux, Rodolphe, 229
LeMoine, James MacPherson, 159, 162, 165, 239, 286, 341, 371, 372
Leo, Ulrich, 549
Leonard, Grace, 673
LePage, John, 117
LePan, Douglas, 773, 795–7, 840, 846
Leprohon, Mrs. J. L., 66, 127, 154, 156, 157–8, 181, 662
LeRossignol, James Edward, 289, 674
Lescarbot, Marc, 11, 238, 652
Leslie, C. W., 570
Leslie, Kenneth, 755, 756, 757
Lesperance, Jean Talon, 429
Lessing, G. E., 440
Lesslie, James, 179
LeSueur, William Dawson, 161, 228, 229, 230, 427, 428, 460
Let Us Compare Mythologies (1956), 812, 814
Lett, William, 368
Letter-Bag of the Great Western (1840), 99, 100, 308
Letters (Hargrave, ed. 1947), 35
Letters from America (R. Brooke, 1916), 348, 363
Letters from Nova Scotia (Moorsom, 1830), 252
Letters of an American Farmer (1776), 96
Letters of a Remittance Man to his Mother (Jarvis, 1909), 297
Letters of Mephibosheth Stepsure (1860), 92, 93, 94, 96, 97, 106, 537

Letters of Sara Hutchinson (1954), 544
Letters on Canada (Curtis, 1911), 362
Letters to a Young Lady Leaving School and Entering the World (1855), 109
Letters to the Family (Kipling, 1908), 357
Lever, Charles, 98
Levine, David A., 816
Levine, Norman, 494, 607, 617, 622, 716
Levy, G. E., 572
Levy, Kurt L., 549
Lewis, C. Day, 741
Lewis, John, 228, 230
Lewis, R. W. B., 511
Lewis, Sinclair, 292, 704
Libby, Walter, 454
Liberal Imagination, The (Trilling), 473
Liberty Asserted (1704), 17, 18
Life after Death (Shaw, 1941), 565
Life and Adventures of John Nicol, Mariner (1822), 46
Life and Adventures of Peter Porcupine (1796), 80
Life and Adventures of Simon Seek (1858), 182
Life and Death (Reynolds ed., 1956), 571
Life and Journal of the Rev. Mr. Henry Alline (1806), 74, 551
Life and Letters of Egerton Ryerson (1937, 1947), 508
Life and Sport on the North Shore (1909), 372
Life and the Universe (1959), 454
Life and Times of Confederation, 1864–1867 (1962), 511
Life and Times of Sir Leonard Tilley (1897), 222
Life and Times of Wm. Lyon Mackenzie (1862), 225
Life and Work of Sir William Van Horne (Vaughan), 229

Life and Writings of Major Jack Downing of Downingsville (1833), 97, 335
Life-Histories of Northern Animals (1909), 382, 453
Life in the Clearings (1853), 144, 618, 623
Life is a Jest (1924), 600
Life of a Little College (1914), 341
Life of Colonel Talbot (1859), 139, 239
Life of Reason series (Santayana), 589
Life of Sir Thomas Roddick (1938), 454
Life, the Question and the Answer, The (1956), 570
Light and the Flame, The (1956), 569, 588
Light and the Lure, The (1897), 306
Light that Failed, The (Kipling), 281
Lighthall, William D., 197, 198, 199, 200, 201, 287, 288, 416, 426, 429, 461, 483
Lillooet (1954), 800
Lily and the Cross, The (1874), 112
Lily of Fort Garry, The (1930), 664, 665
Lincoln, Abraham, 206, 482
Linden Rhymes (1854), 119
Line, John, 565, 569
Lindsay, A. D., 515
Lindsay, Vachel, 724
Lindsey, Charles, 225, 228, 229, 236
Lindsey, G. G. S., 228
Lion the Mastiff (1895), 294, 381
Lippincott, J. S., 628
Lippincott's (magazine), 266
Lipset, S. M., 525
Lismer, Arthur, 653
Literary and Historical Society of Quebec, 128, 131, 133, 162, 209, 447
Literary Club (Halifax), 96
Literary Garland (journal), 65, 136, 142, 144, 145–47, 149, 153, 155, 157, 158, 181, 182
Literary Institute (St. John's), 71
Literary Lapses (1910), 334, 336
Literary Miscellany (journal), 132, 176
Literary Notebooks [Schlegel] *1797–1801* (ed. 1957), 544
Literature of the Middle Western Frontier (1925), 137
Little, David Fleming, 117
Little Admiral, The (1924), 629
Little Black Pony and Other Stories, The (1850), 380
Little Chief of the Gaspé (1955), 631
Little Hearts (1915), 307
Little Organist of St. Jerome, The, and Other Stories (1902), 289
Little Stories of Quebec (1908), 289
Littlewood, Joan, 656
Lives of Game Animals (1925–7), 382, 453
Lives of the Hunted (1901), 382, 453, 626
Lives of the Queens of England (1840–8), 144
Livesay, Dorothy, 471, 472, 480, 488, 494, 687, 729, 738, 740–1, 751, 753, 754, 765, 766, 785
Livesay, Florence Randal, 668
Living Church, The (1940), 568
Living Forest, The (1925), 372
Living Land, The (1961), 386
Living Tide, The (1951), 454
'Lizabeth of the Dale (1910), 330
Lizars, Kathleen and Robina, 142–3, 239, 262, 293, 304
Lloyd, C. F., 480, 614
Lloydminster (1929), 601
Lloyd-Owen, Frances, 380
Lobo, Rag, and Vixen (1899), 382
Lobstick Trail, The (1921), 659
Local Bride, A (1962), 816
Lochead, Douglas, 816
Lock, Clark, 374
Locke, John, 366, 436, 442, 547, 588
Lockhart, John Gibson, 132, 134
Lodge, R. C., 576, 587, 594
Lodging for a Night (1939), 603
Logan, J. D., 484, 536
Logan, John E., 429
Logan, H. A., 523
Logan, Sir William E., 153, 451
Logging with Paul Bunyan (1957), 166
Loghouse Nest, The (1945), 380
Logic of Self-Involvement, The (1963), 596
Logs of the Conquest of Canada, The (1909), 238
Lok, Michael, 41
London, Jack, 283, 298, 301, 362, 381
London and Middlesex Historical Society, 237
London Illustrated News, 265
London Journal, 264–65
Londons Peaceable Estate (1639), 17
Lone Furrow, The (1907), 293, 305, 310, 325
Lonely O'Malley (1905), 293, 325
Lonely Passion of Judith Hearne, The (1955), 717–18
Lonergan, Bernard J. H., 593
Long, Rev. Albert de, 304
Long, Marcus, 587
Long, Morden H., 491
Long House, The: A Poem (1859), 116
Long Patrol, The (1912), 298, 333
Long Pea-Shooter, The (1954), 782
Long Return, The (1959), 628
Longest Way Round, The (1937), 673
Longfellow, Henry Wadsworth, 95, 147, 158, 160,

164, 203, 206, 286, 288, 409, 423, 427, 428, 549
Longley, J. W., 228
Longstaff, Launcelot, 126, 131
Longstreth, T. M., 630
Looking at Architecture in Canada (1958), 508
Looking Backward (1888), 279, 460, 464
Looking Forward: The Strange Experience of the Rev. Fergus McCheyne (1913), 305, 562
Loom of Destiny, The (1899), 325
Loomer, L. O., 308
Loosley, Elizabeth, 528
Lord Dorchester (Bradley), 228
Lord Elgin (Bourinot), 228
Lord Jim (Conrad), 686
Lord of the Silver Dragon (1927), 666
Lord Selkirk of Red River (1963), 506
Lord Shaftesbury (1926), 564
Lord Strathcona (Macnaughton), 229
Lord Sydenham (Shortt), 228, 231
Lords of the North (1900), 296, 629
Lords of the Wilderness (1933), 388
Lorimer, George, 268
Loring Woart Bailey (1925), 454
Lorne, Marquis of, 162, 218, 347, 349, 358, 574
Lorne Pierce Medal, 741
Loss and Gain (Newman), 279
Lost Atlantis, The (1892), 540
Lost Cabin Mine, The (1909), 300
Lost Churches of China, The (1952), 574
Lost Dimensions (1960), 800
Lost for a Woman (1880), 111
Lost in the Backwoods; see, *Canadian Crusoes*
Lost in the Barrens (1956), 631

Lotze, R. H., 578, 581, 582, 583
Love and Salt Water (1956), 709
Love in Manitoba (1912), 297
Love of the Wild (1910), 295, 379
Love the Conqueror Worm (1952), 782
Love Where the Nights are Long (1962), 817
Loved and the Lost, The (1951), 692–3, 703, 841
Lovell, John (publisher), 145, 180, 181,182, 183, 184, 222, 267
Lover in Homespun, A (1896), 289
Lovers in Acadie (1924), 288
Loves of the Poets (1829), 143
Low, F. B., 598
Low, Rev. George Jacobs, 341
Low Life (1926), 639
Low Tide on Grand Pré (1893), 411
Lowell, Amy, 724, 726
Lower, A. R. M., 238, 491, 494, 496, 501, 504, 508, 525, 527, 564
Lower Canada Watchman (journal), 132
Lowlands Low (1935), 755
Lowry, Malcolm, 491, 716–17
Loyal Verses of Joseph Stansbury and Doctor Jonathan Odell (1860), 79
Loyalists of America and Their Times, The (1880), 241
Lucas, Alec, 841, 844
Lucas, Rev. D. V., 351, 358
Lucien (1938), 668
Luck of Ginger Coffey, The, 684, 718
Luck of Roaring Camp, The (1870), 282
Luck of the Mounted, The, 660
Luckyj, G., 542
Ludwig, Jack, 494, 722
Luke Baldwin's Vow (1948), 689

Lumsden, James, 358
Lundy's Lane Historical Society, 237
Lunenburgh, or the Old Eastern District (1890), 241
Luscombe, George, 656
Lutherans in Canada, The (1945), 573
Lyell, Sir Charles, 449, 450
Lynch, Lawrence, 591, 592
Lynch, Mrs. Lawrence, 591
Lyon, Peyton V., 526
Lyrics (McLachlan, 1858), 151
Lyrics of Earth (1893), 389
Lyrics, Songs and Sonnets (Chandler and Mulvaney, 1880), 118
Lyrics Unromantic (1942), 783

M., A.L.O.; *see* Frank, Mrs. M. J.
M., M. A.; *see* Sadlier, Mrs. Mary Anne
Mac, Captain, 350, 352
Macara, Mudie, 533
McArthur, Peter, 344–5, 368, 374–75, 376, 466, 614
Macaulay, Thomas B., 203, 226, 496, 519
Macbeth, 18
Macbeth, Madge, 301, 617, 639, 659, 673
McBride, E. W., 445, 452
MacCallum, H. Reid, 541, 588
McCaul, John, 150, 179, 248, 535
McClelland and Stewart, 270, 511
McClement, W. T., 452
McClintock, Gray, 387
McClintock, Leopold, 38–40
McClung, Nellie, 262, 263, 265, 297, 311, 330, 331, 619, 623
McClure, Robert, 38
McClure, S. S., 268
McClure's (magazine), 268
McCorkell, E. J., 532, 592
McCormick, D. H., 601
McCosh, James, 443
McCourt, E. A., 630, 666, 712

McCowan, Daniel, 368, 373
McCullers, Carson, 722
McCulloch, J. H., 663, 683
McCulloch, Thomas, 62, 92, 93–4, 97, 105, 106, 107, 109, 431–3, 435, 537, 552, 593, 829
MacCulloh, Lewis Luke; see Wilcocke, S. H., 134
McCutcheon, George, 282
MacDermott, H. E., 454
McDiarmid, O. J., 522
MacDonald, Alexander (Bishop), 560
Macdonald, Flora, 308
Macdonald, J. E. H., 363
Macdonald, John (professor), 594
Macdonald, Sir John A., 63, 115, 155, 191, 192, 200, 232, 243, 295, 359, 505, 511, 513, 516, 749
MacDonald, Ralph, 591
McDonald, V. C., 525
MacDonald, W. L., 547
MacDonald, Wilson, 482, 483
Macdonell, Blanche, 287
McDonnell, Constance; see Hammond, Mrs. J. B.
McDougall, Colin, 176
McDougall, D. J., 518
McDougall, E. Jean, 664–66
McDougall, R. L., 532
McDowell, F. D., 629, 663
McDowell, Marjorie, 841
McEvoy, Brian, 358
MacEwen, Gwendolyn, 816
Macfadyen, J. E., 556, 557
McFadyen, J. F., 574
Macfie, Harry, 376
McGee, Katie, 675, 676
McGee, Thomas D'Arcy, 66, 150, 154–6, 155–57, 158, 182, 248, 506
MacGeorge, R. J., 151
MacGibbon, D. A., 523
McGill Daily, 730
McGill Fortnightly Review, 481–2, 730, 731, 732
McGill University Magazine; see *University Magazine*
McGill University Press, 532
McGillen, Pete, 372–3
MacGillivray, C. H., 667
MacGillivray, J. R., 542, 696, 699

McGillivray, James, 663
McGrath, Thomas, 371
MacGregor, D. C., 523
MacGregor, James, 81
MacGregor, John, 141, 212
McGregor, Malcolm F., 518, 543
MacGregor, Mrs. Mary Esther, 262, 263, 292, 305, 330
Machar, Agnes Maule, 162, 196–7, 200, 239, 261, 263, 290, 302, 306, 428, 461, 629
Machel, P., 363
McHenry, E., 525
McIlwraith, Jean Newton, 228, 262, 263, 287, 629
McIlwraith, T. F., 527
McInnes, Graham, 715
MacInnes, Tom, 466
McInnis, Edgar, 504, 510, 526
McIver, R. M., 526
MacIver, Robert W., 597
McIvor, R. Craig, 522
MacKay, Isabel Ecclestone, 294, 632, 639
Mackay, J., 86–7
MacKay, L. A., 546, 637, 665, 751, 753, 754, 755
MacKay, Robert A., 524, 526
McKelvie, B. A., 663
Mackenzie, Alexander (explorer), 25, 28–9, 34, 65, 512, 849
Mackenzie, Alexander (prime minister), 505
Mackenzie, Compton, 312
Mackenzie, W. Roy, 172
Mackenzie, William, 523
Mackenzie, William Lyon, 66, 139, 140, 141, 144, 146, 170, 225, 226, 229, 230, 295, 506, 696
Mackenzie King Record, The: 1939–44, 506
Mackenzie, Selkirk, Simpson (Bryce), 228, 241
McKibbin, Archibald, 293
Mackie, John, 298
McKillican, Janet, 307
Mackinlay, A. W., 179
MacKinnon, Frank, 524
Mackinnon, I. K., 572
McKinnon, William Charles, 116

Mackintosh, W. A., 522, 523
McKishnie, Archibald, 262, 263, 293, 295, 307, 337, 379, 380, 387
McKowan, Evah, 301, 311
MacLachlan, Alexander, 136, 151–2, 154, 206, 847
McLachlan, Mrs., 146
McLaren, Floris Clarke, 759, 760, 766
McLaughlin, T. P., 566
Maclean, H. N., 547
McLean, John, 35
Maclean, John (novelist), 298, 573
MacLean, Kenneth, 547, 588
Maclean's magazine, 269, 271, 674
Maclear, Thomas (publisher), 182, 183, 240
McLelland, J. C., 570
MacLennan, Hugh, 472, 491, 612, 694, 699, 700–2, 703, 711, 719, 845
McLennan, William, 169, 262, 263, 287, 288, 307, 418
McLeod, A. J., 288
McLeod, A. W., 552
Macleod, Donald, 569
Macleod, G. P., 571
MacLeod, Margaret Arnett, 168
McLeod, Robert, 369
McLuhan, Marshall, 518, 541, 829, 848
MacLure, Millar, 719, 831, 832
MacMechan, Archibald, 341, 342, 484, 534, 537, 614, 674, 840
Macmillan Company (Toronto), 511, 630
MacMillan, Alexander, 563, 574
MacMillan, Cyrus, 165, 378, 628
MacMillan, Don, 707
MacMillan, Sir Ernest, 574
McMillan, J. & A. (N.B.), 178
McMillan, John, 178
MacMillan, William, 387
Macmillan's magazine, 265
McMullen, John Mercier, 215–16, 234
MacMurchy, Archibald, 536
MacMurchy, Marjorie, 673

INDEX 915

Macnab, John, 562
McNaught, Kenneth, 506
MacNaughton, John, 229, 534, 609
MacNaughton, Sarah, 601
McNeal, Robert, 518
McNeill, A. D., 108
MacNeill, H. L., 565
McNeill, J. T., 572
MacNutt, W. S., 61, 505, 509
MacPhail, Sir Andrew, 287, 342, 343-4, 346, 452, 534
McPhee, Janet, 639
Macpherson, C. B., 525, 526
McPherson, Hugo, 548, 836, 837
Macpherson, Jay, 494, 788-90, 791, 827, 846
McPherson, John, 118-19
MacQueen, Thomas, 152
McCrae, John, 429
McRae, Robert, 454, 589
Macready, Charles, 651
McRobbie, Kenneth, 816
Mac's of '37, The (1910), 295
Mactaggart, John, 141, 167
McTavish, Newton, 611
McTavish, Simon, 512
McWhinney, Edward, 525
Mad Carews, The (1927), 678
Madame de la Fayette (1922), 549
Madden, J. F., 543
Madden, Mary Anne; *see* Sadlier, Mrs. Mary Anne
Madison, Grant, 376, 379
Madison, James, 248
Madonna of a Day, The (1895), 300, 320
Maeterlinck, Maurice, 653
Maggs, J. T. L., 558
Magic House, The, and Other Poems (1893), 416
Magic Lantern (Montreal), 149
Magic Road, The (1925), 668
Maginn, William, 132, 134
Magnalia, Christi Americana (1702), 12
Magoun, F. P., 543
Magpie, The (1923), 687
Magpie's Nest (1917), 299
Magrath family, 253
Magrath, Thomas William, **141**

Maid of Many Woods, A (1902), 307
Mail (Niagara), 158
Mail (Toronto), 226, 240; *see also, Globe and Mail*
Main Currents of American Thought (Parrington), 486
Main Street (Lewis), 292
Main Travelled Roads (Garland), 282
Mainer, Henry, 293
Mainly about Wolves (1937), 382
Mair, Charles, 66, 154, 158, 159-60, 187, 257, 297, 647, 843
Maitland, Sir Peregrine, 139, 220
Major, The (1917), 311, 323
Major, Charles, 281
Makers of Canada series, 227-30, 231, 232, 234, 236
Makers of Canadian Literature series, 485
Making a Start in Canada (1889), 349
Making Good in Canada (1912), 362
Making of a Man, The (1918), 296
Malaeska; or, The Indian Wife of the White Hunter (Stephen), 278
"Malcolm"; *see* Sinclair, C. M.
Malcolm's Katie, and Other Poems (1884), 158, 406, 408
Malherbe, François de, 545
Mallarmé, Stéphanie, 732
Malloch, A. E., 547
Mallory, J. R., 525
Malvern Essays (1930), 614
Man Forbid, A (1935), 667
Man from Glengarry, The (1901), 270, 292, 322, 323
Man in the Open (1912), 300
Man Who Dared to be God, The (1929), 559
Manby, Thomas, 49
Mandel, Eli, 494, 537, 793, 794
Manitoba (Morton, 1957), 509

Manitoba: Its Infancy, Growth and Present Condition (1882), 219
Manitoba and the North West Territories (1892), 355
Manitoba Chore Boy, A: The Experience of a Young Emigrant (1912), 297
Manitoba Theatre Centre, 656
Manitoban (journal), 207
Manitou Portage (1930), 638
Mann, Stanley, 634
Mann, Thomas, 532, 713, 717
Mann, W. E., 528, **569**
Manning, E., 564
Manning, Zella, 388
Manny, Louise, 172
Manoir de Villerai, Le (1861), 158
Manor House of De Villerai, The (1859), 157
Man's Emerging Mind (1961), 454
Mansfield, Grace **Yarrow**, 172
Mansfield, Katherine, **675**, 689
Manson, William, 565
Mantell, Robert B., 651
Mantley, John, 379
Manual of Christian Theology on the Inductive Method (1900), 556
Manual of Woodcraft Indians (1915), **626**
Many Colored Coat, The (1960), 692-3, 703
Many Moods (1932), 749
"Maple Knott"; *see* Clemo, Ebenezer
Maple Leaf, The; or, Canadian Annual, 150, 179, 180
Maple Leaves (1863-1906) (Le Moine), 159, 286, 341, 371, **372**
Maquinna (Nootka chief), 50
Marcel, G., 597
Marcelle (1905), **287**
March, Bernard: *see* Scott, F. R.
Marchand, Etienne, 46

916 INDEX

Marchbanks, Samuel, 613
Marches of the North (1931), 603
Marching Call, The (1956), 630
Marconi, Guglielmo, 746
Marcus Holbeach's Daughter (1912), 291, 309, 328
Mardi (Melville), 717
Marguerite de Roberval (1899), 288
Marguerite Verne; or, Scenes from Canadian Life (1886), 110, 291
Maria Chapdelaine, 835, 840
Marie Gourdon (1890), 290, 310
Marion (1916), 310
Marion Wilburn (n.d.), 110
Maritain, Jacques, 591, 592, 689, 691
Maritain on the Nature of Man in a Christian Democracy (1955), 592
Maritime Folk Songs (1962), 172
Maritime Monthly (Saint John), 205, 206, 207
Mark, The (1958), 710
Markowitz, J., 452
Marks Brothers, 651
Marlowe, Christopher, 547, 735
Marlyn, John, 472, 495, 711
Marquette, Père Jacques, 21
Marquis, Thomas G., 260, 288, 572, 629
Marriott, Anne, 488, 754, 760, 766
Marryat, Frederick, 141
Marsden, Joshua, 74, 81–3, 573
Marsden, William, 451
Marsh, D. B., 523
Marsh Hay (Denison), 635, 636, 638
Marsh, Louise, 371
Marshall, John G., 450, 555
Marshall, Joyce, 491
Martin, Burns, 544
Martin, Chester, 236, 250, 498–500
Martin, George, 157
Martin, Robert Montgomery, 212
Martinez (of Nootka), 47
Martin-Harvey, Sir John, 651

Martyrs of New France (1909), 574
Marvell, A., 805
Marx, Karl, 458, 466, 469, 472, 490, 691, 769, 770, 787, 833, 834
Mary Melville, the Psychic (1900), 308
Masefield, John, 723, 783
Maseres, Francis, 64, 83–4
Mason, Capt. John, 13, 14
Masque, Entitled "Canada's Welcome," 108, 114
Masque of Aesop, A (1952), 641, 643
Mass Media in Canada (1962), 588
Masses (1932–4), 469, 471, 486, 674
Massey, Raymond, 651
Massey, Vincent, 340, 492, 493, 517, 610, 616, 636, 653; see also Royal Commission on National Development in the Arts, Letters and Sciences
Masson, L. F. R., 29
Master of Life, The: A Romance of the Five Nations (1908), 288
Master of the Mill (1944), 472, 680–1, 833
Master Works of Canadian Authors series, 485
Masters, D. C., 511, 518
Masters, Edgar Lee, 518, 724, 742, 800
Mates of the Tangle (1924), 387
Mather, Cotton, 12
Mathers, D., 570
Matilda Montgomerie; see, Canadian Brothers, The
Matins (Sherman, 1896), 403
Matthew Arnold: A Study in Conflict (1948), 541 (1941), 454
Maude, Cyril, 651
Maude Abbott: A Memoir (1941), 454
Maugham, Somerset, 640
Maupassant, Guy de, 276, 361, 689
Maurer, Armand A., 567, 592
Mavor, James, 249, 520

Maxwell, J. A., 523
Maxwell, William, 363
May, Barbara, 381
May, Paul, 370
Mayer, C. F., 548
Mayo, H. B., 526
Meaning of Christ for Paul, The (1949), 570
Meaning of Poison in Canada, The (1949), 454
Meaning of the Cross, The (1923), 566
Meaning of the Revelation, The (1931), 566
Meanwhile (1927), 683, 684
Meares, John, 29, 47
Measure of a Man, The (1911), 304, 328
Measure of the Rule, The (1906), 294, 314
Measure of the Year (1950), 374, 615
Mechanical Bridge (1951), 541
Medea, 4
Mediaeval Universalism and Its Present Value (1937), 590
Medicine in the Making (1960), 455
Medieval Drama in Chester (1955), 539
Medieval Philosophy (1962), 592
Meek, T. J., 542
Meeting Place of Geology and History, The (1895), 554
Meighen, Arthur, 155, 477, 506
Meisel, John, 525
Melville, Herman, 148, 507, 698, 716, 717, 723
Memoir of the Rev. James MacGregor (1859), 74
Mémoires du capitaine Péron (1824), 46
Mémoires intimes (Fréchette, ed., 1961), 549
Memoirs (Bellot, 1855), 39
Memoirs called Gospels, The (1959), 570
Memoirs of a Canadian Merchant, 616
Memoirs of Celebrated Female Sovereigns (1831), 143

INDEX 917

Memoirs of Odd Adventures (1736), 72
Memoirs of the Administration of Lower Canada ... (three works) (1818, 1820, 1829), 220
Memoirs of the Right Honourable Sir John Alexander Macdonald (1894), 228
Memorial (Cawdell, 1818), 139
Memory, Learning and Language: The Physical Basis of Mind (1960), 456
Men of Kildonan, The (1926), 663
Men of the Last Frontier, The (1931), 376, 628
Mencken, H. L., 272, 704, 734
Mendelssohn, Felix, 206
Mennonites in Manitoba, 1875–1900, The (1900), 573
Menzies, Archibald, 49
Menzies, George, 152
Mercator; *see* Ellice, Edward
Mercenary Match, The (1784), 87
Mercer, S. A. B., 571
Merchant of Venice, The, 657
Meredith, George, 275, 317, 319, 405, 541
Mermaid, The (1895), 320
Merry America (1939), 604
Message of Jesus for the Life of Today, The (1932), 564
Message of Plato, The (1920), 589
Messianic Prophecy Vindicated (1899), 554
Metal and the Flower, The (1954), 770, 785
Metalious, Grace, 699
Metaphysics and Historicity (1961), 588
Metaphysics of Algazel, The (1951), 566
Meteor King, A (1899), 307
Methodism in the Middle West (1946), 572
Methodist Book and Publishing House, 186–7
Methodist Ministry Defended, The (1839), 553

Methodist Ministry further defended (1840), 553
Michael, J. Hugh, 565
Michener, Norah Eveline, 592
Micklem, N., 565
Micmac Indians of Eastern Canada (1955), 164
Middlemarch (Eliot), 279
Midland, The (monthly), 685
Middleton, Christopher, 16
Middleton, J. E., 168, 638, 673
Miegge, Giovanni, 567
Miertsching, J. A., 38
Miles, H. H., 217
Mill, John Stuart, 193, 434, 436, 439, 543
Millar, Margaret, 698
Millay, Edna St. Vincent, 734, 740, 756, 783
Miller, Hugh, 450
Miller, Muriel, 380
Miller, Orlo, 630
Millet, J. F., 288
Millman, R. M., 574
Millman, T. R., 508
Millner, George, 294
Milne, A. A., 632
Milne, Lorus, 369
Milne, Margery, 369
Milne, W. S., 639
Mills, Alan, 169, 172
Mills, Phebe, 107
Milton, Viscount, 35, 256
Milton, John, 75, 148, 156, 193, 480, 529, 539, 540, 541, 543, 544, 546, 548, 744
Milton and the Puritan Dilemma (1942), 546
Milton's Royalism (1943), 541
Mind, its Origin and Goal (1927), 558
Mind, School and Civilization (1952), 594
Mind in Matter (1884), 555
Mine Inheritance (1940), 664
Miracle Man, The (1914), 312
Miraculous Birth of Language, The (1937, etc.), 542
Miramichi (1863), 110
Mirsky, Jeanette, 35
Misadventure of a Working Hobo in Canada (1930), 603
Miserables, Les (Hugo), 281
Miss Dixie: A Romance of the Provinces (1895), 304
Mission, The (1816), 82
Missionary Idea in Life and Religion, The (1928), 574
Missionary Problem, The (1883), 573
Mist of Morning (1919), 294
Mr. Ames against Time (1949), 686
Mr. Crewe's Career (1908), 280
Mr. Perkins of Nova Scotia (1891), 308
Mrs. Falchion (1893), 301
Mrs. Golightly and Other Stories (1961), 721
Mitchell, John, 155, 171, 669
Mitchell, Peter, 348
Mitchell, Roy, 653
Mitchell, Silas Weir, 281, 282
Mitchell, W. O., 491, 711, 720, 828
Mixture of Frailties, A (1958), 705
Moby Dick (Melville), 148, 507, 717
Modern Canadian Poetry (1930), 487
Modern Evangeline, A (1896), 291
Modern Fundamentalism (1927), 563
Modern Humanism and Christian Theism (1939), 571
Modern Ideas of Evolution as related to Revelation and Science (1890), 450, 554
Modern Islam in India (1946), 571
Modern Past and Present (1932), 593
Modern Philosophy, Descartes to Kant (1963), 591
Modern Railroad Structures (1949), 455
Modern Science in Bible Lands (1888), 554
Modern State, The (1926), 526, 597

Modernism, Past and Present (1932), 563
Moir, David Macbeth, 136, 168
Moir, John S., 508, 569
Moiseiwitsch, Tanya, 656
Molière, 11, 549, 642, 653
Molineux globe, 5
Moll Flanders (Defoe), 683
Monarch: The Big Bear of Tallac (1904), 382, 453
Money Master, The (1915), 289, 318
Monro, Alexander, 179, 234
Monsarrat, Nicholas, 606, 698
Montaigne, M., 17, 344, 365, 614
Montcalm, Marquis de, 126
Montcalm and Wolfe (1884), 286
Montesquieu, C. L. de S., 17
Montgomery, Lucy Maude, 262, 263, 268, 331, 479, 625, 626, 627, 631, 632, 672
Montgomery, Gen. R., 86
Monthly Miscellany (London, Eng.), 42
Montreal Natural History Society, 447
Montreal Repertory Theatre, 653
Montreal Witness (journal), 157
Montrealer, 612
Moodie, Susanna, 65, 66, 100, 127, 141, 143, 144, 146, 147, 151–2, 154, 158, 181, 253, 255, 261, 367, 380, 485, 618–23, 825, 827, 839
Moody, James, 60, 78
Moonbeams from the Larger Lunacy (1915), 334
Moonlight and Common Day (1922), 726
Moonstone, The (Collins), 278
Moore, Brian, 494, 684, 698, 702, 711, 713, 717, 718
Moore, Dora Mavor, 655
Moore, G. E., 586
Moore, Marianne, 728, 793, 808
Moore, Mavor, 634, 655
Moore, Philip, 372

Moore, Thomas (poet), 126, 130, 131, 136, 151, 156, 168, 347, 724
Moore, Thomas, 348, 355
Moore, William Henry, 302, 303
Moorhouse, Hopkins, 659
Moorsom, Capt. W., 252, 255
Moose Hunting, Salmon Fishing and Other Sketches of Sport (1902), 372
Mooswa and Others of the Boundaries (1900), 324, 380, 628
Moral Life and Religion, The (1932), 596
Morang, George N., 219, 227–8, 229, 270
More Joy in Heaven (1937), 692
More, Sir Thomas, 6, 543
More Kindred of the Wild (1911), 386, 625
Moresby, Louise; *see* Beck, Lily Adams
Morgan, Henry J., 154, 159, 208, 357, 534
Morgan, W., 556, 558
Morice, A. G., 239, 240, 573
Morley, John, 204, 515
Morley Callaghan's Stories (1959), 689
Mormon Prophet, The (1899), 305
Morning Chronicle (Quebec), 186
Morning Songs in the Night: Poems (1897), 461
Morpurgo, J. E., 5
Morris, Edmund, 418
Morris, Elizabeth Keith, 361
Morris, William, 123, 193, 410, 411, 426, 465, 833
Morrow, E. L., 561
Morrow, T. M., 638
Morton, Arthur S., 501, 561
Morton, Guy E., 312, 659
Morton, James, 297
Morton, W. L., 494, 502, 503, 509, 511, 519, 526
Morven: The Highland United Empire Loyalist (1911), 287
Mosaic Account of Creation of the World . . . Geologically Explained (1856), 449
Moscovitch, Henry, 494
Mossner, D. C., 595
Mother, The (1905), 328
Mother Lode (1930), 638
Mother Nature Stories (1924), 380
Mother of St. Nicholas, The (Santa Claus) (1899), 308
Motley, John L., 249
Motor Scamper 'Cross Canada, A (1922), 599
Motor Tour through Canada, A (1914), 363
Mountain, Bishop George J., 129–30, 132, 448, 553
Mountain, Bishop Jacob, 87, 129
Mountain (magazine), 817
Mountain, The (Williams, 1956), 644
Mountain and the Valley, The (1952), 711–12, 839
Mountain Cloud (1944), 166
Mountain Playhouse, 655
Mounted Police Patrol (1954), 630
Mounty in a Jeep (1949), 630
Mourner's Tribute, The (1840), 136
Movements of Political Protest in Canada (1959), 527
Mowat, Angus, 685, 686
Mowat, Farley, 381, 628, 631, 632
Mowat, J. G., 197
Mower, Nahun, 176
M. Tulli Ciceronis Pro A. Cluentio Oratio (1899), 535
Muckle, J. T., 532, 566, 592
Mud Lark, The (1932), 326
Mürger, Henri, 281
Muir, Thomas, 46
Mulgrave Road, The (1951), 756
Mullins, Rosanna Eleanor; *see* Leprohon, Mrs. J. L.
Mulvaney, Charles Pelham, 118, 185
Munn, Allan M., 596
Munro, Alice, 720, 722
Munro, George, 267, 434
Munro, Kathryn, 574

INDEX

Munro, Norman, 267
Munro, W. B., 238, 244
Munsey, Frank, 268
Munsey's magazine, 268
Munsterhjelm, Eric, 376
Murchison, Sir R. I., 449
Murdoch, Beamish, 80, 221, 222, 223, 234, 236
Murdoch, John A., 378, 379
Murdoch, Robert, 118
Murdoch, William, 117
Murphy, Charles, 156
Murphy, Gardner, 582
Murphy, James, 171
Murray, George, 157, 162
Murray, Gordon, 455
Murray, Hugh, 211, 212
Murray, James (Governor), 499
Murray, John Clark, 435, 442–4, 558, 576, 595
Murray, Robert, 108, 574
Murry, Middleton, 559
Music at the Close (1947), 712
Music on a Kazoo (1956), 782
Muskrat Man (1946), 673
Musson (publisher), 240, 723
Mutable Many, The (1896), 279, 302
My Brave and Gallant Gentleman (1918), 301
My Canada (1915), 297
My Canadian Journal (1891), 353
My Canadian Memories (1920), 601
My Discovery of England (1922), 336
My Discovery of the West (1937), 603
My Dogs of the Northland (1902), 387
My Garden Dreams (1926), 369
My Lady Nell (1889), 307
My Lady of the Snows (1908), 262, 303
My Neighbour (1911), 563
My Spanish Sailor (1889), 320
My Star Predominant (1934), 685
My Strange Rescue and Other Stories (1903), 630

My Travels (1900), 354
My Vision of Canada (1933), 610
My Visit to Canada (1907), 357
Mysterious North, The (1956), 606
Mysterious Stranger, The (1817), 110
Mysterium Fidei, 560
Mystery of Ashton Hall, The (1910), 308, 312
Mystery of Edwin Drood, The (Dickens), 278
Myths and Myth-makers (1872), 161
Myths of Plato, The (Stewart), 577

NAEGELE, KASPAR, 528
Nan and Other Pioneer Women of the West (1913), 299
Nancy McVeigh of the Monk Road (1908), 293
Napoleon (Emperor), 28
Napoleon Tremblay (1939), 668
Narrative, A (Bond Head, 1839), 149
Narrative of a Journey across the Island of Newfoundland in 1822 (Cormack, 1823–4), 70
Narrative of a Journey to the Shores of the Polar Sea (Franklin, 1823), 36–7, 133
Narrative of a Mission, to Nova Scotia . . . (Marsden, 1816, 1827), 74, 81, 573
Narrative of a Second Expedition . . . (Franklin, 1828), 36
Narrative of a Trip to Canada (Bryce, 1881), 349
Narrative of an Expedition to the Shores of the Arctic Sea in 1846 and 1847 (Rae, 1850), 38
Narrative of an Extraordinary Escape (Smethurst, 1760), 73
Narrative of Col. David Fanning (1862), 77

Narrative of his Exertions and Sufferings . . . (Moody, 1782), 78
Narrative of his Explorations in Western North America 1784–1812 (Thompson, 1916), 31–3, 238
Narrative of the Adventures and Sufferings of John R. Jewitt (1815), 50
Narrative of the Arctic Land Expedition to the Mouth of the Great Fish River (Back, 1836), 37
Narrative of the Discoveries on the North Coast of America, 1836–39 (Simpson, 1843), 37–8
Narrative of the Life and Christian Experience of Mrs. Mary Bradley (1849), 74, 81
"Narrow Passage" (Andrew Allan), 655
Nashe, Thomas, 541
Nation (Dublin), 155
Nation (Toronto), 207
National Ballads of Canada (1865), 169
National Film Board, 492, 495, 747, 770
National Policy and the Wheat Economy, The (1957), 522
Native Argosy, A (1929), 674, 689
Natural History of Selborne (White, 1789), 365, 367
Natural History of the Ten Commandments, The (1907), 382
Natural History Society of Montreal, 153, 451
Naturalist in Canada, A (1941), 368–69
Nature and Right of Religion, The (1926), 558
Nature and Human Nature (1855), 99
Nature and the Bible (1875), 554
Nature and Uses of a Liberal Education Illustrated (1819), 432–3
Nature Guide for Farmers, A (1947), 369

Nature Lover in British Columbia, A (1937), 257, 368
Naval History of Great Britain from the Declaration of War by France in 1793 ... (1822–4), 213
Naylor, T. E., 600
Nease, Lilla, 310
Neatby, H. Blair, 506, 510
Neatby, Hilda, 509
Neatby, Leslie H., 39
Need, Thomas, 141, 367
Need of the World, The (1882), 563
Needler, G. H., 540
Neighbours (1922), 676, 677
Neighbours Unknown (1911), 386
Neilson, John, 126, 213
Nelson, Harold, 510
Nelson, V. H., 108
Nerves and Personal Power (1922), 456
Nesbitt, H. H. J., 455
Net and the Sword, The (1953), 796, 846
Neue Mensch, Der: Die Biographie im deutschen Nachkriegsroman (1958), 548
Neville Trueman, the Pioneer Preacher: A Tale of the War of 1812 (1880), 295, 305
New, Chester, 498, 518
New Brunswick; with a Brief Outline of Nova Scotia, and Prince Edward Island (Monro, 1855), 179, 234
New Brunswick; with Notes for Emigrants (1847), 211, 447
New Brunswick and Other Poems (1869), 119
New Brunswick Courier, 114
New Brunswick Magazine (Saint John), 205, 207
New Brunswick Religious and Literary Journal (Saint John), 178
New Canada, The (1903), 359
New Canada and New Canadians (1907), 358

New Canadian Anthology, A (1938), 487
New Canadian Library, 537, 692
New Christianity, The (1920), 563
New Directions, 765
New Dominion Monthly (Montreal), 207
New Empire Company, 652
New Era (1857–8, McGee), 156
New Era, or Canadian Chronicle (1841–2, Richardson), 181, 214
New France (Butterworth, 1885), 350
New Frontier (journal), 469–70, 471, 486, 674, 736, 754, 833
New Gentle Shepherd, The (1798), 80
New Harvesting (1938), 487
New Home, A (1839), 150
New Interlude and a mery of the nature of the iiij elements, A (1519–), 6
New Letters of David Hume (ed. 1954), 595
New Light on the Early History of the Greater North-West (Henry, ed. 1897), 31
New Man and the Divine Society, The (1926), 565
New Materials for the History of Men (1863), 447
New Monthly Magazine, 133
New Play Society, 655
New Philosophical Journal, 70
New Poems (Livesay, 1957), 741
New Provinces: Poems of Several Authors (1936), 472, 473, 487, 753–4, 769, 786
New Testament Evangelism (1911), 557
New Verse (magazine), 732
New World (journal), 439
New Writers series, 769
New York Ledger, 265
New York Nocturnes (1898), 399
New Yorker, 720

Newbiggin, M. I., 599
Newcomer in Canada, A (1924), 600
Newes from Virginia (1610), 10
Newfoundland (Harvey and Hatton, 1883), 71
Newfoundland as it was and as it is (Tocque, 1878), 70
Newfoundland to Cochin, China (1892), 354
Newfoundland to Manitoba (Rae, 1881), 351
Newfoundland Verse (1923), 742–4, 749
Newman, Basil, 605
Newman, Cardinal J. H., 279, 591, 592
Newnes, George, 268
News from Nowhere (Morris), 394
News of the Phoenix (1943), 731, 765
Newton, E., 369
Newton, Sir Isaac, 44, 365, 723
Newton, M. B., 369
Newton, W. D., 598
Newton-White, E., 369
Next of Kin, The (1917), 311
Next Year Country (1951), 528
Nicholls, R. V. V., 454
Nickerson, Moses Hardy, 104, 106, 108, 117
Nickless, Joseph, 176
Nicol, Eric, 611, 719
Nicol, John, 46, 48
Nietzsche, F., 439, 593, 781
Nietzsche and the Ideals of Modern Germany (1915), 593
Nigerian Perspectives: An Anthology (1960), 571
Night Blooming Cereus (1962), 648
Night Hawk, The (1901), 288, 327
Nine Mediaeval Thinkers (1955), 566, 592
Nineteen Poems (Macpherson, 1952), 788
Ninth Circle, The (1928), 660
Ninth Vibration, The (1922), 661

Niven, Frederick, 262, 263, 268, 300, 337, 603, 620, 623, 658, 664
Nixon, Larry, 605
Nkwala (1958), 629
No English Need Apply (1909), 358
No Graven Images (1954), 570
No Man's Meat (1931), 689
No Sect in Heaven (1868), 118
Noel, N. P. R., 362
Nomads of the West (1850), 110
Nonsense Novels (1911), 308, 334, 336
Noreen's Revenge (1875), 111
Norman, Herbert, 518
Norris, Frank, 276, 312
Norris, John, 518
North, Anison; see Wilson, May
North American Review, 266
North American Summer (1939), 604
North and South (Mrs. Gaskell), 279
North Atlantic Triangle: The Interplay of Canada, the United States and Great Britain (1945), 497
North British Review, 149
North Georgia Gazette and Winter Chronicle, 36
North of 55 Degrees (1954), 606
North of Fifty-Three (1914), 300, 332
North Mountain near Grand-Pré (1883), 119
North Overland with Franklin (1901), 630
North West Company, The (1957), 507
North-west Passage by Land, The (1865), 35–256
Northern Approaches (1961), 510
Northern Lights (1909), 296, 317
Northern Lights and Shadows (1900), 291
Northern Review, 489, 490, 536, 767, 768, 785, 795

Northland Footprints (1936), 387, 660
Northland Stories: Tales of Trapping Life in the Canadian Wilderness (1922), 387
Norwood, Gilbert, 480, 533, 538, 539, 611
Norwood, Robert, 479, 559
Notary of Grand Pré, The (1901), 288
Notes, Historical and Critical, to Comte, Mill and Spencer (1898), 440
Notes of a Short Visit to Canada and the States (1885), 350
Notita of New Brunswick (1838), 120–21
Nova Scotia, in its Historical, Mercantile and Industrial Relations (1873), 222
Nova Scotia Archives, 78
Nova Scotia Historical Society, 237
Nova Scotia Literary and Scientific Society, 447
Nova Scotia Magazine, 176
Nova Scotia Minstrel, The (1809), 80
Nova Scotian (newspaper), 94, 96, 106, 178
Now is Time (1945), 762, 787
Now is the Place (1948), 781
Now That April's Here (1936), 674, 689
Nowlan, Alden, 494, 802–3, 846
Noyes, Alfred, 723
Noyes, J. H., 460
Nuki (1953), 628
Nye, E. W. (Bill), 335
Nye, R. B., 5
Nymph and the Lamp, The (1950), 697

O Earth Return (1954), 788
Oakes, Christopher, 297, 303
Object and Event (1953), 776
Oblomoff (Coulter), 640
O'Brien, Lucius, 352
Observations on Hudson's Bay (Isham, ed. 1949), 27

O'Callaghan, E. B., 862
Occident and Orient (1905), 307
Ocean to Ocean (1873), 251, 256
O'Connell, Daniel, 155
O'Connor, Frank, 721
Odd Man's Story, An (1889), 312
Odds and Ends (1836), 135
Odell, Jonathan, 60, 63, 79
O'Donnell, J. R., 566, 592
O'Donnell, Kathleen M., 156
Oedipus Rex, 657
Of Irony, Especially in Drama (1935, 1948), 539
Of Mice and Men (Steinbeck), 688
Of Time and the Lover (1950), 766
Of Walks and Walking Tours (1914), 341, 369
Off to Canada (1888), 348
Off the Rocks (1906), 291
Office of Lieutenant-Governor, The (1957), 510, 524
Ogden, Peter Skene, 34
Ogilvy, Maud, 290, 310
O'Grady, Standish, 135–36
Oh! Canada (1921), 600
O'Hagan, Thomas (1855–1939), 187, 344, 429, 479
O'Hara, John, 721
O'Hara, M. L., 604
O'Higgins, Harvey, 262, 263, 268, 276, 294, 309–10, 312, 337
Old Chieftain, The (1955), 505
Old Church in the New Dominion, The (1929), 563
Old Creole Days (1879),
Old Days on the Farm (1918), 374
Old Documents and the New Bible, The (1890), 559
Old French Lives of St. Agnes (1938), 545
Old Judge, The (1849), 100
Old Lamps Aglow (1957), 135
Old Loyalist, The (1908), 295
Old Man Savarin, and Other

Stories (1895, 1917), 288, 292, 322
Old Mortality (Scott), 93
Old Orchard, The (1903), 293
Old Province Tales (1924), 674
Old Régime in Canada, The (1874), 231, 233, 242, 286
Old Spookses' Pass . . . (1884), 406
Old Testament and Apocalypse (1952), 570
Old Testament Criticism and the Christian Church (1903), 557
Old Testament Vindicated, The (1897), 554
Old-Time Songs of Newfoundland (Doyle), 172
Old Wives' Tale (Bennett), 675, 676
Oldtown Folks (Stowe, (1869), 282
Oleson, T. J., 518
Oliphant, Mrs. Margaret, 141
Oliver Twist (Dickens), 619
Oliver, E. H., 563
Oliver, Michael, 526
On Canada's Frontier (1892), 354
On Canadian Poetry (1943), 490, 538, 752
On Common Ground (1906), 293
On Game Trails in British Columbia (1926), 372
On Golden Wings through Wonderland (1927), 380
On Parliamentary Government in England (1867, 1869), 247
On the Cards and Off (1895), 355
On the Design of Shakespearean Tragedy (1957), 546
On the Division and Methods of the Sciences 1953, 592
On the Governance of Rulers (1935), 591
On the Highest Hill (1949), 379
On the Origin of the Thomistic Notion of Man (1963), 591
On the Pathless West (1904), 299
On the Uses and Abuses of Phrenology (1846), 535
On Understanding Physics (1938), 456
One Act Plays by Canadian Authors (1926), 638
One Generation Away (1931), 663, 675
One Hundred Years of Methodist Missions 1824–1924 (1924), 574
One Mediator, The (1884), 555
One Thing after Another (1948), 611
One Third of a Bill (1925), 637
One-Winged Dragon, The (1951), 629
O'Neil, Charles J., 592
O'Neill, Eugene, 636, 638
O'Neill, James, 651
Only Men on Board (1933), 673
Only World, The (Burgin), 292
Ontario Historical Society, 237
Ontario Workman (newspaper), 462, 464
Ook-pik (1952), 628
Oowikapun; or, How the Gospel Reached the Nelson River Indians (1895), 307
Open House (1931), 610
Open Water (1914), 725
Openway (1922), 380
O'Reilly, Rev. John, 291
Origen's Treatise on Prayer (1954), 567
Origin of Species, The (Darwin, 1859), 366, 449, 455, 553
Origin of Vertebrates, The (1956), 454
Origin of the World according to Revelation and Science, The (1877), 450, 554
Original and Inbred Sin (1896), 555
Original Language of the Apocalypse, The (1928), 566
Orion and Other Poems (1880), 122, 160, 389, 399, 402, 403, 843
Ormsby, Margaret, 509
O'Ruddy, The (1903), 314
Orwell, George, 706–07
Osborn, J. Sherard, 38
Osborne, W. F., 534
Oscar (1857), 154
Osgood, H. L., 246
Osler, Sir William, 340, 342–3, 344, 346, 450, 454
Ostenso, Martha, 484, 666, 676, 678, 683, 688
Other Canadians: An Anthology of the New Poetry in Canada, 1940–1946 (1947), 491, 769, 781, 786, 795
Other Side, The (novel, 1872), 464
Other Side, The; How It Struck Us (1880), 349
Other Side of the "Story", The (1886), 226
Other Paris, The (1956), 721
Ottawa Drama League, 653
Ottawa Past and Present (1871), 216
Ouellet, Fernand, 510
"Ouida," 278, 281, 366
Our Canadian Heritage (1908), 357
Our Canadian Literature (Watson and Pierce, 1922), 536
Our Canadian Literature (anthology, 1935), 487
Our Common Faith (1928), 562
Our Daily Bread (1928), 679, 682
Our Heritage and our Faith (1956), 562
Our Intellectual Strength and Weakness (1893), 260, 271
Our Lady of Sunshine (1910), 361
Our Little Life (1921), 675, 684
Our Living Tradition (series), 408, 532, 539–40

Our Mobile Earth (1926), 456
Our North Land (1885), 218
Our Northern Year (1937), 368
Our Picturesque Northern Neighbour (1899), 353
Our Prophetic Heritage (1945), 570
Our Sense of Identity (1954), 494, 610
Our Western Archipelago (1895), 354
Our Visit to Toronto, Niagara Falls . . . (1898), 354
Our Wonderful Universe (1928), 456
Ourselves in Canada (1960), 607
Out-of-Doors, The (1932), 368
Out of the Earth: The Mineral Industry in Canada (1954), 455
Out with the Birds (1913), 371
Outcasts, The (1901), 324, 380, 628
Outcasts of Canada, The: Why Settlements Fail (1932), 603
Outdoor Rambles (1958), 368
Outdoors (magazine), 268
Outdoors with a Camera in Canada (1945), 373
Outdoors with Pete McGillen (1955), 372-3
Outerbridge, L. M., 574
Outlines of Natural Theology for the Use of the Canadian Student (1859), 449, 553
Outline of Philosophy (Watson, 1898), 440
Outline of Sir William Hamilton's Philosophy (1870), 443
Outposts (English periodical) 766
Outram, James, 358
Over Prairie Trails (1922), 370, 615, 679, 680, 842
Overlaid (Davies, 1949), 642
Overton, Richard, 518

Overture (1945), 733, 765
Owen, Derwyn R. G., 571, 588
Owen, E. T., 533, 546
Owen, Wilfred, 796
Owens, Joseph, 566, 592
Owl Pen (1947), 375
Owls in the Family (1961), 381, 628
Oxford Book of Canadian Verse (1960), 538
Oxley, James Macdonald, 261, 262, 263, 291, 296, 321, 630

PACEY, DESMOND, 491, 495, 530, 536, 537, 632, 720, 828, 837, 841, 844
Pacific Coast Tragedy, A (Fairbairn, 1935), 640
Packard, Frank L., 262, 263, 279, 312, 337, 659
Pagan Love (1922), 659
Page, P. K., 489, 491, 494, 767, 769–773, 781, 785
Paine, T., 306
Painter's Country, A (1958), 622
Painting and Reality (1957), 590
Paley, W., 553
Pall Mall Gazette, 268–69, 515
Palladium of Labor (Hamilton), 463, 464, 465
Palmer, David 104, 119
Palmer, George, 639
Palmerston, Lord, 287
Pamela (Richardson), 547
Pan-ic: A Selection of Contemporary Canadian Poems (1958), 786
Panthea, the Spirit of Nature (1849), 378
Paper Kingdom, The (1936), 673
Papineau, Cartier (DeCelles), 228
Papini, G., 559
Paradise Lost, 539
Paradox and Nirvana (1951), 571
Parham, H. J., 257, 368
Park, Julian, 495, 527, 700
Parker, Dorothy, 740

Parker, Gilbert, 261, 262, 263, 268, 270, 276, 281, 287, 289, 296, 298, 299, 301, 304, 308, 309, 313, 317–19, 320, 325, 332, 477, 483, 632, 662, 837
Parker, J. H., 542
Parkhurst, Anthony, 12
Parkin, Sir George R., 63, 205, 228, 232, 353, 410, 625
Parkman, Francis, 21–22, 27, 159, 231, 232–3, 242, 246, 286, 318, 496, 507
Parks, W. A., 452
Parliamentary Government in the British Colonies (1880), 248
Parrington, V. L., 486
Parry, William, 35–36, 38, 133
Parson John of the Labrador (1924), 673
Parsons, Vivian, 668
The Parts Men Play (1920), 309
Pascal, B., 541, 591
Pascal and the Port Royalists (1902), 249
Passing of Oul-I-But, The (1913), 387, 660
Passing Thoughts on Man's Relation to God and God's Relation to Man (1862), 553
Passion according to St. John, The (1944), 557
Passion in Rome, A (1961), 692–3
Pastoral Epistles, The: Introduction, Translation and Notes (1937), 557
Paterson, Isabel, 299, 662
Path of a Star, The (1899), 316
Pathfinders of the Great Plains: . . . La Vérendrye and his Sons (1915), 224
Pathfinders of the West: Radisson, La Vérendrye, Lewis and Clark (1904), 224
Pathology for the Physician (1958), 454
Patmore, Coventry, 149
Patrick, W., 558

924 INDEX

'Patriotes' of '37, The (1916), 244
Patrol of the Sun Dance Trail, The (1914), 323
Patterson, George, 74, 239, **573**
Patterson, Henry, 182
Patterson Limit, The (1923), 659
Pattillo, Richard, **372**
Paul and Christ (1873), 552
Paulding, James Kirke, 131, 133
Pauli, F. G., 358
Paul's Cross Sermons, 1534–1642, The (1958), 546
Pause (1953), 622
Peace River Country (1958), 707
Peacock, E. A., 247
Peacock, E. R., 459
Peacock, Kenneth, 172
Pearls and Pebbles (1894), 143, 368
Pearson, Carol, 381
Peat, Louisa M., 605
Peckham, Sir George, 12
Pedley, Charles, 221
Pedley, Hugh, 305, 562
Peel, Sir Robert, 95
Peele, George, 542, 543
Peevee (1928), 669, 673
Pegeen and the Pilgrim (1957), 631
Peggy (1924), 601
Pegis, Anton C., 591
Pelts and Powder (1929), 663
Pemberton, R. E. K., 452
Pen and Pencil Club, 157
Penfield, Wilder, 456
Pens and Pirates (1923), 610
Pensionnaires, The (1903), 310
Pentateuch, The (1864), 554
Pentecost (1891), 555
Penton, W. J., 555
People's Life of Christ, The (1920), 559
Pepys, Samuel, 23
Percevals, The, 130
Pericles, 547
Perkins, Simeon, 59
Peron, Capt., 46
Perry, Aaron J., 534
Perry, J. H., 522, 523

Perry, M. Eugene, 674
Perseverance Wins (1880), 307
Personal Memoirs (Richardson, 1838), 180–1
Personal Narrative (J. Edwards), 74
Personal Narrative of the Discovery of the Northwest Passage, A (1857), 38
Personal Note (1941), 756
Peter, John, 547
Peter Bosten: A Story about Realities (1915), 305
Peter the Sea Trout (1954), 380, 628
Peters, Austen, 372
Peter's Adventures in the Out-of-Doors (1940), 380
Petersen, Len, 634, 650, 707
Peterson, Sir William, 535, 543
Petitot, Father, 164
Petitt, Maud, 294, 304, 310
Petrarch, 365
Petronius, 546
Phantom Wires (1907), 312, 325
Pharis, Gwen: see Ringwood, Gwen Pharis
Phelan, G. B., 566, 567, 591
Phelan, Josephine, 506, 629, 630
Phelps, Arthur L., 125, 615, 634, 726
Phelps, Elizabeth, 278
Phenomena of Christianity (1908), 558
Philip Hazelbrook; or, The Junior Curate (1886), 305
Philip Musgrave (1846), 132
Philistia (1884), 313
Phillipps-Wolley, Clive, 262, 263, 300
Phillips, J. A., 182
Phillips, S. G., 563
Philosopher and Theology, The (1962), 590
Philosophical Basis of Religion, The (1907), 441
Philosophical Lectures (Coleridge, ed. 1949), 544
Philosophical Principles of Natural Religion, The (1862), 436

Philosophical Review, 439
Philosophy and the Mass Age (1959), 596
Philosophy in Canada (1952), 587
Philosophy in the Mid-Century (1958–59), 595
Philosophy Made Simple (1956), 597
Philosophy of Business (1945), 594
Philosophy of Education (1937, 1947), 594
Philosophy of Francis Bacon (1948), 586
Philosophy of Gassendi (1908), 577, 582, 583
Philosophy of History (1964), 589
Philosophy of John Stuart Mill (1891), 440
Philosophy of Kant Explained (1908), 440
Philosophy of Plato (1956), 594
Philosophy of Saint Bonaventure (1938), 590
Phips, Sir William, 57
Phoenix (journal), 533, 545
Picher, G. V., 566
Pickanock (1912), 292
Pickard, Humphrey, 434
Picked up Adrift (1872), 112
Picken, Andrew, 141
Pickersgill, J. W., 506
Pickford, Mary, 651
Pickthall, Marjorie, 21, 262, 263, 295, 307, 425, 426, 466, 635, 727, 752
Pickwick Papers (Dickens), 112
Pictorial Review, 678
Pictures of Wild Animals (1901), 382
Picturesque Canada (1882), 256
Pidgeon, George C., 561, 570
Pied Piper of Dipper Creek, The (1939), 697
Piepenburg, W. W., 518
Pieper, Josef, 592
Pierce, Lorne, 159, 346, 483, 484, 485, 487, 536, 609, 741, 768, 832
Pierre (1926), 636–7

Pierre and His People (1892), 296, 317
Piers Plowman, 764
Pilcher, E. W., 557
Pilgrims of the Wild (1935), 376, 628
Pillar, The (1952), 718
Pilot at Swan Creek, The (1905), 300
Pindar, Peter (pseud.), 176
Pindar (Greek Poet), 206
Pindar (1945), 539
Pine, Rose and Fleur-de-lis (1891), 428
Pioneer and Historical Association (Ont.), 237
Pioneer of Imperial Federation in Canada, The (1902), 357
Pioneer Public Service (1955), 510, 524
Pipes of Pan, The (1902–5), 411
Pirandello, L., 653
Pitman, Sir Isaac, 180
Place of Jesus Christ in Modern Theology, The (1929), 560
Place of Meeting: Poems 1958–1960 (1962), 816
Plato, 3, 343, 586, 587, 594, 645, 646
Plato, Sophist and Statesman (1961), 595
Plato's Philebus and Epinoris (1956), 595
Plato's Theory of Art (1953), 594
Plato's Theory of Education (1947), 594
Plato's Theory of Ethics (1928), 594
Plato's Thought (1935), 546, 588
Plays from Hart House Theatre (1926–7), 635–7
Plays from the Pacific Coast (1935), 640
Playter, Maud, 395
Playwrights' Studio Group, 653
Pliny, 364
Plotinus, 580
Plough and the Pen, The, 846
Ploughman of the Moon: An Adventure into Memory (1945), 619

Plummer, Christopher, 657
Plumptre, A. F. W., 523
Pocahontas, 23
Pocock, Roger, 262, 263, 268, 298, 300
Podmore, St. Michael, 358
Poe, Edgar Allan, 140, 159, 423, 720, 723
Poems: "Peter Pindar" (1822), 176; A. K. Archibald (1848), 107, 117; H. L. Spencer (1850), 119; J. Haynes (1864), 119; D. F. Little (1881), 117; A. Lampman (1900), 389; R. Finch (1946), 738, 739, 765; A. J. M. Klein (1944), 736
Poems and Essays (J. Howe, 1874), 115, 121, 340
Poems and Songs (McLachlan, 1874), 151, 154
Poems and Songs (Wm. Murdoch, 1860), 117
Poems by George Murray (1912), 157
Poems, Descriptive and Moral (McPherson, 1852), 119
Poems for People (1947), 741
Poems, Lyrical and Dramatic (J. H. Brown, 1892), 461
Poems of Ten Years (M. R. Knight, 1887), 108, 118
Poems on Methodism (Marsden, 1848), 82
Poems on Various Occasions (Adams, 1745), 73
Poems, Religious, Moral and Sentimental (J. Hogg, 1825), 119, 178
Poems, Written in Newfoundland (Prescott, 1839), 71
Poetic Element in the Scottish Mind, The (1857), 437
Poetic Process (1953), 544
Poetical Account of the American Campaigns of 1812 and 1813 (1815), 80
Poetical Remains of Peter John Allan (1853), 114, 122
Poetical Works (Leprohon, 1881), 157

Poetical Works of Charles Churchill (1956), 544
Poetical Works of John Salter (1852), 118
Poetry: A Magazine of Verse, 724, 726, 730, 766
Poetry and Dogma (1954), 541
Poetry in Canada (1958), 538
Poetry of E. J. Pratt, The (1956), 536
Poetry of Science, The (1854), 378
Poets of the Old Testament, The (1919), 556
Policy Question, The (1963), 526
Political and Historical Account of Lower Canada (1830), 209
Political Annals of Lower Canada (1828), 209
Political Economy in the Modern State (1946), 521
Political Justice (1946), 544
Political Leaders of Upper Canada (1931), 498
Political Theory of Possesive Individualism (1962), 526
Politics of John W. Dafoe and the Free Press (1963), 508
Politics of Labor (1887), 464
Pollock, Francis, 262, 300, 673
Polly Masson (1919), 302–3
Polson's Probation (1897), 297
Polyolbion (Drayton), 139
Pomeroy, Elsie, 404, 491
Pomp of the Lavilettes, The (1896), 289, 318
Ponteach (1766), 138
Pontiac, 22, 138
Pontifical Institute of Mediaeval Studies, 532, 543, 566–7, 590–3, 691
Pool and Rapid: The Story of a River (1932), 378
Pool in the Desert, The (1903), 317
Poole, Thomas W., 239
Poor Man's Rock (1920), **300, 333**

Pope, Alexander, 85, 136, 547, 755
Pope, Sir Joseph, 228, 242, 357
Pope and His Critics (1951), 547
Popery Again Condemned (McCulloch), 552
Popery Condemned by Scripture and the Fathers (1808), 552
Popular History of Ireland, A (1863, 1864), 156, 248
Popular History of the Dominion of Canada, A (1878), 218
Port Folio (Philadelphia), 131
Porteous, Archibald, 354
Porter, Arthur, 456
Porter, G. H., 557
Porter, Gene Stratton, 283
Porter, John, 528
Porter of Baghdad, The, and Other Fantasies (1901), 341
Portlock, Capt. Nathaniel, 46–7
Portlock, Rosa, 304
Portrait of a Dog (1930), 381, 672
Portrait of a Lady, The (James), 281
Portrait of Canada, A (1943), 605
Possession (1923), 670
Post (Washington), 315
Postscript to Adventure (1938), 619
Poteen (1926), 610
Potter, Rev. Austin, 306
Potter, Beatrix, 628
Poule d'eau, La (Roy), 840
Pound, Ezra, 481, 724, 733, 778
Pounder, R. M., 565
Poutrincourt, Sieur de, 11, 652
Powell, E. A., 603
Powell, S. Morgan, 664
Powell, T. P., 350
Power (1925), 326
Powicke, M. R., 518
Practical Reason and Morality (1957), 596
Practical Reasoning (1963), 589

Practice and Privileges of the Two Houses of Parliament (1840), 180, 247
Pragmatism and Idealism (1913), 595
Prairie Child, The (1922), 299, 326
Prairie Mother, The (1920), 299
Prairie Wife, The (1915), 299, 325
Pratt, E. J., 21, 251, 470, 472, 480, 487, 488, 494, 507, 536, 540, 558, 609, 698, 738, 742–50, 752, 754, 765, 766, 768, 785, 787, 808, 829, 830, 834, 843, 844, 846, 848
Pratt, Viola W., 630
Preacher and the Modern Mind, The (1912), 557
Preacher of Cedar Mountain, The (1917), 304, 324
Precipice, The (1948), 701
Preface to Empathy (1956), 588
Prehistoric Man, Researches into the Origin of Civilization in the Old and the New World (1862), 248
Prelude, The (Wordsworth), 397
Preparation of Ryerson Embury, The (1900), 294, 302, 306
Pre-Raphaelites, 63, 147
Presbyterian Church in Canada, 1875–1925, The (1925), 572
Presbyterian Witness (journal), 562
Prescott, Henrietta, 71
Prescott, Sir Henry, 71
Prescott, William H., 249
Preston, R. A., 242, 518
Preston, Sydney, 293
Pretender, The (1914), 310
Preview (magazine), 489–90, 767, 769–70, 771, 774, 776, 785, 834
Price, Daniel, 10
Price, Marjorie, 639
Price-Brown, John, 262, 293, 295
Pride's Fancy (1946), 697
Priestley, F. E. L., 529, 530,

541, 543, 544
Priestley, J. B., 336
Primitive Christian Calendar—related to Mark, The (1952), 566
Primitive Christian Catechism, The (1940), 566
Primitive Culture (1871), 161
Primrose, Hilda S., 604
Prince, S. H., 563
Prince Edward Island Magazine, 207
Prince Rupert's Namesake (1893), 307
Prince Society, 237
Principal Navigations (Hakluyt, 1598–1600), 5, 7, 19
Principalities and Powers (1956), 568
Principle of Official Independence, The (Dawson), 524
Principles of Psychology (James), 578–9
Pringle, Judge J. F., 241
Prism (magazine), 494, 817
Prisoner of Mademoiselle, The (1904), 288, 322
Privacity Agent and Other Modest Proposals, The (1928), 613
Prizewinner, The (1928), 635
Problem of the Unity of the Sciences, The (1961), 454, 589
Prodigal's Brother, The (1899), 298
Professor Conant: A Story of English and American Social and Political Life (1884), 309
Progress and Poverty (1879), 279
Progress of Canada in the Nineteenth Century (1900), 219
Progressive Party in Canada, The (1950), 502
Proletarian Literature (1935), 471
Pronunciation (1930), 542
Propaganda and Psychological Warfare (1926), 526

Prophecy and Eschatology (1926), 565
Prophecy in Islam (1958), 571
Prophecy of Merlin, The, and Other Poems (1870), 157, 429
Prophet, The: A Story of the Two Kingdoms of Ancient Palestine (1911), 308
Prophet in Politics, A (1959), 506
Prophetic Ideas and Ideals (1902), 557
Prophets and Israel's Culture, The (1934), 566
Prophets of the Old Testament (1919), 556
Prospectin' Fools (1927), 660
Prospector, The: A Tale of the Crow's Nest Pass (1904), 294, 300, 323
Protest (Williams, 1956), 644
Protestant Faith and Life (1958), 570
Protestant Spirit, The (1955), 569
Prothero, R. H., 631
Proudfoot, William, 237
Proust, Marcel, 709, 835
Provencher, Paul, 371
Proverb in Ibsen, The (1936), 542
Providential Escape after a Shipwreck, A (1774), 73
Provincials, The (1951), 707
Prowse, D. W., 221
Psychologies of 1930 (1930), 582
Public Archives of Canada, 24, 25
Public Worship of God, The (1927), 563
Pullen-Burry, Mrs. B., 361
Punch, 192
Purchas, His Pilgrimes (1625), 13, 16, 20, 41, 72
Purdy, Alfred W., 816
Pure Celestial Flame, The (1948), 569
Puritanism and Liberty (1938, 1950), 539
Puritanism in the Period of the Great Persecution 1660–1688 (1957), 569
Pusey, E. B., 448
Pyke, Magnus, 674
Pyper, C. B., 611
Pyper, Nancy, 653

QUADRA, B. y, 48
Qualter, Terence H., 526
Quarterly Review (London), 132
Quebec: As it was and As it is (Roger), 216
Quebec Gazette, 87, 88, 90
Quebec Hill; or Canadian Scenery (1797), 86–7
Quebec Literary and Historical Society, 176, 177, 237
Quebec Magazine, 88, 176
Quebec Mercury, 86
Quebec Past and Present (1876), 286
Quebec, 1759 (Stacey), 509
Quebec, The Harp, and Other Poems (1829), 130
Queen's Highway, The (1887), 351
Queen's Quarterly, 439, 441, 451, 459, 481, 530, 534, 609, 665, 674, 680, 786, 816
Quentin Durward (Scott), 133
Quest (1941), 455
Quest of Alistair, The (1921), 659
Quest of the Ballad, The (1919), 172
Quest of the Historical Jesus (Schweitzer), 559
Questioning Mind, The (1937, 1947), 594
Questions of the Day in Philosophy and Psychology (1912), 593
Quinn, Vernon, 599
Quo Vadis, 281
Quodlibets, Lately Come Over from New Britaniola, Old Newfound-land (1628), 14–15

RAABE, Wilhelm, 540, 548
Rabbi's Sons, The: A Story of the Days of St. Paul (1891), 308

Rabcewicz-Zubkowski, Ludwik, 455
Racine, Jean, 11, 549, 649
Radcliff family, 253
Raddall, Thomas, 171, 257, 509, 630, 696, 720, 721
Radisson, Pierre Esprit, 22–4, 50, 57, 296, 629, 630
Radisson Society, 485
Rae, Fraser, 351
Rae, John (explorer), 37–40
Rae, John (economist, 1796–1872), 520
Raftis, J. A., 566
Rahbar, D., 571
Rahman, F., 596
Raid from Beauséjour, The (1894), 288, 322, 625
Railway Notes in the North-West (1884), 351
Rain (Maugham), 640
Raine, Walter, 371
Rainer Maria Rilke: Creative Anguish of a Modern Poet (1957), 548
Raleigh, Sir Walter, 9
Ralph, Julian, 354
Ramage, Kate Douglas, 182
Rambles; see *Nova Scotian*, 209
Rambles of a Canadian Naturalist (1916), 368, 369–70
Ramsay, Allan, 80, 544
Ranching for Sylvia (1912), 299
Rand, Silas, 378
Rand, Silas Tertius, 104, 164
Rand, Theodore, H., 187, 429
Rapaport, Stella F., 631
Rashley, R. E., 538
Rastell, John, 6
Ratcliffe, Walter, 461
Rational and the Real, The (1962), 596
Rattray, William J., 240
Raw Gold (1908), 300, 332
Rawlinson, Richard, 23
Ray, George, 296
Ray, J. E., 599
Ray, John, 365
Rayleigh, Lady Clara, 351
Raymond, W. O., 547
Reade, Charles, 277, 279, 281
Reade, John, 157, 162, 429

Reality of the Divine Movement in Israel (1911), 557
Realms of Being (Santayana), 589
Reaney, James, 408, 494, 537, 635, 648–9, 720, 722, 769, 787–8, 791, 816, 841
Reason and Revelation in the Middle Ages (1938), 566, 590
Rebel, The (magazine), 468, 537
Rebel on the Trail (1953), 629
Rebellion: A Story of the Red River Uprising (1912), 298
Rebels Ride at Night (1953), 630
Rebirth of Ministry, The (1960), 569
Reciprocity Treaty of 1854, The (Masters), 511
Recollections of a Visit to Canada: Experiences of a Member of the Corporation of London (1907), 357
Recorder (Halifax), 446
Recovery of the Teaching Ministry, The (1961), 569
Red Barn Theatre, 656
Red Bill (1929), 660
Red Carpet for the Sun, A (1959), 782, 816
Red Cloud (1882), 298
Red Cow and her Friends, The (1919), 344–5, 375
Red Feathers (1907), 628
Red Fox (1905), 384
Red Heart, The (1949), 648, 787–88
Red River Settlement, The (1856), 34, 239
Red Tarn: A Thrilling Temperance Poem (1873), 107
Red Wilderness (1938), 660
Reddick, David, 371
Redemption (1822), 556
Redemption of Man, The (1920), 557
Redgrave, Michael, 653
Redruff, Raggylug, and Vixen (1900), 382
Reed, Else Porter, 667

Reeve, Winifred, 262, 310
Reeves, John, 646
Reformation, The (1961), 570
Reformation in Europe, The (1844), 552
Régis, Louis-Marie, 595
Reid, A. Howard, 571
Reid, G. B., 452
Reid, J. H. S., 518
Reid, Thomas, 442
Reid, W. S., 518, 572
Reise-Tagebuch (1855), 38
Relation d'un Voyage à la côte du Nord-Ouest de l'Amérique Septentrionale (1820), 33
Relation of Philosophy to Science, The (1873), 439
Relevance of the Prophets, The (1944), 557, 566
Relief (Bicknell), 641
Religion and Theology of St. Paul, The (1918), 558
Religions of the World, The (1894), 555
Remarkable History of the Hudson's Bay Company, The (1900), 241
Remarks and Pamphlet entitled Popery Condemned by Scripture and the Fathers (1809), 552
Reminiscences (L. W. Bailey), 454
Reminiscences (G. Smith, 1911), 233
Reminiscences of a Canadian Pioneer (1884), 180
Remnants (1835), 135
Renaissance (1922), 684
Renascence of Faith, The (1912), 565
Reply to the Report of the Earl of Durham, A (1839), 100
Report on the Geology of Newfoundland (Jukes, 1839), 70
Report upon Canada, A (1883), 348
Reports ... on the Dominion of Canada as a Field for Settlement (1880), 348
Representative Poetry, 483
Resurrection of Christ, The (1920), 565

Return of the Immigrant, The (de la Roche), 639
Return of the Viking (1955), 631
Return to the River (1941), 386
Revell (publisher), 270
Review of Historical Publications Relating to Canada, 220, 224, 227, 235, 239, 242, 243, 246, 480; see also, Canadian Historical Review
Reville, F. D., 298
Revolt of Tartarus (1852), 148
Reynolds, A. G., 571
Reynolds, Lois, 639
Reynolds, Stephen, 50–1
Reynolds Miscellany, 265
Rhodenizer, V. B., 484
Rhymes of the Miner (1937), 171
Rhythm in the Novel (1950), 541
Ricci, V. H., 600
Rice, T. D., 653
Rich, E. E., 24
Rich, R., 10
Rich Man, The (1948), 709
Richard III, King, 307
Richard Carvel (Churchill), 281
Richard Yea-and-Nay (Hewlett), 281
Richardson, C. C., 574
Richardson, John (1787–1865), 37
Richardson, Major John (1796–1852), 66, 127, 137, 138, 139, 145, 180, 181, 214, 483, 485, 617, 697
Richardson, Robert Lorne, 292, 296, 310
Richardson, Samuel, 84
Richey, James Arminius, 106, 117–18
Richler, Mordecai, 494, 684, 694, 699, 702, 707, 708, 711, 712–15, 720, 834
Rickman, John, 45
Rickman, Thomas R., 350
Riddell, J. H., 572
Riddell, W. A., 526
Riddell, Hon. Mr. Justice W. R., 671

Riddle of the Universe Solved, The (1890), 555, 832
Rideau Waterway, The (1955), 455
Ridiculous Courting, A; and Other Stories (1900), 289
Ridley, Hilda M., 487
Ridout, George (1791–1871), 91
Ridout, Thomas (1754–1824), 91
Ridout, Thomas G. (1792–1861), 91
Ried, Leslie, 637
Riel, Louis, 159, 168, 191, 200, 201, 505, 514, 761
Riel (Coulter), 641, 647, 655
Right of Way, The (1901), 270, 290, 318
Rights of Man and Natural Law, The (1945), 691
Riley, James Whitcomb, 723
Riley, Louise, 631
Rilke, Maria Rainier, 548
Ring and the Book, The (Browning), 544
Ringfield (1914), 290, 310
Ringing the Changes (1957), 672
Ringwood, Gwen Pharis, 491, 639, 640
Rink Rat (1949), 707
Rise and Fall of New France, The (1928), 236
Rise and Progress of the Church of England in the British North American Provinces, The (1849), 572
Rise of Canada from Barbarism to Wealth and Civilization, The (1855), 215, 216
Rise of Toronto, The (1947), 518
Rising of the Red Man, The (1902), 298
Rising Village, The (1825), 107, 116, 119–21, 127, 139, 178, 617
Risk, Sidney, 655
Ritchie, C. S., 486
Ritchie, D. L., 574
Ritchie, J. E., 348
Ritchie, P. R., 355

Rival Forts, The; or, The Velvet Side of Beauséjour (1907), 288
River and Empty Sea (1950), 697
River for a Sidewalk (1953), 376, 379
River Never Sleeps, A (1946), 373, 615
Rob McNabb (1923), 672
Robb, J. A., 485
Robbins, William, 546
Robert Elsmere (Ward, 1888), 279
Robert Harding (1938), 668–9
Roberton, T. B., 611
Roberts, Sir Charles G. D., 63–4, 67, 108, 109, 122, 160, 186, 187, 197, 204, 205, 219, 261, 262, 263, 268, 283, 286, 288, 307, 321–2, 325, 329, 340, 371, 379, 381, 382, 383–6, 387, 398, 405, 406, 410, 412, 429, 430, 477, 482, 483, 484, 490, 491, 537, 538, 625, 627, 629, 632, 671, 755, 801, 828, 832, 843
Roberts, Dorothy, 816
Roberts, George Goodridge, 63, 205
Roberts, Leslie, 606
Roberts, Lloyd, 483
Roberts, Richard, 565
Roberts, Theodore Goodridge, 261, 262, 263, 268, 288, 291, 329, 429, 628
Roberts and the Influences of His Time (1930), 537
Robertson, J. K., 452
Robertson, James, 552
Robertson, John Charles, 610–11
Robertson, John Ross, 90
Robertson, Margaret Murray, 261, 278
Robertson, Norman, 239
Robins, John D., 166, 372, 480, 609, 614, 674, 845
Robinson, Edwin Arlington, 755–6, 801
Robinson, Frank, 299
Robinson, James Harvey, 500
Robinson, John Beverley, 229
Robinson Crusoe, 547, 841

Robson, J. M., 543
Robson, Joseph, 24
Rockbound (1928), 668
Rocking Chair and Other Poems, The (1948), 736
Rocky Mountain Journal (ed. 1955), 34
Rocky Mountain Poems (1960), 784
Roderick Hudson (James), 281
Rodomont: A Romance of Mont St. Michel (1926), 661
Roe, E. P., 278
Roger, Charles, 215, 216
Roger Davis, Loyalist (1907), 288
Roger Sudden (1944), 697
Rogers, D. B., 572
Rogers, Grace Dean, 290
Rogers, Grace McLeod, 674
Rogers, Major Robert, 138
Roland Graeme, Knight (1892, 1906), 302, 306, 461
Rolf in the Woods (1911), 380
Rolph, Dr. John, 226
Rolph, Thomas, 141
Rolyat, Jane; *see* McDougall, E. Jean
Roman Letter for Today, The (1959), 570
Roman Singer, A (Crawford), 281
Romance of Labrador, The (1934), 574
Romance of Medicine in Canada, The (1940), 454
Romance of the Halifax Disaster, A (1918), 290, 311
Romance of the Rockies, A (1888), 298, 300
Romance of Toronto, A (1888), 294
Romance of Two Worlds, A (1890), 281
Romantic Canada (1922), 600
Romany of the Snows, A (1896), 296, 317
Rome in Canada: The Ultramontane Struggle for Supremacy over the Civil Power (1877), 225

Romeo and Juliet, 784
Roosevelt and the Antinoe, The, 743, 745, 746
Roosevelt, Franklin D., 488
Roots and Causes of the Wars (1914–1918), The (1924), 249
Roper, Edward, 301, 355
Roper, Gordon, 548, 837, 838
Rorke, Louise, 381
Rose, George M. (publisher), 180, 184
Rose, J. Holland, 5
Rose and the Puritan, The (1958), 802
Rose of Acadie (1898), 290
Rose-Belford's Canadian Monthly (1878–82), 162, 185, 186, 204, 205, 439; see also, *Canadian Monthly and National Review* (1872–8)
Rose à Charlitte: An Acadian Romance (1898), 290, 320
Rose Carney, a Story of Ever Shifting Scenes (1890), 110
Roseharp, The (1835), 139
Ross, Alexander, 25, 33–4, 239
Ross, Frances Arleen, 605
Ross, George W., 229
Ross, Rev. James, 433
Ross, John, 35–37
Ross, Malcolm, 370, 494, 495, 537, 538, 541, 610
Ross, Sinclair, 491, 674, 704, 705, 706, 722, 839
Ross, W. W. Eustace, 728, 730, 732, 785
Rosse, Earl of, 448
Rossetti, Christina, 425
Rossetti, D. G., 205
Rothney, Gordon, 509
Roughing It in the Bush (1852), 100, 144, 181, 204, 253, 485, 618, 718
Rouillard, C. D., 549
Round the World in Strange Company (1915), 362
Round Trip in North America, A (1895), 354
Roundelays (1958), 169
Rousseau, Henri, 848
Rousseau, Jean Jacques, 17, 366, 374, 549–50, 595, 841
Routhier, Judge A. B., 574
Rowan, J. J., 350
Rowat, D. C., 524
Rowell-Sirois Report; see Royal Commission on Dominion-Provincial Relations
Rowland, John, 375
Rowley, O. R., 572
Rowntree, Leonard G., 455
Rowsell, Henry, 179
Roy, Gabrielle, 472, 702, 703, 840
Royal Canadian Institute, 447
Royal Commission on Canada's Economic Prospects (1957), 522
Royal Commission on Dominion-Provincial Relations, 478, 488, 522, 524
Royal Commission on National Development in the Arts, Letters and Sciences, 492–3, 495, 522, 531
Royal Commission on the Relations of Labor and Capital (1889), 458
Royal Power of Dissolution of Parliament in the British Commonwealth (1943), 524
Royal Society of Canada, 25, 157, 162, 186, 218, 250, 271, 403, 452, 484, 516, 530, 531, 532, 536, 546, 661
Royalty in Canada; Embracing Sketches of the House of Argyll (1878), 218
Royce, Josiah, 411
Rudd, W. J. N., 545
Ruddick, Bruce, 489, 767, 769
Rule and Misrule of the English in America (1851), 100
Run through Canada, A (1905), 357
Running Commentary on the Gospel of Mark, A (1960), 566
Rupert of Henzau (Hope), 282

Rusk, Ralph Leslie, 137
Ruskin, John, 193, 413
Russell, Bertrand, 587
Russell, Franklin, 369
Rut, John, 6
Rutherford, E. R., 360
Ryan, Carroll (William Thomas Carroll), 154, 429
Ryan, J. J., 566
Ryerson, Egerton, 66, 140, 146, 180, 229, 232, 241, 508, 552, 617
Ryerson, John, 573
Ryerson Press, 180, 187, 484, 536

S., A., 349
Sabine, Edward, 36
Sabre Thrusts at Free-Thought (1898), 554
Sacred Bullock and Other Stories, The (1939), 381, 672, 675
Sacred Stories of the Sweet Grass Cree (1930), 164
Sacrifice, The (1956), 710
Sacrifice of the Mass, The (1905), 560
Sacrifice of the Shannon, The (1903), 290
Saddlebags for Suitcases (1942), 605
Sadlier, Anna Teresa, 261, 263, 278
Sadlier, James, 156
Sadlier, Mrs. Mary Anne, 156–7, 261, 278
Safarian, A. E., 522
St. Cuthbert's (1905), 293, 305, 329, 330
St. Elmo (Miss Evans), 278
St. Francis, 364
St. James (magazine), 265
Saint Joan (Shaw), 646
St. Lawrence and the Saguenay, The (1856), 148, 154
St. Nicholas (magazine), 453
St. Paul and Epicurus (1954), 570, 589
St. Peter Damiani and his Canonical Sources (1954), 566
Saint-Simon, C. H. de R., comte de, 550

Saint Thomas Aquinas (1935), 590
St. Thomas and Analogy (1941), 566, 591
St. Thomas and Epistemology (1946), 595
St. Thomas and Philosophy (1964), 591
St. Thomas and the Future of Metaphysics (1957), 592
St. Thomas and the Greeks (1939), 591
St. Thomas and the Problem of the Soul in the Thirteenth Century (1934), 591
St. Thomas Aquinas On Being and Essence (1949), 592
St. Ursula's Convent; or, the Nun of Canada (1824), 107, 109–10, 133, 140, 176
Saints in Politics: The Clapham Sect (1952), 569
Salmagundi (Irving), 131, 133
Salmon, E. T., 518, 542
Salmon-Fishing in Canada (1860), 371
Salt Marsh (1942), 760
Salter, F. M., 539
Salter, John, 118
Saltwater Summer (1948), 631
Salverson, Laura Goodman, 621, 622, 623, 658, 664, 666, 667
Sam Slick's Wise Saws and Modern Instances (1853), 99
Sandburg, Carl, 724, 742
Sanderson, Douglas, 698
Sanderson, Elizabeth, 380
Sanderson, J. E., 572
Sandford Fleming (1915), 224
Sandiford, Betti, 638
Sandstone and Other Poems (1945), 760
Sandwell, B. K., 606, 609, 612, 613, 614, 839
Sandys, Edwyn, 296, 371
Sangster, Charles, 147–8, 154, 159, 162, 181, 182, 206, 843

Sansom, Mary J., 361
Santana, the Hero Dog of France (1945), 381
Santayana, G., 589
Santayana: Saint of the Imagination (1961), 589
Sappho, 393, 844
Sarah Binks (1947), 720
Sartre, J. P., 596, 597, 713
Sashes Red and Blue (1956), 631
Saturday and Sunday (1935), 614
Saturday Evening Post, 268, 299, 326
Saturday Night, 265, 271, 481, 611, 612, 613, 724, 742
Saturday Review of Literature, 249
Saul (1857, 1859), 149
Saunders, Margaret Marshall, 261, 262, 263, 290, 307, 320, 366, 380, 381, 383, 572, 627, 671, 672
Saunders, Richard, 369, 371, 518
Saunders, William, 360
Savage, Richard, 547
Savary, A. W., 77
Savigny, Mrs. Annie Gregg, 294, 381
Savonarola, His Life and Times (1890), 249
Savour of Salt (1927), 668
Sawney's Letters and Cariboo Rhymes (1868), 171
Sawtell, Mrs. M. Ethelind, 136
Sawyer, A. Wayne, 434
Saywell, J. T., 510, 524
Sa'-Zada Tales, The (1905), 324, 380
Scadding, Henry, 139, 141, 154, 239, 533
Scaife, Arthur Hodgkin, 300
Scammell, Arthur, 171
Scamper through Some Cities of America, A (1890), 354
Scargill, M. H., 825
Scarlet Letter, The (Hawthorne), 548
Scarlet Sash, The (1925), 667
Scarrow, Howard A., 525
Scenes of the Life of a Halifax Belle (1859), 109
Schelling's Transcendental Idealism (1882), 440
Schlegel, Friedrich, 544
Schnitzler, A., 653
Scholastic Miscellany, A: Anselm to Ockham (1956), 567, 593
Scholefield, E. O. S., 236
Schoolcraft, H. R., 143, 164
School History of Canada, A (1870), 217
Schopenhauer, A., 361
Schull, Joseph, 630, 634
Schurman, Jacob Gould, 434
Schweitzer, Albert, 559
Science and Values (1952), 587
Scientism, Man and Religion (1952), 571, 588
Sclater, J. R. P., 563
Scot in British North America, The (1880–4), 240
Scotchman's Return (1960), 612, 702
Scotsman in Canada, The (1911), 240
Scotsman in Canada, A (1935), 603
Scott, Anthony, 523
Scott, Duncan Campbell, 67, 186, 198, 207, 228, 262, 289, 403, 416–21, 423, 430, 462, 466, 479, 491, 636, 661, 674, 727, 801, 825, 843, 844, 845
Scott, E. F., 556, 561
Scott, Frank R., 472, 480, 481, 488, 489, 494, 525, 687, 732–4, 753, 754, 765, 767, 785, 847
Scott, Frederick George, 187, 403, 429, 574, 732
Scott, H. A., 229
Scott, H. P., 362
Scott, Jack, 611
Scott, Jonathan, 551
Scott, Peter Dale, 713, 719, 816
Scott, R. B. Y., 557, 563, 566, 571
Scott, Sir Walter, 93, 133, 148, 158, 206, 277, 281, 287, 361, 423, 541, 548, 724
Scraps and Sketches; or, The

Album of a Literary Lounger (1831), 135
Scribbler, 129, 132, 134, 139
Scribner's Monthly, 266, 268, 453
Scriptural Rights of the Members of Christ's Visible Church (1854), 552
Scriptural Testimonies to the Doctrines and Duties of Christianity (1873), 555
Scripture Sketches (1829), 553
Scriptures Defended, The (1863), 554
"Scrivener, S.," 348
Sea is Also a Garden, The (1962), 816
Sea Songs and Ballads from Nova Scotia (1928), 172
Seabury, Samuel, 81
Sealed Verdict, The (1947), 716
Search for America, A (1927), 621, 679, 681–2, 841
Search for the Western Sea, The (1908), 224
Searching Image, The (1952), 776
Season Ticket, The (1860), 99, 100
Seasons, The (Thomson), 85
Season's Lovers, The (1958), 775
Seats of the Mighty, The (1896), 281, 287, 318, 632, 841
Second Chance, The (1910), 297, 330
Second Scroll, The (1951), 710–11, 736, 829
Second Silence, The (1955), 774
Secret Trails (1916), 386
Secret World of Og, The (1963), 631
Secrets of the Kingdom, The (1954), 568
Sect, Cult, and Church in Alberta (1955), 528, 569
Sedgewick, G. G., 539
See Canada Next (1940), 605
See the Christ Stand (1945), 562, 569

Seeing Canada (1924), 599
Seeing Canada and the South (1911), 362
Seekers, The (1957), 571
Seeley, J. R., 528
Seigneurs of Old Canada, The (1915), 244
Selected Odes of Horace (1952), 545
Selected Poems: Souster (1956), 779; Livesay (1957), 741, 785; Lowry (1962), 816
Selected Writings (W. L. Mackenzie) (1960), 140
Selections from Canadian Poets (1864), 147, 183, 429, 536
Selections from Kant (1882 etc.), 440
Self-Raised (Southworth), 278
Selkirk, Lord, 34, 134
Sellar, Robert, 239, 287
Selye, Hans, 456
Seneca, 4, 543
Separated to the Gospel (1956), 562
"Seranus"; *see* Harrison, Mrs. J. F.
Seraph on the Sea (1891), 110
Sergeant of Fort Toronto, The (1914), 294–95
Serial Publication in England, before 1750 (1956), 547
Series of Outlines, A; or, Theological Essays . . . (1846), 553
Serious and Pathetic Contemplation (Traherne), 547
Service, Robert W., 171, 262, 263, 301, 310, 362, 424, 425, 426, 466, 303, 316
Servos, L. C., 663
Set in Authority (1906), 619–20, 635
Set Stormy (1931), 673
Seth Jones; or, The Captives of the Frontier (Ellis), 278
Seton, Ernest Thompson, 262, 263, 283, 304, 307, 324, 369, 371, 378, 380–4

passim, 387, 453, 620, 625, 626, 627, 632, 697
Settlement of the Peace River Country, The (1934), 527
Settlements and Churches in Nova Scotia, 1749–1776 (1930), 572
Settlers of the Marsh (1925), 679, 681
Sewell, Anna, 366, 381, 627
Sex and the Nature of Things (1954), 454
Seymour, James, 306
Shack-Locker, The: Yarns of the Deep Sea Fishing Fleets (1916), 291
Shades of the Hamlet, and Other Poems (1852), 119
Shadow, The (1913), 312
Shadow of Tradition, The (1927), 667
Shadow Riders, The (1916), 299
Shaftesbury, Earl of, 366
Shagganappi, The (1912), 256
Shake Hands with the Hangman (1954), 779
Shakespeare, William, 4, 8, 11, 148, 154, 156, 159, 193, 325, 423, 480, 534, 540, 546, 548, 570, 649, 653, 656–7, 704, 735, 783, 823, 838
Shakespeare Club (Montreal), 157
Shakespeare the Seer (1864), 533
Shall I go to Canada? (1912), 362
Shall We Emigrate? (1885), 349
Shanghai Jim (1928), 659
Shanly, C. D., 171
Shanly, Francis, 455
Shanly, Walter, 455
Shapiro, Lionel, 716
Sharp, Edith L., 629
Sharp Brothers (London, Eng.,), 129
Sharpe, John, 178
Shasta of the Wolves (1919), 628
Shaw, Campbell, 298, 300
Shaw, George Bernard, 466, 515, 542, 639, 646, 653, 695, 704

INDEX 933

Shaw, J. E., 549
Shaw, John M., 565
Shaw, Neufville, 489, 767, 769
Shaw, Robert, 555
She (Haggard), 280
She Lived in New York (1894), 309, 321
She Stoops to Conquer, 120
Sheard, Virna, 262, 263, 307, 659
Sheldon, Charles M., 279
Shelley, Percy B., 118, 122, 149, 159, 389, 392, 417, 465, 584
Shepard, Odell, 485
Shepheard's Calendar, 788
Sheppard, E. E., 293, 294, 304, 307, 312
Sheppard, Mrs. William, 128
Sherman, Francis, 403, 426
Sherman, Ralph, 380
Shields, Robert, 354
Shiels, Andrew, 117
Shining Ship (1918), 632
Ship under the Cross, The (1958), 569
Shirley, Governor, 59
Shirreff, Patrick, 141
Shoe and Canoe, The (1850), 31, 167, 254
Shook, L. K., 543
Short Dictionary of Anglo-Saxon Poetry (1960), 543
Short History of the Canadian People, A (1887), 219
Short History of the Dominion of Canada, from 1500–1878... (1878), 217–18
Short History of the Presbyterian Church in the Dominion of Canada (1892), 572
Shortt, Adam, 140, 228, 232, 235, 236, 242, 244, 245, 247, 520
Shrouding, The (1935), 734
Sibbald, Mrs. Susan, 140
Sibbald, William, 140, 179
Sidelights on Canada (1936), 603
Sidney, Sir Philip, 15, 534
Sidomie (1921), 683
Siegfried, André, 243, 528
Sienkiewicz, H., 281

Sign Post (1932), 740, 741
Sigourney, Mrs. Lydia H., 145
Silcox, C. E., 561, 570
Silent Call, The (1930), 387
Silent Man, The (1958), 629
Silken Lines and Silver Hooks (1954), 372
Silver, Arthur P., 256, 371, 372
Silver: The Life of an Atlantic Salmon (1931), 386
Silver Maple, The (1906), 330
Silver Poppy, The (1903), 325
Sim, R. A., 528
Simcoe, Elizabeth, 90, 167
Simcoe, John Graves, 90, 139
Sime, Jessie G., 674, 675, 684
Simple Adventures of a Memsahib, The (1893), 315
Simple Modes in the Philosophy of John Locke (1918), 594
Simpson, George, 34–5, 37
Simpson, Thomas, 37–8
Sinclair, Bertrand William, 262, 263, 276, 300–1, 311, 332–33
Sinclair, Coll MacLean, 295
Sinclair, Sir John, 208
Sinclair, Lister, 634, 645
Sinclair, Upton, 280
Sinden, Margaret, 548
Singer of the Kootenay, The (1911), 300, 329
Singing Season, The (1924), 662
Sinners Twain (1895), 298
Sir Casimir Stanislaus Gzowski (1959), 455
Sir Charles G. D. Roberts (1943), 491
Sir Charles Tupper (Longley), 228
Sir Edmund Head (1954), 505
Sir Frederick Banting (1946), 454
Sir Frederick Haldimand (McIlwraith), 228

Sir James Douglas (1908), 228, 236
Sir John A. Macdonald (Parkin), 228
Sir Wilfrid Laurier and the Liberal Party (1903), 229
Sir William Osler (1920), 454
Sirluck, Ernest, 544
Sissons, C. B., 508, 569
Sister Anne! Sister Anne! (1920), 311
Sister Dominions, The (1896), 354
Sister to Evangeline, A (1898), 288, 322
Sister Woman (1920), 674, 675
Sitwell, Edith, 481, 731, 732
Six Canadian Plays (1930), 638
Six Disquisitions on Doctrinal and Practical Theology (1853), 553
Six Salmon Rivers and Another (1960), 372
Six Young Men in the Wilds of Maine and Canada (1885), 350
Sixth of June, The (1955), 716
Skelton, O. D., 235, 244, 245, 498, 522
Sketch of His Majesty's Province of Upper Canada (1805), 90–1
Sketch of the Early Settlement and Subsequent Progress of the Town of Peterborough (1867), 239
Sketches of New Brunswick (1825), 120, 210
Sketches of the Early Life of a Sailor (1820), 82
Sketches of Upper Canada (Howison), 133
Sketco the Raven (1961), 378
Skilling, Gordon, 526
Skinner, Constance Lindsay, 726–7
Sky Pilot, The (1899), 270, 280, 298, 300, 304, 322, 323
Sky Pilot at Swan Creek, The (1905), 323

934 INDEX

Sky Pilot in No Man's Land, The (1919), 311, 323
Sladen, Arthur, 117
Sladen, Douglas, 348, 355
Slater, Patrick; *see* Mitchell, John
Slater, R. H. L., 571
Sleep My Pretty One (Coulter), 641
Smalacombe, John: *see* MacKay, L. A.
Small, H. Beaumont, 448
Smallwood, Charles, 153
Smart, J. D., 569, 570
Smet, Pierre Jean de, 35
Smethurst, Gemaliel, 73
Smethurst, S. E., 545
Smith, A. J. M., 6, 159, 472, 480, 481, 488, 490–1, 494, 537, 538, 609, 731–2, 734, 739, 753, 762, 765, 768, 769, 775, 785, 816, 837, 844
Smith, Clyde, 305
Smith, Sir Donald, 352, 514
Smith, Douglas Barlow, 110
Smith, Edgar Maurice, 308
Smith, Frank Clifford, 289, 290, 305, 310
Smith, Goldwin, 63, 160, 161, 162, 185, 191, 194, 197, 201, 202, 204, 207, 232, 233–4, 240, 246, 248, 249, 315, 340, 341, 355, 459, 460, 463, 505, 617, 824, 825
Smith, Henry More, 110
Smith, J. C., 357
Smith, Capt. John, 23
Smith, Kay, 767, 769, 795
Smith, Lillian, 632
Smith, Marion B., 547
Smith, Michael, 136
Smith, Minnie, 301
Smith, Piazzi, 447
Smith, Seba, 97, 335
Smith, Sydney, 206
Smith, T. W., 572
Smith, W. C., 571
Smith, Waldo, 567
Smith, William (travel writer), 354
Smith, William (1769–1847), 127–8, 213
Smith, William (1859–1932), 498
Smith, William Peter, 239

Smoking Flax, The (1924), 676, 677
Smoky Days (1901), 322
Smollett, T. B., 95, 99, 141, 549
Smollett et la France (1935), 549
Smyth, John Paterson, 303, 558–59
Snake Country Journals (1950), 34
Snap: A Legend of the Lone Mountain (1890), 300
Snow Birch, The (1958), 379
Snow on the Headlight (1899), 298
So Near is Grandeur (1945), 663
Social Achievements of the Christian Church, The (1930), 563
Social Approach to Economics, A (1939), 523
Social Credit and the Federal Power in Canada (1954), 525
Social Credit Movement in Alberta, The (1959), 528, 587
Social Departure, A (1890), 315
Social Development of Canada, The (1942), 527
Social Good, The (1927), 589
Social Purpose for Canada (1961), 526
Social Romanticism in France (1951), 550
Society and the Housing Crisis (1936), 564
Socrates (1957), 645–46
Socratic Dialogues (ed. 1953), 596
Solberg, P. A., 573
Soldiering in Canada, 616
Soldiers of Liberty (1892), 305, 307
Solo (1924), 683, 685
Solomon Levi (1935), 686–87
Some Animal Stories (1921), 625
Sommerville, William, 554
Son of a Smaller Hero (1955), 713, 714

Son of Courage, A (1920), 379
Son of the Mohawk (1954), 629
Song of Charity, A (1857), 154
Song of Sixpence, 832
Song of the Years, A, and a Memory of Acadia (1889), 119
Songs and Ballads from Nova Scotia (1932), 172
Songs and Ballads of Newfoundland, Ancient and Modern (1902), 171–72
Songs from the Newfoundland Outports (1964), 172
Songs of a Sourdough (1907), 424
Songs of Miramichi (1964?), 172
Songs of Old Canada (1886), 169
Songs of Old Manitoba (1959), 168
Songs of Summerland (1927), 117
Songs of the Church (1854), 574
Songs of the Coast Dwellers (1930), 726
Songs of the Common Day (1893), 802
Songs of the Great Dominion (1889), 197, 416, 426, 429
Songs of the Saguenay and Other Poems (1927), 757
Songs of the Wilderness (1846), 129–30
Sonnets (Heavysege, 1855), 149
Sonnets (W. W. E. Ross, 1932), **728**
Sonnets of William Alabaster (1959), 544
Sophocles, **649**
Sophocles the Playwright (1957), 545
Sordello (Browning), 832
Sort of Ecstasy, A (1954), 731, **785**
Souster, Raymond, 491, 494, 768, 769, 773, 776, 778–81, 785, 786, 816, 834
Southey, Robert, 69
Southworth, Mrs. E. D. E. N., 278

INDEX

Soward, F. H., 510, 526
Sowing Seeds in Danny (1908), 297, 330
Span of Life, The (1899), 287
Spanish John (1898), 308
Sparhawk, Edward V., 135
Spark, Alexander, 87–8
Sparling, C. J., 362
Sparshott, Francis E., 589
Spectator, The (journal), 93
Spedon, A. L., 182
Speech of the Hon. Mr. Justice Haliburton, M.P., in the House of Commons ... 21st of April, 1860 (1860), 100
Speeches and Addresses (McGee) (1937), 156
Spencer, Herbert, 202, 439, 440, 441, 449, 453, 464, 583, 587
Spencer, Hiram Ladd, 119
Spencer, Robert, 510
Spencer, Stanley, 806
Spender, Stephen, 741, 770, 784, 786
Spenser, Edmund, 539, 788
Spettigue, Douglas, 722
Spice-Box of Earth, The (1961), 812
Spinks, J. W. T., 456
Spinoza, B., 411, 434, 443
Spirit of God and the Faith of Today, The (1930), 565
Spirit of Iron (1923), 660
Spirit of Jesus in St. Paul, The (1924), 562
Spirit of Mediaeval Philosophy, The (1936), 590
Spirit of Philosophy, The (1953), 587
Spiritual Experience of St. Paul, The (1901), 558
Spiritual History of Israel, The (1961), 570
Spiritual Values in Shakespeare (1955), 570
Splendid Renegade, The (1928), 663
Spoilers of the Valley, The (1921), 659
Spoon River Anthology, 729
Sporting Adventures in the New World (1855), 371

Sporting Paradise, A (1909), 358
Sporting Sketches (1905), 372
Sportsman in Canada, The (1845), 371
Sportsman Joe (1924), 372
Sportsman's Paradise, The (1888), 350
Spragge, Mrs. Arthur, 351
Sprang, Edward, 381
Sprigge, Elizabeth, 659
Spring Thaw, 655
Stacey, C. P., 494, 509
Stage Society, 655
Stalag 17, 718
Stampede (Pharis), 639
Stampeder, The (1910), 299
Stanley, G. F. G., 494, 505, 509
Stansbury, Joseph, 77, 79
Stanton, Robert, 140, 179
Star (Montreal), 664
Star (Toronto), 689
Starbuck Valley Winter (1943), 631
State in Peace and War, The (1919), 441
Stationers' Register, 9
Statistical Account of Scotland (Sinclair), 208
Statistical Account of Upper Canada (1822), 87, 140, 208
Statistical Sketches of Upper Canada (Dunlop, 1832), 142, 254
Statistics of British North America (1862), 234
Stead, Robert J. C., 257, 262, 263, 268, 276, 299, 304, 311, 337, 466, 666, 676–78, 688
Stead, W. T., 108, 268
Steele, Sir Richard, 18, 92
Steele, Harwood, 630, 660
Steele, John, 118
Stefanson, Vihjalmur, 603, 615, 616, 628
Stein, Gertrude, 709
Steinbeck, John, 688
Steinhauer, H., 548
Steller, G. W., 42
Stembridge, J. H., 605
Stephen, Alexander Maitland, 484, 663, 687
Stephen, Anna, 278

Stephen Leacock Medal, 19
Stephens, C. A., 350
Stephens, Henry, 459
Stephens, William S., 152
Stephenson, Mrs. F. G., 574
Stevens, G. R., 507
Stevens, Wallace, 540, 724, 731, 732, 733, 739, 812
Stevenson, Charles, 597
Stevenson, J. H., 185
Stevenson, Lionel, 484, 536, 537, 768
Stevenson, Lloyd, 454
Stevenson, Orlando John, 374
Stevenson, Robert Louis, 280, 281, 282, 283, 317, 625, 630, 632
Stewart, Basil, 358, 362
Stewart, Charles, 434
Stewart, Charles James, 129, 130, 132
Stewart, David A., 588
Stewart, Dugald, 442
Stewart, Mrs. Frances, 367
Stewart, George, 115, 122, 205–6
Stewart, Herbert L., 481, 563, 576, 593
Stewart, J. A., 577
Stewart, James Livingstone, 571, 659
Stewart's Literary Magazine (Saint John), 115, 205–6
Still Life and Other Verse (1943), 749
Still Stands the House (Pharis), 639
Stone, Edgar, 653
Stone Field, The (1937), 678
Stories of the Canadian Forest (1857), 624
Stories of the Land of Evangeline (1891), 290, 674
Storm and the Silence, The (1949), 718
Storm Below (1944), 716
Story, G. M., 544
Story of Canada, The (1959), 513
Story of Church Union in Canada, The (1930), 561
Story of Lambert, The (1955), 628, 672
Story of Old Kingston, The (1908), 239

Story of Our Language, The (1940), 543
Story of Plants, The (1895), 453
Story of St. Paul's Life and Letters (1924), 559
Story of Sonny Sahib, The (1894), 315
Story of the Canadian Revision of the Prayer Book (1922), 563
Story of the Dominion, The (1899), 219
Story of the Faith, The (1946), 568
Story of the Foss River Ranch, The (1903), 299
Story of the Trapper, The (1902), 629
Story of the Upper Canadian Rebellion, The (1885), 225-6
Story of Troilus, The (1934), 547
Stowe, Harriet Beecher, 108, 151, 152, 279, 282
Strachan, John, 66, 176, 229
Strachey, Lytton, 507
Strack, Lilian H., 605
Strait of Anian, The (1948), 51, 763, 787
Strand (magazine), 268
Strange and Dangerous Voyage (James), 16
Strange Fugitive (1928), 472, 689, 690
Strange Man upon His Cross, The (1934), 565
Strange Manuscript Found in a Copper Cylinder, A (1888), 112, 113
Strange One, The (1959), 379, 387
Stratford Shakespearean Festival, 656-7
Straw Hat Players, 656
Stray Leaves: A Collection of Poems (1865), 118
Streams Run Fast, The (1945), 619
Street Called Straight, The (1912), 326
Streetsville Weekly Review, 151
Strength of the Hills, The (1948), 739

Stress of Life, The (1956), 456
Strickland, Agnes, 144
Strickland, Samuel, 144, 367, 619
Stringer, Arthur, 262, 263, 268, 276, 279, 293, 299, 309, 312, 325, 326, 404, 466, 725
Stroll, Avrum, 597
Structure of Aesthetics, The (1963), 589
Structure of Allegory in the Faerie Queene, The (1961), 546
Stuart, H. C., 572
Studia Varia (1957), 536, 537
Studies in Econometric Method (1953), 523
Studies in Pauline Eschatology (1917), 558
Studies in the Old Testament (1909), 557
Studies in the South and West with Comments on Canada (1889), 350
Studies of Plant Life in Canada (1885), 143, 367
Study of Goethe (1947), 539
Study of Jacques Maritain (1937), 566, 591
Study of Nature and the Vision of God, The (1907), 558
Study with Critical and Explanatory Notes of Lord Tennyson's Poem, The Princess (1884), 533
Stunted Strong, The (1954), 800, 801
Suarez, Francis, 592
Substance of a Journal during a Residence at the Red River Colony, The (1824), 35, 573
Such a Din (1935), 755
Such Harmony (Harris), 641
Such is My Beloved (1934), 691, 692, 828, 841
Suckling, Sir John, 544
Sudbury Basin: The Story of Nickel (1953), 455
Suit of Nettles, A (1958), 788, 841

Suitable Child, The (1909), 328
Sullivan, Alan, 262, 263, 387, 631, 659-60, 663
Sulte, B., 226
Summa Parisiensis on the Decretum Gratiani (1952), 566
Summary of the Laws of Commerce and Navigation, A (1809), 69
Summer on the Canadian Prairie, A (1910), 361
Summer Tour through the Textile Districts of Canada and the United States (1920), 598
Summer Trip to Canada (1885), 349
Sun (Vancouver), 611
Sun and the Moon, The (Reaney), 648
Sun Horse, The (1951), 629
Sun is Axeman, The (1961), 816
Sunlight and Shadow (1928), 614
Sunshine Sketches of a Little Town (1912), 292, 334, 335, 338, 466
Supremacy of the Bible, The, and its Relations to Speculative Science ... (1905), 216
Surgical Pathology (1925), 454
Surtees Society, 237
Susannah: A Little Girl with the Mounties (1936), 630, 673
Susannah of the Yukon (1937), 673
Sutherland, John, 489, 490, 491, 536, 768, 769, 775, 795
Swamp Angel (1954), 709
Swayze, Fred, 816
Swayze, J. F., 629
Sweeney Agonistes, 784
Sweeny, Charlotte, 135
Sweeny, Robert, 135
Swift, Jonathan, 42, 613, 704
Swinburne, Algernon, 149, 205, 410, 411, 415, 423, 723, 752, 812
Swinging Flesh, The (1961), 816

Sykes, E. C., 361
Sylvia Leigh; or, The Heiress of Glenmarle (1880), 110
Symbol of the Apostles, The (1903), 560
Syme, Ronald, 630
Symons, A., 723
Symons, H. L., 614
Synge, J. M., 641, 653
Syntagma Philosophicum (Gassendi), 582
System of Temporal Retribution, A (1841), 553

TABER, Ralph Graham, 291
Table Talk of Samuel Marchbanks, The (1949), 613, 704
Taché, J. C., 286
'Tain't Runnin' No More (1946), 374
Tait, James, 555
Tait, M. D. C., 546
Tait, Michael, 827, 839, 840
Talbot, Edward A., 141
Talbot, F. A., 362
Talbot, Col. Thomas, 139, 143
Tale of Two Cities, A (Dickens), 281
Tales of a Garrison Town (1892), 290, 304
Tales of an Empty Cabin (1936), 376
Tales of Chivalry and Romance (1826), 127, 138
Tales of the Klondike (1898), 301
Tales of the Labrador (1916), 329
Tales of the St. John River (1904), 291
Tales of Western Life, Lake Superior and the Canadian Prairie (1888), 298
Talks on Poetry and Life (1926), 343
Tallman, Warren, 707, 722
Talman, James, 509
Talon, Jean, 512
Tamarac (1957), 707
Tamarack Review, 493, 544, 817, 846
Tambour (1945), 697
Tanghe, R., 542

Tangled Ends (1888), 293
Tanner, Henry, 348
Tanner, John, 23
Tâo (1930), 757
Tarboe (1927), 319
Tartuffe (Molière), 642
Tasso, T., 549
Tate, Frank J., 660
Taylor, A. E., 593, 595
Taylor, Bayard, 723
Taylor, Edward, 12
Taylor, Griffith, 523, 605
Taylor, Henry, 448
Taylor, K. W., 522
Taylor, Nathaniel, 558
Taylor, W. R., 571
Teach Me How to Cry (1955), 644–45
Teachers Trails in Canada (1925), 598
Tecumseh, 137, 138
Tecumseh; or, The Warrior of the West (1828), 127, 137–38
Tecumseh, a Drama (1886), **647**
Teeling, William, 603
Teit, James, 164
Telegram (Toronto), 614
Telescope (newspaper), 134
Temperance Battlefield, The, and How to Gain the Day (1882), 306
Tempest, The, 154, 540, 704, 804
Tempest-Tost (1951), 704, 838
Temple, Thomas, 57
Temple-Bar (magazine), 265
Ten Canadian Legends (1955), 629
Ten Canadian Poets (1958), 495
Ten Nights in a Barroom (1855), 280
Ten Selected Poems (1947) **747**
Ten Thousand Miles Through Canada (1909), 357
Ten Words, The (1960), 570
Ten Years of Upper Canada (Ridout) (1890), 91
Tenny, Edward Payson, 288
Tennyson, Alfred, 122, 147, 148, 154, 158, 161, 204, 206, 389, 396, 399, 402, 408, 423, 489, 541, 723, 724
Tent for April, A (1945), 771
Terence, 535
Terry, Ellen, 651
Tertullian, 590
Teskey, Adeline, 262, 263, 293, 295
Tess of the D'Urbervilles (Hardy), 280
Testament of Cresseid, The (1957), 800
Tests of Life, The (1909), 557
Text-Book of Pathology (1933), 454
Textbook of Popery, A (1831), 552
Thackeray, W.M., 206, 277, 279
Tharp, Louise H., 630
That Summer in Paris (1963), 689
That They May Be One (1929), 574
That Which is Past (1923), 659
Théâtre de Neptune (1606), 11
Theatre of Action, 654
Theatre Studio Group, 653
Theatre under the Stars, 655
Then I'll Look Up (1938), 685
Theory of Economic Change, The (1948), 523
Theory of Knowledge (1951), 595
Theory of Opposition in Aristotle, The (1940), 595
Theory of Politics (1951), 595
They are Returning (1945), 747
They Met at Philippi (1958), 570
They Shall Inherit the Earth (1935), 472, 488, 692, 833
They That Sit in Darkness (1897), 298
They Two; or, Phases of Life in Eastern Canada

Fifty Years Ago (1888), 303, 304
They Who [That] Walk in the Wild (1924), 386
Things Seen in Canada (1927), 599
Think of the Earth (1936), 683
Thirteen Men (1906), 324, 387
Thirty and Three (1954), 612, 702
3800 Miles across Canada (1900), 354, 357
This Citadel in Time (1958), 816
This for Remembrance (1949), 611
This Freedom Whence? (1943), 564
This is our Faith (1943), 562
This Most Famous Stream (1954), 564
This My Son (1923), 668
This Quarter (magazine), 730
This Side Jordan (1960), 715
This Time a Better Earth (1939), 687–88
Thistle, Mel, 380, 628
Thistledown (1875), 115, 116, 123
Thistleton, Hon. Francis, 149
Thomas, Dylan, 646, 771, 772, 792
Thomas, Edward, 740, 798
Thomas, Ernest, 564
Thomas, L. H., 509
Thomas, Lillian, 639
Thomas Chandler Haliburton (1924), 485
Thomas Sterry Hunt (1933), 454
Thomistic Philosophy (1948), 595
Thompson, C. W., 600
Thompson, David (explorer), 25, 31–33, 34, 65, 238
Thompson, David (historian), 213–14
Thompson, Francis, 723
Thompson, H. P., 603

Thompson, Homer, 545
Thompson, Sir John, 219
Thompson, Samuel (publisher), 180
Thompson, S. T., 553
Thompson, Stuart, 368
Thompson, T. Phillips, 464, 465
Thompson, W. P., 452
Thomson, Dale, 505
Thomson, D. F. S., 545
Thomson, Edward William, 262, 263, 268, 288, 292, 322
Thomson, Hugh C., 140, 176
Thomson, James, 79, 85, 139
Thomson, James S., 570, 571, 574, 832
Thomson, Tom, 601, 828
Thorburn, Grant, 142
Thorburn, Hugh G., 524
Thoreau, Henry David, 376, 377, 417, 567, 614, 623, 712, 723, 842, 848
Thorn Apple Tree (1942), 697
Thornton, A. P., 518
Thorold, William, 308
Thoroughbreds (1902), 324
Those Delightful Americans (1902), 309, 315
Thought of C. S. Peirce, The (1950), 587
Thoughts on the Education of Youth (1795), 90
Three Boys in the Wild North Land, Summer (1896), 631
Three Came to Ville Marie (1941), 663
Three Crosses, The (1907), 557
Three Dozen Poems (1957), 803
Three Letters of Credit and Other Stories (1894), 300
Three Mile Bend (1945), 369, 372
Three Months Among the Moose (1881), 371
Three Sapphires, The (1918), 324
Three Thousand Years of Mental Healing (1910), 558
Three Visits to America

(1884), 350
Three Years in Canada (1829), 167
Through Canada in Harvest Time (1903), 358
Through Canada with a Kodak (1893), 353
Through Miramichi with Rod and Rifle (1890), 371
Through the Heart of Canada (1911), 362
Through the Mackenzie Basin (1908), 257
Thrown in (1923), 611
Thunder in the Mountains (1947), 629
Thunderer, The (1927), 661
Thurber, J., 720
Thwaites, R. G., 21, 238, 246
Tiffany, G., 90
Times (London), 138, 351
Times (Winnipeg), 218
Times Literary Supplement, 698
Timlin, Mabel, 523
Tin Flute, The (1947), 472, 703, 840
Tisab Ting; or, The Electric Kiss (1896), 308
Tish (Vancouver), 494, 817
Titanic, The (1935), 747, 749, 844
Titans (1926), 744
Title-Clear (1922), 316
To America and Back, a Holiday Run (1886), 349
To Canada with Emigrants (1886), 348
To Effect an Arrest (1947), 630
To Have and to Hold (Johnston), 281
To Him that Hath (1921), 323
"To Ride a Tiger" (Williams), 644
To the Arctic! (Mirsky), 35
To the Greater Glory (1939), 668
Tocque, Philip, 70–1
Today in America (1881), 350
Todd, Alfred, 180
Todd, Alpheus, 180, 219, 247–48

INDEX 939

Todd, O. J., 545
Token, The (1930), 668
Tolfrey, Frederick, 371
Tom Brown's Schooldays (Hughes), 354
Tom Ellis: A Story of the North-West Rebellion (n.d.), 298
Tom Sawyer (1876), 282, 293, 325
Tomorrow's Tide (1932), 756
Tongue, Griselda, 79
Tongue, William Cotnam, 79–80
Tonnewonte; or, The Adopted Son of America (1831), 110
Tonty of the Iron Hand (1957), 629
Topographical Description of the Province of Lower Canada (1815), 128
Torch for a Dark Journey (1950), 716
Torches through the Bush (1934), 323
Toronto: Past and Present (1884), 185
Toronto of Old (1873), 239
Torquato Tasso (1951), 549
Totem Theatre, 655
Touch of Abner, The (1919), 291, 333
Tour in the States and Canada, A (1883), 350
Tour of their Royal Highnesses the Duke and Duchess of Cornwall and York (1901), 357–8
Tour through Canada, A (1884), 350
Tour through Canada in 1879, A (1880), 348
Towards Christian Unity in Canada (1956), 569
Towards Sodom (1927), 667
Towards the Christian Revolution (1936), 563
Towards the Last Spike (1952), 507, 748, 749, 785, 830
Toye, William, 131
Tracts for Difficult Times (1932), 563
Tracy, Clarence, 547

Tracy, H. L., 545
Traditional Songs from Nova Scotia (1950), 172
Traditions of the Thompson River Indians of British Columbia (1898), 164
Tragedy of Paotingfu, The (1902), 307
Tragedy of Tanoo, The (1935), 640
Tragic Protest, The (1963), 596
Traherne, T., 547
Trail of an Artist-Naturalist (1940), 453, 620
Trail of '98, The (1911), 301
Trail of the Conestoga, The (1924), 667
Trail of the King's Men, The (1931), 667
Trail of the Sandhill Stag, The (1899), 382, 453, 626
Trail of the Sword, The (1894), 318
Trail Tales of Western Canada (1914), 299
Traill, Catherine Paar, 65, 66, 127, 141, 143–44, 151, 154, 181, 187, 254, 367, 368, 370, 380, 619, 624, 625, 825, 844
Train for Tiger Lily (1954), 631
Training of Silas, The (1906), 305
Traits of American Humour by Native Authors (1852), 101
Traits of American Indian Life (1853), 34
Tramp Abroad, A (1880), 281
Transcript (Montreal), 148
Translation of a Savage, The (1893), 309, 318
Translation of John Snaith, The (1926), 637
Translations from Catullus, Horace, etc. (1872), 104
Transparent Sea, The (1956), 777–8
Transplanted, The (1944), 664
Trapper Jim (1903), 296, 372
Traveller's and Sportsman's Guide, The (1880), 350

Travels and Adventures in Canada and the Indian Territories between the Years 1760 and 1776 (1809), 27–8, 30, 88
Travels in Search of a Settler's Guide Book (1884), 348
Travels through Lower Canada and the United States . . . (Lambert, 1810 etc.), 89–90, 126, 175
Travels through the Canadas (Heriot, 1807), 88, 213, 252
Travels through the States of North America . . . (Weld, 1799), 88–9
Treason at York (1949), 630
Treasure of Ho, The (1924), 659
Treasure of the Sea, The (1873), 112
Treasure Trail, The (1906), 300
Treasure Valley (1908), 330
Treasury of Canadian Verse, A (1900), 429
Treatise on Baptism (1835), 552
Treatise on Geology (1845), 449
Treatise on Infant Baptism, A (1836), 552
Treatise on the First Principles of Christianity, A (1808–10), 552
Treatise on the North-West Passage to the South Sea (1622), 16
Treatyse of Fishinge with an Angle (1496), 365
Tree of Dreams, The (1955), 166
Tremaine, Marie, 175
Tremblay, Jack, 629
Trespasser, The (1893), 309, 318
Trespassers (1927), 637
Trethewey, W. H., 545
Trevelyan, G. M., 4
Trevelyan, Kathryn, 602
Trevelyan's Little Daughters (1898), 307
Trial of a City and Other Verse (1952), 764, 847–8

Tribune (Winnipeg), 611
Tribune of Nova Scotia, The: A Chronicle of Joseph Howe (1915), 245
Tricotrin (Ouida), 281
Trifles from my Portfolio (1839), 128
Trilling, Lionel, 473
Trio (1954), 792–94
Trip beyond the Rockies, A (1887), 350
Trip from Buffalo to Chicoutimi, A (1901), 358
Trip to Canada and the Far North-West, A (1886), 349
Trip to the Dominion of Canada, A (1883), 348
Triumph of John Karrs, The (1917), 301
Trollope, A., 273, 326
Trotter, Reginald, 498
Trotter, Thomas, 449
Truth of the Gospel, The (1950), 568
T. S. Eliot et la France (1951), 549
Turgeniev, I., 319
Turk in French History, Thought and Literature, 1520–1660, The (1940), 549
Turkish Nationalism and Western Civilization (1959), 571
Turn Back the River (1938), 662
Turn of the Screw, The (James), 280
Turn of the Year, The (1923), 370, 615, 679, 842
Turnbull, Gael, 794, 816
Turner, Frederick Jackson, 245, 501
Turvey (1949), 655, 716
Tuttle, Charles R., 217–18
Twain, Mark, 101, 113, 206, 228, 279, 280, 282, 300, 325, 335, 347, 515
Tweedsmuir, Lady, 605
Tweedsmuir, Lord, 484, 718
Twelfth Night, 657
Twelve Letters to a Small Town (1962), 816
Twentieth Century Canadian Poetry (Birney, 1953), 494, 761

20th Century Impressions of Canada (1914), 362
Twenty-Five Cents (Harris), 641
Twenty-Five Years' Service in the Hudson's Bay Territory (1849), 35
Twenty-Four Poems (1952), 776
Twenty-one Songs from Prince Edward Island (1964), 172
Twist and Other Stories, The (1923), 674
Two against the North; see, *Lost in the Barrens*
Two Country Walks in Canada (1903), 341, 358
Two Generations (1939), 680, 685
Two Knapsacks (1892), 257
Two Little Savages (1903), 380, 382, 626
Two Mites on Some of the Most Important and Much Disputed Points of Divinity (1781), 75–6, 551, 552
Two Months' Tour in Canada and the United States, A (1889), 350
Two on a Trail (1910), 299
Two on a Trip (1930), 604
Two Saplings, The (1942), 672
Two Sides of the Atlantic (1917), 362
Two Solitudes (1945), 701
Twok: A Novel (1887), 306
Tylor, Sir Edward B., 161
Tyndall, J., 439
Tyrrell, Edith, 380
Tyrrell, J. B., 31, 238

U. E., The: A Tale of Upper Canada in XII Cantos (1846, 1859), 136, 158
Umingmuk of the Barrens (1927), 387
Uncle Tom's Cabin (1852), 151, 279
Under Canadian Skies (1922), 663
Under Groove, The (1908), 325
Under Milk Wood (Thomas), 646

Under the Ice (1961), 802
Under the King's Bastion (1902?), 287
Under the Northern Lights (1926), 660
Under the Red Robe (Wayman), 281
Under the Ribs of Death (1957), 711
Under the Volcano (1947), 711, 717
Under Two Flags (Ouida), 278
Underhill, F. H., 469, 486, 494, 496, 497, 501, 509, 514–18, 526, 609, 825
Undertow, The (1906), 329
Unexpected Bride, The (1895), 293
Unfulfilled, The (1952), 662
Unharboured Heaths (1930), 602
Unheroic North, The (1923), 635
Union of Taste and Science, The, a Poem (1799), 86
Unit of Five (1944), 491, 769, 770, 775–6, 778, 779
United Church of Canada, The (1950), 561
United Kingdom: A Political History, The (1899), 249
United States, The: An Outline of Political History (1893), 249
United States and the Dominion of Canada, The (1879), 234
Unity of Philosophical Experience, The (1937), 590
Universal Difference of the Everlasting Gospel, The (1846), 573
Universalism in its Modern and Ancient Form (1837), 552–3
Universalism Unfounded (1867), 555
Universe, from Crystal Spheres to Relativity, The (1931), 454
University Magazine (McGill), 343, 445, 451, 481, 534
University of Toronto Press, 511, 532, 543

INDEX   941

University of Toronto Quarterly, 451, 481, 486, 487, 532, 533, 536, 537, 538, 539, 542, 546, 548, 577, 696, 698–9, 732, 753, 754, 766
Unknown, The, or Lays of the Forest (1831), 130
Unknown Country, The (1942), 606
Unknown Wrestler, The (1918), 291, 304, 333
Unreformed Senate of Canada, The (1926), 524
Unreluctant Years, The (1953), 632
Untempered Wind, The (1894), 293
Untried Door, The (1921), 565
Up Medonte Way (1951), 375
Upland Game Birds (1902), 371
Upland Trails (1955), 369
Upper Canada: The Formative Years (1963), 511
Upper Canada Herald, 176
Urbanism and the Changing Canadian Society (1961), 528
Ups and Downs in Canada (1922), 600
Urwick, E. J., 587, 589
Utrillo, M., 799

Vacation Rambles (1895), 354
Vaczek, Louis, 697, 698
Vaihinger, Hans, 440
Valeria: A Tale of Early Christian Life in Rome (1882), 308
Valerianos, Apostolos (Juan de Fuca), 41
Valerie Hathaway (1933), 686, 687
Valley of Vision, The (1961), 547
Values of Life, The (1948), 587, 589
Van Gogh, Vincent, 804
Van Horne, Sir William, 249, 355, 360, 749
Vance, Sara, 574
Vancouver, George, 29, 48–9, 51, 58, 764

Vanguard, The (1904), 307
Vanity Fair (Thackeray), 279
Vanzetti, Bartolomeo, 830
Vardon, Roger, 603
Varieties of Religious Experience, The (James), 74, 551
Varley, F. H., 539, 744
Varsity Graduate, 532
Varsity Story, The (1949), 692
Vaughan, H. W., 568
Vaughan, Henry, 418, 825
Vaughan, Leslie, 291
Vaughan, Walter, 229
Vaughan, William, 13–14
Veblen, T., 303, 334
Velvet Paws and Shiny Eyes (1922), 628
Venturing to Canada (1955), 606
Verne, Jules, 113, 204, 284
Vernède, P. E., 362
Vernon, C. W., 563
Vernon's Aunt: Being the Oriental Experiences of Miss Lavinia Moffat (1894), 315
Very House, The (1937), 672
Vesper Chimes (1872), 107
Vicarious Life, The (1946), 570
Vickers, Stephen, 518
Victor, The (1901), 314
Victoria, Queen, 281, 356
Victoria Diamond Jubilee History of Canada, The (1897), 239
Victoria Magazine, 144
Victorian House, The (1951), 787
Victory (Conrad), 699
Vie de sainte Marie l'Egyptienne, La (1949), 545
Views of Canada and the Colonists (1846), 254
Views of Canadian Scenery for Canadian Children (1843), 127
Vignettes of Nature (1881), 369
Viking Heart, The (1923), 666, 667
Village of Souls, The

(1933), 663, 686
Vincent, Mrs. Howard, 354
Vincent, Lady Kitty, 604
Vine of Sibmah, The (1906), 287
Vinton, V. V.; *see* Dale, Mrs. R. J.
Viper's Bugloss (1938), 754
Virgil, 423, 812
Virgin Mary, The (1955), 567
Virginian, The (1902), 283
Visible Word of God, The: An Exposition of Peter Martyn Vermigli (1957), 570
Visit of the Tenant Farmer Delegates to Canada in 1890, The (1891), 355
Vlastos, Gregory, 563
Voaden, Herman, 638, 653
Voice from the Attic, A (1960), 613
Voice of the People, The (1949), 642
Voices (magazine), 730, 766
Voltaire, F. M. A., 203, 204
Voyage of Consolation, A (1898), 309, 315
Voyage of Discovery (Ross, 1819), 35
Voyage of Discovery to the North Pacific Ocean (Vancouver, 1801), 48
Voyage of His Majesty's Ship Rosamond . . . (1818), 70
Voyage of the 'Fox' in the Arctic Seas (1859), 40
Voyage of the New Hazard (ed. 1938), 50
Voyage round the World . . . by Etienne Marchand (1801), 46
Voyage round the World by La Pérouse (1798), 45
Voyage round the World . . . (Dixon; Portlock, both 1789), 46, 47
Voyage to Newfoundland in 1768 (1778), 69
Voyage to the Pacific Ocean, A (1784), 44
Voyages (Hakluyt), 41, 72
Voyages (Radisson), 22
Voyages from Montreal through the Continent of

North America to the Frozen and Pacific Oceans (1801), 28–9
Voyages Made in the Years 1788 and 1789 ... (Meares, 1790), 47
Voyages of the "Columbia" to the Northwest Coast (ed. 1941), 49
Vroom, F. W., 563

Wacousta (1832), 138, 181, 485, 840
Waddington, Miriam, 767, 769, 774, 785
Wade, Allan, 544
Wade, Mason, 518, 528
Waite, P. B., 511
Wakefield, Edward Gibbon, 520
Walden (Thoreau), 376, 623, 712, 842
Walk through the Valley (1958), 712
Walker, Byron Edmund, 237
Walker, David, 494, 711, 718
Walker, Eldred G. F., 362, 600
Walker, F. C., 542
Walker, Frank Norman, 455
Walker, Horatio, 288
Walker, J. H., 603
Walker, John A., 358
Walker, Benson, 381
Walker, William W., 307, 554
Walking Death (1955), 779, 780
Wallace, Elisabeth, 161, 505
Wallace, F. W., 262, 291, 659
Wallace, J. S., 472
Wallace, Lew, 204, 279, 281
Wallace, Malcolm, 534
Wallace, P. A. W., 165, 674
Wallace, W. P., 543
Wallace, W. S., 84, 229, 237, 244, 250, 498
Waller, Edmund, 3
Wallis, R. S., 164
Wallis, W. D., 164
Walpole, Spencer, 247
Walsh, H. H., 508, 551, 569, 572
Walsh, Henry Cecil, 262, 289
Walsh, R. E., 556

Walshe, Elizabeth, 307
Walsingham, Sir Francis, 4
Walter Gibbs, The Young Boss, and Other Stories (1896), 322
Walton, George, 816
Walton, Izaak, 345, 346, 365, 371, 373, 615
Wandering Rhymer, The (1826), 139
Wandering Thoughts, or Solitary Hours (1846), 70–1
Wandering World, The (1959), 816
Wandering Yankee, The (1902), 359
Wanderings of an Artist (1859), 35, 159
War: An Heroic Poem (1762), 72
War of 1812 (1842), 137, 181, 214
Warburton, George, 212, 214
Ward, Artemus, 101, 335
Ward, James, 582
Ward, Mrs. Humphry, 279
Ward, Norman, 524
Warden of the Plains, The (1896), 298
Wardrums of the Skedans, The (1935), 640
Warman, Cy, 262, 263, 297
Warner, C. D., 350
Warr, Bertram, 773–4
Warrington, C. J. S., 454
Wasa-Wasa (1953), 376
Waste Heritage (1939), 472, 488, 688
Waste Land, The (Eliot), 784, 790
Watch That Ends the Night, The (1959), 472, 701, 702, 845
Watchers in the Pond (1961), 369
Watchers of the Trails, The (1904), 383, 384
Water Babies (Kingsley), 204
Water Trio (1948), 387
Waterloo Review, 494
Waterston, Elizabeth, 826, 827
Watkins, Frederick, 595
Watson, A. D., 536, 574

Watson, B., 350
Watson, Homer, 288
Watson, John, 435, 436, 437–42, 444, 555, 556, 576
Watson, Robert, 301, 659, 660
Watson, Sheila, 494, 712
Watson, W. H., 456
Watson, Wilfred, 494, 791, 792
Watson, William, 434
Watson, William R., 605
Watt, E. W., 600
Watt, Frank W., 833
Watters, R. E., 494, 542, 658, 708
Watts, Isaac, 113
Watts-Dunton, Theodore, 426
Wau-nan-gee (1852), 138
Way of the Sea, The (1903), 291, 328
Way of the Strong (1913), 301
Way to Union, The (1912), 562
Wayman, Stanley, 281
"W.C.T.U."; *see* DeWolf, Mrs.
We Keep a Light (1945), 616
Weather Breeder, The (Denison), 635
Weaver, E. P., 362
Weaver, Emily, 262, 263, 305, 307, 308
Weaver, Robert, 720, 721
Weavers, The (1907), 318
Web of Time, The (1908), 329
Webb, Phyllis, 494, 792–3, 816
Webb, Sidney, 466
Webb, W. S., 354
Webling, Peggy, 262, 263, 601
Webster, John, 735, 784
Wedding Gift, The (1947), 697
Wedding Journey, The (1871), 286
Week, The (journal), 64, 150, 162, 185, 186, 194, 197, 201, 236, 260, 266, 285, 315, 340, 341, 346, 403, 536, 616

Weekend Magazine, 611
Wees, Frances Shelley, 698
Weir, R. Stanley, 574
Weld, Isaac, 88–9
Well, The (1958), 706
Welland Canal Company, The (1954), 507
Wells, H. G., 284, 312
Wells, J. E., 530
Wells, Kenneth M., 374, 375, 614
Welty, Eudora, 721
Wesley, Charles, 203
West, Bruce, 611
West, John, 35, 573
West and North-West, The (1880), 348
West from a Car Window, The (1892), 354
Westbury, G. H., 603
Westering Wanderings (1856), 153
Western Angler, The (1947), 373
Western Clarion, 467
Western Wanderings; or, Pleasure Tours in the Canadas (1856), 183
Westminster (magazine), 269
Westminster Press, 303
Westropp, E., 606
Westward with the Prince of Wales (1920), 598
Wetherald, A. Ethelwyn, 295, 430
Wetherell, Elizabeth, 278
Whalley, George, 544
Wharton, Edith, 280
What Christ Means to Me (1927), 560
What God Hath Wrought (1958), 573
What is Civilization? (George), 437
What is My Country? (n.d.), 363
What Necessity Knows (1893), 290, 306, 320
What Our Church Stands for (1932), 562
Whates, H. R., 356
Wheat and Woman (1914), 361
Wheat Economy, The (1939), 522
Wheel Outings in Canada (1895), 354
When Knighthood Was in Flower (Major), 281
When Sparrows Fall (1925), 666
When the Fish are Rising (1947), 372
When the Shadows Flee Away (1891), 303
When the Steel Went Through, 616
When Valmond Came to Pontiac (1895), 289, 318
When We are Young (1946), 778–9
Where the High Winds Blow (1960), 718
Where the Sugar Maple Grows (1901), 293
Which We Did (1936), 612
Whig Interpretation of History, The (Butterfield), 4
Whitbourne, Sir Richard, 13, 14, 16
White Centre, The (1946), 771, 773
White, Gilbert, 365, 366, 367
White, Mary, 518
White, Samuel Alexander, 262, 263, 296, 299, 302, 337, 660
White, Stewart Edward, 283, 298
White Mail, The (1899), 298
White Narcissus (1929), 685
White Savannahs, The (1936), 487, 538
Whitehead, A., 574
Whitehead and the Modern World (1950), 588
Whitehead's American Essays in Social Philosophy (1959), 588
Whitehead's Philosophy of Civilization (1958), 588
Whitehead's Theory of Reality (1952), 588
Whiteoaks (play), 639
Whiteoaks of Jalna, The (1929), 672
Whitman, Walt, 147, 154, 160, 348, 358, 359, 413, 465, 538, 723, 726, 728, 733, 781, 848
Whittier, John G., 203, 206, 423, 723, 801
Whittle too Much, A (1955), 631
Who Has Seen the Wind (1947), 711, 828
"Who's Who" (Mavor Moore), 655
Why and How of Foreign Missions, The (1913), 573–4
Why I am a Presbyterian (1934), 562
Why Not, Sweetheart? (1901), 300
Wickens, G. M., 542
Wicksteed, Gustavus William, 131
Wide, Wide World, The (Wetherell), 278
Widow of the Rock, The (1824), 133, 135
Widower Jones (1888), 293, 304
Wiggins, Ezekiel S., 450, 555
Wilby, T. W., 363
Wilcocke, Samuel Hull, 129, 139
Wilcox, Bailie D., 357
Wild Animal Play for Children, The (1900), 380
Wild Animal Ways (1916), 382
Wild Animals at Home (1913), 369, 626
Wild Animals I have Known (1898), 382, 383, 453, 626
Wild Apples (1927), 756
Wild Geese (1925), 484, 678
Wild Glory (1961), 373
Wild Life Ways (1936), 380
Wild Olive, The (1910), 325
Wild Winter (1954), 380, 631
Wild Youth and Another (1919), 299, 317
Wilderness Camping and How to Enjoy It (1956), 371
Wilderness Champion (1944), 628
Wilderness Walls (1933), 665
Wildlife Friends (1954), 368
Wildlife Sketches (1962), 369

Wildlife Trails (1956), 368
Wildwood Trails (1946), 369
Wiles, R. M., 547
Wilfred Campbell (1942), 491
Wilkie, John, 128
Wilkins, E. H., 549
Wilkinson, Anne, 166, 494, 790–1
Wilkinson, Bertie, 518
Will in Western Thought (1964), 593
Willa Cather: A Critical Biography (1953), 541
Willard, Abijah, 59
William and Mary: A Tale of the Siege of Louisburg (1884), 288
William and Melville (1826), 93, 107, 109
William Lyon Mackenzie (Lindsey), 228–30
Williams, Bealing Stephens, 121
Williams, Bryan, 372
Williams, J. R., 525
Williams, M. B., 369
Williams, Norman, 644
Williams, Roger, 55
Williams, Tennessee, 644, 813
Williams, William Carlos, 729, 733, 808
Willis, John H., 135
Willis, N. P., 143
Willison, Sir John S., 227, 229, 230, 244, 247
Willison's Monthly, 468
Willow Smoke (1928), 668
Willow, the Wisp (1918), 379
Willowdale (1956), 387
Wilmot and Tilley (Hannay, 1903), 223, 228
Wilson, Clifford, 606
Wilson, Sir Daniel, 153–4, 160, 162, 242, 248, 540
Wilson, Edmund, 689
Wilson, Ethel, 472, 491, 494, 694, 702, 707, 708–9, 711, 712, 720, 721, 722
Wilson, H. S., 546
Wilson, J. Tuzo, 455
Wilson, John, 132
Wilson, May, 293, 295
Wilson, Milton, 538

Wilson, R. A., 542
Wind and the Caribou, The (1953), 376
Wind Our Enemy, The (1939), 488, 754, 760
Wind without Rain (1946), 706
Winds of Life (1930), 638
Windsor, Kenneth, 825
Windsor (magazine), 268
Windsor Forest (Pope), 85
Windward Rock (1934), 755
Wine of Life, The (1921), 326
Winesburg, Ohio (Anderson), 712
Winged Words (1953), 593
Winning of the Frontier, The (1930), 563
Winona and Other Stories (1906), 305
Winslow, Edward, 60, 78
Winslow, Joshua, 59
Winslow Papers (ed. 1901), 78
Winsome Winnie (1920), 334
Winson, J. W., 369
Wintemberg, W. J., 166
Winter, Elspeth, 607
Winter, Gordon, 607
Winter, Jack, 634
Winter Adventures of Three Boys (1899), 355
Winter and Summer Excursions in Canada (1892), 355
Winter Studies and Summer Rambles in Canada (1838), 139, 143, 167, 254
Winter Sun (1960), 787, 808–10, 811
Wire Tappers, The (1906), 312, 325
Wisdom and Love in St. Thomas Aquinas (1951), 590
Wisdom of Catholicism, The (1949), 591
Wisdom of St. Anselm, The (1961), 566, 591
Wisdom of the Wilderness (1922), 384
Wiseman, Adele, 494, 710
Wishard, W. T., 553
Wister, Owen, 283, 298

Wiswall, Peleg, 209
Wit and Wisdom of Dewey, The (1949), 588
Wit and Wisdom of Whitehead, The (1947), 588
Witch of Plum Hollow, The (1892), 310, 312
Witches' Brew, The (1925), 609, 744
Witching of Elspie, The (1923), 289, 674
With Flame of Freedom (1938), 668
With Rod and Gun in Canada (1922), 372
With the Birds (1935), 371
With the British Bowlers in Canada (1906), 357
With the Self-Help Emigrants (1888), 348
Wither, George, 14
Witherspoon, John, 72
Within Sea Walls; or, How the Dutch Kept the Faith (1881), 307
Within the Zodiac (1964), 816
Withrow, William H., 218, 249, 294, 295, 305, 308
Wittgenstein, L., 586
Wolf in Sheep's Clothing, A (1905), 304
Wolf King (1933), 628
Wolfe, James, 86, 87, 126, 170, 200, 509, 696
Wolfe, Thomas, 704
Wolfe and Montcalm (Casgrain), 228
Wölfflin, H., 194
Wolverine (1954), 380
Wolves of Cooking Lake, The (1932), 387
Woman as She Should Be; or, Agnes Wiltshire (1861), 109
Woman Hater, The (1912), 290
Woman in Canada, A (1910), 361
Woman in White, The (Collins), 278
Woman Intervenes, The (1895), 314
Woman Who Did, The (1895), 280, 313
Wonder of the Christian Gospel, The (1959), 565

Wonders of the Arctic (1959), 370
Wonders of the West (1825), 140
Wood, A. C., 374
Wood, C. H., 238
Wood, Mrs. Henry, 278
Wood, J. L., 353
Wood, Joanna, 262, 263, 293, 310
Wood, Kerry, 369, 372, 380, 387, 630, 631
Wood, Samuel Thomas, 368, 369
Wood, William C. H., 245
Woodberry, L. E., 546
Woodcarver's Wife, The (1922), 635
Woodcock, George, 494, 529, 535, 719
Woodhead, W. D., 534, 545, 596, 609
Woodhouse, A. S. P., 530, 534, 538, 539, 546
Woodland Tales (1927), 378
Woodley, E. C., 574, 629, 674
Woodling, F. H., 372
Woodmyth and Fable (1905), 378
Woodsmen of the West (1908), 262, 300, 331
Woodstock Herald, 152
Woodsworth, J. S., 469, 477, 506, 515, 563
Woolf, Virginia, 312, 751, 776
Word and Sacrament (1960), 569
Word and the Way, The (1962), 570
Word of God, The (1959), 570
Wordsworth, William, 193, 366, 389–94, 396, 397, 398, 399, 408, 411, 413, 423, 427, 547, 736, 844
Workman, George, 554
Works of Allan Ramsay (1953), 544
Works of Samuel de Champlain, The (ed. 1922–36), 238

World Church: Achievement or Hope (1956), 569
World Encompassed by Sir Francis Drake, The (1628), 41
World for Sale, The (1916), 299, 317, 319
World of Night, The (1948), 369
World Wide, The (journal), 319
Worlds Apart (1956), 644
Wounded Prince, The (1948), 795–96
Wrath of Homer, The (1948), 546
Wreford, James, 491, 769, 775, 776, 785
Wright, Bruce, 369
Wright, R. Ramsay, 452
Wrightman, F. A., 357
Wrong, George MacKinnon, 233, 236, 237, 241–4, 246, 247, 480, 483
Wundt, Wilhelm, 444, 582
Wuorio, Eva-Lis, 631
Wuthering Heights (Bronte), 406, 686, 699
Wyatt, G. H., 350
Wyet, Silvester, 7
Wylie, Elinor, 734, 735, 740

XENOPHON, 545

YALDEN-THOMSON, D. C., 595
Year Book for the Arts in Canada, 634
Year in Canada, and Other Poems, A (1816), 127
Year in Manitoba, A (1883), 348–49
Year in the Great Republic, A (1887), 350
Yeats, W. B., 155, 537, 544, 653, 723, 731, 732, 733, 734, 752, 761, 783, 791, 792, 796, 831, 832
Yeigh, Frank, 362
Yellow Briar, The (1933), 171, 668, 669
Yeomans, Edward, 816

Yet a Little Onward (1941), 773
Yoke of Life, The (1930), 680, 682
Yorkshireman's Trip to the United States and Canada, A (1892), 354
You and the Universe (1958), 454
You Never Know Your Luck (1914), 299, 317, 319
Young, Edward, 75
Young, Egerton Ryerson, 307, 355, 381, 387, 631
Young, Sir Frederick, 357
Young, George Plaxton, 435–6, 444
Young, J. Peat, 600
Young, John, 446
Young Endeavour (1958), 454
Young Fur-Traders, The (1856), 625
Young Lion of the Woods, The (1889), 110
Young Man's Choice (1869), 109
Young Politician, The (1952), 505
Young Seigneur, The (1888), 199
Young Surveyor, The (1956), 629
Young Voyageur (1938), 628, 673
Your Local Government (1955), 524
Youth's Companion (Boston), 322
Yvon Tremblay (1927), 667

ZASLOW, Morris, 509
Zeit-Geist, The (1895), 306, 320
Zerola of Nazareth (1895), 308
Zig-Zag Journeys in Acadia (1885), 350
Zola, Emile, 264, 276, 681, 683
Zubek, J. P., 573
Zuñiga (ambassador), 10